EQUITY AND THE LAW OF TRUSTS IN IRELAND

Equity and the Law of Trusts in Ireland

7th edition

Hilary Biehler
B.A. (Mod.), M.Litt., Ph.D., LL.D., Barrister-at-Law
Fellow of Trinity College Dublin
Professor of Public Law, Trinity College Dublin

ROUND HALL

Published in 2020 by
Thomson Reuters (Professional) Ireland Limited
(Registered in Ireland, Company No. 80867.
Registered Office and address for service:
12/13 Exchange Place, IFSC, Dublin 1, Ireland)
trading as Round Hall

Typeset by
Gough Typesetting Services
Dublin

Printed by
CPI Group (UK) Ltd, Croydon, CR0 4YY

ISBN 978-0-41407-460-6

A catalogue record for this book
is available from the British Library

To my Mother,
and in memory of Douglas

Preface to the Seventh Edition

It is approaching 30 years since I first taught a course in Equity and the Law of Trusts at Trinity College Dublin and nearly 25 years since the publication of the first edition of this textbook. Looking back at the intervening years there have been some important developments in the field but perhaps the most significant development over this time is the general increase in the volume of written judgments delivered. While ground breaking new decisions in relation to equitable jurisdiction and remedies are relatively rare, this area of the law, like others, is increasingly subject to incremental change. Although only four years have passed since the publication of the sixth edition of *Equity and the Law of Trusts in Ireland*, there have been a considerable number of relevant judgments handed down in this area, both in Ireland and England as well as elsewhere in the common law world.

Since the publication of the last edition, some significant judgments have been delivered by the Supreme Court in this jurisdiction relevant to the relationship between Equity and the common law (for example, *ACC Loan Management Ltd v Rickard* [2019] IESC 29 and *McGrath v Stewart* [2016] 2 IR 704). In addition, a number of recent decisions of the Court of Appeal have provided clarification of the principle that it is necessary to establish evidence of undue influence or other wrongdoing in order to succeed in proceedings against a third party financial institution where the latter seeks to enforce a guarantee (see *ACC Loan Management Ltd v Connolly* [2017] 3 IR 629, *Ulster Bank (Ireland) Ltd v de Kretser* [2016] IECA 371 and *Bank of Ireland v Curran* [2016] IECA 399.) Two useful decisions have been delivered recently by the Supreme Court in *Charleton v Scriven* [2019] IESC 28 and *Merck Sharp & Dohme Corporation v Clonmel Healthcare Ltd* [2019] IESC 65 which consider the general principles governing the grant of interlocutory injunctions. A number of judgments relating to the grant of specific performance have also been delivered in the past few years: *JLT Financial Services Ltd formerly known as Liberty Asset Management Ltd v Gannon* [2017] IESC 70 (part performance), *Globe Entertainment Ltd v Pub Pool Ltd* [2016] IECA 272 (test for determining terms which must be included for there to be a concluded agreement), *Thomas Thompson Holdings Ltd v Musgrave Group plc* [2016] IEHC 28 (contracts with covenants which require supervision) and *Leggett v Crowley* [2019] IEHC 182 (hardship as a defence). There have also been some interesting judgments delivered which cast further light on the features of a fiduciary relationship (*Fermoy Fish Ltd v Canestar Ltd* [2015] IESC 93, *ADM Londis plc v Ranzett Ltd* [2016] IECA 290 and *Best v Ghose* [2018] IEHC

376) and on the circumstances in which claims based on unjust enrichment may succeed (*HKR Middle East Architects Engineering LC v English* [2019] IEHC 306 and *Bank of Ireland Mortgage Bank v Murray* [2019] IEHC 306).

In addition, there have been some developments in the jurisprudence in this area in England and Wales which are of interest. One of the most significant decisions delivered by the UK Supreme Court in recent years is *Patel v Mirza* [2017] AC 467, in which the manner in which the defence of illegality operates in private law was reasssessed, and as a result of which it is now clear that the so-called 'reliance principle' and the reasoning underpinning the decision of the House of Lords in *Tinsley v Milligan* [1994] 1 AC 340 will no longer be followed in that jurisdiction. Also noteworthy is the decision of the Privy Council in *Marr v Collie* [2018] AC 631, in which Lord Kerr concluded that the common intention constructive trust principles set out in *Stack v Dowden* [2007] 2 AC 432 and *Jones v Kernott* [2012] 1 AC 776 could be applied to property jointly owned by a co-habiting couple other than a home, such as investment properties and other assets. There have also been a considerable number of decisions relating to proprietary estoppel handed down in that jurisdiction, such as the decision of the Court of Appeal in *Davies v Davies* [2016] EWCA Civ 463 (see also *Moore v Moore* [2018] EWCA Civ 2669), in which Lewison LJ provided useful guidance in relation to how a court should approach the issue of how to satisfy an equity which has arisen in a plaintiff's favour in a claim based on proprietary estoppel, and *Habberfield v Habberfield* [2019] EWCA Civ 890, in which he further clarified the principles set out by Robert Walker LJ in *Jennings v Rice*. The Court of Appeal has also delivered a number of relevant judgments in cases involving the so-called *Pallant v Morgan* equity (*Farrar v Miller* [2018] EWCA Civ 172 and *Generator Developments LLP v Lidl (UK) GmbH* [2018] EWCA Civ 396) and in a case relating to trustee exemption clauses (*Barnes v Noble* [2017] Ch 191).

There have also been some useful decisions delivered by the courts in other parts of the common law world in the past few years. A number of these have been in the area of the administration of trusts, such as the decision of the Supreme Court of New Zealand in *Fenwick v Naera* [2016] 1 NZLR 354, the New Zealand Court of Appeal in *Erceg v Erceg* [2016] 2 NZLR 622 and the Supreme Court of Canada in *Valard Construction Ltd v Bird Construction Co.* (2018) 417 DLR (4th) 1. Other decisions of note are of the High Court of Australia in *Simic v New South Wales Land and Housing Corp* (2016) 339 ALR 200 (rectification), the Supreme Court of Canada in *Cowper-Smith v Morgan* (2017) 416 DLR (4th) 1 (proprietary estoppel) and the Supreme Court of New Zealand in *Proprietors of Wakatū v Attorney-General* [2017] 1 NZLR 423 (certainty of subject matter in express trusts).

I would like to extend my thanks to Dáire McCormack-George and Daragh Troy who assisted me by proofreading the text and to Siobhán Mulholland and Paula Bouwer who compiled the tables and index respectively. I would also like to thank Martin McCann and Pamela Moran of Thomson Reuters Round

Hall for their ongoing support with this project. As ever it has been a pleasure to work with them. I would also like to thank Shane Gough for all his work in typesetting the book. I have been so fortunate over the years to have worked, first with his late father, Gilbert, and now with Shane on all of my book projects for Thomson Reuters Round Hall. Their professionalism, efficiency and good humour have made the task of completing these projects so much easier than they would otherwise have been and I am sincerely grateful to Shane for all his work on this edition.

I have endeavoured to state the law as of 1 August 2019.

Hilary Biehler
1 September 2019

Contents

PREFACE TO THE SEVENTH EDITION vii
CONTENTS xi
TABLE OF CONTENTS xiii
TABLE OF CASES xxvii
OTHER TABLES xcvii

1 Introduction 1

2 Maxims of Equity 20

3 Trusts — An Introduction 68

4 Trusts — Formalities and Essential Elements 86

5 Secret Trusts 112

6 Constitution of Trusts 129

7 Resulting Trusts 157

8 Constructive Trusts 257

9 The Liability of Third Parties to Account in Equity 338

10 Purpose Trusts 380

11 Charitable Trusts 398

12 Void and Voidable Trusts 501

13 The Administration of Trusts 516

14 Injunctions 617

15 Specific Performance 788

16 Rectification 843

17 Rescission 865

18 Equitable Estoppel 922

19 Tracing 993

20 Equitable Doctrines 1018

Index 1045

Table of Contents

CHAPTER 1 INTRODUCTION

General Principles........1
Historical Background........6
Fusion of Law and Equity — a Procedural Fusion Only?........10

CHAPTER 2 MAXIMS OF EQUITY

Introduction........20
Equity Will Not Suffer a Wrong to Be Without a Remedy........20
Equity Follows the Law........22
He Who Seeks Equity Must Do Equity........24
He Who Comes to Equity Must Come With Clean Hands........27
Delay Defeats Equity........36
    Laches and Acquiescence........39
Equality Is Equity........45
Equity Looks to the Intent Rather Than the Form........47
Equity Looks on That as Done Which Ought to have Been Done........49
Equity Imputes an Intention to Fulfil an Obligation........50
Equity Acts In Personam........51
Where the Equities are Equal, the First in Time Prevails........54
Where the Equities are Equal, the Law Prevails........54
    Equitable Interests and Mere Equities........54
    Priorities and the Doctrine of Notice........58
        Actual Notice........60
        Constructive Notice........61
        Imputed Notice........63
        Onus of Proof........64
    Registration of Deeds, Priorities and Notice........64
    Registration of Title and Priorities........66

CHAPTER 3 TRUSTS — AN INTRODUCTION

General Principles 68
The Origins of the Trust Concept 68
Definition of a Trust 70
Trusts Distinguished from Other Forms of Legal Institution 71
Trusts and Bailment 71
Trusts and Agency 72
Trusts and Contract 72
Trusts and Powers 75
Trusts and the Administration of a Deceased's Estate 80
Classification of Trusts 82
Public and Private Trusts 82
Express, Resulting and Constructive Trusts 82
Express Trusts 82
Resulting Trusts 83
Constructive Trusts 83
Simple and Special Trusts 84
Fixed and Discretionary Trusts 84
Protective Trusts 84

CHAPTER 4 TRUSTS — FORMALITIES AND ESSENTIAL ELEMENTS

Formalities 86
Creation of Trusts Inter Vivos 86
Statute Not to be Used as an Instrument of Fraud 87
Dispositions of Equitable Interests Held Under a Trust 90
Creation of Trusts by Will 90
Essential Elements 91
Essential Elements of a Trust 91
Certainty of Intention or Words 92
Sham Trusts 96
Certainty of Subject-Matter 98
Certainty of Objects 103
Test for Fixed Trusts 103
Test for Mere Powers 104
Test for Discretionary Trusts 105
Conceptual and Evidential Certainty 108
Administrative Unworkability and Capriciousness 110

CHAPTER 5 SECRET TRUSTS

Introduction 112
Fully Secret Trusts 113
Secret Trusts Involving Joint Tenants and Tenants in Common 116
Half Secret Trusts 119
The Juridical Nature of Secret Trusts 126

CHAPTER 6 CONSTITUTION OF TRUSTS

Introduction 129
Complete Constitution of a Trust 130
Transfer of Trust Property 130
Declaration of Trust by Settlor 136
Exceptions to the Principle that Equity Will Not Perfect an Incompletely Constituted Gift in Favour of a Volunteer 141
The Rule in *Strong v Bird* 141
Donatio Mortis Causa 144
In Contemplation of Death 147
Delivery of the Subject Matter of the Gift 148
The Gift Must be Conditional upon Death and Revocable 150
The Property Must be Capable of Forming the Subject Matter of a Donatio Mortis Causa 150
Proprietary Estoppel 152
The Position of a Volunteer 152
Possible Alternative Remedies for a Beneficiary Where a Trust is Incompletely Constituted 153

CHAPTER 7 RESULTING TRUSTS

Introduction 157
General Principles 157
Theoretical Basis for Resulting Trusts 158
Automatically Resulting Trusts 160
Failure of the Trust 160
Failure to Exhaust the Beneficial Interest 162
The Distribution of Surplus Funds on the Dissolution of Unincorporated Associations 166
Quistclose Trust 169
Presumed Resulting Trusts 175
Voluntary Conveyance or Transfer 176
Conveyance of Land 177

Transfer of Personalty ... 179
Joint Deposit Accounts ... 180
Joint Bank Accounts of Husband and Wife ... 189
Purchase in the Name of Another ... 191
Rebutting the Presumption of a Resulting Trust ... 193
Evidence of an Intention to Benefit ... 193
Where Fraud or Illegality Exists ... 194
The Presumption of Advancement ... 204
Husband and Wife ... 205
Father and Child ... 209
Persons in Loco Parentis to a Child ... 211
Does the Presumption Apply in other Circumstances? ... 212
Rebutting the Presumption of Advancement ... 215
Evidence that no Gift Intended ... 215
Nature of Evidence Admissible to Rebut Presumption ... 217
Unlawful or Fraudulent Conduct ... 218
Trusts of Family Property ... 223
Introduction ... 223
The Operation of Equitable Principles in Ireland ... 227
The Position in England – the Common Intention Constructive Trust ... 236
Alternative Models ... 251

CHAPTER 8 CONSTRUCTIVE TRUSTS

Introduction ... 257
General Principles ... 257
Institutional and Remedial Constructive Trusts ... 258
Advantages Gained by Persons in Fiduciary Positions ... 259
Fiduciary Relationships ... 259
Introduction ... 259
The Key Obligations – The No-Conflict and No-Profit Rules ... 262
Commercial Relationships ... 267
Liability for Breach of Fiduciary Duty ... 269
The Fiduciary Position of Trustees ... 271
Renewal of a Lease ... 272
Purchase of the Reversion in a Lease ... 275
Competition with Trust Business ... 276
Other Types of Fiduciary Relationships ... 278
Introduction ... 278
The Liability of a Fiduciary to Account for Secret Commissions and Bribes ... 278
The Position of Agents ... 285

The Position of Company Directors 288
Other Situations in Which Institutional Constructive Trusts Arise 297
Mutual Wills 297
Prerequisites for the Imposition of a Constructive Trust 297
The Time at which the Trust Arises 301
Conclusions 302
The Pallant v Morgan Equity 303
The Trustee de Son Tort 308
The Vendor as Constructive Trustee 309
The Mortgagee as Constructive Trustee 314
Where Property is Acquired by a Joint Tenant by the Killing of the Co-Tenant 315
The Remedial Constructive Trust 316
Introduction 316
New Model Constructive Trusts 318
Remedial Constructive Trusts in Ireland 319
Developments Elsewhere in the Common Law World 326
Other Possible Future Developments Relating to the Constructive Trust 331
Introduction 331
The Basis for a Claim in Unjust Enrichment 331
The Role of Unconscionable Conduct 335
Conclusions 336

CHAPTER 9 THE LIABILITY OF THIRD PARTIES TO ACCOUNT IN EQUITY

Introduction 338
Terminology 339
Assisting in the Misappropriation of Trust Property 343
Dishonesty of the Person Assisting in the Breach of Trust 343
The Requirement of Knowledge/Dishonesty 344
The Nature of the Remedies 357
Knowing Receipt of and Inconsistent Dealing With Trust Property 358
General Principles 358
The Threshold for the Imposition of Liability in England 361
The Position in Other Common Law Jurisdictions 367
The Position in this Jurisdiction 368
Possible Future Developments 372
The Liability of Agents of Trustees 375
The Liability of Partners 376

CHAPTER 10 PURPOSE TRUSTS

Introduction....380
Rationale for Policy of Non-Enforcement of Purpose Trusts....381
Enforceability — The Beneficiary Principle....381
Enforceability — Clarity and Certainty....382
The Need for Compliance with the Rules against Perpetual Trusts and Inalienability....384
Exceptional Cases in Which Purpose Trusts have Been Enforced....386
Tombs and Monuments....386
Animals....388
Gifts to Unincorporated Associations....389
A Gift by Way of Endowment for the Benefit of the Association....390
A Gift to the Members of the Association for the Time Being....390
Property Held on Trust to be Applied in Accordance with the Contract Between the Members....394
Conclusion....396

CHAPTER 11 CHARITABLE TRUSTS

Introduction....398
Advantages of Charitable Status....398
Administration of Charities....402
Definition of Charity....406
The Public Benefit Requirement....409
Charitable Purposes....414
Trusts for the Prevention or Relief of Poverty....414
The Meaning of 'Poor'....414
Addition of 'Prevention of' Poverty and 'Economic Hardship'....417
The Element of Public Benefit....418
The Test of Public Benefit in England....419
Trusts for the Advancement of Education....425
The Element of Public Benefit....430
Trusts for the Advancement of Religion....436
Introduction....436
Gifts in General Terms....438
Gifts to Ecclesiastical Office Holders....439
Gifts for the Celebration of Masses....441
Gifts to Religious Orders....444
Gifts for Churches and Other Miscellaneous Purposes....447
Trusts for Other Purposes of Benefit to the Community....449
Introduction....449
Public Benefit....451

For Other Purposes of Benefit to the Community — an Objective or Subjective Test? 457
Specific Types of Trusts which may Qualify as being For Any Other Purpose of Benefit to the Community 459
Gifts for the Aged, the Disabled and the Sick 460
Gifts to Advance Community Development and Promote Harmonious Community Relations and Related Purposes 464
Gifts for the Benefit of Animals 465
Gifts for Sporting and Recreational Purposes 469
Gifts for Political Purposes 474
Conclusions 482
Cy-Près Jurisdiction 483
Introduction 483
Initial Failure of Charitable Purposes 485
Subsequent Failure of Charitable Purposes 490
Legislative Reform of the Cy-près Doctrine 492
The Manner in Which Cy-près Jurisdiction Should be Exercised 498
Sign Manual Procedure 499

CHAPTER 12 VOID AND VOIDABLE TRUSTS

Void Trusts 501
Conditions Precedent and Subsequent 502
Trusts Contrary to Public Policy 503
Trusts in Restraint of Marriage 503
Trusts Tending to Interfere with Parental Duties 504
Voidable Trusts 506
Settlements Defrauding Creditors 506
Voluntary Settlements to Defraud Purchasers 512
Settlements by Bankrupts 513

CHAPTER 13 THE ADMINISTRATION OF TRUSTS

The Office of Trustee 516
Introduction 516
Appointment of Trustees 519
Retirement of Trustees 521
Removal of Trustees 521
The Duties of Trustees 526
Duties on Appointment 526
Duty to Properly Exercise Discretion 527
Introduction 527

Relevant and Irrelevant Considerations 528
Improper Motive 535
Reasonableness 536
Duty to Safeguard the Trust Assets 537
Duty to Invest 541
Duty to Maintain Equality Between Beneficiaries 553
Duty to Convert Trust Property 553
Duty to Apportion 555
Duty to Apportion in Other Circumstances 556
Duty to Distribute 559
Duty to Keep Accounts and Provide Information 561
Duty Not to Profit from the Trust 569
Remuneration and Expenses 570
Purchase of Trust Property 572
Duty Not to Delegate 575
The Powers of Trustees 579
Introduction 579
Power of Sale and to Give Receipts 580
Power of Maintenance 581
Power of Advancement 583
Power to Compound Liabilities 583
Power to Insure 584
Liability of Trustees for Breach of Trust 584
Extent and Measure of Liability 584
Liability of Trustees Inter Se 589
Protection of Trustees from Personal Liability 591
Trustee Exemption Clauses 595
The Position in England 595
The Position in Ireland 598
The Irreducible Core Obligations of Trusteeship 600
Should a Distinction be Drawn between Lay and Professional Trustees? 602
Is There a Need for Statutory Regulation? 604
Variation of Trusts 607
Variation of the Terms of a Trust Without Court Approval 608
Variation of the Terms of a Trust With Court Approval before Legislative Change 608
Legislative Reform 609
Likely Future Developments in Relation to the Administration of Trusts 612

CHAPTER 14 INJUNCTIONS

Introduction 617
The Principles Governing the Grant of Injunctions 620
General Principles Governing the Grant of Perpetual Injunctions 620
Introduction 620
The Inadequacy or Inappropriateness of Damages as a Remedy 621
The Conduct of the Parties 624
Laches and Acquiescence 628
Effect on Third Parties 634
Jurisdiction to Award Damages under Lord Cairns' Act 637
The Measure of Damages Under Lord Cairns' Act 641
Principles Governing the Grant of Interlocutory Injunctions 644
Introduction 644
Undertaking as to Damages 645
The Test for the Grant of an Interlocutory Injunction 649
Circumstances in which a Departure from Cyanamid Guidelines Justified 669
Principles Governing the Grant of Mandatory Injunctions 703
Principles Governing the Grant of Quia Timet Injunctions 716
Specific Circumstances in which an Injunction will be Granted 721
To Restrain a Breach of Contract 721
Particular Considerations which Apply to Contracts for Personal Services 725
Employment Injunctions in this Jurisdiction 731
General Principles 731
Orders Restraining Implementation of Dismissal or Requiring Reinstatement 733
Orders Requiring Payment of an Employee's Salary Pending Trial 737
Injunctions to Restrain the Appointment of a Third Party 740
To Restrain the Commission or Continuance of a Tort 742
To Restrain a Breach of Constitutional Rights 742
To Protect Public Rights 744
Mareva Injunctions and Related Orders 747
Introduction 747
The Duty of Full and Frank Disclosure 752
Prerequisites for the Granting of a Mareva Injunction 757
Extra-Territorial Mareva Injunctions 765
Provisional and Protective Measures 770
Conclusions 773
Anton Piller Orders 775
Bayer Injunctions 785

CHAPTER 15 SPECIFIC PERFORMANCE

General Principles.....788
The Discretionary Nature of the Remedy.....789
Damages in Lieu of or in Addition to Specific Performance.....790
Specific Performance of Particular Types of Contract.....794
Contracts for the Sale of Land.....794
There Must be a Concluded Agreement.....794
Requirements of Note or Memorandum of Agreement.....798
Doctrine of Part Performance.....801
Completion Notices.....807
Contracts for the Sale of Personal Property or to Pay Money.....809
Contracts Requiring Supervision.....811
Contracts to Build or Repair.....818
Contracts for Services.....821
Defences to an Action for Specific Performance.....823
Introduction.....823
Lack of Mutuality.....824
Misrepresentation.....825
Mistake.....827
Hardship.....830
Laches or Delay.....833
Illegality.....836
Impossibility and Frustration.....838

CHAPTER 16 RECTIFICATION

Introduction.....843
Prerequisites for Rectification.....844
Common Mistake.....848
Unilateral Mistake.....852
The Onus of Proof.....857
Discretionary Factors.....859
Types of Instruments Which Can Be Rectified.....860

CHAPTER 17 RESCISSION

Introduction.....865
Mistake.....866
Introduction.....866
Common Law and Equitable Jurisdiction.....867
Unilateral Mistake.....870

General Principles 870
Voluntary Settlements and Similar Instruments 872
Misrepresentation....876
Fraudulent Misrepresentation 876
Innocent Misrepresentation....877
General Principles 878
Undue Influence....878
Introduction....878
Actual and Presumed Undue Influence....880
Undue Influence in the Context of Wills....887
Undue Influence and Third Parties....888
The Position in England....889
The Position in Ireland....898
The Approach in New Zealand....912
Unconscionable Transactions....913
Introduction....913
Elements of a Successful Claim....914
Loss of the Right to Rescind....919
Affirmation....919
If Substantial Restitutio in Integrum is Impossible....920
Third Party Rights....921

CHAPTER 18 EQUITABLE ESTOPPEL

Introduction....922
Promissory Estoppel 923
Proprietary Estoppel....927
Introduction....927
Assurance 928
Reliance....932
Detriment....935
Categories of Cases in which Proprietary Estoppel may Arise....938
Where an Imperfect Gift is Made 938
Common Expectation 939
Unilateral Mistake 942
A Move Towards a Test of Unconscionability....945
The Role of Unconscionability in this Jurisdiction....954
The Extent of the Remedy 956
The Minimum Equity....956
The Expectation-based and Reliance-based Approaches....959
An Approach Based on Proportionality 963
Approaches Elsewhere in the Common Law World 972
The Approach Adopted by the Irish Courts....974

The Relationship between Proprietary Estoppel and Constructive Trusts 975
The Relationship between Proprietary and Promissory Estoppel 985
Likely Future Developments 989

CHAPTER 19 TRACING

Tracing at Common Law 993
Tracing in Equity 995
Introduction 995
General Principles 996
Tracing into a Bank Account 1001
Tracing Through an Overdrawn Bank Account or a Debt 1007
The Requirement of a Fiduciary Relationship 1011
Loss of the Right to Trace 1015

CHAPTER 20 EQUITABLE DOCTRINES

The Doctrine of Conversion 1018
Introduction 1018
Trusts for Sale 1019
Contracts or Conditional Contracts for the Sale or Purchase of Land 1019
Order of the Court 1022
Partnership Property 1022
Settled Land 1023
Failure of Conversion 1023
The Doctrine of Reconversion 1023
By Act of the Party 1023
By Operation of Law 1024
The Doctrine of Election 1025
Introduction 1025
Requirements for Election 1027
Making an Election 1030
Conclusion 1031
The Doctrine of Satisfaction 1031
Satisfaction of Debts by Legacies 1032
Satisfaction of Portion Debts by Legacies 1034
Satisfaction of Legacies by Portions and the Doctrine of Ademption 1037
Satisfaction of Legacies by Legacies 1040
The Doctrine of Performance 1041

By Act of the Party 1042
By Operation of Law 1043

INDEX 1045

Table of Cases

A & N Pharmacy Ltd v United Drug Wholesale Ltd [1996] 2 ILRM 46 ....709, 712
A. Roberts & Co. Ltd v Leicestershire County Council [1961] Ch 555........852–854n
A. v A. [2007] 2 FLR 467 ....96–97n
A. v B. [2008] EWHC 2687 (Ch) 305n, 952n, 953n
A. v C. [1981] 2 All ER 126 752
A.H. v P.H. High Court, 20 June 1989........234n
A.J. Bekhor & Co. Ltd v Bilton [1981] QB 923........751n
A.M.W. v S.W. [2008] IEHC 452 563
Abacus Trust Co. (Isle of Man) Ltd v NSPCC [2001] WTLR 953 529
Abacus Trust Co. (Isle of Man) v Barr [2003] Ch 409 ....529, 532
Abbott v Abbott [2007] UKPC 53 ....164, 238n, 242
Abbott, Re [1934] IR 189 554
Aberdeen Railway Co. v Blaikie Brothers (1854) 1 Macq 461 ....263, 289
Abou-Rahmah v Abacha [2005] EWHC 2662 (QB) 351n
Abou-Rahmah v Abacha [2006] EWCA Civ 1492 ....352, 354
Abrahams, Re [1911] 1 Ch 108 ....581n
ACC Bank plc v McEllin [2013] IEHC 454 ....903n, 905
ACC Bank plc v Walsh [2017] IECA 166 ....899n, 902, 902n, 908
ACC Loan Management Ltd v Browne [2015] IEHC 722 916
ACC Loan Management Ltd v Connolly [2015] IEHC 188, [2017] 3 IR 629 ....4, 21, 898n, 899n, 905, 908–911
ACC Loan Management Ltd v Fryday [2019] IEHC 103 ....36n, 211n
ACC Loan Management Ltd v Rickard [2019] IESC 29........16, 21n, 618
ACC Loan Management Ltd v Sheehan [2016] IEHC 818 ....898n, 903, 909
ACC Loan Management Ltd v Stephens [2015] IEHC 717 ....41n
ACC Loan Management Ltd v Stephens [2017] IECA 229 ....39n
Actionstrength Ltd v International Glass Engineering SpA [2003] 2 AC 541 ......978n
Adams and the Kensington Vestry, Re (1884) 27 Ch D 394........93n
Adams v Director of Public Prosecutions [2001] 2 ILRM 401 ....619n
Adler v Dickson [1955] 1 QB 158........73n
ADM Londis plc v Ranzett Ltd [2016] IECA 290........260, 260n
Aer Rianta cpt v Ryanair Ltd [2001] 4 IR 607 ....899n
Aerospares Ltd v Thompson [1999] IEHC 76........760n, 762
Aforge Finance SAS v HSBC Institutional Trust Services (Ireland) Ltd [2010] 2 IR 688 262
Aga Khan v Firestone [1992] ILRM 31........799n
Agip Africa Ltd v Jackson [1990] Ch 265 ....341n, 344n–346, 359, 359n, 361n, 363, 365n, 377, 993, 993n, 1013
Agnew v Belfast Banking Co. [1896] 2 IR 204........147, 150
Agra Bank Ltd v Barry (1874) LR 7 HL 135 66

Agricultural Credit Corporation of Saskatchewan v Pettyjohn (1991) 79 DLR (4th) 22....1010n
Ahmed v Health Service Executive [2007] IEHC 312....812n, 821n, 822
Ahmed v Ingram [2018] EWCA Civ 519....13n, 588
AIB Finance Ltd v Sligo County Council [1995] 1 ILRM 81....183
AIB Group (UK) plc v Mark Redler & Co. [2015] AC 1503....13n, 14, 587, 588, 588n, 589
Aid/Watch Inc v Commissioner of Taxation (2010) 241 CLR 539....479
Air Canada v M. & L. Travel Ltd (1993) 108 DLR (4th) 592....343n, 347n
Air Jamaica Ltd v Charlton [1999] 1 WLR 1399....159, 167n
AITC Foundation's Application for Registration as a Charity [2005] WTLR 1265....424
Akita Holdings Ltd v Attorney General of the Turks and Caicos Islands [2017] AC 590....367
Al Khudairi v Abbey Brokers Ltd [2010] EWHC 1486 (Ch)....353n
Alacoque v Roche [1998] 2 NZLR 250....486
Albion Properties Ltd v Moonblast Ltd [2011] 3 IR 563....713, 744
Alcock v Soper (1833) 2 My & K 699....554n
Alec Lobb (Garages) Ltd v Total Oil (Great Britain) Ltd [1983] 1 WLR 87, [1985] 1 WLR 173....914, 918
Ali, Re [2012] EWHC 2302 (Admin)....242n
Allcard v Skinner (1887) 36 Ch D 145....40, 878, 880n–882, 886n
Allen v Jackson (1875) 1 Ch D 399....503
Allen v Jambo Ltd [1980] 1 WLR 1252....646n
Allen v Snyder [1977] 2 NSWLR 685....327, 327n
Allen, Re [1905] 2 Ch 400....464n
Allhusen v Whittel (1867) LR 4 Eq 295....556
Allied Irish Bank plc v Burke [2018] IEHC 767....508n
Allied Irish Banks plc v Diamond [2012] 3 IR 549....655, 659n, 662, 668, 669, 715
Allied Irish Banks plc v Hiney [2018] IEHC 325....906n
Allied Irish Banks plc v Smith [2015] IEHC 707....1007n
Allied Irish Banks v Glynn [1973] IR 188....56
Allnut v Wilding [2007] EWCA Civ 412....862
Alsop Wilkinson v Neary [1996] 1 WLR 1220....539
Alstom Transport v Eurostar International Ltd [2010] EWHC 2747 (Ch)....635, 652n
Aluminium Industrie Vassen BV v Romalpa Aluminium Ltd [1976] 1 WLR 676....997n
Amalgmated Investment and Property Co. Ltd v Texas Commerce International Bank Ltd [1982] QB 84....957n, 989, 989n
Amateur Youth Soccer Association v Canada [2007] SCC 42....472
Ambrosiano SPA v Ansbacher & Co. Ltd [1987] ILRM 669....116n
AMEC Group Ltd v Universal Steels (Scotland) Ltd [2009] EWHC 560 (TCC)....691n, 707n
Amedeo Hotels Ltd Partnership v Zaman [2007] EWHC 295 (Comm)....754n
American Cyanamid Co. v Ethicon Ltd [1975] AC 396....650–656, 667–669, 674, 675, 677, 691–693, 697, 698, 706, 707
Ames' Settlement, Re [1946] Ch 217....160, 161
Amin v Amin [2009] EWHC 3356 (Ch)....205n, 245n

AMP (UK) plc v Barker [2001] PLR 77; [2001] WTLR 1237 ....531n, 532n, 533n, 861, 875
An Cumann Peile Boitheimeach Teoranta v Albion Properties Ltd [2008] IEHC 447 ....923n, 956, 983, 984
An Post v Irish Permanent plc [1995] 1 ILRM 336 ....628n, 636n, 668, 742n
Ancient Order of Foresters Friendly Society Ltd v Lifeplan Australia Friendly Society Ltd (2018) 360 ALR 1 358
Ancorde Ltd v Horgan [2013] IEHC 265 ....654n, 662n
Ancorde Ltd v Horgan [2013] IEHC 266 30
Anderson v Finavera Wind Energy Inc [2013] IEHC 489 325
Anderson v Ryan [1967] IR 34 ....921n
Andrew's Trust, Re [1905] 2 Ch 48 ....163, 164, 382n
Angove's Pty Ltd v Bailey [2016] 1 WLR 3179 ....170n, 258n, 284n, 328n, 331
Anketill Jones v Fitzgerald (1930) 65 ILTR 185 ....593n
Anning v Anning (1907) 4 CLR 1049 ....132n
Annulment Funding Co. Ltd v Cowey [2010] EWCA Civ 711 ....891n
Anson v Anson [1953] 1 QB 636 ....204n, 216
Anstis, Re (1886) 31 Ch D 596 49
Anton Piller KG v Manufacturing Processes Ltd [1976] Ch 55 ....776, 776n
Antoni v Antoni [2007] WTLR 1335 ....209n, 217n
Antrim County Land, Building and Investment Co. Ltd v Stewart [1904] 2 IR 357 ....8n
Aquaculture Corporation v New Zealand Green Mussel Co. Ltd [1990] 3 NZLR 299 ....11n, 18n
Aranbel Ltd v Darcy [2010] IEHC 272, [2010] 3 IR 769 ....832, 834n, 839
Archbold v Scully (1861) 9 HLC 360 ....42, 631
Arena Corporation Ltd v Schroeder [2003] EWHC 1089 (Ch) 755
Argyll v Argyll [1967] Ch 302 ....30, 618n, 625, 683
Armitage v Nurse [1998] Ch 241 ....381n, 595–598, 600, 601, 601n, 603, 604n, 605
Armstrong DLW GmbH v Winnington Networks Ltd [2013] Ch 156 ....365n, 366, 993n
Armstrong v Armstrong (1880) 7 LR Ir 207 ....264n, 569
Armstrong v Reeves (1890) 25 LR Ir 325 ....388n, 459n, 466–468
Armstrong v Shepherd & Short Ltd [1959] 2 QB 384 ....30n, 626n
Armstrong, Re (1893) 31 LR Ir 154 1041
Arnold's Trusts, Re [1947] Ch 131 ....76n
Arnott v Arnott (1924) 58 ILTR 145 ....522, 523
Arnott v Arnott (No. 2) [1906] 1 IR 127 438
Aroso v Coutts & Co. [2002] 1 All ER (Comm) 241 ....185n
Arthur Andersen Inc v Toronto-Dominion Bank (1994) 17 OR (3d) 363 ....368n
Arthur v Attorney General of the Turks and Caicos Islands [2012] UKPC 30 ....365n, 366
Article 26 of the Constitution and the Employment Equality Bill 1996, Re [1997] 2 IR 321 .... 407n
Article 26 of the Constitution and the Matrimonial Home Bill 1993, Re [1994] 1 IR 305 ....46n
Ashburn Anstalt v Arnold [1989] Ch 1 ....22n, 319
Ashby, Re [1892] 1 QB 872 ....85n

Ashtiani v Kashi [1987] QB 888 765
Ashton v Pratt (2015) 318 ALR 260 ....958n, 962n, 985n
Ashton, Re [1897] 2 Ch 574 ....1034n
Ashurst v Pollard [2001] Ch 595 53
Aspden v Elvy [2012] EWHC 1387 (Ch) 241n, 242n
Associated Japanese Bank (International) Ltd v Credit du Nord SA
[1989] 1 WLR 255 869
Associated Provincial Picture Houses Ltd v Wednesbury Corporation
[1948] 1 KB 223 536
Association of General Practitioners Ltd v Minister for Health
[1995] 2 ILRM 481 ....926, 986
Astbury v Astbury [1898] 2 Ch 111 ....81n
Astor's Settlement Trusts, Re [1952] Ch 534 ....380n, 381, 383, 384
AT & T Istel Ltd v Tully [1993] AC 45 ....780n, 782n, 782
Atkin v Moran (1871) IR 6 Eq 79 ....754, 755n
Atkinson, Re [1904] 2 Ch 160 557
Atkinson's Will Trusts, Re [1978] 1 WLR 586 ....160n
Attenborough & Son v Solomon [1913] AC 76 81
Attorney General (Boswell) v Rathmines and Pembroke Joint Hospital Board
[1904] 1 IR 161 ....717, 719, 720
Attorney General (O'Duffy) v Appleton [1907] 1 IR 252 745
Attorney General for Dominion of Canada v Ritchie Contracting & Supply Co.
[1919] AC 999 ....717n
Attorney General for Hong Kong v Humphrey's Estate [1987] AC 114 941
Attorney General for Hong Kong v Reid
[1994] 1 AC 324 ....50, 279, 280–284, 320n, 336n, 586n
Attorney General for New South Wales v Perpetual Trustee Co. Ltd
(1940) 63 CLR 209 ....486, 486n
Attorney General for New South Wales v Satwell [1978] 2 NSWLR 200 ....468n
Attorney General for Northern Ireland v Forde [1932] NI 1 ....488n
Attorney General for the United Kingdom v Wellington Newspapers Ltd
[1988] 1 NZLR 129 ....11, 11n
Attorney General of the Cayman Islands v Wahr-Hansen [2001] 1 AC 75 465
Attorney General v Albany Hotel Co. [1896] 2 Ch 696 ....645n
Attorney General v Becher [1910] 2 IR 251 ....458n
Attorney General v Bishop of Chester (1785) 1 Bro CC 444 ....449n
Attorney General v Blake [1998] Ch 439 ....261, 278
Attorney General v Blake [2001] 1 AC 268 ....263, 270, 569n, 642, 643
Attorney General v British Broadcasting Corporation [1981] AC 303 682
Attorney General v Charity Commission for England and Wales
[2012] UKUT 420 (TCC) 410–411n, 419, 420, 424
Attorney General v Chaudray [1971] 1 WLR 1614 746
Attorney General v Delaney (1875) IR 10 CL 104 ....442, 442n, 443
Attorney General v Exeter Corporation (1826) 2 Russ 45 ....417n
Attorney General v Goddard (1929) 98 LJ KB 743 ....278n
Attorney General v Hall [1897] 2 IR 426 443
Attorney General v Lee [2000] 4 IR 298 ....693, 694
Attorney General v Manchester Corporation [1893] 2 Ch 87 ....717, 719, 720

Attorney General v Matthews (1677) 2 Lev 167 ....417n
Attorney General v National Provincial and Union Bank of England Ltd [1924] AC 262 ....412n, 450
Attorney General v Newspaper Publishing plc [1988] Ch 333 683
Attorney General v Nottingham Corporation [1904] 1 Ch 673 ....717n
Attorney General v Paperlink [1984] ILRM 373 ....745–746n
Attorney General v Price (1810) 17 Ves 371 ....420n
Attorney General v Sidney Sussex College (1869) LR 4 Ch App 722 435
Attorney General v Staffordshire County Council [1905] 1 Ch 336 ....704n
Attorney General v Wansay (1808) 15 Ves 231 ....417n
Attorney General's Reference (No. 7 of 2000) [2001] 1 WLR 1879 ....783n
Attwood v Lamont [1920] 3 KB 571 ....837n
Auckland Area Health Board v Television New Zealand [1992] 3 NZLR 406 ....675n, 679n
Australian Hardwoods Pty Ltd v Commissioner for Railways [1961] 1 All ER 737 ....788n
Avondale Printers and Stationers Ltd v Haggie [1979] 2 NZLR 124 328
Ayerst v Jenkins (1873) LR 16 Eq 275 195
Aylward, Re [1955] 5 DLR 753 ....184n

B. & S. Ltd v Irish Auto Trader Ltd [1995] 2 IR 142 ....653n, 656–658n, 664, 698, 742n
B. v B. [1998] 1 WLR 329 786
B. v B. (1976) 65 DLR (3d) 460 ....209n
B. v B. High Court (MacKenzie J) 22 April 1986 ....230n
B.L. v M.L. [1992] 2 IR 77 ....3n, 22, 234
B.P. Exploration Co. (Libya) Ltd v Hunt (No. 2) [1979] 1 WLR 783 ....332n
B2Net Ltd v HM Treasury [2010] EWHC 51 (QB) 665n
Babanaft International Co. SA v Bassatne [1990] Ch 13...747n, 765–766n, 769, 773n
Bacharach's Will Trusts, Re [1959] Ch 245 ....863n
Baddeley v IRC [1953] 1 WLR 84 416
Baden v Société Generale pour Favoriser le Développement du Commerce et de l'Industrie en France SA [1993] 1 WLR 509 ....343n–347n, 349n, 362–369n
Baden's Deed Trusts (No. 2), Re [1973] Ch 9 ....106n–109n
Baden's Deed Trusts, Re [1969] 2 Ch 388 ....106n
Bahin v Hughes (1886) 31 Ch D 390 ....590, 590n
Baillie, Re (1886) 2 TLR 660 127
Baínne Aláinn Ltd v Glanbia plc [2014] IEHC 482 ....645n, 649n, 653n, 659, 756n
Baker v Baker (1993) 25 HLR 408 ....958n
Baker v J.E. Clark Co. (Transport) UK Ltd [2006] EWCA Civ 464 ....597n, 604
Balfe v Halpenny [1904] 1 IR 486 ....121n
Baltic Shipping Co. v Translink Shipping Ltd [1995] 1 Lloyd's Rep 673 ....751n, 766, 766n, 767
Bambrick v Cobley [2006] 1 ILRM 81 ....619, 627, 748, 750n, 753n–756, 764, 775
Banco Ambrosiano v Ansbacher and Co. [1987] ILRM 669 859
Banco Exterior Internacional v Mann [1995] 1 All ER 936 ....896n
Banco Nacional de Comercio Exterior SNC v Empresa de Telecomunicaciones de Cuba SA [2008] 1 WLR 1936 771

Bandon Motors (Bandon) Ltd v Water Sun Ltd [2018] IEHC 191 690
Banister, Re (1879) 12 Ch D 131 826
Bank Mellat v Kazmi [1989] QB 541 ....749n
Bank Mellat v Nikpour [1985] FSR 87 ....752n–755n
Bank of America v Arnell [1999] Lloyd's Rep Bank 399 ....364n
Bank of Baroda v Rayarel [1995] 2 FLR 376 ....896n
Bank of China v NBM LLC [2002] 1 WLR 844 ....766n, 767
Bank of Credit and Commerce International (Overseas) Ltd v Akindele [2001] Ch 437 ....350n, 364, 365n, 366, 371, 373, 373n, 374
Bank of Credit and Commerce International SA v Aboody [1990] 1 QB 923 ....889n, 891
Bank of Ireland Finance Ltd v Rockfield [1979] IR 21 ....60, 62, 63
Bank of Ireland Mortgage Bank v Murray [2019] IEHC 234 334
Bank of Ireland Trustee Co. Ltd v Attorney General [1957] IR 257 ....447, 447n
Bank of Ireland v Cogry Flax Spinning Co. [1900] 1 IR 219 ....56n, 516
Bank of Ireland v Curran [2016] IECA 399 ....898n, 899n, 902n, 905, 907, 908, 911, 911n, 916n
Bank of Ireland v Geoghegan [1955-56] Ir Jur Rep 7 ....609n
Bank of Ireland v O'Donnell [2015] IECA 73 ....710n
Bank of Ireland v O'Toole, High Court 1979 No. 671Sp (Barrington J) 26 June 1980 ....76n, 79
Bank of Ireland v Smyth [1993] ILRM 790 (HC), [1995] 2 IR 459 (SC) 907
Bank of Montreal v Stuart [1911] AC 120 ....881n, 889n
Bank of Nova Scotia v Hogan [1996] 3 IR 239 ....900, 910n
Bank of Scotland plc v Kennedy [2013] IEHC 420 ....927, 927n
Bank of Scotland v Brogan [2012] NICh 21 ....242n
Bank of Scotland v Hickey [2014] IEHC 202 ....899n, 903, 905n
Bank of Tokyo-Mitsubishi UFJ Ltd v Baskan Gida Sanayi Ve Pazarlama AS [2009] EWHC 1276 (Ch) 365n
Bank St Petersburg PJSC v Arkhangelsky [2018] EWHC 1077 (Ch) 200n
Bannatyne v Ferguson: [1896] 1 IR 149 ....1042, 1043
Banner Homes Group plc v Luff Developments Ltd [2000] Ch 372 ....303–306, 308, 975n, 978n, 981n–983, 991
Bannon, Re [1934] IR 701 1035
Banque Belge pour l'Etranger v Hambrouck [1921] 1 KB 321 ....997n
Barber v Houston (1884) 14 LR Ir 273 8
Barclay's Bank Ltd v Quistclose Investments Ltd [1970] AC 567 ....170–175, 321
Barclays Bank plc v Coleman [2001] 1 QB 20, [2002] 2 AC 773 892
Barclays Bank plc v O'Brien [1993] QB 109 889
Barclays Bank plc v O'Brien [1994] 1 AC 180 ....880, 890, 891, 893–895, 897, 898
Barclays Bank plc v Thomson [1997] 4 All ER 816 ....896, 897
Barling v Bishopp (1860) 29 Beav 417 511
Barlow Clowes International Ltd (in liquidation) v Eurotrust International Limited [2006] 1 WLR 1476 ....350, 352–355
Barlow Clowes International Ltd v Vaughan [1992] 4 All ER 22 ....46n, 1002–1006
Barlow's Will Trusts, Re [1979] 1 WLR 278 109
Barnes v Addy (1874) LR 9 Ch App 244 ....343, 343n, 345n, 375
Barnes v Philips [2015] EWCA Civ 1056 248

Barnett v Creggy [2017] Ch 273 ....587n
Barnsley v Noble [2017] Ch 191 ....596, 602
Barraclough v Mell [2006] WTLR 203 ....605n, 1039n
Barrett v Barrett [2008] EWHC 1061 (Ch)....................198
Barrett v Costello High Court 1973 No. 703P (Kenny J) 13 July 1973 ....796n
Barrett v Hartley (1886) LR 2 Eq 789 ....570n
Barrington v ACC Loan Management DAC [2018] IECA 31 ....834n
Barrington's Hospital v Commissioner of Valuation
[1957] IR 299 ....455n, 460n–463, 471, 471n
Barros Mattos Junior v MacDaniels Ltd [2005] 1 WLR 247 ....362n, 1016
Barry v Ennis Property Finance DAC [2018] IEHC 766 ....899, 899n, 901n, 903n, 908
Barry v Harding (1844) 7 Ir Eq R 313 1038
Bartlett v Barclays Bank Trust Co. Ltd (No.1) [1980] Ch 515....................545, 547, 602, 613
Barton v Morris [1985] 1 WLR 1257 ....45n
Basham, Re [1986] 1 WLR 1498....................927n, 935, 951n, 960, 976, 976n, 977, 982n
Bate v Willats (1877) 37 LT 221....................1029n
Bateman's Will Trusts, Re [1970] 1 WLR 1463 123
Bath & North Eastern Somerset Council v Attorney General
[2002] EWHC 1623 (Ch) 451
Bath and North East Somerset District Council v Mowlem
[2015] 2 WLR 785 ....658n
Baumgartner v Baumgartner (1987) 164 CLR 137 ....254n, 327, 335
Bayer AG v Winter [1986] 1 WLR 497 ....785, 786
Bayley v Shoesmith's Contract (1918) 87 LJ Ch 626....................824n
Bayley, Re [1945] IR 224 105
Bayliss v Public Trustee (1988) 12 NSWLR 540 ....150n
Baynes Clarke v Corless [2009] EWHC 1636 (Ch) 975n
Baynes Clarke v Corless [2010] WTLR 751 304
Bayworld Investments v McMahon [2004] 2 IR 199 ....565n
Bayzana Ltd v Galligan [1987] IR 238....................663, 670
Beamish's Estate, Re (1891) 27 LR Ir 326 ....1022, 1035, 1037n
Beaumont, Re [1902] 1 Ch 889 ....144, 151n
Becker v Board of Management of St Dominic's Secondary School Cabra
[2005] 1 IR 561 ....656n, 731n
Beddoe, Re [1892] 1 Ch 547....................539–541n
Beddow v Beddow (1878) 9 Ch D 89....................618
Behbehani v Salem [1989] 1 WLR 723 ....754n
Behnke v Bede Shipping Co. Ltd [1927] 1 KB 649 ....809n
Bekhor Ltd v Bilton [1981] QB 923 ....757, 769
Belair LLC v Basel LLC [2009] EWHC 725 (Comm)....................753n
Bell v Lever Brothers Ltd [1932] AC 161 ....867, 869
Bell v Park [1914] 1 IR 158....................1041
Bell's Indenture, Re [1980] 1 WLR 1217....................377, 377n, 378, 586n, 588
Bellasis v Uthwatt (1737) 1 Atk 426....................1037n
Belletti v Morici [2009] EWHC 2316 (Comm)....................755, 768n
Bellew v Cement Ltd [1948] IR 61....................634, 742n
Belling, Re [1967] Ch 425 ....399n

Belmont Finance Corporation v Williams Furniture Ltd (No. 2) [1980] 1 All ER 393 ....361, 365, 370
Belmont Finance Corporation v Williams Furniture Ltd [1979] Ch 250....343n
Beloved Wilkes' Charity, Re (1851) 3 Mac & G 440 ....527n
Belshaw v Rollins [1904] 1 IR 284....1021n
Beltany Property Finance DAC v Doyle [2019] IEHC 307 ....660n, 669n
Benjamin, Re [1902] 1 Ch 723 559
Bennet v Bennet (1879) 10 Ch D 474....204n, 212–213
Bennett Enterprises Ltd v Lipton [1999] 2 IR 221 ....747n, 760n–763, 769
Bennett v Bennett [1952] 1 KB 249 ....837n
Bennett v Minister for Justice and Equality [2017] IEHC 261....25n, 32
Bentham v Potterton [1998] IEHC 84 ....145, 147
Beresford v Jarvis (1877) 11 ILTR 128 ....384n, 387n, 442n
Beresford v Williamson [2002] EWCA Civ 1632 ....978n
Bergin v Galway Clinic Doughiska Ltd [2008] 2 IR 205....710, 714n, 731, 732, 737, 740
Berry, Re [1962] Ch 97....554
Berryman v Berryman [1913] 1 IR 390....93n
Beshoff Brothers Ltd v Select Service Partner Ireland Ltd [1998] IEHC 122....832n
Best v Ghose [2018] IEHC 376 ....260n–262
Bestobell Paints Ltd v Bigg [1975] FSR 421....674n, 675n, 679
Beswick v Beswick [1966] Ch 538....810n
Beswick v Beswick [1968] AC 58....73n
Betafence Ltd v Veys [2006] WTLR 941 ....533n
Bethal, Re (1971) 17 DLR (3d) 652 ....415n
Bhimji v Chatwani [1991] 1 WLR 989....777, 784n
Bhullar v Bhullar [2003] 2 BCLC 241 ....289, 289n, 290n, 294n
Bhura v Bhura [2014] EWHC 727 (Fam)....242n, 248
Bieber v Teathers Ltd [2012] EWHC 190 (Ch), [2012] EWCA Civ 1466 172
Bigg v Queensland Trustees Ltd [1990] 2 Qd R 11....297
Billson v Crofts (1873) LR 15 Eq 314....85n
Bilta (UK) Ltd v Nazir (No.2) [2016] AC 1 ....198, 198n, 199
Binions v Evans [1972] Ch 359....89n, 318
Birch v Treasury Solicitor [1951] Ch 298....148n–151n
Birdseye v Roythorne & Co. [2015] EWHC 1003 (Ch)....564n
Birmingham and District Land Co. v London and North Western Railway Co. (1888) 40 Ch D 268....924
Birmingham v Kirwan (1805) 2 Sch & Lef 444....1025n, 1027n
Birmingham v Renfrew (1937) 57 CLR 666....297
Biscoe v Jackson (1887) 35 Ch D 460....488n
Bishop, Re [1965] Ch 450 ....191n
Bishopsgate Investment Management Ltd v Homan [1995] Ch 211....1008, 1009n, 1011
Biss, Re [1903] 2 Ch 40....274, 274n, 276n
Black v Kavanagh (1974) 108 ILTR 91....796n
Blackett v Darcy (2005) 62 NSWLR 392....143
Blackwell v Blackwell [1929] AC 318 ....114n, 115n, 122
Blackwood, Re [1953] NI 32....95n

Blake, Re [1955] IR 89 ....502, 505
Blandy v Widmore (1716) 1 P Wms 323 ....1043n
Blathwayt v Baron Cawley [1976] AC 397 505
Blausten v IRC [1972] Ch 256....110n
Blomley v Ryan (1956) 99 CLR 362 913
Bloomfield's Bequest, Re (1920) 54 ILTR 213 ....490n
Blythe v Fladgate [1891] Ch 337....377n
Board of Management of St Patrick's School v O'Neachtain [2018] IEHC 128 ....715n
Boardman v Phipps [1967] 2 AC 46 ....2, 263, 265, 266n, 271, 282, 286, 288, 292, 570, 573
Bobbett's Estate, Re [1904] 1 IR 461 ....58n
Bogg v Raper [1998] EWCA Civ 661 ....604n
Boland v Phoenix Shannon plc [1997] ELR 113 ....733n, 736n, 738
Boles & British Land Company's Contract, Re [1902] 1 Ch 244 ....573n
Boliden Tara Mines Ltd v Cosgrove [2007] IEHC 60 ....533, 861, 875
Boliden Tara Mines Ltd v Cosgrove [2010] IESC 62....843n, 845n, 858
Bonar Law Memorial Trust v IRC (1933) 49 TLR 220....475n
Bond v Hopkins (1802) 1 Sch & Lef 413 ....802n
Bonham v Blake Lapthorn Linell [2007] WTLR 189....540
Bonice Property Corporation v Oakes [2016] IEHC 461 ....763, 764
Bonnard v Perryman [1891] 2 Ch 269....674–680, 682, 684, 684n
Borwick, Re [1933] Ch 657 504
Boscawen v Bajwa [1996] 1 WLR 328 1014
Bostock's Settlement, Re [1921] 2 Ch 469....24
Bouch v Sproule (1887) 12 App Cas 385 558
Boulter, Re [1922] 1 Ch 75....504
Bourke v Lee [1904] 1 IR 280 ....58n
Bourne v Keane [1919] AC 815....442
Boustany v Pigott (1995) 69 P & CR 298....914
Bowden, Re [1936] Ch 71 136
Bowen v Evans (1844) 6 Ir Eq R 569....56
Bowman v Secular Society Ltd [1917] AC 406....381n, 437n, 477, 478
Boy Scouts of Canada v Doyle (1997) 149 DLR (4th) 22....492, 499, 607n
Boyce v Boyce (1849) 16 Sim 476....99
Boyce v Paddington Borough Council [1903] 1 Ch 109 ....742n
Boyes, Re (1884) 26 Ch D 531 ....116n, 121n, 161n
Boyhan v Tribunal of Inquiry into the Beef Industry [1992] ILRM 545....709, 712
Boyle v An Post [1992] 2 IR 437....710
Boyle v Lee [1992] 1 IR 555 ....795, 796, 796n, 799, 801
Boyle, Re [1947] IR 61 583
Boyse v Rossborough (1857) 6 HLC 1 ....887n
Brabourne v Hough [1981] FSR 79 ....674n, 684
Bracken v Byrne [2006] 1 ILRM 91....935
Bradbury v Taylor [2012] EWCA Civ 1208 967–969
Braddon Towers Ltd v International Stores Ltd [1987] 1 EGLR 209 ....813n
Bradshaw v Jackman (1887) 21 LR Ir 12....391n, 392n, 445n
Bradstock Trustee Services Ltd v Nabarro Nathanson [1995] 1 WLR 1405....541

Brady's Estate, Re [1920] 1 IR 170 273
Bray v Ford [1896] AC 44 ....264, 266, 569n
Brazil v Durant International Corporation [2016] AC 297 ....1007, 1010, 1011
Breadner v Granville-Grossman [2001] Ch 523 529
Breakspear v Ackland [2009] Ch 32 567
Brennan v Irish Pride Bakeries [2015] IEHC 665, [2015] IECA 107 ....710n, 712n, 714n, 733n, 740
Brennan v Moran (1857) 6 Ir Ch R 126 ....1040, 1041
Brent LBC v Davies [2018] EWHC 2214 (Ch) 364n
Brereton v Day [1895] 1 IR 518 ....557n
Brett v Attorney General [1945] IR 526 417
Bridgewater v Leahy (1998) 194 CLR 457 ....915n
Brightlingsea Haven Ltd v Morris [2009] 2 P & CR 11 ....980n
Brigid Foley Ltd v Ellott [1982] RPC 433 ....646n
Brikom Investments Ltd v Carr [1979] QB 467 ....927n, 933n
Brink's Mat Ltd v Elcombe [1988] 1 WLR 1350 ....752–755n
Brinks Ltd v Abu-Saleh (No.3) [1996] CLC 133 ....347n
Brisbane City Council v Attorney-General for Queensland [1979] AC 411 ....470n
Bristol and West Building Society v Mothew [1998] Ch 1 ....260, 261, 263, 265n, 271n, 285n
Bristow v Warde (1794) 2 Ves 336 1028
Britain v Rossiter (1879) 11 QBD 123 ....803n
British Midland Tool Ltd v Midland International Tooling Ltd [2003] 2 BCLC 523 ....288n
British Museum v White (1826) 2 Sim & St 594 ....428n
Brocklehurst's Estate, Re [1978] Ch 14 ....884n
Brogden, Re (1888) 38 Ch D 546 ....537, 538
Bromhead's Trusts, Re [1922] 1 IR 75 ....153n
Brooks' Settlement Trusts, Re [1939] Ch 993 ....136n
Broughton v Snook [1938] Ch 505 ....794n
Brown & Root Technology Ltd v Sun Alliance and London Assurance Co. Ltd [1996] Ch 51 132
Brown v Brown (1993) 31 NSWLR 582 ....212n, 221n
Brown v Gellatly (1867) LR 2 Ch App 751 ....556n
Brown v Gregson [1920] AC 860 ....1029n
Brown v Higgs (1803) 8 Ves 561 ....76n, 77n
Brown v Pourau [1995] 1 NZLR 352 ....115, 116n, 127, 127n
Brown, Re [1898] 1 IR 423 ....399n, 439n
Browne v Associated Newspapers Ltd [2007] EWHC 202 (QB), [2008] QB 289 684
Browne v King (1885) 17 LR Ir 448 416
Browne v Maunsell (1856) 5 Ir Ch R 351 593
Browne v Mulligan [1976-77] ILRM 327 ....840n
Browne, Re [1944] IR 90 121
Brownlee, Re [1990] 3 NZLR 243 ....212n
Brownlie v Campbell (1880) 5 App Cas 925 877
Bryanston Finance Ltd v De Vries (No. 2) [1976] Ch 63 ....688, 688n
Bryce v Fleming [1930] IR 376 ....509, 510, 510n

Buckley v Buckley (1888) 19 LR Ir 544 1032
Buckley v National University Maynooth [2009] IEHC 58 ....710n, 732n
Bucks Constabulary Widows' and Orphans' Fund Friendly Society (No.2), Re [1979] 1 WLR 936 ....46, 165n–169
Bula Ltd v Tara Mines Ltd (No. 2) [1987] IR 95....................74n, 704, 708
Bullard v Bullard [2017] EWHC 3 (Ch)....................862n
Burgess v Rawnsley [1975] Ch 429....................45n
Burke v Independent Colleges Ltd [2010] IEHC 412 ....710n
Burke's Estate, Re (1882) 9 LR Ir 24 65
Burke's Estate, Re [1951] IR 216 505
Burley, Re [1910] 1 Ch 215 ....95n
Burnden Holdings (UK) Ltd v Fielding [2018] 2 WLR 885 296
Burns v Burns [1984] Ch 317 ....236n
Burrell v Burrell [2005] STC 569....................529n
Burrough v Philcox (1840) 5 My & Cr 72....................77, 108n
Burroughs-Fowler, Re [1916] 2 Ch 251 ....85n
Bushnell, Re [1975] 1 WLR 1596 475
Butlin's Settlement Trusts, Re [1976] Ch 251 ....862, 863
Butterworth, Re (1882) 19 Ch D 588....................506n
Buttle v Saunders [1950] 2 All ER 193 ....538, 580n
Byrne v Coyle [2014] IEHC 475 ....696, 697
Byrne v Dublin City Council [2009] IEHC 122 ....41n, 651n
Byrne, Re [1935] IR 782....................393, 396n, 444
Byrne's Estate, Re (1892) 29 LR Ir 250 94

C. plc v P. [2008] Ch 1 ....783n
C. & A. Modes v C. & A. (Waterford) Ltd [1976] IR 198....................717n, 742n
C. v C. [1976] IR 254....................46n, 227
C.C. v Minister for Justice and Equality [2016] 2 IR 680....................665
C.C. v N.C. [2012] IEHC 615....................131
C.D. v W.D. [1997] IEHC 23....................231n
C.F. v J.D.F. [2005] 4 IR 154....................233n, 252n, 929
C.H. Giles & Co. v Morris [1972] 1 WLR 307 ....821, 822
C.R v D.R., High Court 1983 No. 228 Sp (Lynch J) 5 April 1984....................230n
CA Pacific Finance Ltd, Re [2000] 1 BCLC 494....................102n
Caborne, Re [1943] Ch 224 ....504n
Cadbury Ireland Ltd v Kerry Co-operative Creamery Ltd [1982] ILRM 77....................74
Cadogan Petroleum plc v Tolley [2011] EWHC 2286 (Ch) 280n
Cadogan v Kennett (1776) 2 Cowp 432 ....510n
Caffoor v Commissioner of Income Tax, Columbo [1961] AC 584....................435
Cahill v Dublin City University [2007] IEHC 20, [2009] IESC 80.....733n, 735, 739n
Cahill v Irish Motor Traders Association [1966] IR 430....................39, 39n, 629
Cain v Moon [1896] 2 QB 283 ....144n, 149n
Callaghan v Callaghan [1995] SASC 5064 214
Callaghan v Independent News and Media Ltd [2008] NIQB 15 ....686n
Callanan v Geraghty [2008] 1 IR 399....................695
Calverley v Green (1984) 155 CLR 242....................215n, 206n, 225n

Cambridge Nutrition Ltd v British Broadcasting Corporation [1990] 3 All ER 523 ....667n, 692
Cameron, Re [1999] Ch 386 ....213n, 1038n
Camille and Henry Dreyfus Foundation v IRC [1956] AC 39 401
Campbell v Griffin [2001] EWCA Civ 990 ....951n, 958n, 965, 966
Campbell v MGN Ltd [2004] 2 AC 457 ....11n
Campbell, Re (1878) 12 ILTR 163 515
Campden Hill Ltd v Chakrani [2005] EWHC 911 (Ch) 1008n
Campus Oil Ltd v Minister for Industry & Energy (No. 2) [1983] IR 88 ....644, 651n–653n, 654, 660n, 663n, 667–669, 671, 672, 674, 677, 678, 688, 689, 691, 694, 697–699, 708, 709, 712, 713, 720, 724, 758
Canadian Aero Service Ltd v O'Malley (1974) 40 DLR (3d) 371 290
Canadian Oil Works Corporation, Re (1875) 10 Ch App 593 ....285n
Cannon v Hartley [1949] Ch 213 ....153n, 156n
Capcon Holdings plc v Edwards [2007] EWHC 2662 (Ch) 937n
Capita Trust Co. (Channel Islands) Ltd v Chatham Maritime J3 Developments Ltd [2006] EWHC 2596 (Ch) 813n
Capital Radio Productions Ltd v Radio 2000 Ltd Supreme Court 1998 No.128 & 129 26 May 1998 726
Capitanescu v Universal Weld Overlays Inc (1996) 141 DLR (4th) 751 ....775n
Capron v Turks & Caicos Islands [2010] UKPC 2 953
Carbin v Somerville [1933] IR 276 ....878n, 920n
Carl B. Potter Ltd v Mercantile Bank of Canada (1980) 112 DLR (3d) 88....368n
Carl Zeiss Stiftung v Herbert Smith & Co. (No. 2) [1969] 2 Ch 276....345, 375, 376n
Carlton v Goodman [2002] EWCA Civ 545 ....247n
Carly v Farrell [1975] 1 NZLR 356 327
Carne v Long (1860) 2 De GF & J 75 ....454n
Carolan v Jordan [2014] IEHC 678 ....485n
Carpenters Estates Ltd v Davies [1940] Ch 160 819
Carr v Connor (1929) 63 ILTR 185 ....576n, 585n
Carreras Rothmans Ltd v Freeman Matthews Treasure Ltd [1985] Ch 207 174
Carrigaline Community Television Broadcasting Co. Ltd v Minister for Transport Energy and Communications [1994] 2 IR 359 ....628n
Carroll Group Distributors Ltd v G. & J.F. Bourke Ltd [1990] 1 IR 481 ....997n, 1009n, 1011n
Carroll v Carroll [1998] 2 ILRM 218 (HC), [1999] 4 IR 241 (SC)....880n, 883n–886, 909n, 913n, 916n–918n
Carroll v Dublin Bus [2005] 4 IR 184 ....739, 822, 823
Carson, Re [1915] 1 IR 321 ....558n
Carter v Ross High Court (Murphy J) 8 December 2000 ....955, 987
Catt v Tourle (1869) LR 4 Ch App 654 724
Caudron v Air Zaire [1985] IR 716....771n
Caus, Re [1934] Ch 162 442
Cavankee Fishing Co. Ltd v Minister for Communication Marine and Natural Resources [2004] IEHC 43....622n
Cave v Cave (1880) 15 Ch D 639 57
Cave v Mackenzie (1877) 46 LJ Ch 564 ....72n

Cawdron v Merchant Taylors School
[2009] EWHC 1722 (Ch) 415n, 416, 418, 431n
Cawley v Lillis [2012] 1 IR 281 ....209n, 315
Cayne v Global Natural Resources plc
[1984] 1 All ER 225 ....667n, 691, 694n, 695, 697
Celanese Canada Inc v Murray Demolition Corp. (2006) 269 DLR 193 ....779n
Celsteel Ltd v Alton House Holdings Ltd [1986] 1 WLR 512 721
Cenac v Schafer (St Lucia) [2016] UKPC 25 ....199n
Central London Property Trust Ltd v High Trees House Ltd
[1947] 1 KB 130...924, 925
Centrepoint Community Growth Trust v Commissioner of Inland Revenue
[1985] 1 NZLR 673 ....437n
Centrepoint Community Growth Trust, Re [2000] 2 NZLR 325..........................416n
Chaine-Nickson v Bank of Ireland [1976] IR 393 ....562, 563
Challinor v Bellis [2015] EWCA Civ 59 ....169, 172
Chambers v Fahy [1931] IR 17...91
Chan v Leung [2002] EWCA Civ 1075 ....237n, 978n
Chan v Zacharia (1984) 154 CLR 178...264, 265, 275n
Channel Tunnel Group Ltd v Balfour Beatty Construction [1992] QB 656..........704n
Chaplin, Re [1933] Ch 115 462
Chapman v Chapman [1954] AC 429...608n, 609
Chapman v Jaume [2012] EWCA Civ 476 ....206n, 215n
Chapman, Re [1896] 2 Ch 763 577
Chappell v Times Newspapers Ltd [1975] 1 WLR 482.................................25, 626
Chardon, Re [1928] 1 Ch 464 ....387n
Charity Commission for England and Wales v Framjees
[2015] 1 WLR 16 ....92n, 1004n
Charles v Fraser [2010] EWHC 2154 (Ch)...300, 302n
Charleton v Scriven [2019] IESC 28 ....668n, 669n, 704, 714, 715
Charrington v Simons & Co. Ltd [1970] 1 WLR 725 ....722n
Chartbrook Ltd v Persimmon Homes Ltd [2009] 1 AC 1101........848–851, 854, 854n
Charter plc v City Index Ltd [2007] 1 WLR 26...............................365n, 366, 373n
Charter plc v City Index Ltd [2008] Ch 313...374
Chartered Trust Ireland Ltd v Healy High Court Circuit Appeal (Barron J)
10 December 1985..925
Chase Manhattan Bank NA v Israel British Bank (London) Ltd
[1981] Ch 105...333n, 1012, 1013, 1013n
Chater v Mortgage Agency Services Number Two Ltd [2003] EWCA Civ 490...892n
Chattock v Muller (1878) 8 Ch D 117 ....303n
Chaudhary v Yavuz [2013] Ch 249..319n
Cheese v Thomas [1994] 1 WLR 129..25, 892
Cheltenham & Gloucester Building Society v Ricketts
[1993] 1 WLR 1545 ....645n–647
Cherny v Neuman [2009] EWHC 1743 (Ch) 761n
Cheshire Foundation in Ireland v Attorney General [2012] 1 ILRM 369 ....492, 497
Chettiar v Chettiar [1962] AC 294..202n, 219, 219n, 220n
Chevalier-Watts [2015] NZLJ 108...479n
Chichester Diocesan Fund and Board of Finance v Simpson [1944] AC 341.......383n

Chichester v Coventry (1867) LR 2 HL 71 ....1039n
Chieftain Construction Ltd v Ryan [2008] IEHC 147 ....654, 655, 667, 698
Childers v Childers (1857) 1 De G & J 482....................87n
Chillingworth v Chambers [1896] 1 Ch 685....................591n
Christ's Hospital v Grainger (1849) 1 Mac & G 460....................400n
Churchill, Re [1909] 2 Ch 431....................581
CIBC Mortgages plc v Pitt [1994] 1 AC 200....................891, 892, 892n
Cigna Life Insurance New Zealand Ltd v Westpac Securities Ltd
[1996] 1 NZLR 80....................347n
Cincinnati Bengals Inc. v Bergey (1974) 453 F Supp 129 ....728n
Citadel General Assurance Co. v Lloyds Bank Canada
(1997) 152 DLR (4th) 411....................338n, 341n, 347n, 361n, 364, 368
City Equitable Fire Insurance Co, Re [1925] 1 Ch 407....................577
Clancy v Commissioner of Valuation [1911] 2 IR 173....................460n, 463n, 470, 471
Clane Hospital Ltd v VHI [1998] IEHC 78....................652n, 653
Clarion Ltd v National Provident Institution [2000] 1 WLR 1888....................14n, 869n
Clark Boyce v Mouat [1994] 1 AC 428....................263
Clark v Clark [2006] EWHC 275 (Ch)....................937n, 957n
Clark v Cutland [2004] 1 WLR 783....................1000n
Clarke v Meadus [2010] EWHC 3117 (Ch)....................329
Clarke v Ramuz [1891] 2 QB 456 ....310n, 311
Clarke, Re [1901] 2 Ch 110....................393
Claystone Ltd v Larkin [2007] IEHC 89 ....819n
Clayton's case (1816) 1 Mer 572....................1001–1007
Cleaver, Re [1981] 1 WLR 939 ....297, 298
Clemens v Clemens Estate (1956) 1 DLR (2d) 625 ....176n
Clements v Meagher [2008] IEHC 258....................260n, 261
Clibborn v Horan [1921] 1 IR 93....................78
Clinam v Cooke (1802) 1 Sch & Lef 22....................806n
Close Invoice Finance Ltd v Abaowa [2010] EWHC 1920 (QB) 213n
Cloutte v Story [1911] 1 Ch 18....................536n
CMS Dolphin Ltd v Simonet [2001] 2 BCLC 704....................288n, 292
Coalport Building Co. Ltd v Castle Contracts (Ireland) Ltd [2004] IEHC 6 689
Coates v Coates [1898] 1 IR 258....................1033
Cobbe v Yeoman's Row Management Ltd [2005] EWHC 266 (Ch)....................951, 979
Cobbe v Yeoman's Row Management Ltd [2006] 1 WLR 2964 (CA)....................801
Cobbe v Yeoman's Row Management Ltd [2008] 1 WLR 1752 (HL)....................305, 307,
336, 934, 949, 952–954n, 979n, 981–983, 987, 991, 992, 992n
Cochrane, Re [1955] Ch 309 ....162, 162n
Cocks v Manners (1871) LR 12 Eq 574 ....392, 445, 446
Coffey v William Connolly & Sons Ltd [2007] IEHC 319 ....710n, 711, 732n,
733n, 737, 740
Cogley v RTE [2005] 4 IR 79....................677, 677n, 678, 681, 682, 687, 688
Cohen v Roche [1927] 1 KB 169....................809
Cohen, Re [1973] 1 WLR 415 ....411n, 417n
Coles v Trecothick (1804) 9 Ves 234....................574
Collier v Collier [2002] EWCA Civ 1095 ....198n, 201, 202, 221n, 222
Collier, Re [1998] 1 NZLR 81....................475, 475n, 477n, 479, 486n

Collings v Wade [1896] 1 IR 340 ....38n, 594n
Collins (1886) 32 Ch D 229....................609n
Collins v Duffy [2009] IEHC 290....................793, 808
Collins v Gharion [2013] IEHC 316....................764
Collins v Gleeson [2011] IEHC 200....................841n
Colohan v Condrin [1914] 1 IR 89 ....190, 206n
Columbia Picture Industries v Robinson [1987] Ch 38....................775, 778, 779, 785
Combe v Combe [1951] 2 KB 215 ....925, 926, 986n
Combe, Re [1925] Ch 210....................76n
Comiskey v Bowring-Hanbury [1905] AC 84....................48n, 95, 95n
Commerzbank Atkiengesellschaft v IMB Morgan plc
[2004] EWHC 2771 (Ch)....................1004
Commission for the New Towns v Cooper (Great Britain) Ltd [1995] Ch 259 ....854n
Commissioner of Inland Revenue v Medical Council of New Zealand
[1997] 2 NZLR 297....................407, 451n
Commissioner of Valuation v Lurgan Borough Council [1968] NI 104....................470
Commissioner of Valuation v O'Connell [1906] 2 IR 479....................449
Commissioner of Valuation v Trustees of the Redemptorist Order
[1971] NI 114....................447n
Commissioners for Special Purposes of Income Tax v Pemsel
[1891] AC 531....................407, 408, 414, 414n, 450, 456, 460, 462, 473
Commissioners of Charitable Donations and Bequests v McCartan
[1917] 1 IR 388....................445
Commissioners of Charitable Donations and Bequests v Walsh
(1828) 7 Ir Eq R 34....................442
Commonwealth of Australia v Verwayen
(1990) 170 CLR 394....................959–963n, 965, 985, 989, 989n
Commonwealth Reserves I v Chodar [2001] 2 NZLR 374 ....259n, 328, 330n 331, 336
Complete Retreats Liquidating Trust v Logue [2010] EWHC 1864 (Ch)...753n–755n
Compton, Re [1945] Ch 123....................402n, 412, 419, 419n, 425, 430, 432, 435, 436, 452n, 456
Congentra AG v Sixteen Thirteen Marine SA
[2008] EWHC 1615 (Comm)....................755, 761
Conlon v Murray [1958] NI 17....................2, 28, 789, 823n, 833
Conn v Ezair [2019] EWHC 1722 (Ch)....................310n, 314n
Conner, Re [1960] IR 67....................385n, 387
Connolly v Byrne Supreme Court 1997 No. 13 23 January 1997....................652n
Connolly v RTE [1991] 2 IR 446....................677, 680
Conservative and Unionist Central Office v Burrell [1982] 1 WLR 522 ......389, 395n
Consul Development Pty Ltd v DPC Estates Pty Ltd (1975) 132 CLR 373 ....368n
Controller of Patents Designs and Trademarks v Ireland [1998] IEHC 224 701
Cook v Deeks [1916] 1 AC 554....................290
Cook v Thomas [2010] EWCA Civ 227....................933n
Cook's Settlement Trusts, Re [1965] Ch 902....................154, 154n, 155
Coomber, Re [1911] 1 Ch 723....................887n
Coombes v Smith [1986] 1 WLR 808....................944n, 946n
Coope v LCM Ligation Fund Pty Ltd (2016) 333 ALR 524....................263n

Cooper and Allen's Contract for Sale to Harlech, Re (1876) 4 Ch D 802............580n
Cooper v Cooper (1874) LR 7 HL 53 ....1025, 1026n, 1028n
Cooper v Phibbs (1867) LR 2 HL 149...25n, 867
Cooper v PRG Powerhouse Ltd [2008] EWHC 498 (Ch).........................171, 171n
Co-Operative Insurance Co. Ltd v Argyll Stores (Holdings) Ltd
[1998] AC 1 ....789n, 811n, 812, 814–817, 820
Copinger v Crehane (1877) LR 11 Eq 429 439
Corbally v Representative Church Body [1938] IR 35..490n
Corbett v Commissioners of Inland Revenue [1938] 1 KB 567...............................557n
Corcoran, Re [1913] 1 IR 1..440n
Corin v Patton (1990) 169 CLR 540...20
Cork Corporation v Rooney (1881) 17 LR Ir 191 ....618n
Corway v Independent Newspapers (Ireland) Ltd [1999] 4 IR 484 ....438n
Cory v Gertcken (1816) 2 Madd 49...27n
Cosma v Minister for Justice Equality and Law Reform [2007] 2 IR 133 665
Cosmoline Trading Ltd v D.H. Burke & Son Ltd [2006] IEHC 38.........................802n
Cotton Box Design Group Ltd v Earls Construction Co. Ltd [2009] IEHC 312.....689
Coulson and Sons v James Coulson & Co. (1887) 3 TLR 846.......................675, 677
Coulson Sanderson & Ward v Ward [1986] 2 BCLC 99 688
Coulson, Re (1953) 87 ILTR 93...93n–94n
Coulthard v Disco Mix Club Ltd [2000] 1 WLR 707 ....339n
Coulthurst, Re [1951] Ch 661...415
Countess of Shelburne v Earl of Inchiquin (1784) 1 Bro CC 338 ....857n
Countyglen plc v Carway [1995] 1 ILRM 481 ....758, 759n, 769
Courtenay v Radio 2000 Ltd [1997] IEHC 129................................733n, 734, 739n
Courtney v McCarthy [2007] IESC 58 ....923n
Courtney v Rumley (1871) IR 6 Eq 99 571
Cowan de Groot Properties Ltd v Eagle Trust plc [1992] 4 All ER 700 .....344n, 363n
Cowan v Scargill [1985] Ch 270..550, 551, 553, 614
Cowper-Smith v Morgan (2017) 416 DLR (4th) 1 ....934, 973
Cowshed Products Ltd v Island Origins Ltd [2010] EWHC 3357 (Ch)...............698n
Cox v Jones [2004] EWHC 1486 (Ch) 244n
Coyle v Finnegan [2013] IEHC 463 ....26n, 956, 974, 985
Cozens, Re [1913] 2 Ch 478 136
Crabb v Arun District Council [1976] Ch 179.............................1n, 927n, 945, 957,
957n, 958, 981, 985n, 986n
Crabb v Crabb (1834) 1 My & K 511 ....209n
Cradock v Piper (1850) 1 Mac & G 664...571
Crane v Hegeman-Harris Co. Inc [1939] 1 All ER 662...844
Cranmer's Case (1701) 2 Salk 508 ....1032n
Cranston, Re [1898] 1 IR 431 ....457–460, 466, 467
Craven's Estate (No. 1), Re [1937] Ch 423 ....144n, 147n, 149n
Crédit Agricole Corpn and Investment Bank v Papadimitrou
[2015] 1 WLR 4265 366
Credit Counselling Services of Atlantic Canada Inc v Minister of National
Revenue (2016) 401 DLR (4th) 375...417
Credit Lyonnais Bank Nederland NV v Burch
[1997] 1 All ER 144 ....894, 895n, 897n, 913n, 915, 919n

Credit Suisse Asset Management Ltd v Armstrong [1996] ICR 882......................693n
Credit Suisse Fides Trust SA v Cuoghi [1998] QB 818..................................771, 772
Creed v Carey (1857) 7 Ir Ch R 295..1043n
Cresswell v Cresswell (1868) LR 6 Eq 69...447n
Crest Homes Ltd v Ascott [1980] FSR 396 ....676n, 679n
Cretanor Maritime Co. Ltd v Irish Marine Management Ltd
[1978] 1 WLR 966 749
Criminal Assets Bureau v P.S. High Court 1997 No. 38R (Finnegan P)
12 April 2002...629
Criminal Assets Bureau v S.H. High Court 1999 No. 235R (O'Sullivan J)
15 March 2000...751n
Criterion Properties plc v Stratford UK Properties LLC [2003] 1 WLR 2108,
[2004] 1 WLR 1846 ....364, 365n, 366, 373n, 374
Crofton v Crofton (1913) 47 ILTR 24 ....518n
Cronin v Minister for Education and Science [2004] 3 IR 205 ....709, 712
Crossco No. 4 Unlimited v Jolan Ltd [2012] 2 All ER 754.....................305, 307, 983
Crossplan Investments Ltd v McCann [2013] IEHC 205......................................653n
Crotty v An Taoiseach [1987] IR 713 ....702, 703, 745
Crowe v Stevedoring Employees Retirement Fund Pty Ltd [2003] VSC 316.......615n
Crowley v O'Sullivan [1900] 2 IR 478...803
Crown Dilmun v Sutton [2004] 1 BCLC 468 ....290n, 294n, 367n
Crown Melbourne Ltd v Cosmopolitan Hotel (Vic) Pty Ltd
(2016) 333 ALR 384...989n
Crown Prosecution Service v Aquila Advisory Ltd [2019] EWCA Civ 588...........284
Crown Prosecution Service v Piper [2011] EWHC 3570 (Admin) 242n
Crownx Inc v Edwards (1994) 120 DLR (4th) 270 ....92n
Cullen v Attorney General for Ireland (1866) LR 1 HL 190 113
Cullen v Cullen [1962] IR 268..925, 938, 944
Cullen v Stanley [1925] IR 73 680
Culliford v Thorpe [2018] EWHC 426 (Ch)...933n
Cullimore's Trusts, Re (1891) 27 LR Ir 18 422
Cummins v Hall [1933] IR 419 ....160n
Cunnack v Edwards [1896] 2 Ch 679 ....167n
Curley v Parkes [2004] EWCA Civ 1515 ....247n
Curran v Collins [2015] EWCA Civ 404...241n
Currie, Re [1985] NI 299 ....487n, 488n
Curtin v Evans (1872) IR 9 Eq 553 1038
Curtis v Birch (2002) 29 EG 139..299
Curtis v Pulbrook [2011] EWHC 167 (Ch) 133n, 135
Curtis v Rippon (1820) 5 Madd 434 ....98n, 99n
Curust Financial Services Ltd v Loewe-Lack-Werk Otto Loewe GmbH &
Co. KG [1994] 1 IR 450....................................31, 35, 621n–623, 626, 658, 659
Custom House Capital Ltd, Re [2014] 1 ILRM 360...........284, 317, 317n, 325, 334n
Custom House Capital Ltd, Re [2017] IEHC 484 1006
Customs and Excise Commissioners v Anchor Foods Ltd [1999] 1 WLR 1139...748n

D.& F. Partnership Ltd v Horan Keogan Ryan Ltd [2011] IEHC 333....................690
D.T. v C.T. [2002] 3 IR 334 ....235n

D'Altroy's Will Trusts, Re [1968] 1 WLR 120 .... 206n
D'Angibau, Re (1880) 15 Ch D 228 .... 153n
Dadourian Group International Inc v Simms [2006] 1 WLR 2499 .... 767, 768
Dadourian Group International Inc v Simms [2007] EWHC 1673 (Ch) 755n
Dagenham (Thames) Dock Co., Ex p. Hulse, Re (1873) LR 8 Ch App 1022 .... 836n
Dagenham Yank Ltd v Irish Bank Corporation Ltd [2014] IEHC 192 .... 651n
Dakota Packaging Ltd v APH Manufacturing BV [2005] 2 IR 54 .... 813n, 815–817
Dale v IRC [1954] AC 11 570
Dale, Re [1994] Ch 31 302
Daly v Attorney General (1860) 11 ICR 41 .... 488n
Daly v Murphy [2017] IEHC 650 .... 103n, 380n, 399
Daniel v Tee [2016] 4 WLR 115 550
Daniels v Dunne (1990) 8 ILT 35 (Circuit Court, 2 February 1989) 182
Dann v Spurrier (1802) 7 Ves 231 .... 928n, 929n
Danske Bank A/S trading as National Irish Bank plc v Madden
[2009] IEHC 319 .... 881n, 899, 900, 909
Danske Bank A/S v Coyne [2011] IEHC 234 .... 845n
Danske Bank v Gillic [2015] IEHC 375 .... 923n
Danske Bank v Madden [2009] IEHC 319 .... 60n, 62, 63
Daraydan Holdings Ltd v Sollard International Ltd [2005] Ch 119 .... 280n
Darby v Shanley [2009] IEHC 459 909
Darlington Properties Ltd v Meath County Council [2011] IEHC 70 42
Daru Blocklaying Ltd v Building and Allied Trades Union
[2003] 1 ILRM 164 .... 672, 673
Daventry District Council v Daventry & District Housing Ltd
[2012] 1 WLR 1333 .... 848–850, 854, 854n, 855n, 857
Davidson, Re [1909] 1 Ch 567 .... 438, 440, 441n
Davies v Davies [2014] EWCA Civ 568 .... 937n, 969n
Davies v Davies [2015] EWHC 1384 (Ch) 968n
Davies v Davies [2016] EWCA Civ 463 .... 970, 971
Davies v Gas Light & Coke Co. [1909] 1 Ch 248 .... 704n
Davies v Hutchinson [2017] IEHC 693 .... 524n, 525n
Davies v O'Kelly [2015] 1 WLR 2725 .... 197, 198, 249n, 250
Davies v Revenue and Customs Commissioners [2009] WTLR 1151 .... 116n
Davis v Richards and Wallington Ltd [1990] 1 WLR 1511 .... 24n, 49, 83n, 167
Davis, Re [1902] 1 Ch 876 488
Dawson v Small (1874) LR 18 Eq 114 .... 417n
Day v Brownrigg (1878) 10 Ch D 294 .... 618n
Day v Day [2014] Ch 114 862
Day v Harris [2014] Ch 211 .... 141n
Day v Mead [1987] 2 NZLR 443 .... 11n
De Bruyne v De Bruyne [2010] 2 FLR 1240 127
De Burca v Wicklow County Council [2000] IEHC 182 .... 709n
De Carteret, Re [1933] Ch 103 .... 415n
De Visme, Re (1863) 2 De GJ & S 17 .... 212n
De Wind v Wedge [2010] WTLR 795 .... 883n
Dean, Re (1889) 41 Ch D 552 388
Delaforce v Simpson-Cook (2010) 78 NSWLR 483 .... 958n, 962n

Delany's Estate, Re (1882) 9 LR Ir 226....................392, 445n
Delius, Re [1957] Ch 299....................429
Dempsey v Ward [1899] 1 IR 463....................273, 274
Den Norske Bank ASA v Antonatos [1999] QB 271....................748n, 782n
Denison, Re (1974) 42 DLR (3d) 652....................423
Denley's Trust Deed, Re [1969] 1 Ch 373....................381n, 382, 384, 390, 396, 398n
Dennehy v Delany (1876) IR 10 Eq 377....................152n
Denny v Hancock (1870) 6 Ch App 1....................829n
Densham, Re [1975] 1 WLR 1519....................515n
Derby & Co. Ltd v Weldon [1990] Ch 48....................766
Derby & Co. Ltd v Weldon (Nos. 3 & 4) [1990] Ch 65....................761n, 765n, 766, 769
Dering v Earl of Winchelsea (1787) 1 Cox 318....................27, 29, 625n
Deslauriers v Guardian Asset Management Ltd [2017] UKPC 34....................137n
Desmond Murtagh Construction Ltd v Hannon [2011] IEHC 276....................825
Deutsche Bank Atkiengesellschaft v Murtagh [1995] 1 ILRM 381....................747n, 769, 770
Devoy v Hanlon [1929] IR 246....................66n, 136
Dewar v Dewar [1975] 1 WLR 1532....................193n
DHJPM Pty Ltd v Blackthorn Resources Ltd (2011) 285 ALR 311....................954, 985n
DHN Food Distributors Ltd v Tower Hamlets LBC [1976] 1 WLR 852....................318
Dillon v Reilly (1875) IR 10 Eq 152....................384n
Dillwyn v Llewelyn (1862) 4 De GF & J 517....................938, 939, 957n
Dingle v Turner [1972] AC 601....................401n, 402, 402n, 410n, 411n, 419n, 421–424n, 432, 453, 455
Diplock, Re [1948] 1 Ch 465, appeal to the House of Lords sub nom Ministry of Health v Simpson [1951] AC 251....................3, 20, 160n, 993, 994n, 996, 998, 998n, 1002, 1012–1015n
Director of Public Prosecutions v B. [2009] IEHC 196....................205n, 209
Director of Public Prosecutions v E.H. High Court (Kelly J) 22 April 1997....................751n
Director of the Serious Fraud Office v Lexi Holdings plc [2009] QB 376....................999n
Diver v McCrea (1908) 42 ILTR 249....................181
Dixon's Trusts, Re (1869) IR 4 Eq 1....................152n
Dobell v Cowichan Copper Co. Ltd (1967) 65 DLR (2d) 440....................810n
Doe v Manning (1807) 9 East 59....................512n
Doherty v Allman (1878) 3 App Cas 709....................721–723
Doherty v Quigley [2015] IECA 297....................509, 511
Dolan v Reynolds [2011] IEHC 334....................25
Donal Rigney Ltd v Empresa de Construcoes Amandio Carvalho SA [2009] IEHC 572....................690
Donnellan v O'Neill (1870) IR 5 Eq 523....................440
Donnelly v Donnelly [2013] IEHC 532....................557, 558
Donohue v Conrahy (1845) 8 Ir Eq R 679....................86
Doolan v Murray High Court 1990 No. 7753 P, 21 December 1993....................877n
Doran v Thompson [1978] IR 223....................923
Dore v Stephenson High Court (Kenny J) 24 April 1980....................796n
Dormeuil Freres SA v Nicolian International (Textiles) Ltd [1988] 1 WLR 1362....................754n
Doueihi v Construction Technologies Australia Pty Ltd (2016) 333 ALR 151....................954
Dougan v Ley (1946) 71 CLR 142....................809n

Douglas and Powell's Contract, Re [1902] 2 Ch 296 ....1024n
Douglas v Hello! Ltd [2001] QB 967 692
Douglas v Hello! Ltd [2006] QB 125 ....11n
Douglas, Re (1887) 35 Ch D 472....................383n, 388n, 466n
Douglas-Menzies v Umphelby [1908] AC 224 ....1025n
Dowding v Matchmove Ltd [2017] 1 WLR 749....................236n, 978, 982
Dowley v O'Brien [2009] 4 IR 752 ....749–750, 774n
Dowling v Minister for Finance [2013] 4 IR 576 ....630, 700
Downes, Re [1898] 2 IR 635 515
Downey v Minister for Education and Science [2001] 2 IR 727....................621n
Downsview Nominees Ltd v First City Corporation Ltd [1993] AC 295....................13
Doyle v Attorney General, High Court 1993 No. 612 Sp (Carroll J)
22 February 1995....................498
Doyle v Byrne (1922) 56 ILTR 125....................181
Doyle v Grangeford Precast Concrete Ltd [1998] ELR 260....................738n
Doyle, Re (1891) Court of Appeal, unreported....................514n
Doyle, Re High Court, 1972 (Kenny J) 502, 504, 506
Drake v Whipp [1996] 1 FLR 826....................243n
Drexel Burnham Lambert UK Pension Plan, Re [1995] 1 WLR 32....................264, 569n
Drimmie v Davies [1899] 1 IR 176 73
Drive Yourself Hire Co. (London) Ltd v Strutt [1954] 1 QB 250 ....73n
Driver v Yorke [2003] EWHC 746 (Ch)....................976n
Drocarne Ltd v Seamus Murphy Properties and Developments Ltd
[2008] IEHC 99....................841
Drohan v Drohan [1981] ILRM 473....................37
Drummond, Re [1914] 2 Ch 90 ....422n
DSG Retail Ltd v PC World Ltd [1998] IEHC 3 ....652n, 660
Dubai Aluminium Co. Ltd v Salaam [1999] 1 Lloyd's Rep 415 ....364n
Dubai Aluminium Co. Ltd v Salaam [2001] QB 113 (CA),
[2003] 2 AC 366 (HL)....................340, 373n, 376, 377, 378
Dublin Airport Authority plc v Services Industrial Professional Technical Union
[2014] IEHC 644....................672n, 674
Dublin City Council v Technical Engineering and Electrical Union
[2010] IEHC 288....................673
Dublin Corporation v Ancient Guild of Incorporated Brick and Stone Layers and
Allied Trades Union, High Court 1991 No. 1556P (Budd J) 6 March 1996;
Sub nom Dublin Corporation v Building and Allied Trade Union
[1996] 1 IR 468 ....319n, 322, 322n, 333, 373n, 1012n
Dublin Port and Docks Board v Britannia Dredging Co. Ltd
[1968] IR 136 722–724
Duckworth v Lee [1899] 1 IR 405....................151n
Duddy v Gresham (1878) 2 LR Ir 442....................502n, 503n, 504n
Duffield v Elwes (1827) 1 Bli 497 ....150n
Duffield v McMaster [1896] 1 IR 370 ....1021n
Duffy v Ridley Properties Ltd [2005] IEHC 314, upheld by Supreme Court at
[2008] 4 IR 282 ....792, 792n, 794n, 808n, 839
Duffy's Estate, Re [2013] EWHC 2395 (Ch)....................454n
Dufour v Pereira (1769) 1 Dick 419 ....297n

Duggan v Allied Irish Building Society High Court 1974 No. 2302P (Finlay P) 4 March 1976.....791, 793n
Duke of Marlborough, Re [1894] 2 Ch 133.....88
Duke of Norfolk's Settlement Trusts, Re [1982] Ch 61.....570
Dullow v Dullow (1985) 3 NSWLR 531.....212n, 221n
Dully v Athlone Town Stadium Ltd [2018] IEHC 209.....522
Dun Laoghaire Rathdown County Council v Shackleton [2002] IEHC 2.....636
Dunbar Bank plc v Nadeem [1998] 3 All ER 876.....892
Dunbar v Dunbar [1909] 2 Ch 639.....206n
Duncuft v Albrecht (1841) 12 Sim 189.....810
Dundee General Hospitals Board of Management v Walker [1952] 1 All ER 896.....536n
Dunlop Pneumatic Tyre Co. Ltd v Selfridge & Co. Ltd [1915] AC 847.....73n
Dunlop, Re [1984] NI 408.....411n, 416n, 423, 453, 455, 461, 461n
Dunne v Byrne [1912] AC 407.....441
Dunne v Duignan [1908] 1 IR 228.....439n
Dunne v Dun Laoghaire-Rathdown County Council [2003] 2 ILRM 147.....652n
Dunne v Dunne [2016] IECA 269.....525
Dunne v Heffernan [1997] 3 IR 431.....524, 525
Dunne v Molloy [1976-77] ILRM 266.....927n, 944n
Dunwoodie, Re [1977] NI 141.....484, 490
Durham Fancy Goods Ltd v Michael Jackson (Fancy Goods) Ltd [1968] 2 QB 839.....924n
DV Bryant Trust Board v Hamilton City Council [1997] 3 NZLR 342.....415n, 423n, 461n
Dyer v Dyer (1788) 2 Cox Eq Cas 92.....191, 192n

E. & L. Berg Homes Ltd v Grey (1979) 253 EG 473.....944n
E.B. v S.S. [1998] 2 ILRM 141.....47
E.N. v R.N. [1990] 1 IR 383 (HC).....234
E.N. v R.N. [1992] 2 IR 116 (SC).....224n, 226n
Eagle Trust plc v SBC Securities Ltd [1993] 1 WLR 484.....346, 363, 365n, 371n
Eaglewood Properties Ltd v Patel [2005] 1 WLR 1961.....311n
Eardley's Will, Re [1920] 1 Ch 397.....1038n
Earl of Chesterfield's Trusts, Re (1883) 24 Ch D 643.....556
Earl of Oxford's Case (1615) 1 Rep Ch 1.....7, 617
Earley v Health Service Executive [2015] IEHC 520.....710n, 732, 732n
East Cork Foods Ltd v O'Dwyer Steel Co. Ltd [1978] IR 103.....332, 334
Eastern Health Board v Commissioners for Charitable Donations and Bequests High Court 1991 No. 207 Sp (Denham J) 17 December 1991.....403
Eastern Services Ltd v No 68 Ltd [2006] 3 NZLR 335.....44n, 834
Easy Loan Corp. v Wiseman (2017) 412 DLR (4th) 155.....1007n
Eaton v Daines [1894] WN 32.....81n
Edge v Pensions Ombudsman [1998] Ch 512, [2000] Ch 602.....263n, 528n, 535n, 536
Edgeworth v Johnston (1877) IR 11 Eq 326.....1039n
Edlington Properties Ltd v J.H. Fenner & Co. Ltd [2006] 1 WLR 1583.....3n, 20
Educational Co. of Ireland Ltd v Fitzpatrick [1961] IR 323.....650n

Edwards, Re [1958] Ch 168....................1028
Edwards, Re [2007] EWHC 1119 (Ch)....................888
Egan, Re [1906] 1 IR 320....................273n
Egerton v Earl Brownlow (1853) HLC 1....................83n
Eichholz, Re [1959] Ch 708....................507n
Eighmie, Re [1935] Ch 524....................387n, 448n
Eircell Ltd v Bernstoff High Court 1999 No. 10182P (Barr J)
18 February 2000....................627
El Ajou v Dollar Holdings plc [1993] 3 All ER 717....................371n
El Ajou v Dollar Land Holdings plc [1995] 2 All ER 213....................1003
Elders Pastoral Ltd v Bank of New Zealand [1989] 2 NZLR 180....................18n, 1014
Elias v George Sahely & Co. (Barbados) Ltd [1983] 1 AC 646....................87n
Ellard v Phelan [1914] 1 IR 76....................1033
Ellingsen (Trustee of) v Hallmark Ford Sales Ltd (2000) 190 DLR (4th) 47....................326n
Elliot v Stamp High Court (Murphy J) 7 November 2006....................884n
Elliott, Re (1910) 102 LT 528....................461n
Ellis, Re (1919) 53 ILTR 6....................120n
Ellison v Ellison (1802) 6 Ves 656....................129
Emery's Investment Trusts, Re [1959] Ch 410....................219
EMI Ltd v Pandit [1975] 1 WLR 302....................776n
Emo Oil Ltd v Oil Rig Supplies Ltd [2017] IEHC 594....................660n
Endacott, Re [1960] Ch 232....................103n, 380n, 381, 381n, 387, 396, 396n
Energy Venture Partners Ltd v Malabu Oil and Gas Ltd [2015] 1 WLR 2309....................774
England's Settlement Trusts, Re [1918] 1 Ch 24....................539n
English PEN's Application for Registration as a Charity [2008] WTLR 1799....................480n
Equiticorp Industries Group Ltd v Hawkins [1991] 3 NZLR 700....................18, 367n
Equiticorp Industries Group Ltd v The Crown
[1998] 2 NZLR 481....................35n, 347n, 367, 373n
ER Ives Investment Ltd v High [1967] 2 QB 379....................957n
Erceg v Erceg [2016] 2 NZLR 622....................565, 568
Erlanger v New Sombrero Phosphate Co. (1878) 3 App Cas 1218....................36n, 866, 920
ESB v Roddy [2010] IEHC 158....................712n
Esso Petroleum Co. (Ireland) Ltd v Fogarty [1965] IR 531....................650, 650n
Estuary Logistics & Distribution Co. Ltd v Lowenergy Solutions Ltd
[2008] 2 IR 806....................645n, 647
European Dynamics SA v HM Treasury [2009] EWHC 3419 (TCC)....................651n, 664n
European Paint Importers Ltd v O'Callaghan [2005] IEHC 280....................623
Evans v IRFB Services (Ireland) Ltd [2005] 2 ILRM 358....................656n, 731n, 741n
Evans, Re [1999] 2 All ER 777....................561
Eves v Eves [1975] 1 WLR 1338....................237n, 318
EVTR, Re [1987] BCLC 646....................171
Ewing v Orr Ewing (No.1) (1883) 9 App Cas 34....................51
Ex p Belchier (1754) Amb 218....................576n
Ex parte James (1803) 8 Ves 337....................265n
Ex parte Lacey (1802) 6 Ves 625....................265n, 572n
Experience Hendrix LLC v PPX Enterprises Inc
[2002] EWHC 1353 (QB)....................43n, 44n
Experience Hendrix LLC v PPX Enterprises Inc [2003] FSR 46....................642, 643

Eykyn's Trusts, Re (1877) 6 Ch D 115 ....206, 225n
Eyre v Dolphin (1813) 2 Ba & B 290 ....65n

F. v F. [1994] 2 ILRM 401 (HC) 224n
F. v Ireland [1995] 2 ILRM 321 (SC) 224n
F.C. Jones & Sons (Trustees) v Jones [1997] Ch 159 994
F.McK. v D.C [2006] IEHC 185 ....754n, 756n
Falcke v Gray (1859) 4 Drew 651 ....809n
Falcon Travel Ltd v Owners Abroad Group plc [1991] 1 IR 175 640
Fanning v University College Cork [2002] IEHC 85 30
Farah Construction Pty Ltd v Say-Dee Pty Ltd
(2007) 230 CLR 89 ....343n, 344n, 368n, 374
Farley v Westminster Bank [1939] AC 430 441
Farquharson v Cave (1846) 2 Coll 356 149
Farrant v Blanchford (1863) 1 De G J & Sm 107 594
Farrar v Miller [2018] EWCA Civ 172 ....307, 928n, 951n, 980
Fastwell Ltd v OCL Capital plc [2018] IEHC 39 ....855n
Fearon v Fearon (1852) 3 Ir Ch R 19 ....1029n
Federal Commerce & Navigation Co. Ltd v Molena Alpha Inc [1978] QB 927 ....12n
Feeney v MacManus [1937] IR 23 ....46, 168, 169
Felan v Russell (1842) 4 Ir Eq R 701 499
Fellowes & Son v Fisher [1976] QB 122 ....644, 652n
Femis-Bank (Anguilla) Ltd v Lazar [1991] Ch 391 ....679n, 683
Fennelly v Anderson (1851) 1 Ir Ch R 706 ....824n
Fennelly v Assicurazioni Generali SPA. High Court 12 March 1985 ....733, 737–739
Fenwick v Naera [2016] 1 NZLR 354 ....572, 572n
Ferguson v Merchant Banking Ltd [1993] ILRM 136 ....828, 846, 871
Ferguson v Wilson (1866) 2 Ch App 77 ....791n
Ferguson, Re (1915) 49 ILTR 110 581
Ferguson's Estate, Re (2018) 424 DLR (4th) 547 ....184n
Fermoy Fish Ltd v Canestar Ltd [2015] IESC 93 ....260n, 261n
Ferris v Ward [1998] 2 IR 194 ....651n
Ffrench, Re [1941] IR 49 ....488n
Ffrench's Estate, Re (1887) 21 LR Ir 283 ....57, 1015n
Ffrench-O'Carroll v Ffrench-O'Carroll [2006] IEHC 220 ....884n
FHR European Ventures LLP v Cedar Capital Partners LLC
[2015] AC 250 ....51, 54, 281–285, 287n, 328n, 331
FHR European Ventures LLP v Mankarious [2016] EWHC 359 (Ch) 1002n
Field Common Ltd v Elmbridge BC [2009] 1 P & CR 1 ....643n
Fielden v Christie-Miller [2015] EWHC 87 (Ch) 932
Fielden v Cox (1906) 22 TLR 411 ....742n
Figgis, Re [1969] 1 Ch 123 ....185, 190n
Films Rover International Ltd v Cannon Film Sales Ltd
[1987] 1 WLR 670 ....706–708, 712, 715
Filshie, Re [1939] NZLR 91 ....385n
Financial Services Authority v Sinaloa Gold plc [2013] 2 AC 28 649
Finegan's Estate, Re [1925] 1 IR 201 1043
Fineland Investments Ltd v Pritchard [2011] EWHC 113 (Ch) 914n

Finnegan v Hand [2016] IEHC 255 ....984, 985
Finnerty, Re [1970] IR 221 ....93n
Fiona Trust Holding Corporation v Privalov
[2007] EWHC 1217 (Comm) 748n, 757n
First City Monument Bank plc v Zumax Nigeria Ltd [2019] EWCA Civ 29....91n
First Commercial Bank plc v Anglin [1996] 1 IR 75....899n
First National Bank plc v Thompson [1996] Ch 231....990
Firstpost Homes Ltd v Johnson [1995] 1 WLR 1567 ....807n
Fishenden v Higgs & Hill Ltd (1935) 153 LT 128....638, 704
Fisher v Brooker [2009] 1 WLR 1764....44, 937n
Fisher v Mansfield [1997] 2 NZLR 230 ....298n
Fisher, Re [1943] Ch 377....554n
Fitzgerald v Fitzgerald [1902] 1 IR 477 862
Fitzgerald's Estate, Re (1957) 92 ILTR 192 ....488n
Fitzgibbon, Re (1959) 93 ILTR 56....93n
Fitzpatrick v Criminal Assets Bureau [2000] 1 IR 217....215
Fitzpatrick v Garda Commissioner [1996] IEHC 24 ....622n
Fitzpatrick v Minister for Agriculture Food and the Marine
[2018] IEHC 77 ....700n, 703, 714
Flanagan v Crosby [2014] IEHC 59 ....15, 16, 21n
Flanagan v Forde High Court (Feeney J) 6 March 2009 ....792n
Fleetwood, Re (1880) 15 Ch D 594....121n
Fleming v Ranks (Ireland) Ltd [1983] ILRM 541 ....751n, 757, 759
Fletcher v Ashburner (1779) 1 Bro CC 497....1018
Fletcher v Eden Refuge Trust [2012] 2 NZLR 227 356
Fletcher v Fletcher (1844) 4 Hare 67....154, 155
Fletcher v Green (1864) 33 Beav 426....589n
Flight v Bolland (1828) 4 Russ 298....824
Flinn, Re [1948] Ch 241 ....440n
Flood v Flood [1999] 2 IR 234 524
Flowermix Ltd v Site Development (Ferndown) Ltd Chancery Divison
(Arden J) 11 April 2000....958n
Foley v Sunday Newspapers Ltd [2005] 1 IR 88....684–686, 688
Foord, Re [1922] 2 Ch 519 162
Forbes v Deniston (1722) 4 Bro PC 189....65
Forde v Birmingham City Council [2009] 1 WLR 2732 ....883n
Foreman v Kingstone [2004] 1 NZLR 841, [2005] WTLR 823 567
Forster v Hale (1798) 3 Ves 696 ....86n, 87n
Fortex Group Ltd v MacIntosh [1998] 3 NZLR 171 ....258, 328, 330, 333n
Foskett v McKeown [1998] Ch 265....1009, 1011n
Foskett v McKeown [2001] 1 AC 102....360, 995–997, 999, 1000, 1000n, 1014
Fossitt's Estate, Re [1934] IR 504 385
Foster Bryant Surveying Ltd v Bryant [2007] BCC 804 293
Foster v Spencer [1996] 2 All ER 672....571
Fountain Forestry Ltd v Edwards [1975] Ch 1 ....81n
Fourie v Le Roux [2007] 1 WLR 320....747, 748, 753n, 774
Foveaux, Re [1895] 2 Ch 501 ....458n, 468
Fowkes v Pascoe (1875) 10 Ch App 343 ....193, 1034n

Fowler v Fowler (1859) 4 De G & J 250 857
Fox v Fox (1863) 15 Ir Ch R 89 ....217n
Francome v Mirror Group Newspapers Ltd [1984] 1 WLR 892 683
Fraser v Evans [1969] 1 QB 349....................674n, 679n, 683
Fraser v Great Gas Petroleum Ireland Ltd [2012] IEHC 523 ....627n
Frawley v Neill [1999] EWCA Civ 875 ....43n, 835
Frederick E. Rose (London) Ltd v William H. Pim Junior & Co. Ltd [1953] 2 QB 450....................844, 851
Frederick Inns Ltd, Re [1994] 1 ILRM 387....................368–371, 374
Freedman v Freedman [2015] EWHC 1457 (Ch)....................534n
Freeland, Re [1952] Ch 110....................142n
French v French [1902] 1 IR 172....................113n, 115
French v Graham (1860) 10 Ir Ch R 522....................27n, 591
Freney v Freney [2008] IEHC 330 ....619n
Fresh 'N'Clean (Wales) Ltd v Miah [2006] EWHC 903 (Ch)....................354n
Freud, Re [2014] EWHC 2577 (Ch)....................123
Friends of the Irish Environment Ltd v Minister for Communications Climate Action and Environment [2019] IEHC 555....................700n
Fry v Densham- Smith [2010] EWCA Civ 1410....................299n
Fry v Fry (1859) 27 Beav 144....................586
Fry v Tapson (1884) 28 Ch D 268 ....576n, 577
Fry, Re [1946] Ch 312 132
Fulton v Gunn (2008) 296 DLR 1....................211n
Funnell v Stewart [1996] 1 WLR 288....................407n, 462
Furey v Lurganville Construction Co. Ltd [2012] IESC 38 925
Furs Ltd v Tomkies (1936) 54 CLR 583....................291n
Futter v Futter [2010] EWHC 449 (Ch)....................530, 532
Fyffes Group Ltd v Templeman [2000] 2 Lloyd's Rep 643....................340n, 357n
Fyffes plc v DCC plc [2009] 2 IR 417....................295, 370

G. & T. Crampton Ltd v Building and Allied Trades Union [1998] 1 ILRM 430....................671
G.R v N.R. [2015] IEHC 856 ....224n
Gabbett v Lawder (1883) 11 LR Ir 295 ....264, 271, 272, 274–276
Gafford v Graham (1998) 77 P & CR 73 ....39, 43, 629, 631n, 633, 633n, 639
Gahan v Boland High Court 1981 No. 4995P (Murphy J) 21 January 1983 and Supreme Court 1983 No. 37, 20 January 1984....................877
Gall v Mitchell (1924) 35 CLR 222....................833n
Gallagher v Tuohy (1924) 58 ILTR 134 680
Gallarotti v Sebastianelli [2012] EWCA Civ 865....................242
Galvin v Devereux [1903] 1 IR 185 1027
Gandy v Gandy (1885) 30 Ch D 57....................74
Gany Holdings (PTC) SA v Khan [2018] UKPC 21 ....175n
Garden Cottage Foods Ltd v Milk Marketing Board [1984] AC 130....................663
Gardiner v Gardiner (1861) 12 ICLR 565 512
Gardiner v Westpac New Zealand Ltd [2015] 3 NZLR 1....................912
Gardner, Re [1923] 2 Ch 230....................114n
Gardom, Re [1914] 1 Ch 662....................415

Gare, Re [1952] Ch 80 ....447n
Garner v Holmes (1858) 8 Ir Ch R 469 ....1032n
Garrahy v Bord na gCon [2002] 3 IR 566 ....720, 741n
Garrard, Re [1907] 1 Ch 382 440
Garth v Meyrick (1779) 1 Bro CC 30....1040n
Gascoigne v Gascoigne [1918] 1 KB 223....29n, 219, 220, 625n
Gaudiya Mission v Brahmachary [1997] 4 All ER 957....398n
GE Capital Woodchester Home Loans Ltd v Reade [2012] IEHC 363....902n
Geary v Rankine [2012] EWCA Civ 555 242
Geary's Trusts, Re (1890) 25 LR Ir 171 490
Geddis v Semple [1903] 1 IR 73....117, 118
Gee v Gee [2018] EWHC 1393 (Ch)....928n, 970n
Gee v Pritchard (1818) 2 Swans 402 8
Gee, Re [1948] Ch 284 ....570n
General Communications Ltd v DFC New Zealand Ltd [1990] 3 NZLR 406....171n
Generator Developments Ltd v Lidl UK GmbH [2018] EWCA Civ 396....306, 307
Geoghegan v Connolly (1859) 8 Ir Ch R 598....827
Geologists Association v IRC (1928) 14 TC 271 429
George Drexler Ofrex Foundation Trustees v IRC [1966] Ch 673....412n
George Wimpey UK Ltd v VI Construction Ltd [2005] EWCA Civ 77....854, 858n
Gestetner Settlement, Re [1953] Ch 672 ....80n, 104
Geys v Société Générale [2013] 1 AC 523 725
Ghost v Waller (1846) 9 Beav 497....594n
Gibb v Promontoria (Aran) Ltd [2018] IECA 95....653n
Gibbard's Settlement Trusts, Re [1967] 1 WLR 42....104n
Gibbon v Mitchell [1990] 1 WLR 1304....872, 875, 876
Gibbons v Doherty [2013] IEHC 109....839n
Gibbons, Re [1917] 1 IR 448....381, 381n, 383, 443n
Giblin v Irish Life and Permanent plc [2010] IEHC 36....733n, 737
Gibson v Representative Church Body (1881) 9 LR Ir 1 440
Gibson v Revenue & Customs Prosecution Office [2009] QB 348....205n, 206n
Gibson v South American Stores (Gath & Chaves) Ltd
[1950] Ch 177....411n, 419n, 421n
Gilead Sciences Inc v Mylan SAS Generics (UK) Ltd [2017] IEHC 666....622n, 661
Gill v Woodall [2009] EWHC 834 (Ch) 887n, 929–932, 937n
Gillett v Holt [1998] 3 All ER 917 (ChD), [2001] Ch 210 (CA)....26n, 928, 930, 933n, 935n–937, 947, 947n, 952n, 956–958, 963, 971, 982n
Gillies v Keogh [1989] 2 NZLR 327 ....255n, 328n
Gillingham Bus Disaster Fund, Re [1958] Ch 300....164, 165
Gilmour v Coats [1949] AC 426....409n, 411n, 437n, 442, 446, 447
Gilmurray v Corr [1978] NI 99....23n, 89, 112n
Gilpin v Legg [2017] EWHC 3220 (Ch) 928n
Gilroy v O'Leary [2019] IEHC 52....687
Gilvarry v Maher [2014] IEHC 694....188
Gisborne v Gisborne (1877) 2 App Cas 300....599
Gissing v Gissing [1969] 2 Ch 85 (CA)....236, 238n, 240
Gissing v Gissing [1971] AC 886 (HL) 247n, 975, 982n
Giumelli v Giumelli (1999) 196 CLR 101....336n, 962, 985n, 989

GKN Bolts & Nuts Ltd (Automotive Division) Birmingham Works, Sports and Social Club, Re [1982] 1 WLR 774 ....46n, 167
Gleeson v Attorney General High Court 1972 No. 2664 Sp (Kenny J) 6 April 1973 ....455n, 461n, 463
Gleeson v Feehan [1993] 2 IR 113 37
Glegg v Bromley [1912] 3 KB 474 ....512n
Glenko Enterprises Ltd v Ernie Keller Contractors Ltd (1996) 134 DLR (4th) 161 ....368n
Globe Entertainment Ltd v Pub Pool Ltd [2016] IECA 272 ....795n, 797
Glyn's Will Trusts, Re [1950] 2 All ER 1150 461
Godley v Power (1961) 95 ILTR 135 ....798n
Golay's Will Trusts, Re [1965] 1 WLR 969 99
Gold v Hill [1999] 1 FLR 54 ....109, 123n
Gold v Rosenberg (1995) 129 DLR (4th) 152 591
Gold v Rosenberg (1997) 152 DLR (4th) 385 ....341n, 347n, 361n, 368
Goldcorp Exchange Ltd, Re [1995] 1 AC 74 ....99–101n, 268, 1008n
Goldschmidt, Re [1957] 1 WLR 524 ....488n
Goldsoll v Goldman [1915] 1 Ch 292 ....837n
Gonin, Re [1979] Ch 16 ....142n, 143n
Gonthier v Orange Contract Scaffolding Ltd [2003] EWCA Civ 873 35
Gooch, Re (1890) 62 LT 384 ....204n, 216
Good Shepherd Nuns v Commissioner of Valuation [1930] IR 646 ....449n
Goodchild v Bradbury [2007] WTLR 463 ....883n
Goodchild, Re [1996] 1 WLR 694 (ChD), [1997] 1 WLR 1216 (CA) 298, 301, 302
Goode Concrete v Cement Roadstone Holdings plc [2011] IEHC 15 ....622n, 658n
Goodier v Edmunds [1893] 3 Ch 455 1019
Goodinson v Goodinson [1954] 2 QB 118 ....837n
Gorbunova v Estate of Berezovsky [2016] EWHC 1829 (Ch) 140n
Gosling, Re (1900) 48 WR 421n
Goulding v James [1997] 2 All ER 239 ....609n, 612n
Gouriet v Union of Post Office Workers [1978] AC 435 ....618n, 745
Governors of Erasmus Smith's Schools v Attorney General (1931) 66 ILTR 57 483
Governors of Royal Victoria Hospital v Commissioner of Valuation (1939) 73 ILTR 236 ....463n
Graf v Hope Building Corporation (1930) 254 NY 1 ....22n
Graham v McCashin [1901] 1 IR 404 ....572n
Graham-York v York [2015] EWCA Civ 72 246
Grangeside Properties Ltd v Collingswood Securities Ltd [1964] 1 WLR 140 ....48n
Grant v Dawkins [1973] 3 All ER 897 ....793n
Grant v Edwards [1986] Ch 638 ....46n, 237, 975
Grant's Will Trusts, Re [1980] 1 WLR 360 ....395n
Gray v Gray (1860) 11 Ir Ch R 218 ....93n
Gray, Re [1925] Ch 362 469
Grealish v Murphy [1946] IR 35 ....913, 916, 917, 919n
Greasley v Cooke [1980] 1 WLR 1306 ....933n, 957n
Great Peace Shipping Ltd v Tsavliris Salvage (International) Ltd [2003] QB 679 ....867, 869, 870
Green v Cobham [2002] STC 820 529

Green v Russell [1959] 2 QB 226..........70n, 74n
Green's Will Trusts, Re [1985] 3 All ER 455..........467n, 559, 560
Greenband Investments v Bruton [2009] IEHC 67..........799n
Greene v Associated Newspapers Ltd [2005] QB 972..........674n, 676n, 679, 681, 682, 683
Greene v Coady [2015] 1 IR 385..........266, 271, 516, 534, 536, 569, 585, 599, 602
Greene, Re [1914] 1 IR 305..........448
Greenpeace of New Zealand Inc, Re [2015] 1 NZLR 169..........476, 479
Greenwood v Lutman [1915] 1 IR 266..........152n
Greer, Re (1877) IR 11 Eq 502..........152
Gregg v Kidd [1956] IR 183..........883, 883n, 884n, 909n
Gresham's Settlement, Re [1956] 1 WLR 573..........104n
Grey v Grey (1677) 2 Swans 594..........216n
Grey v IRC [1960] AC 1..........90n
Griffith v Bourke (1887) 21 LR Ir 92..........1039
Griffith v Ricketts (1849) 7 Hare 299..........1023n
Grimaldi v Chameleon Mining NL (2012) 287 ALR 22..........368, 368n
Grimes, Re [1937] IR 470..........213
Grimond v Grimond [1905] AC 124..........438n
Grist v Bailey [1967] Ch 532..........868
Groom, Re (1977) 16 ALR 278..........171n
Group 4 Securitas (Northern Ireland) Ltd v McIldowney [1997] NIJB 23..........779
Grove-Grady, Re [1929] 1 Ch 557..........458, 466, 468
Grundt v Great Boulder Proprietary Gold Mines Ltd (1937) 59 CLR 641..........961, 989
Grupo Torras SA v Al-Sabah (No. 8) [2004] WTLR 1..........96n
Grupo Torras SA v Al-Sabah (No. 5) [2001] CLC 221..........357
Grupo Torras SA v Sheikh Fahad Mohammad Al-Sabah 16 [2014] 2 CLC 636..........770
Guerin v Heffernan [1925] 1 IR 57..........834
Guest v Guest [2019] EWHC 869 (Ch)..........928n, 929
Guild v IRC [1992] 2 AC 310..........472
Guinness plc v Saunders [1990] 2 AC 663..........292
Gujra v Roath [2018] 1 WLR 3208..........199n
Gulbenkian's Settlement, Re [1970] AC 508..........80n, 104–107
Gulf Oil (Great Britain) Ltd v Page [1987] Ch 327..........683, 684
Gun v McCarthy (1883) 13 LR Ir 304..........866
Gurry v Goff [1980] ILRM 103..........477n
Gustav & Co. Ltd v Macfield Ltd [2008] 2 NZLR 735..........915

Habana Ltd v Kaupthing Singer & Friedlander (Isle of Man) Ltd (2009-10) 12 ITELR 736..........173
Habberfield v Habberfield [2018] EWHC 317 (Ch)..........931n, 932n, 970n, 971, 971n
Habib Bank Ltd v Habib Bank AG Zurich [1981] 1 WLR 1265..........39, 629
Hadden, Re [1932] 1 Ch 133..........470n
Hagger, Re [1930] 2 Ch 190..........301
Haines, Re The Times, 7 November 1952..........389n
Hall, Re [1899] 1 IR 308..........76n, 78n
Hallett's Estate, Re (1880) 13 Ch D 696..........3n, 995n, 997, 1002, 1011
Hallmark Cards Inc. v Image Arts Ltd [1977] FSR 150..........777

Hallows v Lloyd (1888) 39 Ch D 686 526
Halpern v Halpern [2008] QB 195....................879n
Halpin v Hannon (1947) 82 ILTR 74....................440, 440n
Halpin v Tara Mines Ltd [1976-77] ILRM 28....................640
Hamilton v Jackson (1845) 8 Ir Eq R 195....................1027
Hamilton, Re [1895] 2 Ch 370....................93n–95n
Hamilton-Snowball's Conveyance, Re [1959] Ch 308....................312n
Hammond v Mitchell [1991] 1 WLR 1127....................46, 237n
Hammond v Osborn [2002] EWCA Civ 887....................883n, 884n
Hampstead & Suburban Properties Ltd v Diomedous [1969] 1 Ch 248....................722
Hampton v Minns [2002] 1 WLR 1....................38n
Hanchett-Stamford v Attorney-General [2009] Ch 173....................167, 395, 468, 480
Handcock's Trusts, Re (1888) 23 LR Ir 34....................1029n
Hanlon, Re [1933] Ch 254....................503n
Hannon v BQ Investments [2009] IEHC 191....................818n, 840
Hansard v Hansard [2015] 2 NZLR 158....................355n, 973n
Harari's Settlement Trusts, Re [1949] 1 All ER 430....................543
Hardiman v Lawrence Circuit Court 18 December 2002....................937
Harding, Re [2008] Ch 235....................110, 465
Hardy v Hoade [2017] EWHC 2476 (Ch)....................169
Harkins v Shannon Foynes Port Company [2001] ELR 75....................741
Harlequin Property (SVG) Ltd v O'Halloran [2013] IEHC 362....................332n, 172, 370
Harman v Richards (1852) 10 Hare 81....................510
Harnett v Yielding (1805) 2 Sch & Lef 549....................792n
Harries v Church Commissioners [1992] 1 WLR 1241....................552, 553
Harrington v Gulland Property Finance Ltd [2016] IEHC 447....................660n
Harris v Digital Pulse Pty Ltd [2003] NSWCA 10....................18n
Harris v Kent [2007] EWHC 463 (Ch)....................587n, 589n, 947n
Harris v Lord Shuttleworth [1994] ICR 991....................536n
Harris v Swordy High Court 1960 No 71 Sp (Henchy J) 21 December 1967....................879n
Harris v Williams-Wynne [2006] 2 P & CR 27....................44, 44n, 631n, 633n
Harris, Re [1907] 1 IR 32....................554
Harris, Re [1909] 2 Ch 206....................1027n
Harrison v Harrison [2013] VSCA 170....................962n
Hart v McDougall [1912] 1 IR 62....................1024n
Hart v O'Connor [1985] AC 1000....................914
Harte v Kelly [1997] ELR 125....................733n, 736n, 738
Hartigan Nominees Pty Ltd v Rydge (1992) 29 NSWLR 405....................568
Hartlepool Gas & Water Co. v West Hartlepool Harbour & Rly Co. (1865) 12 LT 366....................634n
Hartnett v Advance Tyre Co. Ltd [2013] IEHC 615....................734n
Harwood, Re [1936] Ch 285....................489
Hashem v Shayif [2008] EWHC 2380 (Fam)....................210n
Haslemere Estates Ltd v Baker [1982] 1 WLR 1109....................976n
Hastings-Bass, Re [1975] Ch 25....................528–535, 875
Haughan v Rutledge [1988] IR 295....................941
Havbell Designated Activity Company v Dias [2018] IEHC 175....................660n
Haverty v Brooks [1970] IR 214....................913n, 917

Hawe, Re (1955) 93 ILTR 175 ....448n
Hawkins v Blewitt (1798) 2 Esp 663 ....148n
Hawkins, Re [1924] 2 Ch 47 ....150n
Hawley v Rangitikei District Council [2007] NZHC 1343 ....990n
Hay v Murdoch [1952] WN 145 492
Hay's Settlement Trusts, Re [1982] 1 WLR 202 110
Hayes v Alliance British & Foreign Life & Fire Assurance Co. (1881) 8 LR Ir 149 ....137n
Hayes v Ireland [1987] ILRM 651 ....743n
Hayward, Re [1997] Ch 45 ....53, 53n
Haywood v Cope (1858) 25 Beav 140 789
Hazell v Hammersmith and Fulham LBC [1992] AC 1 1000
Head v Gould [1898] 2 Ch 250 ....585, 590
Headstart Global Fund Ltd v Citco Bank Nederland NV [2011] IEHC 5 ....1002n, 1007
Healey v Brown [2002] WTLR 849 ....127n, 300
Health Service Executive v Keogh [2009] IEHC 419 ....725n
Healy v Attorney General [1902] 1 IR 342 442
Healy v Commissioner of Internal Revenue (1953) 345 US 278 333
Healy v Donnery (1853) 3 ICLR 213 78
Healy v McGillicuddy [1978] ILRM 175 887
Hearn v Younger [2002] WTLR 1317 ....532n, 533n
Hearty v Coleman [1953-54] Ir Jur Rep 73 151
Heavey v Heavey (1974) 111 ILTR 1 227
Heinl v Jyske Bank (Gibraltar) Ltd [1999] Lloyd's Rep Bank 511 ....344n
Helena Housing Ltd v Revenue and Customs Commissioners [2010] UKFTT 71 ....449n–452
Henderson v Merrett Syndicates Ltd [1995] 2 AC 145 ....261n
Heneghan v Davitt [1933] IR 375 64
Hennessy v St Gerard's School Trust High Court 2003 No. 7556P (Smyth J) 30 July 2003 ....733n, 741
Henry v Henry [2010] 1 All ER 988 ....928n, 967, 970
Henry's Estate, Re (1893) 31 LR Ir 158 ....1022n
Hepworth v Hepworth (1870) LR 11 Eq 10 ....175n, 209
Hepworth v Hepworth (1963) 110 CLR 309 337
Herbage v Pressdram Ltd [1984] 1 WLR 1160 ....675n, 679
Herbert v Doyle [2008] EWHC 1950 (Ch) 950n
Herbert v Doyle [2010] EWCA Civ 1095 ....950n, 980
Herrara v An Garda Siochana [2013] IEHC 311 ....694, 744
Hetherington, Re [1990] Ch 1 442
Hewett v First Plus Financial Group plc [2010] 2 FLR 177 ....880n, 883n, 890
Hickey & Co. v Roches Stores (No. 1), High Court 1975 No. 1007P (Finlay P) 14 July 1976 332
Hickey v O'Dwyer [2006] 2 ILRM 81 ....224n, 228, 229, 231n, 1035–1037
Higgins v Argent Developments Ltd [2002] IEHC 171 ....796n, 798n
Higgins v Argent Developments Supreme Court, 13 May 2003 ....799n
High Commissioner for Pakistan in the United Kingdom v Jah [2016] EWHC 1465 (Ch) 341n

Highett and Bird's Contract, Re [1902] 2 Ch 214 ....313n
Highland & Universal Properties Ltd v Safeway Properties Ltd (No. 2)
2000 SC 297 817
Hill v C.A. Parsons & Co. Ltd [1972] Ch 305....................728, 790n, 822
Hill v Hill (1904) 8 OLR 710 ....184n
Hill v Permanent Trustee Co. of New South Wales [1930] AC 720 ....558n
Hillier, Re [1944] 1 All ER 480 ....462n
Hillingdon Estates Co. v Stonefield Estates Ltd [1952] Ch 627....................1019n
Hillsdown Holdings plc v Pensions Ombudsman [1997] 1 All ER 862 ....362n
Hilton v Barker Booth and Eastwood [2005] 1 WLR 567....................271
Hinves v Hinves (1844) 3 Hare 609 ....554n
HKN Invest Oy v Incotrade Pvt Ltd [1993] 3 IR 152....................3n, 22n, 317n, 320, 323
HKR Middle East Architects Engineering LC v English
[2019] IEHC 306....................332n, 334
Hkruk II (CHC) Ltd v Heaney [2010] EWHC 2245 (Ch) 638n
Hoare A Bankrupt, Re [2016] IEHC 345 ....923n, 925n
Hobourn Aero Components Ltd's Air Raid Distress Fund, Re
[1946] Ch 86....................166, 430n
Hobourn Aero Components Ltd's Air Raid Distress Fund, Re [1946] Ch 194....................422n
Hodges, Re (1878) 7 Ch D 754....................536n
Hodgins v Hodgins [2019] IEHC 577 ....622n
Hodgson v Marks [1971] Ch 892....................178
Hoffmann-La Roche v Secretary of State for Trade and Industry
[1975] AC 295 649
Hogan v Byrne (1863) 13 ICLR 166 391
Hogan v Commercial Factors Ltd [2006] 3 NZLR 618....................912
Hogan, Re [1901] 1 IR 168....................1043n
Hogg v Hogg [2008] WTLR 35....................879n, 882n, 893
Holder v Holder [1968] Ch 353 ....573, 591n
Holland v Newbury [1997] 2 BCLC 369....................101, 101n
Holland, Re [1902] 2 Ch 360....................87n, 152n
Holley v Smyth [1998] QB 726....................674n, 676, 676n, 679, 681
Hollis v Rolfe [2008] EWHC 1747 (Ch) 365n
Holloway v Radcliffe (1857) 23 Beav 163 ....1024n
Holman v Howes [2005] EWHC 2824 (Ch)....................244n
Holman v Howes [2008] 1 FLR 1217....................251n, 966
Holmes v Millage [1893] 1 QB 551 21
Holohan v Ardmayle Estates Supreme Court 1966 No. 60, 1 May 1967 ....788n
Honniball v Cunningham [2010] 2 IR 1 ....16n
Hood, Re [1923] 1 IR 109....................190n, 1043n
Hooper v Rogers [1975] Ch 43....................718
Hooper, Re [1932] 1 Ch 38....................387
Hope v Lord Cloncurry (1874) IR 8 Eq 555....................802
Hopgood v Brown [1955] 1 WLR 213 944
Hopkins v Geoghegan [1931] IR 135 ....835n
Hopkins' Will Trusts, Re [1965] Ch 669....................426, 427
Hopkinson, Re [1949] 1 All ER 346....................475
Hopper v Hopper [2008] 1 FCR 557 ....965n

Horlock, Re [1895] 1 Ch 516..1032n
Horne, Re [1905] 1 Ch 76..559n
Horton v Kurzke [1971] 1 WLR 769..808n
Hosking v Runting [2005] 1 NZLR 1..679n
Hospital Products Ltd v United States Surgical Corporation
(1984) 156 CLR 41..71n, 260n, 268
Houghton v Fayers [2000] 1 BCLC 511..364n
Hounga v Allen [2014] 1 WLR 2889..198n
House of Spring Gardens Ltd v Waite [1985] FSR 173..757, 785
Houston v Burns [1918] AC 337..465n
Howard v Commissioner of Taxation (2014) 309 ALR 1..264
Howard v Commissioners of Public Works in Ireland High Court
1992 No. 331JR (O'Hanlon J) 3 December 1992..36n, 630, 635
Howard v UCC [2000] IEHC 138..731n, 740n
Howe v Earl of Dartmouth (1802) 7 Ves 137..554, 580
Howes, Re (1905) 21 TLR 501..179n
Howley's Estate, Re [1940] IR 109..406, 440n, 443n
Howlin v Thomas F. Power (Dublin) Ltd High Court 1977 No.736P
(McWilliam J) 5 May 1978..806
HRH Tessy Prince of Luxembourg v HRH Louis Princess of Luxembourg
[2018] EWFC 77..86n
Hubbard v Pitt [1976] QB 142..652n
Hubbard v Vosper [1972] 2 QB 84..626n, 649n
Hughes v Collins [2017] IECA 93..30n
Hughes v Hitachi Koki Imaging Solutions Europe [2006] 3 IR 457...748n, 762n, 763
Hughes v London Borough of Southwark [1988] IRLR 72..729
Hughes v Metropolitan Railway Co. (1877) 2 App Cas 439..924, 926
Hughes, Re [1970] IR 237..1008, 1011
Huguenin v Baseley (1807) 14 Ves 273..118
Hummeltenberg, Re [1923] 1 Ch 237..407n, 458, 462
Humphrey's Estate, Re [1916] 1 IR 21..48n, 93n–95
Humphreys v Humphreys [2004] EWHC 2201 (Ch)..915
Hunt v McLaren [2006] EWHC 2386 (Ch)..381n, 395
Hunter v Allen [1907] 1 IR 212..274
Hunter v Moss [1993] 1 WLR 934 (DC), [1994] 1 WLR 452 (CA)..100–102
Hunter v Public Trustee [1924] NZLR 882..92n
Hussey v Palmer [1972] 1 WLR 1286..22n, 253, 257n, 318, 320n,
321, 322, 325, 326, 328
Hyett v Stanley [2003] EWCA Civ 942..976n
Hylton v Hylton (1754) 2 Ves Sen 547..882n
Hynes Ltd v Independent Newspapers Ltd [1980] IR 204..1, 12, 13, 15, 835n

IBM (UK) Ltd v Prima Data International Ltd [1994] 1 WLR 719..782, 783n
Ikbal v Sterling Law [2013] EWHC 3291 (Ch)..592n
In Plus Group Ltd v Pyke [2002] 2 BCLC 201..294
Inche Noriah v Shaik Allie Bin Omar [1929] AC 127..884n
Incorporated Council of Law Reporting for England and Wales v
Attorney General [1972] Ch 73..407n, 408n, 413n, 426, 451

Incorporated Law Society of Ireland v Carroll [1995] 3 IR 145 ....744n, 746, 746n
Incorporated Society v Richards (1841) 4 Ir Eq R 177 ....406n, 425n
Independent Newspapers Ltd v Irish Press Ltd [1932] IR 615.....................718, 742n
Independent Trustee Services Ltd v JP Noble Trustees Ltd
[2010] EWHC 1653 (Ch) 365n
Industrial Development Consultants v Cooley [1972] 1 WLR 443........................290
Industrial Yarns Ltd v Greene [1984] ILRM 15 927
Innes, Re [1910] 1 Ch 188 ....142n, 143n
Insol Funding Co. Ltd v Cowlam [2017] EWHC 1822 (Ch)...............................238n
Inspector of Taxes Association v Minister for the Public Service
[1983] IEHC 56 74
International Contract Co, Re (1872) 7 Ch App 485 ....860n
Intrum Justitia BV v Legal and Trade Financial Services Ltd
[2005] IEHC 190 ....870, 877
Inwards v Baker [1965] 2 QB 29..940, 957n, 959n, 986n
Irani v Southampton and South-West Hampshire Health Authority
[1985] IRLR 203 ....729, 730
IRC v Baddeley [1955] AC 572................................411n, 411n, 412n, 415, 452, 471
IRC v Broadway Cottages' Trust [1955] Ch 20..................80n, 103n, 106, 107, 396n
IRC v Educational Grants Association Ltd [1967] Ch 993.................412n, 432, 435n
IRC v McMullen [1981] AC 1 ....401n, 428, 470n
Irish Bank Resolution Corporation Ltd v Quinn [2011] IEHC 470.....881n, 900n, 903
Irish Bank Resolution Corporation Ltd v Quinn [2012] 4 IR 381 ....756n
Irish Bank Resolution Corporation Ltd v Quinn [2013] IEHC 437.....645n, 646, 646n
Irish Life and Permanent plc v Financial Services Ombudsman
[2012] IEHC 367 ....262, 269
Irish Life Assurance Co. Ltd v Dublin Land Securities Ltd [1986] IR 332 (HC),
[1989] IR 253 (SC)................................48n, 843, 845–847, 852, 855, 858, 871
Irish Pensions Trust Ltd v Central Remedial Clinic
[2005] IEHC 87 ....533, 843n, 845n, 861, 875
Irish Shell Ltd v Elm Motors Ltd [1984] IR 200 ....628n, 651n, 652n,
706n, 722n, 723, 725
Irish Shell Ltd v J.H. McLoughlin (Balbriggan) Ltd [2005] IEHC 304 ....656n
Irish Shipping Ltd, Re [1986] ILRM 518 ....317n, 332, 1013
Irish Times Ltd v Times Newspapers Ltd [2015] IEHC 490 630
Irwin v O'Connell [1936] IR 44 ....42n, 205n
Island Export Finance Ltd v Umunna [1986] BCLC 460............................292, 294n
Issac v Defriez (1754) Amb 595 ....411n
Ivey v Genting Casinos (UK) Ltd [2018] AC 391 354

J. Pereira Fernandes SA v Mehta [2006] 1 WLR 1543...86n
J. Trevor and Sons v Solomon Court of Appeal 14 December 1977 675
J.C. v J.H.C. High Court 1982 No. 4931P (Keane J)
4 August 1982...205n, 208, 215n, 225n
J.C. v W.C. [2004] 2 IR 312..802n, 929n
J.C. Williamson Ltd v Lukey and Mulholland (1931) 45 CLR 282 811
J.F. v B.F. High Court (Lardner J) 21 December 1988. ....234n

J.H. v W.J.H. High Court 1977 No. 5831P (Keane J) 20 December 1979........40, 42, 920
J.R., Re [1993] ILRM 657........926, 927, 985–987, 990, 990n
J.R.M. Sports Ltd v Football Association of Ireland [2007] IEHC 67........619n
J.T. Stratford and Sons v Lindley [1965] AC 269........650
Jacklin v Chief Constable of West Yorkshire [2007] EWCA Civ 181........637, 638
Jackson v Attorney General [1917] 1 IR 332........439n
Jackson's Trusts, Re (1874) 8 ILTR 174........518n
Jacob Fruitfield Food Group Ltd v United Biscuits (UK) Ltd [2007] IEHC 368........661, 742n
Jacob v Irish Amateur Rowing Union Ltd [2008] 4 IR 731........695–697
Jacomb v Harwood (1751) 2 Ves Sen 265........81n
Jaffray v Marshall [1993] 1 WLR 1285........588
Jaggard v Sawyer [1995] 1 WLR 269........638, 638n, 642
James Jones & Sons Ltd v Earl of Tankerville [1901] 2 Ch 440........725n
James Roscoe (Bolton) Ltd v Winder [1915] 1 Ch 62........1002n, 1008
James v James [2018] EWHC 43 (Ch)........928n, 931
James v Thomas [2008] 1 FLR 1598........251n
James, Re [1935] Ch 449........142
Jameson v McGovern [1934] IR 758........24
Jan v Torrance [2002] EWCA Civ 431........820n
Jankowski v Pelek Estate (1995) 131 DLR (4th) 717........123, 123n, 125n
Jarvis, Re [1958] 1 WLR 815........277
Jeans v Cooke (1857) 24 Beav 513........176n
Jeffel, Re [2012] IEHC 279........62
Jeffrey v Gretton [2011] WTLR 809........586n
Jenkins's Will Trusts, Re [1966] Ch 249........469
Jennings v Rice [2003] 1 P & CR 8........135, 947n, 948, 952n, 958n, 963–969n, 970, 971, 980
Jerome v Kelly [2004] 1 WLR 1409........310, 313, 313n
Jervoise v Duke of Northumberland (1821) 1 Jac & W 559........24
Jeune v Queens Cross Properties Ltd [1974] Ch 97........819, 820
JLT Financial Services Ltd formerly known as Liberty Asset Management Ltd v Gannon [2017] IESC 70........800n, 806n
Jobling-Purser v Jackman High Court 1992 No. 3808P (Carroll J) 27 July 1999........783n
Jobling-Purser v Jackson High Court (Kinlen J) 27 November 2002........38n, 594n
Jodifern Ltd v Fitzgerald [2000] 3 IR 321........795, 799n, 800, 801
Johnson v Agnew [1980] AC 367........637n, 641, 641n, 642, 792
Johnson v Ball (1851) 5 De G & Sm 85........122n
Johnson v Buttress (1936) 56 CLR 113........883, 883n
Johnson, Re (1881) 20 Ch D 389........510n
Johnson, Re (1905) 92 LT 357........149n
Johnson's Settlement, Re [1944] IR 529........609n
Johnson's Will Trusts, Re [1967] Ch 387........504
Johnston v Lloyd (1844) 7 Ir Eq R 252........543n
Johnston v O'Neill (1879) 3 LR Ir 476........582
Jones v AMP Perpetual Trustee Co. NZ Ltd [1994] 1 NZLR 690........544n, 548n

Jones v Badley (1868) 3 Ch App 362 ....116n
Jones v Coolmore Stud [2016] IEHC 329 ....710n
Jones v Jones [1977] 1 WLR 438 ....957n
Jones v Kernott [2012] 1 AC 776 ....23, 238, 240–243, 246–249, 249n, 251, 306, 983
Jones v Lee [1980] ICR 310 730
Jones v Lock (1865) 1 Ch App 25 140
Jones v Maynard [1951] Ch 572 ....191n
Jones v Watkins Court of Appeal 26 November 1987 ....936, 937, 988n
Jones, Re [1898] 1 Ch 438 ....98n, 99n
Jordan v Roberts [2009] EWHC 2313 (Ch) 134n
Jordan, Re [2014] IEHC 678 489
Jorden v Money (1854) 5 HLC 185 ....922, 924
Joscelyne v Nissen [1970] 2 QB 86 ....844, 845, 858, 859
Joseph Rowntree Memorial Trust Housing Association Ltd v Attorney General [1983] Ch 159 ....416, 423n, 461, 461n
Joseph v Lyons (1884) 15 QBD 280 ....10n
Joyce v Epsom and Ewell Borough Council [2012] EWCA Civ 1398 ....936, 969
Joyce v Health Service Executive [2005] IEHC 174 ....735n
JSC VTB Bank v Skurikhin [2019] EWHC 1407 (Comm) 47n, 86

K.N. v Minister for Justice and Equality [2013] IEHC 566 ....700n
Kane v Cosgrave (1873) IR 10 Eq 211 ....499n
Kane v Radley- Kane [1999] Ch 274 573
Karak Rubber Co. Ltd v Burden (No. 2) [1972] 1 WLR 602 ....345n, 361n
Kasperbauer v Griffith [2000] WTLR 333 ....115n
Kation Pty Ltd v Lamru Pty Ltd (2009) 257 ALR 336 29
Kavanagh v Caulfield [2002] IEHC 67 ....31n, 34, 789n, 838
Kavanagh v Delicato High Court 1989 No. 7536P (Carroll J) 20 December 1996 ....798n
Kavanagh v Lynch [2011] IEHC 348 ....660n, 706n
Kavanagh v Murphy [2016] IEHC 718 ....706n
Kay's Settlement, Re [1939] Ch 329 ....154n, 155
Kayford, Re [1975] 1 WLR 279 ....86n, 93
Keane v Irish Amateur Swimming Association Ltd High Court 2003 No. 8724P (Gilligan J) 4 August 2003 ....739n, 740n
Kearney v Byrne Wallace [2017] IEHC 713 ....710n
Kearney v Ireland [1986] IR 116 ....743n
Kearns Brothers Ltd v Hova Developments Ltd [2012] EWHC 2968 (Ch) 305n
Keating & Co. Ltd v Jervis Shopping Centre Ltd High Court 1995 No. 9606P (Keane J) 1 March 1996 ....669, 670
Keating v Bank of Ireland [1983] ILRM 295 808
Keating v Jervis Shopping Centre Ltd [1997] 1 IR 512 ....660n
Keating v Keating [2009] IEHC 405 ....29n, 913n, 918
Keays v Lane (1869) IR 3 Eq 1 ....593n
Keech v Sandford (1726) Sel Cas T King 61 ....272, 272n, 273, 275, 276, 290
Keefe v Law Society (1998) 44 NSWLR 451 ....1007n
Keegan Quarries Ltd v McGuinness [2011] IEHC 453 ....507, 508n
Keen, Re [1937] Ch 236 ....116n, 122–126n, 161n

Keenan v CIE (1963) 97 ILTR 54 645
Keenan v Iarnród Eireann [2010] IEHC 15 ....710n, 732n, 737, 739n
Kehoe v Wilson (1880) 7 LR Ir 10 ....442, 448n
Kekewich v Manning (1851) 1 De GM & G 176 ....131n
Kelleher, Re [1911] 2 IR 1 511
Kelly v Cahill [2000] 1 IR 56 ....22n, 257n, 317n, 323, 325
Kelly v Kelly (1874) 8 IR Eq 403 ....264n, 273
Kelly v Larkin [1910] 2 IR 550 74
Kelly v Park Hall School Ltd [1979] IR 340 ....799, 800n
Kelly v Simpson [2008] IEHC 374 ....789n, 831n
Kelly, Re [1932] IR 255 ....388, 389
Kelly's Carpetdrome Ltd, Re, High Court (Costello J) 9 May 1983 ....753n
Kemp v Kemp (1801) 5 Ves 849 ....7n
Kennaway v Thompson [1981] QB 88 ....21n, 635, 638
Kennedy v Ireland [1987] IR 587 ....743n
Kennedy v Kennedy [2014] EWHC 4129 (Ch) 874
Kennedy v Panama, New Zealand, and Australian Royal Mail Co. (Ltd) (1867) LR 2 QB 580 ....878n
Kenney v Employers' Liability Assurance Corporation [1901] 1 IR 301 ....74n
Kenny v Kelly [1988] IR 457 ....924n
Kenny v Kenny [2019] IEHC 76 210
Kenny, Re (1907) 97 LT 130 ....439n
Keogh's Estate, Re (1889) 23 LR Ir 257 1033
Keogh's Estate, Re [1945] IR 13 ....392n, 393, 444n, 446, 447
Keren Kayemeth Le Jisroel Ltd v IRC [1931] 2 KB 465 ....437, 460n
Kerr v Baranow (2011) 328 DLR (4th) 577 ....175n, 176n, 254
Kerr v British Leyland (Staff) Trustees Ltd [2001] WTLR 1071 ....532n
Ketchum v Group Public Relations [1997] 1 WLR 4 ....761n
Ketley v Gooden (1996) 73 P & CR 305 ....638n
Keys v Hore (1879) 13 ILTR 58 ....150n
Khan v Health Service Executive [2009] ELR 178 ....710, 710n, 732n
Khan v Minister for Justice and Equality [2013] IEHC 186 ....700n
Khashoggi v IPC Magazines Ltd [1986] 1 WLR 1412 ....676n, 679n
Kieran, Re [1916] 1 IR 289 ....47n, 77, 79n
Kilcarne Holdings Ltd v Targetfollow (Birmingham) Ltd [2005] EWCA Civ 135 ....303n
Kinane v Mackie-Conteh [2005] EWCA Civ 45 ....950n, 978
King v Anderson (1874) IR 8 Eq 625 572
King v Dubrey [2016] Ch 221 ....146, 148, 151n
King v Ulster Bank Ireland Ltd [2013] IEHC 250 ....845n
King's Estate, Re (1888) 21 LR Ir 273 ....117n, 121, 122, 124
Kingham, Re [1897] 1 IR 170 ....557n
Kings v Bultitude [2010] WTLR 1571 489
Kingsley IT Consulting Ltd v McIntosh [2006] BCC 875 ....294n
Kinsella v McAleer High Court 24 April 2009 651
Kinsella v Wallace [2013] IEHC 112 ....658n
Kirby v Barden [1999] IEHC 129 ....522, 522n
Kirklees MBC v Wickes Building Supplies Ltd [1993] AC 227 649

Kiwak v Reiner [2017] EWHC 3018 (Ch) 305n
KLDE Pty Ltd v Commissioner of Stamp Duties (1984) 58 ALJR 545....310n
Kleinwort's Settlements, Re [1951] Ch 860 ....558n
Kliers v Schmerler [2018] EWHC 1350 (Ch)....203n
Klug v Klug [1918] 2 Ch 67 535
Knight v Knight (1840) 3 Beav 148 ....91n
Knight v Knight [2019] EWHC 915 (Ch)....92n, 200n
Knockacummer Wind Farm Ltd v Cremins
[2018] IECA 252 ....848n, 852n, 856, 859n
Koeppler's Will Trusts, Re [1986] Ch 423 ....399n, 475
Koettgen's Will Trusts, Re [1954] Ch 252....435

L. v L. [1992] 2 IR 77 ....231n, 233–235, 252
L'Estrange v L'Estrange [1902] 1 IR 467 ....583n
La Have Equipment Ltd v Nova Scotia (1994) 121 DLR (4th) 67....92n
Lac Minerals Ltd v Chevron Mineral Corporation of Ireland
[1995] 1 ILRM 161 ....845n, 851
Lac Minerals Ltd v International Corona Resources Ltd
(1989) 61 DLR (4th) 14....11n, 14, 326n
Laidlaw Foundation, Re (1984) 13 DLR (4th) 491 472
Laing v Commissioner of Stamp Duties [1948] NZLR 154....469n
Lake v Craddock (1732) 3 P Wms....45n
Lalani v Crump Holdings Ltd [2007] EWHC 47 (Ch) 976, 976n
Lamare v Dixon (1873) LR 6 HL 414 ....789n
Lambert v Lyons [2010] IEHC 29 ....884n, 887
Lancashire Loans Ltd v Black [1934] 1 KB 380 ....882n
Lane's Trusts, Re (1863) 14 Ir Ch R 523....162
Langton v Langton [1995] 2 FLR 890....913n
Lankow v Rose [1995] 1 NZLR 277 ....255n, 328
Lansing Linde Ltd v Kerr [1991] 1 WLR 251 693
Lark Developments Ltd v Dublin Corporation High Court
1992 No. 2888P (Murphy J) 10 February 1993 ....791n
Larkins v National Union of Mineworkers [1985] IR 671 ....759n
Larondeau v Laurendeau [1954] 4 DLR 293....184n
Laskar v Laskar [2008] 1 WLR 2695 ....211, 213
Lassence v Tierney (1849) 1 Mac & G 551 ....96n
Last's Estate, Re [1958] P 137 98
Latec Investments Ltd v Hotel Terrigal Pty Ltd (1965) 113 CLR 265 ....56n
Latimer v Commissioner of Inland Revenue [2002] 3 NZLR 195....432n, 452n
Laurence v Poorah [2008] UKPC 21 919
Lauritzencool AB v Lady Navigation Inc [2005] 1 WLR 3686 ....725n
Lavan v Walsh [1964] IR 87 ....830, 831
Lavelle v Lavelle [2004] EWCA Civ 223....177n, 218
Lavelle, Re [1914] 1 IR 194 ....435, 436
Laverty v Laverty [1907] 1 IR 9 436
Law Society for England and Wales v Habitable Concepts Ltd
[2010] EWHC 1449 (Ch) 365n
Law Society for England and Wales v Issac [2010] EWHC 1670 (Ch) 365n

Law Society of Upper Canada v Toronto-Dominion Bank (1998) 169 DLR (4th) 353....1007n, 1008n
Law Society v Shanks [1988] 1 FLR 504....749n
Lawes v Bennett (1785) 1 Cox 167....1020, 1021
Lawrence v Fen Tigers Ltd [2014] AC 822....639
Lazard Brothers & Co. Ltd v Fairfield Properties Co. (Mayfair) Ltd (1987) 121 SJ 793....834
Le Foe v Le Foe [2001] 2 FLR 970....238n
Leahy v Attorney-General for New South Wales [1959] AC 457....390
Leaper, Re [1916] 1 Ch 579....151n
Learoyd v Whiteley (1886) 33 Ch D 347....544
Lechmere v Lechmere (1735) Cas t Talb 80....1042
Lecky v Walter [1914] 1 IR 378....877n, 878, 878n
Ledgerwood v Perpetual Trustee Co. Ltd (1997) 41 NSWLR 532....126n
Lee v Sankey (1873) LR 15 Eq 204....376
Leeder v Stevens [2005] EWCA Civ 50....881n
Leek, Re [1967] Ch 1061....76n
Legg v Burton [2017] 4 WLR 186....299
Legge v Croker (1811) 1 Ba & B 506....878n
Leggett v Crowley [2019] IEHC 182....831n, 832, 838n, 839n
Legione v Hateley (1983) 152 CLR 406....310n, 835n, 836n
Lehane v Dunne [2017] IEHC 511....762n
Lehman Brothers International (Europe) v CRC Credit Fund Ltd [2010] EWCA Civ 917....98
Lehman Brothers International (Europe), Re [2010] EWHC 2914 (Ch)....102
Lennon v Ganly [1981] ILRM 84....36n, 628, 787
Leo Pharma A/S v Sandoz Ltd [2008] EWHC 541 (Pat), [2008] EWCA Civ 850....663n
Leonard v Leonard [1988] ILRM 245....884n
Leong v Cheye [1955] AC 648....504n
Leopardstown Club Ltd v Templeville Developments Ltd [2010] IEHC152....846–849, 856, 858
Leopardstown Club Ltd v Templeville Developments Ltd [2015] IECA 164....877
Les Laboratoires Servier v Apotex Inc. [2015] AC 430....198, 198n
Lester v Woodgate [2010] EWCA Civ 199....934, 937n, 944, 988
Lester, Re [1940] NI 92....458n
Lett v Lett [1906] 1 IR 618....52
Lewis Securities Ltd v Carter (2018) 355 ALR 703....368n
Lewis v Cotton [2001] 2 NZLR 21....298n
Lewis v Lewis (1876) IR 11 Eq 313....1028
Lewis v Tamplin [2018] EWHC 777 (Ch)....564n, 566n
Lewis, Re [1955] Ch 104....461
Liberty Asset Management Ltd v Gannon [2009] IEHC 468....799n, 804n, 805
Liden v Burton [2016] EWCA Civ 275....931, 931n
Life Association of Scotland v Siddal (1861) 3 De G F & J 58....594n
Lift Manufacturers Ltd v Irish Life Assurance Co. Ltd [1979] ILRM 277....790n, 821, 822

Lillingston, Re [1952] 2 All ER 184 ....149n
Lim Teng Huan v Ang Swee Chuan [1992] 1 WLR 113 ....26n, 946, 957n
Lindsay Petroleum v Hurd (1874) LR 5 PC 221 39
Lindsley v Woodfull [2004] 2 BCLC 131 ....294n
Lingham v Health Service Executive [2006] ELR 137 ....710, 712–714n, 716, 732, 737, 815, 816
Linsen International Ltd v Humpuss Sea Transport Pte Ltd [2010] EWHC 303 (Comm) 761n
Lipinski's Will Trusts, Re [1976] Ch 235 394
Lipkin Gorman v Karpanale Ltd [1987] 1 WLR 987 (QB) 362
Lipkin Gorman v Karpanale Ltd [1989] 1 WLR 1340 (CA) 346n
Lipkin Gorman v Karpanale Ltd [1991] 2 AC 548 (HL) 360n, 362n, 372, 1016, 1016n, 1017
Lissimore v Downing [2003] 2 FLR 308 ....935n
Lister & Co. v Stubbs (1890) 45 Ch D 1 ....279, 279n, 280, 283, 747n
Lister v Hodgson (1867) LR 4 Eq 30 ....863n
Liston v Keegan (1881) 9 LR Ir 539 ....448n
Litchfield-Speer v Queen Anne's Gate Syndicate (No. 2) Ltd [1919] 1 Ch 407 ....717n
Litvinoff v Kent (1918) 34 TLR 298 ....626n
Liverpool Household Stores Association v Smith (1888) 37 Ch D 170 ....676n
Llandudno Urban District Council v Woods [1899] 2 Ch 705 ....742n
Llewellyn's Settlement, Re [1921] 2 Ch 281 ....76n
Lloyd v Banks (1868) 3 Ch App 488 ....60n
Lloyd v Dugdale [2002] 2 P & CR 167 ....937n, 947n
Lloyd v Lloyd (1852) 2 Sim (NS) 255 ....503n
Lloyd v Sutcliffe [2007] EWCA Civ 153 930
Lloyd, Re (1893) 10 TLR 66 ....438n
Lloyds Bank Ltd v Bundy [1975] QB 326 ....887, 918
Lloyds Bank Ltd v Marcan [1973] 1 WLR 339 507
Lloyds Bank plc v Carrick [1996] 4 All ER 630 ....947, 978n
Lloyds Bank plc v Rosset [1991] 1 AC 107 ....237, 238, 238n, 240, 241n, 243, 247, 247n, 251, 978
Lloyds Bowmaker Ltd v Britannia Arrow Holdings plc [1988] 1 WLR 1337 755
Lloyds TSB Bank plc v Markandan & Uddine [2012] EWCA Civ 65 ....592n
Lloyds TSB Bank v Holdgate [2002] EWCA Civ 1543 ....898n
Loan Investment Corporation of Australasia v Bonner [1970] NZLR 724 ....794n, 810n
Locabail International Finance Ltd v Agroexport [1986] 1 WLR 657 706
Local Ireland Ltd v Local Ireland-Online Ltd [2000] 4 IR 567 ....662n, 698, 742n
Lock International plc v Beswick [1989] 1 WLR 1268 ....778n
Lohia v Lohia [2001] WTLR 101 (Ch D); [2001] EWCA Civ 1691 178
London Allied Holdings Ltd v Lee [2007] EWHC 2061 (Ch) 329n, 330
London and Blackwell Railway Co. v Cross (1886) 31 Ch D 354 621
London Borough Council [1996] AC 669 ....1013n
London University v Yarrow (1857) 1 De G & J 72 ....466n
London Wine Co. Ltd, Re [1986] PCC 121 99–101
Londonderry's Settlement, Re [1965] Ch 918 ....566n, 567, 615, 615n
Lonergan v Salter-Townshend [2000] ELR 15 ....739n, 740

Longton v Wilsby (1897) 76 LT 770....................................275
Lonrho plc v Fayed (No.2) [1992] 1 WLR 1....................................257, 316
Lonrho v Shell Petroleum Co. Ltd (No. 2) [1982] AC 173....................................745n
Lord Bellew's Estate [1921] IR 174....................................795n
Lord Chesham, Re (1886) 31 Ch D 466....................................1025n, 1029
Lord Napier and Ettrick v Hunter [1993] AC 713....................................13, 18
Lovell and Christmas Ltd v Wall (1911) 104 LT85....................................843
Lovell, Re [1920] 1 Ch 122....................................504
Lovett v Gogan [1995] 3 IR 132....................................743, 744, 746n
Low v Bouverie [1891] 3 Ch 82....................................562n
Lowe v Lombank Ltd [1960] 1 WLR 196....................................927
Lowry v Reid [1927] NI 142....................................21n, 802, 803, 803n
Lowson v Coombes [1999] Ch 373....................................197, 206n, 215n, 222n, 225n
Lucey v Laurel Construction Co. Ltd High Court 1970 No. 3816 (Kenny J)
18 December 1970....................................844, 845, 852
Lucking's Will Trusts, Re [1967] 3 All ER 726....................................537n
Lumley v Wagner (1852) 1 De G M & G 604....................................726
Luo v Hui [2008] HKEC 996....................................987n
Lynch v Burke [1990] 1 IR 1 (HC), [1995] 2 IR 159 (SC)....181–184, 186–189, 399n
Lynch v Health Service Executive [2010] IEHC 346....................................622n, 624
Lynch v O'Meara, Supreme Court 1974 No. 12, 8 May 1975....................................795
Lynch's Trusts, Re [1931] IR 517....................................542
Lynn v O'Hara [2015] IEHC 689....................................884n, 887
Lysaght v Edwards (1876) 2 Ch D 499....................................310, 311
Lysaght, Re [1966] 1 Ch 191....................................487, 489
Lyus v Prowsa Developments Ltd [1982] 1 WLR 1044....................................89n

M.B. v E.B. High Court 1979 No. 556 Sp (Barrington J) 19 February 1980........230n
M.C. v F.C. [2012] 1 ILRM 1....................................883n, 884
M.D. v Ireland [2009] 3 IR 690....................................702
M.G. v R.D. High Court 1980 No. 423 Sp (Keane J) 28 April 1981....................229
M.K. v J.B. [1999] IEHC 117....................................524
M.P. v Teaching Council [2019] IEHC 148....................................666
M'Court v Burnett (1877) 11 ILTR 130....................................384n, 442n
M'Cracken v M'Clelland (1877) IR 11 Eq 172....................................264n, 273
M'Donogh v Davies (1875) IR 9 CL 300....................................755n
M'Dowell v McNeilly [1917] 1 IR 117....................................190
M'Fadden v Jenkins (1842) 1 Ph 153....................................86n
M'Gonnell v Murray (1869) IR 3 Eq 460....................................151
Macartney, Re [1918] 1 Ch 300....................................1029
Macaulay, Re [1943] Ch 435....................................390, 395
MacDonald v Frost [2009] WTLR 1815....................................932n, 953n, 982n, 988n
MacDuff, Re [1896] 2 Ch 451....................................412n, 426n, 450, 460n
Macedonian Orthodox Community Church St Petka Inc v Diocesan Bishop of the
Macedonian Orthodox Diocese of Australian and New Zealand
(2008) 237 CLR 66....................................541n
Mackenzie v Coulson (1869) LR 8 Eq 368....................................843
Mackey, Re [1915] 2 IR 347....................................515n

Mackie v Wilde [1998] 2 IR 578 ....803, 805, 806
Mackintosh v Pogose [1895] 1 Ch 505 515
Mackreth v Symmons (1808) 15 Ves 329 ....313n
MacLaren's Settlement Trusts, Re [1951] 2 All ER 414 ....558n
MacLaughlin v Campbell [1906] 1 IR 588 439
MacMillan Inc v Bishopsgate Investment Trust plc (No. 3) [1995] 1 WLR 978 ....363n
MacNamara, Re [1943] IR 372 ....400n
Maddison v Alderson (1883) 8 App Cas 467 ....803, 804, 806n
Maddock, Re [1902] 2 Ch 220 ....114n
Madoff Securities International Ltd v Raven [2013] EWHC 3147 (Comm) 354n
Magee v Attorney General [2002] IEHC 87 ....428, 493, 495
Magee v Pennine Insurance Co. Ltd [1969] 2 QB 507 ....868n, 869
Magiera v Magiera [2017] 3 WLR 41 ....53, 54
Maguire v Attorney General [1943] IR 238 ....392, 446, 447
Maguire v Dodd (1859) 9 Ir Ch R 452 86
Maharaj v Johnson [2015] UKPC 28 ....313n
Maher v Irish Permanent Ltd [1998] ELR 77 ....733n, 734
Mahon v Post Publications Ltd [2007] 3 IR 338 685
Mahon v Savage (1803) 1 Sch & Lef 111 ....419n
Mahoney v Purnell [1996] 3 All ER 61 ....892n
Main v Giambrone [2017] EWCA Civ 1193 ....14n, 588
Makeown v Ardagh (1876) IR 10 Eq 445 ....489n
Malayan Credit Ltd v Jack Chia-MPH Ltd [1986] AC 549 45
Malik v Kalyan [2010] EWCA Civ 113 ....964n
Malincross Ltd v Building and Allied Trades Union [2002] 3 IR 607 ....671, 673
Malins v Freeman (1837) 2 Keen 221 ....829n
Malone v McQuaid [1998] IEHC 86 ....205n, 207, 210, 214n, 215n, 224n
Maloney v O'Connor [2015] IEHC 678 ....26, 26n
Manchester Trust v Furness [1895] 2 QB 539 ....62, 364n
Manisty's Settlement Trusts, Re [1974] Ch 24 ....110–111n
Manners, Re [1949] Ch 613 ....1032n
Manser, Re [1905] 1 Ch 68 ....448, 448n
Mara v Browne [1896] 1 Ch 199 ....308, 377, 378, 378n
Marcic v Thames Water Utilities Ltd (No.2) [2002] QB 1003 ....638, 638n
Mareva Compania Naviera SA v International Bulkcarriers SA [1975] 2 Lloyd's Rep 509 747
Margulies v Margulies Court of Appeal, 16 March 2000 ....115n
Mariette, Re [1915] 2 Ch 284 ....428n, 470n
Marks and Spencer plc v Freshfields Bruckhaus Deringer [2004] 1 WLR 2331 ....263n, 265n
Marley v Rawlings [2015] AC 129 ....863, 864
Marr v Collie [2018] AC 631 ....249, 250
Marshal v Crutwell (1875) LR 20 Eq 328 190
Marshall Futures Ltd v Marshall [1992] 1 NZLR 316 ....347n, 367
Marshall v Bourneville [2013] 3 NZLR 766 ....255n
Marshall's Will Trusts, Re [1945] 1 Ch 217 ....70n
Martin v Nationwide Building Society [2001] 1 IR 228 ....731n, 735, 740n

v Nicholson [2004] EWHC 2135 (Ch) 862n
Mascall v Mascall (1984) 50 P & CR 119 132
Masri v Consolidated Contractors (UK) Ltd (No. 2) [2009] QB 450 .... 765n
Masri v Consolidated Contractors International Co. SAL [2007] EWHC 3010 (Comm) 749n
Massey v Midland Bank plc [1995] 1 All ER 929 .... 894, 894n, 895
Massingberd, Re (1890) 63 LT 296 .... 588n
Matharu v Matharu (1994) 68 P & CR 93 .... 944n, 946
Maxwell v Hogg (1867) 2 Ch App 307 .... 620n
Mayor of Lyons v Advocate-General of Bengal (1876) 1 App Cas 91 .... 486n
McAlinden v McAlinden (1877) IR 11 Eq 219 .... 93n
McArdle v O'Donohoe [1999] IEHC 176 .... 129n, 130, 137, 138
McArdle, Re [1951] Ch 669 .... 131n
McBlain v Cross (1871) 25 LT 804 .... 87n
McBrearty v North Western Health Board [2010] IESC 27 .... 38n
McC. v McC. [1986] ILRM 1 .... 46n, 228, 230, 230n, 233n, 234
McCabe v Ulster Bank Ltd [1939] IR 1 213
McCambridge v Winters High Court 1983 No. 486Sp (Murphy J) 28 May 1984 .... 927n
McCann v Morrissey [2013] IEHC 288 .... 628n, 657n
McCarron v McCarron Supreme Court 1995 No. 181 13 February 1997 .... 935, 940n
McCarter & Co. Ltd v Roughan [1986] ILRM 447 .... 798n
McCarthy's Will Trusts, Re [1958] IR 311 .... 455n, 462
McCausland v Young [1949] NI 49 .... 43n
McCormack v McCormack (1877) 1 LR Ir 119 .... 857n
McCormack v Our Lady Queen of Peace Achill House of Prayer Ltd [2018] IEHC 26 .... 40, 878n
McCormick v Grogan (1869) LR 4 HL 82 .... 23n, 87, 112n, 113n, 116n
McCormick v Queen's University of Belfast [1958] NI 1 .... 488n
McCourt v Tiernan [2005] IEHC 268 .... 762n
McCrystal v O'Kane [1986] NI 123 .... 794n, 833
McD. v McD. [1993] ILRM 717 .... 843, 847
McDonagh v Denton [2005] IEHC 127 935
McDonagh v O'Shea [2018] IECA 298 .... 38n
McDonagh v Ulster Bank Ireland Ltd [2014] IEHC 476 .... 628n
McDonald v Horn [1995] 1 All ER 961 614
McDonald v Scott [1893] AC 642 .... 153n
McDonald, Re [2000] 1 ILRM 382 .... 211n
McDonnell v Stenson [1921] 1 IR 80 .... 1018n
McDonogh v Nolan (1881) 9 Lr Ir 262 .... 1019n, 1024
McEneaney v Shevlin [1912] 1 IR 32, [1912] 1 IR 278 .... 175n, 181n
McEnery, Re [1941] IR 323 .... 434, 434n
McEuen, Re [1913] 2 Ch 704 .... 557n
McEvoy v Belfast Banking Co. [1934] NI 67 .... 29n, 220, 625n
McFarlane v McFarlane [1972] NI 59 .... 230n
McGee v Attorney General [1974] IR 284 .... 504n
McGill v S. [1979] IR 238 .... 226n, 229n
McGillycuddy v Joy [1959] IR 189 .... 23n, 89, 112n, 192n

McGonigle v Black High Court (Barr J) 14 November 1988..............881n, 916, 919n
McGovern v Attorney General [1982] Ch 321 ....475n, 476, 478
McGrane v Louth County Council High Court 1983 No. 28F (O'Hanlon J) 9 December 1983..717n
McGrath v Stewart [2008] IEHC 348 (HC); [2016] 2 IR 704 (SC) 17, 31n, 32n, 41, 41n, 789n, 791
McGrath v Wallis [1995] 2 FLR 114 ....210, 215n
McGuane v Welch [2008] 2 P & CR 24..957n
McGuill v Aer Lingus Teo [1983] IEHC 71 ....842n
McGuinness v Allied Irish Banks plc [2014] IEHC 191 ....651n
McGuinness v McGuinness High Court 2001 Nos. 145CA and 147CA (Kinlen J) 19 March 200 ....935n, 937n, 987
McGuinness v Preece [2016] EWHC 1518 (Ch)..928n
McGwire v McGwire [1900] 1 IR 200 1019
McGwire, Re [1941] IR 33 ....486, 488n
McHardy v Warren [1994] 2 FLR 338...243n
McIntosh, Re [1933] IR 69 ....93n, 95n
McKenna, Re [1947] IR 277..504n
McKenna's Estate, Re (1861) 13 Ir Ch R 239 ....593n
McKennitt v Ash [2008] QB 73 ....684n
McKenzie v McKenzie [2003] EWHC 601 (Ch) 247n
McKeown, Re [1974] NI 226 173
McKillen v Times Newspapers Ltd [2013] IEHC 150 686
McKinley v Minister for Defence [1992] 2 IR 333 ....209n, 225n
McLachlan v Taylor [1985] 2 NZLR 277 793
McLoughlin v Setanta Insurance Services Ltd [2011] IEHC 410 ....651n
McMahon v Gaussen [1896] 1 IR 143...583n
McMahon v Kerry County Council [1981] ILRM 419 ....26n, 955
McMakin v Hibernian Bank [1905] 1 IR 306..884n
McManus v Cooke (1887) 35 Ch D 681 ....803n, 806n
McMaster v Byrne [1952] 1 All ER 1362...882n
McMorrow v Morris [2007] IEHC 193 752
McMullen v McGinley [2005] IESC 10 ....260n, 261n
McNally v Ireland [2011] 4 IR 431 444
McNamara v Health Service Executive [2009] IEHC 418....................................731n
McPhail v Doulton [1971] AC 424................................47n, 80, 106–108, 110, 110n
McQuillan v Maguire [1996] 1 ILRM 395 508
McQuirk v Branigan, High Court Circuit Appeal (Morris J) 9 November 1992.....917
Meade v Minister for Agriculture Fisheries and Food [2010] IEHC 105.............710n
Meagher v Dublin City Council [2013] IEHC 474..................15, 16, 18, 39, 629, 791
Meagher, Re [1951] IR 100 558
Medforth v Blake [2000] Ch 86...13n
Medsted Associates Ltd v Canaccord Genuity Wealth (International) Ltd [2018] 1 WLR 314 ....282n
Memory Corporation plc v Sidhu [2000] Ch 645 ....748n
Memory Corporation plc v Sidhu (No. 2) [2000] 1 WLR 1443 753
Mendes v Guedalla (1862) 2 J & H 259 ....577n
Mengel's Will Trusts, Re [1962] Ch 791 1026

Mercedes Banz AG v Leiduck [1996] AC 284 ....749n
Mercier v Mercier [1903] 2 Ch 98 ....206n
Merck Sharp & Dohme Corporation v Clonmel Healthcare Ltd [2018] IECA 177, [2019] IESC 65 ....622, 650, 655, 657, 622n, 660–663n, 667, 691n, 694n, 697, 715n, 744
Meridian Communications Ltd v Eircell Ltd [2001] IESC 42 ....626, 688n
Merrins v Attorney General (1945) 79 ILTR 121 499
Meskell v CIE [1973] IR 121 ....743n
Metall und Rohstoff AG v Donaldson Lufkin & Jenrette Inc [1990] 1 QB 391 ....11, 329
Metro International SA v Independent News and Media plc [2006] 1 ILRM 414 ....656n, 657, 659, 660, 742n
Metropolitan Bank v Heiron (1880) 5 Ex D 319 ....279n, 283
Metropolitan Electric Supply Co. v Ginder [1901] 2 Ch 799 ....724, 725
Mettoy Pensions Trustees Ltd v Evans [1990] 1 WLR 1587 ....528, 614
Meyers v Casey (1913) 17 CLR 90 ....27n
Michael v Phillips [2017] EWHC 614 (QB) 305n
Microdata Information Services Ltd v Rivendale Ltd [1991] FSR 681 684
Microsoft Corporation v Brightpoint Ireland Ltd [2001] 1 ILRM 540 ....775–778, 783, 783n, 785
Midland Bank plc v Cooke [1995] 4 All ER 562 ....46, 238, 243, 247n
Midland Bank plc v Wyatt [1995] 1 FLR 696 ....96, 97
Mietz v Intership Yachting Sneek BV (Case C-99/96) [1999] ECR I–2277 ....770n
Miley v Attorney General for Ireland [1918] 1 IR 455 ....429, 430
Miley v Carty [1927] IR 541 ....1020, 1020n
Miller v Harrison (1871) IR 5 Eq 324 140
Miller v Jackson [1977] QB 966 635
Mills v Shields (No. 1) [1948] IR 367 ....147, 149
Mills v Shields (No. 2) [1950] IR 21 ....151n
Mills, Re [1930] 1 Ch 654 ....76n
Milroy v Lord (1862) 4 De GF & J 264 ....130–134, 137–139, 938n
Minchin v Gabbett [1896] 1 IR 1 1027
Minister for Arts Heritage the Gaeltacht and the Islands v Kennedy [2002] 2 ILRM 94 ....719n
Minister for Justice, Equality and Law Reform v Devine [2007] 1 IR 813 (HC), [2012] 1 IR 326 (SC) 646, 648
Ministry of Health v Simpson [1951] AC 251, see also Diplock, Re 3, 20, 160n, 993, 994n, 996, 998, 998n, 1002, 1012–1015n
Minwalla v Minwalla [2005] 1 FLR 771 ....97n
Miss World Ltd v Miss Ireland Beauty Pageant Ltd [2004] 2 IR 394 ....656n
Mitchelstown Co-Operative Agricultural Society Ltd v Golden Vale Products Ltd [1985] IEHC 51 ....660n
Moate v Moate [1948] 2 All ER 486 ....206n
Mobil Cerro Negro Ltd v Petroleos de Venezuela SA [2008] 1 Lloyd's Rep. 684 772
Moffitt v Bank of Ireland [2000] IEHC 106 ....370n
Moggridge v Thackwell (1803) 7 Ves 36 ....483n
Mollo v Mollo Chancery Division 8 October 1999 ....978n

Moloney v Laurib Investments Ltd High Court 1993 No. 3189P (Lynch J) 20 July 1993 ....757n, 774
Molyneux v Richard [1906] 1 Ch 34 ....819n
Monaghan County Council v Vaughan [1948] IR 306 ....844, 849, 871
Monck v Monck (1810) 1 Ba & B 298 ....1035n
Money Markets International Stockbrokers Ltd, Re [1999] 4 IR 267....1005, 1006
Money Markets International Stockbrokers Ltd (No. 2), Re [2001] 2 IR 17 ....170n
Money Markets International Stockbrokers Ltd, Re [2006] IEHC 349....1001n
Monson v Tussauds Ltd [1894] 1 QB 671 ....675n, 676n
Montagu's Settlement Trusts, Re [1987] Ch 264....361, 363, 365, 372
Moody v Cox [1917] 2 Ch 71 ....29, 30, 625
Moore v Attorney General [1927] IR 569....618
Moore v Butler (1805) 2 Sch & Lef 249....1031n
Moore v Kelly [1918] 1 IR 169 ....512, 513
Moore v McGlynn [1894] 1 IR 74....277, 278, 522, 561, 562
Moore v Moore (1874) LR 18 Eq 474....151n
Moore v Moore [2016] EWHC 2202 (Ch) [2018] EWCA Civ 2669 ....965n, 970n
Moore v Xnet Information Systems Ltd [2002] 2 ILRM 278 ....733n, 734, 739n
Moore, Re (1897) 31 ILTR 5 ....514n
Moran v Heathcote High Court QBD (Eady J) 15 January 2001 ....674n, 677n
Morgan v Morgan (1853) 4 Ir Ch R 606....1029, 1030n
Morgan, Re [1955] 1 WLR 738 470
Moriarty v Martin (1852) 3 Ir Ch R 26....93n, 1029n
Morice v Bishop of Durham (1804) 9 Ves 399....82n, 381, 382, 406n, 439
Morice v Bishop of Durham (1805) 10 Ves 522....110n
Morley v Bird (1798) 3 Ves 628 ....45n
Moroney, Re (1887) 21 LR Ir 27 ....507–511n
Morrin v Morrin (1886) 19 LR Ir 37 ....93n, 94n
Morris v An Bord Pleanala [2017] IEHC 354 ....695n
Morris-Garner v One Step (Support) Ltd [2018] 2 WLR 1353 643
Morrison v Coast Finance Ltd (1965) 55 DLR (2d) 710....914
Morrison v McFerran [1901] 1 IR 360 ....116n
Morrow v M'Conville (1883) 11 LR Ir 236 ....384n, 391–393, 396n, 446n
Mortimer v Bailey [2004] EWCA Civ 1514....633
Mortimer v Beckett [1920] 1 Ch 571....724n
Morton v Tewart (1842) 2 Y & C Cas Ch 67....86n
Moss v Cooper (1861) 1 J & H 367 see also Moss v Taylor 120, 121n
Moss v Taylor (1861) 1 J & H 367 see also Moss v Cooper 120, 121n
Moss, Re [1949] 1 All ER 495....467n
Motor Insurers Bureau of Ireland v Stanbridge [2011] 2 IR 78....508n, 509
Motorola Credit Corporation v Uzan (No. 2) [2004] 1 WLR 113 ....771n
Mouat v Clarke Boyce [1992] 2 NZLR 559 ....11n
Mount Kennett Investment Co. v O'Meara [2007] IEHC 420 ....794n, 839n
Mount Kennett Investment Co. v O'Meara (No.3) [2011] IEHC 210....793
Moyles v Mahon [2000] IEHC 197 ....884n, 917n
Muhammed v ARY Properties Ltd [2016] EWHC 1698 (Ch)....934n
Mulcahy v Mulcahy [2011] IEHC 186 ....883n, 884n, 918n
Mulhall v Haren [1981] IR 364 799

Mulholland v Commissioner of Valuation (1936) 70 ILTR 253 .....449n
Mullarkey v Broad [2007] EWHC 3400 (Ch) 354n
Mullarkey v Irish National Stud Co. Ltd [2004] IEHC 116 .....739n
Muller, Re [1953] NZLR 879 .....179n
Mulligan, Re [1998] 1 NZLR 481 .....548, 548n, 553, 589n
Mulroy, Re [1924] 1 IR 98 .....144n, 148n–149n
Multi Guarantee Co. Ltd, Re [1987] BCLC 257 .....173n
Mungalsingh v Juman [2015] UKPC 38 .....794n
Munster and Leinster Bank Ltd v Croker [1940] IR 185 922
Munster and Leinster Bank Ltd v Attorney General [1940] IR 19 446
Munster and Leinster Bank Ltd v Attorney General (1954) 91 ILTR 34 .....485n, 488n
Murad v Al-Saraj [2005] EWCA Civ 959 .....266, 267, 270, 270n
Murawski's Will Trusts, Re [1971] 1 WLR 707 .....467n
Murgitroyd & Co. Ltd v Purdy [2005] IEHC 110 623
Murless v Franklin (1818) 1 Swans 13 .....192n
Murphy v Abraham (1864) 15 Ir Ch R 371 511
Murphy v Allied Irish Banks Ltd [1994] 2 ILRM 220 .....38n, 594, 594n
Murphy v Attorney General [1982] IR 241 .....332, 334
Murphy v Harrington [1927] IR 339 824
Murphy v Irish Water [2016] IEHC 271 .....719n
Murphy v Launceston Property Finance Ltd [2017] IEHC 65 .....622n, 756n
Murphy v Murphy [1999] 1 WLR 282 .....562, 563
Murphy v Ryan [2009] IEHC 305 .....789n, 794n, 842
Murray Holdings Ltd v Oscatello Investments Ltd [2018] EWHC 162 (Ch) 848n
Murray v Murray [1996] 3 IR 251 .....253, 254, 256, 321, 324
Murray v Newsgroup Newspapers Ltd [2011] 2 IR 431 .....685, 686
Murtagh Properties v Cleary [1972] IR 330 743
Murtagh v Murtagh (1902) 36 ILTR 129 .....93n, 94n
Muschinski v Dodds (1985) 160 CLR 583 .....22n, 254n, 258n, 259, 316, 317, 324, 327, 335, 337, 952n
Mussett v Bingle [1876] WN 170 385–387
Mussoorie Bank Ltd v Raynor (1882) 7 App Cas 321 .....94n, 99n, 102
MWB Business Exchange Centres Ltd v Rock Advertising Ltd [2017] QB 604 .....923n

N. (A Child) (Financial Provision Dependency), Re [2009] EWHC 11 (Fam) 170n
N. v N. [1992] 2 IR 116 232
N.A.D. v T.D. [1985] ILRM 153 .....22n, 231, 233n, 319, 324
N.D. v S.D. [2017] EWHC 1507 (Fam) 139n
Nathan v Leonard [2003] 1 WLR 827 503
National Anti-Vivisection Society v IRC [1948] AC 21 .....413, 458n, 459n, 466n, 468, 469, 477
National Bank Ltd v Behan [1913] 1 IR 512 .....507n, 509n, 512, 513
National Carriers Ltd v Panalpina (Northern) Ltd [1981] AC 675 840–842
National Commercial Bank Jamaica Ltd v Olint Corporation Ltd [2009] 1 WLR 1405 .....650n–652, 656, 664, 705n–707, 716
National Crime Agency v Dong [2017] EWHC 3116 (Ch) 178, 179
National Crime Agency v Robb [2015] Ch 520 1004

National Irish Bank Ltd v Graham [1994] 1 IR 215..16
National Irish Bank Ltd v RTE [1998] 2 IR 465 ....27n, 720
National Mutual Life Association of Australasia Ltd v GTV Corporation Pty Ltd
[1989] VR 747, (1988) 80 ALR 553 ....680n
National Provincial Bank Ltd v Ainsworth [1965] AC 1175......................55, 55n, 59
National Tourism Development Authority v Coughlan
[2009] 3 IR 549 ....400n, 406n, 473
National Westminster Bank plc v Morgan [1985] AC 686.........878n, 887, 891, 919n
National Westminster Bank v Somer International (UK) Ltd [2002] QB 1286 ....991n
Nationwide Building Society v Davisons Solicitors [2012] EWCA Civ 1626......592n
Naujoks v National Institute of Bioprocessing Research and Training Ltd
[2006] IEHC 358, [2007] ELR 25..........................711n, 733n, 735n, 739n, 740
Naylor v Maher [2012] IEHC 408...934, 936, 974
Neal, Re (1966) 110 SJ 549 ....461n
Neale v Willis [1968] 19 P & CR 839 ....89n
Negus v Bahouse [2008] 1 FLR 381...935n, 937n
Neill v Neill [1904] 1 IR 513...609n
Nelson v Nelson (1995) 132 ALR 133 ....201, 212n, 219n, 221, 222
Nelson v Rye [1996] 1 WLR 1378 43
Neptune (Vehicle Washing Equipment) Ltd v Fitzgerald [1996] Ch 274...............289
Neste Oy v Lloyds Bank plc [1983] 2 Lloyd's Rep 658...170
Nestle v National Westminster Bank plc
[1993] 1 WLR 1260 ....526n,546–548, 612n, 613
Nestle v National Westminster Bank plc., Chancery Division, 29 June 1988.........553
Neville & Sons Ltd v Guardian Builders Ltd [1990] ILRM 601 (HC),
[1995] 1 ILRM 1 (SC)..839, 840
Neville Estates Ltd v Madden [1962] Ch 832 ....394, 395, 437n
New v Jones (1883) 1 Mac & G 685n 571n
New Zealand Maori Council v Foulkes [2016] 2 NZLR 337...................................579
New Zealand Mortgage Guarantee Co. Ltd v Wellington Newspapers Ltd
[1989] 1 NZLR 4..679n
Newey (deceased), Re [1994] 2 NZLR 590..297n
Newman v Clarke [2017] 4 WLR 26...573
Newport City Council v Charles [2009] 1 WLR 1884 ....986n
News Datacom Ltd v Lyons [1994] 1 ILRM 450...627
Ni Brudair, Re High Court 1976 No. 93 Sp (Gannon J) 5 February 1979 ....458n, 477
Nicholls v Jessup [1986] 1 NZLR 226 915
Nimmo v Westpac Banking Corporation [1993] 3 NZLR 218...................344n, 347n
Nippon Yusen Kaisha v Karageorgis [1975] 1 WLR 1093......................................747
Niru Battery Manufacturing Co. v Milestone Trading Ltd (No. 1)
[2004] QB 985...362n, 363n, 1016, 1017
Niyazi's Will Trusts, Re [1978] 1 WLR 910...415
Nolan Transport (Oaklands) Ltd v Halligan High Court 1993 No.1008P Keane J 22
March 1994, [1999] 1 IR 128 (SC) 629, 629n, 670n, 671
Nolan v Emo Oil Services Ltd [2009] ELR 122..739n
Nolan v Graves [1946] IR 376..789n, 849, 857, 860
Noonan v O'Connell High Court 1986 No. 2135P (Lynch J) 10 April 1987 916
Norreys v Franks (1874) IR 9 Eq 18...1019

North Devon and West Somerset Relief Fund Trusts, Re [1953] 1 WLR 1260 ....492n
North London Railway Co. v Great Northern Railway Co. (1883) 11 QBD 30 618
Northall (Deceased), Re [2010] EWHC 1448 (Ch) 185n
Northern Bank Finance Corporation Ltd v Charlton [1979] IR 149 ....865, 876, 920
Northern Bank Ltd v Henry [1981] IR 1 ....62, 63
Northern Development Holdings Ltd, Re Chancery Division,
6 October 1978 ....173, 174
Norton's Will Trusts, Re [1948] 2 All ER 842 ....464n
Nottage, Re [1895] 2 Ch 649 469
Nottingham Building Society v Eurodynamics Systems plc [1993] FSR 468 707
Novoship (UK) Ltd v Mikhaylyuk [2015] QB 499 ....342, 358, 360
NRC Holding Ltd v Danilitskiy [2017] EWHC 1431 (Ch) 192n
Nurendale t/a Panda Waste Services v Starrus Eco Holdings Ltd
[2015] IEHC 845 ....660n
NWL Ltd v Woods [1979] 1 WLR 1294 ....691, 694, 695
Nyland v Brennan, High Court 1970 No. 1548P (Pringle J) 19 December 1970....917
NZ Netherlands Society 'Oranje' Inc v Kuys [1973] 2 All ER 1222 ....27n

Ó Domhnaill v Merrick [1984] IR 151 ....37n, 38
O Ltd v Z [2005] EWHC 238 (Ch) 782, 784
Ó Murchú v Eircell Ltd [2001] IESC 15 ....624, 725
O Síodhacháin v O'Mahony [2002] IEHC 175 ....880n
O'Brien v Condon [1905] 1 IR 51 114
O'Brien v Kearney [1998] 2 ILRM 232 808
O'Brien v RTE [2015] IEHC 397 686
O'Brien v Sheil (1873) IR 7 Eq 255 ....210, 217
O'Byrne v Davoren [1994] 3 IR 373 ....80, 92, 107, 384n
O'Callaghan v Ballincollig Holdings Ltd, High Court 1987 No. E202
(Blayney J) 31 March 1993 943
O'Connell v Harrison [1927] IR 330 ....1022n
O'Connor v Harrington Ltd, High Court 1984 No. 69 MCA (Barr J)
28 May 1987 28
O'Connor v McCarthy [1982] IR 161 ....60n, 65, 792n
O'Connor v McNamara [2009] IEHC 190 ....835, 835n
O'Connor v P. Elliott & Co. [2010] IEHC 167 ....800n
O'Connor v Williams [2001] 1 IR 248 743
O'Connor, Re [1913] 1 IR 69 544
O'Connor's Estate, Re [1923] 1 IR 142 ....1023n
O'Dea v O'Briain [1992] ILRM 364 ....709n
O'Doherty v West Limerick Resources Ltd Supreme Court, 14 May 1999 ....30n
O'Donnell v Bank of Ireland [2014] IESC 77 ....371, 374
O'Donnell v Shanahan [2009] BCC 822 289
O'Flaherty v Browne [1907] 2 IR 416 137
O'Flanagan and Ryan's Contract, Re [1905] 1 IR 280 576
O'Flanagan v Ray-Ger Ltd High Court 1980 No. 2858P (Costello J)
28 April 1983 ....880n
O'Flynn v Carbon Finance Ltd [2014] IEHC 458 ....660n
O'G. v Attorney General [1985] ILRM 61 ....209n

O'Gara v Ulster Bank Ireland DAC [2019] IEHC 213....................................622n, 653n
O'Hanlon v Logue [1906] 1 IR 247..384n, 443, 446
O'Hare v Dundalk Racing (1999) Ltd [2015] IEHC 198 ....42, 632
O'Leary v An Post [2016] IEHC 237 ....710n
O'Leary v Volkswagen Group Ireland Ltd [2013] IEHC 318 ....710n
O'Mahony v Examiner Publications (Cork) Ltd
[2010] IEHC 413 ....651n, 708n, 710n
O'Mahony v Horgan [1995] 12 IR 411................747n, 750, 758, 760–763, 773n, 774
O'Mahony v Lowe [2013] IEHC 361 ....658n
O'Mahony v McNamara [2005] 2 IR 519 565
O'Malley v Aravon School Ltd High Court (Costello P)
13 August 1997..733n, 734n
O'Meara v Bank of Scotland plc [2011] IEHC 402......................188–190, 205n, 208
O'Neill v O'Keeffe [2002] 2 IR 1 786
O'Neill v Ryan (No. 3) [1992] 1 IR 166...................791, 829, 832n, 852n, 867n, 870
O'Neill, Re [1943] IR 562 582
O'Neill, Re [1989] IR 544 ....512, 514
O'Regan v White [1919] 2 IR 339...26, 824, 824n
O'Rorke v Bolingbroke (1877) 2 App Cas 814 913
O'Rourke v Darbishire [1920] AC 581...562n
O'Rourke v O'Rourke [2018] IEHC 791...932
O'Rourke v Revenue Commissioners [1996] 2 IR 1 ....333, 334
O'Sullivan v Management Agency & Music Ltd [1985] QB 428...............883n, 920n
Oakes v Turquand (1867) LR 2 HL 325 ....878n
Oatway, Re [1903] 2 Ch 356..1002
OBA Enterprises Ltd v TMC Trading International Ltd [1998] IEHC 169............761
Oblique Financial Services Ltd v The Promise Production Co. Ltd
[1994] 1 ILRM 74 ....622n, 650n
Odstock Private Care Ltd's Application for Registration as a Charity
[2008] WTLR 675 ....463, 464
Official Assignee in Bankruptcy v Wilson [2008] 3 NZLR 45............................93n, 97
Official Custodian for Charities v Mackey [1985] Ch 168...669
Ogilvie v Littleboy (1897) 13 TLR 399...872, 873
OJSC Oil Co. Yugraneft v Abramovich [2008] EWHC 2613 (Comm).................329n
Okunade v Minister for Justice, Equality and Law Reform
[2012] 3 IR 152 ....655n, 658, 663, 665, 668, 668n,
697, 699, 700, 701, 703, 713, 714
Oldham, Re [1925] Ch 75...297, 299
Olins v Walters [2009] 2 WLR 1, [2009] Ch 212 ....299, 301
Ong v Ping [2017] EWCA Civ 2069 ....86n,141n
Ontario (Ontario Securities Commission) v Greymac Credit Corporation
(1989) 52 DLR (4th) 767 (1986) 30 DLR (4th) 1 Ont CA............................1007n
Oosterhuis v Saetrum [2007] NZHC 416 ....258n
Oppenheim v Tobacco Securities Trust Co. Ltd [1951] AC 297 ......402n, 409n, 412n,
423n, 425n, 431, 432, 432n, 434, 435, 451, 452n, 453n, 456
Ormsby, Re (1809) 1 Ba & B 189..570n
Orr v Ford (1989) 167 CLR 316 ....39, 629
Orr v Zomax Ltd [2004] 1 IR 486 ....739n, 741

Orwell's Will Trusts, Re [1982] 1 WLR 1337 ....570n
Osmond Ireland On Farm Business Ltd v McFarland [2010] IEHC 295 ....622n, 623, 651n
Osoba, Re [1978] 1 WLR 791 (ChD), [1979] 1 WLR 247 (CA) 163n, 164, 382n
OT Computers Ltd v First National Tricity Finance Ltd [2007] WTLR 165 103
Ottaway v Norman [1972] Ch 698....115, 127
Ottey v Grundy [2003] EWCA Civ 1176....933n, 948n, 951n, 966
Oughtred v IRC [1960] AC 206....90n
Overton v Banister (1844) 3 Hare 503....27, 592n, 625n
Owen v Owen [1897] 1 IR 580....1019n
Owens v Greene [1932] IR 225 ....181–187n, 399
Owens v Duggan, High Court (Hardiman J) 2 April 2004 ....801, 956
Oxley v Hiscock [2004] 3 WLR 715 ....238, 243–245, 247, 251, 252n, 976n, 980

P & P Property Ltd v Owen White and Catlin LLP [2016] EWHC 2276 (Ch) 592n
P. Elliott & Co. Ltd v Building and Allied Trades Union [2006] IEHC 320....670n, 673, 674
P.D. v R.D. [2015] IEHC 174 ....235n
P.T. v Wicklow County Council [2017] IEHC 623....700n
Padbury v Clarke (1850) 2 McN & G 298....1030n
Padden v Bevan Ashford [2012] 1 WLR 1759 ....896n
Page One Records Ltd v Britton [1968] 1 WLR 157....727, 741
Page v Cox (1852) 10 Hare 163....48n
Pallant v Morgan [1953] Ch 43....35, 303n, 305n–308n, 981
Palmer v Simmonds (1854) 2 Drew 221....93n, 98n
Paradise Motor Co., Re [1968] 1 WLR 1125....212n
Paragon Finance plc v D.B. Thakerar & Co. [1999] 1 All ER 400 ....335, 339–341n, 360
Pardoe, Re [1906] 2 Ch 184....448n
Parfitt v Lawless (1872) LR 2 P & D 462....887n
Parker v McKenna (1874) 10 Ch App 96 ....285, 288
Parker v Moseley [1965] VR 580....492n
Parker, Re [1966] IR 309 ....76n, 77n, 80n, 91, 92, 105n, 107, 108
Parkes v Parkes [1980] ILRM 137....28, 202, 219, 220, 223, 625n
Parkin v Thorold (1852) 16 Beav 59 47
Parol Ltd v Carroll Village (Retail Management) Services Ltd [2010] IEHC 498....815n
Parsons v Kavanagh [1990] ILRM 560 ....743, 744, 746n
Pascoe v Turner [1979] 1 WLR 431 ....939, 957n–960, 976n
Pasko v Pasko [2002] BCSC 435....216n
Pasture Properties Ltd v Evans [1999] IEHC 214 ....645n, 646n, 660
Patel v Ali [1984] Ch 283 ....831, 837n
Patel v Mirza [2017] AC 467 ....13n, 33, 34, 194, 196, 198, 199, 199n, 202, 204, 213, 219, 221n, 223, 250
Patel v Vigh [2013] EWHC 3403 (Ch)....242n
Patel v W.H. Smith (Eziot) Ltd [1987] 1 WLR 853....669, 669n
Paterson v Murphy (1853) 11 Hare 88, 91-2 ....86n
Patten v Hamilton [1911] 1 IR 46....286

Patten, Re [1929] 2 Ch 276......469n
Patterson v Murphy [1978] ILRM 85......21n, 639, 742n
Paul v Constance [1977] 1 WLR 527......86n, 92, 141
Paul v Paul (1882) 20 Ch D 742......136n
Pauling's Settlement Trusts, Re [1962] 1 WLR 86 (ChD)......591
Pauling's Settlement Trusts, Re [1964] Ch 303 (CA)......27n, 37n, 592, 882
Pauling's Settlement Trusts (No. 2), Re [1963] Ch 576......541n
Payman v Lanjani [1985] Ch 457......920
Peacock's Estate, Re (1872) LR 14 Eq 236......1039n
Pechar, Deceased, Re [1969] 1 NZLR 574......315n
Pecore v Pecore (2007) 279 DLR (4th) 513....175n, 176n, 205n, 211, 212, 212n, 218
Peel v Canada (1992) 98 DLR (4th) 140......337n
Pehrsson v Von Greyerz [1999] UKPC 26......132n
Pell Frischmann Engineering Ltd v Bow Valley Iran [2011] 1 WLR 2370......643
Pengelly v Pengelly [2008] Ch 375......24n, 83n
Penn v Lord Baltimore (1750) 1 Ves Sen 444......52
Pennington v Waine [2002] 1 WLR 2075......133–135, 139, 140
Permanent TSB plc v Skoczylas [2013] IEHC 42......690
Pernod Ricard Comrie plc v FII (Fyffes) plc [1988] IEHC 48, [1988] IESC 7.....810n
Perowne, Re [1951] Ch 785......76n
Perrin v Lyon (1807) 9 East 170......503n
Perry v Twomey (1888) 21 LR Ir 480......442n
Persimmon Homes Ltd v Hillier [2018] EWHC 221 (Ch)......848n
Pesca Valentia Ltd v Minister for Fisheries and Forestry [1985] IR 193......701
Peso Silver Mines Ltd (NPL) v Cropper (1966) 58 DLR (2d) 1......290n
Pettigrew v Edwards [2017] EWHC 8 (Ch)......540
Pettingall v Pettingall (1842) 11 LJ Ch 176......388
Pettitt v Pettitt [1970] AC 777......206, 209, 210, 215n, 236
Pettkus v Becker (1980) 117 DLR (3d) 257......254, 317n, 326, 332n
Phelan v BIC (Ireland) Ltd [1997] ELR 208......731n, 733n, 736n, 738
Phelan v Slattery (1887) 19 LR Ir 177......384n
Phillips v Lamdin [1949] 2 KB 33......809n
Phillips v News Group Newspapers Ltd [2013] 1 AC 1......780
Phillips v Phillips (1862) 4 De GF & J 208......56
Philpott v Irish Examiner Ltd [2016] IEHC 62......687
Phipps v Boardman [1964] 2 All ER 187......275n
Phonographic Performance (Ireland) Ltd v Chariot Inns High Court 1992 No. 4673P (Keane J) 7 October 1992......636
Pianta v National Finance and Trustees Ltd (1964) 38 ALJR 232......794n
Pickersgill v Rodger (1876) 5 Ch D 163......1027
Pilkington v IRC [1964] AC 612......583n
Piper, Re [1946] 2 All ER 503......502, 504n
Pipikas v Trayans (2018) 359 ALR 210......803n
Pirbright v Salwey [1896] WN 86......387
Pitcairn, Re [1896] 2 Ch 199......554n
Pitt v Holt [2012] Ch 132 (CA), [2013] 2 AC 108 (SC)......528, 528n, 530, 533–535, 537, 862n, 872–876, 892n
Plimmer v Mayor of Wellington (1884) 9 App Cas 699......940, 944, 957n

Plumptre's Marriage Settlement, Re [1910] 1 Ch 609....................................153, 154n
PMPA Ltd v PMPS Ltd High Court 1992 No. 702Sp (Murphy J)
27 June 1994..1009, 1011n
Polai v Toronto (City) (1970) 8 DLR (3d) 689..29n
Pollock v Ennis [1921] 1 IR 181...519n
Pollock, Re (1885) 28 Ch D 552...1038–1040
Polly Peck International plc (No. 2), Re [1998] 3 All ER 812 ....329, 330, 330n
Polly Peck International plc v Nadir (No. 2) [1992] 4 All ER 769........346n, 773, 774
Ponder, Re [1921] 2 Ch 59...81n
Portman Building Society v Dusangh [2000] 2 All ER (Comm) 221...........914n, 915
Posner v Scott-Lewis [1987] Ch 25..811, 821n
Powell v Benney [2007] EWCA Civ 1283 ....966, 981n
Powell v London Borough of Brent [1987] IRLR 466.................................728n–730
Powell v Powell [1900] 1 Ch 243...884n
Powell v Thompson [1991] 1 NZLR 597 ....18n, 328n, 343n, 373
Power Adhesives v Sweeney [2017] EWHC 676 (Ch)......................................534
Power v Conroy [1980] ILRM 31..226n
Powerscourt Estates v Gallagher [1984] ILRM 123.........................751, 752n, 759, 760
Powerteam Electrical Services Ltd v Electricity Supply Board
[2016] IEHC 87...622n
Powys v Mansfield (1837) 3 My & Cr 359..1034n
Prazic v Prazic [2006] 2 FLR 1128..53
Preedy v Dunne [2015] EWHC 2713 (Ch)...932n
Premier Dairies Ltd v Doyle High Court 1995 No. 7008P (Kinlen J)
29 September 1995, [1996] 1 ILRM 363 723
Prendergast v Joyce [2009] IEHC 199, [2009] 3 IR 519............187, 881, 884n, 885n,
886, 909n, 913n, 918
Prendergast v McLaughlin [2009] IEHC 250..983
Prendiville v Prendiville [1995] 2 ILRM 578..........121n, 122n, 123n, 124, 125, 126n
Prescott, Re [1990] 2 IR 342...488, 489n
Prest v Petrodel Resources Ltd [2013] 2 AC 415 ....178n, 192
Preston v Greene [1909] 1 IR 172 1034
Prevost, Re [1930] 2 Ch 383..454n
Price v Keenaghan Developments Ltd [2007] IEHC 190.....................................802
Price v Strange [1978] Ch 337...818n, 821n, 824
Pride of Derby and Derbyshire Angling Association Ltd v British Celanese Ltd
[1953] Ch 149..620
Pringle v Ireland [2013] 3 IR 1 703
Printers and Transferrers Amalgamated Trades Protection Society, Re
[1899] 2 Ch 184..166
Private Research Ltd v Brosnan [1996] 1 ILRM 27...664
Proctor v Bayley (1889) 42 Ch D 390 ....716n
Production Association Minsk Tractor Works v Saenko [1998] IEHC 36 ....760, 773n
Proprietors of Wakatu v Attorney-General [2017] 1 NZLR 423 ....44n, 100
Protheroe v Protheroe [1968] 1 All ER 1111 276
Provincial Bank of Ireland v McKeever [1941] IR 471 ....574, 575, 884, 884n, 885
Prowting 1968 Trustee One Ltd v Amos-Yeo [2015] EWHC 2480 (Ch) 862n
Prunty v Crowley [2016] IEHC 293 ....800, 956n

Pryce, Re [1917] 1 Ch 234 ... 154n, 155n, 156
Pugh's Will Trusts, Re [1967] 1 WLR 1262 ... 160n
Pullan v Koe [1913] 1 Ch 9 ... 153, 154n
Pulvers v Chan [2007] EWHC 2406 (Ch) ... 365n
Purrunsing v A'Court & Co. [2016] 4 WLR 81 ... 592n
Pym v Lockyer (1841) 5 My & Cr 29 ... 1035, 1039n

Q. v Q. [2009] 1 FLR 935 ... 196, 930n, 948n, 964n, 976n, 981n
Quarter Master UK Ltd v Pyke [2005] 1 BCLC 245 ... 290n, 292n–294n
Quartz Hill Consolidated Gold Mining Co. v Beall
(1882) 20 Ch D 501 ... 617n, 675n, 676n
Quigley v Health Service Executive [2017] IEHC 654 ... 710n, 712n, 715n
Quin v Armstrong (1876) IR 11 Eq 161 ... 1041
Quinlivan v O'Dea [2010] 1 ILRM 72 ... 677n
Quinn v Dean High Court, Wellington, A 123/84 30 July 1986 ... 116n
Quinn v Irish Bank Resolution Corporation Ltd [2016] 1 IR 1 ... 34, 195, 203, 837n
Quinn, Re (1953) 88 ILTR 161 ... 448, 448n, 488n
Quinn's Supermarket v Attorney General [1972] IR 1 ... 437
Quinton v Frith (1868) IR 2 Eq 396 ... 273n

R. (Proctor) v Hutton [1978] NI 139 ... 879, 880, 883n
R. v Advertising Standards Authority Ltd, ex p. Vernons Organisation Ltd
[1992] 1 WLR 1289 ... 674n, 679n
R. v Canadian Broadcasting Corporation (2018) 417 DLR (4th) 587 ... 708n
R. v District Auditor, ex p. West Yorkshire Metropolitan County Council
(1986) 26 RVR 24 ... 110
R. v Ghosh [1982] QB 1053 ... 354n
R. v Kensington Income Tax Commissioners, ex p. de Polignac
[1917] 1 KB 486 ... 753, 755n
R. v Newman (1684) 1 Lev 284 ... 425n
R. v R. High Court 1978 No.574 Sp (McMahon J) 12 January 1979 ... 230n
R. v Radio Authority, ex p. Bull [1998] QB 294 ... 477
R. v Secretary of State for Transport, ex p. Factortame Ltd (No. 2) (Case C-213/89)
[1991] 1 AC 603 ... 707
R. (Hodkin) v Registrar General of Births, Deaths and Marriages
[2014] AC 610 ... 438
R. (Independent Schools Council) v Charity Commission for England and Wales
[2012] Ch 214 ... 409–411n, 414, 431–433
R.F. v M.F. [1995] 2 ILRM 572 ... 205n, 207, 208, 216, 218
R.K. v M.K. High Court 1978 No. 330 Sp (Finlay P) 24 October 1978 ... 233n
Racal Group Services Ltd v Ashmore [1995] STC 1151 ... 862n
Radford v Wexford Corporation (1954) 89 ILTR 184 ... 718
Raftland Pty Ltd v Commissioner of Taxation (2008) 246 ALR 406 ... 97
Rainbow Estates Ltd v Tokenhold Ltd [1999] Ch 64 ... 820, 825n
Raine, Re [1956] Ch 417 ... 448n
Ralli's Will Trusts, Re [1964] Ch 288 ... 136n
Ramsden v Dyson (1866) LR 1 HL 129 ... 939, 942n, 943, 945, 955, 960, 981
Randall v Russell (1817) 3 Mer 190 ... 275n

Rank Film Distributors Ltd v Video Information Centre [1982] AC 380 ....759n, 775n, 780–782
Ras al Khaimah Investment Authority and others v Bestfort Development LLP [2018] 1 WLR 1099 ....750n
Rascal Trucking Ltd v Nishi (2013) 359 DLR (4th) 575 ....176n, 254n
Rathwell v Rathwell [1978] 2 SCR 436 326
Ravenseft Properties Ltd v Stewart's Supermarkets Ltd Chancery Division (Girvan J) 6 May 1997 ....815n
Rawlings v Chapman [2015] EWHC 180 (Ch) 931n
Rawlinson v Ames [1925] Ch 96 ....806n
Rayner v Preston (1881) 18 Ch D 1 312
RBC Trustees Ltd v Stubbs [2017] EWHC 180 (Ch) 862n
Read v Hodgins (1844) 7 Ir Eq R 17 442
Reade v Reade (1880) 9 LR Ir 409 ....1033n
Reading v Attorney-General [1951] AC 507 278
Reading v Reading [2015] EWHC 946 (Ch) 864
Real Estate and Business Brokers (Director) v NRS Mississauga Inc (2000) 194 DLR (4th) 526 ....368n
Recher's Will Trusts, Re [1972] Ch 526 ....381n, 394
Reddy v Fitzmaurice (1952) 86 ILTR 127 440
Redland Bricks Ltd v Morris [1970] AC 652 ....704n, 705, 716, 716n, 818
Rees, Re [1920] 2 Ch 59 ....439n
Rees' Will Trusts, Re [1950] Ch 204 ....162n
Refco Inc. v Eastern Trading Co. [1999] 1 Lloyd's Rep 159 772
Regal (Hastings) Ltd v Gulliver [1967] 2 AC 134 ....266n, 291, 295
Regan v Paul Properties DPF No 1 Ltd [2007] Ch 135 ....638n
Registered Securities Ltd, Re [1991] 1 NZLR 545 ....1007n
Reichenbach v Quinn (1888) 21 LR Ir 138 ....384n
Reid, Re (1921) 50 OLR 595 184
Reidy v McGreevy High Court 1990 No. 11804P (Barron J) 19 March 1993 ....335, 983
Relax Food Corporation Ltd v Brown Thomas & Co. Ltd [2009] IEHC 181 ....622n, 652n, 725n
Relfo Ltd v Varsani [2014] EWCA Civ 360 374
Rennell v IRC [1964] AC 173 ....515n
Reno Engrais et Produits Chemiques SA v Irish Agricultural Wholesale Society Ltd [1976-77] ILRM 179 ....622n
Representative Church Body v Attorney General [1988] IR 19 ....484, 494
Republic Bank Ltd v Lochan [2015] UKPC 26 ....943n
Republic of Haiti v Duvalier [1990] QB 202 ....766, 766n
Resch's Will Trusts, Re [1969] 1 AC 514 ....461n, 463
Reveille Independent LLC v Anotech International (UK) Ltd [2016] EWCA Civ 443 ....952n
Revenue Commissioners v Moroney [1972] IR 372 924
Revenue Commissioners v Sisters of Charity of the Incarnate Word [1998] 2 IR 553 401
Revenue Commissioners v Stapleton [1937] IR 225 ....113n
Reynolds v Malocco [1999] 2 IR 203 ....669n, 677, 680–682

Rice v Rice (1853) 2 Drew 73 56
Richards v Delbridge (1874) LR 18 Eq 11 ....137, 140n
Richards v Wood [2014] EWCA Civ 327 549
Rickerby v Nicholson [1912] 1 IR 343 ....438n
Ringsend Property Ltd v Donatex Ltd [2009] IEHC 568 841
Riordan v Banon (1876) IR 10 Eq 469 ....23n, 119–121n, 125n
Riverlate Properties Ltd v Paul [1975] Ch 133 ....853, 871
Robb v Dorrian (1877) IR 11 CL 292 ....440n
Robb v Hammersmith and Fulham London Borough Council [1991] ICR 514 ....728n–730n
Roberts v Kenny [2000] 1 IR 33 599
Roberts v O'Neill [1983] IR 47 ....830, 831
Roberts, Re [1946] Ch 1 ....209n
Robinson v Crosse & Blackwell Ltd [1940] IR 56 ....274n,275n
Robinson v Moore [1962-3] Ir Jur Rep 29 ....77, 79n
Robinson v Robinson (1877) IR 10 Eq 189 ....543n
Robinson, Re [1951] Ch 198 ....461, 461n
Robison v Killey (1862) 30 Beav 520 ....582n
Rochefoucauld v Boustead [1897] 1 Ch 196 ....23n, 87n–89, 112n
Rochfort v Seaton [1896] 1 IR 18 ....542n
Rogers v An Post [2014] IEHC 412 ....696, 697
Rogge v Rogge [2019] EWHC 1949 (Ch) 874n
Romaine Estate v Romaine (2001) 205 DLR (4th) 320 ....193, 212n
Ron West Motors Ltd v Broadcasting Corporation of New Zealand (No.2) [1989] 3 NZLR 520 ....679n
Rooney and McParland Ltd v Carlin [1981] NI 138 845
Roper's Trusts, Re (1879) 11 Ch D 272 ....536n
Rorke v Abraham [1895] 1 IR 334 ....77n
Rorke's Estate, Re (1865) 15 Ir Ch R 316 ....507n
Rose v Greer [1945] IR 503 507
Rose, Re [1952] Ch 499 ....132–135, 139
Rowe v Prance [1999] 2 FLR 787 ....140n, 141
Rowland v Vancouver College Ltd (2001) 205 DLR 193 29
Rowland v Witherden (1851) 3 McN & G 568 ....577n
Royal Bank of Scotland plc v Chandra [2010] 1 Lloyd's Rep 677 ....880, 893n, 897n, 881n
Royal Bank of Scotland v Etridge (No.1) [1997] 3 All ER 628 ....894, 897, 898n, 901–904, 906, 910, 911, 911n, 912
Royal Bank of Scotland v Etridge (No. 2) [2002] 2 AC 773 ....879–882, 884n, 889–898, 904, 910n
Royal Bristol Permanent Building Society v Bomash (1887) 35 Ch D 390 ....311n
Royal Brunei Airlines Sdn Bhd v Tan Kok Ming [1995] 2 AC 378 ....341n, 343, 344, 347, 348, 350, 350n–353, 355, 356n, 373n
Royal Choral Society v IRC [1943] 2 All ER 101 429
Royal College of Nursing v St Marylebone Borough Council [1959] 1 WLR 1077 ....429n
Royal College of Surgeons of England v National Provincial Bank Ltd [1952] AC 631 ....406n, 430

Royal College of Surgeons of England, Re [1899] 1 QB 871 430
Royal Kilmainham Hospital, Re [1966] IR 451 ....483, 484, 486n, 489, 491, 494
Royal National Lifeboat Institution v Headley [2016] EWHC 1948 (Ch) 539n
Royal North Shore Hospital of Sydney v Attorney General for New South Wales (1938) 60 CLR 396...479n
Royal Society v Robinson [2015] EWHC 3442 (Ch)...863n
Rumball, Re [1956] Ch 105 ....440n
Rushbrooke v O'Sullivan [1908] 1 IR 232 818
Russell v Russell [1903] 1 IR 168 ....581n
Russell v Scott (1936) 55 CLR 440 ....184, 186, 189n
Russell-Cooke Trust Co. v Prentis [2003] 2 All ER 478 1004
Rutherfoord v Maziere (1862) 13 Ir Ch R 204 ....591n
Ryan v Attorney General [1965] IR 294...504n
Ryan v Connolly [2001] 1 IR 627..923n
Ryan v Mutual Tontine Westminster Chambers Association [1893] 1 Ch 116..724n, 811, 821n
Ryanair Ltd v Aer Rianta cpt [2001] IEHC 229 ....621n, 719
Ryanair Ltd v Club Travel Ltd [2012] IEHC 165...651n
Ryanair v Irish Airline Pilots Association High Court (Murphy J) 19 June 2012...630
Rymer, Re [1895] 1 Ch 19 ....490n

S. (A Child), Re [2005] 1 AC 593..873n
S. v J. (Beneficial Ownership) [2016] EWHC 586 (Fam)....................................238n
S.D. v B.D. High Court 1981 No. 194 Sp (Murphy J) 19 March 1982 ....230n
S.V. Nevenas & Co. v Walker [1914] 1 Ch 413...837n
Sabmiller Africa BV v East African Breweries Ltd [2009] EWHC 2140 (Comm)..707n
Sale, Re [1913] 2 Ch 697...557n
Saleh v Romanous [2010] NSWCA 274...985n
Salisbury-Jones, Re [1938] 3 All ER 459 ....216n
Salt v Cooper (1880) 16 Ch D 544 10
Salt v Stratstone Specialist Ltd [2015] 2 CLC 269...866
Salter, Re [1911] 1 IR 289 438
Salvation Army Trustee Co. Ltd v W. Yorkshire Metropolitan County Council (1981) 41 P & CR 179 ....929, 929n
Samad v Thompson [2008] EWHC 2809 (Ch)..980n
Sambach v Dalston (1634) Toth 188..69n
Sandbrook, Re [1912] 2 Ch 471 ....504n
Sanders' Will Trusts, Re [1954] Ch 265, The Times, 22 July 1954........................415
Sanderson's Trusts, Re (1857) 3 K & J 497..163
Sandhu v Sandhu [2016] EWCA Civ 1050...246n
Sanford, Re [1901] 1 Ch 939 98
Sansom v Gardner [2009] EWHC 3369 (QB)..212n
Santander UK v RA Legal Solicitors [2014] EWCA Civ 183 ....592n
Sargeant v National Westminster Bank plc (1990) 61 P & CR 518........................573n
Satnam Investments Ltd v Dunlop Heywood Ltd [1999] 3 All ER 65 ....348n
Satterthwaite's Will Trusts, Re [1966] 1 WLR 277 ....467, 486n

Saul's Trust, Re [1951] Ir Jur Rep 34 ....1027n
Saunders v Al Himaly [2017] EWHC 2219 (Ch) 953n
Saunders v Vautier (1841) Cr & Ph 240 ....608, 609n
Savage v Dunningham [1974] Ch 181 ....275n
Savage v Nolan High Court 1976 No. 2395 P (Costello J) 20 July 1978 24
Sawdon Estate v Watch Tower Bible and Tract Society of Canada
(2014) 370 DLR (4th) 686 ....211n
Sawyer v Sawyer (1883) 28 Ch D 595 593
Sayer, Re [1957] Ch 423 ....108n
Sayers v Collyer (1884) 28 Ch D 103 ....42n, 631
Saylor v Madsen Estate (2007) 279 DLR (4th) 547 ....212n
Sayre v Hughes (1868) LR 5 Eq 376 ....212n
Scally v Rhatigan [2012] IEHC 140 525
Scandinavian Trading Tanker Co. AB v Flota Petrolera Ecuatoriana
[1983] 2 AC 694 ....725n
Scarisbrick, Re [1951] Ch 622 ....76n, 410n, 411n, 417n, 419–420, 421, 424
Schebsman, Re [1944] 1 Ch 83 ....74n
Schmidt v Rosewood Trust Ltd [2003] 2 AC 709 ....107n, 564, 565, 567, 615
Schobelt v Barber (1966) 60 DLR (2d) 519 ....315n
Schomberg v Taylor [2013] EWHC 2269 (Ch) 888n
Schrader v Schrader [2013] EWHC 466 (Ch) 888n
Schwabacher, Re (1908) 98 LT 127 ....810n
Scott v Brownrigg (1881) 9 LR Ir 246 ....120n, 121n, 161n, 439
Scott v Frank F. Scott (London) Ltd [1940] Ch 794 ....860n
Scott v National Trust for Places of Historic Interest or Natural Beauty
[1998] 2 All ER 705 ....526n, 528n, 533n, 535, 567, 576n
Scott v Scott [1924] 1 IR 141 ....58, 1015n
Scottish Burial Reform and Cremation Society v Glasgow City Corporation
[1968] AC 138 ....407n, 408n
Scottish Equitable Life Assurance Society, Re [1902] 1 Ch 282 ....191n
Scowcroft, Re [1898] 2 Ch 638 ....464n, 475, 475n
Scruttons Ltd v Midland Silicones Ltd [1962] AC 446 ....73n
Seager v Copydex Ltd [1967] 1 WLR 923 11
Seaton v Seddon [2012] 1 WLR 3636 ....340n
Sechiari, Re [1950] 1 All ER 417 ....558n
Secure 2013 Corp Inc v Tiger Calcium Services Inc
(2017) 417 DLR (4th) 509 ....779n
Secured Property Loans Ltd v Floyd [2011] 2 IR 652 916
Seddon v North Eastern Salt Co. Ltd [1905] 1 Ch 326 ....878n
Seeley v Jago (1717) P Wms 389 ....1024n
Segelman, Re [1996] Ch 171 ....410n, 411n, 415, 418, 419n, 420
Segelov v Ernst and Young Services Pty Ltd [2015] NSWCA 156 ....569n
Sekhon v Alissa [1989] 2 FLR 94 ....195, 213n
Selangor United Rubber Estates Ltd v Craddock (No. 3)
[1968] 1 WLR 1555 ....309, 339, 340n, 343n, 345
Selkirk v McIntyre [2013] 3 NZLR 265 ....589n, 590, 590n
Sellack v Harris (1708) 5 Vin Abr 521 112
Semelhago v Paramadevan (1996) 136 DLR (4th) 1 ....794n

Sen v Headley [1991] Ch 425 150
Series 5 Software v Clarke [1996] 1 All ER 853 ....650n, 655
Service Corporation International plc v Channel Four Television Corp Ltd [1999] EMLR 83 684
Sewell's Estate, Re (1870) LR 11 Eq 80....554n
Shah v Greening [2016] EWHC 548 (Ch)....831
Shah v Shah [2010] EWCA Civ 1408....139
Shalson v Russo [2005] Ch 281 ....96n, 97n, 1002n, 1008
Shanahan v Redmond High Court 1994 No. 129 Sp (Carroll J) 21 June 1994 50
Shanahan's Stamp Auctions Ltd v Farrelly [1962] IR 386 ....996n, 1001, 1002n, 1004, 1005
Shannon Travel Ltd, Re High Court 1970 No. 3849P (Kenny J) 8 May 1972....1012
Sharpe (a Bankrupt), Re [1980] 1 WLR 219 ....258n
Sharpe v Harrison [1922] 1 Ch 512 ....722n
Shaw v Applegate [1977] 1 WLR 970 ....42n, 631n, 632, 632n, 721n, 945
Shaw v Foster (1872) LR 5 HL 321....313
Shaw, Re [1957] 1 WLR 729 ....396n, 426–429n
Sheane v Fetherstonhaugh [1914] 1 IR 268....1022
Sheehan v Brecccia [2017] IEHC 692 ....659n, 645
Sheehy v Ryan High Court 2002 No. 10338P (Peart J) 29 August 2002....739n
Sheehy v Talbot [2008] IEHC 207....45n, 233, 252n
Shelbourne Hotel Holdings Ltd v Torriam Hotel Operating Co. Ltd [2010] 2 IR 52 ....712, 712n, 714, 715, 715n
Shelfer v City of London Electric Lighting Co. [1895] 1 Ch 287 637–640
Shell UK Ltd v Lostock Garages Ltd [1976] 1 WLR 1187 ....30n, 626n
Shephard v Cartwright [1955] AC 431 ....204, 210, 212n, 217, 218
Shepherd Homes Ltd v Sandham [1971] Ch 340 ....706, 708, 721
Shepherds Investments Ltd v Walters [2006] EWHC 836 (Ch) 288n, 293n
Sheppard v Murphy (1868) IR 2 Eq 544 ....838, 839
Sheridan v Louis Fitzgerald Group Ltd [2006] IEHC 125 ....621n, 622, 622n, 725n, 806n
Sherlock's Estate, Re [1899] 2 IR 561 ....1020, 1021n
Sherrard v Barron [1923] 1 IR 21 ....285, 286n
Shiel v McKeon [2007] 2 ILRM 144....25n, 35, 307
Shillington v Portadown UDC [1911] 1 IR 247 ....458, 471
Shilmore Enterprises Corporation v Phoenix 1 Aviation Ltd [2008] EWHC 169 (QB) 707n
Shipley Urban District Council v Bradford Corporation [1936] Ch 375....844
Shirley Engineering Ltd v Irish Telecommunications Investments plc [1999] IEHC 204....796n, 798n, 799, 799n
Shortill v Grannan (1920) 55 DLR 416 ....184n
Shortt v Data Packaging Ltd [1994] ELR 251....733n, 736n, 738
Sick and Funeral Society of St John's Sunday School, Golcar, Re [1973] Ch 51....166n, 169
Sidebottom Ltd v Leonard High Court (O'Keeffe P) 18 May 1973 808
Sidhu v Van Dyke (2014) 308 ALR 232....962, 985n, 989n
Sidmouth v Sidmouth (1840) 2 Beav 447....217n
Sieff v Fox [2005] 1 WLR 3811 ....528, 530, 531n, 533–534n

Sillett v Meek [2009] WTLR 1065 .... 185, 185n
Silver Wraith Ltd v Siúicre Éireann Cpt [1989] IEHC 34 803
Silverwood v Silverwood (1997) 74 P & CR 453 .... 197, 222n
Sim v H.J. Heinz Co. Ltd [1959] 1 WLR 313 684
Simic v New South Wales Land and Housing Corp (2016) 339 ALR 200 .... 850, 851
Simmons v New South Wales Trustee and Guardian [2014] NSWCA 405 .... 368n
Simson, Re [1946] Ch 299 .... 441n
Sinclair Investments (UK) Ltd v Versailles Trade Finance Ltd [2010] EWHC 1614 (Ch) 329n
Sinclair Investments (UK) Ltd v Versailles Trade Finance Ltd [2012] Ch 453 .... 280, 281, 283, 284, 331
Sinclair v Brougham [1914] AC 398 .... 996n–998, 1001, 1012, 1014
Sinclair v Gogarty [1937] IR 377 677
Singh v Beggs (1996) 71 P & CR 120 807
Singh v Bhasin, Chancery Division, 24 July 1998 540
Singha v Heer [2016] EWCA Civ 424 .... 92n
Singla v Bashir [2002] EWHC 883 (Ch) 914n
Skids Programme Management Ltd v McNeill [2013] 1 NZLR 1 .... 11n, 18n
Sky Petroleum Ltd v VIP Petroleum Ltd [1974] 1 WLR 576 810
Slater v Simm [2007] WTLR 1043 197
Slator v Nolan (1876) IR 11 Eq 367 .... 913n, 916, 917
Slatter, Re (1905) 21 TLR 295 .... 467n
Slattery v Friends First [2015] 3 IR 292 .... 843n, 855, 857, 858n
Slattery v Jagger [2015] EWCA Civ 953 863
Slattery, Re [1917] 2 IR 278 191
Sledmore v Dalby (1996) 72 P & CR 196 .... 963, 963n, 965
Sloane's Estate, Re [1895] 1 IR 146 .... 58n
Small v Oliver & Saunders (Development) Ltd [2006] EWHC 1293 (Ch) 638n
Small v Torley (1890) 25 LR Ir 388 .... 384n
Smelter Corporation of Ireland Ltd v O'Driscoll [1977] IR 305 .... 2n, 28, 625n, 789n, 826
Smith & Snipes Hall Farm Ltd v River Douglas Catchment Board [1949] 2 KB 500 .... 73n
Smith v Clay (1767) 3 Bro CC 639 36
Smith v Cooper [2010] EWCA Civ 722 .... 880n, 883n
Smith v Jones [1954] 1 WLR 1089 .... 860n
Smith v Kay (1859) 7 HLC 750 572
Smith v Matthews (1861) 3 De G F & J 139 .... 86n
Smith v Smith (1875) LR 20 Eq 500 .... 704n
Smith v Tatton (1879) 6 LR Ir 32 .... 506, 511
Smith, Re [1914] 1 Ch 937 .... 393n
Smith's Estate, Re [1894] 1 IR 60 571
Smithkline Beecham plc v Apotex Europe Ltd [2007] Ch 71 635
Smithkline Beecham plc v Genthon BV [2003] IEHC 623 .... 621n, 656, 661n
Smithwick v Smithwick (1861) 12 Ir Ch R 181 544
Smyth v Byrne [1914] 1 IR 53 .... 273n
Smyth v Gleeson [1911] 1 IR 113 .... 1035, 1035n, 1037, 1037n
Smyth v Halpin [1997] 2 ILRM 38 .... 939, 957n, 974, 986n

Smyth v Smyth High Court 1975 No. 4369P (Costello J) 22 November 1978 575
Smyth-Tyrrell v Bowden [2018] EWHC 106 (Ch)............................928n, 929n, 931n
Snowden, Re [1979] Ch 528 116
Soar v Ashwell [1893] 2 QB 390...376n
Soar v Foster (1858) 4 K & J 152...212n
Société des Industries Metallurgiques SA v Bronx Engineering Co. Ltd
[1975] 1 Lloyd's Rep 465...809
Solle v Butcher [1950] 1 KB 671 ....25, 865n, 867–870
Somers v W. [1979] IR 94...61
Sony Music Entertainment Ireland Ltd v UPC Communications Ireland Ltd
[2016] IECA 231 661
Sorochan v Sorochan (1986) 29 DLR (4th) 1 ....254n, 326n, 332n
Soulos v Korkontzilas (1997) 146 DLR (4th) 214..............................259, 270, 270n,
288, 326, 332n, 333n
South Carolina Insurance Co. v Assurance Maatschappij 'de Zeven Provincien' NV
[1987] AC 24...618n
South Place Ethical Society, Re [1980] 1 WLR 1565...451
South Tyneside Metropolitan Council v Svenska International plc
[1995] 1 All ER 545 ....1016n
Southcott Estates Inc v Toronto Catholic School Board
(2012) 351 DLR (4th) 476...794n
Southern Pacific Mortgages Ltd v Scott [2015] AC 385 ....314, 976
Southwell v Blackburn [2014] EWCA Civ 1347..930n
Southwood v Attorney General [2000] EWCA Civ 204...476
Soutzos v Asombang [2010] EWHC 842 (Ch) 171n
Speight v Gaunt (1883) 22 Ch D 727 ....576, 576n, 577n
Speight v Gaunt (1883) 9 App Cas 1 ....537n
Speight, Re (1883) 22 Ch D 727...80n
Spence, Re [1979] Ch 483 489
Spencer v All Souls' College (1762) Wilm 163...435
Spencer v Fielder [2015] 1 WLR 2876...538, 540
Spencer v Kinsella [1996] 2 ILRM 401...523, 524
Spencer v Spencer [2014] 2 NZLR 190...356
Spencer v Strickland [2009] EWHC 3033 (Ch) 213n
Spiller v Maude (1881) 32 Ch D 158...421n
Sports Direct International plc v Minor [2014] IEHC 546 ....659n, 724
Sprange v Barnard (1789) 2 Bro CC 585...98n
Sprange v Lee [1908] 1 Ch 424 ....47n
Spread Trustee Co. Ltd v Hutcheson [2012] 2 AC 194 ....597, 598
Springhill Housing Action Committee v Commissioner of Valuation
[1983] NI 184 ....453n, 472
SPUC v Coogan [1989] IR 734 745
St Andrew's (Cheam) Lawn Tennis Club Trust, Re [2012] 1 WLR 3487 ....161n
Stacey v Branch [1995] 2 ILRM 136.......................................541n, 547–549, 599
Stack v Dowden [2007] 2 AC 432 ....23, 205, 206, 206n, 215n, 236n,
238, 238n–242, 244n, 247n, 248, 249, 251, 252,
252n, 306, 329n, 981, 981n, 983, 991, 992n

Stallion v Albert Stallion Holdings (Great Britain) Ltd
[2010] 2 FLR 78 ....935n, 958n
Standing v Bowring (1885) 31 Ch D 282 ....180, 193
Staniland v Willot (1852) 3 Mac & G 664 ....151n
Stanley deceased, Re [2016] IEHC 8 ....91n, 501n, 569n
Stanley v Kieran [2007] IEHC 272, [2011] IESC 19 ....180, 194
Stannard v Fisons Pension Trust Ltd [1992] IRLR 27 ....532n
Starglade Properties v Nash. [2010] EWCA Civ 1314 354
Starling Securities Ltd v Woods High Court 1975 No. 4044P (McWilliam J)
24 May 1977 ....806, 837
Start Mortgages Ltd v Doyle [2016] IEHC 386 660
Statek Corporation v Alford [2008] EWHC 32 (Ch) 350n
Stead, Re [1900] 1 Ch 237 ....117, 118
Steadman v Steadman [1976] AC 536 ....803, 803n, 804, 806
Steed v Preece (1874) LR 18 Eq 192 ....1022n
Steedman v Drinkle [1916] 1 AC 275 836
Steele v Steele [1913] 1 IR 292 ....1021n
Steele, Re [1976] NI 66 ....494n
Steele's Will Trusts, Re [1948] Ch 603 ....96n
Stern v McArthur (1988) 165 CLR 489 ....835n, 836n
Stewart v Green (1871) IR 5 Eq 470 ....391, 391n, 446n
Stewart v Kennedy (1890) 15 App Cas 75 829
Stewart v Kingsale [1902] 1 IR 496 ....557n
Stewart, Re [1908] 2 Ch 251 141–143
Stewart's Will Trusts, Re [1983] NI 283 ....486n, 487, 489
Stibbe, Re (1946) 175 LT 198 ....1032n
Stileman v Ashdown (1742) 2 Atk 477 511
Stinson v Owens N.I. High Court 1973 noted 107 ILTSJ 239 ....798n
Stinson's Estate, Re [1910] 1 IR 13 1022
Stoffel & Co. v Grondona [2018] EWCA Civ 2031 ....199n, 200n
Stoke-on-Trent City Council v W. & J. Wass Ltd [1988] 1 WLR 1406 ....641n
Stokes v Anderson [1991] 1 FLR 391 976
Stoskus v Goode Concrete Ltd [2007] IEHC 432 ....710n, 711, 714n, 732n, 739
Stott v Milne (1884) 25 Ch D 710 ....539n
Strong v Bird (1874) LR 18 Eq 315 ....141–143n
Strong, Re [1940] IR 382 ....313n
Strydom v Vendside Ltd [2009] EWHC 2130 (QB) 914n
Stump v Gaby (1852) 2 De GM & G 623 56
Suggitt v Suggitt [2012] EWCA Civ 1140 ....967–969n, 971
Suisse v Lord Lowther (1843) 2 Hare 424 ....1034n
Sullivan v Boylan [2012] IEHC 389 744
Sullivan v Sullivan [2006] NSWCA 312 ....958n, 962n
Sullivan, Re [1917] 1 IR 38 ....1026, 1026n, 1027n
Supermacs Ireland Ltd v Katesan (Naas) Ltd [2000] 4 IR 273 ....795n–801
Superwood Holdings plc v Sun Alliance and London Insurance plc
[2002] IEHC 168 751
Surrey County Council v Bredero Homes Ltd [1993] 1 WLR 1361 ....641, 642
Sutcliffe v Lloyd [2008] EWHC 1329 (Ch) 958n

Swain v The Law Society [1982] 1 WLR 17 .... 264n
Swainland Builders Ltd v Freehold Properties Ltd [2002] 2 EGLR 71 .... 848, 859n
Sweeney, Re [1976-77] ILRM 88 .... 48n, 93n, 94
Sweetman v Sweetman (1868) IR 2 Eq 141 .... 1029, 1030
Swifte v Attorney General [1912] 1 IR 133 .... 388n, 466
Swinburne v Geary [2013] IEHC 412 .... 657n
Swindle v Harrison [1997] 4 All ER 705 .... 271, 587
Sykes v Beadon (1879) 11 Ch D 170 837
Sylvan Lake Golf and Tennis Club Ltd v Performance Industries Ltd (2002) 209 DLR (4th) 318 .... 843n, 855, 858
Symes v Hughes (1870) LR 9 Eq 475 194
Symonds Cider and English Wine Co. Ltd v Showerings (Ireland) Ltd [1997] 1 ILRM 481 .... 698, 742n
Szabo v ESAT Digiphone Ltd [1998] 2 ILRM 102 718–720
Szabo v Kavanagh [2013] IEHC 491 .... 628n

T. Choithram International SA v Pagarani [2001] 1 WLR 1 .... 134, 135, 137n–139, 141n
Tabor v Brooks (1878) 10 Ch D 273 599
Tackaberry v Hollis [2008] WTLR 279 .... 244n
Tacon, Re [1958] Ch 447 491
Talbot v Cody (1874) IR 10 Eq 138 .... 190, 206n
Talbot v Duke of Shrewsbury (1714) Prec Ch 394 1032
Tamplin v James (1880) 15 Ch D 215 .... 828, 830
Tang Man Sit v Capacious Investments Ltd [1996] AC 514 .... 271, 586n
Target Holdings Ltd v Redferns [1996] AC 421 .... 13, 14, 586n–589, 613, 614
Tartsinis v Navona Management Co. [2015] EWHC 57 (Comm) 848n, 850n
Tate Access Floors Inc v Boswell [1991] Ch 512 .... 627, 753, 777, 781, 782
Taxback Ltd v Revenue Commissioners [1997] IEHC 8 .... 356n
Taylor v Dickens [1998] 1 FLR 806 .... 8, 941, 947n, 971
Taylor v Plumer (1815) 3 M & S 562 993
Taylor v Revenue and Customs Commissioners [2008] STC (SCD) 1159 .... 116n
Taylor v Taylor (1875) LR 20 Eq 155 1034
Taylor v Taylor [2017] 4 WLR 83 .... 87n, 175n
Taylor, Re (1888) 58 LT 538 486
Taylors Fashions Ltd v Liverpool Victoria Trustees Co. Ltd [1982] QB 133 .... 945–947, 952
Tedcastles Oil Products v Sweeney Oil Retail Ltd High Court (Feeney J) 3 November 2010 724
Tegg, Re [1936] 2 All ER 878 .... 504n
Teichman v Teichman Estate (1996) 134 DLR (4th) 155 .... 608n
Tempany v Hynes [1976] IR 101 .... 49, 49n, 309, 310
Tempest v Lord Camoys (1882) 21 Ch D 571 .... 527, 527n
Templemoyle Agricultural School, Re (1869) IR 4 Eq 295 .... 485, 488n, 492n
Tench v Molyneux (1914) 48 ILTR 48 67
Terry and White's Contract, Re (1886) 32 Ch D 14 826
Tetley, Re [1923] 1 Ch 258 .... 406n

Teva Pharmaceutical Industries Ltd v Mylan Teoranta [2018] IEHC 324 .... 622, 622n, 629n, 661–663n
Texaco Ltd v Mulberry Filling Station Ltd [1972] 1 WLR 814 .... 722n
The Assios [1979] 1 Lloyd's Rep 331 .... 759n
The Barge Inn Ltd v Quinn Hospitality Ireland Operations 3 Ltd [2013] IEHC 387 .... 923, 925n
The Niedersachsen [1984] 1 All ER 398 .... 757n, 761
The Siskina [1979] AC 210 .... 618n, 771n
Thexton v Thexton [2001] 1 NZLR 237 .... 92n
Third Chandris Shipping Corporation v Unimarine SA [1979] QB 645 750
Thomas A Edison Ltd v Bullock (1912) 15 CLR 679 .... 752n
Thomas Bates & Son Ltd v Wyndham's (Lingerie) Ltd [1981] 1 WLR 505 .... 853, 854n, 858, 859, 860n
Thomas Thompson Holdings Ltd v Musgrave Group plc [2016] IEHC 28 .... 816, 817
Thomas v Thomas [1956] NZLR 785 .... 986n
Thompson v Foy [2010] 1 P & CR 16 .... 883, 931n
Thompson v Hurst [2012] EWCA Civ 1752 .... 242n
Thompson v Mechan (1958) 13 DLR (2d) 103 .... 147n
Thompson v Palmer (1933) 49 CLR 507 989
Thompson v Thomas (1891) 27 LR Ir 457 .... 503n
Thompson v Whitmore (1860) 1 J & H 268 .... 863n
Thompson, Re [1934] Ch 342 .... 383, 384
Thompson, Re [1939] 1 All ER 681 .... 504n
Thompson's Estate, Re [1928] IR 606 .... 149, 151n
Thompson's Settlement, Re [1986] Ch 99 .... 574n
Thompson's Trustee v Heaton [1974] 1 WLR 605 .... 276, 278n
Thomson v Eastwood (1877) 2 App Cas 215 .... 574n, 594n
Thomson v Humphrey [2010] 2 FLR 107 .... 245n
Thomson, Re [1930] 1 Ch 203 277
Thornber v Wilson (1858) 4 Dr 350 440
Thorne v Kennedy (2017) 350 ALR 1 .... 881n
Thorner v Major [2009] 1 WLR 776 .... 329, 928, 930–934, 953–954n, 967, 970, 981, 984, 985, 987, 988n, 992, 992n
Thorsteinson Estate v Olson (2016) 404 DLR 453 .... 175n, 176n
Three Stripe International Ltd v Charles O'Neill & Co. Ltd [1989] ILRM 124 .... 742n
Thrupp v Collett (1858) 26 Beav 125 .... 503n
Thynne v Earl of Glengall (1848) 2 HL Cas 131 1034
Tierney v Tough [1914] 1 IR 142 .... 46, 167, 168
Tilley v Thomas (1867) 3 Ch App 61 .... 48n
Tilley's Will Trusts, Re [1967] Ch 1179 .... 999n
Tilson, Infants, Re [1951] IR 1 .... 209n, 214
Timmins v Moreland Street Property Co. [1958] Ch 110 .... 87n
Timmis, Re [1902] 1 Ch 176 .... 82n
Tinker v Tinker [1970] P 136 .... 27n, 219n, 625n
Tinsley v Milligan [1992] Ch 310 (CA), [1994] 1 AC 340 (HL) 13, 13n, 18, 32–35, 196–199, 201n, 202, 215, 218, 221n–223, 250

Tito v Wadell (No. 2) [1977] Ch 106 ....262n, 572, 574, 574n, 575, 790, 812n
TMG Group Ltd v Al Babtain Trading and Contracting Co.
[1982] ILRM 349 ....652n, 722
Toal v Duignan (No. 2) [1991] ILRM 140 38
Todd & Co. v Midland Great Western Rly of Ireland Co. (1881) 9 LR Ir 85........819n
Tola Capital Management LLC v Joseph Linders [2014] IEHC 316 713
Tomkin v Tomkin High Court 1998 No. 6924P (Smyth J) 8 July 2003 535
Tomlinson v Glyn's Executor & Trustee Co. [1970] Ch 112..................................84n
Toole v Hamilton [1901] 1 IR 383...387
Townley v Sherborne (1634) J Bridg 35...585n
Tracey v Bowen [2005] 2 IR 528...762
Traditional Structures Ltd v HW Construction Ltd [2010] EWHC 1530 (TCC) 853
Transvaal Lands Co. v New Belgium (Transvaal) Land & Development Co.
[1914] 2 Ch 488...289
Tribe v Tribe [1996] Ch 107 ....195, 196, 219n–222
Trimmer v Danby (1856) LJ Ch 424 ....386n
Truck and Machinery Sales Ltd v Marubeni Komatsu Ltd [1996] 1 IR 12.....688, 690
Trustees of the Congregation of Poor Clares v Commissioner of Valuation
[1971] NI 174 ....446n
Trustees of the Londonderry Presbyterian Church House v Commissioners of
Inland Revenue [1946] NI 178...412n, 452, 471
Trusts of the Abbott Fund, Re [1900] 2 Ch 326..163
Trusts of the Arthur McDougall Fund, Re [1957] 1 WLR 81..................................475
Trusts of the Rectory of St John (1869) IR 3 Eq 335 492
TSB Bank plc v Camfield [1995] 1 All ER 951...895n
Tubbs v Broadwood (1831) 2 Russ & M 487...1041n
Tuite v Tuite [1978] ILRM 197 ....76n, 79, 79n
Tulk v Moxhay (1848) 2 Ph 774...724n
Turkey v Awadh [2005] 2 P & CR 29 ....883n
Turner v Corney (1841) 5 Beav 515 575
Turner v Jacob [2006] EWHC 1317 (Ch)...............................947n, 948, 978n, 1008n
Turner v O'Reilly [2008] IEHC 92...711n
Turner v Turner [1984] Ch 100...517n, 527
Turton, Re [1926] Ch 96...502n
TV3 Network Services Ltd v Fahey [1999] 2 NZLR 129 ....675n, 679n, 682n
Tweddle v Atkinson (1861) 1 B & S 393..73n
Twinsectra Ltd v Yardley [1999] Lloyd's Rep Bank 438 ....159n, 364n
Twinsectra Ltd v Yardley [2002] 2 AC 164 ....158n, 170–174n, 341n,
347–357, 367n, 373
Tyler, Re [1891] 3 Ch 252...400n
Tynan v County Registrar for Kilkenny [2011] IEHC 250..910
Tyndall's Estate, Re [1941] Ir Jur Rep 51..1019
Tyrrel's case (1557) 2 Dy 1555a...69
Tyrrell v Wright [2017] IEHC 92..660n

UCB Corporate Services Ltd v Williams [2003] 1 P & CR 168...............................898
Ulrich v Treasury Solicitor [2006] 1 WLR 33 ....422n
Ulrich v Ulrich [1968] 1 WLR 180...206n

Ulster Bank (Ireland) Ltd v De Kretser [2016] IECA 371..........4n, 881n, 898n, 899n, 900, 900n, 902n, 904, 905, 907, 910, 911, 911n
Ulster Bank Ltd v Fitzgerald [2001] IEHC 159..............................900, 901, 902, 907
Ulster Bank Ltd v Roche [2012] 1 IR 765....................................901–904, 906, 908, 908n, 910, 911, 911n
Ulster Factors Ltd v Entoglen Ltd [1997] IEHC 34 369
Ultraframe (UK) Ltd v Fielding [2005] EWHC 1638 (Ch)..............289n, 357, 357n, 996n, 999n
Unilever plc v Cussons [1997] 1 NZLR 433 ....35n
Union Eagle Ltd v Golden Achievement Ltd [1997] AC 514 835
United Grand Lodge of Ancient Free and Accepted Masons of England v Holborn Borough Council [1957] 1 WLR 1080..437n
United Scientific Holdings Ltd v Burnley Borough Council [1978] AC 904...11, 12, 18
Universal Thermosensors Ltd v Hibben [1992] 1 WLR 840.................................784
University College Cork v Services Industrial Professional Technical Union [2015] IEHC 282...674
University of Manitoba v Sanderson Estate (1998) 155 DLR (4th) 40 302
US International Marketing Ltd v National Bank of New Zealand [2004] 1 NZLR 589...350n
Uzinterimpex JSC v Standard Bank plc [2008] EWCA Civ 819..........................359n

Valard Construction Ltd v Bird Construction Co. (2018) 417 DLR (4th)..............568
Vallee v Birchwood [2014] Ch 271 ....148–151n
Van Der Merwe v Goldman [2016] 4 WLR 71.................................534n, 874, 874n
Van Laethem v Brooker [2005] EWHC 1478 (Ch) 244n, 948n, 976n
Van Straubenzee, Re [1901] 2 Ch 779 ....554n
Van Uden Maritime BV v Kommanditgesellschaft in Firma Deco- Line [1999] 1 QB 1225...770
Vandervell v IRC [1967] 2 AC 291..90n, 158n, 161, 179
Vandervell's Trusts (No. 2), Re [1974] Ch 269 ....83n, 157
Vanguard Auto Finance Ltd v Browne [2014] IEHC 465.......................................332
Vardon's Trusts, Re (1885) 31 Ch D 275..1026n
Varko Ltd, Re [2012] IEHC 278..22n, 317n, 324, 325
Varsani v Jesani [1999] Ch 219 ....496, 497
Vatcher v Paull [1915] AC 372 ....536n
Vaughan v Cottingham [1961] IR 184 ....81n
Vaughan, Re (1886) 33 Ch D 187...387n, 448n
Verge v Somerville [1924] AC 496...411n, 430n
Verrall v Great Yarmouth Borough Council [1981] QB 202 794
Vickery, Re [1931] 1 Ch 572 577
Victory v Galhoy Inns Ltd [2010] IEHC 459 ....43, 632n
Vinogradoff, Re [1935] WN 68...179, 399n
Viridian Power Ltd v Commission for Energy Regulation [2014] IEHC 4...........700n
Voges v Monaghan (1954) 94 CLR 231 ....116n
Voyce v Voyce (1991) 62 P & CR 290...957n

W. & R. Murrogh, Re [2003] IEHC 95...46n, 1006

W. v M. [2010] IEHC 505, [2011] IEHC 217 ....520n, 611, 612
W. v W. [1981] ILRM 202 ....46n, 207, 226–232
W.B. v J.B. [2019] IECA 58 ....47n
W.J. Alan & Co. Ltd v El Nasr Export and Import Co. [1972] 2 QB 189 ....927n
Wadlow v Samuel [2007] EWCA Civ 155 ....879n
Wait, Re [1927] 1 Ch 606 ....268, 810
Waldron and Bogue's Contract, Re [1904] 1 IR 240 ....557n
Wale, Re [1956] 1 WLR 1346....143
Walker and Elgie's Contract, Re (1919) 53 ILTR 22....93n, 94n
Walker v Stones [2001] QB 902 ....377, 595n, 596
Walker v Symonds (1818) 3 Swans 1 ....28n, 593
Walker's Settlement Trusts, Re [1936] Ch 280....557n
Wall v Feely High Court 1983 No. 7014P (Costello J) 26 October 1983....634n
Wall v Wall High Court 1983 No. 402 Sp (Hamilton P) 10 September 1986 ....224n
Wall, Re (1889) 42 Ch D 510 ....417n
Wall's Estate, Re [1922] 1 IR 59....1039n
Wallace v Irish Aviation Authority [2012] 2 ILRM 345 ....655n, 694, 713n, 732, 744n
Wallace v Kershaw [2019] IEHC 382....669n
Wallbank v Price [2008] 2 FLR 501 ....879n, 880n
Wallgrave v Tebbs (1855) 2 K & J 313....116n
Walsh v Lonsdale (1882) 21 Ch D 9....9, 49n
Walsh v Walsh (1870) IR 4 Eq 396....1041n
Walsh v Walsh (No. 2) [2017] IEHC 177 ....748n, 750, 751
Walters v Northern Coal Mining Co. (1855) 5 De GM & G 629 ....790n
Walton v Walton Court of Appeal 14 April 1994....931
Waltons Stores (Interstate) Ltd v Maher (1988) 164 CLR 387....926, 957n, 958n, 961–963, 985, 989, 989n
Wanze Properties (Ireland) Ltd v Five Star Supermarket High Court (Costello P) 24 October 1997....725n, 811n, 814–817
Ward v Ward (1843) 2 HL Cas 777....538n
Ward, Re [1941] Ch 308 ....425n
Wardle Fabrics Ltd v G. Myristis Ltd [1984] FSR 263 777
Warman International Ltd v Dwyer (1995) 182 CLR 544....270n
Warner Brothers Pictures Incorporated v Nelson [1937] 1 KB 209 ....726, 727
Warnes v Hedley Court of Appeal 31 January 1984 ....928n
Warren v Guerney [1944] 2 All ER 472 216
Warren v Mendy [1989] 1 WLR 853 ....727, 728, 736, 741
Warren v Warren (1783) 1 Bro CC 305 ....1035n
Washington Capitols Basketball Club Inc. v Barry (1969) 304 F Supp 1193 ....728n
Wasserberg, Re [1915] 1 Ch 195 ....149n
Waterman's Will Trusts, Re [1952] 2 All ER 1054....545, 602, 613
Watson v Croft Promo-Sport Ltd [2008] 3 All ER 1171 ....44n, 631, 638n
Watson v Goldsbrough (1986) 1 EGLR 265....960
Watson v Watson (1864) 33 Beav 574....1034n
Watson, Re [1973] 1 WLR 1472....437n
Watters' Will Trusts, Re (1928) 62 ILTR 61 ....120, 125n, 161n
Watts v Public Trustee (1949) 50 SR 130 ....150n
Waverly BC v Hilden [1988] 1 WLR 246 ....745n

Wayling v Jones (1993) 69 P & CR 170 ....933, 951n, 958n
WEA Records Ltd v Visions Channel 4 Ltd [1983] 1 WLR 721 ....777n
Weall, Re (1889) 42 Ch D 674 ....577n
Webb v Ireland [1988] IR 353 926
Webb v Rorke (1806) 2 Sch & Lef 661 ....572n
Webb v Webb [1994] QB 696 ....52, 53, 53n
Webb, Re [1941] 1 Ch 225 ....74n
Webber, Re [1954] 1 WLR 1500 ....499n
Webber's Settlement Trusts, Re [1922] 1 IR 49 ....542n
Webster v Cecil (1861) 30 Beav 62 828
Wedgewood, Re [1915] 1 Ch 113 ....466, 467n
Weeding v Weeding (1861) 1 J & H 424 ....1020n, 1021
Weekes' Settlement, Re [1897] 1 Ch 289 ....76n, 78
Weir v Crum-Brown [1908] AC 162 ....401n
West, Re [1900] 1 Ch 84 162
West End Commercial Ltd v London Troacadero (2015) LLP
[2017] EWHC 2175 (Ch) 928n, 988n
West Sussex Constabulary's Widows, Children & Benevolent (1930) Fund Trusts,
Re [1971] Ch 1 ....165, 166n, 167n
West Sussex Properties Ltd v Chichester DC Court of Appeal, 28 June 2000 869
Westdeutsche Landesbank Girozentrale v Islington Borough Council
[1996] AC 669 ....5, 127, 158, 159, 258, 317, 329,
331n, 335n, 998, 1000, 1012n, 1014
Westland Savings Bank v Hancock [1987] 2 NZLR 21 ....858n
Westman Holdings Ltd v McCormack [1992] 1 IR 151 ......652n, 654n, 657, 670, 698
Weston, Re [1902] 1 Ch 680 ....149n, 151n
Weston's Settlements, Re [1969] 1 Ch 223 607
Westpac New Zealand Ltd v MAP and Associates Ltd
[2011] 3 NZLR 751 ....350n, 355, 355n, 356
Wharton v Masterman [1895] AC 186 ....608n
Wheeler, Re [1896] 1 Ch 315 519
Whelan Frozen Foods Ltd v Dunnes Stores [2006] IEHC 171 ....622n
Whelan v Kavanagh [2001] IEHC 14 837
Whelan v Madigan [1978] ILRM 136 ....21n, 718
Whicker v Hume (1858) 7 HLC 124 ....425n
White Cedar Developments Ltd v Cordil Construction Ltd [2012] IEHC 525 690
White v McCooey [1976-77] ILRM 72 ....791n
White v Shortall [2006] NSWSC 1379 102
White v Williams [2010] EWHC 940 (Ch) 496, 497
White's Will Trusts, Re [1951] 1 All ER 528 ....462n
Whitecross Potatoes (International) Ltd v Coyle [1978] ILRM 31 837
Whiteside v Whiteside [1950] Ch 65 ....860n
Whitlock v Moree [2017] UKPC 44 ....185, 187
Whooley v Merck Millipore Ltd [2018] IEHC 725 ....710n
Wight v Olswang [1999] EWCA Civ 1309 ....602n
Wilcox v Wilcox (2000) 190 DLR (4th) 324 ....254n
Wild v Wild [2018] EWCA Civ 2197 (Ch) 928n, 931n, 937n
Wilkes v Allington [1931] 2 Ch 104 147

Wilkinson v North [2018] 4 WLR 41 ....92n, 102
Wilkinson's Trusts, Re (1887) 19 LR Ir 531 ....392n, 445, 445n, 447
William Sindall plc v Cambridgeshire County Council [1994] 1 WLR 1016 869
Williams v Barton [1927] 2 Ch 9 278
Williams v Central Bank of Nigeria [2014] AC 1189 ....309, 340–344, 360
Williams v Kenneally (1912) 46 ILTR 292 ....788n
Williams v Mayne (1867) IR 1 Eq 519 1025
Williams v Staite [1979] Ch 291 ....957n
Williams v Williams (1881) 17 Ch D 437 376
Williams, Re [1897] 2 Ch 12 ....93n, 95, 95n
Williams' Trustees v IRC [1947] AC 447 ....406n, 410, 450n, 451n, 465n
Williams-Ashman v Price [1942] 1 Ch 219 ....345n, 376
Williamson v Shiekh [2008] EWCA Civ 990 ....245n
Wilmott v Barber (1880) 15 Ch D 96 ....943, 945–947
Wilson Parking New Zealand Ltd v Fanshawe 136 Ltd
[2014] 3 NZLR 567 ....972, 973
Wilson v Law Debenture Trust Corporation plc [1995] 2 All ER 337 ....528n, 614
Wilson v Northampton and Banbury Junction Railway Co.
(1874) 9 Ch App 279 788
Wilson v Paniani [1996] 3 NZLR 378 144
Wilson v Wilson (1848) 1 HLC 538 ....504n
Wilson, Re [1913] 1 Ch 314 ....485n, 489
Wilson, Re [1933] IR 729 ....129n, 131, 142
Windham v Maguire [2009] IEHC 359 ....807n
Wingview Ltd v Ennis Property Finance Designated Area Company
[2017] IEHC 674 ....653n
Winkler v Shamoon [2016] EWHC 217 (Ch) 928n
Winter v Perratt (1843) 9 Cl & F 606 105
Wodzicki v Wodzicki [2017] EWCA Civ 95 249
Wolff v Wolff [2004] EWHC 2110 (Ch) 872n
Wollaston v King (1869) Lr 8 Eq 165 1029
Wolverhampton and Walsall Railway Co. v London and North-Western
Railway Co. (1873) LR 16 Eq 433 ....724, 788n
Wolverhampton Corporation v Emmons [1901] 1 KB 515 ....818, 819
Wood v Sutcliffe (1851) 2 Sim (NS) 163 ....634n
Wood v Watkin [2019] EWHC 1311 (Ch) 204n, 205n, 211
Wood, Re [1949] Ch 498 ....381n
Wood, Re (1872) LR 7 Ch App 302 508
Woodhams, Re [1981] 1 WLR 493 ....487n
Woodleys, Re (1892) 29 LR Ir 304 ....1028, 1028n
Woodward v Hutchins [1977] 1 WLR 760 ....684n
Worth Library, Re [1995] 2 IR 301 ....406, 407n, 427, 428, 431, 434, 454–459,
461n, 463n, 464, 484, 485n, 491, 497, 498
Worthington v Wiginton (1855) 20 Beav 67 1030
Wright v Board of Management of Gorey Community School
[2000] IEHC 37 ....662n
Wright v Hodgkinson [2005] WTLR 435 ....883n, 884n
Wright v Morgan [1926] AC 788 ....572, 573n

Wright, Re [1954] Ch 347 ....491n
Wroth v Tyler [1974] Ch 30 837
Wrotham Park Estate Co. v Parkside Homes Ltd
[1974] 1 WLR 798 ....641–643, 721n
WWF–World Wide Fund for Nature v World Wrestling Federation
Entertainment Inc [2008] 1 WLR 445 643
Wyn Clons Development Ltd v Cooke [2016] IECA 317 792
Wyvern Developments Ltd, Re [1974] 1 WLR 1097 ....538n, 926

X. v A. [2000] 1 All ER 490 ....541n

Yap v Children's University Hospital Temple Street Ltd [2006] 4 IR 298......731, 739
Yaxley v Gotts [2000] Ch 162 ....807, 950n, 977, 978, 981n
Yeates v Minister for Posts and Telegraphs [1978] ILRM 22....................621, 726
Yedina v Yedin [2017] EWHC 3319 (Ch) 853n
Yerkey v Jones (1930) 63 CLR 649....................889n
Young v Sealey [1949] Ch 278 185
Young, Re (1885) 28 Ch D 705 ....190n
Young, Re [1951] Ch 344 ....114n
Young, Re [1955] 1 WLR 1269 ....421n
Z Ltd v A-Z and AA-LL [1982] QB 558 ....748n, 749n

Zamet v Hyman [1961] 1 WLR 1442....................881n
Zeital v Kaye [2010] WTLR 913....................133
Zockoll Group Ltd v Mercury Communications Ltd [1998] FSR 354....................707n
Zuckerfabrik Süderdithmarschen AG v Hauptzollampt Itzehoe and Zuckerfabrik
Soest GmbH v Hauptzollampt Paderborn Joined Cases C-143/88 and
C-92/89 [1991] ECR I-415....................701, 701n

Other Tables

Constitution

Irish Free State Constitution
Article 73 5
Bunreacht na hEireann 1937 ..... 234, 505, 678, 681, 685, 702, 703
Article 15.2.1° 4
Article 34.3.1° 732
Article 38 444
Article 40.3 ..... 504, 750
Article 40.3.1° 732
Article 40.3.2° 732, 744
Article 40.3.3° 745
Article 40.5 ..... 744, 784n
Article 40.6.1°.i 675n
Article 41 209
Article 41.2 234
Article 41.2.2° 234
Article 41.4 ..... 207, 209, 215n
Article 42 ..... 209, 505
Article 44 437
Article 44.1.2° 446n
Article 44.2.1° 444, 506
Article 44.2.3° 444
Article 50 5

Table of Statutes

Acts against Covenous and Fraudulent Conveyances 1584 (27 Eliz., c.4) 512n, 513
Administration of Estates Act 1959 1018
Administration of Justice Act 1982 (UK)
s.20 ..... 863, 863n
Bankruptcy Act 1988
s.3 ..... 514n
s.6 ..... 513n
s.59 ..... 513, 513n, 515
(1), (3) 1988 515
s.124 787
Second Schedule 513n

Bankruptcy (Ireland) Amendment Act 1872
s.52 .... 513, 515
Broadcasting Act 1990
s.92(2)(a)(i) 478, 478n
Capital Acquisitions Consolidation Tax Act 2003
s.76(2) 400
Central Bank and Credit Instiutions (Resolution) Act 2011
s.110 .... 512n
Pt 4, Sch.2 .... 512n
Chancery Amendment Act 1858 (Lord Cairns' Act) 8, 617, 637, 641–644
s.2 790
Charitable Donations and Bequests (Ireland) Act 1844
s.16 .... 117, 429, 429n
Charitable Trusts (Validation) Act 1954 (UK) 422n
Charities Act 1960 (UK)
s.13 493
Charities Act 1961 .... 406n, 429n
s.4 .... 117n
s.21 .... 403n
s.25 .... 403n
s.29 .... 403n, 498n
s.32 .... 403n
s.43 .... 403, 403n
s.45 392
(1) 392n, 412n, 437, 437n, 447
(2) 384n, 441, 443
s.47 .... 493, 494
(1) 493, 494
(e)(iii) 494
(2) 493, 497
s.48(1), (2) 165
s.49(1) 380, 380n, 399, 399n, 400, 430, 441, 444n, 471
s.50 .... 386, 386n, 449, 449n
s.51(1) 427n
Charities Act 1964 (Northern Ireland)
s.22 .... 493n, 494n
Charities Act 1973
s.8 .... 403n, 498n
s.9 .... 403n
s.14 .... 403n
Charities Act 1993 (UK)
s.13 496
(1)
(c), (d) 497
(e)(iii) 496, 497
(1A) 497
(a) 497
s.97 408

Charities Act 2006 (UK)..408n, 413, 417, 423, 424, 433, 480
s.2(2)(a)..417n
s.3(2)..424, 424n
Charities Act 2008 (Northern Ireland)
s.2(2)
(g)..473n
(h)..481n
Charities Act 2009..398, 398n, 402, 403, 405, 411, 412, 413, 431, 434, 435, 459, 481–483, 497
s.1..398n, 402n
s.2..398n, 402n, 409, 436, 460, 474, 482
s.2..481n
(1)..404n, 409n, 481, 483n
(2)..404n
(a)..413n, 418, 456n
(3)..404n
s.3..398n, 402n, 406, 408, 482
(1)..414
(a)..414, 417, 418
(b)..425
(d)..450
(2)..413
(3)..413, 413n
(4)..392n, 411, 413, 413n, 437, 447
(5)..437
(6)..437
(7)..412n–415n, 418, 431n, 436, 456
(b)..418, 431, 464
(8)..412n–415n, 418, 431, 431n, 436, 456
(10)..438
(11)..409, 450, 450n, 459, 460, 465, 474, 482
(a)..460n, 465n
(b)..465n
(c)..465n
(d)..460n
(e)..481n
(f)..481n
(j)..388n, 469
(k)..425
(l)..481n
s.4..398n, 402n
s.5..398n, 402n
s.6-9..398n, 402n
s.7..402, 456
s.10..398n, 402n
(1)..398n, 402n
(2)..398n, 402n
s.11..392n, 398n, 402n, 437n, 441n, 443n, 447n

Charities Act 2009—*contd.*
s.13 .... 403n
s.14 .... 404n
s.38 .... 82n, 380n, 398n, 404n, 494n
s.39 .... 404n
s.43 .... 404n
s.47 .... 404n, 495
s.52 .... 404n
s.55(1) 404n
(2) 405n
s.64 .... 405n
s.66 .... 405n
s.68 .... 405n
s.69 .... 405n
s.74 .... 405n
s.75(1) 404
(2) 404n
s.80 .... 404n
s.81 .... 497n
s.82 .... 404n, 498
s.90 .... 398n, 402n, 405n
s.91 .... 398n, 402n, 405n
s.92 .... 398n, 403n
s.99 .... 398n, 402n, 443, 443n, 444
Pt 2 .... 398n, 402n
Pt 3 .... 398n, 402n, 404
Pt 4 .... 398n, 402n
Pt 5 .... 398n, 402n
Pt 6 .... 398n, 402n
Sch.1 .... 398n, 402n, 404n
Sch.2 .... 392n, 398n, 402n, 437n, 441n, 443n, 447n
Charites Act 2011 (UK) 413, 417
s.2 .... 406, 408
(1)(b) 413
s.3
(1) 473
(a) 417n
(g) 483n
(h) 481
(m) 409
(2)(a) 438
(d) 473
s.4 418
(2) 413, 424, 424n
s.5(1) 471
(3) 472n
s.6 .... 473n

Charites Act 2011 (UK)—*contd.*
s.62
(1)(e)(iii) 496, 496n
(2)(b) 497n
Charities and Trustee Investment (Scotland) Act 2005
s.7(2)
(h) 473n
(j) 481n
Civil Jurisdiction and Judgments Act 1982 (UK)
s.25 772
(2) 771
Civil Law (Presumption of Death) Act 2019 560
s.5(3) 560n
(5)(a), (b) 560n
Civil Liability Act 1961 590
s.2 ....590n
Part III, Ch.1 ....590n
Civil Partnership and Certain Rights and Obligations of Cohabitants Act 2010 ....5n, 223, 224, 226, 235, 255
s.129(2)(f), (g) 235
s.172
(5) 224n
(6) 224n
s.173(3)(g), (h) 235
s.195 ....224n
Common Law Procedure Act 1854 (England) 8n, 617n
Common Law Procedure (Ireland) Act 1856 617
Common Law Procedure Amendment Act (Ireland) 1856 8
Companies Act 1963
s.60 ....60, 203
(14) 60
s.205 829
s.214 690
Companies Act 1985 (UK)
s.434(5) 780n
Companies Act 1990
s.12 758
s.160 ....405n, 690, 691
Companies Act 2006 (UK) 294
s.170(3) 289n, 294n
s.175 295
(4) 295n
Chap.2, Pt 10 ....288n
Companies Act 2014 295
s.82 ....60n
s.227(4) 289n, 295n
s.228 295
(1) 295
(f) 295

Companies Act 2014—*contd.*
s.232 ....295n
s.233 ....295n
ss.839–842 ....690n
Ch.2, Pt 5 ....288n
Ch.4, Pt 14 690
Competition Act 1991 723
ss.4, 5 723
Contracts (Rights of Third Parties) Act (UK) 1999
s.1 ....73, 75
(5)....................811n
Conveyancing Act (Ireland) 1634 (10 Chas 1, sess. 2, c.3)....................507, 509, 512, 513
s.1 512
s.3 512
s.10....................507, 510–512
s.14....................507
Conveyancing Act 1881
s.21(3) 315
s.43....................581
Conveyancing Act 1882 63
s.3(1) 59, 62
(i) 60
(ii) 63
Copyright Act 1963....................636
Copyright Act 2000
s.132....................782n
s.133....................782n
s.143....................781
Corporation Tax Act 2010
Part 13, Chapter 9 ....473n
Court and Court Officers Act 1995
s.52(a) 498n
Courts (Establishment and Constitution) Act 1961 ....9, 12
Courts (Supplemental Provisions) Act 1961
s.45(1) 775n
Third Schedule....................610n
Courts of Justice Act 1924 ....9, 12
Criminal Justice Act 1987 (UK)
s.2....................780n
Criminal Law (Suicide) Act 1993
s.2....................148n
Defamation Act 2009
s.16....................675n, 680n
s.20....................675n
s.33....................687
Dentists Act 1878....................745
Equality Act 2010 (UK) 205
Executors Act 1830 (England) 93n

Family Home Protection Act 1976 ... 61, 907
s.3 ... 55n, 63
s.4 ... 61
Family Law Act 1995 ... 5n, 223, 224, 235
s.16
(1) ... 235
(2) ... 224
(f) ... 235
Family Law (Divorce) Act 1996 ... 5n, 223, 224
s.14 ... 224n
s.20 ... 224n, 235
Finance Act 2001
s.45 ... 401, 474n, 482n
Finance Act 2013
s.15 ... 474n, 482n
s.19 ... 401n
Fisheries (Consolidation) Act 1959 ... 701
Fraudulent Conveyances Act 1571 (13 Eliz., c.5) ... 507n, 511n, 513
Gambling Act 2005 (UK) ... 354
Government of Ireland Act 1920
s.5 ... 444
Guardianship of Infants Act 1964
s.11 ... 582, 583
Human Rights Act 1998 (UK)
s.12(3) ... 693
Income Tax Act 1967
s.333 ... 401
s.334 ... 401
Industrial Relations Act 1990
s.11(1) ... 654, 674
s.14 ... 671-674
(2) ... 674
s.19 ... 670–672, 674, 742
(2) ... 670–674
Pt II ... 673
Inheritance (Provision for Family and Dependents) Act 1975 (UK) ... 298n, 303
s.8 ... 303
Insolvency Act 1986 (UK)
s.291 ... 780n
s.423 ... 508n
Intellectual Property (Miscellaneous Provisions) Act 1988
ss.4, 5 ... 701
Interpretation Act 2005
s.6 ... 17, 618
Irish Bank Resolution Corporation Act 2013
s.21 ... 512
Judicial Separation and Family Law Reform Act 1989 ... 223, 224, 235
s.15 ... 224n

Judicial Separation and Family Law Reform Act 1989—*contd.*
s.20(2) 224
Jurisdiction of Courts and Enforcement of Judgments Act 1998
s.13 .... 771n
Land Act 1965
s.45 .... 28n, 219n
Land and Conveyancing Law Reform Act 2009 .... 177, 315, 609
s.2 .... 59n, 580n
s.3 .... 507, 610
s.8(1) 580n
(3) 59n
s.16 .... 384n, 400n, 501
s.20(1) 580
s.21 59
(1) 59
(2) 59, 60n
(a) 518n
s.23 .... 607n, 609, 611
s.24 .... 607n, 609
(1) 611
(2) 610n
(3) 611
(4) 610, 611
(5) 610n
s.51(1) 791n, 795, 795n, 798, 802, 807
(2) 795n, 807
(3) 796
s.52(1) 49, 309n, 311
(2) 49, 311
(a) 311n
(b) 312
s.57 580
s.58 580
s.62(2), (3) 177
s.74(1) 512, 513
(2) 512, 513
(3) 507, 508n
(4) 507
(a) 507
(5) 512n
(6) 512n
s.86 59
(1)(a) 60
(b) 63
s.107(1), (2) 315
Sch.1 .... 580n
Sch.2, Pt 1 .... 177n
Sch.2, Pt 4 .... 59n, 315n, 518n

Land Registration Act 2002 (UK)....150n
Law of Property Act (England) 1925....177
s.20....518n
s.40....87n
s.47....312n
s.53(1)(b)....86n, 87
(c)....90
s.60....178
(3)....177–179
s.105....315n
s.172....508n
Law of Property (Miscellaneous Provisions) Act 1989 (UK)
s.2....301, 301n, 807, 950, 950n, 977–980n
(1)....801n, 807, 950
(5)....301n, 807n, 950, 950n, 977–979
Limitation Act 1980 (UK)
s.21....296
(1)....342
(a)....296, 342
(3)....296, 342
Local Government (Planning and Development) Act 1976
s.27....28
Lunacy Regulation (Ireland) Act 1871
s.67....1022
Married Women's Property Act 1882
s.17....236
Married Women's Status Act 1957....509
ss.7 and 8....75n
s.12....223, 227
Matrimonial Causes Act 1973
s.37(2)(b)....197
Matrimonial Proceedings and Property Act 1970 (UK)
s.37....233n
Mortmain Act 1391....68
Parish Councils and Burial Authorities (Miscellaneous Provisions) Act 1970 (UK)
s.1....387n
Partnership Act 1890 (UK)....377
s.10....377, 378
s.22....1022, 1022n
Pensions Acts 1990 to 2008....405n
Pensions Act 1995 (UK)
s.35....615
Perpetuities and Accumulations Act 1964 (UK)
s.12....387n
Personal Insolvency Act 2012
s.154....513n, 514n, 515n
Poor Relief (Ireland) Act 1838
s.63....462

Post Office Act 1908 746
Post Office Act 1953 (UK) 745
Presumption of Death Act 2013 (UK) 560
Prevention of Electoral Abuses Act 1923
s.11 ....680n
Proceeds of Crime Act 1996
s. 2 ....756n
Race Relations Act 1976
s.34(1) 465
Real Property Act 1845
s.3 ....9n
Recreational Charities Act 1958 (UK)
s.1
(1) 471n
(2), (a) 472
Registration of Deeds Act (Ireland) 1707 64–66
s.4 64
s.5 64
Registration of Deeds and Title Act 2006 64
s.38 65
(3) 65, 65n
Registration of Title Act 1891
52 ....925n
Registration of Title Act 1964
s.69(1) 313n
s.72 66
Rent Acts 867
Road Traffic Act 1932 743
Roman Catholic Relief Act 1829
s.28 444
s.37 ....444n
Royal Kilmainham Hospital Act 1961 491
Sale of Goods Act 1893
s.52 810
Senior Courts Act 1981 (UK)
s.72 ....780, 783
Settled Land Act 1882
s.22(5) 1023
s.39(1) 518n
Settled Land Acts 1882-1890 1023
Social Welfare (Miscellaneous Provisions) Act 2002
s.16 ....498n
Schedule, Part 2 ....498n
Status of Children Act 1987
s.27(5) 503
Statute Law Revision Act (Ireland) 1878 406
Statute of Chantries 1547 (England) 442

Statute of Charitable Uses 1601 (43 Eliz. 1, c.4) (England)....406, 423, 451, 475, 480
Preamble 451n, 454, 460
Statute of Charitable Uses (Ireland) 1634
(10 Char. 1, Sess. 3, c. 1)....68, 69, 69n, 177, 406, 423n
Preamble 425n
Statute of Frauds 1677
s.1....9
s.7....87n
s.9....90n
Statute of Frauds (Ireland) 1695 ....86n–88, 119n, 128, 802, 804, 805
s.2....87, 790n, 794, 795n, 798, 802
s.4....23n, 86, 87, 90
s.6....90, 90n
Statute of Limitations 1957....16, 18, 37–39, 594, 629, 923
s.2(2) 37n, 594n
s.5....37n
s.9(a) 38
(b)....38
s.13....37, 37n
s.34....37n
s.43....37, 37n, 594
s.44....594
s.45....37, 37n
Statute of Uses (England) 1535....68, 177
Statute of Westminster II 1285....6
Statute of Wills (Ireland) Act 1634 68
Succession Act 1965 ....41, 181, 489, 1018
s.10(3) 81
s.26(2) 524
s.49(2) 559
s.63 1037
(9)....1037
s.78....90
s.82....114n
s.117 ....47, 211n
s.126....37n
Supreme Court Act 1981 (UK) 780n
Supreme Court of Judicature Act 1873 (England)....8, 14, 51
s.25
(7)....12n
(11)....9, 11
Supreme Court of Judicature Act 1875 (England) 8
Supreme Court of Judicature (Ireland) Act 1877....1, 8, 12, 15, 16, 17, 617, 618, 637, 790
s.28....15
(7)....12n
(8)....16, 17, 617, 618, 649n
(11)....9

Taxes Consolidation Act 1997
s.76(6) 400
s.207 401
(1) and (2) 400
s.208 ....400, 401
s.235 ....409, 474, 482n
s.609(1) 400n
s.848A 401, 401n, 474n, 482n
Schedules C, D and F 400
Thirty Fourth Amendment of the Constitution (Marriage Equality) Act 2015 ......209n
Trustee Act 1888
s.8 ....38n
Trustee Act 1893 ....513, 517, 579, 598
s.3 542
s.5(1) 543n
s.8 544
s.10 ....519, 521
(1) 519
s.11 ....82, 521
s.12 519
s.13 580
s.14 580
(2) 580n
s.15 580
s.17 578
(3) 578
s.18 584
(2) 584
s.20 581
s.21 583
s.24 577
s.25 ....520, 521
s.45 593
Part I 542
Trustee Act 1925 (New South Wales)
s.45 ....85n
Trustee Act 1925 (UK)
s.23(1) 578n
s.27 559
s.30 577
(1) 578n
s.33 ....85n
s.34 ....518n
s.36(6) 520n
s.61 ....592, 598
Trustee Act 1931 ....517n
Trustee Act 1956 (New Zealand)
s.42 ....85n

Trustee Act 1958 (Northern Ireland)
s.35 520
Trustee Act 2000 (UK) 548, 578
s.1 .... 601n. 604
(1) 517n, 549, 549n, 578n, 595n
s.4 549
s.5 549
(4) 549n
s.11 579
(1) 578n
(2) 578
s.22(1) 578n
s.23 .... 578n
s.26 .... 578n
s.28 603
(5) 607
s.31 538
s.34 584
Sch.1
para.1 548
para.3 .... 578n
para.7 .... 595, 595n
Trustee (Authorised Investments) Act 1958 .... 517n, 542
s.1 542
s.2 542
Trustee Investment Act 1961 (UK) 555
Trusts (Amendment) (Guernsey) Law 1990 .... 598n
Trusts of Land and Appointment of Trustees Act 1996 (UK) 1019, 1022n
s.3 .... 1022n
Universities Act 1997 736
s.26(5) 735
Valuation Act 2001 449
s.3 449
Fourth Schedule 449
Variation of Trusts Act 1958 (UK) 609
Vendor and Purchaser Act 1874
s.2 580
Wills Act 1837 .... 113n, 114n, 119, 119n, 122, 123n, 126n, 146, 184
s.9 122

Table of Statutory Instruments

Charities Act 2009 (Commencement) Order 2009
(SI No.284 of 2009) 398n, 402n, 443n
Charities Act 2009 (Commencement) Order 2010 (SI No.315 of 2010) 398n, 402n
Charities Act 2009 (Commencement) Order 2014 (SI No.457 of 2014) 398n, 402n
Charities Act 2009 (Commencement) Order 2016 (SI No.350 of 2016) 398n, 402n

Charities Act 2009 (Commencement) (No.2) Order 2016
(SI No.424 of 2016)....398n, 403n
Civil Procedure Rules 1998 (UK)
r.25.1....619n, 649n
Courts Act 1981 (Interest on Judgment Debts) Order 2016
(SI No. 624 of 2016)....
556n, 589
European Communities (Civil and Commercial Judgments) Regulations 2002
(SI No. 52 of 2002)
reg.10....771n
European Communities (Civil and Commercial Judgments) Regulations 2015
(S.I. No. 6 of 2015)
art.8(1), (2)....771
Law Reform (Miscellaneous Provisions) (Northern Ireland) Order 2005
(S.I. 2005 No. 1452 N.I. 7)
art.16....205n
Market Abuse Directive (2003/6/EC) Regulations 2005 (S.I. No. 342 of 2005).....203
Registration of Title Act 1964 (Compulsory Registration of Ownership) (Cork and Dublin) Order 2010 (SI No. 516 of 2010)....66n
Road Traffic (Public Service Vehicles) Regulations 1963 (S.I. No. 191 of 1963)...743
Rules of the Circuit Court 2001
Ord.46, r.1....521n
Rules of the Superior Courts 1986
Ord.3, r.11....521n
Ord.42A....771n
Ord.50 r.6....649n
Ord.52 r.6....752n
Ord.63A....644n
Rules of the Superior Courts (Jurisdiction Recognition and Enforcement of Judgments 2016 SI No. 9 of 2016)....771n
Rules of the Superior Courts (Land and Conveyancing Law Reform Act 2009) 2010 (SI No. 149 of 2010)....610
r.4(iii)....610n
Trustee (Authorised Investments) Order 1990 (SI No. 327 of 1990)....543n
Trustee (Authorised Investments) Order 1998 (SI No. 28 of 1998)....542, 543n
First Schedule....542
Second Schedule, cl.4....543
Trustee (Authorised Investments) Order 1998 (Amendment) Order 2002
(SI No. 595 of 2002)....543

Table of Bills

Charities Bill 2007....481
Charities (Amendment) Bill 2014....482n
Charities (Human Rights) Bill 2018....482n
Charities Regulation Bill 2006....386n, 405, 449n, 482
Civil Law (Miscellaneous Provisions) Bill 2006....609

Courts and Civil Law (Miscellaneous Provisions) Bill 2017
General Scheme, Pt 5 .... 316n
Trustee Bill 2008 (Draft)
s.4(1) 518n
s.5 .... 520n
(2) 519n
s.8(5) 519n
s.9(1) 520n
s.12(1) 606
(2) 549n
(b) 549n
s.13(2) 604n
(b) 604n
(3) 607n
s.14 .... 569n, 607n
s.15 .... 579n
s.19 .... 584n
s.20 .... 543n
s.21 .... 584n
s.22 .... 582n
s.23 .... 583n
Trustee Bill 2000 (UK) 602

Table of EU Legislation

Council Regulation (EC) No. 44/2001 of 22 December 2000 on Jurisdiction and the Recognition and Enforcement of Judgments in Civil and Commercial Matters 764n, 770
art.22 .... 52n
art.31 .... 770n
Regulation (EU) No. 1215/2012 on Jurisdiction and the Recognition and Enforcement of Judgments in Civil and Commercial Matters (Brussels I Regulation (recast) 54, 764, 764n, 770n, 771
art.24 52
art.35 770
art.40 770
Single European Act 1987 .... 702, 745

Table of International Treaties and Conventions

2005 Agreement between the European Community and the Kingdom of Denmark on Jurisdiction and the Recognition and Enforcement of Judgments in Civil and Commercial Matters 764n
Brussels Convention on Jurisdiction and the Recognition and Enforcement of Judgments in Civil and Commercial Matters 1968 .... 53n

art.16 ....52, 52n, 53
art.24 ....770n
European Convention on Human Rights 682, 686, 693, 764
First Protocol, art.1 167
art.8 682
art.10 ....682, 686
(2) 686
art.13 750
European Economic Community Treaty
art.30 652
art.31 652
European Stability Mechanism Treaty 703
Lugano Convention 2007 on Jurisdiction and the Recognition and Enforcement of Judgments in Civil and Commercial Matters which replaced the Lugano Convention of 16 September 1988 ....764n

CHAPTER 1

Introduction

GENERAL PRINCIPLES

Equity can be described as the branch of the law administered by the Court of Chancery prior to the enactment of the Supreme Court of Judicature (Ireland) Act 1877 and is the body of principles which evolved with the aim of mitigating the severity of the rules of the common law. The original objective of the Court of Chancery which operated as a 'court of conscience' was to achieve a fair and equitable result in all cases which came before it and the principles which it developed became known as 'equity'. The court sought to avoid the injustice which might result from a strict application of the common law[1] and to provide a remedy where an existing one might be inappropriate or even lacking altogether.[2]

While equitable jurisdiction developed as a means of mitigating the harshness of the common law, it is important to stress that it is still dependent on the existence of the framework which the common law provides. Equity is essentially a supplementary and fragmentary jurisdiction and as Maitland[3] has suggested it should be regarded as a gloss added to the common law and statute law, rather than as an independent system.[4] More recently Kenny J spoke in similar terms in the course of his judgment in *Hynes Ltd v Independent Newspapers*[5] and referred to equity as being 'a gloss on or an improvement and reform of the common law'. For this reason it is difficult to define its scope and a more useful exercise is to point out the main areas in which equity operates today. However, it should be stressed that equity plays a role in a wide range of different situations and it is not possible to set these out in a fully comprehensive manner. Lord Upjohn's statement in the

1. As Lord Denning MR commented in *Crabb v Arun District Council* [1976] Ch 179, 187, 'Equity comes in true to form, to mitigate the rigours of strict law.'
2. As Sir Anthony Mason, the former Chief Justice of Australia has commented, writing extra-judicially, 'equitable principles were shaped with a view to inhibiting unconscientious conduct and providing for relief against it.' (1997-98) 8 KCLJ 1.
3. Maitland, *Lectures on Equity* Lecture II. See also the comment of Lord Evershed MR to the effect that 'equity never denied the existence of the legal right. It said that the legal position was not the whole position, and added something to it.' (1954) 70 LQR 326, 329.
4. As Kiely states in *Principles of Equity as Applied in Ireland* (1936) p. 7: 'If a conglomeration of miscellaneous rules can be called a system then it is such'.
5. [1980] IR 204, 218.

course of his speech in *Boardman v Phipps*[6] should also be borne in mind, namely that '[r]ules of equity have to be applied to such a great diversity of circumstances that they can be stated only in the most general terms.'

One of the most enduring and still one of its most important creations is the trust, which is the relationship which arises whenever a person, called a trustee, is compelled in equity to hold property for the benefit of some person or persons, termed beneficiaries, or for some object permitted by law, in such a way that the real benefit accrues, not to the trustee, but to the beneficiaries or other objects of the trust.[7] This device is still of enormous practical significance today, particularly in view of the wide-ranging nature of taxation statutes and the desire to avoid or postpone their application whenever this is legally possible. The other area in which the influence of equity can be seen most clearly is in relation to the grant of equitable remedies such as injunctions and specific performance. These remedies which are discretionary in nature continue to play an important role in increasingly diverse areas of the law.

One of the hallmarks of equitable jurisdiction is that it is discretionary in nature, as Black LJ made clear in *Conlon v Murray*[8] in the context of the remedy of specific performance, although his comments could be interpreted as being of more general application. However, he made it clear that '[t]his discretion is not, of course, the arbitrary discretion of the individual judge but is a discretion to be exercised on the principles which have been worked out in a multitude of decided cases'.

To ensure that equitable jurisdiction is not exercised in an arbitrary and unfair manner the courts must strive to reconcile the potentially conflicting aims of achieving justice in an individual case and ensuring an element of consistency in decision-making. It could be argued that the very nature of equitable jurisdiction lends credence to the belief that there is some concept of fairness in equity which renders precedent superfluous. The temptation to seek to do justice in an individual case may be great, but as Lord Evershed has commented extra-judicially, 'there is, I venture to think, great danger in practice in what is, in truth, palm tree justice'.[9] He is correct to the extent that the principles of certainty and consistency form an integral part of the fair administration of justice and the sacrificing of settled principles and precedents in specific cases to meet the demands of justice in the name of equity would result ultimately in the development of an arbitrary and therefore unfair legal system.

One of the key underlying themes in the exercise of equitable jurisdiction is the principle of unconscionability and its application may lead to a tension

6. [1967] 2 AC 46, 123.
7. See Keeton and Sheridan, *The Law of Trusts* (12th ed., 1993) p. 3 and *infra*, Chapter 3.
8. [1958] NI 17, 25. See also the *dicta* of O'Higgins CJ in *Smelter Corporation v O'Driscoll* [1977] IR 305, 310-311.
9. (1954) 70 LQR 326, 329. See also Halliwell (1994) 14 LS 15, 17.

between the aims of certainty and flexibility already referred to. As Virgo has commented, '[a]though doctrine and principle is vital to modern Equity, the very existence of the most important equitable principle might undermine the doctrinal coherence of the subject'.[10] The role which the principle of unconscionability plays in the exercise of equitable jurisdiction is increasingly significant, although in an effort to ensure consistency it tends to be interpreted objectively.

Harding has challenged the view that equity undermines the rule of law by arguing that 'equity's tolerance of indeterminacy constitutes a much smaller threat to the rule of law than is commonly supposed … and … that there are reasons to think that equity makes a particular contribution to the rule of law by performing a function of restraining unconscionable reliance on legal rights.'[11] Harding refers to the fact that Sir Anthony Mason has argued[12] that 'it is characteristic of the development of equitable doctrine that what start their life in equity as unspecific references to the demands of conscience mature into more determinate rules and principles as they are reflected on, refined and applied by judges.'[13] So, it can be said that unconscionability has developed from a concept which often faced the criticism that its use would give rise to uncertainty and lack of consistency into a yardstick which has an objective basis and which underpins the determination of liability in an increasing range of areas in which equitable jurisdiction is exercised.

Another important aspect of the overall development of equity, although it may have been lacking at certain stages of its development, is that equitable principles have been 'altered, improved, and refined from time to time'.[14] Certain areas, such as constructive trusts and the equitable remedy of tracing, have developed considerably in significance over recent decades and are now of primary importance as devices to combat increasingly sophisticated transnational fraud. The extent to which equity itself is still developing is a less straightforward question to answer. Greene MR made it clear in *Re Diplock*,[15] that 'if [a] claim in equity exists, it must be shown to have an ancestry, founded in history and in the practice and precedents of courts administering equity jurisdiction.' Although there have been signs of judicial willingness to extend the reach of existing doctrines in some areas,[16] in others there has been a marked reluctance to do so.[17] Both sides of this argument were considered by Hogan

10. Virgo, *The Principles of Equity and Trusts* (3rd ed., 2018) p. 27.
11. (2016) 132 LQR 278.
12. 'Themes and Prospects' in *Essays in Equity* (Finn ed., 1985) p. 242 at 244.
13. (2016) 132 LQR 278, 287.
14. *Re Hallett's Estate* (1880) 13 Ch D 696, 710 *per* Jessel MR.
15. [1948] Ch 465, 481-482. See also *Edlington Properties Ltd v J.H. Fenner & Co. Ltd* [2006] 1 WLR 1583, 1595-1596.
16. *HKN Invest Oy v Incotrade Pvt Ltd* [1993] 3 IR 152.
17. E.g. the attitude of the Supreme Court in *B.L. v M.L.* [1992] 2 IR 77 in relation to extending the reach of the purchase money resulting trust.

J in *ACC Loan Management Ltd v Connolly*,[18] in which he decided that, given that the settled view of the Court of Appeal was reflected in the judgment of Finlay Geoghegan J in that case, he would for reasons of *stare decisis* agree with it.[19] However, it was clear from his judgment that he favoured an approach which would require a financial institution to take steps to protect the position of vulnerable sureties who undertook to guarantee the debts of another party, regardless of whether evidence of undue influence or other wrongdoing was established.[20]

Hogan J stated as follows:

> One may readily concede that no modern court could justifiably invent or conjure up a new equitable principle by reference to the subjective notions of fairness and equity on the part of individual judges. If the law is considered to be unsatisfactory or inadequate, far-reaching change of this kind is reserved to the Oireachtas by Article 15.2.1° of the Constitution.[21]

However, he was of the view that the approach he was suggesting represented 'simply the application in a modern context of standard principles of equity for which there is much historical precedent'.[22] Hogan J continued as follows:

> If there is no modern willingness to re-fashion and adapt these principles to modern conditions in the case of vulnerable sureties, it may simply be that we the judges who are required to tend to the gardens of equity by ensuring that their verdure remains fresh, vibrant and relevant to the modern world have allowed an ancient path of escape from the gravel paths of the common law to become disused and overgrown.
>
> Yet if equity will not bring that moral element to the common law and ensure that in a modern setting the vulnerable are adequately protected, the principles of equity will in time come to be seen as just another set of rules, as desiccated, inflexible and arid as they were in the days of Lord Eldon in the early 19th century.[23]

So, as is the case in relation to achieving an appropriate balance between flexibility and consistency in the exercise of equitable discretion, judges have to steer a middle course between adapting existing principles where they deem it appropriate to meet the justice of an individual case and avoiding making decisions which have no basis whatsoever in precedent. Where a judge develops

---

18. [2017] 3 IR 629.
19. This decision is considered in detail in Chapter 17.
20. See also the dissenting judgment of Hogan J in *Ulster Bank (Ireland) Ltd v De Kretser* [2016] IECA 371.
21. [2017] 3 IR 629, 653-654.
22. *Ibid.* at 654.
23. *Ibid.*

the law in a manner which should more properly be the subject of legislative change, the uncertainty which this can give rise to may itself cause injustice. This point is well made at a broader level by Keane in the following terms:

> [i]t is the application of settled principles largely contained in precedent which gives the law of equity the virtues of certainty and consistency. It is as true today as in centuries past that hard cases make bad law and that the arbitrary abandonment of principle and precedent to meet what may seem to be the demands of justice in a particular context leads only to uncertainty, inconsistency and in the end, injustice at a more profound level.[24]

Article 73 of the Irish Free State Constitution and Article 50 of the Constitution of Ireland 1937 made provision for the carrying forward of existing laws to the extent to which they were not inconsistent with these Constitutions and the practice has been to treat the established principles of equity as being applicable in our courts. It is fair to say that since the foundation of the State the attitude of the judiciary in this jurisdiction has generally been to follow the approach adopted by their counterparts in England — although there have been notable exceptions to this principle[25] — and equity as it exists in Ireland today plays an ever-increasing role across a broad range of activities, including commercial ones.

As Sir Peter Millett[26] commented in an important article on the way forward for equity in England, '[i]t can no longer be doubted that equity has moved out of the family home and the settled estate and into the marketplace'[27] and in his view 'the intervention of equity in commercial transactions, long resisted by common lawyers, can no longer be withstood'. The growing influence of equitable principles in a commercial context has brought with it its own problems in terms of seeking to ensure sufficient certainty and consistency appropriate to the context. As Lord Browne-Wilkinson commented in *Westdeutsche Landesbank Girozentrale v Islington Borough Council*,[28] 'wise judges have often warned against the wholesale importation into commercial law of equitable principles inconsistent with the certainty and speed which are essential requirements for the orderly conduct of business affairs.' Interestingly, it has recently been

---

24. Keane, *Equity and the Law of Trusts in Ireland* (3rd ed., 2017) pp.27-28.
25. E.g. in relation to half secret trusts (Chapter 5) and the division of family property (Chapter 7).
26. At the time a Lord Justice of Appeal in England, writing extra-judicially. See Millett (1995) 9 Trust Law Int 35.
27. However, it should be noted that equity still plays an important role in resolving property disputes in this jurisdiction where legislation, such as the Family Law Act 1995, the Family Law (Divorce) Act 1996 and the Civil Partnership and Certain Rights and Obligations of Cohabitants Act 2010 does not govern the situation. See further Chapter 7.
28. [1996] AC 669, 704.

suggested that 'care should be taken in the opposite direction too'[29] and that the doctrinal coherence of equitable principles should not be compromised by the 'commercialisation' of equity in judgments delivered in the UK Supreme Court.

It is also fair to say that while the circumstances in which equity intervenes are changing and developing, the underlying rationale for its intervention remains essentially the same. Millett usefully summarises the basis for equity's role as follows:

> The traditional objects of equity have not changed: to relieve against mistake, fraud, accident and surprise; to protect the weak from exploitation and trust and confidence from betrayal; to prevent the unconscionable assertion of legal rights; and to give relief against every kind of unconscionable conduct. It demands not merely honesty and a willingness to meet one's commitments, but integrity, good conscience and fidelity.[30]

HISTORICAL BACKGROUND

The thirteenth century saw considerable progress being made in the development of the common law in England. However, by the end of that century it had grown into a rigid set of principles which were slow to adapt to meet the needs of a developing system of justice and hardship frequently arose as a result. A number of major defects had become apparent, principally that under the common law, many wrongs could not be remedied. An injured party could only bring an action at common law if his claim came within a recognised form of writ. To compound this difficulty, the *in consimili causa* clause in the Statute of Westminster II 1285 was interpreted very restrictively and was confined to varying the form of existing writs.

In addition, even where a remedy was available, it was frequently inappropriate or inadequate. The only remedy available at common law was damages and orders which are of such importance in our modern system of justice, such as specific performance and injunctions, were unknown. A defendant might also suffer because a plaintiff might be entitled to a judgment at common law regardless of mitigating factors which would be relevant to the exercise of equitable jurisdiction as we know it today. A further shortcoming of the common law system as it existed at the end of the thirteenth century was its numerous procedural defects and inadequacies. Often a defendant might not be allowed to give evidence or a jury might be subject to outside influences.

As a result of these defects in the system a practice developed of petitioning the king in situations where a litigant complained that he could not obtain

29. Yip and Lee (2017) 37 LS 647, 669.
30. Millett (1995) 9 Trust Law Int 35, 36-37.

an adequate remedy within the framework of the common law. The Lord Chancellor was the officer responsible for overseeing such matters and as the number of petitions increased, the king delegated his functions to the chancellor with the direction that a petitioner should be given a legal remedy if a litigant was entitled to one and where none existed, to give such a remedy as would be just. The Chancellor and his office took on the role of a court which became known as the Court of Chancery.

The office of Lord Chancellor of Ireland was created in the early thirteenth century,[31] although it should be pointed out that until the seventeenth century Brehon law tended to prevail outside the settled areas in the country. The early chancellors in both jurisdictions were predominantly ecclesiastics and many of the principles which date from this time have their origins in canon law or, to a lesser extent, in Roman law. During the Middle Ages, the Irish parliament seems to have played a significant role in exercising equity jurisdiction and it was not until the sixteenth century that the Lord Chancellor of Ireland started to play a meaningful role in dispensing justice on the basis of equitable principles.

The Court of Chancery never sought to deny a litigant's legal rights but rather aimed to ensure that such rights were not exercised in a manner which would cause undue prejudice to the other party or bring about an unjust or inequitable result to a dispute. The court began to issue injunctions to restrain a party from exercising his legal rights, a practice which effectively curtailed the authority of the common law courts. This caused increasing ill-feeling and matters came to a head during the reign of James I in the *Earl of Oxford's Case*[32] when a bitter dispute about the validity of these 'common injunctions' between the Chief Justice of England, Edward Coke, and the Lord Chancellor, Lord Ellesmere, was resolved in favour of the Court of Chancery.

While in theory the early chancellors acted on a number of settled principles in granting or refusing relief, there was little uniformity in the judgments handed down and the types of remedies varied from one chancellor to the next. By the beginning of the seventeenth century the chancellors were generally common lawyers, rather than ecclesiastics, and while the Court of Chancery remained a 'court of conscience', a system of precedent did begin to develop. Much of this systemisation took place from the time of the chancellorship of Lord Nottingham (1673–1682), sometimes referred to as the 'Father of Equity',[33]

---

31. There is some dispute about the identity and the date of appointment of the first Lord Chancellor. Kiely suggests in *Principles of Equity as Applied In Ireland* (1936) p. 6 that it was John de Worchley appointed in 1219, but other commentators suggest that it was Ralph Neville, appointed in 1232. See Hand (1970) 5 Ir Jur (ns) 291; Ball, *The Judges in Ireland* (1926) pp. 6-7; Wylie, *Irish Land Law* (5th ed., 2013) p. 92 and Keane, *Equity and the Law of Trusts in Ireland* (3rd ed., 2017) p. 12. It should also be noted that J. Roderick O'Flanagan suggests that the first Lord Chancellor was Stephen Ridell, appointed in 1186, see *The Lives of the Lord Chancellors and Keepers of the Great Seal of Ireland from the Earliest Times to the Reign of Queen Victoria* (1870) p.18.
32. (1615) 1 Rep Ch 1. See Baker (1969) 4 Ir Jur (ns) 368.
33. *Kemp v Kemp* (1801) 5 Ves 849, 858 *per* Arden MR.

until the time of Lord Eldon (1801–1806 and 1807–1827). However, the price of systemisation was that by the beginning of the nineteenth century, the principles of equity were nearly as rigid as the common law rules. As Lord Eldon commented in *Gee v Pritchard*,[34] '[n]othing would inflict on me greater pain, in quitting this place [the office of chancellor] than the recollection that I had done any thing to justify the reproach that the equity of this Court varies like the Chancellor's foot.'[35] A further difficulty which had come to the fore by this time was the inconvenience of the fact that two distinct court systems had developed, each applying its own often inconsistent principles. Reforms aimed at tackling this problem were begun in the mid-nineteenth century. In 1856 the Common Law Procedure Amendment Act (Ireland)[36] was passed which gave the common law courts power to grant equitable remedies in limited situations. Subsequently the Chancery Amendment Act 1858 (Lord Cairns' Act) gave the Court of Chancery power to award the common law remedy of damages either in substitution for or in addition to an injunction or a decree for specific performance.

A major reform of the system of the administration of justice was effected in England by the Supreme Court of Judicature Acts 1873 and 1875 (followed in Ireland by the Supreme Court of Judicature (Ireland) Act 1877), which established one Supreme Court of Judicature and replaced the system of separate courts exercising common law and equitable jurisdiction.[37] This court had two divisions, the High Court of Justice, which possessed both original and appellate jurisdiction, and the Court of Appeal, which exercised a purely appellate function. The High Court itself was initially divided into five divisions — Chancery, Queen's Bench, Common Pleas, Exchequer and Probate and Matrimonial. In 1887 the Common Pleas Division was merged with the Queen's Bench and in 1897 so were the Exchequer and Probate and Matrimonial Divisions so that by the end of the century, only the Chancery and Queen's Bench Divisions remained.

Pallas CB summarised the effect of the Judicature Act as follows in *Barber v Houston*,[38] a decision of the Exchequer Division:

> The same system of Jurisprudence now prevails in all Divisions of the High Court; and if, upon the facts pleaded, the Plaintiff could, before the Judicature Act, have had in Equity the relief which he seeks in this

34. (1818) 2 Swans 402, 414.
35. Note that in *Taylor v Dickens* [1998] 1 FLR 806, 820 Judge Weeks in rejecting the suggestion that the court might intervene merely because the assertion of strict legal rights was unconscionable, commented that if it were to do so, 'the days of justice varying with the size of the Lord Chancellor's foot would have returned.'
36. The equivalent legislation in England was the Common Law Procedure Act 1854.
37. See the comments of Palles CB in *Antrim County Land, Building and Investment Co. Ltd v Stewart* [1904] 2 IR 357, 364.
38. (1884) 14 LR Ir 273, 276.

> action, he is now entitled to it in this Court. That Act changed forms of procedure, but did not alter rights or remedies.

The fusion of the administration of legal and equitable jurisdiction was continued with the enactment of the Courts of Justice Act 1924 which established a High Court and Supreme Court to take the place of the Supreme Court of Judicature and this structure was continued by the Courts (Establishment and Constitution) Act 1961. However, as Kiely has stated, '[t]he intrinsic difference between legal and equitable rights and remedies remains unaffected'.[39]

One issue which was bound to lead to difficulties in practice was how this new court system was to deal with any potential conflict between legal and equitable principles. Section 28(11) of the Supreme Court of Judicature (Ireland) Act 1877 addressed this problem by providing that, where any conflict arose between the rules of equity and common law, the equitable rule was to prevail. An illustration of how this provision operated in practice is provided by the decision of the English Court of Appeal in *Walsh v Lonsdale*.[40] The defendant landlord agreed in writing to grant the plaintiff a lease of a mill for seven years although no deed was executed as required by law. The agreement provided that the rent would be paid quarterly in arrears but that a year's rent would be payable in advance if demanded. The plaintiff tenant fell into arrears; the defendant demanded a year's rent in advance and when the plaintiff refused to pay, purported to exercise a right of distress. The plaintiff claimed an injunction and damages for illegal distress but the action failed. At law, the distress would have been illegal, as there was no deed in relation to the seven year lease[41] and the yearly legal tenancy which had arisen because of the entering into possession and the payment of rent by the plaintiff would not have permitted the landlord to demand the payment of a year's rent in advance. However, in equity the agreement for the lease was treated as being as good as a lease and the Court of Appeal, in reliance on section 28(11) (which required that in the event of conflict, the equitable rule must prevail) held that the distress was lawful. As Jessel MR stated, '[t]here are not two estates as there were formerly, one estate at common law by reason of the payment of rent from year to year and an estate in equity under the agreement. There is only one court and equity rules prevail in it.'[42]

---

39. Kiely, *Principles of Equity as Applied in Ireland* (1936) p. 9.
40. (1882) 21 Ch D 9. In this case the equivalent provision, s. 25(11) of the Supreme Court of Judicature Act 1873, was at issue. See Sparkes (1988) 8 OJLS 350.
41. Section 1 of the Statute of Frauds 1677 as amended by s. 3 of the Real Property Act 1845 provided that a lease for a period of time greater than three years would be void unless it was executed by deed.
42. (1882) 21 Ch D 9, 14.

FUSION OF LAW AND EQUITY — A PROCEDURAL FUSION ONLY?

Before exploring the debate about the so-called 'fusion fallacy' it is worth reiterating, as Virgo has pointed out, that Equity 'is not an independent system of law, but it has a distinct identity and function to modify the rigours of the Common Law.'[43] Lord Millett, speaking extra-judicially, explained this fundamental principle well.

> [T]he common law and equity are not two separate and parallel systems of law. The common law is a complete system of law which could stand alone, but which if not tempered by equity would often be productive of injustice; while equity is not a complete and independent system of law and could not stand alone.[44]

The generally accepted opinion at the time of the enactment of the Judicature Acts was that the result of the legislation was to effect a fusion of administration rather than a fusion of the principles of the common law and equity. Jessel MR remarked in *Salt v Cooper*[45] in relation to this issue: 'but it was not any fusion, or anything of the kind, it was the vesting in one tribunal the administration of law and equity in every cause, action or dispute which should come before that tribunal.' Similarly, Ashburner has commented that '[t]he two streams of jurisdiction, though they run in the same channel, run side by side and do not mingle their waters.'[46] This view is also well summarised by Delany in the following terms:[47]

> The Judicature Acts fused the courts of law and equity; they created a substantially uniform system of procedure and pleading; and they provided that in case of 'conflict or variance' the rules of equity should prevail. But there was nothing more than a fusion of jurisdiction, procedure and pleading; the substantive rules themselves remained.

While the development of common law rules since the enactment of the Judicature Acts has in some instances been influenced by equitable principles,

---

43. Virgo, *The Principles of Equity and Trusts* (3rd ed., 2018) p. 22.
44. 'Proprietary Restitution' in *Equity in Commercial Law* (eds. Degeling and Edelman, 2005) p. 309.
45. (1880) 16 Ch D 544, 549. See also *Joseph v Lyons* (1884) 15 QBD 280.
46. Ashburner, *Principles of Equity* (2nd ed., 1933) p. 18.
47. Delany (1961) 24 MLR 116, 117. Delany referred to Maitland's point that equity is not a self-sufficient system in itself and presupposes the existence of the common law. He stressed that the so called 'fusion' effected by the Judicature Acts has not reduced the dependence of equity on the common law. See also the comments of Baker (1977) 93 LQR 529, 531 that 'we may … conclude that it was the intention of the Judicature Acts to preserve the distinction between the rules of law and equity'.

there is no doubt that the distinctions between legal and equitable rights and remedies remain today. For example, to obtain an equitable remedy a litigant must rely on the court's discretion whereas if he seeks a common law remedy, once he has established that a right existing at common law has been breached, a remedy will be granted. There has undoubtedly been greater interaction in this area over the years and it has been accepted that a legal remedy may be given for breach of an equitable right, as in *Seager v Copydex Ltd*,[48] in which damages were assessed in respect of a breach of confidence, which is a right protected by equity. However, as a general rule the courts in England have been reluctant to apply this principle, as in *Metall und Rohstoff AG v Donaldson Lufkin & Jenrette Inc*,[49] in which the Court of Appeal held that damages could not be awarded for a breach of trust. This reluctance has not been evident in some other common law jurisdictions, particularly New Zealand, where damages have been awarded in respect of breach of confidence[50] and breach of fiduciary duty.[51] This more radical view is well summarised by the comments of Cooke P in *Attorney General for the United Kingdom v Wellington Newspapers Ltd*:[52]

> As law and equity are now mingled ... it does not seem to me to matter whether the duty be classified as equitable or not. The full range of remedies deriving historically from either common law or equity should be available.

Such an expansive approach would tend to suggest that the fusion effected by the Judicature Acts was more than merely procedural in nature and that the systems of law and equity themselves have merged as a result. This view was put forward by the House of Lords, and particularly forcefully by Lord Diplock, in *United Scientific Holdings Ltd v Burnley Borough Council*,[53] in which the essential issue was whether a landlord who had failed to adhere strictly to the time requirements laid down by a rent review clause should be deprived of the right to increase the rent. The Supreme Court of Judicature Act provided that stipulations in contracts which would have been deemed to be of the essence in a court of equity prior to the enactment of the legislation should henceforth receive that construction in all courts. The lessee argued that as this question

48. [1967] 1 WLR 923. See also *Campbell v MGN Ltd* [2004] 2 AC 457; *Douglas v Hello! Ltd* [2006] QB 125.
49. [1990] 1 QB 391, 473.
50. *Attorney General for the United Kingdom v Wellington Newspapers Ltd* [1988] 1 NZLR 129; *Aquaculture Corporation v New Zealand Green Mussel Co. Ltd* [1990] 3 NZLR 299; *Skids Programme Management Ltd v* McNeill [2013] 1 NZLR 1. See also the Canadian decision of *Lac Minerals Ltd v International Corona Resources Ltd* (1989) 61 DLR (4th) 14.
51. *Day v Mead* [1987] 2 NZLR 443; *Mouat v Clarke Boyce* [1992] 2 NZLR 559.
52. [1988] 1 NZLR 129, 172. See also his comments in *Day v Mead* [1987] 2 NZLR 443, 451.
53. [1978] AC 904.

had not arisen prior to this, the relevant section[54] could not apply and that time was of the essence. The House of Lords held that the position prior to the enactment of the legislation was not of relevance and that since then a fusion of the rules of law and equity had occurred. It therefore held that the council was entitled to invoke the rent review provisions notwithstanding the fact that the time limits prescribed had expired as time was not normally of the essence under the rules of equity.

In reaching this conclusion Lord Diplock stated that Ashburner's metaphor has become 'both mischievous and deceptive' and if that 'fluvial metaphor is to be retained at all, the waters of the confluent streams of law and equity have surely mingled now'.[55] In his view as a result of the Judicature Acts 'the two systems of substantive and adjectival law formerly administered by courts of law and courts of chancery … were fused.'[56]

The finding in this case appears to have been applied by a number of the members of the Supreme Court in *Hynes Ltd v Independent Newspapers Ltd.*[57] The question at issue was a similar one, namely whether time was of the essence with regard to a rent review provision in a contract. The Supreme Court held that if the time stipulation would not have been deemed to be of the essence of the contract in a court of equity prior to the enactment of the Judicature Act, then it would still receive the same construction. As there were no grounds for implying a term that time was of the essence, the plaintiff tenant's appeal against the validity of the late service of a rent review notice was disallowed. O'Higgins CJ stated that in Ireland 'the fusion of common law and equitable rules … initiated by the Supreme Court of Judicature Act (Ireland) 1877 … was completed by the Courts of Justice Act 1924 and the Courts (Establishment and Constitution) Act 1961.'[58] Kenny J also spoke in terms of the decision of the House of Lords in *United Scientific* as being the 'restoration of a fundamental equitable principle which, unfortunately, has tended to be ignored in many recent decisions.'[59]

However, it would be a mistake to read too much into these comments. Coughlan points out that the statement of O'Higgins CJ quoted above, in which he refers to the legal basis for the existing court structure, may suggest that he was referring instead 'to the uncontroversial principle of procedural fusion'.[60] Keane comments that the opinions expressed by the Law Lords in *United Scientific* must be regarded as *obiter* and argues that it would be unwise

---

54. Section 25(7) of the Supreme Court of Judicature Act 1873. The equivalent provision under the Supreme Court of Judicature (Ireland) Act 1877 was s. 28(7).
55. [1978] AC 904, 925. See also the comments of Lord Denning MR in *Federal Commerce & Navigation Co. Ltd v Molena Alpha Inc* [1978] QB 927, 974.
56. *Ibid.* See also the speeches of Lord Simon at 944-945 and of Lord Fraser at 957-958.
57. [1980] IR 204.
58. *Ibid.* at 216.
59. *Ibid.* at 221.
60. Coughlan, *Property Law* (2nd ed., 1998) p. 49.

to assume that *Hynes* indicates that these views have necessarily been accepted in this jurisdiction.[61]

The better view would certainly seem to be that the substantive distinctions between the two systems of law and equity are still valid and there have been signs of this approach being reasserted in both England and Ireland. So, in *Downsview Nominees Ltd v First City Corporation Ltd*[62] the Privy Council refused to replace or supplement the equitable duties of a mortgagee and a receiver appointed by him by liability in negligence, holding that such a result would lead to 'confusion and injustice'.[63] In *Target Holdings Ltd v Redferns*[64] Lord Browne-Wilkinson, in considering the principles relating to equitable compensation for breach of a traditional trust, stated that the common law rules of remoteness of damage and causation did not apply in this context, although he did also concede that 'the principles underlying both systems are the same'.[65] Similar reluctance to apply the principle of substantive fusion can be discerned from the approach of the House of Lords in *Lord Napier and Ettrick v Hunter*,[66] in which Lord Goff stated that he could see no 'justification for sweeping the line of equity cases under the carpet as though it did not exist'.[67]

In *Tinsley v Milligan*[68] Lord Browne-Wilkinson, although he spoke of the fusion of law and equity,[69] seemed to rely on common law and equitable

61. Keane, *Equity and the Law of Trusts in Ireland* (3rd ed., 2017) p. 26. Keane suggests that until the question is unequivocally resolved, the views expressed 'are most safely regarded as in the nature of premature funeral orations'.
62. [1993] AC 295.
63. *Ibid.* at 316. However, it should be noted that in *Medforth v Blake* [2000] Ch 86 Scott VC held that a receiver managing mortgaged property not only owed a duty to the mortgagor to exercise his powers in good faith and for proper purposes but also owed a duty to manage the mortgaged property with due diligence, which he characterised as an equitable duty of care. This approach avoided the objections to imposing liability in negligence based on the fusion fallacy argument, but the view has also been put forward that 'a self standing equitable duty of care remediable in damages is a novelty – surely tort masquerading under a false label', see Sealy [2000] CLJ 31, 33. See also Frisby (2000) 63 MLR 413.
64. [1996] AC 421, 434.
65. *Ibid.* at 432. See also *Ahmed v Ingram* [2018] EWCA Civ 519 at [35].
66. [1993] AC 713. See further *AIB Group (UK) plc v Mark Redler & Co.* [2015] AC 1503, considered *infra.*
67. *Ibid.* at 743. Although the language employed by Lord Browne-Wilkinson who spoke in terms of 'the fusion of law and equity' (at 749, 751) might have suggested support for the alternative approach, the conclusion which he reached did not.
68. [1994] 1 AC 340. Note the views expressed by members of the Supreme Court in *Patel v Mirza* [2017] AC 467 to the effect that the approach towards the application of the defence of illegality adopted in *Tinsley* should not be followed. This issue is considered in more detail in Chapter 7.
69. *Ibid.* at 375. Although note that this reference appears in the All England Reports as 'the fusion of the administration of law and equity', see [1993] 3 All ER 65, 86. It should also be noted that an earlier reference to 'since law and equity became fused' in the transcript [1993] UKHL 3, appeared at p.371 of the Official Series reports as 'since the administration of law and equity became fused'.

principles which had developed side by side.[70] Somewhat mixed messages also appear evident in the judgments of the Supreme Court of the United Kingdom in *AIB Group (UK) plc v Mark Redler & Co.*,[71] although the predominant one is of substantive distinctions persisting. At the outset of his judgment Lord Toulson JSC acknowledged that '140 years after the Judicature Act 1873 …, the stitching together of equity and the common law continues to cause problems at the seams.'[72] As Davies has suggested, aspects of Lord Toulson's judgment 'appeared to favour a "fusionist" response'[73] and he said that in circumstances such as those which had arisen in *Target Holdings v Redferns Ltd*,[74] 'the extent of equitable compensation should be the same as if damages for breach of contract were sought at common law.'[75] However, Lord Toulson JSC later stated that '[e]quitable compensation and common law damages are remedies based on separate legal obligations. What has to be identified in each case is the content of any relevant obligation and the consequences of its breach.'[76] Lord Reed JSC appeared to place even more emphasis on the distinctions between liability at law and in equity, although he recognised the 'structural similarities'. He stated as follows:

> [T]he liability of a trustee for breach of trust, even where the trust arises in the context of a commercial transaction which is otherwise regulated by contract, is not generally the same as a liability in damages for tort or breach of contract. Of course, the aim of equitable compensation is to compensate: that is to say, to provide a monetary equivalent of what has been lost as a result of a breach of duty. At that level of generality, it has the same aim as most awards of damages for tort or breach of contract. Equally, since the concept of loss necessarily involves the concept of causation, and that concept in turn inevitably involves a consideration of the necessary connection between the breach of duty and a postulated consequence (and therefore of such questions as whether a consequence flows "directly" from the breach of duty, and whether loss should be attributed to the conduct of third parties, or to the conduct of the person to whom the duty was owed), there are some structural similarities

70. This approach is also borne out by the *dicta* of Rimer J in *Clarion Ltd v National Provident Institution* [2000] 1 WLR 1888, 1898 who, in commenting on the type of mistake which will entitle a party to a contract to avoid it, described this as 'an area of law in which even by the end of the twentieth century there has been little merging of the streams of common law and equity'.
71. [2015] AC 1503.
72. *Ibid.* at 1514.
73. (2015) 78 MLR 672.
74. [1996] AC 421.
75. [2015] AC 1503, 1529.
76. *Ibid.* at 1530. See also *Main v Giambrone* [2017] EWCA Civ 1193 at [58].

> between the assessment of equitable compensation and the assessment of common law damages.[77]

Lord Reed JSC went on to add that '[t]hose structural similarities do not however entail that the relevant rules are identical: as in mathematics, isomorphism is not the same as equality.'[78] He also pointed out that, as courts around the world have accepted, a trust imposes different obligations from a contractual or tortious relationship.

Similarly in this jurisdiction, the view has been reasserted that the distinction between legal and equitable rights and remedies remains. This is clear from the judgments of Hogan J in *Meagher v Dublin City Council*,[79] and *Flanagan v Crosby*.[80] In *Meagher* the plaintiff brought a claim for damages for breach of contract arising out of an agreement to provide hostel facilities and other ancillary services for asylum seekers. The court had to consider whether the equitable doctrine of laches could be utilised to defeat a claim for damages for breach of contract at common law which was otherwise not statute-barred. Hogan J stated that it is true that on one view of the judgments in *Hynes Ltd v Independent Newspapers Ltd*, both O'Higgins CJ and Kenny J appeared to suggest that there had been a complete fusion of the two separate streams of the common law and equity. He said that these comments must in the first instance be adjudged to be purely *obiter* because the issue in that case was whether a defendant had validly invoked a rent review clause when the relevant notice had been sent some six weeks too late. He added that 'save for a stray reference by O'Higgins CJ to the "fusion of common law and equitable rules" there is, in fact, little in the judgments to suggest that some broader concept of substantive fusion was actually being embraced or considered.'[81] Hogan J said that one might agree with a statement made in an earlier edition of this book that it 'would be a mistake' to read too much into the comments in *Hynes*.[82] He added that it may in any event be questioned whether fusion with such far-reaching implications could ever really have been legislatively intended. In his view section 28 of the Supreme Court of Judicature Act (Ireland) 1877 assumes that the existing common law rules will continue to apply within their own sphere of influence, even if modified in certain defined instances by reference to pre-existing equitable principles. Hogan J said that despite all the claims which have been made in relation to the fusion of law and equity, there is no authority for the proposition that the court might refuse to award damages for breach of contract or in tort on discretionary grounds such as undue delay or because the claimant has been guilty of bad faith, even though these would

77. *Ibid.* at 1544-1545.
78. *Ibid.* at 1545.
79. [2013] IEHC 474.
80. [2014] IEHC 59.
81. *Ibid.* at [20].
82. *Ibid.* at [21].

be well established grounds for refusing any equitable relief which might otherwise have been granted. He concluded that one may accordingly agree with the observations in *Hanbury and Martin: Modern Equity*[83] that while the two systems of law work ever more closely together and draw mutual inspiration from each other, they 'are not yet fused.' This meant that the doctrine of laches has no application to a claim at common law for damages for breach of contract where that claim is not otherwise barred by the Statute of Limitations. Hogan J concluded that while he deplored the lapse of time and the general delays associated with the proceedings, he would refuse to strike them out on grounds of delay. He considered that the running of the Statute of Limitations had been stopped by reason of the commencement of the proceedings and he did not consider that the equitable doctrine of laches had any application to a common law claim for damages.

The views expressed by Hogan J in *Meagher* were reiterated by him in his judgment in *Flanagan v Crosby*,[84] in which he considered whether a receiver could be appointed by way of equitable execution in respect of the future salary or other emoluments to which an employee was entitled in law. Referring to his findings in *Meagher*, Hogan J commented that 'there continue to be clear and justifiable reasons for the different treatment of the different types of legal and equitable rights.'[85] He expressed some reservations about preserving an ongoing differentiation between legal and equitable rights so far as the power to appoint a receiver by way of equitable execution was concerned and suggested that if the matter were to be viewed afresh from the standpoint of first principles it might be revisited. However, in the circumstances, Hogan J concluded that he felt bound not to depart from the views expressed in other decisions of the High Court[86] to the effect that the appointment of a receiver by way of equitable execution was confined to the enforcement of equitable rights only.

The issue of whether the Judicature Act had effected anything more than procedural fusion was also considered in the context of the jurisprudence relating to the appointment of a receiver by way of equitable execution in the judgment of MacMenamin J in *ACC Loan Management Ltd v Rickard*,[87] where the underlying question was whether the Supreme Court of Judicature (Ireland) Act 1877 had extended the powers of the courts or whether the legislation was purely procedural in nature. The specific issue which the Supreme Court had to address was whether the words 'just or convenient' in section 28(8) of the Act of 1877, which, *inter alia*, made provision for the appointment of a receiver by way of equitable execution, were intended to give the courts wider powers

83. *Hanbury and Martin: Modern Equity* (19th ed., 2012) p.29. Now see Glister and Lee, *Hanbury and Martin: Modern Equity* (21st ed., 2018) p. 24.
84. [2014] IEHC 59.
85. *Ibid.* at [23].
86. *National Irish Bank Ltd v Graham* [1994] 1 IR 215; *Honniball v Cunningham* [2010] 2 IR 1.
87. [2019] IESC 29.

than they had held prior to the enactment of the Judicature Act. An argument had been made that it was not open to the courts to re-interpret or develop the meaning of the phrase 'just or convenient' because it could only be understood in the light of its meaning at the time of the enactment of the legislation in 1877. Referring to the jurisdiction to grant Mareva injunctions, MacMenamin J noted that the courts had felt it appropriate to grant such injunctions having regard to statutory terminology precisely analogous to section 28(8) of the 1877 Act. He pointed out that the courts in this jurisdiction have granted Mareva injunctions and then posed the question that 'if this Court was prepared to countenance incremental development of the terms "just or convenient", in the context of Mareva injunctions, does it not logically equally follow that, by analogy, there may be an incremental development in the law regarding the appointment of receivers?'[88] MacMenamin J stated that there was no doubt that in the former context the courts have given a contemporary interpretation to the term 'just or convenient' and that 'it seems incongruous that, in this one area of law, the terms should be interpreted *only* through the lens of the practice of the Courts of Chancery prior to the 1870s'.[89] He added that it was noteworthy that 'the Judicature Act itself allows for its own modification by rules of court.' MacMenamin J went on to say that he would 'refrain from expressing any concluded view on whether the effect of the 1877 Act was to fuse law and equity' and that 'no such broad assumption is necessary for the narrow and limited conclusion reached in this judgment.'[90] He expressed the view that the interpretation put forward by the appellant would require the court 'to construe the operative parts of an important provision through the lens of a bygone era' and he stated that section 28(8) must now be interpreted in order to make allowances for 'changes in the law' in this State, as provided for in section 6 of the Interpretation Act 2005. On this issue he concluded as follows:

> The persuasive dicta cited from the neighbouring jurisdiction do not, in fact, require this Court to arrive at the conclusion that law and equity have been fused. It is reasonable to have regard to the fact that incremental developments in the law in England and Wales have taken place from 1975 onwards by interpretation of similar words to the s.28(8) of the 1877 Act [sic]. Such an interpretation recognises the reality that our courts have actually implicitly or expressly proceeded on this interpretation in a number of areas critical to commercial life in the 21st Century.[91]

In her judgment in the Supreme Court in *McGrath v Stewart*,[92] Laffoy J also agreed with the view that the two systems 'are not yet fused'. She referred to

88. *Ibid.* at [25].
89. *Ibid.* at [70].
90. *Ibid.* at [71].
91. *Ibid.*
92. [2016] 2 IR 704, 720.

the finding made by Hogan J in *Meagher* and expressed agreement with his conclusion that in consequence, the doctrine of laches has no application to a claim at common law for damages for breach of contract where that claim is not otherwise barred by the Statute of Limitations. Therefore, at this stage it seems that the position in this jurisdiction on the fusion fallacy debate is clear and that there is no recent support for the principle of substantive fusion.

Sir Peter Millett has quite rightly suggested that the opinion that the Judicature Acts had the effect of fusing law and equity to the extent that they have become a single body of law rather than two separate systems of law administered together has been widely discredited,[93] both in England and Australia.[94] While the 'mingled' doctrine has been favoured by some judges in New Zealand[95] this approach has been far from universal in that jurisdiction and in *Equiticorp Industries Group Ltd v Hawkins*[96] Wylie J stated that '[w]e have not yet reached the stage where the conventional ingredients of causes of action can be ignored for the purpose of enabling the courts to arrive at some ill-defined and undisciplined objective of being fair.' However, improvements could be effected particularly where the principles of common law and equity do not co-exist coherently and Burrows has suggested that not enough is being done 'to eradicate the needless differences in terminology used, and the substantive inconsistencies, between common law and equity.'[97]

In reviewing the relevant English decisions, Martin has argued that the view that flexibility and capacity for development is best achieved by disregarding the legal or equitable origins of causes of action, remedies or defences is misconceived.[98] She asserts that it does not seem that the fusion fallacy evidenced in cases such as *United Scientific* has become established in England; on the contrary she claims that there has been a return to orthodoxy. In her view, this is apparent from the decisions of the House of Lords in *Napier* and *Tinsley* which, she says, contain 'meticulous analyses of the separate common law and equitable origins and principles' in the areas concerned. The concluding

93. Millett (1995) 9 Trust Law Int 35, 37.
94. See the judgments of Spigelman CJ and Heydon JA in *Harris v Digital Pulse Pty Ltd* [2003] NSWCA 10 in which the majority of the New South Wales Court of Appeal overturned an award of exemplary damages for a breach of fiduciary duty. See further Edelman (2003) 119 LQR 375.
95. See the *dicta* of Thomas J in *Powell v Thompson* [1991] 1 NZLR 597, 615 where he spoke of the 'happy mingling of law and equity'. See also *Aquaculture Corporation v New Zealand Green Mussel Co. Ltd* [1990] 3 NZLR 299, 301; *Skids Programme Management Ltd v Mc*Neill [2013] 1 NZLR 1, 20.
96. [1991] 3 NZLR 700, 727. A more balanced view is that put forward by Somers J in *Elders Pastoral Ltd v Bank of New Zealand* [1989] 2 NZLR 180, 193: 'Neither law nor equity is now stifled by its origin and the fact that both are administered by one court has inevitably meant that each has borrowed from the other in furthering the harmonious development of the law as a whole.'
97. Burrows (2002) 22 OJLS 1, 5.
98. Martin [1994] Conv 13.

comments in *Hanbury and Martin: Modern Equity*[99] on this subject probably come closest to summing up the existing position:

> What can be said is that more than a century of fused jurisdiction has seen the two systems, whose relationship is 'still evolving', working more closely together; each changing and developing and improving from contact with the other; and each willing to accept new ideas and developments, regardless of their origin. They are coming closer together. But they are not yet fused.

99. Glister and Lee, *Hanbury and Martin: Modern Equity* (21st ed., 2018) p. 24.

CHAPTER 2

Maxims of Equity

INTRODUCTION

The maxims of equity constitute the general principles developed by the Court of Chancery over the years. As Mason CJ stated in *Corin v Patton*,[1] an equitable maxim is 'a summary statement of a broad theme which underlies equitable concepts and principles'. While they are not to be interpreted as positive rules of law which should always be applied in their literal sense, many of them do reflect general trends which can be discerned from the manner in which the equitable jurisdiction of the courts has been exercised. It is important to realise that some of these maxims overlap or may even appear to contradict one another. Others no longer accurately reflect the manner in which equitable jurisdiction operates and they should be treated with a degree of caution. Nevertheless, a brief examination of the maxims and what they mean in practice provides a useful introduction to the manner in which equity operates.

EQUITY WILL NOT SUFFER A WRONG TO BE WITHOUT A REMEDY

The principle which lies behind this maxim is that equity will intervene to protect a recognised right which for some reason is not enforceable at common law and it reflects the basis for the origins of the equitable jurisdiction of the Chancellor. However, as equitable jurisdiction became more established, it also grew increasingly formalised and based on precedent. As Greene MR commented in *Re Diplock*,[2] 'if a claim in equity exists it must be shown to have an ancestry founded in history and in the practice and precedents of the courts administering equity jurisdiction'. Similar sentiments were expressed by Neuberger LJ in *Edlington Properties Ltd v J.H. Fenner & Co. Ltd*,[3] where he said that the fact that a particular type of right or relief may be equitable 'does not … operate as a green light to invent new general or specific rules in order to achieve what one judge might regard as a fair result in a particular case'. However, it has been recognised that equitable principles need to adapt to meet the demands of justice in a modern legal system. As Hogan J stated in

1. (1990) 169 CLR 540, 557.
2. [1948] Ch 465, 481-482.
3. [2006] 1 WLR 1583, 1595-1596.

ACC Loan Management Ltd v Connolly,[4] 'if equity will not bring that moral element to the common law and ensure that in a modern setting the vulnerable are adequately protected, the principles of equity will in time come to be seen as just another set of rules, as desiccated, inflexible and arid as they were in the days of Lord Eldon in the early 19th century.'[5]

Textbook writers have pointed out that this maxim should be treated with considerable caution today. Wylie has commented that 'it is a grossly inaccurate statement of equity's approach in modern times'[6] and it is stressed in *Meagher, Gummow and Lehane's Equity: Doctrines and Remedies*[7] that it is misleading unless one realises that the maxim is now of 'purely historical importance'. It should also be made clear at the outset that in this context the word 'wrong' refers to conduct contrary to the law rather than simply immoral.

Despite its potentially misleading nature, there are nevertheless some important practical illustrations of the operation of the maxim which can still be seen today. Perhaps the most far-reaching of these is the recognition given by equity to the concept of the trust by virtue of which a beneficiary can enforce equitable rights which the common law would not recognise, as it simply regarded the trustee as the legal owner. Other notable illustrations of the maxim can be found in relation to the grant of equitable remedies. The injunction developed as a means of achieving justice where the common law remedy of damages could not provide an adequate remedy and will now issue e.g. to restrain an ongoing nuisance[8] or in *quia timet* form to prevent a threatened wrong from occurring.[9] Similarly, where specific performance of a contract for the sale of land is sought, it can be granted in this jurisdiction despite non-compliance with the necessary statutory formalities provided sufficient acts of part performance can be established.[10] Another illustration is the appointment of a receiver by way of equitable execution which can operate where a creditor is unable to levy execution at law owing to the equitable nature of the property concerned.[11]

Despite the frequency with which the above illustrations of the maxim occur in practice, it would be fair to say that more recent attempts to develop the principle that equity will not suffer a wrong to be without a remedy have proved less successful. As Lindley LJ commented in *Holmes v Millage*,[12] '[i]t

---

4. [2017] 3 IR 629. This judgment is discussed further in Chapters 1 and 17.
5. *Ibid.* at 654.
6. Wylie, *Irish Land Law* (5th ed., 2013) p. 130.
7. Heydon, Leeming and Turner, *Meagher, Gummow and Lehane's Equity: Doctrines and Remedies* (5th ed., 2015) p. 69.
8. *Patterson v Murphy* [1978] ILRM 85; *Kennaway v Thompson* [1981] QB 88.
9. *Whelan v Madigan* [1978] ILRM 136.
10. *Lowry v Reid* [1927] NI 142.
11. See generally the authorities referred to by Hogan J in *Flanagan v Crosby* [2014] IEHC 59 and the judgment of MacMenamin J in *ACC Loan Management Ltd v Rickard* [2019] IESC 29.
12. [1893] 1 QB 551, 555.

is an old mistake to suppose that, because there is no effectual remedy at law, there must be one in equity'. A classic example of how an attempt to develop a new form of equitable relief has met with mixed fortunes is provided by the new model constructive trust,[13] a creature first devised by Lord Denning MR to be imposed 'whenever justice and good conscience require it'.[14] Maudsley criticised this development saying that it was possible to read into the decisions the principle that 'in cases in which the plaintiff ought to win, but has no legal doctrine or authority to support him, a constructive trust in his favour will do the trick.'[15] There was a considerable retrenchment in England from the position laid down in the early decisions[16] and it has been rejected outright in some common law jurisdictions.[17] While there is still evidence of its existence in this jurisdiction,[18] there is certainly no sign of any wholesale adoption of Lord Denning's constructive trust of a 'new model'.

There is also evidence of a reluctance to further extend existing equitable devices for achieving justice between parties which is well illustrated by examining the concept of the purchase money resulting trust and the manner in which it has been used to confer interests in the family home. This type of trust has traditionally been employed to give relief to a party who has no legal interest in the property but has nevertheless contributed financially either directly or indirectly to its purchase. When the Supreme Court was faced with the argument in *B.L. v M.L.*[19] that contributions of a non-financial kind, such as work in the home, should also give rise to a resulting trust, it declined to accept this proposition on the basis that such a step would involve the creation of an entirely new right and instead decided that the issue was one for the legislature.

EQUITY FOLLOWS THE LAW

This maxim might be more accurately stated in the following terms: 'Equity follows the law, but not slavishly nor always'[20] and it is inadvisable to interpret it too strictly. It would be fair to say that although equity does not seek to question the existence of legal rights it will attempt to mitigate the often harsh results caused by their strict enforcement. Equity restricted or modified the application of common law principles where it was in the interests of fairness to do so. A classic illustration of this modification is the principle that equity will not

13. See *infra* Chapter 8.
14. *Hussey v Palmer* [1972] 1 WLR 1286, 1290. See also *N.A.D. v T.D.* [1985] ILRM 153, 160.
15. Maudsley (1977) 28 NILQ 123. See also Oakley (1973) 26 CLP 17, 39.
16. E.g. *Ashburn Anstalt v Arnold* [1989] Ch 1.
17. E.g. in Australia, *Muschinski v Dodds* (1985) 160 CLR 583, 615.
18. *HKN Invest Oy v Incotrade Pvt Ltd* [1993] 3 IR 152; *Kelly v Cahill* [2000] 1 IR 56; *Re Varko Ltd* [2012] IEHC 278.
19. [1992] 2 IR 77.
20. *Graf v Hope Building Corporation* (1930) 254 NY 1, 9 *per* Cardozo CJ.

allow a statute to be used as an instrument of fraud.[21] So, for example, equity would not permit a beneficiary to be deprived of an interest in land under the terms of a trust where this would amount to fraud even if there was insufficient compliance with the requisite statutory formalities,[22] provided that there was some other evidence to establish the nature of his interest.[23] Equally, equity would recognise the existence of secret or half secret trusts[24] by waiving the requirement of strict compliance with the necessary testamentary formalities in the interests of preventing fraud.[25]

Having referred briefly to some of the equitable modifications to common law principles, it should be pointed out that in other situations, equitable interests in land may correspond with legal estates and interests. In addition, there is often a presumption that equity does follow the law. This point is well illustrated by the fact that, as Baroness Hale stated in *Stack v Dowden*,[26] where parties are joint legal owners of property, it will be assumed that equity follows the law and that their beneficial interests reflect their legal interests in this property. It is also clear from the judgments of the members of the Supreme Court of the United Kingdom in *Jones v Kernott*,[27] which clarified the principles that apply in this area, that the starting point or 'default option'[28] is that there is a presumption that where parties are joint tenants in law, they will also be so in equity. A heavy onus of proof will lie on any party seeking to show that equity should not follow the law to establish that the parties held a common intention that their beneficial interests should be different from their legal interests,[29] although on the facts of both *Stack v Dowden* and *Jones v Kernott*, this was successfully established.

A further example of how equity tends to follow the law can be seen in relation to executed as opposed to executory trusts. These expressions refer to the creation of a trust and not to its performance. A trust is said to be executed where the settlor has specified precisely the limits under which the trust property is to be held and where no further instrument is required as the trust has been finally declared in the first instance. A trust is said to be executory where, although a valid trust is created, the settlor has only indicated his general

---

21. *McCormick v Grogan* (1869) LR 4 HL 82, 97 *per* Lord Westbury. See further Chapter 4.
22. Section 4 of the Statute of Frauds (Ireland) 1695 requires that express trusts of land be evidenced in writing and signed by a person able to declare the trust, or by his will.
23. *Rochefoucauld v Boustead* [1897] 1 Ch 196; *McGillycuddy v Joy* [1959] IR 189; *Gilmurray v Corr* [1978] NI 99.
24. See *infra* Chapter 5.
25. E.g. *Riordan v Banon* (1876) IR 10 Eq 469.
26. [2007] 2 AC 432, 453.
27. [2012] 1 AC 776.
28. *Ibid.* at 783 *per* Lord Walker and Baroness Hale.
29. [2007] 2 AC 432 *per* Lord Walker at 447 and Baroness Hale at 459.

intentions as to how the trust property is to be disposed of and the execution of a further instrument is required to define the beneficial interests with precision.[30]

In the case of executed trusts, equity follows the law and generally requires the same precise words of limitation in relation to an equitable interest as would be required for a legal estate. This proposition can be seen from the decision of the English Court of Appeal in *Re Bostock's Settlement*,[31] in which it was held that where an executed trust is created, the requisite legal words of limitation must be used and a general intent to confer an interest in fee simple will not suffice. A similar finding was made by the Supreme Court in *Jameson v McGovern*,[32] where Murnaghan J cited with approval the following *dicta* of Lord Eldon in *Jervoise v Duke of Northumberland*[33] in relation to executed trusts: 'These are cases where the testator has clearly decided what the trust is to be; and as equity follows the law, where the testator has left nothing to be done, but has himself expressed it, there the effect must be the same, whether the estate is legal or equitable.' In *Jameson* by virtue of a marriage settlement freehold premises had been conveyed to a husband for life, to his wife for life, then to any children, or if there were none, to those appointed by the husband and in default of appointment, for the survivor of the husband and wife absolutely. The parties had no children and no appointment was made by the husband. After his death, the question of the extent of the wife's interest under the settlement arose. The Supreme Court held, following *Re Bostock's Settlement*, that the wife only derived a life interest from it, although the court went on to hold that she had an equity independent of the settlement sufficient to give her an equitable fee simple in the property. A similar approach of requiring the necessary words of limitation was followed by Costello J in *Savage v Nolan*,[34] although as in *Jameson* the court was able to find that the parties in question, in this instance children under a marriage settlement, were entitled to an absolute interest independent of the settlement.

HE WHO SEEKS EQUITY MUST DO EQUITY

Equity will only grant relief on terms which ensure that a defendant is treated fairly and to obtain equitable relief, a plaintiff must be prepared to act in an honourable manner. This maxim has many different applications and reflects the fact that equitable remedies are discretionary in nature. It is one of the few maxims that can be interpreted fairly literally; as is pointed out in *Equity:*

---

30. See *Davis v Richards and Wallington Ltd* [1990] 1 WLR 1511, 1537-1538. See also *Pengelly v Pengelly* [2008] Ch 375, 378.
31. [1921] 2 Ch 469.
32. [1934] IR 758.
33. (1821) 1 Jac & W 559.
34. High Court 1976 No. 2395 P (Costello J) 20 July 1978.

Doctrines and Remedies,[35] 'there are many illustrations of, and almost no exceptions to, the maxim'. It in a sense complements the maxim that 'he who comes to equity must come with clean hands' and while the latter principle focuses on the past conduct of the party seeking the intervention of the court, the maxim that 'he who seeks equity must do equity' is concerned with his likely future conduct.[36]

The effect of the maxim is noticeable in the approach of equity towards the granting of remedies and is a feature of equitable jurisdiction which distinguishes it from the common law. An illustration of this is the manner in which equity approaches a claim for rescission of a contract. Rescission will be granted to a plaintiff on terms which the court considers just[37] and relief of an unconditional nature may not achieve this aim. So, in *Cheese v Thomas*[38] an elderly plaintiff who had given the defendant, his great-nephew, approximately half of the purchase price of a house on the understanding that he could live there until he died, sought to have the transaction set aside on grounds of undue influence. Nicholls VC ordered that the property should be sold and that both parties should bear the loss on the sale in the same proportions as they had contributed to the purchase price. He pointed out that the court was concerned to achieve practical justice for both parties and not for the plaintiff alone and stated that 'the plaintiff is seeking the assistance of a court of equity and he who seeks equity must do equity'.[39]

Another illustration of the application of the maxim is that an interlocutory injunction will almost invariably not be granted unless a plaintiff is prepared to give an undertaking as to damages in order to ensure that a defendant may be compensated in the event of the former being successful at the interlocutory stage but ultimately failing at the trial of the action. A specific example of the application of this maxim in the context of a claim for an injunction can be seen in the judgment of Abbott J in *Dolan v Reynolds*.[40] While he held that the plaintiff was entitled to a mandatory injunction requiring the defendant, her brother, to vacate a family property, he also agreed that a declaration should be made that the defendant was entitled to compensation for work carried out by him on the property. In addition, in some cases a court may choose to withhold interlocutory relief where a claimant is unwilling to carry out his side of a contract or arrangement which may exist between the parties. So, in *Chappell v Times Newspapers Ltd*[41] the plaintiffs sought an interim injunction to restrain

35. Heydon, Leeming and Turner, *Meagher, Gummow and Lehane's Equity: Doctrines and Remedies* (5th ed., 2015) p. 75.
36. See also *Bennett v Minister for Justice and Equality* [2017] IEHC 261 at [6]. Although this was not the case in *Shiel v McKeon* [2007] 2 ILRM 144, see further *infra* Chapter 8.
37. *Cooper v Phibbs* (1867) LR 2 HL 149; *Solle v Butcher* [1950] 1 KB 671.
38. [1994] 1 WLR 129.
39. *Ibid.* at 136.
40. [2011] IEHC 334.
41. [1975] 1 WLR 482.

their employers from terminating their contracts of employment, although they refused to give the undertakings sought by the employers not to engage in disruptive behaviour. Although the plaintiffs themselves had not previously been directly involved in these activities, the Court of Appeal refused to grant the relief sought on the grounds that the plaintiffs had failed to establish that they intended to act equitably by abiding by the terms of their contracts of employment. As Lord Denning MR said, 'if one party seeks relief, he must be ready and willing to do his part in it.'[42]

Equally, a claimant will not be granted specific performance of a contract unless he can establish to the satisfaction of the court that he is willing and able to carry out his own contractual obligations. So, in cases where specific performance is sought, 'a court will have regard to the conduct of both parties'.[43] This principle was applied by Barrett J in *Maloney v O'Connor*[44] in refusing an order for specific performance in circumstances where he was satisfied that the plaintiff was seeking performance of the defendants' obligations in a contract whilst himself refusing to perform a central aspect of the agreement. Specific performance may also be refused on the grounds of a lack of mutuality between the parties, a principle set out as follows by O'Connor LJ in *O'Regan v White*:[45] 'Generally speaking, at any rate, it would not be even-handed justice to compel specific performance against the one party, where the same remedy would not be available against the other party in respect of matters to be by him performed under the contract.'

In deciding whether to grant or withhold equitable relief, a court will have regard to the conduct of both parties if it 'is truly to act as a court of conscience'.[46] This principle can be seen in the context of claims which may be defeated by a plea of estoppel and, where it would be unconscionable for a plaintiff to renege on an assumption which he has permitted a defendant to make, he will be estopped from asserting his claim.[47]

The operation of this maxim can also be seen in relation to the mortgagor's equity of redemption. If the mortgagor wishes to use the extension of time permitted by equity to exercise the right of redemption, it can only be exercised on equitable terms; he must be willing to pay all arrears of interest due to the mortgagee and to give him reasonable notice of his intention to redeem.

Finally, the maxim is the basis for the doctrine of election, i.e. that a person cannot take a benefit and reject an associated burden, which will be considered in detail in a later chapter.[48]

---

42. *Ibid.* at 502.
43. *Maloney v O'Connor* [2015] IEHC 678 *per* Barrett J.
44. [2015] IEHC 678.
45. [1919] 2 IR 339, 393.
46. *McMahon v Kerry County Council* [1981] ILRM 419, 421.
47. E.g. *Lim Teng Huan v Ang Swee Chuan* [1992] 1 WLR 113; *Gillett v Holt* [2001] Ch 210; *Coyle v Finnegan* [2013] IEHC 463. See further Chapter 18.
48. See *infra* Chapter 20.

HE WHO COMES TO EQUITY MUST COME WITH CLEAN HANDS

This maxim also reflects the discretionary nature of equity and requires that a person seeking equitable relief must refrain from fraud, misrepresentation or any other form of dishonest or disreputable conduct if he wishes to be granted a remedy.[49] As Halliwell stated, '[t]he unclean hands maxim is often influential in persuading a Court to exercise its discretion in a particular way when considering equitable remedies.'[50] However, unlike the maxim just considered, it refers principally to the past conduct of the plaintiff. The general principle which the maxim lays down was stated by Eyre LCB in *Dering v Earl of Winchelsea*[51] as follows:

> A man must come into a court of equity with clean hands; but when this is said, it does not mean a general depravity; it must have an immediate and necessary relation to the equity sued for; it must be a depravity in a legal as well as in the moral sense.

One classic illustration of the maxim in operation is the decision of Wigram VC in *Overton v Banister*.[52] An infant beneficiary fraudulently misrepresented herself as being of age, although she was only 19, and thereby induced the trustees to give her possession of assets to which she should only have been entitled when she reached the age of 21. When she reached this age, she instituted a suit against the trustees to compel them to reimburse to the trust fund the assets which they had improperly paid to her. Although at common law, her deceit was ineffectual to discharge the trustees of their duty, her claim was disallowed in equity because she had misrepresented her age. It is clear that where a beneficiary has instigated, participated in or in some circumstances consented to a breach of trust, as the decision in *Overton* shows, the beneficiary will not succeed in any action brought against a trustee in respect of this breach.[53] Even where a beneficiary is not involved prior to the breach being committed,

---

49. See generally, Chafee (1949) 47 Mich L Rev 1065 and Pettit [1990] Conv 416. Pettit suggests (at 424) that unclean hands seems to be a 'last resort defence' to be invoked where none of the so called nominate defences are applicable but where it would be unconscionable for the plaintiff to be granted relief by the court. For a restatement of the fact that this maxim applies to a plaintiff seeking equitable relief, see the judgment of Keane J in *National Irish Bank Ltd v RTE* [1998] 2 IR 465, 481-482.
50. Halliwell [2004] Conv 439, 449.
51. (1787) 1 Cox 318, 319-320. Cited with approval by Issacs J in *Meyers v Casey* (1913) 17 CLR 90, 123. See also *Tinker v Tinker* [1970] P 136, 143 *per* Salmon LJ; *NZ Netherlands Society 'Oranje' Inc v Kuys* [1973] 2 All ER 1222, 1227 *per* Lord Wilberforce.
52. (1844) 3 Hare 503. See also *Cory v Gertcken* (1816) 2 Madd 49.
53. *French v Graham* (1860) 10 Ir Ch R 522; *Re Pauling's Settlement Trusts* [1964] Ch 303, 335 *per* Wilmer LJ.

he may still be unable to bring a successful action against the trustees if he subsequently acquiesces in the breach,[54] provided that he does so with full knowledge of the surrounding facts and circumstances.

It is well-established that a plaintiff will be refused a decree of specific performance if his conduct towards the defendant has been less than honest. This point was made in a general way by Black LJ in *Conlon v Murray*,[55] where he stated that the remedy may be withheld in a situation where the conduct of the parties and the circumstances of the case demand it. It was also stressed by the Supreme Court in *Smelter Corporation v O'Driscoll*,[56] in which the plaintiff claimed an order of specific performance of a contract to sell lands. The plaintiff's agent had told the defendant that if she did not sell the land in question, the property would be compulsorily acquired, although, unknown to the agent, this was not in fact the case. The Supreme Court refused a decree of specific performance. O'Higgins CJ said that the remedy was a discretionary one and concluded that by reason of the plaintiff's misrepresentation, the defendant was under a fundamental misapprehension as to the true facts and that it would be unjust to grant specific performance in the circumstances.

While the type of conduct which will disentitle a plaintiff to equitable relief will usually amount to impropriety of a fairly serious nature, because of the discretionary nature of the court's jurisdiction, a claimant would be well advised to follow the advice given by Barr J in the course of his judgment in *O'Connor v Harrington Ltd*,[57] where he concluded that the 'clean hands' principle applies with equal force to applications for injunctions made under section 27 of the Local Government (Planning and Development) Act 1976. Barr J stated that, '[i]n seeking such relief an applicant should put before the court fairly and with candour all facts known to him which are relevant to the exercise of the court's discretion and he should satisfy it about his *bona fides* and the true purpose of his application.'[58]

It has been established that equitable relief may be refused to a plaintiff where his conduct in relation to the transaction at issue has been less than honest even where this conduct has not directly prejudiced the defendant. This proposition is well illustrated by the decision of Costello J in *Parkes v Parkes*.[59] A husband bought land and the conveyance was taken in his wife's name to obviate the need for Land Commission consent.[60] After the parties divorced, the husband registered an inhibition on the land and the wife instituted proceedings

54. *Walker v Symonds* (1818) 3 Swans 1, 64 *per* Lord Eldon.
55. [1958] NI 17, 25.
56. [1977] IR 305.
57. High Court 1984 No. 69 MCA (Barr J) 28 May 1987.
58. *Ibid.* at 14.
59. [1980] ILRM 137.
60. Under s. 45 of the Land Act 1965 this consent would have been required had the conveyance been taken in the husband's name, but as the wife was an Irish citizen, it was not necessary.

claiming that it had been wrongly registered. The husband counter-claimed that he was entitled to the beneficial ownership in the property. It was claimed on behalf of the wife that the husband should not be able to obtain relief in equity 'by setting up his own illegality or fraud'. Costello J referred to other cases where a husband had bought a house and put it in his wife's name to protect it from creditors[61] and where a father had deposited money in his son's name to avoid death duties,[62] and concluded as follows:

> Just as the courts will not grant relief to a person who has allowed property to be placed in a wife's or son's name for the fraudulent purpose of defeating creditors … or for the illegal purpose of evading liability to tax … so it seems to me that the court should not grant relief to a purchaser who has placed property in his wife's name dishonestly and by means of an illegal act performed for the purpose of evading the law relating to the transfer of land.[63]

Therefore, although the husband's dishonest conduct had in no way prejudiced the wife in this instance, it sufficed to disentitle him to the equitable relief which he sought.

One important aspect of the application of this maxim which must be stressed is that a court will decline to intervene on the basis of the 'unclean hands' principle unless there is a sufficient connection between the inequitable conduct and the subject-matter of the dispute.[64] This point was made by Eyre LCB in *Dering v Earl of Winchelsea*[65] and reiterated in the following terms by Scrutton LJ in *Moody v Cox*:[66] 'Equity will not apply the principle about clean hands unless the depravity, the dirt in question on the hand has an "immediate and necessary relation" to the equity sued for.' As Hollinrake JA stated in the decision of the British Columbia Court of Appeal in *Rowland v Vancouver College Ltd*,[67] 'the "clean hands" doctrine relates only to situations in which the alleged act of impropriety being raised against the plaintiff is linked to the very subject matter of the dispute.' Consideration was also given to this principle by Allsop P in his judgment in the decision of the New South Wales Court of Appeal in *Kation Pty Ltd v Lamru Pty Ltd*,[68] where he commented that '[j]ust as the underlying concepts are evaluative and, to a degree, reflective

61. *Gascoigne v Gascoigne* [1918] 1 KB 223.
62. *McEvoy v Belfast Banking Co.* [1934] NI 67.
63. [1980] ILRM 137, 144.
64. See *Keating v Keating* [2009] IEHC 405 at 24.
65. (1787) 1 Cox 318, 319-320.
66. [1917] 2 Ch 71, 87-88. The plaintiff's claim for rescission of a contract succeeded despite the fact that he had given a bribe to the vendor's solicitor, although admittedly in an unconnected matter.
67. (2001) 205 DLR 193, 213. See also *Polai v Toronto (City)* (1970) 8 DLR (3d) 689 *per* Schroeder JA.
68. (2009) 257 ALR 336, 340.

of contemporary social morality, the degree of proximity of the iniquity to the equity is equally necessarily evaluative.'

The effect of this need for a relevant connection between the impropriety and the relief sought is well-illustrated by the decision of Ungoed-Thomas J in *Argyll v Argyll*,[69] where he held that the alleged immorality of the plaintiff's conduct which had led to divorce did not deprive her of her entitlement to an injunction to restrain a breach of confidence by her husband. Ungoed-Thomas J stated that 'the plaintiff's adultery, repugnant though it be, should not in my view license the husband to broadcast unchecked the most intimate confidences of earlier and happier days' and he continued 'a person coming to equity must come with clean hands but the cleanliness required is to be judged in relation to the relief that is sought.'

Another way of approaching this issue is to consider whether the impugned conduct is material to the matter which the court is being asked to adjudicate on. So, in *Ancorde Ltd v Horgan*[70] Laffoy J considered the applicability of the maxim 'he who comes to equity must come with clean hands' in the context of a challenge to interlocutory injunctive relief which had been granted to the plaintiffs. She referred to the *dicta* quoted above from *Moody v Cox* and the importance of there being a sufficient connection between the inequitable conduct and the subject matter of the dispute. She concluded that the information which the defendants relied upon as not having been disclosed to the court at the time the application for the relief was made could not be regarded as material from an objective perspective in determining whether there was a fair issue to be tried. However, Laffoy J added that if she had concluded that there had been a material non-disclosure such as to breach the 'clean hands' principle, it would have been appropriate for her to consider discharging the interlocutory injunctive relief which had been given.

The so-called 'clean hands' principle has been applied in a wide variety of situations where equitable remedies have been sought, e.g. where the plaintiff has acted unfairly and unreasonably,[71] or where he has attempted to mislead the court.[72] However, it will not represent unconscionable behaviour or lead to the application of the clean hands principle where a plaintiff institutes proceedings effectively seeking to simply enforce a legal right by means of an equitable remedy.[73]

It was suggested by Lavan J in *Fanning v University College Cork*[74] that

69. [1967] Ch 302. However, note that in *O'Doherty v West Limerick Resources Ltd* Supreme Court, 14 May 1999 the connection between the appellant's previous convictions for fraud and the relief which he sought was not clear-cut.
70. [2013] IEHC 266.
71. *Shell UK Ltd v Lostock Garages Ltd* [1976] 1 WLR 1187, 1199 *per* Lord Denning MR.
72. *Armstrong v Shepherd & Short Ltd* [1959] 2 QB 384, 397.
73. See the comments of Ryan P in *Hughes v Collins* [2017] IECA 93 at [43].
74. [2002] IEHC 85.

the manner in which a plaintiff puts forward his case to the court may suffice to disentitle him to relief on the grounds that he has failed to come to equity with clean hands. The plaintiff sought to restrain the defendant from taking any steps to discipline, suspend or dismiss him from his post as a professor in the university arising out of an alleged incident which had taken place between the plaintiff and another member of staff. At the outset of his judgment, Lavan J said that the plaintiff's evidence was totally lacking in candour and clarity and that it was delivered in a defensive and limited fashion. He stated that it is an essential rule of law that he who seeks equity must come with clean hands and that with great regret he had to conclude that the plaintiff had signally failed to do this. Lavan J said that for the purpose of completeness he would set out the various submissions made on behalf of the plaintiff and rejected by the defendant, although he added that these seemed to be moot having regard to the findings he had made in relation to the plaintiff and the evidence which he had given. He concluded that the plaintiff had not come to equity with clean hands and that in the circumstances he had disentitled himself to the equitable relief sought. However, the Supreme Court allowed the plaintiff's appeal, quashing the judgment and order of Lavan J and remitting the matter to the High Court to be heard by another judge.[75] Keane CJ concluded that the judgment was entirely unsatisfactory as a judgment of a trial judge disposing of issues between the parties. In his view it was clear that no case had been made that the plaintiff had not come to court with clean hands and this was not the basis on which the case was defended in the High Court.

The Supreme Court gave some consideration to the type of conduct which is necessary to bring the 'clean hands' maxim into operation in *Curust Financial Services Ltd v Loewe-Lack-Werk Otto Loewe GmbH & Co. KG.*[76] There, it had to decide whether the alleged breach by the plaintiff of an exclusive licensing agreement, consisting of its sub-contracting the manufacture of a product without the prior written consent of the first named defendant, should disentitle the plaintiff to relief. As a general principle, Finlay CJ accepted that the court has a discretion, where it is satisfied that a person has come to court otherwise than with 'clean hands,' to refuse equitable relief in the form of an injunction on that ground alone. However, he stated that '[i]t seems to me that this phrase must of necessity involve an element of turpitude and cannot necessarily be equated with a mere breach of contract.'[77] Finlay CJ made reference to the fact that what might be established as a breach by the plaintiff of the agreement not to sub-contract, namely the entering into an arrangement with a third party for this purpose, might also be established as having been provoked by a wrongful repudiation on the part of the first named defendant of its own contractual obligations under the licensing agreement. He therefore concluded that it

75. Supreme Court 2002 No. 284, 30 January 2003.
76. [1994] 1 IR 450.
77. *Ibid.* at 467. Quoted with approval in *Kavanagh v Caulfield* [2002] IEHC 67 at 9; *McGrath v Stewart* [2008] IEHC 348 at 6.

would be unreasonable that such conduct should disentitle the plaintiff to an injunction to which it would otherwise be entitled and he held that this should not constitute a ground for rejecting the claim for relief.[78]

The principle that 'an element of turpitude' would be required in order for the clean hands maxim to apply is also supported by the approach adopted by Barrett J in *Bennett v Minister for Justice and Equality*,[79] in which injunctive relief was sought. Barrett J quoted from the judgment of Finlay CJ in *Curust* and referred to the definition of turpitude, commenting that '"clean hands" need not be spotless hands'.[80] While he pointed out that in seeking to make their case the applicants might have employed somewhat emotive language, Barrett J commented that 'bold assertions and intemperate language do not invariably yield a breach of equitable principle'.[81] In the circumstances, he concluded that more would be required before the principle that 'he who comes to equity must come with clean hands' could be invoked successfully.

This more flexible approach to the application of the maxim was also adopted by the majority of the Court of Appeal and the House of Lords in *Tinsley v Milligan*.[82] This case concerned a dispute in relation to the beneficial ownership of property registered in the sole name of the plaintiff but bought by the parties, who had been in a relationship for a number of years, as part of a business venture on the tacit understanding that both should be joint beneficial owners of the house. The purpose of this arrangement was to assist in the perpetration of fraud on the Department of Social Security, although the defendant subsequently decided to disclose these irregularities to the department. The plaintiff sought possession of the property and the defendant counter-claimed seeking a declaration that the house was held by the plaintiff on trust for both parties in equal shares. The majority of the Court of Appeal held that since both the plaintiff and the defendant had been party to the fraud and since the illegality was not of a continuing nature, it would not be an affront to the public conscience to grant the relief sought by the defendant and that her counterclaim did not arise *ex turpi causa* so as to deny her relief.[83] Lloyd LJ

78. See also *McGrath v Stewart* [2008] IEHC 348 where, although it was suggested that the plaintiff had acted otherwise than in good faith, Murphy J concluded that he did not accept that the plaintiff's conduct 'involved any element of turpitude'. Note that the defendant's appeal was allowed ([2016] 2 IR 704), see further *infra* pp. 41-42.
79. [2017] IEHC 261.
80. *Ibid.* at [7].
81. *Ibid.*
82. [1992] Ch 310 (CA); [1994] 1 AC 340 (HL). See further Lunney (1992) 6 Trust Law Int 110; Martin [1992] Conv 153, 161-166; Halliwell [1994] Conv 62; Buckley (1994) 110 LQR 3. For further analysis of the decision in *Tinsley*, see Thornton [1993] CLJ 394; Stowe (1994) 57 MLR 441; Enonchong (1995) 111 LQR 135; Rose (1996) 112 LQR 386.
83. Lunney comments in (1992) 6 Trust Law Int 110 that the basis of both the maxims *ex turpi causa* and 'he who comes to equity must come with clean hands' is public policy and that it is desirable that public policy achieves the same result whether the interest sought to be protected is legal or equitable.

in considering the possible relevance of the maxim 'he who comes to equity must come with clean hands' seemed to countenance a flexible application of the principle and said that he saw no reason why the court should not in the exercise of its equitable jurisdiction, follow and adopt the more adaptable attitude shown by the common law in cases where issues of public policy have arisen. He continued:

> If the common law can discriminate, so can equity. So far as the joint fraud on the DSS is concerned, the parties were admittedly *in pari delicto*. But when one looks at the overall equities, the balance comes down strongly in favour of the defendant. I do not think that the clean hands maxim should prevent us from giving effect to that balance. We are not obliged to draw up our skirts and refuse all relief.[84]

The majority of the House of Lords agreed with this more flexible approach to the issues of 'clean hands'[85] and illegality. In the opinion of Lord Browne-Wilkinson, illegality may render a proprietary interest unenforceable in certain circumstances but only where the claimant had to rely on the illegality to prove the equitable right and this was not the case in this instance. Lord Goff in his dissenting judgment took a stricter approach towards the equitable maxim and said that '[i]t is founded on the principle that he who has committed iniquity shall not have equity'. In his view, it was not desirable to distinguish between varying degrees of iniquity and he felt that to adopt a more flexible approach would 'open the door to far more unmeritorious cases'.[86]

It should be noted that the UK Supreme Court has now made it clear in *Patel v Mirza*[87] that the reasoning underpinning the approach adopted by the House of Lords in *Tinsley* towards the reliance principle and the doctrine of illegality should not be followed.[88] The view was taken that the rule that a party to an illegal agreement cannot enforce a claim against the other party to the agreement if he has to rely on his own illegal conduct in order to establish the claim does not satisfy the requirements of the coherence and integrity of

84. [1992] Ch 310, 341.
85. Council suggests that the decision of the House of Lords in *Tinsley* leads one to ask whether the maxim 'He who comes to equity must come with clean hands' has now been modified to read 'He who comes to equity should keep unclean hands in his pockets', see (1993) 143 NLJ 1577.
86. [1994] 1 AC 340, 362. Buckley (1994) 110 LQR 3, 5-6 has asserted that many of the cases relied on by Lord Goff in support of the view that the 'clean hands' principle applied in this case were distinguishable as they involved unsuccessful attempts by participants in unlawful schemes to refer to these schemes so as to rebut the presumption of advancement to which their contribution has given rise.
87. [2017] AC 467. See further Lim (2017) 80 MLR 927.This decision is analysed in detail in Chapter 7.
88. *Ibid.* at 502 *per* Lord Toulson JSC. See also *per* Lord Neuberger PSC at 515, Lord Clarke JSC at 530.

the legal system. Lord Toulson JSC, with whom the majority of members of the Supreme Court agreed,[89] suggested that instead, in assessing whether the public interest would be harmed by enforcement of the illegal agreement, 'it is necessary (a) to consider the underlying purpose of the prohibition which has been transgressed and whether that purpose will be enhanced by denial of the claim, (b) to consider any other relevant public policy on which the denial of the claim may have an impact and (c) to consider whether denial of the claim would be a proportionate response to the illegality, bearing in mind that punishment is a matter for the criminal courts.'[90] Lord Sumption JSC and some of the other members of the court[91] did not favour this 'range of factors' approach and advocated more rule based principles. Lord Sumption JSC reiterated that the courts will not give effect, at the suit of a person who has committed an illegal act, to a right derived from that act and he also suggested that the policy basis for the illegality defence is to avoid inconsistency in the law. However, he pointed out that there are exceptions to this where the law regards the parties as not being *in pari delicto*, namely where the claimant's participation in the illegal act is involuntary or where the application of the illegality principle would be inconsistent with the rule of law which makes the act illegal.

In this jurisdiction, while Murphy J referred to the speech of Lord Goff in *Tinsley v Milligan* in *Kavanagh v Caulfield*,[92] the tenor of his judgment does not suggest an unduly strict approach to the concept of illegality. Murphy J stated that the underlying principle is the so-called public conscience test and that the court must weigh up or balance the adverse consequences of granting relief against those which will ensue if relief is refused. In his view the ultimate decision requires the making of a value judgment.[93] On the facts, Murphy J concluded that there had been no illegality such as to render the contract in relation to which specific performance was sought unenforceable and held that he could find no evidence of turpitude on the part of the plaintiff. The issue of illegality has also been considered by the Supreme Court in *Quinn v Irish Bank Resolution Corporation Ltd*,[94] although the principles set out by Clarke J are primarily relevant to a situation where contracts may be considered to be void in the context of a particular statutory regime. However, some parallels may be drawn with the principles identified by Lord Toulson in *Patel v Mirza*, which may have more general application such as '[w]hether the imposition of voidness or unenforceability may be disproportionate to the seriousness of

89. Lady Hale, Lord Kerr, Lord Wilson and Lord Hodge JJSC agreed.
90. *Ibid.* at 504-505.
91. Lord Mance and Lord Clarke JJSC.
92. [2002] IEHC 67.
93. *Per* Nicholas LJ in the decision of the Court of Appeal in *Tinsley v Milligan* [1992] Ch 310, 319.
94. [2016] 1 IR 1. Considered further in Chapter 7.

the unlawful conduct in question in the context of the relevant statutory regime in general.'[95]

It is fair to say that while the earlier authorities suggested a rather rigid approach to the application of the 'clean hands' principle, there is now increasing evidence in England, in this jurisdiction and elsewhere in the common law world[96] of a more flexible attitude being adopted.[97] However, one point which should be made about *Curust* and *Tinsley* is that both parties in these cases had been involved in some form of impropriety. In more recent decisions in England and in this jurisdiction where only one party had been guilty of impropriety, the courts have not taken such a benevolent attitude towards the wrongdoing. In *Gonthier v Orange Contract Scaffolding Ltd*,[98] which involved a claim for possession in which the defendants counter-claimed for the grant of a lease or repayment of its expenditure on the property, the decision to order payment on the counterclaim was reversed by the Court of Appeal. Lindsay J, delivering the judgment of the court, stated that the sole director of the defendant company had asserted a claim for an equity in its favour which depended on expenditure by the company but had very substantially exaggerated that expenditure in ways which were not only inaccurate but misleading and in some respects had the appearance of an intended fraud on the Revenue. The court held that there was abundant evidence to support the claimants' argument that the defendant company's hands were far from clean. Lindsay J stated that its director's hands were 'hopelessly muddied' and in the circumstances concluded that the latter's conduct on the company's behalf was sufficient to lead the court to deny its claim for equitable relief.[99]

A similar result ensued in *Shiel v McKeon*,[100] although the impropriety on the plaintiff's part did not appear to have been so serious. In this case, Clarke J was satisfied that there was at least an informal arrangement entered into between the parties which led the plaintiff to the reasonable belief that the defendant would purchase a property in trust partly on his behalf. This might in the normal course of events have given rise to a so-called *Pallant v Morgan* equity, but as Clarke J commented this was not the end of the matter given that

---

95. *Ibid.* at 66.
96. See *Equiticorp Industries Group v The Crown* [1998] 2 NZLR 480, 527-529; *Unilever plc v Cussons* [1997] 1 NZLR 433, 442.
97. However, Halliwell suggested [1994] Conv 62, 67 that neither the dissenting speech of Lord Goff, nor the majority satisfactorily determined the scope of the underlying principle of unclean hands. She asserts that 'justice … was achieved in the case but the achievement was purely pragmatic and not purposeful'.
98. [2003] EWCA Civ 873.
99. However, as Adams pointed out [2003] Conv 360, 362 this outcome meant that the claimants, who had resiled from their offer of an option, retrieved land on which the defendant had carried out improvement work to a proven cost of £19,500. Halliwell [2004] Conv 439, 451 argued that '[i]t is very difficult to see how this outcome does not offend the concept of unconscionability.'
100. [2007] 2 ILRM 144.

the plaintiff was seeking relief of an equitable nature. He found that it was clear that the plaintiff was aware that he had missed the deadline imposed by the estate agent dealing with the matter for making a higher offer when he met the defendant and that the defendant did not know that the plaintiff had failed to meet this deadline. Clarke J referred to the principle that 'he who seeks equity must do equity'[101] and said that he must have regard to whether it would be inequitable to allow the plaintiff to benefit from an arrangement entered into by him in circumstances where he was aware that the defendant was under a misapprehension as to the plaintiff's negotiating position. He concluded that the plaintiff could not invoke equitable principles when he had procured the arrangement upon which he relied in circumstances where he was aware that the defendant did not know that his position was far weaker than might otherwise be believed.

The future of the so-called 'clean hands' principle is therefore not free from doubt. Halliwell suggested that 'the application of the unclean hands principle and the concept of illegality are producing some very questionable outcomes with respect to equitable property rights and to discretionary remedies.'[102] In some respects the greatest difficulty with the maxim is the lack of consistency in the manner of its application and it is still not easy to predict with any degree of accuracy how it will be applied on the facts of any given case.

DELAY DEFEATS EQUITY

This maxim is enshrined in the phrase *vigilantibus, non dormientibus jura subveniunt*; the law assists the vigilant, not those who sleep. Delay is well established as a discretionary factor which may influence a court's decision to grant or withhold equitable relief.[103] A well known summary of its effect is provided by Lord Camden LC in *Smith v Clay*[104] where he stated that '[a] court of equity … has always refused its aid to stale demands, where a party has slept upon his right and acquiesced for a great length of time. Nothing can call forth this court into activity but conscience, good faith and reasonable diligence.'

Two concepts are of relevance in examining the application of this maxim in practice, namely, laches and acquiescence. The effect of the doctrine of laches is that where there has been unreasonable delay in the bringing of proceedings

---

101. As noted above, this maxim tends to be used to refer to a party's willingness to behave in an equitable manner in the future. However, in this case it appears to have been used to describe the plaintiff's past conduct.
102. Halliwell [2004] Conv 439, 451.
103. See e.g. *Lennon v Ganly* [1981] ILRM 84; *Howard v Commissioners of Public Works in Ireland* High Court 1992 No. 331JR (O'Hanlon J) 3 December 1992. See also *ACC Loan Management Ltd v Fryday* [2019] IEHC 103 at [105] where delay coupled with lack of good faith provided grounds for defeating a claim based on equitable principles.
104. (1767) 3 Bro CC 639, 640n. See also the *dicta* of Lord Blackburn in *Erlanger v New Sombrero Phosphate Co.* (1878) 3 App Cas 1218, 1279.

which would render it unjust to grant relief, a plaintiff may find his claim barred in equity. Acquiescence on the other hand means that where one party infringes another's rights and that other party does nothing, equity infers that the latter has acquiesced in the former's actions and he may not be permitted to pursue his claim. However, before examining these doctrines in more detail, it is first necessary to explain the effect of statutory limitation periods.

As a general principle equitable doctrines will have no application to cases to which the Statute of Limitations 1957 applies,[105] although as is pointed out below, the constitutional right to fair procedures may lead to a claim being dismissed even where it is brought within the requisite period of limitation.[106] In addition, it should be noted that the statute lays down express limitation periods in relation to a number of equitable rights. A six year limitation period is laid down with respect to actions by beneficiaries to recover trust property or in respect of any breach of trust or to recover the estates of deceased persons.[107] A twelve year limitation period is laid down for actions for the recovery of land[108] and actions by a mortgagor to redeem a mortgage.[109] It was held by the Supreme Court in *Gleeson v Feehan*[110] that a limitation period of twelve years as provided for under section 13 of the statute applies to an action by a personal representative of a deceased owner of land seeking recovery of such land in succession to the owner. This was the appropriate limitation period in this context rather than a period of six years as laid down by section 45 as amended, which would apply to an action against a personal representative by a person claiming to be entitled to a share in a deceased's estate. As McMahon J had pointed out in *Drohan v Drohan*,[111] section 45 applied to claims against, and not claims by, personal representatives and it had no application to a claim by a personal representative to recover a deceased's assets against a person holding adversely to the estate.

Section 43 provides that, subject to section 44, an action in respect of a breach of trust, not being an action in respect of which a period of limitation is fixed by any other provision of the legislation, shall not be brought against a trustee[112] after the expiration of six years from the date on which the right of action accrued. However, section 44 excludes from the application of limitation

---

105. Section 5 of the statute provides that 'Nothing in this Act shall afford any equitable jurisdiction to refuse relief on the ground of acquiescence or otherwise' and it would seem in England that where a limitation period is prescribed by statute and a claim is brought within this period a person cannot rely on the doctrine of laches to defeat the claim, see *Re Pauling's Settlement Trusts* [1964] Ch 303.
106. E.g. *Ó Domhnaill v Merrick* [1984] IR 151.
107. Sections 43 and 45 of the Statute of Limitations 1957. Note that a new s. 45 was inserted by s. 126 of the Succession Act 1965.
108. Section 13 of the Statute of Limitations 1957.
109. Section 34 of the Statute of Limitations 1957.
110. [1993] 2 IR 113.
111. [1981] ILRM 473.
112. See s.2(2) of the Statute of Limitations 1957.

periods a claim founded on any fraud or fraudulent breach of trust to which the trustee was party or where the claim is to recover trust property or the proceeds of trust property retained by the trustee or received by him and converted to his own use.[113]

The only exception to the principle that non-statutory considerations will have no application to cases to which the Statute of Limitations 1957 applies, is the reasoning employed by Henchy J in *Ó Domhnaill v Merrick*[114] based on the constitutional right to fair procedures to the effect that in certain circumstances 'inordinate and inexcusable delay' will bar a claim brought within the relevant limitation period where this will place an unfair burden on the person sued. The principle in *Ó Domhnaill* was applied by the Supreme Court in *Toal v Duignan (No.2)*,[115] where Finlay CJ said that the courts have an inherent jurisdiction to dismiss a claim in the interests of justice where the length of time which has elapsed between the events out of which it arises and the time when it comes for hearing is in all the circumstances so great that it would be unjust to call upon a particular defendant to defend himself.[116] These principles are likely to only be applied in a relatively small number of cases in which the limitation period may be particularly long, and the recollection of witnesses of considerable importance, such as those relating to personal injuries allegedly suffered by minors[117] and claims relating to historic physical and sexual abuse.[118]

While some of the most common situations to which express statutory limitation periods apply have been considered, it is important to stress that the principles of laches and acquiescence may also not operate in cases in which limitation periods are applied by analogy.[119] While section 9(a) of the Statute of Limitations 1957 provides that the limitation periods laid down in section 11 for claims in contract and tort shall not apply to any claims for equitable relief, section 9(b) goes on to provide that the provision shall not be construed as preventing a court 'from applying by analogy' any provision of the section.

113. It was suggested by Chatterton VC in *Collings v Wade* [1896] 1 IR 340, 343-344 in considering the earlier provision contained in s. 8 of the Trustee Act 1888 that the scope of the exception 'must be restricted to breaches of trust induced by some corrupt motive of personal gain or advantage to the trustee,' or as Fitzgibbon LJ commented (at 349) 'fraud … must amount to dishonesty.' See also *Murphy v Allied Irish Banks Ltd* [1994] 2 ILRM 220, 228 and *Jobling-Purser v Jackson* High Court (Kinlen J) 27 November 2002 at 39.
114. [1984] IR 151.
115. [1991] ILRM 140.
116. Finlay CJ stated that while the existence of culpable negligence on the part of a plaintiff whose claim has been delayed is of considerable relevance, it is not an essential ingredient for the exercise of the court's inherent jurisdiction to dismiss a claim (at 143). McCarthy J dissented in part by saying that without culpable delay on the part of a plaintiff, the court's inherent jurisdiction to dismiss a claim may not be exercised (at 159).
117. E.g. *McBrearty v North Western Health Board* [2010] IESC 27.
118. E.g. *McDonagh v O'Shea* [2018] IECA 298.
119. This question was left open by the court in *Hampton v Minns* [2002] 1 WLR 1, 33.

One question which remains to be satisfactorily resolved is what the position will be where the cause of action in contract or tort is not statute barred and the claim is for equitable relief. No issue arises where a common law remedy is sought in such a cause of action and it is clear from *Meagher v Dublin City Council*,[120] that the doctrine of laches has no application to a claim at common law for damages for breach of contract which is not otherwise barred by the Statute of Limitations. However, different opinions have been expressed in relation to the position where an equitable remedy is sought in such cases. In *Cahill v Irish Motor Traders Association*[121] Budd J stated that '[m]ere delay will not of itself disentitle a plaintiff to an injunction in aid of his legal rights unless the claim to enforce the right is barred by a statute of limitations.' The effect of this approach would seem to be that where a cause of action is not statute barred and equitable relief is sought in relation to a common law right, the doctrine of laches cannot be applied. This approach seems to have been also followed in Australia and in *Orr v Ford*[122] Deane J said that 'laches … is not available in answer to a legal claim'.

However, in England it was held by the Court of Appeal in *Habib Bank Ltd v Habib Bank AG Zurich*[123] that laches is always relevant where equitable relief is sought and that no distinction should be made between cases where such relief is sought to give effect to legal, as opposed to equitable, rights. This is borne out by the approach taken by Nourse LJ in *Gafford v Graham*,[124] where he stated that he doubted whether a distinction ought to be made between a legal and an equitable right when considering a defence of acquiescence. Given that it is an equitable remedy which is being sought in these cases, there is arguably merit in this approach.[125]

Laches and Acquiescence

The doctrine of laches, which may operate to bar a claim in equity where no statutory period of limitation applies, either expressly or by analogy, has been described as 'an equitable doctrine open to a defendant who can establish that the plaintiff's delay in the manner of their approach to their claim is unfair and unconscionable to the point that they should be denied the relief to which they would otherwise be lawfully entitled'.[126] It was explained in the following terms by Lord Selborne LC in *Lindsay Petroleum v Hurd*:[127]

---

120. [2013] IEHC 474.
121. [1966] IR 430, 449.
122. (1989) 167 CLR 316, 340.
123. [1981] 1 WLR 1265.
124. (1998) 77 P & CR 73, 80.
125. However, note that Keane, *Equity and the Law of Trusts in Ireland* (3rd ed., 2017) p. 47 favours the approach taken by Budd J in *Cahill v Irish Motor Traders Association* [1966] IR 430.
126. *ACC Loan Management Ltd v Stephens* [2017] IECA 229 at [36] *per* Irvine J.
127. (1874) LR 5 PC 221, 239-240.

> [T]he doctrine of laches in Courts of Equity is not an arbitrary or a technical doctrine. Where it would be practically unjust to give a remedy, either because the party has, by his conduct, done that which might fairly be regarded as equivalent to a waiver of it, or where by his conduct or neglect he has, though perhaps not waiving that remedy, yet put the other party in a situation in which it would not be reasonable to place him if the remedy were afterwards to be asserted, in either of these cases, lapse of time and delay are most material.

In deciding whether the defence of laches has been established, a court must first consider whether the plaintiff has delayed unreasonably in bringing his claim and secondly, assess whether prejudice or detriment has been suffered by the defendant as a result.[128] Delay of itself will almost invariably be insufficient and clearly the period of time necessary to invalidate a claim will vary according to the circumstances of each case. Often delay may be interpreted as evidence of an agreement by the plaintiff not to pursue his claim and where a plaintiff has acted in a manner which has induced the defendant to alter his position, it would be inequitable to allow the claim to proceed.

An illustration of the operation of the doctrine of laches is provided by the decision of the English Court of Appeal in *Allcard v Skinner*.[129] The plaintiff, who joined a sisterhood of nuns, made her will in favour of the superior of the order and also transferred large amounts of money and stock to her. When she left the order, she revoked her will but made no attempt to reclaim her property until five or six years later when she instituted proceedings claiming that it had been transferred as a result of undue influence. The majority of the Court of Appeal held that the claim was barred by laches and acquiescence. As Lindley LJ stated, it was a case which by no means rested on mere lapse of time and the plaintiff's conduct amounted in effect to confirmation of the gift. The issue of laches was considered in a related context in *McCormack v Our Lady Queen of Peace Achill House of Prayer Ltd*,[130] although the decision was also based on general principles relating to striking out claims on grounds of delay. The defendant sought to have proceedings struck out which were based on a claim of undue influence involving a transfer to a religious institution brought eleven years after the impugned transfer had taken place. While Faherty J acknowledged that claims based on undue influence do require promptitude, she concluded that she was not persuaded that the circumstances would render it inequitable for the trial to proceed.

A good example of how the doctrine of laches operates in practice is provided by the decision of Keane J in *J.H. v W.J.H.*[131] The plaintiff signed a

128. This principle was referred to in *ACC Loan Management Ltd v Stephens* [2015] IEHC 717 at [23]; [2017] IECA 229 at [43].
129. (1887) 36 Ch D 145.
130. [2018] IEHC 26.
131. High Court (Keane J) 20 December 1979.

document in which she agreed to compromise her rights to her late husband's farm under the Succession Act 1965 in favour of her son. While Keane J accepted that the transaction was an improvident one which the courts would in the normal course of events have set aside, he refused to grant her relief in the circumstances. The plaintiff had delayed for a period of four years in seeking to assert her claim and the defendant claimed to have invested time and money in running the farm on the basis that she had abandoned her rights. Keane J stated as follows:

> I have no doubt that the interval of time which elapsed before the proceedings were issued in the present case could properly be described as substantial. That, however, is not sufficient … there must also be circumstances which render it inequitable to enforce the claim after such a lapse of time.[132]

Keane J concluded that the lapse of time, coupled with circumstances which made it inequitable to enforce the claim, was sufficient to bar the plaintiff's action. A similar conclusion was reached by Murphy J in *McGrath v Stewart*,[133] in which the plaintiff sought specific performance of a contract for the sale of land entered into in 1998 in proceedings instituted just over six years later. He stated that '[w]here the defendant has indicated an intention not to perform the contract, either by express repudiation or otherwise, the plaintiff is expected to pursue his claim with greater expedition. The same is true where, during the period of delay, the plaintiff knew of the manner in which the defendant would be prejudiced by his failure to act expeditiously.'[134] Murphy J found that both of these circumstances had arisen in the case before the court and said that the plaintiff, who was an experienced property dealer in the area, must have been well aware of the steadily increasing value of the properties and the consequent prejudice to the defendant. He expressed the view that any explanation put forward for delay must be a plausible one if it is to defeat an otherwise well-founded defence and he did not accept that the plaintiff had been so intimidated by the defendant's behaviour that he had failed to take action over a period of years. In the circumstances and given the large rise in the value of the properties since the contract had been concluded, he was satisfied that the defence of laches had been made out and that to make an order of specific performance against the defendant would be inequitable. However, on appeal the Supreme Court considered whether the trial judge had been entitled to make an award of damages in lieu of specific performance in

132. *Ibid.* at 35. Quoted with approval in *McGrath v Stewart* [2008] IEHC 348 at 7; *Byrne v Dublin City Council* [2009] IEHC 122 at 6. See also *ACC Loan Management Ltd v Stephens* [2015] IEHC 717 at [29].
133. [2008] IEHC 348.
134. *Ibid.* at 8. Referring to Spry, *The Principles of Equitable Remedies* (5th ed., 1997) pp. 232-233. Now see 9th edition, 2014.

circumstances where he had found that the plaintiffs were not entitled to such an order because the defendant had established laches on their part.[135] Laffoy J concluded that where the court had determined that laches on the part of the plaintiff purchaser, as in the matter before the court, should operate as a bar to an order for specific performance, it was difficult to see how the court could award damages *in lieu* of specific performance. In these circumstances the Supreme Court allowed the defendant's appeal and vacated the order awarding damages in lieu of specific performance.

The principles set out by Keane J in *J.H v W.J.H.* were also relied upon by Hogan J in *O'Hare v Dundalk Racing (1999) Ltd*[136] in refusing to grant injunctive relief in circumstances where almost seven years had elapsed after the events of which the plaintiff complained had taken place. Hogan J concluded that it would be 'manifestly inappropriate' for the court to make an order restoring the plaintiff's original bookmaker's pitch at a racecourse after such a delay in circumstances where this would cause prejudice to a third party who has been awarded the pitch at the time. However, he found that the plaintiff was entitled to damages for breach of contract.

It is clear that a court will be unlikely to accept that a claim should be barred by laches where the delay has effectively been caused by the defendant's conduct. So, in *Darlington Properties Ltd v Meath County Council*,[137] Kelly J concluded that, in circumstances where the defendant had been 'guilty of a catalogue of errors which misled [the plaintiff], failed to inform it of the errors and assumed an ostrich like stance in respect of them', a plea of laches was unjustified.

Acquiescence arises where a plaintiff either expressly or impliedly represents that he does not intend to enforce a claim and as a result of this representation, it becomes unjust in all the circumstances to grant the relief which he subsequently seeks. The principle was summarised as follows by Lord Wensleydale in *Archbold v Scully*:[138]

> If a party, who could object, lies by and knowingly permits another to incur an expense in doing an act under the belief that it would not be objected to, and so a kind of permission may be said to be given to another to alter his condition, he may be said to acquiesce.

It is well-established that acquiescence may bar a claim for equitable relief[139] and it usually arises in circumstances where a party fails to seek a remedy when

135. [2016] 2 IR 704.
136. [2015] IEHC 198.
137. [2011] IEHC 70.
138. (1861) 9 HLC 360, 383.
139. See e.g. *Irwin v O'Connell* [1936] IR 44; *Sayers v Collyer* (1884) 28 Ch D 103; *Shaw v Applegate* [1977] 1 WLR 970.

a violation of his rights is brought to his attention.[140] It has been suggested by McMahon J in *Victory v Galhoy Inns Ltd*[141] that the level of inactivity required to deprive a person of his rights in such circumstances is high and 'must be so reprehensible that it approaches dishonesty'.[142]

Consideration was given by Laddie J in his judgment in *Nelson v Rye*[143] to the circumstances in which the equitable defences of laches and acquiescence operate, although he stressed that it can be misleading to approach them as if they consisted of 'a series of precisely defined hurdles over each of which a litigant must struggle before the defence is made out'. The plaintiff musician sought an account of the moneys received by the defendant, his manager, during the ten year period from 1980–1990 in which the latter had managed his business affairs. Laddie J accepted that the plaintiff's delay in instituting proceedings was such that it would be unreasonable and unjust to allow the plaintiff to assert his right to an account against the defendant for the period prior to December 1985 and that the defences of laches and acquiescence were made out in relation to that part of the claim. Laddie J made the following comment about the circumstances in which the defences will operate:

> [T]hese defences are not technical or arbitrary. The courts have indicated over the years some of the factors which must be taken into consideration in deciding whether the defence runs. Those factors include the period of the delay, the extent to which the defendant's position has been prejudiced by the delay, and the extent to which that prejudice was caused by the actions of the plaintiff. I accept that mere delay alone will almost never suffice, but the court has to look at all the circumstances, including in particular those factors set out above, and then decide whether the balance of justice or injustice is in favour of granting the remedy or withholding it.[144]

The tendency to treat laches and acquiescence as a single defence was also evident in the decision of the Court of Appeal in *Gafford v Graham*[145] and Milne has commented that there is 'no reason for continuing to treat laches and acquiescence as two separate equitable defences'.[146] In *Gafford*, Nourse LJ said that the question which the court must ask is whether in all the circumstances, it would be unconscionable for the plaintiff to continue to seek to enforce the rights which he undoubtedly had.[147] It seems clear from the judgment of

140. *McCausland v Young* [1949] NI 49, 88-89 *per* Andrews LCJ.
141. [2010] IEHC 459.
142. *Ibid.* at [34].
143. [1996] 1 WLR 1378.
144. *Ibid.* at 1392.
145. (1998) 77 P & CR 73.
146. Milne (1998) 114 LQR 555, 557.
147. See also *Frawley v Neill* [1999] EWCA Civ 875; *Experience Hendrix LLC v PPX*

Chadwick LJ in *Harris v Williams-Wynne*[148] that where detriment is present, it will usually suffice to persuade the court that it would be unconscionable for a claimant to seek to pursue his claim in the circumstances. However, in his view in the absence of detriment, it will be necessary to establish some other factor which will make it unconscionable for the party having the benefit of the rights to change his mind.

Further consideration was given to the role of detriment in this context by Lord Neuberger in the decision of the House of Lords in *Fisher v Brooker*.[149] He stated that in order to defeat the claimant's case on the ground of laches, 'the respondents must demonstrate some "acts" during the course of the delay period which result in "a balance of justice" justifying the refusal of the relief to which [the claimant] would otherwise be entitled.'[150] Although Lord Neuberger said that it was not an immutable requirement, he expressed the view that 'some sort of detrimental reliance is usually an essential ingredient of laches'.[151] This was in contrast to the view expressed by Mummery LJ in the Court of Appeal in *Fisher* to the effect that there is 'no requirement of detrimental reliance for the application of acquiescence or laches'.[152] However, as Chadwick LJ acknowledged in *Harris v Williams-Wynne*,[153] if no detriment has been suffered it will be necessary to establish another basis for arguing that it would not be appropriate to grant relief and generally detriment or some form of prejudice will be required. Finally, it should be noted that Lord Neuberger in the *Fisher* case did not seek to draw a distinction between the defences of laches and acquiescence and commented that he was 'not convinced that acquiescence adds anything to estoppel and laches' and that 'laches, failing to raise or enforce an equitable right for a long period, can be characterised as acquiescence'.[154]

Enterprises Inc [2002] EWHC 1353 (QB) at [40]; *Harris v Williams-Wynne* [2006] 2 P & CR 27 at [36]; *Watson v Croft Promo-Sport Ltd* [2008] 3 All ER 1171, 1185.

148. [2006] 2 P & CR 27 at [39].
149. [2009] 1 WLR 1764.
150. *Ibid.* at 1784. This is broadly in line with the approach adopted in New Zealand which requires a 'balancing of equities' (see *Eastern Services Ltd v No 68 Ltd* [2006] 3 NZLR 335, 340, 347). See also the comments of Glazebrook J in the decision of the Supreme Court of New Zealand in *Proprietors of Wakatu v Attorney-General* [2017] 1 NZLR 423, 618 that laches is a defence which requires that the defendant has an equity which on balance outweighs the plaintiffs' rights. While this takes into account the length of delay and the nature of the acts done during this interval of time, ultimately it is a matter of a 'balancing of equities'.
151. *Ibid.* at 1781.
152. [2008] EWCA Civ 287 at [85].
153. [2006] 2 P & CR 27.
154. [2009] 1 WLR 1764, 1780.

EQUALITY IS EQUITY

In circumstances where more than one person is entitled to property, equity favours a principle of equal division. The most common illustration of the maxim in practice is the attitude adopted by equity towards the joint tenancy as a method of holding property. In this case the right of survivorship operates and on the death of a joint tenant, the estate belongs to the surviving joint tenant(s) to the exclusion of the deceased's successors. This can be distinguished from the position in relation to a tenancy in common where the interest of each party devolves upon his personal representatives on his death. Equity tends to lean in favour of a tenancy in common and in certain circumstances, even where persons are joint tenants at law, they may be regarded by equity as tenants in common of the beneficial interest.[155] In such cases, while the survivor(s) may be entitled to the entire estate, he will hold part of it as trustee for the deceased's personal representatives.

This presumption of a tenancy in common in equity arises in three recognised situations. First, where the purchase money for property is provided in unequal shares, equity presumes a tenancy in common proportionate to the contributions made. On the other hand, where the purchase money is advanced equally, the survivor becomes entitled to the entire estate in equity as well as in law. Secondly, where parties lend money on a mortgage, whether equally or unequally, the mortgagees are presumed to be entitled as tenants in common and the survivor is regarded as a trustee for the representatives of the deceased mortgagee to the extent of the amount of the loan advanced by the deceased.[156] Thirdly, where partners acquire property, they are presumed by equity to hold it as tenants in common on the basis that the principle of survivorship is inconsistent with the nature of the partnership relationship.[157] However, these three situations are not the only ones in which equity will presume a tenancy in common, a point made by the Privy Council in *Malayan Credit Ltd v Jack Chia-MPH Ltd*,[158] where it was held that this result will follow where grantees hold premises for several individual business purposes.

Even where an equitable interest in property is held jointly, for example where the purchase money is advanced equally, equity leans in favour of severance and an act of alienation by one tenant or even an agreement to alienate will be sufficient to sever the joint tenancy and create a tenancy in common.[159]

The maxim that equality is equity can also be seen in operation in a number of other circumstances. It has generally been applied where surplus funds remain on the dissolution of an unincorporated association as in *Re Bucks.*

155. See e.g. *Sheehy v Talbot* [2008] IEHC 207.
156. *Morley v Bird* (1798) 3 Ves 628, 631.
157. *Lake v Craddock* (1732) 3 P Wms 158. Although see *Barton v Morris* [1985] 1 WLR 1257.
158. [1986] AC 549.
159. *Burgess v Rawnsley* [1975] Ch 429.

Constabulary Widows' and Orphans' Fund Friendly Society (No.2),[160] where Walton J held that the surplus funds remaining should be distributed equally amongst the members of the association alive at the date of dissolution. There is still a lack of consensus in this jurisdiction on the issue of whether the distribution of surplus funds should be carried out on the basis of equal division or in accordance with the proportion of contributions made and in *Tierney v Tough*[161] O'Connor MR favoured the latter approach. However, subsequently in *Feeney v MacManus*[162] Johnston J supported the principle of distribution on an equal basis and this is the approach which is more likely to be followed.

In addition, there was for some time a tendency in England to apply the maxim in relation to the division of matrimonial property in the absence of any other clear basis for carrying out this exercise. While the principle of equal division might still be applied in England where there is evidence that it was the common intention of the parties that this should be the case,[163] the current approach is based on ascertaining the parties' shared intentions in relation to beneficial ownership of the property.[164] Waite LJ stressed in *Hammond v Mitchell*[165] that 'this is not an area where the maxim that equality is equity falls to be applied unthinkingly'. Subsequently, Waite LJ, delivering his judgment in the Court of Appeal in *Midland Bank plc v Cooke*,[166] said that the court will take into account all conduct which throws light on the question of what shares were intended and that 'only if that search proves inconclusive does the court fall back on the maxim that "equality is equity"'.[167]

However, this approach never found favour with the judiciary in this jurisdiction and instead division is carried out on the basis of an assessment of the respective contributions of the spouses or partners, and the non-owning partner has been held to be entitled to a beneficial interest to the extent of his or her contributions.[168] It should be noted that an attempt to pass legislation providing for automatic joint ownership of the matrimonial home in this jurisdiction proved unsuccessful,[169] and it is fair to say that the maxim no longer

160. [1979] 1 WLR 936. See also *Re GKN Bolts & Nuts Ltd (Automotive Division) Birmingham Works, Sports and Social Club* [1982] 1 WLR 774. The principle may also be applied to the distribution of mixed funds in a bank account in preference to the rule in *Clayton's* case, where there are inadequate monies to meet all claims, see *Barlow Clowes International Ltd v Vaughan* [1992] 4 All ER 22 and *Re W. & R. Murrogh* [2003] IEHC 95.
161. [1914] 1 IR 142.
162. [1937] IR 23.
163. *Grant v Edwards* [1986] Ch 638.
164. See further Chapter 7.
165. [1991] 1 WLR 1127, 1137.
166. [1995] 4 All ER 562.
167. *Ibid.* at 574.
168. *C. v C.* [1976] IR 254; *W. v W.* [1981] ILRM 202; *McC. v McC.* [1986] ILRM 1.
169. *Re Article 26 of the Constitution and the Matrimonial Home Bill 1993* [1994] 1 IR 305.

plays a role in this area and has been superseded by more precise methods of distribution in both jurisdictions.[170]

The Supreme Court commented in *E.B. v S.S.*[171] that the maxim that 'equality is equity' should not necessarily apply where an application is brought under section 117 of the Succession Act 1965 by a child claiming that a parent has failed in his moral duty to make proper provision for the child in accordance with his means. Although the plaintiff's application was dismissed in this case, Keane J stated that it was not necessarily an answer to an application under section 117 that the testator had simply treated all his or her children equally. As he stated, 'the maxim "equality is equity" can have no application where the testator has, by dividing his estate in that manner, disregarded the special needs … of one of the children to such an extent that he could be said to have failed in his moral duty to that child.'[172] However, Keane J acknowledged that the understandable desire of parents to avoid any friction amongst their children by effecting, so far as possible, an equal distribution of their property must also be recognised. In the circumstances the Supreme Court held that the defendant, who had divided her property equally between all her children, had not failed in her moral duty towards the plaintiff.

One other area in which the principle that equality is equity may be of relevance is where a 'trust power' is implied in default of any appointment being made by the donee of a power of appointment. So where a general intention in favour of a class of persons is expressed and no selection is made, a trust in favour of the members of the class in equal shares may be implied.[173]

EQUITY LOOKS TO THE INTENT RATHER THAN THE FORM

While this maxim does not mean that legal formalities will not be required by equity,[174] it looks to the substance rather than the form of a transaction and does not require 'unnecessary formalities'[175] to be observed. Lord Romilly MR laid down this principle in *Parkin v Thorold*[176] in the following terms:

170. See further Chapter 7.
171. [1998] 2 ILRM 141.
172. *Ibid.* at 150. See also *W.B. v J.B.* [2019] IECA 58 at [87].
173. See e.g. *Re Kieran* [1916] 1 IR 289. Although note the comments of Lord Wilberforce in *McPhail v Doulton* [1971] AC 424, 452 to the effect that 'a discretionary trust can, in a suitable case be executed according to its merits and otherwise than by equal division'.
174. As was made clear in *JSC VTB Bank v Skurikhin* [2019] EWHC 1407 (Comm) at [239], maxims such as this 'cannot, of themselves, circumvent mandatory statutory requirements as to fomalities'.
175. *Sprange v Lee* [1908] 1 Ch 424, 430 *per* Neville J.
176. (1852) 16 Beav 59, 66-67.

> Courts of Equity make a distinction in all cases between that which is matter of substance and that which is matter of form; and if it find that by insisting on the form, the substance will be defeated, it holds it to be inequitable to allow a person to insist on such form, and thereby defeat the substance.

This maxim was applied in a number of situations. First, where land was used as security for a loan, equity regarded the transaction as a mortgage even though it might not be described as such.[177] In addition, equity provided relief against the payment of penalties on this basis. Where the parties to a contract agreed that in the event of its breach, a named sum of money would be paid by the defaulting party, equity would ask whether it was a genuine estimate of the damage which would result from the breach or whether it was a penalty to be held over the head of the other party. In deciding this, equity would look at the parties' intention rather than the form of the instrument. Another example of the operation of this maxim is where there has been a failure to complete a contract for the sale of land within the time stipulated. While at law the party who failed to complete was in breach of contract, in equity he would be permitted to complete the contract within a reasonable time thereafter, provided time was not expressed to be of the essence in relation to completion of the contract.[178]

Another illustration of this maxim is the fact that a valid trust may be created without actually using the word 'trust'.[179] In limited circumstances a trust may be created by the use of 'precatory words' where a gift is made and the donee expresses the wish or hope that the property be dealt with in a particular manner. However, the use of such words will only be held to be sufficient to create a trust if this intention is clear from the language used in the instrument as a whole,[180] and they are more usually interpreted as being insufficient to achieve this result.[181]

This maxim is also the basis for the equitable remedy of rectification which allows an instrument to be rectified or corrected where it fails to record the actual intention of the parties to a contract.[182] Equity looks at the substance of the transaction and allows rectification in circumstances where it would be inequitable to allow a party to retain a benefit obtained, e.g. as a result of mistake.[183]

177. *Grangeside Properties Ltd v Collingswood Securities Ltd* [1964] 1 WLR 140.
178. *Tilley v Thomas* (1867) 3 Ch App 61, 67.
179. *Page v Cox* (1852) 10 Hare 163, 169 *per* Turner VC.
180. *Comiskey v Bowring-Hanbury* [1905] AC 84.
181. *Re Humphrey's Estate* [1916] 1 IR 21; *Re Sweeney* [1976-77] ILRM 88.
182. See *infra* Chapter 16.
183. *Irish Life Assurance Co. Ltd v Dublin Land Securities Ltd* [1989] IR 253.

EQUITY LOOKS ON THAT AS DONE WHICH OUGHT TO HAVE BEEN DONE

Where a specifically enforceable obligation exists, equity regards the parties as being in the position in which they would have been had the obligation been performed, and their legal rights and duties are assessed by reference to this position. So, in equity, a specifically enforceable contract for a lease is treated as being equivalent to a lease and the rights and duties of the parties are regarded as being the same as if the lease had actually been executed.[184] Similarly, a specifically enforceable contract for the sale of land transfers the equitable interest to the purchaser as a result of the provisions of section 52(1) of the Land and Conveyancing Law Reform Act 2009 which provides that, subject to section 52(2), the entire beneficial interest in the land will pass to the purchaser on the making of an enforceable contract for sale or other disposition.[185] This provision effected a change to the previous position, as set out by the majority in *Tempany v Hynes*,[186] to the effect that a specifically enforceable contract for the sale of land only transferred the equitable interest to the purchaser to the extent to which the purchase price is paid.

It has traditionally been assumed that the maxim cannot be relied on in this context by a volunteer and equity will regard the obligation as carried out only in favour of persons who are entitled to specifically enforce the contract. Lindley LJ made this point as follows in *Re Anstis*:[187]

> Equity no doubt, looks on that as done which ought to be done; but this rule, although usually expressed in general terms, is by no means universally true. Where the obligation to do what ought to be done is not an absolute duty, but only an obligation arising from contract, that which ought to be done is only treated as done in favour of some person entitled to enforce the contract as against the person liable to perform it.

A similar approach seems to have been adopted by Scott J in *Davis v Richards and Wallington Ltd*,[188] in which he applied the maxim that 'equity looks on that as done which ought to be done' in considering the validity of a definitive trust deed establishing a pension scheme. Scott J said that the effect of the maxim was explained in the following terms in *Snell's Equity*,[189] namely: 'Equity treats a contract to do a thing as if the thing were already done, though only

184. *Walsh v Lonsdale* (1882) 21 Ch D 9.
185. This was also the view taken by Henchy in his minority judgment in *Tempany v Hynes* [1976] IR 101, 109.
186. [1976] IR 101, 114 *per* Kenny J, O'Higgins CJ concurring.
187. (1886) 31 Ch D 596, 605.
188. [1990] 1 WLR 1511.
189. Baker and Langan, *Snell's Equity* (28th ed., 1982) p. 41. Now see McGhee, *Snell's Equity* (33rd ed., 2015), although the statement is not repeated in this edition.

in favour of persons entitled to enforce the contract specifically and not in favour of volunteers.'

However, this requirement does not appear to have been enforced by Carroll J in *Shanahan v Redmond*.[190] The deceased named his cousin as sole beneficiary of a trust, the assets of which comprised a life insurance policy. The parties fell out and the deceased attempted unsuccessfully to exercise a power of appointment over the trust funds in his own favour. Subsequently, he instructed the insurance company to cancel the policy and to replace it with a similar one under which he would be the sole beneficiary. Although this direction had not been carried out when the testator died, Carroll J applied the maxim that equity looks on that as done which ought to be done and held that the existing policy should be treated as if it were a substitute policy in which the deceased was named as sole beneficiary.

Another controversial application of the maxim is contained in the decision of the Privy Council in *Attorney General for Hong Kong v Reid*,[191] where it held that when a fiduciary receives a bribe he holds it under a constructive trust for his principal. Lord Templeman explained this conclusion on the basis of the fiduciary's obligation to account to his principal for the bribe. As he stated, 'Equity considers as done that which ought to have been done. As soon as the bribe was received, whether in cash or in kind, the false fiduciary held the bribe on a constructive trust for the person injured.'[192]

The maxim that equity looks on that as done which ought to be done also underlies the doctrine of conversion which operates by regarding one form of property as being another where there is an obligation to convert it.[193] The effect of the doctrine is that in certain circumstances the nature of property is notionally changed so that realty may be treated as personalty with the legal incidents of personalty and *vice versa*. The reasoning behind this is that where a person is under a duty to convert one form of property into another, it will not be regarded as still being in its original form because the person concerned has failed to perform his obligations.

EQUITY IMPUTES AN INTENTION TO FULFIL AN OBLIGATION

Where a person is under an obligation to perform an act and does some other act which could be regarded as fulfilment of that original obligation, it will be

190. High Court 1994 No. 129 Sp (Carroll J) 21 June 1994.
191. [1994] 1 AC 324. See further Chapter 8.
192. *Ibid.* at 331. This reasoning has been criticised by a number of commentators. Gardner [1995] CLJ 60, 61 has suggested that 'the maxim's cryptic form has apparently led it to be applied in a fashion which cannot be squared with a proper articulation of the law in question.' See also Oakley [1994] CLJ 31 and Watts (1994) 110 LQR 178.
193. See further Chapter 20.

regarded as such. This maxim forms the basis for the equitable doctrines of satisfaction and performance.[194] The effect of the first doctrine is that if a person is under an obligation to another person and subsequently gives that person a benefit, it is presumed that the benefit is intended to satisfy the obligation or debt. Similarly, where a party is under an obligation to carry out a particular act and subsequently does an act which can be considered as performance of his obligation, equity will presume that this subsequent act was carried out in order to fulfil the earlier obligation.

EQUITY ACTS IN PERSONAM

This maxim has been described in *Equity: Doctrines and Remedies*[195] as 'historically of the greatest importance, theoretically the most elusive and practically of the most dubious significance'. While it has been acknowledged that the 'rights and interests evolved in equity were originally conceived as purely personal'[196] it has also been recognised that the view that equitable interests convey no right *in rem* cannot be reconciled with the right of a beneficiary to follow trust property.[197] While equitable relief may often be of a personal nature, equitable proprietary rights are also increasingly being granted and this maxim must be treated with a degree of caution. In this regard it should be noted that Lord Neuberger PSC has commented in *FHR European Ventures LLP v Cedar Capital Partners LLC*[198] that 'it is fair to say that the concept of equitable proprietary rights is in some respects somewhat paradoxical. Equity, unlike the common law classically acts *in personam* …; yet equity is far more ready to accord proprietary claims than common law.'

It was originally one of the most fundamental principles of equity that equitable jurisdiction was exercised against the person of the defendant rather than against his property. This is illustrated by the fact that failure to comply with an order granting equitable relief constitutes contempt of court. Where such a remedy was insufficient, the Court of Chancery had recourse to the writ of sequestration and since the enactment of the Judicature Act, orders can be enforced by any of the legal writs of execution, e.g. *fieri facias*. As Lord Selborne LC stated in *Ewing v Orr Ewing (No.1)*,[199] '[t]he Courts of Equity in England are, and always have been, courts of conscience, operating *in personam* and not *in rem*; and in the exercise of this personal jurisdiction they have always been accustomed to compel the performance of contracts and

194. See *infra* Chapter 20.
195. Heydon, Leeming and Turner, *Meagher, Gummow and Lehane's Equity: Doctrines and Remedies* (5th ed., 2015) p.97.
196. *Re Cuff Knox* [1963] IR 263, 289 *per* Kingsmill Moore J.
197. *Ibid.*
198. [2015] AC 250, 269.
199. (1883) 9 App Cas 34, 40.

trusts as to subjects which were not either locally or *ratione domicilli* within their jurisdiction.'

The maxim also had relevance to disputes relating to property outside the jurisdiction and it was immaterial that the property in question was not within a court's jurisdiction provided that the defendant himself was within its jurisdiction or could be served outside the jurisdiction. So, in *Penn v Lord Baltimore*[200] an English court ordered specific performance of an agreement relating to land boundaries of property in the United States of America although the defendant was in England. When the defendant objected to the jurisdiction of the court, Lord Hardwicke replied that the conscience of the defendant was bound by the agreement and that the dispute was a matter within the jurisdiction of the court which acted *in personam*.

A similar point was made by the Irish Court of Appeal in *Lett v Lett*,[201] in which an injunction was granted to restrain proceedings taken in an Argentine court which amounted to a repudiation of a settlement of divorce proceedings by virtue of which a wife had undertaken not to pursue any further claim against her husband. As Sir Samuel Walker stated, '[t]he jurisdiction asserted is not against the foreign tribunal, but against the person within the jurisdiction, who has made a contract not to resort to proceedings; and whether such proceedings are in a foreign court or not, is immaterial for the purpose of the equity on which the jurisdiction rests — an equity *in personam*.'[202]

An issue which has provoked considerable controversy is whether an interest in land arising under a trust is to be characterised as a right of an *in rem* or *in personam* nature. The practical significance of this classification becomes apparent in the context of the provisions of Article 24 of the Brussels Regulation Recast,[203] which provides, *inter alia*, that in proceedings which have as their object rights *in rem* in immovable property, the courts of the state in which the property is situated shall have exclusive jurisdiction. The failure to clarify the nature of such rights has led to inconsistencies in the application of the Regulation and the previous provisions with similar effect, as an examination of a number of decisions shows. In *Webb v Webb*[204] the claim of a beneficiary under a trust was classified by the European Court of Justice as a right *in personam* rather than *in rem.* A father had bought a flat in France in his son's name and subsequently sought a declaration that the son held the property as a trustee for him. In accordance with the provisions of Article 16 of the Convention on Jurisdiction and the Enforcement of Judgments in Civil and Commercial

200. (1750) 1 Ves Sen 444.
201. [1906] 1 IR 618.
202. *Ibid.* at 635.
203. Regulation (EU) No. 1215/2012 which replaces Article 22 of Council Regulation EC No. 44/2001. This issue was originally dealt with by Article 16 of the Convention on Jurisdiction and the Enforcement of Judgments in Civil and Commercial Matters 1968.
204. [1994] QB 696.

Matters 1968 if the action had been designated as involving rights *in rem*, the French courts would have had exclusive jurisdiction in the matter. However, the European Court of Justice concluded that an action for a declaration that a person holds immovable property as a trustee did not constitute an action *in rem* within the meaning of Article 16 of the Convention which meant that the father was entitled to sue in the English courts.[205] A similar view was taken by the Court of Appeal in *Prazic v Prazic*,[206] in which a wife's proceedings seeking a declaration of beneficial ownership in relation to land in England were classified as being based on *in personam* rights. On the basis of such a finding the English courts did not have exclusive jurisdiction and the Court of Appeal held that as her husband had already petitioned for divorce in France where they had been living, the proceedings before the English courts should be stayed.

The decisions in *Webb* and *Prazic* are difficult to reconcile with that of Rattee J in *Re Hayward*,[207] in which he characterised the claim of a trustee in bankruptcy of a deceased co-owner to a half share of a villa in Spain as of *in rem* nature. As it was a right *in rem* in immovable property within the meaning of Article 16 of the Convention, it was held that the Spanish courts had exclusive jurisdiction in the matter. Rattee J distinguished the decision in *Webb*, asserting that the trustee was in effect claiming the right to legal ownership of half of the villa and said that it was 'difficult to contemplate any right more clearly a right *in rem*'. However, *Re Hayward* was in turn distinguished in *Ashurst v Pollard*,[208] in which the Court of Appeal held that the issues raised in the proceedings were personal issues between the trustee and a bankrupt and his wife as to the beneficial interests in a property and did not have as their object rights *in rem*. In the view of Jonathan Parker LJ, unlike in *Hayward*, the trustee was not seeking to establish or protect, let alone perfect, his title to the bankrupt's interest in the property.

This issue was revisited by the Court of Appeal in *Magiera v Magiera*,[209] in which the decision in *Webb v Webb* was distinguished. The court relied on the decision of the CJEU in *Komu v Komu*,[210] in which it had held that 'an action for termination of the co-ownership of immovable property ... constitutes proceedings which have as their object rights *in rem* in immovable property

---

205. The decision in *Webb* was criticised by Briggs (1994) 110 LQR 526. However, MacMillan [1996] Conv 125, 129 is more supportive of the conclusion reached, asking 'is it not preferable that the determination of a trust created in England be made by an English court?'
206. [2006] 2 FLR 1128.
207. [1997] Ch 45. Stevens has asserted [1998] Conv 144 that while the result in *Hayward* was consistent with the policy of the Convention, namely that matters relating to the ownership of land should be determined by the court of the country in which that land is situated, the inconsistency with the decision in *Webb* is open to criticism.
208. [2001] Ch 595.
209. [2017] 3 WLR 41.
210. [2016] 4 WLR 26 at [28].

falling within the exclusive jurisdiction of the courts of the member state in which the property is situated.' In *Magiera*, Black LJ held that a wife's application for the sale of a property jointly owned by a couple following their divorce had as its object rights *in rem* in immovable property for the purposes of the Brussels Regulation and that, accordingly, the English courts had exclusive jurisdiction.

Stevens has suggested that it is only when it is acknowledged that beneficial interests 'are true proprietary rights *in rem*, albeit of less durability that their legal equivalent'[211] that it will be possible to adopt a consistent approach to issues of jurisdiction in this context. It is difficult to fault the reasoning adopted by Stevens and it will clearly be necessary for the courts to clarify the position of equitable proprietary rights for the purposes of private international law. Despite the traditional classification of such rights as being of an *in personam* nature, this may need to be reassessed in order to achieve a consistency of approach towards issues of jurisdiction where ownership of land is at stake.

WHERE THE EQUITIES ARE EQUAL, THE FIRST IN TIME PREVAILS

WHERE THE EQUITIES ARE EQUAL, THE LAW PREVAILS

These two related maxims are relevant to the question of priorities as between competing interests in land. However, they cannot be looked at in isolation; it is necessary to examine the distinction between equitable interests as opposed to mere equities and the effect of the doctrine of notice on the operation of the maxims. Finally, it is also necessary to consider the impact which registration has had on the question of priorities between competing interests in land.

It should also be pointed out that the courts' increasing willingness to grant equitable proprietary rights means that these maxims should not be interpreted too literally and traditional assumptions about priorities have had to be reassessed. As Lord Neuberger PSC noted in *FHR European Ventures LLP v Cedar Capital Partners LLC*,[212] 'given that equity is far more ready to recognise proprietary rights than common law, the effect of having an equitable right is often to give priority over common law claims — sometimes even those which may have preceded the equitable right.'

Equitable Interests and Mere Equities

It is difficult to define the concept of a 'mere equity' with any degree of clarity

211. [1998] Conv 144, 152.
212. [2015] AC 250, 269.

or to explain the characteristics which distinguish mere equities from equitable interests properly so called. Equitable interests can be categorised as actual rights in property and include interests arising under a trust, equitable mortgages, equities of redemption, restrictive covenants and contracts to convey or create a legal estate in land. On the other hand, mere equities are better described as rights of a procedural nature which are ancillary to a property right and include e.g. the right to have a transaction set aside for fraud or undue influence or a right to have a document rectified for mistake.[213] Delany has suggested that the term extends 'to all personal claims which *may* be converted into equitable estates and interests'[214] and Everton has said that a mere equity might be defined as 'a right of an exclusively personal nature to pursue an equitable remedy'.[215] She suggests that many of the difficulties which have been encountered in endeavouring to distinguish between equities and equitable interests could be overcome if it were accepted that equitable interests can be variable in character and of different quality. Not all mere equities can bind third parties and a category sometimes referred to as a 'naked equity' was identified by the House of Lords in *National Provincial Bank Ltd v Ainsworth*.[216] In the Court of Appeal, Lord Denning MR had held that a deserted wife had a 'licence coupled with an equity' entitling her to remain in possession of the family home and that this took precedence over the rights of the plaintiff bank which had taken a mortgage on the house. However, the House of Lords reversed this decision. As Lord Upjohn stated, the wife was seeking to assert rights over the land of another in relation to which she had no beneficial ownership. He said that he could not see how it was possible for a mere equity to bind a purchaser unless it was ancillary to or dependent on an equitable estate or interest in land. In the case before him the right of the wife was not ancillary to or dependent on an equitable interest and could not bind purchasers; it was a right of a purely personal nature.[217]

The most practical significance of the distinction between mere equities and equitable estates can be seen where a question of priorities arises. As the maxim makes clear, where the equities are equal, the first in time prevails, but where one equity is superior to another, the time of their creation cannot

---

213. See Everton (1976) 40 Conv 209, 210.
214. Delany (1957) 21 Conv 195, 201.
215. *Ibid.* at 220. Wade [1955] CLJ 158, 160 has suggested that another distinction between equitable interests and mere equities lies in the fact that mere equities are discretionary in character but he concedes that a purchaser's right under a contract for the sale of land, which must surely amount to more than a mere equity, depends on the willingness of a court to award specific performance (at 161).
216. [1965] AC 1175.
217. As Keane points out in *Equity and the Law of Trusts in Ireland* (3rd ed., 2017) p. 57 the point decided in *Ainsworth* is now academic in this jurisdiction as a result of the enactment of the Family Home Protection Act 1976, s. 3 of which renders invalid any disposition of the family home by one spouse without the written consent of the other.

govern priority. It would appear that the maxim should only be applied where the equities are in all respects equal. On this point Kindersley VC stated as follows in *Rice v Rice*:[218]

> [I]n a contest between persons having only equitable interests, priority of time is the ground of preference last resorted to; i.e. … a Court of Equity will not prefer the one to the other, on the mere ground of priority of time, until it finds upon an examination of the relative merits that there is no other sufficient ground of preference between them, or in other words that their equities are in all other respects equal; and that, if the one has on other grounds a better equity than the other, priority of time is immaterial.

While a *bona fide* purchaser of a legal estate for value and without notice of an earlier equitable interest may take the property free of that interest, a *bona fide* purchaser of an equitable interest without notice of an earlier equitable interest will take subject to it on the basis of the maxim that where the equities are equal the first in time prevails. However, while such a purchaser does not take free of prior equitable interests, he will take free of any prior mere equities on the basis that the 'equities' are not equal. An example of how this distinction may be of practical importance is provided by the decision of Lord Sugden LC in *Bowen v Evans*.[219] There a dispute arose between the plaintiff, who sought to have a deed set aside for fraud and one of the defendants, who claimed under a settlement for value of the lands which constituted an equitable interest. Sugden LC held that this defendant could raise a plea of purchaser for value against the plaintiff on the basis that the plaintiff's right to have the transaction impeached for fraud was a mere equity and so could not take priority over the defendant's equitable estate acquired for value and without notice of the plaintiff's claim.

This decision is difficult to reconcile with his subsequent judgment as Lord St Leonards in *Stump v Gaby*,[220] in which he found that where a person makes a conveyance in circumstances where it may be set aside for fraud, his equitable right to rescind amounts to a beneficial interest in the land conveyed that is capable of being devised by will. The better view would seem to be that taken subsequently by Lord Westbury in *Phillips v Phillips*,[221] where he confirmed that the right to set aside a deed for fraud or correct it for mistake was a mere equity as distinct from an equitable interest. This is in line with the opinion expressed in this jurisdiction by Kenny J in *Allied Irish Banks v Glynn*,[222] where he stated that '"an equity" does not create or give any estate in the land: it is a

218. (1853) 2 Drew 73, 77. Quoted with approval by Porter MR in *Bank of Ireland v Cogry Flax Spinning Co.* [1900] 1 IR 219, 230.
219. (1844) 6 Ir Eq R 569.
220. (1852) 2 De GM & G 623.
221. (1862) 4 De GF & J 208.
222. [1973] IR 188, 192. See also *Latec Investments Ltd v Hotel Terrigal Pty Ltd* (1965) 113 CLR 265 *per* Kitto and Menzies JJ.

right against persons and is enforceable against those who were parties to the transaction which created it.' In this case the first named defendant conveyed land to his son, the second named defendant, subject to the former's right to remain in residence in a house on the lands. The son deposited the land certificate with the plaintiff bank as security for monies advanced to him by the bank. As a result of proceedings brought by the father, the conveyance was set aside on the grounds of undue influence. The plaintiff bank, which was not aware of these proceedings, then brought a claim to enforce the equitable mortgage. Kenny J held, in giving priority to the bank, that the equitable mortgage took precedence over the prior right of the father to have the deed set aside, a right which was described as a chose in action rather than an equitable interest.[223]

Similarly, there has been some dispute about the status of a beneficiary's equitable right to trace trust property into the hands of third parties and specifically about whether it should be categorised as an equitable interest or as a mere equity. The position in England would appear to be that it is recognised as an equitable interest. In *Cave v Cave*[224] trustees improperly invested trust moneys in the purchase of land, the legal estate in which was conveyed to another party who created both legal and equitable mortgages. Fry J held that the mortgagees took without notice and that as between the beneficiaries and the equitable mortgagee, the beneficiaries took priority because they had a prior equitable estate as opposed to a mere equity. Therefore, although the equitable mortgagee was acting in good faith and took without notice of the beneficiaries' interest, he could not take priority over the prior equitable interest of the beneficiaries. The result in this case is a good illustration of the maxim that where the equities are equal, the first in time prevails, although as the decision of the Irish Court of Appeal in *Re Ffrench's Estate*[225] shows, the result will be different where the equities are not considered to be equal. That decision also concerned a contest as between the right of beneficiaries to trace and that of an equitable mortgagee, although Porter MR reached the opposite conclusion on this issue to that arrived at by Fry J in *Cave v Cave*. Trust funds were mixed by an equitable tenant for life with his own funds and used to buy property. A question of priorities arose between the right of the beneficiaries to trace the trust funds and a bank in whose favour an equitable mortgage had been created, which had no knowledge of the fact that the trust funds had been converted. It was held that the rights of the equitable mortgagee must

223. Kenny J explained the status of the father's interest in the following terms (at 192-193): 'But what was the first defendant's interest in the lands when the deposit with the plaintiffs was made? It cannot be classified accurately as having been "an equity" only for, if the deed was procured by fraud or undue influence, the first defendant would acquire an estate in the lands when he succeeded in setting it aside. What he had was a *chose in action* which could become an estate if he brought proceedings and if they were successful.'
224. (1880) 15 Ch D 639.
225. (1887) 21 LR Ir 283.

prevail over the rights of the beneficiaries who possessed a mere equity only, i.e. the right of tracing. Porter MR said that the equity of the mortgagees was a 'superior equity' to that of the beneficiaries. In his view, the primary right of a beneficiary was against his own trustees and the right to trace the trust fund into its improper investment was ancillary to this. He concluded that such an ancillary right should not prevail against innocent purchasers and said that in this instance he was unable to regard the equities as equal. Porter MR regarded the beneficiaries' right as 'rather in the nature of a chose in action than an estate — an equity as distinguished from an equitable interest and inferior to the equitable interest of the mortgagees.' While Porter MR was the only member of the court who decided the case on the basis that a right to trace was a mere equity, this view has been applied in several decisions in this jurisdiction.[226] In *Scott v Scott*[227] the administratrix of an estate and her son had invested certain assets of the estate in a house and deposited the title deeds with a bank by way of mortgage. When a dispute over priorities arose between the next of kin and the bank, it was held that the former's right was a mere equity which could not prevail over an equitable estate such as was possessed by the bank which amounted to an equitable mortgage on specific items of property.

While this approach to the status of a beneficiary's right to trace appears to be established in Ireland, Wylie has questioned its soundness on the basis that it seems to involve an 'unjustifiable limitation' of the beneficiaries' interests.[228]

Priorities and the Doctrine of Notice[229]

The basic rule at law as in equity is that estates and interests rank in priority according to the order of their creation where they are otherwise equal and so it is important to distinguish legal estates, equitable estates and mere equities for this purpose. The other important factor which affects the question of priorities is the doctrine of notice. This in turn has been affected and to some extent displaced by the modern systems of registration. As regards notice, the rule developed by equity was that a *bona fide* purchaser for value without notice of a legal estate or interest in land would take free of an equitable interest of which he had no notice. Similarly, a *bona fide* purchaser for value of an equitable interest without notice will take free of a mere equity. As Keane[230] points out, there are three major exceptions to this principle, first that a naked equity, such as the right of a spouse to possession considered in *National Provincial Bank*

226. See *Re Sloane's Estate* [1895] 1 IR 146 in which Monroe J confirmed (at 165) that the right to trace was a 'lower one' than the right created by an equitable mortgage by deposit. See also *Bourke v Lee* [1904] 1 IR 280 and *Re Bobbett's Estate* [1904] 1 IR 461.
227. [1924] 1 IR 141.
228. See Wylie, *Irish Land Law* (5th ed., 2013) p. 138.
229. Sheridan (1950) 9 NILQ 33.
230. Keane, *Equity and the Law of Trusts in Ireland* (3rd ed., 2017) p. 69.

v Ainsworth,[231] will not be binding on a subsequent purchaser irrespective of the question of notice as the right is purely personal in nature and cannot be binding on third parties. In addition, a purchaser for value of registered land will not be affected by an unregistered equitable claim even if he has notice of it and a purchaser will not be affected by notice of a prior equitable interest where it is overreached pursuant to section 21 of the Land and Conveyancing Law Reform Act 2009.

For the doctrine of the *bona fide* purchaser without notice to come into effect, the purchaser must be *bona fide*, i.e. there must have been no fraud on his part in relation to the purchase. Secondly, he must have been a purchaser for value although there is authority for the proposition that it need not be shown that the consideration given was adequate. Finally, the purchaser must establish that he took the estate without notice of any prior interest.

It is generally accepted that there are three forms of notice — actual, constructive and imputed — and these can be identified in section 86 of the Land and Conveyancing Law Reform Act 2009, which essentially re-enacted section 3(1) of the Conveyancing Act 1882,[232] in the following terms:

> A purchaser is not affected prejudicially by notice of any fact, instrument, matter or thing unless
>
> (*a*) it is within the purchaser's own knowledge or would have come to the purchaser's knowledge if such inquiries and inspections had been made as ought reasonably to have been made by the purchaser, or
>
> (*b*) in the same transaction with respect to which a question of notice to the purchaser arises, it has come to the knowledge of the purchaser's counsel, as such, or solicitor or other agent, as such, or would have come to the knowledge of the solicitor or other agent if such inquiries and inspections had been made as ought reasonably to have been made by the solicitor or agent.

It should also be noted that section 21 of the Land and Conveyancing Law Reform Act 2009 has affected the operation of the doctrine of notice as it applies to priorities as between competing interests in land. Section 21(1) provides that a conveyance to a purchaser of a legal estate or legal interest in land by the person or persons specified in subsection (2) overreaches any equitable interest in the land so that it ceases to affect that estate or interest, whether or not the purchaser has notice of the equitable interest. The section goes on to provide that a 'person or persons specified' for this purpose:

231. [1965] AC 1175.

232. Repealed by ss. 2, 8(3) and Schedule 2, Part 4 of the Land and Conveyancing Law Reform Act 2009.

(*a*) shall be at least two trustees or a trust corporation where the trust land comprises (i) a strict settlement, or (ii) a trust, including a trust for sale, of land held for persons by way of succession, or (iii) land vested in or held on trust for a minor, (*b*) may be a single trustee or owner of the legal estate or interest in the case of any other trust of land.[233]

However, the section sets out a number of circumstances in which no overreaching will occur and these include any conveyance made for fraudulent purposes of which the purchaser has actual knowledge at the date of the conveyance or to which the purchaser is a party, or any equitable interest to which the conveyance is expressly made subject, or protected by deposit of documents of title relating to the legal estate or legal interest.

Actual Notice

A person will be considered to have actual notice where he discovers information himself, so a subjective standard is imposed. The wording of section 86(1)(a) of the Land and Conveyancing Law Reform Act 2009, which essentially re-enacts section 3(1)(i) of the Act of 1882, shows that unlike in the case of imputed knowledge referred to in paragraph (b), it is not necessary that the actual knowledge was obtained in the course of the transaction in question. However, it is clear that merely hearing a rumour will not amount to actual notice.[234]

The question of actual notice was considered by the Supreme Court in *Bank of Ireland Finance Ltd v Rockfield*[235] although in a different context. The question at issue was whether the plaintiff bank had notice of the fact that monies advanced to a company had been used to purchase its own shares in breach of section 60 of the Companies Act 1963,[236] subsection 14 of which provided that any transaction in breach of section 60 is voidable at the instance of the company against any person who had notice of the facts that constituted the breach of the statute. The Supreme Court held that the company could not invoke section 60(14) as they had failed to establish that the plaintiff had actual notice of the facts alleged to constitute a breach of the section prior to the transaction in question. Kenny J stated that the notice referred to in the subsection was actual notice and not constructive notice and said that there was strong authority to support the view that the doctrine of constructive notice should not be extended to commercial transactions.[237] He said that he was using the term 'actual notice' 'as meaning in this case that the plaintiff bank, or any

233. Section 21(2).
234. *O'Connor v McCarthy* [1982] IR 161, 174. See also *Lloyd v Banks* (1868) 3 Ch App 488, 491 *per* Lord Cairns.
235. [1979] IR 21.
236. Now see the provisions of s.82 of the Companies Act 2014.
237. See also *Danske Bank v Madden* [2009] IEHC 319 at 9.

of its officials, had been informed, either verbally or in writing, that part of the advance was to be applied in the purchase of shares in the defendant company, or that they knew facts from which they *must* have inferred that part of the advance was to be applied for this purpose.'[238]

Constructive Notice

A person will be deemed to have constructive notice where he fails to make the inquiries and inspections which he ought reasonably to have made, judged by reference to standard conveyancing procedures. It is stated in *Snell's Equity*[239] that a purchaser will be treated as having constructive notice 'of all that a reasonably prudent purchaser, acting on skilled advice, would have discovered'.

The question of constructive notice was considered by Henchy J in the Supreme Court in the context of the application of the Family Home Protection Act 1976 in *Somers v W.*[240] The plaintiff had purchased a house from the defendant's husband without the defendant's consent and sought to sell it to a purchaser who insisted on obtaining her written consent. The plaintiff then sought an order dispensing with the defendant's consent under section 4 of the Family Home Protection Act 1976. In finding for the defendant, the Supreme Court held that at the date of the purported assignment, the plaintiff was affected by constructive notice of the defendant's statutory rights as these would have come to the knowledge of the plaintiff's solicitor if such inquiries had been made as ought reasonably to have been made. The Supreme Court therefore concluded that the purported assignment by the defendant's husband to the plaintiff was void. Henchy J stated as follows:

> In earlier times the tendency was to judge a purchaser solely by the facts that actually came to his knowledge. In the course of time it came to be held in the Court of Chancery that it would be unconscionable for the purchaser to take his stand on the facts that had come to his notice to the exclusion of those which ordinary prudence or circumspection or skill should have called to his attention. When the facts at his command beckoned him to look and inquire further, and he refrained from doing so, equity fixed him with constructive notice of what he would have ascertained if he had pursued the further investigation which a person with reasonable care and skill would have felt proper to make in the circumstances.[241]

Further consideration was given to the question of what will constitute making

238. [1979] IR 21, 37.
239. McGhee, *Snell's Equity* (33rd ed., 2015) p. 68.
240. [1979] IR 94.
241. *Ibid.* at 108.

reasonable inquiries by the Supreme Court in *Northern Bank Ltd v Henry*.[242] The second named defendant purchased the leasehold interest in a house with money which belonged to the first named defendant, his wife, but the assignment of the interest was made to him alone. The wife sought a declaration that she was entitled in equity to the leasehold interest. On the same day the husband mortgaged the house to the plaintiff bank which apart from making a search in the Registry of Deeds, made no investigation of the husband's title. The wife succeeded in obtaining a declaration that her husband held the leasehold interest in trust for her and claimed that her interest prevailed over that of the plaintiff bank because, she contended, it had constructive notice of her interest. Henchy J emphasised that section 3(1) of the Conveyancing Act 1882 gave statutory force to the 'existing judicial insistence that constructive notice could be found only when lack of knowledge was due to such careless inactivity as would not be expected in the circumstances from a reasonable man'. He stated:

> In my judgment, the test of what inquiries and inspections ought reasonably to have been made by the plaintiffs is an objective test which depends not on what the particular purchaser thought proper to do in the particular circumstances but on what a purchaser of the particular property ought reasonably to have done to acquire title to it …. [Section 3(1)], because it is laying down the circumstances in which a purchaser is not to be prejudicially affected by notice of any instrument, fact or thing, is setting as a standard of conduct that which is expected from a reasonable purchaser. Reasonableness in this context must be judged by reference to what should be done to acquire the estate or interest being purchased, rather than by the motive for or the purpose of the particular purchase.[243]

There has been some debate in this jurisdiction about the extent to which the doctrine of constructive notice should apply to commercial transactions in this context. In *Bank of Ireland Finance Ltd v Rockfield*[244] Kenny J, referring to the decision of Lindley LJ in *Manchester Trust v Furness*,[245] said that '[t]here is strong authority that the doctrine of constructive notice is not to be extended to commercial transactions'. This statement was applied by McGovern J in *Danske Bank v Madden*,[246] although he acknowledged that the facts of the case before him could be distinguished from those in *Northern Bank v Henry*, examined above. The issue was considered again by Gilligan J in *Re Jeffel*,[247] in which a company receiver sought directions from the court as to whether a debenture held by a bank took priority over the interest in a property claimed by

242. [1981] IR 1.
243. *Ibid.* at 9.
244. [1979] IR 21, 37.
245. [1895] 2 QB 539.
246. [2009] IEHC 319.
247. [2012] IEHC 279.

the respondent, who was the wife of a director and shareholder of the company which was in receivership. The court had to consider whether the bank was a *bona fide* purchaser without notice of the interest in property claimed by the respondent. Gilligan J stated that the Conveyancing Act 1882, as interpreted by the Supreme Court, required a reasonable purchaser to make the necessary inquiries and inspections and where it had not done so, it would be held to be on constructive notice of a transaction. He also considered the question of the extent to which constructive notice would apply to commercial transactions and noted that in both *Bank of Ireland Finance Ltd v Rockfield* and *Danske Bank v Madden* the respective defendants had sought to avoid transactions against their banks. However, he pointed out that in the case before him, as in *Northern Bank v Henry*, the question of notice arose as between a bank and a third party. He continued as follows:

> If either Kenny or Parke JJ, both of whom formed part of the Supreme Court in both *Bank of Ireland v Rockfield* and *Northern Bank v Henry*, which judgments were delivered little more than two years apart, had wanted to clarify that a rule prohibiting the application of constructive notice in all commercial transactions, regardless of the context, existed then they could have done so. Failing same, I am bound to follow the later decision as representing the applicable law in this matter.[248]

Gilligan J concluded that as the bank had failed to conduct proper inquiries into the title to the property, it was fixed with constructive notice of the respondent's interest. He also held that the property constituted the respondent's family home and that the procedures set out in the Family Home Protection Act 1976 for the conveyance of an interest in a family home had not been complied with. Therefore, in accordance with section 3 of that Act, any such purported conveyance was void and the bank consequently did not have any legal interest in the property.

Imputed Notice

This type of notice is referred to in section 86(1)(b) of the Land and Conveyancing Law Reform Act 2009, which essentially re-enacts section 3(1)(ii) of the Conveyancing Act 1882. The effect of the subsection is that all knowledge of which an agent of a purchaser is actually aware, or of which he would have been aware if he had made the inquiries and inspections which he ought reasonably to have made, will be attributed to the purchaser. However, the subsection also stipulates that this notice must have been acquired 'in the same transaction' if it is to bind the purchaser and so any knowledge which an agent may have obtained from previous dealings will not be relevant in this context.

248. *Ibid.* at [68].

Onus of Proof

Finally, it should be noted that the onus of proving that a person had no notice of a prior interest lies on the party claiming that he took without notice. This was confirmed by O'Byrne J in *Heneghan v Davitt*.[249] The plaintiff entered into an agreement for the purchase of lands and while the agreement was awaiting completion the vendors entered into a further agreement for sale with another person which was carried into effect by a conveyance. The plaintiff brought a claim for specific performance. In the Circuit Court, the third party's plea of purchaser for value without notice was upheld but in the High Court it was held that it had been incorrect to impose the onus of proving that the other person had not been a *bona fide* purchaser without notice on the plaintiff. The onus rested instead on the defendant to prove that he was a purchaser for value without notice and since he had not discharged this onus, the plaintiff was granted specific performance of the agreement. O'Byrne J stated as follows:

> In order to defeat a plea of purchaser for value without notice, it is not, in my opinion, necessary that the purchaser should have actual notice. If he has sufficient notice or knowledge to put him upon enquiry, and if he deliberately refrains from making such enquiry, he is thereupon deemed to have constructive notice of such facts as would have come to his knowledge if he had made proper enquiry; and such constructive notice is, in my opinion, sufficient to defeat the plea.[250]

Registration of Deeds, Priorities and Notice

There are two main systems of registration affecting land in Ireland; the registration of deeds system introduced by the Registration of Deeds Act (Ireland) 1707, which was repealed and replaced by the Registration of Deeds and Title Act 2006 which provides for the registration of memorials of deeds and conveyances affecting lands, tenements and hereditaments, and the registration of title system which provides for the registration of ownership of land.

The registration of deeds system did not have any kind of comprehensive application; it was not compulsory and where there was no memorial or written document in existence relating to a disposition, there was nothing to register. However, two provisions of the Act of 1707 were of considerable importance to the question of priorities where a deed had been registered and should be set out. Section 4 provided that registered dispositions ranked in priority according to their date of registration not according to their date of execution, so the maxim that where the equities are equal the first in time prevails has no application in this instance. Section 5 provided that a deed or conveyance of which a memorial was not registered would be deemed 'fraudulent and void'

249. [1933] IR 375.
250. *Ibid.* at 379.

against a deed or conveyance, a memorial of which has been registered and effectively provided that a registered disposition would take priority over a registrable but unregistered disposition. Now section 38 of the Registration of Deeds and Title Act 2006 provides that deeds registered under the Act are taken to be effectual in law and equity and shall rank according to the priority determined by the serial numbers allocated to them. It also provides that a deed which is not registered is void against a registered deed affecting the land concerned. In addition, section 38(3) provides that the section operates without prejudice to the application of any rule of law or equity in cases where a person claiming under a registered deed had knowledge, or was deemed to have knowledge, of a prior unregistered deed.

The Act of 1707 did not govern priorities where an unregistrable disposition was involved, for example the deposit of the title deeds of land to create an equitable mortgage. In this case such a disposition will take priority over a subsequent equitable interest even though the latter is registered. So, in *Re Burke's Estate*[251] it was held that the holder of an equitable mortgage by deposit of title deeds, unaccompanied by any memorandum in writing, took priority over a purchaser for value claiming under a subsequent registered deed, without knowledge of the mortgage.

Where two registered dispositions are involved in a conflict as to priorities, the provisions of section 38 of the Registration of Deeds and Title Act 2006 now apply and they will rank according to the serial numbers allocated to them. The question of notice will not be relevant and a purchaser for value without notice cannot claim priority over a prior registered deed irrespective of whether the estates or interests created are legal or equitable.[252] However, where there is a conflict between a prior unregistered deed and a subsequent registered deed, the issue of notice does become relevant. It was held in *Forbes v Deniston*[253] that the 1707 Act which was intended to prevent fraud should not be used to provide a means of achieving fraud. So, where a purchaser who registers a deed has notice of a prior unregistered deed he will not be permitted to obtain priority.[254] In *Forbes* a subsequent lessee, whose lease was registered and who knew of a prior unregistered lease, was not permitted by the House of Lords to take priority over the holder of the earlier lease.

It has been established that for this qualification to the statutory scheme to operate, the purchaser/lessee must have actual notice of the existence of the prior unregistered deed at the time of the subsequent deed's execution or at least at the time of its registration or else have notice imputed to him by reason of the actual notice of his agent. Therefore, in this context constructive notice will be insufficient, a point re-affirmed by Costello J in *O'Connor v McCarthy*.[255]

---

251. (1882) 9 LR Ir 24.
252. *Eyre v Dolphin* (1813) 2 Ba & B 290.
253. (1722) 4 Bro PC 189.
254. Now see the provisions of s. 38(3) of the Registration of Deeds and Title Act 2006.
255. [1982] IR 161.

A company contracted in writing to sell premises to a purchaser although the memorial of the contract was not registered in accordance with the provisions of the Registration of Deeds Act 1707. It subsequently contracted in writing to sell the premises to a second purchaser and this contract was registered in the Registry of Deeds. The second purchaser's solicitor had no knowledge of the existence of the first contract when he registered the second. However, the second purchaser had heard rumours of a previous contract, but being satisfied that he had in fact bought the premises, did not inform his solicitor of this. Costello J held that the registration of the memorial of the second contract in accordance with the provisions of the 1707 Act conferred priority on it subject to the equitable doctrine of notice. He held that neither the second purchaser nor his solicitor had actual notice of the existence or nature of the first contract and that therefore the second contract must be given its statutory priority. Costello J effectively held that constructive notice was insufficient to defeat the statutory scheme. However, he proceeded to refer to the *dicta* of Lord Cairns in *Agra Bank Ltd v Barry*[256] and suggested that where a purchaser has not acted in good faith, e.g. where he has deliberately refrained from making inquiries, the court might not give effect to the statutory priority even though the purchaser only has constructive notice. In this instance, Costello J was satisfied that neither the second purchaser nor his solicitor had acted in any way *mala fide* and there was no reason to consider whether constructive notice might have sufficed to displace the statutory priority accorded to the second contract.

Registration of Title and Priorities

Under the registration of title system, title to any land may be registered.[257] Compulsory registration of title in the Land Registry has now been extended to all counties in the State.[258] Once land is registered, all dealings relating to it must be effected through the Land Registry. Where title has been registered, the register will to a large extent govern the question of priorities as between competing interests in land. However, certain types of rights and burdens listed in section 72 of the Registration of Title Act 1964 can affect registered land without being registered. In addition, other unregistered rights apart from those referred to in section 72 may be created in or over registered land, although these will not affect the registered owner of a charge created on land for valuable consideration and will only be effective where the transferee is a volunteer.[259] So, where an equitable mortgage is created by the deposit of the land certificate, this equitable charge is subject to any prior equitable interests in accordance

256. (1874) LR 7 HL 135, 149.
257. For more detailed consideration of the registration of title system, see Wylie, *Irish Land Law* (5th ed., 2013) Chapter 23.
258. See the Registration of Title Act 1964 (Compulsory Registration of Ownership) (Cork and Dublin) Order 2010 (SI No. 516 of 2010).
259. *Devoy v Hanlon* [1929] IR 246.

with the maxim that where the equities are equal the first in time prevails. In *Tench v Molyneux*[260] the equitable interest of a purchaser of registered land who had failed to take the necessary steps to effect his registration as owner was held to take priority over a party with whom the vendor had subsequently deposited the land certificate to secure a loan. As the equities were equal in this case, the interest of the purchaser being prior in time prevailed.

260. (1914) 48 ILTR 48.

CHAPTER 3

Trusts — An Introduction

GENERAL PRINCIPLES

The Origins of the Trust Concept

The modern trust developed out of the medieval concept of the use whereby the owner of land would give it to another to hold on his behalf.[1] Initially, when the owner of property put his land in the possession of another person a mere moral obligation was imposed and the original owner had no remedy if his wishes were not carried out. However, the Court of Chancery intervened to provide for the enforcement of the use of land on the grounds that it would be unconscionable not to recognise the device.

The system of the use was adopted for a number of reasons. Perhaps the most significant of these, and the one which ultimately led to legislative intervention to curb its predominance, was that it facilitated the avoidance of certain feudal dues and incidents, e.g. payments to a lord where an heir succeeded to land or the right of escheat where there was no heir. In addition, until the enactment of the Mortmain Act 1391, the concept also enabled property to be effectively transferred to bodies corporate, usually religious institutions, a practice which the earlier mortmain legislation had been designed to prevent. A further advantage was that despite the fact that it was not possible to make a devise of land in Ireland until after the passage of the Statute of Wills (Ireland) Act 1634, a landowner could effectively achieve this result by employing the device of the use. Another often fraudulent practice which grew up was to grant lands to the use of another to defeat the claims of a creditor or to delay actions for the recovery of land.

While the intervention of the Court of Chancery to give effect to the use proved a most useful and beneficial practice from the point of view of tenants of land, it grew increasingly unpopular with feudal lords and especially with the ultimate overlord, the King of England. As a result the Statute of Uses was passed in England in 1535 and the equivalent legislation, the Statute of Uses (Ireland) 1634, was passed by the Irish parliament.[2] The statute provided that

---

1. It became the practice to convey land 'to A to the use of B'. While B had no legal estate in the lands which remained at common law the property of A, the Court of Chancery would recognise B's beneficial or 'equitable' ownership of the land.
2. 10 Chas. I, sess. 2, c.1. It should be noted that this statute has never been repealed. Pearce suggested in an article written in 1990 (see (1990) 41 NILQ 43) that the Statute of Uses could still have effect and that interests in freehold land arising from

where any person or persons were seised of any lands or other hereditaments to the use, confidence or trust of any person(s) or of any corporation, the person or corporation having such use, confidence or trust in fee simple, fee tail, for term of life or for years, or otherwise, should be deemed in lawful seisin and possession of the lands or hereditaments for the same estate as he or they had in the use, confidence or trust.

Prior to the enactment of the statute, it was usual to grant land 'unto A and his heirs to the use of B and his heirs'. Its effect was to provide that the use should be immediately executed with the result that B would become the legal owner and A would have no further interest. As the Statute of Uses (Ireland) 1634 was not passed until nearly a century after the equivalent legislation had taken effect in England, it was recognised by the time of its enactment here that the legislation was far from comprehensive in nature. First, it applied only where a person was seised of land to the use of another, which effectively confined its application to freehold land. Secondly, it did not apply where the person to whom the freehold was conveyed had an active duty to perform, e.g. to collect rent and pay it over.[3] Thirdly, the statute had no application where a body corporate, rather than a person or persons, was seised of lands to the 'use, trust or confidence' of any other person or corporation. However, the most important exclusion, and the one which ultimately led to the creation of the modern concept of the trust as we know it, was that a use upon a use did not come within the ambit of the statute. At common law there could not be a second use in a conveyance of freehold land so if the land was conveyed 'unto A and his heirs to the use of B and his heirs to the use of C and his heirs', the common law would not give effect to the use to C. This was established in *Tyrrel's* case,[4] where it was held that where there was a use upon a use, the second use would not be executed by the statute.

However, the Court of Chancery in England gradually came around to the idea of enforcing this second use in a manner similar to that in which the first use had been enforced prior to the enactment of the Statute of Uses. While some controversy remains about when this practice became established,[5] in time the

---

a contribution to its purchase price should in many cases be treated as executed by the statute. However, in a reply to this article published in 1996 (see (1996) 47 NILQ 367) Mee argued convincingly against such a proposition and submitted (at 376) 'that there is no possibility of the courts in Ireland deciding that the Statute of Uses should execute modern resulting or constructive trusts'.

3. If the statute executed the use in such a case, this person would be left with no interest in the property and would therefore be unable to carry out the duties imposed on him. However, the statute did apply if the use or trust was purely passive, e.g. where land was conveyed to A on trust to permit B to receive the rents, A took no estate since there was no active duty to perform.
4. (1557) 2 Dy 1555a.
5. One view is that the courts had adopted this approach by the time of the enactment of the Statute of Uses (Ireland) 1634 (see Wylie, *Irish Land Law* (4th ed., 2010) p. 189 and Baker (1977) 93 LQR 33, who relies on the authority of *Sambach v Dalston*

second use became known as a trust and it became common to simply convey property 'unto and to the use of B (the trustee) in trust for C (the beneficiary)'.

Definition of a Trust

Since the concept of a trust came to be recognised, numerous attempts have been made both by members of the judiciary and various academic commentators to define in precise terms the nature of the rights and obligations which it gives rise to, often with only a limited degree of success.[6] The following definition is provided in Underhill and Hayton's, *The Law Relating to Trusts and Trustees*:[7]

> [A]n equitable fiduciary obligation, binding a person (called a trustee) to deal with property (called trust property) owned and controlled by him as a separate fund, distinct from his own private property, for the benefit of persons (called beneficiaries or, in old cases *cestuis que trust*), of whom he may himself be one, and any one of whom may enforce the obligation.[8]

This definition is insufficient to cover trusts for various purposes other than for the benefit of persons, so Pettit makes the following addition 'or for a charitable purpose, which may be enforced at the instance of the Attorney-General, or for some other purpose permitted by law though unenforceable'.[9]

Perhaps the most comprehensive definition is that suggested by Keeton and Sheridan:

> A trust is the relationship which arises wherever a person (called the trustee) is compelled in equity to hold property, whether real or personal, and whether by legal or equitable title, for the benefit of some persons (of whom he may be one and who are termed beneficiaries) or for some object permitted by law, in such a way that the real benefit accrues, not to the trustee, but to the beneficiaries or other objects of the trust.[10]

It is not always correct to refer to the trustee as the legal owner and the beneficiary as the equitable owner as the trustee's interest may be equitable only, for instance where a beneficiary under a settlement makes a settlement of his interest where the legal interest remains in the trustees of the original

---

(1634) Toth 188), while another view is that the position was not clarified until later that century (see Strathdene (1958) 74 LQR 550 and Yale [1957] CLJ 72).

6. See Hart (1899) 15 LQR 294 where a number of attempts at definitions dating back to 1734 are set out and analysed.
7. Hayton, Matthews and Mitchell, *Underhill and Hayton: The Law Relating to Trusts and Trustees* (19th ed., 2016) p. 3.
8. This was quoted with approval by Cohen J in *Re Marshall's Will Trusts* [1945] 1 Ch 217, 219 and by Romer LJ in *Green v Russell* [1959] 2 QB 226, 241.
9. Pettit, *Equity and the Law of Trusts* (12th ed., 2012) p. 30.
10. Keeton and Sheridan, *The Law of Trusts* (12th ed., 1993) p. 3.

settlement. So it is more correct to refer to the trustee as the nominal owner of the property and the beneficiary as the beneficial owner.

TRUSTS DISTINGUISHED FROM OTHER FORMS OF LEGAL INSTITUTION

Before examining the trust concept in any detail it is useful to distinguish it from other legal institutions. Some of these may in certain circumstances resemble a trust and the duties and obligations which it gives rise to, although none of them contain all the essential elements necessary to constitute a trust and it is therefore important to be able to distinguish them. It is proposed to examine these in turn.

Trusts and Bailment

Pettit suggests the following definition of bailment:[11]

> [D]elivery of personal chattels upon a condition, express or implied, that they shall be redelivered to the bailor, or according to his directions, when the purpose of the bailment has been carried out.

There are certain similarities between the position of a trustee and bailee in that both are subject to fiduciary obligations, albeit of varying degrees, in relation to the property which is within their control.[12] However, there are a number of basic distinctions between the concepts of a trust and a bailment. The first is that bailment is a creature of common law while trusts are equitable in nature and their enforcement is based on equitable rather than common law principles. Secondly, bailment applies only to personal property whereas a trust can apply to any type of property. Thirdly, while a bailor can enforce or vary the bailment, a settlor cannot carry out the same function in relation to a trust unless he has specifically reserved such a power to himself when setting it up. However, the most important practical significance of the distinction between the concepts of trust and bailment is where the person to whom possession of the property is given disposes of it to a third party. A bailee merely has special property in the goods which constitute the subject-matter of the bailment and cannot generally pass good title to the property which will be valid against the bailor.[13] On the other hand, a trustee can give good title in these circumstances to a person who acquires the legal ownership *bona fide* for value without notice of the trust.

---

11. Pettit, *Equity and the Law of Trusts* (12th ed., 2012) p. 31.
12. See the judgment of Mason J in *Hospital Products Ltd v United States Surgical Corporation* (1984) 156 CLR 41 for a discussion of the nature of the fiduciary obligation owed by a bailee to a bailor.
13. There are exceptions to this general principle, e.g. sale in market overt.

Trusts and Agency

There are some similarities between the relationship of principal and agent and that of trustee and beneficiary to the extent that both the agent and the trustee have fiduciary obligations and must act in the interests of their principal or beneficiaries and not for their own benefit. While the agency relationship is governed mainly by common law principles, equity will intervene in certain circumstances. First, it will impose fiduciary obligations on an agent to make him liable to account where he has made a personal profit out of his position without the consent of his principal. In addition, he will be regarded as a constructive trustee where property has been entrusted to him by his principal for investment or safekeeping.

However, there are also a number of significant ways in which the relationships can be distinguished. First, the agency relationship is personal in nature, whereas the trust is proprietary. Secondly, there must be some form of agreement between an agent and his principal which forms the basis of their relationship, whereas this will hardly ever be either necessary or desirable between a trustee and the beneficiaries of a trust. Thirdly, the agency arrangement is normally terminated by the death of either the principal or the agent; this is not the case in relation to a trust where either a trustee or beneficiary dies. Fourthly, a trustee cannot commit the beneficiaries of a trust to liabilities towards third parties whereas an agent can commit his principal to such liabilities. Fifthly, an agent is bound to carry out his principal's instructions yet a trustee is not subject to such control either by the settlor or the beneficiaries and is simply bound to carry out the terms of the trust and discharge his functions as trustee according to law. A final essential element present in a trust relationship which is lacking in an agency agreement is that while an agent may have his principal's property in his possession, he will not usually have title to it.[14]

Trusts and Contract

From one perspective, contracts and trusts would appear to be completely distinct concepts with few characteristics in common; the former is a creation of the common law, an arrangement which requires valuable consideration for its validity and one which only the parties to it can enforce. A trust, on the other hand, is a species of equitable obligation which can be perfectly valid without the element of consideration being present,[15] and which can be enforced by a beneficiary who is not party to the original arrangement between the testator/settlor and the trustees.

However, in practice it is often difficult to draw a distinction between these

14. *Cave v Mackenzie* (1877) 46 LJ Ch 564, 567 *per* Jessel MR.
15. E.g. where a testator creates a trust in his will or a settlor declares himself trustee of named trusts for the benefit of a volunteer.

concepts and the same transaction may even give rise to both a contract and a trust. Yet important practical consequences may flow from characterising a relationship between parties as either a contract or a trust. For example, where property is vested in A, who then becomes insolvent, the likelihood of B recovering whatever is owed to him is substantially higher if A held the property in trust for him than if he is A's debtor and can only claim in A's bankruptcy. The most far-reaching consequence of the distinction is that beneficiaries can enforce a trust even though not party to its creation whereas only the actual parties to a contract can enforce it.[16] The wisdom of not recognising the right of a third party to a contract to enforce it was often questioned,[17] although it was reasserted on a number of occasions by the House of Lords.[18] Section 1 of the Contracts (Rights of Third Parties) Act 1999 in England now provides that a third party may enforce a term of a contract in his own right if the contract provides that he may or if the term purports to confer a benefit on him, unless on a proper construction of the contract it appears that the parties did not intend such term to be enforceable by a third party.

There have also been sporadic instances of the courts employing the concept of a constructive trust to provide a third party with a remedy by finding that one of the parties to a contract entered into it as a trustee with the intention of benefiting the third party. In *Drimmie v Davies*[19] a dentist and his son agreed by virtue of a deed to become partners for five years; in the event of a dissolution the son was to have the right to purchase the property and, in the event of his father's death, was to pay certain annuities to his brothers and sisters. The father died and his executors and the brothers and sisters succeeded in an action to enforce payment of the annuities on the grounds that the son was bound by the obligation to his father which was now being enforced by his executors. It is clear from the judgment of Chatterton VC, which was upheld by the Irish Court of Appeal, that he felt it was not necessary to decide whether a fiduciary relationship existed between the executors and the beneficiaries for the purpose of maintaining the action. However, Chatterton VC referred to the *dicta* of

16. This latter principle was an accepted feature of the law in this jurisdiction and in England, see e.g. *Tweddle v Atkinson* (1861) 1 B & S 393; *Dunlop Pneumatic Tyre Co. Ltd v Selfridge & Co. Ltd* [1915] AC 847 and has been the subject-matter of much academic debate. See Dowrick (1956) 19 MLR 374; Wylie (1966) 17 NILQ 351; Yates (1977) 41 Conv 49; Andrews (1988) 8 LS 14.
17. See Corbin (1930) 46 LQR 12 and the recommendations of the Law Revision Committee in 1937 Cmd 5449, section D para. 48. In addition, Lord Denning has often advocated a more liberal view, see *Smith & Snipes Hall Farm Ltd v River Douglas Catchment Board* [1949] 2 KB 500; *Drive Yourself Hire Co. (London) Ltd v Strutt* [1954] 1 QB 250; *Adler v Dickson* [1955] 1 QB 158; Denning (1960) 3 Syd Law Rev 209, 214.
18. *Scruttons Ltd v Midland Silicones Ltd* [1962] AC 446; *Beswick v Beswick* [1968] AC 58.
19. [1899] 1 IR 176.

Cotton LJ in *Gandy v Gandy*[20] to the effect that the rule that a contract cannot be enforced except by a party to it is subject to an exception:

> [I]f the contract, although in form it is with A, is intended to secure a benefit to B, so that B is entitled to say that he has a beneficial right as *cestui que trust* under that contract; then B would, in a Court of Equity, be allowed to insist upon and enforce the contract.[21]

This statement was also quoted with approval in *Kelly v Larkin*[22] by Andrews J who stated that, while he did not seek to question the common law doctrine that a contract cannot be enforced except by a party to it, he considered that the facts of the case before him came within the 'equitable exception' to this doctrine expounded in *Gandy*.

It can be argued that such an approach may often be called for to ensure that justice is achieved, yet the courts both in this jurisdiction and elsewhere have shown a marked reluctance to infer the existence of a trust in these circumstances, unless it is clear both from the language used in creating the arrangement and from the surrounding circumstances that this was the clear intention of the parties.[23] In *Cadbury Ireland Ltd v Kerry Co-operative Creamery Ltd*[24] the plaintiffs claimed an entitlement to a quantity of milk at a price to be determined in accordance with a clause in a contract which had been concluded between the defendants because, it claimed, the second named defendants were trustees of the benefit of the clause in question on behalf of the plaintiffs. The defendants pleaded that the plaintiffs were not party to the agreement and denied that they had any rights thereunder. Barrington J held that while the principle that parties to a contract can create a trust of contractual rights for the benefit of a third party which can be enforced by that third party is well-established, in the circumstances, the plaintiffs had failed to establish that the second named defendants were trustees of any contractual rights on their behalf. A similarly unsuccessful attempt to rely on this principle was made by the plaintiffs in *Inspector of Taxes Association v Minister for the Public Service.*[25] Murphy J referred to the judgment of Barrington J in the *Cadbury* case and to the 'well established proposition that parties to a contract can create

20. (1885) 30 Ch D 57.
21. *Ibid.* at 67. Also approved by Walker LJ in *Kenney v Employers' Liability Assurance Corporation* [1901] 1 IR 301.
22. [1910] 2 IR 550, 557. Andrews J held that a person who is not named as a party to a covenant was nevertheless entitled to maintain an action upon it on the basis that he was in a position akin to that of a beneficiary under the covenant.
23. See *Re Webb* [1941] 1 Ch 225, 234 *per* Farwell J; *Re Schebsman* [1944] 1 Ch 83, 104 *per* du Parcq LJ; *Green v Russell* [1959] 2 QB 226, 231 *per* Romer LJ: 'an intention to provide benefits for someone else and to pay for them does not in itself give rise to a trusteeship.'
24. [1982] ILRM 77. See also *Bula Ltd v Tara Mines Ltd (No. 2)* [1987] IR 95, 101.
25. [1983] IEHC 56.

a trust of contractual rights for the benefit of a third party'.[26] However, he said that he would find it very difficult to infer that the various staff associations, which were parties to the original conciliation and arbitration agreement on which the plaintiffs sought to rely, had purported to contract by implication as trustees for the plaintiff association which had been formed subsequently.

Finally, it is worth noting that in some jurisdictions, third parties are given statutory rights against the promisor in a contract which, as has been noted in *Jacobs' Law of Trusts in Australia*,[27] may even put them in a more favourable position than if they had been recognised as beneficiaries under a trust implied by the courts. As noted above, section 1 of the Contracts (Rights of Third Parties) Act 1999 in England now provides that a third party may enforce a term in a contract in his own right in certain circumstances. The Law Reform Commission has also provisionally recommended that the privity of contract rule should be altered so as to allow third parties to enforce rights under contracts made for their benefit.[28] It remains to be seen whether legislation to give effect to this recommendation will be forthcoming and if so, how extensive the reform of the privity rule will be.

Trusts and Powers

There is a fundamental distinction between trusts and powers; while trusts are of an imperative nature, powers are discretionary. A trustee must carry out his functions according to the terms of a trust whereas the donee of a power has considerable discretion as to the manner in which he exercises the power, if indeed he exercises it at all. The beneficiaries under a trust are the owners in equity of the trust property while the objects of a power have only the expectation that the power may be exercised in their favour. The most usual type of power and the one which is relevant in this context is a power of appointment, which authorises the creation or grant of beneficial interests in property and which gives authority to the donee to nominate objects of the power who will generally be chosen from a defined class. It is also relevant at this juncture to draw a distinction between general and special powers of appointment. A power will be characterised as general if the donee may designate any person, even himself, as the object(s) of the power, otherwise it will be termed a special power of appointment.

While these basic distinctions seem clear in theory, they are confused by the fact that a trust may confer a measure of discretion on a trustee, e.g. he may be given a discretion to select beneficiaries from a specified class or to

26. *Ibid.* at 35.
27. Heydon and Leeming, *Jacobs' Law of Trusts in Australia* (8th ed., 2016) para 2.25. See e.g. the position in Western Australia and Queensland. In Ireland, ss. 7 and 8 of the Married Women's Status Act 1957 confer rights on spouses and children to enforce certain types of contracts entered into for their benefit.
28. LRC CP 40-2006, para. 1.172.

decide the proportions in accordance with which the trust property is to be divided; this is known as a discretionary trust. While the beneficiaries under a discretionary trust cannot demand that trustees exercise their discretion in their favour, they can seek to ensure that the trustees make a selection as to who will benefit under the terms of the trust. This compares with the situation in relation to a power of appointment where the donee of the power cannot be compelled to make a selection.

To confuse matters further, there is also a concept known as a power in the nature of a trust or a 'trust power'.[29] This essentially denotes the situation which arises where a court infers the existence of a trust in default of any appointment being made by the donee of a power.[30] A gift over in default of appointment negatives the existence of a trust of this nature for the objects of a power.[31] Where there is no gift over in the event of non-exercise of a power, it may be construed as a trust for all the members of the specified class equally.[32] However, the absence of a gift over is not conclusive[33] and there must be a clear indication that the testator or settlor intended the power to be in the nature of a trust. Where the court is not satisfied that such a trust power exists and the person to whom the power is given has died without exercising it, there will be a resulting trust in favour of the testator's estate.[34]

The manner in which a court should determine whether a mere power or a trust power exists in circumstances where there has been a failure to exercise a power of appointment is, in the words of Evershed MR, a question of deducing the 'intention or presumed intention to be derived from the language of the instrument'.[35] Perhaps the most frequently cited example of such an intention

---

29. For a detailed consideration of these various distinctions, see Unwin (1962) 26 Conv 92; Hopkins [1971] CLJ 68; Cullity (1976) 54 Can Bar Rev 229; Bartlett and Stebbings [1984] Conv 227.
30. Explained in the following terms by Lord Eldon in *Brown v Higgs* (1803) 8 Ves 561, 570: 'there are not only a mere trust and a mere power, but there is also known to this court a power, which the party, to whom it is given, is entrusted and required to execute; and with regard to that species of power the court consider it as partaking so much of the nature and qualities of a trust, that if the person, who has that duty imposed upon him, does not discharge it, the Court will, to a certain extent, discharge the duty in his room and place.' Quoted with approval by Budd J in *Re Parker* [1966] IR 309, 319.
31. *Re Mills* [1930] 1 Ch 654. Note that an ordinary residuary gift is not considered to be a gift over for this purpose, see *Re Hall* [1899] 1 IR 308, 320.
32. See *Re Llewellyn's Settlement* [1921] 2 Ch 281; *Re Arnold's Trusts* [1947] Ch 131.
33. *Re Weekes' Settlement* [1897] 1 Ch 289, applied in *Re Combe* [1925] Ch 210 and *Re Perowne* [1951] Ch 785.
34. See e.g. *Bank of Ireland v O'Toole*, High Court 1979 No. 671Sp (Barrington J) 26 June 1980; *Tuite v Tuite* [1978] ILRM 197.
35. *Re Scarisbrick* [1951] Ch 622, 635. See also the *dicta* of Buckley J in *Re Leek* [1967] Ch 1061, 1073.

being found by the courts is *Burrough v Philcox*,[36] where Lord Cottenham laid down the following principle:

> When there appears a general intention in favour of a class, and a particular intention in favour of individuals of a class to be selected by another person, and the particular intention fails, from that selection not being made, the court will carry into effect the general intention in favour of the class.[37]

A testator gave life estates in certain stock and property to his two children with remainder to their issue and provided that if they should both die without leaving lawful issue, the survivor of the children should have power to dispose by will of the estate amongst his nephews and nieces, or their children, either all to one of them or to as many of them as his surviving child should think proper. There was no gift over in default and it was held by Lord Cottenham that a trust was thereby created in favour of the testator's nephews and nieces and their children, subject to a power of selection and distribution in the surviving child.

A similar result was achieved in *Re Kieran*,[38] where a testator devised and bequeathed his farm and the rest of his property to his brother on trust for the latter's eldest son and, if this son were to die before attaining the age of 21, to such of his other sons as his brother would appoint. The testator's brother's eldest son died before he reached the age of 21 and his brother died without making any appointment amongst his three surviving sons. Pim J held that in the circumstances these three surviving sons were entitled to the farm in equal shares as tenants in common. He commented that 'it is the recognized duty of every court to carry out a trust if it is possible to do so, and if it is possible, a court will avoid a construction which must result in an intestacy and in the carrying of the property, possibly wholly, probably largely, to persons whom the testator never meant to get it.'[39]

The intention of the testator appears to have emerged as the paramount consideration which will influence a court in deciding whether a gift should arise by implication in the absence of any appointment being made in these cases. In *Robinson v Moore*[40] Dixon J was satisfied that the testator intended to deal exhaustively and completely with the property which formed the subject-matter of the power and did not intend that it should devolve as on intestacy or lapse into residue. In these circumstances, he was satisfied that there was an implied gift to the objects of the power in default of appointment.

The rationale behind this approach is that the failure on the part of the

---

36. (1840) 5 My & Cr 72.
37. *Ibid.* at 92. Note also the *dicta* of Lord Eldon in *Brown v Higgs* (1803) 8 Ves 561, 574.
38. [1916] 1 IR 289. This was also the approach adopted by Budd J in *Re Parker* [1966] IR 309.
39. [1916] 1 IR 289, 297. See also *Rorke v Abraham* [1895] 1 IR 334.
40. [1962-3] Ir Jur Rep 29.

donee to exercise the apparent power should not prejudice the donor's intended objects. Instead, the court will substitute its own discretion for that of the donee and in doing so seek to give effect as far as possible to the donor's original intentions.[41] Where the donor of the power has subsequently died, arguably this approach will come much closer to carrying his wishes into effect than if the property were to become the subject-matter of a resulting trust. Despite the existence of the fundamental principle that the courts will seek as far as possible to ascertain and give effect to a testator's intentions, the courts have on a number of occasions decided in such circumstances that no 'trust power' arises and that a resulting trust in favour of a testator's estate should take effect.

In *Healy v Donnery*[42] a testator devised freehold property to his daughter for life and gave her power to dispose of it amongst her children in such shares as she might consider proper. Pennefather B rejected the argument that the power to appoint amongst the children was tantamount to creating a trust in their favour and stated that the power was not coupled with a trust. This approach was confirmed by the English decision of *Re Weekes' Settlement*,[43] in which the following statement of principle was made by Romer J:

> The authorities do not shew … that there is a hard and fast rule that a gift to A for life, with a power to A to appoint among a class and nothing more, must, if there is no gift over in the will, be held a gift by implication to the class in default of the power being exercised. In my opinion, the cases shew … that you must find in the will an indication that the testatrix did intend the class or some of the class to take — intended in fact that this power should be regarded in the nature of a trust — only a power of selection being given, as, for example, a gift to A for life, with a gift over to such a class as A shall appoint.[44]

Here a testatrix bequeathed property to her husband for life and granted him a power of appointment over this property to be exercised in favour of their children. The husband died intestate without having exercised the power and Romer J found that there was no implied gift to the children in default of appointment. A similar result was arrived at in *Clibborn v Horan*,[45] where O'Connor MR stated that 'there must be something in the instrument creating the power from which the intention that the objects shall take in default of

41. Where the court intervenes the objects of the power will take in equal shares as tenants in common, whereas the actual donee might well have exercised his discretion to divide the property in unequal shares.
42. (1853) 3 ICLR 213. See also *Re Hall* [1899] 1 IR 308.
43. [1897] 1 Ch 289.
44. *Ibid.* at 292.
45. [1921] 1 IR 93.

appointment can be gathered'.[46] He concluded that no intention that there should be a trust in favour of the objects of the power was expressed or could be gleaned from the will and in the circumstances there could be no gift by implication to these objects. This principle of giving effect as far as possible to the testator's intentions where these can be extracted from the will resulted in a similar conclusion being reached by McWilliam J in *Tuite v Tuite*.[47] In this instance the testator's intention appeared to the court to be to seek to benefit those persons to whom he had bequeathed his residuary estate and McWilliam J concluded that the proceeds of the property in question should pass under the residuary clause in the will.

A further example of a situation in which a court was satisfied that a testator did not intend a power to operate by implication as a gift to all the potential objects equally in default of appointment is *Bank of Ireland v O'Toole*.[48] A testator had conferred a power of appointment over his property on his widow intending her to exercise it in favour of one of his sons subject to the payment of a number of legacies to the other children. His widow died without exercising the power and Barrington J rejected the argument that it should be construed as a power in the nature of a trust and that the property, which was principally comprised of a farm, should go to the sons equally. He reiterated that the fundamental duty of the court was to attempt to ascertain and give effect to the testator's intentions and that it was clear that the testator intended that the farm should pass to one of his sons alone; it was quite inconsistent with any intention which could be gathered from the will that the sons should take equally.

Despite the conflicting results arrived at by the courts in this jurisdiction even in comparatively recent cases it is possible to deduce some general principles from these decisions. It seems clear that the court will seek to give effect as far as possible to the testator's intentions, which will usually be achieved by construing a power as being in the nature of a trust in default of appointment.[49] However, there must be some intention either expressed or implied in the will that the objects of the power should take a gift by implication in these circumstances. The question which is difficult to answer with certainty is what will constitute sufficient evidence of such intention and this problem of interpretation is to an extent responsible for the divergence in recent authorities in this area.

A final matter of considerable practical significance is that, whether one is dealing with powers or trusts, it is necessary for the objects or beneficiaries to be defined with a sufficient degree of certainty to enable the donees or trustees to carry out their functions in relation to distribution. The position in

---

46. *Ibid.* at 97. This statement was quoted with approval by Dixon J in *Robinson v Moore* [1962-3] Ir Jur Rep 29, 38 a case in which the opposite conclusion was reached.
47. [1978] ILRM 197.
48. High Court 1979 No. 671Sp (Barrington J) 26 June 1980.
49. As in decisions such as *Re Kieran* [1916] 1 IR 289 although, as shown above, not in *Tuite v Tuite* [1978] ILRM 197.

both England and in this jurisdiction in relation to the test of certainty used to differ as between mere powers, on the one hand, and trusts, whether fixed, discretionary or trust powers on the other hand. In the former case the test was whether it could be said with certainty that any given individual was or was not a member of the class.[50] In the latter case the trust was void for uncertainty unless a comprehensive list of the beneficiaries could be drawn up.[51] However, the majority of the House of Lords decided in *McPhail v Doulton*[52] that the test to be applied in ascertaining the validity of a discretionary trust should be the same as that outlined above in relation to mere powers. Clearly the assimilation of the test of certainty in relation to discretionary trusts and powers has from a practical perspective removed to a great extent the need to distinguish between them. While the approach of the House of Lords in *McPhail* is likely to be followed in this jurisdiction in relation to modern discretionary trusts involving significant numbers of potential beneficiaries, this will not necessarily be the case in relation to smaller family trusts. In *O'Byrne v Davoren*[53] Murphy J stated, albeit *obiter*, that a trust for the division of income between members of family to be selected by trustees will be invalid unless the entire class of potential beneficiaries is ascertainable. This issue will be considered in more detail below in the context of the requirement of certainty of objects in relation to express trusts,[54] but for present purposes it suffices to make the point that in this jurisdiction at any rate the distinction between mere powers and discretionary trusts or trust powers may yet be of considerable significance in determining the validity of the trust or power in question.

Trusts and the Administration of a Deceased's Estate

While the roles of a personal representative and trustee are often confused in practice, their origins are quite distinct; the position of the former was regulated by the Ecclesiastical Courts whereas the latter as we have seen was a product of the developments brought about by the Court of Chancery. While the task of the personal representative could be said to be the limited one of realising and distributing assets and the trustee's function is ordinarily of considerably more lasting duration in terms of administering the trust on an ongoing basis, there are nevertheless considerable similarities between the offices.[55]

Both trustees and personal representatives are subject to fiduciary

---

50. *Re Gestetner Settlement* [1953] Ch 672; *Re Gulbenkian's Settlement* [1970] AC 508.
51. *IRC v Broadway Cottages' Trust* [1955] Ch 20, 35-36. Approved by Budd J in *Re Parker* [1966] IR 309.
52. [1971] AC 424. It is interesting to note that a differently constituted House of Lords confirmed the earlier approach only three years earlier in *Re Gulbenkian's Settlement* [1970] AC 508.
53. [1994] 3 IR 373.
54. See *infra* Chapter 4.
55. *Re Speight* (1883) 22 Ch D 727, 742 *per* Jessel MR.

obligations in the performance of their functions and often the same individuals will fulfil both roles at different stages. In the first instance, an individual may act as an executor and once the deceased's estate is administered may take over the role of trustee of the trusts established under the testator's will. It is often difficult to determine precisely when one role ceases and the other commences but the individual concerned will rarely act in both capacities at the same time. Legislative provisions may cause confusion as, for example, section 10(3) of the Succession Act 1965 which provides that a personal representative holds a deceased's estate as a 'trustee' for those entitled to it. Despite the use of such terminology, until the estate is fully administered, the residuary legatee or next of kin will not be regarded as the beneficial owner of the testator's assets and a personal representative does not become a trustee in the strict sense of the word.[56] So when acting as a personal representative, he must be regarded as such for the purposes of deciding on the application of relevant limitation periods to any actions which these parties may take or which may be taken against them.[57]

A distinction between the offices which may have considerable practical significance is that while trustees only have joint authority to deal with or dispose of personal property, personal representatives have joint and several authority to do so and the lawful actions of one will be binding on all.[58] This is illustrated by *Attenborough & Son v Solomon*,[59] where an executor, over thirteen years after the testator's death but before the distribution of the residuary estate had been completed, pledged property which formed part of this residuary estate to a pawnbroker without the knowledge of his co-executor/co-trustee. The pledgor died and when the transaction was discovered an action was brought to recover the property. The result of the case turned on whether the pledgor had been acting as an executor or trustee; if he was adjudged to have been still acting as executor, the pawnbrokers would have obtained good title. However, the House of Lords held that at the relevant date the executors had assented to the trust dispositions under the testator's will taking effect and that the property was held by the pledgor as a trustee. Accordingly he had no authority to act without the assent of his co-trustee and the property could be recovered.

A further distinction which can be made is that a personal representative holds his office for life except where the grant of probate or letters of

---

56. See the *dicta* of Sargant J in *Re Ponder* [1921] 2 Ch 59, 61: 'when the estate has been wound up and the residue ascertained, the executor has ceased to be an executor and has become a trustee for the persons entitled to the residue.' See also *Eaton v Daines* [1894] WN 32 and Ker (1955) 19 Conv 199.
57. See e.g. *Vaughan v Cottingham* [1961] IR 184.
58. *Jacomb v Harwood* (1751) 2 Ves Sen 265, 267. Although note that where one administrator purports to sign a contract on behalf of himself and his co-administrator and warrants that he has the authority to do so when this is in fact lacking, no specifically enforceable contract will exist, see *Fountain Forestry Ltd v Edwards* [1975] Ch 1.
59. [1913] AC 76. See also *Astbury v Astbury* [1898] 2 Ch 111.

administration is for a limited period or the court releases him from such duties.[60] However, by virtue of section 11 of the Trustee Act 1893, provided that there will be at least two trustees remaining to administer the trust, a trustee may by deed declare that he wishes to retire and if the consent of his co-trustees is forthcoming, he will be permitted to do so.

CLASSIFICATION OF TRUSTS

Trusts can be classified in a number of different ways; e.g. according to the manner of their creation, by virtue of the objects which they seek to benefit or from the perspective of the nature of the duties which they impose on the trustee. It is proposed at this point to set out briefly the main classifications which are recognised but it is important to note that these categories are not always mutually exclusive.

Public and Private Trusts

This classification is based on the reason for the creation of a trust. Private trusts are created for the benefit of an individual or a class of individuals irrespective of the benefit which they may confer on the public at large. Public trusts, otherwise known as charitable trusts, are set up for purposes beneficial to the community in general although in most cases they will incidentally confer a benefit on a specific person or class of persons. In the case of the former type of trust the so-called 'beneficiary principle' applies, i.e. there 'must be somebody in whose favour the court can decree specific performance'.[61] However, there is no such requirement in the case of public trusts which may be enforced by the Charities Regulatory Authority.[62]

Express, Resulting and Constructive Trusts

Express Trusts

An express trust is one created by express declaration of the settlor or testator either by instrument *inter vivos* or by will. Certain formalities must be observed in the creation of *inter vivos* trusts of land and all trusts which are set up by means of a will. In addition, all express trusts must contain a number of essential

60. *Re Timmis* [1902] 1 Ch 176, 183 *per* Kekewich J.
61. *Morice v Bishop of Durham* (1804) 9 Ves 399, 405 *per* Grant MR. Note that there is also an anomalous category of 'purpose trusts' which have been upheld as valid despite their failure to adhere to the beneficiary principle. See further, Chapter 10.
62. This function was previously vested in the Attorney General. By virtue of s. 38 of the Charities Act 2009, all the functions of the Attorney General in relation to charitable trusts or organisations were transferred to the Charities Regulatory Authority when this section came into force in 2014. See further Chapter 11.

elements known as 'the three certainties', and these issues will be considered in detail in the following chapter. Further subdivisions in the classification of express trusts can be made; first, according to the form in which the declaration of trust is effected, which can give rise to either executed or executory trusts. A trust is said to be executed where the settlor or testator has delimited precisely the circumstances under which the trust property is to be held and no further instrument is required to effect this. However, in the case of an executory trust, although a valid trust has been created the settlor or testator has only indicated his general intentions as to how the trust property is to be disposed of and a further instrument is required to define the beneficial interests with precision.[63]

Secondly, a subdivision can be made between completely and incompletely constituted trusts. A trust is said to be completely constituted when the trust property has actually been vested in the trustees for the benefit of the beneficiaries; until this has been done the trust remains incompletely constituted. The distinction between these categories and their practical implications will be considered in more detail below in Chapter 6.

Resulting Trusts

A resulting trust[64] is one which arises from the unexpressed but presumed intention of the settlor or testator. They are known as resulting trusts because the beneficial interest in the property reverts or 'results' to the settlor (or if he is dead, to his estate) who transferred the property to the trustee in the first instance. Resulting trusts are often divided into two categories:[65] automatically resulting trusts which arise where a trust has been declared but the beneficial interest fails for some reason or is not disposed of in its entirety and presumed resulting trusts which occur as a result of the inference drawn by the law with regard to the donor's intentions.[66] Due to the informal manner in which they come into being, resulting trusts are exempt from the formalities required in relation to the creation of express trusts.

Constructive Trusts

A constructive trust is a form of trust which arises by operation of law and which comes into being irrespective of the intentions of the parties concerned. The main distinction between resulting and constructive trusts is that in the case of the former, the courts assume that the creation of the trust was intended by the

---

63. *Egerton v Earl Brownlow* (1853) HLC 1, 210. See also *Davis v Richards and Wallington Ltd* [1990] 1 WLR 1511, 1537-1538; *Pengelly v Pengelly* [2008] Ch 375, 378.
64. The term 'implied trust' is sometimes used interchangeably with the term 'resulting trust'.
65. *Re Vandervell's Trusts (No. 2)* [1974] Ch 269, 294 *per* Megarry J. See further Chapter 7.
66. See further Chapter 7.

parties whereas in the latter instance a trust is imposed to satisfy the demands of justice and good conscience and may often be imposed in a manner contrary to the intentions of the individuals concerned. To the extent that there is no requirement to observe the formalities necessary in relation to express trusts in either case, there is often little practical significance in drawing a distinction between the two categories. Constructive trusts are generally regarded as constituting a residual category of trust but as we shall see they are adaptable and often dynamic in nature.[67]

Simple and Special Trusts

This classification distinguishes between different types of trust according to the nature of the duties which are imposed on the trustees in each case. A simple trust[68] is one in which property is vested in a trustee but the trustee is given no active duties to perform and merely holds the legal title to the trust property. A special trust is one in which a trustee is required to carry out duties imposed on him by the settlor or testator which necessitates him taking an active as opposed to a passive role in administering the affairs of the trust.

Fixed and Discretionary Trusts

In a fixed trust each beneficiary has a fixed current entitlement to a specific share or interest in the trust property. However, in the case of a discretionary trust, a beneficiary has no actual entitlement to any part of the trust property; instead the trustees are given the discretion to apply the property for the benefit of specified persons or classes of persons. Therefore, in the latter case a potential beneficiary cannot compel a trustee to exercise his discretion in his favour.[69] Within this category a distinction is sometimes drawn between 'exhaustive discretionary trusts' which impose an obligation on the trustees to dispose of the entire trust income and 'non-exhaustive discretionary trusts' which leave the issue of the extent of any distribution to the trustee.

Protective Trusts

A further category of trust which should be mentioned at this juncture is a protective trust.[70] The essence of such a trust is that the interest of a beneficiary is made determinable on the happening of certain events, usually bankruptcy or an attempt to alienate the trust property. This determinable interest is then

---

67. See further Chapter 8.
68. Also known as a bare trust, see *Tomlinson v Glyn's Executor & Trustee Co.* [1970] Ch 112, 125-126.
69. Although such a trustee can be compelled to at least make a selection amongst the beneficiaries.
70. Sheridan (1957) 21 Conv 110.

followed by the establishment of a discretionary trust, usually in favour of the beneficiary and members of his family or some other class of persons.

While a settlor cannot set up a protective trust to guard against his own bankruptcy,[71] he may do so to protect himself against alienation which will usually be of an involuntary nature. However, the most common type of protective trust will be one in which the interest of a beneficiary, other than the settlor, becomes determinable.[72] It is important to distinguish between such a determinable interest and an interest subject to a condition subsequent. A condition subsequent designed to terminate an interest in the event of bankruptcy or alienation will be void whereas an interest determinable in such cases will be valid.

Although there has been no legislative intervention in this area in Ireland, in a number of other jurisdictions legislation now provides a means whereby a settlor may direct that property be held on protective trusts without the necessity of setting out in detail the circumstances in which the interest will become determinable and the manner in which the discretionary trusts should operate.[73]

71. *Re Burroughs-Fowler* [1916] 2 Ch 251.
72. *Billson v Crofts* (1873) LR 15 Eq 314 and *Re Ashby* [1892] 1 QB 872.
73. E.g. s. 33 of the Trustee Act 1925 in England; s. 42 of the Trustee Act 1956 in New Zealand and s. 45 of the Trustee Act 1925 in New South Wales.

CHAPTER 4

Trusts — Formalities and Essential Elements

FORMALITIES

Creation of Trusts Inter Vivos

Primarily with a view to preventing fraud, legislation has intervened to provide that in specific cases certain formalities must be observed in the creation of express trusts. However, no formalities are required for the creation of an *inter vivos* express trust of personalty and provided that the settlor manifests the intention of creating such a trust,[1] it may be established orally.[2] In relation to the creation of express trusts of land, whether freehold or leasehold,[3] section 4 of the Statute of Frauds (Ireland) 1695 requires that the trust be evidenced in writing and signed[4] by a person able to declare the trust,[5] or by his will.[6] It is important to note that the declaration of trust itself does not need to be in writing but written evidence must exist to prove the declaration and its essential terms.[7]

---

1. *Paul v Constance* [1977] 1 WLR 527, 531 *per* Scarman LJ.
2. While the courts have accepted that such a trust may be validly created in this manner (see *M'Fadden v Jenkins* (1842) 1 Ph 153; *Re Kayford* [1975] 1 WLR 279, 281-282; *Paul v Constance* [1977] 1 WLR 521; *JSC VTB Bank v Skurikhin* [2019] EWHC 1407 (Comm) at [212]), in most cases fairly strong evidence will be required to establish this, see *Paterson v Murphy* (1853) 11 Hare 88, 91-2; *Maguire v Dodd* (1859) 9 Ir Ch R 452, 458.
3. *Forster v Hale* (1798) 3 Ves 696; *Donohue v Conrahy* (1845) 8 Ir Eq R 679.
4. It was suggested by Judge Pelling QC sitting as a Deputy High Court judge in *J. Pereira Fernandes SA v Mehta* [2006] 1 WLR 1543, 1552 that if a party draws up and sends an electronically created document he will be treated as having signed it. However, he also made it clear that the automatic insertion of an email address by an internet service provider should not, in the absence of evidence to the contrary, be intended as a signature.
5. A party who makes a declaration of trust must be entitled to do so. As MacDonald J commented in *HRH Tessy Prince of Luxembourg v HRH Louis Princess of Luxembourg* [2018] EWFC 77 at [115], 'you cannot declare an express trust in a beneficial interest that is not yours'.
6. See Bridge (1986) 64 Can Bar Rev 58 for a comprehensive review of the authorities relevant to the similar evidential requirements imposed by the Statute of Frauds in relation to contracts for the sale of land.
7. *Morton v Tewart* (1842) 2 Y & C Cas Ch 67, 80; *Smith v Matthews* (1861) 3 De G F & J 139, 151. It was accepted in *Ong v Ping* [2017] EWCA Civ 2069 at [62] that written evidence which came into being after the trust was declared would be acceptable for the purposes of the updated provision in England, s.53(1)(b) of the Law of Property Act 1925.

It appears to be accepted that it is possible for an oral declaration of a trust of land to be made on one occasion and evidenced by signed writing on another and that in such a case the oral declaration of trust is rendered enforceable from the former date.[8] So, this written evidence need not come into existence at the time the trust is declared provided that it exists before the commencement of any action in which the validity of the trust is questioned.[9] This written evidence need not be in any precise form,[10] and can even be extracted from two or more separate documents.[11]

The generally accepted view is that section 4 of the Statute of Frauds (Ireland) 1695, or its equivalent,[12] provides an evidential requirement which will only affect the enforceability and not the validity of trusts, so in the absence of any written evidence to prove its existence, such a trust will be valid although unenforceable.[13]

In addition, it should be noted that section 2 of the Statute of Frauds (Ireland) 1695 requires that contracts to create a trust in consideration of marriage must also be evidenced in writing.

Statute Not to be Used as an Instrument of Fraud

Notwithstanding these statutory requirements, the courts will not always insist on strict compliance with the provisions of the Statute of Frauds.[14] Possibly for the reason that these formality provisions which can be considered as merely a means towards an end should be used purposively,[15] the principle has been established that equity will not permit the statute to be used as an instrument of fraud. As Lord Westbury stated in *McCormick v Grogan*:[16]

> The Court of Equity has, from a very early period, decided that even an Act of Parliament shall not be used as an instrument of fraud; and if in the machinery of perpetrating a fraud an Act of Parliament intervenes, the Court of Equity, it is true, does not set aside the Act of Parliament, but it fastens on the individual who gets a title under that Act, and imposes upon

8. *Taylor v Taylor* [2017] 4 WLR 83 at [50].
9. *Rochefoucauld v Boustead* [1897] 1 Ch 196, 206; *Re Holland* [1902] 2 Ch 360, 382.
10. E.g. it can be contained in correspondence *Forster v Hale* (1798) 3 Ves 696; *Childers v Childers* (1857) 1 De G & J 482 or in a telegram *McBlain v Cross* (1871) 25 LT 804.
11. *Forster v Hale* (1798) 3 Ves 696. See also *Timmins v Moreland Street Property Co.* [1958] Ch 110 (Fridman (1958) 22 Conv 275) and *Elias v George Sahely & Co. (Barbados) Ltd* [1983] 1 AC 646 which relate to the requirements imposed by s. 40 of the Law of Property Act 1925 in England in relation to contracts for the sale of land.
12. Section 7 of the Statute of Frauds 1677, replaced by s. 53(1)(b) of the Law of Property Act 1925.
13. See Youdan [1984] CLJ 306, 320-321.
14. See generally, Thompson (1985) 36 NILQ 358.
15. Langbein (1975) 88 Harv L Rev 489, 491-498 and Youdan [1984] CLJ 306, 315.
16. (1869) LR 4 HL 82, 97.

> him a personal obligation, because he applies the Act as an instrument for accomplishing a fraud.

So, the court will not permit a beneficiary to be deprived of an interest in land under a trust in the absence of written evidence of the trust if such a result would amount to a fraud providing that there is some other evidence to establish the existence and nature of the trust. Where there has been a failure to comply with the statutory requirements the court must weigh the desirability of ensuring adherence to these requirements against the likelihood of injustice being caused by insisting on their observance. This balancing exercise is illustrated by the decision in *Re Duke of Marlborough*.[17] The Duchess of Marlborough assigned a leasehold interest in property to the duke and after his death asserted that the transfer was made solely to enable her husband to raise money by mortgaging the lease and that they had agreed that the property would ultimately be re-assigned to her. It was held that the provisions of the Statute of Frauds could not be successfully pleaded in opposition to the duchess's claim to the interest on the basis that the duke's estate would benefit unjustly had the obligation to re-assign the lease not been enforced owing to non-compliance with the statute. Stirling J stated that 'the general principle that the statute is not to be used as a protection to fraud has long been recognised by the courts of equity'[18] but commented that this principle has not always been applied in a uniform manner.

Perhaps the most frequently cited example of the operation of this doctrine is the decision of the English Court of Appeal in *Rochefoucauld v Boustead*.[19] The plaintiff was the owner of mortgaged property which was sold by the mortgagee to the defendant. The defendant had orally agreed to hold the property on trust for the plaintiff subject to repayment to the defendant of the purchase price and other expenses incurred in the transaction. The defendant subsequently sold the land and the plaintiff, who claimed that the land had been conveyed to the defendant as trustee for her, was held to be entitled to obtain an order for an account. Lindley LJ stated:

> [I]t is a fraud on the part of a person to whom land is conveyed as a trustee, and who knows it was so conveyed, to deny the trust and claim the land himself. Consequently, notwithstanding the statute, it is competent for a person claiming land conveyed to another to prove by parol evidence that it was so conveyed upon trust for the claimant, and that the grantee, knowing the facts, is denying the trust and relying upon the form of conveyance and the statute, in order to keep the land himself.[20]

17. [1894] 2 Ch 133.
18. *Ibid.* at 141.
19. [1897] 1 Ch 196.
20. *Ibid.* at 206.

This principle was applied in Ireland in *McGillycuddy v Joy*.[21] The plaintiff and the defendants agreed to purchase a farm jointly and the contract was signed by one of the defendants. The plaintiff paid one-third of the purchase price and the defendants then reneged on the agreement. The plaintiff sought a declaration that the defendant, who had signed the agreement, held the benefit of the contract in trust for him. Budd J held that the principle in *Rochefoucauld* applied even though there was only a contract of sale, as opposed to a conveyance. He concluded that the defendant had purchased that part of the lands previously agreed between them on trust for the plaintiff and that the former's repudiation of that trust constituted a fraud.

Similarly, in *Gilmurray v Corr*[22] the plaintiff had a leasehold interest in lands part of which were used as a golf driving range. After an unsuccessful attempt to buy the freehold, he came to an oral agreement with the defendant whereby the latter would purchase the lands with the plaintiff providing part of the purchase money, on the understanding that the defendant would then transfer the driving range to the plaintiff. The defendant subsequently told the plaintiff that he wished to incorporate in the transfer of the driving range a restrictive covenant that would prevent the use of the site for a licensed restaurant which might compete with the defendant's own premises. The plaintiff would not agree to this and the defendant proceeded with the purchase of the lands and refused to transfer the driving range to the plaintiff. Lowry LCJ held that when the defendant offered to purchase the lands he was acting as a trustee for himself and the plaintiff and that the plaintiff was entitled to prove by parol evidence that the land was conveyed to the defendant as a trustee. Lowry LCJ referred to *Rochefoucauld* and said that the decision had established that it is a fraud in equity for a person to whom land is conveyed as a trustee and who knows that it was so conveyed to deny the trust and claim the land as his own. This principle clearly applied to the facts of the case before him and the defendant could not rely on non-compliance with the statutory requirements to defeat the plaintiff's claim.

A question which has provoked considerable debate in recent years is whether a third party beneficiary can rely on the principle enunciated in *Rochefoucauld* to enforce such an informal trust. Feltham has argued that there is a strong line of authority against allowing a third party to rely on the doctrine and has stated that 'neither precedent nor policy' support the extension of the principle in this way.[23] However, Youdan has asserted that the relevant authorities[24] favour the view that such trusts can be enforced at the instance

21. [1959] IR 189.
22. [1978] NI 99.
23. Feltham [1987] Conv 246.
24. *Neale v Willis* [1968] 19 P & CR 839; *Binions v Evans* [1972] Ch 359; *Lyus v Prowsa Developments Ltd* [1982] 1 WLR 1044.

of a third party beneficiary and on balance this would seem to be the fairer approach.[25]

Dispositions of Equitable Interests Held Under a Trust

Section 6 of the Statute of Frauds (Ireland) 1695 provides that all subsequent dispositions of the beneficial interests held under a trust must be in writing and signed by the person making the disposition, or be included in a will. Two important points should be noted in relation to this requirement. First, it must be remembered that the requirement relating to the creation of trusts of land laid down in section 4 of the statute is that they must be evidenced in writing, whereas this provision, which relates to the subsequent disposition of such interests, requires that the disposition actually be in writing. Secondly, section 6 applies to both personal and real property held under a trust and so while a trust of pure personalty can be created orally and subsequently be enforced, any disposition of this interest must be in writing.

Considerable uncertainty has surrounded the ambit of section 53(1)(c) of the English Law of Property Act 1925[26] and the circumstances in which a 'disposition'[27] takes place within the meaning of the subsection are far from clear.[28] It has been accepted that, where a trustee is directed by a beneficiary to hold his interest on other trusts, this is sufficient to constitute a disposition of the beneficiary's interest.[29] However, the statutory requirement will not apply where the trustee conveys the legal interest to a third party on the instructions of or with the consent of the beneficiary.[30]

Creation of Trusts by Will

Where a trust is created by will, the testator must comply with the statutory requirements laid down by section 78 of the Succession Act 1965 in relation to the making of testamentary dispositions, i.e. that the will be in writing, signed at the foot thereof by the testator or by some other person in his presence and at his direction, and the testator's signature must be made or acknowledged in the presence of two or more witnesses present at the same time, each of whom must attest that signature by his own signature.

However, as with trusts created *inter vivos*, equity will not always strictly enforce the statutory formalities required where the statute is being used as

25. Youdan [1984] CLJ 306; Youdan [1988] Conv 267.
26. This replaced the original equivalent to s. 6 of the 1695 statute, s. 9 of the Statute of Frauds 1677.
27. This phrase replaced the formula used in s. 6 of 'grants and assignments of any trust or confidence'.
28. See e.g. *Oughtred v IRC* [1960] AC 206.
29. *Grey v IRC* [1960] AC 1; Green (1984) 47 MLR 385.
30. *Vandervell v IRC* [1967] 2 AC 291.

an instrument of fraud and it was in obedience to this principle that so called 'secret trusts', which will be considered in Chapter 5, came to be recognised.

ESSENTIAL ELEMENTS

Essential Elements of a Trust

Apart from ensuring compliance with the formalities outlined above, no technical or precise language is necessary to create a valid express trust. However, certain essential elements which have come to be known as 'the three certainties' must be present if such a trust is to be created. These three conditions of substance are as follows: certainty of intention or words, certainty of subject-matter and certainty of objects. These requirements were laid down by O'Byrne J in the decision of *Chambers v Fahy*:[31]

> [I]t has been established that, in order that a trust may be created, the subject matter must be certain, the objects of the trust must be certain and the words relied on as creating the trust must have been used in an imperative sense so as to show that the testator intends to create an obligation.

Before assessing the elements of certainty which must be met in order for a trust to be valid, some general principles should be considered. In his judgment in *Re Parker*,[32] in which the court had to consider whether a trust in a will was void for uncertainty, Budd J set out the following principle:

> The difficulties in interpreting a disposition which is ambiguously expressed are not enough to render the disposition void for uncertainty. To be void for this reason it must be utterly impossible to put a meaning on it.[33]

So, in construing a gift in a will, he stated that 'every endeavour should be made to elicit from the contents of the instrument the intentions of the testator, who, having made a will, has demonstrated that he does not intend to

---

31. [1931] IR 17, 21. This essentially reiterated the statement of Lord Langdale MR in *Knight v Knight* (1840) 3 Beav 148, 173 and these three certainty requirements are still referred to, see *First City Monument Bank plc v Zumax Nigeria Ltd* [2019] EWCA Civ 294 at [18].
32. [1966] IR 308.
33. *Ibid.* at 320. See also *Re Stanley deceased* [2016] IEHC 8 at [17]. An application was made in this case for an order setting aside a trust on the basis that it was void for uncertainty but the *ex parte* application was adjourned in order that the trustees be joined as defendants in circumstances where the applicants would be entitled to the trust property should the trust fail.

die intestate.'[34] These principles were referred to by Murphy J in *O'Byrne v Davoren*,[35] who stated that they imposed 'the duty to seek a construction of the will and an approach to the problems canvassed in relation to the administration of the trust which would resolve ambiguities and uncertainties where this was compatible with the expressed or implied wishes of the testator.' In his view the significance of the judgment of Budd J in *Re Parker* was 'the determination with which he sought to salvage the validity of the particular testamentary trust notwithstanding the difficulties created by the manner in which the testatrix had expressed her intentions'[36] and he agreed that this was the correct approach to adopt. While it should be pointed out that these authorities apply to situations in which it was sought to impugn the validity of trusts set out in a will and that the rationale referred to by Budd J in *Re Parker* that 'having made a will, [the testator] has demonstrated that he does not intend to die intestate' does not apply to *inter vivos* trusts, as a general principle the courts do seek to give effect to a settlor's intentions where this is possible and where there is sufficient evidential and conceptual certainty to allow for this.

Certainty of Intention or Words

The requirement that the words used to create a trust be imperative does not mean that any precise form of wording must be used.[37] So a trust may be validly created without actually using the word 'trust',[38] and conversely the use of that word does not conclusively indicate the existence of a trust.[39] However, as Scarman LJ stated in *Paul v Constance*,[40] 'there must be clear evidence from what is said or done of an intention to create a trust.' In determining whether this requirement of certainty has been met, the court will examine the substance and effect of the words used and a finding that a trust has been created will not be made unless it is satisfied that this was the settlor or testator's actual intention. So even where there is certainty of subject-matter and of objects, no trust can be created unless there is also certainty of intention.[41]

The words used must be examined with a view to ascertaining whether the intention was to make an absolute gift to the donee which he might, in the

34. *Ibid.* at 328.
35. [1994] 3 IR 373, 382.
36. *Ibid.*
37. *La Have Equipment Ltd v Nova Scotia* (1994) 121 DLR (4th) 67, 77 *per* Chipman JA.
38. *Charity Commission for England and Wales v Framjees* [2015] 1 WLR 16, 25; *Knight v Knight* [2019] EWHC 915 (Ch) at [88].
39. *Singha v Heer* [2016] EWCA Civ 424 at [62]; *Hunter v Public Trustee* [1924] NZLR 882. See also the *dicta* of Salmon J in *Thexton v Thexton* [2001] 1 NZLR 237, 247: 'A declaration of trust does not require a technical form of expression, it is a question of construction whether the words used, taking into account the surrounding circumstances, amount to a clear declaration of trust.'
40. [1977] 1 WLR 527, 531. See also *Wilkinson v North* [2018] 4 WLR 41 at [48].
41. *Crownx Inc v Edwards* (1994) 120 DLR (4th) 270, 280.

exercise of his discretion, dispose of in accordance with the settlor or testator's wishes, or whether the latter intended the donee to hold the property on trust. In determining whether the requisite intention to create a trust exists, the court may examine the nature of the transaction and the circumstances surrounding the relationship between the parties.[42] As Megarry J stated in *Re Kayford Ltd*,[43] 'the question is whether in substance a sufficient intention to create a trust has been manifested'.

This question of construction arises most frequently in relation to wills and historically the courts readily inferred the existence of a trust where the words used were hardly of an imperative nature,[44] as for example, where a gift was made by a testator who expressed the hope, wish, expectation or desire that the donee would deal with the property in a particular manner.[45] However, more recently these so called 'precatory words'[46] have usually been interpreted as being insufficient to create a trust. Before examining some of the authorities in this area in more detail, it is important to bear in mind that the type of language used is of itself not conclusive and the question of certainty of intention must be resolved by construing the whole of the instrument in question and thereby endeavouring to ascertain the intention of the settlor or testator.[47]

An examination of the decisions of the courts in this jurisdiction since the last quarter of the nineteenth century shows that the majority favour the conclusion that precatory words will not suffice to create an express trust.[48] Instead they may often be interpreted as merely expressing the motive for the gift[49] or as imposing some form of moral obligation on the donee to carry out the testator's wishes. Certainly there have been numerous statements to the

42. *Official Assignee in Bankruptcy v Wilson* [2008] 3 NZLR 45, 54.
43. [1975] 1 WLR 279, 282.
44. The reason for this approach, as suggested in Glister and Lee, *Hanbury and Martin: Modern Equity* (21st ed., 2018) p. 80 is that prior to the enactment of the Executors Act 1830 in England, the undisposed of residue which remained after an estate was administered might be retained by an executor. Thereafter, the residue was held on trust for the next of kin.
45. *Palmer v Simmonds* (1854) 2 Drew 221; *Moriarty v Martin* (1852) 3 Ir Ch R 26; *Gray v Gray* (1860) 11 Ir Ch R 218.
46. Trusts created by the use of precatory words have sometimes been referred to as 'precatory trusts', although they are in fact ordinary express trusts and the use of this terminology has been criticised as 'misleading' by Rigby LJ in *Re Williams* [1897] 2 Ch 12, 27.
47. *Re Adams and the Kensington Vestry* (1884) 27 Ch D 394, 410 *per* Cotton LJ; *Re Hamilton* [1895] 2 Ch 370, 373 *per* Lindley LJ; *Re Williams* [1897] 2 Ch 12, 14 *per* Romer J.
48. *McAlinden v McAlinden* (1877) IR 11 Eq 219; *Morrin v Morrin* (1886) 19 LR Ir 37; *Murtagh v Murtagh* (1902) 36 ILTR 129; *Berryman v Berryman* [1913] 1 IR 390; *Re Humphrey's Estate* [1916] 1 IR 21; *Re Walker and Elgie's Contract* (1919) 53 ILTR 22; *Re McIntosh* [1933] IR 69; *Re Coulson* (1953) 87 ILTR 93; *Re Fitzgibbon* (1959) 93 ILTR 56; *Re Sweeney* [1976-77] ILRM 88. However, the opposite conclusion was reached in *Re Finnerty* [1970] IR 221.
49. *Re Fitzgibbon* (1959) 93 ILTR 56, 59 *per* Budd J.

effect that the 'tide has turned'[50] and which support the view that the trend is now against permitting the creation of a trust by the use of precatory words.[51] The position now appears to be that such words will not *prima facie* create a trust,[52] so any intention to the contrary must be clearly and unequivocally expressed by the testator. The statement of Monroe J in *Re Byrne's Estate*[53] provides a useful summary of the position:

> [I]t is impossible to lay down any general rule by which all the cases on this subject can be reconciled; but I think it will be found that, in the great majority of cases where the Court of Chancery has refused to establish a precatory trust, there is, in the first place, an absolute gift to a particular individual, the terms of which are sought to be qualified by subsequent words in a subsequent clause. No trust will be established unless the words of qualification are clear and definite, and so expressed as to be regarded as imperative.

In *Re Humphrey's Estate*[54] a testator devised and bequeathed all his property, real and personal, to his wife and added that he wished that she should leave by will or transfer during her life a house and demesne to his son and that the remainder of his property should be left or transferred to his daughters. Ross J held that in the circumstances, the wife took an absolute interest. Similarly, in *Re Coulson*,[55] a testatrix left a farm and the furnishings of the farmhouse to her cousin in her will and went on to state that it was her wish that it should not be sold or divided but should be retained by the cousin for whichever of her children she thought fit. In these circumstances, Dixon J said that while the words used in the will were capable of being imperative they were not necessarily so and that the determining factor was 'what could be gathered from the will as a whole'. He was satisfied that the wording used amounted to no more than an expression of the hope that the cousin would act in the manner intended by the testatrix and held that in the circumstances, she took an absolute interest in the farm and furnishings.

The most recent case to be decided in this area would appear to confirm the approach established in decisions such as *Re Humphrey's Estate* and *Re Coulson*. In *Re Sweeney*[56] the testator devised and bequeathed all his assets to

50. *Re Humphrey's Estate* [1916] 1 IR 21, 24 *per* Ross J.
51. *Re Hamilton* [1895] 2 Ch 370, 374 *per* Lopes LJ; *Mussoorie Bank Ltd v Raynor* (1882) 7 App Cas 321, 330 *per* Sir Arthur Hobhouse; *Murtagh v Murtagh* (1902) 36 ILTR 129, 130 *per* Porter MR; *Re Coulson* (1953) 87 ILTR 93, 94 *per* Dixon J.
52. *Re Walker & Elgee's Contract* (1919) 53 ILTR 22, 23.
53. (1892) 29 LR Ir 250. Note also the *dicta* of Chatterton VC in *Morrin v Morrin* (1886) 19 LR Ir 37 where he stated that where these 'superadded words' do not cut down the interest given, it will not be held without more evidence that a trust has been created.
54. [1916] 1 IR 21.
55. (1953) 87 ILTR 93.
56. [1976-77] ILRM 88.

his wife for her own absolute use and benefit 'subject to the express wish' that she make provision for the payment of certain legacies after her death. The question arose whether the words of the gift to the wife of all the testator's assets could be cut down by these subsequent words. Hamilton J commented that while they were capable of being imperative, if he were to so hold, he would be cutting down considerably the clear words of the gift and quoted with approval the statement of Ross J in *Re Humphrey's Estate*[57] to the effect that: 'after a devise and bequest in clear and express terms, if a trust is intended to be created one would expect that this would be done in terms equally clear and explicit'. He concluded that it was the testator's intention that his wife should enjoy the assets for her own absolute use and benefit and that the words were not intended to create any trust in favour of the other defendants but were merely the expression of his wish for the guidance of his wife as to the manner in which she should dispose of her assets after her death.

Despite the general trend illustrated by these decisions, precatory words may be sufficient to create a trust if it is clear from the language used in the will as a whole that this was the testator's intention.[58] In *Comiskey v Bowring-Hanbury*[59] a testator devised and bequeathed all his real and personal property to his wife absolutely 'in full confidence' that she would make such use of it as he would have made himself and that at her death she would devise it to one or more of the testator's nieces as she might think fit. The majority of the House of Lords held that on the true construction of the will there was an absolute gift of the testator's real and personal estate subject to an executory gift of the same at her death to such of his nieces as survived her, either in accordance with the shares provided for in the wife's will or otherwise equally.

So, it would be incorrect to assume that the use of any particular form of words may or may not be sufficient to create a trust[60] and in any event the courts may find expressions used in other parts of the will which may be employed as a guide in construing the precatory words.[61] Romer J summarised the position aptly in *Re Williams*:[62]

> [T]he rule you have to observe is simply this: 'In considering whether a precatory trust is attached to any legacy, the Court will be guided by the intention of the testator apparent in the will, and not by any particular words in which the wishes of the testator are expressed.'

---

57. [1916] 1 IR 21, 24.
58. *Comiskey v Bowring-Hanbury* [1905] AC 84, 89 *per* Lord Davey.
59. [1905] AC 84. See also *Re Burley* [1910] 1 Ch 215.
60. *Re Hamilton* [1895] 2 Ch 370, 373 *per* Lindley LJ and *Re McIntosh* [1933] IR 69, 71 *per* Kennedy CJ. Contrast the decisions of *Re Williams* [1897] 2 Ch 12 where the words 'in the fullest trust and confidence' were insufficient to create a trust in this case, and *Comiskey v Bowring-Hanbury* [1905] AC 84 where the opposite conclusion was reached where the words 'in full confidence' were employed.
61. *Re Blackwood* [1953] NI 32, 46 *per* Black LJ.
62. [1897] 2 Ch 12, 14.

The only situation where the use of identical language to that employed in a previous case may be decisive is where a testator can be shown to have used this particular language as a precedent with the intention of creating a trust. Where this is shown to be the case, it has been held that a trust may be created even though the words themselves, given a modern interpretation, might not otherwise have been held to be sufficient to create a trust.[63]

Where the test of certainty of intention is not complied with, as where precatory words are interpreted as being insufficient to create a trust, the donee will take an absolute gift of the property.[64] This should be contrasted with the situation which arises where the test relating to certainty of objects is not met, in which case a resulting trust arises in favour of the settlor or testator's estate.

Sham Trusts

It should be noted that even where a settlor executes a declaration of trust, the courts may look behind such a declaration at the settlor's intention to ensure that he genuinely meant to create a trust. In *Midland Bank plc v Wyatt*[65] the defendant and his wife purchased a property in their joint names and the defendant subsequently executed a trust deed giving the equity in the house to his wife and daughters. After the defendant's business ran into difficulties he sought to resist the making absolute of a charging order on the property obtained by the bank relying on the declaration of trust. However, the court held that the declaration upon which the defendant sought to rely was void and unenforceable on the basis that it was a sham and that the deed had been executed by the defendant 'not to be acted upon but to be put in the safe for a rainy day'.[66] The court was satisfied that the defendant had never intended to give his children any interest in the property but had merely sought to protect his family from commercial risk. It was also stated that even if the deed was executed without any dishonest or fraudulent motive but was merely entered into on the basis of mistaken advice, it would still be an unenforceable transaction if it was entered into for some ulterior motive.

It is generally accepted that there must be a common intention to mislead and that both the settlor and the trustee must intend that the true arrangement is otherwise than as set out in the trust deed.[67] It was suggested by the court

63. *Re Steele's Will Trusts* [1948] Ch 603. This decision should not be interpreted as authority for the proposition that if a particular form of wording has been held to create a trust, the use of this wording will necessarily without further evidence also create a trust. See the statement in (1968) 32 Conv 361.
64. *Lassence v Tierney* (1849) 1 Mac & G 551.
65. [1995] 1 FLR 696.
66. *Ibid.* at 707.
67. *Grupo Torras SA v Al-Sabah (No. 8)* [2004] WTLR 1 at [53]; *Shalson v Russo* [2005] Ch 281, 341, 342; *A. v A.* [2007] 2 FLR 467, 481. See further Conaglen (2008) 67 CLJ 176, 187.

in *Midland Bank plc v Wyatt*[68] that a transaction will remain a sham even if one of the parties went along with it neither knowing nor caring what he was signing. As Munby J commented in *A. v A.*,[69] '[w]hat is required is a common *intention*, but reckless indifference will be taken to constitute the necessary intention.' While there have been some suggestions elsewhere to the effect that it is the settlor's intentions alone which should determine the matter,[70] it has been accepted by the New Zealand Court of Appeal in *Official Assignee in Bankruptcy v Wilson*[71] that common intention or at least ignorance and recklessness on the part of a trustee is a necessary prerequisite for there to be a sham. Similarly, in *Raftland Pty Ltd v Commissioner of Taxation*,[72] a decision of the High Court of Australia, Kirby J accepted that the requisite intention to mislead must be a common one and that the test for establishing such intention is subjective.

It has also been generally accepted that a trust which was not initially a sham cannot subsequently become one,[73] but that there is no reason in principle why a trust which was set up as a sham should not subsequently lose that character.[74] A useful summary of the principles which operate in this area is contained in the judgment of Munby J in *A. v A.*[75] as follows:

> Whatever the settlor or anyone else may have intended, and whatever may have happened since it was first created, a trust will not be a sham – in my judgment cannot as a matter of law be a sham – if *either*
>
> i) the original trustee(s), *or*
>
> ii) the current trustee(s),
>
> were not, because they lacked the relevant knowledge and intention, party to the sham at the time of their appointment. In the first case, the trust will never have been a sham. In the second case, the trust, even if it was previously a sham, will have become a genuine – a valid and enforceable – trust as from the date of appointment of the current trustee(s).

If this approach is followed in this jurisdiction, it opens up the possibility of the courts looking behind a whole range of trust declarations with a view to examining the settlor's motives in such cases.

68. [1995] 1 FLR 696, 699. See also *Minwalla v Minwalla* [2005] 1 FLR 771, 788.
69. [2007] 2 FLR 467, 485.
70. See Palmer [2007] NZLRev 81, 94.
71. [2008] 3 NZLR 45.
72. (2008) 246 ALR 406, 443. See further Russell and Jones (2009) 15 (6) Trusts and Trustees 498.
73. *Shalson v Russo* [2005] Ch 281, 342; *A. v A.* [2007] 2 FLR 467, 481.
74. *A. v A.* [2007] 2 FLR 467, 482.
75. [2007] 2 FLR 467, 483-484.

Certainty of Subject-Matter

To ensure the creation of a valid express trust, the subject-matter of the trust must be defined with sufficient certainty. As Arden LJ stated in *Lehman Brothers International (Europe) v CRC Credit Fund Ltd*,[76] '[w]here there is no property which is sufficiently identified to form the subject matter of a trust, no trust is created.' This principle applies not just in a general way to the property which should form the subject-matter of the trust, but also requires that the beneficial interests to be taken by the beneficiaries are defined with sufficient clarity, except in a situation where the trustees are given a discretion to decide what the extent of these beneficial interests should be.

While a testator may leave his residuary estate on trust, where a phrase such as 'the bulk of my … residuary estate' is used no trust will be created.[77] One of the most common examples of a trust failing due to lack of certainty of subject-matter is where a testator gives property to an individual and directs that whatever is not required during that individual's lifetime and remains at the time of his death should go to another person or persons.[78] So, where phrases such as 'the remaining part of what is left'[79] or 'such parts of my … estate as she shall not have sold or disposed of'[80] are employed, these gifts will usually fail to take effect.

However, it would be incorrect to assume that gifts described in this way will invariably be considered too uncertain. As Karminski J commented in *Re Last's Estate*:[81]

> In a matter of construction of this kind, it is clearly essential to pay particular attention to the terms of the instrument which is being construed and to avoid too close comparisons with words used in wills in other cases.

There a testatrix left all her property to her brother and directed that 'anything that is left' should go to her late husband's grandchildren. Karminski J quoted with approval the statement of Joyce J in *Re Sanford*[82] to the effect that 'it is better to effectuate than to frustrate the testator's intentions' and held that when the testatrix's brother died intestate, her husband's grandchildren were entitled to the estate in equal shares.

It must be possible to determine with certainty what will constitute the trust property, so vague expressions such as 'remembering always … the Church of God and the poor'[83] will be insufficient. The most usual result where a purported

76. [2010] EWCA Civ 917 at [171].
77. *Palmer v Simmonds* (1854) 2 Drew 221.
78. *Mussoorie Bank Ltd v Raynor* (1882) 7 App Cas 321.
79. *Sprange v Barnard* (1789) 2 Bro CC 585.
80. *Re Jones* [1898] 1 Ch 438.
81. [1958] P 137.
82. [1901] 1 Ch 939, 944.
83. *Curtis v Rippon* (1820) 5 Madd 434.

trust attached to an absolute gift fails due to the uncertainty of its subject-matter is that the donee takes beneficially,[84] but if it is clear that a trust was intended and the only uncertainty relates to the precise shares which the beneficiaries are to take, the trustees will hold the property on a resulting trust. In *Boyce v Boyce*,[85] a testator devised all his houses in a particular location in trust to his wife for life and after her death in trust to convey whichever of these houses was chosen by her to one of his daughters, the other houses to go to another daughter. The daughter who was to have made the selection predeceased the testator and it was held that the trust failed for uncertainty. Had the trustees been given the authority to make the selection this problem could have been averted but in the circumstances the court felt that it had no choice but to find that all the properties should be held on a resulting trust for the testator's estate.

Where an objective criterion which can be applied by the court is provided by a settlor or testator, a failure to quantify precisely the extent of the subject-matter of a trust will not prove fatal to its validity. In *Re Golay's Will Trusts*[86] Ungoed-Thomas J upheld the validity of a gift directing the testator's executors to allow a beneficiary to use a flat during her lifetime and to receive 'a reasonable income' from his other properties. The question which the court had to consider in such a case was 'whether the testator by the words "reasonable income" has given a sufficient indication of his intention to provide an effective determinant of what he intends so that the court in applying that determinant can give effect to the testator's intention.' Ungoed-Thomas J concluded that the yardstick indicated by the testator was what has been objectively identified as a 'reasonable income' and as the court was constantly involved in making such objective assessments, the direction in the will, in his view, could not be defeated on the grounds of uncertainty.

Difficulties have always arisen where a settlor seeks to create a trust of a definite but still unidentified portion of an asset or assets. It was held by Oliver J in *Re London Wine Co. Ltd*[87] that where wine beneficially owned by certain purchasers and stored in a warehouse had not been segregated no trust could arise over it and the purchasers could therefore not assert proprietary rights over the stock against the holders of a floating charge. The view that where the purported subject-matter of a trust is comprised of goods or chattels these must be properly segregated before there can be a valid trust is borne out by the decision of the Privy Council in *Re Goldcorp Exchange Ltd.*[88] In this case the purchasers of bullion which had not been specifically allocated to them failed to establish proprietary rights over it after the company which had possession of it was put into receivership on the basis that there was no ascertained property

84. E.g. *Re Jones* [1898] 1 Ch 438; *Mussoorie Bank Ltd v Raynor* (1882) 7 App Cas 321; *Curtis v Rippon* (1820) 5 Madd 434.
85. (1849) 16 Sim 476.
86. [1965] 1 WLR 969.
87. [1986] PCC 121.
88. [1995] 1 AC 74.

to which a trust could attach.[89] As Lord Mustill commented, '[i]t makes no difference what the parties intended, if what they intend is impossible: as is the case with an immediate transfer of title to goods whose identity is not yet known'.[90]

These decisions were considered by Elias CJ in her judgment in the decision of the Supreme Court of New Zealand in *Proprietors of Wakatu v Attorney-General*,[91] in which she concluded that it was sufficient to establish certainty of subject matter in a case relating to land that the beneficial interest was in a specific portion of a fixed and predetermined area of this land. She expressed the view that she did not consider that these cases establish any rigid rule that a trust can never exist in non-segregated property.[92] Referring to *Re Goldcorp Exchange Ltd*, she suggested as follows:

> [T]he case should not be taken to stand for a general principle that "unascertained" property cannot form the subject matter of a trust. (Indeed, the Board expressly pointed out how that outcome could be achieved.) Rather, it is authority that legal and equitable title to "generic goods" (that is, those that can be sourced from anywhere by the vendor) cannot pass until the goods are positively identified, because until that point "nobody knows to which goods the title relate".[93]

Where the asset in question is of an intangible nature, the courts in England have accepted that a trust may arise in these circumstances. In *Hunter v Moss*[94] it was confirmed that the requirement of certainty of subject-matter in relation to a trust of intangible assets is not based on any immutable principle which demands segregation or appropriation of the specific property which is to form this subject-matter. The trust in that case was comprised of a number of shares in a company which were of their nature indistinguishable from other shares in the same company. They were all equally capable of satisfying the trust and it was unnecessary to identify any particular shares before determining that the subject-matter requirement was satisfied. In these circumstances, Colin Rimmer QC, giving the judgment of the Divisional Court in *Hunter*, was of the view that 'any suggested uncertainty as to subject matter appears to me to

---

89. Although it should be noted that Lord Mustill drew a distinction (at p. 89) between two types of unascertained goods, namely 'generic' goods and those sold 'ex-bulk' which are stipulated to be supplied from a fixed and pre-determined source.
90. *Ibid.* at 90.
91. [2017] 1 NZLR 423.
92. *Ibid.* at 552.
93. *Ibid.* at 554. Glazebrook J also referred to the fact that there is conflicting authority in relation to whether a trust can arise in a case where the property purportedly subject to a trust is undivided but ascertainable. He stated that cases such as *Re London Wine Co.* and *Re Goldcorp* relate to property that is fungible and expressed the view that they are not applicable to land which is in a special category (at 593).
94. [1993] 1 WLR 934 (DC); [1994] 1 WLR 452 (CA).

be theoretical and conceptual rather than real and practical'[95] and his finding that the trust was not void on the grounds of uncertainty of subject-matter was upheld by the Court of Appeal.[96] However, Dillon LJ made no reference to the distinction drawn between tangible and intangible assets at first instance and simply reasoned that 'just as a person can give by will a specified number of his shares in a certain company, so equally, in my judgment, he can declare himself a trustee of 50 of his ordinary shares'.[97]

The decision in *Hunter* was applied by Neuberger J in *Holland v Newbury*[98] in which he held that it was possible to create a trust of a specified number of shares which constituted a part of unidentified shares of a particular class in a company. While Neuberger J pointed out that the decision in *Hunter* was binding on him unless he was satisfied that it was *per incuriam*, he seemed to accept that a distinction might be drawn between tangible and intangible assets for this purpose.[99] In his view the description of the client's wine in *Re London Wine Co. Ltd*[100] and the customer's bullion in *Re Goldcorp*[101] as 'an unascertained part of a mass of goods' was quite apt whereas it would not be an accurate description of the 50 shares in *Hunter* or those in the case before him.

Prior to the decision in *Hunter* it had been assumed in England that trusts of intangible property would only be valid if the settlor declared a trust of his entire interest in the *chose in action* or of a fixed proportion thereof. The decision provoked controversy; Hayton has been particularly critical of the reasoning employed by Dillon LJ and has suggested that the latter's judgment 'should not be regarded as the last word on the subject'.[102] Martin has stated that critics of the *Hunter* decision do not claim that there is any difference between one ordinary share in a company and another but that difficulties could arise in relation to subsequent dealings with the shareholding of which an unsegregated part is subject to a trust.[103] However, she has submitted that the

---

95. [1993] 1 WLR 934, 946.
96. [1994] 1 WLR 452. It would appear that the decision of the Court of Appeal was made after argument had been concluded but before the decision had been given in *Re Goldcorp* [1995] 1 AC 74, see the decision of Neuberger J in *Holland v Newbury* [1997] 2 BCLC 369, 380.
97. *Ibid.* at 459.
98. [1997] 2 BCLC 369.
99. Although Villiers suggests that he was 'lukewarm' in his support for such a distinction, see (1998-99) 9 KCLJ 112, 113.
100. [1986] PCC 121.
101. [1995] 1 AC 74. It could be argued that the bars of gold bullion in *Goldcorp* were indistinguishable from each other. Villiers has suggested that it might be preferable to reconcile *Hunter* with *Goldcorp* on the basis that the latter concerned generic rather than bulk goods, see (1998-99) 9 KCLJ 112, 114.
102. Hayton (1994) 110 LQR 335, 340. Although as he points out, the House of Lords refused leave to appeal in *Hunter*, see [1994] 1 WLR 614.
103. Martin [1996] Conv 223.

solution achieved in *Hunter* is 'fair, sensible and workable'[104] and welcomed the decision as an example of the court's policy of preventing a clearly intended trust from failing for uncertainty.

It should also be noted that a similar conclusion was reached by Campbell J in the decision of the New South Wales Supreme Court in *White v Shortall*,[105] where he concluded that given the nature of shares in a company it is legitimate to regard an individual as having a beneficial interest in a defined number of shares even if it is not possible to identify the individual shares that are held on trust. However, there has been ongoing criticism of the lack of clarity surrounding the underlying rationale for the decision in *Hunter v Moss*, which as Briggs J has commented in *Re Lehman Brothers International (Europe)*[106] has made it difficult to apply the judgment in any case not involving almost identical facts. His preferred analysis is that such a trust works by creating a beneficial co-ownership share in the identified fund rather than seeking to point to a particular part of the fund which the beneficiary owns outright and this approach appears to be the least problematic from a conceptual point of view.[107]

More recently, in the decision of the Court of Appeal in *Wilkinson v North*[108] David Richards LJ stated that he did 'not see a difficulty in a trust of a share of an indivisible asset, such as real property, intellectual property rights or book debts.' He added that there 'would not be an obstacle to a trust of an undivided share of a holding of securities or of a credit balance on a bank account.' In the circumstances he was satisfied that the claimant's beneficial interest would attach not to the designated percentage of a credit balance on a particular date but to that percentage of such fluctuating credit balance as from time to time existed during the currency of the trust. He concluded that while such a trust would not lack certainty of subject matter, serious issues arose to how it was intended to operate and in his view in the matter before the court there was insufficient intention to create a trust.

A final point which should be made about this certainty requirement is that it should not be regarded as existing in isolation and is often closely connected with the requirement of certainty of words. Sir Arthur Hobhouse made this point in *Mussoorie Bank Ltd v Raynor*[109] in the following terms:

> [T]he uncertainty of the subject of the gift has a reflex action upon the previous words, and throws doubt upon the intention of the testator, and

104. *Ibid.* at 227. See also Glister and Lee, *Hanbury and Martin: Modern Equity* (21st ed., 2018) p. 86; Parkinson [2002] CLJ 657, 669.
105. [2006] NSWSC 1379. See also the decision of Yuen J in the Court of First Instance of the High Court of Hong Kong in *Re CA Pacific Finance Ltd* [2000] 1 BCLC 494.
106. [2010] EWHC 2914 (Ch).
107. See further Goode [2003] LMCLQ 379.
108. [2018] 4 WLR 41 at [21].
109. (1882) 7 App Cas 321, 330.

> seems to shew that he could not possibly have intended his words of confidence, hope, or whatever they may be … to be imperative.

Certainty of Objects

The general principle that 'in order to be valid, a trust must be one which the court can control and execute'[110] has led to the development of a considerable body of case law and academic criticism[111] in relation to the certainty requirements which apply to the objects of a trust. The fundamental rule which must be observed in this context is that the objects or beneficiaries of a trust must be defined with a sufficient degree of certainty to enable the trustees, or if necessary the court, to administer the trust according to the settlor's or testator's intentions.[112] The reason that this area of the law remains clouded by such a degree of uncertainty is that the requirements which must be satisfied will depend on whether the instrument being construed is characterised as a trust or a power and in addition may vary according to the nature of the trust involved.

Test for Fixed Trusts

Under the terms of a fixed trust, the interest which each beneficiary is to take is specified in the trust instrument and the trustees have no discretion to determine either who will benefit or the extent of that individual's share. The requirement in this case is that the persons who are to benefit under a trust must be clearly identified or identifiable by the time it comes into operation; 'the trust must have ascertained or ascertainable beneficiaries'.[113] As Pumfrey J stated in *OT Computers Ltd v First National Tricity Finance Ltd*,[114] 'it must be possible to identify each member of the class of beneficiaries. It is not sufficient to be able to say whether or not any identified person is or is not a member of the class entitled to be considered.'

Clearly where property is to be held on trust to be divided amongst the members of a class either in equal or other specified shares, this task cannot be carried out unless it is possible to draw up a complete list of the members of that class.[115] In addition, the class must be defined with sufficient conceptual

110. *IRC v Broadway Cottages Trust* [1955] Ch 20, 30. See also *Daly v Murphy* [2017] IEHC 650 at [19].
111. See in particular, Hopkins [1971] CLJ 68; Emery (1982) 98 LQR 551. See also Harris (1971) 87 LQR 31; Grbich (1974) 37 MLR 643.
112. This principle was referred to in *Daly v Murphy* [2017] IEHC 650 at [19].
113. *Re Endacott* [1960] Ch 232, 246 *per* Evershed MR.
114. [2007] WTLR 165, 174.
115. *IRC v Broadway Cottages Trust* [1955] Ch 20, 29 *per* Jenkins LJ. While Matthews argued in [1984] Conv 22 that there should be no requirement that all the objects be known in the case of a fixed trust and that the proper test should instead be that the description of the beneficiaries be conceptually certain, there is no sign of any judicial or even academic acceptance of this idea. Hayton argues ([1984] Conv 307)

certainty to enable the trustees or, if they fail to act, the court to be able to decide in principle whether or not a given individual is or is not a member of the class.[116] Where this requirement is met it will not be fatal to the validity of a fixed trust that the whereabouts and even the continued existence of a beneficiary cannot be ascertained; provided that their identity as a member of the class is established, their share can be paid into court.[117]

Test for Mere Powers

The donee of a power of appointment is under no duty to exercise it in a particular manner, if indeed he exercises it at all and to this extent his position differs from that of a trustee.[118] Such a donee can only make a distribution amongst the classes of individuals specified by the settlor and the validity of special powers of appointment depends upon the objects of the power being defined with sufficient certainty. While Harman J sought to lay down a test of certainty in *Re Gestetner Settlement*,[119] it gave rise to some confusion as to the precise meaning intended and in subsequent cases the requirement was variously stated as being that a power would be valid if it could be said with certainty whether any given individual fell within the class of objects,[120] or that it was sufficient that any person should be found who clearly came within the class.[121] Much needed clarification of the position came in the form of Lord Upjohn's judgment in the House of Lords in *Re Gulbenkian's Settlements*[122] where he formulated the test as follows:

> A mere or bare power of appointment among a class is valid if you can with certainty say whether any given individual is or is not a member of the class; you do not have to be able to ascertain every member of the class.

---

that this suggestion is based on a misunderstanding of Lord Upjohn's judgment in *Re Gulbenkian's Settlements* [1970] AC 508 and Martin ([1984] Conv 304) also disputes Matthews' suggestion and instead insists that the test for the validity of a fixed trust should continue to be that it should be possible to draw up a list of potential beneficiaries which is on the balance of probabilities complete.

116. See *infra* pp. 108-109.
117. *Re Gulbenkian's Settlements* [1970] AC 508, 524 *per* Lord Upjohn.
118. Although note the *dicta* of Lord Reid in *Re Gulbenkian's Settlements* [1970] AC 508, 518 in relation to the situation which arises where a power is given to trustees as such and where a settlor or testator must be taken to be relying on them in their fiduciary capacity, sometimes referred to as a 'power fiduciary'. See Emery (1982) 98 LQR 551, 580.
119. [1953] Ch 672, 688.
120. *Re Gresham's Settlement* [1956] 1 WLR 573.
121. *Re Gibbard's Settlement Trusts* [1967] 1 WLR 42 and see the judgments of Lord Denning MR and Winn LJ in *Re Gulbenkian's Settlements* [1968] Ch 126, where the former stated at p. 134: 'if the trustees can say of any particular person that he is clearly within the category the gift is good.'
122. [1970] AC 508, 521.

In *Gulbenkian* a settlement contained a power of appointment in favour of an individual 'any wife and his children or remoter issue … and any person or persons in whose house or apartments or in whose company or under whose care and control or by or with whom [he] may from time to time be employed or residing.' The validity of this power was unanimously upheld by the House of Lords, although four of the Law Lords[123] rejected the broader view which had been put forward by Lord Denning MR and Winn LJ in the Court of Appeal to the effect that a power is valid if any one individual clearly falls within its scope. As Lord Upjohn stated, 'the trustees or the court must be able to say with certainty who is within and who is without the power'.[124]

A similar viewpoint was put forward by Murnaghan J in the Supreme Court in *Re Bayley*,[125] where a power of appointment amongst such of the testator's 'Irish relatives' as his sister should appoint was upheld as valid. Murnaghan J stated:

> It is not, I think, necessary for the valid exercise of a power of appointment that the donee should be able to range in his mind every person capable of taking under the power. It is sufficient if the person chosen as an object comes properly within the description of the class amongst which an appointment may be made.[126]

While the Supreme Court did not go as far as following the broader approach adopted by the members of the Court of Appeal and rejected by the House of Lords in *Re Gulbenkian's Settlements*, Murnaghan J did show his willingness to adopt a flexible attitude by stating that the words of Lord Brougham in *Winter v Perratt*[127] laid down in that case with reference to a devise were equally applicable to the construction of a power; namely: 'we ought not, without absolute necessity, to let ourselves embrace the alternative of holding a devise void for uncertainty. Where it is possible to give a meaning, we should give it, that the will of the testator may be operative.'[128]

Test for Discretionary Trusts

In the case of a discretionary trust, trustees are under an obligation to distribute the trust property to the beneficiaries, although they have a discretion to select which members of the class should benefit and to what extent. Trusts in this category are usually created by a settlor with a view to deriving the

123. Lord Donovan reserved his opinion on the issue although he stated that he was inclined to share this view (at 526).
124. [1970] AC 508, 525.
125. [1945] IR 224.
126. *Ibid.* at 229. See also the *dicta* of Budd J in *Re Parker* [1966] IR 308, 318.
127. (1843) 9 Cl & F 606, 687.
128. [1945] IR 224, 230.

tax advantages which result from divesting himself absolutely of the property and often confer a discretion on trustees to benefit a wide class of potential beneficiaries. Another similar concept, although much less common today, is that of a trust power,[129] which involves the court implying the existence of a trust in default of any appointment being made by a donee of a power.

Considerable doubt still surrounds the question of the correct test of certainty in relation to objects to apply to such discretionary trusts in this jurisdiction. Should the test laid down in *Re Gulbenkian's Settlements* in relation to mere powers apply or must the entire class of potential beneficiaries be ascertained or ascertainable in order for the trust to be valid? The test originally applied in England was as formulated by Jenkins LJ in *IRC v Broadway Cottages Trust*,[130] namely that 'a trust for such members of a given class of objects as the trustees shall select is void for uncertainty unless the whole range of objects eligible for selection is ascertained or capable of ascertainment.' Where this test is applied the validity of a disposition may therefore depend on whether it is classified as a trust or a power.[131] The rationale behind such an approach was twofold: first, that a trustee's duty to distribute could only properly be carried out if he had before him a comprehensive list of the potential beneficiaries,[132] and secondly, that if the court was required to make a distribution where the trustees failed to act, it could only do so on the basis of equal division and this would not be possible without a complete list of the potential beneficiaries.[133]

Although the traditional *Broadway Cottages Trust* test for discretionary trusts was approved *obiter* by the majority of the House of Lords in *Re Gulbenkian's Settlements*,[134] a differently constituted House took the opportunity to reformulate the test of certainty the following year in *McPhail v Doulton*.[135] A deed executed by the settlor provided that a fund was to be held on certain trusts for the benefit of the staff of a company and their 'relatives and dependants'. The House of Lords held that the deed created a trust rather than a power and

---

129. Considered *supra* pp. 75-80.
130. [1955] Ch 20, 35-36.
131. Criticised by Harman LJ in *Re Baden's Deed Trusts* [1969] 2 Ch 388, 397 as 'an absurd and embarrassing result'.
132. This rationale was rejected by Stamp LJ in *Re Baden's Deed Trusts (No. 2)* [1973] Ch 9, 27. Although he accepted, as Lord Wilberforce had indicated in *McPhail v Doulton*, that a 'wider and more comprehensive range of inquiry' was necessary in the case of a discretionary trust than in the case of a mere power, he said that provided an appropriate survey was made it did not matter that it was not absolutely complete.
133. This reasoning was adverted to by Lord Hodson in *McPhail v Doulton* [1971] AC 424, 442, although as he pointed out, such a basis for division may lead to absurdity, particularly in the context of a typical modern discretionary trust. Note also the comments of Lord Wilberforce in *McPhail* at 451 where he pointed out that in the case before him equal division was 'surely the last thing the settlor ever intended.'
134. [1970] AC 508, although not by Lord Reid.
135. [1971] AC 424. Lord Wilberforce, Lord Reid and Viscount Dilhorne formed the majority. Lord Guest and Lord Hodson, who had supported the view of the House in *Re Gulbenkian's Settlements*, dissented.

Lord Wilberforce concluded that the test for discretionary trusts 'ought to be similar to that accepted by this House in *Re Gulbenkian's Settlements* for powers, namely, that the trust is valid if it can be said with certainty that any given individual is or is not a member of the class.'[136] When the matter was remitted to the Court of Appeal,[137] the court concluded that the test of certainty had been satisfied in the circumstances of the case and the trust was valid.

Despite these far-reaching developments in England, there is good reason for supposing that in this jurisdiction, certainly in relation to specific types of discretionary trusts, the law remains as formulated in *IRC v Broadway Cottages Trust*. In *Re Parker*[138] the testator's will provided that certain income from a trust was to be divided amongst his 'necessitous nieces and nephews' and their children in such manner as his executors might think fit. Budd J, in holding that the trust was not void for uncertainty, stated that where trustees have a duty to distribute income under a trust it is essential that they know before performing this duty who the beneficiaries are. He formulated the test as follows:

> [A]n imperative trust for the division of income between such members of the class as the trustees may select is invalid unless the whole class of potential beneficiaries can be ascertained.[139]

This view was approved, albeit in an *obiter* context, by Murphy J in *O'Byrne v Davoren*.[140] The testatrix's will provided that the residue of her estate should be held on trust for the post-primary education of such members of a class consisting of the children, grandchildren and direct descendants of named persons whom the trustees in their discretion should decide would be most likely to benefit therefrom. Murphy J was satisfied that the gift was sufficiently certain but held that it was void because it infringed the rule against perpetuities and the rule against perpetual trusts. Nevertheless, it is interesting to compare the view which he expressed on the question of certainty with those put forward by the House of Lords in *McPhail v Doulton*. Murphy J commented that not only was the judgment of Budd J a precedent of greater authority than that of the House of Lords but he also preferred the reasoning in the former case, namely that an imperative trust for the division of income between such members of a class as the trustees may select is invalid unless the whole class of potential beneficiaries can be ascertained. Murphy J added that he approved Budd J's view to the effect that difficulties in interpretation should not be sufficient to render a gift void for uncertainty; as Budd J had said 'to be void for this reason

136. *Ibid.* at 456. As Lord Walker stated in the decision of the Privy Council in *Schmidt v Rosewood Trust Ltd* [2003] 2 AC 709, 734, 'the differences in this context between trusts and powers are … a good deal less significant than the similarities.'
137. *Re Baden's Deed Trusts (No. 2)* [1973] Ch 9.
138. [1966] IR 308.
139. *Ibid.* at 318.
140. [1994] 3 IR 373.

it must be utterly impossible to put a meaning on it'.[141] Murphy J concluded that the court should endeavour to resolve ambiguities and uncertainties where this was compatible with the expressed or implied wishes of the testator and concluded that this view would have been of decisive importance in upholding the validity of the residuary bequest if the class of relatives had been confined to those living at the date of the testatrix's death.

It can be argued that from a global perspective the *McPhail* approach is much more likely to lead to at least partial fulfilment of a testator's intentions in these circumstances, for the alternative is that the trust will fail for uncertainty. As against this it can also be said that the approach adopted in this jurisdiction, provided an effort is made to give effect to a testator's intentions in as liberal a manner as possible, is more likely to lead to a division of the trust property or income in equal shares amongst *all* potential beneficiaries. However, it is submitted that for a court in this jurisdiction to consider itself faced with a stark choice between the *McPhail* and *Parker* approaches, irrespective of the nature of the discretionary trust involved, is unduly simplistic. As noted above, the rationale of the need for equal division which seems to lie behind *Parker* is far from suitable in the case of many modern discretionary trusts and is based rather on the type of 'trust powers' so common in the nineteenth century.[142] Perhaps before deciding which test is to be preferred in a given case, the question of how the court would exercise its discretion where the trustees fail to do so should be addressed.[143] Where the testator's intentions are likely to be fulfilled by equal division amongst all the potential beneficiaries, clearly the certainty requirement laid down in *Parker* is to be preferred. However, as the judgment of Lord Wilberforce in *McPhail* made clear, this is no longer the case in relation to many modern discretionary trusts which are designed to benefit a much wider class of beneficiary and it is difficult to fault the conclusion reached in the latter case on the basis of the nature of the trust involved.

Clearly such a flexible approach will itself lead to uncertainty and may be as undesirable as a rigid application of principle which fails to take into account the nature and circumstances of a discretionary trust. While it would be impossible to predict how the courts in this jurisdiction will resolve the dilemma, it is to be hoped that they will at least have regard to some of the pragmatic arguments advanced above.

Conceptual and Evidential Certainty

Irrespective of the nature of the trust or power involved,[144] the description used to define the class of potential beneficiaries must be conceptually certain. In some instances, the concepts employed to describe this class may be so precise

141. [1966] IR 308, 320.
142. E.g. *Burrough v Philcox* (1840) 5 My & Cr 72.
143. See Emery (1982) 98 LQR 551, 569.
144. *Re Sayer* [1957] Ch 423, 432 *per* Upjohn J.

that it is most unlikely that any uncertainty could arise, e.g. 'son' or 'daughter'. On the other hand there will be many cases where the terminology used is far from being free from some element of uncertainty, e.g. 'relative' or 'friend'. So, as a general rule, whether one is dealing with a fixed or discretionary trust, the class must be defined with sufficient conceptual certainty to enable the trustees, or if necessary the court, to determine theoretically whether any given individual is or is not a member of that class. Where the words used are sufficiently precise to satisfy this test of conceptual certainty in principle, the question of who falls within this description is a matter of fact. As Sachs LJ commented in *Re Baden's Deed Trusts (No. 2)*,[145] 'it is essential to bear in mind the differences between conceptual uncertainty and evidential difficulties'. This latter concept of evidential certainty relates to the practical question of whether it is possible to establish as a matter of fact that a given individual does or does not fall within the defined class; in the words of Sachs LJ: 'once the class of persons to be benefited is conceptually certain it then becomes a question of fact to be determined on the evidence whether any postulant has on inquiry been proved to be within it; if he is not so proved then he is not in it.'[146]

The point has been made that 'to insist on complete certainty would be to defeat most gifts'[147] and the courts have displayed a relatively flexible attitude towards this issue, as for instance in *Re Baden's Deed Trusts (No. 2)*,[148] where the Court of Appeal accepted that there was no conceptual uncertainty in the words 'relatives' and 'dependants'. Similarly, in *Gold v Hill*[149] Carnwath J rejected the submission that a trust for a named woman with whom the deceased had lived and 'the kids' was insufficiently precise. While he acknowledged that there was potential ambiguity in the words used as the deceased had a number of children from different relationships, in his view the general intention was clear, namely to provide for his partner and her children.

It would appear that the conceptual certainty required in the case of trusts for members of a class subject to the fulfilment of a condition precedent is not as strict, although arguably this is difficult to justify. In *Re Barlow's Will Trusts*[150] a testatrix directed her executors 'to allow any members of my family and any friends of mine who may wish to do so' to purchase any of her paintings at a reduced price. Browne-Wilkinson J upheld the validity of the gift as it was 'possible to say of one or more persons that he or they undoubtedly qualify even though it may be difficult to say of others whether or not they qualify.'[151]

145. [1973] Ch 9, 19.
146. *Re Baden's Deed Trusts (No. 2)* [1973] Ch 9, 20.
147. Glister and Lee, *Hanbury and Martin: Modern Equity* (21st ed., 2018) p. 92.
148. [1973] Ch 9.
149. [1999] 1 FLR 54.
150. [1979] 1 WLR 278.
151. *Ibid.* at 281.

Administrative Unworkability and Capriciousness

Even where a class is defined with sufficient conceptual certainty a trust may still fail for uncertainty 'where the definition of the beneficiaries is so hopelessly wide as not to form "anything like a class" so that the trust is administratively unworkable.'[152] This ground of uncertainty was put forward by Lord Wilberforce in *McPhail v Doulton*,[153] where he suggested that perhaps a discretionary trust for 'all the residents of Greater London' might prove invalid for this reason. While there is no conceptual uncertainty in such a description and it would be theoretically possible to say with certainty whether any given individual is or is not a member of that class, it would arguably not be possible for trustees to exercise their discretion in such a manner so as to give effect to a settlor's intentions when dealing with such a huge number of potential beneficiaries. A discretionary trust in favour of 'any or all or some of the inhabitants of the County of West Yorkshire' was found to be invalid for this reason in *R. v District Auditor, ex p. West Yorkshire Metropolitan County Council*,[154] on the grounds that the definition of the beneficiaries was, in the phraseology used by Lord Wilberforce, so hopelessly wide as to be incapable of forming anything like a class. Similarly, it was suggested by Lewison J in *Re Harding*[155] that a trust for 'the black community' in four London boroughs would be so large as to be unworkable and therefore would have been void had it not been upheld as a valid charitable trust.

It should be noted that while administrative unworkability may invalidate a discretionary trust, the weight of authority[156] supports the view that it will not affect the validity of a mere power. The statement of Templeman J in *Re Manisty's Settlement Trusts*[157] that 'a power cannot be uncertain merely because it is wide in ambit' found favour with Megarry VC in *Re Hay's Settlement Trusts*,[158] where the latter concluded that he did not see how mere numbers could inhibit the donees of a power from considering whether or not to exercise it.

While it has been suggested that this notion of basing a finding of uncertainty on the concept of administrative unworkability is 'incapable of solid justification on the basis of either administrative feasibility or judicial execution',[159] arguably it is a logical and necessary extension of the requirement of evidential certainty. Hardcastle suggested that while the court will not normally permit difficulties in ascertainment to defeat execution of a trust, a point may be reached where its

152. *McPhail v Doulton* [1971] AC 424, 457 *per* Lord Wilberforce.
153. [1971] AC 424. See also the *dicta* of Lord Eldon in *Morice v Bishop of Durham* (1805) 10 Ves 522, 527.
154. (1986) 26 RVR 24.
155. [2008] Ch 235.
156. Although note the contrary view expressed by Buckley LJ in *Blausten v IRC* [1972] Ch 256.
157. [1974] Ch 17.
158. [1982] 1 WLR 202.
159. See McKay (1974) 38 Conv 269, 284.

performance 'becomes an exercise in futility ... when a potentially innumerable class of beneficiaries is coupled with a total lack of provable definitional criteria'.[160]

Another related concept which may form the basis for a finding of uncertainty is that of capriciousness. While the same set of circumstances, such as Lord Wilberforce's example of all the residents of Greater London may at the same time give rise to a finding of administrative unworkability and capriciousness, the latter concept has no necessary connection with width of numbers which is an essential characteristic of the former. A further important distinction which should be drawn is that the notion of capriciousness has been held to apply to mere powers. In *Re Manisty's Settlement Trusts*[161] Templeman J commented that 'a capricious power negatives a sensible consideration by the trustees of the exercise of the power' and contrasted this with a 'wide power' which 'does not negative or prohibit a sensible approach by the trustees to the consideration and exercise of their powers.' So where a settlor seeks to benefit 'an accidental conglomeration of persons'[162] who have no discernible link with him, it may be unrealistic to seek to give effect to his intentions and the instrument, whether construed as a trust or a power, may be found to be invalid on the grounds of capriciousness.

160. Hardcastle [1990] Conv 24, 33.
161. [1974] Ch 17, 27.
162. *Re Manisty's Settlement Trusts* [1974] Ch 24, 27 *per* Templeman J.

CHAPTER 5

Secret Trusts

INTRODUCTION

As we have already seen in relation to trusts created *inter vivos*, equity will not always insist on strict compliance with the statutory formalities required when this would result in a statute being used as an instrument of fraud.[1] Similarly, the statutory formalities which must normally be complied with to create a valid trust which is to take effect after a testator's death may in some circumstances be waived to give effect to what has become known as a 'secret trust'. A fully secret trust usually arises where a testator makes a gift of property to a named person in his will without expressly stating that the latter is to hold it on trust. If either before or after making his will, but during his lifetime, he informs the legatee that he wishes him to hold the property on trust for a third party or for a particular purpose and the legatee either expressly or by his silence impliedly agrees to do so, then he will be bound by the trust.[2] A half secret trust, on the other hand, is said to exist where it is clear from the will that the legatee is to hold the property on trust but neither the terms of the trust nor the identity of the beneficiaries are disclosed in the will.

Historically, the reason for the creation of such trusts was to allow a testator to make provision for a mistress or an illegitimate child or another person whom he wished to benefit for some reason without his family or the world at large being aware of the gift. While this is rarely necessary today, a testator may still employ this device, often to prevent having to specify with precision at the time of making a will how he intends his property to be distributed.[3] The practice of giving effect to secret trusts created for such a purpose has been criticised[4] as it effectively allows a testator to bypass the statutory requirements laid down in relation to the execution of wills where the need for secrecy is not present. However, certainly in the case of a fully secret trust, fraud may still

1. See *supra Rochefoucauld v Boustead* [1897] 1 Ch 196; *McGillycuddy v Joy* [1959] IR 189; *Gilmurray v Corr* [1978] NI 99.
2. Such a trust can also arise where an individual refrains from making a will on the basis of a promise made by his intestate successor that he will carry out the former's wishes, see *Sellack v Harris* (1708) 5 Vin Abr 521 and note the comments of Lord Westbury in *McCormick v Grogan* (1869) LR 4 HL 82, 97.
3. A recent survey conducted into the use of secret trusts by Meager [2003] Conv 203 concludes that 'there is clearly a demand for an instrument which enables testators to make bequests secretly' (at 212).
4. Watkin [1981] Conv 335, 338.

result if effect is not given to these trusts and the principles governing their enforcement are likely to be considered as being too firmly established now to be disregarded for policy reasons.[5]

FULLY SECRET TRUSTS

Historically, the dilemma faced by the courts in deciding whether to enforce a fully secret trust was this: should it be permissible for a testator to disregard or bypass the statutory formalities laid down in relation to testamentary dispositions or should a legatee be permitted to take a gift beneficially when it was clearly intended by a testator to be held on trust? The conclusion reached was that equity should intervene to prevent the perpetration of a fraud[6] and the practice of giving effect to secret trusts developed. The next question was, should the legatee merely hold the property on a resulting trust for the testator's estate, which would be sufficient to prevent fraud, or should the courts go a step further and actually enforce the trust in favour of the beneficiary? It was decided to adopt the latter course and while the avoidance of fraud probably formed the basis for such a development, it is now often justified on the grounds that the testator had declared a valid trust *inter vivos* which merely became constituted on his death by virtue of the testamentary gift to the legatee.[7]

From a practical perspective, it may be of relevance to note that where a testator leaves property to A in his will on the understanding that he will hold it for the benefit of B on a secret trust, B's interest is not considered to have arisen by virtue of the will. This is illustrated in *Cullen v Attorney General for Ireland*,[8] where a residuary legacy was left to an individual to hold it on a secret trust for the benefit of a charity. Although a testamentary gift in favour of a charity would have qualified for an exemption from certain taxes, the House of Lords held that this tax was payable because the testamentary gift was construed as having been made to the individual; 'the charity has no place, and is not to be

---

5. Although Challinor has argued [2005] Conv 492, 493 that the 'continued existence [of the doctrine of secret trusts] divorced from its original function and context, can no longer be justified'. She expresses the view (at 500) that: 'fraud would be better prevented by an insistence upon compliance with the requirements of the Wills Act'.
6. See *McCormick v Grogan* (1869) LR 4 HL 82, 97; *French v French* [1902] 1 IR 172, 230.
7. However, as Kincaid points out [2000] Conv 420, 442, a secret trust relies on the death of the settlor to constitute the trust and the terms of the will or the rules of intestate succession to vest the property in the hands of the secret trustee or legatee. It is generally accepted that a secret trust remains unconstituted until its subject matter is vested in the trustee upon the testator's death. As Pawlowski and Brown point out [2004] Conv 388, 397 this means that a secret beneficiary's expectations will be frustrated if a testator revokes the secret trust during his lifetime unless the former can establish detrimental reliance rendering it unconscionable for the testator to renege on the representations made which would support a claim based on proprietary estoppel.
8. (1866) LR 1 HL 190. See also *Revenue Commissioners v Stapleton* [1937] IR 225.

found either in anything that is expressed in the will, or in anything that is so referred to in the will.'[9] The most important practical result of this principle that such a trust is not regarded as being a testamentary disposition is that a beneficiary will not forfeit his interest merely because he has witnessed the testator's will.[10] Therefore, in *O'Brien v Condon*[11] it was held that a witness to a will was not precluded from benefiting from a secret trust on the grounds that 'what she takes under the trust is something not under the will, but solely by virtue of the secret trust, not disclosed on the will.'[12]

Despite this theoretical independence from the will, the beneficiaries' interests are still dependent on the validity of the initial testamentary disposition.[13] If a testator makes a gift to a legatee in his will intending him to hold it on trust for another and the legatee predeceases the testator, the legacy and therefore the secret trust will fail.[14] However, there is some authority to support the proposition that even if the beneficiary predeceases the testator, his heirs will take the interest created by the secret trust on the testator's death provided that he was alive at the time when the undertaking to enforce the trust was given by the legatee.[15]

To create a valid fully secret trust, the testator must intend to create a trust and its terms must be communicated to the legatee and accepted by him

9. *Ibid.* at 199 per Lord Westbury. However, see Critchley's criticism of this decision and more generally of the 'dehors the will' theory (1999) 115 LQR 631, 641.
10. Section 82 of the Succession Act 1965 provides that a witness to a will may not take a benefit under it.
11. [1905] 1 IR 51. See also *Re Young* [1951] Ch 344, 350 *per* Danckwerts J: 'the whole theory of the formation of a secret trust is that the Wills Act 1837 has nothing to do with the matter.'
12. *Ibid.* at 58 *per* Porter MR.
13. As Viscount Sumner commented in *Blackwell v Blackwell* [1929] AC 318, 334: 'the doctrine must in principle rest on the assumption that the will has first operated according to its terms.'
14. *Re Maddock* [1902] 2 Ch 220, 231 *per* Cozens-Hardy LJ. See further Kincaid [2000] Conv 420, 439-440. On the question of whether a secret trust can be defeated by a secret trustee purporting to renounce or disclaim the legacy, there are conflicting *obiter* statements in *Re Maddock* [1902] 2 Ch 220, 231 (to the effect that renunciation or disclaimer is possible) and *Blackwell v Blackwell* [1929] AC 318, 328 (to the effect that once evidence of the trust is admitted the court would ensure that it could not be renounced). See further Glister [2014] Conv 11, who argues that a legacy cannot be disclaimed in these circumstances.
15. *Re Gardner* [1923] 2 Ch 230. As Wylie has pointed out (see *Irish Land Law* (4th ed., 2010) p. 590) the reasoning in *Gardner* seems to ignore the fact that the trust is unlikely to be completely constituted at this point and some doubt must be cast on the validity of such a proposition for this reason. See also Kincaid [2000] Conv 420, 431-439.

during the testator's lifetime.[16] Brightman J expressed these requirements in the following terms in *Ottaway v Norman*:[17]

> The essential elements which must be proved to exist are: (i) the intention of the testator to subject the primary donee to an obligation in favour of the secondary donee; (ii) communication of that intention to the primary donee; and (iii) the acceptance of that obligation by the primary donee either expressly or by acquiescence.

As Hammond J commented in the New Zealand decision of *Brown v Pourau*,[18] communication of the deceased's intention to create a secret trust is an essential factor because otherwise the devisee can quite reasonably argue that he took the will to mean precisely what it said on its face. Hammond J was of the view that once communication was established, acceptance, though also crucial, could in an appropriate case be inferred from the silence of the devisee. This principle had been laid down in the following terms by Lord Davey in *French v French*,[19] from whose judgment Hammond J quoted with approval:

> It is now well established, and has been settled since the time of Lord Hardwicke, that if a testator communicates in his lifetime to a proposed devisee or legatee that he has left him his property, and expresses a wish that the property should be disposed of in a particular manner, and the legatee or devisee by acquiescence, or even by silence accepts that communication, and the testator dies without any repudiation, a trust is fastened upon his conscience.

Any attempt to communicate the testator's intention after his death, for example by written instructions, will be ineffective as the legatee's conscience will not be affected by the trust at the time the will becomes effective. As Fleming has stated, 'it is not the unilaterally expressed intention of the testator, but the conduct of the legatee in inducing the former, on the faith of his promise, to make or revoke his will, which calls the equitable doctrine into operation.'[20] However, where a testator gives the legatee a sealed envelope during his lifetime containing precise instructions about the terms of the trust and it is not opened until after the testator's death, this will be sufficient to give rise to a trust provided the legatee agrees in principle to carry out its terms during the

16. In the words of Viscount Sumner in *Blackwell v Blackwell* [1929] AC 318, 334 there must be 'intention, communication and acquiescence'.
17. [1972] Ch 698, 711. See also *Kasperbauer v Griffith* [2000] WTLR 333; *Margulies v Margulies* Court of Appeal, 16 March 2000.
18. [1995] 1 NZLR 352. See further Rickett [1996] Conv 302.
19. [1902] 1 IR 172, 230.
20. Fleming (1947) 12 Conv 28, 29.

testator's lifetime.[21] On the other hand, where a testator merely informs the legatee that he intends him to hold the property on trust but does not disclose its terms prior to his death, no secret trust will be created. This will also be the case where it is established that the testator intended to create a trust and the trustee accepted the obligation but the trust fails for some other reason, e.g. because the beneficiaries are unascertainable.[22] Similarly where a legatee agrees to comply with a testator's directions with regard to a trust during the latter's lifetime, but these instructions only come to light following the testator's death.[23] In these situations where the evidence establishes that the testator intended a trust and that the legatee undertook to give effect to it, the legatee will hold the gift on a resulting trust for the testator's estate.[24] However, where the testator never communicated any intention to the legatee during his lifetime that the latter was to hold the legacy on trust, the legatee will take beneficially.[25]

The onus lies on the person seeking to show the existence of a secret trust[26] to establish this on the balance of probabilities. While earlier authorities suggested that a higher standard of proof would be required,[27] it was established in *Re Snowden*[28] that the ordinary civil standard of proof applies. In that case Megarry VC suggested *obiter* that this standard might be higher if any question of fraud arose,[29] although as Keane points out, the Supreme Court has rejected the suggestion that any higher burden of proof should be placed on a plaintiff where an allegation of fraud is made in a civil case.[30]

Secret Trusts Involving Joint Tenants and Tenants in Common

A question which must also be addressed is whether a secret trust will arise

---

21. *Re Boyes* (1884) 26 Ch D 531, 536 and *Re Keen* [1937] Ch 236, 242. See also where the legatee had signed the document containing the testator's instructions although she had not seen its contents; *Morrison v McFerran* [1901] 1 IR 360.
22. See *Brown v Pourau* [1995] 1 NZLR 352.
23. *Re Boyes* (1884) 26 Ch D 531.
24. For the residuary devisees or legatees or if there is no residuary gift, assuming that the residue is the subject-matter of a secret trust, for those entitled on an intestacy.
25. *Wallgrave v Tebbs* (1855) 2 K & J 313.
26. *Jones v Badley* (1868) 3 Ch App 362.
27. *McCormick v Grogan* (1869) LR 4 HL 82, 97 *per* Lord Westbury.
28. [1979] Ch 528, 537. See also *Taylor v Revenue and Customs Commissioners* [2008] STC (SCD) 1159 at [29]; *Davies v Revenue and Customs Commissioners* [2009] WTLR 1151 at [27]. This standard seems to have been accepted elsewhere in the common law world, e.g. see *Quinn v Dean* High Court, Wellington, A 123/84 30 July 1986. The formula adopted by Dixon CJ in his dissenting judgment in *Voges v Monaghan* (1954) 94 CLR 231, 233 was of establishing the elements of the trust 'to the reasonable satisfaction of the court'. Both these formulae were considered by Hammond J in the New Zealand High Court decision of *Brown v Pourau* [1995] 1 NZLR 352.
29. For a criticism of this suggestion, see Rickett [1979] CLJ 260. See also Rickett [1996] Conv 302, 307.
30. Keane, *Equity and the Law of Trusts in Ireland* (3rd ed., 2017) p. 110. See *Banco Ambrosiano SPA v Ansbacher & Co. Ltd* [1987] ILRM 669.

and who will be bound by it where a testamentary gift is made to more than one person but the testator's intentions with regard to the creation of a trust are not communicated to all of these persons during his lifetime. The traditional approach as set out by Farwell J in *Re Stead*[31] involves drawing a distinction between the position of legatees who hold as joint tenants and as tenants in common:

> If A. induces B. either to make, or to leave unrevoked, a will leaving property to A. and C. as tenants in common, by expressly promising or tacitly consenting, that he and C. will carry out the testator's wishes, and C. knows nothing of the matter until after B.'s death, A. is bound, but C. is not bound. … If however the gift were to A. and C. as joint tenants, the authorities have established a distinction between those cases in which the will is made on the faith of an antecedent promise by A. and those in which the will is left unrevoked on the faith of a subsequent promise. In the former case the trust binds both A. and C., … the reason stated being that no person can claim an interest under a fraud committed by another; in the latter case, A. and not C. is bound, … the reason stated being that the gift is not tainted with any fraud in procuring the execution of the will.

On the basis of this statement it seemed that in the case of tenants in common, only those to whom the testator's intentions were communicated during his lifetime were bound and that any other person took free of the trust and was entitled to his share beneficially. However, in the case of joint tenants, a distinction was drawn between a situation where one or more of these joint tenants had accepted the trust prior to the execution of the will and where the acceptance did not take place until after this. In the former case, all the joint tenants were bound and in the latter case only those who had accepted the secret trust were affected by it. Farwell J himself appeared unconvinced by the drawing of such a seemingly arbitrary distinction and admitted that he was unable to see the difference between 'a gift left unrevoked on the faith of antecedent promise and a gift left unrevoked on the faith of a subsequent promise'.[32]

Similar sentiments were expressed by Walker LJ in the Irish Court of Appeal in *Geddis v Semple*,[33] although as the case before him concerned tenants in common, it was not necessary for him to reach any conclusion on the issue. At the time the testator in *Geddis* executed his will, the effect of section 16 of the Charitable Donations and Bequests (Ireland) Act 1844 was to render void gifts of land for charitable purposes unless the testator's will had been executed at least three months prior to his death.[34] With the intention of avoiding

31. [1900] 1 Ch 237, 241. See also the *dicta* of Monroe J in *Re King's Estate* (1888) 21 LR Ir 273, 278.
32. *Ibid.* at 241.
33. [1903] 1 IR 73.
34. This provision was repealed by s. 4 of the Charities Act 1961.

this statutory restriction, the testator devised certain houses and a pecuniary legacy charged on land to three individuals as tenants in common, although at the time the will was executed only one of these individuals was aware of the testator's intention to create a secret trust for a charitable purpose. The Irish Court of Appeal held that while the gift to the individual who knew of the testator's wishes must fail, the other tenants in common, who knew nothing of the intended trust until after the testator's death, became beneficially entitled to their shares. However, there is a suggestion in the judgment of Walker LJ that an 'innocent' tenant in common might be bound in such circumstances if it could be established that the testator was induced to make the gift by the promise of a co-tenant on the basis of the principle laid down in *Huguenin v Baseley*[35] that 'no man may profit by the fraud of another'.

This inducement theory was developed by Perrins who has suggested that Farwell J in *Re Stead* misinterpreted the authorities relied on to support the general principles set out above.[36] In Perrins' view, the only question to which the court must address itself in such circumstances is whether the gift to the legatee who was unaware of the testator's intention to create a secret trust was induced by the promise of the legatee who knew of his intentions in this regard to carry out his wishes. If this approach is accepted, issues such as whether the legatees take as joint tenants or tenants in common and whether the promise was made prior to or after the execution of the will are merely matters of evidence which may be of assistance to the court in deciding on the question of inducement but will not of themselves determine the issue.[37]

There is certainly considerable merit in Perrins' views,[38] and on the basis of the comments of Walker LJ in *Geddis v Semple* they will probably be followed in relation to a situation of tenants in common. Although there is no authority to support this approach in the case of joint tenants, Wylie has put forward the suggestion that a court might regard the creation of a secret trust as severing a joint tenancy, thus allowing the principle of inducement to operate in any event.[39] Until this question is resolved by the courts the result must remain a matter of speculation, but it is submitted that the most equitable result would be to follow the approach laid down by Perrins.

35. (1807) 14 Ves 273.
36. Perrins (1972) 82 LQR 225.
37. As Perrins points out, as a matter of evidence it may be easier to show inducement in the case of a gift to joint tenants and clearly where a secret trust is not communicated to any of the co-tenants until after the testator's death it will be difficult, if not impossible, to show that the gift to the other was induced by any promise made.
38. This is the approach taken in Hayton, Matthews and Mitchell, *Underhill and Hayton: The Law Relating to Trusts and Trustees* (19th ed., 2016) p. 365 although the view is expressed in Glister and Lee, *Hanbury and Martin: Modern Equity* (21st ed., 2018) p. 152 that while the argument is persuasive the case law suggests otherwise.
39. Wylie, *Irish Land Law* (4th ed., 2010) p. 587.

HALF SECRET TRUSTS

A half secret trust arises where a testator leaves property to an individual in a will and expressly directs that this individual is to hold the property on trust without specifying the terms of the trust. The principal advantage to be gained from employing this form of secret trust is that the possibility of the legatee taking the property beneficially and successfully perpetrating a fraud is avoided as it is clear from the face of the will that a trust was intended.[40] However, where a testator manifests his intention to create a trust in this way, the historical justification for non-compliance with the statutory formalities required in the case of secret trusts, namely the prevention of fraud, does not apply as it is clear from the face of the will that a trust is intended.[41] Perhaps for this reason, the courts have adopted a more stringent attitude towards the enforcement of half secret trusts and an examination of the case law in this area in the last century, particularly in England, shows a marked reluctance on the part of the judiciary to overlook non-compliance with the provisions of the Wills Act in the absence of any likelihood of fraud.

This trend was reversed in Ireland by the decision of *Riordan v Banon*[42] and although Chatterton VC acknowledged that 'the same kind of fraud cannot operate'[43] in the case of trusts which appear on the face of the will, he was prepared to extend this principle to half secret trusts as the result of a refusal to enforce such trusts would be to defeat the expressed intention of the testator. In *Riordan*, the testator's will directed that a legacy be disposed by the legatee 'in a manner of which he alone shall be cognizant, and as contained in a memorandum which I shall leave with him'. Prior to executing his will the testator had verbally informed the legatee that he intended to leave the legacy for a named person whom he did not wish to identify in his will and it was

40. So, where a half secret trust fails for any reason the legatee will hold the property on a resulting trust.
41. Virgo, *The Principles of Equity and Trusts* (3rd ed., 2018) pp. 116-117 puts forward the useful suggestion that if fraud were interpreted as also encompassing unconscionable conduct, this broader rationale could form the basis for the enforcement of half secret trusts. In his view the communication, acceptance and reliance could operate as a form of estoppel which would make it unconscionable for the legatee not to carry out the undertaking which he has given.
42. (1876) IR 10 Eq 469.
43. *Ibid.* at 473. Although Chatterton VC also commented (at 478) that the principle which led the courts to hold that the Statute of Frauds and the Wills Act were not to be used as instruments of fraud appeared to apply to cases such as that before him where the will showed that some form of trust was intended.

accepted that the legatee had agreed to carry out this obligation.[44] Chatterton VC held that a valid secret trust had been created.[45] He stated:

> The result of the cases appears to me to be that a testator cannot by his will reserve to himself the right of disposing subsequently of property by an instrument not executed as required by the statute, or by parol; but that when, at the time of making his will, he has formed the intention that a legacy thereby given shall be disposed of by the legatee in a particular manner, not thereby disclosed, but communicated to the legatee and assented to by him, at or before the making of the will, or probably, according to *Moss v Cooper*, subsequently to the making of it, the Court will allow such trust to be proved by admission of the legatee, or other parol evidence and will, if it be legal, give effect to it.[46]

To be valid a half secret trust, like a fully secret trust, must be communicated to and accepted by the legatee prior to the testator's death.[47] This requirement has been strictly enforced as in *Re Watters' Will Trusts*,[48] where a testator directed that his property should be applied for 'charitable purposes and objects known to my executors'. After executing his will but during his lifetime, the testator had a number of general conversations with one of his executors about the manner in which he wished his assets to be applied but failed to specify precisely the particular purposes or objects which he intended to benefit. A memorandum found after his death which contained such specific directions was held not to be admissible as there had not been sufficient communication and acceptance of the trust prior to the testator's death.[49]

One question which has led to considerable controversy and to an apparent divergence in the law as it applies in England and Ireland is whether there can be effective communication and acceptance of a half secret trust after the execution of the testator's will. As can be observed from the portion of Chatterton VC's judgment in *Riordan* set out above, he commented in that decision that such subsequent communication was 'probably' acceptable and this principle was reiterated by Monroe J in the course of his judgment in *Re*

44. One difficulty with this interpretation to which Chatterton VC did not refer was the possibility of inconsistency between the terms of the statement in the will which pointed to some form of subsequent communication and what the court accepted had actually transpired, i.e. communication and acceptance prior to the execution of the will. This ground of inconsistency is considered in more detail *infra*.
45. See also *Re Ellis* (1919) 53 ILTR 6.
46. (1876) IR 10 Eq 469, 477-478.
47. *Scott v Brownrigg* (1881) 9 LR Ir 246.
48. (1928) 62 ILTR 61. There was no evidence to suggest that the trust failed on the grounds of inconsistency. See further *infra* pp. 124-125.
49. Although in the circumstances as a general charitable intention had been manifested by the verbal communication, an order was made that a scheme for the application of the assets should be directed by the court.

King's Estate.[50] While on the facts of that case no secret trust of any nature arose, Monroe J laid down a number of propositions, drawn from the relevant authorities,[51] which it is useful to set out in full:

1. A testator cannot reserve to himself the right of declaring trusts by an instrument informally executed subsequent to the execution of his will. This would be to repeal the statute of wills.
2. If a testator at or before the execution of his will communicate to a person to whom he proposes to give a legacy that the legacy is given upon trust to be applied in a particular way, and if the legatee expressly or tacitly consents to take the legacy on these terms, the Court of Chancery will not permit him to be guilty of a fraud, but will compel the execution of the trust so communicated.
3. This rule applies whether the existence of the trust be indicated on the face of the will, or the legacy by the terms of the instrument be given absolutely.
4. The rule applies when the communication is made subsequently to the execution of the will: *Moss v Taylor*.[52]
5. It is essential to the creation of a valid trust that the communication should be made to the legatee in the testator's lifetime, and that the legatee should not object to execute the trust.
6. If the bequest be to two or more legatees, a valid trust is created if the communication be made to any one of them, before or at the time of the execution of the will. If the communication be made after the execution of the will, it must be made to all the legatees on whom the trust is sought to be imposed.
7. The terms in which the trust is expressed must not be vague or uncertain.[53]

Further confirmation that communication and acceptance of a half secret trust may validly occur after execution of a testator's will provided this is done during his lifetime can be found in the judgment of Overend J in *Re Browne*.[54] Although Overend J found that the reference in the will before the court to the testator's wishes was too ambiguous to disclose a trust on the face of the will and instead decided to enforce a fully secret trust on the basis of the latter's wishes expressed to the legatee during his lifetime, he suggested *obiter* that

50. (1888) 21 LR Ir 273.
51. *Riordan v Banon* (1867) IR 10 Eq 469; *Re Fleetwood* (1880) 15 Ch D 594; *Scott v Brownrigg* (1881) 9 LR Ir 246; *Re Boyes* (1884) 26 Ch D 531.
52. More commonly known as *Moss v Cooper* (1861) 1 J & H 367.
53. (1888) 21 LR Ir 273, 277-278. Quoted with approval by Barron J in *Prendiville v Prendiville* [1995] 2 ILRM 578, 583.
54. [1944] IR 90. Although note the conclusion reached in *Balfe v Halpenny* [1904] 1 IR 486.

that even if he had found the existence of a half secret trust, it would have been immaterial that the trusts in question were communicated to the legatee after the execution of the will so long as they were communicated to him and accepted by him during the testator's lifetime.

The courts in England have not accepted the principle of subsequent communication and indeed it was not until the decision of the House of Lords in *Blackwell v Blackwell*[55] that the validity of half secret trusts was finally recognised in that jurisdiction. A testator gave a sum of money on trust to legatees to apply the income thereof 'for the purposes indicated by me to them' in a codicil to his will. Detailed instructions were given to one of the trustees and the others accepted these terms in outline before execution of the codicil. Viscount Sumner recognised that a half secret trust existed which arose independently of the will: 'it is communication of the purpose to the legatee, coupled with acquiescence or promise on his part, that removes the matter from the provision of the Wills Act and brings it within the law of trusts'.[56] In the course of his speech Viscount Sumner also laid down the following fundamental principle:

> A testator cannot reserve to himself a power of making future unwitnessed dispositions by merely naming a trustee and leaving the purposes of the trust to be supplied afterwards, nor can a legatee give testamentary validity to an unexecuted codicil by accepting an indefinite trust, never communicated to him in the testator's lifetime. ... To hold otherwise would indeed enable the testator to 'give the go-by' to the requirements of the Wills Act, because he did not choose to comply with them.[57]

This statement, although it is in some respects in line with a number of the propositions set out by Monroe J in *Re King's Estate*, has been subsequently interpreted in England as authority for the proposition that the communication and acceptance of a half secret trust cannot be effective if made after the execution of a will. In *Re Keen*[58] a testator gave a legacy to trustees 'to be held upon trust and disposed of among such person, persons or charities as may be notified by me to them or either of them during my lifetime'. Before executing this will the testator had given a sealed envelope to one of the trustees containing the name of the intended beneficiary which the court accepted as 'notification'. The provision in the will was interpreted as the reservation of a power by the testator to make future testamentary dispositions in a manner which would be contrary to section 9 of the Wills Act 1837. However, in the view of Lord

55. [1929] AC 318.
56. *Ibid.* at 339. Quoted with approval by Barron J in *Prendiville v Prendiville* [1995] 2 ILRM 578, 583.
57. *Ibid.* at 339. See also the *dicta* of Parker VC in *Johnson v Ball* (1851) 5 De G & Sm 85, 91.
58. [1937] Ch 236.

Wright MR, even if such subsequent communication had been permitted, the trust would have failed independently on the grounds of inconsistency. On the facts of the case, communication and acceptance of the trust had taken place prior to the execution of the will, when the sealed envelope was handed over, and this was plainly inconsistent with its terms which provided for a future definition of the terms of the trust. While there has been a certain amount of confusion and academic debate about the true *ratio* of *Re Keen*,[59] it was re-affirmed in England in *Re Bateman's Will Trusts*[60] that communication and acceptance of a half secret trust must take place prior to the execution of the will.[61] This view was also accepted on an *obiter* basis in *Re Freud*,[62] although the trust in the matter before the court was found to be fully secret in nature.

It is interesting to note that a refusal to accept the principle of subsequent communication in the context of a half secret trust has more recently manifested itself elsewhere in the common law world. In *Jankowski v Pelek Estate*[63] the majority of the Manitoba Court of Appeal found that the evidence disclosed the existence of a fully secret trust which in their view was valid as communication and acceptance of it had taken place during the testator's lifetime. However, Huband JA was satisfied that any trust intended was a half secret one as there was no possibility that the intended legatee might fraudulently retain the legacy as his own and in his view the rules relating to the enforcement of such trusts are 'much more stringent'. He continued as follows:

> Specifically there must be communication of the terms of the trust to the proposed trustee before or contemporaneously with the making of the will. The word 'contemporaneously' in this context means 'at the same time'. It cannot include 'shortly after'. To have it otherwise would allow

---

59. See the judgment of Barron J in *Prendiville v Prendiville* [1995] 2 ILRM 578; Coughlan (1991) 5 Trust Law Int 69; Mee [1992] Conv 202. Huband JA suggests in the course of his dissenting judgment in *Jankowski v Pelek Estate* (1995) 131 DLR (4th) 717 that *Re Keen* is authority for the proposition that the nature of trust instructions must be consistent with the wording of the will.
60. [1970] 1 WLR 1463. However, it should be noted that in *Gold v Hill* [1999] 1 FLR 54, which concerned the analogous situation of a nomination under a life insurance policy, Carnwath J was prepared to treat communication effected after the execution of the will as valid. He stated that: 'Such doubts as there may be, in the case of testamentary dispositions, as to the effectiveness of an intention communicated after the execution of the will, appear to be derived from the particular rules applying to wills.'
61. This has been justified by Perrins [1985] Conv 248 on the basis that extrinsic evidence of prior communication is admissible as it does not contradict the terms of the will whereas to allow evidence of subsequent communication would be 'to give the go-by' to the Wills Act even where there is no danger of fraud. The suggestion has even been made that this stricter requirement should also apply to fully secret trusts, see Watkin [1981] Conv 335, 340. See also Wilde [1995] Conv 366.
62. [2014] EWHC 2577 (Ch) at [16].
63. (1995) 131 DLR (4th) 717.

> the testator to add to the terms of the will after its execution, in a form which does not comply with statutory requirements.[64]

He concluded that in the case before him the fact that the instructions regarding the trust were given after the will was executed was fatal to its enforcement and said that this could not be redeemed by the fact that these instructions were communicated only minutes after the execution of the will. In his view 'the effect is the same whether the time differential is a few minutes, a few hours, a few weeks or a few years'. This seemed a particularly harsh conclusion to reach and resulted, as Huband JA himself acknowledged, in the intentions of the testatrix being frustrated by purely technical reasons.

The opportunity to resolve the question of whether communication and acceptance of a half secret trust must take place before the execution of the will in order for it to be valid in this jurisdiction was presented to the High Court in the case of *Prendiville v Prendiville*.[65] There, the testator left his estate to his wife for life 'to be used by her according to my wishes — as she has been advised'. Before he died the testator had told one of his sons that he had written out his wishes as to the passing of his estate after his wife's death and had shown him a document containing these instructions which included the provision that a named residence and lands were to be offered for sale to another son at a reasonable valuation. Following the testator's death, his wife made a statutory declaration acknowledging that her husband's instructions had been communicated to and accepted by her. After her death a dispute arose between the next of kin of the testator and the son in whose favour the option to purchase had been made as to whether an enforceable secret or half secret trust existed. Barron J said that *Re Keen* had been relied on as an authority for the proposition that a half secret trust could not be established unless its terms were communicated and accepted prior to the execution of the will. He felt that this proposition could not be taken from that case, which, in his opinion, turned on the construction of the particular clause in the will and the issue of inconsistency. Barron J concluded that the principles of law to be applied to secret and half secret trusts are the same and were those as set out by Monroe J in *Re King's Estate*.[66] He held that in the case before him, a trust existed on the face of the will and found there was sufficient evidence that the terms of the trust in relation to the option to purchase the house had been communicated by the testator to his wife and accepted by her during his lifetime.

Although this judgment would appear to confirm the correctness of the *obiter* views on the timing of communication and acceptance of a half secret trust referred to above, *Prendiville* is not an entirely satisfactory authority for

---

64. *Ibid.* at 730.
65. [1995] 2 ILRM 578.
66. (1888) 21 LR Ir 273. Note that Wilde has asserted in [1995] Conv 366 that there is a justification for the distinctions drawn by the courts between secret and half secret trusts.

a number of reasons. Barron J failed to identify precisely the time at which communication and acceptance of the trust occurred although he did find that this had taken place at some stage during the testator's lifetime. The use of the words 'as she has been advised' would suggest that such communication was intended to take place either before or at the time of execution of the will and yet one must ask why Barron J took the trouble to refute the suggestion that *Re Keen* was authority for the proposition that communication must occur prior to the will, unless on the facts of the case before him, communication did not take place until after its execution.[67] Because of his failure to be more specific about the timing of these events, it is therefore still not clear whether Barron J's rejection of the need for prior communication forms part of the *ratio* of the case. A further possible flaw in his judgment is the failure to address the potential problem of inconsistency. As Andrews has pointed out, the most important requirement with regard to half secret trusts is the need for careful construction, and communication in some other form or at a time other than that contemplated in the will cannot be permissible as it will lead to an attempt to contradict its express terms.[68] Barron J appeared to endorse this ground of inconsistency as being the basis for the decision in *Re Keen* and yet, if as his rejection of the wider ground for that decision suggests, communication in the case before him took place after the execution of the will, this would itself lead to inconsistency with the terms of the instrument.[69] Another simpler explanation is that Barron J was merely clarifying that in his view the *ratio* for the decision in *Re Keen* was based on the inconsistency issue and that he did not make the comments about this decision because he felt it necessary to do so in order to determine the matter before him. On this interpretation, the communication and acceptance in the matter before the court in *Prendiville* could well have taken place before the will was executed and this would mean that there was no inconsistency with its terms and what transpired in practice.

While some questions remain about the basis for the decision in *Prendiville*, it does appear to confirm that in Ireland it is permissible for communication and acceptance of a half secret trust to take place after the execution of a will but during a testator's lifetime provided it does not contradict the terms of the will. Certainly, the view of Barron J that the principles to be applied to fully and half secret trusts should be the same has much to commend it and is based

67. Coughlan (1991) 5 Trust Law Int 69, 72-73.
68. Andrews (1963) 27 Conv 92, 99.
69. See Coughlan (1991) 5 Trust Law Int 69, 73; Mee [1992] Conv 202, 205. It would appear that the possibility of inconsistency was also effectively ignored by Chatterton VC in *Riordan v Banon* (1876) IR 10 Eq 469 and by Meredith J in *Re Watters' Will Trusts* (1928) 62 ILTR 61. However, it appeared to be accepted by Huband JA in his dissenting judgment in *Jankowski v Pelek Estate* (1995) 131 DLR (4th) 717 that inconsistency between the instructions given and the scheme of the will would be fatal. There is probably merit in Mee's argument that inconsistency should be overlooked where it is merely inadvertent (see *infra* n.71).

on sound practical arguments.[70] The passing of the beneficial interest in respect of either type of trust is not a testamentary disposition and so it should not be relevant whether communication and acceptance of the trust occurs prior to the execution of the will.[71] This argument is reinforced if one accepts the modern justification for the enforcement of secret trusts and on this basis the approach of the Irish courts cannot be faulted either on policy grounds.[72]

THE JURIDICAL NATURE OF SECRET TRUSTS

As we have already seen,[73] a secret trust is not considered to have arisen by virtue of a testator's will. While to an extent its existence is dependent on the validity of this instrument and in particular on the disposition which is to form the subject-matter of the trust, it is considered to arise 'dehors' the will.[74]

A related question which has provoked considerable debate, and which can have practical significance, is whether secret trusts are express or constructive in nature. Clearly, if they are characterised as express, where land forms the subject-matter of the trust there should be compliance with the statutory formalities.[75] Fully secret trusts have been variously characterised as implied[76] or sometimes express[77] in nature but the predominant view seems to be that they are constructive and are imposed on a legatee to prevent him from abusing the fiduciary obligations which he assumed on giving an undertaking to the testator that he would enforce the trust.[78] This conclusion would appear to be supported

---

70. It would seem arbitrary to draw a distinction when the overriding reason for enforcing such half secret trusts is to give effect as far as possible to the testator's intention to create a trust. For a view of the academic arguments favouring such an approach, see Holdsworth (1937) 53 LQR 501 and Sheridan (1951) 67 LQR 413.
71. Mee [1992] Conv 202, 206 suggests that where inconsistency occurs as a result of mere inadvertence it would be 'unnecessary and unjust' to base a finding of invalidity on this ground.
72. It is interesting to note that Young J in a decision of the Supreme Court of New South Wales in *Ledgerwood v Perpetual Trustee Co. Ltd* (1997) 41 NSWLR 532 followed *Prendiville v Prendiville* rather than *Re Keen*. Having considered the relevant authorities and academic commentary in some detail, he concluded that: 'I cannot get away from the view that the Irish position is the one which carries out the policy of this part of the law, that is, that it is against the conscience of the donee that the donee should be permitted to have undertaken to the testatrix to carry out her wishes and then not to have done so.'
73. See *supra* pp. 113-114.
74. However, note that Critchley (1999) 115 LQR 631, 641 has suggested that the 'dehors' theory seems to be fatally flawed and that the mistake is to confuse 'outside the will' with 'outside the Wills Act'.
75. See *supra* Chapter 4.
76. Burgess (1972) 23 NILQ 263, 268-273.
77. Perrins [1985] Conv 248, 254. See also Wilde [1995] Conv 366, 371 and Rickett [1996] Conv 302, 305 and 308.
78. Andrews (1963) 27 Conv 92, 98. See also Sheridan (1951) 67 LQR 314, 327.

by the decision in *Ottaway v Norman*,[79] where a fully secret trust of land was upheld as valid on the basis of oral evidence, although it would be incorrect to place too much emphasis on this decision as the issue of the nature of the trust and the need for compliance with the statutory formalities was not discussed. Secret trusts were also characterised as constructive in nature by Patten LJ in *De Bruyne v De Bruyne*,[80] who commented that in such cases although the intended beneficiary does not rely in any sense on an agreement, equity will regard it as against conscience for the owner of the property to deny the terms on which he received it.

Half secret trusts on the other hand have tended to be accepted as being a species of express trust. Support for this proposition is derived from *Re Baillie*[81] where a half secret trust was held not to be enforceable in the absence of adequate written evidence. Burgess has argued that this decision actually turned on the lack of evidence to establish the terms of the trust and that the very essence of a secret trust is that it operates in spite of the requirements as to form.[82] While there is merit in the arguments put forward by Burgess, the most widely held view is that half secret trusts are express in nature. However, more recently it has been suggested that when a secret trust arises the court is imposing trusteeship on the recipient of the gift on the basis that it would be unconscionable for this individual to retain an absolute interest in the property and that 'consequently, the imposition of a secret trust falls four-square within the test for a constructive trust as set out by Lord Browne-Wilkinson in *Westdeutsche Landesbank v Islington Borough Council*'.[83]

The issue of the classification of secret trusts as express or constructive was raised again in the New Zealand decision of *Brown v Pourau*[84] in which Hammond J had to consider whether an oral secret trust of land could be valid. He stated that whatever the correct theoretical explanation, the reported English decisions appeared to recognise that a fully secret trust of land could be valid independent of any requirement of written evidence. In his view contemporary New Zealand jurisprudence required the court to inquire into the obligation which it was being asked to uphold and then make an evaluation of the remedy which would best support or advance that obligation. Applying this reasoning, he concluded that the court should support the intended trust by using a constructive trust as a remedy.[85] While Hammond J's judgment therefore fails to resolve the express/constructive issue in the context in which it has arisen

79. [1972] Ch 698. See also *Healey v Brown* [2002] WTLR 849.
80. [2010] 2 FLR 1240.
81. (1886) 2 TLR 660.
82. Burgess (1972) 23 NILQ 263.
83. Thomas and Hudson, *The Law of Trusts* (2nd ed., 2010) p. 823.
84. [1995] 1 NZLR 352.
85. It should be noted that Rickett [1996] Conv 302 is critical of Hammond J's reasoning and asserts that a secret trust is express in nature and therefore, where necessary, must satisfy the formal requirements in relation to trusts of land. She points out quite correctly (at 306) that if judges persist – as Hammond J did in *Brown v Pourau* – in

in England and in this jurisdiction, it confirms the practical point that for the purposes of compliance with the Statute of Frauds, fully secret trusts can be treated as constructive in nature.

So although this issue of the juridical basis of secret trusts remains to an extent uncertain, it should be remembered that even if a secret trust is characterised as express, compliance with the formality requirements will not be enforced where this would lead to the perpetration of a fraud in a broad sense. This is in line with the views expressed by Virgo who suggests that in relation to a trust of land, regardless of whether it is a fully or half secret trust, it should be valid even if it is not evidenced in writing because 'the trustee's conduct, in consciously allowing the testator to leave them the land in the expectation that the trustee will hold it on trust for another, means that the trustee should not be allowed to use the formality requirements of the Law of Property as an instrument of fraud.'[86]

applying the test of certainty laid down for express private trusts, it is a strong argument in favour of using the express rather than the constructive trust label.

86. Virgo, *The Principles of Equity and Trusts* (3rd ed., 2018) p.113.

CHAPTER 6

Constitution of Trusts

INTRODUCTION

A trust is said to be completely constituted when the trust property has been vested in the trustees for the benefit of the beneficiaries; a trust remains incompletely constituted until this is done. The practical importance of identifying when a trust has been completely constituted lies in the fact that as a general principle, equity will not enforce or perfect an incompletely constituted trust in favour of a volunteer.[1] However, a completely constituted trust will be enforceable at the suit of the beneficiaries irrespective of whether or not they are mere volunteers. This different attitude adopted by equity towards the enforcement of completely and incompletely constituted trusts was summed up by Lord Eldon in *Ellison v Ellison*[2] as follows:

> I take the distinction to be, that if you want the assistance of the Court to constitute you *cestui que trust*, and the instrument is voluntary, you shall not have that assistance for the purpose of constituting you *cestui que trust*; as upon a covenant to transfer stock etc., if it rests in covenant, and is purely voluntary, this Court will not execute that voluntary covenant; but if the party has completely transferred stock etc., although it is voluntary, yet the legal conveyance being effectually made, the equitable interest will be enforced by this Court.

To fully understand the practical implications of this distinction a number of issues must be examined. First, the circumstances in which a trust may be regarded as completely constituted must be clarified and secondly, the question of who will be regarded as a volunteer has to be addressed. Finally, it is necessary to examine the alternative remedies open to beneficiaries of an incompletely constituted trust who are regarded as mere volunteers.

1. *McArdle v O'Donohoe* [1999] IEHC 176 at 17. See also *Re Wilson* [1933] IR 729, 739. Similar principles apply in relation to imperfect gifts.
2. (1802) 6 Ves 656, 662.

COMPLETE CONSTITUTION OF A TRUST

An express trust may be completely constituted either by a transfer of property to trustees to be held on certain trusts, by will or *inter vivos*, or by a settlor declaring himself to be trustee of his own property for the benefit of specified beneficiaries. Since it is important to recognise whether a voluntary trust has been completely constituted if it is to be enforced, it is necessary to set out in some detail the manner in which this may be achieved. These principles were summarised by Turner LJ in the decision of *Milroy v Lord*[3] as follows:

> I take the law of this Court to be well settled, that, in order to render a voluntary settlement valid and effectual, the settlor must have done everything which, according to the nature of the property comprised in the settlement, was necessary to be done in order to transfer the property and render the settlement binding upon him. He may of course do this by actually transferring the property to the persons for whom he intends to provide, and the provision will then be effectual, and it will be equally effectual if he transfers the property to a trustee for the purposes of the settlement, or declares that he himself holds it in trust for those purposes; and if the property be personal, the trust may, as I apprehend, be declared either in writing or by parol, but in order to render the settlement binding, one or other of these modes must, as I understand the law of this Court, be resorted to, for there is no equity in this Court to perfect an imperfect gift.

Transfer of Trust Property

In order to completely constitute a trust by this method, there must be an effective transfer of the property to be included in the trust and an intention on the settlor's part to bring about such a transfer will not suffice. This is illustrated by the decision of O'Donovan J in *McArdle v O'Donohoe*,[4] in which the settlor purported to execute a deed of settlement to make provision for his adopted daughter and her children. O'Donovan J stated that he was satisfied that at the time the deed was executed, it was the settlor's intention that £200,000 invested in a bond would form part of the trust fund. The issue which O'Donovan J had to decide was whether this sum invested in the bond constituted part of the trust fund as defined in the deed of settlement or whether it remained the personal property of the defendant settlor. He concluded that the settlor had never effectively transferred any monies or property which might be included in the 'trust fund' as defined in the deed of settlement and that the trust created by the deed of settlement was not completely constituted. O'Donovan J quoted

3. (1862) 4 De GF & J 264, 274.
4. [1999] IEHC 176.

with approval the following *dicta* of Johnston J in *Re Wilson*, made in the context of an incomplete gift where similar principles apply:[5]

> A gift is a gift, and, of course if a donor, while expressing an intention to give something and taking certain steps in the direction of giving it, has not gone the whole way, the expectant donee has no equity to compel the completion of the gift. It is good sense and good law.

O'Donovan J held that as the trust was not completely constituted,[6] equity would not compel the completion of an incompletely constituted trust in the absence of valuable consideration. He therefore concluded that the sum of £200,000 invested by the settlor in the bond did not constitute part of the trust fund as defined by the deed of settlement but remained his personal property.

It was suggested by Abbott J in *C.C. v N.C.*[7] that there is a lack of clarity in the case law in relation to the question of whether property which is to form the subject matter of a trust must be fully and validly transferred into the ownership of trustees to administer it for the benefit of the beneficiaries. In reality, unless any of the exceptions outlined below apply, a trust will not be regarded as fully constituted where no valid transfer has been effected or declaration of trust made. This was the finding of the court in the *C.C.* case where Abbott J concluded that no steps had been taken to vest the trust property in trustees.

If a trust is to be validly constituted by transfer, it is necessary to comply with whatever formalities apply to the method employed to effect this. A trust created by will can only be regarded as completely constituted provided that the relevant statutory formalities have been complied with. Similarly, where the transfer is effected *inter vivos*, the formalities applicable to the type of interest being transferred must be observed. So where, for example, the subject matter of the trust is a legal estate in unregistered land the transfer must be effective to vest this interest in the trustee and will therefore usually require the execution of a deed. Where the trust property comprises an equitable interest, it will be completely constituted provided that a valid assignment of that interest to the trustees takes place.[8]

In *Milroy v Lord*[9] a settlor executed a voluntary deed purporting to transfer shares in a bank to be held on trust for the plaintiff. Such a transfer could only be properly effected by registration of the name of the transferee in the bank's records. While the trustee held a power of attorney to act on the settlor's behalf, he failed to register the transfer. The Court of Appeal held that no enforceable trust in favour of the plaintiffs had been created.

5. [1933] IR 729, 739.
6. O'Donovan J also held that the settlor had never expressed an intention to constitute himself a trustee. See further *infra* p. 136 *et seq*.
7. [2012] IEHC 615.
8. *Kekewich v Manning* (1851) 1 De GM & G 176; *Re McArdle* [1951] Ch 669.
9. (1862) 4 De GF & J 264.

It should be noted that the statement of Turner LJ in *Milroy* set out above to the effect, *inter alia*, that in order to ensure that a trust is completely constituted, the settlor must have done everything which it is necessary to do to effect the transfer,[10] is subject to some qualification in the following circumstances. Where the settlor has done everything in his power to transfer the title to the property but cannot ensure compliance with some formality which is outside his control, the trust will nevertheless be regarded as completely constituted. In *Re Rose*,[11] a settlor executed a voluntary deed which purported to transfer shares in a private company to trustees but died before the transfer was registered by the company's directors. The question arose whether the settlor was still the owner of the shares at the time of his death for the purpose of determining whether estate duty was payable. The Court of Appeal held that as the settlor had done all in his power to divest himself of the shares, although he remained in law the owner until the transfer was registered, in equity the transfer was regarded as being effective from the date of the deed. The reasoning in *Re Rose* has been criticised[12] and it has been argued that it is difficult to distinguish the circumstances of the case from those in *Re Fry*,[13] in which a donor was not regarded as having done everything in his power to effect a transfer of shares as it could not be registered without treasury consent.

The principle laid down in *Re Rose* has been applied subsequently in England in *Mascall v Mascall*[14] in the context of a transfer of registered land and in *Brown & Root Technology Ltd v Sun Alliance and London Assurance Co. Ltd*,[15] which concerned the assignment of a leasehold interest which had not yet been registered. In *Mascall* the plaintiff had executed a transfer of a property with registered title to his son but before the necessary documents had been sent to the Land Registry for registration, the plaintiff changed his mind about the transfer. The Court of Appeal held that there had been an effective gift to the son; as Lawton LJ commented, 'the plaintiff had done everything in his power to transfer the house to the defendant'.[16] In *Brown & Root* the first named plaintiff, the original lessee, served a notice purporting to terminate the lease after an assignment to the second named plaintiff, its parent company, had taken place but before it had been registered at the Land Registry. The court refused the first named plaintiff a declaration that the notice served was

10. It was suggested by Griffiths CJ in *Anning v Anning* (1907) 4 CLR 1049, 1057 that the words 'necessary to be done' as used by Turner LJ in *Milroy v Lord* mean necessary to be done by the donor.
11. [1952] Ch 499.
12. Sheridan (1955) 33 Can Bar Rev 284 and McKay (1976) 40 Conv 139. See also Lowrie and Todd [1998] CLJ 46.
13. [1946] Ch 312. See also *Pehrsson v Von Greyerz* [1999] UKPC 26.
14. (1984) 50 P & CR 119. However, note the comments of Ollikainen-Read [2018] Conv 63, who suggests that the rule in *Re Rose* should only apply to cases that are analogous to a trustee/beneficiary relationship.
15. [1996] Ch 51.
16. (1984) 50 P & CR 119, 125.

valid to terminate the lease on the basis that the date on which the assignment took place was the date upon which it was completed and so the lease could not have been determined by a notice served by this plaintiff. Paul Barker QC, sitting as a Deputy High Court judge, reiterated that the leading case in this area is *Milroy v Lord* but pointed out that there are exceptions to the rule that 'an attempted but ineffectual or uncompleted conveyance or transfer of property to trustees to hold on certain trusts would not be enforced at the suit of a volunteer'.[17] He accepted the defendant's submission that if it was necessary to fix a date on which the assignment took place, this was the date upon which it was completed. As he pointed out, 'the tenant/assignor gives up the property on that date; he has no control over the stamping of the transfer, or its submission to the Land Registry'.[18]

However, *Re Rose* was distinguished by the Court of Appeal in *Zeital v Kaye*,[19] in which it held that a purported gift of a share in a company, in which the deceased transferor had a beneficial interest, failed in circumstances in which he had neither completed nor dated a share transfer form. Rimer LJ stated that the principle in *Re Rose* required that the deceased should have done all within his power to secure the transfer of the share, but in his view he had not done this and the gift failed as an imperfect one.

In *Pennington v Waine*[20] the Court of Appeal took the opportunity to consider the exception to the principle in *Milroy v Lord* set out in cases such as *Re Rose*[21] in some detail. The donor wanted to transfer shares in a company to her nephew, the second named defendant, and to make him a director of it. The articles of association of this company required that in order for an individual to become a director he must hold at least one share in it. The company's auditors informed the second named defendant of the share transfer and he signed a form of consent to act as a director which was countersigned by the donor. The donor signed a share transfer form but it was retained by the company's auditors and was not sent to the second named defendant. Following the donor's death, in an action brought by her executors, the residuary beneficiaries under her will sought a determination of whether there had been a valid equitable transfer of the shares. Howarth J held that the gift had become effective once the share transfer form was signed and that it was not necessary for the form to have been delivered either to the second named defendant or the company for the gift to be complete. The Court of Appeal agreed that delivery of the share transfer certificate to the donee or the company was not required for there to have been a valid equitable assignment of the shares to the second named defendant. Arden LJ stated that there was a clear finding that the donor

17 [1996] Ch 51, 65.
18 *Ibid.* at 68.
19. [2010] WTLR 913. See further Griffiths [2010] Conv 321. See also *Curtis v Pulbrook* [2011] EWHC 167 (Ch).
20. [2002] 1 WLR 2075.
21. [1952] Ch 499.

intended to make an immediate gift and that a stage had been reached when it would have been unconscionable for her to recall it.[22] In her view delivery of the share transfer before the donor's death was unnecessary so far as the perfection of the gift was concerned.

Clarke LJ agreed that the appeal should be dismissed and held that the execution of the share transfer form took effect as an equitable assignment without the need for delivery. He said that he did not think that the conclusion reached was inconsistent with any of the decided cases like *Milroy v Lord* as in those cases there had been no completed documents evidencing a present transfer of the donor's beneficial interest. He referred to the decision of the Privy Council in *T. Choithram International SA v Pagarani*,[23] in which Lord Browne-Wilkinson had highlighted the contrast between the maxims that equity will not aid a volunteer and that it will not strive officiously to defeat a gift. In his view, if equity refused to help the second named defendant in the case before the court, it would be preferring the former maxim to the latter in a situation where all the circumstances of the case led to the conclusion that it should give effect to the gift which the donor intended. Clearly both judges were in favour of a flexible interpretation being given to the exception to the proposition set out in *Milroy v Lord* and as Arden LJ noted, 'the principle against imperfectly constituted gifts [has] led to harsh and seemingly paradoxical results'.[24]

Garton has commented that 'the effect of *Pennington v Waine* should not be seen as introducing a new exception to the rule against perfecting imperfect gifts; rather it is an opportunity to recast *Re Rose* in a theoretically sound fashion by shifting the focus away from the extent of the formalities completed and into the conscience of the transferor.'[25] He expresses the view that the introduction of the notion of unconscionability in this context has the potential to mitigate the harshness of legal formalities but equally recognises that there is a burden on the courts 'to ensure that the concept is not used in such a way as to grant judges an unfettered discretion to perfect imperfect transactions in an arbitrary and unpredictable fashion.'[26] Halliwell also criticised the decision as representing 'unfettered judicial discretion'[27] and argued that the concept of

22. In contrast, in *Jordan v Roberts* [2009] EWHC 2313 (Ch) it was held that there was no basis for saying that it would be unconscionable to allow a purported donor to refuse to complete a gift of shares in circumstances where no instrument of transfer had ever been executed by her. The court was satisfied that she had not attempted to make a gift which should be viewed as having been perfected or which it would have been inequitable for her to resile from.
23. [2001] 1 WLR 1.
24. [2002] 1 WLR 2075, 2087.
25. Garton [2003] Conv 364, 376.
26. *Ibid.* at 379. Garton adds (at 374) that the introduction of the concept of unconscionability in the absence of any attempt to define what it means in this context or to provide a test for its use gives the court a wide discretion to interfere in incomplete transactions and render them effective.
27. Garton [2003] Conv 192, 200.

unconscionability, while valuable, must be based on principled reasoning. A number of other commentators have criticised the imprecision inherent in the reasoning employed by Arden LJ in *Pennington*[28] and the uncertainty which her use of unconscionability gives rise to[29] and indeed have questioned the justification for employing the concept at all.[30] However, provided the courts heed the words of caution expressed by Robert Walker LJ in *Jennings v Rice*[31] in relation to employing unconscionability, namely that they 'cannot exercise an unfettered discretion according to the individual judge's notion of what is fair in any particular case', it does provide a potential mechanism for perfecting what might otherwise remain an imperfect gift in a manner which effectuates rather than frustrates the clear intention of the donor.

Debate is likely to continue about the basis for the decision in *Pennington v Waine*. Subsequently, in *Curtis v Pulbrook*[32] Briggs J referred to the three routes identified by Arden LJ as 'as methods whereby a court of equity might temper the wind to the shorn lamb' in this context:

> The first is where the donor has done everything necessary to enable the donee to enforce a beneficial claim without further assistance from the donor: see paragraphs 55 to 56 and *Rose v. Inland Revenue Commissioners* [1952] Ch 499. The second is where some detrimental reliance by the donee upon an apparent although ineffective gift may so bind the conscience of the donor to justify the imposition of a constructive trust: see paragraph 59. The third is where by a benevolent construction an effective gift or implied declaration of trust may be teased out of the words used: see paragraphs 60 to 61, apparently based upon *Choithram International SA v. Pagarani* [2001] 1 WLR 1.[33]

Briggs J expressed the view that *Pennington v Waine* appeared to have been an example of sufficient detrimental reliance by the donee, who had agreed to become a director of the subject company upon an assumption that he had received an effective gift of qualifying shares in it. In contrast, on the facts of the case before him, there was no evidence of 'any acts or omissions … in reliance (let alone detrimental reliance) upon having received an apparent gift, so that there is no basis upon which [the defendant] could be treated as a constructive trustee.'[34] While the judgment of Clarke LJ in *Pennington* characterised the trust which arose as express in nature, Arden LJ's reasoning, which appears to be

28. Ladds (2003) 17 Trust Law Int 35, 38.
29. Tijo and Yeo [2002] LMCLQ 296, 303.
30. Doggett [2003] CLJ 263, 266.
31. [2003] 1 P & CR 8.
32. [2011] EWHC 167 (Ch). See further Luxton [2012] Conv 70.
33. *Ibid.* at [43].
34. *Ibid.* at [46].

based on treating the trust as constructive, may as Virgo suggests, be 'consistent with the recognition of the principle of unconscionability.'[35]

The approach taken in these English decisions appears to confirm the *obiter* view expressed in this jurisdiction in *Devoy v Hanlon*.[36] There the owner of registered land executed a voluntary deed transferring land to his son, but the transfer was not registered and was therefore ineffective. He subsequently devised the land to his daughter in his will and she was then registered as the owner. The son's claim to the land failed but only because he could not prove that the deed of transfer was ever delivered. The implication was that the court would have been willing to hold that the son, who was a volunteer and to whom the legal interest had not been transferred, would have been entitled to the land if he could have proved that the deed had been delivered. Once registered, the gift would have been completely constituted and could have been enforced even by a volunteer.

It follows from the proposition that a completely constituted trust is enforceable by a volunteer that such a trust is binding on a settlor and his personal representatives and will be irrevocable unless an express power of revocation is reserved at the time of its constitution. In *Re Bowden*[37] a settlor by means of a voluntary settlement agreed to convey to trustees all the property to which she might become entitled under her father's will. She knowingly allowed this transfer to take place and it was held by Bennett J that she could not subsequently reclaim the property held on trust. As the trust was completely constituted, the fact that the settlement was voluntary did not affect its validity or enforceability. It should also be noted that in England there appears to be authority to support the proposition that a trust may be considered as completely constituted when property is vested in trustees even though it did not come into their possession in their capacity as trustees of that particular trust.[38]

Declaration of Trust by Settlor

The alternative method of completely constituting a trust is for a settlor to declare himself a trustee of property for the benefit of third parties. Neville J made it clear in *Re Cozens*[39] that 'where a declaration of trust is relied on the Court must be satisfied that a present irrevocable declaration of trust has been made.'[40] Traditionally, it has been accepted that there must be a clear

35. Virgo, *The Principles of Equity and Trusts* (3rd ed., 2018) p. 131.
36. [1929] IR 246.
37. [1936] Ch 71. See also *Paul v Paul* (1882) 20 Ch D 742.
38. *Re Ralli's Will Trusts* [1964] Ch 288. However, note the conclusion reached by Farwell J in *Re Brooks' Settlement Trusts* [1939] Ch 993 which was not referred to in *Ralli*.
39. [1913] 2 Ch 478, 486.
40. Agnew and Douglas have argued (2019) 135 LQR 67, 84 that in this context 'the "declaration" is not purely a formality requirement. Rather, it requires proof of a substantive fact, i.e., the settlor's intention.'

manifestation of the intention to create a trust in this way and that where it appears that a settlor's intention was to bring a trust into operation by transfer in the manner outlined above but he fails to achieve this objective, this ineffective attempt to transfer the property will not be construed as a declaration of trust. The general principle was set out by Turner LJ in *Milroy v Lord* as follows:

> [I]f the settlement is intended to be effectuated by one of the modes to which I have referred,[41] the Court will not give effect to it by applying another of those modes. If it is intended to take effect by transfer, the Court will not hold the intended transfer to operate as a declaration of trust, for then every imperfect instrument would be made effectual by being converted into a perfect trust.[42]

This proposition is aptly illustrated by the decision of *Richards v Delbridge*,[43] in which the deceased who was the owner of leasehold premises endorsed and signed on the lease a memorandum in the following terms: 'this deed and all thereto belonging I give to Edwards Benetto Richards from this time forth, with all the stock-in-trade'. He delivered this document to the mother of the intended transferee and after his death the question arose whether the purported transfer was effective. The Court of Appeal concluded that there had been no proper assignment of the lease and in addition, that this ineffective attempt to transfer the interest could not be interpreted as a declaration of trust.[44]

This principle has also been accepted in this jurisidiction as the *dicta* of Fitzgibbon LJ in the decision of the Irish Court of Appeal in *O'Flaherty v Browne*[45] illustrates:

> A voluntary trust may be created by a declaration of trust, or by a complete assignment of the legal ownership to a trustee; but it is impossible to turn an incomplete, conditional, or postponed gift into a trust, where there is no intention to create the relationship of trustee and *cestui que trust*.

This position was also adopted by O'Donovan J in his judgment in *McArdle v*

41. See *supra* n. 3.
42. (1862) 4 De GF & J 264, 274-275. Quoted with approval by Lawson J in *Hayes v Alliance British & Foreign Life & Fire Assurance Co.* (1881) 8 LR Ir 149, 153. See also *T. Choithram International SA v Pagarani* [2001] 1 WLR 1, 11. This principle was also applied by the Privy Council in *Deslauriers v Guardian Asset Management Ltd* [2017] UKPC 34.
43. (1874) LR 18 Eq 11.
44. Jessel MR stated at 15: 'The true distinction appears to me to be plain, and beyond dispute: for a man to make himself a trustee there must be an expression of intention to become a trustee, whereas words of present gift shew an intention to give over property to another, and not retain it in the donor's own hands for any purpose, fiduciary or otherwise.'
45. [1907] 2 IR 416, 434.

O'Donohoe,[46] who stated that in the absence of a stated intention on the part of the settlor to constitute himself a trustee of trust property, and where there has been no effective transfer of the property to trustees, equity will not construe the ineffective transfer as a declaration of trust by the settlor.

However, it is fair to say that the traditional view that what appears to be an ineffective attempt to transfer property by gift can never be construed as a declaration of trust must now be reassessed. The decision of the Privy Council in *T. Choithram International SA v Pagarani*[47] makes it clear that where the settlor is one of a number of co-trustees the trust may be completely constituted by a declaration of trust made by him even though the property has still to be vested in the co-trustees. The donor executed a trust deed establishing a philanthropic foundation, appointing himself one of the trustees, and stated orally that he was giving all his wealth to the foundation. This property was expressed to include his deposit balances and shares in the first to fourth named defendants and the donor told the accountant to those companies that he was to transfer the deposit balances and shares to the foundation, although in some instances his shares in the companies had not been transferred before he died. Some of the other trustees signed the trust deed the day the declaration of trust was made and the others subsequently did so. The Court of Appeal of the British Virgin Islands held that the plaintiffs, who claimed to be entitled to the donor's estate on his intestacy, had succeeded in establishing that the donor had not made a valid gift of the deposit balances and shares to the foundation. However, the defendants' appeal to the Privy Council was allowed. Lord Browne-Wilkinson conceded that while it was understandable that the courts below should have reached the conclusion which they had since the case did not fall squarely within either of the methods normally stated as being the only possible ways of making a gift, he did not agree with this conclusion. In his view, while the words 'I give to the foundation' appeared to be words of outright gift, they were essentially words of gift on trust. He held that there could be no difference in principle between a case where a donor declares himself to be sole trustee and where he declares himself to be one of a number of trustees; in both cases his conscience is affected and it would be unconscionable to allow the donor to resile from the gift. Lord Browne-Wilkinson concluded that in the absence of special factors, where one out of a larger body of trustees has trust property vested in him he is bound by the trust and must give effect to it by transferring the trust property into the name of all the trustees. Therefore, in the view of the Privy Council, the assets included in the gift to the foundation had been properly vested in the trustees.

There was some criticism of this decision on the grounds, *inter alia*, that it might breach the principle laid down in *Milroy v Lord*[48] to the effect that a

46. [1999] IEHC 176 at 19.
47. [2001] 1 WLR 1.
48. (1862) 4 De GF & J 264.

failed transfer will not be interpreted as a successful declaration of the settlor as trustee.[49] However, it has also been welcomed as showing a willingness to depart from strict legal formalities.[50] It is difficult to argue with the conclusion reached by Lord Browne-Wilkinson that it would be unconscionable to allow a donor to resile from his intention to make a gift in such circumstances.[51] In addition, it can be argued that some of the criticisms of the decision in *T. Choithram International SA v Pagarani* are overstated and it is in some respects a less unsatisfactory decision than *Pennington v Waine*. As Davies and Virgo point out, '[i]n *Pagarani*, it was considered to be unconscionable to refuse to transfer title to the other trustees jointly, given that the person was *already* a trustee given his declaration. But in *Pennington*, unconscionability was used to *impose* trusteeship.[52] While the outcomes in *Choithram*, and even in *Pennington*, are arguably supportable as they also gave effect to the settlor's intentions, the use of unconscionability in this way might be less welcome if it were to lead to an outcome which a settlor clearly wished to avoid.

In addition to the *Re Rose* and unconscionability exceptions to the principle in *Milroy v Lord* already examined above, the principle of benevolent construction may, in an appropriate case, lead to a finding that a trust has been fully constituted. This was explained by Arden LJ in *Pennington v Waine*[53] in the following terms:

> [T]he principle that, where a gift is imperfectly constituted, the court will not hold it to operate as a declaration of trust, does not prevent the court from construing it to be a trust if that interpretation is permissible as a matter of construction, which may be a benevolent construction. The same must apply to words of gift. An equity to perfect a gift would not be invoked by giving a benevolent construction to words of gift or, it follows, words which the donor used to communicate or give effect to his gift.

This statement was quoted by Arden LJ in the course of her judgment in *Shah v Shah*[54] where she said that the principle, which used to be referred to as *ut res magis valeat quam pereat*, can apply to trusts in order to effectuate, rather than frustrate, the settlor's intentions. However, on the facts of the case before the Court of Appeal, Arden LJ was satisfied that the words used in a letter were sufficiently clear to enable the court to conclude that there had been a declaration of trust without having recourse to the principle of benevolent

---

49. Rickett [2001] Conv 515, 519.
50. Hopkins [2001] CLJ 483, 485.
51. A possible alternative approach would have been to find that the donor held the property on a constructive trust in which case the requirements in relation to the constitution of an express trust need not have been complied with.
52. *Equity and Trusts: Text, Cases and Materials* (2nd ed., 2016) pp. 159-160.
53. [2002] 1 WLR 2075, 2090. See also *N.D. v S.D.* [2017] EWHC 1507 (Fam) at [236].
54. [2010] EWCA Civ 1408.

construction set out above which she had referred to in *Pennington*. Therefore, the combined effect of *dicta* in recent judgments would appear to be that this principle means that a trust may be found to exist if such a conclusion can be reached as a matter of construction, even where there is also evidence of an imperfectly constituted gift.[55]

Where the trust property is comprised of realty, the declaration of trust must be evidenced in writing and while strictly speaking this is not necessary in relation to personalty,[56] it is clearly desirable from an evidential point of view. While the settlor 'need not use the words "I declare myself a trustee"',[57] he must unequivocally convey that this was his intention. As Lord O'Hagan LC commented in *Miller v Harrison*,[58] the effect of the declaration of trust must be to leave no reasonable doubt about the reason for its execution. In this case a dispute arose about the distribution on intestacy of the property of an individual who had died in America a naturalised US citizen. One of the next of kin executed a deed in which he agreed to share the property equally with the other next of kin and in reliance on this deed, these other individuals allowed a decree in the former's favour to be given by an American court in proceedings to determine ownership of the property. The Court of Appeal held that a subsequent attempt by this person to revoke the deed was invalid as its execution in the first instance had constituted a declaration of trust. As Lord O'Hagan LC stated:

> No future act is contemplated; no promise remains to be fulfilled; there is a gift, and not an engagement to give. The words of the donor denude him equitably of the shares which he bestows, save as a trustee for those so obtaining the beneficial interest, while the legal interest remains in himself … and therefore it binds him, though it states no consideration, and uses no language expressly creating trusts.[59]

In some cases the courts have adopted a fairly rigorous interpretation of this requirement that the intention to declare a trust must be clearly shown. In *Jones v Lock*[60] a father who had been reproved by his family for failing to bring home a present for his baby son on his return from a trip, placed a cheque in the child's hand having expressed the intention that the latter should have the money. The cheque was placed in a safe and six days later the father died. Lord

55. However, note that in *Gorbunova v Estate of Berezovsky* [2016] EWHC 1829 (Ch) Arnold J was not satisfied that words used evidenced an intention to make an immediate disposition of the beneficial interest in specified property. As he stated at [55], 'the words used must show that the settlor intended to dispose of property so that someone else acquired the beneficial interest to the exclusion of himself.'
56. See e.g. *Rowe v Prance* [1999] 2 FLR 787.
57. *Richards v Delbridge* (1874) LR 18 Eq 11, 14 *per* Jessel MR.
58. (1871) IR 5 Eq 324.
59. *Ibid.* at 344.
60. (1865) 1 Ch App 25.

Cranworth LC found that no valid transfer had been effected and stated that there was no evidence of an intention on the father's part to declare himself trustee on his child's behalf.

However, there has been some evidence of a relaxation of this rather restrictive attitude and a more liberal view of the evidence necessary to establish a declaration of trust has been taken in more recent decisions.[61] In *Paul v Constance*,[62] Scarman LJ acknowledged that on the facts it might be thought to be a 'borderline case' as it was not easy to identify a specific moment when the trust was declared. However, the court concluded that the repetition of the words 'the money is as much yours as mine' in relation to funds in a bank account was sufficient to constitute the deceased as trustee of these monies for the plaintiff. Similarly in *Rowe v Prance*,[63] Nicholas Warren QC, sitting as a Deputy High Court judge, held that the regular use of the word 'our' in relation to a boat owned by the defendant and the latter's statement that the plaintiff's security was her interest in it was sufficient to establish that he had effectively constituted himself as an express trustee of the boat for himself and the plaintiff equally.

EXCEPTIONS TO THE PRINCIPLE THAT EQUITY WILL NOT PERFECT AN INCOMPLETELY CONSTITUTED GIFT IN FAVOUR OF A VOLUNTEER

The Rule in *Strong v Bird*

The effect of the rule in *Strong v Bird*[64] is that where an incomplete gift is made during a donor's lifetime and the legal title to this property subsequently becomes vested in the donee, the donor's prior intention to make the gift is regarded as having been perfected provided that the intention has continued until the date of the donor's death. The result of the decision in *Strong* itself was that an executor did not have to account for a debt where a testator had manifested an intention to forgive the debt during her lifetime and this intention had continued until her death. This was extended to a positive application of the principle in *Re Stewart*[65] by a finding that an imperfect gift made by a testator *inter vivos* to his wife was subsequently perfected by her appointment as one of his executors. Neville J stated:

61. As Lord Browne-Wilkinson stated in *T. Choithram International SA v Pagarani* [2001] 1 WLR 1, 11: 'Although equity will not aid a volunteer, it will not strive officiously to defeat a gift.'
62. [1977] 1 WLR 527. See also *Ong v Ping* [2017] EWCA Civ 2069.
63. [1999] 2 FLR 787.
64. (1874) LR 18 Eq 315. For a useful recent analysis of the rule in *Strong v Bird*, see Jaconelli [2006] Conv 432.
65. [1908] 2 Ch 251. See also *Day v Harris* [2014] Ch 211.

> [W]here a testator has expressed the intention of making a gift of personal estate belonging to him to one who upon his death becomes his executor, the intention continuing unchanged, the executor is entitled to hold the property for his own benefit. The reasoning by which the conclusion is reached is of a double character – first, that the vesting of the property in the executor at the testator's death completes the imperfect gift made in the lifetime and secondly, that the intention of the testator to give the beneficial interest to the executor is sufficient to counterveil the equity of beneficiaries under the will, the testator having vested the legal estate in the executor. The whole of the property in the eye of the law vesting in each executor, it seems to me immaterial whether the donee is the only executor or one of several; nor do I think the rule is confined to cases of the release of a debt owing by the donee.[66]

A number of aspects of the principle must be considered in more detail. The legal vesting of the property in the donee commonly occurs when this individual is appointed a personal representative of the donor. So, the rule applies where a donee acquires legal title to the property by becoming an executor[67] of the deceased's estate and has been also held to extend to a situation where the donee is appointed administrator. While the latter principle was laid down in *Re James*[68] and now seems to be accepted, it has been criticised[69] on the basis that the identity of an administrator is often a matter of chance and it would seem unfair that such a person should obtain an advantage over the other beneficiaries by reason of this position.

An intention to make a gift in the future[70] or to make a future testamentary gift[71] will not come within the rule in *Strong v Bird.* The distinction between a present intention to make an immediate gift of property and the intention to make a testamentary gift is well illustrated by the decision in *Re Wilson.*[72] The testator had manifested an intention to make an immediate gift of certain securities to his son, who was the executor of his will, although he did not complete or perfect this gift during his lifetime. Johnston J was satisfied that this intention had been proved and that the principle in *Strong v Bird* applied to perfect the gift. However, the rule did not apply to other properties which the testator had promised to transfer to his son during his lifetime or by his will.

66. *Ibid.* at 254-255.
67. It suffices if a donee is appointed as one of a number of executors. See *supra Re Stewart* [1908] 2 Ch 251, 254.
68. [1935] Ch 449.
69. See the judgment of Walton J in *Re Gonin* [1979] Ch 16, although he did apply the principle as both counsel had accepted it.
70. *Re Freeland* [1952] Ch 110.
71. *Re Innes* [1910] 1 Ch 188.
72. [1933] IR 729.

In relation to the intended testamentary disposition, Johnston J quoted with approval[73] the words of Neville J in *Re Stewart*[74] as follows:

> [T]he intention to give, however, must not be an intention of testamentary benefaction, although the intended donee is the executor, for, in that case the rule cannot apply, the prescribed formalities for testamentary disposition not having been observed.

It is also important that the intention relates to specific property[75] and the gift must be perfected in all respects save for the formalities necessary to effect the proper transfer of the property. In addition, for the rule to apply the intention to make the gift must have continued until the time of the donor's death,[76] and it cannot have any application in cases such as *Re Wale*,[77] where the evidence showed that the settlor appeared to have forgotten the very existence of the settlement and had continued to treat the property as if it were her own. The practical significance of the rule in *Strong v Bird* is that the claim of beneficiaries under a will will be displaced by the donee's prior equity, although it is not clear in this jurisdiction or in England whether this priority will be effective as against creditors.

Jaconelli has characterised the rule in *Strong v Bird* as 'surely the strangest' of the exceptions to the principle that equity will not perfect an imperfect gift and argues that an examination of the rationales underpinning the rule shows each of them to be defective.[78] He points out that the decision in *Strong v Bird* itself did not even establish many of the main features of the rule and asserts that its evolution over the years 'illustrates how, even from inauspicious beginnings, judge-made law is capable of bringing into being a fully developed doctrine that possesses its own internal logic.' [79] The application of the rule has also been considered by the New South Wales Supreme Court in *Blackett v Darcy*,[80] in which Young CJ rejected the argument that it should not apply because only one of two donees had been appointed an executor. However, he did state that the prevailing view is that it is an anomalous rule which should not be extended and he expressed the view that it would be appropriate not to apply it where the whole beneficial interest was not taken by the donee in a real sense.

---

73. *Ibid.* at 748.
74. [1908] 2 Ch 251, 255.
75. *Re Innes* [1910] 1 Ch 188, 193 *per* Parker J.
76. See *Re Gonin* [1979] Ch 16 where the lack of a continuing intention to make the gift resulted in the court's refusal to apply the rule in *Strong v Bird*.
77. [1956] 1 WLR 1346.
78. Jaconelli [2006] Conv 432.
79. *Ibid.* at 450.
80. (2005) 62 NSWLR 392.

Donatio Mortis Causa

A *donatio mortis causa* is the delivery of property to a donee in contemplation of the donor's death which is conditional on this event occurring and the gift is not regarded as complete until the donor dies. It should be regarded as a conditional present gift and must be distinguished from a straightforward gift *inter vivos* which is an absolute present gift, and from a testamentary gift which is a future gift. Buckley J described a *donatio mortis causa* in the following terms in *Re Beaumont*:[81]

> It is an act *inter vivos* by which the donee is to have absolute title to the subject of the gift not at once but if the donor dies. If the donor dies the title becomes absolute not under but as against his executor. In order to make the gift valid it must be made so as to take complete effect on the donor's death.

The general principle that equity will not perfect an imperfect or incomplete gift in favour of a volunteer does not apply to a *donatio mortis causa*, although in practice the assistance of equity will only be required in limited circumstances. Where the subject matter of the *donatio mortis causa* is a chattel which has been delivered to the donee, title to this object is regarded as being complete on the donor's death. However, where the subject matter is a chose in action or land, the legal title to this property will vest in the donor's personal representatives on his death. It is in these circumstances that the exception to the general principle becomes important as equity will compel the donee's personal representatives to take whatever steps are necessary to complete the donor's title.

The essential elements of a *donatio mortis causa* have been laid down in a number of decisions and are now clearly established.[82] There must have been a gift made in contemplation of the donor's death, the subject-matter of the gift must have been delivered to the donee and the gift must have been made on the basis that it becomes absolute only on the donor's death and therefore remains revocable during his lifetime. It is also necessary to consider whether the property is capable of forming the subject matter of a *donatio mortis causa*.

The attitude of the court in relation to these requirements has tended to be quite strict and they must all be satisfied to establish a valid *donatio mortis causa.* As Gallen J commented in the New Zealand High Court decision of *Wilson v Paniani*:[83]

---

81. [1902] 1 Ch 889, 892.
82. See *Cain v Moon* [1896] 2 QB 283, 286 *per* Russell LJ quoted with approval by Molony CJ in *Re Mulroy* [1924] 1 IR 98, 103; *Re Craven's Estate (No. 1)* [1937] Ch 423, 426 *per* Farwell J.
83. [1996] 3 NZLR 378, 384. The court held that on the facts the conditions necessary to establish the existence of a *donatio mortis causa* had not been made out by the plaintiff despite the fact that Gallen J was satisfied that the deceased had wished to benefit her.

> It is important ... that there ought to be stringent requirements in respect of such claims since they are frequently made without any independent evidence to support them and in circumstances where they would be difficult to refute. Accordingly the law ensures that for such a claim to succeed the strict requirements of the law must be adhered to and satisfied.

Another reason why a strict approach has been taken in such cases is that the upholding of a *donatio mortis causa* may mean that the court is giving effect to a distribution of the deceased's property in a manner which may differ considerably from that set out by the deceased in his will. This point is well illustrated by the judgment of Barr J in *Bentham v Potterton*,[84] the most recent decision in this jurisdiction on *donatio mortis causa.* The deceased in her will bequeathed cash legacies varying in amount from £1,000 to £3,000 to nine beneficiaries, including the first and second named plaintiffs, her grandnieces, and a residuary clause provided for the division of the remainder of the estate equally between all but one of the named beneficiaries. The deceased was hospitalised two months before her death and it was discovered that she was suffering from inoperable cancer. Barr J was satisfied that there was no evidence that she had ever been told that her condition was terminal and it was not until a week before she died that she told her niece that she knew she was in fact dying. Three and a half weeks before her death, the deceased asked the first named plaintiff to retrieve bank books from her home and put them in a safe in the latter's house, which she did. The following day, the first named plaintiff informed her great-aunt that she had carried out her wishes and the former deposed that the deceased had then told her that if anything was to happen to her, she was 'to keep the contents of the books and give [her sister] a few bob out of it'. After the deceased's death, an issue arose about whether this transaction amounted to a valid *donatio mortis causa* made in favour of the plaintiffs.

Barr J stressed that the onus lay on the party claiming the gift to prove to the court that the requirements for *donatio mortis causa* had been satisfied. In the first instance, he said that the facts fell short of establishing on the balance of probabilities that the gift had been made by the donor in contemplation of her death. He suggested that if it had been the deceased's intention to make a gift of the funds on deposit to the plaintiffs it seemed probable that she would either have made this clear on the first occasion on which she had referred to the deposit books or alternatively would have made a new will or codicil to give effect to her revised intentions. Barr J concluded that he was not satisfied that the deceased 'positively intended to make a radical change in the disposition of her property in contemplation of her death'. Although this might have been her intention, he said that the surrounding facts raised considerable doubt in this regard and in the circumstances he held that the plaintiffs had not established the validity of the alleged gift on the balance of probabilities.

---

84. [1998] IEHC 84.

The Court of Appeal in *King v Dubrey*[85] has also advocated taking a strict approach towards the concept of *donatio mortis causa* and not permitting any further expansion of the doctrine. Jackson LJ stated that in his view it is important to keep the doctrine within its proper bounds and he suggested that because it is open to abuse, the courts should require strict proof of compliance with the established requirements. Both Jackson and Patten LJJ pointed out that the doctrine allows for the transfer of property on death without the need for compliance with the Wills Act and related legislation. As Jackson LJ put it, 'the doctrine paves the way for all of the abuses which those statutes are intended to prevent.'[86] Similarly, Patten LJ stated:

> The testator's execution of the will and his capacity to make it can be proved objectively by those who witnessed it being done. By contrast, the making of a DMC, as in this case, will usually occur privately between the donor and the donee in circumstances where the potential for fabrication and invention by the donee is high and the prospect of disproving an alleged DMC correspondingly low.[87]

So, it is clear that in assessing whether the conditions for the making of a valid *donatio mortis causa* have been satisfied, the courts are increasingly aware of the fact that in upholding such gifts they are effectively bypassing statutory formalities and safeguards and that there is a possibility that in so doing they may be facilitating the perpetration of a fraud.[88]

The Law Commission in its Consultation Paper, *Making a Will*,[89] has examined the future of the *donatio mortis causa* doctrine. It noted the danger of abuse presented by the doctrine, in particular the risk of fraud and dispute. However, it also expressed the view that the doctrine may continue to serve a useful purpose, 'because it "softens" the hard edges of formalities law.'[90] Taking into account the lack of evidence either way as to problems caused by *donatio mortis causa* in practice, and the arguments that in principle could be made both for and against abolition, it asked for views on whether the doctrine should be abolished or retained.

---

85. [2016] Ch 221. See further Towl [2018] Conv 367, 374 who argues that 'the doctrine is still one mired in conceptual uncertainty.'
86. *Ibid.* at 233.
87. *Ibid.* at 239.
88. Note that Cumber has commented [2016] Conv 56, 61 that '[a]lthough this decision raises questions about the continued utility of the doctrine in English law, it continues to serve a useful function.'
89. Law Commission Consultation Paper 231 (2017) Chapter 13.
90. *Ibid.*, para. 13.47.

In Contemplation of Death

The gift must have been made in contemplation, although not necessarily in the expectation, of death, but not simply in circumstances where the donor is acknowledging the general inevitability of death. So it is usually made where 'death for some reason [is] believed to be impending'[91] as a result of some form of serious illness or because the donor intends to embark on a particularly hazardous journey.[92] However, it is essential that the court is satisfied that the donor knew that he was dying at the time the transaction took place and this point is illustrated by the High Court decision in *Bentham v Potterton*,[93] the facts of which are set out above. Barr J said that he had substantial doubts about whether the donor appreciated the gravity of her medical condition when the transaction in question took place. Although she was elderly and had been gravely ill two years previously, he adverted to the fact that there was no evidence that the deceased had been told that her condition was terminal and pointed out that it was only some two and a half weeks after the transaction had taken place that she had admitted to her niece that she thought she was dying. In these circumstances he said that the facts fell short of establishing on the balance of probabilities that the gift had been made by the donor in contemplation of her death.

Provided that death actually occurs it appears to be immaterial that it does so as a result of a cause different to that contemplated at the time of the gift. This is illustrated by *Wilkes v Allington*,[94] in which a donor made a gift knowing that he was suffering from an incurable disease and then died two months later from pneumonia. It was held that the gift remained valid in such circumstances. A similar result ensued in *Mills v Shields (No. 1)*,[95] where a donor made a gift while suffering from an oppressive form of neurosis and subsequently took his own life while travelling to obtain treatment for this condition. Gavan Duffy P stressed that a *donatio mortis causa* is not defeated by the fact that the donor did not die in the manner he had feared and held that the case was not one of 'intended suicide' within the meaning of that phrase as set out in *Agnew v Belfast Banking Co.*[96] It is therefore important to distinguish *Mills* from the decision in *Agnew* in which it was held that a gift actually made in contemplation of suicide could not form the subject matter of a valid *donatio mortis causa*. Porter MR commented that as suicide was recognised as a crime, it was 'fundamentally opposed to the first principles of our law … that legal rights should be created by the intention to commit suicide followed by the actual commission of it'.[97]

91. *Re Craven's Estate (No. 1)* [1937] Ch 423, 426 *per* Farwell J.
92. The ordinary risks of travel by air will not suffice, see *Thompson v Mechan* (1958) 13 DLR (2d) 103.
93. [1998] IEHC 84.
94. [1931] 2 Ch 104.
95. [1948] IR 367.
96. [1896] 2 IR 204.
97. *Ibid.* at 216.

Fitzgibbon LJ agreed that it would be contrary to public policy to uphold a gift which was intended to take effect as a result of suicide and it is unclear whether the courts would take a different view of this issue today.[98]

The issue of the evidence which must be adduced in order to satisfy the requirement that the gift was made in actual contemplation of impending death has been considered in a number of recent decisions. In *Vallee v Birchwood*[99] the claimant had visited her elderly father in August 2003 when he appeared to be in poor health. At the time he said that he did not expect to live very much longer and that he might not be alive at Christmas. He died that December and the High Court found that in these circumstances the requirement that the gift had been made in contemplation of death had been satisfied. However, in *King v Dubrey*[100] Jackson LJ expressed the view that he did not think that *Vallee v Birchwood* had been correctly decided on the basis that in his opinion the deceased had not had a reason to anticipate death in the near future from a known cause. In *King* Jackson LJ disagreed with the conclusion reached by the trial judge that the deceased had been contemplating her impending death when she made the gift to the claimant. He stated that the requirement that the deceased should be contemplating his impending death meant that he should be contemplating death in the near future for a specific reason. In the matter before the Court of Appeal, while he acknowledged that at the age of 81 most of her life span was behind her, there was no evidence that the deceased was suffering from any specific illness and in his view it could not be said that she was contemplating her impending death in the sense that the authorities in this area required. Patten LJ also found that the evidence before the court, even if credible, came nowhere near satisfying the requirement that the gift should be made in contemplation of death and he concluded that it did not demonstrate that the deceased's death was impending, let alone imminent. Therefore, the judgments in the Court of Appeal suggest that this requirement of establishing 'impending death' in order to make out a claim for a valid *donatio mortis causa* is likely to be more strictly construed in the future.

Delivery of the Subject Matter of the Gift

There must be delivery of the subject matter of the *donatio mortis causa* made by the donor with the intention of parting with dominion over the property[101] and not just mere physical possession.[102] It is insufficient if the property is simply

98. Note that suicide is no longer regarded as a crime; see s. 2 of the Criminal Law (Suicide) Act 1993.
99. [2014] Ch 271.
100. [2016] Ch 221. See further Cumber [2016] Conv 56.
101. There must be 'a complete parting with the dominion over the subject matter by the donor' *per* Molony CJ in *Re Mulroy* [1924] 1 IR 98, 100. See also *Hawkins v Blewitt* (1798) 2 Esp 663.
102. *Birch v Treasury Solicitor* [1951] 1 Ch 298.

handed over for safe keeping and the result of such delivery must be that the donor can no longer exercise any control over the subject matter of the gift.[103] As Evershed MR commented in *Birch v Treasury Solicitor*,[104] delivery must be made 'of the essential indicia or evidence of title, possession or production of which entitles the possessor to the money or property, purported to be given'.

Delivery may be made before[105] or after[106] the appropriate words of gift[107] are used and provided that it is achieved in an effective manner there is no requirement of any written evidence to substantiate it. It was held in *Mills v Shields (No.1)*[108] that where delivery is made to an agent of the donor as trustee for the donee this will suffice. However, this can be contrasted with the finding made in the earlier case of *Re Thompson's Estate*[109] that where the deceased simply handed her servant the property to keep for the donee, this was not sufficient delivery. Meredith J quoted with approval the *dicta* of Knight Bruce VC in *Farquharson v Cave*[110] to the effect that 'a mere delivery to an agent, in the character of agent for the giver, would amount to nothing' and concluded that in the circumstances where insufficient instructions had been given to the agent, no delivery, either actual or constructive, had taken place.

Where the subject matter of the *donatio mortis causa* is a chattel, there must be either delivery of the chattel itself or of something which will enable the donee to obtain effective control over it. So the handing over of a key to a locked container or safe deposit box will constitute delivery,[111] although the reverse is not the case and delivery of a locked box without the key does not meet the requirements of a valid *donatio mortis causa*.[112] A good example of a case where no delivery was found to have taken place was *Re Mulroy*.[113] Shortly before his death, the deceased opened a cash box in the presence of the defendant and took out a deposit receipt and two 'stale' cheques and said to him: 'Here is all belonging to me; I am sorry I have no more to give you. You were very good to me.' He then replaced the documents and locked the box, putting the key in his pocket. The deceased subsequently died intestate and the Irish Court of Appeal held that there was no valid *donatio mortis causa* on the grounds that the deceased, by replacing the documents, had led the court

---

103. *Re Craven's Estate (No. 1)* [1937] Ch 423, 427.
104. [1951] Ch 298, 311.
105. *Cain v Moon* [1896] 2 QB 283.
106. *Re Weston* [1902] 1 Ch 680.
107. Note that words of gift are clearly not in themselves sufficient without actual delivery taking place, see *Re Mulroy* [1924] 1 IR 98, 104 *per* Molony CJ.
108. [1948] IR 367.
109. [1928] IR 606.
110. (1846) 2 Coll 356, 367.
111. *Re Wasserberg* [1915] 1 Ch 195; *Re Lillingston* [1952] 2 All ER 184. Although if the donor retains another key, it will probably not suffice, see *Re Craven's Estate (No. 1)* [1937] Ch 423, 428 *per* Farwell J.
112. *Re Johnson* (1905) 92 LT 357.
113. [1924] 1 IR 98.

to believe that he had never intended to part with them in such a manner as to lose dominion over them during his lifetime.

The Gift Must be Conditional upon Death and Revocable

The gift must have been made on the basis that although it is in form a present gift it is nevertheless conditional on the donor's death and it will remain revocable during his lifetime. As Lord Porter MR stated in *Agnew v Belfast Banking Co.*:[114] 'A *donatio mortis causa* is incomplete till death, and depends upon it. If the sick man recovers it is of no avail. No property passes until death.' Such revocation may occur automatically where, for example, the donor recovers from the illness which led him to make the gift.[115] Equally, the donor may expressly inform the donee that the gift is being revoked, or may recover dominion over it, although recovery of possession for the purposes of safe-keeping will not amount to revocation.[116] Clearly a purported revocation by will cannot be achieved as the instrument will not come into effect until the donor's death at which stage the donee's gift will be regarded as complete.

The Property Must be Capable of Forming the Subject Matter of a Donatio Mortis Causa

Clearly, any property transferable by mere delivery can form the subject matter of a valid gift by way of *donatio mortis causa* and delivery of the documentation appropriate to effect a transfer of property will also suffice.[117] Traditionally, it had been thought that realty could not form the subject matter of a valid *donatio mortis causa*[118] but the Court of Appeal in *Sen v Headley*[119] made it clear that a gift of land by the delivery of deeds should not be excluded.[120] The deceased and the plaintiff lived together for ten years and remained on close terms thereafter. When the deceased was very ill he told the plaintiff that his house was hers and that the deeds to it were in a steel box to which she had the keys. He died intestate and the plaintiff claimed that he had made a valid gift to her in contemplation of death. The defendant, who was the deceased's nephew

114. [1896] 2 IR 204, 216.
115. *Keys v Hore* (1879) 13 ILTR 58.
116. *Re Hawkins* [1924] 2 Ch 47.
117. *Birch v Treasury Solicitor* [1951] Ch 298, 311.
118. See the *dicta* of Lord Eldon in *Duffield v Elwes* (1827) 1 Bli 497 and the Australian decisions of *Watts v Public Trustee* (1949) 50 SR 130 and *Bayliss v Public Trustee* (1988) 12 NSWLR 540.
119. [1991] Ch 425. See Halliwell [1991] Conv 307; Thornley [1991] CLJ 404; Baker (1993) 109 LQR 19.
120. As the Land Registry in England and Wales no longer issues land certificates following the coming into force of the Land Registration Act 2002, it is unlikely that there can now be a valid *donatio mortis causa* of registered land in that jurisdiction. See Roberts [2013] Conv 113; Panesar [2014] Conv 70, 75.

and the administrator of his estate, counterclaimed for the return of the deeds to the house. The Court of Appeal upheld the plaintiff's claim. It seems clear from the decision in *Vallee v Birchwood*[121] that a valid *donatio mortis causa* of land can be made even where the donor retains physical possession of the property for a period of time. So, in this case, delivery of the title deeds and the keys to a house by a father to his daughter in contemplation of his death, which occurred some four months later, was found to be a sufficient delivery of dominion over the house to constitute a valid *donatio mortis causa.*[122]

There is some authority to the effect that stocks and shares cannot form the subject matter of a *donatio mortis causa*[123] on the basis that a share certificate, although it will constitute *prima facie* evidence of good title, is not the vital document which forms 'the fundamental contract between a company and its members'.[124] Similar uncertainty surrounds the position of a savings bank book. In *M'Gonnell v Murray*[125] Walsh MR rejected the argument that it could validly form the subject matter of a *donatio mortis causa* on the grounds that the book did not embody the terms of the contract between the depositor and the bank. However, in the more recent Circuit Court decision of *Hearty v Coleman*[126] it was held by Judge Sheehy that the handing of a post office savings bank book by the testator to the defendant constituted a valid *donatio mortis causa* of the money standing to her credit in the account and other authorities seem to support this conclusion.[127] It would seem that neither an IOU[128] nor a donor's own cheque or promissory note can come within the ambit of the doctrine on the basis that these are respectively merely a revocable instrument and a gratuitous promise.[129]

In the last analysis perhaps the most useful test is that proposed by Evershed MR in *Birch v Treasury Solicitor*,[130] which was set out above; namely whether

---

121. [2014] Ch 271). See further Panesar [2014] Conv 70.
122. However, it should be pointed out, as noted above, that subsequently in *King v Dubrey* [2016] Ch 221 Jackson LJ expressed the view that he did not think that *Vallee v Birchwood* had been correctly decided on the basis that the requirement that the gift be made in contemplation of death had not been satisfied.
123. *Moore v Moore* (1874) LR 18 Eq 474; *Re Weston* [1902] 1 Ch 680, although note *Staniland v Willot* (1852) 3 Mac & G 664.
124. *Mills v Shields (No. 2)* [1950] IR 21, 31 *per* Gavan Duffy J.
125. (1869) IR 3 Eq 460.
126. [1953-54] Ir Jur Rep 73.
127. *Re Weston* [1902] 1 Ch 680; *Birch v Treasury Solicitor* [1951] Ch 298. In addition, in *Re Thompson's Estate* [1928] IR 606 Meredith J, while he held on the facts that there was no valid *donatio mortis causa* on the grounds that there had been no delivery, did not raise any issue as to whether a Post Office savings bank book could have formed the subject matter of such a gift.
128. *Duckworth v Lee* [1899] 1 IR 405.
129. *Re Beaumont* [1902] 1 Ch 889; *Re Leaper* [1916] 1 Ch 579. However, there might be a valid gift if the cheque was paid during the donor's lifetime or even after his death if the bank was not aware of the fact that he had died.
130. [1951] Ch 298, 311.

delivery of the documents concerned amounts to a transfer 'of the essential indicia or evidence of title, possession or production of which entitles the possessor to the money or property, purported to be given'.

Proprietary Estoppel

Where an imperfect gift has been made and the donor knowingly allows the donee to improve the property or act to his detriment in some manner, equity may compel the donor to perfect the gift even where the donee is a volunteer. This will be considered below.[131]

THE POSITION OF A VOLUNTEER

As we have seen, once a trust is completely constituted it can be enforced by any beneficiary, even if he is a mere volunteer. However, where a trust is still incompletely constituted, it may be of crucial importance to determine whether the beneficiaries are volunteers or have given consideration; in these circumstances 'equity will not assist a volunteer' although it will enforce such an incompletely constituted trust if valuable consideration has been given by the beneficiaries.

A beneficiary will be regarded as a volunteer unless he had provided valuable consideration in the sense recognised at common law or he comes within the scope of marriage consideration. It is important to note that what is referred to as 'good consideration' comprised of natural love and affection is not considered to be valuable consideration and will not suffice to make an incompletely constituted trust enforceable in equity. A settlement made before and in consideration of marriage is regarded as being one for valuable consideration. However, a settlement made after marriage will only suffice provided it is made in fulfilment of a pre-nuptial agreement.[132] In any other circumstances a settlement made in consideration of a past marriage will not be regarded as one for valuable consideration. This is illustrated by the decision of *Re Greer*,[133] in which a settlement executed for the benefit of children of a former marriage on the occasion of a second marriage was not found to be a settlement for valuable consideration. The spouses[134] and issue[135] of the marriage are regarded as coming within the marriage consideration. The latter phrase has been variously interpreted as being confined to children[136] and as

131. See Chapter 18.
132. *Re Holland* [1902] 2 Ch 360.
133. (1877) IR 11 Eq 502.
134. *Dennehy v Delany* (1876) IR 10 Eq 377.
135. *Greenwood v Lutman* [1915] 1 IR 266.
136. *Re Dixon's Trusts* (1869) IR 4 Eq 1.

extending to grandchildren[137] but the better view would seem to be that it is usually confined to the children of the marriage.[138]

It has been clearly established that persons coming within the marriage consideration can enforce the settlement even though they might otherwise be regarded as volunteers. In *Pullan v Koe*[139] as part of a marriage settlement in which property was settled on a husband and wife and their prospective children, the wife covenanted to settle after acquired property to the value of £100 or upwards. She subsequently received a gift of £285 which was ultimately used to buy bonds which remained in her husband's name until his death. The question arose whether these bonds could be recovered from his estate and held on the trusts of the settlement. It was held by Swinfen Eady J that the trustees, acting on behalf of the wife and children, could succeed in reclaiming the bonds on the grounds that the money had been subject to a trust in favour of those coming within the marriage consideration. Swinfen Eady J distinguished the circumstances of the case before him from those where it had been held that a court would not intervene to assist a volunteer who did not come within the marriage consideration. In *Re Plumptre's Marriage Settlement*[140] a settlement in consideration of marriage contained a covenant providing for the settlement of property subsequently acquired by the wife on trust for herself and her husband for life, their issue and, in default, for their next of kin. The husband gave some stock to his wife and it was held that after her death the covenant could not be enforced by their next of kin against her personal representative, her husband, on the grounds that the next of kin were volunteers and did not come within the marriage consideration.[141]

POSSIBLE ALTERNATIVE REMEDIES FOR A BENEFICIARY WHERE A TRUST IS INCOMPLETELY CONSTITUTED

Where a beneficiary is a volunteer and does not come within any of the exceptions outlined above, it is necessary to examine whether there are any other means of enforcing an incompletely constituted trust in his favour. A

137. *McDonald v Scott* [1893] AC 642.
138. *Re Bromhead's Trusts* [1922] 1 IR 75. While some early authorities suggested a wider definition of those falling within the marriage consideration, these decisions are now explained on the basis that in the special circumstances of these cases the interests of these parties, often illegitimate children or children of a former marriage, were so closely interwoven with the interests of the children of the marriage that they could not be separated.
139. [1913] 1 Ch 9.
140. [1910] 1 Ch 609. See also *Re D'Angibau* (1880) 15 Ch D 228.
141. It should be noted that a volunteer beneficiary who is party to a covenant may bring an action on the covenant at common law for damages, see *Cannon v Hartley* [1949] Ch 213.

settlor may enter into a covenant to create a trust by transferring existing or so called after acquired property to trustees. This is particularly common in the case of a marriage settlement where the parties may covenant to settle any property which they may subsequently acquire on the trusts of the settlement.[142] Where such a covenant is entered into other than for valuable consideration, there are two main alternatives relating to its possible enforcement which must be examined. First, it may be possible to establish that there is a completely constituted trust of the benefit of the covenant in their favour and secondly indirect enforcement by means of an action by the trustees on the covenant at common law against the settlor may be explored.

The principal difficulty with the first option is in determining the circumstances when such a trust will arise and in particular in assessing whether sufficient intention to create a trust has been established. In the early decision of *Fletcher v Fletcher*[143] a settlor entered into a voluntary covenant with trustees to the effect that if either or both of his natural sons should survive him, his executors should within twelve months of his death pay a sum of £60,000 to the trustees to hold on trust for both or such one of them as might attain the age of 21. One of these sons survived the settlor and reached the age of 21 whereupon he sought to enforce the covenant against the executors who had refused to take any action. The effect of the decision of Wright VC was that there was a completely constituted trust of the benefit of the covenant which could be enforced by the son. On the facts the court in *Fletcher* was satisfied that the testator had manifested a sufficient intention to create a trust, although it has been argued that these same facts would hardly satisfy a more modern approach to the question of certainty of intention.[144] A further difficulty is that *Fletcher* has been distinguished in the case of after acquired property and it has been held in a number of decisions that there can be no enforceable trust of the benefit of the covenant in such cases.[145] In *Re Cook's Settlement Trusts*[146] by virtue of an agreement and subsequent settlement entered into by Sir Herbert Cook and his son, certain pictures became the absolute property of the son, who covenanted that if any of these pictures were to be sold during his lifetime the proceeds of sale should be held on the trusts of the settlement. The son gave one of the pictures to his wife who wished to sell it and the question arose whether the trustees were obliged to take any steps to ensure performance of the covenant. Buckley J distinguished *Fletcher v Fletcher* as follows:

---

142. See *supra Re Plumptre's Marriage Settlement* [1910] 1 Ch 609; *Pullan v Koe* [1913] 1 Ch 9.
143. (1844) 4 Hare 67.
144. See *supra* Chapter 4. While at the time *Fletcher* was decided the use of precatory words was considered to be sufficient to show intention to create a trust, a more stringent approach is now applied.
145. *Re Pryce* [1917] 1 Ch 234; *Re Kay's Settlement* [1939] Ch 329; *Re Cook's Settlement Trusts* [1965] Ch 902.
146. [1965] Ch 902.

> The covenant with which I am concerned did not, in my opinion, create a debt enforceable at law, that is to say a property right, which, although to bear fruit only in the future and upon a contingency, was capable of being made the subject of an immediate trust, as was held to be the case in *Fletcher v Fletcher*. ... In contrast ... this covenant on its true construction is, in my opinion, an executory contract to settle a particular fund or particular funds of money which at the date of the covenant did not exist and which might never come into existence. It is analogous to a covenant to settle an expectation or to settle after-acquired property. The case in my judgment, involves the law of contract, not the law of trusts.[147]

It has been argued that there is no good reason for drawing such a distinction[148] and perhaps the decision in *Cook* is better explained on the grounds that there was clearly no intention to create a trust of the benefit of the covenant in that case.

So, in theory a completely constituted trust of the benefit of a covenant to settle either existing or after acquired property may be found provided the settlor has manifested the appropriate intention and it is likely that in the absence of such a clearly expressed intention no trust will exist. This would allow voluntary covenants to settle property to be enforced where there is sufficient evidence of the settlor's intention to create a trust of the benefit of the covenant; any more radical approach would seem inconsistent with a considerable number of authorities.

A second option, which derives little or no support from the relevant case law, is that where a beneficiary is unable to enforce a covenant to settle in the manner outlined above it might be possible to secure enforcement of the covenant by means of an action on it at common law by the trustees against the settlor. However, the authorities in this area have clearly established that there is no obligation on the trustees to take action in such circumstances; *a fortiori* it has been suggested that they should be restrained from taking any such proceedings.[149] In *Re Kay's Settlement*[150] a spinster executed a voluntary settlement in favour of herself for life and after her death for her issue which contained a covenant to settle after acquired property. She subsequently married, had children and acquired further property and then refused to comply with the trustees' request to bring this additional property into the settlement. The trustees sought the direction of the court on the issue of whether they should take proceedings against the settlor to compel performance of the covenant or to recover damages for her failure to implement it. Simonds J followed the

147. *Ibid.* at 913-914.
148. Barton (1975) 91 LQR 236; Meagher & Lehane (1976) 92 LQR 427; Goddard [1988] Conv 19.
149. *Re Pryce* [1917] 1 Ch 234.
150. [1939] Ch 329.

decision of Eve J in *Re Pryce*[151] and directed the trustees not to take any steps either to compel performance of the covenant or to seek damages in respect of the settlor's failure to implement its terms.

However, even if the courts were to re-appraise their approach, there would be difficulties from the point of view of the beneficiaries in having recourse to this option. First, the extent of the damages to which the trustees would be entitled in these circumstances is far from clear and in any event, any damages which might be recovered would in all likelihood be held by the trustees on a resulting trust for the settlor rather than for the beneficiaries. Therefore, unless a beneficiary is recognised as being an actual party to the covenant, in which case he can maintain an action at common law for its breach,[152] he will not be able to secure a remedy at law for failure to give effect to the terms of the covenant.

151. [1917] 1 Ch 234. Criticised in Heydon and Leeming, *Jacobs' Law of Trusts in Australia* (8th ed., 2016) paras 6.11–6.14.
152. *Cannon v Hartley* [1949] Ch 213.

CHAPTER 7

Resulting Trusts

INTRODUCTION

General Principles

Resulting trusts can be said to arise by implication and are founded on the unexpressed but presumed intention of the settlor.[1] This label is used to describe such trusts because the beneficial interest in the property in question comes back or results to the settlor, or, if he is dead, to those entitled to his estate, on the basis that the law presumes that this was the settlor's intention. They are also sometimes referred to as implied trusts because they are presumed to arise as a result of the settlor's implied intention. Due to the informal manner in which they come into being, such trusts are exempt from the formalities required in relation to the creation of express trusts.

While there are a number of possible bases for the rationale behind resulting trusts, in practice they tend to arise in two distinct factual situations; first, where there has been an apparent gift of property and secondly, where an express trust has failed to dispose of the trust property. Traditionally, a distinction has been made between categories of resulting trusts as suggested by Megarry J in *Re Vandervell's Trusts (No.2)*[2] in the following terms:

> (a) The first class of case is where the transfer to B is not made on any trust. If, of course, it appears from the transfer that B is intended to hold on certain trusts, that will be decisive, and the case is not within this category; and similarly if it appears that B is intended to take beneficially. But in other cases there is a rebuttable presumption that B holds on a resulting trust for A … The presumption thus establishes both that B is to take on trust and also what that trust is. Such resulting trusts may be called 'presumed resulting trusts'.
>
> (b) The second class of case is where the transfer to B is made on trusts which leave some or all of the beneficial interest undisposed of. Here B automatically holds on a resulting trust for A to the extent that the beneficial interest has not been carried to him or others. The resulting trust here does not depend on any intentions or presumptions, but is the automatic consequence of A's failure to dispose of what is vested

1. See generally Chambers, *Resulting Trusts* (1997).
2. [1974] Ch 269, 294. See Clarke (1974) 38 Conv 405; Harris (1975) 38 MLR 557.

> in him… Such resulting trusts may be called 'automatic resulting trusts'.

The extent to which the trusts which may arise by implication in either of these two categories will actually reflect the settlor's real intentions in a given case is open to question and particularly in the context of automatically resulting trusts, the result, which the law presumes, is often quite contrary to that which a settlor could be said to have intended.[3]

Theoretical Basis for Resulting Trusts

A number of potentially unifying theories have been put forward to challenge the orthodoxy of Megarry J's distinction between presumed and automatic resulting trusts.[4] In his speech in *Westdeutsche Landesbank Girozentrale v Islington Borough Council*[5] Lord Browne-Wilkinson suggested that Megarry J was incorrect in his assumption that trusts in category (b) set out above do not depend on intention but operate automatically; in his view all resulting trusts give effect to the presumed intention of the transferor.[6] A further alternative analysis which has been developed in recent years is that resulting trusts arise by virtue of the absence of any intention on the part of the transferor to benefit the transferee. While suggested in the first instance by Birks,[7] this theory has been developed by Chambers,[8] who has stated as follows:

> [A]ll resulting trusts operate on precisely the same principles regardless of the situations in which they arise. They do not depend on an implied intention to create a trust, but neither do they arise completely

---

3. *Vandervell v IRC* [1967] 2 AC 291. See *infra* p. 161.
4. However, Swadling (2008) 124 LQR 72 has reasserted the view that while some resulting trusts arise because of a legal presumption that a trust was declared by the transferor in his own favour, another type of resulting trust arises by operation of law where there is no proof by evidence or presumption of a declaration of trust in favour of a beneficiary.
5. [1996] AC 669.
6. As Rickett and Grantham comment (2000) 116 LQR 15, '[w]hile … describing two sets of circumstances, his Lordship was not convinced that there were two types of resulting trust'.
7. Birks 'Restitution and Resulting Trusts' in *Equity: Contemporary Legal Developments* (ed. Goldstein, 1992) p. 335 *et seq*.
8. Chambers, *Resulting Trusts* (1997) p. 2. As Lord Millett commented in *Twinsectra Ltd v Yardley* [2002] 2 AC 164, 190, '[t]he central thesis of Dr Chambers' book is that a resulting trust arises whenever there is a transfer of property in circumstances in which the transferor (or more accurately the person at whose expense the property was provided) did not intend to benefit the recipient. It responds to the absence of an intention on the part of the transferor to pass the entire beneficial interest, not to a positive intention to retain it.'

> independently of intention. All resulting trusts come into being because the provider of property did not intend to benefit the recipient.

Similar views were expressed by Lord Millett in *Air Jamaica Ltd v Charlton*[9] in the following terms:

> Like a constructive trust, a resulting trust arises by operation of law, though unlike a constructive trust it gives effect to intention. But it arises whether or not the transferor intended to retain a beneficial interest – he almost always does not – since it responds to the absence of any intention on his part to pass a beneficial interest to the recipient.

Once this view of a resulting trust is accepted, the link with a restitutionary response is easy to make[10] and this in itself has led to controversy. Birks has suggested that if and so far as personal restitutionary claims are backed by equitable proprietary claims, we should learn to attribute those proprietary rights to the resulting trust.[11] Similarly, Chambers has put forward the view that the existing resulting trust is capable of a far greater role in proprietary restitution.[12] However, Lord Browne-Wilkinson in *Westdeutsche Landesbank Girozentrale v Islington Borough Council*[13] characterised the resulting trust as an unsuitable basis for developing proprietary restitutionary remedies, and Swadling has rejected such an approach, concluding that 'the resulting trust has little or no part to play in the law of restitution'.[14]

Swadling has also argued that the categories of presumed resulting trust examined below, namely the voluntary conveyance and purchase money resulting trusts, arise 'because of the operation of a true presumption, the fact proved by presumption being that the transferor declared a trust in his own favour.'[15] However, Mee's rationalisation of the basis of presumed resulting trusts is more satisfactory and he suggests that 'the key issue in relation to

---

9. [1999] 1 WLR 1399, 1412. See also the *dicta* of Potter LJ in *Twinsectra Ltd v Yardley* [1999] Lloyd's Rep Bank 438, 457.
10. See Simpson 'On the Nature of Resulting Trusts' in *Restitution and Equity Volume One: Resulting Trusts and Equitable Compensation* (eds. Birks and Rose, 2000) p. 19. He states that: 'In such circumstances, where the evidence (or the reinterpreted presumption) shows that a transfer was made without any intention to benefit the recipient, then the retention of the corresponding enrichment by the recipient will be unjust, in just the same way as in all cases where restitution is the legal response to circumstances of non-voluntary transfer.'
11. Birks 'Restitution and Resulting Trusts' in *Equity: Contemporary Legal Developments* (ed. Goldstein, 1992) pp. 368-369.
12. Chambers, *Resulting Trusts* (1997) p. 7.
13. [1996] AC 669, 716.
14. (1996) 16 LS 110, 111.
15. (2008) 124 LQR 72, 102.

presumed resulting trusts is the intention of the transferor to make the transferee a trustee for the transferor.'[16] In his view:

> The court's task is to identify and give effect to the purpose underlying the transaction, whether it was to make a gift or to create a trust. It makes no difference whether the fact presumed is described as an intention to create a trust for the transferee or, reflecting the influence of the concept of retention, not to pass the beneficial interest to the transferee.[17]

The concept of an 'automatically' resulting trust has also been the subject of considerable academic debate. Swadling has suggested that the use of the term 'automatic' is misleading[18] and puts forward the view that this form of failed trust 'defies legal analysis'.[19] Mee has argued convincingly that automatic resulting trusts can be explained on the basis that where a settlor intends to make the recipient of property a trustee, 'the trust does not truly fail – it simply gives way to a resulting trust'.[20] There is considerable merit in his view that the outcome in such cases, that there should be a resulting trust in favour of the settlor, 'is difficult to fault as a matter of justice' and is 'defensible as a matter of principle'.[21]

AUTOMATICALLY RESULTING TRUSTS

Failure of the Trust

Where an express trust fails completely for any reason, a resulting trust of the trust property will arise in favour of the settlor or his estate.[22] This may occur for a variety of reasons; there may have been a total failure of the beneficiaries, the settlement deed defining the scope of the trust may have been lost,[23] the trust may be void for uncertainty,[24] or may fail to qualify for charitable status in circumstances where it cannot operate as a valid purpose trust.[25] In *Re Ames'*

16. [2014] CLJ 86, 88.
17. *Ibid.* at 112.
18. (2008) 124 LQR 72, 99.
19. (2008) 124 LQR 72, 102. See further Chambers, *Resulting Trusts* (1997) Chapter 2.
20. 'Automatic Resulting Trusts: Retention, Restitution or Reposing Trust?' in *Constructive and Resulting Trusts* (ed. Mitchell, 2010) p. 207 at 209.
21. *Ibid.* at 235.
22. Swadling (2008) 124 LQR 72, 99 suggests that the use of the label 'automatic' in this context is misleading and that a resulting trust does not arise of its own volition in such circumstances but because the courts make an order to this effect.
23. *Cummins v Hall* [1933] IR 419.
24. *Re Pugh's Will Trusts* [1967] 1 WLR 1262; *Re Atkinson's Will Trusts* [1978] 1 WLR 586.
25. *Re Diplock* [1948] Ch 465. Or where the trust is subsequently found to be invalid as

Settlement[26] property was settled on the trusts of a marriage settlement by the husband's father. The marriage was subsequently declared void and it was held that this property should be held on a resulting trust for the settlor's estate after the husband's death, rather than passing to those entitled under the settlement in default of issue.

Another situation in which a resulting trust will arise is where property is given to trustees and yet no trusts are defined. This can arise in the context of a half secret trust,[27] where a testator makes it clear on the face of a will that property is to be held on trust without specifying the nature and extent of the trust and the identity of the beneficiaries. In those circumstances where such a trust fails because there has been no adequate communication and acceptance of the terms of the trust during the testator's lifetime,[28] or if it were to fail on the grounds of inconsistency between the terms of the will and the events which transpired,[29] a resulting trust in favour of the testator's estate would arise. A similar result will ensue where a testator makes an unsuccessful attempt to create a fully secret trust and the intended trustee admits that it was not the testator's intention that he should take as a beneficiary.[30]

One of the most important cases in this area is that of *Vandervell v IRC*,[31] in which the appellant transferred shares in a private company to a college which he wished to endow with the intention of declaring dividends on the shares. The effect of the arrangement was that the college would grant an option to a company which acted as trustee for various family trusts enabling the shares to be acquired by the company, although it was not stated on what trusts these shares were to be held. The House of Lords found that the option was held on a resulting trust for the appellant with the result that not having divested himself completely of his interest in the shares, he was liable for surtax on the dividends paid to the college. As Lord Wilberforce stated, 'the conclusion on the facts found, is simply that the option was vested in the trustee company as a trustee on trusts, not defined at the time, possibly to be defined later. But the equitable, or beneficial interest, cannot remain in the air: the consequence in law must be that it remains in the settlor'.[32]

---

creating a perpetual non-charitable purpose trust, see *Re St Andrew's (Cheam) Lawn Tennis Club Trust* [2012] 1 WLR 3487.

26. [1946] Ch 217.
27. See *supra* Chapter 5.
28. See *Scott v Brownrigg* (1881) 9 LR Ir 246; *Re Watters' Will Trusts* (1928) 62 ILTR 61. This seems to be now accepted as being the requirement in Ireland rather than communication and acceptance prior to the testator's will which still appears to be the position in England, see *supra* Chapter 5.
29. *Re Keen* [1937] Ch 236.
30. *Re Boyes* (1884) 26 Ch D 531.
31. [1967] 2 AC 291.
32. *Ibid.* at 329.

Failure to Exhaust the Beneficial Interest

In practice a trust does not often fail completely but a situation may quite frequently arise where there has been an incomplete disposal of the beneficial interest under a trust. Even though it may appear at the time a trust instrument or will is executed that this interest has been fully disposed of, subsequent events may occur, or fail to occur, which may change this position. In *Re Lane's Trusts*[33] by virtue of a marriage settlement a husband and wife each contributed the sum of £1,000 to a fund to be held on certain trusts with the intention that it would ultimately benefit their children. No issue of the marriage survived the husband and he died before his wife. On her death, it was held that a resulting trust in favour of the husband's administrator and the wife's executor arose. The resulting trust which will arise in such circumstances has been described as 'the last resort to which the law has recourse when the draftsman has made a blunder or failed to dispose of that which he has set out to dispose of'.[34] In *Re Cochrane*[35] a marriage settlement provided that assets were to be held on trust for the wife for life 'so long as she shall reside with [her husband]' and after her death for her husband and then for their issue as they should jointly appoint or in default of appointment at the age of 21, or in the case of daughters, on their marriage. The wife ceased to reside with her husband and her interest under the trust terminated. The income was thereafter paid to the husband until his death and the question then arose whether their children should become entitled to the income during the wife's lifetime. Harman J found that an omission had clearly been made by the draftsman of the settlement as there had been no provision to cover the events which had transpired. In the circumstances he held that a resulting trust should arise for the wife's lifetime.

It may often be difficult to distinguish a gift to a trustee on trust solely to carry out a specified purpose, the implication being that any remaining surplus will be held on a resulting trust, from a situation where a gift is made to a donee subject to the carrying out of some obligation in which case he will be permitted to keep whatever remains after this obligation has been fulfilled. Kekewich J commented in *Re West*[36] that '[i]t is impossible to say that because property is given to persons as trustees they therefore take no beneficial interest … [n]evertheless, there is a presumption that a gift in trust is not a beneficial gift.' This question must be resolved by seeking to ascertain the true intentions of the donor but where the non-beneficial character of the gift is clear from the face of the trust instrument or will, it will be difficult to rebut the presumption of a trust.[37] A good example of a case falling into the latter category outlined above is *Re Foord*,[38] in which a testator left his estate

33. (1863) 14 Ir Ch R 523.
34. *Re Cochrane* [1955] Ch 309, 316.
35. [1955] Ch 309.
36. [1900] 1 Ch 84, 87.
37. *Re Rees' Will Trusts* [1950] Ch 204.
38. [1922] 2 Ch 519.

to his sister absolutely on trust to pay his widow an annuity. Sargant J held that the sister was beneficially entitled to the balance when the income of the estate exceeded the amount of the annuity and that no resulting trust arose.

A number of cases have dealt with the circumstances which arise where property is given on trust for the maintenance or education of specified persons and the difficulties that this leads to when these purposes are fulfilled. Should the intended beneficiaries be permitted to keep the remaining trust property or should a resulting trust in favour of the donor arise once the stated objective has been achieved? Where the specified purposes can be regarded as merely constituting the testator's motive for making the gift, the donee will be permitted to retain the property, but this may be difficult to establish particularly where it is the donee's estate, rather than the donee personally, who stands to benefit. In *Re Trusts of the Abbott Fund*[39] contributions were made to a fund to be used for the maintenance of two distressed ladies. No provision had been made in relation to the disposal of the fund on the death of the survivor and Stirling J held that on her death the balance of the fund should be held on a resulting trust for the subscribers. This can be contrasted with *Re Andrew's Trust*,[40] where a fund was subscribed to by the friends of a deceased clergyman for the education of his children. Kekewich J held that when their formal education was complete, no resulting trust of the remaining balance should arise and that it should instead be divided equally amongst the children. He quoted with approval the following passage from the judgment of Wood VC in *Re Sanderson's Trusts*:[41]

> If a gross sum be given, or if the whole income of the property be given, and a special purpose be assigned for that gift, this Court always regards the gift as absolute, and the purpose merely as the motive of the gift, and therefore holds that the gift must take effect as to the whole sum or the whole income, as the case may be.

Kekewich J felt that he was entitled to construe 'education' in the broadest possible manner and even if a narrow interpretation were to be placed on the meaning of that word, it could be interpreted as being merely the 'motive of the gift' in the sense outlined in the passage above. This approach of treating the trust as being for the benefit of the beneficiaries generally with special reference to a particular purpose was followed in *Re Osoba*,[42] where a testator left property to his widow on trust to be used for her maintenance and for that of his mother and 'for the training of my daughter up to university grade and for the maintenance of my aged mother'. The testator's mother predeceased him and his widow died some years later. When the daughter completed her university education the issue of whether the testator's children from a previous

39. [1900] 2 Ch 326.
40. [1905] 2 Ch 48.
41. (1857) 3 K & J 497, 503.
42. [1978] 1 WLR 791 (ChD); [1979] 1 WLR 247 (CA).

marriage could claim the residue on intestacy arose. Megarry VC set out a number of general principles as follows:

> I think that you have to look at the persons intended to benefit, and be ready, if they can still benefit, to treat the stated method of benefit as merely indicating purpose, and no doubt, as indicating the means of benefit which are to be in the forefront. In short, if a trust is constituted for the assistance of certain persons by certain stated means there is a sharp distinction between cases where the beneficiaries have died and cases where they are still living. If they are dead, the court is ready to hold that there is a resulting trust for the donors; for the major purpose of the trust, that of providing help and benefit for the beneficiaries comes to an end when the beneficiaries are all dead and are beyond earthly help, whether by the stated means or otherwise. But if the beneficiaries are still living, the major purpose of providing help and benefit for the beneficiaries can still be carried out even after the stated means have all been accomplished, and so the court will be ready to treat the stated means as being merely indicative and not restrictive.[43]

The Court of Appeal agreed that the testator's overriding intention was to provide for his wife and daughter and that the specified purposes should be merely regarded as an expression of his motives. In these circumstances no resulting trust arose and it was held by the Court of Appeal, varying the order of Megarry VC, that the beneficiaries took as joint tenants with the result that on her mother's death, the daughter became entitled to the whole of the residue.[44]

Arguably there has been a certain lack of consistency in the case law in this area, although some distinguishing features can be identified. While in *Abbott* it was no longer possible to use the funds for the benefit of the beneficiaries, this was clearly not the case in *Andrews* and *Osoba*, where the beneficiaries were still alive. So while it would be difficult to distinguish between the motives of the subscribers in *Abbott* and *Andrews*, the results in these cases do seem to be justified by the surrounding circumstances.

A further difficulty may arise where a fund is comprised mainly of anonymous contributions. In *Re Gillingham Bus Disaster Fund*[45] donations were made to a fund set up to benefit those injured in an accident and to provide a memorial for those who had been killed. Some of this fund was derived from contributions made by known individuals but it was comprised mainly of donations of an anonymous nature raised by street collections and other means. Harman J concluded that a resulting trust arose despite the obvious practical difficulties involved in drawing such a conclusion and that the Crown's claim

43. *Ibid.* at 795-796.
44. Megarry VC had held that the daughter and the mother's personal representatives were beneficially entitled to the residue in equal shares.
45. [1958] Ch 300. See Atiyah (1958) 74 LQR 190.

to *bona vacantia* could not succeed merely because there were a number of donors whose identity could not be ascertained. He stated:

> The general principle must be that where money is held on trusts and the trusts declared do not exhaust the fund it will revert to the donor or settlor under what is called a resulting trust. The reasoning behind this is that the settlor or donor did not part with his money absolutely out and out but only *sub modo* to the intent that his wishes as declared by the declaration of trust should be carried into effect.[46]

This result was not followed in the later decision of *Re West Sussex Constabulary's Widows, Children & Benevolent (1930) Fund Trusts*,[47] in which Goff J had to determine the manner of distribution of a fund made up partly from the proceeds of entertainments and raffles, from collecting boxes, and from donations and legacies. While Goff J concluded that the gifts in the latter category were to be held on a resulting trust for the donors or their estates, he held that gifts in the first two categories went as *bona vacantia* on the basis that they were absolute out and out gifts. While the logic of the approach in *Gillingham* cannot really be faulted, the practical result of such a finding is often wholly unsatisfactory and to this extent the conclusion reached by Goff J is preferable.[48]

In this jurisdiction, the provisions of section 48(1) of the Charities Act 1961 are of relevance and allow contributions, even those given for non-charitable purposes, to be redistributed in an appropriate manner. It provides that property given for specific charitable or non-charitable purposes which fail may be applied cy-près[49] as if given for charitable purposes generally where it belongs 'to a donor who, after such advertisements and inquiries as are reasonable, cannot be identified or cannot be found; or to a donor who has executed a written disclaimer of his right to have the property returned.' The subsection also provides that in applying property given for specific non-charitable purposes, regard shall be had to the wishes of the trustees or other persons in charge of the property. Section 48(2) provides that it shall be conclusively presumed that the proceeds of case collections, lotteries and other means where it is not possible to distinguish one gift from another, belong to donors who cannot be identified.

46. *Ibid.* at 310.
47. [1971] Ch 1.
48. Although to the extent that it involved the distribution of funds on the dissolution of a club or association, it is not in line with more recent authorities, e.g. *Re Bucks. Constabulary Widows' and Orphans' Fund Friendly Society (No. 2)* [1979] 1 WLR 936, see *infra*.
49. See further Chapter 11.

The Distribution of Surplus Funds on the Dissolution of Unincorporated Associations

Where surplus funds remain on the dissolution of an unincorporated association, some method of distributing these funds must be determined.[50] In *Re Printers and Transferrers Amalgamated Trades Protection Society*[51] on the dissolution of a society formed to provide support for its members and their families, surplus funds were distributed amongst the surviving members in proportion to their contributions by way of a resulting trust. This decision has been criticised on the basis that a proper application of resulting trust principles would have ensured that such distribution would not have been confined to the surviving members on the grounds that 'death does not deprive a man of his beneficial interest'.[52] A less convenient, although more principled, solution was accepted by Cohen J in *Re Hobourn Aero Components Ltd's Air Raid Distress Fund*,[53] in which he held that on the dissolution of the association the assets should be distributed amongst all the members, past and present, in shares proportionate to their contributions.

More recent case law in England has tended to lay considerably more emphasis on the manner in which an association's assets are held prior to its dissolution. Where the funds are considered as being held on trust for the association's purposes, particularly where persons other than members have also contributed, this will usually give rise to a resulting trust in the event of dissolution,[54] or where the donor effectively disclaims it, the assets will go to the Crown as *bona vacantia*.[55] Where, on the other hand, the donor has parted with his money on an absolute basis pursuant to a form of contract, the manner in which any surplus funds will be disposed of in the event of a dissolution will be governed by contract. This may either take the form of an express provision contained in the association's rules or, in the absence of such a provision, in accordance with an implied term, usually to the effect that the surplus is to be divided equally amongst those individuals who are members of the association at the time of the dissolution. In circumstances where an association may have been dissolved due to lack of members this will be impractical and the remaining assets will pass as *bona vacantia*.

The most important case in this area which seems to confirm that the modern trend is to favour a contractual approach is *Re Bucks. Constabulary*

---

50. See further Matthews [1995] Conv 302.
51. [1899] 2 Ch 184.
52. *Re Sick and Funeral Society of St John's Sunday School, Golcar* [1973] Ch 51, 59 *per* Megarry J.
53. [1946] Ch 86.
54. E.g. the category of donations and legacies in *Re West Sussex Constabulary's Widows Childrens & Benevolent (1930) Fund Trusts* [1971] Ch 1.
55. E.g. the category of the proceeds of collection boxes in *Re West Sussex Constabulary's Widows, Childrens & Benevolent (1930) Fund Trusts* [1971] Ch 1.

Widows' and Orphans' Fund Friendly Society (No. 2),[56] which concerned the distribution of a fund established to provide benefits to the widows and orphans of deceased police officers and for the relief of members of the force during sickness or ill-health. When the Bucks. constabulary was amalgamated with others the issue of the proper distribution of the association's assets arose. Walton J held that the surplus funds should be distributed equally amongst the members of the association alive at the date of dissolution.[57] He also expressed the view that it is only where a club or association has become moribund that its assets should go as *bona vacantia*. This approach was followed in *Re GKN Bolts & Nuts Ltd (Automotive Division) Birmingham Works, Sports and Social Club*[58] and now seems to be generally recognised as the most practical way of resolving this question. However, it has not met with universal approval and in *Davis v Richards & Wallington Industries Ltd*,[59] Scott J departed from the more recognised approach of analysing the manner in which the funds are held prior to dissolution and concluded that a resulting trust might still provide the correct solution in certain circumstances.[60]

It now seems clear from the decision of Lewison J in *Hanchett-Stamford v Attorney-General*,[61] despite earlier indications to the contrary,[62] that where an unincorporated association ceases to exist on the death of one of only two members, the last surviving member is entitled to claim the assets of the association which do not vest in the Crown as *bona vacantia*. This conclusion was based in part on the reasoning that to deprive one of two members of an unincorporated association of his share in its assets by reason of the death of the other and without provision of compensation appeared to be a breach of article 1 of the First Protocol of the European Convention on Human Rights which guarantees the peaceful enjoyment of possessions.

The approach favoured in this jurisdiction seems to involve the rejection of the concept of a resulting trust in favour of a contractually based solution. However, there is still a lack of consensus on the issue of whether the distribution of surplus funds should be carried out on the basis of equal division or in accordance with the proportion of contributions made. In *Tierney v*

---

56. [1979] 1 WLR 936.
57. Contrast this with the approach taken in *Cunnack v Edwards* [1896] 2 Ch 679 where it was held that the personal representatives of the members of an association were not entitled to a share in the society's funds when it was dissolved after the death of the widow of the last surviving member on the basis that its members had received all that for which they had contracted. See also *Re West Sussex Constabulary's Widows, Childrens and Benevolent (1930) Fund Trusts* [1971] Ch 1.
58. [1982] 1 WLR 774.
59. [1990] 1 WLR 1511.
60. See Gardner [1992] Conv 41 for an analysis of this decision. See also the comments of Lord Millett in *Air Jamaica Ltd v Charlton* [1999] 1 WLR 1399, 1412.
61. [2009] Ch 173. See further Griffiths [2009] Conv 428; Baughen [2010] Conv 216.
62. *Re Bucks. Constabulary Widows' and Orphans' Fund Friendly Society (No. 2)* [1979] 1 WLR 936, 943.

Tough[63] the manner of distribution of a fund established to provide benefits for the employees of the Grand Canal Company and their families had to be considered. O'Connor MR rejected the suitability of the resulting trust approach to the facts of the case before him in the following terms:

> As I understand that doctrine, it applies only to a case where the trusts or purposes to which a fund or property is dedicated do not exhaust the whole interest, whereupon such part of the fund or property as is not required for carrying out the trusts or the purposes of the settlor results, or, in other words, goes back to the settlor. Now, this principle would give back to the existing members only so much of the funds as represented their own contributions to it ... A resulting trust would have given the fund, so far as subscribed by deceased members, to their personal representatives, and not to other parties.[64]

He concluded instead that the assets were the property of the society which was composed of individual members and that the funds should be distributed amongst the existing members in proportion to the contributions which they had made. In these circumstances he found that the fund could not be regarded as *bona vacantia* and that the Attorney General had no claim to the society's assets. While the basis for O'Connor MR's decision has been upheld as 'wholly convincing' by Walton J in *Re Bucks. Constabulary Widows' and Orphans' Fund Friendly Society (No. 2)*,[65] the manner which he prescribed for distribution of the funds has not met with similar approval.[66] Another relevant authority is the decision of Johnston J in *Feeney v MacManus*,[67] which concerned the dissolution of the General Post Office (Dublin) Dining Club which had a membership comprised of certain classes of post office officials. The club, which provided subsidised refreshments, ceased to function following the destruction of the GPO in 1916 and when the building was re-opened in 1929, a new club was formed with similar objectives and membership. The plaintiffs, who were the secretary and treasurer of the original club, sought directions from the court in relation to the distribution of its remaining property. It was held by Johnston J that the entire fund must be distributed in equal shares amongst the individuals who were members of the club at the time of its dissolution and the

63. [1914] 1 IR 142.
64. *Ibid.* at 155.
65. [1979] 1 WLR 936, 947. Although it could be argued that he decided simply that the inevitable consequence of following resulting trust principles would not yield the result desired, and that an approach which would allow him to distribute proportionately amongst existing members must therefore be arrived at.
66. Rickett [1980] CLJ 88, 116 suggests that it is 'an attempted half-way house which has no basis' and argues that once the manner in which the property was to be held was determined, division on the dissolution of the society ought to have been in accordance with that finding.
67. [1937] IR 23.

personal representatives of those who had died since that date. He concluded that it would be impossible to ascertain the proportions in which each of the members had subscribed to the club's funds and assets and that accordingly, distribution had to be on an equal basis.

This principle of equal distribution would appear to be firmly entrenched in England. In *Re Sick and Funeral Society of St John's Sunday School, Golcar*[68] Megarry J agreed that membership of a club or association is primarily a question of contract and that the sums paid by members cease to be their individual property and capable of forming the subject matter of a resulting trust. He concluded that on dissolution the only interested persons should be the existing members of the club and 'reject[ed] the basis of proportionate division in favour of equality, or division per capita.' Similarly, in *Re Bucks. Constabulary Widows' and Orphans' Fund Friendly Society (No. 2)*[69] Walton J accepted that, provided that there is no other method of distribution prescribed by the terms of the contract, it should be on the basis of equality amongst the existing members. That this is the appropriate approach in the absence of any contractual stipulation to the contrary was confirmed at first instance in *Hardy v Hoade*,[70] where it was suggested that the principle of equal division was particularly apposite in the case of a tennis club where some members have only paid in more because they have been entitled to the benefits of membership for a longer period of time. While it was suggested that different principles might apply in the case of a friendly society in which the purpose of membership is to build the assets of the society for distribution according to the members' contributions, it seems clear that the proper default position in the case of a club is per capita distribution of the net assets amongst the members at the time of the club's dissolution.

Certainly this manner of distribution seems to be more in line with the principle of a contractual relationship which governs members' entitlements and it is likely that the basis of division adopted by the High Court in *Feeney v MacManus* will be applied in Ireland in the absence of any express provision requiring an alternative approach.

Quistclose Trust

A useful explanation of a Quistclose trust is set out by Briggs LJ in the decision of the Court of Appeal in *Challinor v Bellis*[71] as follows.

> Quistclose-type trusts are a species of resulting trust which arise where property (usually money) is transferred on terms which do not leave it at the free disposal of the transferee. That restriction upon its use is usually

68. [1973] Ch 51.
69. [1979] 1 WLR 936.
70. [2017] EWHC 2476 (Ch).
71. [2015] EWCA Civ 59 at [55].

created by an arrangement that the money should be used exclusively for a stated purpose or purposes.

Considerable debate has surrounded the manner in which the so-called 'Quistclose'[72] trust should be classified. While it may be considered to be a form of express trust,[73] the trust which will arise in favour of the lender tends to be classified as a resulting trust[74] and for this reason it is convenient to deal with them at this point. Although there has been little consideration given to the type of trust recognised in the *Quistclose* case in this jurisdiction,[75] trusts of this nature are likely to assume increasing significance in the future and it is proposed to outline the basic principles which relate to them.[76]

While it is possible to identify significant differences between the concepts of a debt and a trust, they are not always mutually exclusive. As Bingham J pointed out in *Neste Oy v Lloyds Bank plc*,[77] the existence of a contractual obligation to pay a debt is not necessarily inconsistent with the parallel existence of a trust in favour of the creditor. If a lender loans money to a borrower subject to the conditions that it is to be kept in a separate bank account and employed for a specified purpose, such an agreement may give rise to a trust.[78] A further question arises when, for whatever reason, the money cannot be used for the purpose laid down. It would appear that in these circumstances, a primary purpose trust coupled with a secondary resulting trust for the benefit of the lender will arise.[79] This reasoning follows from the decision of the House of Lords in *Barclays Bank Ltd v Quistclose Investments Ltd*.[80] A company, R. Ltd, which was in serious financial difficulties, borrowed a sum of money from Quistclose for the purpose of paying a dividend to shareholders under

72. Named after *Barclays Bank Ltd v Quistclose Investments Ltd* [1970] AC 567.
73. Rhodes (2013) 27 Trust Law Int 179, 185 has advocated recognising such trusts as being express in nature. See further Hudson (2017) 80 MLR 775, 783. Glister [2004] CLJ 632, 633 has argued that the theories as to the nature of the *Quistclose* trust are not necessarily mutually exclusive.
74. *Twinsectra Ltd v Yardley* [2002] 2 AC 164, 184 per Lord Millett.
75. Although an argument based on the principles set out in *Barclay's Bank Ltd v Quistclose Investments Ltd* was put forward and rejected in *Re Money Markets International Stockbrokers Ltd (No. 2)* [2001] 2 IR 17.
76. Although Quistclose trusts tend to arise primarily in a commercial context, it has been held that they can also be found in other contexts, e.g. in family proceedings. See *Re N. (A Child) (Financial Provision: Dependency)* [2009] EWHC 11 (Fam) at [30].
77. [1983] 2 Lloyd's Rep 658, 663. However, it should be noted that this decision was disapproved by the Supreme Court in *Angove's PTY Ltd v Bailey* [2016] 1 WLR 3179. See further Wong [2016] Conv 480; Watts (2017) 133 LQR 11.
78. Where the money is used for the authorised purpose, the trust will determine and only the relationship of debtor/creditor, which involves personal liability, will remain. However, where the borrower uses the money for an unauthorised purpose, the lender will be able to employ a proprietary tracing remedy.
79. See Rickett (1991) 107 LQR 608, 617.
80. [1970] AC 567.

an arrangement which spelled out that the money was only to be used for this purpose and which involved this money being paid into a separate bank account in Barclays Bank, to whom R. Ltd was indebted. Before the dividend was paid, R. Ltd went into liquidation and the money in the account was claimed by both Quistclose and Barclays. The House of Lords held that the money had been paid into the account on trust for the purpose of paying the dividend and that since this purpose could not now be carried out, it was held on a resulting trust for Quistclose. As Lord Wilberforce said, the loan for the express purpose of ensuring the payment of the dividend gave rise 'to a relationship of a fiduciary character or trust, in favour, as a primary trust, of the creditors, and secondarily, if the primary trust fail[ed], of the third person',[81] namely the institution which had made the loan. The principle laid down in *Quistclose* was applied by the English Court of Appeal in *Re EVTR*[82] in a situation where the loan was made in order that a company might purchase new equipment rather than to ensure payment of a debt. Dillon LJ concluded that '[o]n *Quistclose* principles, a resulting trust in favour of the provider of the money arises when money is provided for a particular purpose only, and that purpose fails.'

A useful summary of the circumstances giving rise to a Quistclose trust was provided by Lord Millett in *Twinsectra Ltd v Yardley*:[83]

> [I]t is well established that a loan to a borrower for a specific purpose where the borrower is not free to apply the money for any other purpose gives rise to fiduciary obligations on the part of the borrower which a court of equity will enforce. In earlier cases the purpose was to enable the borrower to pay his creditors or some of them, but the principle is not limited to such cases.
>
> Such arrangements are commonly described as creating 'a Quistclose trust' … When the money is advanced, the lender acquires a right, enforceable in equity, to see that it is applied for the stated purpose, or more accurately to prevent its application for any other purpose. This prevents the borrower from obtaining any beneficial interest in the money, at least while the designated purpose is still capable of being carried out.

This explanation has been quoted with approval in other cases[84] and as Evans-Lombe J commented in *Cooper v PRG Powerhouse Ltd*,[85] whether or not

---

81. *Ibid.* at 580. This approach has been applied in other jurisdictions, e.g. in Australia (*Re Groom* (1977) 16 ALR 278) and New Zealand (by the New Zealand Court of Appeal in *General Communications Ltd v DFC New Zealand Ltd* [1990] 3 NZLR 406).
82. [1987] BCLC 646.
83. [2002] 2 AC 164, 184. See further Richardson (2002) 16 Trust Law Int 165; Glister (2002) 16 Trust Law Int 223; Yeo and Tijo (2003) 119 LQR 8.
84. E.g. *Cooper v PRG Powerhouse Ltd* [2008] EWHC 498 (Ch) at [14]; *Soutzos v Asombang* [2010] EWHC 842 (Ch) at [143].
85. [2008] EWHC 498 (Ch).

money has been paid subject to a purpose trust is a question of fact. As he stated, '[i]f a purpose trust is to be established, it is necessary for the payer to show that the arrangement pursuant to which the payment was made defined the purpose for which it was made in such a way that it was understood by the recipient that it was not at his free disposal'.

In the *Twinsectra* case, the plaintiff lent money for the purchase of property after a solicitor gave a personal undertaking that it would be retained by his firm until applied in the acquisition of the property and would not be used for any other purpose. The solicitor who had given the undertaking went bankrupt and the lender commenced proceedings against a number of defendants, including another solicitor, on the grounds that he had dishonestly assisted in a breach of trust. The majority of the House of Lords held that a trust arose because the money had been paid into a solicitor's client account although it did not impose accessory liability. However, Lord Millett concluded that the money was held on a Quistclose trust and went on to hold the solicitor liable for assisting in a breach of trust.[86] It should be noted that Lord Millett made it clear that a Quistclose trust does not necessarily arise merely because money is paid for a particular purpose. As he pointed out, 'a lender will often inquire into the purpose for which a loan is sought in order to decide whether he would be justified in making it. He may be said to lend the money for the purpose in question, but this is not enough to create a trust.'[87] This statement and a useful summary of the principles relating to such trusts contained in the judgment of Norris J in *Bieber v Teathers Ltd*[88] were set out by McGovern J in his judgment in *Harlequin Property (SVG) Ltd v O'Halloran*.[89] However, McGovern J found that, although the plaintiff had paid over funds for completion of a project, it could not be said that there was an intention that the funds in question were for a specific purpose and for no other. In the circumstances, he concluded that the plaintiffs had not established that the facts of the case fitted within the ambit of a *Quistclose* trust.

A further point made clear by Lord Millett in *Twinsectra* is that a party's subjective intentions are not relevant in this context. As he stated, '[i]f he enters into arrangements which have the effect of creating a trust, it is not necessary that he should appreciate that they do so; it is sufficient that he intends to enter into them.' This point was developed by Briggs LJ in *Challinor v Bellis*[90] in the following terms:

> There must be an intention to create a trust on the part of the transferor. This is an objective question. It means that the transferor must have

86. It has been argued by Hughes-Davies [2015] Conv 26, 46 that it seems unlikely that the transaction in *Twinsectra* created a 'true *Quistclose* trust'.
87. [2002] 2 AC 164, 185.
88. [2012] EWHC 190 (Ch) at [16] – [22]. See also [2012] EWCA Civ 1466 at [14].
89. [2013] IEHC 362.
90. [2015] EWCA Civ 59 at [56] – [58].

> intended to enter into arrangements which, viewed objectively, have the effect in law of creating a trust … A person creates a trust by his words or conduct, not by his innermost thoughts. His subjective intentions are, as Lord Millett said, irrelevant. In the *Twinsectra* case, a Quistclose trust was established despite the transferor having no subjective intention to create a trust. But the objectivity principle works both ways. A person who does subjectively intend to create a trust may fail to do so if his words and conduct, viewed objectively, fall short of what is required. As with the interpretation of contracts, this process of interpretation is often called the ascertainment of objective intention. In the contractual context the court is looking for the objective common intention, whereas in the trust context the search is for the objective intention of the alleged settlor.

In such cases, it is not necessary that the term 'trust' is used provided the conditions outlined above, namely in relation to segregation of the funds and specifying the purpose for their use, have been complied with. This point was made clear by Lord MacDermott in the Northern Ireland decision of *Re McKeown*.[91] Here the applicant loaned a sum of money to McKeown, in whose favour an arbitration award had been made, so that the latter might pay the necessary fees and costs to enable him to recover the award. The loan was made on the condition that it would only be used for the purpose of paying these fees and costs, and that the applicant would be paid out of the award. McKeown was adjudicated bankrupt before he received payment of the award and the applicant sought a declaration that the official assignee held the sum of the loan on trust for him. Lord MacDermott upheld the applicant's claim and did not appear to be deterred by the lack of the type of language usually associated with the creation of trusts. However, the words used must be sufficiently certain in nature and must show a sufficient intention to create a trust.[92] It is also clear from the decision of the High Court of the Isle of Man in *Habana Ltd v Kaupthing Singer & Friedlander (Isle of Man) Ltd*[93] that in order for a *Quistclose* trust to arise, it is necessary for new money to be received by a bank for a stated purpose and that neither the routine acceptance of instructions by a bank to make a payment into an account nor the debiting of the account was sufficient in itself to constitute an intention to create a trust.

It is important to point out that in the *Quistclose* case itself, the primary purpose of the trust was no longer capable of being carried out and the question of what the outcome will be where this obligation can still be fulfilled must be considered. Where a trust of this nature is created, a right to compel performance may also be vested in the 'beneficiaries', i.e. those contemplated as the ultimate recipients of the fund. This was the situation which arose in *Re Northern*

91. [1974] NI 226.
92. *Re Multi Guarantee Co. Ltd* [1987] BCLC 257.
93. (2009-10) 12 ITELR 736.

Development Holdings Ltd,[94] where funds were paid into a segregated account for the specific purpose of providing money for the unsecured creditors of a company which was in financial difficulties so that it might continue trading. When the company went into receivership, the question arose of who was entitled to the balance remaining in the account; the banks who had provided the funds, or the company's unsecured creditors. As Millett[95] points out, while Megarry VC might have distinguished the *Quistclose* decision on a number of grounds,[96] he held that the arrangement gave rise to a trust in that mould which might be enforced both by the banks and by the company and its unsecured creditors. This approach was followed by Peter Gibson J in *Carreras Rothmans Ltd v Freeman Matthews Treasure Ltd*,[97] so considerable importance may attach to the question of whether the ultimate beneficiaries are in a position to enforce the obligation involved in the arrangement.

The true nature of a Quistclose trust has given rise to considerable judicial and academic debate and it is possible to identify a number of alternative theories concerning the location of the beneficial interest pending the application of the money for the stated purpose or the failure of that purpose. In *Twinsectra Ltd v Yardley*[98] Lord Millett examined various possibilities although he clearly favoured the position that the beneficial interest remained in the lender throughout.[99] An alternative view put forward by Chambers[100] is that the borrower receives the entire beneficial ownership of the money subject to a contractual right in the lender to prevent its misapplication and if the purpose for which it was lent fails a resulting trust in the latter's favour will come into being. A further alternative adopted by Peter Gibson J in *Carreras Rothmans Ltd v Freeman Matthews Treasure Ltd*[101] is that the beneficial interest remains in suspense until the stated purpose is carried out or fails. However, Lord Millett concluded as follows:

---

94. Chancery Division, 6 October 1978.
95. (1985) 101 LQR 269.
96. *Ibid*. at 278. He suggested that the distinctions were that the fund in *Northern Developments* was established to enable the company to continue trading which would necessarily involve it incurring further liabilities and because the creditors were told of the existence, size and purpose of the fund, unlike in *Quistclose* where the contemplated recipients did not even know of its existence.
97. [1985] Ch 207.
98. [2002] 2 AC 164.
99. See further the criticisms of Penner, 'Lord Millett's Analysis' in *The Quistclose Trust: Critical Essays* (ed. Swadling, 2004) p.56
100. Chambers, *Resulting Trusts* (1997) Chapter 3. See Millett [1998] RLR 283. Lord Millett commented in *Twinsectra Ltd v Yardley* [2002] 2 AC 164, 190 that he did not believe that Chambers' analysis can survive the criticism levelled against it by Ho and Smart (2001) 21 OJLS 267. See further Glister (2004) 63 CLJ 632.
101. [1985] Ch 207, 223. See also the *dicta* of Potter LJ in the Court of Appeal in *Twinsectra* [1999] 1 Lloyd's Rep Bank 438, 456, although he went on to consider what is effectively Chambers' analysis of the position (see *supra*), namely that the beneficial interest was in the borrower. See Tettenborn [2000] LMCLQ 459.

> I would reject all the alternative analyses...and hold the Quistclose trust to be an entirely orthodox example of the kind of default trust known as a resulting trust. The lender pays the money to the borrower by way of loan, but he does not part with the entire beneficial interest in the money, and in so far as he does not it is held on a resulting trust for the lender from the outset.[102]

The doctrinal characterisation of Quistclose trusts continues to give rise to much debate and uncertainty still surrounds the underlying basis for such trusts. Hudson has suggested that while normative justifications grounded in unconscionability, fairness and incentivisation all have weaknesses, in her view the strongest argument is that Quistclose trusts are justified by reference to party intention.[103]

PRESUMED RESULTING TRUSTS

As a general principle, where the ownership of property is transferred to a grantee who gives no consideration, an inference arises that the grantee holds the property by way of a resulting trust for the grantor. However, it must be stressed that this is only a presumption which is 'neither universal nor irrebuttable'.[104] It has been suggested that the presumption rests on the principle that Equity intends bargains not gifts[105] and it can be rebutted by evidence that a gift was intended.[106] The presumption of a resulting trust can also be displaced by the presumption of advancement,[107] which involves the inference being drawn that a gift of property was intended rather than that it should be held on a resulting trust because of the relationship between the parties.[108] Mee has argued that

---

102. [2002] 2 AC 164, 192-193. However, this view has not won universal acceptance. See Payne 'Quistclose and Resulting Trusts' in *Restitution and Equity Volume One: Resulting Trusts and Equitable Compensation* (eds. Birks and Rose, 2000) pp. 88-89.
103. (2017) 80 MLR 775, 811.
104. *Per* Cromwell J in the decision of the Supreme Court of Canada in *Kerr v Baranow* (2011) 328 DLR (4th) 577, 588. See also *Thorsteinson Estate v Olson* (2016) 404 DLR 453 at [25]. In *Taylor v Taylor* [2017] 4 WLR 83 at [41] it was suggested that 'it cannot be too highly stressed that this is merely a presumption, and must yield to evidence requiring a different conclusion.'
105. *Pecore v Pecore* (2007) 279 DLR (4th) 513, 523 *per* Rothstein J. See also *Kerr v Baranow* (2011) 328 DLR (4th) 577, 588.
106. *McEneaney v Shevlin* [1912] 1 IR 32; [1912] 1 IR 278. This is the essence of the distinction between automatically and presumed resulting trusts. As Swadling points out (see (1996) 16 LS 110, 113), 'an automatic resulting trust cannot be rebutted by evidence of an intention to give'.
107. *Hepworth v Hepworth* (1870) LR 11 Eq 10.
108. Considered *infra* pp. 204-215. It has been suggested by Lord Briggs, delivering the judgement of the Privy Council in *Gany Holdings (PTC) SA v Khan* [2018] UKPC 21 at [17] that these presumptions 'are, in modern times, a last resort, now that historic

the continued existence of voluntary transfer resulting trusts is difficult to justify today.[109] However, the presumption continues to apply in many circumstances unless it is rebutted or displaced in the circumstances outlined.

Voluntary Conveyance or Transfer

Where the owner of property makes a voluntary transfer of it to another person, a presumption of a resulting trust arises unless there is sufficient evidence of a contrary intention to rebut the presumption[110] or the presumption of advancement dictates otherwise. The circumstances in which the presumption of a resulting trust may be rebutted have been considered on a number of occasions by the Canadian courts in recent years and these principles provide useful guidance. Once the presumption of a resulting trust is raised, in order to rebut it the transferee must establish on the balance of probabilities that the transferor intended to make a gift.[111] It is the actual intention of the grantor which is the governing consideration if it is sought to rebut the presumption.[112] As a general principle, evidence showing a transferor's intention 'ought to be contemporaneous, or nearly so'[113] to the transaction,[114] and evidence arising subsequently may only be admitted if it is relevant to the transferor's intention at the time of the conveyance.[115] It has also been suggested that 'after the fact evidence can be admitted so long as the trial judge is careful to consider the possibility of self-serving changes in intention over time,'[116] although care clearly needs to be taken in assessing the reliability of such evidence. This is broadly in line with the approach now adopted in England in considering the

restrictions on the admissibility of evidence have been removed, and the forensic tools for the ascertainment and weighing of evidence are more readily available to the court.'

109. Mee (2017) 70 CLP 189, 220-221. See also Mee, '"So, How Should I Presume?": Loan, Resulting Trust, or Discharge of a Prior Obligation' in *Modern Studies in Property Law* Volume 10 (eds. McFarlane and Agnew, 2019) p. 321 at 337.
110. Swadling suggests (see (1996) 16 LS 110, 111) that an examination of the historical origins of the resulting trust reveals that 'any evidence which is inconsistent with the presumption that the transferee is to be a trustee will suffice'.
111. *Pecore v Pecore* (2007) 279 DLR (4th) 513, 529. See also *Thorsteinson Estate v Olson* (2016) 404 DLR 453, 465.
112. *Per* Cromwell J in the decision of the Supreme Court of Canada in *Kerr v Baranow* (2011) 328 DLR (4th) 577, 588. See also *Pecore v Pecore* (2007) 279 DLR (4th) 513, 529.
113. *Jeans v Cooke* (1857) 24 Beav 513, 521, referred to in *Clemens v Clemens Estate* (1956) 1 DLR (2d) 625, 632.
114. *Pecore v Pecore* (2007) 279 DLR (4th) 513, 532. See also *Thorsteinson Estate v Olson* (2016) 404 DLR 453, 465.
115. *Pecore v Pecore* (2007) 279 DLR (4th) 513, 533. See also *Thorsteinson Estate v Olson* (2016) 404 DLR 453, 465.
116. *Rascal Trucking Ltd v Nishi* (2013) 359 DLR (4th) 575, 578 *per* Rothstein J; *Pecore v Pecore* (2007) 279 DLR (4th) 513, 533.

circumstances, examined below, in which the presumption of advancement may be rebutted.[117]

The presumption of a resulting trust in these circumstances applies both to voluntary conveyances and transfers of personal property. The law relating to the transfer of freehold land is now affected by statute, so it is advisable to examine it separately.

Conveyance of Land

A voluntary conveyance of freehold land 'unto the grantee and his heirs' raised a resulting use to the grantor which was executed by the Statute of Uses 1634, with the result that the legal estate reverted to the grantor. As Wylie has stated: 'After the 1634 Statute a voluntary conveyance of land in Ireland without any uses expressed was ineffective and left the legal estate in the land in the grantor.'[118] If the gift of land was 'unto and to the use of the grantee and his heirs' this prevented a resulting use arising and the legal estate became effectively vested in the grantee. However, the Statute of Uses 1634 was repealed by the Land and Conveyancing Law Reform Act 2009[119] and section 62(2) of that Act provides that a deed executed after the coming into effect of that part of the legislation will be fully effective without the need for any conveyance to uses. Section 62(3) goes on to provide that: 'In the case of a voluntary conveyance executed after the commencement of this Chapter, a resulting use for the grantor is not implied merely because the land is not expressed to be conveyed for the use or benefit of the grantee.' There has been some debate about whether the absence of any reference to a 'resulting trust' in this subsection leaves open the question of whether there might still be a presumption of a resulting trust on a voluntary conveyance of land.[120] However, it is likely that the word 'use' was employed rather than 'trust' for the sake of internal consistency in section 62(3) which is a section dealing with conveyances by deed, given that the universal practice in this jurisdiction has been to use the formula 'unto and to the use of'. While there is unlikely to be a difference of any substance between a 'resulting use' and a 'resulting trust' in circumstances where the Statute of Uses has been repealed by the 2009 Act, for the avoidance of doubt it might have been preferable to have used the phrase 'resulting use or trust' in the subsection.

In England, the Law of Property Act 1925 had already repealed the Statute of Uses 1535 and section 60(3) provides that 'in a voluntary conveyance a resulting trust for the grantor shall not be implied merely by reason that the

117. *Lavelle v Lavelle* [2004] EWCA Civ 223 at [19].
118. Wylie, *Irish Land Law* (4th ed., 2010) p. 605.
119. Schedule 2, Part 1.
120. Keane, *Equity and the Law of Trusts in Ireland* (3rd ed., 2017) p. 225. He expresses the view that 'the absence of any reference to a resulting trust in s.62(3) leaves open the question as to whether there is still a presumption of a resulting trust on a voluntary conveyance of freehold land.'

property is not expressed to be conveyed for the use or benefit of the grantee.' The effect of this subsection appeared to be that a voluntary conveyance of land takes effect as expressed unless there is evidence of a contrary intention, although in view of the fact that this question has not been finally determined by the courts[121] it may still be advisable to make it clear that a gift was intended. Russell LJ remarked in *Hodgson v Marks*[122] that it is now a 'debatable question whether on a voluntary transfer of land by A to stranger B there is a presumption of a resulting trust'. Subsequently, in *Lohia v Lohia,*[123] Nicholas Strauss QC, sitting as a Deputy High Court judge, stated that on a plain reading of section 60, the presumption of a resulting trust has been abolished in relation to voluntary conveyances of land. In his view, section 60(3) provides in effect that a voluntary conveyance means what it says and that it is not necessary to use additional words to make it effective.[124] On appeal, the Court of Appeal[125] held that the trial judge's findings that a transfer of the appellant's beneficial interest to his father was intended as part of a family arrangement would rebut any presumption of a resulting trust in any event. For this reason, Mummery LJ and Sir Christopher Slade stated that they would prefer to express no views on the difficult question of whether the presumption of a resulting trust on the voluntary conveyance of land survived the enactment of the section 60(3).

More recently, in *National Crime Agency v Dong*,[126] Chief Master Marsh proceeded on the basis that the presumption of a resulting trust remains.[127] He stated that a literal interpretation of section 60(3), even if this were the right approach, did not inevitably lead to the result that the presumption has disappeared. He commented that while it was surprising that the proper construction of section 60(3) had not been resolved, this was likely to be because presumptions have become less important as the courts have been in a position to consider evidence from wider sources. In his view the presumption in question in any event provides little more than a starting point and may be easily displaced.

There has also been considerable academic debate about the effect of section 60(3). Mee is correct in suggesting that 'the majority view is that section 60(3) must be taken to eliminate the pre-1926 presumption of resulting trust,

121. See the judgments of the Court of Appeal in *Lohia v Lohia* [2001] EWCA Civ 1691.
122. [1971] Ch 892, 933. See Sweeney (1979) 14 Ir Jur (ns) 282.
123. [2001] WTLR 101.
124. See Chambers (2001) 15 Trust Law Int 26. As he points out (at 32): '[T]he conclusion that the presumption of a resulting trust does not apply to a gratuitous transfer of land means only that the donor of land bears the onus of disproving her or his intention to give.'
125. [2001] EWCA Civ 1691.
126. [2017] EWHC 3116 (Ch).
127. He referred to the fact that in *Prest v Petrodel Resources Ltd* [2013] 2 AC 415 Lord Sumption JSC at [49] had taken it as read that Equity would presume a resulting trust upon a voluntary transfer, although he acknowledged that this statement was made without reference to s.60(3) or to the fact there was an alternative view.

although a resulting trust can still arise if the grantee can adduce evidence showing that this was the intention.'[128] He argues convincingly that, although some commentators are attracted by the idea that there should be consistency between the rules in relation to land and personal property, it is difficult to justify a presumption of a resulting trust upon a voluntary conveyance of land today. Mee concludes that '[t]he presumption of resulting trust in this context is an anachronism which should not be tolerated in the modern law.'[129] Mee has held to this view even following the decision in *National Crime Agency v Dong*.[130] He has asserted that the arguments put forward in *Dong* 'do not offer a convincing explanation as to how the wording of section 60(3) could operate to eliminate the presumption of resulting use and yet leave unscathed the presumption of resulting trust (assuming, which is at best a 50/50 proposition, that such a presumption existed prior to 1926).'[131] Therefore, Mee's view, which is likely to be correct, is that no presumption of a resulting trust arises upon a voluntary conveyance of land in England.

Transfer of Personalty

Where there is a voluntary transfer of personalty, the transferee is presumed to hold this property on a resulting trust for the transferor. This presumption will arise most often where there is a voluntary transfer into the joint names of the transferor and transferee but it may also be raised where a transfer is made solely to the transferee.[132] In *Re Vinogradoff*[133] a testatrix had transferred an £800 war loan into the joint names of herself and her four year old granddaughter but continued to receive the dividends until her death. Farwell J held that after her death, the granddaughter held the loan on a resulting trust for the testatrix's estate. This decision illustrates well that presumed resulting trusts can often arise in circumstances where it is highly questionable whether this result would actually reflect the settlor's real intentions, if he had been given an opportunity to decide on the ultimate destination of the property concerned. The importance of the principle that this presumption is rebuttable, and to this extent only operates where no evidence to the contrary has been adduced, was adverted to by Lord Upjohn in *Vandervell v IRC*[134] in the following terms:

> Where A transfers, or directs a trustee for him, to transfer the legal estate in property to B otherwise than for valuable consideration it is a question of the intention of A in making the transfer whether B was to take

128. [2012] Conv 307, 319.
129. *Ibid.* at 325.
130. [2018] Conv 184.
131. *Ibid.* at 192.
132. *Re Howes* (1905) 21 TLR 501; *Re Muller* [1953] NZLR 879.
133. [1935] WN 68.
134. [1967] 2 AC 291, 312.

> beneficially or on trust, and if the latter, on what trusts. If, as a matter of construction of the document transferring the legal estate, it is possible to discern A's intentions, that is an end of the matter and no extraneous evidence is admissible to correct and qualify his intentions so ascertained.
>
> But if, as in this case (a common form share transfer) the document is silent, then there is said to arise a resulting trust in favour of A. But this is only a presumption and is easily rebutted.

This point is well-illustrated in *Standing v Bowring*,[135] where the plaintiff widow transferred stock into the joint names of herself and her godson, the defendant, having been warned that if she made the transfer she could not revoke it. It was held that the plaintiff could not claim a re-transfer on equitable grounds because she had not intended to make the defendant a mere trustee except in relation to the dividends payable on the stock. On the contrary, there was ample evidence to suggest that at the time of the transfer she intended to benefit the defendant and the presumption of a resulting trust was therefore rebutted. Cotton LJ stated:

> [T]he rule is well settled that where there is a transfer by a person into his own name jointly with that of a person who is not his child, or his adopted child, then there is *prima facie* a resulting trust for the transferor. But that is a presumption capable of being rebutted by shewing that at the time the transferor intended a benefit to the transferee.[136]

The manner in which the presumption of a resulting trust may be rebutted was also examined by the Supreme Court in *Stanley v Kieran*,[137] which is considered below in the context of rebutting a resulting trust where property is purchased in the name of another.

Joint Deposit Accounts

One of the most common situations in which a transfer of property takes place into the joint names of the transferor and transferee is where a joint deposit account is opened.[138] This is usually done in a manner which allows the transferor or depositor alone to retain dominion over the money in the account during his lifetime but which displays the intention that the balance should go to the other party should he survive him. Where such an arrangement is put in place the question arises whether the money which remains in the account on the depositor's death should be subject to a resulting trust in favour of his estate

---

135. (1885) 31 Ch D 282.
136. *Ibid.* at 287.
137. [2011] IESC 19.
138. See generally Sheridan (1950-52) 9 NILQ 101; Montrose (1950-52) 9 NILQ 148; Delany (1957) 23 Ir Jur 31; Brady (1990) 12 DULJ (ns) 155; Miller (1992) 6 Trust Law Int 57.

or whether it can be paid over to the other party. The approach traditionally followed was set out by Gordon J in *Doyle v Byrne*[139] as follows:

> Where there is a transfer by a person into his own name jointly with that of a person who is not his child or adopted child, of money on deposit receipt there is, *prima facie*, a resulting trust to the transferor.

If this presumption is to be rebutted, the onus lies on the transferee to show that the transferor intended that the beneficial interest should pass to him.[140] The main policy argument against allowing the survivor or transferee to take a beneficial interest in circumstances where he has made no contribution to the monies in the account is that such an interest may be considered as passing as a form of testamentary disposition which has not complied with the formalities required by the Succession Act 1965.[141] As we have seen above in relation to secret trusts, the courts in this jurisdiction have not always taken such a strict approach to this issue. It is ironic then that in the area of presumed resulting trusts, which are in theory supposed to give effect to a settlor or testator's intentions, the judiciary had, until the Supreme Court decision in *Lynch v Burke*,[142] adopted a more restrictive approach to this policy question and often succeeded in arriving at a result which might be quite contrary to the transferor's actual intentions.

Although it was held in *Diver v McCrea*[143] that no resulting trust arose even in circumstances where the depositor had kept control and dominion over the monies in a joint account during his lifetime, the Supreme Court in *Owens v Greene*[144] declined to follow this approach. In that case, the deceased kept sums of money on deposit in the joint names of himself and a nephew, and of himself and a distant relative. He retained control over these funds during his lifetime but made it clear that he wished the money to go to his co-depositors in the event of his death. The Supreme Court held that these persons, who were volunteers, had failed to rebut the presumption of a resulting trust in favour of the deceased's personal representatives. Kennedy CJ stated that while it was open to the plaintiffs to seek to rebut the presumption of a resulting trust which arose in the circumstances this could only be done by establishing that it was the deceased's intention when putting the money in the accounts to give to the plaintiffs 'then and there and by that act, a right, that is to say an immediate present right to take the monies with which he associated their respective names

139. (1922) 56 ILTR 125, 126-127.
140. *McEneaney v Shevlin* [1912] 1 IR 32, 36 *per* Ross J; *Owens v Greene* [1932] IR 225, 237 *per* Kennedy CJ.
141. Although note that O'Flaherty J in *Lynch v Burke* [1995] 2 IR 159, 167 characterised such dispositions as 'not testamentary' in nature.
142. [1995] 2 IR 159.
143. (1908) 42 ILTR 249.
144. [1932] IR 225.

by survivorship'.[145] It would not suffice to show a testamentary intention on the part of the deceased as a disposition of a testamentary nature could, in the opinion of the Chief Justice, only be made by will. Fitzgibbon J came to the same conclusion on the facts:

> In my opinion the plaintiffs have failed to establish any present intention on the part of [the deceased] to part with his property in, and absolute dominion over, the deposited money during his lifetime, and a disposition, to take effect only upon his death, if he should not have previously disposed of the money, cannot be effected except by a declaration of trust, which is admitted not to have been made by him.[146]

The reasoning in *Owens* was applied by Judge Sheridan in the Circuit Court decision of *Daniels v Dunne*.[147] The deceased opened a joint account in the names of himself and the defendant. Although the words 'payable to either or survivor' appeared in the deposit account book, the customer history card stated that withdrawals were to be signed by the deceased only or his survivor. Judge Sheridan found that the deceased had retained in law total dominion over the money in the account until the time of his death and that *prima facie* the defendant held the monies in the account on a resulting trust in favour of the deceased's estate.

The most significant case in this area is that of *Lynch v Burke*[148] and both the High Court judgment of O'Hanlon J and that of O'Flaherty J in the Supreme Court include a useful analysis of the law in certain other common law jurisdictions in relation to the ownership of monies remaining in a joint deposit account on the death of the depositor. The Supreme Court decision is particularly noteworthy as it reversed the position taken by the courts in this jurisdiction for over six decades. Before examining the reasoning of the Supreme Court in more detail it is useful to explain how pressure to take such a step built up over the preceding years. In *Lynch* the deceased opened a joint account in the names of herself and the first named defendant, her niece. The latter had travelled from Scotland at her aunt's request and both signed the necessary documentation for opening the account. All lodgments were made by the deceased and the account deposit book was endorsed payable to the deceased only or survivor. The deceased bequeathed all her property to the plaintiff and O'Hanlon J held that a resulting trust arose and that therefore the plaintiff was entitled to the money remaining in the joint account. However, it is necessary to examine in more detail precisely how O'Hanlon J arrived at this conclusion. He stated that as a general principle where money is deposited in a joint account by a person who subsequently dies, there is an equitable presumption of a resulting trust

145. *Ibid.* at 237-238.
146. *Ibid.* at 251-252.
147. (1990) 8 ILT 35 (Circuit Court, 2 February 1989).
148. [1990] 1 IR 1 (HC); [1995] 2 IR 159 (SC).

against the survivor in favour of the estate of the deceased in respect of the beneficial interest in the monies remaining on deposit at the time of death. On the facts, O'Hanlon J held that the deceased had intended that the first named defendant would be entitled by right of survivorship to the beneficial interest in this money and the equitable presumption in favour of the deceased's estate was therefore rebutted. However, he felt obliged on the authority of the *Owens* decision to hold that the transaction was an invalid gift and an unsuccessful attempt to make a testamentary disposition otherwise than by will. Despite this conclusion there are definite signs in O'Hanlon J's judgment that he was unhappy with the reasoning in the earlier Supreme Court decision. As he stated:

> I consider that in the present case I am bound to follow and apply [*Owens v Greene*] but having regard to the fact that it is a decision which appears to conflict with the interpretation of this branch of the law in so many other common law jurisdictions it might well be a case where the Supreme Court would be disposed to review again the correctness of that decision, if a suitable opportunity arose for so doing.[149]

This statement was quoted with approval by Morris J in *AIB Finance Ltd v Sligo County Council*,[150] although once again the result in that case was similar to that reached in *Owens v Greene*. The deceased, a priest who wished to benefit his home town in Co. Sligo, had lodged a sum of money in a bank account in the joint names of himself and Sligo County Council with the intention that the money should be used to carry out a specific project under an urban renewal scheme. The priest died and the question arose whether his executor or the county council was entitled to the monies in the account. Although the mandate executed in favour of the bank contained a provision that these monies should be paid to the county council as survivor on the priest's death, there was evidence that the deceased had intended to and had in fact retained control over these funds during his lifetime. Morris J concluded that there was at most an incomplete gift and that the relationship of trustee and beneficiary had not existed as between the deceased and the county council. Therefore, he found that a resulting trust in favour of the deceased's executor arose.

In the circumstances, it was not necessary for Morris J to decide whether the reasoning in *Owens* was correct as there was insufficient evidence to rebut the presumption of a resulting trust in favour of the deceased's estate. Nevertheless it is interesting that he saw fit to expressly approve of O'Hanlon J's *dicta* in *Lynch* set out above[151] and this could be construed as evidence of the fact that the courts were increasingly dissatisfied with the *Owens* approach which was

149. [1990] 1 IR 1, 13.
150. [1995] 1 ILRM 81.
151. See *supra* n. 149.

certainly out of line with the view taken in relation to this question in most other common law jurisdictions.

While some earlier Canadian cases had been decided on the basis of the approach laid down in *Owens*,[152] different reasoning was employed by the Supreme Court of Ontario in *Re Reid*[153] and by the High Court of Australia in *Russell v Scott*.[154] In the latter case an elderly lady transferred money into an account in the joint names of herself and her nephew. Although Dixon and Evatt JJ found that she did not intend her nephew to benefit during her lifetime, they concluded that 'by placing the money in the joint names, the deceased did then and there and by that act give a present right of survivorship'. The court therefore interpreted her actions as giving the nephew an immediate beneficial interest which, however, did not fall into possession until her death and which might be revoked up until that time. This approach, which involved regarding both parties upon the opening of the account as being jointly entitled at common law to a chose in action consisting of their contractual right against the bank which would accrue to the survivor, was a plausible alternative to the reasoning employed in *Owens* and avoided the difficulties inherent in regarding the transaction as a testamentary disposition, namely the need for compliance with the requisite statutory formalities.

O'Hanlon J in *Lynch* certainly seemed to favour this reasoning and Miller suggested that the Supreme Court in *Owens* might not have ruled out reliance on such an approach by speaking in terms of rebutting the presumption of a resulting trust if the plaintiffs had been given 'then and there, a right, that is to say an immediate present right, to take the moneys.'[155]

The position in England would appear to be as set out in Halsbury as follows:

> [T]he fact that the transferor retains control during his lifetime over the property transferred into the joint names does not prevent the gift, even where it appears to be of a testamentary nature and not in conformity with the Wills Act 1837, from being an effective and complete gift *inter vivos* from the time of making, so as to vest the legal title to the property in the donee by survivorship on the death of the transferor.[156]

152. *Hill v Hill* (1904) 8 OLR 710; *Shortill v Grannan* (1920) 55 DLR 416; *Larondeau v Laurendeau* [1954] 4 DLR 293.
153. (1921) 50 OLR 595. See also *Re Aylward* [1955] 5 DLR 753. More recently in *Re Ferguson's Estate* (2018) 424 DLR (4th) 547, the Prince Edward Island Court of Appeal found that the co-depositer, the son of the deceased who had set up the accounts, had adduced sufficient evidence to rebut the presumption of a resulting trust and it was held that he was entitled to the balance in the accounts by right of survivorship.
154. (1936) 55 CLR 440.
155. Miller (1992) 6 Trust Law Int 57, 59.
156. Halsbury, *Laws of England* (4th ed., Volume 20) para. 40. As quoted by O'Hanlon J in *Lynch v Burke* [1990] 1 IR 1, 13.

In *Young v Sealey*,[157] Romer J, although he confessed that the reasoning in *Owens* appealed to him, concluded that the survivor should take free of a resulting trust in these circumstances, an approach which was followed in *Re Figgis*.[158] However, it should be noted that in some more recent first instance decisions, the opposite conclusion has been reached, although no reference was made in these cases to the principle set out in *Young*.[159] In *Sillett v Meek*[160] Michael Furness QC, sitting as a Deputy High Court judge, concluded that the deceased had probably viewed putting the defendant's name on the joint account as a matter of administrative convenience only and that she had not intended the latter to take the contents of the account beneficially.

However, it is clear from the decision of the majority of the Privy Council in *Whitlock v Moree*[161] that where a signed account opening document sets out the account holders' respective beneficial interests, this document will be determinative of these interests. Lord Briggs stated that he was satisfied that in the matter before him there was a sufficiently clear declaration of the parties' respective beneficial interests in the account opening agreement between the joint account holders and the bank to resolve the matter.[162] Lord Briggs stated as follows:

> [T]here is plainly no room for the application of the doctrine of presumed resulting trusts, in favour of an account holder who places money in the account, as [the deceased] did in this case. This is because the account holder is a party to the document which is determinative of the account holders' beneficial interests, and because they have been ascertained by the primary tool for the determination of any dispute as to beneficial interests, namely the terms of the document creating or transferring the property, just as much as beneficial interests in other types of co-owned property are determined by a conveyance, a transfer or a declaration of trust.[163]

He concluded that the matter was one in which the two holders of a joint account had, by an agreement with the bank to which they were both parties, expressly

157. [1949] Ch 278.
158. [1969] 1 Ch 123. See also *Aroso v Coutts & Co.* [2002] 1 All ER (Comm) 241 where Collins J held that sufficient evidence had been adduced to displace the presumption of a resulting trust and to prove that the deceased intended to give his co-depositor a beneficial interest in the assets in the bank account. See further Walford (2001) 31 Tr & Est LJ 9.
159. *Sillett v Meek* [2009] WTLR 1065; *Re Northall (Deceased)* [2010] EWHC 1448 (Ch).
160. [2009] WTLR 1065.
161. [2017] UKPC 44.
162. However, note that Lord Carnwath dissenting concluded at [86] that he could 'see nothing in the language of [the relevant] clause ... to indicate an intention to deal with beneficial interests, rather than simply spell out the consequences of holding a legal estate in a joint bank account.'
163. [2017] UKPC 44 at [31].

set out a declaration as to the beneficial interests in that joint account which, on its true construction, provided for any balance in the account to be the beneficial property of the survivor upon the death of the other account holder, regardless of who had contributed the money to the account before that date.

In this jurisdiction, by the time the Supreme Court was called upon to make a decision in *Lynch v Burke*, it was faced with persuasive arguments requiring it to re-examine the judgment of the former Supreme Court in *Owens.* While it could have been argued that the approach favoured in England and Australia and more latterly in Canada seemed to allow the making of so-called 'nuncupative wills' where there was no real justification for such a course of action, such as avoiding fraud, any policy argument against a more flexible approach was not easily reconcilable with the rationale of a resulting trust which might be said to depend on the implied intention of the donor.[164] It was certainly arguable that insistence on strict compliance with statutory provisions designed to prevent fraud was not necessary or even desirable where no danger of fraud would arise in bypassing their requirements, and where such an approach gave effect to a donor's real intentions about the disposition of his property on his death.

Delivering the judgment of the Supreme Court,[165] O'Flaherty J considered the legal effect of opening a deposit account in joint names. He said that by her presence and signature, it was manifest that the first named defendant was a party to the contract from the outset and she must be entitled to claim as a party to the contract under its terms. He quoted with approval from the judgment of Dixon and Evatt JJ in *Russell v Scott* and stated that since historically, the concept of a resulting trust was an invention of equity to defeat the misappropriation of property as a consequence of potentially fraudulent or improvident transactions, it would be paradoxical if the doctrine was allowed to defeat the clear intention of the donor as found by the trial judge. O'Flaherty J pointed out that in *Owens v Greene*, the Supreme Court had been concerned to emphasise the importance of testamentary dispositions being required to comply with statutory requirements. He commented that if the arrangement in the case before him was not testamentary, which in his view it was not, these statutory requirements had no application. O'Flaherty J also stated that *Owens* had given cause for unease on a number of grounds and concluded that it was wrongly decided and should be overruled. He said that at law the defendant had a legal interest in the monies on deposit either by reason of the contractual relationship of the parties or in the alternative as a gift, which admittedly was not a completed gift in the conventional sense but was one which should be upheld as being a gift subject to a contingency, namely, the donor's death.

One cannot but agree with O'Flaherty J's conclusion that the result arrived at by the Supreme Court will introduce a measure of consistency into this area

164. See Brady (1990) 12 DULJ (ns) 155, 164-165.
165. [1995] 2 IR 159. See further Capper (1996) 47 NILQ 281; Breslin [1996] Comm LP 12; O'Doherty (1996) 14 ILT 167; Mee (1996) 90 GILSI 70.

of the law, and as he suggested, 'restore … equity to the high ground which it should properly occupy to ameliorate the harshness of common law rules on occasion rather than itself be an instrument of injustice'.[166] However, as Capper points out, there are conceptual difficulties with both the 'gift theory' and the 'contract theory' and as he comments, 'the underlying doctrinal principles remain very unclear'.[167] Capper favours the 'contract theory' and it would appear that provided the surviving co-depositor has signed the necessary contractual documents and there is sufficient evidence of the donor's intention to rebut the presumption of a resulting trust, the survivor should benefit. However, Woods points to a number of potential flaws in the contract theory, namely that it may not operate to vest legal ownership in the surviving co-depositor and that even if this can be established, the deceased's intention to confer a right of survivorship on the co-depositor may not operate to rebut the presumption of a resulting trust.[168] She clearly favours the conditional gift theory which, in her view, avoids the rules of privity and the necessity for consideration. Despite Woods' criticisms, the contract theory is in many respects more attractive.[169] It also seems in line with the approach adopted by the Privy Council in *Whitlock v Moree*,[170] in which Lord Briggs commented that '[w]here the parties to a joint account have declared their beneficial interests in it in signed writing, it would be both extraordinary and unsatisfactory for the courts to have to resolve a dispute about their beneficial interests by an open-ended factual inquiry about their subjective intentions, or the subjective intentions of whichever of them provided the money.'

The conclusion arrived at by the Supreme Court in *Lynch v Burke* is clear and it should have laid to rest the rather paradoxical decision of *Owens v Greene* once and for all. This would seem to be borne out by the comments made by Gilligan J in *Prendergast v Joyce*[171] although on the facts of the case it was not necessary to determine whether the co-depositor had acquired her interest by right of survivorship.[172] Gilligan J made reference to the fact that legal title to the chose in action represented by the balance in the accounts would have passed to the co-depositor on her husband's death by survivorship in accordance with the contracts governing the accounts. He stated that unlike the situation in *Lynch*, she had the same rights of access to the accounts as her husband, being able to withdraw funds from them without his consent. In

166. *Ibid.* at 168.
167. Capper (1996) 47 NILQ 281, 293.
168. Woods (2002) 37 Ir Jur 281.
169. It also opens up the interesting idea that if the Supreme Court in *Lynch v Burke* had relied squarely on this theory alone, it might have distinguished *Owens v Greene* rather than overruled it, given that on the facts of the latter case there was no basis for relying on the contractual approach.
170. [2017] UKPC 44 at [33].
171. [2009] IEHC 199.
172. This issue arose in the context of a claim of undue influence made in relation to a transfer from the co-depositor, the widow of the deceased, to the defendant.

those circumstances, although the court did not have evidence before it on the question, he said that it was probable that she was a party to the contracts with the banks in relation to these accounts. Gilligan J added that in any event, the defendant had properly conceded that the sums held in the accounts devolved to the co-depositor as the surviving joint account holder on her husband's death. Similarly in *Gilvarry v Maher*[173] Gilligan J stated that as a result of *Lynch v Burke*, the bank becomes contractually bound to both joint account holders in circumstances such as those before the court where both parties had attended the bank to open the joint account. He held that as a matter of contract the surviving account holder became entitled to the balance in the account on the death of the deceased joint account holder.

However, the comments of Laffoy J in the decision of *O'Meara v Bank of Scotland plc*[174] suggest that there may be some lingering uncertainty about the outcome in joint deposit account cases in the absence of any basis for applying the contract theory outlined above. In that case the court had to determine the beneficial ownership of monies in two joint deposit accounts in the names of the plaintiff widow and her late husband which the defendant bank claimed to be entitled to set off against monies owed to it by the deceased. In relation to the monies lodged in the first account, a presumption of advancement applied which Laffoy J was satisfied had not been displaced. She found that the parties were the joint beneficial owners of the money in the first joint deposit account when it was opened and that the plaintiff was entitled to it by right of survivorship. She went on to express the following view:

> On the authority of [*Lynch v Burke*], the legal effect of the opening of that account in the joint names of [the deceased] and the plaintiff on foot of the application signed by both of them was that the defendant became contractually bound to both account holders and, as a matter of contract between the plaintiff, as surviving joint account holder, and the defendant, she became entitled to the balance in the account on the death of [the deceased].[175]

The relevance of the contractual basis for these conclusions became clearer when the position in relation to the second joint deposit account was analysed. Laffoy J noted that there was no contractual relationship between the plaintiff and the defendant bank in relation to the monies in that account. She found that the 'plaintiff was not a party to it at any time' and commented that 'therefore the decision of the Supreme Court in *Lynch v Burke*, in my view, does not assist the plaintiff.'[176] Laffoy J ultimately concluded that wherever the beneficial ownership was vested, the monies in that joint deposit account were deemed

173. [2014] IEHC 694.
174. [2011] IEHC 402.
175. *Ibid* at [5.7].
176. *Ibid* at [17.1].

to have been impressed with an obligation in equity to fulfil a purpose, namely to top up the monies in the account to the level of a set-off requirement agreed between the bank and the deceased. So, in the circumstances, Laffoy J stated that she did not feel it necessary to determine the question of the plaintiff's beneficial ownership of the monies in the account. However, her references to the lack of any contractual relationship and the view she expressed that the plaintiff could not rely on *Lynch v Burke* in these circumstances suggest that the *ratio* of that case may be being more narrowly construed than might have been anticipated. Realistically, given the requirements which are now applied by financial institutions where a joint account is opened, it is hard to envisage circumstances in which the contractual rationale would not resolve the matter, but some lingering uncertainties remain in the wake of *O'Meara*.

Joint Bank Accounts of Husband and Wife

In the light of the Supreme Court's decision in *Lynch v Burke*[177] it should be possible for either spouse to rebut the presumption of a resulting trust where an account has been opened in their joint names with the intention that the survivor shall take beneficially when the contributing spouse subsequently dies, subject to the residual uncertainty about the scope of the *ratio* of this decision outlined above. Where the sole contributing spouse is a husband, this issue may in any event be resolved by the application of the presumption of advancement, which will be considered in more detail below.[178]

The fact that this presumption might be applied in cases where the sole contributing spouse was a husband led to different principles being applied by the courts even prior to the decision of the Supreme Court in *Lynch* which are worth noting. Dixon and Evatt JJ summarised the position as follows in *Russell v Scott*:[179]

> [T]here is much authority to the effect that where a joint bank account is opened by husband and wife with the intention that the survivor shall take beneficially the balance at credit on the death of one of them that intention prevails, and, on the death of the husband, the wife takes the balance beneficially, although the deceased husband supplied all the money paid in and during his life the property was used exclusively for his own purposes.

So, even prior to *Lynch v Burke*, where money was deposited by a husband in an account in their joint names the presumption of a resulting trust in these circumstances might be rebutted by the presumption of advancement and

177. [1995] 2 IR 159.
178. See *infra* pp. 204-215.
179. (1936) 55 CLR 440, 451.

prima facie the relationship between the parties would usually result in the wife taking the balance remaining in the account beneficially.[180] In *Talbot v Cody*,[181] where a man lodged sums of money in a number of accounts in the joint names of himself and his wife, it was held that his wife, who survived him, was beneficially entitled to these funds. Similarly, in *Colohan v Condrin*,[182] it was held by O'Connor MR that the presumption that a wife should be beneficially entitled to monies in an account in these circumstances was not affected by the fact that the name of her husband's brother was also included on the deposit receipt. As he stated, '[i]t is well settled that if a deposit is made with a bank by a husband of his own money in the names of himself and his wife, there is a presumption that it is intended as an advancement in the event of her surviving her husband.'[183]

However, such a result should not always be assumed and one question which may arise is whether the account was opened merely for the parties' mutual convenience or whether it was intended as a means of making provision for the other spouse.[184] This principle was referred to by Laffoy J in *O'Meara v Bank of Scotland plc*[185] in concluding that, in relation to the first of two joint deposit accounts, there was nothing to suggest that the purpose of the joint investment was for the parties' mutual convenience and that the only reasonable inference which could be drawn was that it was the deceased's intention to make provision for his wife, the plaintiff, should he predecease her.

In certain circumstances, the presumption that the surviving spouse was to benefit may be rebutted by showing that this was not the intention of the spouse who deposited the money. So, in *Marshal v Crutwell*[186] it was held that a wife was not beneficially entitled to monies remaining in a joint account arranged by her husband solely as a matter of convenience to enable her to sign cheques because of his failing health. Alternatively, the depositing spouse may subsequently take some action which will effectively prevent the other from taking a beneficial interest, as in *M'Dowell v McNeilly*,[187] where a husband endorsed a deposit receipt in favour of a third party who subsequently cashed it.

The comments of Laffoy J in the case of *O'Meara v Bank of Scotland plc*,[188] referred to above, should also be noted in this context. On the facts Laffoy J stated that she did not find it necessary to determine the beneficial ownership of monies in a second joint deposit account as between the husband and wife, given that the right of the defendant bank over these monies had priority in

180. *Re Young* (1885) 28 Ch D 705.
181. (1874) IR 10 Eq 138. See also *Re Hood* [1923] 1 IR 109.
182. [1914] 1 IR 89.
183. *Ibid.* at 94-95.
184. *Re Figgis* [1969] 1 Ch 123.
185. [2011] IEHC 402.
186. (1875) LR 20 Eq 328.
187. [1917] 1 IR 117.
188. [2011] IEHC 402.

equity. It was the plaintiff's evidence that the monies were lodged in her and her husband's joint names as 'an advance' to her. Laffoy J later noted that the husband, as the sole contributor to the monies in this account, was the beneficial owner unless the presumption of advancement overrode the doctrine of resulting trust, although in the circumstances outlined she did not find it necessary to decide this question.

One related matter which will more usually be of importance where spouses separate is that where a husband and wife open a joint bank account with the intention of pooling their resources, the monies in this account will not be divided in accordance with their respective contributions but rather on an equal basis.[189] However, either spouse can acquire sole beneficial ownership of assets purchased with monies from such a joint account depending on the surrounding circumstances.[190]

Purchase in the Name of Another

A variation of the principle considered above in relation to voluntary conveyances or transfers of property applies where property is purchased in the name of another. So, where a person provides the purchase money for property, whether real or personal, which is conveyed or transferred to another person or to himself and the other person jointly, it is presumed that the latter holds the property on a resulting trust for the person who provided the purchase money.[191] This principle was set out by Eyre CB in *Dyer v Dyer*[192] as follows:

> The clear result of all the cases, without a single exception, is, that the trust of a legal estate … whether taken in the names of the purchasers and others jointly, or in the names of others without that of the purchaser; whether in one name or several; whether jointly or *successive*, results to the man who advances the purchase money.

The operation of this principle is well illustrated by the decision of Pim J in *Re Slattery*.[193] A policy of insurance was taken out by Lawrence Slattery in the name of and on the life of his brother. He paid the premiums on the policy and

189. *Jones v Maynard* [1951] Ch 572.
190. *Re Bishop* [1965] Ch 450, 456.
191. It was suggested by Pearce (1990) 41 NILQ 43 that the Statute of Uses might still have a role to play in this area and that the Act might execute the trust under which a person with no documentary title to property is held to have a beneficial interest by reason of a contribution to its acquisition. However, Mee argues convincingly against such a proposition (see (1996) 47 NILQ 367), pointing out that the doctrine of the purchase money resulting trust was developed by the courts after the enactment of the Statute of Uses and after the statute had been made a dead letter through the creation of trusts by means of a 'use upon a use'.
192. (1788) 2 Cox Eq Cas 92, 93.
193. [1917] 2 IR 278. See also *Re Scottish Equitable Life Assurance Society* [1902] 1 Ch

retained it in his possession and at no time did his brother have any interest in the policy or make any claim to it. When his brother died it was held that Lawrence Slattery was entitled to the monies payable on the policy; there was no evidence of any intention to make a gift of the interest under the policy to his brother and a resulting trust therefore arose.

The presumption of a resulting trust applies equally where two or more persons advance purchase money jointly but the property is conveyed or transferred to only one of them, in which case there will be a resulting trust in favour of the other party or parties proportionate to the extent of the contributions made.[194] This principle has proved to be extremely important in resolving disputes relating to the beneficial ownership of family property, which will be considered in detail below.[195]

An example of the utility of resulting trust principles in this context is the decision of the Supreme Court of the United Kingdom in *Prest v Petrodel Resources Ltd*,[196] in which they were employed in resolving a dispute about ancillary relief following divorce proceedings. The question for the court was whether it had power to order the transfer of properties to the wife given that they were legally owned not by the husband but by companies which were wholly owned and controlled by him. The Supreme Court held that the only basis on which the companies could be ordered to convey the properties to the wife was that they belonged beneficially to the husband, by virtue of the particular circumstances in which the properties came to be vested in them. The court inferred that the reason for the companies' failure to co-operate with the proceedings was to protect the properties, which suggested that proper disclosure would reveal them to be beneficially owned by the husband as the wife had alleged. There was no evidence to rebut the most plausible inference from the facts which was that the properties were held on a resulting trust by the companies for the husband.[197]

However, it must be stressed that the presumption which arises in any of the above circumstances is liable to be rebutted, either by evidence that the purchaser intended to benefit the other party or because 'the purchaser is under a species of natural obligation to provide for the nominee',[198] known as the presumption of advancement.[199] These two factors, which may lead to the

282 which concerned a similar factual situation and in which the *dicta* of Eyre CB in *Dyer* was cited with approval by Joyce J.

194. E.g. *McGillycuddy v Joy* [1959] IR 189.
195. See *infra* pp. 223-256.
196. [2013] 2 AC 415.
197. See also *NRC Holding Ltd v Danilitskiy* [2017] EWHC 1431 (Ch) at [46].
198. *Murless v Franklin* (1818) 1 Swans 13, 17.
199. It should be pointed out that there is in any event increasing unease about the manner in which these presumptions, particularly the presumption of advancement, operate. Chambers has suggested (2001) 15 Trust Law Int 26, 32 that the courts should rely on a presumption only when it is otherwise impossible to ascertain the intention of

rebuttal of the presumption of a resulting trust in the case of a voluntary transfer, or where property is purchased in the name of another, will now be considered.

Rebutting the Presumption of a Resulting Trust

Evidence of an Intention to Benefit

Where evidence establishes that the transferor or purchaser intended to benefit the donee, no resulting trust will arise. This is well illustrated by *Standing v Bowring*,[200] where evidence showed that the plaintiff transferor had intended to benefit her godson when she transferred stock into his name. The judgment of the Court of Appeal also makes it clear that the relevant time for establishing evidence of intention to make a gift is the time of the transfer and once this is shown, a donor cannot subsequently change his mind and withdraw this intention. A good illustration of this principle is provided by the decision of the British Columbia Court of Appeal in *Romaine Estate v Romaine*,[201] in which an uncle transferred property to his nephew before his death in order to save taxes and subsequently regretted his decision. Levine JA confirmed that 'all of the evidence of the donor's intention, written or oral, at the time a transfer that is claimed to be a gift was made, is admissible to determine whether the transfer was a gift.'[202] However, the Court of Appeal ruled that the trial judge had erred in admitting statements made after the parties fell out to support the presumption of a resulting trust. All the evidence of the uncle's intentions up to that time suggested that he intended to transfer the property to his nephew and it was held that when all the admissible evidence was considered it rebutted the presumption of a resulting trust.

Another decision which casts light on how the presumption of a resulting trust may be rebutted is *Fowkes v Pascoe*,[203] where a Mrs Baker made various purchases of stock in the joint names of herself and the son of her daughter-in-law. After her death, the Court of Appeal upheld this individual's claim to be entitled to the stock on the basis that the purchase had been intended as a gift and the presumption of a resulting trust had therefore been rebutted. The general principle was well set out by Mellish LJ:

> [A] man may make an investment of stock in the name of himself and some other person, although not a child or wife, yet in such a position to him as to make it extremely probable that the investment was intended

---

the donor and that if all the circumstances of a case indicate the probable intention of the apparent donor, a presumption is unnecessary.

200. (1885) 31 Ch D 282 considered above in the context of voluntary transfers. See also *Dewar v Dewar* [1975] 1 WLR 1532 where the presumption was likewise rebutted by evidence of an intention to make a gift.
201. (2001) 205 DLR (4th) 320.
202. *Ibid.* at 335.
203. (1875) 10 Ch App 343.

> as a gift. In such a case, although the rule of law, if there was evidence at all, would compel the Court to say that the presumption of trust must prevail, even if the Court might not believe that the fact was in accordance with the presumption, yet, if there is evidence to rebut the presumption, then, in my opinion, the Court must go into the actual facts.[204]

The principles which apply in relation to rebutting the presumption of a resulting trust were also considered in *Stanley v Kieran*[205] in which the plaintiff sought a declaration that he was the beneficial owner of certain property which as 'a matter of convenience' had been acquired in the first named defendant's name. In the High Court Laffoy J accepted that evidence of the fact that the plaintiff had provided the purchase money on its own would tend to give rise to a presumption of a resulting trust. However, she concluded as a matter of probability that the plaintiff had intended to benefit the first named defendant. The appellant's appeal was allowed by the Supreme Court. Denham J stated that there is a presumption that the provider of funds for the purchase of property is the beneficial owner and that the presumption may be rebutted. This may be done by evidence that the provider of funds intended to benefit the other party or the presumption may be rebutted by the presumption of advancement which did not arise in the case before the court as the parties were not husband and wife. Denham J stated that on the facts the presumption of a resulting trust in favour of the appellant arose and that the respondent had not discharged the burden of rebutting this presumption. In her view the inferences drawn in the High Court that the appellant intended to benefit the respondent were contrary to the evidence. Denham J added that she would not accord weight to the inferences drawn by the High Court and in her view these inferences did not discharge the onus or displace the presumption. Thus Denham J concluded, in allowing the appeal, that she was satisfied that the property was held on a resulting trust for the appellant.

Where Fraud or Illegality Exists

Traditionally, it has been recognised where a trust was intentionally created for an illegal purpose, a resulting trust in favour of the settlor or testator would not arise unless there was a failure to carry out this illegal purpose.[206] The principles which will be applied in this context in England now need to be re-evaluated in the light of the decision of the UK Supreme Court in *Patel v Mirza*,[207] in which the manner in which the defence of illegality operates in private law was reasssessed, and the effect of this case will be examined below. While the issue of illegality in contract has also been considered by the Supreme Court in this

---

204. *Ibid*. at 352-353.
205. [2007] IEHC 272; [2011] IESC 19.
206. *Symes v Hughes* (1870) LR 9 Eq 475.
207. [2017] AC 467.

jurisdiction in *Quinn v Irish Bank Resolution Corporation Ltd*,[208] its specific application in the context of trust law has received little judicial attention here. Therefore, it still remains unclear whether the courts in this jurisdiction will follow a revised approach to the application of the illegality defence in the context of resulting trusts, or continue to apply traditional principles, so for this reason both will need to be examined.

The Traditional Approach to the Operation of the Illegality Defence in this Context

In *Ayerst v Jenkins*,[209] a settlor's personal representatives claimed that a resulting trust arose in circumstances where a settlement had been founded on an illegal consideration, namely the settlor's marriage to his deceased wife's sister, which both parties knew to be illegal at that time. Lord Selborne refused the claim on the basis that a settlor was not entitled to relief in this form on the grounds of illegality of his own intention or purpose unless the direct result of refusing such relief would be 'to effectuate an unlawful object or to defeat a legal prohibition or to protect a fraud.'[210]

Where a transferor had not carried out the illegal purpose which was intended at the time of making the transfer, he might adduce evidence of his repudiated intention so as to recover the property. This principle was confirmed by the decision of Hoffman J in *Sekhon v Alissa*,[211] where a property was conveyed into the sole name of her daughter by a mother with the intention of avoiding liability to capital gains tax when the property was ultimately sold. Hoffman J held that as this unlawful purpose had not yet been carried out, the mother could rely on evidence of this purpose and found that the presumption of a resulting trust in the mother's favour had not been rebutted. This principle was set out by Millett LJ in the following terms in *Tribe v Tribe*:[212]

> [A] person who has transferred property for an illegal purpose can nevertheless recover his property provided that he withdraws from the transaction before the illegal purpose has been wholly or partly performed. This is the doctrine of the *locus poenitentiae* and it applies in equity as well as at law.

The deciding factor in determining whether an illegal purpose has in fact been carried out might be whether any actual deception had been practised

---

208. [2016] 1 IR 1.
209. (1873) LR 16 Eq 275.
210. *Ibid.* at 283.
211. [1989] 2 FLR 94. See Kodilinye [1990] Conv 213.
212. [1996] Ch 107, 124. This is one of the exceptions to the general rule against relying on one's own illegality and is known as the doctrine of *locus poenitentiae*.

on the transferor's creditors.[213] So, in *Q. v Q.*,[214] where a party had made false representations to the Inland Revenue authorities that he had transferred the assets in question, Black J held that that a deception had been effected and an illegal purpose partly carried out. He distinguished the facts of the case before him from those in *Tribe v Tribe*,[215] where the plaintiff was found to have withdrawn from the transaction 'while his dishonesty still lay in intention only'[216] and stated that in this case the party in question could not establish that he had withdrawn from the illegal transaction soon enough.

Even where a transfer of property occurred for an illegal purpose, this would not prevent a resulting trust arising in favour of the transferee where the claim could be made without reliance on this unlawful purpose, sometimes referred to as the 'reliance principle', which was illustrated in this context by the decision of the House of Lords in *Tinsley v Milligan*.[217] Although the UK Supreme Court has now made it clear in *Patel v Mirza*[218] that the reasoning underpinning the decision in *Tinsley* should not be followed,[219] it remains a significant case which needs to be examined. In *Tinsley* two women purchased a house in the plaintiff's sole name but on the understanding that they should be joint beneficial owners of the property in order to assist in the perpetration of a fraud on the Department of Social Security. When the parties quarrelled, the defendant disclosed the fraud to the department and the plaintiff moved out and brought proceedings against the defendant claiming possession and sole ownership of the property. The defendant counter-claimed and sought a declaration that the property was held on trust for the parties in equal shares. The majority of the House of Lords held that a party to an illegality can recover by virtue of a legal or equitable interest in property provided that he can establish his title without relying on his own illegality. In the circumstances it was held that the defendant had established a presumption of a resulting trust by showing that she had contributed to the purchase price of the house and that there was a common understanding between the parties that they owned it jointly. There was no need for her to establish the reason why the house had been conveyed solely into the plaintiff's name and it was held that there was no evidence to rebut the presumption of a resulting trust.[220]

The principles established by the House of Lords in *Tinsley*, although

---

213. Pawlowski [2009] Conv 145, 152.
214. [2009] 1 FLR 935.
215. [1996] Ch 107. Similar principles were applied in this case in the context of rebutting the presumption of advancement.
216. *Ibid.* at 133.
217. [1994] 1 AC 340.
218. [2017] AC 467.
219. [2017] AC 467, 502 *per* Lord Toulson JSC. See also *per* Lord Neuberger PSC at 515, Lord Clarke JSC at 530.
220. However, the position is different where the relationship between the parties gives rise to the presumption of advancement, see *infra*. As Lord Browne-Wilkinson made clear (at 372), in such cases in order to establish any claim, the plaintiff will have

regarded as controversial, were applied by the Court of Appeal in England on a number of occasions. In *Silverwood v Silverwood*,[221] an elderly lady transferred monies into bank accounts in the names of two of her grandchildren and then applied for and received income support from the DSS without disclosing the fact she had made the transfer. After her death her executor claimed that the grandchildren held the monies on a resulting trust for her estate. The Court of Appeal upheld the claim as the executor had not been forced to rely on any illegality in order to establish a resulting trust in favour of the estate.[222] A similar result ensued in *Lowson v Coombes*,[223] in which the plaintiff and defendant both contributed to the purchase price of a house but it was conveyed into the defendant's sole name in order to avoid the plaintiff's wife having any claim on it. The Court of Appeal found that although the house had been conveyed into the defendant's sole name with the illegal purpose of frustrating any potential claim by the plaintiff's wife pursuant to section 37(2)(b) of the Matrimonial Causes Act 1973, the plaintiff was entitled to a declaration that the defendant held half the beneficial interest on a resulting trust for him. In the view of Nourse LJ the case before the court was 'in all material respects … on all fours with [*Tinsley v Milligan*]' and the plaintiff was entitled to relief as he had not been forced to rely on the illegality in order to establish a resulting trust in his favour.[224]

Tinsley v Milligan was also applied by the Court of Appeal in *Davies v O'Kelly*,[225] although in this case the trust which the court accepted arose was a common intention constructive trust.[226] The Court of Appeal held that the trial judge had been correct to find that the claimant was not required to rely on an illegal purpose in order to establish his beneficial interest in property which had been transferred into his partner's name enabling her to fraudulently claim social security benefits. Pitchford LJ stated that 'Equity will not come to the aid of a party who must rely on his unlawful purpose but if his right to an equitable interest in property can be identified without the need to rely on his unlawful purpose it can be enforced.'[227] As he put it, the key question was whether the claimant could prove the existence of a trust without recourse to an

---

to adduce evidence sufficient to rebut the presumption of a gift and in so doing will normally have to plead, and give evidence of, the underlying illegal purpose.

221. (1997) 74 P & CR 453.
222. However, it should be noted that Peter Gibson LJ accepted (at 457) that: 'it would be absurd as well as unjust if a claimant, claiming a resulting trust, could not lead evidence of fraud in order to disprove a spurious defence.'
223. [1999] Ch 373.
224. See also *Slater v Simm* [2007] WTLR 1043.
225. [2015] 1 WLR 2725.
226. This form of trust is considered in detail *infra* pp. 236-251. It is now the well-established basis on which a beneficial interest in family property may be claimed in England.
227. [2015] 1 WLR 2725, 2734.

unlawful agreement.[228] However, in *Barrett v Barrett*,[229] in circumstances where the claimant had made no direct contribution to the purchase price of property but instead had to rely on indirect contributions which he claimed gave rise to a beneficial interest, it was held by David Richards LJ that the *Tinsley* reliance principle could not be availed of. The respondent had bought his brother's house from the latter's trustee in bankruptcy and allowed him to continue living there and pay the mortgage until he sold it as part of what was clearly an agreement or arrangement for an illegal purpose. In these circumstances David Richards LJ concluded that, given that the claimant could not avoid reliance on the unlawful purpose of the agreement in order to put forward his claim to beneficial ownership of the property, he could not succeed. Commenting on this decision in his judgment in *Davies v O'Kelly*,[230] Pitchford LJ explained that *Barrett v Barrett* was distinguishable from the facts of the case before him on the basis that the conduct on which the claimant was relying could not, without more, support an inference of common intention and it could only have that effect if the claimant relied on the express unlawful agreement.

A Re-Assessment of the Operation of the Illegality Defence

In recent years considerable debate has surrounded the issue of the operation of the reliance principle in the context of the broader question of the defence of illegality, particularly in England. Prior to the UK Supreme Court's decision in *Patel v Mirza*,[231] the law in that jurisdiction on this issue was in a state of uncertainty following a number of cases in which conflicting approaches had been adopted.[232] Although its continuing utility was affirmed by a number of members of the Supreme Court in *Les Laboratoires Servier v Apotex Inc.*,[233] Lord Sumption JSC did comment that 'it does not follow that the courts should be insensitive to the draconian consequences which the *ex turpi causa* principle can have if it is applied too widely.'[234] Subsequently, in *Bilta (UK)*

228. Pitchford LJ also gave a useful summary as to how the operation of the presumption of advancement, which did not apply in this case, would have altered the outcome. As he explained at 2734, the effect of the presumption of advancement is the reverse: 'the claimant to an equitable interest had to disprove the evidential presumption of a gift. If, to rebut the presumption the transferor of property was bound to rely on his unlawful purpose in making the transfer he would not be permitted to enforce his interest.'
229. [2008] EWHC 1061 (Ch). See further Evans [2008] Conv 534.
230. [2015] 1 WLR 2725.
231. [2017] AC 467.
232. *Hounga v Allen* [2014] 1 WLR 2889, *Les Laboratoires Servier v Apotext Inc* [2015] AC 430 and *Bilta (UK) Ltd v Nazir (No.2)* [2016] AC 1.
233. [2015] AC 430.
234. *Ibid.* at 444. See also Strauss who suggested (2016) 132 LQR 236, 258 that '[w]hile the reliance test enabled the right result to be achieved in *Tinsley* (but not in *Collier*) a more practical–and equally principled–test might be whether to allow the claim would further or give effect to the illegality, or reward the claimant for it.'

Ltd v Nazir (No.2),[235] Lord Neuberger PSC suggested that the proper approach to the defence of illegality needed to be addressed by the Supreme Court as soon as appropriately possible and the opportunity to do this arose in *Patel v Mirza*, in which nine justices considered the appeal. While some differences of opinion remain following *Patel* in relation to the extent to which the application of the illegality defence should depend on a 'range of factors' or rules based approach,[236] it is now clear that the reasoning adopted by the House of Lords in *Tinsley v Milligan* will no longer be followed[237] and for this reason the judgments in *Patel* are of some significance.[238]

In *Patel v Mirza*[239] the claimant paid a sum of money to the defendant pursuant to an agreement that he would use it to bet on the movement of shares on the basis of inside information and this agreement contravened the statutory prohibition on insider dealing. The agreement could not be carried out because the expected inside information was not forthcoming and the claimant brought proceedings against the defendant seeking the repayment of the money. The trial judge dismissed the claim as being barred by illegality but the Court of Appeal unanimously allowed the claimant's appeal, the majority holding that a party who had withdrawn from an illegal agreement because it could no longer be performed was not prevented by public policy from relying on the agreement provided that no part of it had been carried into effect. The Supreme Court dismissed the defendant's appeal and effectively reassessed the policy basis for and operation of the defence of illegality. Lord Toulson JSC[240] put forward the view that the underlying rationale for the illegality defence is that it would be contrary to the public interest to enforce a claim if to do so would be harmful to the integrity of the legal system, or possibly certain aspects of public morality. He added that in assessing whether the public interest would be harmed by enforcement of the illegal agreement:

> it is necessary to consider (a) to consider the underlying purpose of the prohibition which has been transgressed and whether that purpose will be enhanced by denial of the claim, (b) to consider any other relevant public policy on which the denial of the claim may have an impact and (c) to consider whether denial of the claim would be a proportionate

---

235. [2016] AC 1.
236. See further Lim (2017) 80 MLR 927.
237. See the comments of Sir Kim Lewison in *Cenac v Schafer (St Lucia)* [2016] UKPC 25 at [20] and of Gloster LJ in *Stoffel & Co. v Grondona* [2018] EWCA Civ 2031 at [24]. Martin Spencer J also commented in *Gujra v Roath* [2018] 1 WLR 3208, 3218 that it seemed to him 'that Lord Toulson JSC was, in *Patel v Mirza*, laying down a test that was intended to cover all cases where the common law doctrine of illegality is pleaded as a defence to a civil claim.'
238. Although it should be noted that Nwabueze [2019] Conv 29, 46 has argued that the remit of the illegality principle in the law of trusts is 'very narrow'.
239. [2017] AC 467.
240. With whom Baroness Hale, Lord Kerr, Lord Wilson and Lord Hodge JJSC agreed.

response to the illegality, bearing in mind that punishment is a matter for the criminal courts.[241]

Lord Toulson JSC concluded that a claimant, such as the one before the court, who satisfies the ordinary requirements of a claim for unjust enrichment, should not be debarred from enforcing his claim by reason only of the fact that the money which he seeks to recover was paid for an unlawful purpose. He acknowledged that there might be rare cases where for some reason the enforcement of such a claim might be regarded as undermining the integrity of the justice system, but concluded there were no such circumstances in the matter before the court.[242] Lord Neuberger PSC adopted a similar approach, saying that a claimant in a case such as that before the court should be entitled to the return of money he has paid on the basis that such a rule is consistent with authorities, in accordance with policy and is relatively clear and certain.[243]

Lord Sumption JSC and some of the other members of the court[244] advocated a less flexible and more rules based approach. Lord Sumption JSC considered Lord Toulson's approach to be too uncertain and 'potentially far too wide to serve as the basis on which a person may be denied his legal rights.' In his view, '[i]t converts a legal principle into an exercise of judicial discretion, in the process exhibiting all the vices of "complexity, uncertainty, arbitrariness and lack of transparency" which Lord Toulson JSC attributes to the present law.'[245] Lord Sumption JSC reiterated that the courts will not give effect, at the suit of a person who has committed an illegal act, to a right derived from that act and that the test which has usually been adopted for determining whether this principle applies is the reliance test and he also suggested that the policy basis for the illegality defence is to avoid inconsistency in the law. However, he pointed out that there are exceptions to this where the law regards the parties as not being *in pari delicto*, namely where the claimant's participation in the illegal act is involuntary or where the application of the illegality principle would be inconsistent with the rule of law which makes the act illegal. Lord Sumption JSC concluded that, although the claimant would have to rely on the illegal character of the transaction in order to demonstrate that there was no legal basis for the payment, an order for restitution would not give effect to the illegal act or to any right derived from it.

Lord Toulson JSC said that he agreed with the criticisms made in *Nelson*

241. [2017] AC 467, 504-505. These principles have been applied in a number of cases. See e.g. *Stoffel & Co. v Grondena* [2018] EWCA Civ 2031 at [36]; *Knight v Knight* [2019] EWHC 915 (Ch) at [104].
242. So, as Hildyard J pointed out in *Bank St Petersburg PJSC v Arkhangelsky* [2018] EWHC 1077 (Ch) at [1532], '[w]hat the new approach really introduces is a greater degree of judicial discretion in determining when the illegality defence should apply.
243. [2017] AC 467, 510.
244. Lord Mance and Lord Clarke JJSC.
245. [2017] AC 467, 547.

v Nelson[246] and by academic commentators of the reliance rule as laid down in *Tinsley v Milligan* and that it should no longer be followed. However, it was the reasoning which underpinned the decision of the majority in that case rather than the conclusion with which he and some of the other members of the Supreme Court disagreed.[247] As he stated, '[i]n *Tinsley v Milligan*, even if Miss Milligan had not owned up and come to terms with the DSS, it would have been disproportionate to have prevented her from enforcing her equitable interest in the property and conversely to have left Miss Tinsley unjustly enriched.'[248] In his view the difficulty with the reliance rule set out in *Tinsley* was that it could produce different results according to procedural technicalities which had nothing to do with the underlying policies and he added that the decision of the Court of Appeal in *Collier v Collier*[249] provided a good illustration of this point. In this case the Court of Appeal had rejected a father's claim to the beneficial title in property leased to his daughter on trust for him in order to deceive his creditors because he would have needed to rely on the illegal purpose in order to rebut the presumption of advancement which arose in favour of his daughter.

Similarly, Lord Mance JSC pointed out that a move away from the approach adopted by the majority in *Tinsley* should make it possible to avoid reliance on the artificial procedural concept of the presumption of a resulting trust. He added that '[s]uch a presumption was available in that case to give effect to (though without necessarily referring to) the parties' actual intentions regarding equitable ownership or the reason (although the court was well aware of it) for structuring the transactions as they were. But, as *Collier v Collier* demonstrates, an artificial procedural presumption of this nature cannot be relied upon to be available in every case.'[250] In his view, in future cases the court should be able to simply reverse the effect of a transaction arranged for an illegal purpose. In such cases the underlying equitable interests, which the parties shared based on their contributions and intentions, would be enforceable.

Lord Sumption JSC took the view that the problem with the reliance test was not so much the test itself as the way in which it had been applied in *Tinsley*. He said that it had led to the illegality principle depending on 'adventitious procedural matters, such as the rules of pleading, the incidence of the burden of proof and the various equitable presumptions.'[251] He pointed out that, if the parties had been father and daughter, the outcome would have been different

---

246. (1995) 132 ALR 133.
247. See also *per* Lord Neuberger PSC at 515, Lord Clarke JSC at 530.
248. [2017] AC 467, 502. See also the comments of Lord Neuberger PSC at 519 that 'it seems to me that the justification for the decision of the majority in *Tinsley v Milligan* was, as Lord Toulson JSC says, that it would have been disproportionate to have refused to enforce Miss Milligan's equitable interest in the relevant property on the grounds of her illegal activity, and the policy behind the law making the activity in question illegal was not infringed by acceding to her claim.'
249. [2002] EWCA Civ 1095.
250. [2017] AC 467, 524.
251. *Ibid.* at 536.

because the presumption of resulting trust would have been replaced by a presumption of advancement, as had been in cases such as *Collier v Collier*.[252] As he commented, the distinction between these cases and *Tinsley* is completely arbitrary 'because the equitable presumptions operate wholly procedurally, and have nothing to do with the principle which the court is applying in illegality cases.'[253] He then set out what in his view should be the 'true principle':

> In property cases, as the House held in *Tinsley v Milligan* [1994] 1 AC 340, title is not vitiated by an antecedent illegal arrangement. An equitable interest in property may accordingly arise from a tainted scheme. Whether an equitable interest exists depends on the intentions of the parties. The true principle is that the application of the illegality principle depends on what facts the court must be satisfied about in order to find an intention giving rise to an equitable interest. It does not depend on how those facts are established. Ms Milligan was entitled to the interest which she claimed in the property because she paid half of the price and there was no intention to make a gift. That was all that the court needed to be satisfied about.[254]

So, although Lord Toulson JSC and Lord Sumption JSC took different views in *Patel v Mirza* on the question of whether a 'range of factors' or rules based approach was more suitable in applying the illegality defence,[255] they were in agreement that the outcome should not depend on the applicability or otherwise of equitable presumptions which have led to arbitrary results in the past. This move from an approach to illegality which led to different outcomes depending on whether the presumption of resulting trust (as in *Tinsley v Milligan*[256]*)* or of advancement (as in *Parkes v Parkes*[257]) applied to a more flexible policy based approach is to be welcomed. Even in the light of this revised approach, it is likely that the outcome in the *Tinsley* case would remain the same. If the principles of unjust enrichment on which the approach adopted in *Patel* was based were applied, clearly Ms Tinsley would have been unjustly enriched if Ms Milligan's claim had been denied. In addition, to deny Ms Milligan's claims would not have been a proportionate response given what she had contributed to the purchase price of the property. However, the changes effected by *Patel* do mean that in future, in England in any event, an equitable interest will lie where it falls on the basis of the parties' contributions and intentions, unless

---

252. [2002] EWCA Civ 1095. See also *Chettiar v Chettiar* [1962] AC 294.
253. [2017] AC 467, 536.
254. *Ibid.*
255. See further Lim (2017) 80 MLR 927. Lim favours the approach of Lord Toulson JSC but suggests further refinements to the principles. See also Poulsom [2019] Conv 149, 155.
256. [1994] 1 AC 340.
257. [1980] ILRM 137.

the public interest would be harmed by enforcement of an illegal agreement.[258] Principles which in the past have led to a disproportionate outcome or unjust enrichment of one party will no longer be tolerated.

The operation of the defence of illegality has also been considered in this jurisdiction by Clarke J in the decision of the Supreme Court in *Quinn v Irish Bank Resolution Corporation Ltd.*[259] A preliminary issue was directed to be tried where the plaintiffs claimed that loan transactions were for an illegal purpose, as being in breach of the Market Abuse Directive (2003/6/EC) Regulations 2005 and/or section 60 of the Companies Act 1963, and contended that as a result their guarantees and share pledges were unenforceable and of no legal effect. The High Court found in favour of the plaintiffs but this decision was reversed by the Supreme Court. Clarke J concluded that notwithstanding their illegality, the lending contracts and securities were enforceable. He held that in assessing whether public policy requires that contracts tainted by association with illegality under a statute should be regarded as unenforceable, the first question to be addressed is whether the relevant legislation expressly states that contracts of a particular type are to be treated as void or unenforceable. However, where the relevant legislation is silent on this issue, he said that 'the court must consider whether the requirements of public policy (which suggest that a court refrain from enforcing a contract tainted by illegality) and the policy of the legislation concerned, gleaned from its terms, are such as require that, in addition to whatever express consequences are provided for in the relevant legislation, an additional sanction or consequence in the form of treating relevant contracts as being void or unenforceable must be imposed.'[260] Clarke J added that in assessing the factors to be taken into account in determining whether the balancing exercise requires unenforceability in the context of a particular statutory measure, the court should assess at least the following matters:

(a) Whether the contract in question is designed to carry out the very act which the relevant legislation is designed to prevent
(b) Whether the wording of the statute itself might be taken to strongly imply that the remedies or consequences specified in the statute are sufficient to meet the statutory end
(c) Whether the policy of the legislation is designed to apply equally or substantially to both parties to a relevant contract or whether that policy is exclusively or principally directed towards one party. Therefore, legislation which is designed to impose burdens on one category of persons for the purposes of protecting another category may be considered differently from legislation which is designed to

258. So, in *Kliers v Schmerler* [2018] EWHC 1350 (Ch), an issue of illegality did not bar the claimant's entitlement to relief which had been otherwise established on the basis of resulting trust principles and undue influence.
259. [2016] 1 IR 1.
260. *Ibid.* at 65.

place a burden of compliance with an appropriate regulatory regime on both participants

(d) Whether the imposition of voidness or unenforceability may be counterproductive to the statutory aim as found in the statute itself.[261]

He added that further factors may well be taken into account in an appropriate case and that these include '[w]hether the imposition of voidness or unenforceability may be disproportionate to the seriousness of the unlawful conduct in question in the context of the relevant statutory regime in general.' While the principles set out by Clarke J are primarily relevant to a situation where contracts may be considered to be void in the context of a particular statutory regime, some of these principles, particularly the latter one which is similar to the third factor identified by Lord Toulson in *Patel*, may have more general application to the debate considered above.

Given the arbitrary outcomes which have resulted depending on whether the presumption of a resulting trust or the presumption of advancement apply, there are strong arguments in favour of adopting a more policy based approach in this context.

The Presumption of Advancement

The presumption of advancement arises where because of the relationship which exists between the parties, the donor or purchaser is under an obligation recognised in equity to provide for the person to whom the property is given.[262] Just as the presumption of a resulting trust can be rebutted by evidence showing that a gift was intended, so the presumption of advancement can be rebutted by evidence which establishes that the donor did not intend to benefit or make provision for the donee.[263] The manner in which these presumptions operate was summarised by Viscount Simonds in *Shephard v Cartwright*:[264]

> The law is clear that on the one hand where a man purchases shares and they are registered in the name of a stranger there is a resulting trust in favour of the purchaser; on the other hand, if they are registered in the name of a child or one to whom the purchaser then stood *in loco parentis*, there is no such resulting trust, but a presumption of advancement. Equally it is clear that the presumption [of advancement] may be rebutted but should not … give way to slight circumstances.

The presumption of advancement has been regarded in more recent times as being an outdated concept which can operate in an anomalous and arbitrary

261. *Ibid.* at 66.
262. *Bennet v Bennet* (1879) 10 Ch D 474, 476 *per* Jessel MR.
263. *Anson v Anson* [1953] 1 QB 636; *Re Gooch* (1890) 62 LT 384. See *infra* pp.215-223.
264. [1955] AC 431, 445. See also *Wood v Watkin* [2019] EWHC 1311 (Ch) at [78].

manner and which may be constitutionally suspect. As a result it is fair to say that in circumstances where it has traditionally been held to exist, it has become easier to rebut. In his speech in the decision of the House of Lords in *Stack v Dowden*[265] Lord Neuberger commented that the presumption of advancement 'has now become much weakened, although not quite to the point of disappearance'.[266] In addition, it should be noted that a provision which will abolish the presumption of advancement has been included in the Equality Act 2010 in the United Kingdom[267] and the presumption has already been abolished in Northern Ireland between married and engaged couples.[268]

As will be seen below, the ongoing application of the presumption of advancement in this jurisdiction is a matter on which opinion is divided. In some instances it has continued to be applied[269] and it has been confirmed by the courts in this jurisdiction that the presumption has the status of an equitable doctrine rather than a mere rule of evidence[270] and must be recognised as such. However, there are also increasing signs that the doctrine is regarded as having limited application[271] and that it may be constitutionally suspect.[272]

Traditionally, the presumption of advancement has operated in three types of relationship which will be examined in turn before consideration is given to the question of whether its ambit may extend beyond these categories.

Husband and Wife

The presumption of advancement arises where a husband transfers property to his wife or purchases it in her name.[273] However, traditionally where a wife bought property and put it in her husband's name, this did not give rise to the

---

265. [2007] 2 AC 432, 467. See also *Gibson v Revenue & Customs Prosecution Office* [2009] QB 348, 356; *Amin v Amin* [2009] EWHC 3356 (Ch) at [273].
266. However, note the views expressed at first instance in *Wood v Watkin* [2019] EWHC (Ch) 1311. See also the comment of Rothstein J in the decision of the Supreme Court of Canada in *Pecore v Pecore* (2007) 279 DLR (4th) 513, 523 that the presumptions of a resulting trust and of advancement continue to have a role to play and that they provide a measure of certainty and predictability.
267. This will apply to England, Wales and Scotland. See Richards-Bray (2010) 15 Cov LJ 28. Glister has argued that the provisions of s. 199 are flawed and will not achieve the desired effect, see (2010) 73 MLR 807. See further Andrews and Parsons [2018] Conv 10.
268. Article 16 of the Law Reform (Miscellaneous Provisions) (Northern Ireland) Order 2005.
269. *Malone v McQuaid* [1998] IEHC 86; *O'Meara v Bank of Scotland plc* [2011] IEHC 402.
270. *Per* Henchy J in *R.F. v M.F.* [1995] 2 ILRM 572 and *per* O'Sullivan J in *Malone v McQuaid* [1998] IEHC 86.
271. *J.C. v J.H.C.* High Court 1982 No. 4931P (Keane J) 4 August 1982.
272. *Director of Public Prosecutions v B.* [2009] IEHC 196 at [50] *per* Feeney J.
273. See e.g. *Irwin v O'Connell* [1936] IR 44.

presumption of advancement and instead a resulting trust was presumed.[274] The general principle was set out by Malins VC in *Re Eykyn's Trusts*:[275] 'The law of this Court is perfectly settled that when a husband transfers money or other property into the name of his wife only, then the presumption is, that it is intended as a gift or advancement to the wife absolutely at once. …' As we have seen above in the context of joint bank accounts, this principle traditionally operated where a husband placed money in a bank account in the joint names of himself and his wife.[276] It appears to apply even if the marriage is subsequently dissolved or declared voidable,[277] but not where the marriage is later declared void *ab initio*.[278] The presumption will apply as between engaged couples who subsequently marry,[279] but not between co-habitees.[280]

Lord Diplock in *Pettitt v Pettitt*[281] expressed his view that the presumption was an anachronistic concept in the following terms:

> It would, in my view, be an abuse of the legal technique for ascertaining or imputing intention to apply to transactions between the post war generation of married couples 'presumptions' which are based upon inferences of fact which an earlier generation of judges drew as the most likely intentions of earlier generations of spouses belonging to the propertied classes of a different social era.

It should also be noted that as a result of the decision of the House of Lords in *Stack v Dowden*,[282] where property is transferred into the joint names of a husband and wife, the function of the presumption of advancement is now performed by the presumption of equal beneficial ownership of property held in joint names laid down in that case,[283] at any rate where the attack on one spouse's beneficial interest comes from a third party.[284]

Certainly, in this jurisdiction, in view of the constitutional guarantee of equality, it would seem difficult to justify the continued existence of a principle which undoubtedly seems to benefit a wife and not a husband. As considered

274. *Mercier v Mercier* [1903] 2 Ch 98.
275. (1877) 6 Ch D 115, 118.
276. *Talbot v Cody* (1874) IR 10 Eq 138; *Colohan v Condrin* [1914] 1 IR 89, 94.
277. *Dunbar v Dunbar* [1909] 2 Ch 639.
278. See *Re D'Altroy's Will Trusts* [1968] 1 WLR 120 which establishes this point in another context.
279. *Moate v Moate* [1948] 2 All ER 486; *Ulrich v Ulrich* [1968] 1 WLR 180.
280. *Calverley v Green* (1984) 155 CLR 242; *Lowson v Coombes* [1999] Ch 373. See also *Stack v Dowden* [2007] 2 AC 432, 469; *Chapman v Jaume* [2012] EWCA Civ 476 at [24].
281. [1970] AC 777, 824.
282. [2007] 2 AC 432.
283. See *Gibson v Revenue and Customs Prosecution Office* [2009] QB 348, 356 *per* Arden LJ.
284. *Ibid.* at 357 *per* Wall LJ.

further below, the presumption also appears anachronistic given that Article 41.4 of the Constitution of Ireland now provides that '[m]arriage may be contracted in accordance with law by two persons without distinction as to their sex.' However, the presumption of advancement continues to apply, unless rebutted, where a husband transfers property to his wife or purchases it in her name.

In *W. v W.*,[285] although it was not strictly necessary for his decision, Finlay P took the opportunity to reiterate that where a husband makes a contribution to the purchase of property in his wife's sole name, he will be presumed to have intended to advance his wife unless that presumption is rebutted. One of the most important authorities in the area is the Supreme Court decision of *R.F. v M.F.*,[286] which also concerned a dispute about ownership of property purchased by a husband in the parties' joint names. Henchy J appeared to accept the relevance of the presumption of advancement but went on to hold that it had been clearly rebutted in the circumstances of the case. The evidence established that the wife had refused to live in the house unless it was in their joint names and despite her promise to live there, which Henchy J considered to be an integral part of the arrangement, she had never done so.

Another decision dealing with the application of the presumption of advancement in this context is that of O'Sullivan J in *Malone v McQuaid*.[287] The defendant was the liquidator of a company in which the first and second named plaintiffs, a wife and husband respectively, were one-third shareholders. The defendant obtained a judgment against the husband and registered that judgment as a mortgage against the latter's alleged equitable interest in a property, which was not the family home. This house was registered in his wife's name and she was at the time negotiating a sale to a purchaser which subsequently fell through. In considering the plaintiffs' claim for damages against the defendant in relation to the loss of the sale, it became necessary for the court to establish whether the husband had an equitable interest in the house. O'Sullivan J accepted that assuming that the husband had provided some or all of the monies for the purchase of the house, 'whatever about the [husband's] obligation to provide [the house] for the benefit of his wife, he was clearly under an obligation to provide for his children'.[288] Accordingly, he considered that he should apply the presumption of advancement unless it had been rebutted on the facts. O'Sullivan J pointed to the fact that there was some evidence that the husband had not intended to confer a beneficial interest on his wife and he had allegedly told a third party that he wanted to put the property in her name so that the tenants would not know that he owned the building. However, O'Sullivan J stated that the evidence which tended to rebut the presumption of advancement was of an indirect nature and he concluded that on the overall balance of the evidence it had not been rebutted and applied

285. [1981] ILRM 202, 204.
286. [1995] 2 ILRM 572.
287. [1998] IEHC 86.
288. *Ibid.* at 18.

to the case before him. He therefore held that the entire beneficial interest in the property was vested in the wife, although he found that the registration of the judgment had not caused the abandonment of the sale and accordingly he refused to award damages against the defendant.

The findings made in *O'Meara v Bank of Scotland plc*,[289] considered above in the context of joint deposit accounts, also supports the proposition that a presumption of advancement in favour of a wife may still be applied. In that case the court had to determine the beneficial ownership of monies in two joint deposit accounts in the names of the plaintiff widow and her late husband which the defendant bank claimed to be entitled to set off against monies owed to it by the deceased. In relation to the first account, Laffoy J was satisfied that the defendant had not displaced a presumption of advancement which arose in favour of the wife. She did not find it necessary to determine the beneficial ownership of monies in a second joint deposit account as, in her view, the right of the defendant bank over these monies had priority in equity. However, Laffoy J did note that the husband, as the sole contributor to the monies in this account, was the beneficial owner unless the presumption of advancement overrode the doctrine of resulting trust, which in the circumstances outlined she did not need to decide.

An examination of these decisions would suggest that the courts still tend to proceed on the basis that the presumption of advancement will *prima facie* apply where a husband transfers property to his wife or purchases it in her name. However, as the decision in *R.F. v M.F.* makes clear, the presumption can readily be rebutted by evidence establishing a contrary intention and in practice, it is only likely to directly influence the outcome of a case where there is little or no evidence to show what the parties' intentions in relation to ownership of the property actually were.

This view is also supported by the approach adopted by Keane J in *J.C. v J.H.C.*,[290] in which he held that a husband and wife should share the beneficial interest in property, which although conveyed to them both as joint tenants was purchased entirely out of monies provided by the husband. Keane J stated as follows:

> Where property is taken in the joint names of two or more persons, but the purchase money is advanced by one of them alone, the law presumes a resulting trust in favour of the person who advanced the purchase money. This presumption may however be rebutted; and in particular the circumstance of the person into whose name the property is conveyed being the wife of the person advancing the money may be sufficient to rebut the presumption under the doctrine of advancement.[291]

289. [2011] IEHC 402.
290. High Court 1982 No. 4931P (Keane J) 4 August 1982.
291. *Ibid.* at 3.

However, Keane J went on to refer to the remarks of Lord Diplock in *Pettitt v Pettitt*,[292] which cast doubt on the relevance of the presumption, and he appeared to base his decision on the fact that the evidence 'overwhelmingly' reinforced the presumption of advancement, which he said would arise had there been no other evidence as to the parties' intentions. Therefore, one could argue that Keane J appeared to regard the presumption of advancement as being relevant only where evidence to establish the parties' true intentions was lacking.

One further issue which can no longer be ignored is that the lack of equality inherent in the principle that the presumption of advancement does not extend to circumstances where a wife purchases property in her husband's name. The point has been made in *Kelly: The Irish Constitution* that 'the courts have … identified a principle of equality of spouses within marriage implicit in Articles 41 and 42 which has sounded the death-knell for a number of common law rules reflecting a dominant role for the husband.'[293] This view is also supported by the view expressed by Feeney J in *Director of Public Prosecutions v B.*[294] to the effect that '[i]n this jurisdiction given the constitutional status of spouses and the guarantee of equality, it would be difficult absent particular proved facts to identify circumstances where the continued principle of advancement between a husband and a wife could have any general application.'

It is submitted that the presumption of advancement, a creature of equity, cannot remain immune from constitutional developments over the last few decades in this area of equality of spouses within marriage, not least given that Article 41.4 of the Constitution[295] now provides that '[m]arriage may be contracted in accordance with law by two persons without distinction as to their sex.' It must, therefore, be suggested that the traditional principles referred to above should be regarded with a degree of caution, and that those relating to the presumption as between husband and wife should be regarded as particularly suspect.

Father and Child

Where a father purchases property in the name of his child or transfers it into the child's name, the presumption of advancement will apply. This is illustrated by the decision in *Hepworth v Hepworth*,[296] in which it was held that the voluntary transfer of stock into his son's name by a father operated as an absolute gift

292. [1970] AC 777, 824.
293. Hogan, Whyte, Kenny and Walsh, *Kelly, The Irish Constitution* (5th ed., 2018) p. 1565. See e.g. *Re Tilson, Infants* [1951] IR 1; *O'G. v Attorney General* [1985] ILRM 61; *McKinley v Minister for Defence* [1992] 2 IR 333. See also the comments of Laffoy J in *Cawley v Lillis* [2012] 1 IR 281, 288.
294. [2009] IEHC 196 at [50].
295. See the Thirty Fourth Amendment of the Constitution (Marriage Equality) Act 2015.
296. (1870) LR 11 Eq 10. See also *Crabb v Crabb* (1834) 1 My & K 511; *Re Roberts* [1946] Ch 1; *B. v B.* (1976) 65 DLR (3d) 460; *Antoni v Antoni* [2007] WTLR 1335 at [20].

to the son. As Malins VC commented, '[t]he law is not doubtful that if this had been a transfer to a stranger it would have operated as a trust, but if a gift is made in favour of a child the presumption of law is that it is intended as an advancement or provision for the child'.[297] An important authority in this area is the judgment of Sullivan MR in *O'Brien v Sheil*.[298] There a father lodged securities in a bank in the joint names of himself and his daughter which was held after his death to be an advancement in the daughter's favour, despite evidence which suggested that the father had subsequently intended the securities to be applied to different purposes. Sullivan MR stated that it was 'now settled law that a lodgment by a father in the joint names of himself and his child is as powerful and strong an indication of advancement as a lodgment in the name of the child alone'[299] and stressed that declarations made by the father which were subsequent to the advancement could not constitute evidence to rebut the presumption.[300]

There have been conflicting views expressed on the question of the strength of the presumption of advancement in the case of a father/child relationship. It was suggested by Viscount Simonds in *Shephard v Cartwright*[301] that it should not 'give way to slight circumstances' and by O'Sullivan J in *Malone v McQuaid*[302] that the presumption in such relationships is stronger than in the case of a husband and wife. However, the views of the Law Lords expressed in *Pettitt v Pettitt*[303] would suggest that the presumption of advancement is no longer as strong as it was in any context and it was acknowledged by the Court of Appeal in *McGrath v Wallis*[304] that in the context of a father/son relationship the presumption may be rebutted by 'comparatively slight evidence'.

The presumption of advancement between a father and his adult son was also referred to in *Kenny v Kenny*,[305] in which the plaintiff claimed the proceeds of a mortgage protection policy on a property jointly owned with his deceased son in circumstances in which the plaintiff had made the mortgage repayments. O'Connor J acknowledged that in principle the presumption of advancement could be displaced by evidence that the plaintiff had not intended to make a gift to his son and the plaintiff argued that there was no evidence that he intended to make such a gift. Having considered the evidence, O'Connor J found that the plaintiff had never agreed with his son what would happen to the proceeds

297. *Ibid.* at 12.
298. (1873) IR 7 Eq 255.
299. *Ibid.* at 259.
300. See further *infra* pp. 217-218.
301. [1955] AC 431, 445.
302. [1998] IEHC 86.
303. [1970] AC 777, 815.
304. [1995] 2 FLR 114. See also *Hashem v Shayif* [2008] EWHC 2380 (Fam) at [117] where Munby J commented that 'the practical reality is that the presumption is likely to have decisive effect only if there are no living witnesses and no other relevant evidence'.
305. [2019] IEHC 76.

of the policy and concluded that the height of the plaintiff's case related to the premia paid in relation to the policy rather than the proceeds thereof.

The majority of the Supreme Court of Canada took the view in *Pecore v Pecore*[306] that the presumption of advancement should only apply to transfers to minor children and not to adult children[307] even if they are dependent on their parents. As Rothstein J put it, '[d]ependency is a term susceptible to an enormous variety of circumstances'[308] and would be too difficult to define with sufficient certainty in this context. When this issue arose at first instance in England in *Wood v Watkin*,[309] the view was taken that the position adopted by the majority in *Pecore* was *obiter* and that, in any event, it did not represent the law in that jurisdiction. Judge Barber expressed the opinion that the presumption of advancement can arise in relation to a child who is not a minor and rejected the argument that the latter must be financially dependent in order for the presumption to apply. While he acknowledged, referring to Lord Neuberger's *obiter* comments in *Laskar v Laskar*,[310] that the presumption may be weaker and more readily rebuttable in the case of an adult child who is financially independent, he pointed out that the historic rationale for the presumption is based on parental affection as well as obligation.

As regards the positon in this jurisdiction, Carolan suggests that the view of the majority in *Pecore* is based on the premise that 'a principal justification for the presumption of advancement is parental obligation'[311] and refers to the fact that the authorities in this jurisdiction support this view to an extent.[312] However, he also points out that Irish law appears to take the position that parents continue to owe obligations to their children even after they reach the age of majority,[313] and for this reason he suggests that it is arguable that the logic of the majority in *Pecore* may not be directly applicable in this jurisdiction.[314]

Persons in Loco Parentis to a Child

The presumption also applies where the donor or purchaser of property stands

306. (2007) 279 DLR (4th) 513. See further McInnes (2007) 123 LQR 528; Glister [2007] Conv 370; Carolan (2008) 26 ILT 26.
307. See also *Fulton v Gunn* (2008) 296 DLR 1, 21; *Sawdon Estate v Watch Tower Bible and Tract Society of Canada* (2014) 370 DLR (4th) 686, 699-700.
308. (2007) 279 DLR (4th) 513, 528.
309. [2019] EWHC 1311 (Ch).
310. [2008] 1 WLR 2695, 2700.
311. (2007) 279 DLR (4th) 513, 527.
312. See e.g. *Re McDonald* [2000] 1 ILRM 382, 386.
313. E.g., s. 117 of the Succession Act 1965.
314. It should be noted that in *ACC Loan Management Ltd v Fryday* [2019] IEHC 103, it was submitted by the notice parties in proceedings relating to an application for the cancellation of inhibitions that Irish law should no longer recognise a presumption of advancement as between a parent and child, particularly where transfers are made to a child who is not a minor. However, given that Quinn J was satisfied in any event that the inhibitions should be cancelled, he did not have to determine this issue.

in loco parentis to the person in whose name this property is held or bought.[315] This principle was explained by Jessel MR in *Bennet v Bennet*[316] in the following terms: 'nothing is better established than this, that as regards a child, a person not the father of the child may put himself in the position of one *in loco parentis*[317] to the child and so incur the obligation to make a provision for the child.' Jessel MR stressed that while the presumption of advancement applies to a father because he is under an obligation to provide for his child by virtue of the relationship between the parties, in the case of someone who stands *in loco parentis*, 'you must prove that he took upon himself the obligation.' This principle has been held to apply, *inter alia*, to the relationship between a father and an illegitimate child,[318] or his stepson[319] but not to that between an uncle and his nephew where there was no evidence of the former being *in loco parentis*.[320]

Does the Presumption Apply in other Circumstances?

The position in relation to gifts made by a mother to her child is still not settled in this jurisdiction although it has been largely resolved elsewhere in the common law world and the general trend has been towards recognising that the relationship of mother and child does give rise to the presumption of advancement. The courts in Canada,[321] New Zealand[322] and Australia[323] seem to have all come down in favour of the proposition that the presumption should apply to such relationships. As Rothstein J noted in the decision of the Supreme Court of Canada in *Pecore v Pecore*,[324] '[a]s women now have both the means as well as obligations to support their children, they are no less likely to intend to make gifts to their children than fathers' and the view of the majority of the court was that the presumption of advancement should apply equally to fathers and mothers.

The nineteenth century English authority of *Bennet v Bennet*[325] was based on the reasoning that there is 'no moral legal obligation … no obligation according

---

315. *Shephard v Cartwright* [1955] AC 431, 445.
316. (1879) 10 Ch D 474, 477.
317. Defined by Jessel MR as 'a person taking upon himself the duty of a father of a child to make provision for that child' (at 477). See also *Sansom v Gardner* [2009] EWHC 3369 (QB) at [90].
318. *Soar v Foster* (1858) 4 K & J 152.
319. *Re Paradise Motor Co.* [1968] 1 WLR 1125.
320. *Romaine Estate v Romaine* (2001) 205 DLR (4th) 320, 334.
321. *Pecore v Pecore* (2007) 279 DLR (4th) 51. See also *Saylor v Madsen Estate* (2007) 279 DLR (4th) 547.
322. See *Re Brownlee* [1990] 3 NZLR 243.
323. *Dullow v Dullow* (1985) 3 NSWLR 531; *Brown v Brown* (1993) 31 NSWLR 582; *Nelson v Nelson* (1995) 132 ALR 133.
324. (2007) 279 DLR (4th) 513, 525.
325. (1879) 10 Ch D 474. See also *Re De Visme* (1863) 2 De GJ & S 17. However, note that the contrary conclusion was reached in *Sayre v Hughes* (1868) LR 5 Eq 376.

to the rules of equity … on a mother to provide for her child'.[326] While there has been some further evidence of a reluctance to extend the presumption to gifts made by mothers to their children in that jurisdiction,[327] there has also been growing academic criticism of what is perceived to be an outdated view on this question.[328] In *Laskar v Laskar*[329] the Court of Appeal appeared to accept that the presumption would apply to such a relationship, although Lord Neuberger characterised the approach of counsel in accepting that it did not apply in the circumstances before the court where the child was over 18 and managing her own affairs, as a realistic one. More recently, in *Patel v Mirza*,[330] Lord Toulson JSC appeared to assume that the presumption of advancement would apply as between a mother and her daughter.

The position in this jurisdiction is somewhat unsatisfactory as there have been no recent decisions in this area which might take account of changing perceptions of the parent/child relationship. In *Re Grimes*[331] Johnston J found that the presumption of advancement applied to a gift by a widowed mother to her son, and described the reasoning in *Bennet* as 'singularly unconvincing'. He went on to hold that even if the presumption did not apply, the former's intention to benefit the son in the circumstances of the case was sufficiently strong to rebut any presumption of a resulting trust. However, a different conclusion was reached on this question by the Supreme Court in *McCabe v Ulster Bank Ltd*.[332] The evidence surrounding the circumstances of the gift, which consisted of the lodgment by a widowed mother of sums in a bank account in the names of herself and her three daughters was in the words of Murnaghan J 'very meagre'. After an extensive review of the relevant authorities in the area both in this jurisdiction and in England, Murnaghan J concluded that the application of the presumption of advancement to the relationship between a mother and her child could not be based on any sound principle. He continued:

> I have come to the conclusion that the presumption must be based upon the obligation to make provision which a Court of Equity recognises in the case of a father, or of one who has assumed his obligation in this respect.

---

326. *Ibid.* at 478 *per* Jessel MR.
327. *Sekhon v Alissa* [1989] 2 FLR 94.
328. See Enonchong [1993] RLR 78, 84; Dowling [1996] Conv 274, 283. Andrews [2007] Conv 340, 350-351. See also the views expressed by Lindsay J in *Re Cameron* [1999] Ch 386, 405 in the context of the presumption against double portions, that 'both parties should nowadays be taken to be *in loco parentis* unless the contrary is proved.'
329. [2008] 1 WLR 2695. See also *Spencer v Strickland* [2009] EWHC 3033 (Ch) at [41]; *Close Invoice Finance Ltd v Abaowa* [2010] EWHC 1920 (QB) at [93].
330. [2017] AC 467, 479. Lord Toulson JSC stated that '[i]f the relationship between [the parties] had been that of daughter and mother, and each had contributed to the purchase of a property in the daughter's name, the result would have been different, because there would then have been a presumption of advancement in the daughter's favour.'
331. [1937] IR 470.
332. [1939] IR 1.

> In many cases of widowed mothers very slight circumstances may be sufficient to place the widow *in loco parentis*, i.e., of having assumed the father's obligation to provide. In such cases there will be a basis for the presumption, but in a case such as the present, where there are no circumstances to go upon save the mere relationship of mother and child, there is, in my opinion, no ground for an equitable presumption which will rebut a resulting trust.[333]

On the basis of the facts before the court, the Supreme Court concluded that there was insufficient evidence of the mother's intention to confer a benefit on her daughters to rebut the presumption of a resulting trust. On the one hand, it is difficult to fault the reasoning of Murnaghan J having regard to the historical origins of the doctrine of advancement and if one were to follow his approach it is certainly true that in the majority of cases 'very slight circumstances' would suffice to establish that a widowed mother had assumed the father's traditional obligation to provide for the child. However, it could also be said that the rationale which originally justified the imposition of the presumption as between father and child, namely that the former was under a moral obligation to provide for the latter,[334] is arguably today just as relevant to the position of a mother as to that of a father and it is difficult to justify a principle which continues to result in the drawing of such anomalous and arbitrary distinctions. Equally, if the courts in this jurisdiction were to apply the reasoning employed by the Supreme Court of South Australia in *Callaghan v Callaghan*,[335] namely that the presumption of advancement is based on the relationship between the parties rather than on any obligation on the part of the transferor, it should make no difference whether the parent is a father or a mother.[336]

Keane is correct in suggesting that it is also difficult to reconcile a reluctance to extend the presumption of advancement to mother/child relationships in the light of the position adopted by the Supreme Court in decisions such as *Re Tilson*,[337] which stress the concept of joint parental responsibility towards children.[338] It is therefore likely that if the question arises again, the courts in this jurisdiction will apply the presumption of advancement to transfers between mothers and their children.[339] In any event even if they were to continue to draw such a theoretical distinction between the position of a mother and father in applying the presumption of advancement, it is likely that the evidence available

333. *Ibid.* at 15.
334. See *Bennet v Bennet* (1879) 10 Ch D 474.
335. [1995] SASC 5064.
336. Although the language employed by O'Sullivan J in *Malone v McQuaid* [1998] IEHC 86 at 18 would suggest that the rationale of obligation still subsists.
337. [1951] IR 1.
338. Keane, *Equity and the Law of Trusts in Ireland* (3rd ed., 2017) p. 227.
339. A view shared by Carolan (2008) 26 ILT 26.

to them in any particular case would suffice to ensure that any unjustified presumptions would be rebutted.

As pointed out above, there has been no evidence of a willingness on the part of the judiciary to extend the presumption of advancement to co-habitees, whether of different sexes,[340] or of the same sex.[341]

Finally, it should be noted that in the decision of *Fitzpatrick v Criminal Assets Bureau*,[342] which concerned a dispute about whether a car seized by the first named defendant was in fact the property of an individual or of a company, the High Court refused to contemplate the extension of the presumption of advancement to a relationship of a commercial nature. As Shanley J stated:

> I know of no decided case, and none was opened to me, which suggests that the relationships to which the presumption of advancement extend include those of a shareholder and the company in which he owns shares or the relationship between an individual and the company which he manages, controls or operates.[343]

Rebutting the Presumption of Advancement

As noted above, there has been some erosion of judicial confidence in the concept of the presumption of advancement due in part to the rather anomalous results which it may produce and to significant constitutional developments in the area of equality and the recognition of the fact that 'marriage may be contracted in accordance with law by two persons without distinction as to their sex.'[344] In circumstances where the presumption has traditionally been held to exist, it has generally become easier to rebut.[345] However, in addition to this general development, it is still important to note the circumstances in which the presumption has traditionally been rebutted.

Evidence that no Gift Intended

The presumption of advancement will be rebutted if evidence is adduced to

---

340. *Calverley v Green* (1984) 155 CLR 242; *Lowson v Coombes* [1999] Ch 373. See also *Stack v Dowden* [2007] 2 AC 432, 469; *Chapman v Jaume* [2012] EWCA Civ 476 at [24].
341. *Tinsley v Milligan* [1994] 1 AC 340. See also Thornton [1993] CLJ 394, 395.
342. [2000] 1 IR 217.
343. *Ibid.* at 238.
344. Article 41.4 of the Constitution of Ireland.
345. *Pettitt v Pettitt* [1970] AC 777, 824 *per* Lord Diplock (quoted with approval by Keane J in *J.C. v J.H.C.*, High Court, 1982 No.4931P, 4 August 1982). See also *McGrath v Wallis* [1995] 2 FLR 114. However, there have also been examples of cases where the presumption has not been held to have been rebutted, see *Malone v McQuaid* [1998] IEHC 86.

show that no gift was intended by the donor or transferor.[346] As Henchy J stated in *R.F. v M.F.*:[347]

> If the relevant circumstances show that the paper result achieved by the conveyance conceals the real intention of the husband in entering into the transaction, so that the benefit contended for by the wife was not intended, the court will hold that the presumption of advancement has been rebutted.

In *Anson v Anson*[348] a husband guaranteed his wife's bank account and was obliged to pay a sum of money to the bank on foot of this guarantee. It was held that the husband could recover this amount from the wife and that there was no presumption of advancement in a transaction of this nature. Pearson J stated that the husband had made it clear to his wife that his intention was not to relieve her of the debt, but to solve the immediate problem in which she found herself. Therefore, it would appear that a transaction of this nature cannot be presumed to be an advancement unless the donor makes it clear to the donee at the time of making the guarantee that he does not expect to be reimbursed.

Where the relationship at issue is that of father and child it may be more difficult to identify with any degree of certainty the types of circumstances in which the presumption may be rebutted, particularly where the child is a minor as the father may be more likely to retain some element of control over the property.[349] However, it was held in *Re Gooch*[350] that, where a father bought shares in a company purely to enable the son to become a director, with the latter handing over the dividends received on these shares, and subsequently the share certificates, the presumption of advancement had been rebutted. Similarly in *Warren v Guerney*,[351] where a father arranged for a house to be conveyed into his daughter's name, it was held by the Court of Appeal that the presumption of advancement was rebutted by the fact that the father had retained the title deeds to the property,[352] and by the contemporaneous declarations made by him that it was not his intention that his daughter should be the sole beneficial owner of the house.

---

346. The contesting party must prove on the balance of probabilities that the person who is presumed to have intended a gift actually intended not to make it, see *Pasko v Pasko* [2002] BCSC 435 at [50].
347. [1995] 2 ILRM 572, 577.
348. [1953] 1 QB 636. See also *Re Salisbury-Jones* [1938] 3 All ER 459.
349. See e.g. *Grey v Grey* (1677) 2 Swans 594 where it was held that the fact that a son continued to allow his father to receive the rents on a property was insufficient to rebut the presumption of advancement as it was 'an act of reverence and good manners' (at 600).
350. (1890) 62 LT 384.
351. [1944] 2 All ER 472.
352. It would appear that retention of title deeds alone might be insufficient to rebut the presumption.

Nature of Evidence Admissible to Rebut Presumption

A further important question which must be considered is the type of evidence which will suffice to rebut the presumption of advancement. As Sullivan MR stated in *O'Brien v Sheil*,[353] 'declarations of the [transferor], subsequent to the advancement, if they are not so connected with it as to be reasonably regarded as contemporaneous, cannot be evidence to rebut the presumption of advancement.' In that case, a memorandum found among a father's papers after his death was not admissible in evidence to rebut the presumption of advancement in favour of his daughter in relation to a transfer of securities into their joint names during the father's lifetime.

The most important authority in this area is the decision of the House of Lords in *Shephard v Cartwright*.[354] A father arranged for shares in certain private companies to be allotted to his children. He subsequently dealt with the shares, at one point crediting the profits of these dealings to a bank account in the children's names, but later appropriating these funds to his own purposes. After his death, the children succeeded in establishing that the shares registered in their names must be regarded as an advancement which had not been rebutted by their father's conduct. The House of Lords held that the father's conduct after allotting the shares could not go to prove that he had not intended to make an advancement to his children and laid down a number of important general principles in this regard. Viscount Simonds quoted with approval the following passage from *Snell's Equity*:[355]

> The acts and declarations of the parties before or at the time of the purchase, or so immediately after it as to constitute a part of the transaction, are admissible in evidence either for or against the party who did the act or made the declaration. It has been held that subsequent acts and declarations may only be admissible as evidence against the party who made them, and not in his favour.

These principles would seem to mean that an act or declaration by a donor or transferor at the time of or prior to the transaction may be used by him to rebut the presumption while subsequent acts or declarations cannot be admitted to support his claim but may be used against him by the donee in order to support the application of the presumption. In addition, as pointed out by Oakley, evidence of subsequent acts and declarations by the transferee can be admitted against him in order to enable the transferor to rebut the presumption

353. (1873) IR 7 Eq 255. See also the decisions of *Fox v Fox* (1863) 15 Ir Ch R 89 and *Sidmouth v Sidmouth* (1840) 2 Beav 447 to which Sullivan MR referred.
354. [1955] AC 431.
355. Rivington and Jenkin, *Snell's Equity* (24th ed., 1954) p. 153. Now see McGhee, *Snell's Equity* (33rd ed., 2015) p. 681. See further *Antoni v Antoni* [2007] WTLR 1335 at [20].

of advancement.[356] These principles were confirmed by the Supreme Court in *R.F. v M. F.*,[357] where Henchy J stated as follows:

> The presumption of advancement … is, of course, rebuttable. For a rebuttal to be made out, it is for the husband to show, by reference to acts or statements before or around the transaction, that a beneficial interest was not intended to be conveyed in the circumstances relied on. As to subsequent acts or statements, the authorities show that they are admissible in evidence against the party making them, but not in his or her favour. Thus, subsequent acts or statements on the part of the wife are admissible in evidence to rebut the presumption of advancement.

However, some doubts about the continued application of the principle laid down in *Shepherd v Cartwright* have been expressed. In *Lavelle v Lavelle*,[358] Lord Phillips MR stated that it seemed to him that it was not satisfactory to apply rigid rules of law to the evidence that is admissible to rebut the presumption of advancement, although he acknowledged that clearly 'self-serving statements or conduct of a transferor, who may long after the transaction be regretting earlier generosity, carry little or no weight.'[359]

It should also be noted that Rothstein J expressed the view in the decision of the Supreme Court of Canada in *Pecore v Pecore*[360] that evidence of intention that arises subsequent to a transfer should not automatically be excluded although it must be relevant to the intention of the transferor at the time the transfer is made. In his opinion, '[t]he trial judge must assess the reliability of this evidence and determine what weight it should be given, guarding against evidence that is self-serving or that tends to reflect a change in intention.'[361]

Unlawful or Fraudulent Conduct

As noted above, the law in this area has been complicated by the fact that the UK Supreme Court has held that the approach adopted by the House of Lords in *Tinsley v Milligan*[362] in applying the illegality defence, which led to arbitrary results depending on whether the presumption of advancement applied in a case, should not be followed. While there is little case law on this issue in this jurisdiction, the courts here have tended to follow the approach which previously applied in England. Although reference will be made to the likely outcomes

356. Oakley, *Parker and Mellows: Modern Law of Trusts* (9th ed., 2008) p.308.
357. [1995] 2 ILRM 572, 576-577.
358. [2004] EWCA Civ 223.
359. *Ibid.* at [19].
360. (2007) 279 DLR (4th) 513.
361. *Ibid.* at 533.
362. [1994] 1 AC 340.

which the changes signalled in *Patel v Mirza*[363] will lead to, it is still necessary to consider the manner in which the traditional principles have developed and how they have been applied in this jurisdiction. In summary, the application of these principles has meant that it is not been possible to adduce evidence of an illegal purpose to rebut the presumption of advancement where this illegal purpose has been carried out.

Traditionally, the presumption of advancement could not be rebutted by evidence that a transfer was made for a fraudulent or illegal purpose where this purpose had been wholly or partly carried out.[364] So, where for example, a father transferred land into his son's name with a view to achieving an unlawful purpose or where a husband put property into his wife's name in order to evade the payment of taxes,[365] the transferor could not adduce evidence of the improper purpose to rebut the presumption of advancement. In *Chettiar v Chettiar*[366] a father transferred land into his son's name for an illegal purpose, namely to avoid certain regulations applying to the holding. The Privy Council concluded that the illegal purpose had been carried into effect and held that the father could not rely on evidence of this illegality to rebut the presumption of advancement in order to recover the land. It was not necessary to prove that the transferee was entirely unaware of the illegality in order to prevent the transferor relying on such rebuttal evidence. In *Gascoigne v Gascoigne*[367] a man conveyed property into his wife's name to protect it from his creditors. It was held that he could not rely on this fact to rebut the presumption of advancement and that the wife could retain the property for her own benefit, notwithstanding the fact that she had been aware of the fraudulent purpose behind the transaction.

These principles have also been applied in Ireland. In *Parkes v Parkes*[368] the defendant husband wanted to buy land and arranged for it to be conveyed into his wife's name to obviate the need for Land Commission consent, which would have been necessary had he purchased the property in his own name as he was not an Irish citizen.[369] After the parties divorced, the husband registered an inhibition on the land and the wife instituted proceedings claiming that it had been wrongly registered. The husband counterclaimed that he was entitled to

---

363. [2017] AC 467.
364. *Tribe v Tribe* [1996] Ch 107. See also the *dicta* of Lord Denning MR in *Chettiar v Chettiar* [1962] AC 294, 302. It should be noted at this point that the High Court of Australia rejected this principle in *Nelson v Nelson* (1995) 132 ALR 133 also considered below.
365. *Re Emery's Investment Trusts* [1959] Ch 410.
366. [1962] AC 294.
367. [1918] 1 KB 223. Equally, it is not necessary to establish that the transferor acted fraudulently, and his honest motives may even help to strengthen the presumption against him: see *Tinker v Tinker* [1970] P 136.
368. [1980] ILRM 137.
369. Section 45 of the Land Act 1965 required that the consent of the Land Commission be obtained for the purchase of land to which the section applied by anyone other than a qualified person which means, *inter alia*, an Irish citizen.

the beneficial ownership in the land and the wife put forward the argument that he should not be able to obtain relief in equity by setting up his own illegality or fraud. Costello J referred to *Gascoigne v Gascoigne* and to *McEvoy v Belfast Banking Co.*,[370] where a father had deposited money in his son's name to avoid death duties, and stated:

> Just as the courts will not grant relief to a person who has allowed property to be placed in a wife's or son's name for the fraudulent purpose of defeating creditors ... or for the illegal purpose of evading liability to tax so it seems to me that the court should not grant relief to a purchaser who has placed property in his wife's name dishonestly and by means of an illegal act performed for the purpose of evading the law relating to the transfer of land.[371]

Therefore, the husband was not allowed to adduce evidence of his motives for conveying the land into his wife's name and could not rebut the presumption of advancement which operated in her favour.

However, while this issue did not arise in *Parkes*, it appeared that different considerations would apply where the illegal purpose had not been carried out.[372] As Millett LJ stated in *Tribe v Tribe*,[373] 'a person who has transferred property for an illegal purpose can nevertheless recover his property provided that he withdraws from the transaction before the illegal purpose has been wholly or partly performed.' In *Tribe* this principle was applied specifically to a situation where the presumption of advancement arose.[374] The plaintiff had transferred shares in a family company to his son with a view to defrauding his creditors. The difficulties which might have led to claims being made against him were resolved and when the plaintiff sought to recover the shares from the defendant, the latter resisted his claim. The Court of Appeal held that the plaintiff transferor was entitled to adduce evidence of his intention in order to rebut the presumption of advancement in favour of his son, which he successfully did. Effectively this decision meant that a plaintiff who had made a transfer of property to a person in whose favour the presumption of advancement arises, could withdraw from the transaction before the illegal purpose had been wholly or partly carried out[375] and then recover the property by adducing evidence of

370. [1934] NI 67.
371. [1980] ILRM 137, 144.
372. Note the comments of Denning MR in *Chettiar v Chettiar* [1962] AC 294, 302 to the effect that 'if the fraudulent purpose had not been carried out there might well have been room for repentance and the father might have been allowed to have the land retransferred to him'.
373. [1996] Ch 107, 124. This is one of the exceptions to the general rule against relying on one's own illegality and is known as the doctrine of *locus poenitentiae*.
374. [1986] ILRM 1.
375. Virgo argued in [1996] CLJ 23, 25 that in *Tribe*, although nobody was actually deceived, the father had done all that he could to carry his illegal purpose into effect

his illegal purpose in order to rebut the presumption. However, as Millett LJ stressed, the transferor 'must have withdrawn from the transaction while his dishonesty still lay in intention only. The law drew the line once the intention had been wholly or partly carried into effect.'[376] Millett LJ was of the view that while the withdrawal from the transaction must have been voluntary, genuine repentance in relation to the illegal purpose was unnecessary; as Nourse LJ stated, all that mattered was that no deception should have been practised on the plaintiff's creditors.[377]

The question of whether a transferor should be able to rely on an illegal purpose which has been carried into effect to rebut the presumption of advancement has been considered elsewhere in the common law world. In *Nelson v Nelson*[378] Mrs Nelson transferred a house into the names of her son and daughter so that she could obtain a subsidy for the purchase of a subsequent house. After the sale of the original house her daughter claimed a half-share in it and argued that Mrs Nelson could not adduce evidence of her illegal purpose in order to rebut the presumption of advancement.[379] However, the High Court of Australia accepted evidence to rebut the presumption of advancement even though it was tainted with illegality and despite the fact that the illegal purpose had been carried into effect.[380] In reaching this conclusion the court effectively rejected the distinction drawn by the House of Lords in *Tinsley v Milligan*[381] between cases where the presumption of advancement did or did not apply.[382] As Lord Browne-Wilkinson had stated in *Tinsley*, 'in cases where

---

and that therefore the court should have concluded that his purpose had been partly carried out.

376. [1996] Ch 107, 133. So, in *Collier v Collier* [2002] EWCA Civ 1095, a father could not rely on the principle accepted by the Court of Appeal in *Tribe* in relation to a transfer to his daughter because he had given effect to his dishonest intention and the doctrine of the *locus poenitentiae* described by Millett LJ could not assist him.
377. While this issue did not need to be resolved in *Patel v Mirza* [2017] AC 467, considered above, it is likely that the circumstances which arose in *Tribe* would continue to be determined in a similar way. It should still be possible to rebut the presumption of advancement on the basis of the principles relating to illegality set out in *Patel*.
378. (1995) 132 ALR 133.
379. The court in Australia had already accepted that the presumption of advancement applies between a mother and her child. See *Dullow v Dullow* (1985) 3 NSWLR 531; *Brown v Brown* (1993) 31 NSWLR 582.
380. Rose suggested (1996) 112 LQR 386, 388 that the rules which deny relief to a plaintiff who has been involved in illegality 'are crude and capricious, generally fail to discriminate between the relative demerits of the parties and may penalise a plaintiff disproportionately to the relevant wrongdoing'. It should be pointed out that Mance LJ commented in *Collier v Collier* [2002] EWCA Civ 1095 at [106] that while he had been tempted to take the same approach as Dawson J in *Nelson*, he decided that this was not a course open to him. He concluded that '[i]f English law in this area is to be further refashioned judicially after *Tinsley v Milligan*, it seems to me that it should be at the highest level.'
381. [1994] 1 AC 340.
382. As noted above, the principles laid down in *Tinsley v Milligan* were applied in

the presumption of advancement does not apply, a plaintiff can establish his equitable interest in the property without relying in any way on the underlying illegal transaction'.[383] However, in cases where the presumption of advancement applied, in Lord Browne-Wilkinson's view, 'in order to establish any claim, the plaintiff has himself to lead evidence sufficient to rebut the presumption of gift and in so doing will normally have to plead, and give evidence of, the underlying illegal purpose.'[384] This so-called *Tinsley* distinction had been criticised by academics[385] and in the opinion of Dawson J in *Nelson,* the distinction had no basis in principle and was unjustifiable on policy grounds.[386] In his view, the distinction could not logically be based on the policy of discouraging the transfer of property for an illegal purpose 'because a knowledgeable transferor would choose a transferee other than one who could take advantage of the presumption of advancement'.[387]

As Nourse LJ commented in *Tribe v Tribe,*[388] there seemed to be some perversity in the elevation of the presumption of advancement to a decisive status in the context of illegality, or as Mance LJ put it in *Collier v Collier,*[389] '[w]hy should the presumption of advancement, which depends upon the precise family relationship … play so potentially important a role in determining the enforceability of a transaction between two parties implicated in illegal purpose?' In addition, as Virgo and O'Sullivan[390] pointed out, the elevation of the presumption of advancement to such a conclusive status is problematic because there is no consensus as to which relationships attract it and because it is questionable whether a presumption based on such outdated assumptions should play any role in determining property rights.

The arbitrariness of the distinction drawn in the application of the reliance principle in cases where the presumption of advancement does and does not apply was also criticised by the Law Commission in England and it provisionally recommended that the principle should be abandoned.[391] More recently the

Silverwood v Silverwood (1997) 74 P & CR 453 and *Lowson v Coombes* [1999] Ch 373 although as Thompson [1999] Conv 242, 246 commented in relation to the latter decision, it was central to the result in that case that the relationship between the parties did not give rise to the presumption of advancement. Had it done so, the plaintiff could not have relied on his real motive for putting the house into the defendant's name in order to rebut the presumption and the latter would have retained full beneficial ownership of the property.

383. [1994] 1 AC 340, 371-372.
384. *Ibid.* at 372. See also *Tribe v Tribe* [1996] Ch 107, 117-118 *per* Nourse LJ.
385. See e.g. Enonchong (1995) 111 LQR 133; [1996] RLR 78.
386. (1995) 132 CLR 133, 166.
387. *Ibid.* at 164.
388. [1996] Ch 107, 118.
389. [2002] EWCA Civ 1095 at [97].
390. Virgo and O'Sullivan 'Resulting Trusts and Illegality' in *Restitution and Equity Volume One: Resulting Trusts and Equitable Compensation* (eds. Birks and Rose, 2000) pp. 103-104.
391. Law Com CP No. 154 (1999) *Illegal Transactions: the Effect of Illegality on Contracts*

Commission reiterated this criticism[392] and it subsequently recommended that the courts should be given a statutory discretion to decide the effect of illegality in the case of a limited class of trusts.[393] While statutory intervention in this area is unlikely,[394] this debate has now effectively been superseded by the views expressed by a number of members of the Supreme Court in *Patel v Mirza*,[395] considered in detail above.

It remains to be seen whether the courts in Ireland will decide to follow the so-called *Tinsley* distinction on the basis that this is in line with the decision of Costello J in *Parkes v Parkes*,[396] or whether given the arbitrary nature of the outcomes it can lead to, they will apply the broader principles set out in *Patel v Mirza* which eschew the drawing of such artificial distinctions. Applying the latter principles would lead to more consistent and proportionate outcomes and would also avoid the unjust enrichment of a party simply based on the issue of whether the presumption of a resulting trust or presumption of advancement applied.

Trusts of Family Property

Introduction

The circumstances which give rise to a resulting trust when property is voluntarily conveyed into the name of another or where it is purchased in another party's name have in general terms been outlined above. By far the most common application of these principles today occurs in relation to the question of ownership of family property when recourse to equitable principles is still necessary in the context of property disputes involving spouses, civil partners, cohabitees and other third parties, often financial institutions. While the enactment of legislation in the form of the Family Law Act 1995, the Family Law (Divorce) Act 1996 and the Civil Partnership and Certain Rights and Obligations of Cohabitants Act 2010 has considerably reduced the circumstances in which resulting and constructive trusts continue to play a role in this field, they nevertheless remain significant in some situations.

In the context of property disputes between spouses, section 12 of the Married Women's Status Act 1957 provided a statutory framework for the resolution of such issues, although it made no specific provision in relation to the principles to be applied in carrying out this function. Therefore, until the enactment of the Judicial Separation and Family Law Reform Act 1989,

---

and Trusts, para. 8.12.

392. Law Com CP No. 189 (2009) *The Illegality Defence: A Consultative Report*, para. 6.70. See further Davies [2009] Conv 182.
393. Law Com. No. 320 (2010) *The Illegality Defence*, para.2.22. See further paras. 2.24-2.131.
394. See the comments of Lord Toulson JSC in *Patel v Mirza* [2017] AC 467, 480.
395. [2017] AC 467.
396. [1980] ILRM 137.

equitable principles still governed the manner in which property disputes between spouses who separated were resolved. The 1989 Act provided a scheme for making property adjustment orders in the context of separation proceedings[397] and section 20(2) laid down specific factors which the court should have regard to in resolving these disputes.[398] This legislation was largely re-enacted in the Family Law Act 1995 and the provisions of section 16(2) of the latter Act replace those in section 20(2) of the earlier legislation. In addition, the Family Law (Divorce) Act 1996 has introduced a similar scheme for the making of property adjustment orders in the context of divorce proceedings.[399]

More recently, the Civil Partnership and Certain Rights and Obligations of Cohabitants Act 2010 has provided a mechanism for making property adjustment orders in the context of the breakdown in relationships between civil partners and 'qualified cohabitees'.[400] Where this legislation applies, equitable principles need no longer be relied upon, but there are still a number of situations involving spouses, civil partners and cohabitees where it may be necessary to determine ownership of family property to which the legislative provisions referred to above will not be relevant. So, for example, where spouses decide to separate without obtaining a divorce or judicial separation or where they obtain a civil annulment, or where cohabitees do not come within the scope of the terms of the 2010 Act,[401] equitable principles will still govern any property dispute which may arise between them. In addition, where one spouse, civil partner or cohabitee dies,[402] or is adjudicated bankrupt,[403] or where a judgment mortgage is registered against the interest of one spouse or partner in a property,[404] it may be necessary to rely on equitable principles to determine the respective beneficial shares of the parties. So, bearing in mind the limited

397. Section 15.
398. Note that the constitutionality of other provisions of this legislation was challenged unsuccessfully in *F. v F.* [1994] 2 ILRM 401 (HC); *F. v Ireland* [1995] 2 ILRM 321 (SC).
399. Section 14 of the Act of 1996 provides that a court may make a property adjustment order on granting a decree of divorce or at any time thereafter and s. 20 sets out the factors which the court should have regard to. See e.g. *G.R. v N.R.* [2015] IEHC 856.
400. See s. 172(5) of the Civil Partnership and Certain Rights and Obligations of Cohabitants Act 2010 which provides that a 'qualified cohabitant' means an adult in a relationship of cohabitation with another adult for a period of two years or more, in the case where they are the parents of one or more dependent children, and of five years or more in any other case. Section 172(6) goes on to provide for exceptions to the category of 'qualified cohabitant' in circumstances where one or both cohabitants is or was married to someone else.
401. This may include a situation where the parties would have been classified as 'qualified cohabitants' but the claim is not brought within the two year time period after the ending of the relationship between the cohabitees prescribed by s.195 of the Civil Partnership and Certain Rights and Obligations of Cohabitants Act 2010.
402. *E.N. v R.N.* [1992] 2 IR 116; *Hickey v O'Dwyer* [2006] 2 ILRM 81.
403. *Wall v Wall* High Court 1983 No. 402 Sp (Hamilton P) 10 September 1986.
404. See e.g. *Malone v McQuaid* [1998] IEHC 86.

circumstances in which equity still plays a role in resolving disputes concerning family property, it is useful to reiterate the following general principles.

Where a husband buys property in his wife's name or transfers it into her name, by virtue of the presumption of advancement, she will be regarded as the sole beneficial owner of the property provided that the presumption is not rebutted.[405] Where it is purchased solely by the husband but conveyed or transferred into their joint names, the same presumption of advancement will usually ensure that the parties are beneficially entitled as joint tenants.[406] However, where it is the wife who purchases the property and it is conveyed either solely into the husband's name or into their joint names, in the absence of rebutting evidence, the husband will hold any interest on a resulting trust for his wife.[407] It should be noted that different considerations apply where the parties are not married, or in the context of same sex marriage, as the presumption of advancement does not come into play.[408] In such cases the presumption of a resulting trust will operate and unless it is rebutted, a partner who contributes to the purchase price will acquire a beneficial interest where the property is in the other party's name.

Situations in which property is purchased outright are relatively unusual in practice; more commonly it will be purchased by way of a mortgage and both parties will effectively contribute to the instalments payable. It is important to bear in mind that even where the property is in partners' joint names, this will not necessarily lead to joint beneficial ownership. In this jurisdiction if one partner works and pays the mortgage instalments this is likely to lead to him or her acquiring an increased beneficial interest. Such an arrangement will give rise to a resulting trust in favour of the contributing partner which, if not rebutted, will lead to the conferral of a beneficial interest proportionate to the contribution. Similarly, if property is conveyed solely into one partner's name, the other partner may have a beneficial interest in the property of a proportionate nature arising from any contributions made.

There are fundamental difficulties in employing the traditional concept of the purchase money resulting trust in these circumstances. In theory the beneficial interests of the parties should be assessed at the time the purchase occurs but such an assessment could not accommodate the practical reality of the situation which may involve the repayment of a mortgage loan over a period of years subsequent to the actual purchase. The Irish courts have tended to deal with this difficulty by treating mortgage repayments as the practical equivalent of paying the initial purchase price and as capable of giving rise to a proportionate beneficial interest under a resulting trust. An alternative approach suggested by

---

405. *Re Eykyn's Trusts* (1877) 6 Ch D 115, 118.
406. *J.C. v J.H.C.* High Court 1982 No. 4931P (Keane J) 4 August 1982.
407. However, as noted above, this traditional principle must now be regarded with caution in the light of constitutional developments in the area of equality of spouses within marriage, see e.g. *McKinley v Minister for Defence* [1992] 2 IR 333.
408. *Calverley v Green* (1984) 155 CLR 242; *Lowson v Coombes* [1999] Ch 373.

Finlay P in *W. v W.*[409] is to treat the repayment of the mortgage as the buying back of the equity of redemption from the mortgagee. As he stated:

> [T]he fundamental principle underlying this rule of law is that the redemption of any form of charge or mortgage on property in truth consists of the acquisition by the owner or mortgagor of an estate in the property with which he parted at the time of the creating of the mortgage or charge and ... there can be no distinction in principle between a contribution made to the acquisition of that interest and a contribution made to the acquisition of an interest in property by an original purchase.[410]

As a result it would appear that contributions towards the redemption of any mortgage over property, even if the money was not borrowed to purchase the property, could give rise to a resulting trust.[411] This latter approach in particular may lead to serious anomalies[412] and the more straightforward former theory, although also technically flawed, is less likely to lead to difficulties in its application.

While most of the case law in this jurisdiction in relation to the purchase money resulting trust deals with property disputes between spouses, the rationale behind such a trust as interpreted by the courts is that it should apply because of the circumstances in which the contributions are made, rather than because of the nature of the relationship between the parties. There was no suggestion made in any of the cases decided in this jurisdiction which related to cohabitees[413] that different principles should apply to property disputes between cohabiting partners as opposed to spouses. Now, as a result of the enactment of the Civil Partnership and Certain Rights and Obligations of Cohabitants Act 2010, civil partners and qualified cohabitees should be in a similar position to spouses and should generally no longer need to have recourse to equitable principles to resolve family property disputes. However, it should also be borne in mind that where a relationship is not between qualified cohabitees within the meaning of the 2010 Act, such individuals may not necessarily have the same intentions about sharing beneficial ownership in property and for this reason the presumption of a resulting trust may be more readily rebutted in these cases.

409. [1981] ILRM 202.
410. *Ibid.* at 204-205. Quoted with approval by Finlay CJ in *E.N. v R.N* [1992] 2 IR 116, 123.
411. According to Mee [1993] Conv 359, 363 this reasoning leads to the result that where a person contributes to the repayment of a loan he gains a share, not in what was purchased with the help of the loan, but in the security for the loan.
412. See further Mee [1993] Conv 359, 363. He highlights the difficulty which would arise if someone repaid an unsecured loan which represents a portion of the purchase price of property and argues that in such cases no trust could arise as there could be no question of buying back an estate transferred to the lender in the absence of any security for the loan.
413. See e.g. *Power v Conroy* [1980] ILRM 31; *McGill v S.* [1979] IR 238.

Subject to this caveat, it would appear that the principles established in case law are relevant today where matrimonial property issues between spouses and cohabitees are not governed by legislation, and also to property disputes between spouses and cohabitees and third parties. The difficulties which have arisen in relation to deciding in what circumstances a beneficial interest may be found to exist have largely centred on assessing the worth or suitability of the various types of contributions which can be made and it is proposed to examine these in turn.

The Operation of Equitable Principles in Ireland

(a) Direct Contributions

Where property is purchased in one spouse or partner's name but the other party has made direct contributions to the purchase price or the payment of instalments on the mortgage, the property will be held on a resulting trust to the extent of these contributions in the absence of any agreement to the contrary.[414] The first signs that the concept of a trust would be employed by the courts to resolve disputes about the ownership of matrimonial property emerged from the decision of Kenny J in *Heavey v Heavey*,[415] and subsequently in *C. v C.*,[416] in which he applied this reasoning to the issue of direct contributions. In *C. v C.* the spouses purchased a family home in the husband's sole name although the wife made a direct contribution to the purchase price by paying the deposit and some of the mortgage repayments. When the parties' marriage broke down, the wife made an application pursuant to section 12 of the Married Women's Status Act 1957 claiming that she was entitled to half the beneficial interest in the house. Kenny J said that the correct approach was to apply the concept of a trust to the legal relationship which arises when a wife makes payments towards the purchase of a house or the repayment of mortgage instalments when the house is in the sole name of the husband. He continued by saying that when this is done, the husband then becomes a trustee for her of a share in the house proportionate to the size of her contributions. In view of the size of her contributions, Kenny J therefore granted a declaration that the wife was in the circumstances entitled to one-half of the beneficial interest in the family home.

The principle enunciated in *C. v C.* was reiterated in *W. v W.*[417] by Finlay P in a comprehensive judgment in which he laid down a number of general principles. These included the following:

> Where a wife contributes by money to the purchase of property by her husband in his sole name in the absence of evidence of some inconsistent

414. *W. v W.* [1981] ILRM 202, 204.
415. (1974) 111 ILTR 1.
416. [1976] IR 254.
417. [1981] ILRM 202, 204.

> agreement or arrangement the court will decide that the wife is entitled to an equitable interest in that property approximately proportionate to the extent of her contribution as against the total value of the property at the time the contribution was made.

The position was confirmed by Henchy J in the Supreme Court in *McC. v McC.*[418] and it now seems clear that in this jurisdiction contributions of a direct nature towards the acquisition of the family home will give rise to an equitable interest in the absence of evidence of an agreement to the contrary. This is a sensible and pragmatic approach which recognises the reality that few spouses or partners[419] will think of making any specific agreement to the effect that any contributions they might make will give rise to a beneficial interest. Given that it is equally, if not more, unlikely that spouses or partners will enter into an agreement that such contributions will not lead to the acquisition of any share in the property, it might be thought safe to assume that contributions of a direct or indirect nature will almost invariably give rise to an interest.

However, as the decision of Laffoy J in *Hickey v O'Dwyer*[420] illustrates, a spouse or partner may acquire no beneficial interest even where he or she has made financial contributions in some circumstances. In this case the plaintiff brought proceedings following her husband's death against his personal representatives and his child from another relationship seeking the determination of a number of questions including whether she had any beneficial interest in a house in which she had lived with her husband for a number of years prior to his death. Her husband had been the sole legal owner of the property and it had been purchased by means of a loan from his then employer to pay the deposit and a small state grant, the remainder being financed by a mortgage. When her husband changed jobs and this loan became repayable the plaintiff borrowed the sum necessary to pay off the debt. Both parties' salaries were paid into a joint account and the mortgage and mortgage protection policy, which ultimately discharged the mortgage debt, were paid out of this joint account. Laffoy J stated that it was not in issue that the principles of law to be applied in determining whether the plaintiff's claim was well-founded were those set out by Finlay P in *W. v W.*[421] However, she added that the basis on which a court will decide that a wife is entitled to a beneficial interest in property which is in the sole name of her husband on foot of a contribution to

418. [1986] ILRM 1, 2 *per* Henchy J.
419. As was pointed out above, the same principles should in theory apply to contributions made by either spouses or cohabitees. Some consideration should perhaps be given to the fact that there is a greater likelihood in the case of unmarried couples that the legal owner did not intend his or her partner to derive an equitable interest in the property by making contributions to joint expenses. However, the present position would seem to be that unless there is evidence of an express or implied agreement to this effect, such contributions will be taken into account.
420. [2006] 2 ILRM 81.
421. [1981] ILRM 202.

the purchase price or directly or indirectly towards repayment of the mortgage instalments is subject to the overriding requirement that such a decision will only be made 'in the absence of evidence of some inconsistent agreement or arrangement'.[422] In her view the evidence in the case before the court was not consistent with an understanding between the parties that the plaintiff would have a beneficial interest in the house. Laffoy J took the view that the assistance which the plaintiff had given her husband in relation to repaying the loan he had taken out to pay the deposit could not be construed as a contribution to the purchase price of the property. In addition, it appeared from the plaintiff's own evidence that the understanding between them was that each would own their own house and the plaintiff had in fact subsequently acquired a house in her own name which she had rented out. She added that there was very little concrete evidence to support the plaintiff's claim and that copies of the bank statements which had been furnished were incomplete.

Laffoy J concluded that even if she had been satisfied that the plaintiff's claim for a beneficial interest based on the principles set out in *W. v W.* had been established, she would have found it impossible to calculate the contribution on the basis of the evidence before the court. It can be argued that the plaintiff was unfortunate in failing to obtain any beneficial interest in the property as a result of her contributions. While Laffoy J concluded that the evidence was not consistent with an understanding between the parties that the plaintiff would have a beneficial interest in the house, there was no reference to evidence establishing an express agreement to the effect that the plaintiff's contributions would not give rise to an interest, which on one reading on the *dicta* of Finlay P in *W. v W.* might have seemed necessary. On the authority of *Hickey*, it would appear that something falling short of such an express agreement may suffice. However, it is submitted that this case may well stand on its own facts, particularly given the surrounding circumstances and the underlying rationale of seeking to do justice as between the plaintiff and the deceased's child. Therefore, there is no real argument to support the proposition that this decision altered the well-established principles laid down in *W. v W.*

(b) Indirect Contributions

The issue of whether contributions of an indirect nature, either to the purchase price of property or to mortgage repayments, can give rise to a beneficial interest is one which was the subject matter of considerable uncertainty for a time but now appears to be fairly settled in this jurisdiction. A substantial number of cases relating to this issue came before the High Court in the late 1970s and early 1980s. Two distinct approaches can be identified, the first of which is well illustrated by the decision of Keane J in *M.G. v R.D.*[423] The family home had

422. Referring to the *dicta* of Finlay P in *W. v W.* [1981] ILRM 202, 204.
423. High Court 1980 No. 423 Sp (Keane J) 28 April 1981. See also *McGill v S.* [1979]

been purchased in the sole name of the husband and all mortgage repayments and other expenses directly referable to the house were paid by him. The wife used her salary to purchase items for the house and a car which was used by both parties but Keane J could find no evidence of an agreement of any kind that these outgoings should give her an interest in the property. He concluded that there must be evidence of a common intention that indirect contributions will give the contributor a share in the beneficial interest in property before the court would make such an order and in the circumstances of the case he dismissed the wife's claim.

The alternative approach, and the one which has now found favour with the Supreme Court, can be found in the judgment of Finlay P in *W. v W.*,[424] referred to above. The wife claimed a beneficial interest in the family farm on the basis of the fact that mortgages to which the property was subject had been paid off partly as a result of her contributions and she had also contributed to the carrying out of improvements to the property. Finlay P directed an issue to be tried as to the extent to which the wife had contributed to the repayment of the mortgages but rejected a claim to an equitable interest relating to improvements to which she had contributed after the property had been acquired. In relation to the issue of indirect contributions, he stated as follows:

> Where a wife contributes … to a general family fund thus releasing her husband from an obligation which he otherwise would have permitting him to discharge liabilities out of that fund and permitting him to repay mortgage instalments, she will in the absence of proof of an inconsistent agreement or arrangement be entitled to an equitable share in the property which had been mortgaged and in respect of which the mortgage was redeemed approximately proportionate to her contribution to the mortgage repayments, to the value of the mortgage thus redeemed and to the total value of the property at the relevant time.[425]

This approach of assuming that the wife should be entitled to a beneficial interest proportionate to the extent of her indirect contributions 'in the absence of proof of an inconsistent agreement or arrangement' also found favour with the Supreme Court in *McC. v McC.*[426] The wife had contributed to the cost of

---

IR 283; *S.D. v B.D.* High Court 1981 No. 194 Sp (Murphy J) 19 March 1982; *B. v B.* High Court (MacKenzie J) 22 April 1986.

424. [1981] ILRM 202. See also *R. v R.* High Court 1978 No.574 Sp (McMahon J) 12 January 1979; *M.B. v E.B.* High Court 1979 No. 556 Sp (Barrington J) 19 February 1980; *C.R. v D.R.*, High Court 1983 No. 228 Sp (Lynch J) 5 April 1984, although on the facts the wife's claim did not succeed in this case.
425. *Ibid.* at 204.
426. [1986] ILRM 1. It is interesting to note that the Supreme Court's approach in *McC.* is diametrically opposed to that adopted by Lord McDermott LCJ in the decision of the Northern Ireland Court of Appeal in *McFarlane v McFarlane* [1972] NI 59 in which the Lord Chief Justice said that if an indirect contribution is to result in a wife

a previous family home and when it was sold this amount was put towards the cost of furniture in the new house, the purchase of which was financed by her husband's employers and secured by a mortgage. It was held by the Supreme Court that this original contribution was not applied to the purchase of the second house either directly or indirectly and had not been part of a general family fund. The court upheld the finding of Costello J that the wife was only entitled to a one-third share in the furniture and fittings. However, Henchy J made the following statement about the general effect of indirect contributions:

> When the wife's contribution has been indirect (such as contributing, by means of her earnings, to a general family fund) the court will in the absence of any express or implied agreement to the contrary, infer a trust in favour of the wife, on the grounds that she has to that extent relieved the husband of the financial burden he incurred in purchasing the house.[427]

Therefore, it would seem that where one partner makes an indirect contribution of a financial nature to the purchase of the property in a manner which can be identified as relieving the other party of a burden which he would otherwise bear in relation to these outgoings and thereby allows him to pay the mortgage instalments, this contribution will be recognised in the form of a proportionate beneficial interest in the absence of evidence of an agreement to the contrary.[428]

(c) Improvements to Property

In *W. v W.*[429] Finlay P stated that where a wife expends monies or carries out work in the improvement of a property, the legal ownership of which is vested solely in the husband, she will have no claim by reason of such contributions unless she can establish that it was specifically agreed or that she was led to believe by virtue of the surrounding circumstances that she would be recompensed for it. In addition, he stressed that any claim which she might have was limited to a right to monetary compensation and could not give rise to any beneficial interest. This *dictum* was applied by Barron J in *N.A.D. v T.D.*,[430] a case which shows the limitations of the device of the resulting trust in circumstances

---

acquiring a beneficial interest, it must be the subject of an agreement or arrangement between the spouses.

427. *Ibid.* at 2. This principle was accepted by Finlay CJ in *L. v L.* [1992] 2 IR 77, 107-108 and by McGuinness J in *C.D. v W.D.* [1997] IEHC 23.

428. It should be noted that in *Hickey v O'Dwyer* [2006] 2 ILRM 81 considered in more detail *supra* under the heading 'Direct Contributions', a wife's contributions to the purchase price of property were held not to give rise to a beneficial interest in circumstances where Laffoy J concluded that the evidence before the court was not consistent with such an understanding.

429. [1981] ILRM 202.

430. [1985] ILRM 153.

where a house is built on land which is solely the property of one partner. As Barron J commented:

> The circumstances in which a wife may contribute to the improvement of the property of her husband may obviously vary considerably between minor decorative improvements at the one end of the scale and payment for the erection of an entire dwelling-house at the other end. In each case, since the legal and beneficial ownership of the property was already vested in her husband he is entitled at law in the absence of a contrary agreement to take the entire benefit of the improvement.[431]

So, despite the fact that the plaintiff wife had contributed over one-third of the building costs of the family home, it was held that she was not entitled to any beneficial interest in the property. Barron J also considered the possible application of a constructive trust, which he said was a concept 'imposed by operation of law independent of intention in order to satisfy the demands of justice and good conscience'. However, he was satisfied that there was no evidence of any conduct on the husband's part which would make it inequitable for him to deny his wife's claim and he rejected the argument that she should have any share in the beneficial ownership of the family home.

A slightly less restrictive attitude was adopted by Finlay CJ in his judgment in *N. v N.*,[432] in which the plaintiff widow claimed a beneficial interest in the family home on a number of different grounds. She had for a time applied her earnings from her work as a nurse towards family purposes and had managed bedsitter flats into which part of the house had been converted, the rental income from which was applied either directly or indirectly towards the mortgage repayments. In addition, she claimed that her work in the home as a wife and mother should give her a beneficial interest, an argument which will be considered in more detail below. On the issue of improvements, Finlay CJ appeared to reject the claim that the wife should have any additional percentage increase by virtue of her indirect contributions to a mortgage which was taken out to finance an extension to the property.[433] He stated as follows:

> I do not consider as I indicated in my decision in *W. v W.*, that a direct

---

431. *Ibid.* at 162.
432. [1992] 2 IR 116.
433. He stated (at 122) that the trial judge was correct in rejecting a specific claim that the mortgage, to which the plaintiff contributed by making payments from her earnings to family funds, which was used for the extension of the property, gave rise to an additional percentage interest in the beneficial ownership. However, subsequently (at 123) Finlay CJ stated that having regard to the importance of the contribution made by the wife in managing the bedsitter units and the role which the rental income from them played in the family finances and 'having regard to the fact that I am satisfied she is entitled to credit for contributions towards the redemption of *all* the mortgages' (emphasis added), the share assessed by the trial judge was quite inadequate.

> contribution, even in money's worth, to an improvement made on a family home by a wife, where the husband is the sole owner of it, can, in the absence of express or readily implied agreement, constitute a claim for a beneficial interest in it.[434]

So, while Finlay CJ's statement shows that some form of agreement is necessary if any claim in relation to improvements is to succeed, he at least seems to accept that provided evidence of such an agreement can be established, contributions can give rise to a beneficial interest rather than just an entitlement to monetary recompense.[435] However, it must be pointed out that in the majority of cases it is unlikely that the partner claiming a share as a result of his or her contribution to improvements to the property will be able to provide evidence of the necessary agreement.

Finally, it should be noted that in *Sheehy v Talbot*,[436] which concerned a partition suit in relation to property which the plaintiff and the defendant held in their joint names, Edwards J appeared to take into account the parties' respective contributions to improvements to the property, although he did not explain the basis for this conclusion. He calculated that the parties had contributed in a ratio of 7:1 to these improvements which had added a defined value to the property and apportioned this percentage increase accordingly. However, given the tenor of the judgment of Finlay CJ in *L. v L.*,[437] considered in more detail in the next section, it is likely that further legislative intervention will be necessary to resolve the difficulties created by the restrictive approach currently adopted by the courts in this jurisdiction towards contributions to the renovation or improvement of property.

(d) Other Forms of Contribution

Traditionally, the courts in this jurisdiction refused to accept that a partner's contribution by working in the home, whether in performing housework or looking after children, may give rise to a beneficial interest.[438] As Brady

---

434. [1992] 2 IR 116, 122. Contrast the position in England, where s. 37 of the Matrimonial Proceedings and Property Act 1970 provides that a substantial contribution in money or money's worth to an improvement to property will give rise to a beneficial interest in the absence of evidence of any agreement to the contrary.
435. However, it should be noted that in *C.F. v J.D.F.* [2005] 4 IR 154, 166 McGuinness J, referring to *McC. v McC.* and *N.A.D. v T.D.*, stated that 'the making of improvements to property cannot establish any form of beneficial title'. This statement was made in the context of a dispute about the extent of a husband's assets in judicial separation proceedings and the court rejected the argument that he could have acquired a beneficial interest in property belonging to his father to which he had made improvements.
436. [2008] IEHC 207.
437. [1992] 2 IR 77.
438. *R.K. v M.K.* High Court 1978 No. 330 Sp (Finlay P) 24 October 1978.

commented, while the attitude of the Supreme Court in *McC. v McC.*[439] in relation to the issue of indirect contributions was evidence of a shift towards pragmatism, relief for a wife remained dependent on the fact that she had made a financial contribution to the acquisition of the property and no cognisance was taken of her work in the home.[440] While this rather arbitrary approach was called into question by the High Court, the Supreme Court has declined to change its view on this issue.

In *B.L. v M.L.*[441] the plaintiff wife had made no direct contributions to the purchase of the family home and her only indirect contribution was to its refurbishment and redecoration. However, she spent most of her time running the household and looking after the children of the marriage. Barr J said that it was well-settled that a wife's work in the home and in the care of her children did not amount to an indirect contribution entitling her to a beneficial interest in the family home, nor did work done by her in the maintenance or enhancement of the property. However, Barr J held that having regard to Article 41.2 of the Constitution of Ireland, a woman who elected to adopt the full time role of wife and mother and was thus precluded from contributing directly or indirectly in money or money's worth from independent employment towards the acquisition by the husband of the family home and contents, should have her work in the home taken into account. In these circumstances, Barr J held that the wife was entitled to a 50% beneficial interest in the family home and its contents.[442] However, in *E.N. v R.N.*[443] Barron J said that while he could see the equity in recognising the contribution made by the plaintiff towards the welfare of the family, he did not see Article 41.2.2° as supporting her claim to a share in the family home. He added that in so far as that provision might be construed as a guarantee of financial reward to mothers working in the home, it seemed to him that it must be construed as 'a guarantee of reward from outside the family rather than a re-distribution within the family'. Clearly in view of the differing opinions expressed by High Court judges on the issue, clarification was necessary and this came in the Supreme Court's decision in *L. v L.*,[444] in which the appeal of the appellant husband from the decision of Barr J was allowed. Finlay CJ concluded that to allow the courts to extend the circumstances in which a wife may claim a beneficial interest in the family home to a situation where she has made no direct or indirect financial contribution to the acquisition of the property or to a family fund but has performed the constitutionally preferred role of wife and mother in the home would not be to develop any principle known to the common law but rather would involve

439. [1986] ILRM 1.
440. Brady (1991) 42 NILQ 1, 9.
441. [1992] 2 IR 77.
442. This reasoning was approved *obiter* by Barrington J in *A.H. v P.H.* High Court, 20 June 1989.
443. [1990] 1 IR 383. See also *J.F. v B.F.* High Court (Lardner J) 21 December 1988.
444. [1992] 2 IR 77. See Jackson (1992) 14 DULJ 153.

the creation of an entirely new right. As he said, unless this result was 'clearly and unambiguously warranted by the Constitution or made necessary for the protection of a specified or unspecified right under it, it must constitute legislation and be a usurpation by the courts of the function of the legislature.'[445]

This reasoning was applied by the Supreme Court in the judgment which it delivered on the same day in *E.N. v R.N.*[446] One further anomaly to emerge from this decision was that the court recognised that the wife's activities in managing the bedsitter flats were 'different from and not to be identified with the activities of a wife and mother in the home' and that the income earned from this enterprise which went directly or indirectly towards paying off the various mortgages taken out on the property should be recognised as a contribution which would give her a beneficial interest. Taking all the wife's contributions into account, the Supreme Court held that she was entitled to a half-share in the beneficial interest in the house. As Mee has commented, it is difficult to justify an approach which differentiates between unpaid work in the home which will not give rise to an interest and unpaid work in the legal owner's business which may be recognised.[447]

Although the provisions of the Judicial Separation and Family Law Reform Act 1989 came into effect too late to assist the plaintiff in *L.*, that Act, the provisions of which were substantially re-enacted in the Family Law Act 1995, became relevant where the courts were called upon to make a property adjustment order on the granting of a decree of judicial separation. Section 16(1) of the Family Law Act 1995 now sets out the matters which the court is required to take into consideration in making certain orders including a property adjustment order and these include, by virtue of section 16(2)(f), 'contributions by looking after the home and caring for the family'.[448] Section 20 of the Family Law (Divorce) Act 1996 sets out the same list of factors which the court is required to take into account in making, *inter alia*, property adjustment orders on the granting of a decree of divorce. Similarly, in the context of property adjustment orders or other specified orders made pursuant to the Civil Partnership and Certain Rights and Obligations of Cohabitants Act 2010, a number of factors are set out to which the court shall have regard. While these are formulated slightly differently in so far as they apply to civil partners and cohabitees respectively, section 129(2)(f) and (g) and section 173(3)(g) and (h) of the Civil Partnership and Certain Rights and Obligations of Cohabitants Act 2010 provide that any contributions made in looking after the home and the effect on a civil partner or qualified cohabitant's earning capacity of having foregone the opportunity of remunerative activity in order

445. *Ibid.* at 107.
446. [1992] 2 IR 116.
447. Mee [1993] Conv 359, 366.
448. See the comments of Denham and Murray JJ in *D.T. v C.T.* [2002] 3 IR 334, 381-382 and 407 to which reference was made by Keane J in *P.D. v R.D.* [2015] IEHC 174 at 54.

to look after the home may be taken into account. So, while the legislature has provided for work done by spouses or qualified cohabitees who remain at home to be taken into account in assessing beneficial interest, there is still a lack of recognition of such contributions in circumstances which fall outside the scope of the legislation.

The Position in England – the Common Intention Constructive Trust[449]

(a) Background to the Position in England

While the principle of proportionate interest applied in this jurisdiction which derives from the rationale behind the resulting trust has ensured a degree of consistency in decision-making, this has perhaps been at the expense of an element of flexibility which might in certain circumstances be desirable. In England, the resulting trust analysis has largely been rejected[450] in favour of an approach which involves the imposition of a constructive trust based on the parties' common intentions, and a claimant's share will be measured by reference to such intentions and may give rise to a share in excess of the actual financial contributions made.

A number of decisions of the English Court of Appeal in the late 1960s had established the so-called doctrine of 'family assets' described by Lord Denning MR in the Court of Appeal decision in *Gissing v Gissing*.[451] However, the validity of the doctrine of family assets was questioned by the House of Lords in *Pettitt v Pettitt*,[452] where it was held that section 17 of the Married Women's Property Act 1882, on which Lord Denning had relied, was purely procedural in nature and that the courts did not derive authority from it to transfer property rights from one spouse to another. So, by the time the *Gissing* case reached the House of Lords,[453] the doctrine of family assets had been effectively discredited. While Lord Reid considered that there was no real reason to distinguish between direct and indirect contributions, a distinction which he felt in many cases would be 'unworkable', it was Lord Diplock's more restrictive attitude based on common intention which found favour with the English Court of Appeal during the 1980s.[454]

449. The common intention constructive trust, while largely applied in the context of family property disputes, has also been held to arise in other circumstances, e.g. *Dowding v Matchmove Ltd* [2017] 1 WLR 749 (see further [2017] Conv 146). It is only analysed in the former context in this chapter and the circumstances in which it may arise which overlap with the basis for a claim in proprietary estoppel are examined in Chapter 18.
450. Although note the approach adopted by Lord Neuberger in *Stack v Dowden* [2007] 2 AC 432.
451. [1969] 2 Ch 85, 93.
452. [1970] AC 777. See further Brady (1984) 6 DULJ 1, 7-9.
453. [1971] AC 886.
454. See e.g. *Burns v Burns* [1984] Ch 317, where it was held by the Court of Appeal that since the plaintiff had not made any substantial financial contribution to the acquisition of the house (although she had used her earnings to pay rates, telephone bills etc)

Where there was evidence of an agreement or understanding between the parties that the non-legal owner should have some beneficial interest in property, contributions towards its purchase would ground a claim, as the decision of the Court of Appeal in *Grant v Edwards*[455] illustrates. There the plaintiff was held to be entitled to half the beneficial interest in a house in circumstances where she had made substantial contributions to the household expenses in excess of what would be expected as normal and without which, it was accepted, the defendant would not have been able to pay the mortgage instalments. In the view of Browne-Wilkinson VC the representation made by the defendant to the plaintiff that the house would have been in their joint names but for the plaintiff's matrimonial dispute, was clear evidence of a common intention that she was to have an interest in it. The Court of Appeal held that in such circumstances, equity would infer a trust where, although the house had been purchased in the name of one party, there was a common intention that both parties should have a beneficial interest and the non-proprietary owner had acted to his detriment on the basis of that intention.

However, it seemed clear from the decision of the House of Lords in *Lloyds Bank plc v Rosset*[456] that difficulties would arise where contributions of a purely indirect nature were relied upon to found a claim in circumstances where there was no evidence of an agreement to share the property. In explaining his view of how a common intention constructive trust may arise, Lord Bridge stated that the fundamental question was whether, independently of any inference which might be drawn from the parties' conduct, there had been at any time prior to the acquisition of the house, or exceptionally at a later date, any agreement, arrangement or understanding reached between them that the property was to be shared beneficially. Such a finding of agreement could only be based on evidence of express discussions between the partners and once this was established, it would be necessary for the partner asserting the claim to the beneficial interest to show that he had acted to his detriment or significantly altered his position in reliance on the agreement in such a manner as to give rise to a constructive trust.[457] Alternatively, where there was no evidence to support a finding of an agreement or arrangement to share the property, Lord Bridge stated that the court must rely on the conduct of the parties both as the basis from which to infer a common intention to share the property beneficially and as the conduct relied upon to give rise to a constructive trust. In such a situation,

---

the court could not impute a common intention that she should acquire a beneficial interest.

455. [1986] Ch 638. See also *Eves v Eves* [1975] 1 WLR 1338.

456. [1991] 1 AC 107.

457. This approach was applied in *Hammond v Mitchell* [1991] 1 WLR 1127 (see Lawson [1992] Conv 218). Similarly, in *Chan v Leung* [2002] EWCA Civ 1075 Jonathan Parker LJ reiterated that it was necessary for a claimant to establish that he had acted to his detriment or significantly altered his position in reliance on an alleged promise or agreement in order to establish a constructive trust in such circumstances.

he said, 'direct contributions to the purchase price by the partner who is not the legal owner, whether initially or by payment of mortgage instalments, will readily justify the inference necessary to the creation of a constructive trust'.[458] He added that as he interpreted the authorities, 'it is at least extremely doubtful whether anything else will do.'[459]

These two categories of cases which might give rise to a common intention constructive trust were referred to again by the Court of Appeal in *Oxley v Hiscock*[460] and were labelled as being based on express common intention, where the parties have reached an agreement or understanding that the beneficial ownership in the property will be shared, and on implied common intention, where this is founded on a direct financial contribution to the purchase price.[461] In cases such as *Midland Bank plc v Cooke*[462] and *Oxley v Hiscock*,[463] a direct financial contribution triggered consideration of 'the whole course of dealing' between the parties, and contributions of an indirect nature were taken into account by the court in assessing what it considered fair in terms of the respective beneficial interests. However, in the absence of evidence of an agreement to share or the initial trigger of a direct financial contribution, it was very unlikely that contributions of an indirect nature would be recognised[464] and this was particularly unfair to claimants who had made very large indirect contributions towards the purchase of a property.

However, it is now clear from the decisions of the House of Lords in *Stack v Dowden*,[465] and of the Supreme Court in *Jones v Kernott*,[466] that the law has 'moved on' from the restrictive approach taken towards indirect contributions in *Lloyds* and that such contributions can be taken into account provided they reflect the parties' express, implied or even imputed intention. Effectively there

---

458. [1991] 1 AC 107, 133.
459. *Ibid.* at 133. Note that commenting on this statement in his speech in *Stack v Dowden* [2007] 2 AC 432, 445, Lord Walker stated that he respectfully doubted whether it took full account of the views expressed by the House of Lords in *Gissing v Gissing*. See also the comment of Baroness Hale (at 456) that Lord Bridge in *Rosset* 'may have set that hurdle rather too high in certain respects'.
460. [2004] 3 WLR 715. See Thompson [2004] Conv 496; [2005] Conv 79; Gardner (2004) 120 LQR 541.
461. See Fox (2005) 56 NILQ 83, 96.
462. [1995] 4 All ER 562.
463. [2004] 3 WLR 715.
464. In *Le Foe v Le Foe* [2001] 2 FLR 970, 980 Nicholas Mostyn QC, sitting as a Deputy High Court judge, commented that 'it will only be exceptionally that conduct other than direct contributions to the purchase price, whether in cash to the deposit or by contribution to the mortgage instalments, will suffice to draw the necessary inference of a common intention to share the equity.'
465. [2007] 2 AC 432. See also the decision of the Privy Council in *Abbott v Abbott* [2007] UKPC 53.
466. [2012] 1 AC 776. The joint judgment of Baroness Hale and Lord Walker in this case has been described as 'now regarded as the most authoritative modern guidance as to the proper approach in cases of this sort' per Roberts J in *S. v J. (Beneficial Ownership)* [2016] EWHC 586 (Fam) at [58].

are now two questions which a court must resolve in this context. First, in what circumstances may a common intention constructive trust arise? Secondly, if such a trust may be said to arise, what should the extent of the claimant's beneficial interest be? These questions will now be considered in turn.

(b) The Current Approach

In relation to the question of in what circumstances may a common intention constructive trust arise, Baroness Hale made clear in *Stack v Dowden*[467] that the onus lies on the person seeking to establish that the beneficial ownership in property is different from the legal ownership. So, as she explained, 'in sole ownership cases it is upon the non-owner to show that he has any interest at all' and 'in joint ownership cases, it is upon the joint owner who claims to have other than a joint beneficial interest.' Both the decisions of the House of Lords in *Stack v Dowden* and of the Supreme Court in *Jones v Kernott*[468] concerned family property disputes where the property in question was registered in the parties' joint names. However, many of the principles set out in these cases in relation to the manner in which the courts should deal with such disputes have wider application.

In relation to property which is jointly owned, as Lord Neuberger pointed out in *Stack v Dowden*,[469] 'in the absence of any relevant evidence other than the fact that the property ... acquired as a home for the legal co-owners is in joint names, the beneficial ownership will also be joint, so that it is held in equal shares.' This is the so-called 'default option' referred to by Lord Walker and Baroness Hale in *Jones v Kernott*.[470] Baroness Hale made it clear in *Stack v Dowden* that cases in which joint legal owners are to be taken to have intended that their beneficial interests should be different from their legal interests will be very unusual[471] and a heavy burden will lie on the party seeking to establish this.[472] However, in both *Stack v Dowden* and *Jones v Kernott* a different apportionment of the beneficial interest was ultimately recognised. In *Stack* the House of Lords agreed with the finding of the Court of Appeal that the net proceeds of the sale of the property should be divided 65% to 35% in the defendant's favour. In *Jones* the Supreme Court allowed the claimant's appeal from the decision of the Court of Appeal and restored the order of the trial judge that the claimant was entitled to a 90% beneficial share.

Lord Walker stated in *Stack v Dowden* that he doubted whether Lord

467. [2007] 2 AC 432, 454.
468. [2012] 1 AC 776.
469. [2007] 2 AC 432, 468. See also *Insol Funding Co. Ltd v Cowlam* [2017] EWHC 1822 (Ch) at [86].
470. [2012] 1 AC 776, 783.
471. [2007] 2 AC 432, 459.
472. *Ibid.* at 447 *per* Lord Walker.

Bridge's approach in *Lloyds Bank plc v Rosset*[473] had taken full account of the views expressed, particularly by Lord Reid and Lord Diplock, in *Gissing v Gissing* and added that whether or not Lord Bridge's observation had been justified in 1990, in his opinion the law had now moved on. Baroness Hale similarly commented in *Stack* that '[t]he law has indeed moved on in response to changing social and economic conditions' and she stated that '[t]he search is to ascertain the parties' shared intentions, actual, inferred or imputed, with respect to the property in the light of their whole course of conduct in relation to it.'[474] The position as outlined in *Stack* would seem to be as follows. Where there is an express agreement between the parties as to the apportionment of their beneficial interests, the court will be in a position to identify their actual common intention in relation to how the property is to be shared. However, in practice this will be relatively rare and where an express common intention to share the property in different proportions cannot be established, both Lord Walker and Baroness Hale suggested in *Stack v Dowden* that the court must consider whether such common intention can be inferred or imputed.[475] However, Lord Neuberger took a different position on this issue and said that '[w]hile an intention may be inferred as well as express, it may not, at least in my opinion, be imputed.'[476]

Subsequently, in *Jones v Kernott*[477] Lord Walker and Baroness Hale clarified that 'the search is primarily to ascertain the parties' actual shared intentions, whether expressed or to be inferred from their conduct' and made no reference to the possible imputation of this initial common intention to share the beneficial interest in the property. However, they added that where it is clear that the beneficial interests are to be shared, but it is impossible to divine a common intention as to the proportions in which they are to be shared, the court might be driven to impute an intention to the parties which they may never have had.[478] So, it appears that intention may be imputed where it is clear that the beneficial interests are to be shared but it is not possible to ascertain a common intention as to proportions. In the circumstances the majority of Lord Walker, Baroness Hale and Lord Collins agreed that a common intention that the parties' beneficial interests in the property should change since the acquisition of the property could be inferred.[479] Lord Kerr and Lord Wilson took the view that it was not possible to infer a common intention as to the proportions of the parties' respective beneficial interests and resolved this issue on the basis of

473. [1991] 1 AC 107.
474. [2007] 2 AC 432, 455.
475. *Ibid.* at 447 *per* Lord Walker; at 455 *per* Baroness Hale.
476. *Ibid.* at 472.
477. [2012] 1 AC 776, 788. This decision has been the subject of extensive academic analysis. See Gardner and Davidson (2012) 128 LQR 178; Dixon [2012] Conv 83; Mee [2012] Conv 167; Pawlowski [2012] Conv 149; Yip [2012] Conv 159; Lee [2012] Conv 421; George [2012] CLJ 39.
478. *Ibid.* at 788.
479. *Ibid.* at 792.

imputation.[480] As Lord Kerr stated, 'the court should anxiously examine the circumstances in order, where possible, to ascertain the parties' intention but it should not be reluctant to recognise, when it is appropriate to do so, that inference of an intention is not possible and that imputation of an intention is the only course to follow.'[481] In these circumstances, he suggested that each party is entitled to the share which the court considers fair and in considering this question, it should have regard to the whole course of dealing between the parties.[482] In this case the deposit on a house had been paid by the respondent and while the parties had jointly made the mortgage repayments while they lived there together, for many years the respondent had lived in the property on her own with the parties' children and she had made all the repayments during this time. The majority of the Court of Appeal concluded that the trial judge had in accordance with the reasoning in *Stack* focussed on the parties' intentions which in his view had changed over the years. Wall and Rimer LJJ found that they could not infer from the parties' conduct since their separation a joint intention that the 50-50 legal ownership would be varied. However, this decision was reversed by the Supreme Court and the trial judge's finding that the claimant should have a 90% beneficial interest restored.

The principles set out in *Stack v Dowden* and *Jones v Kernott* have also been adapted to apply to cases of sole legal ownership.[483] However, as Lord Walker and Baroness Hale pointed out in *Jones v Kernott*,[484] the starting point in cases of joint and sole ownership is in a sense different because while the claimant who has no legal ownership has the burden of establishing a common intention constructive trust, the claimant whose name is on the register generally starts with the presumption of a beneficial joint tenancy.[485] As they stated, '[t]he first issue is whether it was intended that the other party have any beneficial interest in the property at all. ... There is no presumption of joint beneficial ownership. But their common intention has once again to be deduced objectively from their conduct.'[486] They continued by saying that if the evidence shows a common

480. *Ibid.* at 800 *per* Lord Kerr; at 803 *per* Lord Wilson. Intention as to the issue of quantification was subsequently imputed in *Aspden v Elvy* [2012] EWHC 1387 (Ch). See further Lee [2012] Conv 421.
481. *Ibid.* at 799 *per* Lord Kerr. Gardner and Davidson (2012) 128 LQR 178, 179 have suggested that the approach of the minority on this issue is 'more realistic'.
482. *Ibid.* at 798.
483. However, note the views expressed by Mills [2018] Conv 350, 351 that the conceptual and practical difficulties between single name and joint name cases mean that *Stack* and *Jones* cannot be said to cover the former type of case. He argues that *Lloyd's Bank v Rosset* is still good law in relation to the 'acquisition question' in this type of case.
484. [2012] 1 AC 776, 784.
485. Lewison LJ stated in *Curran v Collins* [2015] EWCA Civ 404 at [61] that as a result of *Stack* and *Jones*, the starting point is the assumption that beneficial ownership of real property follows the legal title. So, as he stated, 'in a "single name" case ... that means that the sole legal owner is assumed to be the sole beneficial owner unless the contrary is shown.'
486. [2012] 1 AC 776, 794.

intention to share beneficial ownership but does not show what shares were intended, the court will have to proceed in the manner outlined in relation to joint ownership cases. So, the task in terms of quantification of beneficial interest is similar in both cases.[487]

In the Privy Council decision in *Abbott v Abbott*,[488] which involved a property which was vested in the husband's name only, Baroness Hale, who delivered the judgment of the Privy Council, stated that the court's inquiry involved two stages. First, whether it was intended that the wife should share the beneficial interest in the matrimonial home conveyed to the husband only and secondly, if so, the proportionate share intended. Baroness Hale quoted from her speech in *Stack v Dowden*[489] to the effect that 'the search is to ascertain the parties' shared intentions, actual, inferred or imputed, with respect to the property in the light of their whole course of conduct in relation to it.' In this case the husband accepted that his wife did have a beneficial interest in the property although he disputed the amount of this interest. Baroness Hale took into account the parties' whole course of conduct in relation to the property in determining their shared intentions as to its ownership and upheld the trial judge's conclusion that the beneficial ownership should be held equally by the parties.

A number of statements in decisions of the Court of Appeal also support the view that the courts are now applying the *Stack* and *Jones* principles in 'sole name' cases.[490] In *Gallarotti v Sebastianelli*[491] Arden LJ stated that in assessing whether to impose a common intention constructive trust, 'the court looks at the conduct of the parties throughout their relationship'. Similarly, in *Geary v Rankine*[492] Lewison LJ accepted that in such cases '[t]he search is to ascertain the parties' actual shared intentions, whether express or to be inferred from their conduct'. Consistent with the position adopted in *Jones v Kernott* in joint name cases, he stated that '[a]n imputed intention only arises where the court is satisfied that the parties' actual common intention, express or inferred, was that the beneficial interest would be shared, but cannot make a finding about the proportions in which they were to be shared.'[493] Sloan, in analyzing the post-*Jones* decisions in sole legal ownership cases, suggests that

487. *Ibid.* at 794.
488. [2007] UKPC 53 at [4].
489. [2007] 2 AC 432, 455.
490. See also *Crown Prosecution Service v Piper* [2011] EWHC 3570 (Admin); *Aspden v Elvy* [2012] EWHC 1387 (Ch); *Re Ali* [2012] EWHC 2302 (Admin); *Bank of Scotland v Brogan* [2012] NICh 21; *Patel v Vigh* [2013] EWHC 3403 (Ch); *Bhura v Bhura* [2014] EWHC 727 (Fam).
491. [2012] EWCA Civ 865 at [5]. See also *Thompson v Hurst* [2012] EWCA Civ 1752.
492. [2012] EWCA Civ 555. See further Lees [2012] Conv 412.
493. *Ibid.* at [19]. However, it should be noted that Pawlowski has suggested (2015) 29 Trust Law Int 3, 13 that imputation at the acquisition stage is justified 'because it permits the court to arrive at a solution which objectively reflects the parties' reasonable expectations.'

even if the law in England has been liberated from the constraints imposed by the decision of *Lloyd's Bank plc v Rossett*, 'the Supreme Court may still have to clarify precisely how a common intention is to be inferred directly from conduct beyond Lord Bridge's criteria'.[494] However, although there may often be some difficulty in sole ownership cases in establishing a common intention to share beneficial ownership of the property, the fact that the principles set out in *Jones* also apply to such cases appears to be in little doubt.[495]

The second question which must be addressed if a common intention constructive trust has been held to arise in cases of both sole and joint legal ownership is the issue of quantum, namely what should the extent of the parties' respective beneficial interests in the property be? In *Midland Bank plc v Cooke*[496] the Court of Appeal accepted that once a common intention to share beneficial ownership has been established, the court should 'undertake a survey of the whole course of dealing between the parties relevant to their ownership and occupation of the property' and 'the scrutiny will not confine itself to the limited range of acts of direct contribution of the sort that are needed to found a beneficial interest in the first place'.[497] So, in this case, although the wife's initial direct contribution had been only 6.4% of the value of the property,[498] the Court of Appeal took into account 'the whole course of dealing between the parties' and held that she should be entitled to a one-half share in the house.[499]

A similar approach was adopted by the Court of Appeal in *Oxley v Hiscock*,[500] where the issue of determining the extent of the parties' respective beneficial interests was considered in some detail. The purchase price of the property in question had been funded from the proceeds of sale of the claimant's former home which amounted to £61,500 (£25,500 of which was attributable to the defendant's contribution), the sum of £35,500 provided by the defendant and

494. (2015) 35 LS 226, 251.

495. Although note the comments of Gardner [2015] Conv 332, 334-335. However, Gardner acknowledges that 'a significant body of authority applies the joint names rules' in this regard to single name cases.

496. [1995] 4 All ER 562. See O'Hagan (1997) 60 MLR 420; Gardner (1996) 112 LQR 378; Oldham [1996] CLJ 194; Dixon [1997] Conv 66; Wragg [1996] Fam Law 298; Pawlowski [1996] Fam Law 484.

497. *Ibid.* at 574. See also *Drake v Whipp* [1996] 1 FLR 826, where the Court of Appeal found that the female partner's contribution to the actual expenditure on the property amounted to 19.4% of its value, but held on the basis of other contributions which she had made, that she was entitled to a one-third interest in it. See Dunn [1997] Conv 467.

498. A wedding gift of £1,100 was made jointly to Mrs Cooke and her husband by his parents and the court accepted that she had made a direct contribution to the purchase price of the house in the form of her half of the gift. This conclusion was based on the reasoning of the Court of Appeal in *McHardy v Warren* [1994] 2 FLR 338.

499. As O'Hagan has commented (1997) 60 MLR 420, 427 this meant that '[i]f a spouse or cohabitee contributes a proportionately trifling sum directly to the purchase of property, the initial direct contribution opens the door for the scrutiny of the relationship'.

500. [2004] 3 WLR 715.

a mortgage of £30,000. The parties had lived together in the property from the date of its purchase in 1991 until 2001 by which time their relationship had broken down and the mortgage had been paid off as a result of payments made equally by both of them.[501] The Court of Appeal inferred a common intention constructive trust as a result of the financial contributions made by each party and proceeded to determine their respective beneficial interests on the basis of what it considered fair having regard to the whole course of dealing between them in relation to the property. It concluded that having regard to their relative contributions to the purchase price and to all their dealings in relation to the property, a fair division of the proceeds of sale would be 60% to the defendant and 40% to the claimant. Chadwick LJ stated that in many cases the answer to the question of quantum will be provided by evidence of what the parties said and did at the time of the property's acquisition. However, where there was no evidence of any discussion between them as to the amount of the share that each would have, they would be entitled to a share which the court considered fair having regard to the whole course of dealing between them in relation to the property.[502] He added that in this context, this included the arrangements which they had made from time to time in order to meet outgoings such as mortgage contributions, utility and repair bills, insurance and housekeeping expenses. As Fox points out, it appeared from the judgment of Chadwick LJ in *Oxley* that the court felt entitled to assess the parties' shares based on considerations of fairness, irrespective of whether the common intention constructive trust was founded on evidence of express agreement[503] or on a direct financial contribution.[504]

In *Stack v Dowden*[505] Baroness Hale expressed the view that the court must ascertain the parties' shared intention with respect to the property in the light of their whole course of conduct in relation to it.[506] She stated that she

---

501. Chadwick LJ stated (at 752) that on the basis of the trial judge's finding that this was a case of a 'classic pooling of resources' and conduct consistent with an intention to share the burden of the property in relation to outgoings, it would be fair to treat the parties as having made approximately equal contributions to this balance of £30,000.
502. These principles were applied in a number of subsequent cases, see *Van Laethem v Brooker* [2005] EWHC 1478 (Ch); *Holman v Howes* [2005] EWHC 2824 (Ch).
503. Subsequently, in *Cox v Jones* [2004] EWHC 1486 (Ch) Mann J found that there was evidence of an arrangement between the parties that both would have an interest in a property, but in the absence of evidence of an agreement about the extent of their respective shares, he held (at [80]) that the interest must be such as he considered 'fair having regard to the whole course of dealing between them in relation to the property'.
504. Fox (2005) 56 NILQ 83, 96.
505. [2007] 2 AC 432. This decision has been the subject of much academic comment. See further Dixon [2007] Conv 456; Wee [2007] LMCLQ 455; Swadling (2007) 123 LQR 511; Pawlowski [2007] Conv 354; Cloherty and Fox [2007] CLJ 517; Piska (2008) 71 MLR 120; Etherton [2008] CLJ 265; Gardner (2008) 124 LQR 422; Harding [2009] Conv 309; Gardner and Davidson (2011) 127 LQR 13.
506. The *Stack v Dowden* principles have also been applied in cases where property has been acquired in the sole name of one party, see e.g. *Tackaberry v Hollis* [2008] WTLR

preferred the formulation adopted by the Law Commission in *Sharing Homes*[507] on the quantification of beneficial entitlement to that set out by Chadwick LJ in *Oxley v Hiscock*, namely that the court should 'undertak[e] a survey of the whole course of dealing between the parties and tak[e] account of all conduct which throws light on the question what shares were intended', although she acknowledged that this might simply be a 'preferable way of expressing the same thought'. Baroness Hale expressed the view that the court's approach to quantification in cases where the home is conveyed into joint names should certainly be no stricter than the approach in cases where it has been conveyed into the name of one party only although she added that there are differences between sole and joint names cases when trying to divine the common intentions or understanding between the parties. She stated that many factors in addition to financial contributions may be relevant in ascertaining the parties' true intentions and these included the following:

> Any advice or discussions at the time of the transfer which cast light upon their intentions then; the reasons why the home was acquired in their joint names; the reasons why (if it be the case) the survivor was authorised to give a receipt for the capital moneys; the purpose for which the home was acquired; the nature of the parties' relationship; whether they had children for whom they both had responsibility to provide a home; how the purchase was financed, both initially and subsequently; how the parties arranged their finances, whether separately or together or a bit of both; how they discharged the outgoings on the property and their other household expenses.[508]

Baroness Hale added that when a couple are joint owners of a home and jointly liable for the mortgage, it will be easier to draw the inference that they intended that each should contribute as much to the household as they reasonably could and that they would share the eventual benefit or burden equally. She concluded that the case before the court was a very unusual one and that there could not be many unmarried couples who had lived together so long, had four children together and had kept their financial affairs so rigidly separate. She held that the respondent had established her entitlement to the 65% beneficial share awarded to her by the Court of Appeal and that she would dismiss the appellant's appeal, although she also made it clear that the route by which she had arrived at this conclusion was different both in principle and on the facts from that taken by the lower court. Lord Neuberger reached the same conclusion but adopted a resulting trust solution and suggested that the beneficial ownership should be held in the same proportions as the contributions to the purchase price. He

279; *Williamson v Shiekh* [2008] EWCA Civ 990; *Amin v Amin* [2009] EWHC 3356 (Ch); *Thomson v Humphrey* [2010] 2 FLR 107.

507. Law Com. No. 278, 2002, para. 4.27.
508. [2007] 2 AC 432, 459.

added that 'while an intention may be inferred as well as express, it may not, at least in my opinion, be imputed.'[509] This suggests that Lord Neuberger held the view that while the presumption of a resulting trust could be rebutted by a common intention that the beneficial interests should be different from the legal interests, this could only be established expressly or by inference and could not be imputed.

In *Jones v Kernott*[510] Lord Walker and Baroness Hale said that in cases where it was not possible to ascertain by direct evidence or by inference what the parties' actual intentions were as to the shares in which they would own the property, 'each is entitled to a share which the court considers fair having regard to the whole course of dealing between them in relation to the property.' They added that '[t]his phrase should be given a broad meaning, enabling a similar range of factors to be taken into account as may be relevant to ascertaining the parties' actual intentions.' In their view each case will turn on its own facts and while financial contributions are relevant, there are many other factors which may enable the court to decide what shares were either intended or fair.[511]

Further clarification of what 'fair' means in this context was provided by Tomlinson LJ in the decision of the Court of Appeal in *Graham-York v York.*[512] He stated that 'in deciding in such a case what shares are fair, the court is not concerned with some form of redistributive justice' and added that the words 'in relation to the property' in the quotation above from *Jones v Kernott* 'supply the confines of the inquiry as to fairness'.[513] Tomlinson LJ also made the point that 'the judicial evaluation of the fair share is not one in respect of which there is only one right answer'[514] and suggested that an outcome arrived at by a trial judge should only be disturbed if it fell outside the ambit of reasonable decision-making.

Greer and Pawlowski suggest that the decision in *Graham-York* represents a shift away from a holistic approach to quantification and focuses heavily on financial factors and matters which relate directly to the acquisition of the property.[515] However, given the controversial nature of resorting to imputed intention in this context, an approach which focuses on quantifiable contributions and is confined to the course of dealings between the parties specifically related to the property is preferable to one which is too broad and lacks such specificity.

509. *Ibid.* at 472.
510. [2012] 1 AC 776, 794.
511. So, as Floyd LJ noted in *Sandhu v Sandhu* [2016] EWCA Civ 1050 at [12], 'the exercise is not a rigidly arithmetical one'.
512. [2015] EWCA Civ 72.
513. *Ibid.* at [22].
514. *Ibid.* at [25].
515. [2015] Conv 512, 521. See also Gardner (2016) 132 LQR 373.

(c) Doctrinal Issues

The conceptual uncertainty created by decisions in England has given rise to concern on a number of levels. The blurring of the distinctions between resulting and constructive trusts has led to unnecessary uncertainty. While it was traditionally accepted that direct contributions by the non-legal owner to the acquisition of property would give rise to a purchase money resulting trust in his favour,[516] in *Lloyds Bank plc v Rosset*[517] Lord Bridge caused confusion by using the label 'constructive trust' to describe the form of trust which would arise as a result of making a direct contribution towards the purchase of property.[518] This conceptual uncertainty was compounded by the decision of the Court Appeal in *Oxley v Hiscock*,[519] which led Thompson to comment that 'the upshot of this judgment is that all cases now seem set to be decided on the basis of constructive trusts.'[520] He expressed the view that there appear to be two forms of constructive trust being applied in such cases, one the established type and the other based on a concept of fairness, which 'on closer inspection ... seems to be based on resulting trust principles.'[521] Thompson's analysis is certainly correct as far as the *Oxley* case is concerned, given that the court's assessment of what was fair corresponded to the amount of the financial contributions made towards the purchase of the property.[522] Reference was made in other decisions to the difficulties which such conceptual uncertainty can give rise to,[523] but following *Stack v Dowden* and *Jones v Kernott* it is clear

516. However, in *Gissing v Gissing* [1971] AC 886, 905 Lord Diplock commented that it was unnecessary for the purpose of the matter before the court to distinguish between resulting, implied or constructive trusts and this may have sown the seed for the subsequent conceptual uncertainty which now pervades this area of the law in England.
517. [1991] 1 AC 107.
518. See further O'Hagan (1991) 42 NILQ 238, 244 and Thompson [2004] Conv 496, 501 who argued that Lord Bridge wrongly classified the form of trust which arises in such circumstances as constructive. Further confusion was caused as a result of the reference by Ward LJ in *Carlton v Goodman* [2002] EWCA Civ 545 at [32] to the fact that the decision in *Midland Bank plc v Cooke*, itself based on the reasoning of Lord Bridge in *Lloyds*, could only be properly understood when it is appreciated that the court was satisfied that by making a direct contribution a *resulting* trust had been established in the wife's favour.
519. [2004] 3 WLR 715.
520. Thompson [2004] Conv 496, 502.
521. *Ibid.* He added (at 507) that '[t]he role of the resulting trust appears to have been eliminated and replaced by a new form of constructive trust based upon what is perceived to be fair, although the adjudication of fairness appears, paradoxically, to be based upon the principles underlying the resulting trust.'
522. See also the comment of Lord Neuberger in *Stack v Dowden* [2007] 2 AC 432, 468 that the Court of Appeal's decision in *Oxley* 'produced an outcome which would be dictated by a resulting trust solution'.
523. *Carlton v Goodman* [2002] EWCA Civ 545; *McKenzie v McKenzie* [2003] EWHC 601 (Ch); *Curley v Parkes* [2004] EWCA Civ 1515.

that it is the analysis based on the common intention constructive trust which is now firmly established in England.

In *Jones v Kernott*[524] Lord Walker and Baroness Hale stated that '[t]he primary search must always be for what the parties actually intended, to be deduced objectively from their words and their actions. If that can be discovered, then … it is not open to a court to impose a solution upon them in contradiction to those intentions, merely because the court considers it fair to do so.' It is also clear, as Lloyd Jones LJ stated in *Barnes v Philips*,[525] that 'the majority in *Jones v Kernott* held that imputation of intention was permissible only at the stage of ascertaining the shares in which property was held following the demonstration of an actual intention to vary shares in the property.' So, as Mee suggests, 'the decision appears to limit the imputation of openly fictional common intentions to the relatively uncontroversial context of quantifying the parties' shares under a constructive trust in cases where a common intention has been found to exist which does not specify precisely the respective shares.'[526]

However, there has been considerable academic criticism of the concept of imputed common intention. Lee has commented that '[i]n an imputation case, the only common intention is to share in the first place. As to quantification, however, the judge can only impute if it is found that there was *no* common intention as to the precise shares and the 'imputation' of an intention is really a fiction.'[527] Virgo expresses the view that if imputed common intention is simply a smokescreen to enable the court to achieve what it considers to be a fair result, it might have been preferable to state this explicitly, as Lords Kerr and Wilson did in their judgments.[528] He suggests that 'the preferable view is that an imputed common intention cannot be justified doctrinally and should be rejected'[529] and that 'the real danger of the willingness to impute a common intention is that the courts are actually seeking to redistribute the beneficial interests in property to achieve a just result, but without the benefit of any clear principles.'[530]

Virgo's preferred approach is to employ a presumed resulting trust solution as suggested by Lord Neuberger in *Stack v Dowden*.[531] Using this model, there would be a presumption that beneficial interests be based on the financial contribution to the acquisition of the property but this presumption could be rebutted by the parties' express or inferred common intention. However, the

524. [2012] 1 AC 776, 792.
525. [2015] EWCA Civ 1056 at [26].
526. [2012] Conv 167, 168. See further Gardner and Davidson (2012) 128 LQR 178, 178-179; Lee [2012] Conv 421. However, note the comments of Mostyn J in *Bhura v Bhura* [2014] EWHC 727 (Fam) at [8(vii)] analysed by Gardner [2015] Conv 332, 335-337.
527. [2012] Conv 421, 427.
528. *The Principles of Equity and Trusts* (3rd ed., 2018) p.298.
529. *Ibid.* at 336.
530. *Ibid.* at 337.
531. [2007] 2 AC 432, 468.

resulting trust solution for disputes relating to the home of cohabiting partners was rejected by Baroness Hale in *Stack v Dowden*[532] on the basis that the law has 'moved on in response to changing social and economic conditions'. Subsequently in *Jones v Kernott*[533] Lord Walker and Baroness Hale commented that '[t]he time has come to make it clear ... that in the case of the purchase of a house or flat in joint names for joint occupation by a married or unmarried couple, where both are responsible for any mortgage, there is no presumption of a resulting trust arising from their having contributed to the deposit (or indeed the rest of the purchase) in unequal shares.'

As the case law in this jurisdiction has shown, there are drawbacks to utilising a resulting trust model and it is not flexible enough to allow for credit to be given to certain types of contributions which the common intention constructive trust can facilitate. However, the element of uncertainty about which principles should be applied in England is also unsatisfactory and the question of the borderline between circumstances in which the courts there consider it appropriate to apply resulting trust principles on the one hand and the principles developed in *Stack v Dowden* and *Jones v Kernott* on the other hand is an evolving one. The application of resulting trust principles was accepted as appropriate to a dispute between the appellant and her late father's second wife relating to ownership of property by the Court of Appeal in *Wodzicki v Wodzicki*.[534]

However, in the decision of the Privy Council in *Marr v Collie*[535] Lord Kerr concluded that the principles set out in *Stack* and *Jones* could be applied to property jointly owned by a co-habiting couple other than a home. In this case, where investment properties and other assets had been acquired in the parties' joint names, he expressed the view that their respective beneficial interests would depend on their intentions. The Privy Council remitted the matter for determination of the parties' intentions at the time of the purchase of the properties and assets and having regard to their subsequent dealings in relation to them on the basis that the trial judge had failed to make a sufficient examination of this issue. Lord Kerr stated that in *Stack v Dowden* Baroness Hale had set out the fundamental principle that 'the starting point where there is joint legal ownership is joint beneficial ownership'. Although he acknowledged that this statement had been made in a case where the dispute between the parties was in relation to property which was a family home, Lord Kerr expressed the view that she had not intended that the principle should be confined exclusively to the domestic setting and stated that 'there is no reason to doubt its possible

532. *Ibid.* at 455. See also the *dicta* of Pitchford LJ in *Davies v O'Kelly* [2015] 1 WLR 2725, 2741 who commented that a resulting trust approach 'is no longer the appropriate route to the discovery of the parties' common intention'.
533. [2012] 1 AC 776, 786. See also at 794.
534. [2017] EWCA Civ 95.
535. [2018] AC 631. See further Biehler (2018) 32 Trust Law Int 63; Georgiou (2019) 82 MLR 145.

applicability to property purchased by a couple in an enterprise reflecting their joint commercial, as well as their personal, commitment.'[536] The view of the Privy Council in *Marr* was that resulting trust principles should only continue to apply to disputes about beneficial ownership of property when the context is 'wholly non-domestic'.[537] The difficulty is that drawing a line of demarcation between domestic and non-domestic transactions is often far from easy and ultimately the lack of consensus about the underlying rationale for the drawing of lines of this nature will lead to further uncertainty.

In terms of alternative approaches, it should also be noted that the courts in England have applied the reasoning developed by the House of Lords in *Tinsley v Milligan*,[538] in relation to the circumstances in which a resulting trust may arise where a claimant does not need to rely on an illegal purpose to establish it, to a situation in which a common intention constructive trust is at issue. However, the effect of the decision of the UK Supreme Court in *Patel v Mirza*,[539] considered above, in which the manner in which the defence of illegality operates in private law was reassessed, needs to be borne in mind in this regard. In *Davies v O'Kelly*[540] the parties, who were unmarried, transferred the family home in which they lived into the sole name of the defendant. It was later sold to the claimant and the house was let and simultaneously the defendant bought another property where the parties lived together until the relationship ended. The claimant brought proceedings seeking a declaration that the defendant held the house in which they had subsequently lived in trust for the two of them in equal shares. The trial judge found that the properties had been held in the sole name of the defendant in order to enable her to fraudulently claim social security benefits but held that the claimant did not need to rely on the illegality of the transactions to assert his claim to an equitable interest in the property in which the parties had been living together. He found that a common intention could be inferred that the parties were to share the beneficial interest in this property equally, a decision upheld by the Court of Appeal. Pitchford LJ considered whether there was a distinction between a resulting and a constructive trust sufficient to render one enforceable in the face of an illegal purpose and the other not and concluded that there was not. He pointed out that it was not necessary for the claimant to prove the reason why the legal estate in both properties had been conveyed into the defendant's sole name in order to make good his claim to a common intention constructive trust. He accepted that, on the findings of the trial judge, the dealings between the parties during the period in question gave rise to the inference of their common intention without the need to refer to or to rely on the illegal purpose.

There is still evidence of proprietary estoppel principles being employed

536. *Ibid.* at 643.
537. *Ibid.* at 647.
538. [1994] 1 AC 340.
539. [2017] AC 467.
540. [2015] 1 WLR 2725.

in this context in some instances in England,[541] but these cases are relatively rare. In *Oxley v Hiscock*[542] Chadwick LJ stated that once it is recognised that what the court is doing is supplying or imputing a common intention as to the parties' respective shares on the basis of what is shown to be fair, it seemed 'very difficult to avoid the conclusion that an analysis in terms of proprietary estoppel will, necessarily, lead to the same result'. However, in *Stack v Dowden,*[543] Lord Walker stated that he was rather less enthusiastic about the notion that the two doctrines could or should be completely assimilated than he might previously have been. It should also be noted that the requirement that the partner seeking to establish a beneficial share establish detrimental reliance referred to by Lord Bridge in *Lloyds' Bank plc v Rosset* was not referred to in *Stack v Dowden* or *Jones v Kernott* and no longer appears to play any role in establishing a common intention constructive trust. The complex issue of the relationship between constructive trusts and proprietary estoppel is considered in more detail elsewhere[544] but at this point it can be said that the common intention constructive trust is almost invariably used in England as the vehicle to determine property disputes of this nature.

In summary, the 'broad brush' approach adopted by the courts in England, although it has been criticised as arbitrary,[545] can be said to deliver greater flexibility although undoubtedly this comes at the price of increased uncertainty and some inconsistency. However, now that the principles set out in *Stack v Dowden* and *Jones v Kernott* are firmly established, greater consistency may develop over time. Ultimately the courts in both this jurisdiction and in England face similar challenges. As Mee has remarked, '[t]he essential problem is that an approach which conscientiously focuses on genuine intentions would provide a remedy in a very limited set of circumstances, while an approach which moves beyond real intentions seems to involve impermissible judicial law-making.'[546]

Alternative Models

As can be seen from the above discussion of the manner in which recognition is or is not given to different forms of contribution to the purchase price of

541. See e.g. *Holman v Howes* [2008] 1 FLR 1217; *James v Thomas* [2008] 1 FLR 1598.
542. [2004] 3 WLR 715, 748. See further Gardner (2004) 120 LQR 541, 543; Thompson [2005] Conv 79, 87.
543. [2007] 2 AC 432, 448. Etherton also comments [2008] CLJ 265, 286 that his analysis of the reasoning of the majority in *Stack* as being founded on remedial constructive trust principles explains why, contrary to the view expressed by Chadwick LJ in *Oxley,* there was no assimilation between common intention constructive trusts and proprietary estoppel.
544. See *infra* Chapter 18.
545. See Law Commission Discussion Paper, *Sharing Homes* (Law Com No. 278, 2002) para. 2.87. It was pointed out that it is notoriously difficult to ascertain what the parties' necessarily unrecorded common intention really was.
546. [2012] Conv 167, 179.

family property, the principles applied by both the Irish and English courts each have their respective advantages and disadvantages.

The English principles have the advantage of flexibility; there is certainly merit in the 'broad brush' approach adopted in that jurisdiction which permits consideration of the 'whole course of dealing between [the parties] in relation to the property'.[547] In addition, it allows for quantification based on common intention rather than on the amount of the actual contributions made. An issue worth pointing out is that it was accepted in *Stack v Dowden*[548] that the parties' common intentions in relation to the beneficial ownership of the property may change over time, giving rise to what was referred to as an 'ambulatory' constructive trust. Baroness Hale gave as an example a situation where one party has financed or constructed an extension or substantial improvement to the property.[549] Lord Neuberger similarly noted that 'the fact that one party carries out significant improvements to the home will justify an adjustment of the apportionment of the beneficial interest in his favour.'[550] This is potentially significant as the failure of the resulting trust model adopted in this jurisdiction to recognise such contributions has been one of its greatest limitations.[551]

Overall the approach adopted in this jurisdiction has the merit of consistency and comparative simplicity but is also based on reasoning which is theoretically flawed to varying degrees. In addition, the rather limited nature of the contributions which are recognised as giving rise to a beneficial interest is a serious shortcoming. In particular the lack of recognition given to claimants in relation to contributions to improvements to property in the absence of an express or readily implied agreement that this should be the case[552] and the unequivocal rejection of the principle that work in the home can give rise to a beneficial interest gives rise to difficulties. As further judicial development of the resulting trust concept appears to have been ruled out by the Supreme Court's decision in *L. v L.*, it would seem that if the operation of equitable principles in this area is to be extended then the possibility of other approaches must be explored. At this juncture it should be pointed out, as Mee has acknowledged, that the extensive legislative developments in this context over recent decades have meant that the justification for further development of equitable principles

547. *Per* Chadwick LJ in *Oxley v Hiscock* [2004] 3 WLR 715, 750. See also *Stack v Dowden* [2007] 1 AC 432, 448 *per* Lord Walker.
548. [2007] 2 AC 432, 456.
549. *Ibid.* at 459.
550. *Ibid.* at 475.
551. However, as noted above, in *Sheehy v Talbot* [2008] IEHC 207 Edwards J appeared to take into account the parties' respective contributions to improvements to the property, although he did not explain the basis for this conclusion.
552. There is also considerable doubt about whether contributions of this nature can give rise to a beneficial interest at all in the light of the *obiter* comments of McGuinness J in *C.F. v J.D.F.* [2005] 4 IR 154, 166.

has all but disappeared.[553] However, it is worth briefly examining alternative approaches to resolving family property disputes.

The potential of using the constructive trust as a device which will provide a remedy where 'justice and good conscience' demand was illustrated by the decision of Barron J in *Murray v Murray*.[554] The defendant was the legal owner of premises in respect of which he had paid the initial deposit; the remainder, approximately three-quarters of the price, was paid by way of a mortgage. The plaintiff, his nephew, had lived in the premises with his aunt, the defendant's sister, for many years and it was accepted by Barron J that the defendant had intended to transfer the house to his sister. While she was alive she paid the mortgage instalments and most of the outgoings on the property, although there was evidence that she had at one point refused to accept a transfer of the property. After her death the plaintiff claimed a declaration that the entire beneficial ownership in the house was vested in his aunt at the date of her death and the defendant claimed the legal and beneficial ownership himself. The plaintiff claimed that the circumstances were such that it would be unconscionable for the defendant to rely on his legal title and he relied on the decision of *Hussey v Palmer*[555] to support this claim. Barron J stated: 'It is I think quite clear that the law will impose a constructive trust in all circumstances where it would be unjust and unconscionable not to do so.' In his view *Hussey* was authority for the proposition that in certain circumstances where equity so required, 'a debt may be secured by the device of a constructive trust on the property created by the money involved'. He said that in the case before him the equity to create a constructive trust arose from the payment of monies which had resulted in the property being freed from the mortgage and the owner being relieved of other outgoings. Barron J concluded that the aunt was at the date of her death entitled to three-quarters of the beneficial interest in the property so the plaintiff, being her next of kin, was a tenant in common of the premises with the defendant.

It is worth pointing out that the High Court decided not to seek to apply conventional purchase money resulting trust principles to this case. This was probably due to the uncertainty surrounding the issue of whether the plaintiff's aunt made her contributions intending that she would thereby acquire a beneficial interest in the property. Barron J pointed out that there was evidence of the fact that she had not wanted to take a transfer of the legal ownership of the property during her lifetime and so arguably the presumption of a resulting trust might have been rebutted in the circumstances if the court had sought to apply such reasoning. The question remains whether the constructive trust principles employed by the High Court could usefully be employed in other situations involving family property disputes where a claimant will not gain a beneficial

553. (2016) 56 Ir Jur 161, 176.
554. [1996] 3 IR 251.
555. [1972] 1 WLR 1286.

share on the basis of traditional purchase money resulting trust principles. Mee suggests not and argues that a 'simple appeal to abstract notions of equity and fairness will not suffice'.[556] Given the almost universally unfavourable reaction to Lord Denning's new model constructive trust, to which Barron J's trust in *Murray* is undoubtedly related, this is probably an accurate prediction and it is likely that our courts will have to look elsewhere for more acceptable solutions.

It is interesting to also consider briefly the principles employed elsewhere in the common law world to resolve family property disputes.[557] The Canadian Supreme Court relies on the concept of 'unjust enrichment' as a means of resolving such cases. In *Pettkus v Becker*[558] it declined to continue to apply the common intention resulting trust and criticised the 'artificiality'[559] of this approach. It relied instead on the concept of unjust enrichment and will intervene where there is 'an enrichment, a corresponding deprivation and the absence of any juristic reason for the enrichment'.[560] Subsequently, in *Kerr v Baranow*[561] Cromwell J reiterated that '[t]here is no need for any artificial inquiry into common intent.' He concluded that 'as the development of the law since *Pettkus* has shown, the principles of unjust enrichment, coupled with the possible remedy of a constructive trust, provide a much less artificial, more comprehensive and more principled basis to address the wide variety of circumstances that lead to claims arising out of domestic partnerships.'[562] His characterisation of the concept of unjust enrichment as 'the more flexible and appropriate lens through which to view property and financial disputes in domestic situations'[563] and rejection of reliance on common intention as a mechanism for giving rise to a trust is of interest given the continued reliance by the courts in England on the common intention constructive trust.

The Australian approach is founded on the concept of unconscionability and is based on the principles which might apply where a commercial joint venture is terminated.[564] In New Zealand the reasonable expectation principle has been applied and where a claimant has contributed to the acquisition of

556. Mee (1996) 1 CPLJ 9, 13.
557. See Gardner (1993) 109 LQR 263 for an excellent summary of these approaches. See also Wong (1998) 18 LS 369, 380-388.
558. (1980) 117 DLR (3d) 257.
559. *Ibid.* at 270.
560. *Pettkus v Becker* (1980) 117 DLR (3d) 257, 269 per Dickson J. See also *Sorochan v Sorochan* (1986) 29 DLR (4th) 1; *Wilcox v Wilcox* (2000) 190 DLR (4th) 324.
561. (2011) 328 DLR (4th) 577. See further McInnes (2011) 127 LQR 339; Lower [2011] Conv 515.
562. *Ibid.* at 591-592.
563. *Ibid.* at 590. However, it should be noted that the Supreme Court of Canada held in *Rascal Trucking Ltd v Nishi* (2013) 359 DLR (4th) 575 that in a commercial context, the traditional purchase money resulting trust provides 'certainty and flexibility' and it rejected an attempt to abandon it in favour of unjust enrichment. See further McInnes (2013) 129 LQR 473.
564. See *Muschinski v Dodds* (1985) 160 CLR 583; *Baumgartner v Baumgartner* (1987) 164 CLR 137.

the legal owner's property, a constructive trust may be imposed on the basis that this must have been what the parties intended.[565] However, as Gardner points out, in all these jurisdictions there has tended to be 'a gap between the articulated doctrines and the manner in which cases are actually decided'.[566] He quite correctly asserts that all the doctrines make reference to the parties' own ideas but there is often little such thought on their part and in most jurisdictions 'the circle is squared by fabricating the necessary facts'.[567]

All of the approaches adopted in other common law jurisdictions to deal with family property disputes have their relative advantages and disadvantages. Mee has given extensive consideration to the challenges posed in developing a set of principles which would operate in an optimal manner in this context and has suggested as follows:[568]

> A rational modern doctrine would, it is submitted, require the claimant to show a genuine understanding between the parties that the beneficial ownership would differ from the legal ownership. The purchase money resulting trust's focus on the unilateral intention of each contributor would be replaced by a focus on what had been agreed between the parties. The trigger for equitable intervention would then be the fact that the legal owner was acting inconsistently with the agreement on the basis of which he or she had been allowed to obtain the legal ownership of the property.

While Mee acknowledges that this putative doctrine bears some resemblance to the flawed common intention constructive trust, he suggests that some of the difficulties associated with this model might be addressed by avoiding the artificial inference of common intention from conduct. In his view, '[a] doctrine which focused on the existence of genuine agreement between the parties would arguably be the most defensible doctrinal option.'[569]

The current position in this jurisdiction is that a range of legislation now makes provision for a mechanism to determine the beneficial ownership of family property as between spouses, civil partners or qualified co-habitees. The enactment of the Civil Partnership and Certain Rights and Obligations of Cohabitants Act 2010 was significant in this regard and the range of contributions which the courts may have regard to in determining property rights as between civil partners and qualifying cohabitants is significantly broader than heretofore. However, individuals who do not fulfil the criteria laid down for a qualified cohabitee or who live in a domestic relationship such as that

565. *Lankow v Rose* [1995] 1 NZLR 277. See also *Gillies v Keogh* [1989] 2 NZLR 327; *Marshall v Bourneville* [2013] 3 NZLR 766.
566. Gardner (1993) 109 LQR 263, 279.
567. *Ibid.*
568. (2016) 56 Ir Jur 161, 179.
569. *Ibid.*

which existed in *Murray v Murray*[570] will have to continue to rely on equitable principles to provide relief where they seek to have contributions made to the acquisition of property recognised. Such principles will also inevitably continue to be invoked in disputes between financial institutions and spouses or partners in relation to the beneficial ownership of property. For this reason it is likely that reliance will continue to be placed on the purchase money resulting trust and possibly the constructive trust in this context and that the courts will have to persist in grappling with the anomalies to which their application may give rise, albeit in more limited circumstances than heretofore.

570. [1996] 3 IR 251.

CHAPTER 8

Constructive Trusts

INTRODUCTION

General Principles

A constructive trust is one which arises by operation of law and which ordinarily comes into being as a result of conduct and irrespective of the intention of the parties. In general terms it can be described as a trust which is imposed by equity in order to satisfy the demands of 'justice and good conscience'[1] and to prevent a person deriving profit from fraudulent conduct or taking unfair advantage of a fiduciary position.

There can be some degree of overlap between the circumstances in which resulting and constructive trusts can arise[2] and from a practical perspective it makes little difference whether a trust is described as resulting or constructive as there is no requirement that the formalities which apply to express trusts be complied with in either case. In addition, it should be noted that the obligations and liabilities imposed on a constructive trustee will not necessarily be as extensive as those demanded of the trustee of an express trust and may tend to vary according to the nature of the circumstances giving rise to the imposition of the trust.

It is also important not to view the imposition of a constructive trust in isolation; it must often be considered in conjunction with the proprietary remedy of tracing trust property or the personal remedy against a trustee for breach of trust. While these remedies may sometimes prove to be equally effective, where the constructive trustee is insolvent it will be important to pursue a proprietary, rather than a personal, remedy which will ensure that the beneficiary ranks ahead of the trustee's general creditors.

The constructive trust is often regarded as a residual category which arises where fairness demands it. In *Lonrho plc v Fayed (No.2)*[3] Millett J spoke in terms of 'the independent jurisdiction of equity as a court of conscience to grant relief for every species of fraud and other unconscionable conduct' although he stressed that equity's intervention 'must be based on principle; there must

---

1. *Hussey v Palmer* [1972] 1 WLR 1286, 1290 *per* Denning MR. See also *Kelly v Cahill* [2000] 1 IR 56, 61.
2. This can be seen primarily in relation to determining the beneficial interest in family property. See *infra* pp. 223-256.
3. [1992] 1 WLR 1, 9.

be some relationship between the relief granted and the circumstances which give rise to it.'[4] In his view, when appropriate the court will grant a proprietary remedy to restore to the plaintiff property of which he has been wrongly deprived, to prevent the defendant from retaining a benefit which he has obtained through his own wrongdoing and specifically to require a defendant to disgorge property which he should have acquired, if at all, for the plaintiff.

Institutional and Remedial Constructive Trusts

The institutional constructive trust is a device which arises in certain defined situations, for example where there has been a breach of fiduciary duty. It arises by operation of law and the court's role is to effectively recognise a trust which has already arisen. On the other hand, a remedial constructive trust is one which is imposed by the court in the exercise of its discretion as a remedy in circumstances where it considers that fairness requires it. So, in the case of an institutional constructive trust the proprietary interest will be pre-existing,[5] whereas a remedial constructive trust will usually be framed so that the consequences of its imposition operate only from the date of the court order or other specified date.[6]

The distinctions between the institutional and remedial constructive trust were set out in the following terms by Lord Browne-Wilkinson in *Westdeutsche Landesbank Girozentrale v Islington Borough Council*.[7] He stated that '[u]nder an institutional constructive trust, the trust arises by operation of law as from the date of the circumstances which give rise to it: the function of the court is merely to declare that such trust has arisen in the past' and he added that the consequences that flow from such a trust having arisen are determined by rules of law, not as a result of discretion. In contrast, he said that his understanding of a remedial constructive trust was that 'it is a judicial remedy giving rise to an enforceable equitable obligation'[8] and that the extent to which it operates retrospectively to the prejudice of third parties lies in the discretion of the court.

These distinctions have also been explored by Tipping J in the decision of the New Zealand Court of Appeal in *Fortex Group Ltd v MacIntosh*.[9] He stated that an institutional constructive trust is one which arises by operation of the principles of equity and whose existence the court simply recognises in a declaratory way, whereas a remedial constructive trust is one which is imposed by the court in circumstances where before the order of the court, no trust of any kind existed. The difference between the two types of trust in his view is that the former arises upon the happening of the events which bring it

4. *Ibid.* at 9.
5. *Re Sharpe (a Bankrupt)* [1980] 1 WLR 219, 225 *per* Browne-Wilkinson J.
6. *Muschinski v Dodds* (1985) 160 CLR 583, 615.
7. [1996] AC 669, 714. See also *Angove's Pty Ltd v Bailey* [2016] 1 WLR 3179, 3191.
8. *Ibid.*
9. [1998] 3 NZLR 171, 172. See also *Oosterhuis v Saetrum* [2007] NZHC 416 at [21].

into being and its existence is not dependent on any order of the court whereas the latter depends for its very existence on such an order.[10]

While Deane J in *Muschinski v Dodds*[11] has commented that 'for the student of equity there can be no true dichotomy between the two notions' of 'institution' and 'remedy', the question of where the lines of demarcation between them should be drawn has provoked considerable academic comment over the years.[12] A useful description of the difference which exists between the traditional institutional trust and the newer breed of remedial constructive trust which has developed in many parts of the common law world, particularly in Canada, is set out in the judgment of McLachlin J in the Canadian Supreme Court decision of *Soulos v Korkontzilas*:[13]

> The situations which the judge may consider in deciding whether good conscience requires imposition of a constructive trust may be seen as falling into two general categories. The first category concerns property obtained by a wrongful act of the defendant, notably breach of fiduciary obligation or breach of duty of loyalty. The traditional English institutional trusts largely fall under but may not exhaust (at least in Canada) this category. The second category concerns situations where the defendant has not acted wrongfully in obtaining the property, but where he would be unjustly enriched to the plaintiff's detriment by being permitted to keep the property for himself.

ADVANTAGES GAINED BY PERSONS IN FIDUCIARY POSITIONS

Fiduciary Relationships

Introduction

A useful description of a fiduciary relationship and the key attributes of this

10. See also the comments of Glazebrook J in *Commonwealth Reserves I v Chodar* [2001] 2 NZLR 374, 382-383 that generally the institutional constructive trust is a mandatory consequence of certain events while the remedial constructive trust is a discretionary remedy. In addition, while the former exists from the time the events giving rise to it occur, the latter becomes effective at the time of the court order.
11. (1985) 160 CLR 583, 614.
12. See, e.g. Gardner in *Frontiers of Liability* (ed. Birks, 1993) Volume 2 pp. 186-192; Cope, *Constructive Trusts* (1992) pp. 868-870. Lord Millett has commented, writing extra-judicially, that 'while we still insist on the institutional character of the constructive trust, however, we undoubtedly use it as a remedial instrument' (1998) 114 LQR 399.
13. (1997) 146 DLR (4th) 214, 227.

relationship is set out by Millett LJ in *Bristol and West Building Society v Mothew*[14] in the following terms:

> A fiduciary is someone who has undertaken to act for or on behalf of another in a particular matter in circumstances which give rise to a relationship of trust and confidence. The distinguishing obligation of a fiduciary is the obligation of loyalty. The principal is entitled to the single-minded loyalty of his fiduciary. This core liability has several facets. A fiduciary must act in good faith; he must not make a profit out of his trust; he must not place himself in a position where his duty and his interest may conflict; he may not act for his own benefit or the benefit of a third person without the informed consent of his principal. This is not intended to be an exhaustive list, but it is sufficient to indicate the nature of fiduciary obligations. They are the defining characteristics of the fiduciary.

Millett LJ went on to endorse the statement of Finn from his landmark work *Fiduciary Obligations* that a person 'is not subject to fiduciary obligations because he is a fiduciary; it is because he is subject to them that he is a fiduciary'.[15] Or, as Edelman has put it, 'the label "fiduciary" is a conclusion which is reached only once it is determined that particular duties are owed.'[16] As Ryan P explained in *ADM Londis plc v Ranzett Ltd*,[17] where there is a fiduciary relationship one person acts as the fiduciary of another but the duties are not reciprocal and 'only one person in the relationship owes fiduciary obligations to the other'.

The primary feature of a fiduciary relationship is that a fiduciary 'undertakes or agrees to act for or on behalf of or in the interests of another person in the exercise of a power or discretion which will affect the interests of that other person in a legal or practical sense.'[18] Smith has argued that a requirement of loyalty is present in all fiduciary relationships and 'is essential to their categorisation as such'.[19] In his view 'fiduciary relationships arise when a person holds power, but not for his or her own benefit'.[20] Worthington has stated that while modern analysis recognises that fiduciaries typically owe

14. [1998] Ch 1, 18. Quoted with approval by Fennelly J in *McMullen v McGinley* [2005] IESC 10 and by Baker J in *Best v Ghose* [2018] IEHC 376 at [48].
15. *Fiduciary Obligations* (1977) p. 2. See also *ADM Londis plc v Ranzett Ltd* [2016] IECA 290 at [66] and *Clements v Meagher* [2008] IEHC 258 at [3.1], cited with approval in *Fermoy Fish Ltd v Canestar Ltd* [2015] IESC 93 at 5.
16. (2010) 126 LQR 302, 316.
17. [2016] IECA 290 at [67].
18. *Hospital Products Ltd v US Surgical Corporation* (1984) 156 CLR 41, 96-97 *per* Mason J.
19. (2014) 130 LQR 608, 609. Referred to by Baker J in *Best v Ghose* [2018] IEHC 376 at [53].
20. *Ibid.* at 633.

their principals a number of different duties, many of which are of the same type owed by non-fiduciaries in similar contexts, "[o]nly one–the proscriptive fiduciary duty of loyalty–is unique to fiduciaries."[21] The key characteristics of a fiduciary relationship as set out by Millett LJ in *Bristol and West Building Society v Mothew*[22] have also been accepted as applicable in this jurisdiction. In her judgment in *Best v Ghose*[23] Baker J adopted that statement of principle and stated that '[i]t is, therefore, necessary to ascertain whether those elements of loyalty, an obligation to act in the interests of another, and an obligation not to make a secret profit and to act in good faith are present to a sufficient degree before the characteristics of fiduciary relationship can be found.' She continued as follows:

> I consider that the essential material characteristic of a fiduciary relationship arises where a person has both the power to act on behalf of another or to act in a way that impacts on the interests of another, and a responsibility to do so in the interests of that other person. The relevant elements include duties of loyalty, responsibility and control over matters that can impact on the interest of another, and a duty not to make a secret profit.[24]

As Feeney J stated in *Clements v Meagher*,[25] '[i]t is not possible to provide a complete definition of the categories of persons who occupy fiduciary positions. The categories of fiduciary relationships are not closed and it is well recognised that fiduciary duties may be owed notwithstanding the fact that the relationship in question does not fall within one of the settled categories of fiduciary relationships.' In addition, as Lord Woolf MR stated in *Attorney General v Blake*,[26] 'different categories possess different characteristics and attract different kinds of fiduciary obligation'.

While it is not possible to provide an exhaustive definition of the categories of persons who occupy fiduciary positions, generally speaking such individuals can be distinguished from those who are merely bound by contractual obligations by the fact that those in the former category are obliged to act in a completely selfless manner. The most commonly encountered examples of fiduciary relationships are those existing between trustee and beneficiary, agent

---

21. (2018) 32 Trust Law Int 22, 31.
22. [1998] Ch 1, 18. Quoted with approval by Fennelly J in *McMullen v McGinley* [2005] IESC 10 and by Baker J in *Best v Ghose* [2018] IEHC 376 at [48].
23. [2018] IEHC 376 at [66].
24. *Ibid.* at [67].
25. [2008] IEHC 258 at [3.1]. See also *Fermoy Fish Ltd v Canestar Ltd* [2015] IESC 93 at 5; *Best v Ghose* [2018] IEHC 376 at [45].
26. [1998] Ch 439, 454. As Lord Browne-Wilkinson commented in *Henderson v Merrett Syndicates Ltd* [1995] 2 AC 145, 206, 'the phrase "fiduciary duties" is a dangerous one, giving rise to a mistaken assumption that all fiduciaries owe the same duties in all circumstances'.

and principal, director and company and between partners, and although these categories are not closed, some limitations have been imposed on the extension of these obligations.[27] As Hogan J commented in *Irish Life and Permanent plc v Financial Services Ombudsman*,[28] '[w]hile the categories of fiduciaries are never closed, there is, I think, a reluctance to extend their boundaries beyond the traditional categories because to do so would effectively impose super-added duties of utmost good faith and complete disclosure to persons who never contracted to do so and thus potentially frustrate the ordinary workings of the commercial world.'

An example of a situation in which it may be significant to establish the existence of a fiduciary relationship is where a claim is made for an account. As Clarke J made clear in *Aforge Finance SAS v HSBC Institutional Trust Services (Ireland) Ltd*,[29] the trustee relationship is the most common example of a case where a plaintiff beneficiary will be entitled to an account without asserting any wrongdoing on the part of the trustee. However, he also stated that such an obligation will arise where the defendant owes a fiduciary duty to the plaintiff and subsequently in *Best v Ghose*,[30] Baker J agreed that 'an obligation to account is implicit in a fiduciary relationship'. It may therefore be important, as it was in the *Best* case, to establish whether such a fiduciary relationship exists. She stated as follows:

> If the relationship carries with it an obligation and duties equivalent to a duty of loyalty, or what is sometimes called a "duty of trust", then, that relationship is, for the purposes of the calling for an account, a relationship of a fiduciary nature or sufficiently equivalent to import a degree of obligation which may be of a higher order than that express in a contract. The elements may import a duty to account but not always other duties or rights present in a trust in a true sense.[31]

On the facts of the matter before her, Baker J was satisfied that the defendants had undertaken the management of a fund in circumstances which imported a duty of loyalty and an obligation of good faith and she concluded that the management contract contained sufficient elements of a fiduciary nature to import a duty to account.

The Key Obligations – The No-Conflict and No-Profit Rules

Avoiding a conflict between duty and self-interest has been referred to as the

27. See e.g. *Tito v Wadell (No. 2)* [1977] Ch 106.
28. [2012] IEHC 367 at [45].
29. [2010] 2 IR 688.
30. [2018] IEHC 376 at [42].
31. *Ibid.* at [68].

'irreducible core of the fiduciary obligation'.[32] As Lord Cranworth LC stated in *Aberdeen Railway Co. v Blaikie Brothers*,[33] 'It is a rule of universal application, that no one having [fiduciary] duties to discharge, shall be allowed to enter into engagements in which he has, or can have, a personal interest conflicting, or which may possibly conflict, with the interests of those whom he is bound to protect.' In the view of Lord Upjohn in *Boardman v Phipps*[34] this meant 'that the reasonable man looking at the relevant facts and circumstances of the particular case would think that there was a real sensible possibility of conflict; not that you could imagine some situation arising which might, in some conceivable possibility in events not contemplated as real sensible possibilities by any reasonable person, result in a conflict.'[35]

Another aspect of the so-called no-conflict rule is that a fiduciary should avoid placing himself in a situation where his duty to one principal will conflict with his duty to another principal. As Millett LJ commented in *Bristol & West Building Society v Mothew*,[36] '[a] fiduciary who acts for two principals with potentially conflicting interests without the informed consent of both is in breach of the obligation of undivided loyalty; he puts himself in a position where his duty to one principal *may* conflict with his duty to the other'. This principle had been made clear by Lord Jauncey delivering the judgment of the Privy Council in *Clark Boyce v Mouat*.[37] He stated that there is no general rule of law requiring that a solicitor should never act for both parties in a transaction where their interests may conflict, rather the position is that he may act provided that he has obtained the informed consent of both parties to his so acting.[38] In his view such informed consent means 'consent given in the knowledge that there is a conflict between the parties and that as a result the solicitor may be disabled from disclosing to each party the full knowledge which he possesses as to the transaction or may be disabled from giving advice to one party which conflicts with the interests of the other.'[39]

Another key obligation is that a fiduciary may not make any profit out of the fiduciary relationship.[40] As Lord Nicholls stated in *Attorney General v Blake*:[41]

---

32. Weinrib (1975) 25 U Tor LJ 1, 16.
33. (1854) 1 Macq 461, 471.
34. [1967] 2 AC 46, 124. See also *Coope v LCM Ligation Fund Pty Ltd* (2016) 333 ALR 524, 542.
35. Note that a trustee might be authorised either expressly or by implication by a trust instrument to act in a manner which might benefit him where he is also a beneficiary. This could arise, for example, in relation to a pension scheme, see *Edge v Pensions Ombudsman* [2000] Ch 602.
36. [1998] Ch 1, 18.
37. [1994] 1 AC 428.
38. See also *Marks and Spencer plc v Freshfields Bruckhaus Deringer* [2004] 1 WLR 2331, 2334.
39. [1994] 1 AC 428, 435.
40. The operation of the no-profit rule in the context of the trustee/beneficiary relationship is considered in more detail *infra* in Chapter 13 pp. 571-575.
41. [2001] 1 AC 268, 280.

> Equity reinforces the duty of fidelity owed by a trustee or fiduciary by requiring him to account for any profits he derives from his office or position. This ensures that trustees and fiduciaries are financially disinterested in carrying out their duties. They may not put themselves in a position where their duty and interest conflict. To this end they must not make any unauthorised profit. If they do, they are accountable.

It is clear from a number of decisions of the High Court of Australia that liability will only be imposed where the fiduciary obtains the benefit or gain by reason of his fiduciary position. So as Deane J commented in *Chan v Zacharia*,[42] a fiduciary will be liable 'to account for any benefit or gain obtained or received by reason of or by use of his fiduciary position or of opportunity or knowledge resulting from it: the objective is to preclude the fiduciary from actually misusing his position for his personal advantage.' This point was developed by French CJ and Keane J in a joint judgment in *Howard v Commissioner of Taxation*,[43] where they stated that '[i]f there is no possible conflict between personal interest and fiduciary duty, and if the gain or benefit is not obtained by use or by reason of the fiduciary position, the fiduciary is not liable to account for the gain or benefit.'

The fundamental principle that a trustee or other party in a fiduciary position will not be permitted to take advantage of his position to make a personal profit was also laid down in the following terms in this jurisdiction by Chatterton VC in *Gabbett v Lawder*:[44]

> The fundamental position upon which the doctrine of constructive trusts proceeds is, that no person in a fiduciary capacity shall be allowed to retain any advantage gained by him in his character as trustee. His *cestuis que trusts* are entitled to the benefit of any advantage so gained by him, to any addition or accretion to the trust estate which he may have acquired, and to all profit which he may have made by any dealing with it.

The relationship between these two key obligations, the so-called no-conflict and no-profit rules, has been the subject of much debate and they have sometimes been linked. As Lord Herschell stated in *Bray v Ford*,[45] '[i]t is an inflexible rule of a Court of Equity that a person in a fiduciary position … is

42. (1984) 154 CLR 178, 198-199.
43. (2014) 309 ALR 1, 13.
44. (1883) 11 LR Ir 295, 299. See also the *dictum* of Chatterton VC in *Kelly v Kelly* (1874) 8 IR Eq 403, 406: 'It is the great principle that no person in a fiduciary position accepting any benefit attributable in any degree to that fiduciary position can be allowed to enjoy such benefit for himself.' See also *M'Cracken v M'Clelland* (1877) IR 11 Eq 172, 176; *Armstrong v Armstrong* (1880) 7 LR Ir 207, 218.
45. [1896] AC 44, 51. Quoted with approval by Lindsay J in *Re Drexel Burnham Lambert UK Pension Plan* [1995] 1 WLR 32, 37. See also *Swain v The Law Society* [1982] 1 WLR 17, 37 *per* Oliver J.

not, unless otherwise expressly provided, entitled to make a profit; he is not allowed to put himself in a position where his interest and duty conflict.' In *Boardman v Phipps*[46] Lord Upjohn went as far as to suggest that the no-profit rule was merely part of the wider no-conflict rule. However, Conaglen has asserted that Lord Upjohn's observation is incorrect 'insofar as it suggests that the profit rule is merely a subset of the conflict rule, as not all profit cases necessarily involve an identifiable conflict between duty and interest.'[47] The better view certainly seems to be that the principles are distinct. In the decision of the High Court of Australia in *Chan v Zacharia*,[48] Deane J commented that while the no-conflict rule was designed 'to preclude the fiduciary from being swayed by considerations of personal interest', the no-profit rule was designed 'to preclude the fiduciary from actually misusing his position for personal advantage.'[49] More recently Smith has asserted that '[t]he no-conflict rules are about potentially tainted exercises of judgement, and they allow legal acts made in such situations to be set aside. The no-profit rule allows the recovery of profits, regardless of whether there is any legal act that is subject to being set aside.'[50]

Fully Informed Consent

Where fully informed consent has been given to a transaction, a fiduciary's actions are regarded as authorised and he will not be liable to account. So, a trustee can avoid being liable to account where he purchases trust property if he obtains the fully informed consent of all the beneficiaries.[51] However, as Lord Hodson stated in *Boardman v Phipps*,[52] nothing short of 'fully informed consent' could aid a fiduciary who had taken advantage of the opportunity provided by that position to make a profit.[53] Conaglen has suggested in the context of the fair-dealing rule[54] that fiduciary doctrine requires the consent to be of a high quality; 'there must be full disclosure on the part of the fiduciary of all material facts within his control ... before the fiduciary's conflicting personal interest in the transaction is effectively neutralised and the transaction immunised against

---

46. [1967] 2 AC 46, 123.
47. (2005) 121 LQR 452, 467.
48. (1984) 154 CLR 178, 198.
49. *Ibid.* at 199.
50. (2014) 130 LQR 608, 627.
51. *Ex parte Lacey* (1802) 6 Ves 625, 626. See also in the context of a potential conflict of interest between two principals, *Bristol & West Building Society v Mothew* [1998] Ch 1, 18-19; *Marks and Spencer plc v Freshfields Bruckhaus Deringer* [2004] 1 WLR 2331, 2334.
52. [1967] 2 AC 46, 109.
53. See also *Ex parte James* (1803) 8 Ves 337, 353 which suggest that the consent must be 'freely given, after full information'.
54. This is the principle which applies where a trustee purchases property from a beneficiary. See further Chapter 13 pp. 574-575.

the fiduciary conflict principle.'[55] This is in line with the comments of Arden LJ in *Murad v Al-Saraj*,[56] where she said that to obtain a valid consent, 'there would have to have been full and frank disclosure … of all relevant matters.'

The issue of consent was also considered by Charleton J in the context of a trustee/beneficiary relationship in *Greene v Coady*.[57] He said that it is clear that a trustee may proceed to act in a situation where there is a potential conflict between duties or between duty and interest, provided fully informed consent is given by the principals. He added that '[t]his does not require the disclosure of all information which is material to the transaction and the conflict, provided that the consenting party is aware of all material facts and is enabled to make a decision to retain the trustees notwithstanding.'[58] However, given the strict approach generally taken by the courts towards the no-conflict rule, a fiduciary should err on the side of caution in this regard.

Strict Application of the Rules

Both the no-conflict and no-profit rules are strictly applied. So, a fiduciary may be held liable to account for profits made as a result of his fiduciary position even where he has been acting in good faith and where the principal would also not have benefited without the fiduciary's actions.[59] The extent of the rather restrictive approach taken by the courts in this area is well summarised by Jones:[60]

> Once a fiduciary is shown to be in breach of his duty of loyalty he must disgorge any benefit gained even though he acted honestly and in his principal's best interests, even though his principal could not otherwise have obtained the benefit, and even though the benefit was obtained through the use of the fiduciary's own assets and in consequence of his personal skill and judgment.

Lord Herschell suggested in *Bray v Ford*[61] that the no-conflict and no-profit rules were 'based on the consideration that, human nature being what it is, there is danger, in such circumstances, of the person holding a fiduciary position being swayed by interest rather than by duty, and thus prejudicing those whom he was bound to protect.' Arden LJ in *Murad v Al-Saraj*[62] put forward the view

55. [2006] CLJ 366, 391.
56. [2005] EWCA Civ 959 at [71].
57. [2015] 1 IR 385.
58. *Ibid* at 404.
59. *Regal (Hastings) Ltd v Gulliver* [1967] 2 AC 134; *Boardman v Phipps* [1967] 2 AC 46.
60. Jones (1968) 84 LQR 472, 474.
61. [1896] AC 44, 51.
62. [2005] EWCA Civ 959 at [74].

that stringent liability was imposed on a fiduciary as a deterrent and said that 'to provide an incentive to fiduciaries to resist the temptation to misconduct themselves, the law imposes exacting standards on fiduciaries and an extensive liability to account.'

Lowry has questioned the correctness of applying a 'uniform set of inflexible rules to govern all fiduciaries irrespective of the particular circumstances in which they are operating'.[63] Langbein has also advocated allowing a trustee to defend a transaction on the grounds that it was prudently entered into in the best interests of the beneficiaries.[64] In his view, '[a]llowing a best interest defense would cut back on the mischief worked under the sole interest rule while still maintaining the deterrent to trustee disloyalty'.[65] Similarly, in the course of her judgment in *Murad v Al-Saraj*[66] Arden LJ commented that '[i]t may be that the time has come when the court should revisit the operation of the inflexible rule of equity in harsh circumstances, as where the trustee has acted in perfect good faith and without any deception or concealment, and in the belief that he was acting in the best interests of the beneficiary.'

However, Conaglen has argued against any relaxation of the strict standards imposed on fiduciaries.[67] He has suggested that the debate should not be about relaxing the stringency of the accounting obligation required by fiduciary doctrine, but about whether existing mechanisms for obtaining authorisation are sufficient. He rejects the idea of adopting a discretionary approach to liability 'because it would undermine the deterrence that the account of profits represents for fiduciaries.'[68] Conaglen argues that '[i]t would, therefore, be a mistake to allow fiduciaries to hold out hope of retaining some of their unauthorised profits, because that sort of hope is itself the sort of temptation against which fiduciary doctrine is designed to strike.'

Commercial Relationships

As Virgo has commented, '[t]he identification of fiduciary duties, especially in a commercial context, can have profound consequences on the risks inherent in such relationships, since the characterisation of the defendant as a fiduciary will often mean that he or she bears the risk of things going wrong.'[69] While he acknowledges that many of the recognised categories of fiduciary relationship

---

63. Lowry (1994) 45 NILQ 1, 2. Note also the comments of the English Law Commission in Consultation Paper No. 124 (1992) para. 2.4.2.
64. Langbein (2005) 114 Yale LJ 929.
65. *Ibid.* at 990.
66. [2005] EWCA Civ 959 at [82]. Jonathan Parker LJ also said (at [121]) that he could envisage the possibility that at some time in the future the House of Lords might consider relaxing the no-conflict rule in appropriate cases. See further Conaglen [2006] CLJ 278; McInnes (2006) 122 LQR 11.
67. See [2006] CLJ 278; [2011] CLJ 548.
68. [2011] CLJ 548, 577.
69. Virgo, *The Principles of Equity and Trusts* (3rd ed., 2018) p.421.

operate in a commercial context, he points out that there are concerns about attaching fiduciary duties to an *ad hoc* commercial relationship in which they have no legitimate role to play.

Certainly in England and Australia there have been signs of a reluctance on the part of the judiciary to extend the application of fiduciary obligations beyond their recognised categories more broadly to commercial relationships. This attitude is exemplified by the following statement of Lord Mustill in the decision of the Privy Council in *Re Goldcorp Exchange*:[70]

> No doubt the fact that one person is placed in a particular position *vis-à-vis* another through the medium of a contract does not necessarily mean that he does not also owe fiduciary duties to that other by virtue of being in that position. But the essence of a fiduciary relationship is that it creates obligations of a different character from those deriving from the contract itself. Their Lordships have not heard in argument any submission which went beyond suggesting that by virtue of being a fiduciary the company was obliged honestly and conscientiously to do what it had by contract promised to do. Many commercial relationships involve just such a reliance by one party on the other, and to introduce the whole new dimension into such relationships which would flow from giving them a fiduciary character would (as it seems to their Lordships) have adverse consequences far exceeding those foreseen by Atkin LJ in *Re Wait* [1927] 1 Ch 606.

Dawson J in the decision of the High Court of Australia in *Hospital Products Ltd v United States Surgical Corporation*[71] also warned of the 'undesirability of extending fiduciary duties to commercial relationships and the anomaly of imposing those duties where the parties are at arm's length from one another.' Lord Millett, writing extra-judicially, referred to this statement and expressed the view that '[i]f this warning is not observed then equity's place in the commercial world will be put at risk: it will be found to do more harm than good.'[72] He added that '[i]t is of the first importance not to impose fiduciary obligations on parties to a purely commercial relationship who deal with each other at arms' length and can be expected to look after their own interests.'[73]

Mason CJ, the former Chief Justice of Australia, writing extra-judicially, has acknowledged that there has been a disinclination amongst judges to make a finding that a fiduciary relationship exists when the arrangement between the parties is of a purely commercial nature. However, he points out that the courts have affirmed that such a relationship may exist in this context and suggests that 'a fiduciary relationship will arise out of a commercial arrangement when one

70. [1995] 1 AC 74, 98.
71. (1984) 156 CLR 41, 149.
72. (1998) 114 LQR 214, 215.
73. *Ibid.* at 217-218.

party undertakes to act in the interests of the other party rather than in his or her own interests in relation to a particular matter or aspect of their arrangement and that other party, being unable to look after his or her own interests in that matter or aspect of the arrangement, is basically dependent upon the first party acting in conformity with his or her undertaking.'[74]

While there has been little debate on this issue in this jurisdiction, as noted above, Hogan J commented in *Irish Life and Permanent plc v Financial Services Ombudsman*[75] that there is a reluctance to extend the boundaries of fiduciary relationships beyond the traditional categories because this would effectively involve imposing additional duties of utmost good faith and complete disclosure and would 'potentially frustrate the ordinary workings of the commercial world.' So, the position appears to be that while it must be acknowledged that fiduciary obligations do arise in some recognised categories of commercial relationship, such as between a director and a company and in relation to joint ventures, there may be a reluctance to extend these obligations beyond such categories.

Liability for Breach of Fiduciary Duty

A useful summary of the extent of a fiduciary's obligation to account is set out by Conaglen in the following terms:

> It is well-settled that a fiduciary must account for profits that have been generated from his fiduciary position or in circumstances involving a conflict between the fiduciary's duty and his interest. The fiduciary need not account if the profit or conflict was properly authorised, in which case there was no breach of fiduciary duty. But in the absence of such authorisation, the fiduciary must account for all of the profit that has been made in breach of fiduciary duty, other than insofar as the court grants an equitable allowance to the fiduciary for work done in generating that profit.[76]

A question which must also be addressed is whether the opportunity for profit actually derived from the fiduciary relationship. In order to found liability it will be necessary to establish a connection between the fiduciary position and the profit made.

Clearly where a fiduciary has been unjustly enriched at his principal's expense, the imposition of liability can be readily justified. However, where the fiduciary has acted in an honest manner and the principal has not suffered any loss as a result of the former's conduct, the question of whether the fiduciary should be liable to account for any profit made is, in principle,

74. (1994) LQR 238, 245-246.
75. [2012] IEHC 367 at [45].
76. [2011] CLJ 548.

less straightforward. The authorities suggest that unjust enrichment is not a prerequisite for the imposition of liability[77] and 'the liability of a fiduciary to account does not depend on whether the person to whom the fiduciary duty was owed could himself have made the profit'.[78] Equally, as Lord Nicholls stated in *Attorney General v Blake*,[79] '[w]hether the beneficiaries or persons to whom the fiduciary duty is owed suffered any loss by the impugned transaction is altogether irrelevant.'

A further important issue is the nature of the liability which should be imposed and where a fiduciary has acted in breach of his fiduciary duty there are a number of possible forms of remedy. The rationale behind the imposition of a constructive trust in such circumstances was well summarised by McLachlin J delivering the judgment of the majority of the Supreme Court of Canada in *Soulos v Korkontzilas*:[80]

> The constructive trust imposed for breach of fiduciary relationship thus serves not only to do the justice between the parties that good conscience requires, but to hold fiduciaries and people in positions of trust to the high standards of trust and probity that commercial and other social institutions require if they are to function effectively.

However, the proprietary remedy of a constructive trust may have far-reaching consequences for third parties, particularly where the fiduciary has insufficient funds to meet his creditors' demands. The imposition of a constructive trust will also lead to the principal obtaining the benefit of any further increase in value in the profit made by the fiduciary. It has been questioned whether such a proprietary remedy is justified where it leads to the principal obtaining a windfall at the expense of the fiduciary's general creditors.[81]

Personal liability to account for any profits made may be a preferable form of remedy where a fiduciary has acted honestly and has not been unjustly enriched at his principal's expense. If this form of liability is imposed, a fiduciary will be liable to hand over any profit made. It was described by Arden LJ in *Murad v Al-Saraj*[82] as 'a procedure to ensure the restitution of profits which ought to have been made for the beneficiary.' Alternatively, where loss has been suffered, the fiduciary may be liable to pay compensation for this loss. In the latter case,

---

77. This view is supported by the conclusion reached by the majority of the Supreme Court of Canada in *Soulos v Korkontzilas* (1997) 147 DLR (4th) 214. See also the decision of the High Court of Australia in *Warman International Ltd v Dwyer* (1995) 182 CLR 544, 557.
78. *Murad v Al-Saraj* [2005] EWCA Civ 959 at [59] *per* Arden LJ.
79. [2001] 1 AC 268, 280.
80. (1997) 147 DLR (4th) 214, 227.
81. Jones [1994] Conv 156, 164. See also Hicks [2010] CLJ 287, 317. See further *infra* pp. 280-281.
82. [2005] EWCA Civ 959 at [85].

it is clear from the decision of Court of Appeal in *Swindle v Harrison*[83] that it must be established that the loss suffered by the principal would not have occurred 'but for' the breach of fiduciary duty. These remedies are alternatives, so a plaintiff must choose between them. As Lord Nicholls stated delivering the judgment of the Privy Council in *Tang Man Sit v Capacious Investments Ltd*,[84] '[f]aced with alternative and inconsistent remedies a plaintiff must choose, or elect, between them. He cannot have both.'

The uncertainty about the appropriate form of remedy to impose for breach of fiduciary duty has not been helped by the lack of clarity in terminology in many judgments. So, for example, in *Boardman v Phipps*,[85] there were frequent references to a 'liability to account' in the speeches of the House of Lords, but it also affirmed the order of the trial judge, which it is now clear involved the imposition of a constructive trust.[86]

Finally, it should be noted that in some circumstances a transaction entered into by a fiduciary may be voidable and liable to be rescinded by the principal where *restitution in integrum* is possible.[87]

The Fiduciary Position of Trustees

Not all duties of a trustee are fiduciary in nature but express trustees are regarded as being in a fiduciary relationship with the beneficiaries to whom they owe fiduciary duties. In addition, it should be noted that, as Lord Scott commented in *Hilton v Barker Booth and Eastwood*,[88] 'not every breach of duty by a fiduciary is a breach of fiduciary duty'.

The 'fundamental position' referred to above by Chatterton VC in *Gabbett v Lawder*,[89] that no person in a fiduciary capacity shall be allowed to retain any advantage gained by him in his capacity as trustee, applies strictly to trustees and personal representatives. Charleton J explained this principle in the following terms in *Greene v Coady*:[90]

> Since trusts deal with other people's property and since trustees must be faithful to deal properly with trust funds, trustees owe to the trust, and thus to the beneficiaries, a duty of good faith and fidelity. Trustees are not entitled to put themselves into a situation of conflict of interest whereby

83. [1997] 4 All ER 705.
84. [1996] AC 514, 521.
85. [1967] 2 AC 46.
86. See Millett [2012] CLJ 583, 609; Hicks [2013] Conv 232, 236; Hicks (2014) 65 NILQ 1, 2.
87. See further Chapter 17.
88. [2005] 1 WLR 567, 574, referring to the comments of Millett LJ in *Bristol & West Building Society v Mothew* [1998] Ch 1, 16-17.
89. (1883) 11 LR Ir 295.
90. [2015] 1 IR 385, 402.

they may be influenced by how they themselves may profit from any decision which the body of trustees may make.

In the circumstances of the case before him, Charleton J concluded that the trustees had not been influenced by a conflict of interest, that they were conscious of their duties to the beneficiaries and that they had done their best to exercise those duties honestly and in good faith.

These principles also apply to a varying degree to other categories of persons who act in a fiduciary capacity. It is proposed to examine a number of situations which are relevant primarily, although not exclusively, to persons acting as trustees and personal representatives, and then to consider some of the circumstances in which liability will be imposed in the context of other types of fiduciaries.

Renewal of a Lease

A common situation which will give rise to the creation of a constructive trust is where a trustee of leasehold property obtains a renewal of the lease in his own name. It was circumstances such as these which led to the formulation of the so-called rule in *Keech v Sandford*,[91] which has formed the basis for the rather wider principle enunciated by Chatterton VC in *Gabbett v Lawder* above.[92] In *Keech*, a trustee held a lease of the profits of Romford Market on trust for an infant. Before the expiration of the lease he applied for a renewal for the infant's benefit but the lessor refused to renew on the grounds that the infant could not enter into the usual covenants. The lessor indicated that he would be willing to give the trustee the lease instead and the latter accepted the renewal in his own name. It was held that despite the trustee's attempt to obtain a renewal for the infant's benefit, he must be regarded as holding the lease for the latter's benefit and was obliged to pay over to the infant the profits which he received. King LC stated: 'This may seem hard, that the trustee is the only person of all mankind who might not have the lease; but it is very proper that the rule should be strictly pursued'.[93]

This precise principle was outlined as follows by Chatterton VC in *Gabbett v Lawder*,[94] albeit in an *obiter* capacity:

91. (1726) Sel Cas T King 61.
92. A number of commentators have questioned the fairness of a rigid application of the principle in *Keech v Sandford*, which Finn has stated is applied 'in an arbitrary and technical fashion irrespective of any actual conflict of duty and interest, or of any actual misuse of a position of trust.' (see *Fiduciary Obligations* (1977) p. 261). It has also been suggested by Hicks [2010] CLJ 287, 319 that the decision in *Keech v Sandford* offered little to support the broad remedial principle subsequently attributed to it.
93. (1726) Sel Cas T King 61, 62.
94. (1883) 11 LR Ir 295, 299.

> It has long been settled by a current of authorities that a trustee of a leasehold interest who obtains a renewal of the lease, whether by covenant or custom, or by the voluntary act of the reversioner, comes within this principle, and that he cannot hold the interest he so acquired for his own benefit, but as a constructive trustee of it for his *cestuis que trusts*.

In this context any advantage or profit derived by a trustee is deemed by equity to be engrafted onto the property held on trust, a process known in this jurisdiction as the doctrine of graft. The effect and ambit of this doctrine was discussed by Fitzgibbon LJ in *Dempsey v Ward*[95] and it is clear that it extends beyond trustees to other classes of individuals, with executors and administrators being specifically mentioned by Fitzgibbon LJ. Under the rule in *Keech v Sandford*, where a trustee or person in a fiduciary position surrenders an old lease with a view to obtaining a new one, he will be held to be a constructive trustee, and this principle was illustrated in the context of an executor by the decision of *M'Cracken v M'Clelland*.[96] There, an executor surrendered a holding which was subject to the Ulster Custom while the old tenancy was still in existence and, in compliance with the custom, was given a new tenancy on his own behalf. Chatterton VC commented that he was at a loss to understand how the defendant, by virtue of the position which he occupied as executor of the testator's estate, could contend that he was entitled to retain the benefit of the new tenancy for himself and concluded that it was held on a constructive trust for the persons entitled under the will.

The doctrine of graft was also applied in the context of an administrator of an estate in *Kelly v Kelly*,[97] where a widow and administratrix of her husband's estate continued in possession of land held on a tenancy from year to year. The landlord determined the tenancy by serving a notice to quit and the administratrix did not oppose this and was left in occupation at the same rent. It was held that while her conduct did not amount to fraud, the new tenancy was a graft on the old one and she was regarded as being in occupation of the premises as constructive trustee for the next of kin who would have been entitled to the original tenancy on her husband's death. Similarly, the doctrine of graft has been held to apply to the guardian of an infant,[98] and to a person managing the property of a lunatic.[99] A further category of persons to whom the doctrine applies is that of a limited owner, which is illustrated by the decision of the Irish Court of Appeal in *Re Brady's Estate*.[100] A testator bequeathed leasehold premises on trust to permit his wife to use and enjoy these for the remainder of the term so long as she should live and continue to be his widow. The widow,

---

95. [1899] 1 IR 463, 474-475.
96. (1877) IR 11 Eq 172. See also *Re Egan* [1906] 1 IR 320.
97. (1874) IR 8 Eq 403.
98. *Quinton v Frith* (1868) IR 2 Eq 396, 494.
99. *Smyth v Byrne* [1914] 1 IR 53.
100. [1920] 1 IR 170.

who did not remarry, remained on in beneficial possession of the lands for a period of three years after the expiry of the lease and then obtained a new lease of the premises in her own name. The Court of Appeal held that the widow was necessarily in the position of a limited owner only, in addition to being the executor and trustee under the will, and that the renewal of the lease which she obtained in her own name must be deemed to be a graft on the former one.

However, the doctrine of graft is not unlimited in its ambit;[101] although it was applied in *Hunter v Allen*[102] to a case of tenants in common, Barton J commented that *Dempsey v Ward*[103] was a useful decision in that 'it served to remind us that the frontiers of the doctrine of graft have in this country been reached; and that the doctrine should be cautiously applied.' In *Dempsey* it was held that there was no graft when the widow of a previous tenant of an expired lease obtained a new tenancy on her own behalf on the basis that there was nothing to connect these tenancies. Fitzgibbon LJ commented that 'to have a graft at all, there must still be life in the old stock'[104] and said that he entertained grave doubts about the extent to which the doctrine had been developed in this jurisdiction.

The crucial question which must be addressed in determining whether the new interest will be engrafted onto the old is whether the person obtaining the renewal occupies a fiduciary position. In the case of a trustee, there appears to be an almost irrebuttable presumption of a constructive trust arising.[105] This has been confirmed by the following *dicta* of Chatterton VC in *Gabbett v Lawder*:[106]

> Where a trustee obtains a renewal of a lease this Court will not allow the trustee to say that he did not obtain the additional interest as trustee, or that he procured it from personal favour to himself, or from the refusal of the landlord to deal with the *cestuis que trusts*, or for any similar reason. If his position could have caused or even contributed to his obtaining the advantage, it is in my opinion enough; and the Court will not undertake the difficult and often impossible task of investigating the motives of the parties to the transaction. If it results in either gain to the trustee or loss to the *cestuis que trusts*, the trustee is liable to hand over to them the one or make good the other.

However, as Romer LJ stated in *Re Biss*,[107] 'where the person renewing the lease does not clearly occupy a fiduciary position [he] is only held to be a constructive trustee of the renewed lease if, in respect of the old lease, he occupied some

101. *Robinson v Crosse & Blackwell Ltd* [1940] IR 56.
102. [1907] 1 IR 212.
103. [1899] 1 IR 463.
104. *Ibid.* at 474.
105. *Re Biss* [1903] 2 Ch 40, 56 *per* Collins MR.
106. (1883) 11 LR Ir 295, 299-300.
107. [1903] 2 Ch 40, 61.

special position and owed, by virtue of that position, a duty towards the other persons interested,' and so the presumption of a constructive trust will ordinarily be rebuttable.[108] Where the person taking the renewal owes neither a fiduciary obligation nor a special duty, clearly no constructive trust will arise.[109]

Cretney has commented that the distinction between persons who act in a fiduciary capacity and those who do not is a difficult one to draw and while he accepts that it may be justifiable to impose a special onus on trustees, he asks 'why should it be contrary to public policy to allow a trustee to rebut a presumption of misbehaviour?'[110] He argues that while it is quite acceptable that there should be a high onus on a trustee who has obtained a renewal of a lease which may only be discharged in rare cases, this does not justify the principle that the rule in *Keech v Sandford* should be an absolute one. However, as Oakley has commented, although such a 'stringent penal rule' is difficult to justify in a modern context so far removed from the conditions which gave rise to it, there is no evidence of any retrenchment from this position by the judiciary either in England or in this jurisdiction.[111]

Purchase of the Reversion in a Lease

The question of whether a trustee or other person in a fiduciary position may purchase the reversion of a lease held in trust or for his principal for his own benefit has been the subject of some controversy. Traditionally, the rule in *Keech v Sandford* was applied in a limited way to such a purchase and a constructive trust would arise if the lease was renewable by contract or custom or where the trustee obtained the reversion by virtue of his position as lessee.[112] This principle was applied by Chatterton VC in *Gabbett v Lawder*,[113] where the administrator of the estate of an intestate held lands under a lease as trustee. The fee simple reversion of these lands became vested in the Church Temporalities Commissioners who were authorised to sell it but before doing so they were bound to offer it to the lessee at a price to be named by them. The reversion was offered to the lessee who declined to buy it on the ground that the price was too high but he then bought it for himself at a public auction for a lower sum. It was held by Chatterton VC that in the circumstances the administrator became a constructive trustee of the reversion for the persons beneficially

108. *Chan v Zacharia* (1984) 154 CLR 178, 201-202 *per* Deane J.
109. *Robinson v Crosse & Blackwell Ltd* [1940] IR 56, where Johnston J found that the defendants occupied neither a fiduciary nor 'quasi fiduciary' relationship. See also *Savage v Dunningham* [1974] Ch 181.
110. Cretney (1969) 33 Conv 161.
111. Oakley, *Parker and Mellows: The Modern Law of Trusts* (9th ed., 2008) p. 390.
112. See Cretney (1969) 33 Conv 161, 162. See also Jackson (1968) 31 MLR 707, 709. This seems to have been the position originally accepted in England, see *Randall v Russell* (1817) 3 Mer 190; *Longton v Wilsby* (1897) 76 LT 770. See also the *dicta* of Wilberforce J in *Phipps v Boardman* [1964] 2 All ER 187, 201-202.
113. (1883) 11 LR Ir 295.

entitled to the personal estate of the deceased although he was entitled to the costs incurred by him in purchasing the reversion.

The authorities in England now appear to support the imposition of an absolute prohibition against the purchase of the reversion by a fiduciary irrespective of the circumstances in which this occurs and even where the fiduciary is not a trustee or personal representative. In *Protheroe v Protheroe*[114] a husband held the leasehold interest in the family home, which it was agreed he held on trust for himself and his wife in equal shares. After the parties had separated, the husband bought the freehold reversion and it was held by the Court of Appeal that the wife was entitled equally with the husband to the proceeds of sale of the freehold. While it has been argued[115] that this conclusion can also be attributed to a result of a desire on the part of the court to do justice between the spouses rather than by way of application of strict principles which should apply as between trustee and beneficiary, Lord Denning MR made the following general statement: 'There is a long established rule of equity from *Keech v Sandford* downwards that if a trustee, who owns the leasehold, gets in the freehold, that freehold belongs to the trust and he cannot take the property for himself.'[116] This principle was followed without reference to the earlier authorities in this area in *Thompson's Trustee v Heaton*,[117] where Pennycuick VC described Lord Denning's *dictum* as 'an application of the broad principle that a trustee must not make a profit out of the trust estate'.[118]

It is unlikely that the courts in this jurisdiction will take quite such a restrictive view of this position where a fiduciary purchases the reversion on a lease and it is probable that a trust will only arise in the circumstances outlined by Chatterton VC in *Gabbett v Lawder* or where the fiduciary has clearly taken advantage of his position as lessee to obtain this benefit. However, having regard to the tenor of the authorities in the area, the onus will undoubtedly lie on the fiduciary to establish that he has not acted improperly, particularly where he occupies the position of trustee.

Competition with Trust Business

As we have seen above, a trustee must not place himself in a situation where his duty to the trust and his own personal interest may conflict. A fundamental

114. [1968] 1 All ER 1111.
115. Hayton, Matthews and Mitchell, *Underhill and Hayton: The Law Relating to Trusts and Trustees* (19th ed., 2016) p.535.
116. [1968] 1 All ER 1111, 1112.
117. [1974] 1 WLR 605.
118. *Ibid.* at 612. Jackson has criticised this decision on the grounds that in view of the categorisation laid down by Collins MR in *Re Biss* [1903] 2 Ch 40 of the types of relationships which will give rise to an irrebuttable presumption of a constructive trust arising, there should be at most a rebuttable presumption of a trust where a partner as opposed to a trustee obtains the reversion on a partnership lease. See (1975) 38 MLR 226.

principle exists which prevents a trustee or other party in a fiduciary position from taking advantage of his position to make a personal profit and he will be liable to account for any profit made or property acquired as a result to the persons equitably entitled to the property.[119] One situation which will obviously give rise to concern is where a trustee derives profits from a business which can be said to be in competition with any business carried on by the trust and this question was considered in detail by Chatterton VC in *Moore v McGlynn*.[120] The testator, who was a shopkeeper and postmaster, bequeathed all his property to his brother and son to be held on trust and managed by them for the benefit of his wife and children, and he directed that his brother should be entitled to a salary for managing the business. The brother was appointed postmaster and carried on this role in the same premises for a number of years. Subsequently, he set up his own business in the same town and opened the post office there. The question which had to be determined by the court was whether a trust could be imposed for the benefit of the testator's estate in relation to the new premises and business carried on by the testator's brother. Chatterton VC rejected this argument in the following terms: 'I am not prepared to hold that a trustee is guilty of a breach of trust in setting up for himself in a similar line of business in the neighbourhood, provided that he does not resort to deception, or solicitation of custom from persons dealing at the old shop'. However, he continued by saying:

> It is plain that the setting up a shop in a small town to a certain extent in rivalry with another must tend more or less to injure the business of any similar shop in the locality, and I think there would be an inconsistency between the duties of the defendant … as trustee and manager of the testator's business, and the necessary personal interest which he must take in his own … I am of opinion that his new position disqualifies him from remaining any longer a trustee, and it would have been better for him to have procured his removal from the trusteeship before setting up for himself. He should not be continued in a position where his duties and his self interest may conflict.[121]

This rather lenient approach has met with some criticism and can be contrasted with the stricter view taken by Clauson J in *Re Thomson*,[122] where an injunction was granted restraining a trustee from carrying on a yacht brokerage business in the same town as that in which a similar business had been managed by him and his co-trustees on behalf of the trust. Clauson J said that having regard to the special nature of the business which he was pursuing, the defendant trustee would have been entering into engagements which would or might conflict

119. *Re Jarvis* [1958] 1 WLR 815, 819 *per* Upjohn J.
120. [1894] 1 IR 74.
121. *Ibid.* at 89-90.
122. [1930] 1 Ch 203.

with the interests of the beneficiaries as he would be obtaining commission for himself which might otherwise have been obtained on the beneficiaries' behalf. It can be argued that the decision in *Thomson* was influenced by the extremely specialised nature of the business in question. Certainly, it would seem unduly restrictive to impose a constructive trust where a trustee continues to carry on an existing business in competition with one to which he is subsequently appointed trustee. However, it is also doubtful whether it should be necessary to establish a motive of 'deception, or solicitation of custom' in order for a constructive trust to arise and it is arguable that the approach of Chatterton VC in *Moore* was unduly lenient and might not be followed.

Other Types of Fiduciary Relationships

Introduction

As noted above, Woolf MR commented in *Attorney General v Blake*[123] that 'there is more than one category of fiduciary relationship and the different categories possess different characteristics and attract different kinds of fiduciary obligation'. It is now proposed to examine some of the general principles which may apply in more detail, both in relation to the circumstances in which liability may be imposed and with reference to some specific types of fiduciary relationships.

The Liability of a Fiduciary to Account for Secret Commissions and Bribes

As a general principle, a fiduciary may not accept secret commissions or bribes arising out of a transaction in which he is acting on behalf of a principal without the knowledge and consent of his principal. An examination of the authorities in this area shows that the boundaries of the types of relationships which can be categorised as fiduciary are not clear and that such a classification may to an extent depend on the remedy which a court feels is justified in the circumstances of a case. For the purposes of imposing liability to account for any secret profits or commissions received, the interpretation placed on the term 'fiduciary' has always been a fairly liberal one. This is illustrated by the decision in *Reading v Attorney-General*,[124] in which a British Army sergeant was held to be liable to account to the Crown in relation to monies which he received for assisting in the smuggling of goods on the grounds that he had used his uniform and the privileges which attached to it to carry out these activities.

Traditionally, where a fiduciary received a secret commission as a result of his position, he was liable as a constructive trustee of these monies. In *Williams v Barton*[125] a trustee was employed by a stockbroking firm on terms which

123. [1998] Ch 439, 454.
124. [1951] AC 507. See also *Attorney-General v Goddard* (1929) 98 LJ KB 743.
125. [1927] 2 Ch 9.

entitled him to half the commission earned by the firm on business introduced by him. His recommendation that the firm be used to value trust securities was followed and he was held liable to account as a constructive trustee in respect of the commission which he earned from this business. However, it was generally accepted on the authority of the decision of *Lister & Co. v Stubbs*[126] that where a fiduciary received a bribe from a third party, although he was liable to account, he was not regarded as a constructive trustee of this sum.[127] Attempts were made to justify this position on the grounds that the use of the fiduciary position to exact a bribe in these circumstances did not deprive the beneficiary or principal of property which belonged or ought to have belonged to him.[128]

The imposition of a personal, as opposed to a proprietary, remedy has important practical consequences; namely that funds cannot be traced in equity into property into which they might be converted and the beneficiary or principal cannot recover any profit made through the use of the money or acquire any preferential rights should the fiduciary become bankrupt.[129] The rather anomalous result that a person who obtained a bribe might be merely obliged to account for its value, whereas a fiduciary who had earned a commission in good faith might be held to be a constructive trustee of this sum, was the subject of criticism. One view was that the imposition of a proprietary remedy should be confined to situations where a beneficiary has been deprived of property which he would otherwise have obtained. However, the alternative argument was that a constructive trust should be imposed in both sets of circumstances on the grounds that a fiduciary should not be allowed to derive *any* advantage from acting in a manner contrary to his fiduciary obligations or from placing himself in a situation where his duties and personal interests might conflict.

While these issues have yet to be addressed by the courts in this jurisdiction, the decision of the Privy Council in *Attorney-General for Hong Kong v Reid*[130] appeared to have gone some way towards resolving many of the anomalies which had developed in this area. An application to renew the caveats lodged against the titles to properties bought by the first named respondent with bribes which he had accepted in breach of his fiduciary duty was refused by the Court of Appeal of New Zealand but was allowed on appeal by the Privy Council. It was held that when a bribe is accepted by a fiduciary in breach of his duty, he holds it on a constructive trust for the person to whom that duty is owed and to the extent to which they represented bribes received by the first named respondent, the New Zealand properties were held in trust for the Crown. As Lord Templeman stated:

---

126. (1890) 45 Ch D 1.
127. See also *Metropolitan Bank v Heiron* (1880) 5 Ex D 319.
128. Note that Millett commented [1993] RLR 7, 29 that the decision in *Lister* could not be supported 'as a matter of policy, principle or authority'.
129. See further Worthington [2013] CLJ 720, 724.
130. [1994] 1 AC 324. See also Oakley [1995] CLJ 377.

> The rule must be that property which a trustee obtains by use of knowledge acquired as trustee becomes trust property. The rule must, *a fortiori*, apply to a bribe accepted by a trustee for a guilty criminal purpose which injures the *cestui que trust*. The trustee is only one example of a fiduciary and the same rule applies to all other fiduciaries who accept bribes.[131]

Lord Templeman added that if the property representing the bribe decreases in value the fiduciary must pay the difference between that value and the initial amount of the bribe. If the property increases in value, the fiduciary is not entitled to any surplus in excess of the initial value of the bribe because he is not allowed to make a profit out of a breach of duty. The decision of *Lister & Co. v Stubbs* was rejected as being inconsistent with the principle that a fiduciary should not benefit from his own breach of duty and that he should account for the bribe as soon as he receives it. Lord Templeman therefore concluded that '[f]rom these principles it would appear to follow that the bribe and the property from time to time representing the bribe are held on a constructive trust for the person injured.'[132]

This decision was welcomed in some quarters as it resolved the rather arbitrary inconsistency between the remedies imposed in circumstances where a fiduciary received a bribe and earned a commission.[133] However, while it may be reasonable that a fiduciary should not profit from a breach of duty even if this means that the principal receives a windfall, it was argued by Jones that it is not so obvious that a windfall is justified where the contest is between creditors who have given value and a principal who has not.[134] There is certainly merit in the argument that in circumstances where a recipient of a bribe is insolvent the imposition of a more limited form of remedy, such as a claim merely to secure the sum which represents the value of the bribe, might be more equitable given the enormous significance of proprietary remedies and their potential impact on creditors and third parties.

Subsequently, in *Sinclair Investments (UK) Ltd v Versailles Trade Finance Ltd*,[135] where the fiduciary was insolvent and the contest was between the principal and the fiduciary's creditors, the Court of Appeal declined to follow *Attorney-General for Hong Kong v Reid* and held that the beneficiary of a fiduciary's duty could not claim a proprietary interest and was limited to a personal claim in equity. In this case a director had made a secret profit on the sale of shares in a company in circumstances where he had breached his

131. *Ibid.* at 332.
132. *Ibid.* at 336. See also *Daraydan Holdings Ltd v Sollard International Ltd* [2005] Ch 119, 137.
133. Oakley [1994] CLJ 31.
134. Jones [1994] Conv 156, 164. Similarly, Hicks [2010] CLJ 287, 317 has suggested that in many instances there is no clear reason why a principal should fare better than the fiduciary's unsecured creditors. See also Chambers [2013] Conv 241, 251.
135. [2012] Ch 453. See also *Cadogan Petroleum plc v Tolley* [2011] EWHC 2286 (Ch).

fiduciary duty by entering into fraudulent transactions. The question was whether he held the profit on a constructive trust for the company or whether he was personally accountable only, in which case the company would be in competition with other unsecured creditors. Lord Neuberger MR expressed the view that there was a real argument for saying that the decision of the Privy Council in *Reid* was unsound. He said that in cases where a fiduciary takes an asset which he was under a duty to take for a beneficiary, it was easy to see why the asset should be treated as the property of the beneficiary. However, he added that a bribe paid to a fiduciary could not possibly be so described and that there could be said to be a fundamental distinction between a fiduciary enriching himself by depriving a claimant of an asset and by doing a wrong to the claimant. Lord Neuberger MR concluded that the authorities appear to establish that 'a beneficiary of a fiduciary's duties cannot claim a proprietary interest, but is entitled to an equitable account, in respect of any money or asset acquired by a fiduciary in breach of his duties to the beneficiary, unless the asset or money is or has been beneficially the property of the beneficiary or the trustee acquired the asset or money by taking advantage of an opportunity or right which was properly that of the beneficiary.'[136]

This decision was welcomed by a number of commentators,[137] although others did not support it.[138] Millett suggested that it had been incorrect to find that in most cases of this nature there will only be a personal liability to account.[139] His view was that a fiduciary who keeps a profit for himself abuses the trust and confidence placed in him by the principal and that he should be bound to hand it over to his principal the moment he receives it. In his opinion, 'Equity's response to a breach of this duty is to enforce the duty by means of the constructive trust.'[140]

This has been the position taken by the Supreme Court of the United Kingdom in *FHR European Ventures LLP v Cedar Capital Partners LLC*,[141] in what has been described as 'the final instalment of this saga'.[142] It is interesting to note that Lord Neuberger PSC, who in the Court of Appeal in *Sinclair* had taken a different approach, handed down the judgment of the court. The claimants sought recovery of the sum of €10 million which it was alleged had been paid as commission pursuant to an exclusive brokerage agreement made between the second defendant, a company set up by the first named defendant, and the vendor of a hotel, whereby it agreed to facilitate the sale of the hotel by introducing prospective purchasers and to disclose its appointment to

136. *Ibid.* at 482.
137. See Virgo [2011] CLJ 502; Goode (2011) 127 LQR 493.
138. See Hayton (2011) 127 LQR 487; Millett [2012] CLJ 583.
139. [2012] CLJ 583.
140. *Ibid.*
141. [2015] AC 250.
142. Whayman [2014] Conv 518. See also Conaglen [2014] CLJ 490; Gummow (2015) 131 LQR 21; Yip and Lee (2017) 37 LS 647, 657-664.

such purchasers. Following the sale of the hotel to the claimants, the second defendant was paid the commission. The claimants asserted that this sum was a secret profit received by the defendants in breach of their fiduciary duty to the claimants. At first instance Simon J held that the second defendant was liable to account for the sum of the commission but declined to grant the claimants a declaration that they were entitled to a proprietary remedy against the second defendant. The Court of Appeal allowed the claimants' appeal and varied the order, granting a declaration that the second defendant had received the commission on constructive trust for the claimants.[143] The Supreme Court dismissed the second named defendant's appeal in a landmark judgment.

Lord Neuberger PSC stated as follows:

> [T]he centrally relevant point for present purposes is that, at least in some cases where an agent acquires a benefit which came to his notice as a result of his fiduciary position, or pursuant to an opportunity which results from his fiduciary position, the equitable rule … is that he is to be treated as having acquired the benefit on behalf of his principal, so that it is beneficially owned by the principal. In such cases, the principal has a proprietary remedy in addition to his personal remedy against the agent, and the principal can elect between the two remedies.[144]

He pointed out that it would be curious if a principal whose agent wrongly receives a bribe or secret commission were to be worse off than a principal whose agent obtains a benefit in far less dubious circumstances, such as the benefit obtained by the trustees' agents in *Boardman v Phipps*, although that would be the effect if the rule outlined above did not apply to bribes or secret commissions. Lord Neuberger PSC added that wider policy considerations also supported the position that bribes and secret commissions received by an agent should be treated as the property of his principal, rather than merely giving rise to a claim for equitable compensation. He referred to the view expressed by Lord Templeman in *Attorney-General for Hong Kong v Reid* that 'bribery is an evil practice which threatens the foundations of any civilised society'[145] although he commented that secret commissions 'are also objectionable as they inevitably tend to undermine trust in the commercial world.'[146]

---

143. [2013] 3 WLR 466. See Smith [2013] CLJ 260; Chambers [2013] Conv 241; Buckingham (2013) 27 Trust Law Int 102.
144. [2015] AC 250, 262.
145. [1994] 1 AC 324, 330. As Whayman has commented [2014] Conv 518, 520 in relation to the decision in *FHR,* it would be 'paradoxical that a weaker remedy would be awarded in the case of the worse wrongdoing of bribery, where a proprietary remedy would be awarded in the case of a secret profit.'
146. [2015] AC 250, 272. This principle was referred to by Teare J in *Medsted Associates Ltd v Canaccord Genuity Wealth (International) Ltd* [2018] 1 WLR 314, 334. The Court of Appeal concluded that it should not assist the claimant to profit from its breach of fiduciary duty to its clients. If it had granted the claimant judgment for

Lord Neuberger PSC acknowledged that this wide application of the principles outlined will tend to prejudice the agent's unsecured creditors and pointed out that this was seen in *Sinclair* as providing a good reason not to follow *Reid*. However, he said that the argument based on potential prejudice to the agent's unsecured creditors is balanced by the fact that it appears to be just that a principal whose agent has obtained a bribe or secret commission should be able to trace the proceeds of the bribe or commission into other assets and to follow them into the hands of knowing recipients. Lord Neuberger PSC concluded that considerations of practicality and principle appeared to support the respondents' case, 'namely that a bribe or secret commission accepted by an agent is held on trust for his principal.'[147] In his view the law had taken a wrong turn in decisions such as *Metropolitan Bank v Heiron*[148] and *Lister & Co. v Stubbs*[149] and subsequent decisions such as *Sinclair*, at least insofar as they followed these cases, should be treated as overruled.

It should be noted that Lord Neuberger PSC commented in *FHR* that 'it is fair to say that the concept of equitable proprietary rights is in some respects somewhat paradoxical. Equity, unlike the common law, classically acts in personam; yet equity is far more ready to accord proprietary claims than common law.'[150] As Chambers has pointed out, '[a] declaration of constructive trust can have serious, adverse consequences for innocent third parties' and he advocates caution 'before extending the reach of such trusts, especially if they depend on fictions and can operate in favour of principals who have suffered no loss whatsoever from the events that have given rise to the trust.'[151] Some commentators, such as Virgo, were satisfied at the time with the approach of the Court of Appeal in *Sinclair*, the outcome of which was that a fiduciary will only hold assets on a constructive trust either where they have been taken from the principal or where the fiduciary has exploited an opportunity or right of the principal. Virgo asserted then that 'the recognition of a constructive trust in such circumstances is defensible, because the profits made by the defendant can be considered to represent the fruits of the claimant's property'.[152] However, as Smith suggests, 'it is not necessary to say that opportunities or information "belong" to the beneficiary in a legal sense; the rule is activated

---

substantial damages it would be doing this and for this reason the court concluded that the claimant was only entitled to nominal damages for the defendant's breach of contract.

147. *Ibid.* at 273.
148. (1880) 5 Ex D 319.
149. (1890) 45 Ch D 1.
150. [2015] AC 250, 269.
151. [2013] Conv 241, 251.
152. Virgo, *The Principles of Equity and Trusts* (1st ed., 2012) p.524. Now see the discussion in the 3rd edition at pp. 540-542. Virgo comments at p. 540 that the decision in *FHR* 'does at least resolve a long-standing controversy as to the role of the constructive trust where the fiduciary has profited from breach of his or her fiduciary duty.'

when opportunities or information are used to acquire rights'.[153] So, as Patten LJ commented in *Crown Prosecution Service v Aquila Advisory Ltd*:[154]

> It is clear from the approval by the Supreme Court [in *FHR*] of the decision of the Privy Council in *Attorney General for Hong Kong v Reid* [1994] 1 AC 324 that the principal's right to recover the secret profit under a constructive trust applies even when the profit derives from bribery or some other unlawful or disreputable conduct that would not have represented an opportunity which the agent's principal would or should have taken advantage of had its existence been disclosed.

In summary, the result of the decision in *FHR* is that whenever a fiduciary makes a profit as a result of a breach of fiduciary duty, those profits will be held on a constructive trust for the principal, even if they did not derive from interference with the principal's property or from the exploitation of an opportunity which should have been exploited for the principal. Ultimately, the approach in *FHR* is preferable to that adopted by the Court of Appeal in *Sinclair*,[155] as it avoids the outcome that the recipient of a bribe might benefit from conduct which is objectionable. However, it will be harder to justify if the reasoning and conclusions are applied in a case of an 'undeserving' claimant where general creditors lose out as a result.[156] So, in a sense, whether the *FHR* reasoning leads to a 'fair' outcome may depend on whether the secret commission or bribe has been taken by a recipient who is still solvent when the proceedings against him are commenced. Virgo has raised the possibility of modifying the institutional constructive trust applied in *FHR* through the operation of judicial discretion which would allow some of the proprietary implications of the traditional institutional constructive trust to be adapted.[157] While this suggestion, if developed, would lead to greater flexibility and potentially avoid an 'undeserving' principal benefitting at the expense of unsecured creditors, it might also lead to an element of uncertainty which would not be welcome in a commercial context.[158]

Finally, it should be noted that the comments of Finlay Geoghegan J in *Re Custom House Capital Ltd*[159] suggest that there are signs that the courts in

153. [2013] CLJ 260, 262.
154. [2019] EWCA Civ 588 at [16].
155. As Dunne has suggested (2014) 32 ILT 236, 238, '[t]he deterrent effect of fiduciary liability only works where the fiduciary cannot make any profit from the breach.'
156. Yip and Lee (2017) 37 LS 647, 663 also suggest that the decision in *FHR* is difficult to reconcile with Lord Sumption JSC's *obiter* comments in *Angove's Pty Ltd v Bailey* [2016] 1 WLR 3179.
157. Virgo, *The Principles of Equity and Trusts* (3rd ed., 2018) p. 277. See also p. 455.
158. Yip and Lee (2017) 37 LS 647, 659 also argue that Lord Neuberger's change in approach in *FHR* is underlined by commercial considerations, pointing out that disputes about secret commissions and bribes almost invariably arise in a commercial context.
159. [2014] 1 ILRM 360, 373.

Ireland are now taking cognisance of the significance of the imposition of a proprietary remedy in an insolvency situation. Given that the judiciary here have recognised the option of imposing a remedial constructive trust, such a device might provide greater flexibility to address the specific difficulties associated with such situations. However, as will be explored in greater detail below, the lack of a principled basis for the imposition of trusts of this nature has led to considerable uncertainty. For this reason, it might be preferable for the courts in this jurisdiction to simply apply the approach adopted in *FHR* to all situations where a bribe or secret commission is taken. If this were deemed to be unacceptable due to the implications for third parties such as unsecured creditors, an alternative might be to explore the use of the modified institutional constructive trust advocated by Virgo as set out in the paragraph above, which he described as "principled, but also flexible."[160]

The Position of Agents

As Lord Neuberger PSC noted in the course of his judgment in *FHR European Ventures LLP v Cedar Capital Partners LLC*,[161] 'an agent owes a fiduciary duty to his principal because he is 'someone who has undertaken to act for or on behalf of [his principal] in a particular matter in circumstances which give rise to a relationship of trust and confidence.'[162] Where an agent puts himself in a position where his duty to his principal and his own interests may conflict and makes a profit out of his fiduciary position, he will be liable to account for this. Moore LJ summarised the nature of the fiduciary duty owed by an agent to his principal in *Sherrard v Barron*[163] as follows:

> There is no dispute about the law, which is that an agent cannot without the knowledge of his principal make any profit for himself out of services rendered to his principal. Should he do so, he must account. It is equally settled law that it is the duty of the agent to make the fullest disclosure to his principal of all transactions in which the agent is making, directly or indirectly, a profit out of his principal. If this is done and the principal, expressly or by course of conduct, impliedly assents, the agent can retain his profit.

---

160. Virgo, *The Principles of Equity and Trusts* (3rd ed., 2018) p. 277.
161. [2015] 2 AC 250, 261.
162. Referring to the judgment of Millett LJ in *Bristol and West Building Society v Mothew* [1998] Ch 1, 18.
163. [1923] 1 IR 21, 24. Note also the *dicta* of James LJ in *Parker v McKenna* (1874) 10 Ch App 96, 124 that 'no agent in the course of his agency, in the matter of his agency, can be allowed to make any profit without the knowledge and consent of his principal.' See also *Re Canadian Oil Works Corporation* (1875) 10 Ch App 593, 601 *per* Mellish LJ.

The requirement of disclosure and consent is strictly applied in this context as can be seen from *Patten v Hamilton*,[164] where an agent purchased a charge on his principal's estate at an undervalue and continued to collect the interest on the face value of the charge. It was held by the Irish Court of Appeal that in the absence of evidence that the principal had consented to the agent retaining the full benefit of the transaction, the agent should be treated as a trustee for the principal and the extra interest should be applied towards extinguishing the charge.

As Andrews LJ made clear in *Sherrard v Barron*, it is of paramount importance in all transactions between agent and principal and between other parties who stand in a fiduciary relationship to one another that 'there should be nothing in the nature of underhand dealing.'[165] However, liability does not depend on any finding of fraud and applies equally even where it has not been shown that any advantage has been taken. It has also been established that it is irrelevant that the principal does not suffer any loss as a result of the agent's actions and in fact may have benefited, although in such circumstances, the agent may be entitled to remuneration for his endeavours. The best illustration of the rigour with which these principles have been applied is the decision of the House of Lords in *Boardman v Phipps*.[166] Assets were held on trust for the benefit of a testator's children, the trustees being his widow, who was senile, his daughter and an accountant. The trust had a sizable minority shareholding in a textile company and with the consent of the two active trustees, Boardman, the trustees' solicitor, and one of the beneficiaries set about acquiring a majority shareholding in the company in order to make it more profitable. By purporting to act on behalf of the trust they obtained detailed information about the company and succeeded in gaining control of it, making a considerable profit as a result.[167] The House of Lords held that Boardman and the beneficiary were liable to account to the trust for the profits which they had made,[168] although it was held that they were entitled to payment for the work which they had carried out.

The majority view was that the defendants had placed themselves in a position in which their duty and self-interest might conflict and had abused their fiduciary position by utilizing information acquired in a fiduciary capacity. Lord Hodson and Lord Guest agreed that information could be characterised

164. [1911] 1 IR 46. See the general principle set out by Cherry LJ at 60.
165. [1923] 1 IR 21, 26.
166. [1967] 2 AC 46.
167. Bryan has suggested in 'Boardman v Phipps' in *Landmark Cases in Equity* (eds., Mitchell and Mitchell, 2012) p. 580 at 588 that although the majority of the House of Lords used the language of agency, it was in fact intermeddler's liability which was in substance invoked in order to hold the defendants accountable.
168. The order of Wilberforce J, which was upheld by the House of Lords, made it clear that liability to account as a constructive trustee was imposed, although doubt had surrounded this issue for some time. See Millett [2012] CLJ 583, 609; Hicks [2013] Conv 232, 236; Hicks (2014) 65 NILQ 1, 2.

as trust property and found that since the defendants had made a profit out of using this information, they were liable to account for it. Lord Cohen felt that information was not property in the strict sense, and said that the mere use of knowledge which comes to an agent in the course of his agency does not necessarily make him liable,[169] but he will be required to account where, as in the case before him, he purported to act on behalf of the trust. Viscount Dilhorne and Lord Upjohn dissented, holding that the information obtained by the defendants when purporting to act as agents of the trust was not trust property and they found that in the circumstances there was no conflict between their private interests and their fiduciary duty to the trust.

It should be stated that the existence of the conflict of interest identified by the majority has been doubted by some commentators.[170] However, it has been argued that the majority view is preferable as it is more likely to protect the position of a principal or beneficiary who may be unaware of the agent's activities and in any event the agent can avoid liability if he obtains consent for the course of action which he intends to pursue before embarking upon it.

As Lord Neuberger PSC commented in *FHR European Ventures LLP v Cedar Capital Partners LLC*,[171] considered in more detail in the preceding section, the position put forward by the respondents in that case, which the court accepted, was consistent with the fundamental principles of the law of agency. He stated as follows:

> The agent owes a duty of undivided loyalty to the principal, unless the latter has given his informed consent to some less demanding standard of duty. The principal is thus entitled to the entire benefit of the agent's acts in the course of his agency. This principle is wholly unaffected by the fact that the agent may have exceeded his authority. The principal is entitled to the benefit of the agent's unauthorised acts in the course of his agency, in just the same way as, at law, an employer is vicariously liable to bear the burden of an employee's unauthorised breaches of duty in the course of his employment. The agent's duty is accordingly to deliver up to his principal the benefit which he has obtained, and not simply to pay compensation for having obtained it in excess of his authority. The only way that legal effect can be given to an obligation to deliver up specific property to the principal is by treating the principal as specifically entitled to it.[172]

Finally, it is interesting to note that the majority of the Canadian Supreme Court

169. *Ibid.* at 102-103.
170. Jones (1968) 84 LQR 472.
171. [2015] AC 250.
172. *Ibid.* at 270.

held in *Soulos v Korkontzilas*[173] that an agent who acquires property from a third party in breach of his fiduciary obligations to his principal holds this property on a constructive trust despite the fact that the agent had not thereby realised any financial gain.[174] As McLachlin J stated, 'a constructive trust is required in cases such as this to ensure that agents and others in positions of trust remain faithful to their duty of loyalty'.[175] In her view, if the courts did not intervene by imposing a constructive trust in such circumstances the message which that would send out would be that agents might breach their fiduciary duties and the courts would do nothing unless the agent had made a profit. In the opinion of McLachlin J 'this will not do'; as 'courts of equity have always been concerned to keep the person who acts on behalf of others to his ethical mark'.[176]

If the views of the majority of the House of Lords in *Boardman* and of the Supreme Court of Canada in *Soulos* are followed in this jurisdiction, it will lead to particularly strict standards being applied to the conduct of agents and a constructive trust will be imposed even where the principal has not sustained any loss as a result of the agent's actions or where the agent himself has not profited financially from any transaction entered into. It would seem likely that the view of the majority in *Boardman*, which is so firmly entrenched in England, will be followed here. Perhaps more uncertain is whether the slightly controversial principle of imposing a constructive trust in the absence of unjust enrichment will find favour with the courts in this jurisdiction.[177]

The Position of Company Directors[178]

Company directors are treated as being fiduciaries in so far as they owe a duty to their company and they will not be permitted to place themselves in a position where their duty to the company and their personal interests will conflict[179] or to derive a profit from their fiduciary relationship. While statutory provisions now regulate the fiduciary duties of company directors in both Ireland and England,[180] these are largely based on pre-existing common law and equitable

173. (1997) 146 DLR (4th) 214. See further Smith (1997) Can Bar Rev 539; (1998) 114 LQR 14.
174. The view of the minority was that to impose a constructive trust where there had been no unjust enrichment would depart from settled principles, see the judgment of Sopinka J at 236.
175. (1997) 146 DLR (4th) 214, 231.
176. *Ibid.* at 232.
177. See further *infra* pp.331-335 in relation to the role of unjust enrichment.
178. See generally Sealy [1967] CLJ 83; Lowry (1994) 45 NILQ 1.
179. *Parker v McKenna* (1874) 10 Ch App 96, 118. See also *CMS Dolphin Ltd v Simonet* [2001] 2 BCLC 704, 728; *British Midland Tool Ltd v Midland International Tooling Ltd* [2003] 2 BCLC 523, 557; *Shepherds Investments Ltd v Walters* [2006] EWHC 836 (Ch) at [106].
180. See Part 5, Chapter 2 of the Companies Act 2014 and Part 10, Chapter 2 of the Companies Act 2006 respectively.

principles[181] and the courts' interpretation of directors' duties in this regard are still relevant.

As Swinfen Eady J stated in *Transvaal Lands Co. v New Belgium (Transvaal) Land & Development Co.*,[182] referring to the judgment of Lord Cranworth in *Aberdeen Railway Co. v Blaikie*:[183]

> It was there decided that directors of a company have duties to discharge of a fiduciary nature towards their principal, and that it is a rule of universal application, that no one, having such duties to discharge, shall be allowed to enter into engagements in which he has, or can have, a personal interest conflicting, or which possibly may conflict, with the interests of those he is bound to protect.

This view has been echoed by Lightman J in *Neptune (Vehicle Washing Equipment) Ltd v Fitzgerald*,[184] where he stated that 'a director of a company owes a fiduciary duty to the company to act *bona fide* in the best interests of the company and to prefer its interests to his own where they conflict'. It was made clear by Jonathan Parker LJ in *Bhullar v Bhullar*[185] that where a fiduciary has exploited a commercial opportunity for his own benefit, the relevant question is not whether the party to whom the duty was owed, i.e. the company, had some kind of beneficial interest in the opportunity but rather whether the fiduciary's exploitation of the opportunity was such as to attract the operation of the no-conflict rule. He added that he agreed with the trial judge that in this context the test was whether 'reasonable men looking at the facts would think there was a real sensible possibility of conflict'.[186] It is also clear from the judgment of Rimer LJ in *O'Donnell v Shanahan*[187] that liability to account cannot be qualified by reference to whether the impugned transaction was or was not within the scope of the company's business and he confirmed that the authorities do not support a 'scope of business' exception.

It should be noted that no liability will be imposed provided that full disclosure has been made by a director and the informed consent of the company to his activities has been obtained. So, in *Neptune (Vehicle Washing Equipment) Ltd v Fitzgerald*,[188] while Lightman J stated that where a director enters into an arrangement or transaction with himself or with a company in which he is interested, that arrangement may be set aside irrespective of whether the

181. See s.227(4) of the Companies Act 2014; s.170(3) of the Companies Act 2006.
182. [1914] 2 Ch 488, 502.
183. (1854) 1 Macq 461. See also *Bhullar v Bhullar* [2003] 2 BCLC 241, 252; *Ultraframe (UK) Ltd v Fielding* [2005] EWHC 1638 (Ch) at [1307].
184. [1996] Ch 274, 279.
185. [2003] 2 BCLC 241. See further Armour [2004] CLJ 33; Prentice and Payne (2004) 120 LQR 198.
186. *Ibid.* at 256.
187. [2009] BCC 822, 839.
188. [1996] Ch 274.

company has suffered as a result, he stated that it is a defence to such a claim that the company's shareholders have consented to the transaction or the articles of association allow it.

While it has been argued that the rule in *Keech v Sandford* should only apply to trustees in the strict sense, as Lowry has noted, 'it has been taken to be of equal applicability to all types of fiduciaries including company directors, irrespective of the equity of a particular case.'[189] There is no question that liability will be imposed where a director abuses his fiduciary position by diverting to himself a contract which could have been taken up on the company's behalf. So, in *Cook v Deeks*[190] the Privy Council held that directors who had engaged in such conduct held the benefit of those contracts on a constructive trust for the benefit of the company. This principle was succinctly set out by Laskin J in *Canadian Aero Service Ltd v O'Malley*:[191]

> A director or a senior officer … is precluded from obtaining for himself, either secretly or without the approval of the company (which would have to be properly manifested upon full disclosure of the facts), any property or business advantage either belonging to the company or for which it has been negotiating; and especially is this so where the director or officer is a participant in the negotiations on behalf of the company.

Liability will also be imposed where the company itself was not in a position to take on a contract secured by a director where he takes advantage of his fiduciary position to achieve this. So, in *Industrial Development Consultants v Cooley*[192] the defendant managing director of a company which provided construction consultancy services learnt in the course of negotiations with a gas board on its behalf that the board would not enter into an agreement with the company but that it would consider awarding the contract to him in a personal capacity. He secured a release from his employment by falsely claiming ill health and then entered into a contract with the board on his own behalf. Roskill J held that the defendant was a trustee of the benefit of the contract and liable to account for the profits derived from it. As he stated, 'if the defendant is not required to account he will have made a large profit, as a result of having deliberately put himself into a position in which his duty to the plaintiffs who were employing him and his personal interests conflicted.'[193]

189. Lowry (1994) 45 NILQ 1, 2.
190. [1916] 1 AC 554.
191. (1974) 40 DLR (3d) 371, 382.
192. [1972] 1 WLR 443. Similarly, in *Bhullar v Bhullar* [2003] 2 BCLC 241, Jonathan Parker LJ commented that whether the company could or would have taken up the opportunity had it been made aware of it was not the point. See also *Crown Dilmun v Sutton* [2004] 1 BCLC 468, 511; *Quarter Master UK Ltd v Pyke* [2005] 1 BCLC 245, 263.
193. *Ibid.* at 453. However, compare this finding with the decision of the Canadian Supreme Court in *Peso Silver Mines Ltd (NPL) v Cropper* (1966) 58 DLR (2d) 1, in which

In some cases this general principle that a director must not profit from his fiduciary relationship with the company has been inflexibly applied and if a director takes advantage of his position and makes a profit, the court will not look behind his motives for so doing.[194] So, even where a director has acted in an honest and *bona fide* manner in what he believes are the best interests of the company, he will nevertheless be liable to account for any personal profit made as a result of his fiduciary relationship with the company. The harshness of this rule is well illustrated by the decision of the House of Lords in *Regal (Hastings) Ltd v Gulliver*.[195] A company which owned a cinema formed a subsidiary to take up the lease of two additional cinemas so that they might all be sold as a going concern. The landlord insisted on the subsidiary company having a paid up share capital of 5,000 ordinary £1 shares and as the parent company had insufficient resources to subscribe for more than 2,000, the directors of the company agreed to take up the remainder. When the business was transferred to new controllers the directors made a personal profit on the transaction. The purchaser successfully brought an action in the company's name to account for this profit on the grounds that the directors had derived such profit by virtue of their office. Lord Russell stated:

> The rule of equity which insists on those, who by use of a fiduciary position make a profit, being liable to account for that profit, in no way depends on fraud, or absence of *bona fides*; or upon such questions or considerations as whether the profit would or should otherwise have gone to the plaintiff, or whether the profiteer was under a duty to obtain the source of the profit for the plaintiff, or whether he took a risk or acted as he did for the benefit of the plaintiff, or whether the plaintiff has in fact been damaged or benefited by his action. The liability arises from the mere fact of a profit having, in the stated circumstances, been made. The profiteer, however honest and well intentioned, cannot escape the risk of being called upon to account.[196]

This decision seems unduly harsh in that the directors had acted honestly and in the best interests of the company, particularly as the company itself could not have obtained the benefit of the transactions which ultimately took place without the financial input of the directors. As Jones has commented, while the policy issues in *Regal Hastings* were finely balanced, the unquestioning

---

the court appeared to lay down the principle that it would not penalise a director in circumstances where he had acted in a *bona fide* manner and had taken up an opportunity which his company had been unable or unwilling to accept.

194. *Furs Ltd v Tomkies* (1936) 54 CLR 583, 592 *per* Rich, Dixon and Evatt JJ.
195. [1967] 2 AC 134. (Initially reported at [1942] 1 All ER 378). For a detailed analysis of the decision, see Nolan 'Regal Hastings Ltd v Gulliver' in *Landmark Cases in Equity* (eds. Mitchell and Mitchell, 2012) p.499.
196. *Ibid.* at 144.

adherence to the inexorable rule of equity by the House of Lords meant that these factors were never properly weighed against each other.[197]

The fact that a director's liability to account for any profit made as a result of his fiduciary relationship with the company does not depend on *mala fides* but 'on the mere fact of a profit having been made' was restated by the House of Lords in *Guinness plc v Saunders*,[198] in which the court had to consider the question of whether a director might be entitled to remuneration in circumstances where he had made a profit for the company. A committee of the board of directors of the plaintiff company had paid the second named defendant £5.2 million for his services in connection with a takeover bid being made by the plaintiff. Recovery of the money was claimed on the grounds that the second named defendant had received it in breach of his fiduciary duty as director in that he had not disclosed his interest in the agreement to the plaintiff company. The House of Lords agreed that he had failed to disclose his interest and ordered him to repay the money to the plaintiff. In relation to the second named defendant's claim for remuneration, it was argued that *Boardman v Phipps* was authority for the proposition that in exceptional circumstances a court of equity might award remuneration to a trustee and that therefore it might make such payments to a director. However, Lord Goff concluded that the present case was 'very different' to *Boardman* and said that '[w]hether any such an allowance might ever be granted by a court of equity in the case of a director of a company, as opposed to a trustee, is a point which has yet to be decided … In any event I cannot see any possibility of such jurisdiction being exercised in the present case.'[199]

A more flexible approach was adopted by Hutchison J in *Island Export Finance Ltd v Umunna*,[200] in which he held that a former director of a company might secure a contract to supply materials, supplied by the company on a previous occasion, in circumstances where the company was not actively seeking the new contract and where there was no connection between his resignation and the securing of this contract. Hutchison J stated that it would be surprising to find that directors were restrained from exploiting any opportunity of which they had acquired knowledge as directors after they ceased to be such. In his view: 'directors, no less than employees, acquire a general fund of knowledge and expertise in the course of their work, and it is plainly in the public interest that they should be free to exploit it in a new position.'[201] Subsequently, in *CMS Dolphin Ltd v Simonet*,[202] while Lawrence Collins J acknowledged that a director is not precluded following his resignation from a company from using his general fund of skill and knowledge or his personal

197. Jones (1968) 84 LQR 472, 497.
198. [1990] 2 AC 663. See *Goulding* [1990] Conv 296.
199. *Ibid.* at 701. See also *Quarter Master UK Ltd v Pyke* [2005] 1 BCLC 245, 272.
200. [1986] BCLC 460.
201. *Ibid.* at 482.
202. [2001] 2 BCLC 704.

connections, he also made it clear that where he exploits a maturing business opportunity liability will be imposed. The first named defendant, who was the director of an advertising agency, resigned and set up a new business, recruiting all the agency's staff which resulted in its principal clients also switching their business to his new venture. In imposing liability to account Lawrence Collins J stated as follows:

> In my judgment the underlying basis of the liability of a director who exploits after his resignation a maturing business opportunity of the company is that the opportunity is to be treated as if it were property of the company in relation to which the director had fiduciary duties. By seeking to exploit the opportunity after resignation he is appropriating for himself that property. He is just as accountable as a trustee who retires without properly accounting for trust property. In the case of a director he becomes a constructive trustee of the fruits of his abuse of the company's property, which he has acquired in the circumstances where he knowingly has a conflict of interest, and exploited it by resigning from the company.[203]

The difficulties facing a court in assessing whether liability should be imposed on a director who has retired were considered in some detail by Rix LJ in *Foster Bryant Surveying Ltd v Bryant*.[204] He expressed the view that the problem of determining whether a retiring director has or has not breached his fiduciary duty is a highly fact sensitive one. He continued as follows:

> [T]he jurisprudence has shown that, while the principles remain unamended, their application in different circumstances has required care and sensitivity both to the facts and to other principles, such as that of personal freedom to compete, where that does not intrude on the misuse of the company's property whether in the form of business opportunities or trade secrets. For reasons such as these, there has been some flexibility, both in the reach and extent of the duties imposed and in the findings of liability or non-liability. The jurisprudence also demonstrates, to my mind, that in the present context of retiring directors, where the critical line between a defendant being or not being a director becomes hard to

---

203. *Ibid.* at 733. In this case the new company set up by the defendant had gone into liquidation and the proceedings against it has been discontinued. However, in *Quarter Master UK Ltd v Pyke* [2005] 1 BCLC 245, where the defendant directors were found to have acted in breach of fiduciary duty, they were held liable to account not only for personal profits but also for profits made by another company on the basis that they had effectively diverted profits to it. See also *Shepherds Investments Ltd v Walters* [2006] EWHC 836 (Ch) at [133]-[134].
204. [2007] BCC 804.

> police, the courts have adopted pragmatic solutions based on a common-sense and merits-based approach.[205]

It is also clear from the decision of the Court of Appeal in *In Plus Group Ltd v Pyke*[206] that 'there is no completely rigid rule that a director may not be involved in the business of a company which is in competition with another company of which he was a director'. In this case the court was satisfied that the defendant had been effectively excluded from the claimant companies, of which he was a director, some months before he entered into business with one of their customers and that in so doing he was not making use of confidential information which had come to him in his role as director of these companies. In these circumstances, the Court of Appeal concluded that the defendant had committed no breach of fiduciary duty in trading with the companies' former customer.

The tenor of some recent decisions in England such as *In Plus* would seem to be more flexible and as we have seen the courts have recognised the practical reality that a director will inevitably acquire a general fund of knowledge in the course of carrying out his duties and that he cannot be expected to desist from all activities of a commercial nature on leaving his position.[207] However, it is also clear from a number of recent decisions in which liability has been imposed that the no-conflict rule continues to be strictly applied in this context.[208] It has been suggested that the rather inflexible application of this rule is based on public policy considerations[209] and that the purpose of imposing liability in such cases is partly to act as a deterrent.[210] Whatever the motivation there is no real sign of a relaxing of standards, and in the absence of full disclosure and informed consent, a company director may find it difficult to avoid liability to account where profits are made.

Following the enactment of the Companies Act 2006 in England, statutory provisions now govern the fiduciary obligations of company directors in that jurisdiction, although as noted above, these are largely based on pre-existing common law and equitable principles.[211] It has been suggested that the provisions in the English legislation in relation to conflicts of interest tend to

---

205. *Ibid.* at 827.
206. [2002] 2 BCLC 201, 220.
207. *Island Export Finance Ltd v Umunna* [1986] BCLC 460.
208. *Bhullar v Bhullar* [2003] 2 BCLC 241; *Crown Dilmun v Sutton* [2004] 1 BCLC 468; *Quarter Master UK Ltd v Pyke* [2005] 1 BCLC 245; *Kingsley IT Consulting Ltd v McIntosh* [2006] BCC 875.
209. *Quarter Master UK Ltd v Pyke* [2005] 1 BCLC 245, 269.
210. *Lindsley v Woodfull* [2004] 2 BCLC 131, 140 *per* Arden LJ. See also *Kingsley IT Consulting Ltd v McIntosh* [2006] BCC 875, 885. Armour has suggested in [2004] CLJ 33, 35 that the conflict of interest rule is concerned 'not with restoring losses but rather with encouraging disclosure'.
211. See s.170(3) of the Companies Act 2006.

reflect a fairly strict approach to directors' duties.[212] So, section 175 requires a director to avoid a conflict of interest situation even if the company itself could not take advantage of the opportunity, although this duty is not infringed 'if the situation cannot reasonably be regarded as likely to give rise to a conflict of interest' or 'if the matter has been authorised by the directors'.[213]

While there has been little consideration of the relevant principles in this area in this jurisdiction, it would appear that the courts favour a strict approach in accordance with the decision in *Regal Hastings Ltd v Gulliver*.[214] In *Fyffes plc v DCC plc*[215] Laffoy J said that she was satisfied that the following propositions put forward by counsel for the plaintiff were 'amply supported by authority':

> First, the liability to disgorge a profit made from acting in breach of a fiduciary duty arises irrespective of whether the company itself has suffered a loss. Secondly, liability arises irrespective of whether the company itself could have made a profit. Thirdly, the liability is triggered irrespective of considerations of fraud or bad faith.

As with the equivalent English legislation, many of the relevant directors' duties set out in the Companies Act 2014 are based on common law rules and equitable principles.[216] Section 228(1) provides that a director of a company shall not use the company's property, information or opportunities for his own or anyone else's benefit unless this is expressly permitted by the company's constitution or has been approved by a resolution of the company in general meeting. Section 228(1)(f) goes on to provide that a director shall 'avoid any conflict between the director's duties to the company and the director's other (including personal) interests unless the director is released from his or her duty to the company in relation to the matter concerned, whether in accordance with provisions of the company's constitution in that behalf or by a resolution of it in general meeting.' As regards liability, the legislation provides that unless the court grants relief, a director shall be liable to account for any gain made, directly or indirectly, from a breach of duty and/or to indemnify the company for any loss or damage resulting from the breach.[217] It remains to be seen how flexible an approach the courts in this jurisdiction will take to the no-conflict provisions in section 228 of the Act of 2014. However, if the pattern of recent decisions in both this jurisdiction and in England is followed, it is likely to be fairly strictly applied, not least to ensure a form of deterrent effect.

The scope of limitation periods applying to actions for breach of trust as they apply to company directors has been considered in two recent decisions

212. Lim (2013) LQR 242, 243.
213. Section 175(4) of the Companies Act 2006.
214. [1967] 2 AC 134.
215. [2009] 2 IR 417, 660.
216. See s.227(4) of the Companies Act 2014.
217. Sections. 232 and 233 of the Companies Act 2014.

by the courts in England. Section 21(3) of the Limitation Act 1980 prescribes a limitation period of six years for any 'action by a beneficiary to recover trust property or in respect of any breach of trust' not otherwise covered by the Act. However, section 21(1)(a) of the Act provides that no period of limitation prescribed by the Act shall apply to an action by a beneficiary under a trust in respect of any fraud or fraudulent breach of trust to which the trustee was a party or privy. In *First Subsea Ltd v Balltec Ltd*[218] the claimant company sought equitable compensation for alleged breaches of fiduciary duty by the second defendant, a director of the claimant, which had taken place more than six years earlier. The second defendant contended that the claim was barred by the six-year limitation period for actions in respect of breaches of trust contained in section 21(3) of the Act of 1980 but judgment was given for the claimant on the basis that the claim was an action in respect of a fraudulent breach of trust on the part of the second defendant with the consequence that, by virtue of section 21(1)(a) of the 1980 Act, no period of limitation applied. The second defendant's appeal was dismissed on the basis that the trial judge had been entitled to find that the alleged breaches of trust were fraudulent and that the claim was not statute barred. Patten LJ stated that a director who is treated as a trustee of the property of the company for the purposes of section 21 may rely on section 21(3) as a defence to any claim to recover trust property or for breach of trust unless the trust property remains in his possession or his breach of trust was fraudulent. He stated that it seemed to follow that, if a director is a trustee for the purposes of section 21, the phrase 'breach of trust' must encompass any breach of his fiduciary duties as such a director towards the company. Patten LJ added that if a director causes loss to the company as in this case he is accountable in precisely the same way as a trustee would be for any loss caused by his breach of duty to the trust. Subsequently, in *Burnden Holdings (UK) Ltd v Fielding*[219] Lord Briggs JSC stated that while section 21 of the Limitation Act 1980 was primarily aimed at express trustees, it was applicable to company directors by a process of analogy. He expressed the view that '[i]t is common ground (and clear beyond argument) that, as directors of an English company who are assumed to have participated in a misappropriation of an asset of the company, the defendants are to be regarded for all purposes connected with s.21 as trustees.' This was because they were entrusted with the stewardship of the company's property and owed fiduciary duties to the company in respect of that stewardship.

218. [2018] Ch 25.
219. [2018] 2 WLR 885.

OTHER SITUATIONS IN WHICH INSTITUTIONAL CONSTRUCTIVE TRUSTS ARISE

Mutual Wills

Prerequisites for the Imposition of a Constructive Trust

Where two people, usually although not necessarily husband and wife, make an arrangement concerning the disposal of their property and execute mutual wills which are intended to be irrevocable and the survivor subsequently alters his will, his estate will be held by his personal representatives on a constructive trust to give effect to the arrangement provided for in the mutual wills.[220] However, before such a trust will arise, there must be evidence of an agreement to make mutual wills in substantially similar form and not to revoke them. As McPherson J stated in *Bigg v Queensland Trustees Ltd*,[221] '[w]hat matters is proof that the parties made an agreement to execute their wills in that form and that, expressly or by implication, they contracted not to revoke them.'[222]

In determining whether the necessary agreement exists, the court will have regard to the terms of the wills but may also infer evidence of an agreement from the conduct of the parties and the surrounding circumstances. The mere fact that the wills were made simultaneously and in substantially similar terms is not of itself sufficient proof that the parties have entered into a legally binding agreement not to revoke them. This is illustrated by the decision of Astbury J in *Re Oldham*,[223] in which a husband and wife executed mutual wills with similar provisions although there was no evidence of any agreement that they should be irrevocable. After the husband's death the wife remarried and made a new will. Astbury J upheld the second will and stated that the fact that the two wills were made in identical terms did not necessarily mean there was any agreement that they should be irrevocable by the survivor.[224]

While the fact that the wills are made simultaneously and in the same form is not *per se* proof of an agreement sufficient to justify the imposition of a constructive trust, it may be a relevant factor to be taken into account in determining whether such an agreement exists. In *Re Cleaver*,[225] where a husband and wife made similar wills at the same time and subsequently altered them in the same manner, it was held that the trusts set out in these wills would be enforced rather than those set out by the survivor, the wife, in a will made subsequent to her husband's death. In the circumstances, Nourse J was satisfied

220. This principle can be traced to the decision of Lord Camden in *Dufour v Pereira* (1769) 1 Dick 419. See generally Harper [1997] Conv 182, 188-193.
221. [1990] 2 Qd R 11, 13. See Rickett (1991) 54 MLR 581.
222. See also *Re Newey (deceased)* [1994] 2 NZLR 590, 593 *per* Hammond J.
223. [1925] Ch 75.
224. *Ibid.* at 88. See also *Birmingham v Renfrew* (1937) 57 CLR 666, 675 *per* Latham CJ.
225. [1981] 1 WLR 939.

that there was sufficient evidence of an agreement shown by the similarity of the provisions and the fact that the changes were made simultaneously.

However, in *Re Goodchild*,[226] a more recent decision on this question, *Re Cleaver* was distinguished and the importance of having specific evidence as to the testators' mutual intentions at the time of the execution of the wills was stressed.[227] In this case the testator and his wife both simultaneously executed wills in identical terms leaving their estates to each other and after their deaths to the first named plaintiff, their only son. After his wife's death, the testator married the defendant and six weeks after making a new will in which he left his entire estate to her, he died. The plaintiff brought an action seeking, *inter alia*, a declaration that after the death of his first wife, the testator held her estate on trust for the plaintiff, and that after the testator's death, the defendant held his estate similarly on trust. Carnwath J accepted that where there is a clear agreement or other evidence that wills are intended to be mutually binding, the law will give effect to that intention by way of a 'floating trust' which becomes irrevocable after the death of the first testator and crystallises on the death of the second. However, he held that in the circumstances, the evidence fell short of establishing such an agreement between the testator and his first wife and the wills were not mutually binding. Carnwath J stressed that the onus of proof lay on the plaintiff and said that there must be evidence of 'a specific agreement outside the wills not just some loose understanding or sense of moral obligation'.[228] He characterised *Re Cleaver* as an extreme example of the circumstances in which an agreement may be found on the basis of oral evidence but stated that in his view it did not provide any precedent for the case before him.[229]

The Court of Appeal upheld the conclusion that the wills were not mutually binding and affirmed the decision made by Carnwath J. Legatt LJ also distinguished *Re Cleaver* in which he said there had been specific evidence as to the testators' mutual intentions at the time the wills were made, whereas in the case before him, he was satisfied that there was not. He was of the opinion that 'for the doctrine to apply there must be a contract'[230] and stated

226. [1996] 1 WLR 694 (ChD); [1997] 1 WLR 1216 (CA). See Grattan [1997] Conv 153; Richardson (1996) 10 Trust Law Int 88.
227. See also *Fisher v Mansfield* [1997] 2 NZLR 230, where Heron J found that there was evidence of a mutual agreement between the parties at the time of the execution of the wills.
228. [1996] 1 WLR 694, 706.
229. However, Carnwath J went on to hold that the testator's wife's mistaken belief that the terms of the will were mutually binding imposed a moral obligation on him which justified the plaintiff's claim under the Inheritance (Provision for Family and Dependents) Act 1975 and that part of the estate which constituted her share should be available to meet the plaintiff's claim under the Act.
230. Although it should be noted that in the recent decision of the New Zealand Court of Appeal in *Lewis v Cotton* [2001] 2 NZLR 21, 32, Blanchard J stated that a formal legal contract is not needed and that 'a contract made without formality is enough'.

that a key feature of the concept of mutual wills was the 'irrevocability of the mutual intentions'.[231] In his view, what was missing in the case before him was evidence of a mutual intention that both wills should remain unaltered and that the survivor should be bound to leave the combined estates to his son. The decision of the Court of Appeal would seem to mark a return to the stricter approach of Astbury J in *Re Oldham* and shows that the evidential difficulties facing a litigant who seeks to establish that the doctrine of mutual wills applies are not inconsiderable.[232]

The importance of establishing evidence of an agreement that the parties should not revoke their will without the knowledge of the other was stressed again by Rimer J in *Curtis v Birch*[233] in rejecting a claim based on the doctrine of mutual wills. In this case the wills in question had been made less than three months before the death of the wife at a time when both parties knew that she was terminally ill and did not have long to live. However, Rimer J was quite satisfied that this fact in itself did not justify a finding that both testators must be taken to have agreed that the husband's will was to be irrevocable after his wife's impending death. In his view it was essential that there was evidence of an agreement not to revoke their respective wills save with the agreement of the other and this could not be implied by the mere fact that the spouses had agreed to make wills in particular terms. Similarly, in *Olins v Walters*[234] Mummery LJ stated that: '[i]t is a legally *necessary* condition of mutual wills that there is clear and satisfactory evidence of a contract between two testators'. He concluded that, since there had been ample evidence before the trial judge to show on the balance of probabilities that the intention of the defendant and the deceased had been to enter into a contract to create mutual wills, a constructive trust had arisen by operation of law on the death of the first testator which bound the conscience of the surviving testator in relation to the property affected.

It was held by Judge Matthews, sitting as a High Court judge, in *Legg v Burton*[235] that the use of the expression 'absolutely and beneficially and without any sort of trust obligation' in 'mirror' wills made by spouses did not preclude them from being recognised as mutual wills in circumstances where there was sufficient evidence of a legally binding agreement that the wills would not be revoked or changed without notice to the other party sufficient to enable the latter to also change their own will. He said that he agreed with the claimants' submission that if there is a mutual will arrangement giving rise to a trust, it

However, on the facts he concluded that there was insufficient evidence to sustain the mutual wills claim. See further Richardson (2001) 15 Trust Law Int 100.

231. [1997] 1 WLR 1216, 1225.
232. Grattan has pointed out [1997] Conv 153, 159 that it has frequently been advocated that those seeking to execute mutual wills 'would be well advised to ensure that the agreement is recited in the body of the instruments'.
233. (2002) 29 EG 139.
234. [2009] Ch 212, 221. See further Luxton [2009] Conv 498. See also *Fry v Densham-Smith* [2010] EWCA Civ 1410; Griffiths [2011] Conv 511.
235. [2017] 4 WLR 186.

arises *outside* the will, and words such as those used in the wills would not affect it.

A useful summary of the principles relating to mutual wills is contained in the judgment of Jonathan Gaunt QC, sitting as a Deputy High Court judge, in *Charles v Fraser*,[236] in which he held that two sisters had entered into an irrevocable agreement in relation to the disposition of their property in their wills and that the estate of the surviving sister fell to be distributed in accordance with the earlier mutual wills rather then a later will in which she left most of her estate to a different beneficiary. He reiterated that for the doctrine to apply there has to be what amounts to a contract between the two testators that both wills will be irrevocable and remain unaltered and that a common intention, expectation or desire is not enough.[237] In addition, he stressed that the mere execution of reciprocal wills does not imply any agreement either as to revocation or non-revocation and that while the agreement may be oral or in writing, it must be established by clear and satisfactory evidence on the balance of probabilities. As Pawlowski and Brown point out, 'the consequences of the constructive trust imposed upon the survivor may be particularly onerous, given that all of the survivor's property may be locked into the trust and, at the same time, he may have formed additional commitments towards new partners or children'.[238] They suggest that mutual wills are likely to remain unpopular, 'not least because there are other mechanisms which provide far greater flexibility for the devolution of property on death.'[239]

An interesting point was raised in the judgment of David Donaldson QC, sitting as a Deputy High Court judge, in *Healey v Brown*,[240] where the surviving spouse, instead of revoking his will, transferred property into the joint names of himself and the first named defendant which led to the property passing to this defendant by right of survivorship on his death. The wills of the spouses had been made in identical form leaving a named property to the survivor and then to the claimant, who was the wife's niece, with the remainder of the estate going to the first named defendant, the husband's son by an earlier marriage. While it was accepted by the first named defendant that there was sufficient evidence of an agreement that the survivor should not revoke his or her will after the other's death, it was necessary for the court to decide what if any, obligations and restrictions in relation to the property were imposed on a surviving testator who has executed a mutual will and undertaken not to revoke it. Although this point had not been developed in earlier cases, Judge Donaldson was satisfied that where a fiduciary duty is breached by a voluntary disposition *inter vivos* of the property in question, the crystallization of the fiduciary obligation occurs at the moment of that disposition. In his view gifts

236. [2010] EWHC 2154 (Ch). See further Griffiths [2011] Conv 511.
237. *Ibid.* at [59].
238. [2012] Conv 467, 480.
239. *Ibid.* at 483.
240. [2002] WTLR 849. See Davis [2003] Conv 238.

or settlements *inter vivos*, if calculated to defeat the intention of the agreement would be in breach of it and he held that, subject to the provisions of section 2 of the Law of Property (Miscellaneous Provisions) Act 1989,[241] the doctrine of mutual wills would apply so as to impose a constructive trust attaching to the property in the claimant's favour. On the facts, Judge Donaldson held that the claimant was prevented by the provisions of section 2 of the Act of 1989 from establishing the contract which *Re Goodchild*[242] makes clear is necessary for the mutual wills doctrine to apply. However, he was satisfied that, on the basis of an agreement which was only deprived of legal contractual character by section 2 of the 1989 Act to the effect that her share in the flat would be left to her niece, the deceased had left her estate to her husband. In his view it would be entirely inequitable to frustrate her expectation and it was unconscionable for her husband to seek to do so by his actions after her death in seeking to pass the flat to the first named defendant. He therefore concluded that the husband had accepted a trust in favour of the claimant to pass his wife's half share in the property under his will and that the first named defendant held it for himself and the claimant in equal shares.

The Time at which the Trust Arises

While some commentators have argued that the trust may arise either at the date of the agreement or at the time when the survivor dies, the correct view would seem to be that it arises on the death of the first party. This means that the interest of a beneficiary will not lapse if he predeceases the survivor. In *Re Hagger*[243] a husband and wife made joint wills leaving a life interest in their property to the survivor and after that party's death on trust for sale for nine beneficiaries. One of these beneficiaries survived the wife, but predeceased the husband who left the property on different trusts. Clauson J held that the will operated as a trust from the date of the wife's death. In his view, [t]here is, accordingly, no lapse by reason of [the deceased beneficiary's] death in the husband's lifetime, but after the wife's death.'[244] This was also the approach adopted by the Court of Appeal in *Olins v Walters*,[245] where Mummery LJ accepted that the trust is immediately binding and was not postponed so that it would take effect only after the death of the second testator.

Until recently it was unclear whether the trust only arose when the survivor

241. Section 2 of the Law of Property (Miscellaneous Provisions) Act 1989 lays down the requirement that contracts for the sale or other disposition of an interest in land can only be made in writing. However, s. 2(5) provides that nothing in the section shall affect the creation or operation of resulting, implied or resulting trusts, and in the circumstances the court was prepared to impose a constructive trust.
242. [1997] 1 WLR 1216.
243. [1930] 2 Ch 190.
244. *Ibid.* at 195.
245. [2009] Ch 212, 222.

received a benefit under the will of the first party to die.[246] As O'Hagan has pointed out, academic opinion favoured the requirement of benefit 'because to benefit under an agreement and afterwards renege on that same agreement is manifestly fraudulent'.[247] However, the decision of Morritt J in *Re Dale*[248] resolved this question by making it clear that a constructive trust can arise even where the survivor does not take any benefit from the will of the first testator.[249] A husband and wife executed identical wills which both contained a bequest of their property in favour of their daughter and son in equal shares or to the survivor of them. Two months later the husband died and subsequently the wife made a new will in which she revoked all previous wills and bequeathed to the daughter the sum of £300, leaving the son the remainder of her property. The daughter claimed that the mutual wills had been made pursuant to a binding and irrevocable agreement and that the son held the estate of the mother as trustee for both of them in equal shares. The court had to consider as a preliminary issue the question of whether, for the doctrine of mutual wills to apply, it was necessary for the second testator to die to have obtained a personal financial benefit under the will of the first testator to die. In answering this question in the negative, Morritt J held that since the aim of the principle underlying the doctrine of mutual wills was to prevent fraud on the first testator to die, it was not confined to cases in which the surviving testator had benefited under the will of the first testator but extended to cases where the two testators had left their property to beneficiaries other than themselves.[250]

This approach was confirmed by the decision of the Court of Appeal of British Columbia in *University of Manitoba v Sanderson Estate*,[251] in which it was held that the doctrine of mutual wills applied whether or not the survivor received a benefit under the will of the first to die.

Conclusions

Judicial and academic opinion has varied on the issue of the usefulness or otherwise of the doctrine of mutual wills. Morritt LJ described the doctrine as 'anomalous' in the course of his judgment in *Re Goodchild*,[252] while it has been commented that 'the imposition by law of a trust in cases of mutual wills is a clumsy and inadequate way of dealing with a complicated problem'.[253] In

246. See Graham (1951) 15 Conv 28, 35-36.
247. O'Hagan (1994) 144 NLJ 1272.
248. [1994] Ch 31. See O'Hagan (1994) 144 NLJ 1272.
249. See also *Charles v Fraser* [2010] EWHC 2154 (Ch) at [59(iv)].
250. Note that Friel has commented (1996) 1 CPLJ 2, 4 that where a survivor takes no benefit under a mutual will, the use of a constructive trust on property is 'inappropriate and cannot be justified by legal theory'. Instead he suggests that a trust should be imposed not on the property but on the implementation of the contract between the parties.
251. (1998) 155 DLR (4th) 40.
252. [1997] 1 WLR 1216, 1230.
253. Glister and Lee, *Hanbury and Martin: Modern Equity* (21st ed., 2018) p. 277.

addition, Friel has suggested that there is an emerging judicial reluctance to use the device of the constructive trust to resolve 'what are inherently problems within the law of contract'.[254] However, O'Hagan has stated that 'it is in this sphere that the constructive trust is seen in one of its most flexible forms' and the doctrine of mutual wills remains for the present a useful example of how a constructive trust will be imposed by equity to prevent unconscionable or fraudulent conduct.[255] Liew has also suggested that instead of attempting to marginalise or abolish the mutual wills doctrine, attention should be focused on addressing the *practical* problems which may arise in relation to its operation.[256]

It should be noted that in England the Law Commission in its Consultation Paper, *Making a Will*,[257] has examined the operation of the mutual wills doctrine and has noted that it is potentially unfair that claims under the Inheritance (Provision for Family and Dependents) Act 1975 cannot be made against property that is subject to a mutual wills arrangement. It suggests that allowing a claim for financial provision under the 1975 Act against property in a deceased person's estate that is subject to a mutual wills arrangement is a plausible route for reform and that it 'provides a middle ground between abolition and encouragement of the doctrine, while providing some relief from the inflexibility of mutual wills.'[258] It has therefore proposed that section 8 of the Inheritance (Provision for Family and Dependants) Act 1975 be amended to provide that property that is subject to a mutual wills arrangement be treated as part of a person's net estate.

The *Pallant v Morgan* Equity

The so-called '*Pallant v Morgan* equity' is a useful illustration of the innovative and flexible nature of a constructive trust. It is clear from the decision of the Court of Appeal in *Banner Homes Group plc v Luff Developments Ltd*[259] that this so-called *Pallant v Morgan* equity[260] will arise where there is an agreement, arrangement or understanding[261] in relation to the purchase of property between parties which is not necessarily contractually enforceable by virtue of which

254. Friel (1996) 1 CPLJ 2, 4.
255. O'Hagan (1994) 144 NLJ 1272.
256. (2016) 132 LQR 664, 677.
257. Law Commission Consultation Paper 231 (2017) Chapter 12.
258. *Ibid.*, para. 12.34.
259. [2000] Ch 372. See further Thompson [2001] Conv 265; Hopkins [2002] Conv 35; Nield (2003) LS 311; McFarlane (2004) 120 LQR 667.
260. As Hopkins comments [2002] Conv 35, 36, 'although the doctrine was named by reference to an earlier case, the *Pallant v Morgan* equity is the creation of the Court of Appeal in *Banner Homes*'. See further *Pallant v Morgan* [1953] Ch 43; *Chattock v Muller* (1878) 8 Ch D 117.
261. Such an agreement or understanding is crucial and without it no constructive trust can arise, see *Kilcarne Holdings Ltd v Targetfollow (Birmingham) Ltd* [2005] EWCA Civ 135.

it is contemplated that one party will take steps to acquire the property and the other party will thereby obtain some interest in it.[262] It is necessary that in reliance on the arrangement or understanding the non-acquiring party should do, or omit to do, something which confers an advantage on the acquiring party in relation to the acquisition of the property or is detrimental to the ability of the non-acquiring party to obtain the property on equal terms. As Chadwick LJ stated in *Banner Homes*, '[i]t is the existence of the advantage to the one, or detriment to the other, gained or suffered as a consequence of the arrangement or understanding, which leads to the conclusion that it would be inequitable or unconscionable to allow the acquiring party to retain the property for himself in a manner inconsistent with the arrangement or understanding which enabled him to acquire it.'[263] He added that although in many cases the advantage or detriment will be found in the agreement of the non-acquiring party to keep out of the market, this is not a necessary feature; either advantage or detriment would suffice and what is essential is that the circumstances make it inequitable for the acquiring party to retain the property for himself in a manner inconsistent with the arrangement or understanding on the basis of which the non-acquiring party has acted. In the circumstances where the defendant had obtained the benefit of keeping the plaintiff out of the market for the property as a rival bidder and knowing it had the plaintiff's support as a potential joint venturer, the Court of Appeal concluded that it would be inequitable to allow the defendant to treat the property as its own and it held that one half of the property was held on a constructive trust for the plaintiff.

The principles set out in *Banner Homes* were also approved by the Court of Appeal in *Baynes Clarke v Corless*,[264] although on the facts it upheld the trial judge's conclusion that there had been no reliance on an agreement so as to make it unconscionable for the purchaser to retain the land in question in the circumstances. Patten LJ stated as follows:

> The key to the imposition of a constructive trust is that it would be unconscionable for the purchasing party to retain ownership of the land for his own benefit having regard to the prior agreement reached and to the claimants' reliance upon it. Questions of unconscionability are matters for the court which fall to be decided on an objective basis having regard to the terms agreed or the representations made and the effect which they had.[265]

These principles were also considered by Lord Scott in the decision of the

262. It has been argued that the separate treatment of the so-called '*Pallant v Morgan* equity' is not justified and that it is simply an example of a trust arising in response to an agent's breach of fiduciary duty. See Grower [2016] Conv 434.
263. [2000] Ch 372, 389.
264. [2010] WTLR 751.
265. *Ibid.* at [40].

House of Lords in *Cobbe v Yeoman's Row Management Ltd*,[266] although on the facts he was satisfied that a constructive trust such as that imposed in the failed joint venture cases like *Banner Homes* could not be imposed in the case before him. He stated that '[d]espite the unconscionability of the appellant's behaviour in withdrawing from the inchoate agreement immediately planning permission had been obtained, this seems to me a wholly inadequate basis for imposing a constructive trust over the property in order to provide Mr Cobbe with a remedy for his disappointed expectations.'[267] Lord Scott concluded that a claim for the imposition of a constructive trust in order to provide a remedy for a disappointed expectation engendered by a representation made in the context of incomplete contractual negotiations was misconceived and could not be sustained by reliance on unconscionable behaviour on the part of the representor.[268]

As Hopkins has pointed out, since the decision of the Court of Appeal in *Banner Homes*, the so-called *Pallant v Morgan* constructive trust 'has been notable for instances of its rejection, rather than its successful application.'[269] This may be explained, at least in part, by the courts' increasing reluctance to impose a constructive trust in commercial situations where the parties have not entered into a contractually binding agreement. These underlying issues were considered by the members of the Court of Appeal in *Crossco No. 4 Unlimited v Jolan Ltd*,[270] in which it declined to impose a *Pallant v Morgan* constructive trust. Etherton LJ in a dissenting judgment suggested that '[t]he passage of time and developments in the law have ... shown the connection between the common intention constructive trust and the *Pallant v Morgan* equity as explained and applied in *Banner Homes* to be untenable.'[271] He added that, '[i]n a commercial context, it is to be expected that the parties will normally take legal advice about their respective rights and interests and will normally reduce their agreements to writing and will not expect to be bound until a contract has been made,' referring to the *dicta* of Lord Walker in *Cobbe v Yeoman's Row Management Ltd*.[272] In his view it was not necessary to resort to the common intention constructive trust to provide an explanation for the cases

---

266. [2008] 1 WLR 1752.
267. *Ibid.* at 1772.
268. These principles were applied by Jeremy Cousins QC, sitting as a Deputy High Court judge, in *A. v B.* [2008] EWHC 2687 (Ch), where he also held that the claimant had failed to bring her claim within the parameters necessary to establish a *Pallant v Morgan* equity.
269. [2012] Conv 327. This trend has continued, see e.g. *Kiwak v Reiner* [2017] EWHC 3018 (Ch); *Michael v Phillips* [2017] EWHC 614 (QB). However, note the first instance decision of *Kearns Brothers Ltd v Hova Developments Ltd* [2012] EWHC 2968 (Ch) in which it was held that a so-called *Pallant v Morgan* trust arose.
270. [2012] 2 All ER 754. See further Hopkins [2012] Conv 327; Lower [2012] Conv 379; Yip (2013) 33 LS 549.
271. *Ibid.* at 780.
272. [2008] 1 WLR 1752, 1782, 1785.

in which the *Pallant v Morgan* equity had been applied and these situations in his opinion 'ought to be explained in wholly conventional terms by the existence and breach of fiduciary duty'.[273] While the majority judges, Arden and McFarlane LJJ, were at one level sympathetic to this explanation, Arden LJ stated that the reasoning in *Banner Homes* makes it clear that the *ratio* of that case was based on a common intention constructive trust. She added that while the speech of Lord Walker in *Stack v Dowden*[274] and the judgment of Baroness Hale and Lord Walker in *Jones v Kernott*[275] may mean that common intention constructive trusts may be limited in the future to family cases, she did not consider that that position was so clear as to make it possible for the court to treat the *ratio* of *Banner Homes* as not binding on it. On the basis that no finding of unconscionable conduct could be made, she held that the trial judge had been correct to conclude that the claim that a constructive trust arose should be dismissed. However, the tenor of Arden LJ's judgment suggests that a restriction of the application of the *Banner Homes* principles in commercial situations would have advantages and as she pointed out, it 'would be consistent with developments in the law of proprietary estoppel.'[276] She expressed the view that '[f]or the law in general to provide scope for claims in respect of unsuccessful negotiations that do not result in legally enforceable contracts would, in my judgment, be likely to inhibit the efficient pursuit of commercial negotiations, which is a necessary part of proper entrepreneurial activity.'[277]

The judgment of Lewison LJ in the Court of Appeal in *Generator Developments Ltd v Lidl UK GmbH*[278] also supports the view that there will be a reluctance to make a finding that a *Pallant v Morgan* equity arises in what is clearly a wholly commercial context. He stated that the matter before the court 'was a case of commercial parties, advised by lawyers, working at arms' length towards the conclusion of an agreement for a purely commercial enterprise the terms of which were never agreed.'[279] He pointed out that the proposed joint venture had been made 'subject to contract' and said that where negotiations in a commercial context are expressly made in these terms there is no understanding or arrangement capable of satisfying the requirements for a *Pallant v Morgan* equity. Lewison LJ added that 'it cannot be unconscionable to exercise a right which has been expressly reserved to both parties by means of the "subject to contract" formula.'[280] In his view the parties had taken the commercial risk that one or other of them might back out of the proposed transaction and he referred

273. [2012] 2 All ER 754, 780.
274. [2007] 2 AC 432.
275. [2012] 1 AC 776.
276. [2012] 2 All ER 754, 791.
277. *Ibid.* at 791-792.
278. [2018] EWCA Civ 396.
279. *Ibid.* at [78].
280. *Ibid.* at [85].

to the point made by Lord Walker in *Cobbe v Yeoman's Row Management Ltd*[281] that 'equity will not intervene in a case where the parties expressly agree that a putative agreement is binding in honour only.'[282] The only signs of a more flexible approach being taken in a commercial context in recent decisions is in the *dicta* of Kitchin LJ in the Court of Appeal in *Farrar v Miller*,[283] although it should be noted that this judgment was delivered at a preliminary stage in the proceedings which concerned a dispute between property developers. In the course of his judgment concluding that the plaintiff should be entitled to amend the particulars of his claim to allege that a constructive trust arose, Kitchin LJ commented that 'it is not a requirement of a *Pallant v Morgan* equity that the agreement or arrangement between the parties is sufficiently certain to be contractually enforceable.'[284] However, he added that he recognised that the commercial context and the absence of agreement on critical parts of the deal might indicate there was never a common intention to enter into any kind of legal commitment.

Hopkins pointed out, commenting even before the decision of the Court of Appeal in *Generator Developments*, that decisions such as *Crossco* and *Cobbe* illustrated the reluctance of the courts to interfere in commercial situations and he suggested that '[t]he decisions are perhaps indicative of an increasing reluctance to invoke equity where agreements reached in arm's length negotiations are not consigned to legal formality.'[285] However, as Hopkins has argued elsewhere, '[d]espite being presented by the courts as a dichotomy ... in reality, the domestic and commercial lie on a continuum of factual situations.'[286] So, it is fair to say that while there is evidence of an increasing reluctance to impose a constructive trust in the types of commercial scenarios in which the so-called *Pallant v Morgan* equity would typically be invoked, a rigid distinction between commercial and non-commercial cases is not always easy to draw. While the context will undoubtedly be a factor, it would be premature to suggest that this form of constructive trust will no longer be recognised where the parties are involved in a purely commercial relationship.

The concept of the *Pallant v Morgan* equity has been approved of and applied in this jurisdiction by Clarke J in the High Court in *Shiel v McKeon*.[287] In this case a meeting between the parties had taken place as a result of which the plaintiff contended that an arrangement had been entered into whereby the defendant would purchase a property, retaining the rear portion for himself, while holding the front portion consisting of the house and the gardens immediately around it on trust for the plaintiff. However, the existence of such

281. [2008] 1 WLR 1752, 1788-1789.
282. [2018] EWCA Civ 396 at [79].
283. [2018] EWCA Civ 172.
284. *Ibid.* at [46].
285. [2012] Conv 327, 333.
286. (2011) 31 LS 175, 177.
287. [2007] 2 ILRM 144.

an arrangement was strenuously denied by the defendant. Clarke J commented that while there did not seem to be any direct Irish authority on the matter, he saw no reason not to follow the logic of the decisions in *Pallant v Morgan* and *Banner Homes* and to hold that, independent of an entitlement to enforce a contract, there is an equitable entitlement to enforce an arrangement which may not necessarily fulfil all the requirements for the enforcement of a contract. He stated that, as was pointed out in *Banner Homes*, there would be no need for a *Pallant v Morgan* equity in circumstances where there was an enforceable contract because the aggrieved party could simply seek specific performance. In his view 'the *Pallant v Morgan* equity derives from the principle that it would be inequitable for a person who obtains a benefit, such as the withdrawal of a competitor from a bidding process, to retain the benefit without conceding the substance of the arrangement'.[288]

On the facts of the case, Clarke J concluded that there was at least an informal arrangement entered into between the parties which led the plaintiff to the reasonable belief that the defendant would purchase the property on trust partly on his behalf. This led the plaintiff to refrain from attempting to reactivate his bid for the property and led the defendant to believe that the plaintiff would no longer actively pursue it. However, this was not the end of the matter given that the plaintiff was seeking relief of an equitable nature. Clarke J found that it was clear that the plaintiff was aware that he had missed the deadline imposed by the estate agent dealing with the matter for making a higher offer when he met the defendant and that the defendant did not know that the plaintiff had failed to meet this deadline. He referred to the principle that 'he who seeks equity must do equity' and said that he must have regard to whether it would be inequitable to allow the plaintiff to benefit from an arrangement entered into by him in circumstances where he was aware that the defendant was under a misapprehension as to the plaintiff's negotiating position. In the circumstances Clarke J concluded that he was satisfied that equity did not require that the defendant comply with the terms of the informal arrangement which had been procured in circumstances where one party had been, to the knowledge of the other party, unaware of a significant weakness in that party's position.

The Trustee de Son Tort

Where a person intermeddles in the affairs of a trust or performs acts characteristic of a trustee he will become a trustee de son tort, i.e. because of his wrong. This principle was set out by Smith LJ in *Mara v Browne*[289] as follows:

> [I]f one, not being a trustee and not having authority from a trustee, takes upon himself to intermeddle with trust matters or to do acts characteristic

288. *Ibid.* at 151.
289. [1896] 1 Ch 199, 209.

> of the office of trustee he may thereby make himself what is called in law a trustee of his own wrong — i.e., a trustee de son tort, or as it is also termed, a constructive trustee.

As Lord Sumption JSC noted in *Williams v Central Bank of Nigeria*,[290] a distinct head of liability arises where individuals lawfully assume fiduciary obligations in relation to trust property, but without a formal appointment. In such a case he suggested '[t]hey are true trustees, and if the assets are not applied in accordance with the trust, equity will enforce the obligations that they have assumed by virtue of their status exactly as if they had been appointed by deed.'[291]

In essence liability under this heading depends on the voluntary assumption of the obligations of trusteeship followed by actions which amount to a breach of trust. A stranger who purports to act as a trustee will be subject to all the liabilities usually imposed on an expressly appointed trustee and to the fiduciary obligations which preclude him from profiting from his position or from placing himself in a situation where his duty and interests may conflict.

In *Selangor United Rubber Estates Ltd v Craddock (No. 3)*[292] Ungoed-Thomas J identified the following distinguishing features of a trustee de son tort: such persons do not claim to act in their own right but rather for the beneficiaries; their assumption to act is not of itself a ground of liability, except in the sense of liability to account for any failure in the duty so assumed, and their status as trustees precedes the occurrence which may be the subject of a claim against them. This can be contrasted with the situations which will be considered in Chapter 9 where no trusteeship (or more properly now described as liability to account) arises before, but only by reason of the action complained of, and where the individuals involved claim to act in their own right and not for the beneficiaries.

The Vendor as Constructive Trustee

Traditionally, it has been accepted that where a vendor enters into a specifically enforceable contract for sale, equity regards him as a constructive trustee of the property which forms the subject-matter of the contract until completion.[293] This is an example of the equitable doctrine of conversion and the purchaser is regarded as the owner of the property while the vendor is looked upon as the owner of the purchase monies. Contracts which are capable of being

---

290. [2014] AC 1189.
291. *Ibid.* at 1197.
292. [1968] 1 WLR 1555, 1579.
293. Although note how this point was modified by the view taken by the majority of the Supreme Court in *Tempany v Hynes* [1976] IR 101 considered *infra*, to the effect that the vendor only becomes a trustee of the beneficial interest to the extent to which the purchase price is paid. The traditional position was restored by the provisions of s.52(1) of the Land and Conveyancing Law Reform Act 2009, also considered *infra*.

specifically enforced are predominantly contracts for the sale of land, as specific performance will only be granted where a breach of contract cannot be adequately compensated by an award of damages.[294]

The traditional position in England was set out by Jessel MR in *Lysaght v Edwards*[295] in the following terms: 'The moment you have a valid contract for sale the vendor becomes in equity a trustee for the purchaser of the estate sold, and the beneficial ownership passes to the purchaser.'[296] However, more recently it has been accepted, as Lord Walker stated in *Jerome v Kelly*,[297] that 'it would … be wrong to treat an uncompleted contract for the sale of land as equivalent to an immediate, irrevocable declaration of trust' and the view generally accepted in that jurisdiction is that once the vendor has received the full purchase price, he is no more than a bare trustee with limited duties to perform.[298]

The position as set out in *Lysaght* was also the position accepted by Henchy J in a minority judgment delivered in *Tempany v Hynes*.[299] However, the view of the majority[300] of the Supreme Court as set out by Kenny J was as follows:

> [A] vendor who signs a contract with a purchaser for the sale of land becomes a trustee in the sense that he is bound to take reasonable care of the property until the sale is completed, but he becomes a trustee of the beneficial interest to the extent only to which the purchase price is paid. He is not a trustee of the beneficial interest merely because he signs a contract.[301]

The Law Reform Commission considered the issue of the interests of vendors and purchasers of land during the period between contract and completion in a report published in 1995[302] and concluded that the approach adopted by Henchy J in his minority judgment in *Tempany* was the 'only means by which the purchaser's interests prior to completion may be adequately protected'. The

---

294. See further *infra* Chapter 15.
295. (1876) 2 Ch D 499, 506.
296. For a recent analysis defending the vendor/purchaser constructive trust, see Turner (2012) 128 LQR 582.
297. [2004] 1 WLR 1409, 1419.
298. *Conn v Ezair* [2019] EWHC 1722 (Ch) at [54]. See also *Clarke v Ramuz* [1891] 2 QB 456, 459-460.
299. [1976] IR 101, 109. Henchy J stated: 'When a binding contract for the sale of land has been made, the law treats the beneficial ownership as having passed to the purchaser from the time the contract was made … from then until the time of completion, regardless of whether the purchase money has been paid or not, the vendor, in whom the legal estate is still vested, is treated for certain purposes as a trustee for the purchaser.' This also seems to be the view accepted in Australia, see *Legione v Hateley* (1983) 152 CLR 406; *KLDE Pty Ltd v Commissioner of Stamp Duties* (1984) 58 ALJR 545.
300. See the judgment of Kenny J, with whom O'Higgins CJ concurred.
301. *Ibid.* at 114.
302. LRC 49-1995.

Commission, therefore, recommended the enactment of a statutory provision providing that when a binding contract for the sale of land has been entered into, the law should treat the beneficial ownership as having passed to the purchaser from the time the contract was made, subject to the condition that the sale be completed. Section 52(1) of the Land and Conveyancing Law Reform Act 2009 now provides that the entire beneficial interest will pass to the purchaser on the making of an enforceable contract for the sale or other disposition of land, although it goes on to provide in subsection (2) that this will not affect the vendor's obligation to maintain the land so long as possession is retained, his liability for loss or damage under any contractual provision dealing with such risk, or his right to rescind the contract for failure by the purchaser to complete or other breach of contract.

Once the beneficial interest passes, the vendor is recognised as being a trustee of the property in the sense that he must take reasonable care of it.[303] A vendor must maintain the property in a reasonable state of repair,[304] and will undoubtedly incur liability if he wilfully damages the property.[305] The obligation has been described by Lord Coleridge in *Clarke v Ramuz*[306] as being 'to use reasonable care to preserve the property in a reasonable state of preservation and so far as may be, as it was when the contract was made.' In that case while the vendor remained in possession of property, a trespasser removed all the surface soil. It was held that the purchaser could maintain an action against the vendor for breach of trust by reason of the fact that he had taken no care to prevent the removal of the soil. However, it is only where the vendor acts in breach of his trust obligations or fails to take reasonable care that he can be made liable and any damage to the property which occurs without any fault on the part of the vendor is the responsibility of the purchaser.

The traditional position was that when a purchaser enters into a specifically enforceable contract for sale, the risk of accidental damage to the property passes to him and he should insure against such risk. As Jessel MR stated in *Lysaght v Edwards*:[307]

---

303. However, it is clear from the judgment of Lawrence Collins J in *Eaglewood Properties Ltd v Patel* [2005] 1 WLR 1961, 1978 that this obligation to take reasonable care to preserve the property does not extend to a lessor's duty to impose covenants on purchasers of adjoining properties unless that duty is imposed by the contract of sale of the property.
304. *Royal Bristol Permanent Building Society v Bomash* (1887) 35 Ch D 390. See also s. 52(2)(a) of the Land and Conveyancing Law Reform Act 2009, referred to *supra*.
305. *Lysaght v Edwards* (1876) 2 Ch D 499, 507.
306. [1891] 2 QB 456, 459-460.
307. (1876) 2 Ch D 499, 507. Although see Thompson [1984] Conv 43. Note also that the Law Commission in England recommended that the risk should only pass on completion (see Law Commission Report No. 191 para. 2.25 (1990)) and such a provision has also been incorporated in the Standard Conditions of Sale in that jurisdiction.

> [If] anything happens to the estate between the time of the sale and the time of completion of the purchase it is at the risk of the purchaser. If it is a house that is sold, and the house is burnt down the purchaser loses the house. He must insure it himself if he wants to provide against such an accident.

This principle is well illustrated by the decision in *Rayner v Preston*,[308] in which a vendor contracted with a purchaser for the sale of a house which had been insured by the vendor against fire. After the date of the contract but before completion, the property was damaged by fire and the vendor received insurance money in respect of it. It was held that the purchaser was not entitled as against the vendor to the benefit of the insurance money; the risk had passed to the purchaser and it was therefore his responsibility to ensure that the premises were insured.[309] However, this traditional position was regarded as being unfair to purchasers[310] and the effect of the Law Society of Ireland's Conditions of Sale is that, subject to certain exceptions,[311] the risk remains with the vendor between the date of same and completion, although this liability is limited to the amount of the purchase price.[312] It should also be reiterated that section 52(2)(b) of the Land and Conveyancing Law Reform Act 2009 provides that the beneficial interest passing to the purchaser on the making of an enforceable contract shall not affect the liability of the vendor for loss and damage under any contractual provision dealing with such risk.

The decision in *Rayner v Preston* also illustrates the qualified nature of the constructive trusteeship which arises in such cases; while the vendor is a constructive trustee of the land, he is not trustee of anything substituted for the land such as insurance money paid to him under his own insurance policy in relation to damage to the land caused by fire. This point was made by Cotton LJ in *Rayner*, where he said that a vendor was a trustee 'in a qualified sense

308. (1881) 18 Ch D 1. See also *Re Hamilton-Snowball's Conveyance* [1959] Ch 308.
309. Although note that the law on this point has been changed in England by the provisions of s. 47 of the Law of Property Act 1925 which provides that a purchaser may, on completion of the contract, recover from the vendor any insurance money paid in respect of any damage or destruction of the property. See Wellings (1959) 23 Conv 173, 174.
310. The Law Reform Commission pointed out in a report published in 1991 (LRC 39-1991) that it was unsatisfactory that the law as to the passing of risk did not accord with the reasonable expectations of the ordinary person. It recommended (p. 19) that the risk should instead pass to the purchaser 'in all situations where the purchaser goes into possession of the premises, or on completion of the purchase, whichever is the earlier'.
311. See clause 40 of the Conditions of Sale (2019 edition).
312. See clause 39 of the Conditions of Sale (2019 edition).

only'.[313] This fact was also noted by Lord Cairns in *Shaw v Foster*[314] in the following terms:

> [T]he vendor, whom I have called the trustee, was not a mere dormant trustee, he was a trustee having a personal and substantial interest in the property, a right to protect that interest and an active right to assert that interest if anything should be done in derogation of it. The relation therefore, of trustee and *cestui que trust* subsisted, but subsisted subject to the paramount right of the vendor and trustee to protect his own interest as vendor of the property.

The qualified nature of the trust relationship existing between a vendor and purchaser in these circumstances is further illustrated by the fact that the vendor is entitled to keep the rents and profits of the land until completion and is under a duty to discharge all outgoings such as rates and taxes which may be payable in respect of the property until this date.[315] In addition, the vendor may retain possession of the land until the purchase price is paid and if the land is conveyed before this, he will have a lien on the land for the balance of the unpaid purchase money.[316] The view that beneficial ownership of the property is effectively 'split' between vendor and purchaser has been expressed by Lord Walker in *Jerome v Kelly*[317] in the following terms:

> It would therefore be wrong to treat an uncompleted contract for the sale of land as equivalent to an immediate, irrevocable declaration of trust (or assignment of beneficial interest) in the land. Neither the seller nor the buyer has unqualified beneficial ownership. Beneficial ownership of the land is in a sense split between the seller and buyer on the provisional assumptions that specific performance is available and that the contract will in due course be completed, if necessary by the court ordering specific

313. (1881) 18 Ch D 1, 6. See also *Jerome v Kelly* [2004] 1 WLR 1409, 1419 where Lord Walker commented that '[n]either the seller nor the buyer has unqualified beneficial ownership.'
314. (1872) LR 5 HL 321, 338. As Oakley comments, 'the inevitable self interest of the vendor in the successful conclusion of the transaction does not sit very easily with his classification as a trustee.' See Oakley, *Parker and Mellows: Modern Law of Trusts* (9th ed., 2008) p. 483.
315. *Re Highett and Bird's Contract* [1902] 2 Ch 214. However, it would appear that the purchaser is entitled to take the benefit and burden of any gains or losses of a capital nature accruing to the property.
316. *Mackreth v Symmons* (1808) 15 Ves 329. This vendor's lien can be registered as a burden under s. 69(1) of the Registration of Title Act 1964. Similarly, the purchaser will have a lien on the land in respect of any purchase money paid prior to completion, see *Re Strong* [1940] IR 382.
317. [2004] 1 WLR 1409, 1419. See also *Maharaj v Johnson* [2015] UKPC 28 at [17].

performance. In the meantime, the seller is entitled to enjoyment of the land or its rental income.

The nature of the relationship between vendor and purchaser was considered in detail by the Supreme Court of the United Kingdom in *Southern Pacific Mortgages Ltd v Scott*.[318] Lord Collins JSC held that vendors acquired no more than personal rights against purchasers when they agreed to sell their properties on the basis of the purchasers' promises that they would be entitled to remain in occupation. In his view these rights would only become proprietary and capable of taking priority over a mortgage when they were fed by the purchasers' acquisition of the legal estate on completion.[319] Baroness Hale JSC agreed that a 'purchaser was not in a position either at the date of exchange of contracts or at any time up until completion of the purchase to confer equitable proprietary, as opposed to merely personal, rights on the vendor.'[320] However, she expressed the view that this conclusion produced a harsh result and suggested that there should be some middle ground approach between the 'all or nothing' approach of the law.

The relationship which arises between vendor and purchaser has been described as 'a highly self-interested modified form of trusteeship'[321] and some commentators have questioned whether the terms trustee and beneficiary should be used at all to describe the relationship between the vendor and the purchaser in such situations.[322] However, it is also recognised that it is arguably too late to recast the nature of this relationship,[323] and the best approach is to regard the use of such terminology with a certain degree of caution.

The Mortgagee as Constructive Trustee

To a limited extent the liability of a mortgagee to a mortgagor has been described in terms of a trust relationship, although for a number of reasons the drawing of comparisons between the position of a mortgagee and that of a trustee has been described as inappropriate. The strength of the trust analogy

318. [2015] AC 385. See further Televantos and Maniscalco [2015] CLJ 27; Sparkes [2015] Conv 301.
319. See also *Conn v Ezair* [2019] EWHC 1722 (Ch) at [46].
320. [2015] AC 385, 421.
321. Hayton, Matthews and Mitchell, *Underhill and Hayton: The Law Relating to Trusts and Trustees* (19th ed., 2016) p. 602.
322. See Waters, *The Constructive Trust* (1964) where the opinion is expressed that until the purchase price is paid in full, the operation of a relationship of trustee and beneficiary is excluded by the fact that each party continues to guard their own position in a manner quite inconsistent with a trust relationship. Cope has commented in *Constructive Trusts* (1992) p. 970 that the use of the term 'constructive trust' in the context of vendor and purchaser is an 'anomalous and inappropriate analogy'.
323. Glister and Lee, *Hanbury and Martin: Modern Equity* (21st ed., 2018) p. 267 and Cope, *Constructive Trusts* (1992) p. 970.

was never as strong in relation to mortgagees as it was in respect of vendors of property, particularly in view of the fact that a mortgagee did not usually enter into possession of the mortgaged property, while the vendor tended to remain in possession until completion. In addition, the mortgagee's natural desire to protect his own interests in the mortgage transaction and the trustee's obligation to act in the best interests of the beneficiaries were generally regarded as being incompatible.

However, traditionally where a mortgagee retained a surplus after exercising a power of sale over the mortgaged property, he held this on a constructive trust for whoever was entitled to the equity of redemption. This constructive trust was given statutory force by section 21(3) of the Conveyancing Act 1881 which gave effect to previous practice.[324] This provision was repealed by the Land and Conveyancing Law Reform Act 2009[325] and replaced by sections 107(1) and (2) of that Act.

In addition, it should be noted that Cope suggests that one further aspect of the mortgagee's exercise of his power of sale may still give rise to a liability in equity to account as a constructive trustee, namely where a mortgagee purports to exercise this power in favour of himself without the fully informed consent of the mortgagor.[326]

Where Property is Acquired by a Joint Tenant by the Killing of the Co-Tenant

Where property is owned by parties jointly and one of them kills the other, a joint tenancy is severed upon the death of the victim. His or her half share will not form part of the latter's estate and the legal interest will vest in the perpetrator. However, in equity it has been held in a number of common law jurisdictions that this half share should be held on a constructive trust for the victim's estate.

This issue arose in this jurisdiction in *Cawley v Lillis*,[327] in which the defendant had been convicted of the manslaughter of his wife and an application was made to the court to determine the interest, if any, of the defendant in assets owned pursuant to a joint tenancy by the parties. Laffoy J held, following relevant Canadian[328] and New Zealand[329] authorities, that on the death of the deceased, a half share of the joint assets became vested in the defendant upon a constructive trust for the deceased's estate. In her view, 'if the court were to hold that on the date of the death of the deceased the joint assets accrued to the

324. In England, this subsection has been replaced by s. 105 of the Law of Property Act 1925.
325. Schedule 2, Part 4.
326. Cope, *Constructive Trusts* (1992) p. 976.
327. [2012] 1 IR 281.
328. *Schobelt v Barber* (1966) 60 DLR (2d) 519.
329. *Re Pechar, Deceased* [1969] 1 NZLR 574.

defendant solely and were held by him on a constructive trust for himself and the estate of the deceased in equal shares, that outcome, viewed objectively at that time, could not be regarded as conferring a benefit on the defendant as a result of the crime he committed.'[330]

Subsequently in its Report on *Prevention of Benefit from Homicide*,[331] the Law Reform Commission reviewed this issue. The Commission recommended that without prejudice to the presumption that, after severance, the victim holds at least half of the interest in the property, the amount and value of the interest to be held by the offender shall be determined by the court.[332] It proposed that the court should, in determining the amount and value of the interest, make such order as appears to it to be just and equitable, having regard to the fact that the right of survivorship was accelerated by the act of the offender and it set out a number of factors which may be relevant in determining what is just and equitable in this context.[333]

THE REMEDIAL CONSTRUCTIVE TRUST

Introduction

As noted above in the introduction to this chapter, a remedial constructive trust is one which is imposed by the court in the exercise of its discretion as a remedy in circumstances where it considers that fairness requires that a defendant hold property on trust for a plaintiff. As Deane J stated in the Australian decision of *Muschinski v Dodds*:[334]

> Viewed in its modern context, the constructive trust can properly be described as a remedial institution which equity imposes regardless of actual or presumed agreement or intention (and subsequently protects) to preclude the retention or assertion of beneficial ownership of property to the extent that such retention or assertion would be contrary to equitable principle.

The reluctance to embrace the concept of the remedial constructive trust stems from two main sources. First, as Millett J, as he then was, made clear in *Lonrho plc v Fayed (No. 2)*,[335] while equity must be flexible, its intervention must be based on principle and fears have been expressed that the development of

330. [2012] 1 IR 281, 301.
331. LRC 114–2015. For a critique of these proposals, see Mee (2016) 39 DULJ 203. See further Part 5 of the General Scheme of the Courts and Civil Law (Miscellaneous Provisions) Bill 2017.
332. *Ibid.* at 2.80.
333. *Ibid.* at 2.81-2.82.
334. (1985) 160 CLR 583, 614.
335. [1992] 1 WLR 1, 9.

this doctrine might lead to a form of 'palm tree justice'.[336] This argument was addressed by Deane J in *Muschinski v Dodds*[337] in the following manner:

> The fact that the constructive trust remains predominantly remedial does not, however, mean that it represents a medium for the indulgence of idiosyncratic notions of fairness and justice. As an equitable remedy, it is available only when warranted by established equitable principles or by the legitimate processes of legal reasoning, by analogy, induction and deduction, from the starting point of a proper understanding of the conceptual foundation of such principles.

The other main concern about the imposition of a remedial constructive trust relates to the fundamental distinction between the effect of personal and proprietary rights in the context of insolvency.[338] As Lord Millett has commented, speaking extra-judicially, '[t]he potential effect of a proprietary claim on creditors makes it unacceptable that rights of property should depend on vague and ill-defined notions of fairness'.[339] While Lord Browne-Wilkinson suggested in *Westdeutsche Landesbank Girozentrale v Islington Borough Council*[340] that since the remedial constructive trust can be tailored to the circumstances of the particular case, innocent third parties would not be prejudiced and restitutionary defences, such as change of position, could operate, concerns remain about the far reaching effect which such a remedy may have.

There has been a tendency on the part of the judiciary in this jurisdiction not to directly address these concerns, although the comments of Finlay Geoghegan J in *Re Custom House Capital*,[341] considered in more detail below, show that she appreciated the potential difficulties which the imposition of a trust of this nature can give rise to. Despite this, the courts here have been prepared to impose remedial constructive trusts in a number of cases.[342] Before examining these decisions in more detail it is proposed to trace how an earlier form of what is now recognised as the remedial constructive trust has fared and then to consider how it may develop in the future.

---

336. See the dissenting judgments in the Canadian Supreme Court decision of *Pettkus v Becker* (1980) 117 DLR (3d) 257.
337. (1985) 160 CLR 583, 615.
338. See further *infra* p. 336.
339. (1998) 114 LQR 399.
340. [1996] AC 669, 716.
341. [2014] 1 ILRM 360.
342. *Re Irish Shipping Ltd* [1986] ILRM 518; *HKN Invest Oy v Incotrade Pvt Ltd* [1993] 3 IR 152; *Kelly v Cahill* [2001] 1 IR 57; *Re Varko Ltd* [2012] IEHC 278; *Re Custom House Capital* [2014] 1 ILRM 360.

New Model Constructive Trusts

While it has generally been acknowledged throughout the common law world that the concept of 'justice' is too uncertain a basis on which to found a constructive trust which will create proprietary rights which may operate in a wider context than anticipated or required, Lord Denning pioneered just such a development in the English Court of Appeal in the late 1960s and early 1970s. In *Hussey v Palmer*[343] Lord Denning MR stated that a constructive trust would be imposed 'whenever justice and good conscience require it' and he subsequently described this extension of the existing law in *Eves v Eves*[344] as 'a constructive trust of a new model'. These 'new model constructive trusts' were applied in a number of areas, particularly in relation to contractual licences and to family property but almost from the outset they met with academic criticism. Oakley commented that, '[i]t is unsatisfactory for a constructive trust to be imposed whenever the courts feel, on their own individual ideas of justice, that such a remedy will bring about the "right" result'[345] and Maudsley said that it was possible to read into the decisions the principle that 'in cases in which the plaintiff ought to win, but has no legal doctrine or authority to support him, a constructive trust in his favour will do the trick.'[346] Nevertheless, it is interesting to note how this device was utilised in a manner which usually succeeded not only in providing a plaintiff with a remedy, but also in creating proprietary rights which had a consequential effect on third parties.

For a number of years the new model constructive trust played an important role in determining the rights of contractual licensees in a series of cases which attracted considerable criticism. In *Binions v Evans*[347] an employer consented to allowing the defendant, the widow of a former employee, to live rent-free in a cottage for the remainder of her life. The property was sold to the plaintiffs expressly subject to her interest at a lower price than would otherwise have been payable. The plaintiffs then purported to determine the tenancy and the Court of Appeal held that they could not do so. While Megaw and Stephenson LJJ found that the defendant was entitled to a tenancy for life, Lord Denning MR regarded her interest as a licence which was binding on the purchaser under a constructive trust. This approach was endorsed by the Court of Appeal in *DHN Food Distributors Ltd v Tower Hamlets LBC*,[348] where a constructive trust was imposed by the court so as to enable it to make a finding that a contractual licensee had a sufficient interest to qualify for compensation in respect of land which had been compulsorily purchased.

However, the use of the constructive trust as a form of equitable remedy to do justice *inter partes* in order to protect the licensee's possession or occupation

343. [1972] 1 WLR 1286, 1290.
344. [1975] 1 WLR 1338, 1341.
345. Oakley (1973) CLP 17, 39.
346. Maudsley (1977) 28 NILQ 123.
347. [1972] Ch 359. See Martin (1972) 36 Conv 266; Hayton (1972) 36 Conv 277.
348. [1976] 1 WLR 852.

of the premises as against third parties was difficult to justify as they 'let in by the back door contractual licences as full equitable proprietary interests.'[349] As a result of the decision of the Court of Appeal in *Ashburn Anstalt v Arnold*,[350] the ambit of the earlier judgments has been considerably restricted and Fox LJ made it clear that the court would not impose a constructive trust unless it was satisfied that the conscience of the owner of the land had been affected so that it would be inequitable to allow him to deny the claimant an interest.[351] Therefore, it was only in circumstances where a third party sought to renege on the undertaking to honour the licence that he would be liable as a constructive trustee and there was in the circumstances insufficient evidence to infer the existence of a constructive trust. The influence of the new model constructive trust in this context has diminished in England and in view of the rather arbitrary effect which its application has on property rights, it is unlikely to be rekindled in that jurisdiction.

Remedial Constructive Trusts in Ireland

Lord Denning's creation met with some degree of limited approval in this jurisdiction, although recent authority suggests that a more precisely defined doctrine would be preferable.[352] In *N.A.D. v T.D.*[353] Barron J adopted a similar line of reasoning to Lord Denning and he made the following statement:

> The constructive trust is imposed by operation of law independently of intention in order to satisfy the demands of justice and good conscience. Its imposition is dependent upon the conduct of the person upon whom the trust is imposed and prevents him from acting in breach of good faith. There is no fixed set of circumstances in which such a trust is imposed.

The case before Barron J concerned a claim relating to contributions allegedly made by the plaintiff towards the building of a house on a site bought in her husband's name. Barron J said that the essential prerequisite for the imposition of a constructive trust of the type under consideration was that there must be an element in the conduct of the person upon whom it is imposed which would make it inequitable for him to assert his legal rights. He concluded that there was no evidence of conduct on the part of the husband which would make it inequitable to deny the wife's claim and her claim to a share in the

349. See Underhill & Hayton, *Law Relating to Trusts and Trustees* (14th ed., 1987) p. 328. Note that the passage was omitted from the 15th and subsequent editions.
350. [1989] Ch 1.
351. Similar reasoning was applied by the Court of Appeal in *Chaudhary v Yavuz* [2013] Ch 249. See further McFarlane [2013] Conv 74.
352. See *Dublin Corporation v Ancient Guild of Incorporated Brick and Stone Layers and Allied Trade Union* High Court 1991 No. 1556P (Budd J) 6 March 1996.
353. [1985] ILRM 153, 160.

house therefore failed. So while Barron J spoke in general terms in language not dissimilar to that employed by Lord Denning, there was no real sign in his judgment of the flexibility which was the hallmark of this type of trust in England.

Subsequently, in *HKN Invest Oy v Incotrade Pvt Ltd*[354] Costello J stated that a constructive trust will arise when the circumstances of the case are such as to render it inequitable for the legal owner of property to deny another's title to it and agreed that: 'where a person . . . holds property in circumstances which in equity and good conscience should be held or enjoyed by another he will be compelled to hold the property in trust for another'.[355] The case concerned a claim by the plaintiffs who had obtained judgment against the defendants, namely a company and the individuals responsible for conducting its affairs, and who sought to be allowed to complete execution of this judgment. In relation to monies received by way of commission on pre-incorporation contracts, Costello J held that although the individual defendants concerned might not have been fiduciaries at the time they received this commission, these funds were held on trust for the company and could not be the subject of a garnishee order. Costello J held that the monies received after incorporation were held by the individual defendants as fiduciaries on a constructive trust for the company and he made an order declaring that the liquidator was beneficially entitled to the proceeds of both sets of contracts as the assets of the company.

While arguably the result arrived at by Costello J was a just one in the circumstances of the case and ironically had the effect of strengthening the position of the general body of creditors, a class who often fare rather worse where a constructive trust is imposed,[356] it must be said that the reasoning is in some respects open to criticism.[357] Principally, it is difficult to accept the fact that the individual defendants could be constructive trustees of funds which in theory belonged to a company which had not at the time come into existence.[358] In addition, while the ready acceptance of the 'good conscience' approach by Costello J, reminiscent of Lord Denning's 'new model', as already stated, achieved what would be considered by most to be a just result, it is not a

354. [1993] 3 IR 152.
355. *Ibid.* at 162.
356. See, e.g. *Attorney-General for Hong Kong v Reid* [1994] 1 AC 324; Jones [1994] Conv 156.
357. For an excellent critique of the reasoning employed by Costello J, see Steen (2004) 26 DULJ 260.
358. While the post-incorporation commission payments were made at a time when a fiduciary relationship between the individual and corporate defendants had come into existence and the result in this regard could be explained as a form of institutional constructive trust, the court rejected the argument that such a relationship existed prior to incorporation, leaving the court to rely on the remedial or new model constructive trust model employed by Lord Denning MR in *Hussey v Palmer* in resolving the issue of the pre-incorporation payments.

development which will ease the task of those who seek to establish consistent principles in this area of the law.

Steen suggests that the proper analysis of the fact scenario which arose in this case is that the commission payments made by the plaintiffs were in fact subject to a *Quistclose* trust. While on this reasoning the correct decision might have been to uphold the plaintiff's claim, he concedes that in view of the underlying policy considerations identified by Costello J, his decision is 'understandable, if not easily explicable'.[359] Steen refers to the words of Lord Millett, writing extra-judicially, to the effect that 'the potential effect of a proprietary claim on creditors makes it unacceptable that rights of property should depend on vague and ill-defined notions of fairness'[360] and there is considerable merit in his suggestion that if the courts were to rely on the concept of a resulting trust, rather than on the new model constructive trust in such cases, greater certainty and predictability would be introduced into this area of the law.

There have been a number of further examples of constructive trusts being imposed because 'justice and good conscience' demand it. In *Murray v Murray*,[361] considered above in the context of resulting trusts and family property,[362] the plaintiff, the defendant's nephew, had lived in a property belonging to the defendant — who had paid the initial deposit on it — for many years with his aunt, the defendant's sister, who during her lifetime had paid the mortgage instalments and most of the outgoings on the property. After her death the plaintiff, who was her next of kin, claimed that he was entitled to the beneficial interest in the property and argued that in the circumstances it would be unconscionable for the defendant to rely on his legal title. Barron J stated as follows: 'It is I think quite clear that the law will impose a constructive trust in all circumstances where it would be unjust and unconscionable not to do so.' In his view *Hussey* was authority for the proposition that in certain circumstances where equity so required, 'a debt may be secured by the device of a constructive trust on the property created by the money involved'. He concluded that in the circumstances the plaintiff was entitled to three-quarters of the beneficial interest in the property and that he was a tenant in common of the premises with the defendant.

As noted earlier,[363] the lack of any evidence of the fact that the aunt intended to earn a beneficial interest for herself as a result of the contributions she had made seemed to preclude Barron J from finding that these contributions gave rise to a resulting trust and instead he turned to the more flexible constructive trust to provide a remedy. Mee is critical of this approach, stating that *Murray* shows the new model constructive trust in its worst light;[364] in his view the

359. Steen (2004) 26 DULJ 260, 272.
360. Millett (1998) 114 LQR 399, 399-400.
361. [1996] 3 IR 251.
362. See Chapter 7, pp. 223-256.
363. See Chapter 7, pp. 253.
364. Mee (1996) 1 CPLJ 9, 13.

absence of intention should probably have precluded even a constructive trust arising, but its 'inherent vagueness' made it more plausible for Barron J to provide the plaintiff with a remedy.

Further detailed attention was given to the concept of the new model constructive trust in *Dublin Corporation v Ancient Guild of Incorporated Brick and Stone Layers and Allied Trades Union*[365] although it should be noted that when the case came before the Supreme Court, the decision was reversed and the court did not find it necessary to explore the constructive trust issue.[366] The plaintiff corporation issued a compulsory purchase order which affected a hall owned by the defendants. An arbitrator made an award on the basis of the cost of reinstatement of the building and the defendants then substantially demolished the premises making reinstatement impractical. The plaintiff sought a declaration that the union held the sum awarded in trust for the reconstruction of the building and a mandatory injunction requiring the money to be applied for this purpose, or in the alternative, repayment of a sum which represented the difference between the figure awarded and that which would have represented the market value of the premises if reinstatement had not been envisaged. Budd J proceeded to examine the plaintiff's claim for restitution of part of the award on the basis of unjust enrichment. He also considered whether the sum awarded by the arbitrator was impressed with a trust for the plaintiff's benefit. Budd J rejected the contention that a resulting trust arose as he was satisfied that it was the intention of the corporation that the defendants should take the sum awarded beneficially.

In relation to the possibility of a constructive trust arising, the defendants sought to argue that a trust could not be inferred as monies which were not held on a constructive trust at the outset could not subsequently become impressed with such a trust at the behest of the donor on account of some event which occurred after the giving of the money. However, Budd J pointed to Lord Denning MR's statement in *Hussey v Palmer* to the effect that the trust may arise 'later on, as the circumstances require'. Budd J identified two types of constructive trust, one which arises where there is a fiduciary relationship and the other which arises because of the particular circumstances in which a person holds property. While this latter form of constructive trust has been described as arising 'whenever justice and good conscience require it', Budd J commented that the Irish courts have been cautious about adopting such a nebulous touchstone as 'justice and good conscience'. He stated that traditional doctrines of equity permit the imposition of a constructive trust to prevent a person from asserting or exercising a legal right in circumstances where this would amount to unconscionable conduct. In the view of Budd J, 'a system of rules has been evolved which, on the whole, is both practical and just but

365. High Court 1991 No. 1556P (Budd J) 6 March 1996.
366. *Sub nom Dublin Corporation v Building and Allied Trade Union* [1996] 1 IR 468. See further O'Dell (1997) 113 LQR 245.

which cannot claim scientific precision as a whole.' Accordingly he held that the extra money was paid to the defendant under a mistaken assumption and said that while the case was on the outer margins of the circumstances in which the law will imply a constructive trust, it seemed to him that there was strong justification for holding that a constructive trust had arisen.

On appeal to the Supreme Court, the defendants argued that by virtue of the doctrine of *res judicata*, the finality of the arbitration award could not be attacked and submitted that they had not at any stage represented that the hall would be reinstated. The Supreme Court allowed the defendants' appeal and held that the award was final and binding on both parties. Keane J accepted that in certain circumstances a person can be obliged to effect restitution where it would be unjust to retain the property but held that the doctrine of *res judicata* could not be significantly abridged by the invocation of the concept of unjust enrichment.

While Budd J accepted that a constructive trust should 'be imposed by operation of law and independent of the intention of the parties to satisfy the demands of justice and good conscience',[367] he also stressed that the courts in this jurisdiction have been cautious about 'the nebulous touchstone' of justice and good conscience and that the imposition of a constructive trust 'does not leave it open to the court to indulge random notions of what is fair and just as a matter of abstract morality'.[368] Budd J also made it clear that he was conscious of the far-reaching effect which the imposition of a constructive trust might have on third parties. For these reasons, it is fair to say that while Budd J undoubtedly favoured the use of the constructive trust as a remedy for unjust enrichment, it would appear that he was not endorsing the type of 'palm tree justice' with which Lord Denning's new model has often been associated.

One of the decisions in this area which is most difficult to stand over is *Kelly v Cahill*.[369] Although it was nominally based on the *dicta* laid down in decisions such as *HKN Invest Oy v Incotrade Pvt Ltd*, it seemed to involve an even further expansion of existing principles in order to achieve a 'just' result. The deceased informed his solicitor that he wanted to alter his will since he no longer wished to benefit his nephew, the second named defendant, but intended to leave all his property to his wife, the first named defendant. His solicitor advised him to execute a deed transferring his property into the joint names of himself and his wife to avoid a charge to probate tax subsequently arising and the parties believed that the deed executed included all of the lands owned by the deceased. However, through the inadvertence of the solicitor, some of the lands had not been transferred and would pass on the deceased's death to the first named defendant for life with remainder to the second named defendant, subject to her legal right to half of the lands concerned. Barr J stated that the net

367. High Court 1991 No. 1556P (Budd J) 6 March 1996 at 119.
368. *Ibid.* at 116.
369. [2001] 1 IR 56. See O'Dell (2001) 23 DULJ 71 and Hourican (2001) 6 CPLJ 49.

issue in the case before him was whether a constructive trust arose in relation to the lands which were not transferred into joint ownership as intended by the testator. This raised the question of whether a 'new model' constructive trust had been established, and if so whether such a trust had a place in Irish law.

Barr J said that the kernel of the question was whether the evidence established a clear, positive intention on the part of the testator that his wife should inherit all his property, that he took appropriate steps to bring this about and that he could not reasonably have known that through his solicitor's error, the deed of transfer which had been duly executed did not include all his lands. Barr J concluded that it had been established that the deceased had expressed the necessary intention to his solicitor and that he had good reason for believing that the deed of transfer had achieved this intention; in his view it was irrelevant that the second named defendant was neither aware of or had any responsibility for the error which had been made. Barr J expressed the view that 'a "new model" constructive trust…the purpose of which is to prevent unjust enrichment is an equitable concept which deserves recognition in Irish law.'[370] In these circumstances 'justice and good conscience' required that the second named defendant should not be allowed to inherit the property and the interest in remainder under the will should be deemed to be subject to a constructive trust in favour of the first named defendant.

This decision undoubtedly went beyond the circumstances justifying the imposition of a constructive trust contemplated by Barron J in decisions such as *N.A.D.* and *Murray* in that there was no element in the conduct of the person on whom it was imposed which would have made it inequitable for him to assert his legal rights. O'Dell is particularly critical of Barr J's judgment and describes the statement referred to above as 'yet another example of the unfortunate conflation of unjust enrichment and the remedial constructive trust', which has the effect of collapsing the distinction between personal and proprietary claims.[371] In his view, the remedial constructive trust upon which the decision was based, although clearly established in Irish law, is still 'too unfocused and insensitive to issues of policy, priority and timing'[372] and should be deployed with more caution.

Another example of a trust of this nature being imposed is in the decision of Gilligan J in *Re Varko Ltd*,[373] in which the executors of the deceased succeeded in claiming that money belonging to her, which by a series of transactions had found its way into the accounts of a company which was in liquidation, should be held in trust for her estate and was not available for distribution in the winding up of the company. Gilligan J quoted from the decision of Deane J in *Muschinski v Dodds*,[374] in which he had said that '[v]iewed in its modern

370. *Ibid.* at 62.
371. O'Dell (2001) 23 DULJ 71, 83.
372. *Ibid.* at 95.
373. [2012] IEHC 278.
374. (1985) 160 CLR 583, 614.

context, the constructive trust can properly be described as a remedial institution which equity imposes regardless of actual or presumed agreement or intention'. Gilligan J also referred to the decision of Lord Denning in *Hussey v Palmer*[375] and a number of the Irish authorities set out above and said that '[t]his "new model constructive trust" has met with limited approval in this jurisdiction'.[376] Ryan J also referred to decisions such as *Kelly v Cahill* and *Re Varko Ltd* in *Anderson v Finavera Wind Energy Inc*,[377] in which he dismissed a motion to strike out the plaintiff's claim. In his opinion it was at least arguable that the impugned transactions which were alleged to have deprived the plaintiff of his security were of such a nature as to give rise to a constructive trust in his favour.

These decisions suggest that the courts in this jurisdiction appear to continue to be willing to impose a constructive trust where 'justice and good conscience' require it. However, there are also signs of a recognition that a constructive trust, which is a remedy of a proprietary nature, is a potentially far reaching one. So, in *Re Custom House Capital Ltd*[378] Finlay Geoghegan J recognised this in granting a declaration that a company, which was in liquidation, held a sum of money on trust for the applicant. She referred to the fact that counsel for the respondent had drawn attention to the potential effect of a proprietary claim on the rights of other creditors in a winding up and to the importance of avoiding 'palm tree justice'. Finlay Geoghegan J said that in order to make a finding of a constructive trust in her favour the court must be satisfied that it was by reason of fraudulent conduct by or on behalf of the company that it retained the applicant's monies. She concluded that the evidence established as a matter of probability that the applicant made a decision to continue to participate in the company's subordinated loan scheme by reason of fraudulent representations made to her by or on behalf of the company and in these circumstances found in the applicant's favour. This apparent requirement of evidence of fraudulent conduct before a constructive trust will be imposed marks a departure from previous authority. It is suggested that it is certainly justified, particularly in the context of a liquidation where imposing a constructive trust will give an applicant priority over other creditors.[379] It remains to be seen whether fraudulent conduct will also be required in other contexts, but given the proprietary nature of the relief involved, it would probably be desirable for evidence of such conduct to be established before a constructive trust is imposed.

375. [1972] 1 WLR 1286.
376. [2012] IEHC 278 at [39].
377. [2013] IEHC 489.
378. [2014] 1 ILRM 360.
379. For a discussion of this outcome in another context, see Jones [1994] Conv 156; Hicks [2010] CLJ 287.

Developments Elsewhere in the Common Law World

In Canada new model constructive trusts met with some degree of approval although in a 'much modified and more acceptable form'.[380] In *Rathwell v Rathwell*[381] Dickson J approved of the *dicta* of Lord Denning in *Hussey v Palmer*, but held that the formulation of the circumstances in which a constructive trust should be imposed depended on the concept of unjust enrichment. As he stated, 'for the principle to succeed, the facts must display an enrichment, a corresponding deprivation, and the absence of any juristic reason … for the enrichment'.[382] This reasoning was further developed by Dickson J in *Pettkus v Becker*,[383] in which he stated that 'the principle of unjust enrichment lies at the heart of the constructive trust'. However, as the views of the majority in the decision of the Supreme Court of Canada in *Soulos v Korkontzilas*[384] illustrate, the fact that a remedial constructive trust lies to prevent unjust enrichment does not prevent such trusts being imposed in other circumstances. McLachlin J made it clear that she subscribed to the view that while the constructive trust may appropriately apply to prevent unjust enrichment, it is not confined to that role and may be employed even in the absence of an established loss to condemn a wrongful act and maintain the integrity of relationships of trust. She concluded that 'in Canada, under the broad umbrella of good conscience, constructive trusts are recognized both for wrongful acts like fraud and breach of duty of loyalty, as well as to remedy unjust enrichment and corresponding deprivation.'[385]

However, the Canadian courts have also recognised the reality that 'the constructive trust does not lie at the heart of restitution'.[386] So, in *Sorochan v Sorochan*[387] Dickson CJ stated that in determining whether unjust enrichment requires the imposition of the proprietary remedy of a constructive trust, the court must address itself to the specific question of 'whether the claimant reasonably expected to receive an actual interest in property and whether the respondent was or reasonably ought to have been cognizant of that expectation.' Whatever approach is adopted it is important to bear in mind that 'there will be many cases where a plaintiff establishes a cause of action based upon the formula of unjust enrichment but where it will be unjust to remedy a breach of his rights with a remedial constructive trust order.'[388]

380. Hodkinson [1983] Conv 420, 429.
381. [1978] 2 SCR 436.
382. *Ibid.* at 455.
383. (1980) 117 DLR (3d) 257, 273. See also the *dicta* of Lambert JA in the decision of the British Columbia Court of Appeal in *Ellingsen (Trustee of) v Hallmark Ford Sales Ltd* (2000) 190 DLR (4th) 47, 70.
384. (1997) 146 DLR 214. See Smith (1997) 76 Can Bar Rev 539.
385. *Ibid.* at 229.
386. *Lac Minerals Ltd v International Corona Resources Ltd* (1989) 61 DLR (4th) 14, 48 *per* La Forest J.
387. (1986) 29 DLR (4th) 1, 12.
388. Paciocco (1989) 68 Can Bar Rev 315, 350.

The new model constructive trust also met with limited success in Australia. In *Allen v Snyder*[389] a majority of the Court of Appeal of New South Wales rejected it, commenting that 'the legitimacy of the new model is at least suspect: at best it is a mutant from which further breeding should be discouraged'. In *Muschinski v Dodds*[390] Deane J commented that 'there is no place in the law of this country for the notion of a "constructive trust of a new model"' and while the former Australian Chief Justice, Mason CJ, has conceded extra-judicially[391] that Lord Denning's creation may have been a 'shorthand version' of the type of remedial constructive trust now recognised in that jurisdiction, it is arguable that the latter owes little to earlier principles. It is therefore likely that henceforth the new model constructive trust, the underlying objective of which was to prevent a result which was 'inequitable' or contrary to the demands of good conscience, will no longer be applied in this rather flexible form.[392] In *Muschinski*, while Deane J rejected the argument that a constructive trust should be imposed based on broad notions of fairness or unjust enrichment, he found a more specific basis for the imposition of a trust, namely that equity would not permit a person to retain the benefit of property to the extent to which it would be unconscionable for him to do so. This approach was followed in *Baumgartner v Baumgartner*[393] and the notion of unconscionability is now firmly established as the basis for the imposition of what might be termed a 'remedial constructive trust' in Australia.[394]

In New Zealand, Lord Denning's version of the constructive trust met with a rather hostile reaction almost immediately. In *Carly v Farrell*[395] Mahon J commented as follows:

> I am being asked to apply a supposed rule of equity which is not only vague in its outline but which must disqualify itself from acceptance as a valid principle of jurisprudence by its total uncertainty of application and result. It cannot be sufficient to say that wide and varying notions of fairness and conscience shall be the legal determinant. No stable system

389. [1977] 2 NSWLR 685, 701.
390. (1985) 160 CLR 583, 615. See also the comment of Glass JA in the New South Wales Court of Appeal in *Allen v Snyder* [1977] 2 NSWLR 685, 694 that the new model constructive trust was 'without authoritative backing and contrary to principle and authority'.
391. Mason (1994) 110 LQR 238, 250.
392. See Evans [1989] Conv 418.
393. (1987) 164 CLR 137.
394. See further Mason (1997-98) 8 KCLJ 1, 18. Although note that Lord Millett has suggested that such trusts are unlikely to take root in Australia, see (1998) 114 LQR 299. The better view is probably that put forward by O'Dell (2001) 23 DULJ 71, 76 that the form of constructive trust which has developed in that jurisdiction, while distinct from Lord Denning's model, 'plainly has affinities with it'.
395. [1975] 1 NZLR 356, 367.

of jurisprudence could permit a litigant's claim to justice to be consigned to the formless void of individual moral opinion ....

Similarly, in *Avondale Printers and Stationers Ltd v Haggie*[396] Mahon J doubted the correctness of *Hussey v Palmer* and said that the reasoning which Lord Denning had developed was 'vindicated neither by principle nor authority'. However, more recently in *Lankow v Rose*[397] Gault J stated that criticisms of Lord Denning's approach have been 'overstated' and in that decision the court confirmed that a constructive trust may be imposed based on the reasonable expectations of the parties.[398]

The decision of the New Zealand Court of Appeal in *Fortex Group Ltd v MacIntosh*[399] contains some useful discussion of the concept of the remedial constructive trust, although the court held that there were no grounds for its imposition on the facts of the case before it. Tipping J stated that in order to defeat the rights of secured creditors by the imposition of a remedial constructive trust, the plaintiffs must be able to point to something which could be said to make it unconscionable for the secured creditors to rely on their rights in law. He concluded that whether the power to impose a remedial constructive trust exists in New Zealand and if so, on what basis and in what circumstances, must await consideration in another case. The issue was considered again in the decision of Glazebrook J in *Commonwealth Reserves I v Chodar*,[400] in which he commented that as the Court of Appeal in *Fortex* had left open the question of whether a remedial constructive trust should be confirmed in New Zealand law, this suggested to him that 'the doctrine has at least a foot in the door'.[401] He stated that a remedial constructive trust is potentially available as a remedy in cases of unconscionability and unjust enrichment although he stressed that the court must carefully examine whether proprietary relief can be justified in a given case. Glazebrook J was satisfied that there had been unjust enrichment and that retention of the assets in question would be unconscionable and he concluded that it was a suitable case for the imposition of a remedial constructive trust.

The remedial constructive trust has not fared so well in England and appears to have been rejected there,[402] although some *dicta* have suggested that it might be imposed in a suitable case. Slade LJ accepted in the decision of the Court

396. [1979] 2 NZLR 124, 149.
397. [1995] 1 NZLR 277, 288.
398. See also *Gillies v Keogh* [1989] 2 NZLR 327. Note also the *dictum* of Thomas J in *Powell v Thompson* [1991] 1 NZLR 597, 615 that 'the constructive trust has become a broad equitable remedy for reversing that which is inequitable or unconscionable'.
399. [1998] 3 NZLR 171. See Rickett and Grantham [1999] LMCLQ 111.
400. [2001] 2 NZLR 374.
401. *Ibid.* at 383.
402. See e.g. the comments of Lord Neuberger PSC in *FHR European Ventures LLP v Cedar Partners LLC* [2015] AC 250, 274 and of Lord Sumption JSC in *Angove's Pty Ltd v Bailey* [2016] 1 WLR 3179, 3191.

of Appeal *Metall und Rohstoff AG v Donaldson Lufkin & Jenrette*[403] that there is a 'good arguable case' for the existence of the remedial constructive trust in that jurisdiction and Lord Browne-Wilkinson commented in *Westdeutsche Landesbank Girozentrale v Islington LBC*[404] that 'the remedial constructive trust, if introduced into English law [might] provide a more satisfactory road forward'. Warren J expressed the view in *Clarke v Meadus*[405] that while the remedial constructive trust is a 'juridicial beast which English law has set its face against',[406] perhaps the attitude of the courts is changing and he suggested that the opinion of Lord Scott in *Thorner v Major*[407] lent support to this view. However, the traditional reluctance of the courts in England to develop the law in this area should not be underestimated and the vast majority of judicial *dicta* takes the position that the remedial constructive trust is not recognised in English law.

Waters expressed the view that in England 'the constructive trust continues to be seen as an institutional obligation attaching to property in certain specified circumstances'[408] and Lord Millett has commented extra-judicially that the remedial constructive trust is unlikely to take root in England.[409] Similarly, Etherton has expressed the view that the features of subjectivity, retrospective effect and discretion are perceived as undermining the overriding need for certainty in commercial transactions and interfering with the rights of third parties, particularly creditors.[410] This position is also supported by the *dicta* of Mummery and Nourse LJJ in the decision of the Court of Appeal in *Re Polly Peck International plc (No. 2)*.[411] Mummery LJ referred to the decisions in *Metall und Rohstoff AG* and *Westdeutsche* but said that later cases did not take the matter of remedial constructive trusts any further. He concluded that the claim of the applicants that the court should retrospectively confer a proprietary

403. [1990] 1 QB 391, 479.
404. [1996] AC 669, 716.
405. [2010] EWHC 3117 (Ch).
406. *Ibid.* at [82].
407. [2009] 1 WLR 776.
408. Waters, 'The Constructive Trust' in *Equity and Contemporary Legal Developments* (ed. Goldstein, 1992) p. 463.
409. Millett (1998) 114 LQR 399. See also 'Restitution and Constructive Trusts' in *Restitution, Past Present and Future* (ed. Cornish *et al*, 1998) p. 199.
410. Etherton [2008] CLJ 265, 268. It is interesting to note that Etherton (at 283) characterises the constructive trust imposed in *Stack v Dowden* [2007] 2 AC 432 as 'a discretionary remedial constructive trust' although he comments that it should not be seen as 'the full-blown retrospective remedial constructive trust of the US and Canadian model'. See also his judgment in *London Allied Holdings Ltd v Lee* [2007] EWHC 2061 at [273].
411. [1998] 3 All ER 812. See also *OJSC Oil Co. Yugraneft v Abramovich* [2008] EWHC 2613 (Comm) at [378]; *Sinclair Investments (UK) Ltd v Versailles Trade Finance Ltd* [2010] EWHC 1614 (Ch) at [23].

interest on them in the form of a remedial constructive trust in respect of the assets of an insolvent firm was 'not seriously arguable in English law'.[412]

Commenting on the decisions in *Re Polly Peck International plc (No. 2)* and *Fortex Group Ltd v MacIntosh*, Birks stated that they stop short of saying that the remedial constructive trust has no future at all, although he was clearly sceptical about the chance of the concept being developed.[413] Wright in turn was highly critical of Birks' views and suggested that these decisions did not indicate the demise of the remedial constructive trust.[414] He argued that Birks placed undue emphasis on aspects of the judgments which furthered his demise thesis and pointed out that Mummery LJ in *Polly Peck* explicitly confined his comments to an insolvency context.[415]

A useful example of judicial thinking on the question of whether the remedial constructive trust might still have a future in England is contained in the judgment of Etherton J in *London Allied Holdings Ltd v Lee*.[416] Having referred to the views expressed by Birks who warned against the 'rightlessness implicit in discretionary remedialism',[417] he continued as follows:

> An equity lawyer might observe that such language is overly emphatic, having regard, for example, to the strong discretion in the Court to decide upon the appropriate form of relief for proprietary estoppel, including whether it should be personal or proprietary and whether it should be to protect the claimant's expectations or compensate for reliance loss. Moreover, there is no English authority, including *Polly Peck International plc (No. 2)* (in which Mummery LJ, with whom Potter LJ agreed, concentrated on the fact of insolvency), which is binding authority against the remedial constructive trust in principle. Nevertheless, it seems realistic to assume that an English Court will be very slow indeed to adopt the US and Canadian model. On the other hand, there still seems scope for real debate about a model more suited to English jurisprudence, borrowing from proprietary estoppel: namely, a constructive trust by way of discretionary restitutionary relief, the right to which is a mere equity prior to judgment, but which will have priority over the intervening rights

412. *Ibid.* at 823. As he stated (at 827): 'The insolvency road is blocked off to remedial constructive trusts, at least when judge driven in a vehicle of discretion'.
413. Birks (1998) 12 Trust Law Int 202. Although he also stated (1999) 28 UWALR 13, 57 that these decisions can be interpreted 'not merely as throwing cold water on remedial proprietary interests, but as killing them stone dead'. These comments were made prior to the decision in *Commonwealth Reserves I v Chodar* [2001] 2 NZLR 374.
414. Wright [1999] RLR 128. See also (1998-99) 9 KCLJ 140.
415. Rickett and Grantham suggested [1999] LMCLQ 111, 117 that the particularity of the facts in *Polly Peck* coupled with the nature of the judgments mean the case 'cannot be taken to have excluded altogether the remedial constructive trust from the judicial remedial armoury in England.'
416. [2007] EWHC 2061 (Ch).
417. Birks (2000) 20 OJLS 1, 23.

> of third parties on established principles, such as those relating to notice, volunteers and the unconscionability on the facts of a claim by the third party to priority.[418]

It remains to be seen whether this idea of a 'model more suited to English jurisprudence' will develop, although recent judicial comment suggests that this is most unlikely. Lord Neuberger MR stated in *Sinclair Investments (UK) Ltd v Versailles Trade Finance Ltd*[419] that whether a proprietary interest exists or not is a matter of property law and not a matter of discretion and that it followed 'that the courts of England and Wales do not recognise a remedial constructive trust as opposed to an institutional constructive trust.' Lord Neuberger PSC made a similar remark in the course of his judgment in the Supreme Court of the United Kingdom in *FHR European Ventures LLP v Cedar Capital Partners LLC*,[420] where he said that a remedial constructive trust 'has authoritatively been said not to be part of English law'. Similarly, in *Angove's Pty Ltd v Bailey*[421] Lord Sumption JSC commented that 'English law is generally averse to the discretionary adjustment of property rights, and has not recognised the remedial constructive trust favoured in some other jurisdictions.'

Other Possible Future Developments Relating to the Constructive Trust

Introduction

In addition to the traditionally recognised circumstances which may give rise to a constructive trust, it now seems clear from developments in other parts of the common law world that unjust enrichment and unconscionable conduct may also lead to the imposition of such a trust. Glazebrook J expressed the view in the New Zealand decision of *Commonwealth Reserves I v Chodar*[422] that '[t]here appear to be two potential triggers for the exercise of the court's discretion to grant a remedial constructive trust. One is unjust enrichment. The other is unconscionability.'

The Basis for a Claim in Unjust Enrichment

Employing the concept of unjust enrichment as a trigger for a remedial constructive trust can be problematic and it is doubtful whether the proprietary remedy of a constructive trust will be the appropriate form of relief in many cases. Unjust enrichment presupposes '(1) receipt by the defendant of a benefit,

418. [2007] EWHC 2061 (Ch) at [274].
419. [2012] Ch 453, 470.
420. [2015] AC 250, 274. Referring to the *dicta* of Lord Browne-Wilkinson in *Westdeutsche Landesbank Girozentrale v Islington London Borough Council* [1996] AC 669, 714-716. However, note the comments of Gummow (2015) 131 LQR 21, 26.
421. [2016] 1 WLR 3179, 3191.
422. [2001] 2 NZLR 374, 383.

(2) at the plaintiff's expense, (3) in such circumstances that it would be unjust to allow the defendant to retain the benefit'.[423] The two essential preconditions in a claim based on unjust enrichment have been identified by Barton J in *Vanguard Auto Finance Ltd v Browne*[424] as 'the enrichment of the defendant at the expense of the plaintiff and that the enrichment should be regarded as unjust.'

The concept of unjust enrichment was considered by Finlay P in *Hickey & Co. v Roches Stores (No. 1)*,[425] although he did little to clarify whether the principle should be recognised as part of our jurisprudence. The statements of Henchy J in two decisions of the Supreme Court in *East Cork Foods Ltd v O'Dwyer Steel Co. Ltd*[426] and *Murphy v Attorney General*[427] are more significant. In both cases Henchy J appeared to accept that unjust enrichment can form the basis for the imposition of a constructive trust.[428] In the latter case he stated as follows:

> Whether the action be framed at common law for money had and received or (as here) in equity for an account of money held as a constructive trustee for the plaintiffs, I would hold that, in the absence of countervailing circumstances (to which I shall presently refer), such money may be recovered.[429]

However, there is little consideration given to the issue of the circumstances in which unjust enrichment may give rise to a claim in equity in either of these judgments and no discussion of the consequences of the imposition of a proprietary form of remedy.

While no express reference was made to the concept of unjust enrichment it seems to underlie the decision of Carroll J in *Re Irish Shipping Ltd*,[430] which

423. *B.P. Exploration Co. (Libya) Ltd v Hunt* (No. 2) [1979] 1 WLR 783, 839. See also the formulation put forward by McLachlin J in the decision of the Supreme Court of Canada in *Soulos v Korkontzilas* (1997) 146 DLR (4th) 214, 222: '(1) the enrichment of the defendant; (2) the corresponding deprivation of the plaintiff; and (3) the absence of a juristic reason for the enrichment'. Unjust enrichment is a firmly established basis of liability in Canada: see also *Pettkus v Becker* (1980) 117 DLR (3d) 257; *Sorochan v Sorochan* (1986) 29 DLR (4th) 1.
424. [2014] IEHC 465 at [75]. See also *HKR Middle East Architects Engineering LC v English* [2019] IEHC 306 at [395].
425. High Court 1975 No. 1007P (Finlay P) 14 July 1976.
426. [1978] IR 103.
427. [1982] IR 241. See O'Dell (1993) 15 DULJ 27, 29-30.
428. See [1978] IR 103, 111 and [1982] IR 241, 316 *per* Henchy J. These statements of Henchy J were relied upon by counsel for the plaintiffs in *Harlequin Property (SVG) Ltd v O'Halloran* [2013] IEHC 362 as supporting the proposition that the courts can impose a constructive trust where there has been unjust enrichment, although in the circumstances of the case, McGovern J held that it was not appropriate to grant relief of this nature.
429. [1982] IR 241, 316.
430. [1986] ILRM 518.

concerned the imposition of a constructive trust. The former bankers of the company, Citibank, claimed a right of set off in respect of monies paid into the company's account in error by another bank, the Korean Exchange Bank. Carroll J held that Citibank was not entitled to claim such a right and that the money paid in error was subject to a constructive trust and could therefore be traced by the Korean bank. Carroll J quoted with approval the *dicta* of Vinson CJ in the US Supreme Court decision of *Healy v Commissioner of Internal Revenue*[431] to the effect that a 'constructive trust is a fiction imposed as an equitable device for achieving justice'; therefore in the words of Carroll J 'it should not work an injustice'.[432] In addition, the judgment of Budd J in *Dublin Corporation v Ancient Guild of Incorporated Brick and Stone Layers and Allied Trades Union*[433] shows that he favoured the use of a constructive trust as a remedy for unjust enrichment.[434] On appeal, in the Supreme Court Keane J recognised that Irish law recognises the principle of unjust enrichment but given his conclusions about the applicability of the principle of *res judicata*, it was not necessary for him to examine further the basis of the unjust enrichment claim. Unjust enrichment was also accepted as the basis for a cause of action by Keane J in the Supreme Court in *O'Rourke v Revenue Commissioners*[435] where he stated that '[a]s in other common law jurisdictions, the doctrine has been developed incrementally on a case by case basis, so as to ensure that a vague and uncharted area of the law in which 'palm tree justice' flourishes is not judicially encouraged.'

As noted above, O'Dell has been particularly critical of what he terms 'the erroneous equation' of the concepts of unjust enrichment and the remedial constructive trust on the basis that liability in respect of the former in his view should be strict and personal whereas the latter is a form of equitable proprietary remedy.[436] He expresses the view that unjust enrichment is no basis for a constructive trust although it may be that a further element in conjunction with that concept will be sufficient to generate a proprietary remedy of this nature.[437] Virgo also suggests, it is submitted correctly, that 'the better view is

431. (1953) 345 US 278. Also approved by Goulding J in the English case of *Chase Manhattan Bank NA v Israel British Bank (London) Ltd* [1981] Ch 105.
432. [1986] ILRM 518, 522.
433. High Court 1991 No. 1556P (Budd J) 6 March 1996.
434. However, as O'Dell has pointed out (1993) 15 DULJ 27, 45, 'even if an action for restitution in equity is apt, the constructive trust is not the only remedy'.
435. [1996] 2 IR 1, 18.
436. O'Dell (2001) 23 DULJ 71. In his view (at 79): 'much of the misplaced criticism of the principle against unjust enrichment is crossfire from similar but much less misguided critique of the open-textured nature of the remedial constructive trust.'
437. This view is not wholly in line with the authorities in Canada in particular. See the *dicta* of McLachlin J in *Soulos v Korkontzilas* (1997) 146 DLR 214, 229-230. See also the *dicta* of Henry J in *Fortex Group Ltd v MacIntosh* [1998] 3 NZLR 171, 180.

that the doctrine of unjust enrichment should trigger only personal remedies and not the creation of equitable proprietary interests.'[438]

This issue has not been clarified in more recent decisions in this jurisdiction, although there is an increasing recognition of the significance of the distinction between personal and proprietary forms of remedy in this context.[439] In *HKR Middle East Architects Engineering LC v English*[440] McDonald J said that it is clear from the decisions of the Supreme Court in cases such as *East Cork Foods Ltd v O'Dwyer Steel Co.* and *O'Rourke v Revenue Commissioners* that Irish law recognises unjust enrichment as a cause of action where a defendant has received money or some other property belonging to a plaintiff in circumstances where it would be unjust for him to retain it. However, he made it clear that in order to avoid the development of what Keane J in *O'Rourke* described as 'palm tree justice', the courts have generally confined the cause of action to a number of clearly defined categories of case. While he accepted that the requirement that the enrichment of the defendant at the plaintiff's expense must be unjust, McDonald J stressed that this 'does not give the court a licence to apply some subjective notion of injustice.'[441] He found that the matter before the court was a case of unjust enrichment and given the way in which the case had been pleaded and run, identified a specific sum in respect of unpaid liabilities to which the plaintiff was entitled. However, in the light of the circumstances in which he had concluded that the plaintiff was entitled to succeed in this claim, he said that it was unnecessary for him to consider the claims based on a constructive trust or on the remedy for money had and received.

In *Bank of Ireland Mortgage Bank v Murray*[442] Baker J was also satisfied that a claim based on unjust enrichment had been established, although in the circumstances she did not feel that it was necessary to determine whether such a cause of action is rooted in common law or equitable principles. She quoted the passage from the judgment of Henchy J in *Murphy v Attorney General*,[443] set out above, to the effect that it may not always be necessary to determine what the basis for the claim is and continued as follows:

> It does not matter for the purpose of the present case whether the action is one in equity or at common law as the defendants do not raise any equitable principles in defence of the claim and, as there is no question

438. *The Principles of Equity and Trusts* (3rd ed., 2018) p. 254.
439. See e.g. the comments of Finlay Geoghegan J in *Re Custom House Capital Ltd* [2014] 1 ILRM 360, 373 in the context of an imposition of a remedial constructive trust more generally.
440. [2019] IEHC 306.
441. *Ibid.* at [395].
442. [2019] IEHC 234.
443. [1982] IR 241, 316.

> of priority, it is not necessary to consider the question in the context of any proprietary claim.[444]

While Baker J is correct that it may not always matter whether a claim for unjust enrichment is characterised as one arising at common law or in equity, in some cases the difference will be significant and may affect the outcome and the potential impact on third parties. The circumstances in which such claims are brought tend to be ones where a defendant will have insufficient assets to meet the demands of other creditors and the imposition of an equitable remedy of a proprietary nature may have implications for individuals or corporate entities beyond those party to the litigation. For this reason, it would be preferable for the courts to follow the advice of O'Dell and Virgo, referred to above, and characterise claims in unjust enrichment as of a personal nature arising at common law.

The Role of Unconscionable Conduct

As the Australian decisions of *Muschinski v Dodds*[445] *and Baumgartner v Baumgartner*[446] considered above illustrate, it is clear that the need to remedy unconscionable conduct may also justify the imposition of a remedial constructive trust. Millett LJ also appeared to regard unconscionability as a key driving factor when he stated in *Paragon Finance plc v D.B. Thakerar & Co.*[447] that '[a] constructive trust arises by operation of law whenever the circumstances are such that it would be unconscionable for the owner of property … to assert his own beneficial interest in the property and deny the beneficial interest of another.' In this jurisdiction, in *Reidy v McGreevy*[448] Barron J seemed to accept that unconscionable behaviour could give rise to a constructive trust, although the matter before him merely concerned the preliminary issue of whether the plaintiff's claim was statute barred and his brief judgment contains no reasoning on this point.

It should be noted that the former Chief Justice of Australia, Mason CJ, commenting extra-judicially, has identified one significant difference between the notions of unconscionable conduct and unjust enrichment. In his view:

> The former looks to the conduct of the person who takes unconscientious

444. [2019] IEHC 234 at [54].
445. (1985) 160 CLR 583.
446. (1987) 164 CLR 137.
447. [1999] 1 All ER 400, 409. See also *Westdeutsche Landesbank Girozentrale v Islington Borough Council* [1996] AC 669, 705 *per* Lord Browne-Wilkinson.
448. High Court 1990 No. 11804P (Barron J) 19 March 1993. Note that O'Dell has commented (1993) 15 DULJ 27, 50 that 'equity can impose a remedial constructive trust in circumstances other than where the defendant has been unjustly enriched, if the defendant's conduct has nevertheless been unconscionable'.

> advantage of the person in the position of disadvantage and requires an assessment of that conduct whereas the latter looks to the expectations of the parties and inquires whether there was an enrichment, and corresponding deprivation, and the absence of any juristic reason for the enrichment.[449]

Conclusions

Whatever formula is employed as the basis on which liability should be imposed, this post-Denning version of the remedial constructive trust is clearly recognised as being a powerful form of remedy which should be applied only where the circumstances clearly warrant such a course of action,[450] and specifically only where the plaintiff has a higher claim in equity to the property in question than the general creditors of the proposed constructive trustee.[451] Any analysis of the circumstances justifying the imposition of a remedial constructive trust must include a consideration of the position of third parties, particularly unsecured creditors, who may be affected by this form of remedy.[452] As Glazebrook J commented in the decision of the New Zealand High Court in *Commonwealth Reserves I v Chodar*,[453] 'reliability and certainty are primary considerations of any system of property rights, and the unprovoked alteration of those rights is to be avoided where possible … The court must carefully examine the reasons why other forms of relief are inadequate, the interests of any third parties and the other circumstances of the case, and consider whether proprietary relief can be justified.' So, as he made clear in his judgment in *Chodar* a remedial constructive trust should only be imposed where other available remedies are inadequate and the courts will not impose such a remedy if there is an appropriate equitable remedy which falls short of the imposition of a trust.[454]

Lord Scott stated in *Cobbe v Yeoman's Row Management Ltd*[455] that '[i]t is impossible to prescribe exhaustively the circumstances sufficient to create a constructive trust' although he acknowledged that it is possible to recognise particular factual circumstances that will or will not give rise to such a trust. In the last analysis the overriding preoccupation of judges and academic commentators alike is the perennial dilemma of choosing between

449. Mason (1994) 110 LQR 238, 251.
450. Rickett [1991] Conv 125, 135 and see also Fridman (1991) 11 LS 304, 310.
451. Note the criticisms made by Jones [1994] Conv 156 of the decision of the Privy Council in *Attorney-General for Hong Kong v Reid* [1994] 1 AC 324 in relation to the consequences of the imposition of a constructive trust on a fiduciary. See also Hicks [2010] CLJ 287, 317.
452. See, e.g. Goode 'Proprietary Restitutionary Claims' in *Restitution: Past, Present and Future* (ed. Cornish *et al*, 1998) p. 63.
453. [2001] 2 NZLR 374, 384.
454. *Giumelli v Giumelli* (1999) 196 CLR 101, 113.
455. [2008] 1 WLR 1752, 1769. See also the comments of Lord Etherton, speaking extra-judicially, in [2008] CLJ 265.

'predictability in the law and justice in the individual case' and the importance of steering a middle course 'between the extremes of inflexible rules and case-by-case "palm tree" justice'.[456] The difficulties facing the courts in utilising the concept of the remedial constructive trust in a manner which will achieve this objective cannot be underestimated. However, it is submitted that the following statement of Deane J in *Muschinski v Dodds*[457] comes close to summarising present attitudes towards the imposition of such trusts:

> The mere fact that it would be unjust or unfair in a situation of discord for the owner of a legal estate to assert his ownership against another provides, of itself, no mandate for a judicial declaration that the ownership in whole or in part lies, in equity, in that other: cf. *Hepworth v Hepworth* (1963) 110 CLR 309, at pp. 317–318. Such equitable relief by way of constructive trust will only properly be available if applicable principles of the law of equity require that the person in whom the ownership of property is vested should hold it to the use or for the benefit of another. That is not to say that general notions of fairness and justice have become irrelevant to the content and application of equity. They remain relevant to the traditional equitable notion of unconscionable conduct which persists as an operative component of some fundamental rules or principles of modern equity.

---

456. *Peel v Canada* (1992) 98 DLR (4th) 140, 164 *per* McLachlin J.
457. (1985) 160 CLR 583, 616.

CHAPTER 9

The Liability of Third Parties to Account in Equity

INTRODUCTION

Where a trustee or fiduciary has acted in breach of trust or his fiduciary duty, he may be personally liable to account to the beneficiary or principal in the fiduciary relationship. This personal claim against the party responsible for effecting the breach of trust or fiduciary duty may be at law in the form of an action for money had and received, or in equity.[1] Another option is a proprietary remedy at law or in equity to trace the trust property.[2] However, where the trustee or fiduciary is insolvent or where it is no longer possible to trace the trust property, an alternative form of claim may be the only way for a beneficiary or principal to recover misappropriated assets. In certain circumstances, liability to account in equity, often referred to as 'liability to account as a constructive trustee'[3] may be imposed on third parties or 'strangers' to a trust, where they have received trust property with a degree of knowledge sufficient to justify the imposition of liability or have dishonestly assisted in a breach of trust. Where a third party, often a financial institution or professional, has assisted in a breach of trust, experience has shown that such defendants are more likely to be in a position to meet any claim than the individual who was initially responsible for committing the breach.[4] In addition, while a beneficiary may be able to trace trust property into the hands of an innocent volunteer, the latter's liability will be confined to the return of the property or its proceeds while still in his possession. So, where the wrongdoing involves receipt of trust property, personal liability to account may be a more satisfactory remedy than pursuing a tracing claim.

The difference between holding property on a constructive trust, which gives rise to an equitable proprietary interest, and liability to account in equity is relevant in a number of circumstances. The significance of the distinction between constructive trusteeship and liability to account becomes clear where the fiduciary is insolvent, as where a constructive trust arises the principal will

---

1. As La Forest J pointed out in the Canadian Supreme Court decision of *Citadel General Assurance Co. v Lloyds Bank Canada* (1997) 152 DLR (4th) 411, 438, 'where more than one remedy is available on the facts, the plaintiff should be able to choose the one that is most advantageous'.
2. Considered *infra* Chapter 19.
3. This terminology is considered *infra* in the next section.
4. See Oakley, *Parker and Mellows: The Modern Law of Trusts* (9th ed., 2008) p.406.

take in priority to the general creditors. In addition, where assets are profitably invested and increase in value, a constructive trustee will obtain this benefit, whereas where personal liability to account is imposed, the entitlement will be to the original value of the assets or to compensation for their loss.

Terminology

There has been considerable debate in recent years about whether the labels 'constructive trust' and 'constructive trustee' are appropriate at all in this context given that the form of liability at issue is personal and not proprietary in nature.[5] While in more recent decisions these labels have not often been used, it should be borne in mind that this terminology was common in older decisions in particular. A distinction may usefully be drawn between two situations. First, where a stranger to the trust takes it upon himself to act as a trustee and subsequently commits a breach of trust.[6] Secondly, those situations where a third party may incur liability because he has received trust property in an unconscionable manner or with actual or constructive knowledge of the breach of trust, or where he has dishonestly assisted in a breach of trust. In the former case the language of 'trust' and 'trusteeship' may be appropriate but in the latter situations, although the phrase 'liability to account as a constructive trustee' has traditionally been used, this terminology is misleading. As Ungoed-Thomas J remarked in *Selangor United Rubber Estates Ltd v Craddock (No. 3)*,[7] this category of constructive trusteeship 'is nothing more than a formula for equitable relief'.

In the course of his judgment as a member of the Court of Appeal in *Paragon Finance plc v D.B. Thakerar & Co.*,[8] Millett LJ considered this issue in some detail. He said that the phrases 'constructive trust' and 'constructive trustee' have been used by equity lawyers to describe two entirely different situations. The first covers cases where the defendant, although not expressly appointed as a trustee, has assumed the duties of a trustee by a lawful transaction which was independent of and preceded the breach of trust and is not impeached by the plaintiff. In such situations the constructive trustee really is a trustee; he does not receive the trust property in his own right but by a transaction by which both parties intend to create a trust from the outset. The second type of case is where the trust obligation arises as a direct consequence of the unlawful transaction

5. As Virgo has suggested, *The Principles of Equity and Trusts* (3rd ed., 2018) p. 592, 'the language of constructive trusteeship should be avoided because of its proprietary connotations'. However, other commentators, such as Mitchell and Watterson, favour retaining the language of 'personally liable to account as a constructive trustee'. See 'Remedies for Knowing Receipt' in *Constructive and Resulting Trusts* (ed., Mitchell, 2010) p. 115 at 129.
6. Considered in Chapter 8 under the heading 'The Trustee de son Tort'.
7. [1968] 1 WLR 1555, 1582.
8. [1999] 1 All ER 400, 408-409. See also *Coulthard v Disco Mix Club Ltd* [2000] 1 WLR 707, 731.

which is impeached by the plaintiff. These cases arise when the defendant is implicated in a fraud and in such a case the defendant is traditionally, although in the view of Millett LJ, unfortunately, described as a 'constructive trustee'. However, in his opinion, 'such a person is not in fact a trustee at all, even though he may be liable to account as if he were. He never assumes the position of trustee, and if he received the trust property at all it is adversely to the plaintiff by an unlawful transaction which is impugned by the plaintiff.'[9] Lord Millett returned to this theme in the course of his speech in *Dubai Aluminium Co. Ltd v Salaam*,[10] in which he repeated much of what he had said earlier in *Paragon* in relation to the second class of case which he had described in that judgment. In his opinion, in this category of case the expressions 'constructive trust' and 'constructive trusteeship' create a trap and are 'nothing more than a formula for equitable relief'.[11] Lord Millett concluded that he thought the courts should now discard the words 'accountable as a constructive trustee' in this context and substitute the words 'accountable in equity'.[12]

More recently in *Williams v Central Bank of Nigeria*,[13] Lord Sumption JSC set out clearly the distinctions which may be drawn between two classes of cases in this context.

> The first comprises persons who have lawfully assumed fiduciary obligations in relation to trust property, but without a formal appointment. They may be trustees de son tort, who without having been properly appointed, assume to act in the administration of the trusts as if they had been; or trustees under trusts implied from the common intention to be inferred from the conduct of the parties, but never formally created as such. These people can conveniently be called de facto trustees .... In its second meaning, the phrase "constructive trustee" refers to something else. It comprises persons who never assumed and never intended to assume the status of a trustee, whether formally or informally, but have exposed themselves to equitable remedies by virtue of their participation in the unlawful misapplication of trust assets. Either they have dishonestly assisted in a misapplication of the funds by the trustee, or they have received trust assets knowing that the transfer to them was a breach of trust. In either case, they may be required by equity to account as if they

9. *Ibid.* at 409. See also *Fyffes Group Ltd v Templeman* [2000] 2 Lloyd's Rep 643, 671; *Seaton v Seddon* [2012] 1 WLR 3636, 3656.
10. [2003] 2 AC 366.
11. *Per* Ungoed-Thomas J in *Selangor United Rubber Estates Ltd v Craddock (No. 3)* [1968] 1 WLR 1555, 1582.
12. [2003] 2 AC 366, 404-405.
13. [2014] AC 1189. Worthington suggests in 'Exposing Third-Party Liability in Equity: Lessons from the Limitation Rules' in *Equity, Trusts and Commerce* (eds. Davies and Penner, 2017) p. 331 at 358 that the distinctions drawn by the Supreme Court in *Williams* are 'unduly complicated' and that the line between the two classes of cases inadequately defined.

> were trustees or fiduciaries, although they are not. These can conveniently be called cases of ancillary liability. The intervention of equity in such cases does not reflect any pre-existing obligation but comes about solely because of the misapplication of the assets. It is purely remedial. The distinction between these two categories is not just a matter of the chronology of events leading to liability. It is fundamental. In the words of Millett LJ in *Paragon Finance plc v D.B. Thakerar & Co [1999] 1 All ER 400, 413* it is "the distinction between an institutional trust and a remedial formula—between a trust and a catch-phrase".[14]

Within this second class of case, distinctions also need to be drawn. It has been argued that while 'recipient liability is restitution-based, accessory liability is not'[15] and that, given the fundamental distinction between the nature of liability in assistance and receipt cases, it makes sense to impose a different threshold of liability in each category.[16] Specifically, it has been suggested that in cases of assistance in the misappropriation of trust property, which are concerned with the furtherance of fraud, there should be a higher threshold of liability required of the stranger to the trust.[17] However, in cases concerned with the receipt of trust property for the benefit of the recipient, it has been argued that there should be a lower threshold required to found liability. The basis for the imposition of liability in these categories has evolved considerably in recent decades and, as will be explored below, distinct principles have developed in each area.

The description of a third party or stranger in both these contexts as 'not in fact a trustee at all, even though he may be liable to account as if he were'[18] was borne out by the conclusions reached by the majority of the Supreme Court of the United Kingdom in *Williams v Central Bank of Nigeria.*[19] The claimant had participated in a transaction as a result of which he alleged that he had been defrauded. He claimed that a solicitor, who had held the sum of over $6.5 million in his client account in trust for the claimant, had in fraudulent breach of that trust paid just over $6 million into an account maintained by the defendant in England and that the defendant was party to the fraud. The defendant applied to set aside service of the proceedings, contending, *inter alia,*

14. *Ibid.* at 1197-1198.
15. *Royal Brunei Airlines Sdn Bhd v Tan Kok Ming* [1995] 2 AC 378, 386 *per* Lord Nicholls. See also the *dicta* of Lord Millett in *Twinsectra Ltd v Yardley* [2002] 2 AC 164, 194.
16. *Citadel General Assurance Co v Lloyds Bank Canada* (1997) 152 DLR (4th) 411, 433 *per* La Forest J and *Gold v Rosenberg* (1997) 152 DLR (4th) 385, 399 *per* Iacobucci J. See also *Agip Africa Ltd v Jackson* [1990] Ch 265, 292 *per* Millett J.
17. (1997) 152 DLR (4th) 411, 434.
18. *Per* Millett LJ in *Paragon Finance plc v D.B. Thakerar & Co.* [1999] 1 All ER 400, 409.
19. [2014] AC 1189. See also *High Commissioner for Pakistan in the United Kingdom v Jah* [2016] EWHC 1465 (Ch) at [125].

that the claim was barred by the six year limitation period set out in section 21(3) of the Limitation Act 1980 which prescribed such a limitation period for any 'action by a beneficiary to recover trust property or in respect of any breach of trust' not otherwise covered by the Act. However, section 21(1) of the Act further provided that 'no period of limitation prescribed by this Act shall apply to an action by a beneficiary under a trust, being an action in respect of any fraud or fraudulent breach of trust to which the trustee was a party or privy.' The claimant argued that the proceedings should fall within section 21(1)(a) and that no limitation period should apply on the basis that a stranger to a trust can be regarded as a 'trustee' for the purposes of the subsection or that a claim against strangers to a trust may be 'an action in respect of a fraud or fraudulent breach of trust to which the trustee was a party or privy' within the meaning of section 21(1)(a). The trial judge refused the application, a decision upheld by the Court of Appeal, but the majority of the Supreme Court allowed the defendant's appeal. It held that the words 'trust' and 'trustee' in section 21(1)(a) of the Limitation Act 1980 bore their orthodox meaning and that a 'trustee' for the purposes of that subsection did not include a party who was liable to account in equity simply because he was a dishonest assister in a breach of trust and/or a knowing recipient of trust assets. As Lord Neuberger PSC commented, '[t]his is because such a party, while liable to account in the same way as a trustee, is not, according to the law laid down by the courts, a trustee, not even a constructive trustee.'[20]

Lee puts it well when he suggests that '*Williams* should perhaps be seen as confirming not only that strangers to the trust are "not really trustees", but rather that we should now regard them as *really-not-trustees*.'[21] So, as Davies, commenting on the subsequent decision of the Court of Appeal in *Novoship (UK) Ltd v Mikhaylyuk*[22] points out, 'the traditional language of "liability as a constructive trustee" is finally fading from view.'[23]

While there has been relatively little case law in relation to the liability of third parties to account in Ireland, a wealth of authorities has emerged in other jurisdictions. This can be attributed in part to a growth in corporate fraud and to a greater willingness on the part of the judiciary to utilise equitable concepts in a commercial context.

20. *Ibid.* at 1221.
21. (2015) 131 LQR 39, 41. See also Watterson [2014] CLJ 253.
22. [2015] QB 499.
23. (2015) 131 LQR 173, 175. See further Davies, 'Bribery' in in *Equity, Trusts and Commerce* (eds. Davies and Penner, 2017) p.225 at 236-240.

ASSISTING IN THE MISAPPROPRIATION OF TRUST PROPERTY

Dishonesty of the Person Assisting in the Breach of Trust

It was accepted by Lord Selborne in *Barnes v Addy*[24] that strangers will be made liable as constructive trustees where 'they assist with knowledge in a dishonest and fraudulent design on the part of trustees'.[25] However, this view has been discredited and the formulation now accepted of the circumstances in which liability may be imposed under this heading is set out by Lord Nicholls delivering the judgment of the Privy Council in *Royal Brunei Airlines Sdn Bhd v Tan Kok Ming*[26] as follows: 'A liability in equity to make good resulting loss attaches to a person who dishonestly procures or assists in a breach of trust or fiduciary obligation'. This latter formulation focuses on the dishonesty of the person assisting in the breach of trust rather than requiring dishonesty on the part of the trustees as Lord Selborne's principle had done.[27] As Lord Nicholls stated, '[i]n this regard dishonesty on the part of the third party would seem to be a sufficient basis for his liability, irrespective of the state of mind of the trustee who was in breach of trust.'[28] In his opinion it was difficult to see why, if a third party dishonestly assisted in a breach of trust, there should be a further prerequisite to his liability, namely that the trustee must also be shown to have been acting dishonestly.[29] As Lord Sumption JSC recently noted in *Williams*

24. (1874) LR 9 Ch App 244, 252.
25. The requirement of the existence of a fraudulent or dishonest design, which was set out by Lord Selborne in *Barnes v Addy* (1874) LR 9 Ch App 244, 252 meant that the conduct necessary to constitute a person as a constructive trustee under this heading had to be tainted with some kind of fraud or dishonesty. While Ungoed-Thomas J expressed the view in *Selangor United Rubber Estates Ltd v Craddock (No. 3)* [1968] 1 WLR 1555, 1591 that conduct which is morally reprehensible would suffice, this more flexible approach was rejected by the Court of Appeal in *Belmont Finance Corporation v Williams Furniture Ltd* [1979] Ch 250, where the claim in relation to knowing assistance failed on the grounds, *inter alia,* that no sufficiently clear allegations of fraud or dishonesty had been established. This view was echoed by Peter Gibson J in *Baden v Société Generale pour Favoriser le Développement du Commerce et de l'Industrie en France SA* [1993] 1 WLR 509, 574, where he stated that 'the relevant design … must be dishonest and fraudulent'.
26. [1995] 2 AC 378, 392.
27. However, when the Supreme Court of Canada considered this issue in *Air Canada v M. & L. Travel Ltd* (1993) 108 DLR (4th) 592, 617, Iacobucci J made it clear that 'generally there are good reasons for requiring participation in a fraudulent and dishonest breach of trust before imposing liability on agents of the trustees' and the focus seemed to be on whether the breach of trust was itself fraudulent and dishonest rather than the accessory's actions. This is also in line with the approach adopted by the High Court of Australia in *Farah Construction Pty Ltd v Say-Dee Pty Ltd* (2007) 230 CLR 89, 160.
28. *Ibid.* at 385. See also *Powell v Thompson* [1991] 1 NZLR 597, 613.
29. Although Lord Nicholls went on to note (at 392) that this will usually be the case where the third party who is assisting the trustee is acting dishonestly.

v Central Bank of Nigeria,[30] 'it is now clear that that knowing assisters are liable on account of their own dishonesty, irrespective of the dishonesty of the trustees.'

The academic reaction to the approach adopted by the Privy Council in *Royal Brunei Airlines* was overwhelmingly favourable,[31] and it was welcomed as clarifying a number of uncertainties in this area in a purposeful manner. While these issues have not been directly addressed by the courts in this jurisdiction, it seems likely that they would follow the principles laid down by Lord Nicholls and apply the requirement that dishonesty on the part of the accessory must be shown in order to impose liability.

The Requirement of Knowledge/Dishonesty

The decision of the Privy Council in *Royal Brunei Airlines Sdn Bhd v Tan Kok Ming*[32] is also significant in that it marked a shift away from the concept of 'knowledge' being the primary focus of the court's inquiry in weighing up whether liability under this heading may be imposed.[33] Prior to this, a consideration of the degree of knowledge possessed by the assister was crucial to the imposition of liability although the courts in England were far from consistent in their attitude towards this issue over the last few decades.

In his judgment in *Baden v Société Generale pour Favoriser le Développement du Commerce et de l'Industrie en France SA*[34] Peter Gibson J set out five categories of knowledge, which have been referred to in numerous decisions in this area. While considerable reservations have been expressed in relation to this categorisation,[35] and the Privy Council suggested in *Royal Brunei Airlines* that 'the *Baden* scale of knowledge is best forgotten',[36] it would be difficult to examine the relevant authorities without setting out these five categories of knowledge:

---

30. [2014] AC 1189, 1209.
31. See Nolan [1995] CLJ 505; Harpum (1995) 111 LQR 545; Halliwell [1995] Conv 339; McCormack (1995) 9 Trust Law Int 102; Podzebenko (1996) 18 Syd Law Rev 234. However, Berg's reaction is less favourable, see (1996) 59 MLR 443.
32. [1995] 2 AC 378.
33. However, it should be noted that the High Court of Australia has recently reiterated that a knowledge-based approach still represents the law in Australia, see *Farah Construction Pty Ltd v Say-Dee Pty Ltd* (2007) 230 CLR 89, 164. See further Ridge and Dietrich (2008) 124 LQR 26, 30-31.
34. [1993] 1 WLR 509, 575-576.
35. See the comments of Millett J in *Agip (Africa) Ltd v Jackson* [1990] Ch 265, 293 and of Knox J in *Cowan de Groot Properties v Eagle Trust plc* [1992] 4 All ER 700, 761. It has also been described in *Nimmo v Westpac Banking Ltd* [1993] 3 NZLR 218, 228 by Blanchard J as 'unhelpful and … unrememberable'.
36. [1995] 2 AC 378, 392. Although it was suggested by the Court of Appeal in *Heinl v Jyske Bank (Gibraltar) Ltd* [1999] Lloyd's Rep Bank 511, 523 that the classification laid down in *Baden* might well remain a useful guide in identifying different states of knowledge which might or might not result in a finding of dishonesty.

(i) actual knowledge;
(ii) wilfully shutting one's eyes to the obvious;
(iii) wilfully and recklessly failing to make such inquiries as an honest and reasonable man would make;
(iv) knowledge of circumstances which would indicate the facts to an honest and reasonable man;
(v) knowledge of circumstances which would put an honest and reasonable man on inquiry.

While many of the early authorities[37] restricted liability to a stranger who possessed knowledge in one of the first three categories outlined above, a number of first instance decisions in England in the 1960s and 1970s did not follow this approach. So, in *Selangor United Rubber Estates Ltd v Craddock (No. 3)*[38] Ungoed–Thomas J described the type of knowledge which was required to found liability in the following terms: 'knowledge of circumstances which would indicate to an honest reasonable man that such a design was being committed or would put him on inquiry, which the stranger failed to make, whether it was being committed.' However, doubts were expressed about the unfair burden which such a requirement could place on innocent defendants and an alternative view was put forward by the Court of Appeal in *Carl Zeiss Stiftung v Herbert Smith & Co. (No. 2)*,[39] where it was stressed that want of probity should be required to establish liability and the suggestion was made that constructive notice of the impropriety was insufficient.

One of the most important judgments in this area is that of Millett J in *Agip (Africa) Ltd v Jackson*.[40] Although he confirmed that knowledge within the first three categories laid down in the *Baden* case is required, he also suggested that an important distinction must be made between honesty and dishonesty. A senior officer in the plaintiff company fraudulently altered a payment order for £500,000 to a creditor by substituting the name of a company managed by the defendants which had been set up in order to launder the money. The money was credited to the company's bank account and following a series of transactions in which the money was transferred to various recipients, the company was wound up. The plaintiffs brought an action against the defendants to recover the money claiming, *inter alia*, that the defendants were constructive trustees of the funds on the basis of knowing receipt and knowing assistance. Millett J held that none of the defendants could be held liable on the basis of knowingly receiving trust funds for their own benefit but that the defendants were liable

37. E.g. *Barnes v Addy* (1874) LR 9 Ch App 244; *Williams-Ashman v Price* [1942] 1 Ch 219.
38. [1968] 1 WLR 1555, 1590. See also *Karak Rubber Co. Ltd v Burden (No. 2)* [1972] 1 WLR 602.
39. [1969] 2 Ch 276.
40. [1990] Ch 265. See Birks (1989) 105 LQR 528; Harpum [1990] CLJ 217; Millett (1991) 107 LQR 71.

under the heading of knowing assistance as 'they were at best indifferent to the possibility of fraud'. On the question of knowledge, Millett J said that constructive notice of the fraud is not sufficient to make a defendant liable and that 'the true distinction is between honesty and dishonesty'. Millett J continued:

> If a man does not draw the obvious inferences or make the obvious inquiries, the question is: why not? If it is because, however foolishly, he did not suspect wrongdoing or, having suspected it, had his suspicions allayed, however unreasonably, that is one thing. But if he did suspect wrongdoing yet failed to make inquiries because 'he did not want to know' (category (ii)) or because he regarded it as 'none of his business' (category (iii)), that is quite another. Such conduct is dishonest, and those who are guilty of it cannot complain if, for the purpose of civil liability, they are treated as if they had actual knowledge.[41]

The judgment of Fox LJ in the Court of Appeal in *Agip* temporarily confused the issue somewhat and he appeared to accept that all five categories of knowledge as set out in the *Baden* case were relevant.[42] However, subsequently in *Eagle Trust plc v SBC Securities Ltd*,[43] Vinelott J commented that it is implicit in Fox LJ's judgment in *Agip* that he accepted Millett J's conclusion that to establish liability for knowing assistance something amounting to dishonesty and want of probity must be shown.[44] In the view of Vinelott J, '[c]onstructive notice is not enough, though … knowledge may be inferred in the absence of evidence by the defendant if such knowledge would have been imputed to an honest and reasonable man.'[45] Similar views about the knowledge requirement have been

---

41. *Ibid.* at 293. This approach was also advocated by May LJ in *Lipkin Gorman v Karpanale Ltd* [1989] 1 WLR 1340, 1355 in the following terms: 'there is at least strong persuasive authority for the proposition that nothing less than knowledge, as defined in one of the first three categories stated by Peter Gibson J in the *Baden* case, of an underlying dishonest design is sufficient to make a stranger a constructive trustee of the consequences of that design.'
42. The reasoning of the Court of Appeal has been criticised, see Harpum [1991] CLJ 409, 411.
43. [1993] 1 WLR 484.
44. *Ibid.* at 495.
45. *Ibid.* at 496. The position as set out by Vinelott J was later confirmed by Scott LJ in the English Court of Appeal in *Polly Peck International plc v Nadir (No. 2)* [1992] 4 All ER 769, which concerned a claim that the plaintiff company's funds had been misappropriated by the defendant, its former chief executive. The court dismissed the plaintiff's claim for a Mareva injunction against the bank into which these funds had been transferred and Scott LJ approved the statement of Vinelott J that 'a stranger cannot be made liable for knowing assistance in a fraudulent breach of trust unless knowledge of the fraudulent design can be imputed to him'.

adopted in other common law jurisdictions[46] but overall there has been a general movement towards a dishonesty-based test[47] which will now be considered.

The decision of the Privy Council in *Royal Brunei Airlines Sdn Bhd v Tan Kok Ming*[48] is one of the most important authorities on this issue and will be examined in some detail. Lord Nicholls stated that '"knowingly" is better avoided as a defining ingredient of the principle' and that it is 'inapt as a criterion when applied to the gradually darkening spectrum where the differences are of degree and not kind.'[49] Berg has questioned why the Privy Council saw fit to require dishonesty and reject the concept of 'knowingly' as a test of liability[50] and he points out that Lord Nicholls acknowledged that honesty has to be assessed in the light of what a person actually knew at the time.[51] In delivering his opinion in the subsequent decision of the House of Lords in *Twinsectra Ltd v Yardley*,[52] Lord Hutton acknowledged that it was open to their lordships to depart from the principles laid down by Lord Nicholls and to hold that knowledge was a sufficient ingredient of accessory liability.

46. In *Air Canada v M. & L. Travel Ltd* (1993) 108 DLR (4th) 592, 608, a decision of the Canadian Supreme Court, Iacobucci J stated: 'The knowledge requirement for this type of liability is actual knowledge; recklessness or wilful blindness will also suffice'. This approach was approved, albeit in an *obiter* context, by La Forest J in the Supreme Court decision of *Citadel General Assurance Co. v Lloyds Bank Canada* (1997) 152 DLR (4th) 411, 421 where it was stated that in this context 'constructive knowledge will not suffice' (see also *Gold v Rosenberg* (1997) 152 DLR (4th) 365, 394 *per* Iacobucci J).
47. Decisions in New Zealand show a movement towards a test of want of probity (*Equiticorp Industries Group Ltd v Hawkins* [1991] 3 NZLR 700, 728) or dishonesty (*Marshall Futures Ltd v Marshall* [1992] 1 NZLR 316, 326; *Nimmo v Westpac Banking Corporation* [1993] 3 NZLR 218, 228; *Cigna Life Insurance New Zealand Ltd v Westpac Securities Ltd* [1996] 1 NZLR 80, 87; *Equiticorp Industries Group Ltd v The Crown* [1998] 2 NZLR 481, 640).
48. [1995] 2 AC 378. See Halliwell [1995] Conv 339. See also Ashe and Reid (1997) 4 Comm LP 188.
49. *Ibid.* at 391. In the view of Lord Nicholls the *Baden* scale of knowledge should be forgotten and as Halliwell suggested, this might be a particularly welcome development in the context of the proper role of equity in commercial transactions, see [1995] Conv 339, 343.
50. Berg (1996) 59 MLR 443, 451. He argues that it appears that an accessory's liability for assisting in a breach of trust is now based on the same principles as the liability of a third party who induces a breach of contract and that liability for inducing a breach of contract depends not on dishonesty but on knowledge of the existence of the plaintiff's contract and an intention to interfere with its performance.
51. As Gardner points out (1996) 112 LQR 56, 67, '[i]t is doubtful then, that the new law of direct reference to a concept of dishonesty obviates any need for an exegesis upon cognisance'. Berg quite rightly asserts (1996) 59 MLR 443 that the conclusion reached in the subsequent first instance decision of Rimer J in *Brinks Ltd v Abu-Saleh (No.3)* [1996] CLC 133 shows that not only must it be established that the accessory was dishonest, but also that he knew or had reason to suspect that he was assisting a trustee in a manner contrary to the terms of the trust (see also Stevens [1996] Conv 447).
52. [2002] 2 AC 164.

However, he accepted that the latter's statements have been 'widely regarded as clarifying this area of the law'[53] and stated that the principles laid down in *Royal Brunei* should continue to be applied.[54] As we will see below, this issue is far from settled and the use of knowledge as a touchstone of liability may not have been set aside to the extent to which Lord Nicholls clearly intended.

One aspect of the principles set out by Lord Nicholls in *Royal Brunei* which has proved controversial and may continue to be problematic is whether he intended the concept of 'dishonesty' to be interpreted in a purely objective manner or whether it must be established that a defendant was aware that his conduct was dishonest. He stated as follows:

> [I]n the context of the accessory liability principle acting dishonestly, or with a lack of probity, which is synonymous, means simply not acting as an honest person would in the circumstances. This is an objective standard. At first sight this may seem surprising. Honesty has a connotation of subjectivity, as distinct from the objectivity of negligence. Honesty, indeed, does have a strong subjective element in that it is a description of a type of conduct assessed in the light of what a person actually knew at the time, as distinct from what a reasonable person would have known or appreciated. Further, honesty and its counterpart dishonesty are mostly concerned with advertent conduct, not inadvertent conduct. Carelessness is not dishonesty. Thus for the most part dishonesty is to be equated with conscious impropriety.
>
> However, these subjective characteristics of honesty do not mean that individuals are free to set their own standards of honesty in particular circumstances. The standard of what constitutes honest conduct is not subjective. Honesty is not an optional scale, with higher or lower values according to the moral standards of each individual. If a person knowingly appropriates another's property, he will not escape a finding of dishonesty simply because he sees nothing wrong in such behaviour.[55]

Lord Nicholls went on to say that when a court is called upon to decide whether a person is acting honestly, it will look at all the circumstances known to the third party at the time and to personal attributes such as his experience and intelligence.[56] He added that if the concept of honesty is to be judged by objective standards, an accessory will not be able to escape liability by claiming that he did not 'know' that his actions were wrong.

53. *Ibid.* at 174. Although this statement must be questioned in the light of the different interpretations placed on Lord Nicholls' *dicta* by the majority and minority in *Twinsectra Ltd v Yardley*.
54. See, e.g. *Satnam Investments Ltd v Dunlop Heywood Ltd* [1999] 3 All ER 652, 671.
55. [1995] 2 AC 378, 389.
56. Baughen [2000] Conv 351, 356 expressed the view that 'dishonesty' as defined by Lord Nicholls is 'an objective test tailored to the circumstances of the particular defendant.'

However, when the House of Lords was called upon to apply this reasoning in *Twinsectra Ltd v Yardley*,[57] serious differences of opinion arose in relation to whether Lord Nicholls had intended to lay down a purely objective test in relation to dishonesty.[58] In *Twinsectra* a solicitor who was acting for a client in connection with the purchase of land had been unwilling to secure a loan for the client by giving a personal undertaking. A second solicitor was prepared to do so and received the money after the firm gave an undertaking that it would be used solely for the acquisition of property on behalf of the client. The money was released to the first solicitor who paid it out on the client's instructions although he took no steps to ensure that it was only applied in the acquisition of property and a substantial part of it was used for other purposes. The loan was not repaid and the lender sought to impose liability on the first solicitor alleging that he had dishonestly assisted in the breach of trust of the second solicitor, who had gone bankrupt. Carnwath J found that the first solicitor had not been dishonest although he accepted that he had deliberately shut his eyes to the implications of the undertaking. The Court of Appeal reversed this finding, giving judgment against the first solicitor for the proportion of the loan which had not been applied in the acquisition of property, but an appeal against this decision was allowed by the majority of the House of Lords.[59] Lord Hutton stated that there were three possible standards which could be applied to determine whether a person had acted dishonestly, namely a purely subjective standard, a purely objective standard and a combined test which requires that before there can be a finding of dishonesty, it must be established that the defendant's conduct was dishonest by the ordinary standards of reasonable and honest people, and that he himself realised that by those standards his conduct was dishonest. In favouring the third option, the combined objective and subjective test, Lord Hutton said that it would be less than just for the law to permit a finding that a defendant had been dishonest in assisting in a breach of trust where he had not been aware that what he was doing would be regarded by honest men as being dishonest. In his view:

> [D]ishonesty requires knowledge by the defendant that what he was doing would be regarded as dishonest by honest people, although he should not escape a finding of dishonesty because he sets his own standards of honesty and does not regard as dishonest what he knows would offend the normally accepted standards of honest conduct.[60]

---

57. [2002] 2 AC 164.
58. As Garton stated (2001) 15 Trust Law Int 93, 98 – before the decision of the House of Lords was delivered – even if the courts prefer the test of dishonesty, if they are not careful it can involve a similar degree of linguistic confusion as the *Baden* test.
59. Lords Slynn, Steyn, Hoffmann and Hutton.
60. [2002] 2 AC 164, 174. Yeo and Tijo suggested (2002) 118 LQR 502, 507 that the application of a purely objective assessment in this first limb of the combined test can be counter-intuitive and that it may be difficult to determine whether a defendant's

However, Lord Millett dissented and said that in his opinion Lord Nicholls had adopted an objective standard in *Royal Brunei*, according to which the defendant was expected to attain the standard which would be observed by an honest person placed in similar circumstances.[61] While account must be taken of subjective considerations such as the defendant's experience and intelligence and his actual state of knowledge at the relevant time, it was not necessary that he should actually have appreciated that he was acting dishonestly; it was sufficient that he was. So, in the view of Lord Millett, it was unnecessary to consider whether the solicitor realised that honest people would regard his conduct as dishonest and his knowledge that he was assisting the other solicitor to default in his undertaking to the plaintiff was sufficient.

Academic comment following the decision of the House of Lords in *Twinsectra* was almost universally critical of the approach adopted by the majority[62] and the views expressed by Lord Millett were generally welcomed as being more in line with the decision of the Privy Council in *Royal Brunei*.[63] Some measure of clarity was restored by the decision of the Privy Council in *Barlow Clowes International Ltd (in liquidation) v Eurotrust International Limited*,[64] albeit as a result of a judgment which is itself open to criticism.[65] In this case, the defendants had been found liable for dishonestly assisting in the misappropriation of investors' funds. The second named defendant's appeal against the finding of dishonest assistance was allowed and the appellant company appealed to the Privy Council. The trial judge (acting deemster) had stated that if by ordinary standards a defendant's mental state would be characterised as dishonest, it is irrelevant that the defendant judges by different standards. The Court of Appeal had accepted this as a correct statement of the

conduct has breached the objective standard of dishonesty without regard being had to his knowledge and personal attributes.

61. It should be noted that in his judgment in *Bank of Credit and Commerce International (Overseas) Ltd v Akindele* [2001] Ch 437, 447, Nourse LJ spoke about the trial judge in the case before him determining whether the defendant was 'dishonest by the objective standard explained by the Privy Council in *Royal Brunei Airlines Sdn Bhd v Tan*'.
62. Thompson [2002] Conv 387; Thornton [2002] CLJ 524; Yeo and Tijo (2002) 118 LQR 502; Richardson (2002) 16 Trust Law Int 174; Rickett [2002] RLR 112; Andrews [2003] Conv 398; Woodcock (2006) 57 NILQ 494.
63. In the decision of the New Zealand Court of Appeal in *US International Marketing Ltd v National Bank of New Zealand* [2004] 1 NZLR 589 both Anderson and Glazebrook JJ expressed reservations about the practical implications and appropriateness of the subjective element in the test put forward by the majority in *Twinsectra*, while Tipping J preferred to leave open the question of the effect which Lord Millett's 'powerful dissent' might have on the law in New Zealand. Now see the decision of the Supreme Court of New Zealand in *Westpac New Zealand Ltd v MAP and Associates Ltd* [2011] 3 NZLR 751, considered *infra*.
64. [2006] 1 WLR 1476. Applied by Evans-Lombe J in *Statek Corporation v Alford* [2008] EWHC 32 (Ch).
65. Conaglen and Goymour comment [2006] CLJ 18, 20 that while the Privy Council's justification and analysis can be criticised, the amendment to the test is welcome.

law and Lord Hoffmann stated that the Privy Council agreed. The trial judge had found that the second named defendant strongly suspected that the funds passing through his hands were monies which the company had received from members of the public who thought that they were subscribing to a scheme of investment in gilt-edged securities but that he consciously decided not to make inquiries because he preferred not to run the risk of discovering the truth. Lord Hoffmann stated that their Lordships considered that by ordinary standards such a state of mind is dishonest. Counsel for the second named defendant submitted that a state of mind was not dishonest unless the individual was aware that it would by ordinary standards be regarded as dishonest and only in such a case could he be said to be consciously dishonest. However, the trial judge had made no finding about the second named defendant's opinions about normal standards of honesty; the only finding was that by normal standards he had been dishonest but that his own standard was different. Counsel for the second named defendant had relied on the statement by Lord Hutton in *Twinsectra Ltd v Yardley* set out above. Lord Hoffmann commented as follows:

> Their Lordships accept that there was an element of ambiguity in these remarks which may have encouraged a belief, expressed in some academic writing, that *Twinsectra* had departed from the law as previously understood and invited inquiry not merely into the defendant's mental state about the nature of the transaction in which he was participating but also into his views about generally acceptable standards of honesty. But they did not consider that this is what Lord Hutton meant. The reference to 'what he knows would offend normally accepted standards of honest conduct' meant only that his knowledge of the transaction had to be such as to render his participation contrary to normally acceptable standards of honest conduct. It did not require that he should have had reflections about what those normally acceptable standards were.[66]

The Privy Council, therefore, rejected counsel's submission that the judge had failed to apply the principles of liability for dishonest assistance which had been laid down in *Twinsectra.* In their opinion these were no different from the principles stated in *Royal Brunei Airlines v Tan* which had been correctly summarised by the judge. Lord Hoffmann stated that someone can know, and can certainly suspect, that he is assisting in a misappropriation of money without knowing that the money is held on trust or what a trust means.[67] The Privy

66. [2006] 1 WLR 1476, 1481. See also the *dictum* of Treacy J at first instance in *Abou-Rahmah v Abacha* [2005] EWHC 2662 (QB) at [43] that '[a] dishonest state of mind on the part of the person assisting is required in the sense that that person's knowledge of the relevant transaction had to be such as to render his participation contrary to normally acceptable standards of honest conduct.'
67. *Twinsectra Ltd v Yardley* [2002] 2 AC 164, 170 *per* Lord Hoffmann and at 202 *per* Lord Millett. See also *Abou-Rahmah v Abacha* [2005] EWHC 2662 (QB) at [43].

Council accordingly considered that there was abundant evidence on which the judge was entitled to make the findings of fact which she did and that the Court of Appeal of the Isle of Man (Staff of Government Division) should not have set them aside. They therefore held that the appeal should be allowed and the decision of the trial judge (acting deemster) restored.

Yeo has commented that the distinction between the majority and minority positions in *Twinsectra* was explained away by the Privy Council in *Barlow Clowes* as a difference of view on the standards of objective dishonesty.[68] However, it is difficult to accept the assertion of the Privy Council that there was no difference between the principles laid down by the majority in *Twinsectra* and those set out by Lord Nicholls in *Royal Brunei*. One simple solution is to accept the conclusions reached by the Privy Council in *Barlow Clowes* at face value without over analysing how these were arrived at.[69] However, following the Privy Council's decision academic controversy continued about the extent to which *Barlow Clowes* had actually clarified the law. Ryan commented that the decision has 'brought closure to the ambiguity engendered by *Twinsectra* as to the true test posited by Lord Nicholls in *Royal Brunei*'[70] and he correctly stated that the interpretation of *Royal Brunei* put forward in *Barlow Clowes* is a more accurate reading of the former decision than that put forward by the majority in *Twinsectra*. However, Halliwell and Prochaska expressed the view that it was 'entirely dubious' to suggest that *Barlow Clowes* may at last have brought clarity to this area of the law and suggested that 'we are creeping full circle, slowly but inexorably to the plague of "knowledge" as an ingredient of accessory liability.'[71]

A further opportunity to clarify the principles which should be applied in this area arose before the Court of Appeal in *Abou-Rahmah v Abacha*[72] and while the comments of the members of the court are of an *obiter* nature, they do provide some useful guidance on this issue of significant practical importance.[73] The claimants had made payments into the account of the fourth named defendant bank as part of a fraudulent scheme orchestrated by the first

68. Yeo (2006) 122 LQR 171.
69. While the question of the status of *Barlow Clowes* in terms of precedent in English law has been raised given that it represents the view of the Privy Council, it was suggested that it would be preferable for the courts in that jurisdiction to follow it notwithstanding the technical difficulty with precedent, see Conaglen and Goymour [2006] CLJ 18, 21. Bryan also commented (2006) 17 KCLJ 105, 107 that the judgment 'deserves to be applied as an authoritative exposition of equitable principle.'
70. Ryan [2006] Conv 188, 196. See also the comments of Bryan who asserted (2006) 17 KCLJ 105, 110 that the decision 'will put equitable principles governing accessory liability back on track.'
71. Halliwell and Prochaska [2006] Conv 465, 466. See also the comments of Woodcock (2006) 57 NILQ 494, 511.
72. [2006] EWCA Civ 1492. See further Virgo [2007] CLJ 22.
73. As Arden LJ commented at [64], a claim based on liability for assisting in a breach of trust can arise in the context of ordinary commercial transactions, making it particularly desirable that the principles to be applied should be clear.

three named defendants. The money was then transferred into the account of a client company, the principals of which were involved in the fraud and the trial judge accepted that the bank's branch manager probably suspected that these individuals might have been assisting in money laundering from time to time. The money and the fraudsters disappeared and despite the trial judge's finding, he dismissed the claims of the appellants on all grounds. On appeal, they pursued the claims based on the 'equitable tort of knowing or dishonest assistance'[74] and in restitution for money had and received but they were unsuccessful in the former claim and the Court of Appeal upheld the bank's defence of change of position in respect of the latter. Rix LJ concluded that it would not be correct to reverse the trial judge's finding so as to conclude that the bank manager had been dishonest 'in the *Twinsectra* sense, even as clarified in *Barlow Clowes*'[75] and while he did not agree with the conclusions of his fellow judges that the defence of change of position had been made out by the bank, he declined to dissent on this ground having regard to the 'state of flux in the fundamental analysis of restitutionary claims'. Despite the above comment, Rix LJ appeared reluctant to enter more fully into the *Barlow Clowes* 'controversy' and Pill LJ similarly commented that he did not feel that it was 'necessary in this appeal to resolve the question of the impact of *Barlow Clowes* upon *Twinsectra*',[76] although he did acknowledge the value of the former decision in its explanation of the latter. However, the comments of Arden LJ, although of an *obiter* nature, do appear to endorse the *Barlow Clowes* 'restatement' of the law in this area and she stated that in her opinion, 'this Court should follow the decision of the Privy Council'.[77]

Arden LJ confirmed that the test of dishonesty in this context is 'predominantly objective' and that it is not a requirement of the standard of dishonesty that the defendant should be conscious of his wrongdoing.[78] In her view, before the Court of Appeal or the High Court could decide to follow a decision of the Privy Council rather than a decision of the House of Lords, the circumstances must be quite exceptional, which she concluded was the case in the matter before her. She expressed the opinion that while *Twinsectra* was binding on the court, *Barlow Clowes* did not involve a departure from, or refusal to follow, the former case. As she stated, '[r]ather, the *Barlow Clowes* case gives guidance as to the proper interpretation to be placed on it as a matter of English law. It shows how the *Royal Brunei* case and the *Twinsectra* case

74. [2006] EWCA Civ 1492 at [1] *per* Rix LJ.
75. *Ibid.* at [40].
76. *Ibid.* at [91].
77. *Ibid.* at [59].
78. This approach was approved by Newey J in *Al Khudairi v Abbey Brokers Ltd* [2010] EWHC 1486 (Ch) at [134], who said that the court should proceed on the basis that a person can be dishonest regardless of whether he appreciates that his conduct would be considered dishonest by ordinary honest people.

can be read together to form a consistent corpus of law.'[79] Arden LJ concluded that she considered that the trial judge had been correct to proceed on the basis that the law as laid down in *Twinsectra*, as interpreted in the Privy Council in *Barlow Clowes*, represented the law of England and Wales.[80]

Further support for the view that it is the position adopted by the Privy Council in *Barlow Clowes* which will be applied by the courts in England can be found in the judgment of Sir Andrew Morritt C in the decision of the Court of Appeal in *Starglade Properties v Nash*.[81] He stated that there is no suggestion either that the standard of dishonesty is flexible or determined by anyone other than by the court on an objective basis having regard to the ingredients of the combined test as explained by Lord Hutton in *Twinsectra* and Lord Hoffmann in *Barlow Clowes*. He continued as follows:

> The relevant standard … is the ordinary standard of honest behaviour. Just as the subjective understanding of the person concerned as to whether his conduct is dishonest is irrelevant so also is it irrelevant that there may be a body of opinion which regards the ordinary standard of honest behaviour as being set too high. Ultimately, in civil proceedings, it is for the court to determine what that standard is and to apply it to the facts of the case.[82]

As Ryan has correctly pointed out, 'merely because the courts accept that a particular judicial development has clarified the correct interpretation of previous authorities does not rid the law of complexity or doubt'.[83] However, it would be reasonable to assume that the judgments of Arden LJ in *Abou-Rahmah* and of Sir Andrew Morritt C in *Starglade Properties* may help to resolve any outstanding questions about the appropriate test to apply in such cases.

It has been stated by Lord Hughes JSC in the decision of the UK Supreme Court in *Ivey v Genting Casinos (UK) Ltd*[84] in the context of a case relating to cheating under the Gambling Act 2005, that 'there can be no logical or principled basis for the meaning of dishonesty (as distinct from the standards of proof by which it must be established) to differ according to whether it arises in a civil action or a criminal prosecution.'[85] This is a pragmatic approach given that, as Lord Hughes pointed out, the same behaviour by the same person may fall to be examined in both civil and criminal proceedings. He referred to the test of

---

79. [2006] EWCA Civ 1492 at [68].
80. See also *Fresh 'N' Clean (Wales) Ltd v Miah* [2006] EWHC 903 (Ch) at [18]; *Mullarkey v Broad* [2007] EWHC 3400 (Ch) at [36].
81. [2010] EWCA Civ 1314. See also *Madoff Securities International Ltd v Raven* [2013] EWHC 3147 (Comm) at [353].
82. *Ibid.* at [32].
83. Ryan [2007] Conv 168, 174.
84. [2018] AC 391. This marked a change in the law from that as set out in *R. v Ghosh* [1982] QB 1053.
85. *Ibid.* at 411.

dishonesty as set out by Lord Nicholls in *Royal Brunei* and by Lord Hoffmann in *Barlow Clowes* and stated as follows:

> When dishonesty is in question the fact-finding tribunal must first ascertain (subjectively) the actual state of the individual's knowledge or belief as to the facts. The reasonableness or otherwise of his belief is a matter of evidence (often in practice determinative) going to whether he held the belief, but it is not an additional requirement that his belief must be reasonable; the question is whether it is genuinely held. When once his actual state of mind as to knowledge or belief as to facts is established, the question whether his conduct was honest or dishonest is to be determined by the fact-finder by applying the (objective) standards of ordinary decent people. There is no requirement that the defendant must appreciate that what he has done is, by those standards, dishonest.[86]

The courts in New Zealand have also followed the approach of the Privy Council in *Barlow Clowes*, which was described by Tipping J in the judgment of the Supreme Court of New Zealand in *Westpac New Zealand Ltd v MAP and Associates Ltd*[87] as representing 'a significant volte-face from the decision of the House of Lords in *Twinsectra*'. Tipping J said that the court would accept the position as set out by Lord Hoffmann in *Barlow Clowes* but added some elaboration about the circumstances in which suspicion would amount to dishonesty. He stated as follows:

> The key ingredient in the cause of action for dishonest assistance is the need for a dishonest state of mind on the part of the person who assists in the breach of trust. We agree with the statement in *Barlow Clowes* that such a state of mind may consist in actual knowledge that the transaction is one in which the assistor cannot honestly participate. But it may also consist in what we would describe as a sufficiently strong suspicion of a breach of trust, coupled with a deliberate decision not to make inquiry lest the inquiry result in actual knowledge. For the purpose of this alternative, it is necessary that the strength of the suspicion that a breach of trust is intended makes it dishonest to decide not to make inquiry. That state of mind, which equity equates with actual knowledge, is usually referred to as wilful blindness. It involves shutting one's eyes to the obvious and can thus fairly be equated with the dishonesty involved when there is actual knowledge.[88]

86. *Ibid.* at 416-417.
87. [2011] 3 NZLR 751, 762.
88. *Ibid.* This statement was set out in a decision of the New Zealand Court of Appeal in *Hansard v Hansard* [2015] 2 NZLR 158 where Lang J described *Westpac*, on an *obiter* basis, as the leading authority in the jurisdiction in relation to knowing assistance.

This statement was quoted with approval by White J delivering the judgment of the New Zealand Court of Appeal in *Fletcher v Eden Refuge Trust*.[89] He added that 'a dishonest state of mind consists of actual knowledge that the transaction is one in which the assistor cannot honestly participate or a sufficiently strong suspicion of a breach of trust that it is dishonest to decide not to inquire, coupled with a deliberate decision not to make inquiry lest the inquiry result in actual knowledge.'[90] The standard set out in *Westpac* was also considered by Randerson J in the decision of the New Zealand Court of Appeal in *Spencer v Spencer*,[91] in which the court was assessing the meaning of 'dishonesty' for the purposes of trustee exemption clauses, which he suggested was analogous with the state of mind necessary to establish accessory liability in knowing assistance cases. Randerson J concluded that 'the assessment of a trustee's honesty comprises both subjective and objective elements.'[92] He added that the court must first establish what the trustee actually knew and this knowledge might include constructive knowledge arising from wilful blindness in the sense described in the *Westpac* case. Then the court must decide whether, in the light of what the trustee knew, he acted in the way an honest person would in the circumstances. As Randerson J made clear, this assessment is to be made on an objective basis and '[a] trustee who believes his or her actions or omissions were in the best interests of the beneficiaries will not necessarily be entitled to protection'.[93]

The courts in this jurisdiction have yet to address properly the question of the standard to be applied in such cases.[94] However, it appears likely that the test which would be adopted is whether by ordinary standards the defendant's conduct would be characterised as dishonest. The arguments in favour of applying what is in effect the position adopted by Lord Millett in his dissent in *Twinsectra* are compelling. As Tipping J pointed out in *Westpac*, 'although a dishonest state of mind is a subjective mental state, the standard by which the law determines whether it is dishonest is objective'.[95] To opt for the more

89. [2012] 2 NZLR 227.
90. *Ibid.* at 243.
91. [2014] 2 NZLR 190.
92. *Ibid.* at 218.
93. *Ibid.*
94. O'Dell suggested in *Annual Review of Irish Law 1997* p. 632 that the decision of McCracken J in *Taxback Ltd v Revenue Commissioners* [1997] IEHC 8 'might well constitute the Irish adoption of the principle in *Tan*'. Although *Royal Brunei Airlines Sdn Bhd v Tan Kok Ming* is referred to in the course of the judgment, it is submitted that there are no real grounds for O'Dell's assertion. The case concerned a dispute between the parties about the withholding by the Revenue Commissioners of refunds payable to the applicant VAT refunding agency. The Revenue contended on the authority of *Royal Brunei Airlines* that if they made payments to the applicant they might be assisting in the applicant's dishonesty and incur liability themselves. However, McCracken J rejected this argument and stated that unless they had statutory authority to withhold monies during an investigation of this type they must discharge their statutory obligations in relation to payment.
95. [2011] 3 NZLR 751, 762.

subjective approach favoured by Lord Hutton in *Twinsectra* would allow the balance to shift too far in favour of potentially unmeritorious defendants and it is therefore likely that the courts in this jurisdiction will follow the approach adopted by the Privy Council and the Supreme Court of New Zealand.

The Nature of the Remedies

Where a loss has been incurred by a party as a result of dishonest assistance, the assister will be liable to provide compensation for this loss.[96] It was accepted by the Court of Appeal in *Grupo Torras SA v Al-Sabah (No. 5)*[97] that 'the relevant enquiry is ... what loss or damage resulted from the breach of trust or fiduciary duty which has been dishonestly assisted' and that it is not necessary to assess the causative significance of the dishonest assistance. This means that the dishonest assister is jointly and severally liable with the trustees for any loss caused as a result of the breach of trust or fiduciary duty.[98]

However, the nature of the third party assister's liability to account in relation to any profits made as a result of the breach of duty is different. It is clear that where a profit has been made as a result of the dishonest assistance, the assister will be liable to account for the profits he has made derived from this assistance.[99] However, the third party will only be liable to account for any profit he *himself* has made as the following statement of Lewison J in *Ultraframe (UK) Ltd v Fielding*[100] makes clear:

> I can see that it makes sense for a dishonest assistant to be jointly and severally liable for any *loss* which the beneficiary suffers as a result of a breach of trust. I can see also that it makes sense for a dishonest assistant to be liable to disgorge any profit which he *himself* has made as a result of assisting in the breach. However, I cannot take the next step to the conclusion that a dishonest assistant is also liable to pay to the beneficiary an amount equal to a profit which he did not make and which has produced no corresponding loss to the beneficiary.

This issue was explored in some detail in the decision of the Court of Appeal

96. *Fyffes Group v Templeman* [2000] 2 Lloyds's Rep 643.
97. [2001] CLC 221, 225.
98. However, as Virgo points out in *The Principles of Equity and Trusts* (3rd ed., 2018) p. 623, there are doctrinal difficulties with this characterisation. He argues that the preferable view of an accessory's liability is that it is derivative in nature in that it depends on the wrong committed by the trustee or fiduciary, but that once this is established, the accessory will be regarded as personally liable for their *own* wrongdoing. If Virgo's approach were followed, as he points out, it would mean that no artificial distinction need be drawn between compensatory and gain based remedies.
99. *Ultraframe (UK) Ltd v Fielding* [2005] EWHC 1638 (Ch) at 1594.
100. [2005] EWHC 1638 (Ch) at [1600].

in *Novoship (UK) Ltd v Mikhaylyuk*.[101] The Court of Appeal concluded that, in the circumstances of the case before it, the remedy of an account of profits was available against a party who had dishonestly assisted a fiduciary to breach his fiduciary obligations, even if that breach did not involve a misapplication of trust property. However, Longmore LJ made clear that this remedy is only available where there is a causal connection between the dishonest assistance and the profit for which the third party is asked to account. In the matter before the court, while the assister had profited from the dishonest assistance, he was satisfied that there was no sufficiently direct causal link between the wrongdoing and the profits and that the defendant was not liable to account for them. Longmore LJ also stated that as the claim was made against a defendant who was not a fiduciary, the court would in any event have a discretion to withhold or grant a remedy and it might be withheld where liability to account would be disproportionate to the form and extent of the wrongdoing.[102] This decision is significant; as Davies points out, it 'creates the conceptual space for the remedies to differ as between the primary wrongdoer and accessory; only the former and not the latter has assumed fiduciary obligations towards the claimant.'[103]

It should be noted that there is some debate about the nature of the causation test which should apply in relation to liability for claims based on dishonest assistance. While Longmore LJ in *Novoship* referred to whether this assistance was the 'real or effective cause' of the loss, a different approach has been adopted in Australia. So, in *Ancient Order of Foresters Friendly Society Ltd v Lifeplan Australia Friendly Society Ltd*,[104] in which the High Court of Australia examined the issue of the necessary causal connection in such cases, it was held that it is sufficient to establish that the profit would not have been made but for the dishonest wrongdoing.

KNOWING RECEIPT OF AND INCONSISTENT DEALING WITH TRUST PROPERTY

General Principles

A recipient of property which has been misappropriated in breach of trust or fiduciary duty may be liable to account provided that he possesses the necessary degree of knowledge of the breach of trust or he receives it in circumstances

101. [2015] QB 499.
102. *Ibid.* at 535.
103. (2015) 131 LQR 173, 174. See further Gummow [2015] CLJ 405; Devonshire [2015] CLJ 222; Campbell [2015] Conv 160. See also Glister, 'Account of Profits and Third Parties' in *Equitable Compensation and Disgorgement of Profit* (eds. Degeling and Varuhas, 2017) p. 175 at 193-195.
104. (2018) 360 ALR 1 at [9]. See further Douglas (2019) 135 LQR 214; Ridge and Dietrich [2019] CLJ 383.

in which it will be regarded as unconscionable for him to retain it. Similarly, where a recipient of trust property deals with it in a manner which he knows to be inconsistent with the terms of the trust, he will be liable to account for the property. This second category of liability covers situations in which the recipient might not be liable for 'receipt' as such, because he does not possess the requisite degree of knowledge at the relevant time, but subsequently deals with the property in a manner inconsistent with the trust after acquiring such knowledge. Millett J described these categories in his judgment in *Agip (Africa) Ltd v Jackson*[105] as follows:

> [I]t is necessary to distinguish between two main classes of case under this heading.
>
> The first is concerned with the person who receives for his own benefit trust property transferred to him in breach of trust. He is liable as a constructive trustee if he received it with notice, actual or constructive, that it was trust property and that the transfer to him was a breach of trust; or if he received it without such notice but subsequently discovered the facts.
>
> The second and in my judgment distinct class of case is that of the person, usually an agent of the trustees, who receives the trust property lawfully and not for his own benefit but who then either misappropriates it or otherwise deals with it in a manner which is inconsistent with the trust. He is liable to account as a constructive trustee if he received the property knowing it to be such, though he will not necessarily be required in all circumstances to have known the exact terms of the trust.

As Millett J pointed out, in either class of case outlined it is immaterial whether the breach of trust was fraudulent or not and the most controversial question associated with these categories of liability is the degree of knowledge or unconscionability required. It is also clear from Millett J's judgment that 'the recipient must have received the property for *his own* use and benefit.'[106] The traditional view has been that monies paid into a bank account, other than those paid into an overdrawn account,[107] will be regarded as having been received magisterially rather than beneficially and so will not be considered as having been 'received' in a sense necessary to trigger potential liability under this heading. However, some uncertainty surrounds this question,[108] and Lord

105. [1990] Ch 265, 291.
106. *Ibid.* at 292. Emphasis added.
107. In such cases the money is regarded as having been received beneficially by the bank as it goes to reducing or discharging the customer's overdraft. See *Agip (Africa) Ltd v Jackson* [1990] Ch 265, 292 per Millett J.
108. Note also the *obiter* comments of Moore-Bick J in *Uzinterimpex JSC v Standard Bank plc* [2008] EWCA Civ 819 at [39]-[40]. See further the discussion in Virgo, *The Principles of Equity and Trusts* (3rd ed., 2018) pp. 598-599.

Millett suggested in his speech in *Foskett v McKeown*[109] that 'money paid into a bank account belongs legally and beneficially to the bank and not to the account holder'.

As Lord Sumption JSC commented in *Williams v Central Bank of Nigeria*,[110] '[t]he essence of a liability to account on the footing of knowing receipt is that the defendant has accepted trust assets knowing that they were transferred to him in breach of trust and that he had no right to receive them'. However, he pointed out that it is clear 'that a knowing recipient is not a trustee'.[111] This is in line with the view expressed by Millett LJ in *Paragon Finance plc v D.B. Thakerar & Co.*, [112] that while a knowing recipient is 'not in fact a trustee at all', he may be liable to account as if he were.

Before examining this question in more detail, it should be pointed out that the principles which apply in this area are still far from certain, and given their increasing use in a commercial context, this has become a cause for considerable concern. Furthermore there have been some signs of a move away from equitable principles as a means of resolving questions of this nature.[113] The irony of such a development has not been lost on Lord Nicholls as the following comment shows:

> Whatever may ultimately emerge either from the courts or from the legislature, one point is clear. Traditionally equity has supplemented the common law, giving a remedy where the common law was rigid and harsh. With its emphasis on conscience and flexibility, equity went to the heart of the matter affording new rights, new remedies, new procedures. Now, ironically, part of the heartland of equity is itself under siege from the encroaching influence of the common law in the guise of restitution. A vigorous new force is at large.[114]

At one level there are similarities between the type of liability imposed in cases of both dishonest assistance and knowing receipt. So, for example, in *Williams v Central Bank of Nigeria*,[115] Lord Sumption JSC did not consider that there should be any difference between the two categories so far as limitation periods were concerned. Similarly, in *Novoship (UK) Ltd v Mikhaylyuk*,[116] Longmore LJ suggested that it would be inappropriate to differentiate between the availability in principle of remedies relating to profits made by a knowing

109. [2001] 1 AC 102, 128.
110. [2014] AC 1189, 1208.
111. *Ibid.* at 1213-1214.
112. [1999] 1 All ER 400, 409.
113. See e.g. the decision of the House of Lords in *Lipkin Gorman v Karpanale Ltd* [1991] 2 AC 548.
114. Nicholls, 'Knowing Receipt: the Need for a New Landmark' in *Restitution: Past, Present and Future* (ed. Cornish *et al,* 1998) p. 243.
115. [2014] AC 1189, 1208.
116. [2015] QB 499. See further Davies (2015) 131 LQR 173, 174.

recipient and by a dishonest assistant. However, at another level there is a fundamental difference between the nature of liability in cases of assistance in the misappropriation of trust property and knowing receipt.[117] It has been argued that given this distinction, it makes sense to impose liability on a different basis in each category.[118] The threshold for the imposition of liability in cases of knowing receipt will now be explored.

The Threshold for the Imposition of Liability in England

Traditionally, it has been accepted that in cases of knowing receipt, which are concerned with the receipt of trust property for the benefit of the recipient, there should be a lower threshold of knowledge required than in cases of assistance in the misappropriation of trust property in order to found liability.[119] However, the principles in this area are far from settled and it is proposed to trace developments in a number of jurisdictions with a view to suggesting the attitude which the courts are likely to take in the future.

It was held by Buckley LJ in *Belmont Finance Corporation v Williams Furniture Ltd (No. 2)*[120] that where a stranger to a trust receives trust property with either actual or constructive knowledge of the breach of trust, he will be regarded as a constructive trustee of this property. Liability was imposed in that case on the basis of a receipt of trust monies by a company, the directors of which knew or ought to have known belonged to the trust.[121]

However, subsequently in *Re Montagu's Settlement Trusts*,[122] Megarry VC favoured the imposition of liability only in circumstances where the recipient possessed actual knowledge of the breach of trust. The trustees in that case had transferred certain chattels to a beneficiary (the tenth Duke of Manchester) in breach of trust and he had disposed of a number of these during his lifetime, although his solicitor had been aware of the terms of the settlement. After his death, the eleventh duke claimed that the tenth duke was a constructive trustee of the chattels. Megarry VC held that while the estate of the tenth duke was liable to return any remaining chattels or their traceable proceeds, the duke himself was not liable as constructive trustee as he had no actual knowledge that the chattels were trust property transferred in breach of trust. Megarry

117. As Iacobucci J stated in the Canadian Supreme Court decision of *Gold v Rosenberg* (1997) 152 DLR (4th) 385, 396, 'participation in a fraud underlies liability in cases of knowing assistance; unjust enrichment is the essence of a claim in knowing receipt'.
118. *Citadel General Assurance Co v Lloyds Bank Canada* (1997) 152 DLR (4th) 411, 433 *per* La Forest J; *Gold v Rosenberg* (1997) 152 DLR (4th) 385, 396 *per* Iacobucci J. See also *Agip Africa Ltd v Jackson* [1990] Ch 265, 292 *per* Millett J.
119. See the *dictum* of La Forest J in *Citadel General Assurance Co v Lloyds Bank Canada* (1997) 152 DLR (4th) 411, 434 to the effect that 'more is expected of the recipient, who unlike the accessory, is necessarily enriched at the plaintiff's expense'.
120. [1980] 1 All ER 393.
121. See also *Karak Rubber Co. Ltd v Burden (No. 2)* [1972] 1 WLR 602.
122. [1987] Ch 264. See Hayton [1987] CLJ 395; Harpum (1987) 50 MLR 217.

VC was of the view that the imposition of a constructive trust should depend primarily on the actual knowledge of the recipient and not on whether he is deemed to have constructive notice of the trust. He stated:

> I do not see why one of the touchstones for determining the burdens on property should be the same as that for deciding whether to impose a personal obligation on a man. The cold calculus of constructive and imputed notice does not seem to me to be an appropriate instrument for deciding whether a man's conscience is sufficiently affected for it to be right to bind him by the obligations of a constructive trustee.[123]

Megarry VC held that in considering whether a constructive trust has arisen in the context of the knowing receipt of trust property, the basic question is whether the conscience of the recipient is sufficiently affected to justify the imposition of such a trust.[124] He stated that, for this purpose, knowledge extends to the first three categories outlined in *Baden*, for in such cases there is a want of probity which justifies the imposition of a constructive trust.

A similar view was taken by Alliot J at first instance in *Lipkin Gorman v Karpanale Ltd*,[125] in which liability for both knowing assistance and knowing receipt was at issue. A partner in the plaintiff firm of solicitors had withdrawn money mostly from the clients' account and lost it gambling at a club. The plaintiff firm brought an action against the club on the basis of knowing receipt and against their bank on the grounds of knowing assistance. The plaintiff failed to establish liability on the part of the club on this basis and the finding of liability against the bank was reversed on appeal to the Court of Appeal. The solicitors' appeal from the dismissal of their claim against the club was ultimately allowed by the House of Lords[126] but on a different basis. It was held that the innocent recipient of stolen money was obliged to pay an equivalent sum to the true owner where full consideration for it had not been given and where this party had been unjustly enriched at the expense of the true owner. However, Lord Goff stressed that such a claim would be subject to a defence of change of position which will be available 'to a person whose position has so changed that it would be inequitable in all the circumstances to require him to make restitution, or alternatively to make restitution in full.'[127] In this case although the solicitors had no proprietary rights in the money in their bank

123. *Ibid.* at 273.
124. This approach has been approved by Knox J in *Hillsdown Holdings plc v Pensions Ombudsman* [1997] 1 All ER 862, 902-903.
125. [1987] 1 WLR 987.
126. [1991] 2 AC 548. See Birks [1991] LMCLQ 473; McKendrick (1992) 55 MLR 377.
127. *Ibid.* at 580. It is clear that the defence is not open to a person who has changed his position in bad faith or to a wrongdoer, see *Lipkin Gorman v Karpanale Ltd* [1991] 2 AC 548, 580. As Laddie J commented in *Barros Mattos Junior v MacDaniels Ltd* [2005] 1 WLR 247, 257, '[t]he recipient cannot put up a tainted claim to retention against the victim's untainted claim for restitution.' See further *Niru Battery Manufacturing*

account, at common law they were owners of a chose in action constituted by the indebtedness of the bank to them and could trace their property into its direct product, namely, the money drawn from the bank account by the gambler, and follow it into the hands of the club.

In *Agip (Africa) Ltd v Jackson*[128] Millett J stated at one point in his judgment that a person who receives for his own benefit trust property transferred to him in breach of trust is liable as a constructive trustee if he received it 'with notice, actual or constructive' that it was trust property transferred in breach of trust. Later in his judgment he referred to the doubts expressed by Megarry VC in *Montagu* about whether constructive notice is sufficient in relation to knowing receipt and appeared to reserve the question of whether these doubts were well-founded. However, Gardner's suggestion that 'taken with Millett J's other remarks, this passage seems a reflection rather of courtesy towards a brother judge than of uncertainty on Millett J's part over his own view'[129] is probably accurate.

It has been argued that the principle of constructive notice imposes too high a burden in a commercial context and in *Eagle Trust plc v SBC Securities Ltd*[130] Vinelott J distinguished between the type of knowledge which would be required to found liability in commercial and non-commercial types of transactions. In relation to the former category he stated that in order to make a defendant liable as a constructive trustee, it must be shown that he knew in one of the senses set out in the first three categories identified in *Baden* that the property was misapplied trust property, or the circumstances must be such that, in the absence of any evidence or explanation by the defendant, that knowledge can be inferred.[131] In the view of Vinelott J this inference may be drawn 'if the circumstances are such that an honest and reasonable man would have inferred that the moneys were probably trust moneys and were being misapplied, and would either not have accepted them or would have kept them separate until he had satisfied himself that the payer was entitled to use them in discharge of the liability'.[132] However, it has been argued by Millett J that judges who have warned against extending constructive notice to commercial dealings 'were obviously referring to the doctrine in its strict conveyancing sense'.[133] Fox has suggested that this longstanding policy against extending constructive

Co. v Milestone Trading Ltd [2004] QB 985, 999-1000 *per* Clarke LJ (see also Birks (2004) 120 LQR 373).

128. [1990] Ch 265, 293.
129. Gardner (1996) 112 LQR 64, 69-70.
130. [1993] 1 WLR 484.
131. Vinelott J was of the opinion that a difference remains between inferred knowledge and notice and stated (at 494) that 'the term "notice" is often used in a sense or in contexts where the facts do not support the inference of knowledge'.
132. [1993] 1 WLR 484, 506. See also the judgment of Knox J in *Cowan de Groot Properties Ltd v Eagle Trust plc* [1992] 4 All ER 700, 759, although in the circumstances of the case, no liability arose.
133. *MacMillan Inc v Bishopsgate Investment Trust plc (No. 3)* [1995] 1 WLR 978, 1000.

notice to commercial transactions[134] can be circumvented and that the same objections would not necessarily apply to an 'appropriately adjusted commercial standard of notice'.[135] In his view, 'there are no compelling economic reasons why constructive notice, set at the proper commercial standard, should not become a basis of liability for knowing receipt arising out of a commercial transaction'. Certainly there have been decisions in other jurisdictions which have not displayed the same unwillingness to confine the basis of liability for knowing receipt in commercial cases to knowledge in the sense of the first three categories set out in *Baden*. In *Citadel General Assurance Co v Lloyds Bank Canada*[136] the Canadian Supreme Court was willing to impose liability on a banker in respect of knowing receipt where he only possessed constructive knowledge of the breach of trust.

The decision of the Court of Appeal in *Bank of Credit and Commerce International (Overseas) Ltd v Akindele*[137] has clarified and simplified the law in England in this area. Although it initially received a fairly cautious welcome,[138] it is now well established as setting out the appropriate test for liability in this context in that jurisdiction. The claimants, who were the liquidators of two banking companies, contended that the defendant was liable to account to them for a sum of money as a constructive trustee on the basis that he had knowingly assisted in a breach of trust or had received trust monies with knowledge of the breaches. Carnwath J dismissed the claim on the basis that dishonesty by the defendant, which in his view was the essential foundation of the claimants' case, whether under the head of knowing assistance or knowing receipt, had not been established. The claimants' appeal to the Court of Appeal was dismissed, although Nourse LJ clarified the basis for establishing liability on the grounds of knowing receipt and held that Carnwath J had erred in insisting on dishonesty in this context.[139]

Nourse LJ agreed that as the defendant had not acted dishonestly, the claim of knowing assistance was bound to fail. However, he stated that dishonesty was not a prerequisite to liability under the head of knowing receipt and that

134. See *Manchester Trust v Furness* [1895] 2 QB 539.
135. Fox [1998] CLJ 391, 396.
136. (1997) 152 DLR (4th) 411.
137. [2001] Ch 437.
138. Nolan [2000] CLJ 447; Jaffey (2001) 15 Trust Law Int 151; Barkehall Thomas (2001) 21 OJLS 239. However, other commentators, e.g. Penner (2000) 14 Trust Law Int 229, are more critical of this approach. See also the criticisms voiced by Lord Nicholls in an *obiter* context in *Criterion Properties plc v Stratford UK Properties LLC* [2004] 1 WLR 1846, 1848.
139. Confusion appears to have arisen in relation to whether dishonesty was a prerequisite to establishing liability for knowing receipt as a result of a number of decisions (see *Twinsectra Ltd v Yardley* [1999] Lloyd's Rep Bank 438, 466-467 *per* Potter LJ; *Bank of America v Arnell* [1999] Lloyd's Rep Bank 399, 406-407 *per* Aikens J; *Dubai Aluminium Co. Ltd v Salaam* [1999] 1 Lloyd's Rep 415, 453 *per* Rix J). However, in *Houghton v Fayers* [2000] 1 BCLC 511 Nourse LJ reaffirmed that knowledge was the determining factor. See also *Brent LBC v Davies* [2018] EWHC 2214 (Ch) at [559].

the trial judge had been incorrect to proceed on this assumption.[140] He referred to *Belmont Finance Corporation Ltd v Williams Furniture (No.2)*[141] which he said was clear authority for the proposition that dishonesty is not a necessary ingredient of liability for knowing receipt. Nourse LJ stated that while the categorization of knowledge laid down in the *Baden* case has been influential in many decisions relating to knowing receipt, it was not formulated with that head of liability in mind. While he acknowledged that it might often be helpful in identifying different states of knowledge which may or may not lead to a finding of dishonesty for the purpose of establishing liability for knowing assistance, he stated that he had 'grave doubts' about its utility in cases of knowing receipt. Nourse LJ then posed the question of what purpose could be served by a categorization of knowledge in the context of knowing receipt. In his view it could only be to enable the court to determine, in the words of Megarry VC in *Re Montagu's Settlement Trusts*,[142] whether the claimant's conscience was sufficiently affected for it to be right to bind him with the obligations of a constructive trustee. So, if this were the purpose, there was no need for categorization and all that was necessary was that 'the recipient's state of knowledge should be such as to make it unconscionable for him to retain the benefit of the receipt.'[143] In his view such a test, although it could not any more than any other avoid difficulties of application, ought to deal with the problems of definition and allocation which previous categorizations had given rise to. He added that it should also make it easier for the courts to adopt a common sense approach in the commercial context in which claims in knowing receipt are now frequently made.[144] Nourse LJ concluded that Carnwath J's findings of fact supported the conclusion that the defendant's knowledge was not such

140. See also *Charter plc v City Index Ltd* [2007] 1 WLR 26, 31.
141. [1980] 1 All ER 393. This proposition was supported by other more recent *dicta*, e.g. *per* Millett J in *Agip (Africa) Ltd v Jackson* [1990] Ch 265, 292; Vinelott J in *Eagle Trust plc v SBC Securities Ltd* [1993] 1 WLR 484, 497.
142. [1987] Ch 264, 273.
143. [2001] Ch 437, 455. This test has been approved in numerous cases. See, e.g., *Charter plc v City Index Ltd* [2007] 1 WLR 26, 31; *Pulvers v Chan* [2007] EWHC 2406 (Ch) at [377]; *Hollis v Rolfe* [2008] EWHC 1747 (Ch) at [173]; *Bank of Tokyo-Mitsubishi UFJ Ltd v Baskan Gida Sanayi Ve Pazarlama AS* [2009] EWHC 1276 (Ch) at [990]; *Law Society for England and Wales v Habitable Concepts Ltd* [2010] EWHC 1449 (Ch) at [15]; *Independent Trustee Services Ltd v JP Noble Trustees Ltd* [2010] EWHC 1653 (Ch) at [51]; *Law Society for England and Wales v Issac* [2010] EWHC 1670 (Ch) at [6]; *Arthur v Attorney General of the Turks and Caicos Islands* [2012] UKPC 30 at [33]; *Armstrong DLW GmbH v Winnington Networks Ltd* [2013] Ch 156, 193.
144. See also *Criterion Properties plc v Stratford UK Properties LLC* [2003] 1 WLR 2108, 2119 *per* Carnwath LJ. This decision was affirmed by the House of Lords ([2004] 1 WLR 1846) on different grounds and the concept of unconscionability did not form the basis for the decision. However, it should be noted that Lord Nicholls expressed the view on an *obiter* basis that the Court of Appeal in *Akindele* had erred in basing liability for knowing receipt on unconscionability.

as to make it unconscionable for him to retain the benefit of the receipt and dismissed the appeal.

The relative simplicity of the approach adopted by Nourse LJ was welcomed[145] and it was suggested by Carnwath LJ in the decision of the Court of Appeal in *Criterion Properties plc v Stratford UK Properties LLC*[146] that 'the purpose of the new formulation was to give greater flexibility for the application of common sense in commercial situations.' It has also been stated by Sir Andrew Morritt C in *Charter plc v City Index Ltd*[147] that it is common ground that the decision of the Court of Appeal in *Akindele* 'reflects what the law now is' in that jurisdiction.

Some uncertainty remains about the role which knowledge should continue to play in the imposition of liability in this context. In delivering the opinion of the Privy Council in *Arthur v Attorney General of the Turks and Caicos Islands*[148] Sir Terence Etherton stated that '[k]nowledge, in the knowing receipt sense, means not merely notice, but, in accordance with *Akindele*, such knowledge as to make the recipient's conduct unconscionable and to give rise to equitable fraud.' More specific reference to knowledge was made in a first instance decision in *Armstrong GmbH v Winnington Networks Ltd*,[149] where Stephen Morris QC, sitting as a High Court judge, expressed the view that, in a commercial context, knowledge of types (1) to (3) on the *Baden* scale on the part of a defendant would render receipt of trust property unconscionable. In his view knowledge of types (4) and (5) on this scale would also render receipt unconscionable, 'but only if, on the facts actually known to this defendant, a reasonable person would either have appreciated that the transfer was probably in breach of trust or would have made inquiries or sought advice which would have revealed the probability of the breach of trust.' This issue was also considered by the Privy Council in *Crédit Agricole Corpn and Investment Bank v Papadimitrou*,[150] in which Lord Sumption suggested that the question of what constitutes notice or knowledge is the same irrespective of whether a person claims to be a *bona fide* purchaser of assets without notice of a prior interest in them or disputes a claim to make him accountable as a constructive trustee on the basis of knowing receipt. The primary judgment in this case was delivered by Lord Clarke who suggested that in order to avoid constructive notice, a defendant must make inquiries if the facts known to him would give a reasonable person in the position of the particular individual

145. Breslin, 'Unbundling constructive trusteeship' in *Liber Memorialis James C. Brady* (eds. Breen and Casey, 2001) p. 95.
146. [2003] 1 WLR 2108, 2119. However, note the criticisms voiced by Lord Nicholls in an *obiter* context in the House of Lords, see [2004] 1 WLR 1846, 1848.
147. [2007] 1 WLR 26, 32.
148. [2012] UKPC 30 at [36]. See further Dixon [2012] Conv 439; Hopkins [2013] Conv 61.
149. [2013] Ch 156.
150. [2015] 1 WLR 4265.

serious cause to question the propriety of the transaction. While the case did not relate directly to knowing receipt, the view expressed by Lord Sumption, that the test for establishing whether a finding should be made of constructive notice of proprietary rights should be the same as in relation to knowing or unconscionable receipt, is potentially significant.[151]

Finally, it should be noted that liability for knowing or unconscionable receipt tends to be restitutionary in nature[152] and a defendant will be liable to account for any profits received or which he will make.[153] The Privy Council accepted in *Akita Holdings Ltd v Attorney General of the Turks and Caicos Islands*[154] that the remedies available against a knowing recipient of property acquired at an undervalue from a person acting in breach of a fiduciary duty included the personal remedy of seeking an account of profits and that this liability to account arose from the mere fact of a profit having been made. However, it should be noted that Glister has argued that knowing recipients should not automatically be liable to disgorge discrete profits.[155] Specifically, he suggests that where the recipient's conduct cannot be characterised as anything other than mere receipt and he has a relatively low level of knowledge, liability to account for such discrete profits should not be assumed.

The Position in Other Common Law Jurisdictions

It is interesting to note that there has been some inconsistency in other common law jurisdictions in relation to the circumstances in which liability will be imposed in cases of knowing receipt. In the New Zealand decision of *Marshall Futures Ltd v Marshall*[156] Tipping J stated that, in cases of knowing receipt, 'where the person alleged to be a constructive trustee will usually have benefited personally from the breach of trust there are good policy reasons for allowing constructive knowledge in the form of categories (iv) and (v) to be sufficient to make him responsible'.[157] In the subsequent decision of *Equiticorp Industries Group v The Crown*[158] Smellie J found that the defendant had either wilfully shut its eyes to the obvious or if not, had wilfully and recklessly failed to make the inquiries which a reasonable and honest commercial party would have made and therefore the need to make a decision about the knowledge of types (iv) and (v) on the *Baden* scale did not arise.

The issue has also been considered in detail in two significant decisions of

---

151. See further Pearce [2015] Conv 522.
152. *Twinsectra v Yardley* [2002] 2 AC 164, 194 *per* Lord Millett.
153. *Crown Dilmun v Sutton* [2004] 1 BCLC 468 at [204].
154. [2017] AC 590. See further Turner [2018] CLJ 255.
155. 'Account of Profits and Third Parties' in *Equitable Compensation and Disgorgement of Profit* (eds. Degeling and Varuhas, 2017) p. 175 at 196.
156. [1992] 1 NZLR 316, 326.
157. A similar view was expressed by Wylie J in *Equiticorp Industries Group v Hawkins* [1991] 3 NZLR 700, 728.
158. [1998] 2 NZLR 480.

the Canadian Supreme Court. In *Citadel General Assurance Co v Lloyds Bank Canada*[159] La Forest J expressed the view that in cases of knowing receipt there should be a lower threshold of knowledge required of the stranger to the trust than in cases of knowing assistance. As he stated, '[m]ore is expected of the recipient, who unlike the accessory, is necessarily enriched at the plaintiff's expense. Because the recipient is held to this higher standard, constructive knowledge (that is, knowledge of facts sufficient to put a reasonable person on notice or inquiry) will suffice as the basis for restitutionary liability.'[160] Similarly, in *Gold v Rosenberg*,[161] Iacobucci J, albeit in a dissenting judgment,[162] stated that in cases of knowing receipt, a person need not have actual knowledge and that notice would suffice.

In Australia, while knowledge in the first four categories has been required to establish liability for knowing assistance,[163] there has been some uncertainty about whether knowledge or notice encompassing any of the five *Baden* categories would suffice in relation to knowing receipt,[164] although the weight of authority suggests that knowledge in categories (i) to (iv) but not category (v) will suffice.[165] In *Grimaldi v Chameleon Mining NL*,[166] in concluding that knowledge within category (iv) would suffice for the imposition of liability for knowing receipt, the Federal Court of Australia suggested that '[a]s with assistance liability, recipient liability should be seen as fault based and as making the same knowledge/notice demands as in assistance cases'.

The Position in this Jurisdiction

In this jurisdiction the Supreme Court appears to be prepared to accept that constructive knowledge will suffice to ground liability for knowing receipt even in a commercial context. In *Re Frederick Inns Ltd*,[167] payments were made by a group of associated companies to the Revenue Commissioners in the six

159. (1997) 152 DLR (4th) 411. See Smith (1998) 114 LQR 394.
160. *Ibid.* at 434. See also *Carl B. Potter Ltd v Mercantile Bank of Canada* (1980) 112 DLR (3d) 88; *Arthur Andersen Inc v Toronto-Dominion Bank* (1994) 17 OR (3d) 363; *Glenko Enterprises Ltd v Ernie Keller Contractors Ltd* (1996) 134 DLR (4th) 161; *Real Estate and Business Brokers (Director) v NRS Mississauga Inc* (2000) 194 DLR (4th) 526.
161. (1997) 152 DLR (4th) 385.
162. The view of the majority was that the bank had not actually received the trust property. However, the minority found that there had been receipt and went on to consider whether the requisite degree of knowledge existed.
163. *Farah Constructions Pty Ltd v Say-Dee Pty Ltd* (2007) 230 CLR 89, 163. See also e.g. *Lewis Securities Ltd v Carter* (2018) 355 ALR 703, 743.
164. See the discussion in *Grimaldi v Chameleon Mining NL* (2012) 287 ALR 22, 85.
165. See, e.g., *Consul Development Pty Ltd v DPC Estates Pty Ltd* (1975) 132 CLR 373, 412; *Simmons v New South Wales Trustee and Guardian* [2014] NSWCA 405 at [90]; *Lewis Securities Ltd v Carter* (2018) 355 ALR 703, 742-743.
166. (2012) 287 ALR 22, 85.
167. [1994] 1 ILRM 387.

months immediately preceding the commencement of the winding up of four of these companies out of the proceeds of sale of various licensed premises which had belonged to these four companies. This sum was appropriated by the commissioners in reduction of the tax liabilities of not only the four companies involved in the proceedings but also those of six other companies in the group. The liquidator challenged these payments as being *ultra vires* in so far as they had effected an alienation of the companies' assets when they were insolvent. Lardner J held that the payments made by the companies which exceeded their liabilities and were intended to reduce the liabilities of the other companies in the same group were *ultra vires* on the grounds that each company was a separate entity. The commissioners' appeal was dismissed by the Supreme Court which held that no clause in the memoranda of association of any of the companies, properly construed, gave them power to pay the debts of an associated company and that the payments were therefore *ultra vires*. Blayney J held that the *ultra vires* payments constituted a misapplication by the directors of company funds in breach of their fiduciary duties. These monies had been received by the Revenue Commissioners with constructive knowledge of this breach as the memoranda of association of the four companies, which were documents of public record, revealed the absence of capacity. So, apart from the monies which the Revenue Commissioners had originally appropriated towards the discharge of the respective tax liabilities of the four companies involved in the proceedings, the payments made were held by them on a constructive trust and had to be repaid to the official liquidator.[168] The Supreme Court therefore ordered that the sums involved should be repaid by the Revenue Commissioners.

The question of the degree of knowledge required to establish liability for knowing receipt was also considered by the High Court in *Ulster Factors Ltd v Entoglen Ltd*.[169] The first named defendant entered into a factoring agreement with the plaintiff whereby it agreed to assign all its debts to the plaintiff by way of sale or assignment and the plaintiff agreed to make payment to or to the order of the first named defendant of a sum not exceeding the 'availability balance' as defined in the agreement. After the first named defendant went into liquidation, the plaintiff instituted proceedings against the company and its liquidator, the second named defendant, claiming the balance which it alleged was due to it. What remained at issue at the hearing of the action was one payment made to a third party by the plaintiff which the liquidator claimed had not been properly paid. The defendants submitted that this payment was *ultra vires* the company and that it had been made without the company's authority. Laffoy J did not accept that the payment by the plaintiff was *ultra vires* the company. However, she went on to say that even if the liquidator had established that the payment

168. As O'Dell has asserted, the application of principle by Blayney J in *Re Frederick Inns Ltd* seemed to go even further than the fifth point on the *Baden* scale and he has commented that: 'even if the *Baden* scale does not reach notice properly so-called, *Frederick Inns* certainly seems to'. See *Annual Review of Irish Law 1997* p. 644.
169. [1997] IEHC 34.

was *ultra vires*, he had not made out any basis on which the plaintiff should be required in effect to make restitution of this payment. Laffoy J quoted with approval from the judgment of Blayney J in *Re Frederick Inns Ltd* in which he had applied the principle set out in *Belmont Finance Corporation Ltd v Williams Furniture Ltd (No.2)*[170] and stated that 'what renders the recipient of or the dealer with funds which are being misapplied in breach of the fiduciary duties of the directors of a company liable as a constructive trustee is knowledge, actual or constructive, of the breach of trust'.[171] She found that the plaintiff did not have actual knowledge of any breach of duty and concluded that 'there was no obligation on the plaintiff to enquire as to the purpose for which any payment which the company requested the plaintiff to make to a third party was being made or to satisfy itself that the payment was *intra vires* the company and, even if the payment was *ultra vires*, constructive knowledge of a breach of trust cannot be imputed to the plaintiff for failure to make such inquiries'. Laffoy J also rejected the liquidator's contention that the payment was made without the company's authority and she held that the plaintiff was entitled to judgment in the amount claimed.

The alternative approaches to the imposition of liability in cases of knowing receipt were also considered in some detail by Laffoy J in *Fyffes plc v DCC plc*.[172] She expressed the view that in putting forward the unconscionability test in *Akindele*, 'Nourse LJ was positing a stricter, not a laxer, test than constructive notice'.[173] Laffoy J concluded that in the circumstances it was not necessary for her to decide between the application of the *Akindele* unconscionability test or the *Belmont/Frederick Inns* actual or constructive knowledge test, although earlier in her judgment she did refer to *Frederick Inns* as 'a decision by which this court is bound'.[174] McGovern J also gave consideration to the appropriate test for the imposition of liability in this context in *Harlequin Property (SVG) Ltd v O'Halloran*.[175] Although in the circumstances of the case before him he did not consider it necessary to impose a constructive trust, he referred to the test accepted by the Supreme Court in *Re Frederick Inns* and also said that regard should be had to the comments of Keane to the effect that on the basis of this decision 'the threshold for finding a person accountable as a constructive trustee for the knowing receipt of misapplied trust property has been set at a significantly lower level in Ireland.'[176]

170. [1980] 1 All ER 393.
171. [1997] IEHC 34 at 8.
172. [2009] 2 IR 417. The *Akindele* decision was also mentioned by Finnegan J in *Moffitt v Bank of Ireland* [2000] IEHC 106 but he expressed no view on whether it might be applied as it was not necessary to do so on the facts of the case.
173. *Ibid.* at 670.
174. *Ibid.*
175. [2013] IEHC 362.
176. Keane, *Equity and the Law of Trusts in the Republic of Ireland* (2nd ed., 2011) p.245. Now see 3rd ed., 2017, p. 256.

The Supreme Court revisited this issue in *O'Donnell v Bank of Ireland*,[177] although in the circumstances Laffoy J concluded that the trial judge had been correct in finding that the defendants had no knowledge of or reason to believe that there had been a breach of trust and she held that the claim that a property was subject to a constructive trust on the basis of knowing receipt failed. Laffoy J noted that the Supreme Court had not considered the test for the imposition of liability in this context since the modification put forward by the Court of Appeal in England in *Akindele*. She continued as follows:

> While, on the current state of the law on the equitable principle of "knowing receipt", there is a divergence between this jurisdiction and the United Kingdom in that "knowledge, actual or constructive" of the breach of trust is an ingredient of the test for establishing liability as a constructive trustee in this jurisdiction, whereas in the United Kingdom the corresponding ingredient of the test is whether the recipient had sufficient knowledge of the circumstances of the transfer to make it "unconscionable" for him to retain the benefit of the receipt, the Court does not have to address that divergence, because it was not urged on behalf of the appellants that this Court should adopt the approach which has been adopted in the United Kingdom.[178]

Therefore, there is currently nothing to suggest that the courts in this jurisdiction will adopt the *Akindele* unconscionability approach whatever the context. So, the threshold for the imposition of liability continues to be lower in this jurisdiction. As Keane has pointed out, 'the conduct of the Revenue in *Re Frederick Inns* could not conceivably be described as unconscionable'.[179] Arguably the test in *Re Frederick Inns* imposes an unnecessarily high onus on persons or bodies dealing with a company and it is interesting to note that the Supreme Court made no attempt to distinguish the standard required in relation to commercial and non-commercial transactions. Fox has put forward the argument that there is no reason 'why constructive notice, set at the proper commercial standard, should not become a basis of liability for knowing receipt arising out of a commercial transaction.'[180] However, this is an area fraught with difficulty[181] and some doubt must remain about whether the courts in this jurisdiction may see fit to revisit this question in the future.

177. [2014] IESC 77.
178. *Ibid.* at [117].
179. Keane, *Equity and the Law of Trusts in Ireland* (3rd ed., 2017) p.257.
180. [1998] CLJ 391, 405.
181. It is interesting to note the divergence of opinion on the meaning of the term 'notice' between Vinelott J in *Eagle Trust plc v SBC Securities Ltd* [1993] 1 WLR 484 and Millett J in *El Ajou v Dollar Holdings plc* [1993] 3 All ER 717. While the approach of Vinelott J appears to assume that a reasonable person 'must always behave as rigorously as he does in the land transfer context', Millett J accepts the idea that 'the reasonable person behaves differently in different contexts' (see Gardner (1996) 112 LQR 56,

POSSIBLE FUTURE DEVELOPMENTS

It has been argued that neither the restricted view of fault set out in *Re Montagu's Settlement Trusts*[182] nor the broader view of liability encompassing constructive knowledge provides a wholly satisfactory answer and that 'each will produce an unattractive result in some situations'.[183] In addition, it has been suggested that in the light of the approach taken by the House of Lords in *Lipkin Gorman v Karpanale Ltd*,[184] liability in this area might in future be decided in terms of common law principles in an action for money had and received, based on the concept of strict liability but subject to the defence of change of position. Such a remedy possesses the distinct advantage that its imposition does not depend on the state of mind or degree of knowledge of the recipient.[185]

An interesting alternative theory was also put forward by Lord Nicholls, writing extra-judicially, who suggested that personal liability should be based on a combination of two separate principles.[186] First, recipient liability should cover all third party recipients. This would be a principle of strict liability in that it would apply to every recipient with an impeachable title irrespective of fault, but it would be restitutionary in nature. It would be confined to restoring an unjust gain. Change of position would accordingly be available as a defence. Secondly, dishonest recipients should be personally liable to make good losses as well as accounting for benefits. Harpum welcomed this model as seeking to reconcile the views of those who consider that receipt-based liability should be founded on restitutionary principles and those who consider that it should be based upon equitable wrongdoing.[187] As he pointed out, it involves a move away from fault-based liability, which might be a welcome step, but this would be balanced by the availability of the defences of change of position and *bona fide* purchase.

However, both judicial and academic opinion is divided about the wisdom of a movement away from a fault-based approach in this area. Some judges have

---

62). Gardner believes that Millett J's approach is probably the better founded (at p. 63) and suggests that it is the formula to the effect that 'notice is a function of how the reasonable person would have behaved in the relevant circumstances . . . rather than the standards set in the land transfer cases, that truly defines notice'. It would certainly be useful if the courts in this jurisdiction were to consider this question and clarify what their understanding of 'notice' is, particularly in a commercial context.

182. [1987] Ch 264.
183. *Per* Nicholls, 'Knowing Receipt: the Need for a New Landmark' in *Restitution: Past, Present and Future* (ed. Cornish *et al*, 1998) p. 241.
184. [1991] 2 AC 548.
185. However, as Oakley points out in *Parker and Mellows: Modern Law of Trusts* (9th ed., 2008) p. 440, the introduction of strict liability would have an adverse impact on innocent volunteers.
186. Nicholls, 'Knowing Receipt: the Need for a New Landmark' in *Restitution: Past, Present and Future* (ed. Cornish *et al*, 1998) p. 244.
187. 'Knowing Receipt: the Need for a New Landmark: Some Reflections' in *Restitution: Past, Present and Future* (ed. Cornish *et al*, 1998) p. 247 at 248.

commented that although the cause of action is compensatory in nature, it may also be described as restitutionary.[188] It was suggested by Thomas J in the New Zealand decision of *Powell v Thompson*[189] that liability in the knowing receipt category is based on the concept of unjust enrichment, which is receipt-based and not fault-based.[190] If one accepts this approach, it should therefore follow that the degree of knowledge possessed by the recipient should not be the decisive factor.[191] Similar views were expressed by Lord Millett in the course of his speech in *Twinsectra Ltd v Yardley*,[192] in which he stressed that liability for knowing receipt is receipt-based and does not depend on fault. He added that there is powerful academic support for the proposition that the liability of the recipient is the same as in other cases of restitution, that is to say, strict but subject to a defence of change of position.

However, there have also been equally strong judicial and academic views expressed in favour of retaining a fault-based approach in equity. In *Bank of Credit and Commerce International (Overseas) Ltd v Akindele*[193] Nourse LJ admitted that no argument had been made before the court based on the views put forward by Lord Nicholls[194] and acknowledged that at Court of Appeal level this would have been a fruitless exercise. However, he doubted whether strict liability coupled with a change of position defence would be preferable to fault-based liability in many commercial transactions. In his view the courts must continue to do their best with the accepted formulation of liability for knowing receipt, simplifying and improving it where possible. Academic opinion has tended to support the views put forward by Nourse LJ and Jaffey has commented that it is fortunate that the Court of Appeal in *Akindele* resisted the temptation to effect a radical reform of the law on the basis of a restitutionary analysis of knowing receipt.[195] Similarly, Smith has concluded that fault-based liability in equity is the appropriate vehicle for the courts to apply in this context; in his

188. *Charter plc v City Index Ltd* [2007] 1 WLR 26, 39 *per* Sir Andrew Morritt C.
189. [1991] 1 NZLR 597, 607. See also *Equiticorp Industries Group Ltd v The Crown* [1998] 2 NZLR 481.
190. See also *Royal Brunei Airlines Sdn Bhd v Tan* [1995] 2 AC 378, 386; *Dublin Corporation v Ancient Guild of Incorporated Brick and Stone Layers and Allied Trades Union* High Court 1991 No. 1556P (Budd J) 6 March 1996 at 51.
191. McGrath suggests [1999] LMCLQ 343, 351 that 'the flood waters are clearly amassing behind the fault-based barrier for knowing receipt claims'.
192. [2002] 2 AC 164, 194. See also his comments in *Dubai Aluminium Co. Ltd v Salaam* [2003] 2 AC 366, 391.
193. [2001] Ch 437. See also *Charter plc v City Index Ltd* [2007] 1 WLR 26, 32.
194. See *supra*, Nicholls 'Knowing Receipt; The Need for a New Landmark' in *Restitution: Past, Present and Future* (ed. Cornish *et al*, 1998). See also his *obiter* comments in *Criterion Properties plc v Stratford UK Properties LLC* [2004] 1 WLR 1846, 1848.
195. Jaffey (2001) 15 Trust Law Int 151, 152. Hayton has also commented (2007) Trust Law Int 55, 60 with reference to *Akindele* that 'Equity has always been concerned only to impose liability on defendants whose consciences are sufficiently affected'. Hayton also supported the view expressed by Nourse LJ in *Akindele* that an extension to receipt based liability would be commercially unworkable.

opinion 'knowing receipt counts as equitable wrongdoing and cannot be made to fit into the mould of unjust enrichment'.[196]

It is interesting to note that when this issue was discussed by the High Court of Australia in *Farah Construction Pty Ltd v Say-Dee Pty Ltd*[197] the decision of the New South Wales Court of Appeal to adopt a strict liability approach was characterised as 'a grave error'. The view was expressed by the High Court that the reasoning of the Court of Appeal did not demonstrate any inconsistency or other reason which would justify changing the law in the manner proposed and it was stated that an unjust enrichment claim should not be used to 'cut down traditional equitable protection'.[198] It should be stressed that this debate is far from over and it is entirely possible that the courts may revisit the issue of the imposition of a restitutionary model.[199] Certainly, the *obiter* comments of Lord Nicholls in *Criterion Properties plc v Stratford UK Properties LLC*[200] show that he still favoured a strict liability approach subject to a defence of change of position. In addition, a strict liability personal claim in unjust enrichment was the preferred approach of the Court of Appeal in *Relfo Ltd v Varsani*.[201] Gardner has also advocated an alternative approach, namely the imposition of a personal liability in restitution and suggests that '[t]his personal extension of the restitutionary liability of a recipient of illicitly transferred trust property might render his liability for "knowing receipt" irrelevant'.[202]

However, for the present, equitable principles continue to be relevant and the *dicta* of Carnwath LJ in *Charter plc v City Index Ltd*[203] makes it clear that *Akindele* still represents the law in England and that 'liability for "knowing receipt" depends on the defendant having sufficient knowledge of the circumstances of the payment to make it "unconscionable" for him to retain the benefit or pay it away for its own purposes.' It should also be borne in mind that as the law stands at present in this jurisdiction, on the basis of the approach in *Re Frederick Inns*, which was accepted in *O'Donnell*, actual or

196. Smith (2000) 116 LQR 412, 430. See also Barkehall Thomas (2001) 21 OJLS 239, 250; Sheehan [2008] RLR 41, 62; Low [2008] RLR 96, 106; Bryan, 'The Liability of the Recipient: Restitution at Common Law or Wrongdoing in Equity' in *Equity in Commercial Law* (eds. Degeling and Edelman, 2005) p. 327 *et seq*; Mitchell and Watterson, 'Remedies for Knowing Receipt' in *Constructive and Resulting Trusts* (ed. Mitchell, 2010) p.115 at 157; Salmons [2017] CLJ 399, 429.
197. (2007) 230 CLR 89, 149. See further Conaglen and Nolan [2007] CLJ 515; Hayton (2007) Trust Law Int 55; Ridge and Dietrich (2008) 124 LQR 26.
198. *Ibid.* at 157.
199. Note that Lord Walker expressed support, commenting extra-judicially (2005) 27 Syd L Rev 187, 202 for Lord Nicholls' receipt-based model, although he acknowledged that 'it is not yet established law, or anywhere close to it, in any jurisdiction.'
200. [2004] 1 WLR 1846, 1848.
201. [2014] EWCA Civ 360.
202. Gardner (2009) 125 LQR 20, 24.
203. [2008] Ch 313, 321. See further Gardner (2009) 125 LQR 20; Virgo [2008] CLJ 254; Goymour [2008] RLR 113.

constructive knowledge is still required before liability under the heading of knowing receipt can be imposed.

THE LIABILITY OF AGENTS OF TRUSTEES

An agent of a trustee will not be liable to account provided that in receiving trust property or in dealing with it, he has acted honestly and within the scope of his usual authority as an agent. So where he is acting in the capacity of agent, he will not be accountable to the beneficiaries, but only to his principal, provided that he does not act outside the scope of his authority. This general rule was laid down by Lord Selborne in *Barnes v Addy*[204] as follows:

> [S]trangers are not to be made constructive trustees merely because they act as the agents of trustees in transactions within their legal powers, transactions, perhaps of which a Court of Equity may disapprove, unless those agents receive and become chargeable with some part of the trust property, or unless they assist with knowledge in a dishonest and fraudulent design on the part of the trustees.

In that case solicitors advised against the appointment of a sole trustee although they prepared the documentation necessary for his appointment. When the trustee in question sold the trust property and misapplied the proceeds it was held that the solicitors could not be treated as constructive trustees as they had acted honestly in the course of their agency and had merely carried out the instructions of the trustees.

One of the most important authorities in this area is the decision of the Court of Appeal in *Carl Zeiss Stiftung v Herbert Smith & Co. (No. 2)*,[205] in which a solicitor who was given money by a client, which the plaintiff claimed was held by the client on trust for the plaintiff, was found not to be accountable for this money since there had been no want of probity on the solicitor's part. Edmund Davies LJ summarised his view of an agent's position as follows:

> A solicitor or other agent who receives money from his principal which belongs at law or in equity to a third party is not accountable as a constructive trustee to that third party unless he has been guilty of some wrongful act in relation to that money. ... To act 'wrongfully' he must be guilty of (i) knowingly participating in a breach of trust by his principal; or (ii) intermeddling with the trust property otherwise than merely as an agent and thereby becomes a trustee *de son tort*; or (iii) receiving or dealing with the money knowing that his principal has no right to pay

204. (1874) 9 Ch App 244, 251-252.
205. [1969] 2 Ch 276.

> it over or to instruct him to deal with it in the manner indicated; or (iv) some dishonest act relating to the money.[206]

It would appear that agents of trustees who are in receipt of trust property or who deal inconsistently with it, are to an extent regarded more favourably than a beneficial recipient of trust property and an agent's duty to inquire is less strictly interpreted.[207] This point is well illustrated by the decision of Kay J in *Williams v Williams*,[208] in which a solicitor disposed of lands which were subject to a settlement on the settlor's behalf in accordance with the latter's instructions. It was held that the solicitor was not liable to account since he neither knew of the settlement nor had wilfully shut his eyes to its existence although the facts disclosed that he should have been put on inquiry as to its existence. So where an agent acts honestly in following his principal's instructions, he will not be liable. This was confirmed by the judgment of Bennett J in *Williams-Ashman v Price*,[209] in which solicitors who had followed the instructions of a trustee in making an unauthorised loan and other investments were found not to be liable as constructive trustees as they had acted honestly on the trustee's instructions and had not intermeddled in the affairs of the trust.

However, where an agent receives trust property and, knowing that he is acting in breach of trust, deals with it in a manner inconsistent with its terms, he may be personally liable. This is evident from the decision of *Lee v Sankey*,[210] in which Bacon VC made it clear that where an agent receives trust monies and deals with them in a manner inconsistent with the trust of which he is aware, he is personally liable for the consequences. Solicitors who were employed by trustees to receive the proceeds of the sale of a testator's property and improperly paid over the money to only one of the two trustees, who dissipated the fund and subsequently died insolvent, were held liable to account to the beneficiaries in respect of the loss which had occurred.

THE LIABILITY OF PARTNERS

Where a partner in a solicitors' firm is found to have dishonestly assisted in a breach of trust, the firm will also be vicariously liable in certain circumstances where the partner is acting in the ordinary course of the firm's business. The decision of the House of Lords in *Dubai Aluminium Co. Ltd v Salaam*[211] has clarified a number of issues which had led to difficulties in this area and it is clear that earlier authorities on this issue must now be treated with caution.

---

206. *Ibid.* at 303-304.
207. *Carl Zeiss Stiftung v Herbert Smith & Co. (No. 2)* [1969] 2 Ch 276, 297.
208. (1881) 17 Ch D 437.
209. [1942] Ch 219.
210. (1873) LR 15 Eq 204. See also *Soar v Ashwell* [1893] 2 QB 390.
211. [2003] 2 AC 366.

In *Mara v Browne*[212] it was suggested *obiter* by Lord Herschell that it was not within the scope of the implied authority of a solicitor who is a partner in a firm to act so as to make himself a constructive trustee and thereby subject his partner to the same liability. This *dictum* was applied by Vinelott J in *Re Bell's Indenture*[213] in which it was sought to impose liability on a partner in a firm of solicitors whose co-partner had knowingly assisted in a breach of trust. Although in this case the monies had actually passed through the firm's client account, it was held that the innocent partner was not liable as a constructive trustee and it was further held that no liability could arise under the Partnership Act 1890.[214] Subsequently, it was held by Millett J and the Court of Appeal in *Agip (Africa) Ltd v Jackson*,[215] that where the court found that an accountant had dishonestly assisted in a breach of trust, liability could also be imposed on his partner, although there was no discussion of the basis for such a finding.

The terms of section 10 of the Partnership Act 1890 provide as follows:

> Where, by any wrongful act or omission of any partner acting in the ordinary course of business of the firm, or with the authority of his co-partners, loss or injury is caused to any person not being a partner in the firm, or any penalty is incurred, the firm is liable therefor to the same extent as the partner so acting or omitting to act.

It was held by the majority of the Court of Appeal and by Lord Millett in *Dubai Aluminium Co. Ltd v Salaam*[216] that the words 'any wrongful act or omission' in section 10 of the Act of 1890 are not limited to tortious acts or wrongs actionable at common law but are wide enough to encompass all wrongful acts or omissions. In the view of Aldous LJ the conclusion reached in *Agip Africa* could only have been arrived at on the basis that section 10 applied to the facts of that case. In *Dubai* the Court of Appeal concluded that the partner's acts could not have been carried out 'in the ordinary course of business' within the meaning of the section and that vicarious liability could not be imposed on other partners in the circumstances of the case. This approach was followed by the Court of Appeal in *Walker v Stones*,[217] in which Sir Christopher Slade

---

212. [1896] 1 Ch 199.
213. [1980] 1 WLR 1217.
214. Vinelott J distinguished the earlier decision in *Blythe v Fladgate* [1891] Ch 337 on the basis that in that case there had been no trustees at the time the breach of trust had been committed and the partners in the firm of solicitors could not claim that they had received the moneys as agents of the trustees. Luxton [1981] Conv 310 is critical of *Re Bell's Indenture* and suggests that as a result of that decision, the liability of the partners of a solicitor who is liable as a constructive trustee, depends on whether there were validly appointed trustees at the time, a distinction which he argues should not be relevant to the co-partner's liability.
215. [1990] Ch 265, 296; [1991] Ch 547.
216. [2001] QB 113 (CA); [2003] 2 AC 366 (HL).
217. [2001] QB 902.

further accepted that breaches of trust committed by a trustee-partner would fall outside the ordinary business of any partnership and would be incapable of giving rise to vicarious liability under section 10.

However, it is clear in the light of the conclusions reached by the House of Lords in *Dubai*, which overturned the findings of the Court of Appeal[218] and upheld the decision of the trial judge,[219] that the *dictum* of Lord Herschell in *Mara v Browne* which has been relied upon on so many occasions must be reassessed. Lord Nicholls stated that the acts done by the partner were so closely connected with the acts he was authorised to do that they might properly and fairly be regarded as having been done by him while he was acting in the ordinary course of the firm's business. He made it clear that the liability of a firm of solicitors in respect of acts of a partner which render him liable depends on an application of the ordinary principles relating to vicarious liability and that there is no special rule of law applicable to this head of equitable liability. He stated that he did not think that Lord Herschell or the other members of the Court of Appeal in *Mara* could be taken to have suggested otherwise,[220] and in so far as Vinelott J did so in *Re Bell's Indenture*, he must have fallen into error. Lord Millett expressed the view that deliberate and dishonest conduct committed by a partner for his sole benefit is legally capable of being in the ordinary course of the business of his firm and that the conclusion that the solicitor was acting in the ordinary course of the firm's business would have been open to the trial judge. In his opinion, Lord Herschell had used the expression 'constructive trustee' to mean 'trustee de son tort'. However, unlike the solicitor in *Mara*, the partner allegedly guilty of wrongdoing in this case had not assumed the position of trustee on behalf of others. Lord Millett continued as follows:

> The distinction between the two kinds of constructive trustee is of crucial importance in the present context. If, as I think, it is still not within the ordinary scope of a solicitor's practice to act as a trustee of an express trust, it is obviously not within the scope of such a practice voluntarily to assume the obligations of a trustee and so incur liability as a *de facto* trustee or a constructive trustee of the first kind. But given that a solicitor may be guilty of deliberate and dishonest conduct while acting within the ordinary scope of his practice, there is no conceivable reason why his firm should not thereby incur vicarious liability for loss caused by the conduct which constituted him a constructive trustee of the second kind.[221]

Lord Millett agreed that *Re Bell's Indenture* had been wrongly decided and

218. See Mitchell (2001) 15 Trust Law Int 164.
219. [1999] Lloyd's Rep Bank 415. See McGrath [1999] LMCLQ 343.
220. In the view of Lord Nicholls the statements in *Mara* were directed at a different question, namely whether acting as a trustee, although not having been so appointed, can be regarded as conduct within the scope of the business of a solicitor.
221. [2002] 2 AC 366, 405.

concluded that the order of the Court of Appeal should be set aside and the decision of the trial judge upheld.

CHAPTER 10

Purpose Trusts

INTRODUCTION

As we have seen a private trust may be established in favour of specified or ascertainable individuals. In addition, a trust for purposes which are treated in law as charitable will be recognised as valid. The distinctive feature of such trusts is that they are regarded as being for the public benefit and are enforceable by the Charities Regulatory Authority.[1] It should be noted that section 49(1) of Charities Act 1961 provides that where the purposes of a gift include charitable and non-charitable objects, its terms will be construed so as to exclude the non-charitable objects. This means that provided a trust for purposes can be interpreted to include charitable objects, the non-charitable objects are dispensed with and the trust will be considered to be valid.[2] However, trusts for non-charitable purposes will not generally be regarded as valid as they are considered to lack the human beneficiaries necessary to secure their enforcement, to be too uncertain in nature, and will often offend the rules against perpetual trusts and inalienability. These potential difficulties do not prevent attempts being made to establish so-called 'purpose trusts'; as Sheridan has commented: 'distributors of largesse … generally give because they want to, and not because giving can be accomplished with legal ease.'[3] In certain limited circumstances purpose trusts have been recognised as valid, although these cases have tended to be regarded as 'concessions to human weakness or sentiment'[4] which 'ought not to be increased in number, nor indeed followed, except where the one is exactly like another'.[5] Therefore, it is necessary first to consider the objections raised in relation to the enforcement of non-charitable purpose trusts and then to consider the limited exceptions to the general rule that they will not be enforced.

---

1. By virtue of s. 38 of the Charities Act 2009, all the functions of the Attorney General in relation to charitable trusts or organisations were transferred to the Charities Regulatory Authority.
2. Note the very broad interpretation placed on s.49(1) of the Charities Act 1961 by Gilligan J in *Daly v Murphy* [2017] IEHC 650 in applying it to a residuary bequest in a will for 'such purposes as my executor in his absolute discretion shall think fit.' This decision is considered in more detail in Chapter 11.
3. Sheridan (1953) 17 Conv 46.
4. *Re Astor's Settlement Trusts* [1952] Ch 534, 547 *per* Roxburgh J.
5. *Re Endacott* [1960] Ch 232, 251 *per* Harman LJ.

RATIONALE FOR POLICY OF NON-ENFORCEMENT OF PURPOSE TRUSTS

Enforceability — The Beneficiary Principle[6]

As stated above the Charities Regulatory Authority is charged with the responsibility of enforcing charitable trusts, and private trusts in favour of individuals can be enforced by the beneficiaries themselves. One of the principal objections to non-charitable purpose trusts is that there is no one who can ensure that the court will secure performance of the trust if this should become necessary. As Grant MR stated in *Morice v Bishop of Durham*,[7] 'there must be somebody in whose favour the court can decree performance'. This principle was explained by Roxburgh J in *Re Astor's Settlement Trusts*[8] in the following terms: a trustee would not be expected to be subject to an equitable obligation unless there was somebody who could enforce a correlative equitable right.

There seems little doubt about the relevance of the beneficiary principle in this jurisdiction, although some anomalous exceptions to the requirement that there should be human beneficiaries capable of enforcing the trust remain. These are largely confined to the categories of gifts for tombs and monuments and for specific animals which will be considered below, although occasionally decisions have been made which are difficult to justify and for this reason are unlikely to be followed. In *Re Gibbons*[9] a testator directed that the residue of his estate should be disposed of by his executors, who were fellow priests 'to my best spiritual advantage, as conscience and sense of duty may direct'. While Barton J held that the bequest was not charitable in nature he found that it could be upheld as a valid private trust and rejected arguments that it was too indefinite and lacked the beneficiaries necessary for it to be so regarded. The rationale employed by Barton J in reaching this decision is far from clear and it could be said to fall within the category of 'troublesome, anomalous and aberrant cases' which Harman LJ suggested in *Re Endacott*[10] should not be added to.

It is important to note that the objection raised in this regard is not that the trust is for a purpose or object *per se* but rather that there is a lack of beneficiaries in whose favour the court can enforce the trust obligations.[11] Often it may be

---

6. See generally McKay (1973) 37 Conv 420.
7. (1804) 9 Ves 399. This principle was reiterated by Lord Parker in *Bowman v Secular Society Ltd* [1917] AC 406, 441 where he said that with the exception of charitable trusts 'a trust to be valid must be for the benefit of individuals'. See also *Re Wood* [1949] Ch 498, 501 *per* Harman J; *Re Endacott* [1960] Ch 232, 246; *Re Recher's Will Trusts* [1972] Ch 526, 538; *Hunt v McLaren* [2006] EWHC 2386 (Ch) at [89].
8. [1952] Ch 534, 541. See also *Armitage v Nurse* [1998] Ch 241, 253.
9. [1917] 1 IR 448.
10. [1960] Ch 232, 251.
11. *Re Denley's Trust Deed* [1969] 1 Ch 373, 383. Although note the comments of Barton J in *Re Gibbons* [1917] 1 IR 448, 453 in reply to such an argument that '[t]he Court is not asked to compel enforcement of this trust. The executors are willing to carry

a matter of construction to determine whether a given trust is for the benefit of persons or purposes and what might appear at first glance as a purpose trust may be upheld as a discretionary trust for the benefit of individuals. So, for example, a trust for the education of certain children might be construed as a trust of which these children are the beneficiaries, with the purpose of providing for their education being interpreted merely as an expression of motive for the gift.[12] This reasoning was developed by Goff J in *Re Denley's Trust Deed*[13] in a manner which resulted in the following principle being laid down:

> Where, then, the trust, though expressed as a purpose, is directly or indirectly for the benefit of an individual or individuals, it seems to me that it is in general outside the mischief of the beneficiary principle.

However, such a construction will not always be possible and Goff J stressed that there were limitations to the application of such a principle:

> I think that there may be a purpose or object trust, the carrying out of which would benefit an individual or individuals, where that benefit is so indirect or intangible or which is otherwise so framed as not to give those persons any *locus standi* to apply to the court to enforce the trust, in which case the beneficiary principle would, as it seems to me, apply to invalidate the trust, quite apart from any question of uncertainty or perpetuity.[14]

Therefore, it would seem that a trust even if it is expressed in terms of a purpose may be valid and enforceable provided that it can be construed as directly or indirectly conferring a benefit on an ascertained or ascertainable individual or individuals and provided that it does not fall foul of the other objections to the enforcement of such trusts which will now be considered.

Enforceability — Clarity and Certainty

If non-charitable purpose trusts are to be recognised as valid they must be expressed in terms which are sufficiently clear and certain to enable a court to oversee their performance. So, for example, in *Morice v Bishop of Durham*[15] a gift for 'such objects of benevolence and liberality as the Bishop of Durham in his own discretion shall most approve of' was considered to be too uncertain.

---

it out; and I see no sufficient ground for refusing to allow them to effectuate, as they propose to do, the expressed intentions of the testator.'

12. This type of approach can be found in *Re Andrew's Trust* [1905] 2 Ch 48; *Re Osoba* [1979] 1 WLR 247.
13. [1969] 1 Ch 373, 383-384.
14. *Ibid.* at 382-383.
15. (1804) 9 Ves 399.

As Grant MR stated, 'there can be no trust over the exercise of which this Court will not assume a control; for an uncontrollable power of disposition would be ownership, and not trust'.[16]

This principle is well illustrated by the decision in *Re Astor's Settlement Trusts*,[17] where an *inter vivos* settlement, expressly limited to the perpetuity period, provided that shares were to be held on trust for specified non-charitable objects including 'the establishment, maintenance and improvement of good understanding, sympathy and co-operation between nations' and 'the preservation of the independence and integrity of newspapers'. Roxburgh J held that the trusts fell foul of the beneficiary principle but he also made it clear that they would have failed as being too uncertain in nature. He stated:

> If (contrary to my view) an enumeration of purposes outside the realm of charities can take the place of an enumeration of beneficiaries, the purposes must, in my judgment, be stated in phrases which embody definite concepts and the means by which the trustees are to try to attain them must also be prescribed with a sufficient degree of certainty.[18]

The question of what will constitute a sufficient degree of certainty is itself not an issue altogether free from doubt. In *Re Gibbons*[19] Barton J described the direction that a gift should be applied to the best spiritual advantage of the testator, 'as conscience and sense of duty may direct' as 'wide' but 'not indefinite'. While Barton J may have been influenced by the willingness of the executors to carry out the testator's wishes in a manner which they were satisfied would comply with his intentions, a decision of this nature does little to clarify the approach which should be followed in this area.

It might be argued on the basis of *Re Thompson*[20] that there is authority to support the proposition that where the purposes or object of a trust are defined with sufficient clarity and certainty, a lack of human beneficiaries will not be fatal. There the testator gave a legacy of £1,000 to a friend to be applied towards the promotion and furtherance of fox hunting. Clauson J said that 'the object of the gift has been defined with sufficient clearness and is of a nature to which effect can be given'[21] and upheld its validity. However, such a view appears to be directly in conflict with the principles laid down by Roxburgh

16. *Ibid.* at 404-405. On appeal Lord Eldon stated as follows (1805) 10 Ves 522, 539: 'As it is a maxim, that the execution of a trust shall be under the control of the Court, it must be of such a nature, that it can be under that control; so that the administration of it can be reviewed by the Court.' See also *Chichester Diocesan Fund and Board of Finance v Simpson* [1944] AC 341.
17. [1952] Ch 534. See Marshall (1953) 6 CLP 151.
18. *Ibid.* at 547.
19. [1917] 1 IR 448.
20. [1934] Ch 342.
21. *Ibid.* at 344. See also *Re Douglas* (1887) 35 Ch D 472, 486 *per* Cotton LJ.

J in *Re Astor's Settlement Trusts*,[22] and the better view would seem to be that unless the beneficiary principle can be overcome in the manner suggested by Goff J in *Re Denley's Trust Deed*,[23] the certainty of any purposes expressed will not cure the difficulty caused by the lack of beneficiaries. For this reason, *Re Thompson* is perhaps best considered as a rather anomalous decision which should not be followed.

The Need for Compliance with the Rules against Perpetual Trusts and Inalienability

While the first two objections to the enforcement of purpose trusts arise out of the principle that a trust for non-charitable purposes should fail if it cannot be properly controlled and, if necessary, administered by a court, this objection is based on considerations of public policy, which dictate that property should not be tied up for excessive periods of time. Essentially, before a purpose trust will be enforced, the court must be satisfied that its terms will not offend the rule against trusts of undue duration and that the property included in the trust will not be rendered inalienable.[24] So, even where a purpose trust might be interpreted as complying with the requirements of the beneficiary principle and as being sufficiently certain, it must be limited to the period of perpetuity[25] if it is to be valid.

It should be noted at this point that the terminology employed by judges in this area can be confusing. In this context what is at issue is essentially an application of the rule against inalienability or the rule against perpetual trusts rather than the rule against perpetuities,[26] although an examination of the authorities shows that judges tend to employ these phrases interchangeably.[27] The effect of the rule against inalienability is to render void a trust which comprises property which might remain inalienable beyond the perpetuity

22. [1952] Ch 534.
23. [1969] 1 Ch 373.
24. It was for this reason that numerous bequests for the saying of masses (now recognised as a valid charitable purpose, see *O'Hanlon v Logue* [1906] 1 IR 247 and s. 45(2) of the Charities Act 1961) were held to be void in the last century. See *Dillon v Reilly* (1875) IR 10 Eq 152; *Beresford v Jarvis* (1877) 11 ILTR 128; *M'Court v Burnett* (1877) 11 ILTR 130; *Morrow v M'Conville* (1883) 11 LR Ir 236; *Small v Torley* (1890) 25 LR Ir 388. Although note that the contrary conclusion was reached in *Phelan v Slattery* (1887) 19 LR Ir 177 and *Reichenbach v Quinn* (1888) 21 LR Ir 138.
25. The period of a life or lives in being plus 21 years or, if there is no life in being, a period of 21 years only.
26. The rule against perpetuities was abolished in this jurisdiction by virtue of s. 16 of the Land and Conveyancing Law Reform Act 2009. However, the rule against inalienability persists so, where property is tied to a specific non-charitable purpose for a period of time in excess of a perpetuity period, the trust will be void.
27. E.g. *O'Byrne v Davoren* [1994] 3 IR 373.

period and it is concerned with the duration of an interest which is already vested rather than with the time at which vesting occurs.[28]

Clearly one of the most important factors in determining whether a gift is void on these grounds will be whether the obligation involves merely the application of the income from the gift to the stated purpose. However, even where the application of the gift is not limited to income only and there is no direction that the capital be maintained indefinitely, it may still offend the rule against inalienability. This is illustrated by the decision of the Supreme Court in *Re Fossitt's Estate*,[29] in which a bequest to the 'Orange Institution of Ireland' for the upkeep of a hall was held to be void for perpetuity, despite the fact that there was no evidence that the income alone was to be employed for this purpose. Fitzgibbon J stated:

> In my opinion it was the intention of the testator that the capital might be applied from time to time, if occasion should arise and the income of the fund was insufficient, towards the upkeep of the Hall, but I am satisfied that the testator contemplated the continued existence of the fund, in whole or in part, for an absolutely indefinite period, which might far exceed that fixed by law of a life or lives in being and twenty-one years after.[30]

Where a phrase such as 'so long as the law allows' or 'such period as the law permits' has been employed, a gift will be regarded as being valid for a period of 21 years. However, where no such qualification is included, a gift will be void unless it comes to a determination before the end of the perpetuity period. On the other hand, in some respects a fairly flexible attitude has been taken towards the need for compliance with the rule against inalienability and the courts have assumed that the requirements of the rule will be met where it appears that this is a reasonable interpretation of a gift. So, in *Mussett v Bingle*,[31] where a testator gave a legacy of £300 to be applied in the erection of a monument to his wife's first husband and a further sum of £200, the interest on which was to be used for its maintenance, Hall VC upheld the validity of the former gift presumably on the assumption that the monument would be erected within the perpetuity period. The latter gift was clearly of a perpetual nature and therefore void.

Finally, it should be noted that the Law Reform Commission in its Report on *The Rule Against Perpetuities and Cognate Rules*[32] considered the effect of

---

28. See Coughlan, *Property Law in Ireland* (2nd ed., 1998) p. 178.
29. [1934] IR 504. This can be compared to the decision of Haugh J in *Re Conner* [1960] IR 67, in which a gift to a cemetery company for the upkeep of a family vault was upheld in circumstances where there was nothing to prevent the company 'resorting to the capital if and when, they think proper in their discretion to do so'.
30. *Ibid.* at 513.
31. [1876] WN 170. See also *Re Filshie* [1939] NZLR 91.
32. LRC 62-2000 paras. 5.08-5.13.

the rule against trusts of undue duration but did not recommend its abolition. The Commission noted that the rule is just one of the devices employed to regulate non-charitable purpose trusts and concluded that it would be preferable to postpone any detailed consideration of the rule until it could be examined in the context of a review of the entire area of unincorporated associations.[33]

EXCEPTIONAL CASES IN WHICH PURPOSE TRUSTS HAVE BEEN ENFORCED

Tombs and Monuments

At common law a trust for the erection of a tomb, gravestone or monument was not regarded as being charitable in nature. In this jurisdiction legislation has intervened in a limited way and section 50 of the Charities Act 1961 now provides that gifts for the maintenance or improvement of a tomb, vault, grave, tombstone or any other memorial to a deceased person are deemed to be charitable gifts in so far as they do not exceed £60 a year in the case of income and £1,000 in any other case. However, these monetary limits have not been increased in the years since the enactment of the legislation and in many cases gifts for such purposes will exceed these limits.[34] In these circumstances a bequest for such a purpose will have to come within the rather anomalous exception which has developed at common law, the effect of which is that gifts for the erection of a tomb or monument or for its maintenance will be upheld as valid purpose trusts provided that they do not offend the rule against inalienability.

As illustrated by the decision of Hall VC in *Mussett v Bingle*,[35] the courts appear to assume that directions of this nature will be carried out within the perpetuity period. However, to come within this limited exception the trust must

33. This echoes the view put forward by the Law Commission of England and Wales in its Report on *The Rules Against Perpetuities and Excessive Accumulations* (1998 Law Com No. 251) at para. 1.14 to the effect that the rule against inalienability is in reality just one of the devices that is employed to keep the development of non-charitable purpose trusts in check. In the view of the Commission, any consideration of the rule belongs more properly to a review of the law governing such trusts and unincorporated associations.
34. The Law Reform Commission recommended (*The Rule Against Perpetuities and Cognate Rules* LRC 62-2000 para. 5.15) that these sums be increased to a limit of £1,000 (€1,270) per year in the case of income and to a limit of £16,000 (€20,316) on the capital sum (as of the year 2000). Section 50 was restated in head 82 of the General Scheme for the Charities Regulation Bill 2006, published by the Department of Community, Rural and Gaeltacht Affairs in March 2006, but this provision was not included in the draft Bill published in April 2007.
35. [1876] WN 170. See also *Trimmer v Danby* (1856) LJ Ch 424 where a bequest of £1,000 to erect a monument to the testator in St Paul's Cathedral was upheld.

also be expressed with sufficient certainty to be carried out. In *Re Endacott*[36] a testator bequeathed his residuary estate valued at £20,000 to a specified parish council 'for the purpose of providing some useful memorial to myself'. The gift was held void by the Court of Appeal. Harman LJ stated as follows: 'I cannot think a case of this kind, the case of providing outside a church an unspecified and unidentified memorial, is the kind of instance which should be allowed to add to those troublesome, anomalous and aberrant cases'.[37]

In circumstances where the statutory limits specified above have been exceeded, the issue of compliance with the rule against inalienability becomes of crucial importance in relation to gifts for the maintenance of graves and monuments, and if trusts of this nature are to be regarded as valid at common law they must be confined to the perpetuity period. *Mussett v Bingle* illustrates that a gift for the maintenance of a monument without any words of qualification will be void and in *Toole v Hamilton*[38] it was held by Porter MR that a bequest which was to be invested and the income thereof applied in maintaining an enclosure around a grave was also void. However, in *Pirbright v Salwey*[39] a gift for the upkeep of a grave for so long as the law for the time being permitted was upheld as valid for a period of 21 years. Similarly, in *Re Hooper*[40] a testator bequeathed a sum of money to trustees to apply the income to the maintenance of family graves and monuments 'as far as they can legally do so'. Maugham J held that this trust was valid for a period of 21 years from the testator's death.

A number of devices can be employed to avoid the difficulty of complying with the rule against inalienability. Where a gift is given for the maintenance of an entire churchyard, this will be upheld as a valid charitable gift and so not subject to the rule,[41] and at common law this will provide an effective means of indirectly securing the maintenance of a particular grave or monument.[42] A further method appears to be to make a gift to a cemetery company, where one exists, to be applied for the maintenance of a grave or tomb.[43] In *Re Conner*[44] a bequest of £1,000 was made 'to the General Cemetery Company of Dublin to be applied for the maintenance and care of the family vault at Mount Jerome'.

36. [1960] Ch 232.
37. *Ibid.* at 251.
38. [1901] 1 IR 383. See also *Beresford v Jarvis* (1877) 11 ILTR 128.
39. [1896] WN 86.
40. [1932] 1 Ch 38.
41. *Re Vaughan* (1886) 33 Ch D 187.
42. *Re Eighmie* [1935] Ch 524.
43. Such an approach seems to have been justified in England in *Re Chardon* [1928] 1 Ch 464 on the basis that a determinable interest was not subject to the rule against perpetuities although by virtue of s. 12 of the Perpetuities and Accumulations Act 1964 this is no longer the case. Note that s. 1 of the Parish Councils and Burial Authorities (Miscellaneous Provisions) Act 1970 now authorises local and burial authorities in England to conclude agreements for the maintenance of graves for a period of up to 99 years.
44. [1960] IR 67.

Haugh J said that the testatrix clearly bequeathed the money to the company with the sole limitation that it should be spent in the maintenance of the family vault and concluded that there was nothing to prevent the company from resorting to the capital if and when it was found necessary to do so for the purposes outlined in the will. In the circumstances, he was satisfied that the gift was a valid non-charitable one which did not offend the rule against inalienability and which should therefore be enforced.

Animals

A gift to provide for the welfare of animals generally or for the care and maintenance of a class of animals is regarded as being charitable in law.[45] Gifts to provide for the care of specified animals, while they are admittedly not of a charitable nature and would *prima facie* seem to fall foul of the beneficiary principle, have been upheld as coming within the limited class of exceptions to the principle that non-charitable purpose trusts will not be enforced. So, the lack of human beneficiaries is overlooked provided the purposes are sufficiently clear in nature and the trust is of a limited duration. In *Pettingall v Pettingall*[46] a gift of £50 a year for the maintenance of the testator's favourite black mare was upheld as valid. In *Re Dean*[47] North J upheld a gift of £750 per annum for a period of 50 years for the care and maintenance of the testator's horses and hounds. He rejected the view that the court would not recognise the validity of a trust unless it is capable of being enforced by someone. In what has been recognised as a rather unsatisfactory judgment, North J then proceeded to virtually ignore the potential problem of violating the rule against inalienability and remarked that he would uphold a gift of this nature 'provided that it is not to last for too long a period'.[48] Such an approach to the perpetuity question is unlikely to be followed in England and has been rejected in this jurisdiction. In *Re Kelly*[49] a testator bequeathed a sum of money to be applied in the care and maintenance of his dogs with a gift over should any surplus remain on the death of the last dog. Meredith J upheld the gift as being valid for a period of 21 years following the testator's death, although it would have been technically void thereafter and the gift over was found to be void for remoteness. A number of points in his judgment are worth noting. It clearly emerges that only a human life can be used as a measuring life for the purpose of applying the rule against perpetuities. Meredith J expressed this point unequivocally in colourful language:

---

45. *Re Douglas* (1887) 35 Ch D 472; *Swifte v Attorney General* [1912] 1 IR 133; *Armstrong v Reeves* (1890) 25 LR Ir 325. See further *infra* Chapter 11 and s. 3(11)(j) of the Charities Act 2009.
46. (1842) 11 LJ Ch 176.
47. (1889) 41 Ch D 552.
48. *Ibid.* at 557.
49. [1932] IR 255.

> If the lives of the dogs or other animals could be taken into account in reckoning the maximum period of lives in being and twenty-one years afterwards any contingent or executory interest might be properly limited, so as only to vest within the lives of specified carp, or tortoises, or other animals that might live for over a hundred years, and for twenty-one years afterwards, which of course is absurd. 'Lives' means human lives. It was suggested that the last of the dogs could in fact not outlive the testator by more than twenty-one years. I know nothing of that. The Court does not enter into the question of a dog's expectation of life. In point of fact neighbour's dogs and cats are unpleasantly long-lived; but I have no knowledge of their precise expectation of life ... there can be no doubt that 'lives' means lives of human beings, not of animals or trees in California.[50]

On the basis of this statement it would also appear that the court will not take judicial notice of the fact that certain animals will not live for a period of more than 21 years although authority in England suggests the contrary.[51] Meredith J rejected the suggestion that he should read into the will an implied limitation to a period of 21 years or 'so long as the law permits'. However, he stressed that this did not prevent him from analysing a provision which was 'manifestly not good in its entirety' for the purpose of determining whether it included a severable part which did not offend the rule against perpetuities, which in the case before him, amounted to expenditure for a period of 21 years. Therefore, in the light of *Re Kelly* it can be said with a fair degree of certainty that in this jurisdiction purpose trusts for the care and maintenance of specified animals will be upheld for a period of 21 years provided that they are expressed with sufficient clarity. In the interests of certainty it is probably preferable that such trusts are clearly limited to a period of 21 years or 'so long as the law allows', although if one accepts the approach of Meredith J such an omission will not be fatal.

Gifts to Unincorporated Associations[52]

An unincorporated association has been defined by Lawton LJ in *Conservative and Unionist Central Office v Burrell*[53] as follows:

> [T]wo or more persons bound together for one or more common purposes, not being business purposes, by mutual undertakings, each having mutual duties and obligations, in an organisation which has rules which identify

50. *Ibid.* at 260-261.
51. *Re Haines, The Times*, 7 November 1952. See Sheridan (1953) 17 Conv 46, 60.
52. See generally Rickett [1980] CLJ 88, 90-111.
53. [1982] 1 WLR 522, 525.

in whom control of it and its funds rests and on what terms and which can be joined or left at will.

While a gift to a body corporate even for non-charitable purposes will be valid because such a body has a separate legal personality and therefore can enforce it, difficulties arise where it is sought to confer a gift of a non-charitable nature on an unincorporated association. An unincorporated association has no separate personality in law and is regarded as a collection of individuals and the potential difficulties which must be considered are that gifts of this nature may fall foul of the beneficiary principle or may contravene the rule against inalienability.

A number of different methods of conferring a benefit on unincorporated associations have been devised, the final two of which have been recognised as essentially overcoming the potential problems referred to above.

A Gift by Way of Endowment for the Benefit of the Association

Where a gift is construed as an endowment for the benefit of the association, it will almost inevitably be found to be void as infringing the rule against inalienability. This point emerged from the decisions of the House of Lords in *Re Macaulay*[54] and of the Privy Council in *Leahy v Attorney-General for New South Wales*.[55] However, if the wording of the gift is such that it satisfies the requirement of the rule against inalienability, the decision of Goff J in *Re Denley's Trust Deed*[56] would seem to confirm that the difficulties posed by the beneficiary principle can be overcome.

A Gift to the Members of the Association for the Time Being

A gift to an unincorporated association may be enforced if it is recognised as a gift to the members of the association alive at the time of the disposition, or in the case of a will, at the date of the testator's death. The beneficiary principle is satisfied as it is possible to ascertain who these members are and the rule against inalienability will not be infringed provided that the members are free to dispose of the property, both income and capital, at any time. This principle is explained as follows by Lovell:[57]

> In the context of trusts for unincorporated associations, it is submitted that the fact that the association can last forever is of no significance. … Once there has been an effectual dedication to the purpose or enterprise, and provided that there is no restriction on the use of the capital, then

---

54. [1943] Ch 435n.
55. [1959] AC 457. Although note that on the facts of the case the gift was saved by the provisions of a New South Wales statute.
56. [1969] 1 Ch 373.
57. Lovell (1970) 34 Conv 77, 96.

> there is no reason to argue that any principle of perpetuity is offended. Quite clearly the association may last for a period of time longer than the perpetuity period, but the property together with all other association assets is vested according to the trusts of the association and the latter can dissolve at any time if the members so wish it.

However, it must be possible to construe the gift as being for the individual members of the association for the time being and as some of the authorities have shown such an interpretation is not always possible. So, in *Hogan v Byrne*[58] Christian J held that to put such a construction on the testator's bequest to 'monks named Christian Brothers' would be to defeat his real intention. He stated: 'If you do that you disappoint the testator's intentions. He intended that the land should be held by one body, and not that it should be divided into an indefinite number of parts each to belong to a different person.' As Christian LJ subsequently stated in *Stewart v Green*,[59] sitting as Lord Justice of Appeal, two distinct interpretations of gifts of this nature are possible:

> First a trust for the [individuals] who happened to compose the community at the moment of the testator's death in their natural capacities. Second, a trust for the community in its communal character, of whomsoever it should from time to time and for ever consist. The first would, of course, be good and effectual in law; and … practically his purpose would be achieved. … The other intent — that of giving to the community in a communal or quasi corporate character — would mean the *form* undoubtedly most accordant with the testator's ideas; but would labour under the disadvantage of being utterly incapable of legal realization; for as the community, as such, has no legal personality, it is incapable of taking in that character.

In the case before the court, counsel arguing in favour of the validity of the gift repudiated the first possible construction, relying instead on an argument based on its charitable nature which was not made out, and as a result the bequest was declared void.[60] Similarly in *Morris v M'Conville*,[61] Chatterton VC stressed that: 'the court must act upon the intention of the testator as expressed in the words he has used'.[62] The Vice-Chancellor said that he found the terms of the testator's will impossible to reconcile with the theory of the gift in the case before him being to the individual members of a convent, and found that

---

58. (1863) 13 ICLR 166.
59. (1871) IR 5 Eq 470, 481.
60. As Porter MR commented in *Bradshaw v Jackman* (1887) 21 LR Ir 12, 22 the decision in *Stewart v Green* might well have been different if counsel had insisted upon, rather than repudiated, the first of the two possible constructions of the will.
61. (1883) 11 LR Ir 236.
62. *Ibid.* at 247.

it was instead intended as a 'permanent contribution *de anno in annum* to the funds of the convent in its aggregate and quasi corporate capacity'[63] which he held to be void.

Despite such setbacks this approach of construing a gift to an association as being for the benefit of the members for the time being was successfully employed on a number of occasions towards the end of the nineteenth century particularly in the context of gifts to associations of a religious nature which were not considered at the time to be charitable in law. It was of particular importance in relation to gifts to contemplative religious orders, which were considered not to possess the necessary element of public benefit to qualify for charitable status. The decision of Gavan Duffy J in *Maguire v Attorney General*[64] marked a change in judicial attitudes to the question of the public benefit inherent in gifts of this nature, and the provisions of section 45 of the Charities Act 1961 seemed to confirm that gifts to contemplative religious orders are valid charitable gifts.[65] However, the principles developed in these decisions are important and can be considered as being of general application.

In *Cocks v Manners*[66] a gift to a contemplative order of nuns was treated as a gift to the superior of the community for the time being and in this manner was upheld on the basis that it did not infringe the rule against inalienability. This principle was applied in Ireland in *Re Delany's Estate*,[67] where a gift to a convent was upheld as being for the benefit of the nuns who comprised the community at the time of the testator's death. A useful summary of this reasoning was set out in *Morrow v M'Conville*,[68] although as noted above, it was not accepted as applying in the case before the court:

> [A] gift, not charitable, to a religious community, including not only the existing members, but also all persons who should be, or become thereafter members of it, during a period capable of extending beyond the legal limits prescribed by the rule against perpetuities is void; but … if such gift, according to its true construction, is one to the individuals composing the community at the death of the testator, or some other

63. *Ibid.* at 250.
64. [1943] IR 238. Although note the decision of Overend J in *Re Keogh's Estate* [1945] IR 13.
65. Section 45(1) provided: 'In determining whether or not a gift for the purpose of the advancement of religion is a valid charitable gift it shall be conclusively presumed that the purpose includes and will occasion public benefit.' It was repealed by s.11 and Schedule 2 of the Charities Act 2009, and replaced by s. 3(4) of the Charities Act 2009 which provides that '[i]t shall be presumed, unless the contrary is proved, that a gift for the advancement of religion is of public benefit'.
66. (1871) LR 12 Eq 574.
67. (1882) 9 LR Ir 226. See also *Re Wilkinson's Trusts* (1887) 19 LR Ir 531 and *Bradshaw v Jackman* (1887) 21 LR Ir 12.
68. (1883) 11 LR Ir 236.

> time, within legal limits, appointed for ascertaining the class of such individuals, the gift is valid.[69]

The main consideration which must be taken into account by a court in applying this approach is that there must be nothing to indicate that any form of 'perpetual endowment' was contemplated and this was one of the major difficulties faced by Chatterton VC in *Morrow*, where the trust was clearly treated as being 'a continuing one'. This point was stressed by Overend J in his decision in *Re Keogh's Estate*,[70] where a testator made a bequest to the superioress for the time being of a convent and left the residue of his estate to the prior of an order, neither of which qualified as charitable gifts. Overend J was satisfied that there was nothing in the testator's will which suggested that he had contemplated that the money would be applied for a perpetual endowment and he upheld the gifts to the superioress and the prior to be used for the purposes of their orders.

This principle was applied in a different context in *Re Clarke*,[71] where a bequest was made to the Committee of the Corps of Comissionaires in London to aid in the purchase of a barracks or in any other way beneficial to the corps. Byrne J upheld the bequest as a valid gift to the members of the corps for the time being as they could at any time dispose of it. He stated:

> The test, or one test, appears to be, will the legacy when paid be subject to any trust which will prevent the existing members of the association from spending it as they please? If not, the gift is good. So also if the gift is to be construed as a gift to or for the benefit of the individual members of the association. On the other hand, if it appears that the legacy is one which by the terms of the gift, or which by reason of the constitution of the association in whose favour it is made, tends to a perpetuity, the gift is bad.[72]

The Supreme Court considered this issue in *Re Byrne*,[73] in which a testator left his residuary estate for the use and benefit of the Jesuit Order in Ireland. The majority of the Supreme Court[74] held that the work of the order, while largely charitable in nature, was not exclusively so and that it did not qualify as a charitable gift. As Murnaghan J stated, if the testator meant his gift to enure for the benefit of 'a continuing body whose existence has not received legal recognition', it would fail. If on the other hand, his intention was to divide the money amongst individuals forming a class, there would be no legal objection

69. *Ibid.* at 246-247.
70. [1945] IR 13.
71. [1901] 2 Ch 110. See *Re Smith* [1914] 1 Ch 937.
72. *Ibid.* at 114.
73. [1935] IR 782.
74. Murnaghan and Fitzgibbon JJ. Kennedy CJ dissented and held that the gift was charitable in nature.

to its validity. Murnaghan J reiterated the point that 'the language of the testator must in each case be the guide' and upheld the bequest as a valid gift of a non-charitable nature for the benefit of an ascertainable class of persons.

The only real theoretical difficulty with such an approach is that any member who leaves the association can take his share with him unless he assigns it to the other members and a new member will have no share in the property. More recently in England an alternative theory has been developed which has found favour with the courts in that jurisdiction and which may well also prove to be the most suitable approach for the courts here to employ.

Property Held on Trust to be Applied in Accordance with the Contract Between the Members

This manner of construing a gift was summarised by Cross J as follows in *Neville Estates Ltd v Madden*:[75]

> [I]t may be a gift to the existing members not as joint tenants, but subject to their respective contractual rights and liabilities towards one another as members of the association. In such a case a member cannot sever his share. It will accrue to the other members on his death or resignation, even though such members include persons who became members after the gift took effect. If this is the effect of the gift it will not be open to objection on the score of perpetuity or uncertainty unless there is something in its terms or circumstances or in the rules of the association which precludes the members at any given time from dividing the subject of the gift between them on the footing that they are solely entitled to it in equity.

This 'contract-holding theory' was applied by Brightman J in *Re Recher's Will Trusts*,[76] which concerned the validity of a gift to the 'London and Provincial Anti-Vivisection Society'. Brightman J concluded that it was not a gift to the members of the society at the date of the testator's death, nor an attempted gift to present and future members beneficially, nor a gift in trust for the purposes of the society. Instead he held that the legacy ought to be construed as a gift to the members beneficially as an accretion to their funds subject to the contract which they made between themselves. As he stated: 'In the absence of words which purport to impose a trust, the legacy is a gift to the members beneficially, not as joint tenants or as tenants in common so as to entitle each member to an immediate distributive share, but as an accretion to the funds which are the subject matter of the contract which the members have made *inter se*.'[77] A similar approach was applied by Oliver J in *Re Lipinski's Will Trusts*,[78]

75. [1962] Ch 832, 849. See Warburton [1985] Conv 318, 322-325.
76. [1972] Ch 526.
77. *Ibid.* at 539.
78. [1976] Ch 235. See Widdows (1977) 41 Conv 179 and Gravells (1977) 40 MLR 231.

where a testator bequeathed half of his residuary estate to trustees to the 'Hull Judaeans (Maccabi) Association' in memory of his late wife, to be used in the work of constructing new buildings for the association and/or improving them. Oliver J held the gift valid as an absolute gift to the members of the association beneficially as an accretion to its funds subject to the rules of the association. It was not open to objection on the grounds of perpetuity as Oliver J was satisfied that there was nothing in the will which suggested any intention to create a permanent endowment and he pointed out that the members could if they wished divide the gift between themselves. In this regard he distinguished the decision of the House of Lords in *Re Macaulay*,[79] where a gift was made for the 'maintenance and improvement' of a building on the grounds that in the case before him it was, in his view, quite evident that the association was free to spend the capital of the legacy if it chose to do so.

Other, more recent, cases in which the courts have held that a gift fits within the construction outlined by Cross J in *Neville Estates Ltd v Madden* set out above include *Hunt v McLaren*[80] and *Hanchett-Stamford v Attorney-General*.[81] In the latter case Lewison J stated that under normal circumstances a gift to an unincorporated association will fall into this category and that the members for the time being of the association will be beneficially entitled to its assets subject to the contractual arrangements between the parties.[82] In addition, as pointed out in *Hunt*, since the members of an unincorporated association own its assets subject to the contractual obligations owed by them to each other, they can vary these contractual arrangements.[83]

Essentially this contract-holding theory involves the idea of property being held on trust to be applied in accordance with the contract existing between the members contained in the rules of the association and it will satisfy the requirements of the rule against inalienability provided that the members are entitled to wind up the association and divide its property between them at any time. One clear advantage of this approach is that compliance with the beneficiary principle is not an issue as the property is held subject to the terms of a contract rather than on trust. In addition, a member who leaves the association or dies will lose his share in the property and any new member will automatically acquire one without the need for any formalities. However, it is important to emphasise that the rules of the association must provide the necessary contractual element in the relationship between the members[84] and it is also necessary that the members have the requisite authority to divide the assets between themselves.[85]

79. [1943] Ch 435n.
80. [2006] EWHC 2586 (Ch). See further Luxton [2007] Conv 274.
81. [2009] Ch 173. See further Griffiths [2009] Conv 428; Baughen [2010] Conv 216.
82. *Ibid.* at 183.
83. [2006] EWHC 2386 (Ch) at [113].
84. *Conservative and Unionist Central Office v Burrell* [1982] 1 WLR 522, 525.
85. *Re Grant's Will Trusts* [1980] 1 WLR 360.

Conclusion

While the categories of trusts for the erection and maintenance of tombs and monuments and for the care of specified animals seem to be accepted as enforceable provided that they do not offend the rule against inalienability, doubt remains about the validity of other forms of non-charitable purpose trusts. Provided that the certainty requirement is met it would appear that trusts for unincorporated associations can be enforced if one of the constructions outlined above is applied, and the reasoning of Goff J in *Re Denley's Trust Deed*[86] should ensure that difficulties raised by the need for compliance with the beneficiary principle and the rule against inalienability will effectively be overcome. As the cases make clear, if a construction is to be applied which will result in the gift being legally enforceable, it is important that such a construction can be ascertained from the words used by a donor or testator.[87] While recent decisions show a greater willingness to place a favourable construction on gifts of this nature, the warning given by the Court of Appeal in *Re Endacott*[88] that the categories of these 'anomalous' cases should not be extended should also be heeded.

In a general context the suggestion has been made that what might appear as an invalid purpose trust could be saved if it were construed as a power rather than a trust on the basis that there is no requirement that the beneficiary principle be satisfied in relation to powers. While this option has been explored,[89] it has been rejected on the basis that a valid power cannot 'be spelt out of an invalid trust'.[90]

Apart from in the exceptional cases of tombs and monuments and specified animals, the lack of beneficiaries has proved to be a major stumbling block to the enforcement of non-charitable purpose trusts. As Lord Evershed MR commented in *Re Endacott*,[91] '[n]o principle, perhaps, has greater sanction or authority behind it than the general proposition that a trust by English law, not being a charitable trust, in order to be effective must have ascertained or ascertainable beneficiaries.' However, Hayton has put forward the suggestion that an 'enforcer' might be appointed under the terms of a trust in order to oversee its enforcement and he suggests that there is no reason why equity should not permit a settlor to confer additional enforcement rights on other persons, including himself.[92] If such an approach were approved, non-charitable purpose trusts should not be automatically void and could be valid if the settlor had appointed an enforcer as long as they were administratively workable and

86. [1969] 1 Ch 373.
87. E.g. *Morrow v M'Conville* (1883) 11 LR Ir 236, 247; *Re Byrne* [1935] IR 782, 818.
88. [1960] Ch 232.
89. By Harman J in *Re Shaw* [1957] 1 WLR 729, 746.
90. *IRC v Broadway Cottages Trust* [1955] Ch 20, 36 *per* Jenkins LJ; *Re Shaw* [1957] 1 WLR 729, 746; *Re Endacott* [1960] Ch 232, 246.
91. [1960] Ch 232, 246.
92. Hayton (2001) 117 LQR 96.

restricted to a valid perpetuity period. Hayton's suggestion is an interesting one and may be developed, particularly given that the courts cannot legitimately refuse to give effect to a foreign non-charitable purpose trust which is valid in another jurisdiction where trust instruments may expressly provide for the appointment of an enforcer.[93] This suggestion has been taken up by a number of other academic commentators, including Brown, who also advocates a statutory system of enforcement, supervision and incentives.[94] He suggests that the residuary legatees could be given rights of supervision and enforcement by deed and that they would have an incentive to supervise the trust as in the event of its failure, they would benefit under a resulting trust. However, Pawlowksi and Summers, who also advocate an enforcement mechanism, suggest, it is submitted correctly, that a person independent of the trustees and beneficiaries should be appointed as the enforcer.[95] More generally they recommend a more robust approach towards the reform of private purpose trusts involving a general recognition that such trusts should be valid save in exceptional cases where the purpose is clearly unlawful or contrary to public policy.

From a practical perspective, where advance planning is feasible, the incorporation of an association which a donor or testator wishes to benefit will undoubtedly provide a method of ensuring that the gift will be carried into effect. However, in the majority of cases, this will not be achieved and the courts will still be faced with the difficult policy question of whether to continue to extend the principle which allows for the enforcement of non-charitable purpose trusts in limited circumstances. It could be argued that a refusal to enforce non-charitable purpose trusts should in theory lead to a greater preponderance of gifts of a charitable nature more likely to provide real benefit to the community. However, it has been suggested that 'capricious trusts are the rare ones' and that '[t]he fact that settlors may attempt to create them is no reason for failing to establish a rational method of validating the useful ones.'[96] Certainly the present approach is in many respects far from rational and lacks any real consistency.[97] In the final analysis, in the absence of any legislative intervention in this area, we must continue to rely on the rather haphazard principles and devices developed at common law when it is sought to establish the validity of a non-charitable purpose trust.

---

93. See further *ibid.* at 100.
94. Brown [2007] Conv 148.
95. Pawlowski and Summers [2007] Conv 440, 454.
96. Glister and Lee, *Hanbury and Martin: Modern Equity* (21st ed., 2018) p. 449.
97. See the views expressed by Baxendale-Walker in *Purpose Trusts* (1999). He criticises the present legal position as 'uncertain and unsatisfactory' (at p. 284) and contends that the rule against purpose trusts was unknown in earlier centuries and that the authorities which support such a view have largely been ignored in more recent decisions.

CHAPTER 11

Charitable Trusts

INTRODUCTION

Advantages of Charitable Status

While as a general rule, subject to the exceptions examined above,[1] trusts for purposes rather than for the benefit of persons are invalid, charitable trusts which are considered to be for the public benefit are an exception to this principle. Charitable trusts are considered to be for the benefit of the public generally or at least for an appreciable section of it and for this reason have traditionally enjoyed a number of advantages over other types of trust.[2] The provisions of the Charities Act 2009, most of which came into force in 2014,[3] gave legislative force to many common law principles relating to charitable status but also introduced some significant changes to the law in this area.

Before examining in more detail the types of trusts which will qualify for such favourable treatment it is useful to set out briefly the advantages to be gained from establishing charitable status. Charitable trusts do not depend on the existence of beneficiaries to enforce them;[4] they are considered to be of a public nature and as such are enforceable by the Charities Regulatory Authority[5]

---

1. *Supra* Chapter 10.
2. As Mummery LJ commented in the Court of Appeal decision in *Gaudiya Mission v Brahmachary* [1997] 4 All ER 957, 963, '[u]nder English law charity has always received special treatment. . . . It is, therefore, subject to special rules governing registration, administration, taxation and duration'. See also Warburton [1999] Conv 20, who states (at 29) that 'charitable trusts operate in a different legal, fiscal and social environment from family and commercial trusts'.
3. The bulk of the Charities Act 2009 came into force on 16 October 2014. See the Charities Act 2009 (Commencement) Order 2014 (SI No. 457 of 2014) which brought into force ss. 3, 6-9, 10 (insofar as not already commenced), 11, Parts 2, 3, 5, 6 and Schedules 1 and 2. The following sections of the Charities Act 2009 came into force earlier: ss. 1, 2, 5, 10(1) and (2), 99 (see the Charities Act 2009 (Commencement) Order 2009, SI No. 284 of 2009); ss. 4, 90 (see the Charities Act 2009 (Commencement) Order 2010, SI No. 315 of 2010). Part 4 came into force on 8 July 2016 (see the Charities Act 2009 (Commencement) Order 2016, SI No. 350 of 2016); ss.91, 92 came into force on 5 August 2016 (see the Charities Act 2009 (Commencement) (No.2) Order 2016, SI No. 424 of 2016).
4. While the decision in *Re Denley's Trust Deed* [1969] 1 Ch 373 has made it possible for the beneficiary principle to be effectively by-passed in certain circumstances, a considerable number of purpose trusts will still fall foul of this principle.
5. By virtue of s. 38 of the Charities Act 2009, all the functions of the Attorney General in

(known as the Charities Regulator). The corollary of this proposition is that those individuals who might benefit from a trust considered to be legally charitable will not be recognised as having the right to enforce such trusts.[6]

A further advantage is that charitable trusts are not subject to the same requirements relating to certainty of objects which must be complied with if a private trust is to be considered valid.[7] Originally, provided that a trust could be identified as being exclusively[8] charitable in nature, such a trust would be enforced even if the nature of these charitable objects was not expressly delimited.[9] In such circumstances a cy-près scheme[10] could be framed to ensure that the charitable intention of the donor or testator was given effect to. From a general perspective, charitable status is also desirable as it will facilitate the operation of cy-près jurisdiction should this become necessary. If a trust fails to qualify as charitable, this jurisdiction cannot be exercised and a bequest may fail, allowing a resulting trust to operate in favour of the donor or his estate. While resulting trusts are intended in theory to give effect to the unexpressed but presumed intention of the donor, this may not always be the case,[11] and it is certainly preferable to find a means of perpetuating the donor's charitable intention in as close a form as possible to that originally expressed by him.

Prior to the intervention of statute, a trust could only be construed as charitable in nature if its purposes were exclusively so. However, section 49(1) of Charities Act 1961 provides that where the purposes of a gift include charitable and non-charitable objects, its terms will be construed so as to exclude the non-charitable objects. It had been assumed, as Keane suggests, that this provision required that 'the language used should at least indicate a general charitable intention'[12] before section 49(1) could be applied. However, in *Daly v Murphy*[13] Gilligan J applied it to a residuary bequest in a will to an executor

---

relation to charitable trusts or organisations were transferred to the Charities Regulatory Authority.

6. *Re Belling* [1967] Ch 425.
7. See the *dicta* of Porter MR in *Re Brown* [1898] 1 IR 423, 427.
8. Note that s. 49(1) of the Charities Act 1961 now provides as follows: 'Where any of the purposes of a gift include, or could be deemed to include, both charitable and non-charitable objects, its terms shall be so construed and given effect to as to exclude the non-charitable objects and the purpose shall, accordingly, be treated as charitable.'
9. *Re Koeppler's Will Trusts* [1986] Ch 423.
10. Where a gift is made to charity, it may be impossible to give effect to the intentions of the donor in the precise terms that he intended or it may be impractical or inconvenient to do so. The cy-près doctrine, where it applies, allows for the making of a scheme for the application of such property for other charitable purposes as near as possible to those intended by the donor. This is considered in detail below.
11. E.g. *Re Vinogradoff* [1935] WN 68. See also the approach taken by the former Supreme Court in *Owens v Greene* [1932] IR 225 in relation to the question of the beneficial ownership of money held in joint deposit accounts which persisted until it was reversed in the Supreme Court decision in *Lynch v Burke* [1995] 2 IR 159.
12. Keane, *Equity and the Law of Trusts in Ireland* (3rd ed., 2017) p. 182.
13. [2017] IEHC 650.

'to apply same for such purposes as my executor in his absolute discretion shall think fit'. He held that the matter before him was one in which extrinsic evidence should be admitted to establish the testator's intention and that he was satisfied on the balance of probabilities that his intention was that the residue of his estate was to be used for charitable and non-charitable purposes. Gilligan J concluded that section 49(1) of the Charities Act 1961 applied and as the objects of the trust could be deemed to include both charitable and non-charitable purposes, the non-charitable purposes fell away and the residuary bequest could be applied for charitable purposes. While this conclusion undoubtedly was the one most likely to accord with the wishes of the testator and avoided the result of the distribution of the residue by way of intestacy, the very broad interpretation placed by the court on the provisions of section 49(1) was unexpected and raises questions about the enforcement of what might have appeared to be a non-charitable purpose trust.

Another crucial distinction between charitable and non-charitable trusts is that the former may be perpetual in nature in so far as the rule against inalienability, which has proved such a major stumbling block in any attempts to enforce non-charitable purpose trusts, does not apply to them. Although charitable trusts may be of perpetual duration, they were in the past subject to the rule against perpetuities[14] to the extent that the initial vesting had to take place within the relevant perpetuity period.[15]

It should be noted that charitable trusts also enjoy a number of significant fiscal immunities in terms of exemptions from liability to various forms of taxation. Section 207(1) and (2) and section 208 of the Taxes Consolidation Act 1997 grant certain exemptions from income tax under Schedules C, D and F in respect of income accruing to charitable bodies or trusts established for charitable purposes to the extent that such income is applied for charitable purposes.[16] Section 76(6) of the Taxes Consolidation Act 1997 provides for the carrying over of any exemptions which would apply under income tax provisions to corporation tax. Exemptions also apply in respect of capital taxes, and a capital gain which accrues to a charity is not chargeable to capital gains tax provided that it is applied for charitable purposes.[17] In addition, section 76(2) of the Capital Acquisitions Consolidation Tax Act 2003 provides that a gift or inheritance taken for public or charitable purposes will be exempt from capital acquisitions tax provided that the Revenue Commissioners are satisfied that it has been or will be applied to such purposes. Finally, it should be noted

14. Now abolished by s.16 of the Land and Conveyancing Law Reform Act 2009.
15. *Re MacNamara* [1943] IR 372, 379; *National Tourism Development Authority v Coughlan* [2009] 3 IR 549, 562. This principle was subject to the limited exception that a gift over from one charity to another was not subject to the rule against perpetuities, see *Christ's Hospital v Grainger* (1849) 1 Mac & G 460; *Re Tyler* [1891] 3 Ch 252.
16. See further Maguire, *Irish Income Tax 2018* pp. 2355-2376 and Corrigan, *Revenue Law* (2000) pp. 757-770.
17. Section 609(1) of the Taxes Consolidation Act 1997.

that by virtue of section 848A of the Taxes Consolidation Act 1997, inserted by section 45 of the Finance Act 2001, charities can reclaim the tax paid on such donations.[18]

The scope of the exemption from income tax provided by sections 333 and 334 of the Income Tax Act 1967, which have been replaced by sections 207 and 208 of the Taxes Consolidation Act 1997, was considered by the High Court in *Revenue Commissioners v Sisters of Charity of the Incarnate Word.*[19] The appellants contended that sections 333 and 334 applied to bodies or persons established for charitable purposes but only if they were established within the State and they claimed that the respondents in this case were not established within the State. The respondents claimed that there was no justification for giving the exemption provisions the restricted interpretation contended for by the appellants and argued that even if the appellants' interpretation was correct, the charity was in fact established within the State through one of its branches. Geoghegan J accepted the conclusions reached by the Court of Appeal and the House of Lords in *Camille and Henry Dreyfus Foundation v IRC*[20] in relation to the equivalent English provisions to the effect that a limited geographical meaning should be given to the expression 'established'. Geoghegan J then went on to consider whether the charity was in fact established in the State. He stated that 'a foreign charity with no activities base (for want of a better expression) in Ireland is not entitled to an exemption but a foreign charity which does have such a base is entitled to it in respect of funds applied towards Irish charitable activities'. Geoghegan J concluded that having regard to the fact that the respondents owned and managed a nursing home in the State there was sufficient 'establishment' in Ireland to give rise to the exemption and he upheld the decision of the Circuit Court that the respondents were entitled to the benefit of the provisions of sections 333 and 334 of the Income Tax Act 1967 as amended.

In view of the extensive advantages enjoyed by charitable trusts, it has been argued that some limitation must be placed on their proliferation. While certain judicial statements show a tendency to adopt a benign attitude to this question,[21] the perceived benefit of undeserved fiscal immunity has proved a rather thorny issue over the years. An examination of the case law in England would suggest that this motive has led to a restrictive attitude being adopted to the wider question of whether certain trusts should qualify as being legally charitable.[22] Traditionally, the concepts of fiscal immunity and charitable

---

18. Amended by s.19 of the Finance Act 2013. Tax relief under s.848A in respect of donations made on or after 1 January 2013 by individuals to an eligible charity or other approved body is now allowed to the charity or body rather than to the donor.
19. [1998] 2 IR 553.
20. [1956] AC 39.
21. *Weir v Crum-Brown* [1908] AC 162, 167 *per* Lord Loreburn; *IRC v McMullen* [1981] AC 1, 14 *per* Lord Hailsham.
22. See the comment of Lord Cross in *Dingle v Turner* [1972] AC 601, 624 to the effect

status were said to 'march hand in hand'[23] although, as Lord Cross commented in *Dingle v Turner*,[24] such a state of affairs was 'unfortunate' given that the question of whether a trust was so unlikely to benefit the public that it ought to be declared invalid and the question of whether it was likely to confer such substantial benefits to the community that it ought to enjoy fiscal immunity were, in his view, two distinct issues.[25] An alternative approach favoured by the Radcliffe Commission[26] was to sever the connection, which would allow a more liberal approach to develop towards the question of the type of trusts which should qualify as being legally charitable unhindered by the baggage of perceived undeserved fiscal immunity.

The Law Reform Committee of the Law Society of Ireland in its report *Charity Law: The Case for Reform*[27] recommended that tax relief should continue to be an automatic consequence of obtaining charitable status, subject to the Revenue Commissioners' right of appeal to the High Court, although it was also suggested that the option of tiered tax relief[28] depending on the type of charitable purpose being undertaken should be given further consideration. However, the view that a distinction should be drawn between the determination of charitable status and entitlement to tax exemption has won out in this jurisdiction and section 7 of the Charities Act 2009 provides that nothing in the legislation will operate to affect the law in relation to the levying or collection of tax or the determination of eligibility for exemption from liability to pay tax.

Administration of Charities

The Charities Act 2009 was passed by the Dáil in February 2009, although very few of its sections were commenced until 2014.[29] Under the terms of the

---

that such considerations 'pretty obviously influenced' the decisions of the courts in *Re Compton* [1945] Ch 123 and *Oppenheim v Tobacco Securities Trust Co. Ltd* [1951] AC 297.

23. *Dingle v Turner* [1972] AC 601, 624 *per* Lord Cross.
24. [1972] AC 601.
25. Note also the comments of Lord MacDermott in *Dingle v Turner* [1972] AC 601, 614 in which he doubted whether consequential fiscal privileges had much relevance to the substantive question of whether a trust should be considered charitable in law, a view shared by Viscount Dilhorne and Lord Hodson.
26. Cmd. 9474. See Chapter 9, paras. 170 and 173. These recommendations were not implemented.
27. July 2002, p. 94.
28. See also Chesterman (1999) 62 MLR 333, 340.
29. Sections 1, 2, 5, 10(1) & (2) and 99 came into force as a result of the Charities Act 2009 (Commencement) Order 2009 (SI No. 284 of 2009); ss. 4 and 90 came into force as a result of the Charities Act 2009 (Commencement Order) 2010 (SI No. 315 of 2010); ss. 3, 6-9, 10 (insofar as not already commenced), 11, Parts 2, 3, 5, 6 and Schedules 1 and 2 came into force on 16 October 2014 (see the Charities Act 2009 (Commencement) Order 2014 (SI No. 457 of 2014); Part 4 came into force as a result of the Charities Act 2009 (Commencement) Order 2016 (SI No. 350 of 2016); ss.91

Charities Act 2009, a new regulatory framework has been put in place under a Charities Regulatory Authority,[30] known as the Charities Regulator. Prior to this the Attorney General had the function of overseeing the enforcement of charities in Ireland and was joined in any court proceedings brought in relation to such matters to ensure that the interests of charities are safeguarded. In addition, a statutory body, known as the Commissioners of Charitable Donations and Bequests, was responsible for the proper administration of trusts on a day-to-day basis.

The Commissioners had the role of advising charity trustees in relation to the administration of trusts[31] and a general power to authorise or direct the institution of legal proceedings in relation to any charitable matter.[32] In addition, the Commissioners had powers in relation to the investment of funds held on charitable trusts[33] and to frame a scheme applying property cy-près.[34] A further power, the exercise of which was considered by the High Court, had been to appoint new trustees to a charity.[35] In *Eastern Health Board v Commissioners for Charitable Donations and Bequests*[36] an order was made by the Commissioners pursuant to section 43 of the Charities Act 1961 as amended appointing new trustees of trusts established in respect of the Worth Library which had been housed in Dr Steevens' Hospital under the terms of a will which directed that the books concerned should not be removed from the room in the hospital in which they were kept. The hospital was closed in 1988 and while the Commissioners prepared a cy-près scheme, the books were temporarily housed in Trinity College Dublin. The plaintiff subsequently purchased the hospital and sought an order annulling the order of the Commissioners appointing Trinity College and the director of the National Library to be trustees in place of the existing trustees. Denham J held that the appointment of the new trustees was not premature and had not prejudiced the plaintiff's position and stated that she was satisfied that it was the correct decision to move the books to Trinity College for safekeeping at the time when the hospital was being sold. She also rejected the claim that the Commissioners had not complied with the procedures laid down by section 43 and held that the notice of the intention to appoint new trustees had been adequate.

In accordance with the Charities Act 2009, the Charities Regulatory Authority has taken over the functions exercised both by the Attorney

---

and 92 came into force as a result of the Charities Act 2009 (Commencement) (No.2) Order 2016 (SI No. 424 of 2016).

30. Established by s. 13 of the Act of 2009.
31. Section 21 of the Charities Act 1961.
32. Section 25 of the Charities Act 1961.
33. Section 32 of the Charities Act 1961 as substituted by s. 9 of the Charities Act 1973.
34. Section 29 of the Charities Act 1961 as amended by s. 8 of the Charities Act 1973.
35. Section 43 of the Charities Act 1961 as substituted by s. 14 of the Charities Act 1973.
36. High Court 1991 No. 207 Sp (Denham J) 17 December 1991.

General[37] and the Commissioners of Charitable Donations and Bequests.[38] The Authority possesses extensive powers to oversee the administration of charitable trusts and its functions include increasing public trust and confidence in the management and administration of charitable trusts and organisations and ensuring the accountability of charitable organisations to donors and beneficiaries of charitable gifts and the public.[39] Its functions also include establishing and maintaining a register of charitable organisations, ensuring and monitoring compliance by such organisations with the legislation and carrying out investigations in accordance with the provisions of the Act.[40] The Charities Regulatory Authority is required to consist of not less than nine and not more than twenty members[41] including the chairperson who is appointed by the Minister for Justice and Equality from amongst the members with the approval of the government.[42]

A Charity Appeals Tribunal has also been established to consider appeals from decisions of the Charities Regulatory Authority.[43] The legislation provides that any party to proceedings before the Tribunal may appeal a decision of the Tribunal to the High Court on a point of law, although an appeal shall not be brought without the permission of the Tribunal, or if it refuses permission, the High Court.[44] A Register of Charitable Organisations has been set up pursuant to Part 3 of the Act which contains information about registered charities. The Charities Regulatory Authority is required to ensure that such a register is maintained[45] and the Authority may remove a charitable organisation from the register in specified circumstances.[46] The trustees of a charitable organisation are required, *inter alia*, to keep proper books of account[47] and to prepare an annual report and submit it to the Authority.[48] Individuals may be disqualified from acting as a trustee of a charitable organisation in certain circumstances,[49]

---

37. Section 38.
38. Section 82.
39. Section 14.
40. *Ibid.*
41. Schedule 1, s. 2(1). Not less than three of these members shall hold or formerly have held judicial office in the Superior Courts or shall be barristers or solicitors of not less than 10 years standing.
42. Schedule 1, s. 2(2) and (3).
43. Section 75(1). It shall consist of five members of whom two shall hold or formerly have held judicial office in the Superior Courts or shall be barristers or solicitors of not less than 10 years standing, see s. 75(2).
44. Section 80.
45. Section 39.
46. Section 43.
47. Section 47.
48. Section 52.
49. Section 55(1) provides that a person shall be disqualified from acting as a charity trustee where he is adjudicated bankrupt, makes a composition or arrangement with creditors, is a company that is in the course of being wound up, is convicted on indictment of an offence, is sentenced to a term of imprisonment by a court of competent jurisdiction,

although a person who is not qualified or has ceased to be a trustee may apply to the High Court for an order that he may hold the position of charity trustee of a particular organisation and such an order may be made where the court is satisfied that this course of action is in the public interest and in the best interests of the charitable organisation in question.[50] The Charities Regulatory Authority may appoint an inspector to investigate a charitable organisation and to prepare a report for the Authority on its affairs.[51] The Authority may require a charitable organisation to produce specified books, documents or other records[52] and if a District Court judge is satisfied that there are reasonable grounds for believing that there has been a failure to comply with such a requirement, he may issue a warrant authorising a named inspector or officer of the Authority to search the organisation's premises and take possession of all necessary material.[53]

The legislation also provides that the High Court has power to relieve a charity trustee from personal liability for breach of trust if it considers that this trustee has acted honestly and reasonably and ought fairly to be excused for the breach of trust.[54] In addition, it provides that a charitable organisation may enter into an agreement with a charity trustee for the purchase of indemnity insurance against personal liability out of the charity's funds in respect of any act done or omitted to be done by the trustee in good faith and in the performance of his functions as a charity trustee.[55]

A number of measures originally proposed in the General Scheme for the Charities Regulation Bill published in March 2006 were not included in the legislation. These included a statutory duty of care to be imposed on charity trustees which would have required them, *inter alia*, to seek in good faith to ensure that the charity acts in a manner which is consistent with its purposes and to act with the care and diligence that it is reasonable to expect of an individual who is managing the affairs of another person.[56]

While the Charities Act 2009 addresses some important issues which were in great need of legislative intervention, it is disappointing that many of the provisions in the General Scheme for the Charities Regulation Bill 2006 dealing with various matters relating to charity trustees were not included in the Bill, or ultimately in the Act, and it would be helpful if some of these issues are addressed in any future legislation dealing with the role and powers of trustees generally. However, the legislation was broadly welcomed and it should ensure

---

is the subject of an order under s. 160 of the Companies Act 1990 or is prohibited or suspended from being a trustee under the Pensions Acts 1990 to 2008 or has been removed from the position of charity trustee by the High Court pursuant to s. 74 of the Charities Act 2009.

50. Section 55(2).
51. Sections 64 and 66.
52. Section 68.
53. Section 69.
54. Section 90.
55. Section 91.
56. Head 108 of the draft Heads of Bill.

greater accountability and lead to more transparency in the conduct of the affairs of charitable organisations. While greater regulation in this area was clearly necessary to improve public confidence in the sector, the increased reporting and accounting obligations may prove onerous for smaller charities in particular.

Definition of Charity

Gavan Duffy J remarked in *Re Howley's Estate*[57] that '"charity" is in law an artificial conception, which during some 300 years, under the guidance of pedantic technicians, seems to have strayed rather far from the intelligent realm of plain common sense'. Whether such a colourful comment can be justified is open to debate but it is certainly arguable that the meaning of the term 'charity' in law often bears no necessary relationship to a lay person's conception of the word.[58]

A statutory definition of 'charitable purpose' was provided for the first time in this jurisdiction by section 3 of the Charities Act 2009 and it is also now defined in England by section 2 of the Charities Act 2011. A list of charitable purposes was also contained in legislation passed in both jurisdictions in the seventeenth century, although these statutes were never intended to define charitable objects in a legal sense but rather to enumerate a variety of purposes recognised as being legally charitable.[59] In addition, this list was never intended to be exhaustive and as Keane J reiterated in *Re Worth Library*,[60] a trust might be considered charitable if it fell within the 'spirit or intendment'[61] of the statute. While the Irish Statute of Charitable Uses 1634[62] was repealed by the Statute Law Revision Act (Ireland) 1878, it is nevertheless useful to set out the terms

---

57. [1940] IR 109, 114.
58. See also the comments of Lord Sterndale MR in *Re Tetley* [1923] 1 Ch 258, 266 and of Charleton J in *National Tourism Development Authority v Coughlan* [2009] 3 IR 549, 562.
59. As Lord Sugden LC commented in *Incorporated Society v Richards* (1841) 4 Ir Eq R 177, 202, 'I consider that the object of the statute of Elizabeth was to remedy the abuses that then existed in the management of charitable property …' and he accepted that the legislation in both jurisdictions was of similar effect. The comment has also been made by Lord Morton in *Royal College of Surgeons of England v National Provincial Bank Ltd* [1952] AC 631, 650-651 that this was directed towards reforming abuses in the application of property devoted to charitable uses, rather than to defining the concept of a charity.
60. [1995] 2 IR 301, 333. See generally Delany (1994) 45 NILQ 364; Brady (1994) 16 DULJ 153.
61. See *Morice v Bishop of Durham* (1804) 9 Ves 399, 405. This phrase has also been interpreted on occasion in a negative way to mean that a purpose might only be considered charitable if it fell within the 'spirit or intendment of the legislation'. See *Williams' Trustees v IRC* [1947] AC 447, 455.
62. 10 Char. 1, Sess. 3, c. 1. The English version, the Statute of Charitable Uses 1601, 43 Eliz. 1, c.4, preserved in subsequent legislation, was also finally repealed by the Charities Act 1961.

of the Preamble as the decisions given regarding its scope provide a useful insight into the question of what was regarded as legally charitable at that time.[63]

> [T]he erection, maintenance, or support of any college, schoole, lecture in divinity or in any of the liberall arts or sciences; or for the reliefe of any manner of poore, succourlesse, distressed, or impotent persons; or for the building, re-edifying, or maintaining in repaire any church, college, schoole or hospitall; or for the maintenance of any minister and preacher of the Holy Word of God; or for the erection, building, maintenance, or repair of any bridges, causeyes, cashes, paces and highways within this realme; or for any other like lawfull and charitable use and uses, warranted by the laws of this realme now established and in force....

Although these words have provided a useful guide over the years, as Bright has commented, its wording was 'clearly not tailored to current social problems.'[64] Thomas J stated in the decision of the New Zealand Court of Appeal in *Commissioner of Inland Revenue v Medical Council of New Zealand*[65] that in applying the 'spirit and intendment' of the Preamble, it was important to be guided by principle rather than by a detailed analysis of decisions in particular cases, and it should be pointed out that judicial perceptions of what is charitable in law have altered over the years.[66] In his judgment in *Commissioners for Special Purposes of Income Tax v Pemsel*,[67] Lord Macnaghten identified four broad categories of charitable trust and following this decision a claim to charitable status was generally determined by considering whether a particular purpose came within one of these categories which are as follows:

1. Trusts for the relief of poverty
2. Trusts for the advancement of education

---

63. In the context of the English statute, see the comments of Lord Wilberforce in *Scottish Burial Reform and Cremation Society v Glasgow City Corporation* [1968] AC 138, 154.
64. Bright [1989] Conv 28, 31.
65. [1997] 2 NZLR 297, 314. See also the *dicta* of Sachs LJ in *Incorporated Council of Law Reporting for England and Wales v Attorney General* [1972] Ch 73, 95.
66. Contrast for example *Re Hummeltenberg* [1923] 1 Ch 237 and *Funnell v Stewart* [1996] 1 WLR 288. The former case, according to Fletcher (1996) 112 LQR 557 'tended to indicate that "faith healing" was not a charitable purpose'. By the time that the latter case was decided in 1996 it was accepted by the court that faith healing 'had become a recognised activity of public benefit' (at 297) although as Hazel Williamson QC, sitting as a Deputy High Court judge, acknowledged: 'this would not necessarily have been the case when *Re Hummeltenberg* was decided'. She held in the alternative that the purpose in any event qualified as charitable on the basis of the religious nature of the faith healing movement.
67. [1891] AC 531, 583. These categories were approved by Keane J in *Re Worth Library* [1995] 2 IR 301, 334. See also *Re Article 26 of the Constitution and the Employment Equality Bill 1996* [1997] 2 IR 321, 355.

3. Trusts for the advancement of religion
4. Trusts for other purposes beneficial to the community.

As a result it was generally accepted that trusts which were considered to be charitable in law fell into these four separate, although not necessarily mutually exclusive, categories. While it was recognised that this classification was one of convenience only and that there might be purposes which did not fit neatly into one or other of these categories,[68] or which fitted into one or more categories at the same time,[69] for more than a century it nevertheless provided the basis on which the courts both in this jurisdiction and in England approached the question of whether a trust should be accorded charitable status.

For some time consideration was given in England to the question of providing further statutory guidance in this area.[70] While section 97 of the Charities Act 1993 provided that 'charitable purposes' was defined to mean 'purposes which are exclusively charitable according to the law of England and Wales', section 2 of the Charities Act 2011[71] now defines 'charitable purposes' more specifically in terms loosely based on the Macnaghten classification. It refers to purposes such as 'the prevention or relief of poverty', 'the advancement of education' and 'the advancement of religion' as well as enumerating some of the purposes previously recognised as falling within the category of 'other purposes beneficial to the community'. It also recognises as charitable purposes aims such as 'the advancement of amateur sport' and 'the advancement of human rights' which might not have been recognised as charitable prior to the enactment of the legislation.

In this jurisdiction, the Law Reform Committee of the Law Society of Ireland in its report *Charity Law: The Case for Reform*[72] stopped short of recommending a statutory definition although it did favour the introduction of guidelines in statutory form in order to facilitate decision making in this area whether by the courts or bodies such as the Revenue Commissioners. However, a definition of 'charitable purpose' is now set out in section 3 of the Charities Act 2009, which closely mirrors the four categories identified in *Pemsel's* case. These purposes are 'the prevention of relief of poverty or economic hardship', 'the advancement of education', 'the advancement of religion' and 'any other purpose that is of benefit to the community'.

A charitable trust is defined as a trust 'established for a charitable purpose

68. *Scottish Burial Reform and Cremation Society Ltd v Glasgow Corporation* [1968] AC 138, 154 *per* Lord Wilberforce.
69. See, e.g. *Incorporated Council of Law Reporting for England and Wales v Attorney General* [1972] Ch 73.
70. See the Report of the Committee on the Law and Practice Relating to Charities 1952 Cmd. 8710 (The Nathan Report) at para. 697. Note that the Committee on Charity Law and Voluntary Organisations 1976 (The Goodman Committee) suggested 'guidelines' which might be followed.
71. This Act replaces the Charities Act 2006.
72. July 2002 at p. 85.

only'.[73] Section 2 of the Act of 2009 provides that a charitable organisation shall not include an excluded body which is defined to include a body that promotes purposes which are unlawful, contrary to public morality or public policy or support terrorist activities or which are for the benefit of an organisation, membership of which is unlawful. More controversially, as will be examined in more detail below, an excluded body also includes 'a body that promotes a political cause, unless the promotion of that cause relates directly to the advancement of the charitable purposes of that body' and 'an approved body of persons within the meaning of section 235 of the Taxes Consolidation Act 1997, which is 'any body of persons established for and existing for the sole purpose of promoting athletic or amateur games or sports'.

It should be noted that while section 3(1)(m) of the English Charities Act 2011 extends the meaning of 'charitable purpose' to any purposes which may reasonably be regarded as analogous to, or within the spirit of, any of those specifically listed or those recognised under existing charity law, there is no equivalent provision in the Irish legislation. This has led some commentators to speculate about whether this omission will lead to a less dynamic approach being taken by the courts to extending the definition of charitable purpose in this jurisdiction.[74] However, given that the word 'includes' is used before the list of specific purposes set out in section 3(11), there is no real reason why the courts should depart from their traditional practice of treating the concept of charitable purpose as a constantly evolving one.

The Public Benefit Requirement

What the Macnaghten classification failed to make clear explicitly was that for a trust to be regarded as legally charitable, it had to be of a public character and had to contain some element of benefit to the public generally.[75] Lord Simonds remarked that no court would be rash enough to attempt to define precisely or exhaustively what the content of the test of public benefit must be[76] and that '[n]o one who has been versed for many years in this difficult and very artificial branch of the law can be unaware of its illogicalities.'[77] An examination of the various judicial interpretations of the types of trust which have been regarded as legally charitable shows that there have in effect been two hurdles to overcome, first, an element of benefit, e.g. the relief of poverty, and secondly, an element of *public* benefit.

The Upper Tribunal acknowledged in its judgment in *R. (Independent*

73. Section 2(1).
74. See Breen (2008) 59 NILQ 223, 229. See also O'Halloran, *Charity Law* (2009) p. 113.
75. See O'Halloran (2001) 23 DULJ 97, where the differences in approach towards the public benefit test as between this jurisdiction and Northern Ireland are analysed.
76. *Gilmour v Coats* [1949] AC 426, 446-447.
77. *Oppenheim v Tobacco Securities Trust Co. Ltd* [1951] AC 297, 307.

Schools Council) v Charity Commission for England and Wales[78] that the authorities do not provide a comprehensive statement of the elements of the public benefit requirement but rather a series of examples of when the requirement is or is not satisfied. It pointed out that '[t]he courts have adopted an incremental and somewhat ad hoc approach in relation to what benefits the community or a section of the community'.[79] It is also clear that 'as society changes, so too perceptions of what is for the public benefit can change in the future just as much as they have changed in the past'.[80] However, the Upper Tribunal in *Independent Schools Council* did set out the following principles in the course of its judgment:

> There has never been an attempt comprehensively to define what is, or is not, of public benefit. It is possible, however, to discern from the cases two related aspects of public benefit. The first aspect is that the nature of the purpose itself must be such as to be a benefit to the community: this is public benefit in the first sense. … The second aspect is that those who may benefit from the carrying out of the purpose must be sufficiently numerous, and identified in such manner as, to constitute what is described in the authorities as "a section of the public": this is public benefit in the second sense.[81]

As Lord Simonds put it in *Williams' Trustees v Inland Revenue Commissioners*,[82] it has been stated consistently that in order to be charitable a trust must be of a public character and not merely for the benefit of particular private individuals. So, the true question must be whether the gift really is for the relief or advancement of the charitable purpose amongst a class of persons or merely a gift to individuals, albeit with the relief or advancement of the purpose amongst those individuals as the motive for the gift.[83]

There have been real difficulties over the years in determining whether a gift benefits a sufficient section of the public or an 'appreciably important class

78. [2012] Ch 214, 236. See also *Attorney General v Charity Commission for England and Wales* [2012] UKUT 420 (TCC) at [34].
79. *Ibid.*
80. *Attorney General v Charity Commission for England and Wales* [2012] UKUT 420 (TCC) at [77]. See also *R. (Independent Schools Council) v Charity Commission for England and Wales* [2012] Ch 214, 229: 'In that context, it must be remembered that the concept of what is and is not for the public benefit (as seen by society generally, and as reflected in judicial recognition of the views of society) changes over time. As we will see, changing social perceptions have, in the past, resulted in changes in what is seen as for the benefit of society and, accordingly, of what is properly to be accorded charitable status.'
81. [2012] Ch 214, 235-236. See also *Attorney General v Charity Commission for England and Wales* [2012] UKUT 420 (TCC) at [32]–[33].
82. [1947] AC 447, 457.
83. *Re Scarisbrick* [1951] Ch 622 655 *per* Jenkins LJ. See also *Dingle v Turner* [1972] AC 601, 617; *Re Segelman* [1996] Ch 171, 188.

of the community'[84] in order to qualify as charitable. However, an analysis of the case law shows that there has tended to be a link between what is a sufficient section of the public or the community for this purpose and the type of charitable purpose under consideration.[85] Lord Cross commented in *Dingle v Turner*[86] that '[i]n truth the question whether or not the potential beneficiaries of a trust can fairly be said to constitute a section of the public is a question of degree and cannot be by itself decisive of the question whether the trust is a charity'; as he put it '[m]uch must depend on the purpose of the trust'.[87] This point was also made in the following terms by the Upper Tribunal in *Attorney General v Charity Commission for England and Wales*:[88]

> [W]hether or not an institution satisfies the public benefit requirement must be assessed by reference to the criteria which are relevant to its purposes. For instance, as is clear from the cases, what is or is not a sufficient section of the public to satisfy the second aspect of public benefit varies depending on the nature of the charity: a sufficient section of the public in relation to an educational institution may not be sufficient in relation to a religious institution and *vice versa*.

So, this concept of public benefit has varied considerably as between the different categories of charitable trusts.[89] In the case of trusts for the relief of poverty it had, until the enactment of the Charities Act 2009, been greatly modified as a result of judicial intervention.[90] In addition, in this jurisdiction in the case of trusts for the advancement of religion, section 3(4) of the Charities

---

84. *Per* Lord Wrenbury in *Verge v Somerville* [1924] AC 496, 499.
85. As the Upper Tribunal stated in its judgment in *R. (Independent Schools Council) v Charity Commission for England and Wales* [2012] Ch 214, 263, *IRC v Baddeley* [1955] AC 572 highlights the issue that what constitutes a sufficient section of the public cannot be considered separately from the particular nature of the charitable purpose.
86. [1972] AC 601, 624. Quoted with approval in *Attorney General v Charity Commission for England and Wales* [2012] UKUT 420 (TCC) at [58].
87. Sanders has suggested (2007) 10(2) CL & PR 33, 42 that, according to this view, 'the question of the *benefit* a charity offers and the question whether a sufficient section of the *public* has access to this benefit as intermingled.'
88. [2012] UKUT 420 (TCC) at [64].
89. See the statements of Lord Simonds in *Gilmour v Coats* [1949] AC 426, 449; Lord Somervell in *IRC v Baddeley* [1955] AC 572, 615 (see further Atiyah (1958) 21 MLR 138, 139); Carswell J in *Re Dunlop* [1984] NI 408, 425-426 and the Upper Tribunal in *Attorney General v Charity Commission for England and Wales* [2012] UKUT 420 (TCC) at [34].
90. The so called 'poor relations' trusts were recognised in a number of decisions handed down in the eighteenth century, see e.g. *Issac v Defriez* (1754) Amb 595, and the modification of the public benefit requirement in this category is well recognised today, see *Gibson v South American Stores (Gath & Chaves) Ltd* [1950] Ch 177; *Re Scarisbrick* [1951] Ch 622; *Dingle v Turner* [1972] AC 601; *Re Cohen* [1973] 1 WLR 415; *Re Segelman deceased* [1996] Ch 171. However, as a result of the enactment of

Act 2009 provides that 'it shall be presumed, unless the contrary is proved, that a gift for the advancement of religion will occasion public benefit'.[91]

In the other categories, the position has tended to be as laid down by Lord Greene MR in *Re Compton*,[92] namely that 'a gift under which the beneficiaries are defined by reference to a purely personal relationship to a named *propositus* cannot on principle be a valid charitable gift.' As he put it, '[t]he inherent vice of the personal element is present however long the chain'.[93]Trusts for the advancement of education often failed to qualify for charitable status because they did not satisfy the public benefit requirement. In England, the factors which prevented the public benefit test being satisfied in the context of trusts for the advancement of education extended beyond blood ties or a personal nexus to a 'nexus of contract',[94] and trusts for the education of persons, or relatives of persons, in common employment were found not to be charitable in nature.[95]

In addition, while the requirement has tended to differ as between the various types of trusts in the fourth category, it was often to this residual category that the most rigorous interpretation of the public benefit test has been applied.[96] Perhaps due to the apparent latitude which this category allows for, the courts traditionally took a relatively strict view in interpreting what constitutes a trust for 'other purposes beneficial to the community'.[97] Greater flexibility towards

---

subss.3(7) and (8) of the Charities Act 2009, such trusts are unlikely to be recognised in this jurisdiction in the future. See further *infra*.

91. This section replaced s. 45(1) of the Charities Act 1961 which went further and provided that it shall be conclusively presumed that a trust for the advancement of religion will occasion public benefit.
92. [1945] Ch 123, 131.
93. *Ibid.*
94. Plowright (1975) 39 Conv 183, 185.
95. *Oppenheim v Tobacco Securities Trust Co. Ltd* [1951] AC 297. See also *George Drexler Ofrex Foundation Trustees v IRC* [1966] Ch 673; *IRC v Educational Grants Association Ltd* [1967] Ch 993. This approach was in line with the recommendations of the Goodman Committee Report on Charity Law and Voluntary Organisations (1976) paras. 38 and 50(b).
96. See the comments of Babington LJ in *Trustees of the Londonderry Presbyterian Church House v Commissioners of Inland Revenue* [1946] NI 178, 196; of Viscount Simonds in *IRC v Baddeley* [1955] AC 572, 592 and of Lord Somervell in *Baddeley* (at 615), although note the different conclusion reached by Lord Reid in *Baddeley* at 612-613.
97. As Viscount Cave pointed out in *Attorney General v National Provincial and Union Bank of England Ltd* [1924] AC 262, 265, 'Lord Macnaghten did not mean that all trusts beneficial to the community are charitable, but there are certain charitable trusts which fall within that category, and accordingly to argue that because a trust is for a purpose beneficial to the community it is therefore a charitable trust is to turn round his sentence and give it a different meaning. . . . It is not enough to say that a trust is for public purposes beneficial to the community or for the public welfare, you must also show it to be a charitable trust.' See also the comments of Lindley LJ (at 466-467) and Rigby LJ (at 476) in *Re Macduff* [1896] 2 Ch 451 and Andrews LJ in *Trustees of the Londonderry Presbyterian Church House v Commissioners of Inland Revenue* [1946] NI 178, 187.

this question can be seen in more recent decisions[98] but evidence of the more demanding approach can often still be identified in terms of the application of the public benefit requirement to this category.

The concept of public benefit is retained by section 3(2) of the Charities Act 2009 which provides that a purpose shall not be regarded as a charitable purpose for the purposes of the Act unless it is of public benefit.[99] Section 3(3) provides that subject to subsection (4), which makes separate provision in relation to gifts for the advancement of religion, a gift shall not be regarded as being of public benefit unless it is intended to benefit the public or a section of the public, and that in a case where it confers a benefit on a person other than in his capacity as a member of the public or a section of the public, any such benefit must be reasonable in all the circumstances and ancillary to and necessary for the furtherance of public benefit.[100] The Act further provides in section 3(7) that in determining whether a gift is of public benefit, account shall be taken of any limitation imposed by the donor of the gift on the class of persons who may benefit and whether this limitation is justified and reasonable having regard to the nature and purpose of the gift, and also the amount of any charge payable for any service provided in furtherance of the purpose for which the gift is given and whether it is likely to limit the number of persons or classes of persons who will benefit from the gift. Another significant provision which has changed how the public benefit requirement will be applied, in particular in relation to trusts for the relief of poverty, is section 3(8), which provides that a limitation on the persons who may benefit 'shall not be justified and reasonable if all of the intended beneficiaries of the gift or a significant number of them have a personal connection[101] with the donor of the gift'.

In many respects the statutory provisions relating to the public benefit test introduced by the English Charities Act 2006 and Charities Act 2011 are less likely to effect a change in practice than those contained in the Charities Act 2009. Section 2(1)(b) of the Act of 2011 requires that a charitable purpose be one which is for the public benefit and section 4(2) provides that in determining whether that requirement is satisfied in relation to any purpose, 'it is not to be presumed that a purpose of a particular description is for the public benefit'. It seems to be generally accepted that this provision was designed to reverse the so-called presumption of public benefit suggested by Lord Wright in *National Anti-Vivisection Society v IRC*[102] and when the effect of this *dicta* was

---

98. See, e.g. the *dictum* of Lord Russell in *Incorporated Council for Law Reporting for England and Wales v Attorney General* [1972] Ch 73, 88, where he suggested that if a purpose is beneficial to the community it is *prima facie* charitable in law.
99. Although, as noted above, s. 3(4) provides that it shall be presumed, unless the contrary is proved, that a gift for the purpose of the advancement of religion will occasion public benefit.
100. Section 3(3).
101. See further s. 2(2)(a) of the Act discussed in more detail in the context of trusts for the prevention or relief of poverty.
102. [1948] AC 21, 42.

considered by the Upper Tribunal in *R. (Independent Schools Council) v Charity Commission for England and Wales*,[103] it stated that '[i]t is apparent from that passage that Lord Wright was here concerned with what we have described as public benefit in the first sense.'[104] There has been extensive academic debate about the effect of these provisions[105] but they do not appear to have altered the law in relation to the so-called second aspect of the public benefit test in England and Wales.

CHARITABLE PURPOSES

Trusts for the Prevention or Relief of Poverty

The purpose of trusts for 'the relief of poverty' was the first category of charitable trust enumerated in the so-called Macnaghten classification in *Pemsel's*[106] case. This has been modified to 'the prevention or relief of poverty or economic hardship' in section 3(1) of the Charities Act 2009 which defines charitable purposes. The existing case law interpreting the meaning of 'poverty' or 'poor' for the purposes of the Macnaghten classification remains a useful guide in this context but should be read with some caution given the expanded definition now used in section 3(1)(a). In addition, aspects of any relevant decisions relating to the public benefit test under this heading must now be read in the light of sections 3(7) and (8) of the Charities Act 2009 which will be considered in more detail below and the requirement of public benefit will undoubtedly be more rigorously applied in the future as a result.

The Meaning of 'Poor'

The point was made in *Tudor on Charities* that '"poor" is a relative term'[107]

103. [2012] Ch 214, 241.
104. This first sense was interpreted as meaning that the nature of the purpose had to be such as to be a benefit to the community. The second sense was 'that those who may benefit from the carrying out of the purpose must be sufficiently numerous, and identified in such manner as, to constitute what is described in the authorities as "a section of the public".' See [2012] Ch 214, 235-236.
105. See particularly Sanders (2007) 10(2) CL & PR 33; Luxton (2009) 11(2) CL & PR 19. See also Luxton, 'Public Benefit and Charities: the Impact of the Charities Act 2006 on Independent Schools and Private Hospitals' in *Contemporary Perspectives on Property, Equity and Trusts Law* (ed. Dixon, 2007) p. 201; Hackney, 'Charities and Public Benefit' (2008) 124 LQR 347; Warburton (2008) 10(3) CL & PR 1; Morris, 'Public Benefit: The Long and Winding Road to Reforming the Public Benefit Test for Charity: A Worthwhile Trip or "Is Your Journey Really Necessary?"' in *Modernising Charity Law: Recent Developments and Future Directions* (eds. McGregor-Lowndes and O'Halloran, 2010), p.103; Synge [2011] CLJ 649.
106. *Commissioners for Special Purposes of Income Tax v Pemsel* [1891] AC 531.
107. Henderson and Fowles, *Tudor on Charities* (10th ed., 2015) p. 134.

and the authorities have shown that it was not necessary for a class of persons to be destitute in order for a trust for their relief to qualify as charitable in nature. This point was made by Evershed MR in *Re Coulthurst*[108] as follows:

> It is quite clearly established that poverty does not mean destitution; it is a word of wide and somewhat indefinite import; it may not unfairly be paraphrased for present purposes as meaning persons who have to 'go short' in the ordinary acceptation of that term, due regard being had to their status in life and so forth.

There the Court of Appeal held that a trust for the benefit of the widows and children of deceased officers of a bank, who by reason of their financial circumstances were the most deserving, was a valid charitable trust. As Viscount Simonds commented in *IRC v Baddeley*,[109] 'there may be a good charity for the relief of persons who are not in grinding need or utter destitution' and a trust to provide for persons of limited or reduced means may come within the ambit of this category. So, in *Re Gardom*[110] a gift for the provision of a temporary residence for 'ladies of limited means' was held to be charitable. As Eve J commented, although such persons were not destitute, 'there are degrees of poverty less acute than abject poverty or destitution.'[111] However, there is often a fine line to be drawn between cases which will satisfy the requirement as being for the relief of poverty and those which will not. In *Re Sanders' Will Trusts*[112] Harman J held that a bequest to provide housing for the 'working classes' and their families resident in a certain district did not qualify, while in *Re Niyazi's Will Trusts*[113] Megarry VC upheld as a valid charitable trust a gift 'for the construction of or as a contribution towards the cost of a working men's hostel' in the town of Famagusta in Cyprus.

More recent pronouncements on this issue would suggest that a more flexible attitude is now being taken towards the degree of poverty which must be established. In *Re Segelman deceased*[114] Chadwick J accepted that a gift to poor and needy members of a class of the testator's relatives was a valid charitable gift for the relief of poverty.[115] He stated that the evidence suggested that 'most members of the class are comfortably off, in the sense that they are

---

108. [1951] Ch 661, 665-6. See also *Re De Carteret* [1933] Ch 103, 108; *Re Bethal* (1971) 17 DLR (3d) 652, 666; *DV Bryant Trust Board v Hamilton City Council* [1997] 3 NZLR 342, 349; *Cawdron v Merchant Taylors School* [2009] EWHC 1722 (Ch).
109. [1955] AC 572, 585.
110. [1914] 1 Ch 662.
111. *Ibid.* at 668.
112. [1954] Ch 265. The case was settled on appeal (see *The Times*, 22 July 1954).
113. [1978] 1 WLR 910.
114. [1996] Ch 171.
115. It should be noted that such a limited class would be likely to fail the public benefit test if a similar case were to arise now in this jurisdiction as a result of the provisions of ss. 3(7) and (8) of the Charities Act 2009.

able to meet their day-to-day expenses out of income, but not affluent' and that 'like many others in similar circumstances, they need a helping hand from time to time in order to overcome an unforeseen crisis'. Histed has commented that 'the court has come perilously close to implying that an occasional problem of expenditure exceeding income is sufficient to qualify a class member as "poor"'.[116] She states that even though this was presumably not the implication intended, 'the tone of the judgment does suggest a more flexible approach to the poverty requirement than has obtained in earlier cases'.[117] Subsequently, in *Cawdron v Merchants Taylors' School*,[118] Blackburne J concluded that the provision of financial assistance to dependent relatives of old boys of a school killed or disabled in the First World War in order to pay fees at the school was a charitable purpose for the relief of poverty. He was satisfied that it was to those who would otherwise 'go short' that the assistance was to be directed. In considering the object of the trust Blackburne J weighed up whether the aims set out proceeded from motives of general benevolence towards the dependents of the classes of persons identified, in which case its validity was to be decided as a matter of charity law, or from motives of personal bounty towards the persons so identified, in which case the validity of the gift was to be determined as a matter of private trust law, and concluded that he had no doubt that it fell into the former category.

A further limitation which should be noted is that the need which is to be relieved by the charitable gift must be attributable to the condition of the person to be benefited. This point was made by Peter Gibson J in *Joseph Rowntree Memorial Trust Housing Association Ltd v Attorney General*[119] in the context of schemes to provide accommodation for disabled and elderly people, but it would have equal application to trusts for the poor and would seem to rule out any gift which does not go towards alleviating their condition of poverty. An earlier illustration of this principle was provided by Harman J in *Baddeley v IRC*,[120] where he commented that a gift to amuse the poor would not relieve them and therefore would not be considered charitable. A further consideration is the fact that potential beneficiaries are young and therefore may not themselves have a means of support does not necessarily fulfil the poverty requirement. In *Browne v King*[121] a gift to be applied for the benefit of the children of the tenantry of an estate under the age of twelve years did not qualify as charitable. As Porter MR stated, '[t]here is nothing to guide me in deciding that the gift

116. [1996] Conv 379, 386.
117. This approach can also be discerned in other jurisdictions, e.g. in New Zealand, where in *Re Centrepoint Community Growth Trust* [2000] 2 NZLR 325, Cartwright J stated that 'in contemporary New Zealand poverty can quite readily be equated with lack of affordable accommodation.'
118. [2009] EWHC 1722 (Ch).
119. [1983] Ch 159, 171. See also *Re Dunlop* [1984] NI 408, 414-416.
120. [1953] 1 WLR 84, 88. As he stated, '[r]elief seems to connote need of some sort … and not merely an amusement however healthy it is.'
121. (1885) 17 LR Ir 448.

is for children of poor persons, or persons in great need. The law imposes on parents the duty of supporting their children and there is nothing to satisfy me that the tenantry … are not able to fulfil that obligation.'[122]

A gift of this kind may be expressed in either general or particular terms. So, a gift to the poor in a general way will be upheld,[123] or a gift to the poor of a particular area,[124] or a particular religious denomination.[125] It has been established that the fact that the recipients of the testator or donor's bounty are to be chosen by his executors or trustees does not present any difficulties.[126] Similarly, in *Brett v Attorney General*,[127] it was held by the Supreme Court that a trust for 'such poor persons in the County of M. as the executor shall select and consider worthy of assistance' was charitable and that the power of selection conferred on the executor could not alter the essentially charitable nature of the gift.

Addition of 'Prevention of' Poverty and 'Economic Hardship'

When the Charities Act 2006 was enacted in England, the reference relating to poverty was expanded from the established 'relief of poverty' criteria to the 'prevention or relief of poverty' and this was repeated in the Charites Act 2011.[128] This extended formula has also been adopted in section 3(1)(a) of the Charities Act 2009 in this jurisdiction. The addition of the word 'prevention' may in some circumstances be significant as the decision of the Canadian Federal Court of Appeal in *Credit Counselling Services of Atlantic Canada Inc v Minister of National Revenue*[129] illustrates. Webb JA stated that 'to satisfy the requirement that a purpose is for the relief of poverty, the person receiving the assistance must be a person who is then in poverty'.[130] However, the assistance provided by the appellant extended to individuals who were in employment and had assets and would not necessarily be considered to be 'in poverty' in the sense understood by the court. The court concluded that while the activities of the appellant could be described as related to the prevention of poverty they did not extend to the 'relief of poverty'. In the view of Webb JA it would require legislation as was forthcoming in England and now in Ireland, to extend the criteria to include 'prevention of poverty' as a charitable purpose.

---

122. *Ibid.* at 456.
123. *Attorney General v Matthews* (1677) 2 Lev 167.
124. *Attorney General v Exeter Corporation* (1826) 2 Russ 45.
125. *Attorney General v Wansay* (1808) 15 Ves 231; *Dawson v Small* (1874) LR 18 Eq 114; *Re Wall* (1889) 42 Ch D 510.
126. *Re Scarisbrick* [1951] Ch 622 and *Re Cohen* [1973] 1 WLR 415 where a trust 'for the maintenance and benefit of any relative of mine whom my trustees shall consider to be in special need' was upheld as charitable.
127. [1945] IR 526.
128. See s.2(2)(a) of the Charities Act 2006 and s.3(1)(a) of the Charities Act 2011.
129. (2016) 401 DLR (4th) 375.
130. *Ibid.* at [16].

The other way in which the statutory definition under this heading was extended by section 3(1)(a) of the Charities Act 2009 was by the inclusion of the concept of 'economic hardship'. The addition of these words may well also be significant in consolidating the extension of the scope of this heading of charitable purpose which was already underway. While there was evidence in decisions such as *Re Segelman*[131] and *Cawdron v Merchants Taylors' School*,[132] considered above, of an expansion of the traditional meaning of 'poverty' in this context, the addition of the words 'economic hardship' should remove any doubts about whether such an approach would find favour with the courts in this jurisdiction. It may in time even lead to a more expansive approach being adopted by the judiciary here in relation to this category of charitable purpose than that taken by their counterparts in England.

The Element of Public Benefit

Before statutory intervention it is fair to say that the public benefit test in the context of trusts for the relief of poverty in this jurisdiction had been relatively easy to satisfy. However, the provisions of section 3(7) of the Act of 2009 make clear that in determining whether a gift is of public benefit, account shall be taken of '(a) any limitation imposed by the donor of the gift on the class of persons who may benefit from the gift and whether or not such limitation is justified and reasonable, having regard to the nature and purpose of the gift.' Section 3(7)(b) provides that account shall also be taken of the amount of any charge payable for any service provided in furtherance of the purpose for which the gift is given and whether it is likely to limit the number or classes of persons who will benefit from the gift. Section 3(8) goes on to provide that a limitation on the persons who may benefit 'shall not be justified and reasonable if all of the intended beneficiaries of the gift or a significant number of them have a personal connection with the donor of the gift'. Section 2(2)(a) of the Act sets out a number of circumstances in which a person is connected with another for this purpose and includes where the former is the 'parent, brother, sister, spouse, grandparent or grandchild of the individual or a child of the spouse of the individual' or is employed by them under a contract for service. A person is also considered to be connected with an individual in this context if they are in a trustee/beneficiary relationship, in partnership or linked through a body corporate.

As a result the so-called 'poor relations' or 'poor employees' trusts are most unlikely to qualify for charitable status in the future in this jurisdiction given the personal connection between the donor of the gift and the intended beneficiaries.[133] However, section 4 of the English Charities Act 2011 imposes

131. [1996] Ch 171.
132. [2009] EWHC 1722 (Ch).
133. See also Keane, *Equity and the Law of Trusts in Ireland* (3rd ed., 2017) p.183.

no similar limitation and simply provides that it is not to be presumed that a purpose is for the public benefit and that the phrase is to be interpreted 'as that term is understood for the purposes of the law relating to charities in England and Wales'. For this reason it is likely that the case law in this area in England which has built up over the years will continue to be followed in that jurisdiction[134] and it is useful to set out the main principles relating to the public benefit test as it applies there.

The Test of Public Benefit in England

It has always been important to distinguish a gift to specified poor individuals from a gift to a class of the poor. Trusts in the former category have not been regarded as charitable in nature, while those in the latter have been, even where this class is of limited scope. As Jenkins LJ stated in *Re Scarisbrick*,[135] 'I think the true question in each case has really been whether the gift was for the relief of poverty amongst a class of persons … or was merely a gift to individuals, albeit with relief of poverty amongst those individuals as the motive of the gift.'

This position has come about largely as a result of the development of the category of so-called 'poor relations' trusts, whereby a donor or testator may create a valid charitable trust to benefit those of his relatives who are in straitened financial circumstances.[136] These cases have been recognised as forming an exception to the general principle laid down by Lord Greene MR in *Re Compton*[137] that 'a gift under which the beneficiaries are defined by reference to a purely personal relationship to a named *propositus*, cannot on principle be a valid charitable gift.'

A justification for these types of trust was suggested by Evershed MR in *Re Scarisbrick*[138] in the following terms:

> The 'poor relations' cases may be justified on the basis that the relief of poverty is of so altruistic a character that the public element may necessarily be inferred thereby; or they may be accepted as a hallowed, if illogical, exception.

These types of trusts came to be regarded as anomalous exceptions to the public benefit requirement which attaches to charitable trusts generally.[139] When this issue was considered again by the Upper Tribunal in *Attorney General v*

---

134. See further Rahmatian [2009] Conv 12.
135. [1951] Ch 622 655. See also *Dingle v Turner* [1972] AC 601, 617; *Re Segelman* [1996] Ch 171, 188.
136. See *Mahon v Savage* (1803) 1 Sch & Lef 111.
137. [1945] Ch 123, 131.
138. [1951] Ch 622, 639. See also *Gibson v South American Stores (Gath & Chaves) Ltd* [1950] Ch 177, 197 *per* Evershed MR.
139. See *Re Compton* [1945] Ch 123, 139 *per* Lord Greene MR.

Charity Commission for England and Wales,[140] it was acknowledged that the 'poor relations' cases represent an exception to the general rule or an anomaly and are not to be extended but the tribunal added that 'within the exception, logic and coherence must prevail'.[141]

A good illustration of such a trust is provided in the *Scarisbrick* case itself, where a trust to benefit such relations of the testatrix's son and daughters who in the opinion of the survivor of her children 'shall be in needy circumstances' was upheld as a valid charitable trust. Jenkins LJ, having set out the general requirement of public benefit in charitable trusts, continued as follows:

> There is, however, an exception to the general rule, in that trusts or gifts for the relief of poverty have been held to be charitable even though they are limited in their application to some aggregate of individuals ascertained as above, and are, therefore, not trusts or gifts for the benefit of the public or a section thereof. The exception operates whether the personal tie is one of blood (as in the numerous so called 'poor relations' cases) or of contract, e.g., the relief of poverty amongst the members of a particular society … or amongst employees of a particular company or their dependants.[142]

A further point which was made by the Court of Appeal in *Scarisbrick* is that no distinction should be drawn between trusts for the poor which are to have perpetual continuance and those which provide for immediate distribution amongst the recipients.[143] As Jenkins LJ stated, 'I see no sufficient ground in the authorities for holding that a gift for the benefit of poor relations qualifies as charitable only if it is perpetual in character.'[144]

Another example of a trust for poor relations being upheld in England is *Re Segelman deceased*,[145] in which Chadwick J accepted that a gift to poor and needy members of a class of the testator's relatives, which was not to close until 21 years after his death, was a valid charitable gift for the relief of poverty and that it was not disqualified from being such by the restricted nature of the class. At the time of the hearing, there were 26 members of the class and Chadwick J stated that it was reasonable to assume that at the end of the period of 21 years from the testator's death, the class would be substantially larger. Chadwick

140. [2012] UKUT 420 (TCC) at [70].
141. This reflects the view expressed by Evershed MR in *Re Scarisbrick* [1951] Ch 622, 640 that '[i]f there must be an anomaly, let it be itself logical and coherent'.
142. [1951] Ch 622, 649.
143. In so doing the Court of Appeal reversed the finding of Roxburgh J at first instance in which he had held that the bequest was not charitable on the basis that a gift for immediate distribution lacked the necessary public character to render it charitable. This finding was in the opinion of the Court of Appeal based on a mistaken interpretation of the decision of Grant MR in *Attorney General v Price* (1810) 17 Ves 371.
144. [1951] Ch 622, 655.
145. [1996] Ch 171.

J stated that *prima facie* a gift for the benefit of poor and needy persons is a gift for the relief of poverty and that such a gift is no less charitable because those whose poverty is to be relieved are confined to a particular class limited by ties of blood or employment. He quoted a statement from the judgment of Jenkins LJ in *Scarisbrick*, which had been approved by the House of Lords in *Dingle v Turner*,[146] to the effect that the true question must be whether the gift was really for the relief of poverty amongst a class of persons or merely a gift to individuals, albeit with the relief of poverty amongst those individuals as the motive for the gift. Chadwick J continued by saying that the basis for disqualification as a charitable gift must be that the restricted nature of the class leads to the conclusion that the gift is really one to the individual members of a class. In his view the gift which he was required to consider was not of that character and had, in common with the gift in *Scarisbrick*, the feature that the class of those eligible to benefit was not closed on the testator's death but remained open for a further period of 21 years. Chadwick J stated that during that period issue of the named individuals born after the testator's death would become members of the class. In his opinion it was impossible to attribute to the testator an intention to make a gift to those after-born issue as such and his intention must therefore be taken to have been the relief of poverty amongst the class of which they would become members.

While Chadwick J did not address this point directly, the implication might be taken from his judgment that if the class of persons to benefit was confined to those of the testator's relatives living at the date of his death, the gift might have been construed as one to individual members of the class which would not qualify as being for the relief of poverty. Histed has commented that Chadwick J's opinion seemed to be that 'the more restricted the class, the more probable that the gift was one to individuals' and in her view the gift was saved by the inclusion of potential after-born issue.[147] She also expressed the view that the basis for the selection of the class appeared to depend not so much on the degree of relationship to the testator but on the possibility of future need and suggested that this factor also influenced the court's decision that the gift was a charitable one.

The relaxation of the public benefit requirement in England has been extended to other categories or classes of persons and so trusts for 'poor employees'[148] and 'poor members'[149] have also been recognised despite the existence of some personal nexus between the donor or testator and those whom he seeks to benefit. However, the existence of the quality of poverty amongst those whom it is sought to benefit must be clear and trusts for employees have

146. [1972] AC 601.
147. [1996] Conv 379, 385.
148. The validity of such trusts was recognised in England in *Re Gosling* (1900) 48 WR 300. See also *Gibson v South American Stores (Gath & Chaves) Ltd* [1950] Ch 177.
149. *Spiller v Maude* (1881) 32 Ch D 158n (members of mutual benefit society); *Re Young* [1955] 1 WLR 1269 (members of a social club).

failed to qualify as charitable where this has not been evident.[150] So, in *Re Cullimore's Trusts*,[151] a trust for the benefit and maintenance of the families of employees of a firm was found not to be charitable. As Porter MR stated:

> Mere kindness, generosity, or benevolence on the testator's part is not enough to constitute a charitable purpose; there must also be an element of poverty or need on the part of the object, or else the gift must be dedicated to some purpose, such as education, religion or the like which the law regards as charitable. There is nothing here to show that the persons whom the testator meant to benefit were to be poor persons.[152]

However, the decision of the House of Lords in *Dingle v Turner*[153] clearly confirmed that trusts for the benefit of 'poor employees' will be recognised in England as valid charitable trusts.[154] The testator directed trustees to apply the income of a fund for the purpose of paying pensions to poor employees of a firm who were at least 60 years of age, or who were at least 45 years of age and incapacitated from earning a living, and the House of Lords upheld the gift as being a charitable trust. Lord Cross rejected the argument that the trust in the case before him should not be recognised as charitable despite the fact that the company was in some respects relatively small, employing around 600 people at the date of the testator's death. He stated:

> [T]he 'poor members' and 'poor employees' decisions were a natural development of the 'poor relations' decisions and to draw a distinction between different sorts of 'poverty' trusts would be quite illogical and could certainly not be said to be introducing 'greater harmony' into the law of charity. Moreover, though not as old as the 'poor relations' trusts, 'poor employees' trusts have been recognised as charities for many years; there are now a large number of such trusts in existence; and assuming, as one must, that they are properly administered in the sense that the benefits under them are only given to people who can fairly be said to

150. See *Re Drummond* [1914] 2 Ch 90, where a trust to provide for the holiday expenses of employees in a department in a certain company was found not to be charitable. See also *Re Hobourn Aero Components Ltd's Air Raid Distress Fund* [1946] Ch 194.
151. (1891) 27 LR Ir 18.
152. *Ibid.* at 24.
153. [1972] AC 601.
154. Note that in *Ulrich v Treasury Solicitor* [2006] 1 WLR 33, where the evidence was that the income of a trust for employees and widows and children of employees of named companies had always been applied for 'hardship' purposes, Hart J stated that he did not think that anyone could have complained if the trustees had from the outset regarded the trust as being one for the relief of poverty. In the circumstances he held that the trustees had regarded the trust as one for exclusively charitable purposes, even though non-charitable applications could also have been contemplated, and he declared that it had been validated by the Charitable Trusts (Validation) Act 1954.

be according to current standards, 'poor persons', to treat such trusts as charitable is not open to any practical objection.[155]

The principle laid down by Lord Cross is now well-established in England and has been extended to include poor members of a profession. In *Re Denison*[156] the High Court of Ontario found that a bequest for the relief of 'impoverished or indigent members of the Law Society [of Upper Canada] and of their wives and widows and children' was charitable. While the extension of the exception to the public benefit requirement in cases of this nature has been criticised,[157] it is submitted that it is too firmly entrenched to be overturned at this stage in England.

It should be noted that the preamble to the English Statute of Charitable Uses referred to 'the relief of aged, impotent and poor people'.[158] While it was recognised that these purposes were to be construed in a disjunctive manner,[159] prior to the coming into force of the Charities Act 2006 judges tended to consider them as being grouped under one heading.[160] In England, trusts for the aged and the sick were characterised as falling into the first rather than the fourth category in Lord Macnaghten's classification and some residual doubt remained about whether the exception to the public benefit requirement could be extended to such trusts. This question seems to have been settled by Carswell J in *Re Dunlop*,[161] where he stated that the House of Lords in *Dingle v Turner* intended to circumscribe the scope of the exception and 'to confine it to cases concerning the relief of actual poverty.'[162]

The courts in England have taken the view that it is unrealistic to enforce the requirement that there should be no personal tie or nexus between a donor or testator and the class of individuals which he seeks to benefit in this category, as the charitable gift will usually be motivated by this connection, and to enforce it strictly would not be practicable.[163] As the Charity Commissioners made clear

155. [1972] AC 601, 623.
156. (1974) 42 DLR (3d) 652.
157. E.g. by the Report of the Goodman Committee on Charity Law and Voluntary Organisations, Chapter II, para. 37.
158. The version contained in the Statute of Charitable Uses (Ireland) 1634 referred to 'the relief ... of poor, succourless, distressed or impotent persons'.
159. *Joseph Rowntree Memorial Trust Housing Association Ltd v Attorney General* [1983] Ch 159; *DV Bryant Trust Board v Hamilton City Council* [1997] 3 NZLR 342, 349.
160. Lord Simonds in *Oppenheim v Tobacco Securities Trust Co. Ltd* [1955] AC 297, 308.
161. [1984] NI 408. Considered in more detail *infra* pp. 453-454.
162. *Ibid.* at 424. The judgment of Carswell J, considered in more detail below, would suggest that while potential beneficiaries of trusts for the aged and the sick must constitute 'a particular section of the community at large', a less strict public benefit test is applied to such categories than that which he suggested should apply to the fourth category.
163. Although as Plowright comments (1975) 39 Conv 183, 187: 'there are limits to the acceptable width of class even within this exception beyond which the court will not allow that the trust can properly be regarded as a charitable trust, but will conclude

in *AITC Foundation's Application for Registration as a Charity*,[164] in assessing whether the class of beneficiaries constituted a section of the public, the purpose of the trust and its relationship to the size of the class were as relevant as the numerical size of the class. In addition, the Commissioners noted that in cases concerning the relief of poverty, a connection between beneficiaries was not determinative of the issue of public benefit.

However, given the growing unease surrounding the lack of rigour in enforcing the public benefit in that jurisdiction, there has been some uncertainty about whether the so-called poor relations/employees trusts had been affected by legislation.[165] In *Attorney General v Charity Commission for England and Wales*[166] the Upper Tribunal concluded that 'we do not think that the abolition of the presumption of public benefit in section 3(2) of the 2006 Act has had any impact on whether a trust for the relief of poverty is charitable or not.' Later in its judgment it commented as follows:

> In order that a trust for the relief of poverty with a narrow class of beneficiary should be charitable, the public benefit requirement *as applied to such a trust* required only that public benefit in the first sense be established. The 2006 Act has not, in our judgment, changed that.[167]

So, it seems clear that section 3(2) of the Act of 2006 and its successor, section 4(2) of the Act of 2011, have not had any impact on the way in which the public benefit aspect of the 'poor relations/employees' trusts are regarded by the courts.

The Upper Tribunal acknowledged in its judgment in *Attorney General v Charity Commission for England and Wales* that in the poverty cases, the class of potential direct beneficiaries may be very small and not sufficient to satisfy the public benefit requirement in the second sense of benefit to a section of the public.[168] It confirmed in answering the questions put to it, that trusts for the relief of poverty could be upheld as charitable even if confined to a restricted class defined by personal relationship or contract of employment.[169]

Rahmatian suggests that it is by no means impossible that the House of Lords may decide to overrule *Re Scarisbrick* and *Dingle v Turner*.[170] It is also difficult to disagree with the view that if the 'poor relations/employees'

---

that it is nothing more than a private trust. It is this … qualification that makes it unwise to assert that trusts for the relief of poverty form a complete exception to the requirement of public benefit.'

164. [2005] WTLR 1265.
165. As noted above, s.3(2) of the Charities Act 2006 and s.4(2) of the Charities Act 2011 provide that in determining whether the public benefit requirement has been met, 'it is not to be presumed that a purpose of a particular description is for the public benefit.'
166. [2012] UKUT 420 (TCC) at [39].
167. *Ibid.* at [64].
168. *Ibid.* at [43].
169. See the responses to questions 2.1 and 2.2 in the Annex to the judgment.
170. He refers to the *dicta* of Lord Cross in *Dingle v Turner* [1972] AC 601, 625 to the

exception were abolished and a unitary public benefit test adopted, the law would be more coherent.[171] As Lord Greene pointed out in *Re Compton*,[172] at the time the 'poor relations' exception was established, the essential nature of the public benefit requirement as we know it now was not clearly appreciated.[173] The anomalous treatment of trusts of this nature developed in an era of very different social conditions and political influences which have radically altered over the intervening years. So, while for the moment, this anomalous category of charitable trusts survives in England and Wales, this issue may well be revisited by the courts or in legislation in that jurisdiction.

Trusts for the Advancement of Education

Trusts for the advancement of education in the formal sense have long been recognised as charitable in nature,[174] and section 3(1)(b) of the Charities Act 2009 expressly provides that the advancement of education is a charitable purpose. It should also be noted that section 3(11)(k) of the Charities Act 2009 specifically provides that 'the advancement of the arts, culture, heritage or sciences' is included in the heading of purposes that are of benefit to the community, which should ensure that any gifts of this nature that are not found to come within the meaning of 'education' may still qualify as charitable in nature.

The concept of what is 'educational' in the sense of what will be recognised as legally charitable has been widened considerably by a process of judicial interpretation. A gift for the advancement of education in a general manner will be recognised as charitable; so a bequest for 'educational … purposes',[175] or a gift 'for the benefit, and advancement, and propagation of education and learning in every part of the world'[176] will be upheld. Similarly, a gift to schools,[177] or to colleges, either generally or to found a scholarship,[178] will be recognised as charitable under this heading. In addition, more recent authorities have established that the ambit of trusts recognised as being for the advancement

---

effect that the question of the validity of these trusts ought some day to be considered by the House of Lords.

171. See Sanders (2007) 10(2) CL & PR 33, 48. See also Warburton (2008) 10(3) CL & PR 1, 20. However, Lord Simonds' comments in *Oppenheim v Tobacco Securities Trust Ltd* [1951] AC 297, 309 to the effect that it would be unwise to cast doubt on well-established authorities in this area in order to introduce greater harmony into the law of charity as a whole should also be borne in mind.
172. [1945] Ch 123, 129.
173. See also Warburton (2008) 10(3) CL & PR 1, 15.
174. The Preamble to the Statute of Charitable Uses (Ireland) 1634 made reference to 'the erection, maintenance or support of any college, school, lecture in divinity, or on any of the liberal arts or sciences, the building, re-edifying, or maintaining in repair any college [or] school'.
175. *Re Ward* [1941] Ch 308.
176. *Whicker v Hume* (1858) 7 HLC 124.
177. *Incorporated Society v Richards* (1841) 4 Ir Eq R 177.
178. *R. v Newman* (1684) 1 Lev 284.

of education is not confined to those which are educational in the formal sense of the word.

In England it is possible to discern two distinct approaches to the question of what constitutes 'education'. A rather narrow view was taken by Harman J in *Re Shaw*,[179] which concerned a direction under the will of George Bernard Shaw that his trustees should use his residuary estate to provide for research, *inter alia*, into the advantages of reform of the alphabet. Harman J stated that 'if the object be merely the increase of knowledge that is not in itself a charitable object unless it be combined with teaching or education'.[180] He found that these latter elements were lacking in the case before him and also concluded that the objects were not beneficial to the community in a way regarded as charitable in law.

A more expansive interpretation of what should qualify as 'education' was put forward by Wilberforce J in *Re Hopkins' Will Trusts*,[181] where a gift to a society to be applied to the task of finding the Bacon-Shakespeare manuscripts was held to be a valid charitable trust. Wilberforce J stated:

> I think, therefore, that the word 'education' as used by Harman J in *Re Shaw* must be used in a wide sense, certainly extending beyond teaching, and that the requirement is that, in order to be charitable, research must either be of educational value to the researcher or must be directed as to lead to something which will pass into the store of educational material, or so as to improve the sum of communicable knowledge in an area which education may cover — education in this last context extending to the formation of literary taste and appreciation.[182]

Wilberforce J said that he would be unwilling to treat Harman J's words as meaning that the promotion of academic research is not a charitable purpose unless the researcher were engaged in teaching or education in the conventional sense. While he accepted that research of a purely private nature would not normally be educational, research of the character proposed in the case before him did not fall into this category as it was 'inherently inevitable and manifestly intended' that the results of such research should fall into the public domain. This point that education requires more than just the accumulation of knowledge and must involve some element of sharing or publication was reiterated by Buckley LJ in *Incorporated Council for Law Reporting for England and Wales v Attorney General*.[183] The majority of the Court of Appeal found that the activities of the council fell within the second head of Lord Macnaghten's

---

179. [1957] 1 WLR 729.
180. *Ibid.* at 737. See also *Re Macduff* [1896] 2 Ch 451, 472-3 *per* Rigby LJ.
181. [1965] Ch 669.
182. *Ibid.* at 680.
183. [1972] 1 Ch 73.

classification[184] and Buckley LJ commented in the course of his judgment that the concept of the advancement of education must extend 'to the improvement of a useful branch of human knowledge and its public dissemination'.[185]

In considering these divergent approaches in *Re Shaw* and *Re Hopkins* in *Re Worth Library*,[186] Keane J commented that the views of Harman J in *Re Shaw* might not command universal acceptance today and that it was possible that they would exclude from the legal definition of charity certain trusts for the encouragement of academic research which might reasonably be regarded as being for the public benefit. Keane J concluded by saying that if this was the likely interpretation of the views of Harman J, he would prefer those of Wilberforce J.

A closer examination of the judgment of Keane J in *Worth* confirms that he favoured an interpretation at the liberal end of the spectrum. In this important decision, the High Court was called upon to decide whether to approve a cy-près scheme proposed by the trustees of the 'Worth Library' which consisted of a bequest of a large and valuable collection of books originally made in the eighteenth century to Dr Steevens' Hospital in Dublin. When the hospital was closed in 1988, the trustees of the library decided to transfer the books temporarily to Trinity College, Dublin for safekeeping and appointed the college as trustees in their place.[187] The Eastern Health Board, which had purchased the hospital premises that year, took the view that the library should be returned to its original location and when the Attorney General gave his consent to the trustees' application to the High Court for an order framing a cy-près scheme,[188] the board was joined as a defendant to the proceedings. At the outset of legal arguments in the case, Keane J indicated to counsel for the various parties the fundamental issues which he felt required resolution, namely the question of whether the initial bequest of the Worth Library was in law a charitable trust, and if so, the type of charitable bequest which it represented. If this first question was answered in the affirmative, the court would then proceed to consider whether the conditions necessary for the exercise of its cy-près jurisdiction had been satisfied and decide what form of scheme should be approved. In considering the first submission of counsel on behalf of the plaintiff, that the initial bequest should qualify as being for the advancement of education, Keane J made the following general statement:

> [G]ifts for the advancement of education … would embrace, not merely

184. Sachs and Buckley LJJ. Russell LJ found that the purposes were charitable under the fourth heading alone.
185. [1972] 1 Ch 73, 102.
186. [1995] 2 IR 301, 337.
187. The Attorney General took the view that an appropriately qualified independent person should also be appointed as a trustee and the Director of the National Library agreed to act in that capacity.
188. As he was required to do by s. 51(1) of the Irish Charities Act 1961.

> gifts to schools and universities and the endowment of university chairs and scholarships: 'education' has been given a broad meaning so as to encompass gifts for the establishment of theatres, art galleries and museums and the promotion of literature and music. In every case, however, the element of public benefit must be present and, if the benefit extends to a section of the community only, that section must not be numerically negligible.[189]

Keane J rejected the argument that the trust might qualify as being one for the advancement of education on the basis of the lack of an element of public benefit. However it is interesting to note that he stated that in any event a finding that the library was for educational purposes would involve 'some straining of the concept of "education" even beyond the liberal limits of the modern decisions', given the insignificant portion of the library devoted to topics of medical interest.

A broad approach towards the meaning of 'educational' in this context was also adopted by Lavan J in *Magee v Attorney General*,[190] which concerned a cy-près application. Having referred to the *dicta* of Keane J in *Re Worth Library*[191] to the effect that the word 'education' has been given a broad meaning and to the words of Vaisey J in *Re Shaw's Will Trusts*[192] set out above, Lavan J stated that: 'these … sentiments tend to confer a stamp of approval on attempts to contribute to the betterment of a class of persons or a community, even if not in a classroom setting.'[193] He concluded that the activities carried on in the local community hall, which largely consisted of the running of a number of self-help groups, must be deemed to be 'educational' in nature.

A number of decisions have illustrated that the ambit of education for this purpose is not limited to education of the mind and extends to the physical education of those attending a school or college. So, in *IRC v McMullen*[194] the House of Lords upheld as charitable under this heading a trust 'to organise or provide or assist in the organisation or provision of facilities which will enable and encourage pupils at schools and universities in any part of the United Kingdom to play association football and other games or sports and thereby to assist in ensuring that due attention is given to the physical education and development of their minds'.

Similarly, the concept of education has been found to extend to aesthetic education and to such purposes as the support of museums[195] and the promotion

189. [1995] 2 IR 301, 336.
190. [2002] IEHC 87.
191. [1995] 2 IR 301, 337.
192. [1952] Ch 163, 172.
193. [2002] IEHC 87, 24.
194. [1981] AC 1. See also *Re Mariette* [1915] 2 Ch 284.
195. *British Museum v White* (1826) 2 Sim & St 594.

of an appreciation of art[196] and music.[197] In *Re Shaw's Will Trusts*[198] Vaisey J upheld the validity of a gift for 'bringing the masterpieces of fine art within the reach of the people of Ireland of all classes in their own country', and stated that he thought that 'education' included 'not only teaching, but the promotion and encouragement of those arts and graces of life which are after all, perhaps the finest and best part of the human character.'[199] In *Royal Choral Society v IRC*[200] the English Court of Appeal upheld a trust to promote the performance of choral works. Lord Greene MR said that he disagreed with the narrow conception of education as meaning a teacher instructing a class and concluded that in his opinion, 'a body of persons established for the purpose of raising the artistic state of the country … is established for educational purposes.'[201]

Gifts to professional bodies can qualify as being for the advancement of education provided that their objects are truly educational in nature rather than being the promotion of the status of the profession or the safeguarding of the welfare of its members. However, in practice such bodies and associations will frequently have ancillary objects which fall into the latter category. In *Miley v Attorney General for Ireland*[202] the Irish Court of Appeal was required to determine whether a legacy to the Royal College of Surgeons in Ireland was one for 'charitable uses' within the meaning of section 16 of the Charitable Donations and Bequests Act 1844.[203] The court found that there were two main objects contemplated by the charter of the college, one being the promotion of the science of surgery, and the other being the regulation of the profession and the promotion of the interests of those practising it. The court concluded that the latter object was not a charitable one and that as the testatrix had not impressed her gift with a charitable purpose, the bequest should not be considered to be one for 'charitable uses' within the meaning of section 16 of the Act of 1844.

However, the courts in England have tended to take a more pragmatic approach to this issue by adopting reasoning well summarised by Greer LJ in *Geologists Association v IRC*:[204]

---

196. *Re Shaw's Will Trusts* [1952] Ch 163.
197. *Re Delius* [1957] Ch 299.
198. [1952] Ch 163.
199. *Ibid.* at 172.
200. [1943] 2 All ER 101.
201. *Ibid.* at 105.
202. [1918] 1 IR 455.
203. Section 16 (now repealed by the Charities Act 1961) rendered void gifts of land for charitable uses unless the instrument conferring the gift was executed at least three months prior to the death of the donor. The testatrix had died four days after the execution of her will and therefore the validity of her bequest, which would have been payable partly out of realty, would have been affected by the provisions of s. 16 if it had been found to be charitable in nature.
204. (1928) 14 TC 271, 283. See also *Royal College of Nursing v St Marylebone Borough Council* [1959] 1 WLR 1077, 1085.

> If you come to the conclusion, as you may in many cases, that one of the ways in which the public objects of an association can be served is by giving special advantages to the members of the association, then the association does not cease to be an association with a charitable object because incidentally and in order to carry out the charitable object it is both necessary and desirable to confer special benefits upon the members.

A similar principle was applied by the House of Lords in *Royal College of Surgeons of England v National Provincial Bank Ltd.*[205] It was held that the main object of the college was the promotion and encouragement of the study and practice of surgery and that the professional protection of its members was ancillary to this overall objective and did not alter the charitable status of the college.

It can be said with a fair degree of certainty that the decision of the Irish Court of Appeal in *Miley* is now unlikely to be followed for a number of reasons. First, the surrounding circumstances of the case and the consequences of a finding of charitable status to the outcome must be borne in mind. Secondly, the court laid considerable emphasis on the earlier English decision in *Re Royal College of Surgeons of England*,[206] which was subsequently distinguished by the House of Lords in *Royal College of Surgeons of England v National Provincial Bank Ltd.* In any event, legislation would seem to have resolved the question in a manner which should ensure that the decision in *Miley* would not now be followed. As noted above, section 49(1) of Charities Act 1961 provides that where the purposes of a gift include charitable and non-charitable objects, its terms will be construed so as to exclude the non-charitable objects. On this basis gifts such as that considered in *Miley* would probably be interpreted in such a way that they would be applied solely in furtherance of the charitable purposes of such a professional body.

The Element of Public Benefit

It is well-established that a gift for the advancement of education will only qualify as charitable provided that it is for the benefit of the public generally or of an 'appreciably important class'[207] of the public. This principle was stressed in *Re Compton*,[208] in which the Court of Appeal held that a trust for the education of the descendants of three named individuals was not a valid charitable trust. As Lord Greene MR stated, 'a gift under which the beneficiaries are defined by reference to a purely personal relationship to a named *propositus* cannot on

205. [1952] AC 631.
206. [1899] 1 QB 871.
207. *Verge v Sommerville* [1924] AC 496, 499 *per* Lord Westbury.
208. [1945] Ch 123. See also *Re Hobourn Aero Components Ltd's Air Raid Distress Fund* [1946] Ch 86.

principle be a valid charitable gift.'[209] So, in England,[210] it will still be easier for a trust to qualify as charitable in nature if is construed as being for the relief of poverty rather than the advancement of education.[211]

The courts both in this jurisdiction and in England have tended to be consistent in rejecting a claim to charitable status on the basis of the purpose of the advancement of education where there is a personal connection between the donor and the intended beneficiaries and to this extent the provisions of section 3(8) of the Charities Act 2009 are unlikely to effect any real change in practice here. As can be seen from a review of the relevant case law in both jurisdictions, the key issues are that the number of potential beneficiaries must not be numerically negligible and their membership of the class must not depend on their relationship to a particular individual. While the provisions of the 2009 Act focus on the second requirement, there is no reason to believe that the courts in this jurisdiction will depart from the *dicta* of Keane J in *Re Worth Library*[212] to the effect that the section of the community to benefit must not be 'numerically negligible' if the trust is to qualify as charitable under this heading.

One element of the Act of 2009 which may lead to a stricter approach being taken in this context in future is section 3(7)(b) which provides that in determining whether a gift is of public benefit, account shall be taken of 'the amount of any charge payable for any service provided in furtherance of the purpose for which the gift is given.' While a considerable number of private fee-paying schools in this jurisdiction continue to enjoy charitable status, as Keane points out, 'it may prove difficult for fee-paying schools to demonstrate that they provide access to a sufficient proportion of the public to justify their educational role being described as for the public benefit.' On this basis the reasoning set out by the Upper Tribunal in *R. (Independent Schools Council) v Charity Commission for England and Wales*,[213] considered below, is likely to become relevant in this jurisdiction too and such schools may be expected to do more in terms of providing scholarships and bursaries and promoting wider access if they are to retain their charitable status.

One of the most important English authorities in this area is the decision of the House of Lords in *Oppenheim v Tobacco Securities Trust Co. Ltd*,[214]

---

209. *Ibid.* at 131.
210. This distinction is no longer relevant in this jurisdiction as a result of the provisions of ss. 3(7) and (8) of the Charities Act 2009 which apply to both classes of trust.
211. In *Cawdron v Merchants Taylors' School* [2009] EWHC 1722 (Ch) Blackburne J concluded that the provision of financial assistance to dependent relatives of old boys of a school killed or disabled in the First World War to pay fees at the school was a charitable purpose for the relief of poverty and that the issue of whether the class of potential beneficiaries constituted a sufficient section of the public did not therefore arise.
212. [1995] 2 IR 301, 336.
213. [2012] Ch 214, 294. See further Synge (2012) 75 MLR 624; Sloan [2012] CLJ 45; Mullender (2012) 128 LQR 188; Jaconelli [2013] Conv 96.
214. [1951] AC 297.

which concerned the validity of a trust set up to provide for the education of the children of employees or former employees of a tobacco company and its subsidiaries. Despite the fact that the number of such employees exceeded 110,000 at the date of the settlement, it was held that the trust must fail as the distinguishing quality of the class of beneficiaries was a relationship with a named *propositus* and for this reason they could not constitute a section of the public. Lord Simonds stated as follows:

> These words 'section of the community' have no special sanctity, but they conveniently indicate first, that the possible (I emphasise the word 'possible') beneficiaries must not be numerically negligible, and secondly, that the quality which distinguishes them from other members of the community, so that they form by themselves a section of it, must be a quality which does not depend on their relationship to a particular individual.[215]

Lord MacDermott in his dissenting judgment considered that the '*Compton* test',[216] while it might often prove of value could equally, if a personal or impersonal relationship remained the criterion, prove to be 'a very arbitrary and artificial rule'. The reasoning of the majority in *Oppenheim* has not met with universal approval[217] and the decision of Lord Cross in *Dingle v Turner*[218] shows an element of empathy with the views expressed by Lord MacDermott. In the view of Lord Cross the question of whether the beneficiaries under a trust constitute a section of the community is essentially one of degree and cannot of itself prove decisive in determining whether the trust is charitable in nature.[219] A further important reason for questioning the validity of the majority view in *Oppenheim* put forward by Lord Cross in *Dingle v Turner* was his view that the decisions in both *Compton* and *Oppenheim* appeared to him to have been 'pretty obviously influenced by considerations of a perceived undeserved fiscal immunity which would be the result of a finding of charitable status.' Such concerns can also be seen to lie behind the comments made by Harman LJ in the course of his judgment in *IRC v Educational Grants Association*[220] that 'it is an admirable thing that the children of employees should have a higher education, but I do not see why it should be at the expense of the taxpayer.'

This issue was also referred to by the Upper Tribunal in its judgment in *R.*

---

215. *Ibid.* at 306.
216. See *supra* n. 209.
217. See, e.g. the comments of Blanchard J in the decision of the New Zealand Court of Appeal in *Latimer v Commissioner of Inland Revenue* [2002] 3 NZLR 195.
218. [1972] AC 601.
219. It is interesting to note that Lord Simonds in *Oppenheim* criticised the dissenting judgment of Lord MacDermott for the very reason that it made the question one of degree; an objection which Geoffrey Cross QC (later Lord Cross) writing in (1956) 72 LQR 189-190 said was not an objection which he believed to be very cogent.
220. [1967] Ch 993, 1013.

(Independent Schools Council) v Charity Commission for England and Wales[221] in the following terms:

> [P]olitical debates must have political conclusions, and it should not be expected of the judicial process that it should resolve the conflict between deeply held views. We venture to think, however, that the political issue is not really about whether private schools should be charities as understood in legal terms but whether they should have the benefit of the fiscal advantages which Parliament has seen right to grant to charities. It is for Parliament to grapple with this issue.

It also suggested that 'the fact that fiscal privileges are given underlines the need for genuine public benefit'.[222] In this case the Upper Tribunal addressed a wide range of issues relating to the public benefit requirement in the context of trusts for the advancement of education.[223] The decision and the consequent changes to the guidance of the Charity Commission[224] have been the subject of considerable academic debate.[225] The Upper Tribunal expressed the view that the Charities Act 2006 made little, if any, difference to the legal position of the independent schools sector. The question it had to consider was whether the public benefit in the first sense which the provision of education gives was outweighed by disbenefits arising from the charging of fees. It made it clear that there is no requirement in considering the public benefit in the second sense that all beneficiaries or potential beneficiaries of a charitable purpose should be poor unless the purpose is itself the relief of poverty, although it acknowledged that a trust which excluded the poor from benefiting could not be charitable in nature. The Upper Tribunal concluded that a hypothetical school, which had as its sole object the advancement of the education of children whose families could afford to pay fees, did not have purposes which provided the element of public benefit necessary to qualify as a charity. In its view the primary focus in considering whether a school was operating for the public benefit had to be on the direct benefits it provided, such as scholarships or other forms of direct assistance but it was permissible to take into account indirect or wider benefits as a result of the particular way in which the educational object was carried out by a particular school. It stated as follows:

221. [2012] Ch 214, 294. See further Synge (2012) 75 MLR 624; Sloan [2012] CLJ 45; Mullender (2012) 128 LQR 188; Jaconelli [2013] Conv 96.
222. *Ibid.* at 273.
223. The proceedings involved an application for judicial review of guidance issued by the Charity Commission for England and Wales and a reference by the Attorney General comprising a series of specific questions about the operation of charity law in relation to a hypothetical independent school.
224. Now see Charity Commission Guidance, *Public Benefit: The Public Benefit Requirement* (September 2013).
225. See e.g. Synge (2012) 75 MLR 624; Sloan [2012] CLJ 45; Mullender (2012) 128 LQR 188.

> Nobody has suggested that fee-paying schools are not entitled to charitable status provided that they do enough to promote access whether by way of scholarships, bursaries or other provision, but paying regard to the need to charge fees to operate at all. Nobody complains that the schools are educating fee-paying students; the concern is that they must be seen to be doing enough for those who cannot afford fees.[226]

In the view of the Upper Tribunal it was not possible to be prescriptive about the nature of the benefits which a school must provide to the poor nor the extent of them and it was for the charity trustees of the school to address how their obligations might best be fulfilled in the context of their own particular circumstances.

Prior to the coming into force of the Charities Act 2009, there was no evidence in any decisions made by the courts in this jurisdiction of a more relaxed attitude being applied towards this question of public benefit in the context of trusts for the advancement of education, although it should be pointed out that the authorities here involved a considerably smaller number of potential beneficiaries than in *Oppenheim*. In *Re McEnery*[227] Gavan Duffy J concluded that a bequest to enable the nephews and nieces of the testator and their male descendants to obtain professions was too narrow in scope to be charitable and that the intention of the testator was to benefit specific individuals. As he stated, 'Courts of Equity generally have been consistently insistent on the public character of legal charity, importing a benefit to the community, or a section of the community.'[228]

When the question came before Keane J in *Re Worth Library*, he had no hesitation in finding that the trust could not qualify as being for the advancement of education as the library was clearly expressed to be for the use and benefit of three named office holders in the hospital alone. It is to an extent unfortunate that the question of whether a gift framed in slightly wider terms might have satisfied this requirement did not arise for consideration. Keane J nevertheless expressed some views on the issue which are of relevance. He commented that, in the context of trusts for the advancement of education, 'in every case ... the element of public benefit must be present and, if the benefit extends to a section of the community only, that section must not be numerically negligible.'[229]

The effect of a consistently strict approach to the public benefit test in this category of charitable trust has been mitigated to a limited degree by what are sometimes referred to as the 'founder's kin' decisions. So, while a trust simply to educate a donor's relatives would not qualify as being charitable in nature,[230] a gift to an educational institution which contained a direction that preference

226. [2012] Ch 214, 282.
227. [1941] IR 323.
228. *Ibid.* at 326.
229. [1995] 2 IR 301, 336.
230. E.g. *Re McEnery* [1941] IR 323.

be given to the 'founder's kin' might constitute a charitable trust. The effect of this principle was summarised in a general context as follows by Atiyah:[231]

> Where there is a charitable trust for the benefit of a section of the community the trust is not invalidated because the trustees are directed to give preference to certain beneficiaries who would not by themselves have constituted a section of the community.

This principle would seem to be supported by two English decisions, *Spencer v All Souls' College*[232] and *Attorney General v Sidney Sussex College*.[233] It was also given recognition by Upjohn J in *Re Koettgen's Will Trusts*,[234] where a trust established to further the commercial education of British born persons, which included a direction that preference be given to employees of a particular firm, was upheld as charitable. However, subsequently in *Caffoor v Commissioner of Income Tax, Columbo*,[235] the Privy Council showed a reluctance to adopt such an approach and found that the trust before them conferred such a priority on the donor's own relatives and descendants that 'the only fair way to describe [it was] as a family trust'.[236] Lord Radcliffe commented that *Koettgen* 'edges very near to being inconsistent with *Oppenheim*'[237] and Atiyah similarly comments that the decision of Upjohn J 'opens the way to serious evasion of the *Oppenheim* ruling'.[238]

In this jurisdiction an example of a particularly liberal construction of the founder's kin principle is the decision of O'Connor MR in *Re Lavelle*,[239] in which he upheld a bequest to a college which contained a direction that the income should be used to educate the testator's relatives there. While the facts of this case arguably fit within the 'founder's kin' exception established in the cases referred to above, the decision was one which should have been regarded with a degree of caution even before the coming into force of the Charities Act 2009. In the course of his judgment O'Connor MR stated that 'gifts for the advancement of education are undoubtedly charitable and it has been decided that bequests for the education of the donor's descendants and kinsmen are also charitable', referring to the English authorities. This is misleading and as Lord Greene MR made clear in *Re Compton*,[240] if a gift were to come within this limited exception, the primary object of the donor must be to endow a

231. (1958) 21 MLR 138, 148.
232. (1762) Wilm 163.
233. (1869) LR 4 Ch App 722.
234. [1954] Ch 252.
235. [1961] AC 584.
236. *Ibid.* at 603.
237. *Ibid.* at 604. See also *IRC v Educational Grants Association Ltd* [1967] Ch 993, 1010 *per* Lord Denning MR.
238. (1958) 21 MLR 138, 148.
239. [1914] 1 IR 194.
240. [1945] Ch 123, 132.

college for educational purposes and the preference afforded to his own family must be 'merely a method of giving effect to this intention'. This issue was also considered by Barton J in *Laverty v Laverty*,[241] who stated *obiter* that in his opinion 'a valid charitable trust might be created for the advancement of education, with a preference for persons of a particular surname, either by the endowment of, or gift to, a school or college or by a gift, as in the present case, to trustees, if sufficiently definite.'[242] However, on the facts of the case before him, Barton J held that, having regard to the discretion vested in the trustees, a gift for the support and education in Ireland of Roman Catholic boys and men with specified surnames was not charitable in nature as it 'might have been intended to work, as a mere matter of private bounty' and might have been used for 'support' and not just 'education'.

On the basis that the comments of O'Connor MR in *Re Lavelle* do not seem to be supported by the authorities on which he placed reliance, and having regard to the fact that Barton J's suggestion in *Laverty* was merely *obiter*, some doubt must have surrounded the validity of the 'founder's kin' exception in this jurisdiction, although such trusts were likely to be valid provided that the gift was expressed in the terms suggested by Lord Greene in *Re Compton*. However, the coming into effect of sections 3(7) and (8) of the Charities Act 2009 means that these founder's kin trusts are now unlikely to be regarded as charitable. Wording such as that employed in *Lavelle* is likely to be regarded as a 'limitation' on the class who might benefit which is not 'justified and reasonable'. While a broadly drafted founder's kin clause might arguably still fall within the reasoning in *Re Compton* outlined above, where a testator's close relatives, namely those coming within the scope of the 'personal connection' definition in section 2 of the Act of 2009 are included, the limiting provisions will not be considered justified and reasonable and the trust will not be charitable.

Trusts for the Advancement of Religion

Introduction

Trusts purporting to fall into this category have been numerous in this jurisdiction in the past and the historical aspect of these trusts in particular has been well charted elsewhere.[243] Legislative intervention has helped to clarify what had been a most complex and uncertain area of the law which, until comparatively recently, was notable for the significant divergences which existed between the attitudes adopted in England and in this jurisdiction in relation to certain

241. [1907] 1 IR 9.
242. *Ibid.* at 13.
243. Delany, *The Law Relating to Charities in Ireland* (1957) and Brady, *Religion and the Law of Charities in Ireland* (1976).

types of trusts which fall into this category.[244] It should be noted that section 3(4) of the Charities Act 2009 provides that '[i]t shall be presumed, unless the contrary is proved, that a gift for the advancement of religion is of public benefit'. This continues the presumption of public benefit originally provided for by section 45(1) of the Charities Act 1961, although this presumption is no longer conclusive.[245] Section 3(5) provides that the Charities Regulatory Authority shall not make a determination that a gift for the advancement of religion is not of public benefit without the consent of the Attorney General. In addition, section 3(6) provides that a charitable gift for the purpose of the advancement of religion shall have effect and shall be construed 'in accordance with the laws, canons, ordinances and tenets of the religion concerned'.

The advancement of religion has been described by Lord Hanworth MR in *Keren Kayemeth Le Jisroel Ltd v IRC*[246] as 'the promotion of spiritual teaching in a wide sense, and the maintenance of the doctrines on which it rests and the observances that serve to promote and manifest it ....' Certainly in England the judiciary has not tended to prefer one religion to another in determining the question of whether a trust falls into this category,[247] and as Cross J has commented, '[a]s between different religions, the law stands neutral, but it assumes that any religion is at least better than none'.[248] An examination of more recent authorities would suggest that judicial attitudes are becoming increasingly flexible and that, provided the religion in question is considered to be *bona fide*, the limited nature of its support or following will not preclude it from qualifying for charitable status.[249]

The predominant view in common law jurisdictions is that it is not necessary that a religion be monotheistic in this context,[250] and it is likely that the courts in this jurisdiction will take a similarly progressive approach. Certainly, Walsh J made it clear in *Quinn's Supermarket v Attorney General*[251] that, despite the references to the Christian nature of the State in Article 44 of the Constitution, religion is not confined to the Christian faith. In his view Article 44 expressly recognises the separate co-existence of different religious denominations. As he

244. For analysis of the current position in that jurisdiction, see Harding (2008) 71 MLR 159; Iwobi (2009) 29 LS 619.
245. Section 45(1) of the Charities Act 1961 provided that: '[i]n determining whether or not a gift for the purpose of the advancement of religion is a valid charitable gift it shall be conclusively presumed that the purpose includes and will occasion public benefit.' It was repealed by s.11 and Schedule 2 of the Charities Act 2009.
246. [1931] 2 KB 465, 477. See also the *dicta* of Donovan J in *United Grand Lodge of Ancient Free and Accepted Masons of England v Holborn Borough Council* [1957] 1 WLR 1080, 1090.
247. See *Gilmour v Coats* [1949] AC 426, 458-459 *per* Lord Reid.
248. *Neville Estates Ltd v Madden* [1962] Ch 832, 853.
249. *Re Watson* [1973] 1 WLR 1472; *Centrepoint Community Growth Trust v Commissioner of Inland Revenue* [1985] 1 NZLR 673.
250. Despite the views expressed by Lord Parker in *Bowman v Secular Society* [1917] AC 406, 449. See further Edge and Loughrey (2001) 21 LS 36, 38-40.
251. [1972] IR 1.

stated, 'it does not prefer one to the other and it does not confer any privilege or impose any disability or diminution of status upon any religious denomination, and it does not permit the State to do so.'[252]

In England, section 3(2)(a) of the Charities Act 2011 now provides that "'religion' includes (i) a religion which involves belief in more than one god, and (ii) a religion which does not involve belief in a god.' This has led Lord Toulson to comment in *R. (Hodkin) v Registrar General of Births, Deaths and Marriages*[253] that 'the understanding of religion in today's society is broad', although it should be noted that the case arose in a context outside the scope of the law relating to charities.

A limitation is placed on what may be treated as a gift for the advancement of religion by section 3(10) of the Charities Act 2009 which provides that a gift cannot qualify under this heading if it is made to or for the benefit of an organisation or cult the principal object of which is the making of profit or that employs oppressive psychological manipulation of its followers or for the purpose of gaining new followers.

Gifts in General Terms

A gift for 'religious purposes' has been held to be charitable on the basis that this will *prima facie* mean charitable purposes unless the context suggests otherwise. As O'Connor MR stated in *Arnott v Arnott (No. 2)*,[254] it has been held that 'a gift for religious purposes and not more will be construed by the court as confined to such religious purposes as are in their nature charitable.' On the basis of this reasoning, it had been argued that a gift for 'charitable or religious purposes' should fail on the grounds that the use of the word 'charitable' shows that the word 'religious' means something distinct from charitable.[255] However, such an interpretation has been rejected in this jurisdiction and it was held by Barton J in *Re Salter*[256] that a gift framed in these terms will be charitable in nature. This can be distinguished from the wording employed in *Re Davidson*,[257] where a gift for 'charitable, religious or other societies, institutions, persons or objects' was found not to be charitable on the grounds that the words 'or other societies' would have enabled the trustees to apply the gift to societies or institutions which were neither charitable nor religious in character. A gift confined to a

---

252. *Ibid.* at 23. Quoted with approval by Barrington J in *Corway v Independent Newspapers (Ireland) Ltd* [1999] 4 IR 484, 502.
253. [2014] AC 610, 627.
254. [1906] 1 IR 127, 134. See also the *dictum* of Ross J in *Rickerby v Nicholson* [1912] 1 IR 343, 347 that 'according to our law a bequest for a religious purpose is *prima facie* charitable'.
255. See *Rickerby v Nicholson* [1912] 1 IR 343, 348. See also *Grimond v Grimond* [1905] AC 124 which relates to an interpretation of Scots law.
256. [1911] 1 IR 289. See also *Rickerby v Nicholson* [1912] 1 IR 343; *Re Lloyd* (1893) 10 TLR 66.
257. [1909] 1 Ch 567.

specified religion may also be charitable, so in *Copinger v Crehane*,[258] a gift for 'the advancement and benefit of the Roman Catholic religion' was upheld as a valid charitable bequest on the grounds that its terms limited it strictly and exclusively to charitable purposes. The test in determining the validity of such bequests would appear to be that laid down by Grant MR in *Morice v Bishop of Durham*,[259] which was summarised as follows by Chatterton VC in *Copinger*:[260] '[W]here the trustee is bound to apply the bequest to charitable purposes, the bequest shall not fail on account of the uncertainty of the object, but … where there is a discretion to apply it to charitable purposes or to other purposes not charitable, and the trust is indefinite, the gift fails.'

The latter interpretation was placed on a bequest for 'such Roman Catholic purposes in the parish of Coleraine and elsewhere' as the trustees might deem proper by the Irish Court of Appeal in *MacLaughlin v Campbell*,[261] and the gift was held to be void on the basis that it might be applied for a purpose other than a charitable one. The distinction is a fine one as the *dictum* of Fitzgibbon LJ makes clear:

> If the gift were made to 'the Church' e.g. the 'Church of Rome' or the 'Church of Ireland', I should think that it would import — at least *prima facie* — the operative institution which ministered religion and gave spiritual edification to its members; a gift in such terms would exclude objects which would be included in a gift for the 'purposes' of the individual members of a religious body.[262]

A bequest to 'the Christian Brethren' has been upheld as charitable,[263] as has a gift to 'foreign missions',[264] and 'to Presbyterian missions and orphans'.[265] However, a gift for 'missionary purposes' was held by Sullivan MR in *Scott v Brownrigg*[266] to be too vague and wide to be upheld, although it would appear that where there is sufficient evidence to connect the words 'purposes' or 'objects' with the preaching of religion, such a gift may be charitable.[267]

Gifts to Ecclesiastical Office Holders

It would appear that a gift for the benefit of the incumbent of an ecclesiastical

258. (1877) LR 11 Eq 429.
259. (1804) 9 Ves 399.
260. (1877) LR 11 Eq 429, 431.
261. [1906] 1 IR 588.
262. *Ibid.* at 597.
263. *Re Brown* [1898] 1 IR 423.
264. *Dunne v Duignan* [1908] 1 IR 228.
265. *Jackson v Attorney General* [1917] 1 IR 332.
266. (1881) 9 LR Ir 246.
267. *Re Kenny* (1907) 97 LT 130; *Re Rees* [1920] 2 Ch 59. See also *Jackson v Attorney General* [1917] 1 IR 332, 335.

office for the time being is charitable, whereas a gift for the particular individual who happens to hold that office at the time of the gift will not be. So, in *Gibson v Representative Church Body*[268] a bequest to the chaplain of the Rotunda chapel at the time of the testatrix's death and his successors was upheld as charitable. This can be contrasted with a separate gift in a codicil to the testatrix's will to the chaplain for his own personal use and with the decision in *Donnellan v O'Neill*,[269] in which a bequest to a cardinal absolutely for his own use and benefit was held to be a gift to the latter in his private capacity and not to be charitable in nature. The test was described by Kindersley VC in *Thornber v Wilson*[270] as being 'whether the testator designates the individual as such, or as being the person who happens to fill the office'.

So, a gift to a minister for the time being or to a minister for the time being and his successors without more will be considered charitable in nature on the basis that the character of the office-holder is such that it is inevitable that he will apply the gift for strictly charitable purposes. As Cozens-Hardy MR stated in *Re Davidson*,[271] while a court does not hold a trust charitable merely because the trustee has a religious office, 'if you find in a will words indicating that a distribution is to be made by persons in succession as holders of a particular religious or charitable office, that goes far to establish — and, it may be, goes sufficiently far to establish — the fact that the whole gift is charitable.' So, in *Reddy v Fitzmaurice*,[272] a residuary gift to a bishop for the time being and his successors without any further words of qualification was interpreted as being of a charitable nature. However, where additional words were attached to the gift which indicated the trusts on which the donee was to hold the property, the gift would fail at common law if the purposes could be construed as not being exclusively charitable ones.

A gift to an ecclesiastical office-holder followed by words which did no more than confer a complete discretion on him or impose a specific limitation which fell within the scope of the charitable nature of his office would be charitable. This is illustrated by the decision of Joyce J in *Re Garrard*,[273] where a gift to the vicar and churchwardens for the time being of a certain parish 'to be applied by them in such manner as they shall in their sole discretion think fit' was upheld as a valid charitable gift. Similarly, in *Halpin v Hannon*[274] a bequest to a named priest or his successor 'for such purposes in the diocese as he wishes'

268. (1881) 9 LR Ir 1. See also *Robb v Dorrian* (1877) IR 11 CL 292; *Re Corcoran* [1913] 1 IR 1.
269. (1870) IR 5 Eq 523.
270. (1858) 4 Dr 350, 351. Quoted with approval by Barton J in *Re Corcoran* [1913] 1 IR 1, 6.
271. [1909] 1 Ch 567, 569. Quoted by Gavan Duffy J in *Re Howley* [1940] IR 109. See also the *dicta* of Black J in *Halpin v Hannon* (1947) 82 ILTR 74, 77.
272. (1952) 86 ILTR 127.
273. [1907] 1 Ch 382. See also *Re Flinn* [1948] Ch 241; *Re Rumball* [1956] Ch 105.
274. (1947) 82 ILTR 74.

was found to be charitable. In the course of his judgment, after a consideration of some of the English authorities, Maguire CJ is reported as saying:

> From these decisions it was clear that it was necessary to distinguish the case where a gift to the holder of a religious office was followed by words which made it clear that the gift might be applied to non-charitable purposes and that such was the testator's intention, and cases where later words do not clearly indicate an intention to widen a field of selection so as to include non-charitable objects.[275]

However, where the words of qualification are wide enough to include purposes which might not be charitable in law, the position at common law was that the gift must fail, notwithstanding the charitable nature of the office generally. This proposition was established in a number of cases including *Dunne v Byrne*,[276] where a residuary bequest to an archbishop and his successors to be applied wholly or in part as the archbishop might judge 'most conducive to the good of religion' in the diocese was held by the Privy Council to be void. Similarly, in *Farley v Westminster Bank*[277] the House of Lords held that a gift to the vicar and churchwardens of a parish for 'parish work' was too wide to be valid.

Therefore, unless the gift was given in unqualified terms or on trusts which were unequivocally charitable in nature, the gift might fail. It is likely that the provisions of section 49(1) of the Charities Act 1961 which provides that 'where any of the purposes of a gift include, or could be deemed to include, both charitable and non-charitable objects, its terms shall be so construed and given effect to as to exclude the non-charitable objects and the purpose shall, accordingly, be treated as charitable' may now have resolved this problem of construction.

Gifts for the Celebration of Masses

Delany commented more than 60 years ago that '[s]o much property is devoted to this type of gift in Ireland that it has become by far the most common object of benevolence.'[278] This statement may be less accurate today but gifts of this nature have certainly led to an extensive amount of litigation over the last century. The charitable nature of such gifts was confirmed by section 45(2) of the Charities Act 1961,[279] but it is an area which for a long time provoked considerable uncertainty and controversy.

Historically, the legal principles applicable differed considerably between

275. *Ibid.* at 75.
276. [1912] AC 407. See also *Re Davidson* [1909] 1 Ch 567.
277. [1939] AC 430. However, note that this decision was distinguished by Romer J in *Re Simson* [1946] Ch 299.
278. Delany, *The Law Relating to Charities in Ireland* (1957) p. 53.
279. Now repealed by s.11 and Schedule 2 of the Charities Act 2009.

England and Ireland. The legality of such gifts was doubtful in England as a result of the interpretation placed on the Statute of Chantries 1547 but a majority of the House of Lords held in *Bourne v Keane*[280] that gifts for the saying of masses were not illegal without holding that they were charitable bequests. Subsequently, in *Re Caus*,[281] Luxmoore J held that such gifts were charitable, although the findings of the House of Lords in *Gilmour v Coats*[282] led to doubts being expressed about the validity of this decision. However, more recently in *Re Hetherington*,[283] Browne-Wilkinson VC confirmed that a gift for the saying of masses is *prima facie* charitable since it is for a religious purpose and contained the necessary element of public benefit because in practice the masses would be celebrated in public. While he stressed that the celebration of a religious rite in private would not contain this essential public element, the Vice Chancellor made it clear that where either construction was possible, the gift was to be construed as one to be carried out only by charitable means, *viz.*, celebrated in public.

In Ireland the Statute of Chantries never applied and the validity of a gift for the saying of masses was recognised by Lord Manners LC in *Commissioners of Charitable Donations and Bequests v Walsh*,[284] a finding confirmed by the judgment of Blackburne MR in *Read v Hodgins*.[285] However, the charitable nature of such gifts was examined in detail by the Court of Exchequer in *Attorney General v Delaney*,[286] in which it was held that a bequest for masses to be said for the repose of the soul of the testatrix and her brother was not charitable on the basis that there was no stipulation that the masses be said in public. Palles CB commented that if the will had prescribed that the masses should be celebrated in public, he would have accepted them as being charitable. This reasoning suggested that the charitable nature of such gifts depended on whether a stipulation was made that they be said in public, although in a number of subsequent cases, gifts of this nature failed even where the inference was that they should be celebrated in public.[287] This misinterpretation of the judgment of Palles CB was particularly evident in the decision of *Kehoe v Wilson*,[288] where a bequest for masses 'to be celebrated in Ireland in a church open for public worship at the time of such celebration' was held not to be charitable. The view

280. [1919] AC 815.
281. [1934] Ch 162.
282. [1949] AC 426.
283. [1990] Ch 1. See Hopkins [1989] CLJ 373; Parry [1989] Conv 453.
284. (1828) 7 Ir Eq R 34n.
285. (1844) 7 Ir Eq R 17.
286. (1875) IR 10 CL 104.
287. *Beresford v Jarvis* (1877) 11 ILTR 128; *M'Court v Burnett* (1877) 11 ILTR 130.
288. (1880) 7 LR Ir 10. This decision was followed, albeit unwillingly, by Porter MR in *Perry v Twomey* (1888) 21 LR Ir 480 although Chatterton VC subsequently pointed out in *Healy v Attorney General* [1902] 1 IR 342, that it was never his intention to depart from the view expressed by Palles CB in *Delaney's* case in relation to the validity of masses celebrated in public.

that where a gift contained a direction that the masses be celebrated in public such gifts should be regarded as charitable was, however, re-affirmed by the decision of the Irish Court of Appeal in *Attorney General v Hall*.[289]

The question of the charitable nature of gifts for the saying of masses, whether in private or in public, was finally resolved by the Irish Court of Appeal in *O'Hanlon v Logue*.[290] A testatrix devised and bequeathed her property on certain trusts and then on trust to sell it and invest the proceeds and pay the income thereof from time to time to the Roman Catholic Primate of all Ireland for the time being for the celebration of masses for the repose of the souls of her late husband, her children and herself, the will containing no direction that these masses be said in public. The Court of Appeal upheld the charitable nature of the gift and made it clear that a bequest for the saying of masses, whether in public or not, constituted a valid charitable gift. In what was described by Brady[291] as 'a remarkable *volte face*' since his judgment in *Delaney*, Palles CB concluded that the view which he had expressed in the earlier case, that the only element of public benefit in the celebration of the mass is the edification of the congregation, was too narrow and failed to appreciate it 'as a gift from God'. This decision has been followed on a number of occasions,[292] and the issue was put beyond doubt by the enactment of section 45(2) of the Charities Act 1961,[293] which read as follows:

> For the avoidance of the difficulties which arise in giving effect to the intentions of donors of certain gifts for the purpose of the advancement of religion and in order not to frustrate those intentions and notwithstanding that certain gifts for the purpose aforesaid, including gifts for the celebration of Masses, whether in public or private, are valid charitable gifts, it is hereby enacted that a valid charitable gift for the purpose of the advancement of religion shall have effect and as respects it having effect, shall be construed in accordance with the laws, canons, ordinances and tenets of the religion concerned.

Finally, the provisions of section 99 of the Charities Act 2009 in relation to the sale of mass cards should be noted.[294] It provides that a person who sells a

289. [1897] 2 IR 426.
290. [1906] 1 IR 247.
291. Brady, *Religion and the Law of Charities in Ireland* (1976) p. 81.
292. *Re Gibbons* [1917] 1 IR 448 and *Re Howley* [1940] IR 109, although in *Re Howley* Gavan Duffy J made some rather confusing remarks (at 116) to the effect that a gift for masses, though charitable, might nonetheless fail if too remote. This suggestion would seem to be at odds with the charitable nature of the gift.
293. Now repealed by s.11 and Schedule 2 of the Charities Act 2009.
294. Section 99 came into force on 1 September 2009 by virtue of the provisions of the Charities Act 2009 (Commencement) Order 2009.

mass card other than pursuant to an arrangement with a recognised person[295] shall be guilty of an offence. A challenge to the validity and constitutionality of section 99 was rejected by the High Court in *McNally v Ireland*.[296] The plaintiff's claim that the section contravened EC competition law or the terms of Council Directives governing 'industrially manufactured products' was dismissed and his primary argument was that it was inconsistent with Articles 38 and 44 of the Constitution. His claim based on Articles 44.2.1° and 44.2.3° failed on the grounds of lack of *locus standi* and his challenge pursuant to Article 38 was also dismissed. MacMenamin J was satisfied that there was a rational connection between the means and the objective of the legislation and that it was minimally intrusive into the constitutional rights of a potential accused.

Gifts to Religious Orders

Historically, there were a number of differences between gifts in favour of male religious orders and female ones. The effect of section 28 of the Roman Catholic Relief Act 1829 was that certain male religious orders such as the Jesuits were regarded as illegal, with the consequence that any gift to these orders was also tainted with illegality and void at law. These disabilities were not removed until the enactment of section 5 of the Government of Ireland Act 1920, which impliedly repealed them. The question of whether gifts to such orders could be considered charitable in nature arose in the case of *Re Byrne*,[297] where a testator directed that his residuary estate be given 'for the absolute use and benefit of the Jesuit Order in Ireland.' It was held by Johnston J that the bequest was not illegal but that it was not a charitable bequest and was void for uncertainty. On appeal, the majority of the Supreme Court held that the gift to the order was not a charitable legacy on the basis that the work of the order while largely charitable, was not exclusively so, although the gift was upheld as a valid gift of a non-charitable nature for the benefit of an ascertainable class of persons.[298] Kennedy CJ dissented, stating that bequests to religious institutions for religious purposes were *prima facie* charitable and concluded that the activities carried out by the Jesuits were clearly charitable in a legal sense.

While the disabilities imposed by the Roman Catholic Relief Act 1829 did not apply to religious orders of women,[299] gifts to such orders of a continuing nature might still fail at common law if the purposes of the order were not exclusively charitable. This problem was particularly evident in relation to

295. This is defined to mean a bishop of the Roman Catholic church or a provincial of an order of priests established under the authority of, and recognised by, that church.
296. [2011] 4 IR 431.
297. [1935] IR 782. See also *Re Keogh's Estate* [1945] IR 13.
298. See further *supra* Chapter 10. This result would now probably be avoided as a result of the operation of s. 49(1) of the Charities Act 1961.
299. See s. 37 of the Act of 1829.

contemplative orders on the grounds that they did not fulfil the necessary public benefit requirement. In these circumstances, the only possible solution was to uphold the gift on the basis that it was a valid gift for the benefit of those members of the community alive at the time of the testator's death. This point is well-illustrated by the decision of Wickens VC in the English case of *Cocks v Manners*,[300] which also proved to be of considerable importance in this jurisdiction. A testatrix directed that her property should be sold and after the payment of certain legacies that the proceeds should be distributed among certain specified religious institutions. Wickens VC held that a gift to the Sisters of Charity at a specified place payable to the superior for the time being was a good charitable gift. He considered that it was a 'voluntary association for the purpose of teaching the ignorant and nursing the sick' and said that it could not be distinguished in this respect from other types of voluntary associations performing charitable functions. However, the other bequest to a Dominican convent payable to the superior for the time being was held not to be charitable on the basis that the community had 'none of the requisites of a charitable institution' whether the word was used in its popular or legal sense. As Wickens VC commented, '[i]t is said … that religious purposes are charitable, but that can only be true as to religious services tending directly or indirectly towards the instruction or the edification of the public'.[301] However, he held that this gift was valid as a good non-charitable gift, payable to the superior for the time being for the benefit of the existing members of the order, on the grounds that there was nothing to prevent them spending it as they pleased.

This finding that contemplative religious orders were not charitable in nature was applied in Ireland. As O'Connor MR stated in *Commissioners of Charitable Donations and Bequests v McCartan*:[302]

> Monasteries of men and women are often, if not mostly, institutions, the members of which devote their lives exclusively to acts of piety such as pious meditation, prayer and self denial. Such institutions, however praiseworthy, are not charitable in the sense recognised by this Court.

In view of this approach the only way of establishing the validity of gifts to contemplative orders at that time was to apply the reasoning of Wickens VC in *Cocks v Manners* and to interpret them as being to the community as it existed at the time of the testator's death, i.e. as a gift to the individual nuns of whom the community happened to consist at that time. This approach can be seen in *Re Wilkinson's Trusts*,[303] where the Irish Court of Appeal upheld a

---

300. (1871) LR 12 Eq 574.
301. *Ibid.* at 585. See also the *dicta* of Fitzgibbon LJ in *Re Wilkinson's Trusts* (1857) 19 LR Ir 531, 539.
302. [1917] 1 IR 388, 396.
303. (1887) 19 LR Ir 531. See also *Re Delany's Estate* (1882) 9 LR Ir 226; *Bradshaw v Jackman* (1887) 21 LR Ir 12.

bequest to a superioress of a convent solely for the purposes of the convent on this basis. However, as has been seen, it was not always possible to place such a construction on a gift and where it is interpreted as being a gift to those individuals who may successively become members of the community it will be void on the grounds of perpetuity.[304]

The view that contemplative religious orders did not provide some benefit to the community was questioned by Black J in *Munster and Leinster Bank Ltd v Attorney General*,[305] and the issue arose directly before the High Court in the case of *Maguire v Attorney General*.[306] The testatrix directed in her will that a sum of money be spent founding a convent 'of perpetual adoration' in a specified place or elsewhere as the trustees might determine. In the course of a detailed examination of the issues involved, Gavan Duffy J stated that it was a 'grave discredit to the law that there should, in this Catholic country, be any doubt about the validity of [such a bequest].'[307] He said that it had been assumed that the decision in *Cocks v Manners* had decided as a matter of law that a testamentary gift to a contemplative order of nuns could not be charitable on the grounds that the public was not edified by the gift. However, Gavan Duffy J regarded it as a decision on a question of fact; that while at that time the public would not have been edified by private prayer unaccompanied by external works of charity, there was no reason for attributing the same outlook to public opinion in Ireland at the time when he was considering the case. As he stated, '[t]he finding, or assumption, in *Cocks v Manners* that the convent of a contemplative community tended neither directly nor indirectly towards public edification has no scintilla of authority as a determinant of the actual position among us.'[308] Gavan Duffy J, therefore, upheld the gift as charitable by employing the reasoning of Palles CB in *O'Hanlon v Logue*, without directly overruling *Cocks v Manners*.[309]

Doubts were raised about the validity of the decision of Gavan Duffy J when the House of Lords held in *Gilmour v Coats*[310] that a gift to a Carmelite priory which consisted of a community of cloistered nuns was not charitable as it lacked the necessary element of public benefit.[311] In addition, in *Re Keogh's*

304. *Stewart v Green* (1871) IR 5 Eq 470. See also *Morrow v M'Conville* (1883) 11 LR Ir 236. See further *supra* Chapter 10.
305. [1940] IR 19, 30.
306. [1943] IR 238.
307. *Ibid.* at 244.
308. *Ibid.* at 248-249.
309. It is interesting to note that Brady, while he acknowledged the provisions of Article 44.1.2° of the Constitution as it then existed, commented that '[i]t is difficult to avoid the inference that while all recognised religions might now be equal before the law, the Roman Catholic religion, in Gavan Duffy J's view, was more equal than all the others.' Brady, *Religion and the Law of Charities in Ireland* (1976) p. 92.
310. [1949] AC 426.
311. This approach was applied by Lord MacDermott LCJ in *Trustees of the Congregation of Poor Clares v Commissioner of Valuation* [1971] NI 174, 176. See also the *dictum* of

Estate,[312] in considering the validity of gifts to the superioress of a Carmelite convent and to the prior of an order of Carmelite fathers, Overend J said that whether or not these gifts could be supported as charitable gifts, they could be upheld as valid gifts to the individuals comprising the communities in the manner laid down in *Re Wilkinson's Trusts*.[313] As a result of this uncertainty, legislation drafted in 1954 included a provision to confirm the charitable status of contemplative religious orders, although as Brady pointed out, the legislation never progressed beyond its formal introduction in the Dáil.[314]

The subsequent decision of Dixon J in *Bank of Ireland Trustee Co. Ltd v Attorney General*[315] allayed these fears to an extent when he declined to follow the decision in *Gilmour* and held that a gift to be applied to the repair and/or improvement of a convent of a contemplative order of nuns was charitable. However, it was still felt that the matter should be put beyond doubt by legislation and section 45(1) of the Charities Act 1961 provided that in determining whether or not a gift for the purpose of the advancement of religion was a valid charitable gift it should be 'conclusively presumed' that the purpose included and would occasion public benefit.[316] As noted above, section 3(4) now provides that '[i]t shall be presumed, unless the contrary is proved, that a gift for the advancement of religion is of public benefit.' While this statutory presumption is rebuttable and no longer conclusive in nature, there is no reason to suggest that this rewording will lead to any significant change in practice, particularly given the tenor of decisions such as *Maguire v Attorney General*.[317]

Gifts for Churches and Other Miscellaneous Purposes

Gifts for the erection or maintenance of the fabric of a church building or its fixtures and fittings will be upheld as charitable. So a gift to a named church,[318] or to build a parsonage in connection with a church,[319] or for such purposes as

---

Lowry J in *Commissioner of Valuation v Trustees of the Redemptorist Order* [1971] NI 114, 169 that '[i]t is….clear that an order which has no other purpose than to achieve its own sanctification by private prayer and contemplation is not an association with charitable objects'. However, it should be noted that the majority of the Court of Appeal (Lord MacDermott LCJ and Lowry J; Curran LJ dissented) held that the apostolic functions carried out by the orders in question possessed the necessary public quality.

312. [1945] IR 13.
313. (1887) 19 LR Ir 531.
314. Brady, *Religion and The Law of Charities in Ireland* (1976) p. 92. See 184 *Dáil Debates* cols 555-557.
315. [1957] IR 257.
316. Repealed by s.11 and Schedule 2 of the Charities Act 2009.
317. [1943] IR 238. See also *Bank of Ireland Trustee Co. Ltd v Attorney General* [1957] IR 257.
318. *Re Gare* [1952] Ch 80.
319. *Cresswell v Cresswell* (1868) LR 6 Eq 69.

the erection of a new altar and altar rails,[320] or the provision and maintenance of seating in a church will be regarded as valid.[321] It was held by O'Connor MR in *Re Greene*[322] that a gift 'for the decoration or improvement of the Roman Catholic Church of the Carmelite Fathers at Clarendon Street, in the City of Dublin' was charitable, although difficulties still existed at that time about gifts to benefit such purposes,[323] and in a number of earlier cases gifts for the repair and maintenance of churches belonging to monastic orders had been declared void.[324] O'Connor MR reasoned that the gift in the case before him was not a gift to a monastic community for its own purposes but rather was 'given for the decoration or improvement of a church whose purpose is public worship.'[325] Certainly today there would be no doubts about the legality or charitable nature of such gifts and they would undoubtedly be recognised as valid.

Similarly, gifts for the upkeep of a churchyard or cemetery will be regarded as charitable in nature,[326] whether it is open to persons of all denominations,[327] or possibly, as has been held in England, confined to those of a specific religion.[328] In *Re Quinn*[329] Budd J stated that he could see no real distinction between a gift for the repair and improvement of a church and for a churchyard and concluded that a gift given for the upkeep of a cemetery, open to persons of all denominations, was a gift for the advancement of religion. Even if this were not the case, Budd J was satisfied that the bequest would fall into the fourth category of Lord Macnaghten's classification, as being a gift for other purposes beneficial to the community.

Often this device of making a bequest for the upkeep of an entire churchyard is used as an indirect means of achieving an object of a more specific nature which might otherwise fail.[330] The general view is that gifts for the maintenance or repair of specific vaults or tombs, if these are not part of the fabric of a church, will not be regarded as charitable at common law. As we have seen above,[331] these may be upheld as valid purpose trusts provided they do not infringe the rule against inalienability or if they are of limited nature and fall within the

320. *Re Hawe* (1955) 93 ILTR 175. Although on the facts, the gift failed for remoteness, it was contemplated as taking effect on the occurrence of events which might not necessarily occur within the perpetuity period.
321. *Re Raine* [1956] Ch 417.
322. [1914] 1 IR 305.
323. See *supra* on gifts to male religious orders at pp. 444-445.
324. *Kehoe v Wilson* (1880) 7 LR Ir 10; *Liston v Keegan* (1881) 9 LR Ir 539.
325. [1914] 1 IR 305, 319.
326. *Re Vaughan* (1886) 33 Ch D 187; *Re Pardoe* [1906] 2 Ch 184.
327. *Re Quinn* (1953) 88 ILTR 161.
328. *Re Manser* [1905] 1 Ch 68.
329. (1953) 88 ILTR 161.
330. E.g. *Re Eighmie* [1935] Ch 524. Although often where a gift is given for such a general purpose there will be no means of enforcing any specific direction regarding the upkeep of family graves or tombs. See the *dicta* of Budd J in *Re Quinn* (1953) 88 ILTR 161, 166 and *Re Manser* [1905] 1 Ch 68.
331. Chapter 10.

statutory financial limits they will be regarded as charitable by virtue of section 50 of the Charities Act 1961.[332]

The question of whether residences for priests, clergy and other persons connected with the church qualify as charitable is a difficult one to answer with accuracy, primarily because many of the cases in this area have arisen in the context of whether these premises should be exempt from rates. As Wylie has commented, 'the tests for exemption from rates on the ground of charity are much narrower than those for determining whether or not an object is otherwise charitable.'[333] There is limited authority to support the proposition that gifts for the repair or upkeep of a residence of this nature may be charitable,[334] but the decisions made in a rating context would suggest otherwise. So, in *Commissioner of Valuation v O'Connell*,[335] Palles CB held that a house built by parishioners and used as a residence by a Roman Catholic priest was not exclusively used for charitable purposes so as to be exempt from rates. A similar finding was made in respect of a convent[336] and a basement portion of a church, used as a residence for a sexton on the grounds that it was a separate unit and not indispensably part of the fabric of the church.[337] It should be noted that the changes made by the Valuation Act 2001 to the rating exemptions enjoyed by charities should ensure that a more flexible attitude will be adopted in such cases in the future. 'Charitable organisation' as defined in section 3 of the Act extends to bodies the main objects of which are charitable provided any secondary objects are the attainment of the main objects and an extensive list of property which is not rateable is set out in the Fourth Schedule to the legislation.

Trusts for Other Purposes of Benefit to the Community

Introduction

This category can be described as the most difficult of Lord Macnaghten's classes of charitable trust to define and delimit, and embraces purposes which do not fall within any of the three categories already considered but which are nevertheless beneficial to the community in a way recognised by the law as charitable.[338] This fourth category of charitable trust has been reworded to

---

332. These limits are £60 *per* year in the case of income, or in any other case, £1,000. The Law Reform Commission has recommended (*The Rule Against Perpetuities and Cognate Rules* LRC 62-2000 para. 5.15) that these sums be increased to a limit of £1,000 (€1,270) *per* year in the case of income and to a limit of £16,000 (€20,316) on the capital sum (as of the year 2000). Section 50 was restated in head 82 of the General Scheme for the Charities Regulation Bill 2006, published in March 2006 but this provision was not included in the draft Bill published in April 2007.

333. Wylie, *Irish Land Law* (4th ed., 2010) p. 638. See also Brady (1968) 3 Ir Jur (ns) 215.

334. *Attorney General v Bishop of Chester* (1785) 1 Bro CC 444.

335. [1906] 2 IR 479.

336. *Good Shepherd Nuns v Commissioner of Valuation* [1930] IR 646.

337. *Mulholland v Commissioner of Valuation* (1936) 70 ILTR 253.

338. It was suggested by the First Tier Tribunal Tax in *Helena Housing Ltd v Revenue*

read 'any other purpose that is of benefit to the community' in section 3(1)(d) of the Charities Act 2009. There are a number of well-established charitable purposes under this heading and section 3(11) of the Act of 2009 provides that a 'purpose that is of benefit to the community' includes the purposes which are specifically set out. These are as follows:

a) the advancement of community welfare, including the relief of those in need by reason of youth, age, ill-health or disability,
b) the advancement of community development, including rural or urban regeneration,
c) the promotion of civic responsibility or voluntary work,
d) the promotion of health, including the prevention or relief of sickness, disease or human suffering,
e) the advancement of conflict resolution or reconciliation,
f) the promotion of religious or racial harmony and harmonious community relations,
g) the protection of the natural environment,
h) the advancement of environmental sustainability,
i) the advancement of the efficient and effective use of the property of charitable organisations,
j) the prevention or relief of suffering of animals,
k) the advancement of the arts, culture, heritage or sciences, and
l) the integration of those who are disadvantaged, and the promotion of their full participation, in society.[339]

The view was expressed by Lindley LJ in *Re MacDuff*[340] that Lord Macnaghten did not intend to lay down in *Pemsel's* case that every object of 'public general utility' must necessarily be charitable and this point was developed by Viscount Cave in *Attorney General v National Provincial and Union Bank of England Ltd*[341] in the following terms:

> Lord Macnaghten did not mean that all trusts beneficial to the community are charitable, but that there were certain charitable trusts which fell within that category; and accordingly to argue that because a trust is for a purpose beneficial to the community it is therefore a charitable trust is to turn round his sentence and to give it a different meaning. So here it is not enough to say that the trust in question is for public purposes

and Customs Commissioners [2010] UKFTT 71 that the fourth category should be sufficiently flexible to allow the evolution of the law of charity to meet the needs of a changing society.

339. Section 3(11).
340. [1896] 2 Ch 451, 466.
341. [1924] AC 262, 265. See also *Williams v IRC* [1947] AC 447, 455 *per* Lord Simonds.

beneficial to the community or is for the public welfare; you must also show it to be a charitable trust.

A more flexible interpretation was placed on the *dicta* of Lord Macnaghten more recently by Russell LJ in *Incorporated Council for Law Reporting for England and Wales v Attorney General*,[342] where he suggested that in substance the position is that if a purpose is shown to be of sufficient benefit or utility to the community, it is *prima facie* charitable in law.[343] Here the Court of Appeal held unanimously that the purpose of providing law reports was charitable under the fourth head of Lord Macnaghten's classification; as Russell LJ commented such an object 'cannot be thought otherwise than beneficial to the community and of general public utility'.

However, the view expressed by Russell LJ has not met with universal approval and Dillon J subsequently commented in *Re South Place Ethical Society*[344] that it was not in line with earlier judicial statements[345] and that the approach to be adopted in considering whether something is within the fourth category 'is the approach of analogy from what is already stated in the preamble to the Statute of Elizabeth or from what has already been held to be charitable within the fourth category.' So, it is probably correct to say that if a trust is to qualify under this heading, it is necessary, but not necessarily sufficient, that the purpose is of general public utility.[346]

Public Benefit

One of the primary difficulties in laying down guidelines as to the type of trust which may qualify under this heading is the perennial question of the necessary element of public benefit. A trust may appear to be one of general public utility but difficulties may arise when its application is confined to a limited group of persons. Hart J drew attention to this difficulty when he commented in *Bath & North Eastern Somerset Council v Attorney General*[347] that in order to satisfy the public benefit test in this fourth category, '[f]irst, the purpose itself must be beneficial as one of public utility; and secondly, the benefit of the purpose must be available to a sufficient section of the community.' As we have seen above, the test laid down by Viscount Simonds in *Oppenheim v Tobacco Securities*

342. [1972] Ch 73.
343. As Gault J commented in *Commissioner of Inland Revenue v Medical Council of New Zealand* [1997] 2 NZLR 297, 302 few institutions having objects of general public utility have been held not to be within the 'spirit and intendment' of the Preamble of the Statute of Charitable Uses 1601.
344. [1980] 1 WLR 1565, 1574.
345. Dillon J referred to the *dicta* of Lord Simonds in *Williams v IRC* [1947] AC 447, 455.
346. *Helena Housing Ltd v Revenue and Customs Commissioners* [2010] UKFTT 71 at [115].
347. [2002] EWHC 1623 (Ch).

Trust Co. Ltd[348] required that for a group of persons to constitute a 'section of the community', it must not be numerically negligible, and the quality which distinguishes these persons from other members of the community must be one which does not depend on their relationship to a particular individual.[349]

One view is that the application of the public benefit requirement to trusts falling within this fourth category should be more strictly enforced than in the other categories. This view is illustrated by a statement made by Babington LJ in *Trustees of the Londonderry Presbyterian Church House v Commissioners of Inland Revenue*[350] to the effect that in this category 'there can be no charity until it is shown that the gift is to or for the benefit of the public or a section of the public'. Similar sentiments were expressed by Lord Somervell and Viscount Simonds in *IRC v Baddeley*,[351] in which the majority of the House of Lords held that a trust to provide, *inter alia*, for recreational facilities for Methodists resident in a particular area of London did not fulfil the public benefit requirement and so was not a valid trust. Lord Somervell stated as follows:

> I cannot accept the principle submitted by the respondents that a section of the public sufficient to support a valid trust in one category must as a matter of law be sufficient to support a trust in any other category. I think that difficulties are apt to arise if one seeks to consider the class apart from the particular nature of the charitable purpose. They are, in my opinion, interdependent. There might well be a valid trust for the promotion of religion benefiting a very small class. It would not follow that a recreation ground for the exclusive use of the same class would be a valid charity.[352]

An alternative view was favoured by Lord Reid in his dissenting opinion which is founded on the premise that the definition of the class of persons necessary to constitute a sufficient section of the community to satisfy the public benefit requirement should not vary from one category to another. Lord Reid rejected the suggestion that, for example, the members of one particular religion might constitute a 'section of the community' for one charitable purpose and yet

---

348. [1951] AC 297, 306. See also the *dicta* of Lord Greene MR in *Re Compton* [1945] Ch 123, 131.
349. It should be noted that in the decision of the New Zealand Court of Appeal in *Latimer v Commissioner of Inland Revenue* [2002] 3 NZLR 195 Blanchard J stated that the common descent of the Maoris was 'a relationship poles away from the kind of connection which the House of Lords must have been thinking of in the *Oppenheim* case'. In his view there was no indication that the House of Lords had tribal or clan groups in contemplation when laying down this test and the Court of Appeal was satisfied that the Maori beneficiaries constituted a section of the community.
350. [1946] NI 178, 196-197.
351. [1955] AC 572.
352. *Ibid.* at 615. See also the *dicta* of Viscount Simonds at 592.

be regarded merely as 'a fluctuating body of private individuals' for another charitable purpose.[353]

An attempt to rationalise this whole question was made by Lord Cross in *Dingle v Turner*,[354] where he stated as follows:

> In truth, the question of whether or not the potential beneficiaries of a trust can fairly be said to constitute a section of the public is a question of degree and cannot be, by itself, decisive of the question whether the trust is a charity. Much must depend on the purpose of the trust. It may well be that, on the one hand, a trust to promote some purpose, *prima facie* charitable, will constitute a charity even though the class of potential beneficiaries might fairly be called a private class, and that on the other hand, a trust to promote another purpose, also *prima facie* charitable, will not constitute a charity even though the class of potential beneficiaries might seem to some people fairly describable as a section of the public.[355]

This approach has met with both academic[356] and judicial approval and as Carswell J stated in *Re Dunlop*,[357] if it is recognised that the manner in which the essential benefit to the public is effected varies as between the different categories of charity, it becomes easier to determine the existence of this element when examining a trust. Carswell J continued:

> The essence of the charitable nature [of trusts within Lord Macnaghten's fourth category] is that the beneficiaries should not be a private class, nor should any limitations be placed upon the gift which would prevent the public as a whole from enjoying the advantage which the donor intends to provide for the benefit of all of the public. It would be quite consonant with this concept that it should be more difficult for a trust under the fourth head to satisfy the requirements of public benefit, and that a bridge to be used only by Methodists should fail to qualify where a gift for the education of the children of members of that church might be a valid charity.[358]

In *Dunlop* Carswell J was required to consider the validity of a trust to found or assist in the founding of a home for 'Old Presbyterian Persons'. He held that the object was, subject to the satisfaction of the requirement of public benefit, a

---

353. *Ibid.* at 612-613.
354. [1972] AC 601. See also the dissenting judgment of Lord MacDermott in *Oppenheim v Tobacco Securities Trust Co. Ltd* [1955] AC 297, 318.
355. *Ibid.* at 624. Quoted with approval by Gibson LJ in *Springhill Housing Action Committee v Commissioner of Valuation* [1983] NI 184, 191.
356. See Jones [1974] CLJ 63, 65.
357. [1984] NI 408. See Dawson [1987] Conv 114.
358. *Ibid.* at 426.

valid charitable gift for the relief of the aged as it relieved a need attributable to the condition of the persons to be benefited. Carswell J concluded that the public benefit requirement had been satisfied and that the gift could not be regarded as a private benefaction. The fact that the people who would derive benefit from the trust were to be Presbyterians rather than any other denomination did not, in his view, negative the paramountcy of the public purpose of assistance for the aged.[359] In the opinion of Carswell J, the members of the Presbyterian Church were 'sufficiently defined and identifiable by a common quality of a public nature' and accordingly constituted a section of the public at large 'certainly for the purposes of a gift under Lord Macnaghten's first head'. It should be pointed out that in England the words aged, impotent and poor in the Preamble to the Statute of Charitable Uses were read disjunctively and Carswell J had earlier expressed the view that the almost non-existent public benefit test in relation to trusts for poor relations and poor employees should not extend 'to the whole of Lord Macnaghten's first head' *viz.*, trusts for the aged and impotent as well. However, the manner in which he stated his conclusion would suggest that the gift in the case before him probably qualified as a charitable trust under this first heading, to which a less strict public benefit test applied than that which he had suggested should be employed in relation to trusts falling into Lord Macnaghten's fourth category.[360]

The extent of the public benefit requirement in this fourth category of charitable trusts has been considered in this jurisdiction in *Re Worth Library*,[361] in which Keane J examined two alternative submissions advanced by counsel for the plaintiff as to why the original gift should qualify as being within the fourth category of Lord Macnaghten's classification. While Keane J accepted that a gift for a library might be charitable in nature as being for the public benefit, he was satisfied that the relevant authorities had made it clear that such a gift was not charitable *per se*.[362] The bequest therefore failed to satisfy the public benefit requirement as it was to provide a library for the physician, surgeon and chaplain of the hospital 'who alone would have access to the room in which the library was housed'.[363] Keane J then proceeded to consider whether a gift of a library such as the one at issue, which was expressed to be for the benefit

359. It should be noted that by the time of the testator's death it was no longer practicable to use the properties envisaged by him for the purpose suggested and the court directed the preparation of a cy-près scheme.
360. However, note the conclusion reached by Roth J in *Re Duffy's Estate* [2013] EWHC 2395 (Ch) that a gift to the amenity fund of a residential home for the elderly which never had more than 33 residents did not meet the public benefit requirement as that number of beneficiaries could not be regarded as a sufficient section of the community. See further Synge (2016) 132 LQR 303.
361. [1995] 2 IR 301.
362. In this context, he referred to *Carne v Long* (1860) 2 De GF & J 75 and *Re Prevost* [1930] 2 Ch 383.
363. Keane J concluded that the wording used by Dr Worth in directing that catalogues of the books contained in the library be compiled suggested that his primary concern

of named office holders in the hospital only, could be regarded as being for the benefit of the hospital generally and hence charitable.[364] Keane J rejected counsel's suggestion that the directions contained in the will regarding access to the books being restricted to named office holders was a precatory condition only and concluded that these were directions 'which the testator wished to be complied with to the letter'.

Given the tenor of his approach to the whole question of public benefit, Keane J then reached a somewhat surprising conclusion. While the library itself would not have been of significant practical benefit to the office holders given the nature of the topics to which these books related, Keane J was of the view that the library itself 'in its beautiful setting would have provided a haven of quiet intellectual relaxation for the beneficiaries.'[365] He therefore concluded that the bequest of the library played a role in the advancement of the charity represented by the hospital and as such constituted a valid charitable bequest for the benefit of that institution within the fourth category of Lord Macnaghten's classification. In a sense, it is difficult to justify the finding that a bequest for the benefit of three named office holders in a hospital could be of real benefit to the community generally. The 'charitable' nature of the bequest in a popular, as opposed to a legal, sense and the desirability of framing a cy-près scheme in the *Worth* case was never called into question and yet the fact that Keane J found it necessary to go through the motions of applying and ultimately satisfying the public benefit requirement illustrates the anomalies which the current legal position may create.

It is fair to say that the conclusion in *Worth* is not in keeping with the general principles laid down by Carswell J in *Re Dunlop*, and that the result in that decision, as in *Worth*, was not altogether in line with the strictness of the public benefit requirement which it is theoretically necessary to overcome. One must question the reason why Keane J saw fit effectively to modify this stringent public benefit requirement in relation to trusts 'for other purposes beneficial to the community' in finding that the bequest in *Re Worth Library* was a valid charitable bequest for the benefit of the hospital. At this point the question of the rationale behind applying such a stringent public benefit requirement should also be raised. The answer probably lies in the statement made by Lord Cross in the course of his judgment in *Dingle v Turner*,[366] that 'in answering the question whether any given trust is a charitable trust, the courts … cannot avoid having regard to the fiscal privileges accorded to

---

was to ensure the security of the books rather than to facilitate scholars who might wish to peruse them.

364. It has been accepted that a gift for the benefit of a hospital is charitable in nature. See *Barrington's Hospital v Commissioner of Valuation* [1957] IR 299; *Re McCarthy* [1958] IR 311; *Gleeson v Attorney General* High Court 1972 No. 2664 Sp (Kenny J) 6 April 1973.
365. [1995] 2 IR 301, 340.
366. [1972] AC 601, 624.

charities'. As we have seen above, Lord Cross commented that the issues of validity and fiscal immunity were closely connected and he seemed to accept that the decisions in cases such as *Re Compton*[367] and *Oppenheim v Tobacco Securities Trust Co. Ltd*[368] were influenced by the fact that if the trusts at issue had been declared valid charitable trusts, they would have enjoyed a perceived 'undeserved fiscal immunity'.

Certainly it would appear that the overriding consideration in the mind of Keane J when deciding the question of the charitable status of the bequest in *Worth* seemed to be the desirability of finding it to be a charitable trust so that the court could apply the property cy-près, rather than the issue of the fiscal privileges which would accompany such status. The suggestion of the Radcliffe Commission,[369] namely to provide that only certain charities which are clearly of obvious benefit to the public at large should enjoy the fiscal privileges associated with charitable status, might lead to a more consistent application of principle. In this context, it should be noted that section 7 of the Charities Act 2009 now provides that 'nothing in this Act shall operate to affect the law in relation to the levying or collection of tax or the determination of eligibility for exemption from liability to any tax.'

Finally, it should be pointed out that although the provisions of sections 3(7) and (8) of the Charities Act 2009 appear to rule out the imposition of a limitation on the class of intended beneficiaries where they all, or a significant number of them, have a personal connection[370] with the donor, section 3(7)(a) allows for some flexibility in relation to the public benefit test as between various categories of charitable trust to be retained. It expressly states that account shall be taken of whether any limitation imposed on the class to benefit is justified and reasonable 'having regard to the nature of the purpose of the gift'. So, although this will remain an open question until the courts in this jurisdiction have an opportunity to express a view on it, the statutory provisions would appear to allow for the continued application of a more stringent test of public benefit in the category of any other purpose of benefit to the community on the basis that the type of purpose demands it. It remains to be seen whether the courts will adopt a one size fits all approach to the question of the public benefit test in the first, second and fourth *Pemsel* categories or whether the terms of section 3(7)(a) will be relied on to preserve some of the existing distinctions.

367. [1945] Ch 123.
368. [1951] AC 297.
369. Cmnd 9474, Chapter 7. The Commission stated as follows: 'In our view what is amiss in the present system is not the idea of giving income tax relief in respect of charity but the undue width of the range of what ranks as a charity for this purpose.' (para. 170). 'We conclude … that there would be no insuperable difficulty in producing a statutory definition of charity for tax purposes that would at any rate correspond more closely than the present with the accepted idea of what charity is.' (para. 173).
370. See further the provisions of s. 2(2)(a) of the Act.

For Other Purposes of Benefit to the Community — an Objective or Subjective Test?

There has traditionally been a divergence in the position adopted by the judiciary in Ireland and England in relation to the test which should be applied by the courts in determining whether a purpose satisfies the requirement of being 'beneficial to the community' to the extent that it may be regarded as being charitable in law. The Irish authorities suggest that a subjective test should be applied and that due weight should be given to the donor's view of the charitable nature of his bequest provided that this purpose is not obviously illegal or immoral. However, the accepted approach now in England and Northern Ireland is to adopt an objective test and allow the court to form an opinion on the issue based upon the evidence before it. Keane J remarked in *Re Worth Library* that as the objects under consideration in the case before him were such that an appreciable number of reasonable people would consider them to be charitable, it was not necessary for him to express any firm view on the divergence of opinion referred to above. However, it is interesting to note that the comments which he made would support the view that the court should give due weight to a donor's intentions in these circumstances.

The most important authority in the area in an Irish context is the decision of *Re Cranston*,[371] in which the Irish Court of Appeal was required to decide whether gifts for certain vegetarian societies were charitable in nature. The majority of the court upheld the conclusion reached by Porter MR that the objects of the societies could be said to be charitable within the legal sense of the term. Fitzgibbon LJ clearly believed that the view of the donor should be decisive in determining whether a gift fell within the category of 'other purposes beneficial to the community', provided that this purpose is not immoral nor illegal. He stated:

> What is the tribunal which is to decide whether the object is a beneficent one? It cannot be the individual mind of a judge, for he may disagree, *toto caelo*, from the testator as to what is or is not beneficial. On the other hand, it cannot be the *vox populi*, for charities have been upheld for the benefit of insignificant sects, and of peculiar people. It occurs to me that the answer must be — that the benefit must be one which *the founder* believes to be of public advantage, and his belief must be at least rational, and not contrary either to the general law of the land, or to the principles of morality. A gift of such a character, dictated by benevolence, believed to be beneficent, devoted to an appreciably important object, and neither *contra bonos mores* nor *contra legem*, will in my opinion, be charitable in the eye of the law, as settled by decisions which bind us. It is not for us to say that these have gone too far.[372]

371. [1898] 1 IR 431.
372. *Ibid.* at 446-447. Walker LJ also placed emphasis on the fact that the motive of the

A similar view was taken by Barton J in *Shillington v Portadown UDC*,[373] in which he concluded that benefits which the testator wished to confer on residents of his native town and its locality were 'such as he believed to be of public advantage'. As, in his view, this belief was rational and not illegal nor immoral, Barton J accepted that the bequest constituted a valid charitable gift.

While this subjective approach was at one time favoured in England,[374] it would now appear in that jurisdiction that the donor's intentions and beliefs as to the charitable nature of the bequest which he is making are not factors which a court may take into consideration. This view is well-illustrated by the statements made by Russell J in *Re Hummeltenberg*.[375] He referred to the views of the majority judges in the Irish Court of Appeal in *Re Cranston*, and stated that although he agreed with them in so far as they declared that the personal or private opinion of the judge was immaterial, he disagreed with them to the extent that they suggested that it was for the creator of the trust to determine whether the purpose is beneficial to the public. In the view of Russell J, 'the question whether a gift is or may be operative for the public benefit is a question to be answered by the court by forming an opinion upon the evidence before it.'[376] This approach was endorsed by Lord Hanworth MR in *Re Grove-Grady*,[377] where he said that the court must decide whether benefit to the community had been established and the courts in Northern Ireland have also adopted this objective approach.[378]

Although the views expressed by Keane J in *Re Worth Library* on this question were merely *obiter* and the objects put forward to the court, of the advancement of learning and of hospitals, would probably have been seen as being of benefit to the community irrespective of whether a subjective or objective approach had been applied, it is nevertheless of interest to note his views because the same result will not always be arrived at by applying these divergent tests. Keane J stated:

> In every case, the intention of the testator is of paramount importance. If

donor in making the bequest was to benefit mankind generally. He did comment that there may be cases in which the court might allow its own views to override those of a donor, even where the gift was not illegal, immoral or contrary to public policy, but he was satisfied that this was not such a case (at 450).

373. [1911] 1 IR 247. See also *Attorney General v Becher* [1910] 2 IR 251; *Re Ni Brudair* High Court 1976 No. 93 Sp (Gannon J) 5 February 1979.
374. *Re Foveaux* [1895] 2 Ch 501, 507.
375. [1923] 1 Ch 237.
376. *Ibid.* at 242. Cited with approval by Megaw J in *Re Lester* [1940] NI 92, 103. See also the *dicta* of Lord Simonds in *National Anti-Vivisection Society v IRC* [1948] AC 31, 65-66.
377. [1929] 1 Ch 557, 572. In this regard he cited with approval the statement made by Holmes LJ in his dissenting judgment in *Re Cranston* that the issue 'does not depend on the view entertained by any individual — either by the judge who is to decide the question, or by the person who makes the gift'.
378. *Re Lester* [1940] NI 92, 101-105.

> he intended to advance a charitable object recognised as such by the law, his gift will be a charitable gift. In the case of gifts which do not come within the first three categories, the fact that the testator's view as to the public utility of his favoured object — e.g. vegetarianism — is not shared by many people will not of itself prevent it from being, in the eyes of the law, a valid charitable object within the fourth category, provided it is not illegal, irrational or *contra bonos mores*. That, as I understand is the effect of the majority decision of the Irish Court of Appeal in *In re Cranston*.[379]

It is not difficult to envisage circumstances in which a donor's intentions and motives cannot be easily reconciled with those of the court, and public policy and an appreciation of what may be immoral are concepts which may undergo significant change over a period of time. This is aptly illustrated by changing judicial attitudes towards trusts created for the purpose of seeking to bring about the abolition of vivisection.[380]

While the courts in this jurisdiction are unlikely to take a liberal attitude towards the question of what types of trusts might be of an illegal or immoral nature, it would appear that they will continue to apply the *dicta* of Fitzgibbon LJ in *Re Cranston* and give due weight to a donor's intention in deciding the question of whether a trust is likely to benefit the community. This may yet prove to be of crucial importance if they are called upon to make a pronouncement on the charitable nature of bequests to organisations which an appreciable number of so-called 'objective' members of society would not consider charitable. Clearly in such circumstances, the divergence of view which Keane J rightly characterised as 'not material' in *Worth* might become highly relevant.

Specific Types of Trusts which may Qualify as being For Any Other Purpose of Benefit to the Community

The range of trusts for other purposes beneficial to or of benefit to the community has always been broad. Prior to the coming into force of the Charities Act 2009 it was possible to group many of the cases in this area under certain headings, although the emergence of previously unrecognised heads of charity was also always a possibility. By setting out a non-exhaustive list in section 3(11), the legislation has, in a sense, preserved this approach. In addition, by specifically enumerating purposes such as 'the protection of the natural environment' and 'the advancement of environmental sustainability' any doubts about whether such aims, which the courts might not previously have considered in this context, are charitable in nature will be dispelled. 'The advancement of the efficient and effective use of the property of charitable organisations' is also

379. [1995] 2 IR 301, 335.
380. Considered in detail *infra*, see *Armstrong v Reeves* (1890) 25 LR Ir 325; *National Anti-Vivisection Society v IRC* [1948] AC 31.

specifically listed which should also further broaden the scope of 'charitable purpose'. It is important to stress that the absence of a specific purpose from this list does not mean that it cannot be considered charitable, unless it falls within the scope of an 'excluded body' as defined in section 2 of the Act.

One general point which was clarified by Lord Macnaghten in *Pemsel's*[381] case in a manner which seems to have met with subsequent judicial approval is that 'trusts [in this fourth category] are not the less charitable in the eye of the law, because incidentally they benefit the rich as well as the poor ....' This approach was confirmed in this jurisdiction by the Irish Court of Appeal in *Re Cranston*.[382] So, while it would appear that a trust which will benefit a category of persons under the fourth heading does not need to benefit the poor to the exclusion of the rich,[383] and the fact that rich and poor alike may benefit does not generally appear to be an issue,[384] a trust of this nature which will exclusively benefit the rich will not be charitable.[385]

At this point it is useful to consider a number of purposes which have traditionally been considered charitable, those in relation to which some doubt remains and also to identify purposes which are not regarded as legally charitable in nature.

Gifts for the Aged, the Disabled and the Sick

These types of purpose are now specifically referred to in section 3(11) of the Charities Act 2009 which provides that a purpose that is of benefit to the community includes 'the advancement of community welfare including the relief of those in need by reason of youth, age, ill-health, or disability'[386] and 'the promotion of health, including the prevention or relief of sickness, disease or human suffering'.[387] The fact that trusts of this nature should be considered legally charitable was already well-established. While the preamble to the English Statute of Charitable Uses referred to 'the relief of aged, impotent and poor people' the Irish statute specifically mentioned 'the relief or maintenance of any manner of poor, succourless, distressed or impotent persons.' In the context of the English statute, it was held that these words should be read

381. [1891] AC 531, 583.
382. [1898] 1 IR 431. See also *Barrington's Hospital v Commissioner of Valuation* [1957] IR 299.
383. See *Keren Kayemeth le Jisroel Ltd v IRC* [1931] 2 KB 465, 492. Provided that the poor are not excluded from the ambit of the trust, *Re MacDuff* [1896] 2 Ch 451, 464 *per* Lindley LJ.
384. Although note the findings of Palles CB in *Clancy v Commissioner of Valuation* [1911] 2 IR 173.
385. *Re MacDuff* [1896] 2 Ch 451, 471 *per* Rigby LJ.
386. Section 3(11)(a).
387. Section 3(11)(d).

disjunctively.[388] In *Re Robinson*[389] Vaisey J upheld the validity of a bequest to 'old people over 65 years' in a certain district on the basis that 'old people over 65 years in a particular parish are a class of persons just as much objects of charity as the poor of the parish or the sick of the parish.'[390] Similarly, in *Re Glyn's Will Trusts*,[391] Danckwerts J confirmed that elderly people need not necessarily be poor to benefit from a charitable trust.

This issue did not arise in relation to the interpretation of the Irish statute as the words themselves were framed disjunctively.[392] Although some decisions appeared to support the view that it was a sufficient charitable purpose simply to benefit the aged or the sick without more,[393] it was generally accepted that the trust must be for the relief of a need attributable to the condition of the persons to be benefited,[394] a point emphasised by Peter Gibson J in *Joseph Rowntree Memorial Trust Hospital Association Ltd v Attorney General*,[395] in which a scheme to build self-contained dwellings for the elderly was found to be charitable in nature. Carswell J laid similar stress on the concept of 'relief' in *Re Dunlop*[396] in considering the charitable nature of a trust to the Presbyterian Residential Trust to found or help to found a home for 'Old Presbyterian persons'. He emphasised that the concept of relief and its connotation of meeting a need was in his view 'preferable to one which would admit as beneficiaries any aged persons, whatever may be the amount of their resources and irrespective of their needs arising from their condition of advancing years'.[397] Carswell J concluded that the gift was designed to serve the purpose of benefiting the public by providing accommodation for the relief of a class of persons who require it by reason of their age and that it was therefore charitable in nature.

Similarly, it was held that gifts for the relief of the disabled or the sick qualified under the fourth head of Lord Macnaghten's classification. In *Re Lewis*[398] a bequest to 10 blind girls and 10 blind boys resident in a certain area was upheld by Roxburgh J who stressed that poverty was not an essential ingredient in order for the bequest to qualify as charitable in nature. A gift to

388. *Joseph Rowntree Memorial Trust Hospital Association Ltd v Attorney General* [1983] Ch 159, 171. As Peter Gibson J commented, '[i]t would be as absurd to require that the aged must be impotent or poor as it would be to require the impotent to be aged or poor, or the poor to be aged or impotent.' See also *Re Dunlop* [1984] NI 408, 414.
389. [1951] Ch 198.
390. *Ibid.* at 201.
391. [1950] 2 All ER 1150n; [1950] 2 TLR 510.
392. *Barrington's Hospital v Commissioner of Valuation* [1957] IR 299, 320 *per* Kingsmill Moore J. See also *Gleeson v Attorney General* High Court 1972 No.2664 Sp (Kenny J) 6 April 1973 at 11; *Re Worth Library* [1995] 2 IR 301, 339.
393. E.g. *Re Robinson* [1951] Ch 198.
394. E.g. *Re Neal* (1966) 110 SJ 549; *Re Resch's Will Trusts* [1969] 1 AC 514.
395. [1983] Ch 159. See also *DV Bryant Trust Board v Hamilton City Council* [1997] 3 NZLR 342.
396. [1984] NI 408.
397. *Ibid.* at 414.
398. [1955] Ch 104. See also *Re Elliott* (1910) 102 LT 528.

the 'sick and wounded' has been found to be charitable[399] and in *Re Chaplin*[400] a gift 'to provide a home of rest that shall afford the means of physical and/or mental recuperation to persons in need of rest by reason of the stress and strain caused or partly caused by the conditions in which they ordinarily live and/or work' was accepted as being charitable as was a gift to a hospital to be applied for the purposes of providing a 'home of rest' for the nurses who worked there.[401]

In *Funnell v Stewart*[402] the testatrix left her residuary estate to the first and second named defendants to further the spiritual work of a faith healing group. Her executors sought to determine whether the disposition created a valid charitable trust. Hazel Williamson QC, sitting as a Deputy High Court judge, was satisfied that the substance of the group's work was faith healing. She accepted that it was charitable, either on the basis that faith healing has become a recognised activity of public benefit (although she acknowledged that this might not necessarily have been the case when *Re Hummeltenberg* was decided), or on the basis that the religious nature of the faith healing movement renders its purposes charitable and a sufficient element of public benefit is assumed so as to enable the charity to be recognised by law. On the issue of religion and public/private services she stated that the inclusion of the possibility of private services, 'which could clearly not themselves be charitable' did not prevent the gift from being charitable.

A number of cases in this jurisdiction established that gifts for the sick or to hospitals are charitable in nature. In *Re McCarthy's Will Trusts*[403] Budd J upheld as valid charitable gifts under this heading a bequest to a society which had as its principal object the care of the sick making pilgrimages to Lourdes and a bequest to a hospital at Lourdes which he described as being for the benefit of the sick and therefore 'clearly charitable'. The most important authority in this area is *Barrington's Hospital v Commissioner of Valuation*,[404] in which the plaintiff hospital sought to challenge the changing of its exemption from rating valuation on the basis that its purposes were exclusively charitable in nature within the meaning of section 63 of the Poor Relief (Ireland) Act 1838. While Kingsmill Moore J accepted that 'charitable purposes' within the meaning of the section has a less extensive meaning than that given to those words in *Pemsel's* case,[405] his judgment nevertheless contains some important statements of general principle. He found that the term 'impotent' includes sick and injured persons and that 'a trust for the care of the sick or the maintenance of

399. *Re Hillier* [1944] 1 All ER 480.
400. [1933] Ch 115.
401. *Re White's Will Trusts* [1951] 1 All ER 528.
402. [1996] 1 WLR 288.
403. [1958] IR 311.
404. [1957] IR 299.
405. *Ibid.* at 333.

a hospital is a charity in the legal meaning of that term.'[406] The real issue which had to be resolved by the Supreme Court was whether the fact that the hospital admitted a number of fee-paying patients could alter this position. The court found that the presence in the hospital of a limited number of patients falling into this category did not detract from the charitable purpose of the institution and concluded that it was used exclusively for charitable purposes within the meaning of the section.[407] However, it is interesting to note that Kingsmill Moore J commented that 'if a hospital is being conducted exclusively for the well-to-do it ceases to be charitable'[408] and later in his judgment he modified this statement to read 'exclusively or predominantly'.[409]

In practice, the more important issue is probably the destination of any profits which may be derived from the hospital's activities and O'Daly J laid emphasis in *Barrington's* case on the fact that no private profit was derived from the premises by its occupiers. The non-profit making nature of a private hospital also proved to be of relevance in *Re Resch's Will Trusts*,[410] where a gift of the testator's residuary estate to a private non-profit making hospital was upheld as charitable despite the objection that it only provided for 'persons of means'. Lord Wilberforce confirmed that a hospital does not lose its charitable status 'because charges are made to the recipients of benefits' but stressed that a certain type of hospital might not qualify as charitable in nature, either because it 'is carried on commercially, i.e. with a view to making profits for private individuals, or that the benefits it provides are not for the public, or a sufficiently large section of the public to satisfy the necessary tests of public character.'[411]

The destination of the profits derived from a private hospital also appeared to be of relevance in *Gleeson v Attorney General*,[412] which concerned the charitable status of St Vincent's Private Hospital in Dublin which operated in conjunction with a public hospital. Kenny J stated that 'there is ... much to be said for the view that a private nursing home which charges fees and which is run in conjunction with a hospital and whose profits are applied for the purposes of the hospital is a legal charity'.[413] He reiterated that an institution does not cease to be charitable in nature because its activities benefit 'the rich as well as the poor' and concluded that the private hospital was a legally charitable institution. However, it should be noted that in *Odstock Private Care Ltd's*

---

406. *Ibid.* at 321.
407. See also *Re Worth Library* [1995] 2 IR 301, 339-340. Although note the findings made by Palles CB in *Clancy v Commissioner of Valuation* [1911] 2 IR 173 in relation to the charitable status of a hall where a majority of the persons using it paid for the use of the facilities.
408. [1957] IR 299, 322.
409. *Ibid.* at 334. Relying on *Governors of Royal Victoria Hospital v Commissioner of Valuation* (1939) 73 ILTR 236.
410. [1969] 1 AC 514.
411. *Ibid.* at 540-541.
412. High Court 1972 No. 2664 Sp (Kenny J) 6 April 1973.
413. *Ibid.* at 11.

Application for Registration as a Charity[414] the Charity Commissioners held that a company which provided private health care at an NHS hospital could not be registered as a charity where its services were not available to the public at large, because those living in poverty could not afford the fees.

Section 3(7)(b) of the Charities Act 2009, which provides that account shall be taken of the amount of any charge payable for any service provided in furtherance of the purpose for which the gift is given and whether it is likely to limit the number or classes of persons who will benefit from the gift, will now be relevant in this context. So, as Keane has suggested, '[h]ospitals and nursing homes are unlikely to satisfy this test if they are financed exclusively by fees for admissions.'[415]

Finally, it should be noted that Keane J placed a fairly flexible interpretation on the concept of a gift for the benefit of a hospital in *Re Worth Library*.[416] As noted above, Keane J concluded that the bequest of the library played a role in the advancement of the charity represented by the hospital by providing 'a haven of quiet intellectual relaxation' for the named office holders and as such constituted a valid charitable bequest for the benefit of that institution within the fourth category of Lord Macnaghten's classification. While Keane J commented that he did not feel that there was any ground for scepticism as to the capacity of Dr Worth's bequest to play a part in the advancement of the charity represented by the hospital, his conclusion is difficult to reconcile with his earlier attitude towards the public benefit question and undoubtedly extends the prior understanding of what might constitute a gift for the benefit of a hospital.

Gifts to Advance Community Development and Promote Harmonious Community Relations and Related Purposes

Traditionally, it has been accepted that trusts for the benefit of a particular locality or community are charitable in nature. So, trusts which make provision for the carrying out of public works or the provision of public facilities such as a village club and reading room in a specified area,[417] will be recognised as charitable. In addition, gifts to a particular locality have traditionally been upheld provided they are of a general character or, where purposes are specified, where these are exclusively charitable in nature. A gift to a church council,[418] or to a town[419] will be upheld where the purposes are confined to general or public purposes beneficial to the community, although a gift to a parish to be applied to 'such public, benevolent or charitable purposes' as the trustees might

414. [2008] WTLR 675.
415. Keane, *Equity and the Law of Trusts in Ireland* (3rd ed., 2017) p. 197.
416. [1995] 2 IR 301.
417. *Re Scowcroft* [1898] 2 Ch 638.
418. *Re Norton's Will Trusts* [1948] 2 All ER 842.
419. *Re Allen* [1905] 2 Ch 400.

think proper was construed disjunctively and was not regarded as charitable in nature.[420] It was reiterated by Lewison J in *Re Harding*[421] that a gift to the inhabitants of a locality, without specifying a particular purpose for which it was to be applied, is a valid charitable gift and that the same principle applies to a gift to a particular class of inhabitants within a locality on the basis that the court construes it as implicitly limited to charitable purposes. However, he stressed that if an express purpose is stated, that purpose must itself be charitable and that 'a non-charitable purpose trust cannot be validated by localising the gift'.[422] In the circumstances he concluded that a gift to the Diocese of Westminster for 'the black community' of specified London boroughs should in accordance with the provisions of section 34(1) of the Race Relations Act 1976 be construed as if the restriction by reference to colour had been removed and took effect as a gift to the diocese on charitable trusts, the precise nature of which could be dealt with by a scheme.

It was suggested by Lord Browne-Wilkinson delivering the judgment of the Privy Council in *Attorney-General of the Cayman Islands v Wahr-Hansen*[423] that gifts for the benefit of a named locality or its inhabitants have been 'benevolently construed'. The Privy Council rejected the submission that a gift for 'organisations or institutions operating for the public good' not limited to a particular locality should attract such a benevolent construction. In the view of Lord Browne-Wilkinson, to apply the principles developed in relation to gifts to a locality to all cases where there are general statements of benevolent or philanthropic objectives so as to restrict the meaning of the words to such objects as are in law charitable would not be permissible.

A number of purposes related to community welfare and development are now included in the list of purposes of benefit to the community set out in section 3(11) of the Charities Act 2009. It refers to 'the advancement of community welfare',[424] 'the advancement of community development, including rural or urban regeneration',[425] and 'the promotion of civic responsibility or voluntary work'.[426]

Gifts for the Benefit of Animals

Gifts for the benefit of particular animals are not considered charitable, although as we have seen above,[427] they may be upheld if limited to the perpetuity period

420. *Houston v Burns* [1918] AC 337.
421. [2008] Ch 235.
422. *Ibid.* at 240. See also *Williams Trustees v Inland Revenue Commissioners* [1947] AC 447.
423. [2001] 1 AC 75.
424. Section 3(11)(a).
425. Section 3(11)(b).
426. Section 3(11)(c).
427. See *supra* Chapter 10.

as an anomalous exception to the principle that purpose trusts will not be enforced. However, gifts for the welfare of animals generally or for a particular type of animal are recognised as charitable in law.

The rationale behind this finding has varied. In England, the motive of public utility appeared to underlie some of the early decisions in this area,[428] but more recently the idea that kindness towards animals tends to promote the morality of human beings seems to be fundamental to the reasoning employed. In *Re Wedgewood*[429] Swinfen Eady LJ stated as follows:

> A gift for the benefit and protection of animals tends to promote and encourage kindness towards them, to discourage cruelty, and to ameliorate the condition of the brute creation, and thus to stimulate humane and generous sentiments in man towards the lower animals, and by these means promote feelings of humanity and morality generally, repress brutality and thus elevate the human race.

In an Irish context, there was evidence in the judgment of Chatterton VC in *Armstrong v Reeves*[430] that the motive of safeguarding the welfare of the animals themselves might be sufficient to bring such trusts within the fourth heading of Lord Macnaghten's classification. However, the approach in *Wedgewood* appears to have been taken by members of the Irish Court of Appeal in *Re Cranston*,[431] in which Holmes LJ commented that '[i]f it is beneficial to the community to promote virtue and to discourage vice, it must be beneficial to teach the duty of justice and fair treatment to the brute creation, and to repress one of the most revolting kinds of cruelty.'[432] Certainly in England the establishment of some benefit to human beings was considered to be of paramount importance as was stressed by Russell LJ in *Re Grove-Grady*,[433] where he said that the validity of gifts in favour of animals depended on the question of whether they produce a benefit to mankind.

Whatever the rationale for enforcing trusts of this nature, a variety of different types of gifts have been upheld. These include trusts for the care of specific categories of domestic animals; for example, gifts to a 'Home for Lost Dogs',[434] to 'the Dublin Home for Starving and Forsaken Cats',[435] and

428. *London University v Yarrow* (1857) 1 De G & J 72.
429. [1915] 1 Ch 113, 122. See also the comments of Cozens-Hardy MR to the effect that a trust of this nature tends to 'promote public morality by checking the innate tendency to cruelty.' (at 117).
430. (1890) 25 LR Ir 325.
431. [1898] 1 IR 431.
432. *Ibid.* at 457.
433. [1929] 1 Ch 557, 582. See also *National Anti-Vivisection Society v IRC* [1948] AC 31, 45.
434. *Re Douglas* (1887) 35 Ch D 472.
435. *Swifte v Attorney General* [1912] 1 IR 133.

'for the welfare of cats and kittens needing care and attention'[436] have been upheld as charitable. Similarly, gifts of a general nature for the protection and benefit of animals,[437] or to a society which possesses such aims,[438] were upheld, irrespective of whether its activities were confined to the protection of domestic animals or of animals useful to man.[439] In addition, a gift to institutions such as a sanctuary which provides refuge for sick and unwanted animals[440] were regarded as charitable in nature. However, it is important that such institutions are not intended to be profit-making if they are to qualify for charitable status. As Russell LJ stated in *Re Satterthwaite's Will Trusts*,[441] '*prima facie*, an animal hospital is a charity, as being calculated to promote public morality by encouraging kindness, discouraging cruelty and stimulating humane sentiments to the benefit of mankind; but it lacks the quality of legal charity if it be carried on for private profit as a profession or occupation or trade.'

The object of promoting vegetarianism has been recognised as charitable and in *Re Cranston*[442] the Irish Court of Appeal upheld a gift to named vegetarian societies on the basis of a subjective test as to the element of public benefit which these involved.[443] Clearly the members of the Court of Appeal were not fully convinced of the benefit of such organisations but were satisfied that the testator appreciated the benefit to be derived from their activities. As Fitzgibbon LJ commented:

> It is hard to see why the promotion of total abstinence from flesh should not be a 'charitable' object in the legal sense, if we are at liberty to recognise the promotion of total abstinence from intoxicants as charitable; moderation and temperance may be carried to excess, and though the benefits and drawbacks may differ in degree, they seem to be the same in kind. The motives of the promoters of teetotalism and of vegetarianism are equally unselfish, and equally benevolent, and the efforts of vegetarians, so far as I can form a judgment, seem less likely to do mischief than those of anti-vivisectionists, or even than those of the promulgators of the works of Joanna Southcote.[444]

In certain cases trusts which might appear to benefit animals have not been

436. *Re Moss* [1949] 1 All ER 495.
437. *Re Wedgewood* [1915] 1 Ch 113. See also *Re Green's Will Trusts* [1985] 3 All ER 455.
438. *Armstrong v Reeves* (1890) 25 LR Ir 325.
439. *Ibid.* at 341 *per* Chatterton VC.
440. *Re Murawski's Will Trusts* [1971] 1 WLR 707.
441. [1966] 1 WLR 277, 284.
442. [1898] 1 IR 431.
443. This finding that vegetarianism was a charitable object was applied in England by Joyce J in *Re Slatter* (1905) 21 TLR 295, without any reference to the different nature of the test employed in this jurisdiction.
444. [1898] 1 IR 431, 447.

found to be charitable in nature. In *Re Grove-Grady*[445] a testatrix left her residuary estate on trust to found an animal benevolent society the objects of which included the provision of a refuge for the preservation of 'all animals, birds and other creatures not human'. The majority of the Court of Appeal held that the trust was not charitable as it lacked the necessary element of benefit to the community, Russell LJ stating that 'it is merely a trust to secure that all animals within the area shall be free from molestation or destruction by man. It is not a trust directed to ensure absence or diminution of pain or cruelty in the destruction of animal life.'[446] It is likely that such a decision would not be followed given the intervention of statute, particularly in view of the increased importance attached to preserving different species of wildlife,[447] or that alternatively such a trust might be upheld on the basis of its educational value. It was also held by Lewison J in *Hanchett-Stamford v Attorney-General*[448] that the Performing and Captive Animals Defence League was not a charitable trust. While he accepted that a trust which had as its sole object the prevention of cruelty to performing animals would be capable of being charitable, nonetheless he concluded that its purpose was not charitable in nature as one of the objects of the league was to secure an outright ban on performing animals, which would involve a change in the law.

Another category of trust which might be said to be of direct benefit to animals and which has met with differing judicial reaction over the last century is that of trusts which aim to abolish vivisection. In *Armstrong v Reeves*[449] a legacy to the Society for the Abolition of Vivisection was held to be charitable on the grounds that the society was for the public benefit as it tended to correct and prevent cruelty to animals. Chatterton VC rejected the argument that there was something illegal in the nature of the society as one of its aims was to secure the suppression of vivisection by changing the law. In his view it was instead 'a society for the purpose of inducing the legislature by legitimate means, by bringing public opinion to bear, to make certain alterations in the law.'[450]

A similar view was taken by Chitty J in *Re Foveaux*,[451] although the House of Lords held in *National Anti-Vivisection Society v IRC*[452] that the society was not entitled to income tax relief on the grounds that its object was not a charitable one. Faced with a finding of fact made in the lower court that the benefit to humanity in allowing vivisection outweighed the incidental suffering to animals, the House of Lords concluded that a trust which had been found to

445. [1929] 1 Ch 557.
446. *Ibid.* at 585.
447. Note the more recent decision of Holland J in *Attorney General of New South Wales v Satwell* [1978] 2 NSWLR 200.
448. [2009] Ch 173. See further Griffiths [2009] Conv 428; Baughen [2010] Conv 216.
449. (1890) 25 LR Ir 325.
450. *Ibid.* at 339.
451. [1895] 2 Ch 501.
452. [1948] AC 31.

be detrimental to society could not be charitable merely because of the testator's opinion. The reasoning behind such a conclusion would seem to be that while the protection of animals from cruelty is a charitable purpose, vivisection is a necessary element in medical research and its suppression could not therefore be considered to be beneficial to the community. This point is evident in the judgment of Buckley J in *Re Jenkins's Will Trusts*,[453] where he stated as follows:

> [T]he prohibiting of any forms of cruelty inherent in vivisection, however admirable that may be from an ethical point of view, is not a charitable activity in the contemplation of the law because the court cannot weigh the benefits to the community which result from using animals for vivisection and research against the benefits which would result to the community from preventing such practices.

Section 3(11)(j) of the Charities Act 2009 now specifically includes 'the prevention or relief of suffering of animals' in the list of purposes of benefit to the community. However, given that the 'prevention or relief of sickness, disease or human suffering' is also included in this list of charitable purposes it is unlikely that the rationale underlying decisions such as *National Anti-Vivisection Society v IRC*[454] and *Re Jenkins's Will Trusts*[455] will be revisited.

Gifts for Sporting and Recreational Purposes

In this context it may be necessary to draw a distinction between trusts to promote and encourage a particular sport or sports, which have traditionally not been regarded as charitable, and trusts to provide facilities for recreational purposes, which will almost invariably be upheld. So, in *Re Nottage*,[456] where a testator had sought to establish a trust to provide a prize for the most successful yacht of the season in order to encourage the sport of yacht racing, the Court of Appeal emphasised that a gift to encourage sport for its own sake was not in itself a charitable one. However, a gift of this nature may be upheld where it is part of a more general charitable purpose such as improving the effectiveness of the armed forces. In *Re Gray*[457] a gift to a regimental fund for the promotion of sport[458] was upheld on the basis that it would improve the efficiency of the army. As Romer J commented, 'it is to be observed that the particular sports specified were all healthy outdoor sports, indulgence in which might reasonably

453. [1966] Ch 249, 255.
454. [1948] AC 31.
455. [1966] Ch 249.
456. [1895] 2 Ch 649. See also *Re Patten* [1929] 2 Ch 276 (a gift to encourage the playing of cricket) and *Laing v Commissioner of Stamp Duties* [1948] NZLR 154 (rowing, swimming and athletics).
457. [1925] Ch 362.
458. Limited to shooting, fishing, cricket, football and polo.

be supposed to encourage physical efficiency.'[459] Similarly, gifts to provide for the promotion of sport in a school,[460] or in educational institutions generally,[461] as we have seen will be regarded as being for the advancement of education.[462]

The provision of recreational or leisure facilities such as parks[463] or playing fields[464] have been recognised as charitable objectives and in *Re Morgan*[465] a gift for 'a public recreation ground for amateur activities' for the benefit of a particular parish was upheld. The suggestion was made by Lord MacDermott LCJ in *Commissioner of Valuation v Lurgan Borough Council*[466] that a distinction must be drawn between the provision of indoor and outdoor facilities and he commented that 'the law does not regard the mere provision of recreational facilities charitable unless they are provided in the open air on land dedicated to the use and enjoyment of the public.' However, this distinction is not supported by authority in this jurisdiction as an examination of the decision of a Divisional Court in *Clancy v Commissioner of Valuation*[467] shows. The point at issue was whether a hall built with the object of 'promoting temperance among the poor and labouring classes of the town of Sligo and neighbouring districts' and used for such diverse activities as playing billiards and cards and taking baths, was used for exclusively charitable purposes. Persons using the hall were expected to pay an entrance fee; thereafter they were 'put on their honour' to make small contributions if they could afford to do so and the evidence established that more than half of the patrons made such contributions. Palles CB expressed the view that while the user of the hall might have been regarded as being exclusively charitable, the fact that its facilities were open to all, rich and poor alike, posed a difficulty and he concluded that its use by persons not falling within the ambit of the charitable purpose was not 'insignificant or insubstantial'. Gibson J found that the primary object of the institution was charitable as being 'for the moral and educational improvement of its visitors' but he agreed with the finding of Palles CB that its user was not exclusively charitable in nature. While the question was not expressly considered, it would appear that the court implicitly recognised that the provision of recreational facilities for the benefit of the public, whether outdoor or indoor, would be regarded as charitable.

A number of points should be noted about *Clancy's* case which would suggest its general value as a precedent is now limited. First, it was made in

459. [1925] Ch 362, 365.
460. *Re Mariette* [1915] 2 Ch 284.
461. *IRC v McMullen* [1981] AC 1.
462. See *supra* p. 428.
463. *Brisbane City Council v Attorney-General for Queensland* [1979] AC 411.
464. *Re Hadden* [1932] 1 Ch 133. The gift was for 'playing fields, parks, gymnasiums or other plans which will give recreation to as many people as possible'.
465. [1955] 1 WLR 738.
466. [1968] NI 104, 125.
467. [1911] 2 IR 173.

the context of a decision on rating which, as has been acknowledged,[468] often involves a more restrictive view of the concept of charitable status than might be employed in relation to a trust or gift. In addition, the fact that certain patrons of the hall paid for the use of the facilities should no longer appear to cause the same difficulty if one accepts by analogy the reasoning employed by the Supreme Court in the context of a hospital which took in fee-paying patients in *Barrington's Hospital v Commissioner of Valuation*,[469] although it must be acknowledged that these individuals constituted a smaller percentage of the whole than the paying patrons in *Clancy*. A further consideration which would now be of relevance is the potential application to such cases of section 49(1) of the Charities Act 1961 which provides that where the purposes of a gift include charitable and non-charitable objects, its terms shall be construed so as to exclude the non-charitable objects.

A decision in this jurisdiction which shows a more flexible approach is *Shillington v Portadown UDC*,[470] where a gift to an urban council for the purpose of encouraging and providing 'means of healthy recreation' for the residents of an area was found to be charitable, aided by the application of a subjective test to the question of whether the trust was one beneficial to the community. As Barton J stated:

> The testator's purpose was a charitable or public purpose. He wished to benefit the residents of his native town and of its immediate neighbourhood. The benefits which he intended to confer on them were such as he believed to be of public advantage. That belief was rational and not contrary to the laws of the land or the principles of morality.[471]

It should also be noted that legislation was introduced in England to regulate the status of trusts for recreational purposes, partly to restore the perceived *status quo* which was threatened by a number of restrictive decisions such as those of the House of Lords in *IRC v Baddeley*[472] and by the Court of Appeal in Northern Ireland in *Trustees of the Londonderry Presbyterian Church House v IRC*.[473] Section 5(1) of the Charities Act 2011 provides that subject to the provisions of the Act, 'it is charitable (and is to be treated as always having been charitable) to provide, or assist in the provision of, facilities for (a) recreation, or (b) other leisure-time occupation, if the facilities are provided in the interests of social welfare.'[474] The latter requirement will not be met unless the facilities are provided 'with the object of improving the conditions

468. *Barrington's Hospital v Commissioner of Valuation* [1957] IR 299, 333.
469. [1957] IR 299.
470. [1911] 1 IR 247.
471. *Ibid.* at 256-257.
472. [1955] AC 572.
473. [1946] NI 178.
474. Replacing s.1(1) of the Recreational Charities Act 1958.

of life' of those whom they are primarily intended for and '(i) those persons have need of the facilities because of their youth, age, infirmity or disability, poverty or social and economic circumstances or (ii) the facilities are to be available to the members of the public at large or to male, or female, members of the public at large.'[475]

The meaning of these provisions was considered by the House of Lords in *Guild v IRC*,[476] in which a testator left the residue of his estate to a town council for use in connection with the town's sport centre or for some similar purpose in connection with sport. The House of Lords held that on the true construction of section 1(2)(a) of the Recreational Charities Act 1958,[477] facilities for recreation or other leisure time activities could be provided with the object of improving people's conditions of life, notwithstanding that such people were not in a position of relative social disadvantage or suffering from some degree of deprivation. It concluded that the testator's bequest would come within the ambit of section 1(2) of the Act of 1958 and was therefore charitable in nature on the basis that people from all walks of life may have their condition of life improved by the provision of suitable recreational facilities. Similar legislation was introduced in Northern Ireland and was applied in *Springhill Housing Action Committee v Commissioner of Valuation*,[478] in which a community centre in the Springhill estate in Belfast was found to be used wholly or mainly for charitable purposes. Gibson LJ stated that he was satisfied that the centre was occupied for a purpose which is normally charitable and the class of persons for whose benefit it was occupied, being the residents of a sizeable estate, was not so insignificant in number as to deprive it of its *prima facie* public character.

The issue of whether amateur sport generally should be regarded as a charitable purpose has provoked considerable debate in a number of common law jurisdictions. The Goodman Committee in England recommended that the encouragement of sport and recreation should in itself be recognised as a charitable object, provided that the requirement of benefit to the community is satisfied.[479] This issue was also considered in some detail by the High Court of Ontario in *Re Laidlaw Foundation*,[480] which agreed with the finding made in the lower court that the promotion of amateur athletic sports was charitable in that under controlled circumstances it promoted health and was in itself educational. However, more recently in *Amateur Youth Soccer Association v Canada*,[481] the Supreme Court of Canada upheld a decision not to register the appellant as a charity. Rothstein J accepted that the case law has established that a sporting activity may be charitable when connected to another recognised head

475. Section 5(3) of the Charities Act 2011.
476. [1992] 2 AC 310. See further Norman [1992] Conv 361.
477. Now s.5(3)(a) of the Charities Act 2011.
478. [1983] NI 184.
479. The Goodman Committee Report on Charity Law and Voluntary Organisations (1976).
480. (1984) 13 DLR (4th) 491. See further Breen (2001) 6 CPLJ 76.
481. [2007] SCC 42.

of charity such as education but had to consider the appellant's contention that it was time for the courts to acknowledge that the promotion of amateur sports involving the pursuit of physical fitness could stand on its own as a purpose within the fourth *Pemsel* category. While he was sympathetic to the proposition that organisations promoting fitness should be considered charitable, he was satisfied that the appellant association's main objective was the promotion of soccer and he stated that the fact that a purpose happens to have a beneficial by-product is not enough to make it charitable in nature. He concluded that while it might be desirable as a matter of policy to give sports associations the tax advantages of charitable status, in his view this was a task better suited to the legislature than the courts.

The approach towards the question of whether the advancement of amateur sport should be a charitable purpose in England is now clear. In 2003 the Charity Commission recognised as charitable 'the promotion of community participation in healthy recreation by providing facilities for playing particular sports' and 'the advancement of the physical education of young people not undergoing formal education'.[482] Now section 3(1) of the English Charities Act 2011, which lists purposes which qualify as 'charitable purposes', includes '(g) the advancement of amateur sport'[483] and section 3(2)(d) defines sport in this context as 'sports or games which promote health by involving physical or mental skill or exertion'.[484]

However, both recent case law and legislative provisions make it clear that the advancement of amateur sport will not qualify as a legally charitable purpose in this jurisdiction. This issue was considered by Charleton J in *National Tourism Development Authority v Coughlan*,[485] in which he had to consider whether a trust, the subject matter of which was golf courses, could be charitable in nature. At the outset Charleton J acknowledged that the definition of charity in law differs from that generally applied in the wider community and he said that while one would imagine that trusts for sporting objects would be held to be beneficial to the community, that is not how the law has regarded charitable gifts for the promotion of any particular sport. Charleton J referred to the fact that in some of the decided cases, no importance was attached to the fact that a fee was charged for membership of an organisation existing for a charitable purpose, although he said that the more exclusive the enterprise, the less likely it is to have as its sole purpose the betterment of society in general. He expressed the view that the trust had been set up by the plaintiff in order

482. Research Report 11 – Charitable Status and Sport (April 2003) p.1.
483. Section 2(2)(g) of the Charities Act (Northern Ireland) 2008 makes the same provision and s. 7(2)(h) of the Charities and Trustee Investment (Scotland) Act 2005 lists 'the advancement of public participation in sport' as a charitable purpose.
484. Community amateur sports clubs registered as such were already afforded tax relief (see Chapter 9 of Part 13 of the Corporation Tax Act 2010) and s. 6 of the Charities Act 2011 provides that if such a club is registered for this purpose it is not a charity.
485. [2009] 3 IR 549.

to benefit tourism in the relevant area and said that it was difficult to imagine a trust for the purposes of tourism as being of itself of sufficient benefit to the community to attract charitable status. In summarising his observations on the issues raised Charleton J stated, *inter alia*, as follows:

> Sport has never been recognised to be an object of sufficiently wide benefit to the community as to enjoy charitable status. The law has traditionally regarded sport as a form of recreation and, in consequence, trusts and bequests for sporting purposes are not recognised as charitable.[486]

Applying his observations to the facts of the case before him, Charleton J concluded that he did not regard the activity being carried on by the defendants as being anything other than sport and recreation. In his view the subject matter of the trust, a golf course, could not be the subject of a charitable trust under ordinary circumstances, although he said that an exception might arise if the trust had been set up for the use of a golf course by members of the army or by people with disabilities. He therefore concluded that the trust could not be regarded as a charitable one.

The omission of any reference to the advancement of any form of sporting activity in the list of purposes set out in section 3(11) of the Charities Act 2009 has justifiably given rise to criticism in the light of the importance now attached to engaging in exercise from a health perspective. While it was contended that the legislation merely sought to preserve the *status quo* in relation to sporting activities and charitable status,[487] it has effectively ruled out any incremental change in the law in this area as section 2 defines an 'excluded body' to include an approved body of persons within the meaning of section 235 of the Taxes Consolidation Act 1997, which is 'any body of persons established for and existing for the sole purpose of promoting athletic or amateur games or sports'. Although this means that such bodies can qualify for exemptions from income tax and corporation tax, the lack of charitable status may lead to them being less likely to attract donations from third parties.[488] To this extent the rationale behind the manner in which the legislation dealt with the status of amateur sporting bodies is open to question.

Gifts for Political Purposes

It is well-established that trusts for the advancement of political purposes are

486. *Ibid.* at 569.
487. 192 Seanad Debates col.728, 4 December 2008, John Curran TD.
488. It may in any event reduce their income from donations. Pursuant to s.848A of the Taxes Consolidation Act 1997, inserted by s.45 of the Finance Act 2001 and as amended by s.15 of the Finance Act 2013, charities can reclaim tax paid on donations.

not charitable and as a result gifts for the benefit of specific political parties will clearly not qualify for charitable status.[489]

It is often not easy to distinguish trusts which will be accepted as being *bona fide* for the advancement of education from those which are merely disguised as being for such a purpose and are in fact designed to promote political purposes. In *Re Trusts of the Arthur McDougall Fund*[490] a trust for the teaching of political theory was accepted as being educational in nature and in *Re Koeppler's Will Trusts*[491] a bequest to fund the holding of conferences with political themes was also upheld. However, a more borderline case is *Re Scowcroft*,[492] in which a gift for the maintenance of a village club and reading room 'for the furtherance of Conservative principles and religious and mental improvement' was found to be charitable, the reasoning employed by Stirling J suggesting that he felt able to make this finding because the purposes of the trust were not predominantly political. A different conclusion was reached in *Re Hopkinson*,[493] where a trust for the advancement of adult education with particular reference to education in the Labour Party's doctrines was found not to be charitable. As Vaisey J commented, '[p]olitical propaganda masquerading — I do not use that word in any sinister sense — as education is not education within the statute of Elizabeth ... In other words it is not charitable.'[494] This reasoning was applied by Goulding J in *Re Bushnell*,[495] in which a bequest for 'the advancement and propagation of the teaching of socialised medicine' was found to have predominantly political rather than educational objectives and was therefore not charitable in nature. Provided that the predominant motive for a trust is not political, it may often be upheld and as Goulding J commented, '[t]he existence of some political motive is not necessarily fatal to a good charitable trust'.[496]

A number of decisions suggest that the purpose of aiming to secure peace by a particular means will not be considered charitable as it is political in nature. In the New Zealand decision of *Re Collier*[497] a bequest for the promotion of world peace failed as being overtly political, Hammond J adding that to the extent that soldiers were being encouraged to 'down arms' it also pursued an

489. In relation to trusts to support a political party Hammond J commented in the New Zealand decision of *Re Collier* [1998] 1 NZLR 81, 90 that the conclusion that trusts for their benefit are not charitable 'appears to be the agreed position throughout the common law world' and stated that he was not aware of any suggestion that any change to this position should be effected.
490. [1957] 1 WLR 81.
491. [1986] Ch 423.
492. [1898] 2 Ch 638.
493. [1949] 1 All ER 346. See also *Bonar Law Memorial Trust v IRC* (1933) 49 TLR 220.
494. *Ibid.* at 350.
495. [1975] 1 WLR 1596.
496. *Ibid.* at 1603. Approved by Slade J in *McGovern v Attorney General* [1982] Ch 321, 343. See also *Re Scowcroft* [1898] 2 Ch 638.
497. [1998] 1 NZLR 81.

unlawful aim. In *Southwood v Attorney General*[498] the Court of Appeal held that 'the advancement of education of the public in the subject of militarism and disarmament' was not a charitable purpose. Referring to the *dicta* of Slade J in *McGovern v Attorney General*,[499] Chadwick LJ stated that cases in which the court will regard the element of public benefit as incapable of proof one way or the other include gifts for 'political objects'. He said that while he would have no difficulty in accepting the proposition that it promotes public benefit for the public to be educated in the differing means of securing peace and avoiding war, there are divergent views on how best to achieve this aim. Chadwick LJ stated as follows:

> The court is in no position to determine that promotion of one view rather than the other is for the public benefit. Not only does the court have no material on which to make that choice; to attempt to do so would be to usurp the role of government. So the court cannot recognize a charitable trust to educate the public to an acceptance that peace is best secured by demilitarization…Nor conversely could the court recognize a charitable trust to educate the public to an acceptance that war is best avoided by collective security through the membership of a military alliance ….[500]

Santow's comment that the line between educational and political has become blurred in this context is a fair one.[501] Recently in *Re Greenpeace of New Zealand Inc*,[502] considered in more detail below, the Supreme Court of New Zealand, although it rejected the 'political purpose' exclusion, voiced concerns about how a court might assess the public benefit of trusts which purported to promote peace. It found that the Court of Appeal had applied an incorrect approach to the assessment of charitable purposes when it concluded that an object 'to promote nuclear disarmament and the elimination of weapons of mass destruction' was charitable and remitted the application for charitable status for reconsideration. Elias CJ expressed the view that the achievement of nuclear disarmament would require a change in the policy pursued by certain states and in the dealings of the New Zealand government towards other nations. She said that for the reasons discussed by Slade J in *McGovern v Attorney General*, the court would have no adequate means of judging the public benefit of promoting nuclear disarmament and the elimination of all weapons of mass destruction. In her view, '[w]hether promotion of these ideas is beneficial is a matter of opinion in which public benefit is not self-evident and which seems unlikely to be capable of demonstration by evidence.'[503] She added that where

498. [2000] EWCA Civ 204. See Garton (2000) 14 Trust Law Int 233.
499. [1982] Ch 321, 333-334.
500. *Ibid.* at [29].
501. (1999) 52 CLP 255, 276.
502. [2015] 1 NZLR 169.
503. *Ibid.* at 206.

a charity promotes an abstraction, such as 'peace' or 'nuclear disarmament', 'the focus in assessing charitable purpose must be on *how* such abstraction is to be furthered.'[504]

The principle that a trust which essentially has political objectives will not be regarded as charitable was confirmed in this jurisdiction in *Re Ní Brudair*,[505] where a gift for the benefit of republicans according to the objects of that movement as they were in the years 1919–1921 was found to be too vague and uncertain to constitute a valid charitable gift. Gannon J concluded that taking an overall view of the express directions of the testatrix and the 'latitude of apparent duty imposed on her trustees' he was satisfied that there was no charitable intention nor charitable gift in the legal sense in her will. He also commented that even if the testatrix had presented her trustees with the democratic programme of the Dáil of January 1919 by way of directions as to how the money was to be spent this was essentially a statement of broad political objectives and would not constitute a valid charitable trust.

Often trusts for the advancement of political purposes will involve advocating a change in the law and this latter objective provides one of the primary reasons why trusts of this nature will not be regarded as charitable.[506] Lord Parker laid down the reasons for this general principle in *Bowman v Secular Society Ltd*[507] as follows:

> [A] trust for the attainment of political objects has always been held invalid, not because it is illegal, for everyone is at liberty to advocate or promote by any lawful means a change in the law, but because the court has no means of judging whether a proposed change in the law will or will not be for the public benefit, and therefore cannot say that a gift to secure the change is a charitable gift.

This principle was approved by Lord Simonds in *National Anti-Vivisection Society v IRC*,[508] where it was held by the House of Lords that the main object of the society was political, namely the abolition of vivisection by means of an alteration in the law, and that for this reason it could not be considered as a body established for charitable purposes only. Similarly, in *R. v Radio Authority, ex p. Bull*,[509] it was held by the Court of Appeal that the promotion of the observance of fundamental human rights by campaigning to change the

---

504. *Ibid.*
505. High Court 1976 No. 93 Sp (Gannon J) 5 February 1979. See also *Gurry v Goff* [1980] ILRM 103.
506. As Hammond J stated in the New Zealand decision of *Re Collier* [1998] 1 NZLR 81, 89, 'the conventional view in the British Commonwealth is that charitable trusts to change the law itself are invalid'.
507. [1917] AC 406, 442.
508. [1948] AC 31.
509. [1998] QB 294.

law or government policy was a political object within the meaning of section 92(2)(a)(i) of the Broadcasting Act 1990.[510]

The *dictum* of Lord Parker in *Bowman v Secular Society Ltd* was analysed further by Slade J in *McGovern v Attorney General*,[511] which concerned the question of whether a trust created by Amnesty International to achieve certain stated purposes could be registered as a charity. These purposes included the relief of needy persons who were or had been prisoners of conscience and their families, attempting to secure the release of such prisoners, procuring the abolition of torture or inhuman or degrading treatment or punishment, the promotion of research into the maintenance and observance of human rights and the dissemination of the results of such research. Slade J concluded that a trust, the main objective of which was to secure a change in the laws of a foreign country, could not be regarded as charitable because the court would have no means of knowing whether such a change would be for the public benefit and because of public policy considerations based on the risk of prejudicing relations between the countries concerned. Slade J stated that a trust for political purposes falling within the spirit of Lord Parker's pronouncement in *Bowman's* case can never be regarded as being for the public benefit in the manner which the law regards as charitable. He laid down the following general principle:

> Trusts for political purposes falling within the spirit of this pronouncement include, *inter alia*, trusts of which a direct and principal purpose is either (i) to further the interests of a particular political party; or (ii) to procure changes in the laws of this country; or (iii) to procure changes in the law of a foreign country; or (iv) to procure a reversal of government policy or of particular decisions of governmental authorities in this country; or (v) to procure a reversal of government policy or of particular decisions of governmental authorities in a foreign country.[512]

One further point of importance to be derived from the judgment of Slade J is his comment that if all the main objects of a trust are exclusively charitable, the fact that the trustees may have incidental powers to employ political means to further these objects will not deprive the trust of its charitable status.

Hammond J in the decision of the High Court of New Zealand in *Re Collier*[513] questioned 'why is it that the law allows existing charities to make "political" statements; yet … impugns *ab initio* those which are proposed to be set up to campaign for reform'. Clearly the notion that a 'coherent system

510. Section 92(2)(a)(i) of the Act of 1990 provided that a licensed independent radio service could not include advertisements inserted by or on behalf of a body whose objects were wholly or mainly of a political character.
511. [1982] Ch 321. See Watkin [1982] Conv 387; Nobles (1982) 45 MLR 704; Walton [2014] Conv 317.
512. *Ibid.* at 340.
513. [1998] 1 NZLR 81, 90.

of law can scarcely admit that objects which are inconsistent with its own provisions are for the public welfare'[514] is increasingly being called into question and as Hammond J pointed out in *Re Collier*, judges themselves often make suggestions for changes in the law.

There has recently been a change in attitude in parts of the common law world in relation to the issue of whether trusts which have political purposes may have charitable status. It has been held in Australia that there is no general rule excluding 'political objects' from charitable purposes in that jurisdiction. In *Aid/Watch Inc v Commissioner of Taxation*[515] the High Court of Australia had to consider whether an organisation involved in campaigning for effective foreign aid policies through the generation of public debate was a charitable institution for the purpose of obtaining tax exemption. The majority of the High Court[516] accepted that generating public debate about the best methods for the relief of poverty by the provision of foreign aid has characteristics indicative of charitable status, as these activities were apt to contribute to the public welfare and did not fall within any area of disqualification from such status.

Similarly, in New Zealand, the majority of the Supreme Court held in *Re Greenpeace of New Zealand Inc*[517] that the political purpose exclusion should no longer be applied in that jurisdiction. The matter before the Supreme Court of New Zealand was an appeal against the refusal to register Greenpeace New Zealand Inc as a charity, the objects of which included 'to promote the adoption of legislation, policies, rules, regulations and plans which further the objects of the Society and support their enforcement or implementation through political or judicial processes, as necessary.' The majority of the court agreed that political and charitable purposes are not mutually exclusive and suggested that a blanket exclusion is unnecessary and distracts from the inquiry of whether a purpose is of public benefit within the sense recognised by the law as charitable. Elias CJ also noted that a strict exclusion policy 'risks rigidity in an area of law which should be responsive to the way society works.'[518] In her view, the better approach is not a doctrine excluding 'political' purpose but to accept that an object which entails advocacy for change in the law is simply one aspect of the question of whether a purpose advances the public benefit. She stated that 'assessment of whether advocacy or promotion of a cause or law reform is a charitable purpose depends on consideration of the end that is advocated, the means promoted to achieve that end and the manner in which the

---

514. *Per* Dixon J in *Royal North Shore Hospital of Sydney v Attorney General for New South Wales* (1938) 60 CLR 396, 426.
515. (2010) 241 CLR 539. See Chia, Harding and O'Connell (2011) 35 Melb ULR 353, who welcomed the decision (at 377) as 'a clear and strong rejection of the political purposes doctrine. It removes a doctrinal anomaly and the muddle it engendered.' See further Turner [2011] CLJ 504; Chevalier-Watts (2014) 19 Canterbury L Rev 52.
516. French CJ, Gummow, Hayne, Crennan and Bell JJ.
517. [2015] 1 NZLR 169. See further Harding (2015) 131 LQR 181; Chevalier-Watts [2015] NZLJ 108.
518. *Ibid.* at 196.

cause is promoted in order to assess whether the purpose can be said to be of public benefit within the spirit and intendment of the 1601 Statute.'[519] Harding suggests that while the majority was 'vague' in relation to the manner in which the pursuit of a political purpose might generate public benefit, they had more to say about ways in which the achievement of a purpose of this nature might create such a benefit.[520] He expresses the view that '[i]n jurisdictions where it is still recognised, the rule against political purposes is bound to come under increasing pressure as charities both seek and are compelled to engage more and more in politics.'[521]

Some useful guidance on how the law in this area is developing in England has been provided by the Charity Commission and in case law. The Commission has stated that while political means should not be the dominant method by which an organisation pursues its charitable objectives, a charity may engage in political activities in furtherance of its charitable purposes provided that these do not dominate what it does.[522] More recently the Commission has reiterated that political campaigning or activity may be undertaken by a charity only in the context of supporting the delivery of its charitable purposes.[523] It has made clear that 'a charity cannot exist for a political purpose, which is any purpose directed at furthering the interests of any political party, or securing or opposing a change in the law, policy or decisions either in this country or abroad.'[524] Whilst accepting that 'political activity, including campaigning for a change in the law, is an entirely legitimate activity and can be an effective means of supporting a charitable purpose', it has stressed that 'it is not a charitable purpose to campaign for changes to the law whether in the UK or overseas'.[525] This view was also expressed by Lewison J in *Hanchett-Stamford v Attorney-General*,[526] where he stated that '[t]he Charities Act 2006 has not changed the fundamental principle that if one of the objects or purposes of an organisation is to change the law, it cannot be charitable.' However, he also acknowledged that it was not necessarily unlawful for a charity to promote or oppose changes in the law, provided that its purposes were exclusively charitable.[527] These distinctions may

519. *Ibid.* at 198.
520. (2015) 131 LQR 181, 183.
521. *Ibid.* at 186.
522. *The Promotion of Human Rights* RR12 (January, 2005) paras. 33-34. So, in *English PEN's Application for Registration as a Charity* [2008] WTLR 1799 the Charity Commissioners held that where an organisation established for the promotion of the education and human rights of a class of beneficiaries and for the relief of poverty also pursued some political activities, it was still eligible for registration as a charity where these activities engaged less than 20% of its resources and were ancillary to its charitable purposes.
523. *Speaking Out – Guidance on Campaigning and Political Activity by Charities* CC9 (March 2008) B1.
524. *Ibid.*
525. *Ibid.* at D7.
526. [2009] Ch 173, 181-182. See further Griffiths [2009] Conv 428.
527. *Ibid.* at 180.

be difficult to draw in practice and inevitably it may still be easier for a body with existing charitable status to engage in political campaigning in support of its purpose than for an organisation which intends to use these methods to obtain such status.

Current practice in England seems broadly in line with that in this jurisdiction as an examination of the relevant provisions in the Charities Act 2009 shows.[528] Section 2(1) provides that a charitable organisation shall not include an 'excluded body' which is defined to include: '(a) a political party, or a body that promotes a political party or candidate, (b) a body that promotes a political cause, unless the promotion of that cause relates directly to the advancement of the charitable purposes of that body.' In commenting on the wording ultimately included in the legislation at the Report Stage of the Dáil Debate on the Bill, John Curran TD stressed that it was designed to allow a charity to engage in valid political work as a means of achieving its charitable aims but that it could not be its primary activity. He stated as follows:

> [C]harities will not be permitted to support either a political candidate or a party .... They will be permitted to promote a political cause but only one relating directly to their charitable purpose. A charity must take care not to become a political organisation, however, and should always remain focused on its charitable purpose, which must be, by definition, its only purpose.[529]

A related issue which provoked considerable debate during the passage of the Charities Bill 2007 through the Oireachtas is the extent to which the protection or advancement of human rights may be a valid charitable purpose. The setting out of specific purposes such as 'the advancement of conflict resolution or reconciliation', [530] 'the promotion of religious or racial harmony and harmonious community relations'[531] and 'the integration of those who are disadvantaged, and the promotion of their full participation in society'[532] undoubtedly illustrates the importance attached to the aim of fostering greater social inclusion in the legislation. However, section 3(1)(h) of the Charities Act 2011 in England specifically includes 'the advancement of human rights'[533] in the list of charitable purposes. The advancement of human rights and social justice was also included in Head 3(1)(d)(v) in the General Scheme for the

528. As Breen comments (2008) 59 NILQ 223, 227, s. 2 of the Charities Act 2009 does not exclude organisations that have otherwise charitable objects from using political means to achieve charitable ends and if the principal object of the organisation is charitable, it falls outside the ambit of s. 2.
529. 666 Dáil Debates col. 28, Report Stage, 5 November 2008.
530. Section 3(11)(e).
531. Section 3(11)(f).
532. Section 3(11)(l).
533. It is also included in s. 2(2)(h) of the Charities Act (Northern Ireland) 2008 and in s. 7(2)(j) of the Charities and Trustee Investment (Scotland) Act 2005.

Charities Regulation Bill published in March 2006 although this was deleted from the Bill as published in April 2007. Commenting on this issue during the Report Stage of the debate before the Dáil, John Curran TD stated that while the Bill did not seek to narrow charitable purposes, it did not seek to expand them either and that the advancement of human rights or social justice was not a charitable purpose at common law.[534] He commented that many of the charitable purposes listed in section 3 were closely related to human rights and were activities in which human rights groups engaged.[535] However, the omission of any specific reference to the advancement of human rights met with considerable criticism in both the Dáil and the Seanad. As Breen has suggested, given the undefined nature of the term 'political causes', section 2 of the Act will make it more difficult for human rights organisations to qualify for charitable status in the absence of any express reference to human rights as a charitable purpose.[536] More recently she has commented that '[t]he answer to the … question – are human rights too political to be charitable – seems, unfortunately, to be yes for the time being in Ireland.'[537] Two private members Bills have been introduced over the past few years with a view to adding 'the advancement of human rights' to the list of charitable purposes set out in section 3(11) but these have not been enacted.[538]

Conclusions

While the approach of largely preserving Lord Macnaghten's categories and setting them out in statutory form is to be welcomed, some of the omissions from the list of other purposes of benefit to the community in the Charities Act 2009 are surprising. An example of this is the promotion of amateur sport, and the decision to designate an organisation which has such a purpose as an 'excluded body' is difficult to justify. While the tax exemptions that these bodies may avail of are useful,[539] their exclusion from charitable status is still likely to lead to a reduction in their income.[540] Given the obvious health benefits of encouraging such activities, the approach of the legislature in this jurisdiction is open to question and the inclusion of the advancement of amateur sport as a

534. 666 Dáil Debates col. 38, Report Stage, 5 November 2008. He added that the Revenue Commissioners operate a separate tax exemption scheme for human rights bodies which have consultative status with the United Nations, such as Amnesty International, and that this position would not be affected by the legislation.
535. 192 Seanad Debates col. 750, Committee Stage, 4 December 2008.
536. Breen (2008) 59 NILQ 223, 227.
537. Breen [2012] PL 268, 285.
538. The Charities (Amendment) Bill 2014 and the Charities (Human Rights) Bill 2018.
539. See s.235 of the Taxes Consolidation Act 1997.
540. It means that the recipient body cannot reclaim tax paid on donations, as it could if the body had charitable status. See s.848A of the Taxes Consolidation Act 1997, inserted by s.45 of the Finance Act 2001 and as amended by s.15 of the Finance Act 2013.

charitable purpose in the Charities Act, as is the case in England and Wales,[541] would have been a better option.

Similarly, the omission of any reference to the advancement of human rights and social justice in the Act of 2009 is difficult to explain. The explanation that the legislature was not seeking to expand the definition of existing charitable purposes is not particularly satisfactory,[542] and an incremental development to include the advancement of human rights was in any event likely to happen over time. Given that the list of specified purposes is non-exhaustive such a development may still take place, provided that an organisation seeking charitable status can avoid being characterised as one which promotes a political cause unless it relates directly to the advancement of its otherwise charitable purposes.[543]

CY-PRÈS JURISDICTION

Introduction

Where a gift is made to charity, it may be impossible or impracticable to give effect to the intentions of the donor in the precise terms which he intended. The cy-près doctrine, where it applies, allows for the making of a scheme for the application of such property to other charitable purposes as near as possible to those intended by the donor. As Budd J stated in *Re Royal Kilmainham Hospital*,[544] '[t]he principle is applied where the method indicated by the donor of carrying out his charitable intentions becomes impracticable, or his intentions cannot be executed literally, most frequently owing to altered circumstances.' The rationale behind the operation of this doctrine is that provided a clear charitable intention is expressed, a gift should not be allowed to fail because the mode of effecting this intention, if specified, cannot be carried out, or no longer provides the most useful and effective manner of applying the bequest. From a practical perspective it will not be possible for a donor to forecast how circumstances affecting his gift will change over a period of time and this difficulty can be also said to underlie the cy-près doctrine. As Meredith J stated in *Governors of Erasmus Smith's Schools v Attorney General*:[545]

541. Section 3(1)(g) of the Charities Act 2011.
542. 666 Dáil Debates col. 38, Report Stage, 5 November 2008, John Curran TD.
543. Section 2(1) of the Charities Act 2009.
544. [1966] IR 451, 469.
545. (1931) 66 ILTR 57, 61. See also the *dictum* of Lord Eldon in *Moggridge v Thackwell* (1803) 7 Ves 36, 69 as follows: 'If the testator has manifested a general intention to give to charity, the failure of the particular mode in which the charity is to be effectuated shall not destroy the charity; but if the substantial/general intention is charity, the law will substitute another mode of devoting the property to charitable purposes, though the formal intention as to the mode cannot be accomplished.'

> To apply without modification a charitable intention that is only expressed in relation to assumed facts and under different conditions is obviously not to carry out the real intention at all. It is on this principle that Courts of Law adapt the statement of a charitable intention to suit altered circumstances and conditions with a view to giving effect to the real intention. Donors cannot be expected to provide expressly for more than the world and the times with which they are familiar.

Therefore, for a trust to attain charitable status is a most desirable aim, not only because of the advantages already considered, but also because it will facilitate the operation of cy-près jurisdiction should this become necessary. If a trust does not qualify as charitable, this jurisdiction cannot be exercised and a bequest may fail as contravening the rule against perpetual trusts, allowing a resulting trust to operate in favour of the donor or his representatives. Such resulting trusts will often not reflect the donor's wishes, and it is certainly preferable to find a means of perpetuating the donor's charitable intention in as close a form as possible to that originally expressed by him.

An examination of the judgment of Keane J in *Re Worth Library*[546] would seem to confirm that, as a prerequisite to the exercise of cy-près jurisdiction, a court must satisfy itself that the purpose for which the bequest was originally made was charitable. Despite the fact that counsel were in agreement that the bequest in question was a charitable one, Keane J expressed the view that, as the court was being invited to exercise its jurisdiction to approve a cy-près scheme, a jurisdiction which could only operate in relation to charitable bequests, he felt it necessary to investigate the issue of the charitable status of the original bequest fully. However, it is interesting to note that in another case of a similar nature, *Representative Church Body v Attorney General*,[547] in which O'Hanlon J was called upon to approve a cy-près application in relation to a collection of books in the Old Library of St. Canice's Cathedral, Kilkenny, he proceeded to grant the order sought without raising the question of the charitable nature of the bequest.

In practice, an important distinction must be drawn between circumstances where the gift fails *ab initio*, in which case the property can only be applied cy-près where the donor has manifested a general charitable intention, and cases of subsequent failure where it is not necessary to show such an intention provided that the donor has made an absolute and perpetual gift to a particular charity. This distinction has been well summarised by Murray J in *Re Dunwoodie*[548] in the following terms:

546. [1995] 2 IR 301.
547. [1988] IR 19. See further Osborough (1989) 24 Ir Jur (ns) 50.
548. [1977] NI 141, 145. This principle was expressed in a different manner by Budd J in *Re Royal Kilmainham Hospital* [1966] IR 451, 469 although the effect is the same. 'The cy-près principle is confined … to cases where property is given with a general intention to charity with this exception, that where property is given absolutely and

> There is an important distinction between a charitable trust which is initially impossible or impracticable, i.e. impossible or impracticable as at the death of the testator, and a charitable trust which becomes impossible or impracticable after his death. As regards the former type, the property involved will not be applied cy-près unless the court finds that the testator had a general charitable intention, but as regards the latter type — usually referred to as a case of supervening impossibility — the court will direct a cy-près application whether or not a general charitable intention on the part of the testator can be found in the relevant will.

It has been argued by Garton that the traditional justification put forward for the cy-près doctrine, namely that it gives effect to a donor's charitable intentions, is inadequate and incoherent.[549] He correctly points out that this rationale does not account for the distinction which is drawn between cases of initial and subsequent failure. Garton suggests that the better view is that the cy-près doctrine is simply a vehicle for the redistribution of wealth and should be exercised on this basis by the Charity Commission 'with the aim of addressing philanthropic insufficiency and particularism as part of its broader regulatory strategy for the charitable sector'.[550]

Initial Failure of Charitable Purposes

In cases where the charitable purposes of a gift fail for one of the reasons which will be examined below, the doctrine of cy-près can be applied 'where, in form, the gift is given for a particular charitable purpose, but it is possible, taking the will as a whole, to say that, notwithstanding the form of the gift, the paramount intention, according to the true construction of the will, is to give the property in the first instance for a general charitable purpose rather than a particular charitable purpose. . . .'[551] Numerous attempts have been made by the judiciary to describe the meaning of the phrase 'general charitable intention'. In *Re Templemoyle Agricultural School*[552] Chatterton VC commented as follows:

> It does not mean merely an intention to give charity [sic] generally, without reference to any specified object, but it means an intention the

---

perpetually to charity for a particular purpose and has vested in the charity the fund can be applied cy-près irrespective of the donor's particular intention.' Quoted with approval by Keane J in *Re Worth Library* [1995] 2 IR 301, 341.

549. Garton (2007) 21 Trust Law Int 134.
550. *Ibid.* at 149.
551. *Re Wilson* [1913] 1 Ch 314, 320-321 *per* Parker J. Quoted with approval by Budd J in *Munster and Leinster Bank Ltd v Attorney General* (1954) 91 ILTR 34, 39 and by White J in *Carolan v Jordan* [2014] IEHC 678 at [15].
552. (1869) IR 4 Eq 295, 301. It should be noted that this decision concerned a case of supervening failure, where arguably it was not necessary to establish a general charitable intent. See *infra* pp. 490-492.

> substance of which is charitable, whether generally and without any specified object, in which case the Crown will prescribe the mode of effectuating it, or for an object more or less accurately specified, but with a mode of benefiting that object superadded, which cannot be lawfully or at all carried into execution, in which case the Court will carry out the substantial intention.

An alternative formulation was put forward by Kay J in *Re Taylor*:[553] 'if upon the whole scope and intent of the will you discern the paramount object of the testator was to benefit not a particular institution, but to effect a particular form of charity, independently of any special institution or mode, then, although he may have indicated the mode in which he desires that to be carried out, you are to regard the primary paramount intention chiefly. . . .' A useful distinction was drawn by Dixon and Evatt JJ in *Attorney General for New South Wales v Perpetual Trustee Co. Ltd*[554] between cases in which every element in the description of the trust is indispensable to its validity and operation and cases 'where a further and more general purpose is disclosed as the true and substantial object of the trust'. A good example of a case falling into the former category is the decision of the New Zealand Court of Appeal in *Alacoque v Roche*,[555] in which the court concluded that the benefit to the convent named by the testatrix, which had closed some months before her death, was 'the sole and indispensable purpose of the gift' and that no general charitable intention could be found.

While the view has been expressed that in seeking to ascertain whether a general charitable intention can be found in a will, the court should look only at the particular gift,[556] the position would seem to be that such an intention may be discerned from other gifts contained in the will.[557] This was made clear in *Re McGwire*[558] by Black J who stressed that 'a general charitable intention may be collected from the will as a whole'. It has also been suggested that because of a reluctance to establish a construction which will lead to intestacy, the courts may lean in favour of finding a general charitable intention.[559]

Whether a donor has displayed sufficient charitable intention is inevitably a question of construction of the relevant document;[560] clearly the more detailed the donor's directions, the less likely it will be that a general charitable intention can be discerned from the terms of the instrument. However, the English

553. (1888) 58 LT 538, 543. See *Re Royal Kilmainham Hospital* [1966] IR 451, 469.
554. (1940) 63 CLR 209, 225. Quoted with approval by Murray J in *Re Stewart's Will Trusts* [1983] NI 283, 297.
555. [1998] 2 NZLR 250.
556. *Mayor of Lyons v Advocate-General of Bengal* (1876) 1 App Cas 91, 114.
557. *Re Satterthwaite's Will Trusts* [1966] 1 WLR 277, 286 *per* Russell LJ.
558. [1941] IR 33, 38.
559. *Per* Hammond J in *Re Collier* [1998] 1 NZLR 81, 95.
560. Dixon and Evatt JJ suggested in *Attorney General for New South Wales v Perpetual Trustee Co. Ltd* (1940) 63 CLR 209, 226 that this question must be approached on the basis of the circumstances of the failure of the initial trust.

decision of *Re Lysaght*[561] would appear to have widened considerably the scope of the concept of general charitable intention. A testatrix made provision in her will for funds to be applied for medical studentships within the gift of the Royal College of Surgeons of England. One of the clauses provided that qualifying students must be male, British-born subjects, the sons of British-born doctors registered in the UK 'and not of the Jewish or Roman Catholic faith'. The college declined to accept the bequest in the terms set out in the will but expressed its willingness to do so provided the offending clause was deleted. It was held by Buckley J that to insist on enforcing the discriminatory provision would defeat the paramount intention of the testatrix, and a scheme was ordered which would enable implementation of the trust omitting the words 'and not of the Jewish or Roman Catholic faith'.[562] As Buckley J commented, '[a] general charitable intention, then, may be said to be a paramount intention on the part of a donor to effect some charitable purpose which the court can find a method of putting into operation, notwithstanding that it is impracticable to give effect to some direction by the donor which is not an essential part of his true intention — not that is to say, part of his paramount intention.'[563] As Warburton has commented, this reasoning involves asking whether the impugned direction is essential to the donor's purpose and 'allows a far narrower and more detailed intention to amount to a "general" intention'.[564] Although this more liberal approach will be beneficial in circumstances where a good charitable gift might otherwise fail, it is not so justifiable where it appears to defeat the real intention of a donor.

The former consideration applied in *Re Stewart's Will Trusts*,[565] in which a liberal approach to the concept of general charitable intention can also be discerned. The testator left the residue of his estate to a fund established by the Non-Subscribing Presbyterian Church of Ireland for the purpose of supplementing the income of ministers of that church and directed that the income from the residue of his estate should be used for the support of ministers whose congregations complied with certain conditions, one of which, relating to the use of unaltered and unabridged hymn books, was impossible to fulfil. Murray J ordered a cy-près scheme to remove this condition from the trust, holding that the paramount intention of the testator was to increase the salary of ministers of a Christian church. He stated that he could not see how it would be right to regard such an 'ill-considered' provision as an essential part of the

561. [1966] 1 Ch 191.
562. A similar approach was taken by Vinelott J in *Re Woodhams* [1981] 1 WLR 493 where a scheme to found music scholarships confined to orphans from named homes was altered to omit the latter restriction.
563. [1966] 1 Ch 191, 202. Quoted with approval by Carswell J in *Re Currie* [1985] NI 299, 306.
564. [1981] Conv 231, 232.
565. [1983] NI 283.

charitable scheme particularly when the result of so doing would be to make the trust completely unworkable and frustrate the testator's paramount intention.

This can be contrasted with a decision of the High Court in this jurisdiction which suggests that a more restrictive approach may be applied, although there was no discernible attempt to lay down any such general principle. In *Re Prescott*[566] a testatrix bequeathed her house to a Dublin parish of the 'Russian Orthodox Church abroad' and directed that if there were no parishioners or members of that church living in Ireland that it should be sold and the proceeds applied for the general purposes of the said church in England. At the time of the testatrix's death, the parish had ceased to exist and the executor applied to the court for directions as to the manner in which the proceeds of the sale of the house were to be distributed. MacKenzie J held that the gift of the house had lapsed as it was to a body which did not exist either at the time of making the will or at the death of the testatrix and the gift over, being dependent on the validity of this gift, also lapsed. While MacKenzie J accepted that there may be cases where a court can find a general charitable intention even in a case of a single gift,[567] he concluded that there was no indication that the testatrix had any intention other than to benefit the named institution in the case before him and he held that the doctrine of cy-près could not be applied. This appears to be a rather restrictive decision given the terms of the gift over in the testatrix's will and it would certainly appear to be out of line with other authorities in this area. On the whole, it would be fair to say that the Irish courts have generally leaned in favour of a fairly flexible attitude to this issue.[568]

Initial impossibility in relation to a charitable trust may arise in a number of circumstances. The gift may have been made to a non-existent institution and as Buckley J commented in *Re Davis*,[569] 'where you find a gift to a charitable institution which never existed, the Court, which always leans in favour of charity, is more ready to infer a general charitable intention than to infer the contrary.' While such an intention will not always be found in cases of non-existent institutions,[570] it is likely to be easier to establish in such cases than in circumstances where the object once existed but ceased to do so before the

566. [1990] 2 IR 342.
567. See, e.g. *Biscoe v Jackson* (1887) 35 Ch D 460; *Re Currie* [1985] NI 299.
568. A general charitable intention was found in the following cases: *Daly v Attorney General* (1860) 11 ICR 41; *Munster and Leinster Bank Ltd v Attorney General* (1954) 91 ILTR 34; *Re Templemoyle Agricultural School* (1869) IR 4 Eq 295; *Re McGwire* [1941] IR 33; *Re Quinn* (1953) 88 ILTR 161; *Re Fitzgerald's Estate* (1957) 92 ILTR 192; *Re Currie* [1985] NI 299. Cases where no such intention was found include *Re Ffrench* [1941] IR 49n; *Attorney General for Northern Ireland v Forde* [1932] NI 1; *McCormick v Queen's University of Belfast* [1958] NI 1.
569. [1902] 1 Ch 876, 881. See, e.g. *Daly v Attorney General* (1860) 11 ICR 41.
570. *Re Goldschmidt* [1957] 1 WLR 524.

gift took effect.[571] This point was made by Megarry VC in *Re Spence*,[572] where he commented that 'the court is far less ready to find [a general charitable] intention where the gift is to a body which existed at the date of the will but ceased to exist before the testator died, or as I have already held, where the gift is for a purpose which, though possible and practicable at the date of the will, has ceased to be so before the testator's death.'

This view would seem to be borne out by the conclusion reached by Proudman J in *Kings v Bultitude*,[573] in which a gift had been made to a church organisation which had ceased to exist as such prior to the testatrix's death. She was satisfied that the case was one of initial failure of the gift and that there was nothing in the testatrix's will to indicate a general charitable intention which might save it.

The distinction referred to in *Re Spence* was not drawn in the most recent decision on this point in this jurisdiction, although it confirms the difficulty in either case of establishing general charitable intention where the testator seeks to make a charitable gift of a specific nature and this aim fails. In *Re Jordan*[574] the testator left four fifths of his estate to a memorial fund which it transpired had never been set up and one fifth to a charity which had been wound up after the will had been made but before the testator's death. Having referred to the *dicta* of Parker J in *Re Wilson*[575] and of Budd J in *Re Royal Kilmainham Hospital*[576] White J said that when the specific bequest in the deceased's will was examined, no general charitable intention was discernible. He stated as follows:

> Even if the court leans in favour of a flexible attitude, as applied in *Re Lysaght* [1966] 1 Ch 191 and in *Re Stewart's Will Trusts* [1983] NI 283, where in both cases discriminatory additions to a charitable bequest were ignored in order to implement a *cy-près* scheme, that would still not be sufficient in this case as no general charitable intention has been expressed in the will.[577]

In these circumstances White J said that the court could not go beyond the will and that the words used were not sufficient to infer general charitable intention. He concluded that the court could not apply the cy-près doctrine and that the residuary estate would have to be distributed in accordance with the provisions of the Succession Act 1965.

One reason for initial failure of a gift is that the body or institution which

571. *Re Harwood* [1936] Ch 285, 287 *per* Farwell J. See also *Makeown v Ardagh* (1876) IR 10 Eq 445, 452; *Re Prescott* [1990] 2 IR 342.
572. [1979] Ch 483, 495.
573. [2010] WTLR 1571. See Picton [2011] Conv 69.
574. [2014] IEHC 678.
575. [1913] 1 Ch 314, 320.
576. [1966] IR 451, 469.
577. [2014] IEHC 678 at [18].

the testator intended to benefit may have been amalgamated with or absorbed into another institution by the time the gift is to take effect. Such a gift may lapse if the court considers that on its true construction it is intended to have been for the originally specified purpose or institution alone.[578] However, it has been established that where a named parish ceases to exist as a separate entity and amalgamates with another, a gift to such a parish may be applied for the purposes of the new unit.[579] Another common difficulty which arises is that the institution may be misdescribed. As Chatterton VC commented in *Re Geary's Trusts*,[580] '[t]he Court, however, will not allow a charitable legacy to fail because of misdescription, but will endeavour to carry out the testator's intention as nearly as possible.'

Finally, the possibility that the consent of the intended recipient to an acceptance of the trust in its original terms may not be forthcoming must be considered. In *Re Dunwoodie*[581] the testatrix bequeathed the residue of her estate on trust for a particular Presbyterian Church with a direction that the bequest should be used for the installation of bells at that church. The committee of the church decided not to install the bells and the question arose whether the residuary bequest should devolve as on an intestacy or be applied cy-près. Murray J held that the trust for the installation of the bells must be treated as initially impossible to fulfil because the consent of the relevant church authority which was essential to the fulfilment of the trust had never been given. However, he was satisfied that the testatrix had shown a general intention to further the general purposes of the particular church and that the initial failure of the trust in no way invalidated the general trust for the church which remained perfectly good. In the circumstances, he ordered that the property should be applied cy-près.

Subsequent Failure of Charitable Purposes

A gift may be capable of being carried out in the precise terms laid down by the donor or testator at the time it takes effect but may subsequently fail or become impossible or impracticable to enforce. In such circumstances, it is not necessary to establish a general charitable intention provided that the gift is given 'absolutely and perpetually to charity'. The material date for deciding whether a general charitable intention is necessary is therefore the date on which the trust comes into effect, which in the case of a will, is the date of the

578. *Re Rymer* [1895] 1 Ch 19.
579. *Corbally v Representative Church Body* [1938] IR 35. See also *Re Bloomfield's Bequest* (1920) 54 ILTR 213, where a clergyman was found to be entitled to an endowment originally intended for the incumbent of a parish which had merged with his.
580. (1890) 25 LR Ir 171.
581. [1977] NI 141.

testator's death.[582] The effect of the distinction between initial and supervening impossibility was set out by Evershed MR in *Re Tacon*[583] as follows:

> It is well established that in the case of a gift to charity ... where no general charitable intention is present, then (1) if the charity has ceased to exist before the will comes into operation the gift lapses, but (2) if the charity is still in existence at the date mentioned, it is effective as a gift to the extent that the interests of the next-of-kin (or of whoever else take in default of the charitable interest taking effect) are for ever excluded, notwithstanding the later dissolution or disappearance of the charity.

One of the most important decisions establishing this principle in this jurisdiction is that of Budd J in *Re Royal Kilmainham Hospital*.[584] A hospital founded by Charles II in 1684 for the support and maintenance of old soldiers of his army and those of his successors gradually ceased to function after the setting up of the Irish Free State and the Irish government took over control of the lands and buildings. In 1961, the Royal Kilmainham Hospital Act was passed which provided, *inter alia*, for the settling of a scheme for some specified charitable purposes or purpose for the benefit of some classes of members of the defence forces. It was held by Budd J that since it was no longer possible to carry out the founder's intentions the available funds should be applied cy-près and he directed that they should be used to benefit organisations of former members of the defence forces and the British Army. Budd J stated as follows:

> There was no controversy as to the general principles applicable when charitable gifts, which have taken effect, subsequently fail for want of objects. If there is an absolute perpetual gift to a charity, even though the trusts declared are only for the accomplishment of a particular charitable purpose, the subject-matter is applicable cy-près upon failure of the trusts.[585]

Similarly, in *Re Worth Library*[586] Keane J found that the original bequest of the library in the will of Dr Worth was 'undoubtedly an absolute and perpetual gift' and for this reason could be applied cy-près when the hospital ceased to exist, notwithstanding his finding that no general charitable intention could be inferred on the facts before him.

In certain circumstances surplus funds may remain where a charitable purpose has been completed or where full provision has been made for its requirements and provided that it is an absolute and perpetual gift to charity,

---

582. *Re Wright* [1954] Ch 347.
583. [1958] Ch 447, 453.
584. [1966] IR 451.
585. *Ibid.* at 472.
586. [1995] 2 IR 301, 342.

these funds may be applied cy-près. In *Trusts of the Rectory of St John*[587] a surplus remained after providing for the maintenance of the choir and choral service at a cathedral church in Cork City as required by the terms of a trust. Chatterton VC held that as part of these monies was not required for the literal fulfilment of the donor's intentions, some of the fund might be applied cy-près in the purchase of an organ for the church, a purpose which was essential for carrying that intention into effect.

Finally, it should be pointed out that there have been sporadic examples throughout the common law world of courts determining whether general charitable intent exists in cases of supervening failure,[588] although Picarda has characterised such judgments as examples of the courts searching unnecessarily for such an intent and finding it.[589] In the decision of the Newfoundland Court of Appeal in *Boy Scouts of Canada v Doyle*,[590] which was a case of supervening failure, Marshall JA still went on to consider whether the requirement of general charitable intent was satisfied. However, he also considered the arguments in favour of dispensing with this latter requirement and concluded that whichever approach was followed, the conditions for cy-près were satisfied in the case before him. His judgment certainly cannot be taken as authority for the proposition that he was insisting on a requirement of general charitable intent even in cases of supervening impossibility or failure and the overwhelming weight of opinion is against such a proposition.[591] Similarly, in *Cheshire Foundation in Ireland v Attorney General*,[592] considered further below, which was a case of a subsequent failure of a charitable purpose, Laffoy J referred to the fact that 'as is pointed out in O'Halloran's *Charity Law* (2nd ed., 2009) at para.31–39, subs. [47](2) retains the established common-law requirement that a general charitable intention is an essential prerequisite for a cy-près scheme.' She concluded that the requirement of general charitable intention had in any event been satisfied in the matter before the court and made a cy-près order.

Legislative Reform of the Cy-près Doctrine

At common law this jurisdiction could only be exercised where it was

587. (1869) IR 3 Eq 335.
588. E.g. *Re Templemoyle Agricultural School* (1869) IR 4 Eq 295 (Ireland); *Re North Devon and West Somerset Relief Fund Trusts* [1953] 1 WLR 1260 (England); *Parker v Moseley* [1965] VR 580 (Australia); *Hay v Murdoch* [1952] WN 145 where the House of Lords suggested that in Scotland a general charitable intent was required in all cases.
589. Picarda, *The Law and Practice Relating to Charities* (4th ed., 2010) p. 461.
590. (1997) 149 DLR (4th) 22.
591. See, e.g. the statement In Henderson and Fowles, *Tudor on Charities* (10th ed., 2015) p. 525 to the effect that: 'it is now clear that it is not necessary for the donor to have had a general or paramount charitable intention before an outright gift can be applied cy-près on a subsequent failure'.
592. [2012] 1 ILRM 369, 373.

impossible or impracticable to give effect to the wishes of a donor in the precise terms which he intended. However, the doctrine as it developed at common law was criticised as being too restrictive in nature and section 47 of the Irish Charities Act 1961 laid down much broader parameters for the exercise of this jurisdiction,[593] allowing a cy-près order to be made in circumstances where there were difficulties in implementing the original terms or where more effective use might be made of the trust property by framing an alternative scheme. It is helpful to set out in full the terms of section 47(1) which enumerates the circumstances in which a cy-près order may now be made.

> (1) Subject to subsection (2), the circumstances in which the original purposes of a charitable gift may be altered to allow the property given or part of it to be applied cy-près shall be as follows:—
> (a) where the original purposes, in whole or in part—
> (i) have been as far as may be fulfilled; or
> (ii) cannot be carried out, or cannot be carried out according to the directions given and to the spirit of the gift; or
> (b) where the original purposes provide a use for part only of the property available by virtue of the gift; or
> (c) where the property available by virtue of the gift and other property applicable for similar purposes can be more effectively used in conjunction, and to that end can suitably, regard being had to the spirit of the gift, be made applicable for common purposes; or
> (d) where the original purposes were laid down by reference to an area which then was but has since ceased to be a unit for some other purpose, or by reference to a class of persons or to an area which has for any reason since ceased, either to be suitable, regard being had to the spirit of the gift, or to be practical in administering the gift; or
> (e) where the original purposes, in whole or in part, have since they were laid down—
> (i) been adequately provided for by other means; or
> (ii) ceased as being useless or harmful to the community or for other reasons, to be in law charitable; or
> (iii) ceased in any other way to provide a suitable and effective method of using the property available by virtue of the gift, regard being had to the spirit of the gift.

Lavan J noted in his judgment in *Magee v Attorney General*[594] that, although

593. See also s. 13 of the Charities Act 1960 in England and s. 22 of the Charities Act (Northern Ireland) 1964 which introduced similar reforms.
594. [2002] IEHC 87.

section 47 of the Charities Act 1961 has caused substantial inroads to be made into the restrictive common law approach to the cy-près doctrine, it was still desirable and necessary to have due regard to the wishes of the donor 'so as to avoid the threat of making the practice of donating to charity a veritable shot in the dark'.[595] He stated that the primary rule to be observed in the application of the cy-près doctrine is that the intention of the donor must be served as far as possible and regard must be had to the spirit of the gift. Thus, he added, if the donor names a particular object which is capable of taking effect, any application cy-près which becomes necessary must be restricted to the limits of that object and the mode of application must as far as possible coincide with the donor's wishes.

The provisions of section 47(1) have been applied in a number of cases. In *Re Royal Kilmainham Hospital* Budd J found that the original purposes of the gift could no longer be carried out according to the directions given and the spirit of the gift and that these original purposes had, at least in part, ceased to provide a suitable and effective method of using the property available. Subsection (1)(e)(iii) was again considered by O'Hanlon J in *Representative Church Body v Attorney General*,[596] in which the plaintiff sought a cy-près order under section 47 in relation to a collection of books kept in the Old Library attached to St Canice's Cathedral, Kilkenny. The plaintiff claimed ownership of the books and wished to sell them and apply the proceeds to the maintenance and repair of the cathedral. It was argued that the books were no longer used in the manner envisaged in the original bequests but the application was opposed by the Attorney General[597] on the grounds that the collection was an important cultural asset for Kilkenny and that if it were sold there was no effective legal restriction on its exportation. O'Hanlon J held that the original purposes of the charitable gifts had ceased to provide a suitable or effective method of using the property available, regard being had to the spirit of the gift. He held further that it was permissible to alter the original purposes of the bequests and to allow the property to be applied cy-près and he made an order authorizing the sale of the collection by the plaintiff so that the proceeds might be applied to the repair and maintenance of the cathedral.

This decision provides a good illustration of how the original common law requirements in relation to the exercise of cy-près jurisdiction have now been relaxed. While it could be argued that section 47 was applied in an unduly lenient manner in this case, the requirement that the property be applied in

595. *Ibid.* at 3.
596. [1988] IR 19. See further Osborough (1989) 24 Ir Jur (ns) 50. The equivalent provision in s. 22 of the Charities Act (Northern Ireland) 1964 was applied in *Re Steele* [1976] NI 66.
597. By virtue of s. 38 of the Charities Act 2009, all the functions of the Attorney General in relation to charitable trusts or organisations were transferred to the Charities Regulatory Authority.

conformity with the 'spirit of the gift' should ensure that due regard will be given to the wishes of a donor.

However, where the original purposes, or those substituted by a subsequent cy-près scheme, have not been fulfilled and have not ceased to provide a suitable and effective method of using the property available, section 47 will not permit the further application of the property cy-près. This is made clear by the decision of Lavan J in *Magee v Attorney General*,[598] in which the plaintiff trustees brought an application seeking to have the proceeds of sale of trust property, originally given to provide primary Catholic education for male Catholics in an area, applied cy-près. The plaintiffs contended that the original purposes of the charitable trust had been fulfilled as there was adequate schooling for Catholics in the area and sought to have the proceeds of sale of a monastery, the remainder of the trust property, applied cy-près in order to discharge part of the parish debt. The Attorney General contended that the scheme proposed by the plaintiffs was not as close as possible to the original objects of the donor as it had failed to have sufficient regard to the educational nature of those objects and it was further submitted that the proposed scheme had been framed without sufficient consideration being given to the educational needs of the locality. In 1997 the trustees had reluctantly agreed with the Commissioners of Charitable Donations and Bequests to the framing of a cy-près scheme concerning the sale of a school, which together with the monastery, made up the trust property. This provided that the trustees should retain the money received from the sale strictly for educational use for all children attending primary or secondary schools in the parish. In the light of this, the question which the court had to decide was whether the proceeds of sale, the subject-matter of the application before it, could now be used for the purposes advanced by the plaintiffs. In the view of Lavan J it was therefore necessary to answer the question of whether the advancement of educational facilities in all the schools of the parish was closer to the spirit of the gift than the discharge of a parish debt incurred in the pursuit of enhancing the community. He accepted that the activities carried on in the local community hall, the refurbishment of which had contributed so significantly to the incurring of the parish debt, must be deemed to be 'educational' in nature. However, he added that this view of the activities and functions did not solve the very complicated issues raised by the application. Lavan J stated that there was no evidence before him that the cy-près scheme of 1997 was sufficient to meet the needs of all the schools in the parish and added that he considered that there were various types of educational aids which these schools might need. Furthermore, he noted that given his acceptance of the fact that the activities carried on in the community centre were educational in nature, the court might otherwise have been sympathetic to the plaintiffs' case. Lavan J was satisfied that the trust established in 1892 had been superseded by the cy-près scheme of 1997 and that the application to apply the proceeds of

598. [2002] IEHC 87.

the sale of the monastery could not be severed from the latter scheme. In these circumstances, Lavan J concluded that he was unable to grant the plaintiffs the relief which they sought.

The equivalent English provision, section 13(1)(e)(iii) of the Charities Act 1993, now replaced by section 62(1)(e)(iii) of the Charities Act 2011,[599] was considered by the Court of Appeal in *Varsani v Jesani*.[600] A charitable trust had been established with the purpose of promoting the faith of a particular Hindu sect and the charity's assets included a temple in London. The members of the sect split into two groups and this produced a situation in which neither group would worship in the same temple as the other. Carnwath J held that the court had jurisdiction under section 13 of the Charities Act 1993 to make a regulatory scheme and ordered that the sect's assets be held on separate trusts for the furtherance of the faith as practised by each group.

The minority group's appeal was dismissed by the Court of Appeal. Morritt LJ concluded that if the original purposes of the charity had led to the impasse which in his view could not be resolved as a matter of faith, then it was self-evident that the original purposes had ceased to be a suitable and effective method of using the available property. He concluded that the spirit of the gift supported the submission that the court should exercise the jurisdiction conferred on it by section 13(1)(e)(iii) of the 1993 Act by directing a scheme for the division of the property of the charity as between the majority and minority groups. Chadwick LJ agreed that the appeal should be dismissed for the reasons set out by Morritt LJ. In relation to the manner in which the spirit of the gift could be identified, he stated as follows:

> The need to have regard to the spirit of the gift requires the court to look beyond the original purposes as defined by the objects specified in the declaration of trust and to seek to identify the spirit in which the donors gave property upon trust for those purposes. That can be done, as it seems to me, with the assistance of the document as a whole and any relevant evidence as to the circumstances in which the gift was made.[601]

The manner in which the Court of Appeal had interpreted section 13(1)(e)(iii) in the context of a schism in a religious organisation in *Varsani* was considered by Briggs J in *White v Williams*,[602] which also involved a cy-près application in relation to property used by a church. He stated as follows:

> [I]n relation to property donated to a religious charity prior to the relevant schism, the spirit of the gift is to be ascertained as at the time when the gift

599. In s.62(1)(e)(iii) of the Charities Act 2011 the phrase 'the appropriate considerations' is substituted for the phrase 'the spirit of the gift'.
600. [1999] Ch 219.
601. *Ibid.* at 238.
602. [2010] EWHC 940 (Ch).

> was made, and the schism will, of itself, commonly lead to the results (i) that the appropriation of the whole of the property to the use and control of one of the emerging factions will be contrary to the spirit of the gift, and (ii) that the use of the donated property for the advancement of the religion of one of those factions, to the exclusion of any others, will no longer be a suitable and effective method of using that property.[603]

The provisions of section 13(1A) of the Charities Act 1993,[604] which provided that the phrase 'the appropriate circumstances' substituted for the phrase 'the spirit of the gift' in the original section 13(1)(c), (d) and (e) (iii) meant on the one hand the spirit of the gift concerned and on the other hand the social and economic circumstances prevailing at the time of the proposed alteration of the original purposes, were also considered by Briggs J in the course of his judgment in *White v Williams*. He stated that the 'spirit of the gift', for the purposes of section 13(1A)(a) is to be ascertained more broadly than by a slavish application of the language of the relevant trust deed. He referred to the *dictum* of Morritt LJ in *Varsani v Jesani*[605] to the effect that 'the concept is clear enough, namely, the basic intention underlying the gift or the substance of the gift rather than the form of the words used to express it or conditions imposed to effect it.'

In this jurisdiction, section 47(2) of the 1961 Act provides that its provisions are not 'to affect the conditions which must be satisfied in order that property given for charitable purposes may be applied cy-près except insofar as these conditions require a failure of the original purposes'. So, the importance of establishing a general charitable intention where this would have been required prior to the enactment of the legislation remains. This understanding of section 47(2) appears to have been confirmed by Laffoy J in *Cheshire Foundation in Ireland v Attorney General*,[606] where she stated that it retained the established common law requirement that a general charitable intention is an essential prerequisite for a cy-près scheme. However, she did not acknowledge that this requirement has not been applied in cases of subsequent failure, as arose on the facts of the case, provided there has been an absolute and perpetual gift to charity, which was the approach taken Keane J in *Re Worth Library*.[607] In the circumstances, Laffoy J said that she was satisfied that the requirement of general charitable intention had been satisfied and she made the cy-près order sought by the applicant subject to one amendment to the proposed scheme.

Finally, it should be noted that prior to the coming into force of the Charities Act 2009 the Commissioners of Charitable Donations and Bequests[608] had

603. *Ibid.* at [19].
604. Now see s.62(2)(b) of the Charities Act 2011.
605. [1999] Ch 219, 234.
606. [2012] 1 ILRM 369.
607. [1995] 2 IR 301, 342.
608. Section 81 of the Charities Act 2009 provided that this body should be dissolved.

jurisdiction to frame a cy-près scheme without being subject to any financial limits in this regard.[609] This function has now been taken over by the Charities Regulatory Authority by virtue of section 82 of the Charities Act 2009 which transferred the functions of the Commissioners to that authority.

The Manner in Which Cy-près Jurisdiction Should be Exercised

As the word 'cy-près' suggests, in determining new purposes for which property should be applied, the court should seek to ensure that these purposes are as near as possible to those originally set out in the gift. In addition, as Keane J stated in *Re Worth Library*,[610] it is also 'desirable that the original intentions of the testator should be adhered to so far as is possible', although as Keane J himself acknowledged, the difficulties in both ascertaining and giving effect to such intentions will be obvious where there has been a considerable lapse of time since the making of the initial gift. In the context of the facts in the case before him, he therefore stated that it would be futile to transport the donor in some form of time machine from the early eighteenth century to the present day and all that the court could do was 'to apply the gift as it might be applied by a late twentieth century equivalent of [the donor]'. In the circumstances, Keane J concluded that any cy-près scheme framed by the court must provide for the retention of the books and portraits which formed the subject-matter of the gift in their original setting, which after it ceased to be a hospital, became a health board headquarters.

Another example illustrating the importance of adhering to the original purposes as closely as possible is provided by the decision of Carroll J in *Doyle v Attorney General*.[611] A fund was set up to benefit a child who suffered from a rare genetic skin disease and some of the money raised was used for her benefit. Following her death, the plaintiffs proposed the division of the funds between seven named charities which were institutions, all but one of which were located in the area in which the funds were raised, which treated the sick, the elderly and the handicapped. The scheme was opposed by the Attorney General on the grounds that many of the proposed beneficiaries were not as near as possible to the original purposes of the fund. Carroll J stated that the care of the elderly, the handicapped and the sick was not sufficiently close to the original purpose of the fund and said that she agreed with the submission that there should be some connection with the disease from which the original beneficiary had suffered, 'either by way of research, or treatment, or palliative

609. Section 16 and Schedule, Part 2 of the Social Welfare (Miscellaneous Provisions) Act 2002. Section 29 of the Charities Act 1961 originally limited the jurisdiction of the Commissioners to circumstances where the value of the charitable gift did not exceed £5,000, a figure extended by s. 8 of the Charities Act 1973 to £25,000, and by s. 52(a) of the Court and Court Officers Act 1995 to £250,000.
610. [1995] 2 IR 301, 343.
611. High Court 1993 No. 612 Sp (Carroll J) 22 February 1995.

care'. In her opinion, the requirement that regard should be had to the wishes of the trustees or other persons in charge of the property did not override the requirement that the property should be applied cy-près. Carroll J concluded that a proportion of the fund should be spent on a specialist clinic set up to treat sufferers of the disease and that a lesser proportion should be given to research into the disease, which was being carried out in a specified location, on condition that the court could be provided with information as to what would constitute a meaningful contribution to research. Carroll J suggested that the plaintiffs might give their opinion as to the division of the fund as between these two purposes but added that if it was not possible to provide a meaningful sum for research, then the entire fund should go the specialist clinic.

Further light was thrown on the process of deciding how to apply property cy-près by the judgment of Marshall JA in the decision of the Newfoundland Court of Appeal in *Boy Scouts of Canada v Doyle*.[612] The court had to determine how trust property should be applied cy-près when a particular boy scout troop in whose favour it had been established ceased to exist.[613] Marshall JA stated that the first step in the process required 'an examination of the trust settlement's general intent as a prelude to defining the mode which in substance will as nearly as possible execute the general charitable intent'.[614] He concluded that as the particular troop no longer existed, the trust should be applied for the benefit of the local scouting movement which was represented by the provincial council. In his view by making it possible for all scouting to benefit in place of one particular troop, the court could ensure that: 'the general object will not be defeated but will continue to be executed in substance through the offices of the scouting movement'.[615]

Sign Manual Procedure

Where money or property is given to charity generally without provision being made for the appointment of trustees the government is considered to be the trustee and is required to ensure the administration of the gift under the 'sign manual procedure'. In *Felan v Russell*[616] property was bequeathed for 'pious purposes' and although it was accepted as being for charitable purposes, the trustee died before a scheme to apply the gift was settled. It was held that the gift vested in the Crown and that it should be disposed of under the sign manual procedure. Similarly, in *Merrins v Attorney General*,[617] Black J held

612. (1997) 149 DLR (4th) 22.
613. The court accepted that there was no difficulty in holding that a trust for the benefit of a scouting troop fell within the parameters of the advancement of education and referred to the decision of Vaisey J in *Re Webber* [1954] 1 WLR 1500 on this point.
614. (1997) 149 DLR (4th) 22, 79.
615. *Ibid.* at 81.
616. (1842) 4 Ir Eq R 701. See also *Kane v Cosgrave* (1873) IR 10 Eq 211.
617. (1945) 79 ILTR 121.

that a gift in remainder to charity generally in relation to which no trustee had been appointed, should be applied at the 'will and pleasure' of the government.

CHAPTER 12

Void and Voidable Trusts

As set out in Chapter 4, a private trust will not be valid where it does not comply with any necessary formalities or the requirements of certainty.[1] It may also fail in circumstances where, although it appears to be otherwise valid, it is in fact illegal or contrary to public policy. In such cases, where the trust is void, it is regarded as being invalid *ab initio* and never comes into effect. Alternatively, a trust may be voidable in certain circumstances; these trusts are not void *ab initio* and will remain in operation unless or until their validity is successfully challenged.

VOID TRUSTS

A trust may be void because it offends statutory provisions or the common law or because it may be contrary to public policy. Where a trust is declared void, the property which it was intended to include in it will be held on a resulting trust for the settlor or where such a trust arises under a will, it will lapse into the testator's residuary estate.

Where a trust involves the creation of a future interest it has traditionally been subject to the rules against perpetuities and inalienability. The rule against perpetuities was abolished by section 16 of the Land and Conveyancing Law Reform Act 2009 so a trust will no longer be void *ab initio* where it might vest outside the perpetuity period, i.e. that of a life or lives in being plus a further period of 21 years allowing additionally for periods of gestation. However, the rule against inalienability persists so where property is tied to a specific non-charitable purpose, for a period of time in excess of a perpetuity period, the trust will be void. These issues are considered in detail elsewhere and it is not proposed to consider them in this context.[2]

---

1. An application may be made for an order setting aside a trust on the basis that it is void for uncertainty. Such an application was made in *Re Stanley deceased* [2016] IEHC 8 but the *ex parte* application was adjourned in order that the trustees be joined as defendants in circumstances where the applicants would be the persons entitled to the trust property should the trust fail.
2. Wylie, *Irish Land Law* (5th ed., 2013) Chapter 5. On the rule against inalienability, see *infra* Chapter 10 in relation to purpose trusts.

Conditions Precedent and Subsequent

Often the question of whether a trust is void relates to the issue of the validity of any condition to which the trust may be made subject and illegality often arises as a result of a condition imposed on what might otherwise be a valid gift. Such conditions fall into two categories; conditions precedent, which preclude the trust from coming into effect unless and until the condition is fulfilled and conditions subsequent which do not prevent the gift vesting but render it liable to be divested if and when the condition is satisfied. Gifts which incorporate a void condition subsequent can still be enforced without the application of this condition,[3] whereas traditionally certain distinctions have to be made in the case of conditions precedent. Generally where a gift of realty is made dependent on a condition precedent which is found to be void, the gift will fail in its entirety.[4] In England a distinction was drawn in the case of gifts of personalty between situations where the condition was *malum in se* (intrinsically wrong in itself) as opposed to *malum prohibitum* (wrong in the eyes of the law).[5] In the former case, the gift would fail but in the latter case, the gift would be considered good and would pass unfettered by the terms of the invalid condition. The distinction was applied in that jurisdiction in cases such as *Re Piper*,[6] where a condition that children should not reside with their father was categorised as *malum prohibitum* with the result that the gift took effect free of the illegal condition.

However, this principle was described as 'archaic' by Dixon J in *Re Blake*[7] who commented as follows: 'this is a curious and somewhat pedantic distinction to introduce in ascertaining the wishes of testators who, in the vast majority of cases, would be quite unaware of the existence of the distinction, and, even if they were aware of it, might be unable to obtain from lawyers any very precise idea of the nature and limits of the distinction.'[8] In the circumstances of the case, Dixon J found that the condition precedent which he was required to consider fell into neither category and concluded that the gift failed in its entirety. However, some doubt still surrounds the effect of an invalid condition precedent attached to a gift in this jurisdiction, particularly as Kenny J appears to have held subsequently in *Re Doyle*[9] that 'when a condition precedent attached to a gift is in violation of the donee's constitutional rights, the donee takes the benefit of the gift without complying with the condition'.

---

3. *Duddy v Gresham* (1878) 2 LR Ir 442.
4. *Re Turton* [1926] Ch 96.
5. See Delany (1955) 19 Conv 176.
6. [1946] 2 All ER 503.
7. [1955] IR 89.
8. *Ibid.* at 100. See the comments of Delany in (1955) 19 Conv 176, 177 that 'the distinction … is both obsolete and inherently unsound' and 'can no longer be said to be based on any rational foundation — if indeed, it ever possessed one.'
9. High Court, 1972 (Kenny J). See Wylie, *Irish Land Law* (4th ed., 2010) p. 615.

Trusts Contrary to Public Policy

Trusts which have as their object an illegal or immoral aim will be regarded as void on this ground. So, trusts for such diverse objects as to provide for the payment of fines of convicted poachers[10] have been held to be void. Trusts in favour of future illegitimate children were considered to be void at common law as tending to promote immoral conduct[11] and were regarded as being contrary to public policy. However, this is no longer the case as a result of the intervention of statute and section 27(5) of the Status of Children Act 1987 repealed the common law rule which rendered trusts in favour of future illegitimate children void in relation to wills or settlements made after the commencement of the Act.

Many trusts will be of doubtful validity because they contain conditions which may be vulnerable on public policy grounds. It was suggested by John Martin QC, sitting as a Deputy High Court judge, in *Nathan v Leonard*[12] that a condition subsequent in a will would only be struck down where it was truly repugnant to or inconsistent with the nature of the gifts made by the will. In this case the court upheld the validity of a codicil to the testatrix's will which contained a condition that if any beneficiary took action to contest or disagree with the will, all the dispositions in it would be forfeit and the entire estate left to the first and second defendants. Judge Martin commented that: 'although the condition may well have an arbitrary effect, that is not of itself enough to render it invalid: a testator may dispose of his property as he wishes, however capriciously'.[13]

It is now proposed to examine some of the categories of conditions generally struck down on public policy grounds in greater detail.

Trusts in Restraint of Marriage

A condition in a trust which amounts to a general restraint on marriage is *prima facie* void.[14] However, it was made clear by Mellish LJ in *Allen v Jackson*[15] that this principle does not apply to conditions which come into effect only upon a second marriage. It would also appear that in England at any rate, conditions which operate as a partial restraint on marriage, for example prohibiting marriage with certain classes of persons,[16] may be valid. Traditionally, a distinction has been drawn in that jurisdiction between a partial restraint imposed in relation

---

10. *Thrupp v Collett* (1858) 26 Beav 125.
11. *Thompson v Thomas* (1891) 27 LR Ir 457. As Keane comments in *Equity and the Law of Trusts in Ireland* (3rd ed., 2017) at p. 277, this common law rule was in any event of doubtful constitutional validity.
12. [2003] 1 WLR 827.
13. *Ibid.* at 831.
14. *Lloyd v Lloyd* (1852) 2 Sim (NS) 255; *Re Hanlon* [1933] Ch 254.
15. (1875) 1 Ch D 399. See also the judgment of Ball C in *Duddy v Gresham* (1878) 2 LR Ir 442.
16. *Perrin v Lyon* (1807) 9 East 170.

to realty on the one hand and to personalty on the other hand. In the case of realty a partial restraint never appears to be regarded as invalid, whereas in respect of personalty the condition is considered to be *in terrorem* only and invalid if there is no gift over on the happening of the marriage.[17]

In view of the fact that the right to marry has been recognised as an unspecified personal right which derives from Article 40.3 of the Constitution,[18] it is likely that even partial restraints on marriage would now be considered void in this jurisdiction and on the basis of the *dicta* of Kenny J in *Re Doyle* referred to above, it appears that a donee would take the gift free from any such condition.

A corollary of this principle is that trusts made in contemplation of or which might encourage the future separation of a husband and wife are void. So, in *Re Johnson's Will Trusts*[19] a trust which cut down the testator's daughter's interest to a nominal amount so long as she was married and living with her husband was considered to be void on that basis. This decision can be distinguished from that in *Re Lovell*,[20] where the object of the trust was found to be to make provision for a woman during her separation until she might return to her husband or remarry and where the parties are already separated no objection should arise.[21] However, in view of the constitutional status of the institution of marriage in this jurisdiction, it is likely that a strict attitude will be taken by the courts here towards any trust which might have the effect of directly or indirectly weakening the marriage bond.

Trusts Tending to Interfere with Parental Duties

Trusts which seek to weaken the ties between parents and children by requiring that children reside apart from their parents have been held to be void as being contrary to public policy. So, in *Re Boulter*[22] a condition in a gift to the testator's grandchildren which provided that it should be forfeited if either or both of them should live with or be under the custody or control of their father was held to be void as contrary to public policy and tending to encourage the separation of parents from their children. In addition, trusts which interfere with parental duties in relation to the upbringing of their children will also be considered void on policy grounds. In *Re Borwick*[23] a condition subsequent

17. *Duddy v Gresham* (1878) 2 LR Ir 442; *Leong v Cheye* [1955] AC 648, 660.
18. *Ryan v Attorney General* [1965] IR 294, 313; *McGee v Attorney General* [1974] IR 284, 301. Note also the comments of Gavan Duffy P in *Re McKenna* [1947] IR 277.
19. [1967] Ch 387. See also *Re Caborne* [1943] Ch 224. Although note the decision of *Re Thompson* [1939] 1 All ER 681 in which Bennett J came to the contrary conclusion.
20. [1920] 1 Ch 122.
21. *Wilson v Wilson* (1848) 1 HLC 538.
22. [1922] 1 Ch 75. See also *Re Sandbrook* [1912] 2 Ch 471 and *Re Piper* [1946] 2 All ER 503 where the fact that the father was divorced did not affect the court's finding on this issue.
23. [1933] Ch 657. See also *Re Tegg* [1936] 2 All ER 878.

in a trust which provided that an interest should be forfeited if the beneficiary should before attaining the age of 21 'become a Roman Catholic or not be openly or avowedly Protestant' was found to be void as it interfered with the exercise of parental duty in relation to the religious upbringing of the child. Some doubt was thrown on the validity of this approach by the decision of the House of Lords in *Blathwayt v Baron Cawley*,[24] in which a clause in a trust which provided for forfeiture of an interest if the beneficiary should become a Roman Catholic was upheld. The majority of the House of Lords acknowledged that such conditions would tend to influence or interfere with parental responsibilities but took the view that they should not be categorised as contrary to public policy.

The validity of this type of condition has been considered by the courts in this jurisdiction on a number of occasions. In *Re Burke's Estate*[25] Gavan Duffy P held that a condition in the testatrix's will that her nephew should be educated in a Roman Catholic school to be selected at the absolute discretion of the trustees, 'however well meaning from the standpoint of an anxious benefactor' was inoperative as it tended to override the rights and duties of parents in relation to the education of their children provided for in Article 42 of the Constitution. Perhaps the most important authority in this area is the judgment of Dixon J in *Re Blake*,[26] in which he had to consider the validity of a trust in favour of the testator's grandchildren but subject to a condition that they be brought up as Roman Catholics. Dixon J referred to the relevant English authorities and to Article 42 of the Constitution and stated as follows:

> This Article puts the matter on a different and higher plane in this country, as the parental right and duty is declared and guaranteed by our fundamental law. Under it, the State 'guarantees to respect the inalienable right and duty of parents to provide, according to their means, for the religious and moral, intellectual, physical and social education of their children.' It is clear that any attempt to restrict or fetter that right would be contrary to the solemnly declared policy and conceptions of the community as a whole and therefore such as the Courts established under that Constitution could not and would not lend their aid to.[27]

The effect of such a finding was considered in detail by Dixon J. The distinction between a finding of invalidity in relation to conditions precedent and subsequent had been outlined as follows by Gavan Duffy P in *Re Burke's Estate*:[28]

24. [1976] AC 397.
25. [1951] IR 216.
26. [1955] IR 89.
27. *Ibid.* at 97.
28. [1951] IR 216, 224.

> The practical effect of the distinction is of the utmost importance: a gift made subject to a condition precedent fails altogether, as a rule, if the condition is found to be void, but if a gift is made subject to a condition subsequent which is found to be void or inapplicable, the condition disappears and the gift takes effect independently of the condition.

While Dixon J acknowledged that Gavan Duffy P had left open the possibility of there being an exception to the general rule in the case of conditions precedent, he concluded that the conditions in the case before him were void and unenforceable and that the gifts were dependent on their being carried out and were also void. Some doubt must be raised about such a conclusion in the light of the decision of Kenny J in *Re Doyle*, where it appears to have been stated that where a condition precedent to a gift is found to be in violation of the donee's constitutional rights the donee may take the benefit of the gift without complying with the condition. However, it should be pointed out that the condition in that case, which was found to be contrary to the provisions of Article 44.2.1° of the Constitution, was held in any event to be invalid on the grounds that it was impossible to perform.

VOIDABLE TRUSTS

Trusts falling within this category come into operation and will remain effective unless and until they are set aside in court proceedings. A trust may be voidable for a variety of reasons, often because it comes into being as a result of mistake, misrepresentation, fraud, duress or undue influence. In addition, a trust may be set aside where it amounts to an attempt to defraud a settlor's creditors or subsequent purchasers or where the settlor becomes bankrupt within a specified period of settling the property. In this context it is proposed to examine these latter situations, which are governed by specific statutory provisions, in more detail.

Settlements Defrauding Creditors

In practice a person may often be tempted to settle property, usually on his family or close associates, in circumstances where he fears that his creditors may otherwise succeed in obtaining control over his assets. However, as Fitzgerald B commented in *Smith v Tatton*,[29] '[a] man must be honest before he is generous'. The issue of settlements which might defraud creditors was dealt with by the

29. (1879) 6 LR Ir 32, 41. See also the comments of Jessel MR in *Re Butterworth* (1882) 19 Ch D 588, 598: 'a man is not entitled to go into a hazardous business, and immediately before doing so, settle all his property voluntarily, the object being this: "if I succeed in business, I make a fortune for myself. If I fail, I leave my creditors unpaid. They will bear the loss".'

provisions of sections 10 and 14 of the Conveyancing Act (Ireland) 1634. This legislation was repealed and replaced by subsections 74(3) and (4) of the Land and Conveyancing Law Reform Act 2009. Section 10 of the Conveyancing Act (Ireland) 1634[30] provided that any gift or conveyance of property, real or personal, made for the purpose of delaying, hindering or defrauding creditors was 'void' as against such creditors, although this phrase was interpreted as meaning 'voidable'[31] and this is now expressly provided by section 74(3) of the Act of 2009 which provides that 'subject to subsection (4), any conveyance of property made with the intention of defrauding a creditor or other person is voidable by any person thereby prejudiced.' As Finlay Geoghegan J pointed out in *Keegan Quarries Ltd v McGuinness*,[32] the scope of section 74(3) is not confined to the defrauding of creditors, but includes the phrase 'or other person' and a transaction is expressed to be voidable by 'any person thereby prejudiced'. She held that on a proper construction of the section, it appeared that a person from whom a potential claim is contemplated by a transferor is a person intended to be protected by section 74(3) and comes within the class of 'other persons' referred to in the subsection.

Section 14 of the 1634 Act went on to provide that this provision would not extend to conveyances *bona fide* made for good consideration without notice of any fraud. Although the section referred to 'good consideration' it was interpreted to mean 'valuable consideration'[33] and this is the phrase used in section 74(4)(a). However, it should be noted that section 3 of the Act of 2009 provides that 'valuable consideration' does not include marriage or a nominal consideration in money.

The general object of the relevant sections of the Conveyancing Act (Ireland) 1634 was summarised by Palles CB in *Re Moroney*[34] in the following terms: 'The object of the statute was to protect the rights of creditors as against the property of their debtor. It was no part of its object to regulate the rights of creditors *inter se*, or to entitle them to an equal distribution of that property.' The extent of the fraudulent intent required by the statute is far from clear; in *Rose v Greer*[35] Overend J stated that the class of fraud against which the statute is directed is 'one in which the debtor attempts to defeat his creditors by bogus or colourable transactions under which the debtor retains a benefit to himself'. While it was suggested by Pennycuick VC in *Lloyds Bank Ltd v Marcan*[36] in

30. 10 Chas 1, sess. 2, c.3. The original equivalent in England was 13 Eliz., c.5.
31. *Re Eichholz* [1959] Ch 708.
32. [2011] IEHC 453.
33. This requirement was interpreted to mean valuable consideration including marriage, but natural love and affection did not suffice, see *Re Rorke's Estate* (1865) 15 Ir Ch R 316.
34. (1887) 21 LR Ir 27, 62. See also the comments of O'Connor MR in *National Bank Ltd v Behan* [1913] 1 IR 512, 516, to the effect that: 'the deed must be fraudulent in its conception or execution'.
35. [1945] IR 503, 510.
36. [1973] 1 WLR 339, 344.

the context of the then-equivalent English provision,[37] that the word 'defraud' was not intended to be confined to cases involving actual deceit or dishonesty, Cairns LJ disagreed with this view when the matter was considered by the Court of Appeal[38] and said that fraud involves dishonesty, so that while deceit is not a necessary element, dishonest intention is required, at any rate when the conveyance is one for consideration.

However, the view expressed by Pennycuick VC seems to be more in accord with the position adopted in this jurisdiction. In *Re Moroney*[39] Palles CB appeared to accept that there might be cases falling within the ambit of the statute where no fraudulent intention actually exists in the settlor's mind but can be assumed as a matter of law from the consequences of his actions. At this point it is useful to set out the Chief Baron's comments in full:

> Therefore to bring a conveyance within the statute, first, it must be fraudulent; secondly, the class of fraud must be an intent to delay, hinder or defraud creditors. Whether a particular conveyance be within this description may depend upon an infinite variety of circumstances and considerations. One conveyance for instance, may be executed with the express intent and object in the mind of the party to defeat and delay his creditors, and from such an intent the law presumes the conveyance to be fraudulent, and does not require or allow such fraud to be deduced as an inference of fact. In other cases, no such intention actually exists in the mind of the grantor, but the necessary or probable result of his denuding himself of the property included in the conveyance, for the consideration, and under the circumstances actually existing, is to defeat or delay creditors, and in such a case, as stated by Mellish LJ in *Re Wood* LR 7 Ch App 302, the intent is, as a matter of law, assumed from the necessary or probable consequences of the act done.[40]

This view that it is not necessary to establish that the agreement was motivated by actual fraud provided that the necessary or probable result of the agreement was to defeat or delay creditors was approved by Costello P in *McQuillan v Maguire*.[41] A decree in favour of the plaintiffs against the first named defendant in relation to a building contract had been converted into a judgment mortgage over the latter's interest in a property. A month after the decree had been

37. Section 172 of the Law of Property Act 1925. Subsequently replaced by s. 423 of the Insolvency Act 1986.
38. [1973] 1 WLR 1387, 1391.
39. (1887) 21 LR Ir 27.
40. *Ibid.* at 61-62. See also *Motor Insurers Bureau of Ireland v Stanbridge* [2011] 2 IR 78, 93-94; *Allied Irish Bank plc v Burke* [2018] IEHC 767 at [23]. These principles were also quoted by Finlay Geoghegan J in *Keegan Quarries Ltd v McGuinness* [2011] IEHC 453 at [151] who stated that in her view they also applied to s.74(3) of the Land and Conveyancing Law Reform Act 2009.
41. [1996] 1 ILRM 395.

obtained, the second named defendant, who was the wife of the first named defendant, instituted proceedings under the Married Women's Status Act 1957 and an order was made by consent declaring that she was entitled to the entire beneficial interest in this premises. When the plaintiffs learnt of the order they instituted proceedings seeking a declaration that the first named defendant was at all material times the beneficial owner of the premises and that the judgment mortgage was well charged on that beneficial interest. The plaintiffs submitted that the order had been obtained by collusion and with the intention of defrauding them and argued that it should be set aside in accordance with the provisions of the Conveyancing Act (Ireland) 1634. Costello P referred to *Re Moroney* and reiterated that the court did not have to find that the agreement had been motivated by actual fraud in order to set it aside. If it could be shown that the necessary or probable result of the agreement was to defeat or delay creditors, it could be avoided. He concluded that the agreement entered into between the defendants in the proceedings taken under the 1957 Act was void as it had the effect both of hindering and delaying the payment of a debt due by the first named defendant to the plaintiffs. He therefore held that the plaintiffs were entitled to a well charging order over the first named defendant's 50% of the premises on the basis that the wife had a 50% beneficial interest by virtue of contributions she had made to earlier family homes.

Similarly, in *Motor Insurers Bureau of Ireland v Stanbridge*,[42] Laffoy J held that the necessary or probable result of the defendants disclaiming their respective shares of deceased's estate on intestacy was to delay, hinder and defeat the payment of the debt due by them to the plaintiff as the assignee of the deceased's judgment against them and that, therefore, fraud had been proved. In *Doherty v Quigley*[43] Peart J also agreed that a finding that the natural and probable consequence of transfers of property by the first defendant was to delay or hinder his creditors was sufficient to satisfy the second limb of the test for a finding of fraudulent intent as set out by Palles CB in *Re Moroney*. He concluded that the finding of fraudulent intent made by the trial judge by way of inference for satisfying this test was in his view irresistible and correct on the facts of the case.

The onus lies on the party alleging fraud,[44] and this will be particularly relevant where it appears that the transfer or conveyance of the property was made in a *bona fide* manner for good consideration. The latter point emerges clearly from the decision of the High Court in *Bryce v Fleming*.[45] The first named defendant assigned lands to the second named defendant at a price which reflected the estimate which the parties placed on the value of the lands. The plaintiff had three days previously obtained judgment against the first named defendant and was a creditor of his to nearly half the value of the lands in

42. [2011] 2 IR 78.
43. [2015] IECA 297.
44. *National Bank Ltd v Behan* [1913] 1 IR 512, 516 *per* O'Connor MR.
45. [1930] IR 376.

question. The second named defendant stated in evidence that she had paid the full value of the lands and that she had no knowledge of the judgment which had been obtained against the vendor. The Circuit Court judge declared the deed void as against the first named defendant's creditors on the grounds that he did not believe the evidence of the second named defendant that she had no knowledge of the fraudulent nature of the transaction. On appeal the plaintiff's action was dismissed on the basis that the assignment was for valuable consideration and the evidence of the plaintiff did not establish that there was any knowledge of fraud on the part of the second named defendant nor did it show that she had sought to acquire the land other than as a *bona fide* purchaser.

So, even where a conveyance is for valuable consideration, this fact alone will not suffice to prevent the application of section 10 of the Conveyancing Act (Ireland) 1634.[46] This point was developed by Palles CB in *Re Moroney*[47] in the following manner:

> If, however, in such a case, the intent were not only to sell the property, but forthwith to abscond with the proceeds, so as in effect to withdraw the property from the fund available for the creditors without providing an equivalent, I should entertain no doubt that in such a case there would be an intention to defraud creditors, which, if the purchaser had notice of, would avoid the sale, and which, whether he had notice or not, would be an act of bankruptcy by the vendor.

However, it will clearly be more difficult to impugn the validity of a deed made for valuable consideration; as Turner LJ stated in *Harman v Richards*:[48] 'those who undertake to impeach for *mala fides* a deed which has been executed for valuable consideration, have, I think, a task of great difficulty to discharge'. As Johnston J made clear in *Bryce v Fleming*,[49] where there is a *bona fide* purchase for valuable consideration it cannot be impeached unless the purchaser is shown to be privy to the vendor's intention.

A further point to note is that the mere fact that an individual with debts is selling property is not necessarily evidence that he intends to defeat his creditors rather than to obtain the means to satisfy these debts.[50] *A fortiori*, knowledge of such a fact will not be a sufficient ground for imputing to a purchaser knowledge of a fraudulent intention on the part of the vendor. From a practical perspective a sale of this nature often provides the means necessary to satisfy existing debts; while the property itself ceases to be available for the

46. *Cadogan v Kennett* (1776) 2 Cowp 432, 434-435 *per* Lord Mansfield.
47. (1887) 21 LR Ir 27, 63.
48. (1852) 10 Hare 81, 89. See also *Re Johnson* (1881) 20 Ch D 389, 393; *Bryce v Fleming* [1930] IR 376, 379-380, 385.
49. [1930] IR 376.
50. *Bryce v Fleming* [1930] IR 376, 380 *per* Johnston J.

purpose of satisfaction, the consideration derived from the sale can be regarded as a 'substantial equivalent'.[51]

It is now clear that a settlement entered into with the intention of defrauding future creditors will come within the ambit of these provisions. In *Stileman v Ashdown*[52] Lord Hardwicke accepted that this could be the case: 'It is not necessary that a man should actually be indebted at the time he enters into a voluntary settlement, to make it fraudulent; for, if a man does it with a view to his being indebted at a future time, it is equally fraudulent, and ought to be set aside.'

This principle was confirmed in this jurisdiction in *Murphy v Abraham*,[53] where it was held by Smith MR that a voluntary deed in the form of a post-nuptial settlement entered into by a trader prior to embarking upon a partnership arrangement was executed with a view to defrauding his future creditors and could be set aside. Subsequently, in *Smith v Tatton*[54] Fitzgerald B concluded that there was no evidence of future indebtedness being in the contemplation of the grantor, although he seemed to accept that, in principle at least, a deed might be impeached if this had been the case. He stated that there were two classes of cases in which a deed might be set aside on this ground, first where there were existing debts and secondly, where 'either by the provision of the deed or other circumstances, it is shown that future indebtedness was at least in the contemplation of the grantor, so as to point whatever other evidence there may be of fraud to future creditors.'[55] Doubt was cast on the validity of this principle by some of the *dicta* of the Irish Court of Appeal in *Re Kelleher*,[56] including the statement of Holmes LJ that once the debts of creditors existing at the date of a deed have been discharged, a later creditor cannot take advantage of what might have been relied on by previous creditors as an implied fraud on them. However, a closer reading of the decision suggests that the decisive factor was the lack of any proof of an actual intention to defraud and it appears that where such an intention can be established the principle laid down in *Murphy v Abraham*[57] remains intact. This view is confirmed by the conclusions drawn by Peart J in the decision of the Court of Appeal in *Doherty v Quigley*.[58] He stated that the plaintiff was a creditor, in the sense of a future creditor, and said that it was noteworthy that section 10 refers not only to 'creditors' but to 'creditors and others' who may be delayed, hindered or defrauded by a fraudulent transfer of property. He also referred to the *dicta* of Romilly MR in *Barling v Bishopp*[59]

51. *Re Moroney* (1887) 21 LR Ir 27, 63.
52. (1742) 2 Atk 477, 481 in relation to the initial equivalent English provision (13 Eliz., c.5). See also *Barling v Bishopp* (1860) 29 Beav 417.
53. (1864) 15 Ir Ch R 371.
54. (1879) 6 LR Ir 32.
55. *Ibid.* at 42-43.
56. [1911] 2 IR 1, 9.
57. (1864) 15 Ir Ch R 371.
58. [2015] IECA 297.
59. (1860) 29 Beav 417.

and said that this establishes that section 10 of the Act of 1634 applied 'not just to existing creditors, but also to persons who by reason of facts existing at the date of transfer might become a creditor in the future'.[60]

Finally, it appears to be well-settled that merely preferring one creditor over another does not come within the mischief which the statute was designed to prevent[61] and that a debtor who gives a creditor security with the intention of preferring him to other creditors does not possess the necessary illegal intention.[62]

Voluntary Settlements to Defraud Purchasers

The issue of voluntary settlements which might defraud a purchaser was originally dealt with by the provisions of the Conveyancing Act (Ireland) 1634 which was repealed and the provisions of sections 74(1) and (2) of the Land and Conveyancing Law Reform Act 2009 now govern this area.[63] Section 1 of the Conveyancing Act (Ireland) 1634 provided that any voluntary conveyance made with the intention of defrauding subsequent purchasers was void (interpreted as meaning voidable), as against subsequent purchasers for value, and section 3 of the Act went on to exclude *bona fide* conveyances for good consideration from the ambit of the section. The meaning of the term '*bona fide*' in this context was considered by Hamilton P in *Re O'Neill*,[64] who said that it must be taken to mean 'without notice of the intention to delay, hinder or defraud creditors of their lawful debts, rights and remedies.'

This legislation was interpreted strictly from the point of view of the person conveying the property and as Monahan CJ stated in *Gardiner v Gardiner*:[65] 'from the fact of the deed being voluntary, we are justified in drawing the inference that the deed was made with intent to defraud purchasers.' The corresponding English enactment[66] was similarly interpreted,[67] and as Ronan LJ commented in *Moore v Kelly*,[68] 'this principle plainly treated as fraudulent perfectly honest transactions, and was found, particularly in the case of settlements making provision for families, to operate very harshly and unjustly.' As a result, the Voluntary Conveyances Act 1893 was passed which provided in the words of O'Connor MR in *National Bank Ltd v Behan*,[69] 'that no voluntary

60. [2015] IECA 297 at [22].
61. *Glegg v Bromley* [1912] 3 KB 474, 484 *per* Vaughan Williams LJ.
62. [1912] 3 KB 474, 492 *per* Parker J.
63. As amended by s. 110 and Part 4, Schedule 2 of the Central Bank and Credit Instiutions (Resolution) Act 2011 which inserts a new subs. (5) and s.21 of the Irish Bank Resolution Corporation Act 2013 which inserts a new subs. (6).
64. [1989] IR 544.
65. (1861) 12 ICLR 565, 575.
66. 27 Eliz., c.4.
67. *Doe v Manning* (1807) 9 East 59.
68. [1918] 1 IR 169, 181.
69. [1913] 1 IR 512, 517.

conveyance, if in fact made *bona fide* and without any fraudulent intent, should thereafter be deemed fraudulent or convinous within the meaning of the Act 10 Chas. 1, Sess. 2, c.3, by reason of any subsequent purchase for value.' However, it was held in *Behan* that despite these provisions, the onus of proving the *bona fides* of a voluntary settlement still lay on the person seeking to uphold it. O'Connor MR held that as infants were unable to prove affirmatively the *bona fides* of a voluntary conveyance of lands executed in their favour by their father, the conveyance was void as against a subsequent purchaser for value. He stated that in his view there could be no doubt as to the onus of proof under the Act of 1893 and that the words 'if *in fact* made *bona fide* and without any fraudulent intent' clearly placed the onus on the party seeking the protection of the statute. This would seem to be an unduly restrictive approach and serious doubts about its validity were voiced by O'Brien LC in *Moore v Kelly*.[70] Although he referred to the *Behan* decision and said that he would never overrule the judgment of the Master of the Rolls unless he considered that he was 'absolutely bound to reach a different conclusion', he went on to comment as follows:

> [O]rdinarily, I should have thought that the person on whom the onus of proof would lie under 27 Eliz. c.4, once the irrebuttable presumption to which I have referred was swept away, was the person alleging fraud, just as under 13 Eliz., c.5, where an actual intent to defraud the grantor's creditors is alleged, the burden of proving such intent falls on the person alleging it.[71]

As noted above, sections 74(1) and (2) of the Land and Conveyancing Law Reform Act 2009 have replaced the provisions of the Conveyancing Act (Ireland) 1634 and section 74(1) now specifically provides that a voluntary disposition of land made with the intention of defrauding a subsequent purchaser of land is 'voidable by that purchaser'. As Wylie points out, this means that: '[a]rguably … the courts will, in future, take the view that the burden rests firmly on the purchaser seeking to challenge the voluntary conveyance'.[72]

Settlements by Bankrupts

Section 52 of the Bankruptcy (Ireland) Amendment Act 1872, which made provision for the setting aside in certain circumstances of settlements made by persons subsequently adjudicated bankrupt, was repealed[73] and replaced by section 59 of the Bankruptcy Act 1988 as amended.[74] Section 59 as amended

70. [1918] 1 IR 169.
71. *Ibid.* at 179.
72. Wylie, *Irish Land Law* (4th ed., 2010) pp. 622-623.
73. By s. 6, Second Schedule of the Bankruptcy Act 1988.
74. Section 59 was amended by s. 154 of the Personal Insolvency Act 2012. On this issue, see generally Sanfey & Holohan, *Bankruptcy Law and Practice* (2nd ed., 2010) pp. 183-186 and Forde & Simms, *Bankruptcy Law* (2nd ed., 2009) pp. 128-132.

now provides that any settlement of property,[75] not being a settlement before and in consideration of marriage, or made in favour of a purchaser or incumbrancer in good faith and for valuable consideration, shall be void as against the official assignee if the settlor is adjudicated bankrupt within three years[76] of the date of the settlement and, if the settlor is adjudicated bankrupt within five years of the date of the settlement, shall be void unless the parties claiming under the settlement prove that the settlor was, at the time of making the settlement, able to pay all his debts without the aid of the property comprised in it and that the interest of the settlor in such property passed to the trustee of the settlement on its execution.

As in the case of the sections considered above, the reference to the settlement being void as against the official assignee has been interpreted as meaning voidable and therefore valid unless steps are taken to have it set aside.[77] There is no requirement to prove any fraudulent intent on the part of the settlor and it is the mere fact of him becoming bankrupt within the period of time laid down in the statute which brings the section into operation.[78] To secure protection against its provisions, as Hamilton P commented in *Re O'Neill*,[79] 'it is necessary that the conveyance should be both for valuable consideration and *bona fide*' or that the settlement should be one in consideration of marriage.

In *Re O'Neill* the bankrupt conveyed his interest in premises to his daughter for slightly below the market value less than two years prior to being adjudicated bankrupt. The official assignee applied to have the conveyance set aside on the grounds that it had not been entered into *bona fide* and for valuable consideration. Hamilton P stated that the onus was on the official assignee to establish as a matter of probability that the conveyance was made with intent to delay, hinder or defraud creditors of their lawful debts, rights and remedies and that it was possible for the court to infer such intent from the circumstances of the case. In relation to the question of on whom the onus lay to establish that the conveyance was not made in good faith or for valuable consideration, Hamilton P stated that without deciding this question finally, he was prepared to deal with the particular case before him on the basis that the onus was on the official assignee to establish a lack of good faith on the part of the bankrupt's daughter. He concluded that while she must be regarded as a purchaser for valuable consideration, she did not purchase the premises in good faith as she must have been aware of her father's financial position and of the fact that the object of the transaction was to hinder, delay and defraud his creditors.

One further point to note about the judgment of Hamilton P in *Re O'Neill*

---

75. Defined in s. 3 of the Act of 1988 to include real and personal property.
76. 'Three years' was substituted for 'two years' by s. 154 of the Personal Insolvency Act 2012.
77. *Per* Palles CB in *Re Doyle* (1891) Court of Appeal, unreported, quoted in Kiely, *The Principles of Equity as applied in Ireland* (1936) pp. 70-71.
78. *Re Moore* (1897) 31 ILTR 5.
79. [1989] IR 544, 551.

is that he accepted as applying with equal validity to the Irish legislation the statement of Stirling J in *Mackintosh v Pogose*[80] to the effect that to come within the saving clause in the section, it is sufficient that the purchaser acts in good faith and it is not necessary that both parties should have so acted.[81]

The other ground on which the application of the section may be avoided is where the settlement is made 'before and in consideration of marriage'. It was confirmed in *Re Campbell*[82] that this wording cannot extend to a post-nuptial settlement not made in pursuance of an ante-nuptial agreement. It has been held in England that for a settlement to be regarded as being in consideration of marriage, it must be made on the occasion of the marriage, must be conditioned only to take effect on the marriage taking place and it must be made by a person for the purpose of, or with a view to, encouraging or facilitating the marriage.[83] In addition, it was held by the Irish Court of Appeal in *Re Downes*[84] that the exception in relation to settlements made before or in consideration of marriage is not confined to settlements made on the marriage of the settlor and in that case was held to extend to a settlement made on the marriage of the settlor's sister.

While section 59 of the Bankruptcy Act 1988 as amended essentially reproduces the important features of section 52 of the Bankruptcy (Ireland) Amendment Act 1872, there are a number of important changes to note. Section 52 only applied to traders, a distinction which was criticised[85] and not retained in section 59. The 10-year period originally specified was reduced to five years in section 59(1) and the relevant date from which the three-[86] and five-year periods specified are to be calculated is now the date of adjudication of bankruptcy, whereas formerly it was reckoned from the date when an act of bankruptcy was committed.[87] In addition, the phrase 'and that the interest of the settlor in such property passed to the trustee of such settlement on the execution thereof' was included so that a settlement to take effect in the future would fall within the section. In addition, section 59(3) renders void as against the official assignee any transfer of property made in pursuance of a contract or covenant for the settlement of property acquired after its execution unless the payment or transfer comes within certain conditions set out in the subsection.[88]

80. [1895] 1 Ch 505, 509.
81. [1989] IR 544, 551.
82. (1878) 12 ILTR 163.
83. *Rennell v IRC* [1964] AC 173, 202 *per* Lord Cohen. See also *Re Densham* [1975] 1 WLR 1519, 1527 *per* Goff J in the context of equivalent English legislation.
84. [1898] 2 IR 635.
85. See Bankruptcy Law Committee Report (1972; Prl. 2714) Chapter 23.
86. 'Three years' was substituted for 'two years' by s. 154 of the Personal Insolvency Act 2012.
87. *Re Mackey* [1915] 2 IR 347.
88. This subsection was inserted to meet the criticisms made in the Bankruptcy Law Committee Report (1972; Prl. 2714) Chapter 23.10.1 (5).

CHAPTER 13

The Administration of Trusts

THE OFFICE OF TRUSTEE

Introduction

Wylie has commented that 'the position of a trustee is an extremely exacting one and, all too frequently, a thankless one.'[1] This statement is an accurate reflection of the view which might be expressed by many who agree to undertake such a role. Trustees are required to carry out duties and obligations which can often be of considerable complexity and in doing so are expected to display a high degree of honesty and integrity. Referring to the danger that the interests of innocent beneficiaries may be jeopardised by those appointed to safeguard them, Porter MR stated as follows in *Bank of Ireland v Cogry Flax Spinning Co.*:[2]

> That is why it is so important to select an honourable and upright, as well as an intelligent and capable man for the office of trustee. If the selection is unfortunate, so may be the results.

As Charleton J suggested in *Greene v Coady*,[3] the settlor/testator and the beneficiaries will have an expectation that cannot be departed from, namely that the trustees will pursue the aims of the trust honestly and in good faith. In his view:

> Clarity of conscience and ability to think both clearly and objectively is thus required on any decision that impacts on the management of the trust for the benefit of those for whom it was set up. No matter what is said in a trust deed, this fundamental obligation can never be departed from.[4]

Trustees are only entitled to payment for their endeavours if the trust instrument itself makes provision for remuneration and they are precluded from making any form of personal profit out of the affairs of the trust or as a result of placing themselves in a position where their own interests and those of the trust might conflict. By undertaking to act in this capacity, in addition to incurring the wrath

1. Wylie, *Irish Land Law* (4th ed., 2010) p. 659.
2. [1900] 1 IR 219, 236.
3. [2015] 1 IR 385.
4. *Ibid.* at 405.

of the beneficiaries should he fail to exercise his duties in a manner which they might consider appropriate, a trustee may also face the prospect of personal liability to account where he is found to have been in breach of duty.

In view of these considerations, it may reasonably be asked why any right-minded individual would ever agree to act as a trustee, and it is the onerous nature of the responsibilities which go with the office which is primarily responsible for the growth in the numbers of professional trustees. Traditionally, trustees have fallen into two categories: non-professional trustees, who are often family members or close associates of the settlor or testator who agree to act out of a sense of duty, and professional trustees, usually banks and financial institutions, who undertake the role only in circumstances where suitable provision is made for their remuneration. Arguably it is preferable when creating a trust to ensure that a combination of these categories of trustees are appointed; it is often unwise to nominate only non-professional trustees,[5] for although they may and indeed should seek professional assistance where this is required, they may not always be aware of the circumstances in which this will be necessary.

Some aspects of the law relating to the administration of trusts are set out in legislation, primarily the Trustee Act 1893.[6] As will be seen below, this legislation made provision in relation to such issues as the appointment, retirement and removal of trustees and some of the powers of trustees but it was far from comprehensive in nature. As the Law Reform Commission commented in its Consultation Paper *Trust Law: General Proposals*[7] 'trustee legislation has not kept up to date with the changing economic and social nature of trusts' and many key aspects of this area of the law now covered by legislation in England, such as a trustee's duty of care[8] and the delegation of trustees' functions, remain governed by principles developed in case law. A wholesale overhaul of the statutory scheme in the area of the administration of trusts in this jurisdiction is therefore necessary. In the course of this chapter reference will be made to the proposals put forward by the Law Reform Commission in its Report

5. See, e.g. *Turner v Turner* [1984] Ch 100.
6. See also the Trustee Act 1931; the Trustee (Authorised Investments) Act 1958.
7. LRC CP 35-2005 Introduction para. 2. See also Law Reform Commission Report *Trust Law: General Proposals* LRC 92-2008.
8. Section 1(1) of the English Trustee Act 2000 provides that whenever the duty set out in the subsection applies to a trustee, he must exercise such care and skill as is reasonable in the circumstances having regard in particular '(a) to any special knowledge or experience that he has or holds himself out as having, and (b) if he acts as a trustee in the course of a business or profession, to any special knowledge or experience that it is reasonable to expect of a person acting in the course of that kind of business or profession.' The Law Reform Commission in its Report *Trust Law: General Proposals* LRC 92-2008, para. 3.15 recommended the introduction of a statutory duty of care.

Trust Law: General Proposals,[9] to which a draft Trustee Bill is appended, and comprehensive statutory reform is long overdue.[10]

Any person can be appointed a trustee in this jurisdiction, even a minor,[11] although in practice it is desirable to appoint a person who will be capable of carrying out the functions required of him. A corporation may act as a trustee provided that its memorandum and articles of association confer on it express authority to carry out this role. It is preferable that the trustees appointed reside in the jurisdiction but exceptions may have to be made. In the past the court has sanctioned the appointment of persons resident outside the jurisdiction where there is no practical alternative.[12] While a beneficiary or the close relative of a beneficiary[13] may be appointed a trustee, arguably this is undesirable in practice in view of the potential conflict of interest which might result. However, there may be difficulties in finding sufficient suitable persons who do not stand to benefit from the trust to act and it has also been argued that provided a beneficiary does not act as a sole trustee, it may even be preferable to appoint such a person as he will have an added incentive to ensure that the affairs of the trust are effectively and profitably conducted.

There is generally no minimum number of trustees necessary: one trustee will suffice except where statute requires otherwise,[14] although for practical reasons it is more desirable to have two or more.[15] In this jurisdiction there is no upper limit on the number of trustees who may be appointed,[16] but for reasons of administrative workability it is obviously undesirable to have more than a reasonable number to facilitate the process of decision-making and to avoid the machinery of the trust becoming unwieldy.

---

9. LRC 92-2008.
10. A Trusts Bill had been listed in Section C of the Government Legislation Programme for some years up until 2016 as 'Publication expected – not possible to indicate at this stage'. However, there is no longer any reference to it.
11. Although in England, s. 20 of the Law of Property Act 1925 provides that the appointment of a minor to be a trustee of an express trust shall be void. In addition, The Law Reform Commission in its Report *Trust Law: General Proposals* LRC 92-2008, para. 2.12 recommended that a minor should be prohibited from acting as a trustee.
12. *Crofton v Crofton* (1913) 47 ILTR 24.
13. *Re Jackson's Trusts* (1874) 8 ILTR 174.
14. Two trustees are required under s. 39(1) of the Settled Land Act 1882 (repealed by the Land and Conveyancing Law Reform Act 2009, Schedule 2, Part 4, now; see s. 21(2)(a) of that Act) in order to give a receipt for capital money on a sale by a tenant for life unless the settlement authorises otherwise.
15. The Law Reform Commission in its Report *Trust Law: General Proposals* LRC 92-2008, para. 2.22 recommended that in the case of non-charitable trusts, two trustees or a corporate trustee should be required. See s. 4(1) of the draft Trustee Bill 2008.
16. Note that in England, s. 34 of the Trustee Act 1925 restricts the number of trustees in trusts of land to four. The Law Reform Commission in its Report *Trust Law: General Proposals* LRC 92-2008, para. 2.25 recommended that there should not be any restriction on the number of trustees.

Appointment of Trustees

The first trustees are ordinarily appointed by the settlor or testator in the trust instrument and where this is a will, the executors and trustees will often be the same persons. Where none are appointed or where those nominated predecease the testator or refuse to act, the court has jurisdiction to appoint trustees.[17] These trustees will hold as joint tenants, so where one or more dies, the survivors continue to act as trustees and on the death of a sole trustee, the trust property will vest in his personal representatives pending the appointment of new trustees.

As regards the appointment of new or additional trustees, this power of appointment may be exercised by persons nominated for that purpose in the trust instrument in the circumstances laid down in that document. Usually, this power will be framed so that it is exercisable whenever the persons nominated deem it necessary but where limitations are imposed these may be strictly construed. In *Re Wheeler*[18] a power to appoint a new trustee in circumstances where an existing trustee was 'incapable' of acting was held not to be exercisable where an incumbent became bankrupt on the grounds that while he might as a result have been deemed 'unfit' to act, this did not mean that he was 'incapable' of performing his duties. In addition to any express power contained in the trust instrument, a statutory power to appoint new trustees is contained in section 10 of the Trustee Act 1893. This statutory power must be exercised in writing and, in practice, it is desirable that it is exercised by deed to facilitate the application of section 12 of the Act of 1893 which makes provision for the vesting of trust property in new or continuing trustees. Section 10(1) provides that this power may be exercised by 'the person or persons nominated for the purpose of appointing new trustees by the instrument, if any, creating the trust, or if there is no such person or no such person able and willing to act, then the surviving or continuing trustees or trustee for the time being, or the personal representatives of the last surviving or continuing trustee'. The Law Reform Commission recommended in its Report *Trust Law: General Proposals* that the non-judicial power of appointment should be extended to include a liquidator where a corporate trustee is in liquidation or has been wound-up and there is no person nominated in the trust instrument and to the beneficiaries where they are *sui juris* and together absolutely entitled to the entire beneficial interest under the trust.[19] It also recommended that a trustee who is being compulsorily removed should not be permitted to exercise the non-judicial power of appointment[20] and that any new legislative provision governing the appointment of trustees

17. *Pollock v Ennis* [1921] 1 IR 181.
18. [1896] 1 Ch 315.
19. LRC 92-2008, paras. 2.94, 2.98. See s. 5(2) of the draft Trustee Bill 2008.
20. *Ibid.* at para. 2.83. See s. 8(5) of the draft Trustee Bill 2008.

should make clear that a person who has disclaimed the position of trustee is excluded from exercising the power to appoint new trustees.[21]

This power to appoint new trustees can at present be exercised where a trustee:

(i) is dead, or
(ii) remains out of the jurisdiction for more than twelve months,[22] or
(iii) desires to be discharged from his duties, or
(iv) refuses to act,[23] or
(v) is unfit to act, or incapable of acting.[24]

This power is confined to the appointment of replacements for original or substituted trustees, although where trustee(s) are being replaced the number may be increased. However, it should be noted that it does not confer a power to appoint additional trustees except in these circumstances and in this respect the law differs from that in Northern Ireland and England.[25] The Law Reform Commission in its Report *Trust Law: General Proposals* has recommended the introduction of a non-judicial power to appoint additional trustees without recourse to the courts.[26] This would allow for the appointment of additional trustees where a replacement is not being sought and would bring the law in this jurisdiction more into line with that elsewhere in the common law world.

In addition, section 25 of the Trustee Act 1893 confers a power on the court to appoint new or additional trustees whenever it is expedient to do so and would be 'inexpedient, difficult or impracticable so to do without the assistance of the court'.[27] The procedure for bringing an application under section 25 is set out

---

21. *Ibid.* at para. 2.85. See s. 9(1) of the draft Trustee Bill 2008.
22. The Law Reform Commission in its Report *Trust Law: General Proposals* LRC 92-2008, para. 2.54 expressed the view that this ground should be deleted as it was no longer appropriate.
23. The Law Reform Commission in its Report *Trust Law: General Proposals* LRC 92-2008, para. 2.58 recommended that the statutory power of appointment should not apply to situations where trustees refuse to act subsequent to accepting trusteeship.
24. The Law Reform Commission in its Report *Trust Law: General Proposals* LRC 92-2008 recommended the inclusion of additional categories, namely where a minor has been invalidly appointed (para. 2.63) and where a trustee is made a ward of court or an enduring power of attorney comes into effect (para. 2.65) but it specifically recommended that the non-judicial power of appointment should not be exercisable in circumstances where one of the trustees has been declared bankrupt (para. 2.68). See s. 5 of the draft Trustee Bill 2008.
25. See s. 35 of the Trustee Act (NI) 1958 and s. 36(6) of the Trustee Act 1925.
26. LRC 92-2008, para. 2.49. See s. 5 of the draft Trustee Bill 2008.
27. See e.g. *W. v M.* [2011] IEHC 217.

by Keane;[28] it must be brought by special summons grounded on affidavit if it is brought to the High Court,[29] or by civil bill if it is made to the Circuit Court.[30]

Retirement of Trustees

A trustee may disclaim his appointment and refuse to take up the office at the outset and if he wishes to do this, to avoid any possible uncertainty, he should preferably express his intention by deed.[31] However, once a trustee has accepted the office and has failed to disclaim it within a reasonable time, he can only retire in specified circumstances. First, he can retire if there is an express clause in the trust instrument permitting him to do so or if he receives the consent of all the beneficiaries, provided that they are all *sui juris* and between them entitled to the entire beneficial interest in the trust property. In addition, statutory provision is made for retirement by virtue of section 11 of the Trustee Act 1893 which lays down that provided there will be at least two trustees left to administer the trust, a trustee may by deed declare that he wishes to retire and if his co-trustees consent by deed, he will be permitted to do so.[32] Alternatively, an existing trustee may retire as a result of the exercise of the statutory power to appoint new trustees provided in section 10 of the Trustee Act 1893. In addition, a trustee may seek a court order under section 25 of the Act of 1893 which empowers the court to appoint new trustees for existing ones whenever it is expedient, or would be difficult or impractical to do so without the court's assistance.

Removal of Trustees

A trustee may be removed from his office where express provision is made for this in the trust instrument or by the beneficiaries where they are *sui juris* and between them absolutely entitled to the trust property. In addition, a trustee may be removed where the court exercises the power conferred on it by section 25 of the Trustee Act 1893 to appoint a new trustee where an existing trustee refuses or is unfit to act. The Law Reform Commission in its Report *Trust Law: General Proposals* recommended that removal without replacement should not be permitted by statute unless at least two trustees or a corporate trustee remains.[33] It also recommended that bankruptcy of a trustee, liquidation of a corporate trustee, conviction of an indictable offence, or where an individual

28. Keane, *Equity and the Law of Trusts in Ireland* (3rd ed., 2017) p. 132.
29. Order 3, rule 11 of the Rules of Superior Courts 1986.
30. Order 46, rule 1 of the Rules of the Circuit Court 2001.
31. While disclaimer may be implied, in view of the limited circumstances in which a trustee may retire, it is preferable that an intention to disclaim should be unambiguously expressed.
32. The Law Reform Commission in its Report *Trust Law: General Proposals* LRC 92-2008, para. 2.141 recommended that a trustee should not be permitted to retire unless at least two trustees or a corporate trustee remains.
33. LRC 92-2008, para. 2.153.

is sentenced to a term of imprisonment by a court of competent jurisdiction, should all form grounds for the removal of a trustee and the appointment of a replacement by the court.[34]

The court also has an inherent jurisdiction to remove trustees where they act dishonestly or incompetently or even where their conduct is deliberately obstructive. This point was confirmed by Murnaghan J in *Arnott v Arnott*.[35] The defendant was removed from the position of trustee to which she had been appointed on the basis that the business, the subject-matter of the trust, was to be managed by the plaintiff in circumstances where her persistent non-cooperation rendered the trust virtually unworkable. Murnaghan J stated that the jurisdiction of the court to remove a trustee should be exercised if the welfare of the beneficiaries demanded it, even though no dishonesty or incompetence had been alleged or proved against the trustee in question. He said that the jurisdiction of the court was usually resorted to when a trustee has mismanaged a trust or has been proved dishonest or incompetent but the guiding principle to which all others must be subordinate was the welfare of the beneficiaries.

A further ground on which a court may exercise its inherent jurisdiction to remove a trustee is where there is a clear conflict of interest between the trustee's duty to the trust and his own personal interests. In *Moore v McGlynn*[36] the defendant was discharged from further performance of the duties of trustee where he had set up a rival business in competition with that of which he was trustee for the benefit of the family of his deceased brother. Although Chatterton VC held that the new business should not be affected by a trust for the benefit of his brother's estate, he was satisfied that it would be improper for the trustee to continue in a position where his personal interests and his duty to the trust might conflict. As he stated, 'his new position disqualifies him from remaining any longer a trustee, and it would have been better for him to have procured his removal from trusteeship before setting up for himself. He should not be continued in a position where his duties and his self-interest may conflict.'[37] Conflict of interest also formed the basis for the decision of Carroll J in *Kirby v Barden*,[38] in which the defendant's actions, both in retaining a gift of a questionable nature for herself and in acquiescing in giving up a claim to the property which should have formed part of the deceased's estate, appeared to have been driven by self-interest. While Carroll J concluded that the jurisdiction of the court to remove a trustee should be exercised with caution, in her view the circumstances of the case amply justified the defendant's removal both as trustee and personal representative. Humphreys J also made an order removing the defendant as a trustee in *Dully v Athlone Town Stadium Ltd*,[39]

34. *Ibid.* at para. 2.156.
35. (1924) 58 ILTR 145.
36. [1894] 1 IR 74. See also *Kirby v Barden* [1999] IEHC 129.
37. *Ibid.* at 90.
38. [1999] IEHC 129.
39. [2018] IEHC 209.

where he was satisfied that numerous breaches of trust had been committed and in circumstances where he found that the defendant's approach had been obstructive and that a conflict of interest arose. Humphreys J rejected the submission that the court should focus on the conduct of the defendant from the time of the issuing of the proceedings and not on any matters before then and stated that '[i]n deciding whether a trustee should be removed, regard must be had to all relevant circumstances including conduct of the defendant prior to the proceedings.'[40]

The fact that the primary issue which the court should have regard to in deciding whether to order the removal of a trustee is the welfare of the beneficiaries was confirmed by Barron J in *Spencer v Kinsella*[41] in a judgment which, although ultimately failing to resolve some of the problems faced by the plaintiffs, did provide useful guidance in relation to the circumstances in which a trustee may be removed from his office. Showgrounds in Gorey were vested in trustees on trust so that they might be used as a sports ground, park or pleasure ground subject to conditions as to payment or otherwise to be prescribed by the trustees. In recent years the grounds had been used by a local football club and coursing club and the land had also been used for the grazing of sheep. Complaints against the trustees were made by the football club which had spent money on the repair and maintenance of the grounds, and it was alleged that they were neglecting their duties and that the grounds were being allowed to fall into a state of disrepair. The plaintiffs sought the removal of the trustees on the basis that they had persistently refused to act when called on to do so and submitted that the welfare of the beneficiaries required this course of action. They were supported in their claims by the second named defendant but the remaining trustees submitted that they had at all times acted in a *bona fide* manner and argued that the exercise of their powers should not be interfered with by the court unless they had acted *mala fide*, capriciously or outside the terms of the trust. Barron J accepted that the existing situation could not be allowed to continue and said that a reorganisation must take place, either with or without the assistance of the court. While he acknowledged that it was difficult to find local people who had no affiliation with any organisation seeking to use the grounds, he stated that 'in all cases of trust, it is a truism to say that no trustee should allow his interest to conflict with his duty'. Barron J referred to the *Arnott* case and said that a trust is set up for the welfare of beneficiaries and before determining whether or not any trustee should be removed it is necessary to determine whether his continuation in office will be detrimental to such welfare. He concluded that the welfare of the beneficiaries was being affected by the difficulties which had been brought to the court's attention and said that in view of the existing conflict of interest some of the trustees who found themselves in such a position of conflict should step down and allow a

40. *Ibid.* at [55].
41. [1996] 2 ILRM 401.

general reorganisation to take place. Barron J stated that what was required was the appointment of trustees who were as far as possible impartial as between the various users of the grounds. However, he decided not to exercise the powers of the court at that time and to adjourn the matter for six months to enable the administration of the trust to be placed on a proper footing.[42]

Barron J's judgment is useful in that it confirms that the overriding principle to which the court must have regard in exercising its power to remove trustees is the welfare of the beneficiaries. This is also borne out by the decision of Carroll J in *M.K. v J.B.*,[43] in which she held, in refusing to remove a trustee, that there would be no grounds for doing so unless the latter's decision to sell a property was not for the welfare of the beneficiary, which in her opinion it would be. Clearly the court can act where, although there has been no breach of trust or actual misconduct, the conflict of interest existing amongst the trustees is such that the trust can no longer function effectively. From a practical perspective conflict of interest can be as damaging to the welfare of the beneficiaries of a trust as actual misconduct and by placing the interests of the beneficiaries at the forefront of the matters to which the court should have regard, the decision of Barron J in *Spencer* should ensure that sufficient attention is given to this point. His pragmatic approach is to be welcomed and it is submitted that while it is important that trustees seek to work together to resolve their differences, it is also crucial that the court retains a power to intervene where the welfare of the beneficiaries is not being adequately protected.

The circumstances in which an order may be made removing an executor from that position pursuant to section 26(2) of the Succession Act 1965 have also been considered by the courts in this jurisdiction on a number of occasions. In *Dunne v Heffernan*[44] Lynch J stated that an order removing an executor is a very serious step to take and that it is not justified because one of the beneficiaries appears to have felt frustrated and excluded from what he considered to be his legitimate concerns. In the view of Lynch J, '[i]t would require serious misconduct and/or serious special circumstances on the part of the [executor] to justify such a drastic step'.[45] In the circumstances, the Supreme Court was satisfied that there were no grounds justifying the removal of the defendant as executrix pursuant to section 26(2) of the Act of 1965. These principles were reiterated by Macken J in *Flood v Flood*,[46] where she stated that a court is

42. Hamilton CJ in the course of a Supreme Court judgment delivered on 13 January 1999 ([1999] IESC 16) stated that the matter was re-entered before Barron J on 11 November 1996 and that the order which he made on that date recited that the court was informed that the issues between the parties had been resolved save as to the costs of the proceedings. In its judgment, the Supreme Court allowed an appeal brought by the sixth named defendant, the Minister for Agriculture, Food and Forestry, in relation to the order for costs made against him by the trial judge.
43. [1999] IEHC 117.
44. [1997] 3 IR 431.
45. *Ibid.* at 443. See also *Davies v Hutchinson* [2017] IEHC 693 at [15].
46. [1999] 2 IR 234.

not justified in removing an executor from his role simply because one of the beneficiaries appears to have felt frustrated and excluded, but that it 'requires serious misconduct and/or serious special circumstances on the part of the executor to justify such a drastic step.'[47] However, she concluded that as a very serious matter had arisen in the administration of the estate, the only way in which it could be dealt with was by removing the defendant as executor. The principles set out in *Dunne* were also applied by Laffoy J in *Scally v Rhatigan*,[48] where it was claimed by the defendant in a counterclaim that the plaintiff executor was conflicted in a professional capacity and was not an appropriate person to act as executor in relation to the testator's estate. Laffoy J was satisfied that the plaintiff would be in a position of having irreconcilable duties to the beneficiaries of the estate assets and of the non-estate assets if a grant of probate issued to her. She concluded that she had no doubt that this conflicted position amounted to 'serious special circumstances' in the sense outlined by Lynch J in *Dunne v Heffernan* and that the welfare of the beneficiaries of the estate assets would not be protected by the testator's estate being administered by the plaintiff.

The Court of Appeal revisited this issue in *Dunne v Dunne*[49] in the context of an application to remove a legal personal representative. In reversing the decision of Cregan J to replace the legal personal representative,[50] Peart J stated that even where such a person stands to gain depending on how an issue is determined, which may occur quite frequently where the administrator is a family member, this does not mean that it will be necessary to replace him even though such a situation might be characterised as one giving rise to a conflict of interest. Peart J added as follows:

> In my view, absent some serious misconduct … the conflict must be one which has the capacity to hinder or prevent the proper and fair determination of the issue that has arisen. One could describe this as an operative conflict – in other words it is a conflict which operates unfairly against the interests of another party who is therefore at a meaningful or significant disadvantage or prejudice in the resolution of the issue, and where the appointment of another representative would remove that disadvantage or prejudice.[51]

Peart J went on to say that one reason why a legal personal representative should not be replaced unless it is necessary in the sense he had outlined is that

---

47. *Ibid.* at 244.
48. [2012] IEHC 140.
49. [2016] IECA 269.
50. [2015] IEHC 607.
51. *Ibid.* at [44]. See also *Davies v Hutchinson* [2017] IEHC 693 at [20]. On the facts of this case, O'Regan J concluded that the asserted conflicts of interest did not amount to special circumstances or serious grounds for the removal of an executrix.

to do so will impose additional expense on the estate. As he pointed out, the new independent replacement is likely to be a professional person, or at least somebody who will be entitled to be paid for his services and particularly where litigation is involved, this will lead to a considerable drain on the resources of the estate to the detriment of the beneficiaries.

Similar considerations may arise in the context of a small family trust, or one with limited assets. Therefore, the cardinal principle that, in considering applications to remove a trustee, the welfare of the beneficiaries is of paramount importance means that sometimes it may be necessary for the court to have regard to this broader context in weighing up potential conflicts of interest.

THE DUTIES OF TRUSTEES

Duties on Appointment

The first duties of a trustee once appointed are to ascertain the nature and extent of the property comprised in the trust and to ensure that he understands the terms of the trust instrument. As Kekewich J stated in *Hallows v Lloyd*:[52]

> I think that when persons are asked to become new trustees, they are bound to inquire of what the property consists that is proposed to be handed over to them, and what are the trusts. They ought also to look into the trust documents and papers to ascertain what notices appear among them of incumbrances and other matters affecting the trust.

Trustees are required to act in good faith and in a responsible and reasonable manner in performing their functions and they must inform themselves, before making a decision, of matters that are relevant to that decision.[53] It is essential that a trustee is aware from the outset of the precise nature of the powers conferred on him by the instrument, e.g. in relation to investment and he should seek legal advice if there is any reasonable doubt about the ambit of these powers.[54] A trustee must also ensure that the property which is subject to the trust is under his control and, where necessary, he must arrange for the property to be conveyed or transferred into the joint names of himself and his co-trustees. He must collect in any assets which are part of the trust and ensure that the trust fund is properly invested. In addition, a trustee should satisfy himself that there is no evidence of a breach of trust committed by a previous

52. (1888) 39 Ch D 686, 691.
53. *Per* Robert Walker J in *Scott v National Trust for Places of Historic Interest or Natural Beauty* [1998] 2 All ER 705, 717.
54. In *Nestle v National Westminster Bank plc* [1993] 1 WLR 1260, in which the plaintiff bank claimed to have had doubts about the precise scope of its investment powers, Dillon LJ stated (at 1265) that: 'it was inexcusable that the bank took no step at any time to obtain legal advice as to the scope of its power'.

trustee which ought to be investigated or rectified. He must make all reasonable inquiries in this regard, and if the circumstances suggest that such a breach has occurred, he should take whatever steps may be necessary to remedy the breach, or he may find himself liable also.

Duty to Properly Exercise Discretion

Introduction

Where trustees have discretion in relation to the management of a trust, the court will not take this discretion out of their hands,[55] but it will intervene if necessary if it is exercised improperly. So, as Jessel MR stated in *Tempest v Lord Camoys*,[56] 'It is settled law that when a testator has given a pure discretion to trustees as to the exercise of a power, the Court does not enforce the exercise of the power against the wish of the trustees, but it does prevent them from exercising it improperly.' It is clear that trustees are under an obligation to apply their minds to the exercise of any discretion vested in them and a failure to do so may result in a decision made being challenged successfully. In *Turner v Turner*[57] purported appointments made by trustees were set aside by the court in circumstances where the trustees were unaware that they had any discretion and had not read or understood the effect of the documents they had signed. As Mervyn Davies J stated, the court can set aside the exercise of a fiduciary power if satisfied that the trustees never applied their minds at all to the exercise of the discretion entrusted to them and he concluded that: '[t]he trustees therefore made the appointments in breach of their duty in that it was their duty to "consider" before appointing and this they did not do'.[58]

However, as a general principle, provided the trustees do give proper consideration to the exercise of their discretionary powers, it has been suggested that 'the duty of supervision on the part of this Court will … be confined to the question of the honesty, integrity and fairness with which the deliberation has been conducted and will not be extended to the accuracy of the conclusion arrived at, except in particular cases.'[59] This is a rather simplistic view of the true position as a more detailed survey of the case law in this area will show but it is probably accurate to state that in the absence of evidence that a trustee

55. *Tempest v Lord Camoys* (1882) 21 Ch D 571, 579 *per* Brett LJ.
56. (1882) 21 Ch D 571, 578.
57. [1984] Ch 100.
58. *Ibid.* at 110.
59. *Re Beloved Wilkes' Charity* (1851) 3 Mac & G 440, 448.

has acted improperly,[60] or in breach of duty,[61] the court will not interfere with the exercise of discretion.

Relevant and Irrelevant Considerations

As a general principle trustees are under an obligation to inform themselves before making a decision of all matters relevant to that decision.[62] Thus, in exercising a discretionary power it has been suggested that they should take into account all relevant considerations and ignore all irrelevant or extraneous matters.[63]

This area of the law has been reviewed by the Supreme Court of the United Kingdom in *Pitt v Holt*[64] and the relevant principles considerably amended so earlier authorities in this area should be treated with a degree of caution. What had become known as the principle in *Re Hastings-Bass* was set out by Buckley LJ in the decision of that name in the following terms:

> [W]here by the terms of a trust … a trustee is given a discretion as to some matter under which he acts in good faith, the court should not interfere with his action notwithstanding that it does not have the full effect which he intended, unless (1) what he has achieved is unauthorised by the power conferred upon him, or (2) it is clear that he would not have acted as he did (a) had he not taken into account considerations which he should not have taken into account, or (b) had he not failed to take into account considerations which he ought to have taken into account.[65]

However, it is important to note that the *Hastings-Bass* case itself involved a negative rather than a positive formulation of the principle. Subsequently, in *Mettoy Pensions Trustees Ltd v Evans*,[66] Warner J effectively reformulated the principle in positive terms so that it was interpreted as meaning that the courts should intervene in certain circumstances rather than that they should not intervene unless certain requirements were met. In *Sieff v Fox*[67] Lloyd LJ, sitting as a judge of first instance, summarised the so-called rule in *Hastings-Bass* in the following terms:

---

60. 'Improperly' was interpreted in this context as meaning acting on the basis of an improper motive, taking into account irrelevant factors or not taking into account factors which should have been taken into account, see *Wilson v Law Debenture Trust Corporation plc* [1995] 2 All ER 337, 343 *per* Rattee J.
61. *Pitt v Holt* [2013] 2 AC 108.
62. *Scott v National Trust for Places of Historic Interest or Natural Beauty* [1998] 2 All ER 705, 717.
63. *Edge v Pensions Ombudsman* [2000] Ch 602, 627.
64. [2013] 2 AC 108.
65. [1975] Ch 25, 41.
66. [1990] 1 WLR 1587.
67. [2005] 1 WLR 3811. See further Nolan and Conaglen [2006] CLJ 15.

> Where trustees act under a discretion given to them by the terms of the trust, in circumstances in which they are free to decide whether or not to exercise that discretion, but the effect of the exercise is different from that which they intended, the court will interfere with their action if it is clear that they would not have acted as they did had they not failed to take into account considerations which they ought to have taken into account, or taken into account considerations which they ought not to have taken into account.[68]

So, as Lee has commented, the principle set out in the *Hastings-Bass* case 'somehow metamorphosed into a positive proposition'.[69] This interpretation of the principle in *Hastings-Bass* was invoked successfully by trustees themselves in a number of cases where the exercise of their powers led to the unforeseen consequence of giving rise to a significant tax liability. In *Green v Cobham*[70] Parker J accepted that had the trustees directed their minds as they should have done to the tax implications of their actions, they would not have made the impugned appointment and, holding that this was a clear case for the application of the principle in *Hastings-Bass*, he declared the deed in question to be void in its entirety. Similarly, in *Abacus Trust Co. (Isle of Man) Ltd v NSPCC*,[71] Patten J, having referred to the decision in *Green* concluded that: 'that decision is clear authority that trustees, when exercising powers of appointment, are bound to have regard to the fiscal consequences of their actions and that where it can be demonstrated that a proper consideration of these matters would have led to the appointment not going ahead the court is entitled to and should treat that as an invalid exercise of power in the sense of it being void *ab initio*.'[72] These decisions were the subject of considerable academic and judicial criticism.[73] As Park J suggested in *Breadner v Granville-Grossman*,[74] '[t]here must surely be some limits. It cannot be right that whenever trustees do something which they later regret and think that they ought not to have done, they can say that they never did it in the first place.' In his view, the courts could not extend the principle in *Hastings-Bass* by treating as valid something which the trustees had not done, but, it was argued, would have done if they had taken all proper considerations into account.

In *Abacus Trust Co. (Isle of Man) v Barr*[75] Lightman J expressed the view that it was not sufficient to bring the principle in *Hastings-Bass* into play that a

68. *Ibid.* at 3847.
69. [2014] Conv 175, 176. See also Davies [2011] Conv 406, 408.
70. [2002] STC 820.
71. [2001] WTLR 953.
72. *Ibid.* at 964-965. See also *Burrell v Burrell* [2005] STC 569.
73. See Dawson [2002] Conv 67; Walker [2002] PCB 226.
74. [2001] Ch 523, 543. Lord Neuberger has commented extra-judicially (2009) 15 Trusts and Trustees 189, 192 that 'it is hard to see why the principle does not amount to just that'.
75. [2003] Ch 409.

trustee had made a mistake or by reason of ignorance or mistake had not taken a relevant consideration into account or had taken an irrelevant consideration into account. He added that if a trustee has used all proper care and diligence in obtaining relevant information and advice, there could be no breach of duty and his decision could not be impugned merely because this information turned out to be incorrect. However, Lloyd LJ in *Sieff v Fox*[76] stated that it did not seem to him that the principle applied only in cases where there had been a breach of duty by the trustees, or by their advisers or agents. In this case trustees succeeded in having the exercise of a power of appointment set aside in circumstances where they had received erroneous professional advice about potential tax liability on the basis that they would not have exercised the power had they known of the liability this would give rise to. As Davies has pointed out, the way in which the rule in *Hastings-Bass* had developed was particularly significant from the perspective of beneficiaries in circumstances where an exemption clause in a trust deed might absolve trustees from liability.[77]

Subsequent academic comment about the manner in which the rule in *Hastings-Bass* was being employed was overwhelmingly critical[78] and two Law Lords made comments extra-judicially which suggested that they had serious doubts about the manner in which the principle was being applied and developed. Lord Walker commented that the law in this area was 'in considerable doubt and disarray' and said that the unrestrained extension of the principle in *Hastings-Bass* would lead to huge uncertainty.[79] Lord Neuberger also commented extra-judicially that 'the consequences of the principle are unclear, arbitrary and wide'[80] and he characterised it as a 'get-out-of-gaol-free card for trustees'.[81]

It is interesting that it was Lloyd LJ, who had delivered the first instance judgment in *Sieff v Fox*, who ultimately took the step of stating in the decision of the Court of Appeal in *Pitt v Holt*[82] that 'the principle known as the rule in *Hastings-Bass* … is not a correct statement of the law.'[83] The Supreme Court considered appeals in two cases, *Pitt v Holt* and *Futter v Futter*. In the first, the claimant, who had been appointed as receiver for her husband after he sustained serious injuries in an accident, placed money from a compensation award into a discretionary trust acting upon professional advice which she had obtained.

---

76. [2005] 1 WLR 3811.
77. [2011] Conv 406, 410.
78. As Davies commented [2011] Conv 406, 'the "rule" in *Hastings*-Bass allowed Equity to interfere with completed transactions solely on the ground that trustees had erred regarding the financial consequences of their transactions.' See also Wu (2007) 21 Trust Law Int 62, 73; Molloy (2009) 15 Trusts and Trustees 200, 218.
79. (2002) PCB 226, 238.
80. Neuberger (2009) 15 Trusts and Trustees 189, 190.
81. *Ibid.* at 192.
82. [2012] Ch 132 (CA); [2013] 2 AC 108 (SC).
83. Longmore LJ expressed agreement with this view and commented (at 203) that the law had taken 'a seriously wrong turn'.

On her husband's death, his estate was liable to inheritance tax which could have been avoided if a clause had been included in the trust providing that half the fund would be applied for his benefit during his lifetime, which had been the case in any event. In the second case, trustees had exercised powers of advancement under a discretionary trust with a view to avoiding liability to capital gains tax although the transaction did not achieve this purpose as they had acted on the basis of incorrect advice received from professional advisers. In both cases the claimants argued that they had not taken into account a relevant consideration, namely the financial consequences of the transactions. However, the Court of Appeal was satisfied that they had not acted in breach of duty as they had made their decisions on the basis of professional advice, albeit advice which turned out to be wrong, and so the transactions were not voidable.[84]

Lloyd LJ drew a distinction between a transaction which is void where trustees act outside the scope of their powers and one which is voidable where trustees exercise their discretionary powers in breach of duty.[85] He made it clear that a transaction would only be rendered voidable in this context where a trustee had acted in breach of duty.[86] Lloyd LJ stated as follows:

> The trustees' duty to take relevant matters into account is a fiduciary duty, so an act done as a result of a breach of that duty is voidable. Fiscal considerations will often be among the relevant matters which ought to be taken into account. However, if the trustees seek advice (in general or in specific terms) from apparently competent advisers as to the implications of the course they are considering taking, and follow the advice so obtained, then, in the absence of any other basis for a challenge, I would hold that the trustees are not in breach of their fiduciary duty for failure to have regard to relevant matters if the failure occurs because it turns out that the advice given to them was materially wrong.[87]

The conclusions reached by the Court of Appeal were welcomed in academic circles[88] and the Supreme Court upheld its decision on the so-called rule in *Hastings-Bass*,[89] which it has been suggested might now be better described

---

84. As Nolan and Cloherty (2011) 127 LQR 499, 502 commented, 'taking bad advice into account is no longer regarded as taking an irrelevant matter into account.'
85. This issue had been considered in a number of earlier decisions. In *AMP (UK) plc v Barker* [2001] WTLR 1237, 1266 Lawrence Collins J had characterised the impugned appointment as voidable. In *Sieff v Fox* [2005] 1 WLR 3811 Lloyd LJ suggested that to hold that a defect makes the appointment voidable, rather than void, is attractive but concluded that he did not have to decide between 'void' or 'voidable' in order to determine the case before him.
86. [2012] Ch 123, 205.
87. *Ibid.* at 179.
88. Davies [2011] Conv 406; Nolan and Cloherty (2011) 127 LQR 499.
89. See further Nolan (2013) 129 LQR 469; Watterson [2013] CLJ 501; Ng [2013] BTR 566; Lee [2014] Conv 175; Evans [2015] Conv 61.

as the rule in *Pitt v Holt*.[90] Lord Walker JSC indicated his general agreement with the judgment of Lloyd LJ on the *Hastings-Bass* issue and said that he agreed that Buckley LJ's statement of the supposed rule in *Hastings-Bass* was wider than the true principle laid down in the actual decision. Lord Walker JSC stated as follows:

> In my view Lightman J [in *Abacus Trust Co. (Isle of Man) v Barr* [2003] Ch 409] was right to hold that for the rule to apply the inadequate deliberation on the part of the trustees must be sufficiently serious as to amount to a breach of fiduciary duty. Breach of duty is essential (in the full sense of that word) because it is only a breach of duty on the part of the trustees that entitles the court to intervene (apart from the special case of powers of maintenance of minor beneficiaries, where the court was in the past more interventionist: see para 64 above). It is not enough to show that the trustees' deliberations have fallen short of the highest possible standards, or that the court would, on a surrender of discretion by the trustees, have acted in a different way. Apart from exceptional circumstances (such as an impasse reached by honest and reasonable trustees) only breach of fiduciary duty justifies judicial intervention.[91]

So, in the *Pitt* case, the claimant lost her appeal on the *Hastings-Bass* issue as she had followed professional advice in the creation of the settlement and had committed no breach of duty although her appeal was allowed on the basis of mistake.[92] In the *Futter* case, the trustees had not acted in breach of duty as they had taken and acted on professional advice in relation to the applicability of capital gains tax and the claimants' appeal was dismissed.

The *Hastings-Bass* rule as originally formulated made it clear that the failure to take into account relevant considerations or the taking into account of irrelevant matters must have been significant. As Buckley LJ stated in *Re Hastings-Bass*, it must be clear that the trustee 'would' not otherwise have acted as he did. However, in two subsequent decisions of the Court of Appeal the question was reformulated in terms of the less stringent requirement of whether the trustees 'might' have acted differently,[93] and this approach was followed in a number of cases at first instance.[94] When this issue arose in *Abacus Trust Co. (Isle of Man) v Barr*[95] Lightman J expressed the view that the rule does

90. Nolan and Cloherty (2011) 127 LQR 499, 501.
91. [2013] 2 AC 108, 139.
92. See further Chapter 17. Ng [2015] Conv 266, 267 has suggested that while prior to this decision mistaken trustees relied on the rule in *Hastings-Bass* rather than the doctrine of mistake, the outcome of *Pitt v Holt* has been to reverse this trend.
93. *Kerr v British Leyland (Staff) Trustees Ltd* [2001] WTLR 1071 (decided in 1986); *Stannard v Fisons Pension Trust Ltd* [1992] IRLR 27.
94. *AMP (UK) plc v Barker* [2001] WTLR 1237; *Hearn v Younger* [2002] WTLR 1317.
95. [2003] Ch 409.

not require that the relevant issue not considered by the trustee should make a fundamental difference between the facts as actually perceived by the trustee and as they should have been perceived and that '[a]ll that is required in this regard is that the unconsidered relevant consideration would or might have affected the trustee's decision'.[96] However, subsequently in *Sieff v Fox*,[97] Lloyd LJ, sitting at first instance, distinguished the Court of Appeal decisions in which the formula of 'might' as opposed to 'would' had been used as being cases relating to pension trusts where trustees were under an obligation to act. In these cases the beneficiaries' rights arose in the context of a contract of employment and it seemed to Lloyd LJ to be 'logical that a relatively low threshold of relevance ("might") should have been adopted by the courts as the test'.[98] On the other hand, in cases where the trustees have exercised a power voluntarily, in his view the more stringent test of 'would' was justified in order to determine whether the exercise of discretion could be set aside.[99] The issue was also considered in *Pitt v Holt*,[100] where Lord Walker referred to this distinction and said that in practice the court may sometimes decide to proceed in this way. However, he said that as a matter of principle there must be a high degree of flexibility in the range of the court's possible responses and he concluded that '[t]o lay down a rigid rule of either "would not" or "might not" would inhibit the court in seeking the best practical solution in the application of the *Hastings-Bass* rule in a variety of different factual situations.'[101]

There has been little judicial consideration of the rule in *Hastings-Bass* in this jurisdiction. When the issue arose before Kelly J in *Irish Pensions Trust Ltd v Central Remedial Clinic*[102] he preferred the formulation of 'would' rather than 'might' have acted differently. This approach was also followed by Finlay Geogeghan J in *Boliden Tara Mines Ltd v Cosgrove*,[103] although on the facts of the case she concluded that it had not been established that the trustees had

---

96. *Ibid.* at 417. See also *Scott v National Trust for Places of Historic Interest or Natural Beauty* [1998] 2 All ER 705, 718.
97. [2005] 1 WLR 3811. See further Nolan and Conaglen [2006] CLJ 15.
98. *Ibid.* at 3828. See also *Betafence Ltd v Veys* [2006] WTLR 941, 964.
99. This was characterised by Mitchell (2006) 122 LQR 35, 40 as a 'neat and principled way of reconciling the cases'. An issue arises about the appropriateness of applying the test of 'might' have acted differently in the context of decisions made by the trustees of a pension fund involving a freedom whether to exercise discretion, see *AMP (UK) plc v Barker* [2001] WTLR 1237 and *Hearn v Younger* [2002] WTLR 1317. In *Sieff v Fox* [2005] 1 WLR 3811, 3836, Lloyd LJ stated that he respectfully disagreed with the view that the 'might' test could be applied to any voluntary exercise of power. Subsequently, in *Betafence Ltd v Veys* [2006] WTLR 941, 964 Lightman J said that despite his reservations on the issue, he would follow the guidance laid down by Lloyd LJ in *Sieff* and leave it to the appellate court to review the law. See also Hayton [2005] Conv 229, 237-239.
100. [2013] 2 AC 108.
101. *Ibid.* at 145.
102. [2006] 2 IR 126.
103. [2007] IEHC 60.

failed to take relevant considerations into account or that if they had considered certain factors that they would not have acted as they had done. More detailed consideration was given to these issues by Charleton J in *Greene v Coady.*[104] He agreed that trustees must take all relevant matters into account, exclude irrelevant matters and direct themselves properly in law and in interpreting the provisions of a trust deed.[105] Once trustees are shown to have acted honestly and in good faith, having taken account of all relevant considerations and excluded all irrelevant considerations, in his view only decisions which can be characterised as being ones that no reasonable body of trustees could have made may be impugned. He also stated that there was no authority for the proposition that a pension trust should be treated any differently in this respect from family trusts or a charitable trust. It is clear from the judgment of Charleton J that once it is established that a factor is one which could be taken into account, unless the weight attached to it can be said to be outside the range of what any reasonable body of trustees would give to it, the decision of the trustees must stand. He also stated that 'once a consideration is relevant, it is a matter for the trustees as to how factors are to be weighed in the balance in the exercise of their discretion.'[106]

It is becoming increasingly apparent in England that the decision of the Supreme Court in *Pitt v Holt* has not had the effect which might have been anticipated in terms of limiting the scope of remedying the unintended tax consequences of decisions made by trustees. First instance judgments such as in *Power Adhesives v Sweeney*[107] suggest that a flexible approach is being taken towards the application of the principles set out in *Pitt v Holt* and the former decision was described by Davies and Douglas as 'a very generous approach, reminiscent of the "get-out-of-gaol-free card" provided by the rule in *Hastings-Bass* prior to *Pitt v Holt.*'[108] There is also evidence of a more expansive approach being taken towards granting rescission for mistake in this context.[109] Lee has gone as far as to state that recent developments 'may suggest that the doctrine of equitable mistake has merely replaced the rule in *Hastings-Bass* and that dispositions with unintended consequences are set aside as easily as

104. [2015] 1 IR 385.
105. Charleton J referred to the fact that two of these propositions were derived from the decision of *Re Hastings-Bass* [1975] Ch 25 which had been affirmed in *Sieff v Fox* [2005] 1 WLR 3811. He made no reference to the reformulation of the rule in *Hastings-Bass* made by the Supreme Court of the United Kingdom in *Pitt v Holt* [2013] 2 AC 108 but this would have made no difference to the outcome in the case before him.
106. [2015] 1 IR 385, 399.
107. [2017] EWHC 676 (Ch).
108. (2018) 32 Trust Law Int 3, 9.
109. See e.g. *Freedman v Freedman* [2015] EWHC 1457 (Ch); *Van Der Merwe v Goldman* [2016] 4 WLR 71. Davies and Douglas (2018) 32 Trust Law Int 3, 15 suggest that '[t]he breadth of rescission for mistake has drawn some of the venom from the decision of the Supreme Court in *Pitt v Holt*.'

before.'[110] There has also been increasing evidence of the use of rectification as a remedy for tax planning errors and Davies and Douglas suggest that 'by curtailing the rule in *Hastings-Bass*, the decision of the Supreme Court [in *Pitt v Holt*] may well have pushed a series of tax mistake claims down the rectification route.'[111] These developments have met with academic criticism and it has been suggested that the jurisdiction to grant relief under the rule in *Hastings-Bass* should remain narrow and that attempts to expand it again should not be encouraged.[112]

Improper Motive

As Robert Walker LJ stated in *Scott v National Trust for Places of Historic Interest or Natural Beauty*,[113] 'trustees must act in good faith, responsibly and reasonably'. So, where it is established that a trustee has acted in bad faith or has been motivated by an improper motive, the court may intervene to set aside the exercise of his discretion.[114] This is clear from the decision of Neville J in *Klug v Klug*,[115] where one of the trustees declined to exercise her discretion under a power of advancement to enable a beneficiary to pay legacy duty because this beneficiary, her daughter, had married without her consent. In the circumstances, where he was satisfied that the trustee's letters showed that she had effectively not exercised her discretion at all, Neville J stated that it was the duty of the court to interfere and direct a sum to be paid out of the trust capital to meet the beneficiary's obligations. These principles were also applied by Smyth J in *Tomkin v Tomkin*,[116] where the plaintiff beneficiary sought relief in circumstances where he claimed that the defendant trustee, who was also a beneficiary, was failing to manage the trust property in the interests of all the beneficiaries and to maximise its potential. Smyth J upheld that plaintiff's claim, concluding that 'in circumstances where the defendant has failed to exercise that discretion and has, in effect, renounced, or purported to renounce such discretion … for an improper motive … the court is obliged to intervene and direct the defendant to sell the trust property.'

It should be noted that there is a degree of overlap between the rationale underlying the principles set out above and what is known as the doctrine of 'fraud on a power'. A power must be exercised in an honest manner and any

110. [2018] Conv 45, 61.
111. (2018) 32 Trust Law Int 3, 15.
112. Davies and Douglas (2018) 32 Trust Law Int 3, 21.
113. [1998] 2 All ER 705, 717.
114. As Scott VC stated in *Edge v Pensions Ombudsman* [1998] Ch 512, 535, 'trustees are under a duty to exercise their discretionary power honestly and for the purpose for which the power was given and not so as to accomplish any ulterior purposes.'
115. [1918] 2 Ch 67.
116. High Court 1998 No. 6924P (Smyth J) 8 July 2003.

exercise for an improper purpose will be considered to constitute a fraud on those entitled in default.[117]

Reasonableness

The question of the circumstances in which a court will intervene on the grounds that a trustee has exercised his discretion unreasonably is a complex one and will depend to an extent on the nature of the trust. While some nineteenth century decisions suggested that the court might set aside a decision where trustees had not exercised a 'proper'[118] or 'sound'[119] discretion, more recent decisions show a greater reluctance to intervene provided this discretion is exercised in good faith.[120] This view is borne out by the approach adopted by Charleton J in *Greene v Coady*[121] where, as already noted, he stated that once trustees are shown to have acted honestly and in good faith and to have taken into account all relevant considerations and excluded all irrelevant considerations, 'only decisions which are properly to be characterised as being ones that no reasonable body of trustees could have made may in law be condemned.'[122] Scott VC spoke in similar terms in *Edge v Pensions Ombudsman*,[123] where he stated as follows:

> The judge may disagree with the manner in which trustees have exercised their discretion but, unless they can be seen to have taken into account irrelevant, improper or irrational factors, or unless their decision can be said to be one that no reasonable body of trustees properly directing themselves could have reached, the judge cannot interfere.

The decision of Scott VC not to interfere with the discretion exercised by the trustees was upheld by the Court of Appeal[124] and Chadwick LJ commented that it was no coincidence that courts considering the exercise of discretionary powers, albeit in different contexts, should reach similar and consistent conclusions. Having quoted extensively from the judgment of Lord Greene MR in *Associated Provincial Picture Houses Ltd v Wednesbury Corporation*,[125] he stated that it was unnecessary to consider to what degree an analogy should be drawn between the principles applicable in public law cases and in the context of discretion exercised by trustees of a private pension scheme, although in

117. *Cloutte v Story* [1911] 1 Ch 18; *Vatcher v Paull* [1915] AC 372.
118. *Re Hodges* (1878) 7 Ch D 754, 761.
119. *Re Roper's Trusts* (1879) 11 Ch D 272, 273.
120. See the comments of Lord Normand in *Dundee General Hospitals Board of Management v Walker* [1952] 1 All ER 896, 901.
121. [2015] 1 IR 385.
122. *Ibid.* at 398. See also *Harris v Lord Shuttleworth* [1994] ICR 991, 999.
123. [1998] Ch 512, 534.
124. [2000] Ch 602.
125. [1948] 1 KB 223.

both cases discretion is vested in the decision maker because of his knowledge and experience. There has been little evidence of a willingness to draw such an analogy in other cases.[126] More recently in *Pitt v Holt*,[127] the Court of Appeal specifically advised against referring to public law principles in the context of trust law. As Mummery LJ stated:

> [A]nalogies with judicial review in public law are unhelpful and unnecessary … [t]here are surface similarities in the language of discretion and in the debates about the limits of discretionary power, but the contexts are so different that it is dangerous to develop the private law of fiduciaries by analogy with public law on curbing abuse of power.[128]

Subsequently, Lord Walker JSC delivering the judgment of the Supreme Court of the United Kingdom said that while there are superficial similarities between what the law requires of trustees in their decision-making and what it requires of decision-makers in the field of public law, this 'analogy cannot however be pressed too far.'[129]

Duty to Safeguard the Trust Assets

It is generally accepted that in relation to the management and administration of a trust, unpaid trustees are expected to use such due diligence and care as an ordinary prudent man would use in the management of his own affairs.[130] This obligation will be examined in more detail in the specific context of a trustee's duty of investment but in this section it is proposed to consider it in more general terms and also to consider the importance of preserving the trust assets, and the circumstances in which a trustee may be indemnified in relation to litigation.

The trustee's duty to safeguard trust assets has been interpreted as imposing fairly strict standards and would seem to require him to obtain payment of monies owing to the trust as soon as they become due. In *Re Brogden*[131] liability was imposed upon trustees of a marriage settlement who, although they had taken reasonable steps to obtain payment of a sum due, had stopped short of instituting proceedings because of the effect which they feared this would have on a family partnership. As Lopes LJ stated, when a trust is owed money, the trustee is bound to demand payment and if this demand is not met within a reasonable time, he must 'take active measures to enforce its payment,

126. Although see generally Evans (2012) 26 Trust Law Int 55.
127. [2012] Ch 123.
128. *Ibid.* at 204. See also the *dicta* of Lloyd LJ at 164.
129. [2013] 2 AC 108, 123.
130. *Speight v Gaunt* (1883) 9 App Cas 1, 19; *Re Lucking's Will Trusts* [1967] 3 All ER 726, 733.
131. (1888) 38 Ch D 546.

and if necessary, … institute legal proceedings'.[132] He continued by saying that he knew of nothing which would excuse not taking action 'unless it be a well-founded belief that such action on his part would result in failure and be fruitless, the burden of proving such well-founded belief lying on the trustee setting it up in his own exoneration'.

A trustee is bound to do the best he can from a financial point of view for the beneficiaries and this principle can in certain circumstances, particularly in relation to the sale of trust assets, require him to act in a manner which an ordinary prudent business man would not deem appropriate.[133] So, in *Buttle v Saunders*,[134] Wynn-Parry J stated that trustees 'have an overriding duty to obtain the best price which they can for their beneficiaries'. However, he went on to say that it would be an unfortunate simplification of the problem to state that the mere production of an increased offer at no matter how late a stage in the negotiations would impose an obligation upon a trustee to accept this offer, and stated that 'trustees have such a discretion in the matter as will allow them to act with proper prudence'. Wynn-Parry J therefore accepted that there might be cases where a trustee could properly refuse a higher offer and proceed with the lower one, although he was satisfied that this was not such a case and the tenor of his judgment undoubtedly suggests that it will be difficult for a trustee not to accept the best offer from a financial point of view irrespective of ethical or other considerations.

As a general principle, a trustee is entitled to the costs of litigation properly entered into when acting on behalf of the trust out of trust funds, or to reimbursement of such costs. This principle is enshrined in section 31 of the Trustee Act 2000 in England and in *Spencer v Fielder*[135] Sir Terence Etherton C reiterated that the starting point is that 'trustees are entitled to be reimbursed out of trust assets all expenses properly incurred by them when acting on behalf of the trust.' While there is no equivalent legislative provision in this jurisdiction, some useful guidelines in relation to the operation of this general principle may be deduced from the case law in England.

If a trustee believes that it is necessary to institute or defend litigation in order to safeguard the trust assets, he would be well advised to seek the approval of the court before determining what course of action to take. On the one hand, as noted above, Lopes LJ stated in *Re Brogden*[136] that where a debt is owed to the trust and has not been paid within a reasonable time, the only thing which

132. *Ibid.* at 574. The decision in *Ward v Ward* (1843) 2 HL Cas 777 would suggest that an exception to this principle exists where the taking of legal proceedings would impose financial hardship on a beneficiary.
133. As Templeman J stated in *Re Wyvern Developments Ltd* [1974] 1 WLR 1097, 1106 in relation to the obligations of a fiduciary, in this case an official receiver '[h]e must do his best by his creditors and contributories. He is in a fiduciary capacity and cannot make moral gestures, nor can the court authorise him to do so.'
134. [1950] 2 All ER 193. See Bodkin (1950) 14 Conv 228; Samuels [1975] Conv 177.
135. [2015] 1 WLR 2876, 2792.
136. (1888) 38 Ch D 546.

would excuse a trustee from not taking legal action would be a 'well-founded belief that such action on his part would result in failure and be fruitless'. On the other hand, there is also authority to the effect that a trustee can only be indemnified in relation to expenses properly incurred for the benefit of the trust and as Bowen LJ made clear in *Re Beddoe*,[137] in this context the word 'properly' means 'reasonably as well as honestly incurred'.[138] Bowen LJ went on to state as follows:

> While I agree that trustees ought not to be visited with personal loss on account of mere errors in judgment which fall short of negligence or unreasonableness, it is on the other hand essential to recollect that mere *bona fides* is not the test, and that it is no answer in the mouth of a trustee who has embarked in idle litigation to say that he honestly believed what his solicitor told him, if his solicitor has been wrong-headed and perverse.[139]

Similarly, Lindley LJ stated that if a trustee brings or defends an action unsuccessfully and without the leave of the court, it is for him to show that the costs so incurred were 'properly' incurred and that while the fact that the trustee acted on counsel's opinion is a factor which ought to be in his favour, it will not provide him with indemnity.[140]

The importance of acting on the basis of court authorisation if a trustee is to ensure that he will receive an indemnity was reiterated in a number of first instance decisions. In *Alsop Wilkinson v Neary*[141] Lightman J stated that a trustee's right to be indemnified extends in the case of a dispute with third parties to the costs of proceedings properly brought or defended for the benefit of the trust estate. However, he went on to say that '[v]iews may vary whether proceedings are properly brought or defended, and to avoid the risk of a challenge to their entitlement to the indemnity … trustees are well advised to seek court authorisation before they sue or defend'. In the view of Lightman J, provided trustees make full disclosure as to the strengths and weaknesses of their case, if they act as authorised by the court, their entitlement to an indemnity

137. [1892] 1 Ch 547. See also *Re England's Settlement Trusts* [1918] 1 Ch 24 where Eve J stated that the trustee's failure to obtain any sanction from the court was 'grievously aggravated by his deplorable conduct' in prosecuting an action in the names of himself and his co-trustee without any authority from the latter. In the circumstances the court held that the trustee was not entitled to his costs out of the trust estate.
138. So, where a court concludes that a trustee has acted unreasonably and that his expenses in relation to litigation were not 'properly incurred', he will not be entitled to be reimbursed in respect of them from the trust fund, see *Royal National Lifeboat Institution v Headley* [2016] EWHC 1948 (Ch) at [40].
139. *Ibid.* at 562.
140. *Ibid.* at 558. See also *Stott v Milne* (1884) 25 Ch D 710; *Re England's Settlement Trusts* [1918] 1 Ch 24.
141. [1996] 1 WLR 1220.

will be secure. Similarly in *Singh v Bhasin*,[142] Alan Boyle QC, sitting as a Deputy High Court judge, stressed that where a trustee omits to apply for court authorisation, sometimes referred to as a *Beddoe* order, he defends an action at his own risk as to costs and may find at the conclusion of the proceedings that the court will hold that his conduct in so doing was unreasonable. He said that the court is entitled to examine the entirety of the trustee's conduct in defending the proceedings for the purpose of assessing whether it was reasonable to take this course and that matters which may be taken into account include the nature and merits of the proceedings brought and the legal advice on the basis of which the trustee took the steps which he did. Judge Boyle accepted the submission of counsel that a trustee cannot look to a trust fund for the costs incurred by him in consequence of a failure to act with the prudence and good sense of an ordinary prudent man and concluded that the trustee had acted unreasonably in defending the proceedings.

In *Pettigrew v Edwards*[143] Master Matthews accepted that an application for a *Beddoe* order may serve a useful purpose where there is a third party dispute, such as a claim by or against a third party in relation to trust assets, as the trustees cannot be sure at the outset whether the proceedings will turn out to be for the benefit of the fund. However, in a case where it is claimed that trustees have acted in breach of trust, the court will probably be in no position at that stage to judge the reasonableness or propriety of the trustees' defence of their position and a *Beddoe* order will not serve any useful purpose. In addition, he stated that where the dispute is in substance between individuals claiming a beneficial interest in the trust, the trustees' duty is to remain neutral and while they will as trustees be entitled to nominal costs, there is no need for a *Beddoe* order. In the matter before the court Master Matthews declined to make such an order as the litigation was being carried out by two trustees against a life tenant in their capacity as capital beneficiaries. He concluded that as they were adults and *sui juris* they must decide whether to take the risk of litigation and making a *Beddoe* order would risk injustice to the life tenant by insulating the trustees from the consequences of the litigation.

As the judgment of Kitchin J in *Bonham v Blake Lapthorn Linell*[144] illustrates, where the court subsequently concludes that it has been proper and reasonable for trustees to commence and pursue litigation, a failure to first obtain a *Beddoe* order may not amount of a breach of trust. Kitchin J stated that he was satisfied that the claim had had a reasonable prospect of success and concluded that the costs of the litigation had been properly and reasonably incurred and that a failure to apply for a *Beddoe* order did not constitute a breach of trust.

In *Spencer v Fielder*[145] Sir Terence Etherton C clarified that there are clearly types of case in which trustees will not usually be entitled to be indemnified in

142. Chancery Division, 24 July 1998.
143. [2017] EWHC 8 (Ch).
144. [2007] WTLR 189.
145. [2015] 1 WLR 2786.

respect of their costs, for example if they are successfully sued for compensation for past breaches of trust or where they take an unsuccessful partisan position in hostile litigation between rival claimants to a beneficial interest in the subject matter of the trust. In contrast, they are likely to be entitled to an indemnity where the substance of the litigation is to clarify a matter of uncertainty in relation to the administration of a trust or where the conduct of the trustees in the litigation is otherwise in the best interests of the beneficiaries as a body rather than for the personal benefit of the trustees themselves. In his view, 'what matters is whether, in substance, trustees who are parties to litigation are acting in the best interests of the trust rather than for their own benefit.'[146] Sir Terence Etherton C added that in limited circumstances trustees may be entitled to an indemnity for costs even though they will incidentally secure a personal benefit from a successful claim or defence or where there are allegations of breach of trust.[147]

A further consideration which must be borne in mind where the trust fund is small and likely to be easily dissipated is that litigation is probably better avoided 'unless there is such a chance of success as to render it desirable in the interests of the estate that the necessary risk should be incurred'.[148] So, in *Bradstock Trustee Services Ltd v Nabarro Nathanson*[149] it was held that trustees had not failed in their duty to protect the trust estate when they discontinued litigation in circumstances where the trust fund was likely to have been exhausted in indemnifying them.

Duty to Invest

Trustees are under a duty to invest the trust property with a view to ensuring a steady income for the beneficiaries currently entitled to an interest while at the same time preserving the value of the capital for the benefit of those who may subsequently become entitled to an interest in the property.[150] They are under no obligation to consult the beneficiaries about their investment decisions, unless required to do so under the terms of the trust, and 'should not be bound in any way to act on the wishes of the beneficiaries'.[151]

---

146. *Ibid.* at 2793.
147. Referring to *Macedonian Orthodox Community Church St Petka Inc v Diocesan Bishop of the Macedonian Orthodox Diocese of Australian and New Zealand* (2008) 237 CLR 66.
148. *Per* Bowen LJ in *Re Beddoe* [1892] 1 Ch 547, 562.
149. [1995] 1 WLR 1405.
150. See *Stacey v Branch* [1995] 2 ILRM 136, 142 *per* Murphy J.
151. *Per* Arden J in *X. v A.* [2000] 1 All ER 490, 496. While Arden J clearly accepted that a trustee is under no obligation to consult, she noted that at the conclusion of his judgment in *Re Pauling's Settlement (No. 2)* [1963] Ch 576, 586, Wilberforce J had expressed the hope that the trustees would give consideration to suggestions made by the beneficiaries with regard to investments and would not object to any suggestion that was in reasonable terms.

Some important principles must be noted at the outset. A trustee is only permitted to invest in authorised securities and even where he adheres to this requirement, he must display impartiality and act with ordinary prudence in deciding which investments to make. So, the fact that a form of investment is authorised by the trust instrument or by statute will not absolve a trustee from liability if he does not exercise the requisite degree of care in deciding which investments to make.

The question of whether an investment is authorised is governed in the first instance by the terms of the trust instrument, which will usually include an investment clause detailing the trustees' powers in this regard. Where a clause in the trust instrument expressly delimits the ambit of a trustee's power of investment, its provisions must be adhered to and investment in unauthorised securities will amount to a breach of trust.[152] However, in certain circumstances, the court may sanction the overriding of express directions as to powers of investment where these are found to be in conflict with a settlor or testator's implied intentions. So, in *Re Lynch's Trusts*,[153] it was held by Johnston J that the court had jurisdiction to disregard a direction in a trust as to the lodgment of monies on deposit receipt and to direct these funds to be invested instead in suitable trustee securities. This finding was made as the predominant motive of the testator, as expressed in his will, was to make provision for the support and maintenance of his family and he concluded that the direction that the funds should remain on deposit receipt was subsidiary to this overall objective.

In the absence of an express investment clause, or subject to its terms, a trustee may invest the trust property in accordance with the statutory scheme laid down in Part I of the Trustee Act 1893 as amended by the Trustee (Authorised Investments) Act 1958. Section 3 of the Act of 1893 provides that this statutory power of investment is to be exercised according to the discretion of the trustees. Section 1 of the Act of 1958 as amended specifies what are authorised investments and section 2 of the 1958 Act empowers the Minister for Finance to vary this list. Until recently, the ambit of investments authorised by statute remained limited and was generally confined to investments such as Irish and British government securities, real securities, stock in semi-state bodies, debentures or debenture stock, in publicly quoted industrial and commercial companies registered in Ireland which met certain requirements, and in deposit accounts in specified financial institutions. However, the scope of authorised investments has been extended by statutory instrument and the Trustee (Authorised Investments) Order 1998[154] varies the list of investments set out in section 1 of the Act of 1958 by deleting those specified in the section and substituting those set out in the First Schedule to the order. These investments now include units or shares in certain unit trust or collective investment

152. *Rochfort v Seaton* [1896] 1 IR 18; *Re Webber's Settlement Trusts* [1922] 1 IR 49.
153. [1931] IR 517.
154. SI No. 28 of 1998.

schemes, specified annuity and life assurance contracts and the equity of companies listed on the Irish Stock Exchange and other recognised exchanges which meet certain financial requirements. One interesting innovation is clause 4 of the Second Schedule to the order which provides that where any part of the trust fund is invested in equities, the trustee shall review those investments at intervals of not more than six months.[155] Further amendments have been effected by the Trustee (Authorised Investments) Order 1998 (Amendment) Order 2002,[156] which provides that in making an investment of trust funds, a trustee shall take due account of the nature of the liabilities of the trust, an appropriate diversification[157] and liquidity of investments.

The Law Reform Commission in its Report *Trust Law: General Proposals* recommended the introduction of a revised list of authorised investments and suggested that consideration should be given to determining suitable parameters for the selection process for authorised investments, for example, the provision of dividend income, bearing in mind the interests of both current and future beneficiaries.[158] It also recommended that the existing market capitalisation threshold should be reviewed and that investment in land should be permitted as an authorised investment in a revised list of authorised investments.

It is now quite common to authorise trustees to invest in such a manner as they think fit and in *Re Harari's Settlement Trusts*[159] a clause in a trust which gave trustees power to invest 'in or upon such investments as to them may seem fit' was held by Jenkins J to mean that the trustees should be empowered to invest in any investments which they honestly thought were desirable. Jenkins J said that to hold otherwise would be to read words into the settlement which were not there and he saw no reason to impose any restriction on the plain and ordinary meaning of the words employed.

A power to invest in 'real securities' has been interpreted to cover investment in mortgages of land,[160] but not in its purchase.[161] It should be noted that such a power does not authorise trustees to lend trust funds on the security of a judgment mortgage.[162] In addition, in relation to the investment in mortgages

---

155. See SI No. 327 of 1990, SI No. 75 of 1992 and SI No. 28 of 1998. The Law Reform Commission in its Report *Trust Law: General Proposals* LRC 92-2008, para 8.46 recommended that the existing duty to review the investments of trust funds at intervals of not more than 6 months should be replaced with a duty to review investments at intervals of not more than 12 months. The Commission further recommended that it should be clarified that the duty to review applies also where the trust funds have been left in their original form.
156. SI No. 595 of 2002.
157. See generally Panico (2009) 15 Trusts and Trustees 96.
158. LRC 92-2008, paras. 8.30, 8.38. See s. 20 of the draft Trustee Bill 2008.
159. [1949] 1 All ER 430.
160. This extends to mortgages of certain leasehold land, see s. 5(1) of the Trustee Act 1893.
161. *Robinson v Robinson* (1877) IR 10 Eq 189.
162. *Johnston v Lloyd* (1844) 7 Ir Eq R 252.

of land, Smith MR stressed in *Smithwick v Smithwick*[163] that 'it may be that a trustee lending on a second mortgage should exercise greater caution than if there was no prior encumbrance.' A degree of statutory protection is afforded to trustees who lend funds on the security of any property by section 8 of the Trustee Act 1893 which provides that no liability shall arise 'by reason only of the proportion borne by the amount of the loan to the value of the property at the time when the loan was made' provided that certain conditions laid down in the section are met.

It is important to stress that even where a trustee does not stray outside the ambit of investments authorised either by the terms of the trust or by statute, he must nevertheless observe certain standards in carrying out his duties in this regard. As O'Connor MR pointed out in *Re O'Connor*,[164] 'however unlimited the power of investment may be, the trustee remains subject to the jurisdiction of the court. The trustee has no power to act dishonestly, negligently or in breach of trust to invest on insufficient security'. O'Connor MR continued by saying that subject to the power of the court to compel a dishonest or grossly incompetent trustee to account, it is in the power of the settlor or testator to place funds in the hands of the trustee to be invested in the fullest sense of the word and it was held in the instant case that a clause which permitted the trustees to invest in property 'as they think most desirable, but not in British funds' authorised them to invest in freehold land in Ireland and England.

The standard of care and prudence which must be employed by a trustee in exercising his powers of investment has been considered by the courts on numerous occasions, although it has not always been expressed in a consistent manner. In *Learoyd v Whiteley*[165] Lindley LJ stated in the Court of Appeal that a trustee would have to take not only such care as a prudent man would take if he had only himself to consider but the care that an ordinary prudent man would take if he were making investments for the benefit of those for whom he felt morally bound to provide.[166] When the matter reached the House of Lords, Lord Watson spoke along the same lines and stated that 'business men of ordinary prudence may, and frequently do, select investments which are more or less of a speculative character; but it is the duty of a trustee to confine himself to the

163. (1861) 12 Ir Ch R 181, 196.
164. [1913] 1 IR 69, 75-76.
165. (1886) 33 Ch D 347, 355.
166. In interpreting this obligation, Thomas J commented in a decision of the New Zealand High Court in *Jones v AMP Perpetual Trustee Co. NZ Ltd* [1994] 1 NZLR 690, 706 that: 'This duty includes the duty to seek advice on matters which the trustee may not understand, such as the making of investments, and in receiving that advice to act with the same degree of prudence. It is not enough to act in good faith and with sincerity. Consequently, although a trustee may take advice on investments, he or she is not bound to accept and act on that advice. They must, in addition to being honest and sincere in relation to the advice which is received, continue to act as an ordinary prudent person would act.'

class of investments which are permitted by the trust, and likewise to avoid all investments of that class which are attended with hazard'.[167]

These statements would suggest that the degree of care which a trustee might exercise in relation to the investment of his own money may be insufficient; a greater duty of care is required. However, despite the fact that these principles were apparently quoted with approval by Brightman J in *Bartlett v Barclays Bank Trust Co. Ltd*,[168] a more flexible approach seems to have been applied in that case, at any rate as regards non-professional trustees. The defendant bank was trustee of a trust, the only assets of which were nearly all the shares in a family property company. It was thought that funds might be more readily raised to pay taxes due on the death of the life tenants if the company went public and that a public issue would be more successful if the company was also involved in property development. One speculative purchase resulted in large losses to the trust fund, and the plaintiff beneficiaries succeeded in their claim against the bank for breach of trust. Brightman J stated as follows:

> The cases establish that it is the duty of a trustee to conduct the business of the trust with the same care as an ordinary prudent man of business would extend towards his own affairs .... That does not mean that the trustee is bound to avoid all risk and in effect act as an insurer of the trust fund .... The distinction is between a prudent degree of risk on the one hand, and hazard on the other. Nor must the court be astute to fix liability upon a trustee who has committed no more than an error of judgment, from which no business man, however prudent can expect to be immune.[169]

A further important principle which was confirmed by Brightman J was that in his opinion a higher duty of care is expected of a professional trustee, such as a trust corporation which carries on the specialised business of trust management. This point had been made *obiter* by Harman J in *Re Waterman's Will Trusts*,[170] where he stated that a paid trustee is expected to exercise a higher standard of diligence and knowledge than an unpaid trustee. Brightman J concluded that a professional corporate trustee is liable for breach of trust if loss is caused to the trust fund because it neglects to exercise the special care and skill which it professes to have. He held that the bank had wrongfully and in breach of trust neglected to ensure that it received an adequate flow of information concerning the activities of the boards of the companies concerned and that it had failed in its duty whether it was judged by the standard of the prudent man of business or of the skilled trust corporation.[171]

The application of the standard of 'an ordinary prudent man of business'

167. (1887) 12 App Cas 727, 733.
168. [1980] Ch 515.
169. *Ibid.* at 531.
170. [1952] 2 All ER 1054, 1055.
171. [1980] Ch 515, 535.

had more disturbing consequences from the point of view of the beneficiary in *Nestle v National Westminster Bank plc*.[172] By virtue of the terms of a settlement made in 1922 the defendant bank, the successor to the original trustee, was given wide powers to invest in equities. However, the bank never obtained legal advice about the scope of its powers of investment and assumed that these were narrower than they in fact were. The plaintiff, the remainder beneficiary, contended that the trust fund which was worth approximately £269,000 when she became absolutely entitled in 1986 should have been worth well over £1 million by then if the fund had been properly invested. Hoffmann J rejected the plaintiff's claim and concluded that the bank had acted conscientiously, fairly and carefully throughout its administration of the trust. The Court of Appeal dismissed the plaintiff's appeal and concluded that the plaintiff had not succeeded in establishing that she had suffered loss. Legatt LJ stated that it had not been established that a prudent trustee, knowing the true scope of the power of investment and having conducted regular reviews, which the bank had not done, would have invested the fund in such a manner that it would have been worth more than it was when the plaintiff became entitled to it.[173] The Court of Appeal applied the traditional test; as Legatt LJ stated, 'the essence of the bank's duty was to take such steps as a prudent businessman would have taken to maintain and increase the value of the trust fund. Unless it failed to do so, it was not in breach of trust.'[174]

Although the Court of Appeal did not find the bank liable, the judges did not agree with the trial judge's conclusion that the bank had acted conscientiously and as Legatt LJ commented, '[n]o testator, in the light of this example, would choose this bank for the effective management of his investment.'[175] Kenny has rightly suggested that it is a sad reflection on the present state of trust law that a bank which 'no testator … would choose … for the effective management of his investment' should be found not to be liable for mismanagement of the trust.[176] The law in this area in England at any rate would seem to unduly favour the position of the trustee.[177] As Doyle has commented, there is no reported case in which a trustee has been found liable for a breach of trust arising from investment within the ambit of that authorised by the trust instrument or the

172. [1993] 1 WLR 1260.
173. Similarly Staughton LJ stated that it must be shown that the bank's failure to appreciate the scope of its powers or to conduct periodic reviews led it to make decisions which it should not have made or to fail to make decisions which it should have made, and that loss thereby resulted.
174. [1993] 1 WLR 1260, 1283.
175. *Ibid.* at 1284. See Martin (1992) 142 NLJ 1279.
176. Kenny [1993] Conv 63, 67.
177. Watt and Stauch have commented [1998] Conv 352, 361 that the reasoning of the Court of Appeal in *Nestle* showed an 'erroneous conflation of the quite distinct processes of determining breach of trust and determining the loss caused by that breach'. In their view, the effect of this has been 'to leave the English courts unduly reluctant to review the exercise of investment discretions, no matter how imprudently discharged'.

general law where the trust capital has simply continued to erode as a result and he concludes that 'the burden of proof facing potentially litigious beneficiaries is prohibitively high.'[178] Certainly in the case of professional trustees, the reasoning which surfaced in *Bartlett* of applying a stricter standard might be developed further to avoid a result such as that arrived at in *Nestle*.

The extent of the duty imposed on a trustee in relation to investment of trust property was considered in this jurisdiction by Murphy J in *Stacey v Branch*.[179] The plaintiff beneficiary brought a claim against the defendant trustee alleging a breach of trust on the grounds that the latter had not managed a trust property with the necessary degree of care and claimed specifically that if this house had been let over a period of 14 years rather than maintained by a caretaker, it would have yielded a substantial rental income. The trust deed conferred on the defendant the power to deal with this property 'as he in his absolute discretion shall think fit' pending the attainment of 21 years by the plaintiff. Murphy J made it clear that words such as 'absolute discretion' would not necessarily relieve a trustee from his duty to exercise reasonable care and prudence. However, he was satisfied that the defendant's decision to place the caretaker in occupation of the premises was one made *bona fide* in the exercise of his discretion and he dismissed the plaintiff's claim. Murphy J also gave some consideration to the nature of a trustee's duty of investment in general terms and it is worth setting this *dicta* out in full.

> What is the nature of the duty imposed on a trustee? A trustee must, of course, invest trust funds in the securities authorised by the settlement or by statute. To invest in any other securities would be of itself a breach of trust; but, even with regard to those securities which are permissible, the trustee must take such care as a reasonably cautious man would take having regard not only to the interest of those who are entitled to the income but to the interest of those who will take in the future. In exercising his discretion a trustee must act honestly and must use as much diligence as a prudent man of business would exercise in dealing with his own private affairs; in selecting an investment he must take as much care as a prudent man would take in making an investment for the benefit of persons for whom he felt morally bound to provide. Businessmen of ordinary prudence may, and frequently do, select investments which are more or less of a speculative character; but it is the duty of a trustee to confine himself not only to the class of investments which are permitted by the settlement or by statute, but to avoid all such investments of that class as are attended with hazard.[180]

---

178. Doyle (1991) 5 Trust Law Int 138, 142.
179. [1995] 2 ILRM 136. See Buttimore (1996) 14 ILT (ns) 48.
180. *Ibid.* at 142.

This statement which requires a trustee in selecting investments to exercise the care which a prudent man would take in making an investment for the benefit of persons for whom he felt morally obliged to provide imposes a relatively stringent standard on trustees. However, it can also be said that the degree of care which a prudent man would exercise in these circumstances has altered over the years.[181] As Panckhurst J commented in the New Zealand decision of *Re Mulligan*,[182] 'prudence provides a flexible standard, one which will change with economic conditions and in the light of contemporary thinking and understanding'. Dillon LJ made a similar comment in the course of his judgment in *Nestle v National Westminster Bank plc*[183] to the effect that '[t]rustees should not be reckless with trust money but what a prudent man should do at any time depends on the economic and financial conditions at that time — not on what judges of the past, however eminent, held to be prudent in the conditions of 50 or 100 years before'.[184] Therefore, there is probably merit in Curran's suggestion that 'it could certainly be argued that some speculative investment e.g. hedging and support of an overall portfolio policy would be perfectly acceptable today'.[185]

Finally, it should be stressed that where the default on the part of the trustees, as in *Nestle* and *Stacey*, is due to lack of initiative rather than to speculative investment decisions, it would still seem to be extremely difficult for a beneficiary to succeed in establishing a breach of trust on the part of the trustee. Beneficiaries may legitimately have concerns that the law as it stands at present does not adequately protect them from the trustee who is guilty of inactivity or even neglect in relation to his investment duties. However, whether one views the law from the perspective of beneficiary or trustee, it is clear that any attempt to change existing principles will be problematic in view of the need to avoid encouraging trustees to engage in excessive speculation.

It is important to note that the provisions of the Trustee Act 2000 in England are now relevant to the standards which apply to trustees' investment powers in that jurisdiction. Schedule 1 paragraph (1) of the Act of 2000 applies the statutory duty of care to powers of investment which requires that a trustee 'must exercise such care and skill as is reasonable in the circumstances having regard in particular to any special knowledge or experience that he has or holds himself out as having, and if he acts as trustee in the course of a business or

181. There is certainly some evidence of a more pragmatic approach to the question of the degree of risk which a trustee may take in making investment decisions elsewhere in the common law world. As Thomas J stated in *Jones v AMP Perpetual Trustee Company NZ Ltd* [1994] 1 NZLR 690, 707, '[n]either prophecy or prescience is expected of trustees and their performance must be judged, not by hindsight, but by facts which existed at the time of the occurrence'. Similarly, in *Re Mulligan* [1998] 1 NZLR 481, 501 Panckhurst J stated that 'a trustee is neither a surety, nor an insurer of the fund for which he is responsible'.
182. [1998] 1 NZLR 481, 500.
183. [1993] 1 WLR 1260.
184. *Ibid.* at 1268.
185. Curran (1996) 90 GILSI 340.

profession, to any special knowledge or experience that it is reasonable to expect of a person acting in the course of that kind of business or profession.'[186] However, in the course of his judgment in *Richards v Wood*[187] Lewison LJ stated that he did not consider that these provisions materially altered the test that a trustee should be required to use the same degree of prudence and diligence as a person of ordinary prudence would have done if he had been conducting his own affairs.

Section 4 of the Act of 2000 sets out the concept of 'standard investment criteria' which a trustee must have regard to in exercising any power of investment. These criteria are the suitability to the trust of investments of the same kind as any particular investment proposed to be made or retained and the need for diversification of trust investments in so far as is appropriate to the circumstances of the trust. In addition, a trustee is required to review trust investments from time to time and consider whether, having regard to the standard investment criteria, they should be varied. This provision should go some way towards ensuring that trustees cannot simply invest trust property at the outset and then fail to show any interest in their investments and will require them to carry out periodic reviews of their decisions. Section 5 of the Act of 2000 also requires a trustee to obtain and consider 'proper advice'[188] in relation to the exercise of his power of investment unless he reasonably concludes that in all the circumstances it is unnecessary and inappropriate to do so.

Legislation along these lines might provide welcome clarification to the law in this jurisdiction and there is clearly growing unease about the message which decisions such as *Stacey v Branch* may be sending to trustees. The Law Reform Commission in its Report *Trust Law: General Proposals* recommended that a statutory duty of care similar to that set out in section 1(1) of the Trustee Act 2000 should apply to the exercise of trustee's powers on investment.[189] The Commission recommended that the statutory duty of care should allow for a distinction to be drawn between professional and non-professional trustees by demanding a higher standard of care from trustees who are qualified professionals,[190] and that the statutory duty of care should be of general application.[191]

The principles which should be applied in establishing loss and in calculating compensation where a trustee's investment decisions lead to a breach of trust were considered by Richard Spearman QC, sitting as a Deputy

186. Section 1(1) of the Trustee Act 2000.
187. [2014] EWCA Civ 327.
188. This is the advice of a person who is reasonably believed by the trustee to be qualified to give it by his ability in and practical expertise of financial and other matters relating to the proposed investment, see s. 5(4) of the Trustee Act 2000.
189. LRC 92-2008, paras. 3.15, 8.40. See s. 12(2) of the draft Trustee Bill 2008.
190. *Ibid.* at para. 3.23. See s. 12(2)(b) of the draft Trustee Bill 2008.
191. *Ibid.* at para. 3.26.

High Court Judge, in *Daniel v Tee*,[192] although on the facts he concluded that while the claimants had established some breaches of duty, they had failed to prove that they suffered loss as a result of those breaches. He stated as follows:

> [I]t will not be sufficient to establish liability unless any breach of duty resulted in investment choices which were imprudent, and then only to the extent of the difference between the position to which those choices gave rise and the position which would be likely to have resulted from prudent investment choices. For example, if the trustees decide on an inappropriate investment strategy, but either they do not implement that strategy or when it is implemented it results in investments being made which are no more disadvantageous to the beneficiaries than those which would have been made in accordance with an appropriate investment strategy, then that decision will not have occasioned any loss.[193]

He stated that in a case where the trustees have misunderstood or misapplied their investment powers in some radical way and this has plainly resulted in loss, for example, by investing in fixed interest securities and failing to invest in equities at all, it may be appropriate to measure fair compensation, namely what a prudent trustee would have been likely to achieve, by reference to the performance of an appropriate index of equities. However, he added that it seemed to him that where trustees are alleged to have been at fault in making particular investments or in failing to make particular investments then it is necessary to establish on the balance of probabilities what loss has resulted from each breach.

Another question which arises in relation to investment is the extent to which trustees are entitled to take into account non-financial considerations in making investment decisions. In *Cowan v Scargill*[194] it was made clear that trustees should not be influenced in their choice of investment by such considerations. A mineworker's pension fund was managed by ten trustees, five of whom were members of the National Union of Mineworkers. These five trustees refused to agree to a revised investment plan put forward on the basis, *inter alia*, that it contemplated increased overseas investment and investment in forms of energy such as oil and gas which were in competition with coal. It was held by Megarry VC that these trustees were in breach of duty in refusing to concur in the adoption of this investment plan. Megarry VC stated:

> Trustees may have strongly held social or political views. They may be firmly opposed to any investment in South Africa or other countries, or they may be opposed to any form of investment in companies concerned

192. [2016] 4 WLR 115.
193. *Ibid.* at [156].
194. [1985] Ch 270.

> with alcohol, tobacco and armaments or many other things. In the conduct of their own affairs, of course, they are free to abstain from making any such investments. Yet under a trust, if investments of this type would be more beneficial to the beneficiaries than other investments, the trustees must not refrain from making the investments by reason of the views that they hold.[195]

It should be noted that Megarry VC seemed to accept that trustees might pursue an ethical investment policy provided that the financial implications of doing so were equally advantageous from the point of view of the beneficiaries.[196] Lord Nicholls, writing extra-judicially, has also accepted this point in the following terms:

> The range of sound investments available to trustees is so extensive that very frequently there is scope for trustees to give effect to moral considerations, either by positively preferring certain investments or negatively avoiding others, without thereby prejudicing beneficiaries' financial interests.[197]

The approach adopted in *Cowan* can arguably be justified on the basis that if the criteria of the most sound decision from a financial point of view is qualified in any way, the court will lose the means of judging investment decisions on the basis of an objective standard and will instead move into the realm of a purely subjective one. However, Megarry VC also accepted that in an exceptional case where the only actual or potential beneficiaries of a trust are all adults, it might not be for the 'benefit' of such beneficiaries to know that they were obtaining larger financial returns under the trust by reason of investments in what they might view as morally or socially dubious activities than they would have otherwise received. He expressed the view that '[t]he beneficiaries might well consider that it was far better to receive less than to receive more money from what they consider to be evil and tainted sources.'[198] As he put it, '[b]enefit' is a word with a very wide meaning, and there are circumstances in which arrangements which work to the financial disadvantage of a beneficiary may yet be for his benefit.

The question of the extent to which trustees may pursue an ethical

---

195. *Ibid.* at 287-288.
196. Megarry VC also pointed out that he was not suggesting that the benefit of the beneficiaries meant solely their financial benefit and said that if they hold strong views on certain moral and ethical issues, it might not be for their benefit to know that they were obtaining financial returns from sources which they would not consider morally acceptable. However, Megarry VC stressed that in his view cases in which such considerations might arise would be 'very rare'.
197. Nicholls (1995) 9 Trust Law Int 71, 75.
198. [1985] Ch 270, 288.

investment policy is clearly even more relevant in relation to charitable trusts and this issue was considered by Nicholls VC in *Harries v Church Commissioners*.[199] The plaintiffs sought declarations that the commissioners were obliged to have regard to the object of promoting the Christian faith and not to act in a manner which would be incompatible with that object when managing the assets of which they were trustees. The plaintiffs contended that the commissioners in making investment decisions attached overriding importance to financial considerations and that they were only prepared to take non-financial considerations into account to the extent that they did not significantly jeopardise or interfere with accepted investment principles. It was held by Nicholls VC in refusing the declarations sought that it was axiomatic that charity trustees were concerned to further the purposes of the trust of which they had accepted the office of trustee. When property was held by trustees for the purpose of generating money, *prima facie* the purposes of the trust were best served by the trustees seeking to obtain the optimum return which was consistent with commercial prudence and in most cases the best interests of the charity required that the trustee's choice of investments be made solely on the basis of well-established investment criteria. The circumstances in which charity trustees were bound or entitled to make a financially disadvantageous investment decision for ethical considerations were extremely limited and there was no evidence that such circumstances existed in the case before the court. Nicholls VC stated as follows:

> The law is not so cynical as to require trustees to behave in a fashion which would bring them or their charity into disrepute. … On the other hand, trustees must act prudently. They must not use property held by them for investment purposes as a means for making moral statements at the expense of the charity of which they are trustees.[200]

However, he did accept that in rare cases, 'when the objects of the charity are such that investments of a particular type would conflict with the aims of the charity',[201] trustees should not invest in particular types of business.

The judgment of Nicholls VC in *Harries* has been criticised by Nobles, who argues that the investment policy of charitable trusts, like the manner in which they distribute funds, should be governed by the charitable purposes which they purport to further.[202] Thornton has also drawn attention to the

199. [1992] 1 WLR 1241. See Buttimore (1995) 13 ILT (ns) 141.
200. *Ibid.* at 1247.
201. *Ibid.* at 1246. He gave as examples 'cancer research companies and tobacco shares, trustees of temperance charities and brewery and distillery shares, and trustees of charities of the Society of Friends and shares in companies engaged in production of armaments'.
202. Nobles [1992] Conv 115.

mismatch between practical considerations[203] and the principles established in cases like *Cowan* and *Harries*.[204] However, she concludes that if a trust is to protect the interests of all beneficiaries then trust property should not be used to forward the views, however socially desirable these may be, of the trustees or the majority of the beneficiaries.

Duty to Maintain Equality Between Beneficiaries

A trustee is obliged to balance what may often be the competing interests of a life tenant and remainderman in relation to the trust property. As Panckhurst J stated in the decision of the New Zealand High Court in *Re Mulligan*,[205] '[i]t is elementary that a trustee must act with strict impartiality and endeavour to maintain a balance between the interests of life tenant and remaindermen. Put another way, a trustee must be even-handed as between income and capital beneficiaries.' Hoffmann J also acknowledged the importance of ensuring that a trustee acts in a fair manner in making investment decisions which may have different consequences for different classes of beneficiaries in the course of his judgment at first instance in *Nestle v National Westminster Bank plc*.[206] However, he stressed that trustees must have a wide discretion in this regard and stated that he preferred the formulation that a trustee must act fairly rather than one which required strict equality between tenant for life and remainderman. As he stated, '[i]t would be an inhuman law which required trustees to adhere to some mechanical rule for preserving the real value of capital when the tenant for life was the testator's widow who had fallen upon hard times and the remainderman was young and well off'.[207]

It should be noted that in seeking to ensure that a fair result is achieved, a trustee may be obliged to convert certain types of trust investment into an alternative form and this in turn may necessitate apportionment of the beneficiaries' interests.

Duty to Convert Trust Property

This duty arises specifically in two situations. First, where there is an express trust for sale an obligation is imposed on a trustee to sell the property as soon as practicable. It should be noted that a mere power to sell the trust property

203. She gives as an example the *Legal Framework for the Integration of Environmental Social and Governance Issues into Institutional Investment* (UNEPFI Asset Management Working Group 2005) which identifies various mechanisms for incorporating ethical factors.
204. Thornton [2008] CLJ 396.
205. [1998] 1 NZLR 481, 501.
206. Chancery Division, 29 June 1988.
207. *Ibid.* at 5.

is not sufficient to give rise to such an obligation to convert.[208] In addition, a duty to convert may arise under what is known as the rule in *Howe v Earl of Dartmouth*,[209] which effectively provides that where residuary personalty is settled by will in favour of persons who are to enjoy it in succession, subject to a contrary provision in the will, all assets of a wasting, future or reversionary nature or which consist of unauthorised securities should be converted into property of a permanent or income bearing character.[210]

The effect of the rule was summarised by Walker LC in *Re Harris*[211] as follows:

> The general rule is, that where there is a general residuary bequest of personal estate, including chattels real, to be enjoyed by persons in succession, the Court puts upon the bequest the interpretation that the persons indicated are to enjoy the same thing in succession, and converts the property as the only means of giving effect to that intention.

The rule only applies to a residuary bequest in a will, not to a specific bequest nor where there is an *inter vivos* settlement on the basis that the settlor was assumed to have had an accurate idea of the state of the assets when he created the trust.[212] In addition, the application of the rule will be excluded where the will provides otherwise or where it was clearly the testator's intention that the property should be enjoyed *in specie*. The latter finding was made by Meredith J in *Re Abbott*,[213] where he held that the testator had contemplated the trustees retaining the bulk of the property and must be presumed to have intended the tenants for life to enjoy it in the form in which it was left. In the circumstances, Meredith J was satisfied that the rule in *Howe v Earl of Dartmouth* was excluded by virtue of the language employed by the testator himself. This can be compared with the decision in *Re Harris*,[214] where the Irish Court of Appeal found insufficient evidence of intention on the part of the testatrix that the property should be enjoyed *in specie*. Walker LC stated that the rule must be applied unless 'upon the fair construction of the will, you find a sufficient indication of intention that it is not to be applied'[215] and he held that the burden should be on the person seeking to exclude its application.

The purpose of the rule is to maintain equality between present and future beneficiaries; to prevent the tenant for life from enjoying the benefit

208. *Re Pitcairn* [1896] 2 Ch 199.
209. (1802) 7 Ves 137.
210. See *Hinves v Hinves* (1844) 3 Hare 609, 611.
211. [1907] 1 IR 32, 35.
212. *Re Van Straubenzee* [1901] 2 Ch 779.
213. [1934] IR 189. See also *Alcock v Soper* (1833) 2 My & K 699; *Re Sewell's Estate* (1870) LR 11 Eq 80; *Re Fisher* [1943] Ch 377.
214. [1907] 1 IR 32. See also *Re Berry* [1962] Ch 97.
215. *Ibid.* at 35.

of unauthorised or wasting securities to the detriment of the remainderman and to prevent the latter benefiting from future or reversionary assets to the detriment of the tenant for life. The apportionment rules were considered by the Law Commission in England in a report published in 1982[216] and it was acknowledged that in practice the rules of apportionment are almost always excluded in well-drafted settlements. While its conclusions must be read in the light of more flexible statutory investment powers in both jurisdictions, it is worth quoting some of the comments contained in the report in relation to rules which existed then:

> It is quite clear that in present day investment conditions the rules both of conversion and apportionment pending conversion have little if any relevance. When they do apply they require, in effect, the sale of equities, other than those authorised by the Trustee Investment Act 1961, and re-investment in gilt-edged securities. At a time when investment in equities may be the only way in which the capital value of the fund can in fact be maintained the traditional theory that re-investment is necessary to protect those interested in the capital no longer holds good. Conversely, the yield on fixed interest investments is now such as to provide the tenant for life with an income which is as high as and may be higher than the average yield on unauthorised equities.[217]

Duty to Apportion

Where a duty to convert arises in either of the above situations, in the absence of any indication that the tenant for life is to enjoy the income until the conversion is effected, a duty also arises to apportion the original property between the tenant for life and the remainderman pending conversion. Where the assets are of a wasting, hazardous or otherwise unauthorised nature, this is presumed to benefit the tenant for life at the expense of the remainderman as this property may produce a high level of income to the detriment of its capital value. In making any apportionment, the trustee should ensure that the beneficiary currently in possession only receives income equivalent to the current yield on authorised investments and that any additional monies should be added to the trust capital.

In assessing when the capital should be valued for the purpose of calculating this yield, a distinction must be drawn between situations where there is a power to postpone conversion and cases where there is no such power. In the former case, the date of valuation is considered to be the date of the testator's death and in the latter case, if no sale is effected in the meantime, a date one year

---

216. *The Powers and Duties of Trustees* (23rd Report) Cmnd 8733.
217. *Ibid.* para. 3.31.

after his death is employed.[218] This principle is adopted on the basis that the testator's personal representatives are deemed to have an 'executor's year' in which to effect the administration of the estate. Whichever date is deemed to be the valuation date, the tenant for life is entitled to interest on the value of the assets at that date from the date of death until the date of the actual conversion.

The opposite problem to that referred to above in relation to wasting or hazardous securities arises in the context of future, reversionary or other non-income bearing assets. In the latter case, the life tenant will obtain no benefit from these types of security until the interest falls into possession and it may be necessary to sell such property and re-invest it in securities which will ensure a more equitable division as between the life tenant and the remainderman. The question of determining the manner of such apportionment is calculated in accordance with the rule in *Re Earl of Chesterfield's Trusts*.[219] The effect of this rule is well-summarised by Wylie:[220]

> The trustees should calculate what sums invested at 4% interest at the date of the testator's death, accumulating at compound interest at that rate with yearly rests, would, after deduction of income tax at the standard or basic rate, produce the actual sum raised by sale of the future or reversionary interest. The sum so calculated should be treated as the capital and the difference between it and the sum received from the sale of future or reversionary interest should be paid to the tenant for life as income.

Keane has suggested that there is no reason why the interest rate payable on judgment debts, currently fixed at 2%,[221] should not apply in this jurisdiction in relation to the application of this principle.[222] It should also be noted that this rule will not apply where the settlor or testator manifests a contrary intention.

Duty to Apportion in Other Circumstances

A duty to apportion may arise in other circumstances, some of which will now be considered.

Under the Rule in Allhusen v Whittell[223]

The purpose of this rule is to achieve equity between the tenant for life and remainderman in relation to the payment of debts and other duties due out of

218. This distinction is illustrated in *Brown v Gellatly* (1867) LR 2 Ch App 751.
219. (1883) 24 Ch D 643.
220. Wylie, *Irish Land Law* (4th ed., 2010) p. 697.
221. Reduced from 8% by the Courts Act 1981 (Interest on Judgment Debts) Order 2016 (SI No. 624 of 2016).
222. Keane, *Equity and the Law of Trusts in Ireland* (3rd ed., 2017) p. 144.
223. (1867) LR 4 Eq 295.

an estate. Often debts will not be paid for a considerable period after the death of a testator and in the meantime the tenant for life will continue to enjoy the income from the estate, including that portion which is owed to creditors. The effect of the rule is to charge the tenant for life with interest on the monies subsequently used to meet whatever debts may be payable out of the estate and so put him in the same position as if these debts had actually been paid at the time of the testator's death. The manner in which this apportionment is achieved is set out in *Parker and Mellows: Modern Law of Trusts* as follows:[224] 'the rule requires a calculation of the average income of the estate from the date of death to the date of payment, taken net after the deduction of income tax at the basic rate.' It is important to note that the application of this rule may be excluded where the contrary intention is expressed by the testator.[225]

Under the Rule in Re Atkinson[226]

This rule governs the manner in which an apportionment is made where an authorised mortgage security is sold and the proceeds received are insufficient to satisfy the amounts of the outstanding principal and interest in full. By virtue of the rule, these proceeds are apportioned between the tenant for life and the remainderman in the proportion which the amount due for arrears bears to the amount due in respect of the principal.[227] The circumstances in which the rule applies are still uncertain. It has been held that it applies to monies due under a holding of debenture stock,[228] but not to arrears of dividends on preference shares.[229]

Where Repairs or Improvements are Carried Out

Where repairs which are necessitated by ordinary wear and tear and which can be considered merely as maintenance are effected to trust property, the cost of such work should come out of the income of the trust and must be borne by the tenant for life.[230] However, where work can be regarded as effecting a permanent improvement to property, it is considered that the cost should be deducted from the trust capital,[231] and therefore this will have a greater effect on the interest of the remainderman. These principles were applied by Hedigan J in *Donnelly*

224. Oakley, *Parker and Mellows: Modern Law of Trusts* (9th ed., 2008) p. 760. See also *Corbett v Commissioners of Inland Revenue* [1938] 1 KB 567, 584-585 *per* Romer LJ.
225. *Re McEuen* [1913] 2 Ch 704.
226. [1904] 2 Ch 160.
227. See also *Stewart v Kingsale* [1902] 1 IR 496.
228. *Re Walker's Settlement Trusts* [1936] Ch 280.
229. *Re Sale* [1913] 2 Ch 697.
230. *Re Kingham* [1897] 1 IR 170; *Re Waldron and Bogue's Contract* [1904] 1 IR 240.
231. *Brereton v Day* [1895] 1 IR 518.

v Donnelly,[232] where there was no income from the trust to pay for repairs to a house in which the plaintiff tenant for life resided. In these circumstances he directed that if possible the house should be repaired and the cost of so doing should be a charge on the trust and ultimately recovered to the benefit of the trustees upon the demise of the plaintiff. In the event that this could not be done, he directed that the house should be sold and the proceeds invested so as to maintain the capital integrity of the trust while providing some income to benefit the plaintiff.

Purchase or Sale of Shares Cum Dividend

As a general rule, there will be no apportionment in relation to shares purchased or sold just before or after the payment of a dividend and the entire amount received is deemed to be capital. This may prove to be unjust, e.g. where shares are sold just before the dividend is declared, the price reflects the amount which will be paid, although if they had been retained until the payment was actually made the amount of the dividend would have been treated as income. This principle of non-apportionment may therefore be inequitable and it has been held that where it gives rise to a 'glaring injustice'[233] it may not be applied.

Distribution of Accumulated Profits in the Form of Bonus Shares

It was decided by the House of Lords in *Bouch v Sproule*[234] that such shares should be treated as capital except where a company has no power under its articles of association to create new shares in this manner, in which case they will be treated as income.

Distribution of Capital Profit

Where a company makes a capital profit and distributes it in the form of a cash bonus or capital dividend, it is regarded as a distribution of income to which the tenant for life is entitled.[235] So, in *Re Meagher*,[236] where a company decided to allot stock to its shareholders in the form of a 'special capital profits dividend', it was held by Kingsmill Moore J that it should be treated as income and paid to the tenant for life.

232. [2013] IEHC 532.
233. *Re MacLaren's Settlement Trusts* [1951] 2 All ER 414, 420.
234. (1887) 12 App Cas 385. See also *Re Carson* [1915] 1 IR 321; *Hill v Permanent Trustee Co. of New South Wales* [1930] AC 720, 730-732.
235. *Re Sechiari* [1950] 1 All ER 417; *Re Kleinwort's Settlements* [1951] Ch 860.
236. [1951] IR 100.

Duty to Distribute

A trustee is under an obligation to ascertain the identity of those who are entitled under the trust instrument and to take the necessary steps to ensure that the trust property is distributed in accordance with its terms. In England, section 27 of the Trustee Act 1925 as amended provides that trustees may advertise for potential beneficiaries and provided that certain requirements specified in the section are complied with, they may proceed to distribute the trust property amongst the beneficiaries whose identities are known to them. There is no equivalent statutory power in this jurisdiction, although section 49(2) of the Succession Act 1965 lays down a procedure whereby personal representatives of a deceased person may advertise for claimants and may distribute the estate amongst those who have lodged claims within the period specified. While trustees have no statutory power to assist them in carrying out this task, it would seem to be good practice for them to follow a similar course where doubts arise as to the identity of those entitled under the terms of a trust.

A beneficiary who is underpaid or who receives no payment at all has a right of action against the trustees for breach of trust, although the trustee in turn will have a right of recovery against any person who has been overpaid or paid in error. There is authority in England to support the proposition that where a trustee who is also a beneficiary underpays himself, he has no remedy[237] but this has been criticised and it is unlikely that such a harsh principle would be followed in this jurisdiction.

Where a reasonable doubt exists about the respective claims of the beneficiaries, a trustee may apply to the court for directions and will be protected from liability in this regard provided he follows these directions.[238] Such an application may be brought before the High Court by special summons grounded on affidavit and it is prudent for a trustee to take such a course of action where legitimate doubt exists about the manner in which the trust assets should be distributed.

In circumstances where the whereabouts or continued existence of a beneficiary are unknown, the court may authorise distribution of the trust property to proceed after a specified period of time. Such an order is known as a 'Benjamin order' and may be made after a period of seven years on the authority of the decision of Joyce J in *Re Benjamin*.[239] The testator's son disappeared in 1892 and under the will of his father, who died the following year, he was entitled to a share in the latter's estate if he survived the testator. Joyce J concluded that the son must be presumed dead and the court gave the trustees liberty to distribute his share on the basis that he had predeceased the testator.

The principles laid down in *Re Benjamin* were applied in *Re Green's Will*

237. *Re Horne* [1905] 1 Ch 76.
238. *Re Londonderry's Settlements* [1965] Ch 918.
239. [1902] 1 Ch 723.

Trusts.[240] The testatrix's son went missing in 1943 while on a wartime bombing raid and was certified by the Air Ministry as presumed dead. She bequeathed the residue of her estate to trustees for her son's benefit and directed that if he had not come forward to claim the property by the year 2020 the trustees were to establish a charitable foundation for the benefit of cruelly treated animals. The court gave the executors liberty to deal with the estate on the basis that the son had predeceased the testatrix and made a Benjamin order, the effect of which was to enable the charity to enjoy the testatrix's estate as from the date of her death. This decision has been criticised by Luxton[241] on the ground that such an order was contrary to the intention of the testatrix. However, from the point of view of the trustees, bringing an application to court is undoubtedly the most prudent course of action in such cases and while the order made may not always accurately reflect the wishes of a testator, it will at least have the advantage of absolving them from any personal liability.

It should be noted that the Law Reform Commission recommended that, for the purpose of the civil law aspects of the law of missing persons, a statutory framework should be put in place which would provide for the making of a presumption of death order in respect of categories of missing persons.[242] The Civil Law (Presumption of Death) Act 2019 will provide that a presumption of death order may be made by a court at any time after a person has gone missing where the circumstances indicate that his death is virtually certain or no earlier than one year after the person has gone missing where the circumstances indicate that his death is highly probable.[243] It will also provide that it shall continue to be presumed that a person is dead where, by reason of absence from the State or otherwise, it remains uncertain for a period of at least seven years as to whether a missing person is alive.[244] The combined effect of these subsections is to make clear that it will not be necessary to wait for seven years before applying for a presumption of death order, but also that after seven years' absence, where it is uncertain that a person is alive, it can still be presumed that he is dead. In the UK, the Presumption of Death Act 2013 came into force in 2014 and sets out a procedure for seeking a declaration that a person missing for seven years is presumed dead. However, this legislation is not as far reaching as that to be brought into force in this jurisdiction and may leave trustees concerned about the whereabouts or continued existence of beneficiaries in a state of uncertainty for the duration of this seven-year period.

An alternative to seeking a Benjamin order, which might prove a sensible option where the funds available are of a limited nature, is to take out a missing beneficiary insurance policy. This course was followed by the defendant trustee/

240. [1985] 3 All ER 455.
241. Luxton [1986] Conv 138.
242. *Civil Law Aspects of Missing Persons* LRC 106-2013.
243. Subsections 5(3) and (5)(a).
244. Subsection 5(5)(b).

beneficiary in *Re Evans*[245] in circumstances where the other beneficiary, her brother, had not been heard of for 30 years. Richard McCombe QC, sitting as a Deputy High Court judge, held that the premium payable on such a policy was a proper and allowable expense. He stated as follows:

> In my view, personal representatives, particularly of small estates, should not be discouraged from seeking practical solutions to difficult administration problems, without the expense of resort to the court. Further, in small intestate administrations, where frequently the representative will have a personal interest, sizeable sums should not have to be tied up indefinitely for fear of the re-emergence of a long lost beneficiary. The missing beneficiary policy does provide, at relatively small cost, a practical answer to such problems. Such a policy provides a fund to meet the claim of such a beneficiary in exoneration of the representative and of the overpaid beneficiary. The policy is to the advantage of all and is to some extent more effective than the limited protection provided by the more costly application to court for a Benjamin order.[246]

The policy taken out by the defendant only yielded up sufficient funds to cover the capital sum to which the plaintiff was entitled and the court also had to consider his claim to interest. In the circumstances, the court concluded that it would be wrong not to satisfy this claim to the extent to which it was capable of being realised out of property from the deceased's estate still at the defendant's disposal, although it was also held that the defendant should be relieved against the claim to the extent that it could not be satisfied out of the proceeds of sale of that property.

Duty to Keep Accounts and Provide Information

A trustee is obliged to keep clear and accurate accounts of the trust property and a beneficiary is entitled to inspect these accounts, although in theory if he wants a copy of them he must pay for them. This obligation to keep accounts arises independently of any question that a breach of duty may have occurred as was made clear by Chatterton VC in *Moore v McGlynn*,[247] where he pointed out that the obligation arises merely by virtue of the relationship of trustee and beneficiary. It is not strictly necessary for a trustee to have these accounts audited although it may be prudent where the complexity of the trust demands it and it would usually be wise for a trustee to obtain professional assistance in this area where he does not possess the relevant expertise himself.

It has also been established that a beneficiary is entitled to inspect documents

245. [1999] 2 All ER 777.
246. *Ibid.* at 785-786.
247. [1894] 1 IR 74, 86.

relating to the assets of the trust,[248] although it would seem that beneficiaries should only be permitted to have access to information relating to their interest in the trust property so, for example, a remainderman would only be entitled to information relevant to capital transactions. The obligation on trustees to provide information is well-established,[249] and the extent of the entitlement was set out as follows in *The Law Relating to Trusts and Trustees*[250] and quoted with approval by Kenny J in *Chaine-Nickson v Bank of Ireland*:[251]

> When a beneficiary has a vested interest in a trust fund so that he has a right to payment of the income, the trustees must at all reasonable times at his request give him full and accurate information as to the amount and state of the trust property and permit him or his solicitor, to inspect the accounts and vouchers and other documents relating to the trust.

There was some doubt about whether this entitlement extended to beneficiaries under a discretionary trust but this was resolved by Kenny J in *Chaine-Nickson*. The plaintiff was one of a number of potential beneficiaries under a settlement of property vested in the defendants as trustees on discretionary trusts. The plaintiff sought an order directing the defendants to give him particulars of matters relating to the administration of the trust. The defendants argued that in the case of a discretionary trust, none of the potential beneficiaries were entitled as of right to any information relating to the management of the trust. As Kenny J pointed out, the logical result of this argument was that the trustees were not under an obligation to account to anyone in relation to their actions, a proposition he could not accept. He therefore concluded as follows:

> Legal principle and the one relevant authority [*Moore v McGlynn*] establish that a potential beneficiary under a discretionary trust is entitled to copies of the trust accounts and to details of the investments representing the trust funds.[252]

The entitlements of potential beneficiaries under a discretionary trust were also considered by Neuberger J in his judgment in *Murphy v Murphy*,[253] in which he referred to the fact that the decision in *Chaine-Nickson* has been accepted in the leading English textbooks as stating the correct position on this issue. Neuberger J held that the plaintiff was entitled to know the names and addresses

248. *O'Rourke v Darbishire* [1920] AC 581, 626 *per* Lord Wrenbury.
249. *Low v Bouverie* [1891] 3 Ch 82, 99 *per* Lindley LJ.
250. Underhill, *The Law Relating to Trusts and Trustees* (11th ed., 1959) p. 401. Now see Hayton, Matthews and Mitchell, *Underhill and Hayton: Law of Trusts and Trustees* (19th ed., 2016).
251. [1976] IR 393, 396.
252. *Ibid.* at 399.
253. [1999] 1 WLR 282.

of the trustees of settlements under which he was identified as a specific potential beneficiary although he was not entitled to such information in relation to settlements under which he was, along with the rest of the world, merely a potential beneficiary. He agreed that in relation to the former type of settlement, a potential beneficiary does have the right to ask the trustees for 'information as to the nature and value of the trust property, the trust income, and as to how the trustees have been investing and distributing it'.[254] However, it is clear from the judgment of Neuberger J that the extent of this obligation will depend on the nature of the discretionary trust and the number of potential beneficiaries. He stated that while a trustee of a discretionary trust must appreciate that he will have duties 'it would be most undesirable for this court to make orders which would be likely to result in trustees of discretionary private trusts being badgered with claims by many beneficiaries for consideration to be given to their claims for trust moneys, or for accounts as to how trust moneys have been spent: the duties of a trustee are, it may fairly be said, quite onerous enough without such added problems'.[255] Mitchell has commented that these distinctions leave the law in a state of uncertainty since it cannot be confidently predicted that the courts will hold that a given class of beneficiaries is so large as to make it undesirable to allow its individual members to enforce their rights.[256] However, despite this element of uncertainty, the approach of Neuberger J is to be welcomed to the extent that it has clarified the potentially open-ended obligations which the decision of Kenny J in *Chaine-Nickson* might have been interpreted as imposing, irrespective of the size of the class of potential beneficiaries. While the obligations set out in *Chaine-Nickson* and *Murphy* may well be reasonable in relation to discretionary trusts of a relatively limited nature, these burdens could prove unduly onerous where the number of potential beneficiaries is large and it is helpful that the courts have recognised this fact.

Some useful comments about the considerations which may be of relevance to a court in deciding on the extent to which disclosure of information relevant to a trust should be ordered is contained in the judgment of Abbott J in *A.M.W. v S.W.*,[257] although the application before the court related to motions brought by opposing parties in judicial separation proceedings seeking disclosure of information relating to trusts which both parties alleged should have been taken into account in the proceedings. Abbott J commented that the law, as set out in decisions such as *Murphy v Murphy*, requires that 'considerations of justice and proportionality'[258] should inform the court in weighing up what obligations should be placed on trustees. This broad requirement of justice, in his view, amounted to taking a cost benefit analysis, both in monetary and human terms, towards the question of disclosure. On the facts before him, Abbott J

254. *Ibid.* at 290.
255. *Ibid.* at 293.
256. Mitchell (1999) 115 LQR 206, 208.
257. [2008] IEHC 452.
258. *Ibid.* at [7.3].

concluded that while the respondent had disclosed a wide range of documents, his disclosure had been inadequate in some respects and he expressed the view that it would be more cost effective to seek further documents from the respondents rather than from the trustee given that their obligation to provide information would be more circumscribed.

Further clarification on this general issue was provided by the Privy Council in *Schmidt v Rosewood Trust Ltd*,[259] in which the petitioner sought disclosure of documents relating to trusts under which he claimed discretionary interests both in his own capacity and as the administrator of his father's estate. His appeal against a decision setting aside an order for disclosure was allowed by the Privy Council and the matter was remitted for further consideration by the High Court. Lord Walker stated that in his view there were three areas in which the court might have to form a discretionary judgment: whether a discretionary object should be granted relief at all, what classes of documents should be disclosed, either completely or in a redacted form, and what safeguards should be imposed to limit the use which might be made of documents or information disclosed. He stated that a beneficiary's right to seek disclosure of trust documents, although sometimes not inappropriately described as a proprietary right, is best approached as one aspect of the court's inherent jurisdiction to supervise, and where appropriate intervene in, the administration of trusts.[260] There was therefore in his view no reason to draw any stark distinction either between discretionary and non-discretionary interests, or between the rights of an object of a discretionary trust and those of the object of a mere power. He added as follows:

> However, the recent cases also confirm that no beneficiary (and least of all a discretionary object) has any entitlement as of right to disclosure of anything which can plausibly be described as a trust document. Especially when there are issues as to personal or commercial confidentiality, the court may have to balance the competing interests of different beneficiaries, the trustees themselves, and third parties. Disclosure may have to be limited and safeguards may have to be put in place. Evaluation of the claims of a beneficiary (and especially of a discretionary object) may be an important part of the balancing exercise which the court has to perform on the materials placed before it. In many cases the court may

259. [2003] 2 AC 709.
260. See also *Lewis v Tamplin* [2018] EWHC 777 (Ch) at [40]. This principle was also quoted by Newey J in *Birdseye v Roythorne & Co.* [2015] EWHC 1003 (Ch) at [24] although he went on to say that 'it must remain the case that a person must, at least normally, establish as a minimum a prima facie case that he is a beneficiary before there can be any question of the Court requiring a trustee or executor to disclose documents which would be protected by privilege if the applicant were not a beneficiary.'

> have no difficulty in concluding that an applicant with no more than a theoretical possibility of benefit ought not to be granted any relief.[261]

The underlying rationale of the court's inherent jurisdiction to supervise the administration of trusts identified by the Privy Council in *Schmidt* was also applied by Carroll J in *O'Mahony v McNamara*[262] in granting the plaintiffs, who were members of a staff benefit retirement scheme, an order for disclosure of trust documents against the trustees of the scheme. Carroll J reiterated that the right to seek disclosure of documents is one aspect of the court's inherent jurisdiction to supervise, and if necessary to intervene in, the administration of a trust and stated that in determining such an application, the court may have to balance the competing interests of the beneficiaries, the trustees and third parties.

A useful summary of the factors which should be weighed up by a trustee in considering whether to make disclosure of trust documents or information relating to the trust was set out by Wild J, delivering the judgment of the New Zealand Court of Appeal in *Erceg v Erceg*,[263] although he stressed that the balancing of these factors and any other relevant considerations is a matter for the exercise of the trustees' discretion.

> (a) Whether there are issues of personal or commercial confidentiality;
> (b) The nature of the interests held by the beneficiary or beneficiaries seeking disclosure;
> (c) The competing interests of – and therefore the impact on – the beneficiary or beneficiaries seeking disclosure, the trustee(s) themselves, other beneficiaries and any affected third parties;
> (d) Whether some or all of the documents can be withheld in full, or disclosed only in a redacted form;
> (e) Whether safeguards should be imposed on the use of the disclosed trust documentation (for example, undertakings or professional inspection) to avoid illegitimate use;
> (f) Whether (in the case of a family trust) disclosure would be likely to embitter family feelings and the relationship between the trustee and applicant beneficiary to the detriment of the beneficiaries as a whole. …
> (g) The nature and context of the application for disclosure.

Wild J said that in making a decision about disclosure, the question for a trustee should be what will best ensure the sound administration of the trust,

261. [2003] 2 AC 709, 734-735.
262. [2005] 2 IR 519. See also *Bayworld Investments v McMahon* [2004] 2 IR 199, 220.
263. [2016] 2 NZLR 622, 629-630.

discharge the fiduciary duties which the trustee owes the beneficiaries and meet the trustee's obligation to fulfil the settlor's wishes.

It would appear on the authority of the decision of the English Court of Appeal in *Re Londonderry's Settlement*,[264] that trustees exercising a discretionary power are not bound to disclose to the beneficiaries the reasons which motivate them in reaching a decision as to the manner in which the trust property should be distributed. In this case the trustees of a discretionary family trust decided to distribute the capital of the trust. The defendant, a daughter of the settlor, was dissatisfied with the provision made for her and her children and sought access to the minutes of the trustees' meetings, documents prepared for the meetings and correspondence entered into between those involved in the administration of the trust. The trustees only supplied her with copies of the intended appointments of capital and copies of the trust accounts, and sought clarification from the court in relation to the extent of their duty of disclosure. The Court of Appeal held that the trustees were not under an obligation to disclose the reasons for their decisions on the basis that they could not otherwise properly exercise their confidential role. As Danckwerts LJ stated:

> It seems to me that where trustees are given discretionary trusts which involve a decision upon matters between beneficiaries, viewing the merits and other rights to benefit under such a trust, the trustees are given a confidential role and they cannot properly exercise that confidential role if at any moment there is likely to be an investigation for the purpose of seeing whether they have exercised their discretion in the best possible manner.[265]

However, Danckwerts LJ continued by saying that this position might be otherwise if a case were made of lack of *bona fides* and it has been suggested that a beneficiary determined to discover the grounds on which a trustee's discretion has been exercised might do so by instituting litigation alleging that this discretion has been exercised *mala fides* and then obtaining an order for discovery.[266]

The result in *Re Londonderry's Settlement* has been criticised on the grounds that it allows the trustees to be effectively unaccountable in the exercise of their decision-making functions in relation to the distribution of the assets of a discretionary trust.[267] There is considerable merit in the principle that trustees in these circumstances should disclose, at least in outline, the reasons which have motivated them in coming to their decisions, if only to avoid unnecessary

264. [1965] Ch 918.
265. *Ibid.* at 935-936.
266. Megarry (1965) 81 LQR 192, 196.
267. The Court of Appeal made clear that this decision related to the *dispositive* powers of trustees and not their administrative powers, a point confirmed in *Lewis v Tamplin* [2018] EWHC 777 (Ch) at [47].

allegations of bad faith. There has been no sign to date of courts in other jurisdictions questioning the authority of *Re Londonderry's Settlement*, at least in the context of family trusts, and in *Foreman v Kingstone*,[268] a decision of the High Court of New Zealand, Potter J reiterated that trustees are not obliged to disclose to beneficiaries their reasons for exercising discretionary powers. However, as Robert Walker J pointed out in *Scott v National Trust for Places of Historic Interest or Natural Beauty*,[269] where a decision taken by trustees is directly attacked in legal proceedings, the trustees may be compelled either legally or practically to disclose the substance of the reasons for their decision. In addition, as noted below, Hayton has suggested that the courts, taking their lead from *Schmidt v Rosewood Trust Ltd*,[270] should insist on pension trustees providing reasons for their decisions and be more prepared to intervene in the affairs of such trusts.[271] It could also be argued that following the decision in *Schmidt* the emphasis has shifted from confidentiality to accountability.[272] There are certainly strong arguments supporting greater accountability generally, particularly in the context of pension trusts, but it remains to be seen how the courts in this jurisdiction will deal with the matter.

While the decision of Briggs J in *Breakspear v Ackland*[273] suggests that the principle of confidentiality laid down in *Londonderry* is still good law, the increasing significance of accountability may lead to a greater degree of disclosure than might previously have been contemplated. The case is also significant as it provided the courts with the opportunity to clarify the status of so-called 'wish letters' written by settlors for the guidance of trustees of discretionary trusts. In the matter before the court the claimants sought disclosure of a wish letter in order to evaluate their future expectations under such a trust. Briggs J reiterated that '[a]t the heart of the *Londonderry* principle is the unanimous conclusion ... that it is in the interests of beneficiaries of family discretionary trusts, and advantageous to the due administration of such trusts, that the exercise by trustees of their dispositive discretionary powers be regarded, from start to finish, as an essentially confidential process.'[274] He also stated that the question of disclosure should be addressed primarily on the basis of an assessment of its objective consequences rather than by reference to the subjective purpose for which disclosure was sought. In his view it was axiomatic that a document brought into existence for the sole or predominant purpose of being used to further an inherently confidential process should itself properly be regarded as confidential, to substantially the same extent and effect as the process which it was intended to serve. However, he concluded that

---

268. [2004] 1 NZLR 841 (also reported in [2005] WTLR 823).
269. [1998] 2 All ER 705, 719.
270. [2003] 2 AC 709.
271. Hayton [2005] Conv 229, 245.
272. Griffiths [2008] Conv 322, 327.
273. [2009] Ch 32. See further Griffiths [2008] Conv 322; Fox [2008] CLJ 252.
274. *Ibid.* at 51.

the fact that the trustees intended to seek the court's sanction for a scheme of distribution of the trust fund was of real significance to the question of whether disclosure should be ordered and that the wish letter was a key document to be taken into account by the trustees and relevant to the court's approval of the scheme. Briggs J found that in the circumstances the trustees had necessarily surrendered any form of confidentiality protection against a full disclosure and examination of their reasoning by seeking the court's sanction and he ordered disclosure of the wish letter to the claimants.

The status of wish letters was also considered by the New Zealand Court of Appeal in *Erceg v Erceg*,[275] in which Wild J said that the court would include 'any document recording wishes or instructions conveyed by the settlor to the trustees – any so-called "wish list"' in the description of trust documents in considering the correct approach to disclosure of such documents. He referred to the point made by Kirby P in *Hartigan Nominees Pty Ltd v Rydge*[276] to the effect that such documents do not give an insight into the minds of the trustees and therefore to allow disclosure does not encroach on the principle that trustees are not required to provide reasons for their discretionary decisions.

Finally, although the issue of the extent of a trustee's duty to account and provide information in relation to a trust usually arises in circumstances where a beneficiary is already aware of the trust, the broader question of whether beneficiaries have the right to be informed about the existence of a trust should also be addressed. This issue was considered by the Supreme Court of Canada in *Valard Construction Ltd v Bird Construction Co*,[277] where Brown J stated that Equity imposes a duty on trustees to disclose the existence of a trust to its beneficiaries in a number of circumstances. He continued as follows:

> In general, wherever 'it could be said to be to the unreasonable disadvantage of the beneficiary not to be informed' of the trust's existence, the trustee's fiduciary duty includes an obligation to disclose the existence of the trust. Whether a particular disadvantage is *unreasonable* must be considered in light of the nature and terms of the trust and the social or business environment in which it operates, and in light of the beneficiary's entitlement thereunder. For example, where the enforcement of the trust requires that the beneficiary receive notice of the trust's existence, and the beneficiary would not otherwise have such knowledge, a duty to disclose will arise. On the other hand, 'where the interest of the beneficiary is remote in the sense that vesting is most unlikely, or the opportunity for the power or discretion to be exercised is equally unlikely', it would be rare to find that the beneficiary could be said to suffer unreasonable disadvantage if uninformed of the trust's existence.[278]

275. [2016] 2 NZLR 622, 627.
276. (1992) 29 NSWLR 405.
277. (2018) 417 DLR (4th) 1.
278. *Ibid.* at [19]. Footnotes omitted.

Brown J added that in considering what would be required in this regard in a particular case, the court should be careful not to ask in hindsight what could ideally have been done to inform potential beneficiaries of the trust. In his view 'the proper inquiry is into what steps, *in the particular circumstances* of the case–including the trust terms, the identity of the trustee and of the beneficiaries, the size of the class of potential beneficiaries and pertinent industrial practices–an honest and reasonably skilful and prudent trustee would have taken in order to notify potential beneficiaries of the existence of the trust.'[279] So, where a trustee can reasonably assume that the beneficiaries knew of a trust's existence or where the circumstances of the case would make notification 'entirely impractical', few if any steps may be required of a trustee.[280]

It should also be noted that the Law Reform Commission in its Report *Trust Law: General Proposals* recommended that beneficiaries should be given a statutory right to be provided with a trust deed of settlement, although no specific reference was made to any entitlement to be informed of the existence of the trust. The Commission also recommended that disclosure of documents other than the deed of settlement should be a matter for the discretion of the trustees or the courts.[281]

Duty Not to Profit from the Trust

It is a well-established rule that a person who occupies a fiduciary position is not entitled to make a profit from that position unless expressly authorised to do so, or to place himself in a situation where his interest and duty may conflict.[282] Charleton J explained this principle in the following terms in *Greene v Coady*,[283] namely that '[t]rustees are not entitled to put themselves into a situation of conflict of interest whereby they may be influenced by how they themselves may profit from any decision which the body of trustees may make.'

As we have seen above,[284] this principle is strictly applied to the relationship between a trustee and beneficiary and a trustee is not entitled to retain any financial benefit which he has gained as a result of his fiduciary position. This point was made in the following terms by Lord O'Hagan C in *Armstrong v Armstrong*:[285]

> I think it is plain that a trustee, so making a commodity of his position,

279. *Ibid.* at [26].
280. See further *Segelov v Ernst and Young Services Pty Ltd* [2015] NSWCA 156 at [138]–[142].
281. LRC 92-2008, para. 5.60. See s. 14 of the draft Trustee Bill 2008.
282. *Bray v Ford* [1896] AC 44, 51 *per* Lord Herschell. See also *Re Drexel Burnham Lambert UK Pension Plan* [1995] 1 WLR 32, 37; *Attorney-General v Blake* [2001] 1 AC 268, 280; *Re Stanley Deceased* [2016] IEHC 8 at [13].
283. [2015] 1 IR 385, 402.
284. See *supra* Chapter 8.
285. (1880) 7 LR Ir 207, 218.

and gaining a profit which but for it he would not have secured, must be held, on general principles and for the safety of *cestuis que trusts*, to retain that profit for the benefit of the trust estate.

In addition, the operation of this principle can be seen in relation to the issue of charging fees for work done on behalf of the trust and also arises where a trustee attempts to purchase trust property.

Remuneration and Expenses

As a general principle, a trustee is not entitled to remuneration for work carried out by him in his capacity as trustee.[286] This principle has been applied even where a trustee has expended considerable time and energy in performing the duties imposed upon him by the trust instrument.[287] However, it is not without exceptions and as Lord Normand commented in *Dale v IRC*,[288] it does not mean 'that reward for services is repugnant to the fiduciary duty, but that he who has the duty shall not take any secret remuneration or any financial benefit not authorised by the law, or by his contract, or by the trust deed under which he acts, as the case may be.' Clearly where the trust instrument itself makes provision for remuneration, this will be paid and if a settlor or testator wishes to appoint a professional trustee, it is essential that satisfactory provision be made in this regard.[289] Although such clauses are often strictly construed,[290] much will depend on the precise wording employed. It has been held in England that provided the instrument expressly authorises it, a trustee may employ a company which he controls to provide services for the trust and the company may be paid for such services.[291]

In addition, the court has an inherent jurisdiction to order that a trustee be remunerated for his services where no provision for payment has been made in the trust instrument or to allow a trustee to receive payment in excess of what was originally laid down or agreed. So, in *Re Duke of Norfolk's Settlement Trusts*,[292] the Court of Appeal agreed to increase the rate of remuneration authorised by the settlor. It would appear that such payment will only be ordered by the court in fairly exceptional cases where the trustee's efforts have resulted in considerable profit accruing to the trust, as in *Boardman v Phipps*,[293] where remuneration on a generous scale was permitted in recognition

286. *Re Ormsby* (1809) 1 Ba & B 189.
287. *Barrett v Hartley* (1886) LR 2 Eq 789.
288. [1954] AC 11, 27.
289. The Law Reform Commission in its Report *Trust Law: General Proposals* LRC 92-2008, para. 2.184 recommended against introducing a statutory default provision.
290. *Re Gee* [1948] Ch 284, 292 *per* Harman J.
291. *Re Orwell's Will Trusts* [1982] 1 WLR 1337.
292. [1982] Ch 61, 78 *per* Fox LJ.
293. [1967] 2 AC 46.

of the results achieved. Remuneration for trustees was also ordered pursuant to the court's inherent jurisdiction for past, although not for future services in *Foster v Spencer*[294] on the basis that the services rendered by the trustees were wholly outside their contemplation when appointed. In addition, Paul Baker QC, sitting as a Deputy High Court judge, stressed that the right of a trustee to remuneration for past services cannot depend upon the fact that, at the time he seeks it, his services are still required so that he is in a position to demand payment for the past as a condition of continuing in office.

A further exception to the general principle of no remuneration will also be made where a trustee makes an arrangement to this effect with all the beneficiaries, provided that they are *sui juris*. Where they are not all of full age and capacity, such as where some of the beneficiaries may be minors or as yet unborn, application must be made to the court to authorise any payment.

The position of a trustee who is also a solicitor gives rise to some difficulties. As a general rule such a person is not entitled to charge for his services and it has even been suggested that if he were, it might encourage the institution of unnecessary litigation.[295] However, where a solicitor/trustee acts for himself and his co-trustees in litigation relating to the trust and the costs of his so acting do not exceed the costs which would have been incurred had he acted for his co-trustees only, he is entitled to be paid these costs. This principle is known as the rule in *Cradock v Piper*[296] and has been applied in this jurisdiction in *Re Smith's Estate*.[297]

A trustee is entitled to be reimbursed for expenses properly incurred in the administration and management of the trust. This principle was set out as follows by Chatterton VC in *Courtney v Rumley*:[298]

> The principle upon which this Court acts in reference to the allowance of expenses to trustees is, that the trust property shall reimburse them all the charges and expenses incurred in the execution of the trust, and in this the Court will always deal liberally with a trustee acting *bona fide*. But when the costs or expenses claimed have been incurred through the misconduct or negligence of the trustee, he will not be allowed them.

This principle is given statutory confirmation by section 24 of the Trustee Act 1893 which provides that a trustee 'may reimburse himself, or pay or discharge out of the trust premises all expenses incurred in or about the execution of his trusts or powers.' As Chatterton VC made clear in *Courtney v Rumley*, the fact

294. [1996] 2 All ER 672.
295. *New v Jones* (1883) 1 Mac & G 685n.
296. (1850) 1 Mac & G 664.
297. [1894] 1 IR 60.
298. (1871) IR 6 Eq 99, 106.

that a trustee proves unsuccessful in litigation will not prevent him from being reimbursed provided that he is acting in good faith.[299]

Purchase of Trust Property

Subject to strictly limited exceptions, it is an established principle that a trustee may not purchase trust property from himself and his co-trustees because if this were permitted the trustee would effectively be both vendor and purchaser.[300] This rule, sometimes referred to as the 'self-dealing rule' was summarised as follows by Megarry VC in *Tito v Wadell (No. 2)*:[301] 'The self-dealing rule is (to put it very shortly) that if a trustee sells the trust property to himself, the sale is voidable by any beneficiary *ex debito justitiae*, however fair the transaction.' Thus any sale is voidable at the option of a beneficiary, who should take steps to have the transaction set aside within a reasonable time.[302] As Lord Kingsdown stated in *Smith v Kay*,[303] in a portion of his judgment quoted with approval by Napier CS in *King v Anderson*,[304] in the case of the trustee/beneficiary relationship, 'the Court presumes confidence put and influence exerted'. Therefore, there appears to be an almost irrebuttable presumption in such cases that undue influence has been exercised and it is unlikely to be sufficient to establish that the trustee was acting honestly and that the price paid was a fair one. Equally, it has been established that the right of the beneficiaries to have a transaction of this nature set aside does not depend on the fact that the trustee has made a profit.[305]

The inflexible manner in which the self-dealing rule is applied is well illustrated by the decision of the Privy Council in *Wright v Morgan*.[306] Property was left to two trustees on trust for sale to only one of them. This trustee assigned his right to the other who retired from his office and then purchased the property at a price fixed by independent valuers. The Privy Council held that this sale must be set aside as only a sale to the other trustee had been authorised by the terms of the will. A strict liability approach was adopted in applying the self-dealing rule by the Supreme Court of New Zealand in *Fenwick v Naera*.[307] Glazebrook J stated that '[t]he use of strict liability in the context of a fiduciary relationship stems from fiduciary law's traditional prophylactic approach: it is thought that prevention is better than cure in that this provides

299. *Graham v McCashin* [1901] 1 IR 404.
300. In the decision of the Supreme Court of New Zealand in *Fenwick v Naera* [2016] 1 NZLR 354, 378 Glazebrook J stated that 'we do not accept the submission that in equity the self-dealing rule applies only to purchases.'
301. [1977] Ch 106, 241.
302. *Webb v Rorke* (1806) 2 Sch & Lef 661, 672 *per* Lord Redesdale.
303. (1859) 7 HLC 750, 779.
304. (1874) IR 8 Eq 625, 628.
305. *Ex p. Lacey* (1802) 6 Ves 625.
306. [1926] AC 788.
307. [2016] 1 NZLR 354.

good protection to beneficiaries and removes temptation from fiduciaries.'[308] However, as he went on to say, referring to the view expressed by Lord Upjohn in *Boardman v Phipps*,[309] '[t]here must … be a "real sensible possibility" of a conflict and not just a remote, speculative, or negligible risk' and the standard to be applied in this regard is objective.

As a general principle this rule cannot be evaded by selling the trust property to a relative or associate of the trustee or to a company controlled by him; at the very least, in such circumstances the transaction will be closely scrutinised by the court to ensure that it is not merely a colourable device to preclude the application of the self-dealing rule. It would also appear that the principle applies where a trustee has recently retired,[310] although not where he has retired a considerable time before purchasing the trust property.[311]

The self-dealing rule was applied by analogy by Scott VC in *Kane v Radley-Kane*[312] to a situation where a personal representative had appropriated shares in satisfaction of a statutory legacy due to her as the deceased's widow, without the consent of the beneficiaries or the sanction of the court. He stated that such an appropriation was 'in clear contravention of the self-dealing rule' and was equivalent to a purchase by the personal representative of the appropriated assets. Scott VC concluded that the appropriation could not stand against an objection by one of the beneficiaries and that the proceeds of the sale of the shares formed part of the assets of the estate for which the widow as personal representative was accountable.

There are three main exceptions to the principle that a trustee may not purchase trust property from himself and his co-trustees. First, he may do so where the trust instrument expressly permits this,[313] although any such authorisation will be strictly construed. Secondly, the court may sanction a purchase in a suitable case or thirdly the beneficiaries may consent provided that they are *sui juris* and all agree to this course of action. It is also clear from the decision in *Newman v Clarke*[314] that the rule against self-dealing will not apply to the unilateral exercise of a right granted to a trustee before the trusteeship came into existence. In addition, there are borderline cases where the court may feel that it is inappropriate to apply the self-dealing rule, as in *Holder v Holder*.[315] There, one of the executors of a will, who had renounced his executorship soon after his appointment and had taken little part in the administration of the estate prior to doing so, purchased trust property at an auction for a price above the

308. *Ibid.* at 377. Referring to Butler, "Fiduciary Law" in *Equity and Trusts in New Zealand* (ed. Butler, 2nd ed, 2009) at [17.2.4].
309. [1967] 2 AC 46, 124.
310. *Wright v Morgan* [1926] AC 788.
311. *Re Boles & British Land Company's Contract* [1902] 1 Ch 244.
312. [1999] Ch 274.
313. *Sargeant v National Westminster Bank plc* (1990) 61 P & CR 518.
314. [2017] 4 WLR 26.
315. [1968] Ch 353.

reserve fixed by an independent valuer. The Court of Appeal declined to set aside the sale on the application of one of the beneficiaries. However, it would be fair to say that the circumstances of this case were exceptional and it would be incorrect to assume that this decision marks the beginning of any general trend towards a watering down of the self-dealing rule.[316]

However, a less strict approach has always been adopted by the courts where a trustee purchases property from a beneficiary rather than from the trust itself, sometimes referred to as the 'fair-dealing rule'.[317] While a presumption of undue influence will arise because of the nature of the relationship, this is rebuttable and the onus lies on the trustee to show that the transaction should be upheld.[318] Megarry VC laid down this principle in *Tito v Wadell (No. 2)* in the following terms:[319]

> [I]f a trustee purchases the beneficial interest of any of his beneficiaries, the transaction is not voidable *ex debito justitiae*, but can be set aside unless the trustee can show that he has taken no advantage of his position and has made full disclosure to the beneficiary, and that the transaction is fair and honest.

Similarly, in *Coles v Trecothick*,[320] Lord Eldon commented that a trustee may buy from a beneficiary provided that 'there is a distinct and clear contract, ascertained to be such after a jealous and scrupulous examination of all the circumstances' and provided that there is no evidence of fraud, concealment or of advantage being taken by the trustee of information acquired by him as a result of his position.

In such circumstances where a trustee is seeking to establish that he gave full value for the property, it will obviously be desirable that an independent valuation is obtained. In addition, in order to establish that a trustee did not take unfair advantage of the beneficiary, it may be advantageous to prove that independent legal advice has been given, although it has been established that a lack of such advice or an independent valuation will not necessarily prove fatal from the point of view of the trustee. In *Provincial Bank of Ireland v*

316. See, e.g. *Re Thompson's Settlement* [1986] Ch 99, 115 *per* Vinelott J.
317. Conaglen has suggested [2006] CLJ 366, 395 that the distinction drawn between the self-dealing rule and the fair-dealing rule by Megarry VC in *Tito v Wadell (No.2)* is not technically as accurate as had been supposed and that these rules 'are more appropriately understood as applications of the general fiduciary conflict principle'.
318. *Thomson v Eastwood* (1877) 2 App Cas 215, 236 *per* Lord Cairns. See generally Nolan, 'Conflicts of Interest, Unjust Enrichment and Wrongdoing' in *Restitution, Past Present and Future* (eds. Cornish *et al,* 1998). As Nolan states at p. 95, a fiduciary faced with an action under the fair-dealing rule as opposed to the self-dealing rule can successfully defend the action by showing that he acted with 'objective' fairness.
319. [1977] Ch 106, 241.
320. (1804) 9 Ves 234, 247.

McKeever[321] it was stated by Black J that where a trustee takes a voluntary benefit from a beneficiary there is a presumption that the benefit was obtained by undue influence. However, he also made it clear that this presumption may be rebutted, irrespective of whether the beneficiary has had independent advice, if it is shown that the transfer was the result of the free exercise of an independent will. This point was also made by Costello J in *Smyth v Smyth*.[322] The deceased gave a life interest in a field to his brother, who was one of the trustees of his will, and the remainder interest to his nephew. The nephew agreed to sell this interest to his uncle and subsequently sought to have the sale set aside on the grounds of undue influence and on the basis that as trustee the defendant should not have purchased the plaintiff's interest in this manner. Costello J confirmed that the onus of proving the *bona fides* of the transaction lay on the defendant and said that he was required to examine the surrounding circumstances 'with very great care' with a view to ascertaining whether any unfair advantage had been taken by the defendant. Costello J held that the price paid by the defendant was in fact a fair one and that the defendant had not sought to take advantage of his position as trustee or to influence the plaintiff's decision to sell. He further concluded that the defendant was not under any obligation to ensure that the plaintiff received independent legal advice, nor was he under a duty to procure an independent valuation as, in his view, both the defendant and his solicitor were correct in their assessment that the price agreed was a fair one.

Conaglen has considered the fiduciary self-dealing and fair-dealing rules in some detail.[323] He acknowledges that the primary difference between the rules appears to be the relevance of substantive fairness to the validity of a transaction which is caught by the fair-dealing rule, compared with transactions which fall within the self-dealing rule where such considerations appear to be irrelevant. However, he suggests that the supposed distinction between the two rules is not as clear as Megarry VC suggested in *Tito v Wadell* and that they are most appropriately both understood as applications of the fiduciary conflict principle.[324]

Duty Not to Delegate[325]

The general principle in relation to delegation by a trustee of his powers and functions was summarised by Lord Langdale MR in *Turner v Corney*[326] as follows:

> [T]rustees who take on themselves the management of property for the

321. [1941] IR 471.
322. High Court 1975 No. 4369P (Costello J) 22 November 1978.
323. [2006] CLJ 366.
324. *Ibid.* at 367. See also at 390.
325. See generally Jones (1959) 22 MLR 381, 381-385.
326. (1841) 5 Beav 515, 517.

> benefit of others have no right to shift their duty on other persons; and if they employ an agent, they remain subject to the responsibility towards their *cestuis que trust*, for whom they have undertaken the duty.

The rationale behind the principle of non-delegation of a trustee's duties is that the office is viewed as one where confidence is placed in the abilities of the particular individual appointed and it is therefore expected that he should personally look after the interests of the beneficiaries. So, in *Re O'Flanagan and Ryan's Contract*,[327] where a testator appointed his wife as trustee of property to hold for herself and their children, it was held by Porter MR that she had no power to delegate this role.

It has been suggested that while trustees will often be required to take advice from appropriate experts, '[i]t is for advisers to advise and for trustees to decide'.[328] However, this proposition should be read with a degree of caution and the principle of *delegatus non potest delegare* cannot be applied inflexibly to the position of trustees. Indeed, it has long been recognised that a trustee may delegate in situations of 'legal necessity' or 'moral necessity'.[329] Provision may be made for delegation in the trust instrument, and provided that the delegation does not exceed what is authorised, it will be permissible. In addition, it has been recognised that the proper administration of a trust would not be practicable if a trustee was not free to delegate the performance of certain functions to professional agents, such as solicitors and brokers. So, a trustee may employ a qualified professional person as his agent where the exercise of his office demands that these services be obtained and, as Wylie has commented, it may even in certain circumstances amount to a breach of trust not to delegate.[330]

The general principle is that where an ordinary prudent man of business would employ an agent to act on his behalf, a trustee will be entitled to delegate his functions and will not be liable for the default of an agent employed in these circumstances.[331] In *Speight v Gaunt*[332] the defendant trustee had employed a broker at the request of the beneficiaries to purchase stock. When the broker absconded with the monies provided for the purchase, the beneficiaries sought to make the defendant liable for breach of trust. It was held by the Court of Appeal and confirmed by the House of Lords that the defendant had acted

327. [1905] 1 IR 280. See also *Carr v Connor* (1929) 63 ILTR 185, 189 where Fitzgibbon J commented that a trustee is 'bound to exercise his own judgement'.
328. *Scott v National Trust for Places of Historic Interest or Natural Beauty* [1998] 2 All ER 705, 717 *per* Robert Walker J.
329. *Ex p. Belchier* (1754) Amb 218.
330. Wylie, *Irish Land Law* (4th ed., 2010) p. 673.
331. *Speight v Gaunt* (1883) 22 Ch D 727, 762 *per* Lindley LJ; *Fry v Tapson* (1884) 28 Ch D 268, 280.
332. (1883) 22 Ch D 727.

prudently as a reasonable man of business would have acted in employing a broker to act in such a situation and that he was not liable.

A number of further points should be noted about the circumstances in which a trustee may delegate to an agent. First, a trustee must exercise his own discretion in appointing an agent; he cannot delegate the making of this choice.[333] So, in *Fry v Tapson*[334] trustees did not exercise their own judgment in relation to the appointment of a valuer to advise them in a transaction where money was lent on a mortgage, but instead relied on the recommendation of their solicitor. This individual was in fact an agent of the mortgagor and when loss subsequently occurred, it was held that the trustees were liable as they had not made the decision in relation to who should be appointed themselves. It is also important to note that an agent should not be entrusted with responsibilities not normally undertaken by that class of agent[335] so, for example, a solicitor should not be employed to carry out work which should properly be within the remit of a broker's functions.[336]

In addition, even where an agent is properly appointed in the circumstances, a trustee must still exercise a reasonable degree of supervision over the agent's activities.[337] Some indemnity is afforded by section 24 of the Trustee Act 1893 which provides that a trustee shall be liable only for his own acts and defaults and not for those of any other trustee or banker or broker unless any loss occurs as a result of 'wilful default' on his part. The meaning of the latter term was considered by Lindley LJ in *Re Chapman*,[338] where he commented that 'trustees acting honestly, with ordinary prudence and within the limits of their trust, are not liable for mere errors of judgment'. Subsequently, in *Re Vickery*,[339] in construing the phrase 'wilful default' in section 30 of the Trustee Act 1925, which replaced section 24 of the Act of 1893 in England, Maugham J said that the words implied, as suggested by Romer J in *Re City Equitable Fire Insurance Co.*,[340] 'either a consciousness of negligence or breach of duty, or a recklessness in the performance of a duty'.[341] However, this subjective

333. *Re Weall* (1889) 42 Ch D 674. Kekewich J pointed out that 'a trustee is bound to exercise discretion in the choice of his agents' but went on to state that provided he selects properly qualified persons he cannot be made responsible for their intelligence or honesty.
334. (1884) 28 Ch D 268. See also *Speight v Gaunt* (1883) 22 Ch D 727, 756 *per* Lindley LJ.
335. Trustees must ensure that they select persons who are 'properly qualified' to carry out the function at issue: *Re Weall* (1889) 42 Ch D 674, 678 *per* Kekewich J.
336. *Rowland v Witherden* (1851) 3 McN & G 568.
337. In terms of the degree of supervision required in such circumstances, trustees are expected to exercise the 'ordinary prudence which a man uses in his own affairs'; *Mendes v Guedalla* (1862) 2 J & H 259, 277 *per* Page Wood VC.
338. [1896] 2 Ch 763, 776.
339. [1931] 1 Ch 572.
340. [1925] 1 Ch 407.
341. [1931] 1 Ch 572, 584.

approach has been criticised,[342] and the standard of the ordinary prudent man of business is probably preferable in this context.

A further relevant statutory exemption is provided by section 17 of the Trustee Act 1893 which sets out that a solicitor may be entrusted with the receipt of purchase money deriving from the sale of trust property and either a solicitor or banker may receive insurance monies. The validity of the power of delegation is dependent in the former case on the solicitor having custody of a deed containing a receipt for the money and in the latter case on the solicitor or banker having the insurance policy with a receipt signed by the trustees. The effect of the section is that in these defined circumstances a trustee will not be liable merely because he has delegated his functions, although subsection (3) goes on to provide that liability may be imposed where the trustees allow the monies received to remain in the hands of or under the control of the solicitor or broker for a period longer than is reasonably necessary.

The law in England in relation to the delegation of trustees' functions has been extended and clarified by the provisions of the Trustee Act 2000.[343] Trustees may now, subject to any restriction or exclusion imposed by the trust instrument or by other legislation,[344] authorise an agent to exercise any of their 'delegable functions'.[345] These constitute functions other than those listed in section 11(2), such as functions relating to the manner in which trust assets should be distributed or the power to appoint a person to be a trustee, and trustees may now delegate decision-making in relation to investments. A trustee is required to keep the arrangements under which an agent acts under review[346] but is not liable for any act or default of an agent unless he has failed to comply with the statutory duty of care laid down in the legislation in entering into the arrangement or in keeping it under review.[347] This requires that he must exercise such care and skill as is reasonable in the circumstances having regard, in particular, to any special knowledge or experience that he has or holds himself out as having and, if he acts as trustee in the course of a business or profession, to any special knowledge or experience that it is reasonable to expect of a person acting in the course of that kind of business or profession.[348]

It is fair to say that the present position in relation to delegation by trustees in this jurisdiction is far from satisfactory and clearly it needs to be addressed as

342. See Stannard [1979] Conv 345; Dal Pont [2001] Conv 376.
343. Formerly s. 23(1) of the Trustee Act 1925 provided that a trustee might employ an agent to do any act required to be done in the execution of the trust and that he should not be responsible for the default of such an agent if employed in good faith. In addition, s. 30(1) of the Act of 1925 provided that a trustee should not be liable for the acts or defaults of a co-trustee or agent or for any other loss unless this was caused by his own wilful default.
344. Section 26 of the Trustee Act 2000.
345. Section 11(1) of the Trustee Act 2000.
346. Section 22(1) of the Trustee Act 2000.
347. Section 23 and Schedule 1, para. 3 of the Trustee Act 2000.
348. Section 1(1) of the Trustee Act 2000.

a matter of some urgency. As Kenny has commented, 'delegation of some or all of the acts of trusteeship is an inevitable consequence of modern trusteeship'[349] and legislation along the lines of that enacted in England would both clarify the law and ease the burden on trustees. The Law Reform Commission in its Report *Trust Law: General Proposals*[350] recommended the introduction of legislation in terms similar to the provisions of section 11 of the Trustee Act 2000 and also recommended that the proposed statutory duty of care should apply to trustees' powers of delegation. It recommended that the following functions should be non-delegable:

(a) any function relating to whether or in what way the assets of the trust should be distributed or otherwise dealt with during the period of the trust,
(b) any power to decide whether any fees or other payment due to be made out of the trust funds should be made out of income or capital,
(c) any power to appoint a person to be a trustee of the trust, or
(d) any power conferred by any other enactment or the trust instrument which permits the trustees to delegate any of their functions or to appoint a person to act as a nominee or custodian.

In relation to point (c) above, the power to appoint new trustees, the New Zealand Court of Appeal in its decision in *New Zealand Maori Council v Foulkes*[351] has characterised it as being of a fiduciary nature and one which cannot be delegated. As Harrison J put it, 'as it resposes the settlor's personal trust and confidence in the done to exercise its own judgment and discretion, the power cannot be delegated to a third party.'[352]

THE POWERS OF TRUSTEES

Introduction

Before the intervention of statute in this area, where a trust instrument was being drafted it was necessary to ensure that sufficient powers were conferred on the trustees by the instrument to enable them to carry out their duties in the manner envisaged by the settlor or testator. The Trustee Act 1893 confers a number of basic powers on trustees but this legislation was only intended to augment the powers conferred by the trust instrument, which will often still determine the precise extent of the trustees' powers. It is now proposed to examine some of the more important statutory powers conferred on trustees but it should be

349. Kenny [1997] Conv 372, 373.
350. LRC 92-2008, para. 6.25. See s. 15 of the draft Trustee Bill 2008.
351. [2016] 2 NZLR 337.
352. *Ibid.* at 344.

borne in mind that in the final analysis the terms of the instrument itself are still of overriding importance.

Power of Sale and to Give Receipts

A trustee may be authorised to sell trust property by virtue of an express power contained in a trust instrument or alternatively such a power may be implied, e.g. in circumstances where the rule in *Howe v Earl of Dartmouth*[353] applies. The only other circumstances in which a trustee may sell trust property is where he is authorised to do so by the court or where a power of sale is conferred on him by statute.

Where a trustee holds property on trust for sale or with a power of sale, statutory powers are conferred on him in relation to the conduct of the sale by section 13 of the Trustee Act 1893. The section provides that, subject to a contrary intention being expressed in the trust instrument, a trustee is empowered to sell the trust property in whole or in part and either by public auction or by private contract subject to such conditions as he thinks fit.

The overriding duty of a trustee selling trust property is to obtain the best price for the beneficiaries,[354] although it should be noted that section 14 of the Trustee Act 1893 provides that a sale may not be impeached by a beneficiary on the grounds that any of the conditions of sale were unduly depreciatory unless it appears that the consideration for the sale was thereby rendered inadequate. In such cases, the position of the purchaser is also protected unless it appears that he was acting in collusion with the trustee at the time the contract for sale was concluded.[355]

A further relevant power is contained in section 15 of the Act of 1893 as amended which provides that a trustee who is either a vendor or purchaser may sell or buy trust property without excluding the application of sections 57 and 58 of the Land and Conveyancing Law Reform Act 2009.[356]

Section 20(1) of the Land and Conveyancing Law Reform Act 2009 now provides that subject to the duties of a trustee and any restrictions imposed by statute, the law of trusts generally, or any instrument or court order, a trustee of land has the full power of an owner to convey or otherwise deal with the land. It should also be noted that the Law Reform Commission in its Report *Trust Law: General Proposals*[357] recommended that trustees should be provided with a statutory power of sale and that this proposed statutory power should be subject to the duties of trustees under the general law of trusts.

353. (1802) 7 Ves 137. See *supra* pp. 554.
354. *Buttle v Saunders* [1950] 2 All ER 193, 195. See also *Re Cooper and Allen's Contract for Sale to Harlech* (1876) 4 Ch D 802, 815 *per* Jessel MR.
355. Section 14(2) of the Act of 1893.
356. Substituted for the reference to s. 2 of the Vendor and Purchaser Act 1874 by ss. 2, 8(1) and Schedule 1 of the Land and Conveyancing Law Reform Act 2009.
357. LRC 92-2008, paras. 11.18, 11.21.

A statutory power is conferred on trustees by section 20 of the Trustee Act 1893 to give receipts and it provides that a written receipt given by a trustee for the money, securities or property sold is a sufficient discharge to the person paying and effectively exonerates him from being answerable for any loss or misapplication of the property.

Power of Maintenance

Express provision can be and often is made in the trust instrument empowering the trustees to apply the income of the trust property for an infant's benefit.[358] Statutory powers of maintenance are also conferred on trustees by section 43 of the Conveyancing Act 1881 which empowers them to use trust income towards the maintenance or education of infant beneficiaries in certain circumstances. In situations where this power is exercisable, trustees may pay maintenance to an infant's parent or guardian or otherwise apply the income for the maintenance, education or benefit of an infant. Section 43 can be applied where property is held on trust for an infant beneficiary for life or for any greater interest, whether absolutely or contingently, on attaining the age of 18 or on the occurrence of any specified event before attaining that age. However, if the vesting of the interest is contingent on reaching a greater age or on the happening of some future event, the statutory power cannot be employed.

A further limitation on this statutory power is that it only applies where the trust property 'carries the intermediate income', i.e. the income which arises between the time of the coming into effect of the trust and the time the infant attains his majority, or the contingency occurs. As a general principle, a future or contingent gift will not be regarded as carrying the intermediate income which could be applied for maintenance except where it is a gift of residuary personalty, as in such cases the income can go to no one except the residuary legatee. However, other types of future or contingent legacies will only carry the intermediate income in limited circumstances, as set out by Ker.[359] First, they will be regarded as carrying the income where the testator was the parent of, or *in loco parentis* to, the infant beneficiary, except where the contingency is the attaining of some age greater than the age of majority,[360] or where the testator has provided another fund out of which the infant is to be maintained. So, in *Re Ferguson*,[361] it was held by O'Connor MR that a contingent specific bequest carried the intermediate income as the testator was *in loco parentis* and had made no alternative provision for the maintenance of the legatee before the bequest vested. The second exception is where the testator has manifested an intention that the infant is to be maintained as in *Re Churchill*,[362] where the

358. E.g. *Russell v Russell* [1903] 1 IR 168.
359. Ker (1953) 17 Conv 273, 276-278.
360. *Re Abrahams* [1911] 1 Ch 108.
361. (1915) 49 ILTR 110.
362. [1909] 2 Ch 431.

testatrix had given a legacy to her grand nephew and directed that any part of it should be paid towards his advancement in life or otherwise for his benefit. The third exception is where the testator segregates a fund for the legatee and is set out in the following terms by Chatterton VC in *Johnston v O'Neill*:[363]

> It is, no doubt, the general rule that general legacies payable at a future day, even though vested, do not carry interest before the day of payment, except legacies given to a child by a parent, or a person *in loco parentis*. But to this general rule there are exceptions, one of which is, that where a fund is directed to be presently separated from the general personal estate for the purpose of providing for the future payment of certain legacies, it carries the interest accruing up to the time of payment, to the legatees, with the capital sum. In such cases, the rule that the interest follows the capital prevails, and the legatee gets his legacy with its interim accretions.

A statutory power to permit the court to make payments of income or capital is conferred by section 11 of the Guardianship of Infants Act 1964 which provides that an application may be brought by the guardian of an infant where such a payment is necessary for his maintenance or education. The Law Reform Commission in its Report *Trust Law: General Proposals* recommended that trustees should be provided with a general statutory power to apply income for the maintenance of beneficiaries in appropriate cases[364] and that the power of maintenance should be subject to the proposed statutory duty of care.[365]

In addition, the court also has an inherent jurisdiction to make an order sanctioning the use of capital by trustees for the maintenance of infants where they have no other means of support.[366] In *Re O'Neill*[367] Maguire P directed that a payment be made out of the trust capital for the maintenance and education of the testator's children, although he made it clear that it was a jurisdiction which should only be exercised where it was really necessary. He stated:

> I must be satisfied that such a course is not only beneficial but necessary to the welfare of the minors. … The jurisdiction to make an advance out of capital is not to be exercised lightly. Where a minor is actually destitute the way is clear, but where the minors, as here, are not destitute, the question of the existence of a sufficient element of necessity becomes a difficult problem.[368]

363. (1879) 3 LR Ir 476, 480-481.
364. LRC 92-2008, para. 10.23. See s. 22 of the draft Trustee Bill 2008.
365. *Ibid.* at para. 10.38.
366. *Robison v Killey* (1862) 30 Beav 520, 521.
367. [1943] IR 562.
368. *Ibid.* at 564-565.

Power of Advancement

While 'maintenance' usually refers to the payment of income for the benefit of infant beneficiaries, the term 'advancement' is used to describe payments made out of the trust capital to a beneficiary before he becomes entitled to an interest under the trust. Traditionally, 'the word "advancement" meant ... the establishment in life of the beneficiary who was the object of the power or at any rate some step that would contribute to the furtherance of his establishment'.[369] A power to make advancements out of capital may be expressly conferred by the trust instrument.[370] In addition, as seen above, a statutory power exists under section 11 of the Guardianship of Infants Act 1964 whereby the court can sanction capital payments for the support of an infant beneficiary where an application is made by the infant's guardian.

The Law Reform Commission in its Report *Trust Law: General Proposals* recommended the introduction of a statutory power to advance capital.[371] It also recommended that the amount advanced should not exceed half of the presumptive or vested share of the beneficiary,[372] and that the power of advancement should be subject to the proposed statutory duty of care.[373]

Power to Compound Liabilities

By virtue of section 21 of the Trustee Act 1893, trustees may 'compromise, compound, abandon, submit to arbitration or otherwise settle' any debt or claim without being responsible for any loss occasioned by any act done by him in this regard in good faith. As Overend J stated in *Re Boyle*[374] in relation to this power, which is also conferred on executors and administrators, '[t]here is no question that an executor has power to compromise even a doubtful claim, if he *bona fide* believes it to be in the interest of the estate.'

The Law Reform Commission in its Report *Trust Law: General Proposals* recommended that new powers concerning debts, settling and compounding liabilities should provide that trustees may:

(a) accept any property before the time at which it is transferable or payable;
(b) sever and apportion any blended trust funds or property;
(c) pay or allow any debt or claim on any evidence they may reasonably deem sufficient;
(d) accept any composition or security for any debt or property claimed;
(e) allow time for payment of any debt;

369. *Pilkington v IRC* [1964] AC 612, 634.
370. *McMahon v Gaussen* [1896] 1 IR 143; *L'Estrange v L'Estrange* [1902] 1 IR 467.
371. LRC 92-2008, para. 10.27. See s. 23 of the draft Trustee Bill 2008.
372. *Ibid.* at para. 10.30.
373. *Ibid.* at para. 10.38.
374. [1947] IR 61, 69.

(f) compromise, compound, abandon, submit to arbitration, or otherwise settle, any debt, account, dispute, claim or other matter relating to the trust;

and for any of those purposes may enter into such agreements or arrangements and execute such documents as seem to them expedient, without being personally responsible for any loss occasioned by any act or thing so done by them if they have discharged the statutory duty of care.[375]

Power to Insure

While trustees originally had no power to insure unless this was conferred by the trust instrument, section 18 of the Trustee Act 1893 provides that they may insure trust property 'against loss or damage by fire' to an amount not exceeding three-quarters of the full value of the property. In addition, section 18(2) provides that this power does not apply to any building or property which the trustees are bound to convey absolutely to any beneficiary on being requested to do so.

It should be noted that in England section 34 of Trustee Act 2000 now provides that a trustee may insure any property which is subject to a trust against risks of loss or damage due to any event and that a trustee may pay the premiums out of the trust funds.[376] The Law Reform Commission in its Report *Trust Law: General Proposals* recommended that any new legislation should not impose upon trustees a duty to insure trust property.[377] However, it recommended that a new statutory power to insure should confer upon trustees a discretion to pay insurance from the 'trust funds', with trust funds defined as comprising either trust income or capital.[378]

LIABILITY OF TRUSTEES FOR BREACH OF TRUST

Extent and Measure of Liability

A trustee will be found to be acting in breach of trust if he fails to perform the duties required of him or if he acts in an unauthorised manner. A breach may occur in a variety of circumstances such as where trust monies are invested in unauthorised investments, where a trustee fails to distribute the trust estate to the beneficiaries in the correct proportions, or where he fails to exercise a proper degree of supervision over the management of the trust by his co-

375. LRC 92-2008, para.9.16. See s. 21 of the draft Trustee Bill 2008.
376. See para. 6.4 of Law Commission Report No. 260 1999 on *Trustees' Powers and Duties*.
377. LRC 92-2008, para. 7.18. See s. 19 of the draft Trustee Bill 2008.
378. *Ibid.* at para. 7.23.

trustees. However, it will be necessary for the beneficiaries to establish conduct which in the opinion of the court amounts to a breach of trust.[379] The tenor of the judgment of Charleton J in *Greene v Coady*[380] suggests that 'counsels of perfection cannot be applied to the decisions of trustees'. He stated as follows:

> In making any decision as to the liability of trustees it is not for the court to be cleverer or better informed or more astute or more enquiring or better in its judgment than the trustees. The court must also avoid the temptation to listen to the evidence and to make its own conclusion as to what should have been done by the trustees on the date of the impugned decision.[381]

Where a trustee fails to comply with the duties imposed on him by the trust instrument he is liable to make good the loss to the trust estate or, where he makes an unauthorised profit for himself, even if this does not cause loss to the trust, he must account for it. As a general rule, a trustee is liable only in respect of the breaches of trust which he has himself committed and not those committed by his co-trustees; liability is personal and not vicarious.[382] However, this indemnity will not apply where his conduct amounts to wilful default on his part, and inactivity on the part of a trustee in circumstances where he ought to have intervened can often be regarded as sufficient grounds for imposing liability.

A trustee is not liable for breaches of trust committed before his appointment unless there is evidence indicating such a breach which requires him to investigate further. It is therefore important that on appointment, a trustee takes whatever steps are necessary to ensure that the trust affairs are in order and investigates anything which causes him suspicion. When a trustee retires from a trust he remains liable for breaches committed by him during his term of office and his estate remains liable after his death. Where a breach occurs shortly after his retirement he will be liable if he retired in order to facilitate a breach of trust which he foresaw would take place or if he contemplated at the time that a breach of trust would be effected and decided to retire to avoid direct involvement. This issue was considered by Kekewich J in *Head v Gould*,[383] where he held that to make a retiring trustee liable for a breach of trust committed by his successor, it must be proved that the breach committed was not merely the outcome of the retirement and new appointment but was contemplated by the former trustee when the retirement took place; as he said,

379. See *Carr v Connor* (1929) 23 ILTR 185, where Fitzgibbon J concluded at 191 that: 'the plaintiffs had failed to prove that the defendant was guilty even of an error of judgment still less of any wilful default.'
380. [2015] 1 IR 385, 398.
381. *Ibid.* at 396.
382. *Townley v Sherborne* (1634) J Bridg 35, 37.
383. [1898] 2 Ch 250.

the former trustees 'must be proved to have been guilty as accessories before the fact of the impropriety actually perpetrated.'[384]

The measure of a trustee's liability where an unlawful profit has been made as a result of his breach of trust is that he should account for the profit.[385] It should be noted that the Privy Council has held that where such an unlawful profit has been made, a plaintiff is entitled either to an account of the profits made by the defendant in breach of his fiduciary obligations or to damages for the loss suffered by the plaintiff by reason of the breach; the plaintiff must make an election between these remedies.[386]

In other cases where there has been a breach of trust or fiduciary duty, the measure of a trustee's liability is the loss caused to the trust estate either directly or indirectly.[387] Where the breach consists of a trustee making an unauthorised investment, the measure of damages will be the loss incurred by the trust in selling this investment if this is the course of action agreed on by the beneficiaries. Where trustees improperly retain an unauthorised investment, they will be liable for the difference between the price which the property would have fetched if sold at the proper time and the price actually received for it. This point is well illustrated by the decision of Romilly MR in *Fry v Fry*.[388] A testator had directed that an inn should be sold 'as soon as convenient' after his death. The trustees refused an initial offer of £900 and nine years after the testator's death the value of the property was greatly depreciated by the opening of a railway which deprived it of its coach traffic. The inn still remained unsold some 26 years after the testator's death. The estates of the trustees who had died in the interim were held liable for the difference between the original offer of £900 and the amount of the proceeds of the sale which the court directed should take place.

Where trustees improperly sell an authorised investment they may be liable either to account for the proceeds of sale or to repurchase the investment at its value at the date of the judgment.[389] In addition, where the trustees pay out trust funds to the wrong person, they will be liable to make good this amount so that the correct beneficiary can be paid.[390]

The principles relating to equitable compensation where loss has been caused as a result of a breach of trust or fiduciary duty were considered in

---

384. *Ibid.* at 274.
385. As the Privy Council made clear in *Attorney General for Hong Kong v Reid* [1994] 1 AC 324, in such circumstances, if assets are bought with trust monies, any increase in their value will be held on a constructive trust, whereas if they decrease in value the trustee will be personally liable in relation to such loss.
386. *Tang Man Sit v Capacious Investments Ltd* [1996] 1 AC 514.
387. So, where there has been a breach of trust but it causes no loss to the beneficiary, there will be no liability, see e.g., *Jeffrey v Gretton* [2011] WTLR 809.
388. (1859) 27 Beav 144.
389. *Re Bell's Indenture* [1980] 1 WLR 1217.
390. See *Target Holdings Ltd v Redferns* [1996] 1 AC 421.

some detail by the House of Lords in *Target Holdings Ltd v Redferns*.[391] As Lord Browne-Wilkinson commented:

> Equitable compensation for breach of trust is designed to achieve exactly what the word compensation suggests: to make good a loss in fact suffered by the beneficiaries and which, using hindsight and common sense, can be seen to have been caused by the breach.[392]

Lord Browne-Wilkinson stated that the equitable rules of compensation for breach of trust have largely been developed in relation to so-called traditional trusts, where the only way to properly protect the rights of the beneficiaries is to restore to the trust fund what ought to be in it. In such cases, he said that the basic rule is that 'a trustee in breach of trust must restore or pay to the trust estate either the assets which have been lost to the estate by reason of the breach or compensation for such loss'.[393] However, Lord Browne-Wilkinson stressed that there does have to be some causal connection between the breach of trust and the loss to the trust estate for which the compensation is recoverable. So, as the decision of the House of Lords made clear, a trustee will not be required to compensate for loss which would have occurred in any event even if there had been no breach of trust.[394]

Lord Browne-Wilkinson then went on to consider what the position would be where, at the time of the bringing of an action claiming compensation for breach of trust, those trusts had come to an end. In such circumstances, he stated, the court will not order restitution to be made to the trust estate, but rather will direct that payment of compensation be made directly to the beneficiaries. In such cases the measure of compensation will be the same, i.e. 'the difference between what the beneficiary has in fact received and the amount he would have received but for the breach of trust'.[395]

A compensatory analysis was also adopted by the Supreme Court of the United Kingdom in *AIB Group (UK) plc v Mark Redler & Co.*,[396] in which it followed the reasoning adopted in *Target Holdings* in dismissing the claimant's appeal. Lord Reed JSC stated as follows:

---

391. [1996] 1 AC 421.
392. *Ibid.* at 439. See further *Harris v Kent* [2007] EWHC 463 (Ch) at [140].
393. *Ibid.* at 434. See also *Barnett v Creggy* [2017] Ch 273, 284.
394. This so-called stringent test of causation or measure of loss was applied by the Court of Appeal in *Swindle v Harrison* [1997] 4 All ER 705 in the context of breach of fiduciary duty. See further Ho (1997) 11 Trust Law Int 72 and (1998) 12 Trust Law Int 66.
395. [1996] 1 AC 421, 435. See also *Swindle v Harrison* [1997] 4 All ER 705, 717.
396. [2015] AC 1503. See Davies (2015) 78 MLR 681; Ho (2015) 131 LQR 213; Turner [2015] CLJ 188; Carn (2014) 28 Trust Law Int 226; Yip and Lee (2017)37 LS 647, 652–657. See further Millett (2018) 32 Trust Law Int 44, who argues that 'the proper remedy for breach of trust is account and payment, not equitable compensation.'

> [T]he model of equitable compensation, where trust property has been misapplied, is to require the trustee to restore the trust fund to the position it would have been in if the trustee had performed his obligation. If the trust has come to an end, the trustee can be ordered to compensate the beneficiary directly. In that situation the compensation is assessed on the same basis, since it is equivalent in substance to a distribution of the trust fund. If the trust fund has been diminished as a result of some other breach of trust, the same approach ordinarily applies, mutatis mutandis.[397]

He said that the foreseeability of the loss is generally irrelevant, but that the loss must be caused by the breach of trust, 'in the sense that it must flow directly from it'.[398] Lord Reed JSC added that the requirement that the loss should flow directly from the breach is also the key to determining whether causation has been interrupted by the acts of third parties.

So, as Gloster LJ stated in *Ahmed v Ingram*,[399] 'as *AIB* and *Target Holdings* demonstrate, liability in equity is fault based, and the relevant loss for which compensation is payable must be *caused by the actions or omissions of the relevant trustee*.' She added that as the decision in *Target Holdings* makes clear, in order to recover equitable compensation the trustee must show actual loss caused by the breach, 'thus equating the equitable principle for calculating compensation, with the common law principle of assessing loss.' In addition, it should be noted that in *Main v Giambrone*[400] Jackson LJ distinguished the outcome from that in *Target Holdings* and *AIB*. In the matter before the court, there was a causal link between the breach of trust and the loss sustained and the Court of Appeal held that the trial judge had been correct in awarding equitable compensation. As Jackson LJ stated, '[i]n *Target* the plaintiff's claim failed on the "but for" test. In the present case the claimants' claim passes the "but for" test.' [401]

Another question which must be addressed is the date at which the actual loss to the trust should be assessed. Traditionally, it was accepted that the loss should be ascertained at the date proceedings commenced,[402] but Vinelott J disputed this in *Re Bell's Indenture*,[403] where he stated that the loss should be ascertained instead at the date of judgment. Further confusion was caused when it was stated in *Jaffray v Marshall*[404] that the trustees were liable to pay compensation at the highest intermediate value of the property between the date

397. *Ibid.* at 1400-1401. See also the *dicta* of Lord Toulson JSC at 1384.
398. *Ibid.*
399. [2018] EWCA Civ 519 at [35].
400. [2017] EWCA Civ 1193. See further Davies (2018) 134 LQR 165, 167, who suggests that the distinction between *Target* and *AIB* on the one hand and the matter before the Court of Appeal on the other hand was 'very thin indeed'.
401. *Ibid.* at [63].
402. *Re Massingberd* (1890) 63 LT 296.
403. [1980] 1 WLR 1217, 1233.
404. [1993] 1 WLR 1285.

of the breach and the date of judgment. However, as a result of the consideration given by the House of Lords to this issue in *Target Holdings Ltd v Redferns*[405] it now seems clear that liability is to be assessed at the date of judgment. As Lord Browne-Wilkinson stated:

> [T]he fact that there is an accrued cause of action as soon as the breach is committed does not in my judgment mean that the quantum of compensation payable is ultimately fixed as at the date when the breach occurred. The quantum is fixed at the date of the judgment at which date, according to the circumstances then pertaining, the compensation is assessed at the figure then necessary to put the trust estate or the beneficiary back into the position it would have been in had there been no breach.[406]

This approach was also followed in *AIB Group (UK) plc v Mark Redler & Co.*,[407] where Lord Reed JSC commented that '[t]he measure of compensation should therefore normally be assessed at the date of trial, with the benefit of hindsight.'

Finally, it should be noted that where a trustee is under an obligation to replace trust funds, he is charged with interest on the sum due. At common law this figure was 4% but the rate now prescribed for interest on judgment debts payable is 2% as set out in the Courts Act 1981 (Interest on Judgment Debts) Order 2016.[408]

Liability of Trustees Inter Se

Where two or more trustees are involved in a breach of trust, liability is joint and several, so each is liable in respect of the whole loss although all may not have been equally blameworthy.[409] In such circumstances, a decree against all the trustees involved may be enforced against one or more of them,[410] and those against whom execution is levied may claim contribution from the other trustees involved in the breach of trust. The effect of the operation of this principle is that while all the trustees may not be equally blameworthy, they may still be held to be equally liable. The fact that this is arguably not always fair in practice

405. [1996] 1 AC 421. See Ulph (1995) 9 Trust Law Int 86; Nolan [1996] LMCLQ 161; Rickett (1996) 112 LQR 27; Capper [1997] Conv 14.
406. *Ibid.* at 437. See further *Harris v Kent* [2007] EWHC 463 (Ch) at [140].
407. [2015] AC 1503, 1544.
408. SI No. 624 of 2016.
409. As Panckhurst J stated in the decision of the New Zealand High Court in *Re Mulligan* [1998] 1 NZLR 481, 502, 'it is elementary that a duty of diligence rests on each trustee' and that: 'the starting point is that where a breach of trust has been committed, the trustees are jointly and severally liable to the beneficiaries for any loss caused by the breach' (at 511). See also *Selkirk v McIntyre* [2013] 3 NZLR 265, 268-269.
410. *Fletcher v Green* (1864) 33 Beav 426, 430.

is well illustrated by the decision of the Court of Appeal in *Bahin v Hughes*.[411] A testator gave a legacy to his three daughters on trust to pay the income to the plaintiff for life and after her death to her children. One of the daughters and the husband of another effected an unauthorised investment in leasehold property and when this security proved insufficient, the plaintiff sought to impose liability on all the trustees. The Court of Appeal held that they were jointly and severally liable and all equally responsible for indemnifying the beneficiaries. In the opinion of the court, the money had been lost just as much as a result of the default of the inactive trustees as by the innocent, though erroneous, action of their co-trustee. Cotton LJ remarked:

> It would be laying down a wrong rule to hold that where one trustee acts honestly, though erroneously, the other trustee is to be held entitled to indemnity who by doing nothing neglects his duty more than the acting trustee.[412]

As Katz J has commented in the decision of the New Zealand High Court in *Selkirk v McIntyre*,[413] '[a] "passive" trustee is not entitled to simply delegate their responsibilities to the "active" trustee.' In his view, 'Equity simply does not recognise the concept of an "active" trustee or a "passive" trustee'.[414] So, all trustees are accountable to the beneficiaries for the proper administration of the trust unless they can demonstrate that the case falls within one of a limited number of exceptions.

Even where a breach of trust has occurred, a trustee may escape liability or may be entitled to indemnity from a co-trustee in certain circumstances. Where one trustee acts in a fraudulent manner his co-trustees may be entitled to an indemnity. In addition, where one trustee alone receives the benefit of a breach of trust, he will be liable to provide an indemnity[415] and to first contribute the amount of the personal benefit received.[416] Similarly, where one trustee has exercised a controlling influence over the others which has effectively prevented his co-trustees from exercising independent judgment, they may successfully claim indemnity. This type of influence may be found to exist, e.g. where there is one professional trustee such as a solicitor, although Kekewich J stressed in *Head v Gould*[417] that there is no rule that 'a man is bound to indemnify his co-trustee against loss merely because he [is] a solicitor.' Certainly in that case

411. (1886) 31 Ch D 390.
412. *Ibid.* at 396. Note that the provisions of the Civil Liability Act 1961 apply to a breach of trust. See the definition of 'wrong' in s. 2 and see also Part III Chapter 1 of the Act on the liability of concurrent wrongdoers.
413. [2013] 3 NZLR 265, 273.
414. *Ibid* at 274.
415. *Bahin v Hughes* (1886) 31 Ch D 390, 395.
416. *Selkirk v McIntyre* [2013] 3 NZLR 265, 270.
417. [1898] 2 Ch 250, 265.

where the co-trustee had been shown to be an active participant and not merely to have acted on the solicitor's advice, no indemnity could be obtained. Finally, where a trustee is also a beneficiary and has participated in a breach of trust, he must indemnify his co-trustees to the extent of his beneficial interest.[418]

Protection of Trustees from Personal Liability

A trustee who has committed a breach of trust may escape personal liability if he can establish certain circumstances. Where the beneficiary has instigated, participated in or even consented to the breach of trust, the trustee will not be liable for any breach which occurs. Some of the factors which may influence the court in deciding whether the beneficiary's conduct will be such as to afford protection to the trustee were considered by Wilberforce J at first instance in *Re Pauling's Settlement Trusts*,[419] where he stated as follows:

> The court has to consider all the circumstances in which the concurrence of the *cestui que trust* was given with a view to seeing whether it is fair and equitable that, having given his concurrence, he should afterwards turn round and sue the trustees; that, subject to this, it is not necessary that he should know what he is concurring in is a breach of trust, provided that he fully understands what he is concurring in, and that it is not necessary that he should himself have directly benefited by the breach of trust.

A similar view was expressed by Laskin JA, delivering the judgment of the Ontario Court of Appeal in *Gold v Rosenberg*,[420] to the effect that in order for a beneficiary's consent to be valid, he must be capable of giving approval and must understand what is being approved. However, Laskin JA agreed that it was not necessary for the trustee to show that the beneficiary knew that the act or omission in question constituted a breach of trust.

A good example of a case in which a breach of trust was committed at the instigation of a beneficiary is *French v Graham*.[421] Two trustees, one of whom was a solicitor, lent trust funds at the request of the tenant for life of a settlement on a security which proved totally inadequate. The non-professional trustee stood in the opinion of Brady LC in the 'ordinary position of a trustee who has been induced to commit a breach of trust at the request of one of his *cestuis que trust*' and was entitled to be indemnified by the tenant for life in respect of his liability for breach of trust. However, the Lord Chancellor was satisfied that the tenant for life had relied on the trustee solicitor advising him in the transaction in his professional capacity and as the latter had made no

---

418. *Chillingworth v Chambers* [1896] 1 Ch 685.
419. [1962] 1 WLR 86, 108. Approved by the Court of Appeal in *Holder v Holder* [1968] Ch 353.
420. (1995) 129 DLR (4th) 152, 157.
421. (1860) 10 Ir Ch R 522. See also *Rutherfoord v Maziere* (1862) 13 Ir Ch R 204.

sufficient investigation of the title of the property involved, he was not entitled to be indemnified by the tenant for life.

The decision of a beneficiary to participate in or consent to a breach of trust will only usually[422] be relevant in this context where he is of full age and capacity and his participation or consent must have been freely given with full knowledge of the surrounding facts and circumstances. As Wilmer LJ stated in *Re Pauling's Settlement Trusts*,[423] if the trustee can establish 'a valid request or consent by the beneficiary' to an advance made in breach of trust, that will provide the trustee with a good defence against any claim by the beneficiary. In *Pauling* the trustees of a marriage settlement made a number of advancements to the children of the marriage with their mother's consent and, although nominally paid to the children, this money was applied to family purposes. The children subsequently brought an action claiming that these sums had been improperly paid out and the trustees relied on the consent and acquiescence of the beneficiaries to whom advancements had been made. However, in the view of the Court of Appeal this was not effective to absolve the trustees from liability in every case and it was held that some of the payments to the beneficiaries had constituted breaches of trust for which the trustees were liable.

It should be noted that a statutory defence is available in England by virtue of section 61 of the Trustee Act 1925 which provides that if it appears to the court that a trustee is or may be personally liable for a breach of trust but has acted 'honestly and reasonably' and ought fairly to be excused for the breach, the court may relieve him wholly or partly from personal liability.[424] In a recent review of the operation of the section, Haley has suggested that the changing nature of trusteeship, the availability of liability insurance and the widespread use of exemption clauses mean that consideration should be given to the question of whether this discretionary relief is still necessary or desirable.[425] While he accepts that there may be a continuing need for this jurisdiction in relation to unpaid trustees, he suggests that a 'major overhaul' of the discretionary power conferred by the section is needed.[426]

The Law Reform Commission in its Report *Trust Law: General Proposals* also recommended the introduction of a provision which would confer a discretion on the courts to relieve trustees from liability for breach of trust in circumstances where they have acted honestly and reasonably and ought

---

422. However, in *Overton v Banister* (1844) 3 Hare 503 the court refused to allow an infant who had fraudulently misrepresented her age to succeed in arguing that any assent was ineffective.
423. [1964] Ch 303, 335.
424. See further *Lloyds TSB Bank plc v Markandan & Uddine* [2012] EWCA Civ 65; *Nationwide Building Society v Davisons Solicitors* [2012] EWCA Civ 1626; *Ikbal v Sterling Law* [2013] EWHC 3291 (Ch); *Santander UK v RA Legal Solicitors* [2014] EWCA Civ 183; *Purrunsing v A'Court & Co.* [2016] 4 WLR 81; *P & P Property Ltd v Owen White and Catlin LLP* [2016] EWHC 2276 (Ch).
425. [2017] CLJ 537. See also Lowry and Edmunds (2017) 133 LQR 223.
426. *Ibid.* at 565.

fairly to be excused for the breach of trust.[427] It further recommended that the proposed statutory provision providing for the relieving of liability for breach of trust should not distinguish between professional and lay trustees.[428]

The court has an inherent jurisdiction where a beneficiary has been instrumental in effecting a breach of trust to require the beneficiary to indemnify the trustee in respect of the latter's liability to make good any loss incurred.[429] This principle was reiterated by Chitty J in *Sawyer v Sawyer*[430] in the following terms:

> [E]ach person at whose instance the trustees have committed a breach of trust is liable to recoup the subject of that breach of trust to the trustees … it must be shown that the breach of trust was committed at the instance and request of the *cestuis que trust*. I make no distinction between instance and request, but it must be shown clearly that the breach of trust was instigated by them and that they were acting and moving parties to it.

However the proposition that 'a *cestui que trust* is bound to make good to the trustee every loss occasioned by an investment made with his privity' was rejected by Brady LC in *Browne v Maunsell*,[431] and it would appear that where a beneficiary has merely consented to the breach of trust, his beneficial interest can only be impounded in this way where he has obtained a personal benefit from the breach. This power to impound a beneficiary's interest was given statutory authority by section 45 of the Trustee Act 1893 which provides that where it can be established that a beneficiary has instigated or requested or consented in writing to a breach of trust, the court may order that the interest of the beneficiary should be impounded with a view to indemnifying the trustee. This power will not normally be exercised in favour of the trustee unless it can be established that the beneficiary was aware at the time that the conduct which he instigated or consented to amounted to a breach of trust.

Even where a beneficiary is not involved prior to the breach being committed, a trustee may still be protected from liability where the beneficiary subsequently acquiesces in the breach or executes a release absolving the trustee from liability. As Lord Eldon stated in *Walker v Symonds*,[432] 'either concurrence in the act or acquiescence without original concurrence will release the trustees' but he went on to state that this is only a general rule and that the court must investigate the circumstances which induced the concurrence or acquiescence. For acquiescence to be effective in this context, the beneficiary must be *sui*

---

427. LRC 92-2008, para. 4.45.
428. *Ibid.* at para. 4.47.
429. *Keays v Lane* (1869) IR 3 Eq 1.
430. (1883) 28 Ch D 595, 598. Quoted with approval by Johnston J in *Anketill Jones v Fitzgerald* (1930) 65 ILTR 185, 191.
431. (1856) 5 Ir Ch R 351.
432. (1818) 3 Swans 1, 64. See also *Re McKenna's Estate* (1861) 13 Ir Ch R 239.

juris and have consented freely to the trustee's actions with full knowledge of the surrounding facts and circumstances and it appears that the onus lies on the party alleging acquiescence to prove facts from which the beneficiary's consent can be inferred.[433]

Similarly, a release even of an informal nature may be effective to absolve a trustee from liability,[434] but it is essential that the beneficiary executed such a release with full knowledge of the facts and of the consequences of his actions.[435] Westbury LC summarised the position in *Farrant v Blanchford*[436] as follows:

> Where a breach of trust has been committed, from which a trustee alleges that he has been released, it is incumbent on him to show that such release was given by the *cestui que trust* deliberately and advisedly with full knowledge of all the circumstances, and of his own rights and claims against the trustee.

Finally, it should be noted that a trustee may be protected from an action for breach of trust by virtue of the provisions of the Statute of Limitations 1957. Section 43 provides that, subject to section 44, an action in respect of a breach of trust, not being an action in respect of which a period of limitation is fixed by any other provision of the legislation, shall not be brought against a trustee[437] after the expiration of six years from the date on which the right of action accrued. Section 44 goes on to provide that no limitation period fixed by the Act will apply to an action against a trustee where the claim is founded on any fraud or fraudulent breach of trust to which the trustee was party or where the claim is to recover trust property or the proceeds of trust property retained by the trustee or received by him and converted to his own use.[438] In *Murphy v Allied Irish Banks Ltd*[439] the plaintiff succeeded in claiming interest on monies retained by the defendant following the sale of mortgaged property only for a period of six years from the date of the institution of proceedings. It was made clear by Murphy J in the course of his judgment that the fact that a trustee admits liability for trust moneys and is accountable for them does not prevent the statute running.

433. *Life Association of Scotland v Siddal* (1861) 3 De G F & J 58, 77.
434. *Ghost v Waller* (1846) 9 Beav 497.
435. *Thomson v Eastwood* (1877) 2 App Cas 215.
436. (1863) 1 De G J & Sm 107, 119.
437. See s. 2(2) of the Statute of Limitations 1957.
438. It was suggested by Fitzgibbon LJ in *Collings v Wade* [1896] 1 IR 340, 349 that in this context 'fraud ... must amount to dishonesty.' See also *Murphy v Allied Irish Banks Ltd* [1994] 2 ILRM 220, 228 and *Jobling-Purser v Jackson* High Court (Kinlen J) 27 November 2002 at 39.
439. [1994] 2 ILRM 220.

Trustee Exemption Clauses

A further issue which has attracted considerable judicial and academic attention in both England and Ireland recently is the extent to which an exemption clause in a trust instrument may protect a trustee from liability.[440] It has become increasingly common to insert provisions in trust instruments which protect a trustee from liability for breach of trust or restrict the scope of this liability. It has been suggested that '[a]s the powers of trustees have increased … so has the breadth of trustee exemption clauses'[441] and a question which must be addressed is whether such clauses undermine to too great an extent the interests of the beneficiaries which a trust is designed to protect.

The Position in England

It should be noted that in England Schedule 1, paragraph 7 of the Trustee Act 2000 provides that the statutory duty of care[442] 'does not apply if or in so far as it appears from the trust instrument that the duty is not meant to apply'. The current position in relation to the recognition of trustee exemption clauses in that jurisdiction was set out by the Court of Appeal in *Armitage v Nurse*,[443] where it upheld a clause in a settlement which provided that no trustee should be liable for any loss or damage unless it was caused 'by his own actual fraud'. In agreeing with the trial judge's conclusion that the trustees were absolved from liability in the circumstances by this clause, Millett LJ expressed the view that it would exempt a trustee from liability 'no matter how indolent, imprudent, lacking in diligence, negligent or wilful he may have been, so long as he has not acted dishonestly'.[444] While he agreed that there is an irreducible core of obligations owed by trustees to beneficiaries, he did not accept that these core obligations included the duties of skill and care, prudence and diligence. Millett LJ stated that the duty of the trustees to carry out their obligations honestly and

440. It should be noted that Schedule 1, para. 7 of the Trustee Act 2000 provides that the statutory duty of care 'does not apply if or in so far as it appears from the trust instrument that the duty is not meant to apply.'
441. Law Commission Consultation Paper No. 171 on *Trustee Exemption Clauses* (2003) para. 2.2.
442. Section 1(1) of the Trustee Act 2000 provides that whenever the duty set out in the subsection applies to a trustee, he must exercise such care and skill as is reasonable in the circumstances having regard in particular '(a) to any special knowledge or experience that he has or holds himself out as having, and (b) if he acts as a trustee in the course of a business or profession, to any special knowledge or experience that it is reasonable to expect of a person acting in the course of that kind of business or profession.'
443. [1998] Ch 241.
444. *Ibid.* at 251. Sir Christopher Slade expressed the view in *Walker v Stones* [2001] QB 902, 941 that Millett LJ's analysis clearly illustrates the need, as a matter of policy, for the courts to construe clauses of this nature 'no more widely than their language on a fair reading requires'.

in good faith for the benefit of the beneficiaries is the minimum necessary to give substance to the trust but in his view it was sufficient. However, Millett LJ himself acknowledged that there is a widely held view that exemption clauses of this nature have gone too far and that professional trustees, who would not think of excluding liability for ordinary professional negligence, should not be able to rely on a trustee exemption clause covering gross negligence.[445] It was subsequently held by the Court of Appeal in *Walker v Stones*,[446] in which the exemption clause was described as not being materially different to that in *Armitage*, that a solicitor-trustee[447] could not escape liability where he deliberately commits a breach of trust in the genuine belief that this course of action is in the interests of the beneficiaries, if no reasonable solicitor-trustee could have held that belief.

In *Barnsley v Noble*[448] Sales LJ held that the phrase 'wilful … fraud' in an exoneration clause should be interpreted as meaning 'a knowing and deliberate breach of a relevant equitable duty or reckless indifference to whether what is done is in breach of such duty'.[449] Similarly, Sir Terence Etherton stated that that the word 'wilful' imports a requirement of conscious wrongdoing. The Court of Appeal held that the trial judge had correctly concluded that the defendant had not deliberately kept things back knowing that he ought to disclose them and had not deliberately or consciously acted in a way which he knew to be wrong. In these circumstances, the court was satisfied that the exoneration clause applied to protect the defendant in respect of the claim for equitable compensation.

The Trust Law Committee in its Consultation Paper *Trustee Exemption Clauses*[450] expressed the provisional view that a trustee remunerated for his services should not be able to rely on an exemption clause excluding liability for negligence and worse, at all events where the trustee cannot prove that prior independent advice was given to the settlor. The Law Commission in its Consultation Paper on *Trustee Exemption Clauses*[451] subsequently concluded that it did not consider that an outright prohibition on trustee exemption clauses was justified or necessary but suggested that some legislative regulation was required.[452] The Commission proposed drawing a distinction between lay and professional trustees and suggested that lay trustees should in general continue to be able to rely on trustee exemption clauses.[453] It invited views

445. See also Millett (1998) 114 LQR 214, 216.
446. [2001] QB 902.
447. Sir Christopher Slade said (at 939) that he was limiting this proposition to solicitor-trustees because he accepted that the test of honesty may vary from case to case, depending on, among other things, the role and calling of the trustee.
448. [2017] Ch 191.
449. *Ibid.* at 204.
450. (1999) para. 8.1.
451. Law Commission Consultation Paper No. 171 (2003).
452. *Ibid.* at para. 4.19-4.20.
453. *Ibid.* at para. 4.39.

on the suggestion that professional trustees should be unable to rely on an exemption clause where their conduct has been so unreasonable, irresponsible or incompetent that in fairness to the beneficiaries their conduct should not be excused.[454] It provisionally proposed that a professional trustee should not be able to rely on any provision excluding liability for breach of trust arising from negligence[455] and invited views on whether professional trustees should not be able to exclude liability for breach of trust where it was not reasonable for the trustees to rely on an exemption clause by reference to all the circumstances, including the nature and extent of the breach of trust.[456]

However, in its Report on *Trustee Exemption Clauses*[457] published in July 2006, the Law Commission stated that the general message to emerge from its consultation process was that the Consultation Paper had failed to take adequate account of the likely adverse consequences of legislative regulation in this area. It concluded that there was an unacceptably high risk that the type of statutory reform envisaged by the Consultation Paper would give rise to significantly damaging consequences and expressed the view that such reform could lead to increased costs, delays in trust administration, a greater tendency towards defensive trusteeship and a general loss of flexibility in the operation of trusts.[458] As an alternative, the report focussed on the relationship between trustees and settlors and considered the viability of regulation aimed at ensuring that settlors were aware of the meaning and effect of exemption provisions when settling assets on trust. It recommended that a rule of practice should be recognised and enforced by regulatory and professional bodies along the following lines: 'Any paid trustee who causes a settlor to include a clause in a trust instrument which has the effect of excluding or limiting liability for negligence must before the creation of the trust take such steps as are reasonable to ensure that the settlor is aware of the meaning and effect of the clause.'[459]

The conclusion reached by the Law Commission in its report means that statutory regulation of this area in England is now unlikely and unless the matter comes before the Supreme Court, the law in that jurisdiction will remain as set out by Millett LJ in *Armitage v Nurse*.[460] However, there are signs in the judgments of some of the members of the Privy Council in *Spread Trustee Co. Ltd v Hutcheson*[461] that, if a suitable opportunity presented itself, the Supreme

454. *Ibid.* at para. 4.78.
455. *Ibid.* at para. 4.85.
456. *Ibid.* at para. 4.86.
457. Law Commission Report No. 301 (2006).
458. *Ibid.* at para. 5.99.
459. *Ibid.* at para. 6.65. This conclusion has been described as an 'astonishing result' by Kenny and Smules [2007] Conv 103, who suggest that that rejection of a legislative solution undermines the concept of a trust.
460. As Tuckey LJ commented in *Baker v J.E. Clark & Co.* [2006] EWCA Civ 464 at [21]: 'it is now settled law in England and Wales that trustee exemption clauses can validly exempt trustees from liability for breaches of trust, except fraud.'
461. [2012] 2 AC 194.

Court of the United Kingdom might well take a different view from that adopted in *Armitage*. In this case the majority of the Privy Council held that Guernsey customary law and the Trusts (Guernsey) Law 1989, which provided that 'nothing in the terms of a trust shall relieve a trustee of liability for a breach of trust arising from his own fraud or wilful misconduct', did not prohibit trustee exemption clauses excluding liability for gross negligence.[462] The trustees argued that the content of Guernsey customary law should be taken as similar to that of England and that English law permitted exclusion of liability for gross negligence. Lord Clarke, one of the majority, agreed with Millett LJ's conclusion in *Armitage* that a clause may exempt from liability 'no matter how indolent, imprudent, lacking in diligence, negligent or wilful [a trustee] may have been, so long as he has not acted dishonestly.'[463] However, Baroness Hale, who dissented on this issue, expressed the view that the reasoning in *Armitage* was open to serious question. She said that there was a body of opinion which considered that the law was not clear, and suggested that it was not 'an eccentric or unusual view' to find that the exclusion of liability for gross negligence was 'repugnant to the nature of a trust or contrary to public policy'.[464] Aitken has suggested that '[i]t seems clear that the blanket protection at present provided by *Armitage* itself to the delinquent trustee is likely to come under sustained attack when a suitable vehicle for the Supreme Court presents itself.'[465] It is also worth noting that even Lord Clarke, who acknowledged in *Spread Trustee* that *Armitage* correctly stated English law at the time the Privy Council delivered its decision, suggested that there was much to be said as a matter of policy for it not being permissible to exclude liability for breach of the duty to act with reasonable care and skill and without negligence.[466]

The Position in Ireland

At present there is no legislative regulation of trustee exemption clauses in Ireland. There is no reference to such clauses in the Trustee Act 1893 which still applies in this jurisdiction and there is no equivalent to section 61 of the Trustee Act 1925 which provides that if it appears to the court that a trustee is or may be personally liable for a breach of trust but has acted 'honestly and reasonably' and ought fairly to be excused for the breach, then the court may relieve him wholly or partly from personal liability.

Some indication of the likely attitude of the Irish courts towards this issue can be gleaned from the comments of Geoghegan J in the High Court decision

462. The Trusts (Amendment) (Guernsey) Law 1990 had come into force in 1991 and added the words 'or gross negligence'.
463. [2012] 2 AC 194, 223.
464. *Ibid.* at 244.
465. (2011) 127 LQR 503, 505. See also Loi [2011] Conv 521, 529.
466. *Ibid.* at 225.

of *Roberts v Kenny*[467] in relation to a clause in a will which directed that the defendant, who was a trustee of part of the testatrix's property, should not be accountable in any way for breaches of trust or misappropriation of assets. Although the issue did not arise in the context of the application before the court, Geoghegan J commented that while it might be that the defendant would be exempt from liability for negligent misappropriation of assets, he could not construe the will as exempting him from liability for deliberate dissipation. However, the tenor of the judgment of Murphy J in *Stacey v Branch*,[468] while it did not involve construction of an exemption clause, suggests that a settlor should be given a considerable degree of autonomy and flexibility in weighing up the extent of the obligation to be imposed on a trustee by the trust instrument. Having quoted a passage from *Snell's Equity*[469] which suggested that, however wide the language used, a trustee must act honestly and with ordinary prudence, Murphy J commented as follows:

> It is true to the extent that words such as 'absolute discretion' would not necessarily relieve a trustee from his duty to exercise reasonable care and prudence. On the other hand there is no doubt that an absolute owner of property can settle his affairs in such a way and on such terms as would relieve his trustees from the responsibility to exercise the degrees of care and prudence which would otherwise be inferred (see *Gisborne v Gisborne* (1877) 2 App Cas 300 and *Tabor v Brooks* (1878) 10 Ch D 273). At the end of the day the extent of the obligations imposed on a trustee or the degree to which he is relieved from responsibilities ordinarily assumed is a matter of the construction of the terms of the document under which the trustee is appointed.[470]

The most useful Irish authority on exemption clauses is the judgment of Charleton J in *Greene v Coady*.[471] The plaintiffs were the beneficiaries or potential beneficiaries of a company pension fund and claimed damages for breach of trust against the trustees for accepting an offer from the company to close its liability to contribute to the fund. They claimed, *inter alia*, that the failure of the trustees to seek a contribution demand for a higher sum to make up the funding deficit amounted to wilful default on their part. An exemption clause in the trust instrument provided that the trustees should not be liable in any manner whatsoever including for negligence,[472] but that any trustee should

467. [2000] 1 IR 33.
468. [1995] 2 ILRM 136. See further Buttimore (1996) 14 ILT (ns) 48.
469. Baker, *Snell's Equity* (29th ed., 1990) p.225. Now see McGhee, *Snell's Equity* (33rd ed., 2015).
470. [1995] 2 ILRM 136, 143.
471. [2015] 1 IR 385.
472. Although it provided that a trustee who was engaged in the business of providing a trusteeship service for payment should be liable for negligence.

be liable for wilful default. Charleton J rejected the plaintiffs' submission that the defendant trustees were not exonerated by the exemption clause set out in the trust deed. He stated that '[i]t is always possible for a trust deed to provide in advance for exemption from anything except the core obligation of trustees to exercise fidelity to the objects of the trust for the ultimate good of the beneficiaries through acting honestly and objectively and in good faith.'[473] He expressed the view that for the trustees to be liable for wilful default, the beneficiaries must show that the default 'can be truly characterised as a conscious breach of duty or a reckless breach of duty, in the sense of conscious awareness that is dismissed'.[474] Charleton J added that if that was wrong and wilful default simply meant a failure that was voluntary, then the judgment of Millet LJ in *Armitage v Nurse* confirmed that for liability to be established, that default must infringe the core duty of trustees to manage the trust honestly and in good faith for the benefit of the trustees. In the circumstances, he concluded in dismissing the plaintiffs' claim that the decision of the trustees to accept the company's offer in winding up the pension scheme was within the range of what might be considered a reasonable response to a very difficult situation and 'not one with which any court could take issue'.[475]

The Irreducible Core Obligations of Trusteeship

In view of the need for legislative reform in relation to trust law, the Law Reform Commission decided to embark on a comprehensive review of this whole area and the issue of the extent to which a trustee may be protected from liability by an exemption clause in a trust instrument was considered in detail in Chapter 7 of its Consultation Paper *Trust Law: General Proposals*.[476] Having set out and weighed up the arguments for and against statutory regulation in this area, the Law Reform Commission recommended that there was a need for regulation of trustee exemption clauses 'such that liability for breach of the irreducible core obligations of trustees may not be excluded.'[477] It concluded that approaches based on the distinction between negligence and gross negligence or on the conduct of the trustee would be of little practical assistance because of the difficulty in defining this distinction. It added that it considered that a preferable approach was for the issue of trustee exemption clauses to be addressed in relation to the standard of the irreducible core obligations of trusteeship in conjunction with the statutory duty of care which the Commission had recommended should be introduced.[478] The Law Reform Commission's recommendation that there should be regulation of trustee exemption clauses

473. [2015] 1 IR 385, 444.
474. *Ibid.* at 419.
475. *Ibid.* at 461.
476. Law Reform Commission Consultation Paper LRC CP 35-2005.
477. *Ibid.* at para.7.59.
478. The Commission recommended at para. 3.43 that a statutory duty of care founded on

such that liability for breach of the irreducible core obligations of trustees may not be excluded was repeated in its Report *Trust Law: General Proposals*[479] which was published in December 2008.

Some consideration has already been given to the concept of 'the irreducible core obligations of trustees' by both academics and members of the judiciary. Hayton has suggested that a duty of confidence imposed on a trustee and enforceable in a court is central to the trust concept.[480] As he stated, 'the beneficiaries' rights to enforce the trust and make the trustees account for their conduct with the correlative duties of the trustees to the beneficiaries are at the core of the trust'.[481] Hayton referred to the fundamental interrelated obligations of the trustees to disclose information and trust documents and to account to the beneficiaries and added that the duty to act in good faith cannot be excluded as this 'would make a nonsense of the trust relationship as an obligation of confidence'[482] and 'would empty the area of obligation so as to leave no room for any obligation'.[483] Hayton concluded as follows:

> There seems no reason in principle why a settlor should not have freedom to exempt his trustees from liability for losses flowing from negligence, covering ordinary and gross negligence, but not extending to losses flowing from recklessness in the sense of deliberate indifference to one's responsibilities because the latter would enable the trustees to act in bad faith and negate a core duty of the trustees.[484]

Millett LJ in his judgment in *Armitage v Nurse*[485] also accepted the submission that there is an irreducible core of obligations owed by trustees to beneficiaries and enforceable by them which is fundamental to the concept of a trust. However, in his view the duty of the trustees to perform the trusts honestly and in good faith for the benefit of the beneficiaries was all that was required and he did not accept that the core obligations included the duties of skill and care, prudence and diligence.

The Law Reform Commission's view of the irreducible core obligations of trusteeship was broadly similar to those of Hayton and of Millett LJ in *Armitage*. It recommended that it should not be possible to absolve a trustee from the duty to perform the obligations of trusteeship honestly and in good

---

a hybrid objective and subjective standard be introduced and suggested that section 1 of the English Trustee Act 2000 provided a useful model in this regard.

479. Law Reform Commission Report, *Trust Law: General Proposals* LRC 92-2008.
480. Hayton, 'The Irreducible Core Content of Trusteeship' in *Trends in Contemporary Trust Law* (ed. Oakley, 1996) p.47.
481. *Ibid.* See also *Armitage v Nurse* [1998] Ch 241, 253.
482. *Ibid.* at 57.
483. *Ibid.* at 58.
484. *Ibid.* at 59.
485. [1998] Ch 241.

faith.[486] In its view the honesty or dishonesty of the trustee's conduct will be a matter to be assessed by the court considering all the circumstances, including the role of the trustee and his experience, the nature of the trustee's conduct and the role of any other trustees. This recommendation is in line with the views expressed by Charleton J in *Greene v Coady*[487] that it is possible for a trust deed to provide an exemption from liability for anything except the core obligations of trustees to exercise fidelity to the objects of the trust 'through acting honestly and objectively and in good faith.'

It should be noted that in *Barnsley v Noble*[488] the Court of Appeal held that the exoneration clause as it applied to lay trustees should be construed as covering all categories of personal liability for loss to the trust including loss suffered as a result of breach of the self-dealing rule, in circumstances where there had been no wilful default in the sense of deliberately or consciously acting in a way which a defendant knew to be wrong. This suggests, as Virgo has stated, 'a blurring of the distinction between the nature of the breach and the fault relating to a particular breach of duty'[489] and is, in his view, inconsistent with a strict interpretation of fiduciary duties.

Should a Distinction be Drawn between Lay and Professional Trustees?

In the course of the debate before the House of Lords on the Trustee Bill 2000, Lord Goodhart expressed particular concern about the failure to limit reliance on exemption clauses by professional trustees. As he stated, '[h]owever negligent, lazy or misguided the trustees may have been, they cannot be held liable for the loss that they have caused to the trust fund'.[490] He added that if a friend or family member is acting as a trustee without remuneration, it may be fair to allow him to be exempted from personal liability for negligence but that 'there can be no justification, save in the most exceptional circumstances, for extending such an exemption to a paid professional trustee.'[491]

There is also judicial support for the principle, as Harman J put it in *Re Waterman's Will Trusts*,[492] that 'a paid trustee is expected to exercise a higher standard of diligence and knowledge than an unpaid trustee'. This concept was developed by Brightman J in *Bartlett v Barclays Trust Co. (No.1)*,[493] where he stated that a higher duty of care is clearly due from a trust corporation which carries on the specialised business of trust management and 'holds itself out …

---

486. Law Reform Commission Report, *Trust Law: General Proposals* LRC 92-2008 para. 4.29. It also recommended that it should not be possible to absolve a trustee from the duty to account to the beneficiaries of the trust (para. 4.32).
487. [2015] 1 IR 385, 444.
488. [2017] Ch 191.
489. Virgo, *The Principles of Equity and Trusts* (3rd ed., 2018) p.476.
490. Hansard (HL) Vo. 612, col. 383, 14 April 2000.
491. *Ibid.*
492. [1952] 2 All ER 1054, 1055. See also *Wight v Olswang* [1999] EWCA Civ 1309 at 6.
493. [1980] Ch 515.

as being above ordinary mortals'.[494] So, as Millett LJ commented in *Armitage v Nurse*,[495] the view is widely held that trustees who charge for their services and who as professionals 'would not dream of excluding liability for ordinary professional negligence' should not be able to rely on a trustee exemption clause which excludes liability for gross negligence.

The issue of whether a distinction should be drawn between professional and non-professional trustees in the context of statutory regulation of exemption clauses has been addressed by a number of law reform bodies. The Trust Law Committee,[496] in its Consultation Paper published in 1999, suggested that there was merit in trust corporations and professional trustees accepting the price of liability for negligence and insuring against such risk, with the premiums being reflected in the fees for the services provided.[497] The Law Commission in considering this question initially expressed the view that the current law was too deferential to trustees, particularly professional trustees, and it provisionally proposed that any statutory regulation of trustee exemption clauses should draw a distinction between professional and lay trustees[498] and that the former should not be able to rely on such a clause which excluded liability for breach of trust arising from negligence.[499] In reviewing the results of the consultation process in its subsequent Report *Trustee Exemption Clauses*[500] the Law Commission reported that most consultees agreed with the view that there should be some distinction between different types of trustee. However, rather than basing this distinction on the legislative definition contained in section 28 of the Trustee Act 2000 as had been suggested in the Consultation Paper,[501] it recommended that a distinction should be drawn between professional and lay trustees solely on the basis of remuneration.[502] Its final recommendation, that a rule of practice designed to secure settlor awareness of trustee exemption clauses be introduced, referred to a situation where 'any paid trustee' caused a clause excluding or limiting liability for negligence to be included in a trust.

When this issue was addressed by the Law Reform Commission in its Consultation Paper, although it gave extensive consideration to the practice advocated in other jurisdictions of drawing a distinction between professional and lay trustees, it ultimately concluded that this was not necessary as in its

494. *Ibid.* at 534.
495. [1998] Ch 241, 256.
496. A Committee set up in 1994 by a group of leading academics and practitioners to research weaknesses in trust law in England and Wales and to suggest ways to improve the law in this area. The consultation paper may be accessed at www.kcl.ac.uk/schools/law/research/tlc/consult.html.
497. (1999) para. 7.8.
498. Law Commission Consultation Paper No. 171 (2003) para. 4.39.
499. *Ibid.* at para. 4.85.
500. Law Commission Report No. 301 (2006).
501. Consultation Paper No. 171 (2003) para. 4.37 distinguished trustees 'acting in a professional capacity' from those not so acting.
502. Law Commission Report No. 301 (2006) para. 4.29.

view the issue was addressed by the flexible standard of care recommended by it.[503] The different standards of care, knowledge and expertise expected of professional and non-professional trustees are reflected in the statutory duty of care set out in section 1 of the English Trustee Act which the Law Reform Commission also favoured adopting.[504] This section provides that a trustee will be expected to exercise such care and skill as is reasonable in the circumstances having regard in particular 'to any special knowledge or experience that they have or hold themselves out as having, and if they act as trustee in the course of a business or profession, to any special knowledge or experience that it is reasonable to expect of a person acting in the course of that kind of business or profession.' A similar conclusion to that set out above was reached by the Law Reform Commission in its final report in 2008 where it simply set out that the proposed statutory provision providing for the relieving of liability for breach of trust should not distinguish between professional and lay trustees.[505]

Is There a Need for Statutory Regulation?

As Tuckey LJ correctly pointed out in *Baker v J.E. Clark Co. (Transport) UK Ltd*,[506] trustee exemption clauses 'are common in trust deeds nowadays'. The arguments for and against statutory regulation in this area are fairly clear. It is certainly likely that it would lead to the imposition of higher charges for the work of professional trustees and it could result in a reluctance on the part of such trustees to act in this capacity. It has also been suggested that a trust as a private law institution derives its terms from the directions of the settlor[507] and that settlors should have autonomy to dictate the terms of a trust which they set up.[508] Furthermore, it can be asserted that the current judicial attitude is that exemption clauses should be restrictively construed and that therefore liability will only be excluded by clear and unambiguous words.[509]

However, as against this, it can also be argued that there may be a lack of awareness on the part of settlors that trustee exemption clauses are routinely included in trust instruments.[510] While it might have been thought that greater

503. Consultation Paper LRC CP 35-2005, para. 7.74.
504. *Ibid.* at para. 3.43; Report No. 92 (2008) para. 3.15.
505. Report No. 92 (2008) para. 4.47.
506. [2006] EWCA Civ 464 at [5].
507. Law Commission Consultation Paper No. 171 (2003) para. 2.8.
508. Law Reform Commission Consultation Paper LRC CP 35-2005 para. 7.57.
509. *Armitage v Nurse* [1998] Ch 241, 255; *Bogg v Raper* [1998] EWCA Civ 661 at [28]. This principle has been specifically set out in the provisions of s. 13(2) of the draft Trustee Bill 2008 annexed to the Law Reform Commission Report No. 92 of 2008 which provides that 'any exclusion or limitation … (a) shall be drafted in clear, unequivocal and unambiguous terms'.
510. It should be noted that s. 13(2)(b) of the draft Trustee Bill 2008 provides that any exclusion or limitation 'shall be brought to the attention of the settler prior to the execution of the instrument creating the trust.'

regulation would lead to a transfer of trusts to jurisdictions which do not restrict reliance on exemption clauses, the experience in Jersey and Guernsey, which have already imposed statutory regulation, would appear to suggest that this is not the case.[511] In addition, it can be questioned whether as a matter of policy trustees, particularly professional trustees, should be able to escape liability for grossly negligent or even negligent acts. As the Law Commission commented in its Consultation Paper, 'if the terms of the instrument do not impose sufficiently stringent obligations on the persons referred to as trustees, it may be that the instrument cannot be accurately described as a trust at all.'[512] A similar point was made by McCormack when he commented that clauses in a trust instrument which permit trustees to engage in wrongdoing to the detriment of the beneficiaries are at odds with the key concept of trusteeship.[513]

While the Law Commission in England ultimately recommended that there should be no statutory regulation of trustee exemption clauses,[514] there are convincing arguments to support the contrary view as set out above. On balance it is submitted that there is a strong case for some form of statutory regulation and the Law Commission's earlier assertion that the current legal position is too deferential to professional trustees in particular is one that has commanded support from both academics and members of the judiciary.[515]

It is likely that statutory regulation will follow in Ireland, perhaps along the lines suggested by the Law Reform Commission and set out in the draft Trustee Bill 2008 annexed to the Report.[516] However, it must be asked whether the model of regulation proposed is the most workable in practice and whether it will strike an appropriate balance between protecting the rights and interests of settlors and beneficiaries. There are two key questions which must be addressed in this context, first whether regulation should prevent reliance on exemption clauses specifically on the basis of a trustee's conduct or whether the focus instead should be on the irreducible core obligations of trusteeship. Secondly, it will be necessary to determine whether to draw a distinction between the position of lay and professional trustees and if so, by what mechanism.

In relation to this first issue both options give rise to difficulties of definition and there is no consensus on the question of whether it would be appropriate in this context to draw a distinction between negligence and gross negligence. In the course of his judgment in *Armitage v Nurse*[517] Millett LJ said that it would be very surprising if the law drew the line between liability for ordinary

511. See the comments in Law Commission Consultation Paper No. 171 (2003) p.vii.
512. No. 171 (2003) para. 2.9.
513. McCormack [1998] Conv 100, 113.
514. Report No. 301 (2006).
515. Smith has commented (2004) 26 DULJ 129, 143 that 'there is a strong case for curbing the use of trustee exemption clauses by professional trustees.' As noted above, in *Barraclough v Mell* [2006] WTLR 203, 218 Judge Behrens stated that this was an area of law ripe for reform.
516. Law Reform Commission Report, *Trust Law: General Proposals* LRC 92-2008.
517. [1998] Ch 241, 254.

negligence and gross negligence as the difference had been regarded as merely one of degree and 'English lawyers have always had a healthy disrespect for [this] distinction.' The Scottish Law Commission in its Discussion Paper on *Breach of Trust*,[518] although it expressed the view that gross negligence was a workable concept, suggested that it might be impossible to draw a hard and fast line between negligence and gross negligence. It concluded that allowing lay trustees immunity for gross negligence would go too far and it ultimately recommended that such trustees should only be able to rely on clauses which excluded liability for negligence and not gross negligence.[519] The Law Commission was of the view that the definition of gross negligence was 'at best imprecise'[520] and concluded that it did not consider the concept sufficiently clear or distinctive so as to form the basis of regulation of trustee exemption clauses.[521] However, it concluded that the expansion of professional negligence in many areas made it logical and consistent to deny professional trustees resort to exemption clauses when their conduct can be so characterised. The Law Reform Commission suggested that while it might be said that the distinction between negligence and gross negligence presents little difficulty, in practice it is difficult to define with precision and it suggested that a clearer formula be introduced to distinguish between classes of trustees' conduct.[522] Despite these divergent views it has not been suggested that the concept of negligence *simpliciter* gives rise to definitional difficulties and the Law Commission provisionally recommended in its Consultation Paper that professional trustees should not be able to rely on any clause excluding liability for breach of trust arising from negligence.[523] This is in many respects the clearest solution and one which is in line with the standards expected of professionals in other fields of work.

The alternative approach, namely to provide for regulation of trustee exemption clauses so that liability for breach of the irreducible core obligations of trustees may not be excluded, also gives rise to difficulties of definition. However, as pointed out above, there is some consensus that this should be interpreted as involving at a minimum a duty to perform the obligations of trusteeship honestly and in good faith and to account to the beneficiaries of the trust. Ultimately the question, certainly in relation to professional trustees, will be of where to draw the line in terms of their conduct and the approach suggested by the Law Reform Commission appears to strike the right balance. It recommends in section 12(1) of the draft Trustee Bill 2008 annexed to its Report that: '[e]very trustee shall, as a fiduciary, perform the trust honestly

518. Discussion Paper No. 123 (2003).
519. *Ibid.* at para. 3.46.
520. Consultation Paper No. 171 (2003) para. 4.77.
521. *Ibid.* at para. 4.78.
522. Consultation Paper LRC CP 35-2005 para. 7.78.
523. Consultation Paper No. 171 (2003) para. 4.85.

and in good faith for the benefit of the beneficiaries, and any provision that purports to exclude or limit this fiduciary duty is void.'[524]

The second and related question is whether and, if so, how to distinguish between lay and professional trustees in this context. There seems little doubt that the drawing of some distinction is desirable and the real question is whether to impose separate standards or to simply link the question of liability to the statutory duty of care. If the former approach is adopted, the question of how to define a 'professional trustee' arises. As noted above, while the Law Commission provisionally favoured the definition of a trustee acting in a professional capacity adopted in section 28(5) of the Trustee Act 2000,[525] it ultimately opted for a distinction being drawn solely on the basis of remuneration.[526] Again, the Law Reform Commission's recommendation to take the latter approach avoids difficult definitional issues and should ensure that higher standards will be expected of professional trustees. It remains to be seen whether the draft legislation proposed will be enacted but it is submitted that if so it will go some way towards restoring an appropriate measure of confidence in the conduct of professional trustees in particular.

VARIATION OF TRUSTS

As a general principle a trustee must administer a trust according to the terms laid down in the trust instrument and any deviation will constitute a breach of trust.[527] Until recent legislative reform in this area[528] a court could not, except in limited circumstances, sanction the performance of acts by the trustees which were not authorised by the trust instrument or any variation in its terms and this led to enormous practical problems.

The question of variation of the terms of a trust instrument after it has come into operation is one which has assumed increasing importance especially in view of the need to adapt the terms of trusts to meet changing taxation requirements. As Lord Denning MR commented in *Re Weston's Settlements*,[529] '[n]early every variation that has come before the court has tax avoidance for

524. Section 13(3) also provides that any provision in a trust which purports to exclude or limit the duty to provide information to beneficiaries set out in section 14 of the Bill shall be void.
525. *Ibid.* at para. 4.37.
526. Law Commission Report No. 301 (2006) para. 4.29.
527. As Marshall JA commented in the decision of the Newfoundland Court of Appeal in *Boy Scouts of Canada v Doyle* (1997) 149 DLR (4th) 22, 63, '[i]t is, therefore, a basic tenet of law that, in the absence of authorization conferred upon them in the trust settlement, trustees may not appropriate to themselves the right to vary the terms of the trust settled upon them, or assume powers that have not been conferred upon them'.
528. Sections 23 and 24 of the Land and Conveyancing Law Reform Act 2009.
529. [1969] 1 Ch 223, 245.

its principal object'. In addition, it may be necessary, or in any event, highly desirable to alter the original terms of a trust for a variety of other reasons and the courts must attempt to steer a path between giving effect to the intentions of a testator or settlor expressed in the trust instrument and seeking to envisage how these individuals might have wished the instrument to be altered in the light of changed circumstances.

Variation of the Terms of a Trust Without Court Approval

In certain situations the terms of the trust may be varied without court approval. Where the beneficiaries are all of full age and capacity and together are absolutely entitled to the trust property, they may terminate the trust and require that it be distributed in accordance with their directions, a principle sometimes referred to as the rule in *Saunders v Vautier*,[530] although the decision in that case is expressed in slightly narrower terms.[531] There the testator bequeathed stock on trust to accumulate the dividends until a beneficiary attained the age of 25 and directed that the capital and the accumulated dividends should then be transferred to the beneficiary. When the latter reached the age of 21, he successfully claimed that he was entitled to call for the immediate transfer of the entire fund.

In practice this principle has been interpreted as meaning that any one or more adult beneficiaries who are of sound mind and entitled to the whole beneficial interest under a trust can direct the trustees to transfer the trust property to them and put an end to the trust.

A further situation in which the terms of the trust may be varied without the sanction of the court is where an express power of advancement contained in the trust instrument is exercised by the trustees in order to secure a capital advance to the remainderman.

Variation of the Terms of a Trust With Court Approval before Legislative Change

Before recent legislative intervention in this area, as a general principle a court would not permit trustees to deviate from the terms of a trust in performing their duties. However, variation of a trust scheme might be sanctioned by the court in certain limited circumstances.[532] Court approval might be sought to vary the terms of a trust where there were unborn or minor beneficiaries who could not consent to a variation which might be desirable,[533] or to permit the

530. (1841) Cr & Ph 240.
531. See *Wharton v Masterman* [1895] AC 186, 198 *per* Lord Davey.
532. *Chapman v Chapman* [1954] AC 429, 445 *per* Lord Simonds LC. See also *per* Lord Asquith at 469.
533. As Huband JA commented in delivering the judgment of the Manitoba Court of Appeal in *Teichman v Teichman Estate* (1996) 134 DLR (4th) 155, 157 in relation to the rule

payment of maintenance to minor beneficiaries where no provision was made to this effect by the trust instrument.[534] The court also had an inherent power to sanction variation of a trust instrument in cases of necessity to avoid the destruction of, or ensure the preservation of, trust property, e.g. to effect essential repairs to a building to save it from collapse. This 'emergency or salvage' jurisdiction might be exercised where some crisis unforeseen by the settlor or testator arose and it was necessary for the trustees to vary the terms of the trust so as to enable them to take action where the consent of the beneficiaries could not be obtained, often because they were not yet in existence or were under a disability.[535]

In addition, the court had authority to sanction a variation in the terms of a trust in order to effect a compromise of disputes as between the claims of various beneficiaries. It should be noted that in *Chapman v Chapman*[536] the majority of the House of Lords adopted a narrow definition of the word 'compromise' in this context and partly as a result of this decision, legislation was introduced in England in the form of the Variation of Trusts Act 1958. This legislation provides that a court may, if it thinks fit, approve an arrangement varying or revoking a trust or enlarging the powers of the trustees on the application of defined classes of beneficiaries or potential beneficiaries.[537]

Legislative Reform

In its Report *The Variation of Trusts*[538] published in 2000, the Law Reform Commission recommended the introduction of legislation broadly similar to that introduced in England by the Variation of Trusts Act 1958. The government intended to provide legislation permitting the variation of trusts by means of an amendment to the Civil Law (Miscellaneous Provisions) Bill 2006[539] but it was ultimately introduced in the Land and Conveyancing Law Reform Act 2009.

Section 23 of the Act of 2009 contains the required definitions, while section 24 provides the courts with a statutory mechanism for approving variations of

in *Saunders v Vautier*, 'unanimity [is] required, except that the court could consent on behalf of the beneficiaries who were minors or otherwise lacked capacity or who were as yet unborn, so long as the arrangement was for the benefit of those beneficiaries'.

534. *Re Collins* (1886) 32 Ch D 229.
535. See, e.g. *Neill v Neill* [1904] 1 IR 513; *Re Johnson's Settlement* [1944] IR 529; *Bank of Ireland v Geoghegan* [1955-56] Ir Jur Rep 7.
536. [1954] AC 429.
537. As Mummery LJ commented in the decision of the Court of Appeal in *Goulding v James* [1997] 2 All ER 239, although the jurisdiction provided for in the Act has been invoked 'thousands of times' there have been 'remarkably few reported cases on its construction'. In *Goulding,* the court approved an arrangement varying the terms of a trust which was undoubtedly for the benefit of unborn beneficiaries although extrinsic evidence had been given to the effect that this variation would run contrary to the testatrix's original intentions. See further Luxton (1997) 60 MLR 719.
538. LRC 63-2000.
539. 184 Seanad Debates col. 285, 20 June 2006.

the terms of trusts.[540] Applications should be brought by special summons as required by the Rules of the Superior Courts (Land and Conveyancing Law Reform Act 2009) 2010.[541]

The application to the court must be made by an appropriate person in relation to a relevant trust,[542] namely a trustee, a beneficiary or any other person who the court considers appropriate to approve an 'arrangement' for the benefit of a 'relevant person'. The nature of the arrangement must be specified in the application and in this context 'arrangement' means varying, revoking or resettling the trust or varying, enlarging or restricting the powers of the trustees. For this purpose 'relevant person' means a person who has a vested or contingent interest under a trust but who is incapable of assenting to an arrangement by reason of lack of capacity, an unborn person, a person whose identity, existence or whereabouts cannot be established by taking reasonable measures, or any other person with a contingent interest. The court shall not hear an application made to it in respect of a relevant trust unless it is satisfied that the applicant has given notice in writing of the application to the Revenue Commissioners and to such persons as may be prescribed by Rules of Court at least two weeks before the hearing of the application.[543]

Section 24(4) provides that the court may make an order approving the arrangement specified in the application if it is satisfied that the carrying out of the arrangement would be for the benefit of the relevant person specified in the application and any other relevant person, or may refuse the application where the court is not satisfied that the arrangement would be for the benefit of such persons, or where 'the Revenue Commissioners have satisfied the court that the application is substantially motivated by a desire to avoid, or reduce the incidence of, tax.' In determining whether an arrangement would be for the benefit of a relevant person, the court may have regard to any benefit or detriment, financial or otherwise, that may accrue to that person directly or indirectly in consequence of the arrangement.[544] It remains to be seen how often the Revenue Commissioners will seek to oppose proposed arrangements on the grounds set out above. However, where they can establish that an application is 'substantially motivated' by a desire to avoid tax, it would appear that the court will have to refuse it and this provision may significantly curtail the extent to which variation schemes may be approved.

Laffoy J considered aspects of the operation of this statutory power to

540. By virtue of s. 3 of the Act of 2009. In this context 'court' means the High Court, or the Circuit Court when exercising the jurisdiction conferred on it by the Third Schedule to the Courts (Supplemental Provisions) Act 1961.
541. See rule 4(iii) of SI No. 149 of 2010.
542. This definition extends to trusts whether arising before or after the introduction of the legislation but does not include a charitable trust or an occupational pension scheme.
543. Section 24(2) of the Land and Conveyancing Law Reform Act 2009.
544. Section 24(5) of the Land and Conveyancing Law Reform Act 2009.

approve variations to a trust in her judgments in *W. v M.*[545] She noted that section 24(3) of the Act of 2009 provides that the court might hear an application made to it under the section otherwise than in public and given that the position of a person of unsound mind not so found and of infants was under consideration in the proceedings, she considered it appropriate to hear the matter *in camera* and to redact the judgments delivered appropriately. Laffoy J concluded that the trust created by the trust document in the matter before the court was a 'relevant trust' within the meaning of section 23 and that, in accordance with section 24(1), the court had jurisdiction to entertain an application for an order to approve an arrangement to vary, revoke or resettle the trust for the benefit of a relevant person, 'provided the arrangement has been assented to by all of the persons beneficially interested in the trust who, in broad terms, are identifiable and capable of assenting.'[546]

The trust in question related to a life assurance policy in which the lives assured were a married couple with children, two of whom were named as beneficiaries in default of the exercise of a power of appointment by the survivor of the couple. The father died and the mother, who suffered from dementia, lacked the capacity to exercise the power of appointment.[547] The premiums, which were substantial, were paid in equal shares by the children who stood to benefit. When one of these children died, his widow, the plaintiff, continued to pay a half share of the premiums. However, in accordance with the terms of the original trust, on the death of the mother, the share which would have gone to the deceased child would revert to the mother's estate. The application for a variation was brought to ensure that the widow of the deceased child would benefit as his personal representative. All the relevant parties, the plaintiff and the couple's remaining children, including one who was prepared to assent on behalf of her mother, consented to the proposed variation. However, the initial variation proposed did not, in the view of Laffoy J, achieve the result which the parties intended and the fact that the mother was the 'relevant person' for whose benefit the plaintiff was seeking to have the arrangement approved was not specified in the application, as required by section 24(1). She said that it was open to the court to permit an application of this nature to be amended and an amended scheme was submitted. In a subsequent judgment Laffoy J made an order approving the arrangement embodied in the amended scheme of arrangement pursuant to section 24(4) of the Act of 2009.[548] She accepted that the plaintiff, as personal representative of the deceased child, was an 'appropriate person' within the meaning of section 23 and concluded that the evidence before the court indicated beyond the balance of probabilities that, if

---

545. [2010] IEHC 505 and [2011] IEHC 217.
546. [2010] IEHC 505 at [2.2]
547. This power of appointment could not in any event under the terms of the original trust have been exercised in favour of the plaintiff, who was the deceased child's widow. See [2010] IEHC 505 at [6.1].
548. [2011] IEHC 217.

she had the capacity to do so, the mother would have assented to the amended scheme of arrangement. While some uncertainty surrounded the question of the ultimate destination of the mother's assets after her death, Laffoy J referred to the fact that whether she died testate or intestate her surviving children would benefit and they had all assented to the proposed variation.

The judgments of Laffoy J in *W. v M.* illustrate that some flexibility may be necessary if the legislation is to function effectively, particularly where a beneficiary is incapable of assenting to a variation. Her pragmatic yet careful approach is to be welcomed and her judgments provide useful guidance in relation to how some of the difficulties which may occur in practice in relation to such applications may be resolved. This legislative reform should address one of the most pressing issues of concern in this area and the fact that it was introduced on its own before the long awaited comprehensive trust law reform legislation gives some indication of how urgently it was needed. While it may take some time for the various aspects of the legislation to be tested before the courts, if experience in England is anything to go by,[549] it will be a most welcome innovation.

LIKELY FUTURE DEVELOPMENTS IN RELATION TO THE ADMINISTRATION OF TRUSTS

Lord Nicholls writing extra-judicially has commented that, '[t]imes change and with them the problems confronting trustees'.[550] The Law Commission of England and Wales has also pointed out that 'trusteeship is an increasingly specialised task that often requires professional skills that … trustees may not have'.[551] As the range of choices in relation to investment of trust funds has increased, so have the difficulties inherent in the management of trust investments which is becoming an increasingly technical area requiring specialist expertise. However, as was noted above, the circumstances in which a trustee may delegate have not kept pace with such developments, with the result that a trustee may find himself trying to make investment decisions in

549. As noted above in *Goulding v James* [1997] 2 All ER 239, 246, Mummery LJ commented that the equivalent legislation has been invoked 'thousands of times'.
550. Nicholls (1995) 9 Trust Law Int 71. As Legatt LJ commented in *Nestle v National Westminster Bank plc* [1993] 1 WLR 1260, 1281, 'in Victorian times . . . little was demanded of a trustee beyond the safeguarding of the trust fund by refraining from improvident investment. This process was no doubt also intended to save beneficiaries from trouble and anxiety, or what is now called "hassle"'.
551. Consultation Paper No. 146 on *Trustees' Powers and Duties* (1997) para. 1.1. The Commission commented that 'as a result of changes both in the way in which financial markets operate and the purposes for which trusts are now employed, the present law is no longer always adequate to enable trustees to administer a trust to the best advantage of the beneficiaries or the objects of the trust'.

circumstances where he lacks the knowledge to make them in a fully informed way.

Partly as a result of such factors, increasing numbers of professionals are being appointed to act as trustees. This in itself leads to difficulties and as Kenny has commented, 'Equity's rules are unsuited to modern professional trusts'.[552] As she points out, no professional trustee would act unless paid for doing so and despite this fact trusts are still governed 'by rules derived from a social era when trustees were generously donating their time and skill to the administration of another's property'. Undoubtedly the tasks performed by professional trustees require considerable skill and experience for which they are well remunerated and as Kenny suggests, in view of this, beneficiaries of modern trusts should be regarded as entitled to a high standard of professionalism.

There have been suggestions made in the context of a trustee's duty to invest to the effect that a higher standard of care is expected of a professional trustee. So, in *Re Waterman's Will Trusts*[553] Harman J stated *obiter* that a higher standard of diligence and knowledge is required and this was confirmed by Brightman J in *Bartlett v Barclays Bank Trust Co. Ltd*,[554] in which he said that a greater duty of care is owed by a professional trustee such as a trust corporation which carries on the specialised business of trust management. However, in *Nestle v National Westminster Bank plc*,[555] while the defendant was a professional institution, Legatt LJ merely stated that 'the essence of the bank's duty was to take such steps as a prudent businessman would have taken to maintain and increase the value of the trust fund'.[556] When one considers the skill which a professional trustee professes to have and the fact that such a trustee will be financially rewarded, often quite substantially, for acting in this capacity, the reluctance of the Court of Appeal to impose a higher standard is surprising.

It should also be stressed that there have been some signs to indicate that the judiciary are aware that traditional principles developed in the context of family trusts are no longer adequate or suitable to deal with modern commercial trusts. The most useful statement to this effect is contained in the speech of Lord Browne-Wilkinson in *Target Holdings Ltd v Redferns*[557] in the following terms:

> [I]n my judgment it is in any event wrong to lift wholesale the detailed rules developed in the context of traditional trusts and then seek to apply them to trusts of a quite different kind. In the modern world the trust has become a valuable device in commercial and financial dealings. The fundamental principles of equity apply as much to such trusts as they do to the traditional trusts in relation to which those principles were originally

552. Kenny (1996) 146 NLJ 348.
553. [1952] 2 All ER 1054, 1055.
554. [1980] Ch 515.
555. [1993] 1 WLR 1260.
556. *Ibid.* at 1283.
557. [1996] 1 AC 421, 435.

> formulated. But in my judgment, it is important, if the trust is not to be rendered commercially useless, to distinguish between the basic principles of trust law and those specialist rules developed in relation to traditional trusts which are applicable only to such trusts and the rationale of which has no application to trusts of a quite different kind.

As Nolan has commented, drawing a distinction between different types of trusts might be justifiable in principle as it recognises that the relationship between trustee and beneficiary and therefore their correlative rights can vary widely from one context to another.[558] Hayton has also suggested that 'the species of pensions trust should be regarded as having evolved from the trust genus as a drastically different species from the species of traditional family trust'.[559] On the other hand Ulph argues that the unity of trust principles is already under threat due to the wide variety of contexts in which these principles operate and suggests that the approach in *Target* strains this unity even further.[560] Finally, it should be noted that while the House of Lords in that case concluded that traditional principles should not apply to the case before them, as Capper points out the *dicta* of Lord Browne-Wilkinson offers little real insight into how the rules relating to commercial trusts should differ from those applicable to traditional trusts.[561]

One distinct area in which the established principles relating to the administration of trusts are clearly of doubtful utility is in relation to pension trusts. However, even in this context there has been considerable judicial debate in England about the efficacy of developing new principles which will take into account the different nature of such trusts. In *McDonald v Horn*[562] Hoffmann LJ acknowledged that 'pension funds are a special form of trust' and in *Mettoy Pension Trustees Ltd v Evans*[563] Warner J pointed out that beneficiaries under a pension scheme are not volunteers and said that in construing the trust instrument it was important to bear in mind the origin of the beneficiaries' rights under it. However, in *Cowan v Scargill*,[564] Megarry VC stated that he could 'see no reason for holding that different principles apply to pension fund trusts from those which apply to other trusts'. This point was reiterated by Rattee J in *Wilson v Law Debenture Trust Corporation plc*,[565] where he commented that 'in general the principles applicable to private trusts as a matter of trust law apply equally to pension schemes'. In *Wilson* counsel for the plaintiffs submitted that in the case of a pension scheme, in the absence of express provision to

558. Nolan [1996] LMCLQ 161, 163.
559. Hayton [2005] Conv 229, 245.
560. Ulph (1995) 9 Trust Law Int 86, 88.
561. Capper [1997] Conv 14, 22.
562. [1995] 1 All ER 961, 973.
563. [1990] 1 WLR 1587, 1618.
564. [1985] Ch 270, 290.
565. [1995] 2 All ER 337, 347.

the contrary, a trustee should be bound to give reasons for the exercise of the discretion conferred upon him, as it would seem unreasonable that members of the scheme who had bought their interests could not see whether the trustee had exercised his discretion properly. However, Rattee J rejected this argument in the following terms:

> It would in my judgment be wrong in principle to hold that the long-established principles of trust law as to the exercise by trustees of discretions conferred on them by their trust instruments, in the context of which parties to a pension scheme such as the present entered into those schemes, no longer apply to them and that the trustees are under more onerous obligations to account to their beneficiaries than they could have appreciated when appointed, on the basis of the relevant trust law as it has stood for so long.[566]

Despite the rather restrictive terms of this judgment, it can be argued that the proposition put forward by counsel for the plaintiffs seemed eminently reasonable in the context of a pension scheme in which the 'beneficiaries' were individuals who had paid for their interest in the trust. The decision of the Court of Appeal in *Re Londonderry's Settlement*[567] to the effect that trustees are not obliged to disclose to the beneficiaries their reasons for acting seems out of touch with the commercial realities of modern pension trusts and it is likely that the question will be revisited in this context.[568] As noted above, the approach of the Privy Council in *Schmidt v Rosewood Trust Ltd*[569] was to suggest that the greater the strength of the claimant's interest in the trust, the more likely it is that a court would exercise its 'inherent jurisdiction to supervise, and if necessary to intervene in, the administration of trusts'. Hayton has suggested that the courts, taking their lead from *Schmidt*, should insist on pension trustees providing reasons for their decisions and be more prepared to intervene in the affairs of such trusts.[570] It should also be noted that in England, section 35 of the Pensions Act 1995 now requires pension fund trustees to disclose their investment policy and this move towards greater accountability is clearly a desirable step.

---

566. *Ibid.* at 348. However, note the comments of Lord Walker writing extra-judicially, 'Some Trust Principles in the Pensions Context' in *Trends in Contemporary Trust Law* (ed. Oakley, 1996) p. 131 that this conclusion seems 'to treat *Re Londonderry's Trusts* as a rather more precise and definitive statement of principle than it may be'.
567. [1965] Ch 918.
568. See the comments of Lord Browne-Wilkinson in a paper published in February 1992 by the Leo Cussen Institute (referred to by Balmford J in *Crowe v Stevedoring Employees Retirement Fund Pty Ltd* [2003] VSC 316 at [34]) where he suggested that the principles set out in *Re Londonderry's Settlement* were wholly inappropriate to pensions schemes.
569. [2003] 2 AC 709, 729.
570. Hayton [2005] Conv 229, 245.

Finally, it is submitted that any piecemeal attempts at reform which can be effected by judicial decisions are likely to be insufficient to properly address the substantial practical difficulties facing trustees required to administer modern trusts. Furthermore, it is clearly necessary to introduce a greater degree of accountability for the benefit of beneficiaries of certain types of trusts who are not volunteers and who are effectively paying for the trustees' services; as Kenny has argued such individuals should be regarded as 'clients, entitled to a high level of service'.[571] While there is some merit in the argument that for the sake of certainty the same principles should apply to all types of trust, it must also be borne in mind that the reality is that modern trusts are now called upon to fulfil many diverse functions. This is just one of the many thorny issues which will have to be addressed when the long-awaited legislative reform of trust law is undertaken.

571. Kenny (1996) 146 NLJ 348.

CHAPTER 14

Injunctions

INTRODUCTION

At common law the usual remedy where a plaintiff succeeded in his action was an award of damages; this form of relief was often inadequate or inappropriate and equity supplemented the legal remedies available by developing alternative types of remedy such as the injunction. An injunction is an order restraining the person to whom it is directed from carrying out a specified act or requiring him to perform such an act; it is a most flexible and versatile form of remedy and is used with increasing frequency today.

The injunction developed initially as a means of doing justice in cases where the traditional common law remedy of damages could not achieve such an aim. As the Court of Chancery grew in stature, the device of the injunction was even employed to restrain the enforcement of the judgments of the common law courts. This led to a bitter dispute between the two systems, a dispute which was resolved by King James I, following the *Earl of Oxford's case*,[1] in favour of the Court of Chancery. A distinction was drawn between the grant of equitable injunctions in the so-called 'exclusive jurisdiction', i.e. in circumstances where it is sought to protect an equitable right, for example the right of a beneficiary under a trust, and the grant of injunctions in the 'auxiliary jurisdiction' where the remedy is used to protect a legal right. Over a period of time this auxiliary jurisdiction became widely used and eventually power was given to the common law courts themselves to grant injunctions by the Common Law Procedure (Ireland) Act 1856.[2] Around this time jurisdiction was also given to the Court of Chancery to award damages in addition to or in lieu of an injunction by the Chancery Amendment Act 1858, known as Lord Cairns' Act, and from a procedural point of view the two systems grew even closer together. The enactment of the Judicature (Ireland) Act 1877 effectively brought about a fusion of procedure and section 28(8) provided that the court was empowered to grant interlocutory relief 'whenever it was just and convenient to do so'.

Debate has raged ever since over the question of whether the Judicature Act and its successors effected any enlargement of the court's power to grant an

1. (1615) 1 Rep Ch 1.
2. The suggestion was made in the context of the equivalent English legislation, the Common Law Procedure Act 1854, that it resulted in the common law courts having more extensive jurisdiction in this area than the Court of Chancery: *Quartz Hill Consolidated Gold Mining Co. v Beall* (1882) 20 Ch D 501, 509 *per* Baggallay LJ.

injunction. In *Moore v Attorney General*[3] Murnaghan J expressed the view that the Act 'extends the principles upon which jurisdiction was formerly exercised by the Court of Chancery' and Jessel MR commented in *Beddow v Beddow*[4] that the courts now had unlimited power to grant an injunction whenever it was just and convenient to do so. However, the better view would seem to be that the legislation did not confer any additional jurisdiction on the court. As Brett LJ commented in *North London Railway Co. v Great Northern Railway Co.*,[5] 'if no court had the power of issuing an injunction before the Judicature Act, no part of the High Court has power to issue an injunction now'. This view has been accepted by the House of Lords in England,[6] and despite the comment of Murnaghan J in *Moore* it would seem to be the logical conclusion to reach.

This issue was also considered by MacMenamin J in his judgment in the Supreme Court in *ACC Loan Management Ltd v Rickard*,[7] where he addressed the question of whether the words 'just or convenient' in section 28(8) of the Supreme Court of Judicature (Ireland) Act 1877, which, *inter alia*, made provision for the appointment of a receiver by way of equitable execution, were intended to give the courts wider powers than they had held prior to the enactment of the Judicature Act. In the course of his judgment, he pointed out that the courts in this jurisdiction have allowed for incremental development of the terms 'just or convenient' in the context of the grant of Mareva injunctions and he said that section 28(8) must now be interpreted in order to make allowances for 'changes in the law' in this State, as provided for in section 6 of the Interpretation Act 2005. However, in resolving the issue before the court he stated that '[t]he persuasive dicta cited from the neighbouring jurisdiction do not, in fact, require this Court to arrive at the conclusion that law and equity have been fused.'[8]

Injunctions may be classified in a number of ways, first as between those which impose negative and positive obligations. The most common form of injunction falls into the former category and is known as a prohibitory injunction, namely one which restrains the performance or continuance of a wrongful act. The latter form of order is known as a mandatory injunction and has the effect of requiring the performance of an act.

A further classification can be made between interim and interlocutory injunctions on the one hand and perpetual injunctions on the other hand.[9]

---

3. [1927] IR 569, 580. See also the *dicta* of Chatterton VC in *Cork Corporation v Rooney* (1881) 17 LR Ir 191, 200.
4. (1878) 9 Ch D 89, 93. See also *Argyll v Argyll* [1967] Ch 302.
5. (1883) 11 QBD 30, 36-37. See also *Day v Brownrigg* (1878) 10 Ch D 294, 307 *per* James LJ.
6. *Gouriet v Union of Post Office Workers* [1978] AC 435; *The Siskina* [1979] AC 210; *South Carolina Insurance Co. v Assurance Maatschappij 'de Zeven Provincien' NV* [1987] AC 24.
7. [2019] IESC 29.
8. *Ibid.* at [71].
9. It should be noted that in England and Wales the term 'interim injunction' is now

The former are granted prior to the trial of an action; an interim injunction is obtained for a limited period and will have effect only until a further order is made and is often, although not invariably, sought on an *ex parte* basis.[10] It is well established that an order such as an interim or occasionally an interlocutory injunction, obtained on the basis of an *ex parte* application, may be set aside on the ground of breach of the duty of full and frank disclosure.[11] In determining whether there has been a failure to make sufficient disclosure, the court will have regard to the factors set out by Clarke J in his judgment in *Bambrick v Cobley*,[12] considered in more detail below in the context of Mareva injunctions, which include the materiality of the facts not disclosed and the extent to which it may be said that the plaintiff is culpable in respect of the failure to disclose.

An interlocutory injunction will have effect until the final hearing of the action takes place and its purpose is to maintain the *status quo* between the parties as far as possible until the final determination of the issues in dispute by the court. A perpetual injunction on the other hand will only be granted at the trial of the action where a plaintiff has established a right and the actual or threatened infringement of that right by the defendant. In practice, the order amounts to a final determination of the issues in dispute by the court although it does not mean that the injunction will necessarily last perpetually as its name suggests.

Finally, a distinction may be drawn between *quia timet* injunctions which are granted in respect of wrongs which are merely threatened or apprehended and other forms of injunction which are designed to prevent the continuance of a wrong or to guard against its repetition.[13]

---

generally used to describe what is referred to as an 'interlocutory injunction' in this jurisdiction as a result of the terminology employed in Rule 25.1 of the Civil Procedure Rules 1998.

10. Where a matter is particularly urgent a plaintiff may apply for such an order on an *ex parte* basis and the order will generally continue until the next motion day when the defendant will have the opportunity of putting his side of the case.
11. This principle was set out in *Adams v Director of Public Prosecutions* [2001] 2 ILRM 401 and applied in the context of applications to set aside injunctive relief in *J.R.M. Sports Ltd v Football Association of Ireland* [2007] IEHC 67; *Freney v Freney* [2008] IEHC 330.
12. [2006] 1 ILRM 81, 89.
13. However, it should be noted that where a plaintiff fears that the earlier actions of the defendant may lead to future causes of action, the term mandatory *quia timet* injunction may be used to describe what is sought.

THE PRINCIPLES GOVERNING THE GRANT OF INJUNCTIONS

General Principles Governing the Grant of Perpetual Injunctions

Introduction

An injunction will only be granted to protect a right of the plaintiff whether a legal right deriving from the common law, an equitable right (e.g. the right of a beneficiary under a trust), a constitutional right, or a right deriving from a specific statutory power. The plaintiff must establish a sufficient interest in the protection of this right,[14] and an injunction will not issue to remedy mere inconvenience or where the interference with the plaintiff's rights is trivial. Traditionally, it was thought that the grant of an injunction was limited to circumstances where a proprietary right had been infringed or threatened but this is certainly no longer the general rule. As Spry has commented, 'any attempt to found the jurisdiction to grant injunctions exclusively on the existence of property or proprietary rights is not justified'.[15]

A further cardinal principle which must be borne in mind is that injunctions, like other forms of equitable remedy, are discretionary in nature. So, while a plaintiff may establish the infringement of a right and a *prima facie* entitlement to relief he may still be denied this relief on discretionary grounds. However, this discretion cannot be exercised in an arbitrary manner but rather in accordance with well established principles which have been considered in detail by the courts. So, as Evershed MR stated in *Pride of Derby and Derbyshire Angling Association Ltd v British Celanese Ltd*:[16]

> It is, I think, well settled that if A proves that his proprietary rights are being wrongfully interfered with by B, and that B intends to continue his wrong, then A is *prima facie* entitled to an injunction, and he will be deprived of that remedy only if special circumstances exist, including the circumstance that damages are an adequate remedy for the wrong that he has suffered.

It is now proposed to examine the operation of some of these discretionary factors in practice. It should be pointed out that many cases never progress beyond the interlocutory stage and in general the same discretionary principles operate irrespective of whether a perpetual or interlocutory order is being sought. The specific factors relevant to the grant of interlocutory relief will be considered in detail below.

---

14. *Maxwell v Hogg* (1867) 2 Ch App 307, 311 *per* Turner LJ.
15. Spry, *The Principles of Equitable Remedies* (9th ed., 2014) p. 350.
16. [1953] Ch 149, 181.

The Inadequacy or Inappropriateness of Damages as a Remedy

Historically, the main reason for the intervention of the Court of Chancery was the inadequacy or inappropriateness of damages or other remedies at common law. Therefore, in the context of the grant of an injunction, a plaintiff was required to satisfy the court that the right which he sought to protect was of such a nature that an award of damages would not leave him in all respects in as good a position as if he had obtained enforcement of this right.

As Lindley LJ stated in *London and Blackwell Railway Co. v Cross*,[17] '*prima facie* you do not obtain injunctions to restrain actionable wrongs, for which damages are the proper remedy'. This principle still operates today, although arguably in a slightly more modified form and no injunction will be granted where an injury can be properly compensated in monetary terms.[18] So, where a plaintiff seeks injunctive relief, he must, as a matter of probability, demonstrate the risk that damages would not be an adequate remedy.[19] Clearly where it appears that wrongdoing will continue into the future, such as where there is a continuing nuisance, damages are unlikely to provide an adequate remedy and in such circumstances the grant of an injunction will often prove to be the only just form of relief.

However, it may be considered fair to confine a plaintiff to an award of damages where the wrongdoing of which he complains has ceased and is not likely to re-occur, and where his loss is quantifiable. A question which has often arisen, particularly in the context of interlocutory applications, is the extent to which difficulties in quantifying a plaintiff's loss may make damages an inadequate form of relief. In *Yeates v Minister for Posts and Telegraphs*[20] Kenny J commented that 'an injunction is granted before the hearing of an action only when damages will not be an adequate remedy or when the assessment of damages will be extremely difficult'.

This issue of difficulty in the quantification of damages was considered by the Supreme Court in *Curust Financial Services Ltd v Loewe-Lack-Werk Otto Loewe GmbH*,[21] in which the court had to consider whether the alleged breach by the plaintiff of an exclusive licensing agreement, consisting of its sub-contracting the manufacture of a product without the prior written consent of the first named defendant, should disentitle it to relief. Finlay CJ expressed the view that, '[d]ifficulty, as opposed to complete impossibility, in the assessment of …

---

17. (1886) 31 Ch D 354, 369. See also *Downey v Minister for Education and Science* [2001] 2 IR 727.
18. In *Ryanair Ltd v Aer Rianta cpt* [2001] IEHC 229 Kelly J stated that the fact that in the affidavit evidence before the court damages had actually been quantified was fatal to the applicant's claim for an interlocutory injunction.
19. *Per* Kelly J in *Smithkline Beecham plc v Genthon BV* [2003] IEHC 623 referring to the *dicta* of Finlay CJ in *Curust Financial Services Ltd v Loewe-Lack-Werk* [1994] 1 IR 450, 471. See also *Sheridan v Louis Fitzgerald Group Ltd* [2006] IEHC 125 at 12.
20. [1978] ILRM 22, 24.
21. [1994] 1 IR 450.

damages should not, in my view, be a ground for characterising the awarding of damages as an inadequate remedy.'[22] He pointed out that the loss which would be incurred by the plaintiff if no interlocutory injunction were granted and it ultimately succeeded in the action was 'clearly and exclusively a commercial loss in … a stable and well-established market' and that it should *prima facie* be capable of assessment in damages both in terms of the loss already sustained up to the date of assessment and probable future loss. In the circumstances, the Supreme Court concluded that the quantum of damages could be assessed and that no interlocutory injunction should be granted. So, as Barniville J stated in *Teva Pharmaceutical Industries Ltd v Mylan Teoranta*,[23] '[t]herefore, difficulty in measuring damages is not sufficient. It must be established as a matter of probability that the assessment of damages will be impossible by reason of the particular harm which may be suffered by the plaintiff.' The effect of this principle was also considered by O'Donnell J in *Merck Sharp & Dohme Corporation v Clonmel Healthcare Ltd*,[24] where he cautioned that it 'should not be understood as establishing a rule of general application that if damages may be awarded an injunction must be refused.'

The *Curust* principles were applied by Clarke J in *Sheridan v Louis Fitzgerald Group Ltd*,[25] in which the plaintiff sought an interlocutory injunction in circumstances where the defendant had entered into an arrangement with a third party to provide for the continuation of restaurant and catering services at the defendant's public house which had previously been provided by a company in which the plaintiff had an interest. Having quoted with approval from the judgment of Finlay CJ in *Curust*, Clarke J said that there was no reason in principle why the plaintiff would not be entitled to damages to compensate

22. *Ibid.* at 469. Quoted with approval in *Fitzpatrick v Garda Commissioner* [1996] IEHC 24 at 14; *Sheridan v Louis Fitzgerald Group Ltd* [2006] IEHC 125 at 12; *Relax Food Corporation Ltd v Brown Thomas & Co. Ltd* [2009] IEHC 181 at 6; *Osmond Ireland On Farm Business Ltd v McFarland* [2010] IEHC 295 at 16; *Lynch v Health Service Executive* [2010] IEHC 346 at 8; *Goode Concrete v Cement Roadstone Holdings plc* [2011] IEHC 15 at [23]; *Powerteam Electrical Services Ltd v Electricity Supply Board* [2016] IEHC 87 at [41]; *Murphy v Launceston Property Finance Ltd* [2017] IEHC 65 at [28]; *Gilead Sciences Inc v Mylan SAS Generics (UK) Ltd* [2017] IEHC 666 at [26]; *Teva Pharmaceutical Industries Ltd v Mylan Teoranta* [2018] IEHC 324 at [70]; *Merck Sharp & Dohme Corporation v Clonmel Healthcare Ltd* [2018] IECA 177 at [69] *per* Whelan J; *O'Gara v Ulster Bank Ireland DAC* [2019] IEHC 213 at [49]; *Hodgins v Hodgins* [2019] IEHC 577 at [30]. See also *Reno Engrais et Produits Chemiques SA v Irish Agricultural Wholesale Society Ltd* [1976-77] ILRM 179, 184; *Oblique Financial Services Ltd v The Promise Production Co. Ltd* [1994] 1 ILRM 74, 79; *Cavankee Fishing Co. Ltd v Minister for Communication, Marine and Natural Resources* [2004] IEHC 43 at 7; *Whelan Frozen Foods Ltd v Dunnes Stores* [2006] IEHC 171 at 17; *Goode Concrete v Cement Roadstone Holdings plc* [2011] IEHC 15 at [23].
23. [2018] IEHC 324 at [124].
24. [2019] IESC 65 at [40].
25. [2006] IEHC 125.

him for any loss which he could establish was likely to arise subsequent to the date of assessment of damages. If he could persuade the court that, as a matter of probability, the business was less successful financially at that date than it would have been had he been operating it, he would be entitled to damages to compensate for losses sustained during whatever period would be necessary to enable it to reach the position it would have been in had the plaintiff been running it from the outset. Clarke J stated that while there would undoubtedly be difficulties in making such a calculation, it seemed to him that any such difficulty fell far short of the impossibility identified by Finlay CJ in *Curust.* In these circumstances he was satisfied that damages would be an adequate remedy and it did not seem to him to be appropriate to grant the interlocutory injunction sought.

Inevitably, it will not be an easy task for the court to distinguish situations where damages will or will not be capable of assessment. In *Murgitroyd & Co. Ltd v Purdy*[26] Clarke J concluded that if a plaintiff failed to obtain an interlocutory injunction to prevent breach of a 'non-competition' clause in a service agreement but ultimately succeeded at trial, it would suffer a potential loss of clients and intervening financial loss which might in practice not be capable of recovery. In these circumstances he found that damages would not be an adequate remedy for the plaintiff although he concluded that the balance of convenience did not favour the grant of an interlocutory injunction provided that the issue in question could be ready for trial within a short time frame. Similarly, in *European Paint Importers Ltd v O'Callaghan*,[27] in which the plaintiff sought an interlocutory injunction to restrain breach of a 'non-solicitation' clause in a contract, Peart J was satisfied that damages would not be capable of assessment as it would be impossible to determine which orders the defendants had obtained as a result of solicitation. However, in *Osmond Ireland On Farm Business Ltd v McFarland*,[28] in which the plaintiff also sought to restrain the breach of a non-solicitation clause, Laffoy J expressed the view that it would be possible to assess the impact of the loss of orders on the plaintiff's business and to quantify such loss in damages given the highly regulated nature of the sector in which the parties were operating. Applying the principles set out by the Supreme Court in *Curust*, she concluded that the plaintiff had not demonstrated that damages would be an inadequate remedy if it were refused interlocutory relief but subsequently succeeded at trial.

A further specific issue which has arisen in this context is whether insolvency or going out of business *per se* will be regarded as a form of harm which cannot be adequately compensated by an award of damages. In *Curust Financial Services Ltd v Loewe-Lack-Werk Otto Loewe GmbH*[29] Finlay CJ concluded that the plaintiff had not established a real risk of insolvency if the interlocutory

---

26. [2005] IEHC 110.
27. [2005] IEHC 280.
28. [2010] IEHC 295.
29. [1994] 1 IR 450.

injunction sought was not granted and he was not required to consider the broader issue of whether going out of business would constitute a form of irreparable harm for which damages would not provide an adequate remedy. In *Ó Murchú v Eircell Ltd*,[30] in which the Supreme Court was satisfied that damages would be an adequate remedy if no injunction were granted at the interlocutory stage, Geogeghan J appeared satisfied that even if the plaintiff did go out of business pending the trial, his losses could be assessed in monetary terms.

This issue was addressed in some detail by Irvine J in *Lynch v Health Service Executive*,[31] in which the plaintiff dentists sought an interlocutory injunction restraining the defendant from giving effect to a circular which capped the budget for a dental services treatment scheme. Having considered the relevant authorities, Irvine J concluded that she was satisfied that 'there is no principle of law which establishes that insolvency or going out of business *per se* should be deemed to amount to proof that irreparable harm will necessarily be occasioned and that damages will not provide the plaintiff with an adequate remedy should an interlocutory injunction be refused.'[32] As she pointed out, whether irreparable harm is likely to be sustained is a decision that will depend on the facts of each individual case and may rest on factors such as the precise nature of the plaintiff's business and the market in which it is trading. Irvine J concluded that the only circumstance in which damages would not be an adequate remedy in the case before her would be if she was satisfied as a matter of probability that the plaintiffs would be forced to cease practising for a significant period of time if an interlocutory injunction were withheld. On the facts she found that, while it might be difficult to calculate precise losses with one hundred percent accuracy, they could not be considered incapable of calculation. Irvine J concluded that she was not satisfied that the plaintiffs had established that they were likely to sustain loss which was incapable of being adequately remedied by an award of damages if she refused to grant the interlocutory injunction sought and they were ultimately successful at trial and she refused their application.

The Conduct of the Parties

The discretionary considerations which are taken into account by a court in deciding whether to grant an injunction relate not only to the nature of the right which a plaintiff seeks to enforce and to the potential consequences of the decision to grant or refuse relief, but may also include factors relating to the conduct of the person invoking the jurisdiction of the court and, to a lesser extent, the conduct of the defendant. In this regard, two of the maxims considered earlier are relevant, namely 'he who comes to equity must come

30. [2001] IESC 15.
31. [2010] IEHC 346.
32. *Ibid.* at [42].

with clean hands' and 'he who seeks equity must do equity'.[33] While these maxims should be treated with caution, they do reflect the general principles which operate in relation to a plaintiff's conduct.

Where an injunction is sought by a plaintiff in furtherance of the perpetration of fraud, a court will not hesitate to refuse relief but conduct falling far short of fraud may also disentitle a plaintiff to an equitable remedy. The effect of the maxim 'he who comes to equity must come with clean hands'[34] is such that where a plaintiff who has been guilty of some impropriety or disreputable conduct seeks relief in the form of an equitable remedy, it may be refused by the court on discretionary grounds.[35] However, the court will decline to intervene on the basis of the 'clean hands' principle[36] unless there is a sufficient connection between the inequitable conduct and the subject matter of the dispute. As Scrutton LJ commented in *Moody v Cox*:[37]

> Equity will not apply the principle about clean hands unless the depravity, the dirt in question on the hand, has an immediate and necessary relation to the equity sued for.

This proposition is well-illustrated by *Argyll v Argyll*,[38] where it was held by Ungoed-Thomas J that the alleged immorality of the plaintiff's conduct which had led to divorce did not deprive her of her entitlement to an injunction to restrain a breach of confidence by her husband. As Ungoed-Thomas J stated, '[a] person coming to equity for relief … must come with clean hands, but the cleanliness required is to be judged in relation to the relief that is sought.'[39] The so called 'clean hands' principle has been applied in a wide variety of situations

33. See *supra* Chapter 2.
34. For a statement of this general principle, see *Dering v Earl of Winchelsea* (1787) 1 Cox 318, 319-320, where Eyre LCB stated that 'a man must come into a Court of Equity with clean hands; but when this is said, it does not mean a general depravity; it must have an immediate and necessary relation to the equity sued for; it must be a depravity in a legal as well as in the moral sense'. See also *Tinker v Tinker* [1970] P 136, 143 *per* Salmon LJ.
35. See *Overton v Banister* (1844) 3 Hare 503; *Gascoigne v Gascoigne* [1918] 1 KB 223; *McEvoy v Belfast Banking Co. Ltd* [1934] NI 67; *Smelter Corporation of Ireland Ltd v O'Driscoll* [1977] IR 305; *Parkes v Parkes* [1980] ILRM 137. The latter case illustrated the proposition that a plaintiff may be refused equitable relief where his conduct in relation to the transaction at issue has been less than honest even where this conduct has not directly prejudiced the defendant.
36. See generally Pettit [1990] Conv 416. Pettit suggests (at 424) that unclean hands seems to be a 'last resort defence' to be invoked where none of the so called nominate defences are applicable but where it would be unconscionable for the plaintiff to be granted relief by the court.
37. [1917] 2 Ch 71, 87-88. The plaintiff's claim for rescission of a contract succeeded despite the fact that he had given a bribe to the vendor's solicitor, although admittedly in an unconnected matter.
38. [1967] Ch 302.
39. *Ibid.* at 332.

where an injunction has been sought, e.g. where the plaintiff's conduct has been 'unfair and unreasonable',[40] where he has sought to safeguard his rights by 'deplorable means',[41] where he has committed a breach of covenant,[42] or where he has attempted to mislead the court.[43] In some cases the conduct of the defendant may effectively cancel out any wrongdoing of the plaintiff, as in *Meridian Communications Ltd v Eircell Ltd*,[44] where Lavan J had rejected the plaintiff's application for an interlocutory injunction on the basis that it had not come to court with clean hands. However, on appeal McGuinness J concluded that neither party had been entirely free of fault and she stated that in the circumstances the court would not refuse relief on the grounds relied on by Lavan J.

This principle was also referred to by the Supreme Court in *Curust Financial Services Ltd v Loewe-Lack-Werk Otto Loewe GmbH*,[45] in which Finlay CJ accepted that as a general principle the court has a discretion, where it is satisfied that a person has come to court otherwise than with 'clean hands', to refuse equitable relief in the form of an injunction on that ground alone. However, he continued by saying that 'it seems to me that this phrase must of necessity involve an element of turpitude and cannot necessarily be equated with a mere breach of contract.'[46] Finlay CJ made reference to the fact that what might be established as a breach by the plaintiff of the agreement not to sub-contract, namely the entering into an arrangement with a third party for this purpose, might also be established as having been provoked by a wrongful repudiation on the part of the first named defendant of its own contractual obligations under the licensing agreement. He therefore concluded that it would be unreasonable that such conduct should disentitle the plaintiff to an injunction to which it would otherwise be entitled and this would suggest that the Supreme Court appears willing to take on board the flexible approach adopted in England in recent years towards the application of the 'clean hands' principle.

The application of the maxim 'he who seeks equity must do equity' can be seen where the court will decline to grant an injunction to a party who, for example, seeks to enforce contractual rights while at the same time refusing to perform his own contractual obligations or to give an assurance that he will do so in the future. This proposition is well-illustrated by the decision of the Court of Appeal in *Chappell v Times Newspapers*,[47] which concerned a dispute which had arisen between unions and employers in the printing

40. *Shell UK Ltd. v Lostock Garage Ltd* [1976] 1 WLR 1187, 1199 *per* Lord Denning MR.
41. *Hubbard v Vosper* [1972] 2 QB 84, 101 *per* Megaw LJ.
42. *Litvinoff v Kent* (1918) 34 TLR 298.
43. *Armstrong v Sheppard & Short Ltd* [1959] 2 QB 384, 397.
44. [2001] IESC 42.
45. [1994] 1 IR 450, 468.
46. *Ibid.* at 467.
47. [1975] 1 WLR 482.

industry. Following selective industrial action, the employers threatened to terminate their employees' contracts unless normal production was resumed. The plaintiffs, who were individual union members who had not personally been involved in any industrial action, sought an interim injunction to restrain their respective employers from terminating their contracts of employment, although they refused to give the undertakings sought by the employers not to engage in disruptive activities. The Court of Appeal refused to grant an interim injunction on the grounds that the plaintiffs had failed to establish that they themselves intended to act equitably by abiding by the terms of their contracts of employment. As Lord Denning MR said, 'it has long been settled both at common law and in equity that in a contract where each has to do his part concurrently with the other, then if one party seeks relief, he must be ready and willing to do his part in it.'[48]

The issue of the influence which the conduct of the defendant may have on the decision of a court to grant or withhold relief of this nature is one which has been considered less frequently. In *News Datacom Ltd v Lyons*,[49] in which the plaintiff sought an interlocutory injunction to restrain an alleged breach of copyright in software used to decode satellite television signals, Flood J said that the mere fact that the conduct of one of the parties, in this case the defendant, might be questionable as a matter of ethics or morality was not a reason to grant relief in the absence of any other accepted grounds for making the order sought. However, in *Eircell Ltd v Bernstoff*[50] the defendant's conduct seemed to constitute a significant factor in deciding where the balance of convenience lay. Barr J referred to what he termed the 'reprehensible' conduct of the defendants in seeking to intimidate other people and contrasted it with what he described as the 'fair and reasonable behaviour' of the plaintiff. In view of this and having regard to the fact that damages would not constitute an adequate remedy from the plaintiff's point of view, he concluded that the balance of convenience favoured the granting of the interlocutory injunction sought.

Finally, the importance of the duty of full and frank disclosure on the plaintiff's part where an interim injunction is sought on an *ex parte* basis should be referred to. This was described by Browne-Wilkinson VC in his judgment in *Tate Access Floors Inc v Boswell*[51] as 'the golden rule', namely that a plaintiff applying for *ex parte* relief must disclose to the court all matters relevant to the exercise of the court's discretion. Where an application is brought to discharge an interim injunction on the grounds of lack of candour, the following factors set out by Clarke J in *Bambrick v Cobley*,[52] considered in more detail below in the context of Mareva injunctions, will be relevant. These are the materiality

---

48. *Ibid.* at 502.
49. [1994] 1 ILRM 450.
50. High Court 1999 No. 10182P (Barr J) 18 February 2000.
51. [1991] Ch 512, 532.
52. [2006] 1 ILRM 81, 89. See also *Fraser v Great Gas Petroleum Ireland Ltd* [2012] IEHC 523 at [36]; *Camden Street Investments Ltd v Vanguard Property Finance Ltd*

of the facts not disclosed, the extent to which it might be said that the plaintiff is culpable in respect of a failure to disclose – so deliberately misleading the court is likely to weigh more heavily in favour of the discretion being exercised against the continuance of an injunction than an innocent omission – and the overall circumstances of the case which led to the application in the first place.

Laches and Acquiescence

The court may also refuse to grant an injunction on the grounds of laches or acquiescence. The defence of laches is said by Spry to arise if two conditions are satisfied:[53]

> [F]irst, there must be unreasonable delay on the part of the plaintiff in the commencement or prosecution of proceedings, and secondly, in view of the nature and consequences of that delay it must be unjust in all the circumstances to grant the specific relief that is in question, whether absolutely or on appropriate terms or conditions.

The length of the delay will be judged from the time the plaintiff had sufficient knowledge of the facts giving rise to the claim or where he had a reasonable suspicion of the infringement of his rights. Delay by itself is unlikely to bar a claim for equitable relief but when coupled with other circumstances, often relating to the conduct of the plaintiff, it may be sufficient to lead to an equitable remedy being refused. Clearly once a plaintiff is appraised of the facts which would lead him to seek the intervention of the court he should proceed without undue delay and should not wait until the eleventh hour before bringing proceedings. This point was stressed by O'Hanlon J in *Lennon v Ganly*,[54] in which he refused the plaintiff an injunction restraining the defendants from embarking on a rugby tour to South Africa, because, *inter alia* he had delayed until just before the tour was due to commence and because a considerable period of time had elapsed since news of it had first been announced. However, the courts will take a realistic view of what constitutes undue delay and unless it is of appreciable length or some serious prejudice has been suffered by reason of it, it will not be a bar to relief.[55]

[2013] IEHC 478 at [48]; *Szabo v Kavanagh* [2013] IEHC 491 at [44]; *McDonagh v Ulster Bank Ireland Ltd* [2014] IEHC 476 at [34].

53. Spry, *The Principles of Equitable Remedies* (8th ed., 2010) p. 431. (Now see 9th ed., 2014, p. 446). Quoted with approval by Laffoy J in *McCann v Morrissey* [2013] IEHC 288 at [40].
54. [1981] ILRM 84.
55. See e.g. *An Post v Irish Permanent plc* [1995] 1 ILRM 336 where Kinlen J found that any delay in bringing an application for interlocutory relief was insufficient to influence the decision to grant relief. See also *Irish Shell Ltd v Elm Motors Ltd* [1984] IR 200, 216; *Carrigaline Community Television Broadcasting Co. Ltd v Minister for Transport, Energy and Communications* [1994] 2 IR 359.

While it is clear from the decision of Hogan J in *Meagher v Dublin City Council*[56] that the doctrine of laches has no application to a claim at common law for damages where that claim is not otherwise barred by the Statute of Limitations, different views have been taken in relation to the position where an equitable remedy such an injunction is sought. In *Cahill v Irish Motor Traders' Association*[57] Budd J expressed the opinion that delay by itself will not disentitle a plaintiff to an injunction to protect a legal as opposed to an equitable right unless the claim is barred by statute. This view would also seem to prevail in Australia where Deane J commented in *Orr v Ford*[58] that '[l]aches is an equitable defence and is not available in answer to a legal claim'. However, the Court of Appeal in *Habib Bank Ltd v Habib Bank AG Zurich*[59] drew no distinction between legal and equitable rights in this context and made it clear that the defence of laches can apply whenever an injunction is sought. Similarly, in *Gafford v Graham*,[60] Nourse LJ commented that he doubted whether a distinction ought to be made between a legal and equitable right when considering a defence of acquiescence. While this issue is far from settled, the better view would seem to be that it should be possible for laches and acquiescence to provide a defence whenever an equitable remedy such as an injunction is sought.

As Finnegan P made clear in *Criminal Assets Bureau v P.S.*,[61] where a party has obtained an interim injunction he has an obligation to prosecute the proceedings promptly both in relation to the interlocutory injunction and the substantive action. He added that delay on the part of a plaintiff will entitle a defendant to seek to have the interim or interlocutory injunction discharged, although he stressed that an interim injunction which has been obtained by a plaintiff on an *ex parte* basis will be more susceptible to being discharged for delay than an interlocutory injunction.

The general principles which apply to delay in the context of applications for interlocutory injunctions are well summarised by Keane J in his judgment in *Nolan Transport (Oaklands) v Halligan*[62] in the following terms:

> In all cases of this nature, where interlocutory relief is sought, the courts expect the parties to move with reasonable expedition where they are seeking interlocutory relief, because it is the essence of such relief that if it turns out that it has been wrongly granted, one party has suffered an

56. [2013] IEHC 474.
57. [1966] IR 430, 449.
58. (1989) 167 CLR 316, 340 *per* Oliver LJ.
59. [1981] 1 WLR 1265, 1285.
60. (1998) 77 P & CR 73, 80. See further infra p. 633.
61. High Court 1997 No. 38R (Finnegan P) 12 April 2002.
62. *Nolan Transport (Oaklands) Ltd v Halligan* High Court 1993 No.1008P, Keane J) at 6. See also *Teva Pharmaceutical Industries Ltd v Mylan Teoranta* [2018] IEHC 324 at [181].

> injustice. It is, therefore, a remedy that should not be lightly invoked; and, if invoked, it should be invoked rapidly, and where a party simply awaits events as they unfold, they cannot expect to find the court amenable to the granting of this relief, as it would where a party moves expeditiously to protect his rights.

A shorter period of inactivity will defeat a claim for an interlocutory injunction than is required to defeat an action for a perpetual injunction. This is clear from the judgment of Clarke J in *Dowling v Minister for Finance*,[63] who stated that the courts will scrutinise the expedition with which a party seeks interim or interlocutory injunctive relief, as 'failure to do so runs a significant risk both to the court having a reasonable opportunity to give adequate consideration to the issues and the defendant having a reasonable opportunity to be heard as to why the measures sought should not be imposed.' He stated as follows:

> The factors, therefore, which come into play in assessing whether a party has moved with reasonable expedition in applying for an interim or an interlocutory injunction are different, and are governed by much stricter scrutiny, than those which apply when the court is considering whether a party has lost all entitlement to bring proceedings at all, as a result of *laches* or delay, or where it is said that a party has been guilty of inordinate or inexcusable delay in the conduct of proceedings once commenced.[64]

There have been examples of cases in this jurisdiction in which relief in the form of an interlocutory injunction has been refused, either partly or wholly as a result of the plaintiff's delay in seeking a remedy. In *Howard v Commissioners of Public Works in Ireland*,[65] which involved a claim for an interlocutory injunction to restrain the respondents from proceeding with development work on a proposed visitor centre and national park in the Burren, O'Hanlon J placed emphasis, *inter alia*, on the conduct of the parties. He concluded that the application should be refused because he believed that the balance of convenience lay in favour of allowing the work to proceed and also because the applicants had delayed unduly in seeking the relief while the respondents had behaved in an 'irreproachable manner'. In *Ryanair v Irish Airline Pilots Association*[66] Murphy J held that a delay of three months on the part of the plaintiff in seeking an interlocutory injunction to restrain alleged trademark infringement and passing off was sufficient to lead the court to exercise its discretion to refuse the application. In *Irish Times Ltd v Times Newspapers Ltd*,[67] in which the plaintiffs sought an interlocutory injunction to restrain

63. [2013] 4 IR 576, 599.
64. *Ibid.*
65. High Court 1992 No. 331JR (O'Hanlon J) 3 December 1992.
66. High Court (Murphy J) 19 June 2012.
67. [2015] IEHC 490.

the defendant from launching its new digital newspaper in Ireland pending the resolution of proceedings relating to alleged trademark infringement and passing off, Hedigan J concluded that the plaintiffs had not acted with the reasonable expedition required of a moving party for interlocutory relief and for that reason he refused the relief sought.

Acquiescence is described as arising in the following circumstances by Spry:[68] 'first, there must, on the part of the plaintiff, be an assent or lying by in relation to the acts of another person; and secondly, in view of the assent or lying by and consequent acts it must be unjust in all the circumstances to grant the specific relief that is in question.' Similarly, in *Archbold v Scully*[69] Lord Wensleydale said that 'if a party, who could object, lies by and knowingly permits another to incur an expense in doing an act under the belief that it would not be objected to, and so a kind of permission may be said to be given to another to alter his condition, he may be said to acquiesce.' A good example of the operation of the principle of acquiescence as a defence to a claim for an injunction is *Sayers v Collyer*,[70] where the plaintiff failed to obtain an injunction to restrain the use of a house as a beer shop in breach of covenant as he had been aware of this breach for a number of years and had even bought beer there himself. As Baggallay LJ commented, 'I can hardly imagine a stronger case of acquiescence than this.'[71]

More recently acquiescence has been linked increasingly to the concept of unconscionability. A useful summary of this approach is contained in the judgment of Simon J in *Watson v Croft Promo-Sport Ltd*[72] in the following terms:

> Acquiescence is an equitable doctrine under which equitable relief (whether by way of injunction or equitable damages) will be barred on the ground that there has been delay coupled with matters which, in all the circumstances, makes it unconscionable for a party to continue to seek to enforce rights which he had at the date of the complaint.

He added that if detriment is present it will usually lead the court to conclude that it would be unconscionable for the claimant to seek to enforce his rights. However, in the absence of detriment the court will need to establish some other factor which makes it unconscionable for the party having the benefit of the rights to change his mind.[73]

Acquiescence has sometimes been held to be sufficient to bar a claim for

---

68. Spry, *The Principles of Equitable Remedies* (9th ed., 2014) p. 456.
69. (1861) 9 HLC 360, 383.
70. (1884) 28 Ch D 103.
71. *Ibid.* at 107.
72. [2008] 3 All ER 1171, 1185. This principle is derived from the judgments of the Court of Appeal in *Shaw v Applegate* [1970] 1 WLR 970, 978 and in *Gafford v Graham* (1998) 77 P & CR 73, 81.
73. See *Harris v Williams-Wynne* [2006] 2 P & CR 27 at [39].

an injunction but not a remedy in damages as the decision of the Court of Appeal in *Shaw v Applegate*[74] illustrates. The defendant purchased property and covenanted not to use it as an amusement arcade and the vendor subsequently assigned the benefit of the covenant to the plaintiffs. Three years after the defendant had started to install amusement machines the plaintiff sought an injunction to restrain the breach of covenant. The Court of Appeal held that to deprive the possessor of a legal right of that right on the ground of his acquiescence the situation must have been such that it would be dishonest or unconscionable to seek to enforce it. Since the plaintiffs had been confused about whether the defendants' activities constituted a breach of covenant, it could not be said that the plaintiffs would be acting dishonestly or unconscionably in seeking to enforce their rights under the contract when they did and the court held that their acquiescence had not been such as to deprive them of any remedy at all.[75] The Court of Appeal concluded that in view of the goodwill built up by the defendant over a period of years and the expenditure incurred by him, while the plaintiff's acquiescence was sufficient to bar him from relief in the form of an injunction, in the circumstances he had not disentitled himself to an award of damages.

This decision was relied upon by Hogan J in deciding not to award an injunction but to confine the plaintiff to a remedy in damages for breach of contract in *O'Hare v Dundalk Racing (1999) Ltd.*[76] Almost seven years after the events of which the plaintiff complained had taken place, he brought proceedings against the defendant racecourse operator and sought, *inter alia*, injunctive relief restoring his original bookmaker's pitch at the racecourse. Hogan J concluded that it would be 'manifestly inappropriate' for the court to make this order after such a lapse of time given the prejudice this would cause a third party. He said that the plaintiff had by his inactivity allowed the admittedly wrongful transfer of the licence to become an accomplished fact so far as the present pitch holder was concerned and made reference to the consequences for this individual if the court were to restore the pitch to the plaintiff. Hogan J commented that '[t]here is a long line of authority to the effect that the courts should not make an order of this nature where the plaintiff has delayed in a manner which would be prejudicial to another party'.[77] In the

74. [1977] 1 WLR 970. In *Victory v Galhoy Inns Ltd* [2010] IEHC 459, McMahon J stated that the level of inactivity necessary to prevent a person asserting his rights is high and must be so reprehensible that it approaches dishonesty. Commenting on the approach adopted in *Shaw*, he stated that a lower standard might be seen as encouraging and promoting litigation before the claimant is sure of his entitlement to relief or likelihood of success.
75. Goff LJ made a connection between the nature of the relief claimed and the effect of the acquiescence and stated (at 979) that he thought that it was 'easier to establish a case of acquiescence where the right is equitable only'.
76. [2015] IEHC 198.
77. *Ibid.* at [40].

circumstances he declined to grant injunctive relief although he awarded the plaintiff damages for breach of contract.

The plaintiff's conduct led to the court withholding all relief in *Gafford v Graham*,[78] which concerned a claim for relief in respect of building works carried out by the defendant in breach of a restrictive covenant. The Court of Appeal was satisfied that the plaintiff had known of his rights and had made no attempt to complain for some three years after this building work had taken place. In these circumstances Nourse LJ stated that the plaintiff's acquiescence was a bar to all relief in respect of these matters.[79] He said that he doubted whether a distinction ought to be drawn between claims to enforce legal and equitable rights when considering a defence of acquiescence[80] and that the real test was whether the situation had become such that it would be unconscionable for the plaintiff to seek to enforce his rights.[81] As Nourse LJ stated, '[a]s a general rule, someone who, with the knowledge that he has clearly enforceable rights and the ability to enforce them, stands by while a permanent and substantial structure is unlawfully erected, ought not to be granted an injunction to have it pulled down.' However, this aspect of the decision in *Gafford* was distinguished by the Court of Appeal in *Mortimer v Bailey*,[82] in which the claimants sought a mandatory injunction requiring the removal of an extension built onto a house in breach of a restrictive covenant. Peter Gibson LJ referred to the fact that Nourse LJ had stated in *Gafford* that '[the claimant's] willingness to settle the dispute on payment of a cash sum can properly be reflected by an award of damages' whereas in the case before the court there was no suggestion that the claimants would have been willing to accept damages in settlement of the dispute. In addition, he stated that he would not characterise what had occurred in the case before him as the claimants 'standing by' while the extension was built. While Peter Gibson LJ accepted that the claimants had been slow to seek an interim injunction, he concluded in upholding the decision to grant a mandatory injunction, that having promptly put the defendants on notice of their intention to take proceedings, their conduct did not disentitle them from obtaining the relief sought.

78. (1998) 77 P & CR 73.
79. It should be noted that the Court of Appeal awarded damages in respect of other development and building work where the plaintiff had acted promptly in complaining about it, although it declined to grant an injunction.
80. See also the comments of Chadwick LJ in *Harris v Williams-Wynne* [2006] 2 P & CR 27 at [54].
81. See also *Harris v Williams-Wynne* [2006] 2 P & CR 27 at [36]. However, the Court of Appeal distinguished the facts of the case before it from those that had arisen in *Gafford v Graham* and held that in the circumstances it would not be unconscionable for the defendant to continue to seek to enforce his rights under a restrictive covenant.
82. [2004] EWCA Civ 1514. See further Watt [2005] Conv 460.

Effect on Third Parties

There have been judicial statements made suggesting that the courts in deciding whether to grant an injunction should have regard to the surrounding circumstances and to the rights of those who may be peripherally involved,[83] and that an injunction should not be granted where this will have the effect of 'very materially injuring the rights of third parties'.[84] However, Spry has stated that 'it is not generally appropriate that specific private rights should be denied in order to give rise to an indefinite advantage to the general public'[85] and this view has tended to prevail. The question was considered by the Supreme Court in *Bellew v Cement Ltd*,[86] in which the majority of the court concluded that the general public convenience should not be taken into account in weighing up whether to grant relief in the form of an injunction. The plaintiffs sought an interlocutory injunction to restrain the defendants, who were the sole manufacturers of cement in the State, from carrying out blasting operations in a quarry which it was alleged constituted a nuisance. The defendants argued that in view of the importance of the defendants' products to the building industry and having regard to the fact that because of the impending long vacation blasting operations would have to cease for several months, an injunction should not be granted. It was held by the Supreme Court in granting the order sought that the plaintiff had made out a *prima facie* case[87] of nuisance and that the court was not entitled to take the public convenience into consideration when dealing with the rights of private parties. As Maguire CJ stated, '[t]his matter is a dispute between private parties and I think that the court should be concerned, only, to see that the rights of the parties are safeguarded.'[88] Black J dissented and stated that while the concept of public convenience cannot justify the refusal of a remedy for a nuisance, it is a different matter to say that it cannot, or ought not to, affect the way in which a nuisance should be dealt with.[89]

In England there have been somewhat conflicting authorities on this question but it would seem that while the public interest may be a factor to be weighed up by the court, where significant damage would be caused to the claimant if an injunction were withheld the claimant's individual rights should take priority.

83. *Wood v Sutcliffe* (1851) 2 Sim (NS) 163, 165.
84. *Hartlepool Gas & Water Co. v West Hartlepool Harbour & Rly Co.* (1865) 12 LT 366, 368.
85. Spry, *The Principles of Equitable Remedies* (9th ed., 2014) p. 416.
86. [1948] IR 61.
87. This was the accepted test in relation to the granting of an interlocutory injunction at the time. It has now been replaced by the requirement of establishing that there is a fair question to be tried. See *infra* pp. 650-652.
88. [1948] IR 61, 64.
89. Note that in *Wall v Feely* High Court 1983 No. 7014P (Costello J) 26 October 1983, Costello J appeared to take the public convenience into account albeit to the limited extent of considering how this would affect the defendant local authority, although it did not ultimately influence his decision.

In *Miller v Jackson*[90] the owner of a house situated beside a cricket ground sought an injunction to prevent the club continuing with its activities which involved a risk of injury from cricket balls landing on the property. While two members of the Court of Appeal agreed that these activities constituted a nuisance, Cumming-Bruce LJ agreed with the view of Lord Denning MR that an injunction should not be granted in these circumstances and that the plaintiff should be confined to a remedy in damages. In his view 'a court of equity must seek to strike a fair balance between the right of the plaintiffs to have quiet enjoyment of their house and garden without exposure to cricket balls occasionally falling like thunderbolts from the heavens, and the opportunity of the inhabitants of the village in which they live to continue to enjoy the manly sport which constitutes a summer recreation for adults and young persons, including one would hope and expect, the plaintiff's son.'[91] This view was unanimously disapproved of several years later by a differently constituted Court of Appeal in *Kennaway v Thompson*.[92] The plaintiff sought an injunction to restrain a nuisance which consisted of excessive noise caused by power boat racing on a lake in the vicinity of her house. The Court of Appeal granted an injunction which greatly restricted the club's activities on the grounds that the public interest in allowing the racing to continue uninterrupted could not prevail over the plaintiff's entitlement to enjoy her home free from the tortious interference which this racing caused.

More recently, in *Smithkline Beecham plc v Apotex Europe Ltd*,[93] Jacob LJ suggested that the position of third parties or the public who may be affected by an interlocutory injunction is a matter which the court may take into account, and this may be the case in limited circumstances where a perpetual injunction is sought. Vos J also expressed the view in *Alstom Transport v Eurostar International Ltd*[94] that particularly in cases 'at the interface of public law and private law', the public interest should be taken into account in determining the balance of convenience where an interlocutory injunction is sought.

There is a greater tendency to look beyond the rights of the parties actually involved in an action in assessing whether to grant an injunction at the interlocutory stage. In *Howard v Commissioners for Public Works*[95] the applicants sought an interlocutory injunction to restrain the respondents from proceeding with development work on a proposed interpretative centre in the Burren. O'Hanlon J concluded that the evidence was sufficient to satisfy him that major disruption of a very serious kind would occur if the project were to be brought to a standstill. He said that he had no doubt that the financial loss would be very substantial, that the respondents might find themselves

90. [1977] QB 966.
91. *Ibid.* at 988.
92. [1981] QB 88.
93. [2007] Ch 71, 84.
94. [2010] EWHC 2747 (Ch).
95. High Court 1992 No.331JR (O'Hanlon J) 3 December 1992.

facing serious liabilities for breach of contract and that many people would lose their employment. In addition, O'Hanlon J was of the view that the loss and damage which would be sustained by the applicants if the interlocutory relief were refused did not fall within the category of what he could regard as irreparable damage and he concluded that the interlocutory order should be refused. While other factors, such as the conduct of the parties, were also referred to, it is difficult to avoid the conclusion that O'Hanlon J was influenced at least in part by the wider public convenience which involved primarily the employment prospects of those working on the project, in deciding to refuse the relief sought. Similarly, in *Dun Laoghaire Rathdown County Council v Shackleton*,[96] O'Sullivan J stated that, in reaching the conclusion that the plaintiff had made out a good cause of action and that interlocutory relief should be granted preventing an arbitrator from embarking on hearing a claim for compensation, he had been influenced by public interest considerations.[97]

A related question is whether the activities of third parties should have any effect on the decision of a court to grant or refuse an injunction. Arguably this should not be a factor and the court should confine itself to an examination of the issues which affect the parties directly involved, although the approach adopted by Keane J in *Phonographic Performance (Ireland) Ltd v Chariot Inns*[98] suggests that this will not always be the case. The plaintiff sought an interlocutory injunction restraining the defendants from permitting certain sound recordings from being played in public when the defendant refused to pay an amount claimed by the plaintiff by way of 'equitable remuneration' within the meaning of the Copyright Act 1963. Keane J concluded that there were 'unquestionably serious issues at stake between the parties involving difficult questions of law' and held that as more damage would be caused by refusing than by granting an injunction the order sought should be granted. However, in the course of his judgment, Keane J made reference to the fact that if the interlocutory injunction was refused and the plaintiff was ultimately successful, large sums would have to be recovered from other operators who might follow the defendants' example and refuse to pay and he said that it was unlikely, given the number of businesses involved, that all these sums would be recovered. While the conclusion reached by Keane J was probably correct in the circumstances, as Coughlan has pointed out, the question should arguably have been decided solely by reference to the infringement of the plaintiff's rights allegedly committed by that defendant and the defendant could hardly be held accountable for the activities of independent third parties.[99]

---

96. [2002] IEHC 2.
97. Note that the question of whether the court could take into account the wider question of public convenience was raised also in *An Post v Irish Permanent plc* [1995] 1 ILRM 336, 349 but Kinlen J said that he would express no view on the matter at the interlocutory stage as it was one more properly to be determined at trial.
98. High Court 1992 No. 4673P (Keane J) 7 October 1992.
99. Coughlan [1993] EIPR D-10.

Jurisdiction to Award Damages under Lord Cairns' Act

While originally the Court of Chancery had no jurisdiction to award damages, the Chancery Amendment Act 1858 (Lord Cairns' Act) authorised the court in all cases where it had jurisdiction to grant an injunction or an order of specific performance to award damages either in addition to or in substitution for the other remedies. This power to award damages in equity declined in significance after the enactment of the Judicature Act which conferred jurisdiction on the courts to make an award of damages in any case where this could have been done previously by the common law courts. However, it is still necessary to rely on Lord Cairns' Act in circumstances where no entitlement to damages lies at common law, e.g. where the right in question is equitable in nature, or where a breach of the plaintiff's rights has not yet occurred and is merely anticipated.[100] The discretion granted by Lord Cairns' Act is similar to that exercised since the enactment of the Judicature Act to make an award of damages in lieu of granting an injunction and it does not seem necessary to draw any distinction in relation to the general principles involved.

An attempt to lay down a 'good working rule' in relation to the principles governing the award of damages in lieu of an injunction under Lord Cairns' Act was made by Smith LJ in *Shelfer v City of London Electric Lighting Co.*[101] An electric lighting company caused considerable discomfort and annoyance to the lessee of premises by carrying out excavation work. At first instance Kekewich J held that while the defendants had created a continuing nuisance, damages should be the only remedy, although the Court of Appeal allowed the plaintiff's appeal against the refusal of an injunction. Smith LJ laid down the general principle that damages should only be awarded in lieu of an injunction or specific performance in the following circumstances:[102]

(1) If the injury to the plaintiff's legal rights is small,
(2) And is one which is capable of being estimated in money,
(3) And is one which can be adequately compensated by a small money payment,
(4) And the case is one in which it would be oppressive to the defendant to grant an injunction.

Smith LJ continued by saying that even where these four principles are satisfied, an injunction may still be awarded if the defendant has acted in reckless disregard of the plaintiff's rights. A further point stressed by Lindley LJ which is of particular importance is that the court in exercising this jurisdiction will not allow a wrong to continue simply because the wrongdoer is able and willing to pay for the injury he may inflict. It should also be noted that, as Lloyd LJ pointed out in the course of his judgment in *Jacklin v Chief Constable of West*

100. *Johnson v Agnew* [1980] AC 367, 400.
101. [1895] 1 Ch 287.
102. *Ibid.* at 322-323.

Yorkshire,[103] the four principles are cumulative and it will not be sufficient for a defendant to satisfy the first three and there has to be some additional factor, characterised in *Shelfer* as oppression, to justify withholding the injunctive remedy. In addition, as the decision in *Marcic v Thames Water Utilities Ltd (No.2)*[104] makes clear, the *Shelfer* principles only apply where it is the defendant who seeks to avoid an injunction being granted and not where the plaintiff seeks damages rather than an injunction.

The application of the *Shelfer* principles did not meet with universal approval in England, so, in *Fishenden v Higgs & Hill Ltd*,[105] Hanworth MR said that they were for guidance only and Romer LJ made it clear that if one of the four requirements was not fulfilled, it did not mean that an injunction must be granted. The Court of Appeal, while upholding a finding of nuisance with regard to interference with a right to light, held that in the circumstances damages were a sufficient remedy. However, in general these principles tended to be applied, as in *Kennaway v Thompson*,[106] where the plaintiff sought an injunction to restrain power boat racing on a lake near her house. The Court of Appeal held that the principles in *Shelfer's* case applied and awarded her an injunction limiting the racing activities on the grounds that the injury to the plaintiff was not small or capable of estimation in monetary terms nor could the sum awarded by the High Court judge, who had decided to award damages in lieu, be considered a small payment. Lawton LJ said that he considered that *Shelfer's* case was binding on him and stressed that in cases of continuing nuisance the jurisdiction to award damages in lieu should only be exercised in very exceptional circumstances.

The 'good working rule' laid down in *Shelfer* was again applied by the Court of Appeal in *Jaggard v Sawyer*[107] to support the conclusion that the plaintiff should have been awarded damages in lieu of an injunction in respect of a breach of covenant and trespass. However, Millett LJ made it clear that it should not be assumed that these principles will cover every potential situation and they should be applied where appropriate. As he commented, 'A.L. Smith LJ's check-list has stood the test of time; but it needs to be remembered that it is only a working rule and does not purport to be an exhaustive statement of the circumstances in which damages may be awarded instead of an injunction.'[108] Millett LJ added that the outcome of any particular case usually turns on the

103. [2007] EWCA Civ 181 at [48]. See also *Hkruk II (CHC) Ltd v Heaney* [2010] EWHC 2245 (Ch) at [61].
104. [2002] QB 1003.
105. (1935) 153 LT 128.
106. [1981] QB 88. See also *Jaggard v Sawyer* [1995] 1 WLR 269, 277-278 *per* Bingham MR.
107. [1995] 1 WLR 269. See also *Ketley v Gooden* (1996) 73 P & CR 305; *Small v Oliver & Saunders (Development) Ltd* [2006] EWHC 1293 (Ch); *Regan v Paul Properties DPF No 1 Ltd* [2007] Ch 135.
108. *Ibid.* at 287. See also *Marcic v Thames Water Utilities Ltd (No.2)* [2002] QB 1003, 1008; *Watson v Croft Promo-Sport Ltd* [2008] 3 All ER 1171, 1188.

question of whether it would in all the circumstances be oppressive to the defendant to grant the injunction to which the plaintiff is *prima facie* entitled. This certainly seemed to form the basis for the decision of the Court of Appeal in *Gafford v Graham*,[109] where Nourse LJ applied the *Shelfer* principles and concluded in awarding damages in lieu of an injunction that it would be oppressive and therefore unfair to the defendant to grant an injunction.[110]

More recently, in *Lawrence v Fen Tigers Ltd*,[111] further reservations were expressed about the application of the *Shelfer* principles by a number of members of the Supreme Court and the court ordered that injunctive relief granted by the trial judge in relation to nuisance caused by motor sports activities should be restored. Lord Neuberger PSC suggested that the approach to be adopted when considering whether to award damages instead of an injunction should be more flexible and that a mechanical application of A L Smith LJ's four tests in *Shelfer*, and an approach involving damages being awarded only in 'very exceptional circumstances', are both wrong in principle and give rise to a serious risk of injustice in practice. In his view, 'the court's power to award damages in lieu of an injunction involves a classic exercise of discretion, which should not, as a matter of principle, be fettered.'[112] Lord Carnwath JSC also agreed that the opportunity should be taken to signal a move away from the strict criteria derived from *Shelfer*. Lord Sumption JSC in a sense went further and said that in his view the decision in *Shelfer* was out of date, and that it was 'unfortunate that it has been followed so recently and so slavishly'.[113]

The leading Irish authority in this area is *Patterson v Murphy*,[114] in which the plaintiffs sought damages and an injunction arising out of alleged acts of nuisance caused by blasting and quarrying activities carried on by the defendants in a field adjoining their house. Costello J found that these activities did constitute acts of nuisance and held that the plaintiffs were entitled to an injunction. He said that the infringement of their rights was most serious; the injury which they had suffered and would continue to suffer if the nuisance were allowed to continue had been and would be considerable and he was satisfied that damages would not adequately compensate them. Costello J laid down a number of 'well established principles' on which the court exercises its discretion in deciding whether to grant an injunction and it is worth setting them out in full.

1. When an infringement of the plaintiffs' right and a threatened further infringement to a material extent has been established, the plaintiff is *prima*

109. (1998) 77 P & CR 73.
110. However, it should be noted that Nourse LJ also stated that: '[the claimant's] willingness to settle the dispute on payment of a cash sum can properly be reflected by an award of damages.'
111. [2014] AC 822.
112. *Ibid.* at 855.
113. *Ibid.* at 864. See also *per* Lord Clarke JSC at 866.
114. [1978] ILRM 85, 99-100.

facie entitled to an injunction. There may be circumstances, however, depriving the plaintiff of this *prima facie* right but generally speaking the plaintiff will only be deprived of an injunction in very exceptional circumstances.

2. If the injury to the plaintiffs' rights is small, and is one capable of being estimated in money, and is one which can be adequately compensated by a small money payment and if the case is one in which it would be oppressive to the defendant to grant an injunction, then these are circumstances in which damages in lieu of an injunction may be granted.
3. The conduct of the plaintiff may be such as to disentitle him to an injunction. The conduct of the defendant may be such as to disentitle him from seeking the substitution of damages for an injunction.
4. The mere fact that a wrong-doer is able and willing to pay for the injury he has inflicted is not a ground for substituting damages.

Costello J distinguished the decision of Gannon J in *Halpin v Tara Mines Ltd*,[115] in which the plaintiffs had been refused an injunction and awarded damages in respect of a nuisance caused by the defendant's prospecting activities. In *Halpin*, while Gannon J had found that these activities had amounted to a nuisance, he was satisfied that the defendant had modified its operations and improved its working practices to such an extent by the time of the trial of the action that the court should decline to grant an injunction.

While the point made by Lindley LJ in *Shelfer* that a court will not allow a wrong to continue simply because the wrongdoer is able and willing to pay for the injury he may inflict is an important one, where the wrongdoing is unintentional and the plaintiff has suffered no loss in its trading position, a remedy in damages may meet the justice of the situation. In *Falcon Travel Ltd v Owners Abroad Group plc*[116] the plaintiff, a retail travel agent in the Wicklow and Dublin areas, sought an injunction against the defendants who had opened an office in this country on the grounds of alleged passing off. Due to the similarity in the companies' names, confusion arose and there was bad publicity for the plaintiff on one occasion, although in general their turnover increased because of the confusion. Murphy J accepted that while the defendant was aware of the plaintiff's business, he was satisfied that it had not intended to exploit its reputation or business. While it did not appear that the plaintiff's business had suffered, Murphy J accepted that the plaintiff had suffered damage in that its reputation had become submerged into that of the defendant and he concluded that the tort of passing off had been established. Although he said that an injunction would ordinarily be the most suitable means of protecting the plaintiff's property rights, he took into account the fact that the wrongdoing was unintentional and that the plaintiff had suffered no loss in its trading position

115. [1976-77] ILRM 28.
116. [1991] 1 IR 175.

as well as the fact that an injunction would cause the defendant enormous expense. In view of these factors, Murphy J decided to exercise his discretion to award damages in lieu of an injunction, calculated with a view to organising an advertising campaign to make it clear to the public that the plaintiff and defendant were separate businesses.

The Measure of Damages Under Lord Cairns' Act

The question of the measure of damages which can be awarded under Lord Cairns' Act is one which has provoked considerable uncertainty in England[117] and this controversy is not one which the courts in this jurisdiction have directly addressed. In *Johnson v Agnew*[118] the House of Lords held that there was no difference in the measure of damages which could be awarded under Lord Cairns' Act and at common law, Lord Wilberforce stated that the Act 'does not provide for the assessment of damages on any new basis'.[119] However, no reference was made by the House of Lords in *Johnson* to the earlier decision of Brightman J in *Wrotham Park Estate Co. v Parkside Homes Ltd*,[120] in which he had considered the measure of damages to be awarded in equity in lieu of an injunction for breach of a restrictive covenant. As the plaintiff had sustained no loss, any damages which would have been awarded at common law would have been purely nominal,[121] but Brightman J concluded that a 'just substitute' for the injunction sought would be the sum which the plaintiff might have obtained in return for modifying the covenant.

Subsequently, in *Surrey County Council v Bredero Homes Ltd*,[122] in which the plaintiff only sought common law damages as the grant of an injunction had become impossible before proceedings were issued, the Court of Appeal expressed different views about the earlier decisions. Dillon LJ stated that in his opinion the award of significant damages in *Wrotham Park* was inconsistent with *Johnson* and said that the conclusion of Brightman J involved the assumption that Lord Cairns' Act had effected a substantive and not merely a procedural change in the law, a finding which ran contrary to what had been stated by the House of Lords. However, the majority of the Court of Appeal on an *obiter* basis expressed the view that the conclusion reached in *Wrotham Park* was a fair and just one in the circumstances.

---

117. Some of the factors which the courts will weigh up in assessing quantum are considered by Halpern [2001] Conv 453.
118. [1980] AC 367.
119. *Ibid.* at 400.
120. [1974] 1 WLR 798. It should be noted that *Wrotham Park* appears to have been approved by the Court of Appeal in *Stoke-on-Trent City Council v W. & J. Wass Ltd* [1988] 1 WLR 1406 in which the House of Lords decision in *Johnson* was not referred to.
121. Although it should be stressed that on the facts of this case, as a restrictive covenant was involved, damages could only be awarded under Lord Cairns' Act.
122. [1993] 1 WLR 1361.

More recently the Court of Appeal in *Jaggard v Sawyer*[123] has addressed the question of whether it is possible to reconcile the earlier decisions. The Court of Appeal concluded that the trial judge had been correct to apply the *Wrotham Park* approach to the assessment of damages to compensate the plaintiff for a continuing breach of her rights, and it was clearly of significance to this decision that the damages included compensation for future injury. Millett LJ adverted to this fact when he stated that 'when the court awards damages in substitution for an injunction, it seeks to compensate the plaintiff for loss arising from future wrongs that is to say, loss for which the common law does not provide a remedy'. He also rightly pointed out that in *Johnson v Agnew* the plaintiff was claiming damages for loss occasioned by a single, once-off, past breach of contract. He continued as follows:

> In my view Lord Wilberforce's statement [in *Johnson v Agnew*] that the measure of damages is the same whether damages are recoverable at common law or under the Act must be taken to be limited to the case where they are recoverable in respect of the same cause of action. It cannot sensibly have any application where the claim at common law is in respect of a past trespass or breach of covenant and that under the Act is in respect of future trespasses or continuing breaches of covenant.[124]

The *Wrotham Park* principle, which allows damages to be awarded in lieu of an injunction even where the plaintiff has sustained no loss, won the support of the House of Lords in *Attorney General v Blake*.[125] Although the case did not involve the application of Lord Cairns' Act, the House of Lords, in holding that a claim for an account of profits might be made in a case of breach of contract, was required to consider whether a court might award substantial damages for an infringement when no financial loss flowed from such infringement. Lord Nicholls stated that in his opinion Brightman J had been correct in the conclusion which he had reached in *Wrotham Park* and that, in so far as the decision in *Surrey County Council v Bredero Homes Ltd* was inconsistent with the approach adopted in the former case, the view of Brightman J was to be preferred. Lord Nicholls commented that 'the *Wrotham Park* case, therefore, still shines, rather as a solitary beacon, showing that in contract as well as tort damages are not always narrowly confined to recoupment for financial loss.'[126]

The principles set out by the House of Lords in *Blake* were applied and developed further by the Court of Appeal in *Experience Hendrix LLC v PPX*

123. [1995] 1 WLR 269. See also Ingman [1995] Conv 141.
124. *Ibid.* at 291. It is interesting to note that while Millett LJ characterised the *Wrotham Park* decision as one concerning a single past breach of covenant (at 291), Bingham MR considered it to involve a 'continuing invasion' of the plaintiff's rights (at 281).
125. [2001] 1 AC 268.
126. *Ibid.* at 283.

Enterprises Inc,[127] in which it was held that the court may, in addition to granting an injunction to the beneficiary of a restrictive covenant to restrain further breaches, also award damages for past infringement even though he cannot establish any actual financial loss. Chadwick LJ added in an *obiter* context in *WWF–World Wide Fund for Nature v World Wrestling Federation Entertainment Inc*[128] that in his view the speech of Lord Nicholls in *Blake* led to the conclusion that in a case where a covenantor has acted in breach of a restrictive covenant, the court may award damages on a *Wrotham Park* basis notwithstanding that there could not be any claim for an injunction. In his view the power to award damages on such a basis does not depend on Lord Cairns' Act but exists at common law.[129]

The basis for the awarding of damages under Lord Cairns' Act continues to give rise to debate. A number of general principles relating to the awarding of damages in this context were set out by Lord Walker in the judgment of the Privy Council in *Pell Frischmann Engineering Ltd v Bow Valley Iran*,[130] where he stated that although damages under Lord Cairns' Act are awarded in lieu of an injunction 'it is not necessary that an injunction should actually have been claimed in the proceedings, or that there should have been any prospect, on the facts, of it being granted.'

More useful guidance about the manner in which damages awarded under Lord Cairns' Act should be quantified is provided by Lord Reed JSC in his judgment in the Supreme Court in *Morris-Garner v One Step (Support) Ltd*.[131] He reiterated that damages may be awarded under Lord Cairns' Act in substitution for specific performance or an injunction, 'where the court had jurisdiction to entertain an application for such relief at the time when the proceedings were commenced' and that such damages are a monetary substitute for what is lost by the withholding of such relief. Lord Reed JSC set out the following general principles:

> One possible method of quantifying damages under this head is on the basis of the economic value of the right which the court has declined to enforce, and which it has consequently rendered worthless. Such a valuation can be arrived at by reference to the amount which the claimant might reasonably have demanded as a quid pro quo for the relaxation of

127. [2003] FSR 46 at [34]. See also *Field Common Ltd v Elmbridge BC* [2009] 1 P & CR 1 at [74].
128. [2008] 1 WLR 445, 473. See further Cunnington [2007] CLJ 507; Rotherham [2008] LMCLQ 25.
129. See [2017] Conv 339 has suggested that instead of explaining the award on the basis of restitutionary principles, both Chadwick and Mance LJJ asserted that it was compensatory in nature but without identifying the claimant's loss. In his view, this 'deprived the award of plausible compensatory reasoning' (at 346).
130. [2011] 1 WLR 2370, 2386.
131. [2018] 2 WLR 1353. See further Burrows (2018) 134 LQR 515; Chew [2018] Conv 386; Bartscherer (2019) 82 MLR 367.

> the obligation in question. The rationale is that, since the withholding of specific relief has the same practical effect as requiring the claimant to permit the infringement of his rights, his loss can be measured by reference to the economic value of such permission.[132]

However, he added that this is not the only approach to assessing damages under Lord Cairns' Act and that '[i]t is for the court to judge what method of quantification, in the circumstances of the case before it, will give a fair equivalent for what is lost by the refusal of the injunction.'[133]

Principles Governing the Grant of Interlocutory Injunctions

Introduction

The essential aim of an interlocutory injunction is to preserve the *status quo* existing between the parties to an action until the trial of the issues in dispute can take place and it will have effect until the final determination of the rights of the parties by the court.[134] The rationale behind the grant of such injunctions is primarily the need to protect the rights of a plaintiff as they exist at the time he institutes proceedings to prevent him suffering irreparable prejudice by reason of the delay which must necessarily occur between the institution of proceedings and the trial of the action. O'Higgins CJ summarised these principles as follows in *Campus Oil Ltd v Minister for Industry & Energy (No. 2)*:[135]

> Interlocutory relief is granted to an applicant where what he complains of is continuing and is causing him harm or injury which may be irreparable in the sense that it may not be possible to compensate him fairly or properly by an award of damages. Such relief is given because a period must necessarily elapse before the action can come for trial and for the purpose of keeping matters *in statu quo* until the hearing.

In practice the courts grant far more injunctions of an interlocutory than a perpetual nature as many disputes are resolved after the interlocutory stage and do not proceed to trial for various other reasons.[136] In certain circumstances, where the parties consent, the court may even treat the application for an interlocutory order as the trial of the action. While this procedure will inevitably

132. *Ibid.* at 1382-1383.
133. *Ibid.*
134. However, as Zuckerman suggests in *Zuckerman on Civil Procedure: Principles of Practice* (2013) p. 399, such injunctions are 'not directly concerned with the preservation of physical states of affairs but with the preservation of rights.'
135. [1983] IR 88, 105.
136. *Fellowes & Son v Fisher* [1976] QB 122, 129 *per* Lord Denning MR. It should be noted that Kirwan suggests (2008) 15 DULJ 325, 351 that the more speedy hearing of cases entered into the Commercial List pursuant to Order 63A may diminish the need to seek injunctions of an interlocutory nature.

lead to a more expeditious resolution of the issues to be determined, it will only be a suitable course to take where there is no dispute about the facts as an interlocutory hearing is conducted on the basis of affidavit evidence alone.

A court also has a wide discretion to vary or discharge injunctive relief granted by it. In *Sheehan v Breccia*,[137] while Haughton J referred to a number of circumstances in which an order to vary may be made such as 'where there has been a fundamental breach of an express agreement between the parties, where there has been inordinate delay on behalf of the party obtaining the injunction, or where there has been a subsequent judicial decision which alters the position of the law' he also accepted that the courts are not limited to acting in these circumstances and he stated that 'the underlying consideration is that the approach taken is that which the Court deems to be just or convenient.'[138] While in the circumstances he declined to make an order discharging the interlocutory injunction which had been granted in the proceedings, this decision was reversed by the Court of Appeal and Peart J concluded that, as there was no serious or fair issue which might have resulted in the grant of a permanent injunction, the interlocutory injunction must be discharged.[139]

Undertaking as to Damages

Where an interlocutory injunction is sought, a plaintiff will almost invariably be required to give an undertaking as to damages.[140] This means that if it transpires at the hearing of the action that an injunction has been wrongly granted at the interlocutory stage, the plaintiff will have undertaken to adequately indemnify the defendant against any loss incurred by the defendant by reason of this.[141] It would appear that the giving of an undertaking will only be dispensed with in 'special circumstances',[142] and it was stressed by Budd J in *Keenan v CIE*[143] that such an undertaking is a *sine qua non* where a mandatory interlocutory injunction is sought. While it is required for the defendant's benefit to ensure that he can be recompensed, if it is subsequently shown that no interlocutory order should have been made, the undertaking is given to the court[144] and not

137. [2017] IEHC 692 at [44].
138. *Ibid.* at [45].
139. [2019] IECA 234.
140. However, note the comment of Barrett J in *Bainne Aláinn Ltd v Glanbia* [2014] IEHC 482 at [27] that in this context, 'just because something is typically done does not mean that it must always be done.'
141. *Pasture Properties Ltd v Evans* [1999] IEHC 214 at 8.
142. *Attorney-General v Albany Hotel Co.* [1896] 2 Ch 696, 700 *per* North J.
143. (1963) 97 ILTR 54.
144. *Cheltenham & Gloucester Building Society v Ricketts* [1993] 1 WLR 1545, 1550. See also *Estuary Logistics & Distribution Co. Ltd v Lowenergy Solutions Ltd* [2008] 2 IR 806, 809-810; *Irish Bank Resolution Corporation Ltd v Quinn* [2013] IEHC 437 at [40].

to the party enjoined and accordingly non-compliance with any undertaking will constitute contempt of court.[145]

Generally the court will have to be satisfied about the plaintiff's ability to honour an undertaking as to damages should this become necessary[146] and an interlocutory injunction may be refused where the court considers that an undertaking given is of no real value.[147] However, it would appear that the court may have some discretion in this regard and this issue was considered by O'Donnell J in his dissenting judgment in *Minister for Justice, Equality and Law Reform v Devine*.[148] He stated that '[t]he picture which emerges … is not of a mechanical rule, but rather of the exercise of the discretionary jurisdiction in which the presence or absence of an undertaking as to damages may be significant, and in many cases decisive.'[149] O'Donnell J noted that it is well established that a court can grant an interlocutory injunction notwithstanding the fact that the undertaking as to damages is of little or no worth because of the lack of means of the applicant,[150] and said that it would clearly be wrong that a deserving plaintiff with a good claim would be denied an injunction simply because he was without assets. In such circumstances he said that the court must take into account the fact that a party would be unlikely to be able to satisfy an undertaking as to damages as one of the factors in considering the grant of an interlocutory injunction and that it may proceed to grant an injunction even without such an undertaking.

There is also a useful consideration of some of the underlying factors in relation to the court's discretion in this area in *Irish Bank Resolution Corporation Ltd v Quinn*[151] and as Peart J noted in the course of his judgment, the court has a discretion not to enforce an undertaking as to damages if the defendant's conduct would make it unjust or inequitable to do so.[152] In this case the personal defendants sought to have the injunctions granted against them discharged on the basis that the undertakings as to damages given by the plaintiff were now worthless as it was in liquidation. The joint special liquidators of the plaintiff had confirmed the undertakings as to damages previously given to the court and offered a fortified undertaking by ring-fencing a sum in the liquidation assets. Peart J made it clear that the onus lay on the defendants to

145. *Irish Bank Resolution Corporation Ltd v Quinn* [2013] IEHC 437 at [76].
146. *Brigid Foley Ltd v Ellott* [1982] RPC 433, 435-436 *per* Megarry VC.
147. *Pasture Properties Ltd v Evans* [1999] IEHC 214.
148. [2012] 1 IR 326. The view of the majority, considered in more detail below, was that an undertaking in damages should almost invariably be required where an interim injunction is sought, as was the case in the matter before the court.
149. *Ibid.* at 360.
150. *Allen v Jambo Ltd* [1980] 1 WLR 1252.
151. [2013] IEHC 437.
152. *Ibid.* at [77]. He referred to the examples given by Peter Gibson LJ in his judgment in *Cheltenham & Gloucester Building Society v Ricketts* [1993] 1 WLR 1545 which include delay by the defendant in seeking to enforce the undertaking, the unmeritorious conduct of the defendant, and the 'inequitable conduct' of a defendant.

satisfy the court that the balance of convenience lay in their favour in seeking to have the injunctions discharged and also as to the extent of the likely losses to them as a result of the injunctions having been granted if it transpired that they should not have been. He expressed the view that the court might well have been justified in considering that the balance of convenience was so clearly in favour of the plaintiffs at the time the injunctions were sought that the absence of a solid undertaking as to damages could have been overlooked in the interests of justice. He concluded that he had no doubt that the balance of convenience remained in favour of leaving the injunctions in place and said that this view was enhanced by the existence of the fortified undertaking although this was not a decisive point.

The factors which the court should consider in deciding whether to enforce an undertaking as to damages where an injunction is discharged prior to trial were considered by Clarke J in *Estuary Logistics & Distribution Co. Ltd v Lowenergy Solutions Ltd.*[153] He quoted from the judgment of Neill LJ in *Cheltenham & Gloucester Building Society v Ricketts*,[154] in which the latter had considered the possible options facing the court in such circumstances. It could determine that the undertaking as to damages should be enforced and proceed at once to make an assessment of such damages, or direct an inquiry as to damages in which issues of causation and quantum would be considered. Alternatively, the court could adjourn the application for the enforcement of the undertaking until the trial or further order or could determine that the undertaking was not to be enforced. In the view of Clarke J these principles seemed to comply with the justice and equity of the type of situation which could arise in such circumstances and he stated that it seemed to him that they also represented the law in this jurisdiction. He added as follows:

> Where the choice rests between immediate enforcement and a postponement of a determination to the trial, it seems to me that the Court has to balance all material factors. These include:
>
> (a) Whether there is a significant possibility that the trial judge may be in a better position to assess all relevant factors;
>
> (b) Whether the nature of the damage alleged is such that it will fall to be considered at the trial in any event; and
>
> (c) Whether the immediate payment of any damages might give rise, in the circumstances of the case under consideration, to a risk of injustice.[155]

Clarke J stated that it seemed to him that there would potentially be an injustice if he were to direct the enforcement of the undertaking as to damages at that stage of the proceedings. He referred to the fact that while the events which

153. [2008] 2 IR 806.
154. [1993] 1 WLR 1545, 1551-1552.
155. [2008] 2 IR 806, 814.

gave rise to the discharge of the injunction were discrete and unconnected with the underlying merits of the substantive case, the losses claimed in respect of the undertaking as to damages were intimately connected with the issues which arose in the proceedings. He pointed out that in that regard the case before him was very different from one where the damages claimed in respect of an undertaking as to damages were wholly separate from the underlying issues which would be debated at the trial. Clarke J concluded that he was satisfied that the justice of the case required that a decision as to whether to enforce the undertaking as to damages should be reserved to the trial judge who would be in a much better position to take account of all appropriate factors.

The principles which apply where an undertaking is sought in relation to an injunction of an *ex parte* nature which is claimed against the State were considered by the Supreme Court in *Minister for Justice, Equality and Law Reform v Devine*.[156] The Minister had applied *ex parte* for an order restraining the respondent from dealing with property in the State in aid of confiscation proceedings taken in the United Kingdom brought to recoup the proceeds of crime so found by the courts in that jurisdiction. The respondent sought to have the restraint order made by the High Court set aside on the basis that the court had not required the Minister to furnish an undertaking as to damages when applying for the order. O'Sullivan J refused to set aside the interim restraint order but held that an undertaking should be given. The Minister's appeal on the ground that, in circumstances where he was enforcing the law of the land, he should not be required to give an undertaking as to damages, was dismissed by the majority of the Supreme Court. Fennelly J stated as follows:

> There cannot, I think, be any room for doubt about the general rule. It is that a party who seeks the aid of the court by way of injunction restraining another person from acting in any particular specified way is required, as a condition of the grant of any injunction, to undertake to the court that he or she would be liable for any damage or loss sustained by the person so restrained, if it should transpire that the injunction should not have been granted. The undertaking is an integral part of the process of seeking to maintain the *status quo*, of maintaining a just balance.[157]

At a general level Fennelly J also commented that there are very powerful reasons for requiring an applicant for an interim, as distinct from an interlocutory, injunction almost invariably to provide an undertaking as to damages as an essential part of the system of balancing rights. However, in a strong dissenting judgment O'Donnell J suggested that there was no automatic requirement of an undertaking as to damages, that the issue was a matter for the court's discretion and that the presumption should be against an undertaking being required in such cases.

156. [2007] 1 IR 813 (HC); [2012] 1 IR 326 (SC).
157. *Ibid.* at 341.

The principles which apply in England where an undertaking in damages is sought against the Crown or a public authority in proceedings where an application for an injunction is made should also be noted. The main authority is *Hoffmann-La Roche v Secretary of State for Trade and Industry*[158] which established that the Crown could in certain circumstances be required to give an undertaking in damages in such cases. However, where an injunction is sought to enforce the 'law of the land', it would be necessary to show very good reason why an undertaking as to damages should be required and in the case before the court this had not been established. This principle that the court had a discretion not to require an undertaking to be given was extended to other public authorities exercising law enforcement functions in certain circumstances in *Kirklees MBC v Wickes Building Supplies Ltd.*[159] More recently in *Financial Services Authority v Sinaloa Gold plc*,[160] the principle that an undertaking in damages might not be required was further extended to apply to innocent third parties, in this case the bank acting for one of the defendants against which the Financial Services Authority sought injunctions to restrain breaches of legislation. However, the decision has been criticised and it has been suggested that '[p]ublic entities, like other persons, ought to do equity in return for seeking equity.'[161]

The Test for the Grant of an Interlocutory Injunction

In principle, a court may grant an injunction of an interlocutory nature whenever it is 'just and convenient'[162] to do so and it has been stressed that the remedy 'should be kept flexible and discretionary … and must not be made the subject of strict rules.'[163] However, in practice recognised guidelines have generally been applied by the courts in deciding whether to grant or refuse this form of relief. It has been acknowledged that there is 'no significant difference' between the principles which apply to the granting or withholding of interlocutory injunctions in this jurisdiction and in England,[164] with the proviso that in this

158. [1975] AC 295.
159. [1993] AC 227.
160. [2013] 2 AC 28.
161. Varuhas and Turner (2014) 130 LQR 33, 37.
162. Section 28(8) of the Supreme Court of Judicature (Ireland) Act 1877 and Order 50, rule 6 of the Rules of the Superior Courts 1986.
163. *Hubbard v Vosper* [1972] 2 QB 84, 96 *per* Denning MR. See also the comments of Barrett J in *Baínee Aláinn Ltd v Glanbia plc* [2014] IEHC 482 at [23] that '[t]his necessary flexibility and discretion is reflective, at least in part, of the fact that the life of the law is not logic, it is experience, and experience teaches that even ostensibly similar facts can sometimes require entirely dissimilar treatment when viewed through the prism of context.'
164. It should be noted that in England and Wales the term 'interim injunction' is now often used to describe what is referred to an 'interlocutory injunction' in this jurisdiction as a result of the terminology employed in Rule 25.1 of the Civil Procedure Rules 1998.

jurisdiction a court cannot by its order abridge or in any way diminish the constitutional rights enjoyed by any of the parties to the action.[165]

The American Cyanamid/Campus Oil formulation

Traditionally, a plaintiff would be granted an interlocutory injunction only if he could establish a '*prima facie* case', i.e. a probability that he would succeed in his claim at the hearing of the action, and the effect of this requirement was that a plaintiff had to show that it was more likely than not that he would succeed. This test was accepted by the House of Lords in *J.T. Stratford and Sons v Lindley*[166] and by the majority of the Supreme Court in *Esso Petroleum Co. (Ireland) Ltd v Fogarty*.[167] However, there was evidence of a different approach being suggested in some cases based on whether there was a fair or substantial question to be decided[168] and the *prima facie* test was criticised on the basis that it led to confusion as to the object sought to be achieved by this form of relief.

The *prima facie* test was finally rejected by the House of Lords in 1975 in favour of a less rigid requirement in the landmark decision of *American Cyanamid Co. v Ethicon Ltd*.[169] In considering the significance of this decision for future case both in England and in Ireland, it is important not to lose sight of the fact that, as O'Donnell J commented in *Merck Sharp & Dohme Corporation v Clonmel Healthcare Ltd*,[170] 'the underlying theme of the decision

165. *Oblique Financial Services Ltd v The Promise Production Co. Ltd* [1994] 1 ILRM 74, 76-77.
166. [1965] AC 269, 338 *per* Lord Upjohn.
167. [1965] IR 531, 538 *per* Ó Dálaigh CJ.
168. *Educational Co. of Ireland Ltd v Fitzpatrick* [1961] IR 323, 337 *per* Lavery J and *Esso Petroleum Co. (Ireland) Ltd. v Fogarty* [1965] IR 531, 541 *per* Walsh J.
169. [1975] AC 396. This test met with approval in a number of other common law jurisdictions, see further Kerr (1983) 18 Ir Jur (ns) 34, 39, footnote 25. It is still generally applied in England, apart from in a number of exceptional cases. However, it should be noted that Laddie J suggested in *Series 5 Software v Clarke* [1996] 1 All ER 853, 865 that 'Lord Diplock did not intend … to exclude consideration of the strength of the cases in most applications for interlocutory relief.' He continued as follows: 'It appears to me that what is intended is that the court should not attempt to resolve difficult issues of fact or law on an application for interlocutory relief. If, on the other hand, the court is able to come to a view as to the strength of the parties' case on the credible evidence, then it can do so. … If it is apparent from that material that one party's case is much stronger than the other's then that is a matter the court should not ignore. To suggest otherwise would be to exclude from consideration an important factor and such exclusion would fly in the face of the flexibility advocated earlier in *American Cyanamid*.' Lord Hoffmann also made reference in delivering the opinion of the Privy Council in *National Commercial Bank Jamaica Ltd v Olint Corporation Ltd* [2009] 1 WLR 1405, 1409 to the fact that amongst the matters which the court may take into account is the likelihood that the injunction will turn out to have been wrongly granted or withheld, 'that is to say, the court's opinion of the relative strength of the parties' cases'.
170. [2019] IESC 65 at [33].

was to reassert the flexibility of the remedy and the essential function of an interlocutory injunction in finding a just solution pending the hearing of the action.'

In *American Cyanamid* the plaintiff sought and obtained an interlocutory injunction to restrain the defendant from marketing surgical products in alleged infringement of the plaintiff's patent. The modified test propounded by Lord Diplock required a plaintiff to show that the claim was not frivolous or vexatious, in other words that there was 'a serious question to be tried', and where this was established, the court had to go on to consider the balance of convenience which involved assessing the probable implications for both parties should the relief sought be granted or refused. He added that '[i]t is no part of the court's function at this stage of the litigation to try to resolve conflicts of evidence on affidavit as to facts on which the claims of either party may ultimately depend nor to decide difficult questions of law which call for detailed argument and mature considerations. These are matters to be dealt with at the trial'.[171] Or, as Clarke J put it in *Kinsella v McAleer*,[172] '[i]t is not practical, therefore, for the courts to become involved in deciding contentious issues of fact or complicated legal questions as to the rights of the parties at this stage because the information and evidence is not available.'

Although an assessment of where the balance of convenience lay involved consideration of a number of factors, the most important of these was recognised as being the question of the adequacy of damages.[173] In Lord Diplock's view the court was required to consider first, if an interlocutory order was refused and the plaintiff were to succeed at the trial in establishing an entitlement to a permanent injunction, whether he would be adequately compensated by an award of damages. The court also had to consider whether the defendant would be adequately compensated by an award of damages if the decision went against him at the interlocutory stage but he was ultimately successful at the trial. However, as Lord Hoffmann pointed out in *National Commercial*

---

171. *Ibid.* at 407. See also *European Dynamics SA v HM Treasury* [2009] EWHC 3419 (TCC) at [12]. This principle is also well established in this jurisdiction, see e.g. *Campus Oil Ltd v Minister for Industry and Energy (No.2)* [1983] IR 88, 110-11; *Irish Shell v Elm Motors Ltd* [1984] IR 200, 224; *Ferris v Ward* [1998] 2 IR 194, 200; *Byrne v Dublin City Council* [2009] IEHC 122 at 8; *Osmond Ireland On Farm Business v McFarland* [2010] IEHC 295 at 11; *O'Mahony v Examiner Publications (Cork) Ltd* [2010] IEHC 413 at 12; *McLoughlin v Setanta Insurance Services Ltd* [2011] IEHC 410 at [3]; *McGuinness v Allied Irish Banks plc* [2014] IEHC 191 at [39]; *Dagenham Yank Ltd v Irish Bank Corporation Ltd* [2014] IEHC 192 at [56].

172. High Court, 24 April 2009 at [10]. See also *Ryanair Ltd v Club Travel Ltd* [2012] IEHC 165 at [8].

173. As Lord Diplock stated at 408, '[i]t would be unwise to attempt even to list all the various matters which may need to be taken into consideration in deciding where the balance lies, let alone to suggest the relative weight to be attached to them.' See also *National Commercial Bank Jamaica Ltd v Olint Corporation Ltd* [2009] 1 WLR 1405, 1409.

Bank Jamaica Ltd v Olint Corporation Ltd,[174] it will often be difficult to assess whether damages or a cross-undertaking will be an adequate remedy and in his view the court has to engage in trying to predict whether granting or withholding an injunction is more or less likely to cause irremediable prejudice, and if so, to what extent, if it turns out that the injunction should not have been granted or withheld. As he put it, '[t]he basic principle is that the court should take whichever course seems likely to cause the least irremediable prejudice to one party or the other.'[175]

While these *American Cyanamid* principles received a mixed reception in this jurisdiction in the years immediately following the decision of the House of Lords,[176] they were approved in *Campus Oil Ltd v Minister for Industry and Energy (No.2)*,[177] which was a case dealing with an application for an interlocutory injunction of a mandatory nature, and have been applied since in numerous decisions.[178] The plaintiff claimed a declaration that the obligation imposed on it by statutory instrument to buy a specified portion of its petroleum oil supplies from a state-owned refinery was contrary to Articles 30 and 31 of the EEC Treaty. The issue was referred to the European Court of Justice and the defendants sought an interlocutory injunction compelling the plaintiff to comply with the terms of the order pending determination of the plaintiff's claim at the trial of the action. It was held by Keane J in granting an interlocutory injunction that the probability of success at the trial was not the proper test to be applied by the court in deciding whether to grant such an injunction. Instead an applicant must establish that there is a fair question to be determined and that the balance of convenience lies on the side of granting the injunction. This finding was upheld by the Supreme Court and O'Higgins CJ stated as follows:

> In my view, the test to be applied is whether a fair *bona fide* question has been raised by the person seeking the relief. If such a question has been raised, it is not for the Court to determine that question on an interlocutory application; that remains to be decided at the trial. Once a

174. [2009] 1 WLR 1405.
175. *Ibid.* at 1409. See also *Alstom Transport v Eurostar International Ltd* [2010] EWHC 2727 (Ch) at [78].
176. See Kerr (1983) 18 Ir Jur (ns) 34, 39-40. Note that in *TMG Group Ltd v Al Babtain Trading and Contracting Co.* [1982] ILRM 349, 353, Keane J stated that 'insofar as the decision of the House of Lords in *American Cyanamid Co. v Ethicon Ltd* suggests the application of different principles to applications of this nature, it does not represent the law in this country'. While they were applied at first with some reluctance by the Court of Appeal in *Hubbard v Pitt* [1976] QB 142 and *Fellowes & Son v Fisher* [1976] QB 122 they are now generally accepted in England.
177. [1983] IR 88. See also *Irish Shell Ltd v Elm Motors Ltd* [1984] IR 200.
178. Some examples include *Westman Holdings Ltd v McCormack* [1992] 1 IR 151; *Connolly v Byrne* Supreme Court 1997 No. 13, 23 January 1997; *DSG Retail Ltd v PC World* [1998] IEHC 3; *Clane Hospital Ltd v VHI* [1998] IEHC 78; *Dunne v Dun Laoghaire-Rathdown County Council* [2003] 2 ILRM 147; *Relax Food Corporation Ltd v Brown Thomas & Co. Ltd* [2009] IEHC 181.

> fair question has been raised … then the Court should consider the other matters which are appropriate to the exercise of its discretion to grant interlocutory relief. In this regard, I note the view expressed by Lord Diplock in *American Cyanamid Co. v Ethicon Ltd.* I merely say that I entirely agree with what he said.[179]

The following useful summary of the principles which the court should adhere to when considering applications for interlocutory relief is set out in the judgment of Quirke J in *Clane Hospital Ltd v Voluntary Health Insurance Board*,[180] in which the plaintiffs sought an interlocutory injunction restraining the defendants from replacing their scheme of charges for medical services. He stated that the court should adopt the following sequence of issues for consideration:[181]

1. Whether or not the applicant has raised a fair, substantial[182] *bona fide* question for determination.
2. Whether, if the applicant were to succeed at the trial in establishing his right to a permanent injunction, he could be adequately compensated by an award of damages.
3. Whether, if the respondent were to be successful at the trial, he could be adequately compensated under the applicant's undertaking as to damages for any loss which he would have sustained by reason of the grant of interlocutory relief.
4. If either party or both have, by way of evidence, raised a real and substantial doubt as to the adequacy of the respective remedies in damages available to either party, then where does the 'balance of convenience' lie?
5. In some instances are there any 'special factors' (usually technical in nature) which may influence the exercise of discretion and the grant of the relief sought?

---

179. [1983] IR 88, 107. It was suggested by Laffoy J in *Crossplan Investments Ltd v McCann* [2013] IEHC 205 at [21] that 'it is generally recognised that the threshold for compliance with the "a fair bona fide question" test is a low threshold.' See also *Wingview Ltd v Ennis Property Finance Designated Area Company* [2017] IEHC 674 at [14] and *O'Gara v Ulster Bank Ireland DAC* [2019] IEHC 213 at [42], where Barniville J stated that this 'low threshold' means that 'unless the case is unstateable, it is generally not a difficult threshold to meet.'
180. [1998] IEHC 78. See further the list of considerations set out by McCracken J in *B. & S. Ltd v Irish Auto Trader Ltd* [1995] 2 IR 142, 154 and Barrett J in *Baínne Aláinn Ltd v Glanbia plc* [2014] IEHC 482 at [29]. See also the useful summary of principles drawn from case law in this area set out by Barrett J in *Baínne Aláinn Ltd* at [42].
181. *Ibid.* at 10. See also *Gibb v Promontoria (Aran) Ltd* [2018] IECA 95 at [23] *per* Whelan J.
182. On the same page of his judgment, Quirke J spoke in terms of the plaintiff establishing 'a fair *bona fide* question' and it is unlikely that he was deliberately seeking to make the test harder to satisfy by inserting the word 'substantial'. However, in view of the fact that the latter term did not appear in either the *American Cyanamid* or *Campus Oil* decisions, it is probably better omitted.

Quirke J concluded that the plaintiffs had raised a fair, substantial and *bona fide* question for determination, but he was satisfied that if the plaintiffs succeeded at the trial in establishing their right to a permanent injunction, they could be adequately compensated by an award of damages and in the circumstances, he decided to refuse the relief sought by the plaintiffs.

A Serious or Fair Question to be Tried?

The question of what is meant by a serious or fair question to be tried was considered by Edwards J in *Chieftain Construction Ltd v Ryan*,[183] in which the plaintiff building contractors sought interlocutory injunctions to restrain the defendants from carrying on certain activities at their sites which they alleged amounted to trespass and nuisance, although the defendants claimed that their conduct was peaceful picketing which was lawful by virtue of section 11(1) of the Industrial Relations Act 1990. Edwards J posed the question of whether the court's assessment should be confined to an issue of substance in the narrow sense, namely the utility of the argument, or whether the substance of the point should be considered in the broad sense, namely as encompassing both the utility and the strength of the case put forward. He said that he could derive no clear guidance from the judgments in *Campus Oil* as to whether regard could be had to the strength of the case in considering whether the plaintiff had raised a fair or substantial or serious issue to be tried but added that the interchangeability of the adjectives employed suggested strongly to him that what was required was a consideration of the 'substance' of the point raised in the broad sense. Edwards J concluded as follows:

> It seems to me that any evaluation of a plaintiff's prospects of success must necessarily involve a consideration of both the utility and the strength of the point in question. Moreover, the use of the adjective 'real' imports a need to evaluate the 'reality' of the prospects of success and that requires an examination, if it be possible, of the strength of a plaintiff's case.[184]

It has tended to be generally accepted that the strength of the plaintiff's claim should not be a relevant factor in determining whether an injunction should be granted once it has been accepted that a fair question has been raised,[185]

183. [2008] IEHC 147.
184. *Ibid.* at 9.
185. *Westman Holdings Ltd v McCormack* [1992] 1 IR 151, 157. See also *Ancorde Ltd v Horgan* [2013] IEHC 265 at [36]. However, note the views expressed by Lord Diplock in *American Cyanamid Co. v Ethicon Ltd* [1975] AC 396, 409 to the effect that 'if the extent of the uncompensatable disadvantage to each party would not differ widely, it may not be improper to take into account in tipping the balance the relative strength of each party's case as revealed by the affidavit evidence adduced on the hearing of the application.' However, he stressed that this should be done only where it is apparent that there is no credible dispute that the strength of one party's case is disproportionate

save in an exceptional case such as where the trial of the action is unlikely to take place.[186] In *Allied Irish Banks plc v Diamond*[187] Clarke J commented that while the approach of having regard to the weight of the case on either side might have a 'superficial attraction', the counter arguments were much stronger. In his view the significant additional evidence that would need to be filed and the much more detailed legal submissions on the merits of the case which would be required would lead to such a delay that it would in many cases defeat the whole purpose of the interlocutory jurisdiction. However, the comments of O'Donnell J in *Merck Sharp & Dohme Corporation v Clonmel Healthcare Ltd*,[188] should also be noted in this context. He suggested that 'in cases where the balance of convenience may be finely balanced, it may be appropriate to have regard, even on a preliminary basis, to the strength of the rival arguments as they may appear to the court.'[189] He also referred to the fact that it had been recognised in *American Cyanamid* that if the question of the adequacy of damages is evenly balanced, it 'may not be inappropriate to consider the relative strengths and merits of each party's case as it may appear at the interlocutory stage.'

The court will inevitably consider a plaintiff's prospects of success to some extent in determining the threshold question of whether he has established a serious or fair question to be tried. The reality, as Edwards J adverted to in *Chieftain*, is that in many cases there will be conflicts of evidence which cannot effectively be resolved on the basis of affidavits alone and in such cases a court must be wary of making a determination based on the strength or otherwise of a plaintiff's claim.[190] However, there is certainly merit in the view expressed by Laddie J in *Series 5 Software Ltd v Clarke*[191] to the effect that where a court is in a position to form a clear view as to the relative strengths and weaknesses of the parties' cases on the basis of credible evidence adduced at the interlocutory stage it may take this into account, at least in assessing whether a serious or fair question has been made out. The broader view expressed by Laddie J in *Series 5* to the effect that in his view Lord Diplock in *American Cyanamid* had not

---

to that of the other party and stated that 'the court is not justified in embarking upon anything resembling a trial of the action upon conflicting affidavits in order to evaluate the strength of either party's case.'

186. See further *infra* pp. 691-699.
187. [2012] 3 IR 549, 574. Clarke J reiterated in *Okunade v Minister for Justice, Equality and Law Reform* [2012] 3 IR 152, 183 that there are strong reasons for not placing greater weight on the strength or weakness of the parties' cases. See also *Wallace v Irish Aviation Authority* [2012] 2 ILRM 345, 352.
188. [2019] IESC 65.
189. *Ibid.* at [62].
190. Although Edwards J did suggest that where there are serious conflicts in the affidavit evidence, or a serious uncertainty as to the law, a court should accept the fact that it may not be possible to accurately evaluate the strength of the plaintiff's case and give the benefit of the doubt to the plaintiff. As he put it, '[t]he very existence of such serious conflicts would suggest "a fair issue to be tried"'.
191. [1996] 1 All ER 853.

intended to exclude consideration of the strength of cases in most applications for interlocutory relief has proved somewhat controversial. However, it is submitted that there is some merit in the view expressed by Lord Hoffmann in *National Commercial Bank Jamaica Ltd v Olint Corporation Ltd*[192] that the court should take whichever course seems likely to cause the least irremediable prejudice to one party or the other and that amongst the factors which it may take into account is the likelihood that the injunction will turn out to have been wrongly granted or withheld, 'that is to say the court's opinion of the relative strengths of the parties' cases'.

Are the Adequacy of Damages and Balance of Convenience Distinct Issues?
Considerable debate has surrounded the question of whether the adequacy of damages and the balance of convenience are two distinct issues for the court to consider or whether the latter is simply an aspect of the former. Some confusion was sown by Lord Diplock himself in *American Cyanamid* on this point when he appeared to consider the adequacy of damages question at the outset of the inquiry into where the balance of convenience lay but went on to add that 'it is where there is doubt as to the adequacy of the respective remedies in damages available to either party or to both, that the question of balance of convenience arises'.[193] Commenting on this *dictum* in *B & S Ltd v Irish Auto Trader Ltd*,[194] McCracken J said that he would be more inclined to the view that the entire test rests on a balance of convenience but that the adequacy of damages is a very important and frequently decisive element in considering where this lies. As against this, in *Smithkline Beecham plc v Genthon BV*[195] Kelly J commented that reference had been made before him to decisions of the High Court in which there appeared to have been a conflation of the two issues of adequacy of damages and balance of convenience and he expressed the opinion that this approach was not justified on the basis of either the *American Cyanamid* case or the Supreme Court authorities in the area. In his view, where he was satisfied, as he was in the case before him, that damages would be an adequate remedy for the plaintiff, he did not have to proceed to consider the balance of convenience.

A common approach is to ask, as Clarke J has done in a number of cases,[196] whether the plaintiff has made out a fair case to be tried, whether damages would be an adequate remedy and only if the answer to this question is in the

192. [2009] 1 WLR 1405, 1409.
193. [1975] AC 396, 408.
194. [1995] 2 IR 142, 146. See also *Miss World Ltd v Miss Ireland Beauty Pageant Ltd* [2004] 2 IR 394, 404; *Metro International SA v Independent News and Media plc* [2006] 1 ILRM 414, 422.
195. [2003] IEHC 623.
196. *Evans v IRFB Services (Ireland) Ltd* [2005] 2 ILRM 358, 361; *Irish Shell Ltd v J.H. McLoughlin (Balbriggan) Ltd* [2005] IEHC 304 at 5; *Becker v Board of Management of St Dominic's Secondary School Cabra* [2005] 1 IR 561, 569.

negative, then to ask where the balance of convenience lies. It can also be argued, as Clarke J suggested in *Metro International SA v Independent News and Media plc*,[197] that whether the criteria referred to above are viewed as a single test of the balance of convenience of which the adequacy of damages is a potentially significant part or as two separate tests is 'more a matter of semantics than substance'. In this regard he stated that it is clear from the judgment of McCracken J in *B & S Ltd v Irish Auto Trader Ltd*[198] that in a case where the plaintiff could be adequately compensated in damages and the defendant was a mark for such damages, the balance of convenience would inevitably favour the rejection of the application for an injunction. However, as Finlay CJ pointed out in *Westman Holdings Ltd v McCormack*,[199] the question of whether a plaintiff could, in the event of being refused an injunction and succeeding in the action, be adequately compensated by damages raises two separate issues, namely, 'whether damages would be an adequate remedy, and …whether there is a defendant liable to pay such damages who is able to do so, and thus the appropriate compensation could actually be realised.'

This question has recently been reconsidered by O'Donnell J in *Merck Sharp & Dohme Corporation v Clonmel Healthcare Ltd.*[200] While he referred to the comment of Clarke J in *Metro* to the effect that the issue is largely a semantic one and agreed that in most cases either approach would lead to the same conclusion, he stated that in his view, 'the preferable approach is to consider adequacy of damages as part of the balance of convenience, or the balance of justice, as it is sometimes called.'[201] In his opinion, such an approach tends to reinforce the essential flexibility of the remedy and adopting it means that it is not simply a question of asking whether damages are an adequate remedy. He continued as follows:

> As observed by Lord Diplock, in other than the simplest cases, it may always be the case that there is some element of unquantifiable damage. It is not an absolute matter: it is relative. There may be cases where both parties can be said to be likely to suffer some irreparable harm, but in one case it may be much more significant than the other. On the other hand, it is conceivable that while it can be said that one party may suffer some irreparable harm if an injunction is granted or refused, as the case may be, there are nevertheless a number of other factors to apply that may tip the balance in favour of the opposing party. This, in my view,

197. [2006] 1 ILRM 414, 423.
198. [1995] 2 IR 142, 145.
199. [1992] 1 IR 151, 158. See also *McCann v Morrissey* [2013] IEHC 288 at [43]; *Swinburne v Geary* [2013] IEHC 412 at [15].
200. [2019] IESC 65.
201. *Ibid.* at [35].

> reflects the reality of the approach taken by most judges when weighing up all the factors involved.[202]

So, in the view of O'Donnell J, 'while the question of the adequacy of damages to either party and the capacity of the parties to pay them is often the largest single element in the balance of convenience, and will often be decisive in most cases, there are other factors which are relevant and which, in a closely balanced case, may tip the balance.'[203]

Issues which Arise in Assessing Whether Damages Would be an Adequate Remedy

If damages would not be an adequate remedy for a plaintiff who is refused interlocutory relief but succeeds at trial, then a further issue as set out by Clarke J in the decision of the Supreme Court in *Okunade v Minister for Justice, Equality and Law Reform*[204] in the following terms must be considered:

> If damages would not be an adequate remedy for the plaintiff, then the court must consider whether, if it does grant an injunction at the interlocutory stage, a plaintiff's undertaking as to damages will adequately compensate the defendant, should the latter be successful at the trial of the action, in respect of any loss suffered by him due to the injunction being enforced pending the trial. If the defendant would be adequately compensated by damages, then the injunction will normally be granted. This last matter is also subject to the proviso that the plaintiff would be in a position to meet the undertaking as to damages in the event that it is called on.

So, where it is not possible to conclude that an undertaking in damages given by the plaintiff would be likely to adequately compensate the defendant should the plaintiff be granted an interlocutory injunction but ultimately not succeed in the action,[205] or where the court cannot conclude that the plaintiff will be in a position to make good its undertaking as to damages,[206] injunctive relief will often be refused at the interlocutory stage.

In weighing up whether damages would be an adequate remedy, one of the key issues is whether it will be possible to properly assess the amount of damages which might compensate for loss suffered.[207] As noted above, in *Curust*

202. *Ibid.*
203. *Ibid.* at [60].
204. [2012] 3 IR 152, 180-181. This is an explanation of the position set out in *B. & S. Ltd v Irish Auto Trader Ltd* [1995] 2 IR 142, 145. See further *O'Mahony v Lowe* [2013] IEHC 361 at [18].
205. *Kinsella v Wallace* [2013] IEHC 112 at [37].
206. *Goode Concrete v Cement Roadstone Holdings plc* [2011] IEHC 15 at [28].
207. As Mance LJ commented in *Bath and North East Somerset District Council v Mowlem*

Financial Services Ltd v Loewe-Lack-Werk Otto Loewe GmbH,[208] Finlay CJ expressed the view that, '[d]ifficulty, as opposed to complete impossibility, in the assessment of …damages should not, in my view, be a ground for characterising the awarding of damages as an inadequate remedy.' Barrett J considered the effect of this statement in *Baínne Aláinn Ltd v Glanbia plc*[209] in the context of cases where the alleged loss could conceivably be reduced to damages but where the quantification of those damages was not capable of reasonably precise estimate. He stated as follows:

> In this last regard, nothing is impossible to an accountant or an actuary: if asked to quantify a loss he or she will do so but such estimates may and sometimes will be little more than informed guesswork. In other words one will reach a point where it is possible still to quantify the amount of damages but impossible to do so with any meaningful accuracy. It is this type of impossibility that the court understands Finlay C.J. to refer to when he speaks of "[d]ifficulty, as distinct from complete impossibility, in the assessment of…damages", *i.e.* damages that are completely impossible to calculate with such a degree of accuracy as to represent the probable loss that a person will suffer absent injunctive relief.[210]

It should also be noted that as Clarke J pointed out in *Metro International SA v Independent News and Media plc*,[211] it can be important to have regard to the nature of the loss which may be suffered in order to assess whether it might be compensatable in damages and the context in which relief is sought may be significant. He stated that there are types of cases where the courts have traditionally not been prepared to award damages even though any relevant loss could be calculated in monetary terms and, by way of example, said that the mere fact that a property right or a diminution in such a right can be valued in financial terms does not of itself mean that damages for infringement of that right can be said to be an adequate remedy.[212] Therefore, as Clarke J commented

---

[2015] 2 WLR 785, 794, the courts ought to recognise that 'the assessment of the totality of any likely loss *before* the event is an even more rough and ready and difficult exercise than after the event; and that such an assessment may prove in the event not to give rise to adequate compensation.'

208. [1994] 1 IR 450, 469.
209. [2014] IEHC 482.
210. *Ibid.* at [33].
211. [2006] 1 ILRM 414, 423. See also *Sports Direct International plc v Minor* [2014] IEHC 546 at [31].
212. Similarly, in *Allied Irish Banks plc v Diamond* [2012] 3 IR 549, 590 Clarke J stated that '[t]he mere fact that it may, therefore, be possible to put a value on property rights lost does not, of itself, mean that damages are necessarily an adequate remedy for the party concerned is entitled to its property rights instead of their value.' See also the comments of Kirwan, *Injunctions: Law and Practice* (2nd ed., 2015) para. 6.38, quoted with approval in *Sheehan v Brecccia* [2017] IEHC 692 at [57], that when property

in *Metro*, in assessing the adequacy or otherwise of damages as a remedy 'the court can and should have regard to the question of whether the right sought to be enforced or protected by interlocutory injunction is one which is of a type that the court will normally protect by injunction even though it might, in one sense, be possible to value the extinguishment or diminution of that right in monetary terms.'[213]

The significance of the fact that property rights are at stake where an injunction is sought to restrain trespass has been regarded as significant. So, in *Pasture Properties Ltd v Evans*[214] Laffoy J stated that 'it is axiomatic in trespass cases that damages are not an adequate remedy' and in *Start Mortgages Ltd v Doyle*,[215] Murphy J stated that the principle that damages are not an adequate remedy in such cases arises as 'a logical consequence of the particular status of property rights within our constitutional framework.' It should also be noted that it has been accepted that a plaintiff whose title is not at issue will *prima facie* be entitled to an injunction to restrain trespass.[216] In such cases the onus will shift to a defendant to satisfy the courts that there is a serious question to be tried as to whether the defendant had a right to act in a manner which would otherwise constitute a trespass.[217]

The issue of the inadequacy of damages as a remedy has also arisen in relation to passing off actions and intellectual property disputes. In *DSG Retail Ltd v PC World Ltd*[218] Laffoy J referred to 'the normal axiom in passing off actions, that damages would not be an adequate remedy for the plaintiff'. Similarly, in his dissenting judgment in the Court of Appeal in *Merck Sharp and Dohme Corporation v Clonmel Healthcare Ltd*,[219] Hogan J stated that 'where an established property right – such as an intellectual property right – has been infringed, that holder is *prima facie* entitled to an injunction to restrain such an infringement.' However, this outcome is likely simply as a result of the factors

rights are at issue, the starting point is in the main that damages would not afford an adequate remedy.

213. [2006] 1 ILRM 414, 424-425. See also *O'Flynn v Carbon Finance Ltd* [2014] IEHC 458 at [172].
214. [1999] IEHC 214. See also *Harrington v Gulland Property Finance Ltd* [2016] IEHC 447 at [35].
215. [2016] IEHC 386 at [10].
216. *Keating v Jervis Shopping Centre Ltd* [1997] 1 IR 512, 518. See also *Kavanagh v Lynch* [2011] IEHC 348 at [7.2]; *Tyrrell v Wright* [2017] IEHC 92 at [56]; *Havbell Designated Activity Company v Dias* [2018] IEHC 175 at [43]; *Beltany Property Finance DAC v Doyle* [2019] IEHC 307 at [49].
217. *Nurendale t/a Panda Waste Services v Starrus Eco Holdings Ltd* [2015] IEHC 845 at [16]-[17]; *Tyrrell v Wright* [2017] IEHC 92 at [56]; *Havbell Designated Activity Company v Dias* [2018] IEHC 175 at [44]. However, note that in some instances the *Campus Oil* principles have continued to be applied in such cases, see e.g *Emo Oil Ltd v Oil Rig Supplies Ltd* [2017] IEHC 594.
218. [1998] IEHC 3. See also *Mitchelstown Co-Operative Agricultural Society Ltd v Golden Vale Products Ltd* [1985] IEHC 51.
219. [2018] IECA 177 at [10].

which tend to arise in such cases and as Clarke J made clear in *Jacob Fruitfield Food Group Ltd v United Biscuits (UK) Ltd*,[220] he did not consider that there is a rule of law to this effect. As he commented, '[w]hat the cases indicate is that a proper application of the principles applicable to a consideration of the balance of convenience and the adequacy of damages will normally, in a passing off case, lead to the conclusion that the plaintiff will suffer uncompensatable damages and that the balance of convenience will favour the grant of an injunction.'[221] However, an injunction will not necessarily be the only appropriate remedy where property rights are at stake, and in *Sony Music Entertainment Ireland Ltd v UPC Communications Ireland Ltd*[222] Hogan J accepted that there is nothing to suggest that a right to intellectual property is 'inviolable'.

Subsequently, in *Gilead Sciences Inc v Mylan SAS Generics (UK) Ltd*,[223] McGovern J made it clear that whether a case involves property rights is not determinative of the question of whether interlocutory relief should be granted and it is no more than a factor to be taken into account. This issue was also considered by Barniville J in *Teva Pharmaceutical Industries Ltd v Mylan Teoranta*,[224] where he made it clear that the fact that a property right is at issue is merely a factor to be taken into account and also that it should be considered rather as an issue in assessing where the balance of convenience lies. He stated as follows:

> It is clear that there is no rule of law or presumption that in a case where the plaintiff who seeks to protect a property right an interlocutory injunction should be granted as a matter of course. It is quite clear that the test to be applied in considering an application for an interlocutory injunction in a patent infringement case is the same as that to be applied in other cases not involving the invocation of a property right. … The fact that a property right is in issue is a factor to be taken into account as part of the balance of convenience assessment. However, it is only one such factor. The weight to be given to that factor in the overall consideration of where the greater risk of injustice lies will very much depend on the circumstances of the case.[225]

This is also in line with the approach taken by O'Donnell J in the Supreme Court in *Merck Sharp & Dohme Corporation v Clonmel Healthcare Ltd*,[226] in considering the appropriate principles relating to the grant of interlocutory

220. [2007] IEHC 368
221. *Ibid.* at [4.2].
222. [2016] IECA 231 at [41]. See also *Smithkline Beecham plc v Genthon* BV [2003] IEHC 623.
223. [2017] IEHC 666.
224. [2018] IEHC 324 at [124].
225. *Ibid.* at [169].
226. [2019] IESC 65.

injunctions in the context of the protection of patents and supplementary protection certificates. He expressed the view that *Teva* had been correctly decided and added that this and other decisions could not be understood, in his view, as 'establishing some general principle that interlocutory injunctions are inappropriate in the field of patents, [special protection certificates], or intellectual property more generally.'[227]

The Balance of Convenience

As Barniville J noted in *Teva Pharmaceutical Industries Ltd v Mylan Teoranta*,[228] '[i]t is normally only when damages would not adequately compensate the plaintiff or the defendant that it is necessary to go on to consider the question of the balance of convenience.' In addition, as Whelan J commented in the Court of Appeal in *Merck Sharp and Dohme Corporation v Clonmel Healthcare Ltd*,[229] '[i]n determining where the balance of convenience lies various issues may require consideration by a trial judge. These will vary from case to case and be case specific.'

In circumstances where the court concludes that damages would not be an adequate remedy for either party, it may then consider whether on the facts the damage which would be suffered by the plaintiff should the court decline to make the order sought would, on the balance of probability, be greater than the damage suffered by the defendant should the court grant the interlocutory relief.[230] This is explained well by Clarke J in his judgment in *Allied Irish Banks plc v Diamond*[231] in the following terms:

> The balance of convenience is, perhaps, the factor that is most closely and directly associated with the risk of injustice. Where both plaintiff and defendant have established arguable cases for respectively the claim and the defence and where neither could be adequately compensated in damages, the court turns to the balance of convenience. In substance, the court has to assess how serious the consequences for the respective parties would be in the event that an injunction is granted which ultimately, again with the benefit of hindsight after a trial, should not have been granted or is refused where ultimately, with the benefit of hindsight after a trial, it is determined that it should have been granted. In both cases the parties will, on the hypothesis that leads to a consideration of the balance of convenience, be at risk of suffering consequences for which damages would not be an adequate remedy. There will, therefore, either

227. *Ibid.* at [52].
228. [2018] IEHC 324 at [124].
229. [2018] IEHC 177 at [76].
230. *Local Ireland Ltd v Local Ireland-Online Ltd* [2000] 4 IR 567. See also *Wright v Board of Management of Gorey Community School* [2000] IEHC 37.
231. [2012] 3 IR 549, 571. See also *Ancorde Ltd v Horgan* [2013] IEHC 265 at [75].

> way, be irremediable consequences of either the granting or refusal of the interlocutory order sought. The court has to form a view as to which of those consequences, on balance, would be the lesser.

This issue was also considered by Clarke J in his judgment in the Supreme Court in *Okunade v Minister for Justice, Equality and Law Reform*,[232] where he observed that '[t]he test of the balance of convenience is, of course, itself expressly directed to deciding where the least harm would be done by comparing the consequences for the plaintiff in the event that an interlocutory injunction is refused but the plaintiff succeeds at trial with the consequences for the defendant in the event that an interlocutory injunction is granted but the plaintiff fails at trial.'

Preserving the Status Quo

Where there is doubt as to the adequacy of the respective remedies in damages, the court may also consider other factors, such as the taking of whatever measures would be necessary to preserve the *status quo*.[233] The concept of the *status quo* was considered by Lord Diplock in *Garden Cottage Foods Ltd v Milk Marketing Board*[234] where he said that 'the relevant *status quo* … is the state of affairs existing during the period immediately preceding the issue of the writ claiming the permanent injunction or, if there be unreasonable delay between the issue of the writ and the motion for an interlocutory injunction, the period immediately preceding the motion.' This interpretation is arguably correct but it has not always been strictly followed. This statement was quoted by Whelan J in the Court of Appeal in *Merck Sharp and Dohme Corporation v Clonmel Healthcare Ltd*, [235] although she added that 'it is for the trial judge to determine what constitutes the status quo in any given case rather than adhering slavishly to pre-determined formulae lacking the legal resilience that is a pre-requisite for a strict legal principle.'

In *Bayzana Ltd v Galligan*[236] the plaintiff sought an injunction restraining the defendants from picketing a factory premises which it had bought with notice of the dispute. The majority of the Supreme Court concluded that there was a fair question to be tried and was satisfied that the balance of convenience favoured the plaintiff employers. However, McCarthy J in his dissenting

232. [2012] 3 IR 152, 181. See also *Teva Pharmaceutical Industries Ltd v Mylan Teoranta* [2018] IEHC 324 at [163]; *Merck Sharp & Dohme Corporation v Clonmel Healthcare Ltd* [2018] IECA 177 at [51] *per* Whelan J.
233. As O'Higgins CJ stated in *Campus Oil Ltd v Minister for Industry and Energy (No.2)* [1983] IR 88, 106, '[i]nterlocutory relief is intended to keep matters *in statu quo* until the trial and to do no more'.
234. [1984] AC 130, 140. See also *Leo Pharma A/S v Sandoz Ltd* [2008] EWHC 541 (Pat) at [96], affirmed on appeal [2008] EWCA Civ 850.
235. [2018] IECA 177 at [125].
236. [1987] IR 238.

judgment pointed out that in this instance the *status quo* to be preserved was that pertaining when the plaintiff became involved in the matter when it was aware of the dispute and of the picket and upheld the order of Hamilton P which merely restricted the number of pickets.

As McCracken J commented in *Private Research Ltd v Brosnan*,[237] '[w]eighing heavily in favour of the plaintiff is the general rule that, where possible, the court should strive to maintain the *status quo*. However, this is only one element in considering the balance of convenience and there is no absolute rule that the *status quo* must be maintained'. In some cases, the balance of convenience will lie in favour of refusing an interlocutory injunction, notwithstanding that this may result in the alteration of the parties' respective positions. An example of this is the decision of McCracken J in *B. & S. Ltd v Irish Auto Trader Ltd*,[238] in which he refused to grant an injunction restraining the defendant from publishing, printing and distributing its magazine 'Auto Trader' in Ireland despite the plaintiff's claim that the tort of passing off had been established. While McCracken J acknowledged that '[i]t is normally a counsel of prudence, although not a fixed rule, that if all other matters are equally balanced, the court should preserve the *status quo*',[239] he held that in view of the fact, *inter alia*, that the defendant had acted in a *bona fide* manner and that there was unlikely to be confusion between the parties' magazines, he was satisfied that the balance of convenience lay in refusing the relief sought notwithstanding that this altered the *status quo*.

It should also be borne in mind, as Lord Hoffmann pointed out in *National Commercial Bank Jamaica Ltd v Olint Corporation Ltd*[240] that the reality is that it may be impossible to simply preserve the *status quo* and any order made is likely to have consequences, both for the parties and possibly for third parties. As he stated:

> It is often said that the purpose of an interlocutory injunction is to preserve the status quo, but it is of course impossible to stop the world pending trial. The court may order a defendant to do something or not to do something else, but such restrictions on the defendant's freedom of action will have consequences, for him and for others, which a court has to take into account. The purpose of such an injunction is to improve the chances of the court being able to do justice after a determination of the merits at the trial. At the interlocutory stage, the court must therefore assess whether granting or withholding an injunction is more likely to produce a just result.[241]

237. [1996] 1 ILRM 27, 32.
238. [1995] 2 ILRM 152.
239. *Ibid.* at 156.
240. [2009] 1 WLR 1405.
241. *Ibid.* at 1409. Quoted with approval in *European Dynamics SA v HM Treasury* [2009]

Finally, the comments of Clarke J in *Okunade v Minister for Justice, Equality and Law Reform*[242] should be noted in this regard; 'even that part of the test which suggests that maintaining the *status quo* might be determinative where all other factors are evenly balanced is in itself a recognition that, in order to interfere with the situation as it currently stands, the court requires a justification. Therefore the risk of injustice from not acting must be greater than that from acting in order that the court depart from the *status quo*.'

Principles Relating to Grant of Injunctions Pending Appeal

The issue of whether the same principles apply where an injunction is sought pending an appeal, which will operate in a manner akin to a stay, has been considered on a number of occasions. In *Cosma v Minister for Justice, Equality and Law Reform*[243] the Supreme Court held that it had jurisdiction to grant an interlocutory order pending appeal which would prevent the continued operation of a valid order of the High Court and in effect operate as a form of stay. The decision of the Supreme Court in *C.C. v Minister for Justice and Equality*[244] confirms that at a level of principle, the guidelines which should be applied on an application for a stay, or the grant of an interlocutory injunction pending the determination of an appeal, are the same as those applied to an application for interlocutory injunctive relief. However, the fact that a trial has already taken place means that in practice the issues before the court may be narrower or more refined and it will in the first instance be required to focus on whether there is any stateable or arguable basis for the appeal.

In *C.C. v Minister for Justice and Equality*[245] Clarke J said that the problem of what to do pending an appeal gives rise to the same type of issue as arises in the context of the grant or refusal of a stay or interlocutory injunction pending trial because the court does not necessarily know what the ultimate result of the appeal will be. In his view, the overarching principle is to identify the regime which runs the least risk of injustice. He held that, as in all cases, the first question is whether there is any stateable or arguable basis for the appeal itself. If there is, then the court has to assess the potential injustice which may result from, on the one hand, intervening in favour of the appellant only to find that the appellant loses, as opposed to not intervening in favour of the appellant only to find that the appeal is successful. He continued as follows:

> What is the logic of applying a different standard to the assessment of the strength or weakness of a party's case pre-trial or post-trial and

EWHC 3419 (TCC) at [13]. See also *B2Net Ltd v HM Treasury* [2010] EWHC 51 (QB) at [5].

242. [2012] 3 IR 152, 181.
243. [2007] 2 IR 133.
244. [2016] 2 IR 680.
245. *Ibid.*

> pending appeal. In principle, the risk of injustice is just the same if one grants or rejects an application for a stay or injunction pending trial or if one grants or rejects an application for a stay or injunction post-trial and pending appeal. The risk is that the case will ultimately turn out in such a way that, with the benefit of hindsight, a party will have had its rights interfered with by the presence or absence of an order. In one case what may confer that hindsight may be the result of a trial. In the other case hindsight may be conferred by the result of an appeal. But there is no difference in principle.[246]

Clarke J concluded that he could not see any legitimate basis for suggesting that a different principle or test applies which is dependent on whether the applicant seeks an appropriate order pending trial, on the one hand, or pending appeal, on the other. However, he did go on to accept that the fact that the case was at an appellate stage and had been the subject of a determination at first instance could influence the application of that general principle. He noted that, in at least some cases, there will be significant issues of fact in dispute pre-trial. At trial the facts will be found and the circumstances in which the facts so found can be revisited on appeal are very limited. Likewise, legal issues can fall away precisely because of the way in which the facts are found or as a result of developments or clarifications which occur at the trial. Thus, the issues which may remain legitimately for decision on appeal may, at least in many cases, be narrower and significantly refined compared with those issues which it might properly be said were before the court at the trial stage. Therefore, the assessment of whether there are stateable or arguable grounds for an appeal, while in principle giving rise to the same question as might arise in the context of deciding whether there were stateable or arguable grounds for a claim, might in practice be very different. Furthermore, where, as is often the case, the issues which potentially arise on appeal are narrow and concerned with questions of law, it is much more likely that the court will be able to assess the strength or weakness of a pending appeal. It followed that the very process of a trial could easily lead to a significant narrowing and refinement of the kind of issues which remain open on an appeal such that it might well be possible for a court to place much greater weight on the strength or weakness of the potential appeal compared to the situation which would have pertained were the court attempting to assess the strength or weakness of the underlying case pre-trial.

These principles were also considered by Allen J in *M.P. v Teaching Council.*[247] In relation to the question of the extent to which the court may engage in an assessment of the strength of the case, he reiterated that the court 'at least in the majority of cases, should not go beyond assessing whether

246. *Ibid.* at 696-697.
247. [2019] IEHC 148.

there is an arguable ground of appeal'[248] He stated that 'it seems to me that this application is not to be approached as an application for the continuation of the interlocutory injunction granted pending the trial of the action, but rather as a new application which takes into account how the case unfolded at trial. The initial test to be applied at this stage is whether there is a *bona fide* ground or grounds for appeal.'[249] So, while it is clear that at a level of principle the *Campus Oil* guidelines also apply where an interlocutory injunction is sought pending an appeal, the fact that a trial has already taken place will lead to a court, in approaching the first limb of this test, focusing on whether there is an arguable legal basis for an appeal.

These Principles are Only Guidelines

At this point it should be reiterated that an interlocutory injunction, like any other type of equitable remedy, is a discretionary form of relief and it has been stated by Edwards J in *Chieftain Construction Ltd v Ryan*[250] 'that the *Campus Oil* criteria only represent guidance, albeit guidance that should not be deviated from lightly'. Similarly, in *Merck Sharp and Dohme Corporation v Clonmel Healthcare Ltd*,[251] Whelan J commented in her judgment in the Court of Appeal that '[t]he principles set out in *American Cyanamid* and *Campus Oil* are important and helpful guidelines but are not to be treated as though written on a tablet of stone to be slavishly and blindly followed.' A similar approach was also adopted by O'Donnell J in the Supreme Court in this case on this issue, where although he acknowledged that the established principles remain a valuable guide, he stressed that the *American Cyanamid* decision 'should not … be approached as though it were the laying down of strict mechanical rules for the control of future cases.'[252] So, it has been accepted that while the so called '*Cyanamid/Campus Oil* principles' have provided the basis for the exercise of the courts' jurisdiction in this area for some time, they should be regarded as guidelines[253] rather than rules which must be strictly adhered to. As Gray has pointed out, in so far as Lord Diplock's formulation suggests that an applicant faces a series of hurdles and that once he has surmounted them he is guaranteed success, it is unfortunate.[254] As she states, this approach goes beyond the provision of assistance to a judge in the exercise of his discretion and in fact amounts to a significant restriction of that discretion.

---

248. *Ibid.* at [21].
249. *Ibid.* at [24].
250. [2008] IEHC 147 at 7.
251. [2018] IEHC 177 at [37] *per* Whelan J.
252. [2019] IESC 65 at [33].
253. *Cayne v Global Natural Resources plc* [1984] 1 All ER 225, 237 *per* May LJ. See also *Cambridge Nutrition Ltd v British Broadcasting Corporation* [1990] 3 All ER 523, 535.
254. Gray [1981] CLJ 307, 313.

Lord Diplock himself acknowledged that there may be special factors which should be taken into consideration in individual cases, although the fact that a trial is likely to take place within a short space of time is not one of them. This point was made by Kinlen J in the course of his judgment in *An Post v Irish Permanent plc*,[255] in which the plaintiff sought an interlocutory injunction to restrain alleged passing off in relation to the use of the term 'savings certificate' by the defendant to describe a financial savings product which it was issuing in competition with the plaintiff. Kinlen J granted an interlocutory injunction as he found that there was a serious question to be tried and that the balance of convenience favoured the granting of the order and rejected the argument that the fact the matter was likely to be tried quickly was an important consideration.[256]

Before examining the specific circumstances in which the courts consider it appropriate to depart from the *Cyanamid/Campus Oil* guidelines it is worth assessing to what extent they have evolved over time. In his judgment in *Allied Irish Banks plc v Diamond*[257] Clarke J gave consideration to this issue and suggested that while the criteria for the grant of interlocutory injunctions are well settled in this jurisdiction, 'a high value might be placed on an assessment of where the greatest risk of injustice might lie in future applications for interlocutory injunctions.' He added that it seemed more appropriate to characterise the 'greatest risk of injustice' criteria 'not so much as a different test to that which has become established in the *Campus Oil v Minister for Industry (No.2)* jurisprudence but rather as the underlying principle which informs the more detailed rules which have been worked out in accordance with that jurisprudence.' Clarke J is correct in suggesting that the elements in the traditional test are closely associated with the risk of injustice, in particular the factor of the balance of convenience. It can also, as he points out, provide a useful way of assessing whether a different approach is required in some of the particular types of cases considered in the next section. Clarke J returned to this issue in his judgment in the Supreme Court in *Okunade v Minister for Justice, Equality and Law Reform*[258] and, although the case itself concerned the grant of an interlocutory injunction in the context of judicial review proceedings, he also gave consideration to the principles underlying the grant or refusal of such injunctions generally.[259] Having reviewed the relevant authorities in which the *Campus Oil* guidelines had been applied, Clarke J noted that they involved the

255. [1995] 1 ILRM 336.
256. Note that the case was settled prior to trial with the defendant giving an undertaking that it would not sell products bearing the name 'savings certificates'.
257. [2012] 3 IR 549, 570.
258. [2012] 3 IR 152.
259. *Ibid.* at 181. Subsequently, in *Charleton v Scriven* [2019] IESC 28, Clarke CJ commented at [4.1] that '[w]hile it is the case that *Okunade* had a particular focus on the criteria to be applied in respect of interlocutory injunctions or similar orders in a public law context, it is also clear that much of the analysis in the judgment in that case applies equally to private law injunction proceedings.'

application of the basic principle 'under which the court is required to minimise the risk of injustice'.[260] He also reiterated the point which he made in *Diamond* that many of the refinements of and variations to the so-called 'pure' *Campus Oil* principles which have developed can be seen as a response to the need to minimise the risk of injustice in particular types of cases and this should be borne in mind in considering the examples below.

Circumstances in which a Departure from Cyanamid Guidelines Justified

It is now acknowledged that departure from the *Cyanamid* principles is justified in certain circumstances.[261] The most obvious of these is where the parties agree that the hearing of the interlocutory application will constitute the trial of the action. Other exceptions have developed and while it would not be wise to attempt to set these out in an exhaustive manner, the following situations have been recognised.

Where there is no Arguable Defence to the Plaintiff's Claim

This principle is almost self-explanatory and as Scott J made clear in *Official Custodian for Charities v Mackey*,[262] the *Cyanamid* principles are not applicable in a case where there is no arguable defence as there will clearly be no serious question to be tried in such a case. So, e.g. where a plaintiff has clear title and the defendant's trespass is indisputable, the balance of convenience will play no part in the court's decision and the plaintiff may obtain an interlocutory injunction to restrain the trespass, even where it has caused no damage.[263] This principle was confirmed by Keane J in *Keating & Co. Ltd v Jervis Shopping Centre Ltd*,[264] where he stated that '[i]t is clear that a landowner, whose title is not in issue, is *prima facie* entitled to an injunction to restrain a trespass and … this is also the case where the claim is for an interlocutory injunction only'.[265] However, as Keane J pointed out, this principle is subject to the following qualification, set out by Balcombe LJ in the Court of Appeal decision in *Patel v W.H. Smith (Eziot) Ltd*[266] as follows: 'However, the defendant may put in evidence to seek to establish that he has a right to do what would otherwise be a trespass. Then the court must consider the application of the principle set out in *American Cyanamid Co. v Ethicon Ltd* in relation to the grant or refusal

260. *Ibid.* See also *Charleton v Scriven* [2019] IESC 28 at [4.2].
261. As Kelly J pointed out in *Reynolds v Malocco* [1999] 2 IR 203, 209 'these principles have a wide but not a universal application'. See generally Martin (1993-94) 4 KCLJ 52.
262. [1985] Ch 168, 187.
263. *Patel v W.H. Smith (Eziot) Ltd* [1987] 1 WLR 853.
264. High Court 1995 No. 9606P (Keane J) 1 March 1996.
265. *Ibid.* at 9. See also *Beltany Property Finance DAC v Doyle* [2019] IEHC 307 at [49]; *Wallace v Kershaw* [2019] IEHC 382 at [41].
266. [1987] 1 WLR 853, 859.

of an interlocutory injunction'. In the *Keating* case, Keane J stated that it was clear that the defendants were asserting a right to operate a crane in the airspace above the plaintiff's premises. In his opinion there was a serious question to be tried as to whether they had such a right and it followed that the plaintiff would not be entitled to an interlocutory injunction unless it could satisfy the court that damages would not be an adequate remedy. Keane J concluded that the plaintiff had not established that damages would be an inadequate remedy and decided for this and other reasons to refuse the injunction sought.

Where an Interlocutory Injunction is Sought in the Context of a Trade Dispute

The conclusions reached by the Supreme Court in both *Bayzana Ltd v Galligan*[267] and *Westman Holdings Ltd v McCormack*[268] made it clear that the common law position clearly favoured the employer where proceedings were brought seeking to restrain picketing by means of an interlocutory injunction. An employer could usually establish that the balance of convenience favoured the preservation of the *status quo* pending the trial of the action and the courts were often influenced by the potential inability on the part of some of the defendants to pay damages. In addition, they placed little emphasis on the loss of the defendants' right to picket, stressing instead that they could if necessary be subsequently compensated in respect of any loss of wages which they might suffer.[269]

Attempts were made to redress this imbalance by means of legislation and section 19 of the Industrial Relations Act 1990 has qualified the effect of common law principles in the context of trade disputes.[270] The effect of section 19(2) is that once a plaintiff establishes an entitlement to an interlocutory injunction by showing that there is a fair question to be tried, the court must consider whether the defendants can establish a fair case that they were acting in furtherance or contemplation of a trade dispute. If they can, the injunction will not be granted; if they cannot, the court will go on to consider, as it does at common law, whether the balance of convenience favours the grant of an injunction.[271] This statutory provision can only be availed of by defendants where they have complied with the formalities laid down in the statute in relation to such matters as the holding of secret ballots and the giving of adequate strike notice, and the consequence of failing to abide by such procedures is that the

267. [1987] IR 238.
268. [1992] 1 IR 151.
269. As Keane J commented in *Nolan Transport (Oaklands) Ltd v Halligan* High Court 1993 No.1008P, 22 March 1994 it was common knowledge that the use by employers of the procedure of seeking an interlocutory injunction 'meant that the use of what were otherwise legitimate methods sanctioned by law by trade unions of advancing their interests were effectively neutralised by the way in which the law operated'.
270. See the comments of Clarke J in *P. Elliott & Co. Ltd v Building and Allied Trades Union* [2006] IEHC 320 at [6.4] to similar effect.
271. See Kerr (1990) ICLSA 90/19-33.

restrictions on an employer's ability to obtain an interlocutory injunction do not apply.[272]

This point is well-illustrated by a number of decisions in which those involved in industrial action were unable to rely on the provisions of section 19 as they had failed to comply fully with the requirements contained in the Act. In *Nolan Transport (Oaklands) Ltd v Halligan*,[273] which concerned an application to restrain picketing, the court had to consider whether the defendants could invoke the statutory protection afforded to them by the section. Both Keane J and on appeal Murphy J in the Supreme Court agreed that the onus lies on the party resisting an application for an interlocutory injunction to show that a secret ballot has been held in compliance with the terms of section 14 of the Act of 1990. In his view the express reference in section 19 to a secret ballot 'held in accordance with the rules of a trade union as provided for in section 14' suggests that those engaged in industrial action cannot rely on the protection afforded by the section unless the secret ballot has been held in accordance with the requirements laid down in section 14.

A similarly strict approach to the application of section 19(2) of the 1990 Act was taken both by the High Court and the Supreme Court in *G. & T. Crampton Ltd v Building and Allied Trades Union*,[274] in which the plaintiff sought an interlocutory injunction to restrain the defendants from picketing its premises. The plaintiff argued that a precondition to the operation of section 19(2) of the Industrial Relations Act 1990 had not been complied with as there had been no effective secret ballot held sufficient to comply with the requirements of section 14 of the Act. Laffoy J granted the interlocutory injunction sought and the defendants appealed. The Supreme Court held that the trial judge had been entitled to come to the conclusion that a condition precedent to the implementation of section 19 had not been satisfied and upheld the conclusions which she had reached in deciding the matter on the basis of the principles set out in the *Campus Oil* case, namely that a fair question had been raised, that damages would be an inadequate remedy and that the balance of convenience lay in favour of granting the injunction.

In *Malincross Ltd v Building and Allied Trades Union*[275] the plaintiff sought an interlocutory injunction to restrain picketing by the defendants at a building site, in circumstances where the employer with whom the defendants were in dispute no longer carried on business at the site. In relation to the question of whether the defendants might rely on the provisions of section 19(2) of the Act of 1990, McCracken J stated that he was satisfied that the union had held a secret ballot in accordance with its rules and that it had given the appropriate notice to the employer of its intention to take industrial action. However, an issue arose as to the extent to which the proposals in the ballot had to identify

---

272. See Kerr [1993] ELR xi.
273. High Court 1993 No.1008P (Keane J) 22 March 1994; [1999] 1 IR 128 (SC).
274. [1998] 1 ILRM 430.
275. [2002] 3 IR 607.

the nature of the industrial action, and specifically a question remained as to whether the ballot authorised the placing of pickets at a site when it ceased to be the company site of the employer. McCracken J stated that the sufficiency of the secret ballot is clearly a condition precedent to the right of the defendants to resist an interlocutory injunction under section 19(2). In his view the purpose of the Act appeared to be to ensure that, if a union is to be entitled to the protection of section 19, it must have the clear support of its members. He concluded that a serious issue remained as to the whether the picketing of the plaintiff's premises, once the employer had left those premises, was authorised by the ballot and that until that question had been determined, a condition precedent to section 19(2) had not been satisfied by the defendants. Accordingly, McCracken J felt obliged to apply the *Campus Oil* principles. He concluded that any loss or disadvantage which might be incurred by the defendants if an interlocutory order were granted would be far outweighed by the enormous damage which would be caused to the plaintiff should the injunction be wrongly refused. He was therefore satisfied that the balance of convenience strongly favoured the plaintiff and decided to grant the interlocutory injunction sought.

A slightly different point arose in *Daru Blocklaying Ltd v Building and Allied Trades Union*,[276] although the difficulty was still related to purported non-compliance with the secret ballot requirements imposed by section 14. Kelly J expressed the view that the ballot ought to have been conducted in circumstances where the entitlement to vote was accorded equally to all members whom it was reasonable at that time for the union to believe would be called upon to engage in industrial action. It appeared that only three people had been balloted although it was accepted by the defendants that on the day the picketing commenced there might have been as many as nine individuals attending the picket. Kelly J stated that the union is obliged to ensure that all members whom it was reasonable for it to believe at the time of the ballot would be called upon to engage in the industrial action would be balloted and that there was no evidence before the court that this had been done. The onus lay on the defendants to satisfy the court as to compliance with the provisions of section 14 and he said that this onus was not discharged by a bald assertion that a ballot had been carried out in accordance with the rules of the union and the provisions of the Act. Kelly J concluded that the defendants had not discharged the onus of demonstrating full and complete compliance with section 14, particularly having regard to the choice of just three people who were asked to ballot.

However, in a number of subsequent decisions, the courts have found that the provisions of section 19(2) have been complied with, which would perhaps suggest that lessons have been learned from the rather strict approach taken

276. [2003] 1 ILRM 164. See further *Dublin Airport Authority plc v Services Industrial Professional Technical Union* [2014] IEHC 644 where the legal validity of the secret ballot was also at issue.

in cases such as *Malincross* and *Daru*. In *P. Elliott & Co. Ltd v Building and Allied Trades Union*[277] Clarke J made it clear that the proper approach of the court in considering whether the conditions necessary for the application of section 19(2) have been established must be determined once and for all at the interlocutory stage with the court doing its best on the evidence available. In the case before him he was satisfied that the only issue in relation to whether section 19(2) applied concerned whether a proper ballot had been conducted in accordance with the requirements of section 14. He stated that in his view a practical approach should be taken towards the text of issues put to ballot by trade unions and '[t]he test must be as to whether a reasonable member of the trade union concerned would know what they were voting for or against'.[278] Clarke J concluded that the ballot in the case before him had been conducted in accordance with the requirements of section 14 and that the provisions of section 19(2) applied. Given that he had concluded that the defendants had established a fair case to the effect that the industrial action in question was in contemplation or furtherance of a trade dispute, he said that it seemed to him that it was not open to him to grant an injunction restraining picketing generally. However, given that he was satisfied that there was evidence to suggest that the picket had not been properly conducted both as to its composition and the manner in which the pickets had acted, he granted a limited form of injunction restraining those aspects of the picketing which might be unlawful.

In *Dublin City Council v Technical, Engineering and Electrical Union*[279] Laffoy J also took a pragmatic approach towards the interpretation of the legislation and stated that in considering whether the interlocutory relief sought by the plaintiff to restrain picketing by the defendants should be granted, the court must consider the application of section 19 against the provisions of Part II of the Act of 1990 as a whole. She found that the pre-conditions to engaging in industrial action stipulated in section 19(2) had been fulfilled by the union before the industrial action had been commenced and that the union had established a fair case that it was acting in contemplation or furtherance of a trade dispute. Laffoy J stated that the consequence of these findings was that, by reason of section 19(2), the court must not grant an injunction restraining the industrial action even though the injunction was sought by the plaintiff who was not, and never had been, the employer of the members of the union involved and was not a party to the trade dispute. She acknowledged that she was conscious that, although there was very little difference between the circumstances which existed in *Malincross* and the circumstances of the case before her, her approach towards the application of section 19(2) and the result reached differed from that in the former case. However, she stated that she was satisfied that the conclusion she had reached that the plaintiff's application

277. [2006] IEHC 320.
278. *Ibid.* at [6.15].
279. [2010] IEHC 288.

for an interlocutory injunction must be dismissed, even though it had raised a serious issue to be tried on the application of section 11(1), accorded with the intention of the Oireachtas in enacting section 19(2), which had been explained by Clarke J in *P. Elliott & Co. Ltd.*

However, in two more recent decisions of Gilligan J the defendant trade unions failed to rely successfully on the provisions of section 19(2). In *Dublin Airport Authority plc v Services Industrial Professional Technical Union*[280] Gilligan J found that the legal validity of the secret ballot which had been conducted was clearly at issue. He pointed out that the onus lay on the defendant to show that a secret ballot in compliance with section 14 of the Act of 1990 had been held and that no evidence had been adduced to assist the court in this regard. He concluded that he was satisfied that the defendant was not entitled to rely on section 19(2) and applying the *Campus Oil* principles, he granted the injunctive relief sought. Similarly, in *University College Cork v Services Industrial Professional Technical Union*,[281] there was an issue about the adequacy of the secret ballot as the defendants' members, who were employees of the plaintiff on its main campus which the defendant intended to picket, had not been involved in the ballot which led to the industrial action. He therefore concluded that the *Campus Oil* principles applied and in the circumstances granted the interlocutory injunctions sought. These decisions illustrate once again the importance of full compliance with the secret ballot requirements in section 14(2) of the Act of 1990 if the provisions of section 19 are to be relied upon by defendants who intend to engage in industrial action.

Where an Interlocutory Injunction is Sought in Proceedings for Defamation or Where the Right to Freedom of Expression is at Issue

The principles which apply where an interlocutory injunction is sought in proceedings for defamation are firmly established and predate the *American Cyanamid* principles by nearly a century. As Lord Coleridge CJ stated in *Bonnard v Perryman*:[282]

> [T]he subject matter of an action for defamation is so special as to require exceptional caution in exercising the jurisdiction to interfere by injunction before the trial of an action to prevent an anticipated wrong. The right of free speech is one which it is for the public interest that individuals should

280. [2014] IEHC 644.
281. [2015] IEHC 282.
282. [1891] 2 Ch 269, 284. See also *Fraser v Evans* [1969] 1 QB 349, 360; *Bestobell Paints Ltd v Bigg* [1975] FSR 421, 432; *Brabourne v Hough* [1981] FSR 79, 84; *R. v Advertising Standards Authority Ltd, ex p. Vernons Organisation Ltd* [1992] 1 WLR 1289, 1293; *Holley v Smyth* [1998] QB 726, 739; *Moran v Heathcote* High Court QBD (Eady J) 15 January 2001; *Greene v Associated Newspapers Ltd* [2005] QB 972, 988.

> possess, and indeed, that they should exercise without impediment, so long as no wrongful act is done.

It was argued in *J. Trevor and Sons v Solomon*[283] that the decision in *American Cyanamid* might have modified the principles which traditionally applied in this context. However, Lord Denning MR rejected this suggestion out of hand and commented that he was quite sure that the House of Lords had no intention whatsover of altering the well-established principles on which the courts would grant, or refuse to grant, injunctions in libel actions. Therefore, it is clear that a more onerous task faces a plaintiff seeking an interlocutory injunction to restrain publication of alleged defamatory matter, largely due to a traditional reluctance on the part of the courts to interfere unduly with an individual's right to freedom of expression, a right which is given constitutional protection in this jurisdiction.[284] A further reason for such caution is that, while a statement might appear defamatory, a defendant may intend to plead a variety of defences such as 'truth'[285] or 'honest opinion'[286] at the trial, or he may seek to establish that he is protected by privilege.

It is not disputed that the courts have jurisdiction in an appropriate case to restrain the further publication of defamatory material by means of an interlocutory injunction[287] but this jurisdiction will only be exercised 'for clear and compelling reasons'.[288] In *Coulson and Sons v James Coulson & Co.*[289] the jurisdiction to grant an interim injunction in a libel case was described by Esher MR as one of a 'delicate nature' which ought only to be exercised on the 'rarest occasions'. In his view:

> It ought only to be exercised in the clearest cases, where any jury would say that the matter complained of was libellous, and where if the jury did not so find the court would set aside the verdict as unreasonable.[290]

He added that the court must be satisfied that in all probability the alleged libel

283. Court of Appeal, 14 December 1977. See also *Herbage v Pressdram Ltd* [1984] 1 WLR 1160, 1162. In *Bestobell Paints Ltd v Bigg* [1975] FSR 421, 430 Oliver J accepted the suggestion of counsel that the established doctrine in this area 'cuts right across the *American Cyanamid* case'.
284. Article 40.6.1°.i of the Constitution of Ireland.
285. See s. 16 of the Defamation Act 2009.
286. See s. 20 of the Defamation Act 2009.
287. *Quartz Hill Consolidated Gold Mining Company v Beall* (1882) 20 Ch D 501, 507.
288. *TV3 Network Services Ltd v Fahey* [1999] 2 NZLR 129, 132. See also *Auckland Area Health Board v Television New Zealand* [1992] 3 NZLR 406, 407.
289. (1887) 3 TLR 846.
290. *Ibid.* at 846. Quoted with approval in *Bonnard v Perryman* [1891] 2 Ch 269, 284; *Monson v Tussauds Ltd* [1894] 1 QB 671, 693, 696-697; *Bestobell Paints Ltd v Bigg* [1975] FSR 421, 431.

was untrue, and if written on a privileged occasion that there was malice on the part of the defendant.

The language of Lord Esher MR was adopted and approved by Lord Coleridge CJ in *Bonnard v Perryman*[291] who stated that '[u]ntil it is clear that an alleged libel is untrue, it is not clear that any right at all has been infringed'[292] and he added that the importance of leaving free speech unfettered is a strong reason in cases of libel for being most cautious in relation to the granting of interim injunctions. In the case before him he was satisfied that the libellous nature of the publication was beyond dispute but its effect could only be determined by a jury and he said that the court could not feel sure that the defence of justification was one which, on the facts before them, the jury might find unfounded. In the circumstances, the majority of the court held that the decision of North J to grant an interim injunction should be reversed.[293]

The proposition that the court should not intervene by granting an interlocutory injunction in such situations except in 'a clear case' was subsequently approved and applied[294] and it was accepted that the court in *Bonnard* had laid down a binding 'rule of practice' as to the circumstances in which the court might grant an interlocutory injunction pending trial in cases of libel.[295] A useful summary of the position in England is provided in the judgment of Sir Christopher Slade in *Holley v Smyth*.[296] He accepted that the court might be left with a residual discretion, which must be exercised in accordance with established principles, to decline to apply the rule in *Bonnard* in exceptional circumstances and that one exception, recognised in that case itself, was where the court was satisfied that the defamatory statement was clearly untrue. However, both he and Auld LJ made it clear in that decision that neither the would-be libeller's motive, nor the manner in which he threatened publication, nor the potential damage to the plaintiff would normally be a basis for making an exception to the rule.[297] As Auld LJ stated, 'motive is logically

291. [1891] 2 Ch 269. See also *Liverpool Household Stores Association v Smith* (1888) 37 Ch D 170, 181; *Greene v Associated Newspapers Ltd* [2005] QB 972, 988.
292. *Ibid.* at 284. Quoted with approval in *Khashoggi v IPC Magazines Ltd* [1986] 1 WLR 1412, 1416. See also the *dictum* of Jessel MR in *Quartz Hill Consolidated Gold Mining Company v Beall* (1882) 20 Ch D 501, 508 that '[a]s a general rule the plaintiff who applies for a interlocutory injunction must shew the statement to be untrue'. Quoted with approval by Lord Denning MR in *Crest Homes Ltd v Ascott* [1980] FSR 396, 398.
293. Kay LJ dissented, stating that while he agreed that in order to justify the court in granting an interlocutory injunction in such a case there must be strong *prima facie* evidence that the statement made was untrue; in his opinion on the basis of the affidavits before the court there was such evidence.
294. *Monson v Tussauds Ltd* [1894] 1 QB 671, 689 *per* Lord Halsbury.
295. *Ibid.* at 697 *per* Davey LJ.
296. [1998] QB 726. Quoted with approval by Brooke LJ in *Greene v Associated Newspapers Ltd* [2005] QB 972, 990.
297. *Ibid.* at 744, 749. In *Holley* the defendant threatened that unless the plaintiff paid him a sum of money he would publish damaging allegations. The Court of Appeal

irrelevant to the defendant's entitlement to exercise his right to freedom of speech if what he has to say is true'[298] and he pointed out that motives of vindictiveness or pecuniary gain have been rejected as grounds for creating an exception to the rule.

In this jurisdiction, the principles laid down in *Coulson* and *Bonnard* were also followed. As Sullivan CJ stated in *Sinclair v Gogarty*,[299] an interlocutory injunction should only be granted in the clearest cases where any jury would say that the matter complained of was libellous and where, if the jury did not make such a finding, the court would set aside the verdict as unreasonable. Interestingly, this was one of very few cases in which the principles in *Coulson* and *Bonnard* were applied in which the plaintiff succeeded in obtaining the relief sought and the Supreme Court held that statements made in relation to the plaintiffs were clearly so defamatory that an injunction should be granted to prevent the continued sale of a book which contained them. In *Connolly v RTE*,[300] Carroll J concluded that, while she was satisfied that there was an issue to be tried and that damages would not be an adequate remedy, the balance of convenience favoured not granting an injunction and she suggested that injunctions were 'very rarely granted' in such matters. In *Reynolds v Malocco*[301] Kelly J referred to the *American Cyanamid/Campus Oil* principles and stated that they have a 'wide but not universal application', adding that in a number of cases special rules apply. He stated that the plaintiff must show 'that there is no doubt [the words] are defamatory'[302] and added that if a defendant intended to plead justification or another defence, normally an injunction would be refused. Despite this test marking 'the high water mark' from the perspective of those seeking injunctions,[303] the plaintiff succeeded in obtaining an interlocutory injunction in that case on the basis that the court was satisfied that the defendant had gone nowhere near demonstrating the existence of an arguable prospect of making out the defence of justification and that it would be virtually impossible for the plaintiff to ever recover any sum of damages which might be awarded.

Subsequently, in *Cogley v RTE*[304] Clarke J stated that the first question that needed to be addressed in any interlocutory application in which a plaintiff sought prior restraint on the publication or broadcast of material on the grounds that it was defamatory was whether on the evidence available at the interlocutory stage, it was clear that the plaintiff would ultimately succeed at trial. On the basis of the reasoning in *Campus Oil Ltd v Minister for Industry*

concluded that on the material before it, it had not been established that the contents of the threatened publication were plainly untrue and discharged the interlocutory injunction granted at first instance.

298. *Ibid.* at 744. See also *Moran v Heathcote* High Court QBD (Eady J) 15 January 2001.
299. [1937] IR 377, 384. See also *Quinlivan v O'Dea* [2010] 1 ILRM 72, 75.
300. [1991] 2 IR 446, 448.
301. [1999] 2 IR 203.
302. *Ibid.* at 209-10. See also *Quinlivan v O'Dea* [2010] 1 ILRM 72, 75.
303. *Per* Clarke J in *Cogley v RTE* [2005] 4 IR 79, 85.
304. [2005] 4 IR 79.

and Energy (No. 2),[305] he said that it did not seem to be appropriate to ask the court at the interlocutory stage to attempt to weigh up the likelihood of a plaintiff succeeding or failing or of the defendant succeeding in maintaining any defence in defamation proceedings. In his view the plaintiff would fail to cross the first hurdle if, on the basis of the argument and materials before the court, it appeared that there was any reasonable basis for contending that the defendant might succeed at the trial of the action. He was satisfied that the reference in the authorities to a 'clear case' meant a case where it is obvious that the plaintiff would succeed and where it was equally clear that none of the possible lines of defence which might be open to a defendant could reasonably succeed. Clarke J added that even in a case where it can be clearly shown that the defendant would have no defence, the court will retain a discretion which can be exercised having regard to all the circumstances of the case. He concluded that on the basis of the established jurisprudence in this area it did not seem that the plaintiff in the first proceedings had crossed the initial threshold referred to above and he refused her application for interlocutory relief to prevent the broadcast of a programme which she alleged defamed her going ahead. He also refused to grant an interlocutory injunction to the plaintiffs in the second proceedings which would have had the effect of restraining the broadcast. This decision is therefore in line with earlier authorities in this area and reaffirms how difficult it will be to obtain interim or interlocutory injunctive relief to restrain alleged defamation.

Clarke J also spoke about the importance of encouraging and preserving public debate on issues of importance. He commented that one of the underlying reasons for the reluctance of the courts to grant interlocutory injunctions in defamation cases stemmed from the fact that if the traditional basis for the grant of such injunctions was sufficient, there would be a disproportionate effect on public debate and indeed it would be largely stifled in respect of many issues. He added that 'it is important to note that both the Constitution itself and the law generally recognised the need for a vigorous and informed public debate on issues of importance'.[306] The key in such cases is to achieve the correct balance between encouraging public debate and preserving the freedom of the press on the one hand and protecting the reputation of an individual on the other hand. The approach adopted by Clarke J in *Cogley* seeks to achieve this and shows a willingness to consider the underlying interests of both parties in defamation proceedings.

While the relevance of a plea of justification had not been considered in detail by the court in *Bonnard*, its view on this issue took hold and it came to be interpreted as authority for the proposition that 'if the defendant in a libel action says that he is going to justify the words complained of – that is to prove that they are true in substance and in fact – then an interlocutory

305. [1983] IR 88.
306. [2005] 4 IR 79, 94.

injunction ought not to be granted against him.'[307] It was suggested that all that it is necessary for a defendant to do in this context is to assert that he intends to justify the statement at issue[308] and it was stated by Griffiths LJ in *Herbage v Pressdram Ltd*[309] that the principle that no injunction will be granted if the defendant raises the defence of justification is a 'rule so well established that no elaborate citation of authority is necessary'. However, this is certainly open to question and a more accurate statement which better reflects the contemporary approach to this issue is set out in the following terms by Oliver J in *Bestobell Paints Ltd v Bigg*:[310]

> [N]o interlocutory injunction will be granted in defamation proceedings, where the defendant announces his intention of justifying, to restrain him from publishing the alleged defamatory statement until its truth or untruth has been determined at the trial, except in cases where the statement is obviously untruthful and libellous.

Subsequently, in *Holley v Smyth*,[311] Auld LJ stated that the exercise of the court's discretion to grant interlocutory relief to restrain a libel where a defence or claim of justification is made is guided by the principle that it is not normally just and convenient to intervene unless the plaintiff has proved that the libel is plainly untrue. An alternative approach, suggested by Brooke LJ in *Greene v Associated Newspapers Ltd*,[312] is to state that in an action for defamation a court will not impose a prior restraint on publication 'unless it is clear that no defence will succeed at trial'. Either way it is clear that the courts in England no longer view the so-called rule in *Bonnard v Perryman* as an absolute one and

---

307. *Crest Homes Ltd v Ascott* [1980] FSR 396, 397 *per* Lord Denning MR.
308. *Fraser v Evans* [1969] 1 QB 349, 360. See also *R. v Advertising Standards Authority Ltd, ex p. Vernons Organisation Ltd* [1992] 1 WLR 1289, 1293. A similar view was expressed by Browne-Wilkinson VC in *Femis-Bank (Anguilla) Ltd v Lazar* [1991] Ch 391, 396-397.
309. [1984] 1 WLR 1160, 1162. See also *Khashoggi v IPC Magazines Ltd* [1986] 1 WLR 1412, 1414. In that decision Sir John Donaldson MR even went as far as to say that the court should not intervene if it thinks that the case before it is one in which 'the plea of justification might, not would, succeed.'
310. [1975] FSR 421, 430. This statement was approved by the New Zealand Court of Appeal in *New Zealand Mortgage Guarantee Co. Ltd v Wellington Newspapers Ltd* [1989] 1 NZLR 4 where Cooke P suggested that one way of establishing this might be to show that there was no reasonable foundation for the defence. See also *Ron West Motors Ltd v Broadcasting Corporation of New Zealand (No.2)* [1989] 3 NZLR 520; *Auckland Area Health Board v Television New Zealand Ltd* [1992] 3 NZLR 406. Subsequently, in *TV3 Network Services Ltd v Fahey* [1999] 2 NZLR 129, 132 Richardson P stated that, where a publisher intends to justify an alleged defamatory statement, the circumstances must be exceptional to warrant an injunction. See also *Hosking v Runting* [2005] 1 NZLR 1, 39.
311. [1998] QB 726.
312. [2005] QB 972, 990.

accept that even where a defence of justification is raised, the plaintiff should be afforded the opportunity to seek to establish that the words complained of are plainly untrue or that the defence of justification cannot succeed.

The approach in this jurisdiction towards the relevance of a plea of justification, now replaced by the defence of truth,[313] has tended to be more flexible and the principle established in *Bonnard* is now treated with a considerable degree of caution. In *Gallagher v Tuohy*[314] Murnaghan J concluded that where a plea of justification has been raised, the court cannot prejudge the issue and decide that it is erroneous. This is in line with the approach later adopted by Carroll J in *Connolly v RTE,*[315] where she commented that injunctions would 'never' be granted where a defendant claimed justification as a defence. However, in *Cullen v Stanley*[316] O'Connor J commented that he did not think that the Court of Appeal in *Bonnard* intended to lay down a rule which should be rigidly applied in every case.[317] In his view, the court should inquire whether there was any evidence that the defendant had any material to support the plea of justification which he intended to make. O'Connor J stated that the court had been given nothing but 'the baldest affidavit' which contained no statement that the defendant had any information to support his plea and he concluded that there was no satisfactory evidence that the defendant had any justification for the publication complained of.[318]

When the matter came before Kelly J in *Reynolds v Malocco,*[319] he had to address directly the question of whether a bald statement of intent to plead justification was sufficient to debar a plaintiff who might otherwise be entitled to an injunction from such relief. The plaintiff sought an interlocutory injunction to restrain the defendants from publishing an article which he alleged defamed him. While Kelly J acknowledged that if the defendant intends to plead justification or any other recognised defence, normally an injunction of this type will be refused, he proceeded to analyse the authorities in this area in some detail. He concluded that he preferred the approach adopted by O'Connor J in *Cullen v Stanley* and said that he did not think that 'a rule which permits a defendant to

313. See also s. 16 of the Defamation Act 2009.
314. (1924) 58 ILTR 134.
315. [1991] 2 IR 446.
316. [1925] IR 73.
317. The majority of the Supreme Court (Kennedy CJ and Fitzgibbon J) held that the plaintiff as a candidate for a parliamentary constituency was entitled to the protection of s. 11 of the Prevention of Electoral Abuses Act 1923 and granted an interim injunction on that basis.
318. This is in line with the approach adopted by the Supreme Court of Victoria in *National Mutual Life Association of Australasia Ltd v GTV Corporation Pty Ltd* [1989] VR 747 (see also the decision of the High Court of Australia in the matter, reported at (1988) 80 ALR 553) where Ormiston J said that he did not accept that it was necessarily sufficient for a defendant to assert that it proposed to plead justification and prove the truth of its allegations at trial.
319. [1999] 2 IR 203.

in effect oust the ability of this Court to intervene by way of injunction in an appropriate case by the simple expedient of expressing an intention to plead justification at the trial of the action is consistent with the obligations imposed on the court under the Constitution'.[320]

Applying these principles, Kelly J concluded that the innuendo to the effect contended for by the plaintiff was clear and he stated that in the absence of a successful plea of justification, a jury would say that the matter complained of was libellous, a verdict which he did not believe the Supreme Court would set aside as unreasonable. In relation to the question of a plea of justification, he was satisfied that the first named defendant's averment did not go anywhere near demonstrating the existence of an arguable prospect of making out the defence. It followed that in his view the plaintiff had made out a sufficiently strong case to satisfy the test required for the grant of an interlocutory injunction. However, Kelly J pointed out that it did not automatically follow that an injunction should be granted, as such relief was of a discretionary nature. He repeated that the jurisdiction was 'of a delicate nature' and that the court must be circumspect to ensure that it does not unnecessarily interfere with the right to freedom of expression. Kelly J added that he did not want to set out in a hard and fast manner the factors which the court should take into account in the exercise of its discretion. In his view, it was sufficient if he identified one issue of particular importance which had influenced the exercise of his discretion in the case before him and this was that it was unlikely that the plaintiff would be able to recover any damages from the defendants if the interlocutory injunction were refused but he later succeeded at the trial. In these circumstances, Kelly J was satisfied that his discretion must be exercised in favour of granting an interlocutory injunction rather than refusing it.

Although this issue did not arise directly in *Cogley v RTE*,[321] Clarke J appeared to favour the attitude adopted by Kelly J on this point. He reiterated that Kelly J had rejected the proposition that a mere assertion of an intention to justify the words complained was of itself sufficient and said that it was 'necessary for a defendant to put forward some basis which was credible and potentially sustainable to suggest that the plaintiff might not succeed at trial.'[322] It is submitted that the attitude adopted by Kelly J in *Reynolds* and Clarke J in *Cogley* on this issue is certainly preferable to the rather inflexible approach adopted by the courts in England until relatively recently. While the tests suggested by the Court of Appeal in *Holley* and *Greene* show evidence of a retreat from the hardline approach taken in earlier cases, the greater flexibility and pragmatism suggested by the courts in this jurisdiction is to be welcomed. While there is no requirement for the defendant to establish more than a 'credible and potentially sustainable' case to suggest that the plaintiff

320. *Ibid.* at 212.
321. [2005] 4 IR 79.
322. *Ibid.* at 85.

might not succeed at trial, this is a significant shift in the plaintiff's favour from the position that all the defendant was obliged to do was make a bald statement of intent to plead justification, now replaced by the defence of truth.

The relevance of the provisions of the European Convention on Human Rights must also be considered in this context. Counsel for the claimant in *Greene v Associated Newspapers Ltd*[323] contended that the rigidity of the rule in *Bonnard v Perryman* ran roughshod over the right to reputation protected by Article 8 of the Convention and gave the court no power to weigh up competing rights and give a proportionate response. However, the Court of Appeal was satisfied that the Article 8 rights of the claimant in the case before it could not be accorded great weight before the trial of the action took place when compared with the importance to be attached to the freedom of the press to report matters of public interest. In this regard the court stressed the distinction between a defamation case, where the claimant's right to a reputation had been put in issue and could not be effectively resolved before the trial, and a case which raised issues of privacy or confidentiality.

While the courts in this jurisdiction have not explored the relevance of the provisions of the Convention to cases where prior restraint orders are sought in defamation cases in the same degree of detail, they clearly favour the primacy of Article 10 in such situations. In *Reynolds v Malocco*[324] Kelly J explained that the reason for the court's reluctance to grant interlocutory injunctions in cases of alleged defamation is grounded in the importance attached to the right of free speech, which he described as a right now fortified by Article 10. Similarly in *Cogley v RTE*,[325] in considering the application by the plaintiffs in the second proceedings before him for an interim injunction, Clarke J stated that it was necessary to consider the position pursuant to the European Convention on Human Rights in relation to the grant of prior restraint orders, which restrain in advance the broadcast or publication of material. He added that there is an obligation on a court only to grant such orders after what he described as 'careful scrutiny'.

It is clear that prior restraint orders will be issued very sparingly even outside the context of defamation proceedings; as Lord Scarman stated in *Attorney-General v British Broadcasting Corporation*,[326] 'prior restraint of publication, though occasionally necessary in serious cases, is a drastic interference with freedom of speech and should only be ordered where there is a substantial risk of grave injustice'. However, it should be noted that where a prior restraint order is sought, the nature of the cause of action may play a significant role in the outcome of the application and a distinction has traditionally been drawn between defamation cases on the one hand and cases raising issues of national

323. [2005] QB 972.
324. [1999] 2 IR 203.
325. [2005] 4 IR 79.
326. [1981] AC 303, 362. See also *TV3 Network Services Ltd v Fahey* [1999] 2 NZLR 129, 132.

security, conspiracy to injure, confidentiality and privacy on the other.[327] As Sir John Donaldson MR commented in *Attorney-General v Newspaper Publishing plc*,[328] if the court allows publication of confidential information pending trial, there is no point in proceeding with the trial as the cloak of confidentiality can never be restored. He added that '[c]onfidential information is like an ice cube … Give it to the party who has no refrigerator or will not agree to keep it in one, and by the time of the trial you just have a pool of water which neither party wants.'[329] So, in *Argyll v Argyll*[330] the plaintiff succeeded in obtaining interlocutory injunctions restraining the publication of revelations about her private life on the grounds that this would have amounted to a breach of confidence in circumstances where a claim simply based on defamation would in all likelihood have failed. This approach is supported by the *obiter* comments of Lord Denning MR in *Fraser v Evans*,[331] where he stated that although there may be cases where it would be wrong to grant an injunction on the grounds of breach of confidence when it would not be granted on the basis of libel, there will also be cases of breach of confidence which are defamatory where the court might intervene even though the defendant asserts that he intends the justify the comments.

This has led to the granting of injunctions to restrain the publication of damaging material based on causes of action other than defamation. An example of this is the decision of the Court of Appeal in *Gulf Oil (Great Britain) Ltd v Page*,[332] which overturned the decision of Warner J who declined to grant an injunction restraining the defendants from displaying an airborne sign on the grounds that the truth of the words used was not in issue. The Court of Appeal held that the general principle in defamation cases that there was no wrong done if the words published were true did not apply to the matter before it which instead concerned conspiracy to injure. Parker LJ expressed the view that the court should proceed on the same principles as it would in the case of any other tort and commented that 'the prospect that this would open the floodgates and reverse the principle applicable in libel actions is, in my view, unreal'.[333] However, this strategy was not successful in *Femis-Bank (Anguilla) Ltd v Lazar*,[334] where the plaintiff claimed that allegations published by the defendants amounted to conspiracy to injure. Browne-Wilkinson VC stated that even if a case is brought on the basis of conspiracy, the question of whether an injunction should be granted as a matter of discretion remains and the fact

327. See the comments of Brooke LJ in *Greene v Associated Newspapers Ltd* [2005] QB 972, 994-995.
328. [1988] Ch 333.
329. *Ibid.* at 358.
330. [1967] 1 Ch 302. See also *Francome v Mirror Group Newspapers Ltd* [1984] 1 WLR 892.
331. [1969] 1 QB 349, 362.
332. [1987] Ch 327.
333. *Ibid.* at 333.
334. [1991] Ch 391.

that any injunction would interfere with freedom of speech was an important factor to be taken into account. He concluded that only in the very clearest cases such as *Gulf Oil* would interference with the public interest be justified and he declined to grant the relief sought.

As Eady J commented in *Browne v Associated Newspapers Ltd*,[335] it is important that the policy underlying *Bonnard v Perryman* is not undermined too readily by claimants opting for alternative causes of action and it is clear that where the court perceives a claim to be an attempt to bypass the strictures of the rule against prior restraint in cases of defamation the claim will fail. As Griffiths LJ commented in *Microdata Information Services Ltd v Rivendale Ltd*,[336] '[i]f the court were to conclude that though the plaintiff had framed his claim in a cause of action other than defamation but nevertheless his principal purpose was to seek damages for defamation, the court will refuse interlocutory relief'. In *Sim v H.J. Heinz Co. Ltd*[337] an interlocutory injunction to prevent the broadcasting of a voice purporting to be the plaintiff's in advertisements was refused on the grounds of passing off, the plaintiff having abandoned his application for an injunction based on the claim that the broadcast was defamatory. McNair J was satisfied that the question of whether the plaintiff's reputation had been damaged raised issues similar to those which would have to be tried in the libel action. This would ultimately have to be decided by a jury and he held that it was undesirable in the absence of evidence that the plaintiff would suffer irreparable damage that this matter should be decided in advance by a judge. A similar result ensued in *Service Corporation International plc v Channel Four Television Corp Ltd*,[338] where Lightman J refused an injunction to restrain the broadcast of a programme on grounds of breach of confidence and copyright and trespass in circumstances where he expressed the view that he had great difficulty in seeing the alternative claims made as other than an attempt to circumvent the rule in *Bonnard v Perryman*.

An important decision in this context in this jurisdiction is *Foley v Sunday Newspapers Ltd*,[339] where the plaintiff sought an interlocutory injunction

335. [2007] EWHC 202 (QB) at [28]. The decision of Eady J was varied by the Court of Appeal, see [2008] QB 289. See also *McKennitt v Ash* [2008] QB 73, 101 *per* Buxton LJ.
336. [1991] FSR 681, 688.
337. [1959] 1 WLR 313. See also *Brabourne v Hough* [1981] FSR 79 where Slade LJ refused to grant an interlocutory injunction on the basis that the plaintiff's claims in so far as they were based on passing off and unlawful interference with trade were very closely allied to claims based on injurious falsehood which in his view were governed by the *Bonnard v Perryman* principle.
338. [1999] EMLR 83. See also *Woodward v Hutchins* [1977] 1 WLR 760 where the Court of Appeal declined to grant an interlocutory injunction on the grounds of breach of confidence where it found it would have the same effect as an injunction which the court would not grant in a libel action. As Lord Denning MR stated (at 765): 'I cannot help feeling that the plaintiff's real complaint here is that the words are defamatory'.
339. [2005] 1 IR 88.

restraining the defendant from publishing material which he alleged constituted a real and serious risk to his life and bodily integrity. The explanation put forward for the nature of the proceedings brought was that the plaintiff was 'a citizen whose reputation and character is blemished and who, for that reason, is unlikely to have an effective remedy available to him in the law of defamation even when matters that are materially untrue and highly prejudicial are published about him'. Kelly J stated that if the case before him had been an action in defamation, having regard to the averments made on behalf of the defendant to the effect that it stood over the allegation made, an injunction would not have been granted. It was submitted on behalf of the defendant that the plaintiff ought not to be entitled to an injunction in the case before the court where he had not brought libel proceedings and that as the injunction being sought would amount to just as much of an incursion into the freedom of the press, it should not be granted. Kelly J stated that he was satisfied that, before an injunction of this type should be granted, the plaintiff would have to demonstrate a convincing case to bring about a curtailment of the freedom of expression of the press and that this was particularly so having regard to the strongly expressed guarantees in the Constitution in favour of freedom of expression. He concluded that the evidence before him was such that he would not be justified in restricting the defendant's right to publish material about the plaintiff prior to the trial, provided that it did not exhort anyone to act violently towards him.

These principles were also considered in *Murray v Newsgroup Newspapers Ltd*,[340] in which the plaintiff, who had a number of convictions for serious sexual offences, sought interlocutory injunctive relief restraining the further publication of photographs of him and details of his whereabouts. Irvine J reiterated that in cases where it is sought to restrict freedom of expression by means of an interlocutory order she was satisfied that the plaintiff was required, as Kelly J had said in *Foley v Sunday Newspapers Ltd*,[341] 'to demonstrate, by proper evidence, a convincing case to bring about a curtailment of the freedom of expression of the press'. In her view, this was the same as saying that the plaintiff had to demonstrate at the interlocutory stage that he was likely to establish at the trial of the action that the publication complained of should not be allowed. She added that in order to demonstrate a 'convincing case', or that such prohibition was 'likely' to be ordered, the applicant had to show that the interference with freedom of expression sought was justified by one of the recognised exceptions to that right and that the proposed restriction would be proportionate to the aim to be achieved. Furthermore, she said, as Fennelly J had noted in *Mahon v Post Publications Ltd*,[342] the court must scrutinise an application for an injunction seeking prior restraint of a publication 'with

340. [2011] 2 IR 431.
341. [2005] 1 IR 88, 102.
342. [2007] 3 IR 338, 381.

particular care'. Irvine J stated that she had not been furnished with what could be described as proper or cogent evidence to demonstrate that the plaintiff was likely to prove that any potential infringement of his right to life or that any interference with his rights to privacy could not be justified in the public interest.[343] She concluded that he had not demonstrated by the necessary evidence that there was a real risk to his life or that he was likely to succeed at the trial of the action in further prohibiting the publication of information concerning him by the defendant newspapers.

Subsequently, in *McKillen v Times Newspapers Ltd*[344] MacEochaidh J quoted the principles set out by Irvine J in *Murray* and said that he considered that this was the proper test to apply to an application to restrain publication. In the circumstances of the case before him he said that balancing the competing interests involved and bearing in mind the weighty importance that is attached to a free press, he had decided to permit publication of some of the information in question. However, he also concluded that an injunction should be granted restraining publication of information of an opinion nature communicated internally within a financial institution which the plaintiffs had conducted business with, and information relating to the commercial relationship between the plaintiffs. The 'convincing case' test favoured in *Foley* and *Murray* was also part of the approach applied by Binchy J in *O'Brien v RTE*,[345] in which the plaintiffs sought, *inter alia*, injunctions restraining the defendant from publishing confidential documents or information relating to the first plaintiff's personal banking arrangements with the second plaintiff and communications between them in the course of the parties' banker/customer relationship. Binchy J stated that on any application for an interlocutory injunction seeking prior restraint of publication, the requirements of Article 10(2) of the European Convention on Human Rights must be addressed, in addition to the relevant principles applicable for interlocutory relief, which in this context involved the 'convincing case' test. Having referred to the *McKillen* case, to some of the Convention jurisprudence and to the competing constitutional considerations, Binchy J concluded that the plaintiffs had established a convincing case that they would succeed at trial. He was also satisfied that the balance of convenience favoured the plaintiffs and that the relief sought fell within the scope of Article 10 and he concluded that the plaintiffs were entitled to orders restraining publication.[346]

343. Irvine J distinguished the facts of the case before her from those which had arisen in *Callaghan v Independent News and Media Ltd* [2008] NIQB 15 in which interlocutory relief was granted to a plaintiff serving a life sentence for murder preventing the publication of an unpixelated photograph of him.
344. [2013] IEHC 150.
345. [2015] IEHC 397.
346. It should be noted that Binchy J in an *ex tempore* judgment varied the original order on 12 June 2015 ([2015] IEHC 379) made to take account of developments in relation to information that had been put into the public domain since the original order was made.

Finally, the provisions of section 33 of the Defamation Act 2009 should be borne in mind, although the section reflects the common law principles already considered. It provides that '(1) The High Court … may upon the application of the plaintiff, make an order prohibiting the publication or further publication of the statement in respect of which application was made if in its opinion (a) the statement is defamatory, and (b) the defendant has no defence to the action that is reasonably likely to succeed.' In *Philpott v Irish Examiner Ltd*[347] the plaintiff sought interlocutory orders prohibiting the defendant from continuing to publish articles online relating to proceedings in the Circuit Court which had been appealed and subsequently settled. Barrett J expressed the view that the provisions of section 33 of the Defamation Act 2009 'by reducing the test to a matter of judicial opinion … appear to have lowered the bar for plaintiffs in this regard'.[348] However, he later stated that '[u]nder that provision, the court must be of the opinion that an impugned statement "is defamatory", not that it is arguably or even unarguably so, but that, in the court's opinion, it "is" so. This is a high threshold for a plaintiff to satisfy.'[349] Barrett J also noted that the position at common law was similar and that the jurisdiction to make a section 33 type order 'should only be exercised in the clearest cases' which is in line with the formula adopted in *Cogley v RTE*. On the facts of the matter before the court, Barrett J concluded that none of the statements complained of were defamatory and he refused the relief sought.

Subsequently, in *Gilroy v O'Leary*,[350] Allen J concluded that the threshold under section 33 is the same as that which applied at common law. Having considered the language used in the legislation, he stated as follows:

> After careful consideration, I have come to the conclusion that there is no difference between an 'opinion' and a 'finding' or the court being 'satisfied'. It seems to me that the key to understanding what the test in s. 33 is, is that the same test is applicable to interim, interlocutory, and permanent orders. The jurisdiction of the court to make prior restraint orders is as delicate post 2010 as it previously was. I cannot conceive that the court would permanently interfere with free speech or the free expression of opinion unless in a case where is was satisfied and/or had made a finding that the statement was defamatory of the plaintiff and that the defendant had no defence.[351]

He added that the onus is on a plaintiff applying for an order pursuant to section 33 to establish that the statement *is* defamatory and expressed the view that this is the same as the common law standard expressed as a requirement that

---

347. [2016] IEHC 62.
348. *Ibid.* at [5].
349. *Ibid.* at [27].
350. [2019] IEHC 52.
351. *Ibid.* at [53].

the plaintiff must show that it was clear that he would succeed at trial, as in *Cogley*, or it that was clear that no defence would succeed at trial, as in *Foley*.

Where an Interlocutory Injunction is Sought to Restrain the Presentation of a Petition for the Winding Up of a Company

This exception has been accepted in England for some time,[352] and the approach taken there was followed by the High Court in this jurisdiction in *Truck and Machinery Sales Ltd v Marubeni Komatsu Ltd*.[353] However, the outcome in more recent cases also makes it clear that where the company in good faith and on substantial grounds disputes any liability in respect of the alleged debt, the petition will be dismissed.

In *Truck and Machinery Sales Ltd v Marubeni Komatsu Ltd*[354] the plaintiff sought an injunction to restrain the defendant from presenting a petition to wind up the company. Counsel for the plaintiff sought to rely on the *Campus Oil* principles and argued that the plaintiff had raised a serious question as to whether the sum claimed was due and owing by it and that the balance of convenience lay in favour of restraining the petition until the hearing of the action. Counsel for the defendant argued that in order to obtain such relief, the plaintiff would have to establish that the presentation of the petition was an abuse of process and that it was bound to fail or, at least, that there was an alternative remedy available. Keane J stated that he was satisfied that the jurisdiction to restrain the presentation of a petition to wind up a company is one which should only be exercised with great caution. He referred to the principles set out by the Court of Appeal in *Bryanston Finance Ltd v De Vries (No. 2)*[355] and in *Coulson Sanderson & Ward v Ward*[356] and said that he was satisfied that this was the approach which should also be adopted in this jurisdiction. He continued as follows:

> The constitutional right of recourse to the courts should not be inhibited, save in exceptional circumstances, and this applies as much to the presentation of a petition for the winding up of a company by a person with the appropriate *locus standi* as it does to any other form of proceedings. The undoubted power of the courts to restrain proceedings which are an abuse of process is one which should not be lightly exercised. In the

352. *Bryanston Finance Ltd v De Vries (No.2)* [1976] Ch 63.
353. [1996] 1 IR 12. See also *Meridian Communications Ltd v Eircell Ltd* [2001] IESC 42.
354. *Ibid.*
355. [1976] Ch 63.
356. [1986] 2 BCLC 99. As Slade LJ had commented, 'the court should not, on the hearing of an interlocutory motion, interfere with what would otherwise appear to be the legitimate presentation of a winding up petition by someone qualified to present it unless the evidence before it is sufficient to establish *prima facie* that the plaintiff company will succeed in establishing that the proceedings sought to be restrained would constitute an abuse.'

> context of winding-up petitions, I have no doubt that it should be exercised only where the plaintiff company has established at least a *prima facie* case that its presentation would constitute an abuse of process. In many cases, a *prima facie* case will be established where the plaintiff company adduces evidence which satisfies the court that the petition is bound to fail, or at the least, that there is a suitable alternative remedy. It would not be appropriate to apply the principles laid down by the Supreme Court in *Campus Oil Ltd v Minister for Industry and Energy (No.2)* in cases of this nature where it is the creditors' right to have recourse to the courts, rather than any right of the plaintiff company, which is under threat.[357]

Keane J concluded that the plaintiff company had failed to establish a *prima facie* case that the presentation of the petition would be an abuse of process or that it would be bound to fail. In addition, there was no alternative remedy open to the defendant and he held that the injunction sought should be refused. The key finding made by Keane J is set out in the following terms:

> It is clear that where the company in good faith and on substantial grounds, disputes any liability in respect of the alleged debt, the petition will be dismissed, or if the matter is brought before the court before the petition is issued, its presentation will in normal circumstances be restrained. This is on the ground that a winding-up petition is not a legitimate means of seeking to enforce payment of a debt which is *bona fide* disputed.[358]

This statement has provided the basis for the conclusion reached by the courts in a number of subsequent cases. In *Coalport Building Co. Ltd v Castle Contracts (Ireland) Ltd*[359] the court addressed the question of whether the plaintiff was acting in good faith in, and had substantial grounds for, disputing the alleged debt. While it was contended on behalf of the defendant that there was no genuine *bona fide* dispute in relation to the alleged debt, this argument was rejected by the court. Laffoy J therefore made an order restraining the defendant from taking any steps to advertise or otherwise publicise a petition for the purpose of seeking the winding up of the plaintiff company until further order on condition that the plaintiff lodge in court a sum as security for the alleged debt.

Similar findings have been made in a number of subsequent decisions. In *Cotton Box Design Group Ltd v Earls Construction Co. Ltd*[360] Laffoy J found that it was impossible to conclude on the basis of the evidence other than that the company was acting in good faith and on substantial grounds in disputing the petitioner's claim. She stated that she was satisfied that the company had established at least a *prima facie* case that the prosecution of

357. [1996] 1 IR 12, 27.
358. *Ibid.* at 24.
359. [2004] IEHC 6.
360. [2009] IEHC 312.

the petition would constitute an abuse of process and concluded that this was a sufficient basis on which to restrain its further prosecution. In *Donal Rigney Ltd v Empresa de Construcoes Amandio Carvalho SA*[361] Laffoy J concluded that notwithstanding that the affidavit evidence gave rise to some uncertainty as to the facts, she did not see any basis for finding that the plaintiff was not acting *bona fide*. In these circumstances, she said that she could not rule out the prospect of a very serious injustice being caused to the plaintiff if the petition for winding up was allowed to proceed and she made an order restraining the defendants from proceeding with it. Similarly, in *White Cedar Developments Ltd v Cordil Construction Ltd*,[362] Laffoy J found that not only had the plaintiff disputed the debt claimed to be due by it to the defendant in good faith and on substantial grounds, but it had done so in a very convincing manner. She was also of the view that presentation of a petition to wind up the plaintiff would constitute an abuse and in the circumstances Laffoy J made an order restraining the defendant pending the trial of the action from advertising, presenting or otherwise proceeding with the petition to wind up the plaintiff.

However in *D.& F. Partnership Ltd v Horan Keogan Ryan Ltd*[363] Ryan J applied the principles set out in *Truck and Machinery Sales Ltd* to find in favour of the defendant. He held that there was no basis for concluding that there was a substantial *bona fide* dispute as to the existence or the amount of the debt in the case before him. He found that the defendant had not adopted the procedure under section 214 of the Companies Act 1963 in respect of a legitimately disputed claim and that it was not an abuse of process. In these circumstances, he held that the application for an interlocutory injunction must be refused. Similarly, in *Bandon Motors (Bandon) Ltd v Water Sun Ltd*,[364] Keane J refused the application for an interlocutory injunction restraining the presentation of a winding-up petition. He concluded that the company had failed to establish that its denial of liability for the debt claimed by the petitioners was made in good faith or on substantial grounds and that it had not established a *prima facie* case that the petition was bound to fail.

Finally, it should be noted that Cooke J held in *Permanent TSB plc v Skoczylas*[365] that the principles set out by Keane J in *Truck and Machinery Sales Ltd* do not apply to an application for an interlocutory injunction to restrain the initiation by the defendants of applications under section 160 of the Companies Act 1990[366] for orders disqualifying the plaintiffs as company directors. He stated that there were important distinctions to be drawn between the issue considered in *Truck and Machinery Sales Ltd* and the circumstances

361. [2009] IEHC 572.
362. [2012] IEHC 525.
363. [2011] IEHC 333.
364. [2018] IEHC 191.
365. [2013] IEHC 42.
366. Now, see generally Part 14, Chapter 4 of the Companies Act 2014 and in particular, ss. 839-842.

of the matter before the court. Cooke J pointed out that unlike the creditor who has a legitimate property interest in the assets of an insolvent company, the defendants had no equivalent personal interest in obtaining the disqualification of the plaintiffs. A further important distinction was that the grant of the injunction sought did not deprive the defendants of access to the court for the assertion of the claims which they wished to pursue. Cooke J concluded that the *Campus Oil* principles applied and held that an interlocutory injunction should be granted restraining the defendants, until the trial of the action, from issuing proceedings or presenting any application under section 160 of the Companies Act 1990 against the plaintiffs.

Where the Trial of the Action is Unlikely

It is now well-established that one of the situations in which it is not appropriate to apply the *Cyanamid/Campus Oil* guidelines is where it is unlikely that a trial will in fact take place. This principle was laid down in England by Lord Diplock in the decision of *NWL Ltd v Woods*,[367] where he stressed that *American Cyanamid* was not dealing with a case where the grant or refusal of an injunction would in effect dispose of the action finally in favour of whichever party was successful, and that where these circumstances exist an important additional element must be brought into the assessment of the balance of convenience. He continued as follows:

> Where … the grant or refusal of the interlocutory injunction will have the practical effect of putting an end to the action because the harm that will have been already caused to the losing party by its grant or refusal is complete and of a kind for which money cannot constitute any worthwhile recompense, the degree of likelihood that the plaintiff would have succeeded in establishing his right to an injunction if the action had gone to trial is a factor to be brought into the balance by the judge in weighing the risks that injustice may result from his deciding the application one way rather than the other.[368]

This approach has been followed by the Court of Appeal in England in a number of cases. In *Cayne v Global Natural Resources plc*[369] the plaintiff shareholders sought an interlocutory injunction to restrain the defendant company from implementing a merger agreement and proceeding with the allotment of shares prior to the company's impending annual general meeting. If the injunction was granted the balance of power in the company would remain the same until

367. [1979] 1 WLR 1294.
368. *Ibid.* at 1307. See also *AMEC Group Ltd v Universal Steels (Scotland) Ltd* [2009] EWHC 560 (TCC) at [7]-[8]; *Merck Sharp & Dohme Corporation v Clonmel Healthcare Ltd* [2018] IECA 177 at [93] *per* Whelan J.
369. [1984] 1 All ER 225.

after the crucial vote was taken and the plaintiffs would therefore obtain the result which they sought; on the other hand if the injunction was refused the votes of the new shareholders would ensure that the plan of the incumbent directors succeeded. As Kerr LJ commented, 'the practical realities … are that, if the plaintiffs succeed in obtaining an injunction, they will never take this case to trial'.[370] May LJ stated that in a case such as that before the court, where the grant or refusal of an injunction will effectively dispose of the action in favour of the successful party, the 'balance of the risk of doing an injustice' better described the process involved. The Court of Appeal concluded that in these circumstances it would not be appropriate to apply the *American Cyanamid* guidelines which were based on the assumption that a proper trial would determine the issues at a later stage, and instead justice required that the defendant should be entitled to dispute the plaintiff's claim at the trial of the action and if an injunction would preclude this it should not be granted at an interlocutory stage.

A similar finding was made by the Court of Appeal in *Cambridge Nutrition Ltd v British Broadcasting Corporation*,[371] in which the plaintiff sought an injunction to prevent the broadcast of a TV programme about low calorie diets which focused particularly on its activities, claiming that the BBC had undertaken not to broadcast the programme until after an official report on the subject had been published. The nature of the programme was such that it was only suitable for transmission in its existing form before publication of the report and the defendant resisted the plaintiff's claim. As Kerr LJ stated, 'the subject matter concerns the right to publish an article, or to transmit a broadcast, whose importance may be transitory but whose impact depends on timing, news value and topicality.'[372] The Court of Appeal reiterated that where the decision on an application for an interlocutory injunction was the equivalent of giving final judgment the court should not grant the order merely because the plaintiff was able to show a good arguable case and the balance of convenience lay in favour of granting an injunction. Instead the court should assess the relative strength of each party's case before deciding whether the injunction should be granted. Kerr LJ stressed that the *American Cyanamid* principles were no more than a set of useful guidelines and 'must never be used as a rule of thumb, let alone as a strait-jacket'.[373] He concluded that the case before him was not an appropriate one for the application of these guidelines 'because the crucial issues between the parties do not depend on a trial, but solely or mainly on the grant or refusal of the interlocutory relief.'

Similar issues were considered in the decision of the Court of Appeal in *Douglas v Hello! Ltd*,[374] in which the claimants sought an injunction restraining

370. *Ibid.* at 235.
371. [1990] 3 All ER 523.
372. *Ibid.* at 535.
373. *Ibid.* at 535.
374. [2001] QB 967.

the defendants from publishing photographs taken at their wedding on the grounds that any publication would be in breach of confidence. Keene LJ pointed out that the third named claimant, who had exclusive rights to the photographs, and the defendants which both published weekly magazines, were undoubtedly concerned with material whose topicality was crucial and said that in such cases where the parties are principally interested in the grant or refusal of the interlocutory relief, the court must look beyond conventional *American Cyanamid* principles and seek to establish where the balance of justice lies. In addition, in his view section 12(3) of the Human Rights Act 1998, which provides that where any relief might affect the Convention right to freedom of expression it should not be granted so as to restrain publication before trial 'unless the court is satisfied that the applicant is likely to establish that publication should not be allowed', requires the court to look at the merits of the case and not merely to apply the *American Cyanamid* test. However, the Court of Appeal concluded that, although the claimants were likely to establish at trial that publication should not be allowed, in its view damages were an adequate remedy and the balance of convenience came down against prior restraint.

A further example of a case where the decision at the interlocutory stage was crucial is that of *Lansing Linde Ltd v Kerr*,[375] where the Court of Appeal confirmed that a trial judge may properly take into account a plaintiff's prospects of success at trial where the grant or refusal of interlocutory relief will effectively determine the matter. In this case the plaintiff company sought an interlocutory injunction to enforce a clause in the defendant's contract of employment which stipulated that he would not work for any of its competitors for a period of 12 months after termination of his employment with the company. The defendant, who occupied a senior position in the company, had given six months' notice and a month later accepted the position of managing director of a competitor. It was held by the Court of Appeal in refusing the injunction that the trial judge had properly taken into account the plaintiff's prospects of success at the trial, having regard to the fact that it would not be possible to hold a trial before the period for which the plaintiff claimed to be entitled to an injunction had expired, or substantially expired, and that in those circumstances it was not enough to decide merely that there was a serious issue to be tried.

It has also been accepted in a number of cases in this jurisdiction that different principles should apply where the order granted at the interlocutory stage will effectively dispose of the action, both in relation to orders of a mandatory and prohibitory nature. An example of the former is *Attorney General v Lee*,[376] in which the plaintiff sought a mandatory interlocutory injunction to direct the defendant to attend an inquest into the death of her husband as a witness. The

375. [1991] 1 WLR 251. See also *Credit Suisse Asset Management Ltd v Armstrong* [1996] ICR 882.
376. [2000] 4 IR 298.

Supreme Court discharged the interlocutory injunction granted by the High Court. Keane CJ expressed the view that, because any interlocutory relief granted by the court would effectively dispose of the matter in advance of a trial, it was not appropriate to resolve the interlocutory matter by reference to the usual test of whether the plaintiff had established that there was a fair question to be tried. He pointed out that if it should emerge at the plenary hearing of the proceedings that the defendant was entitled to succeed, it was difficult to see how justice could be done to that party where the interlocutory order had effectively disposed of the case. These principles were referred to by Hogan J in *Herrara v An Garda Siochana*,[377] who stated that the approach which had been taken in *Lee* was effectively to ask whether the defendant had any potentially sustainable defence to the application. In this case the plaintiff, whose passport had been taken by the gardaí when he had been arrested by them, sought an interlocutory injunction compelling them to return it so that he could travel abroad to take up an offer of employment. Hogan J stated that the court must ask whether the defendants could show that they had any potentially sustainable defence to the plaintiff's action. In his view the defendants had not advanced any arguable defence to the plaintiff's claim based on statute or common law and he granted the interlocutory injunction sought. A further decision of Hogan J relevant in this context in which the interlocutory injunction sought was mandatory in substance is *Wallace v Irish Aviation Authority*,[378] in which the plaintiff sought an interlocutory injunction restraining the defendant from placing her on administrative leave pending the outcome of an appeal against a decision to dismiss her from her employment. Hogan J characterised the matter before him as one where the grant or refusal of the interlocutory relief would effectively determine the proceedings and reiterated that in such cases the court is permitted, by way of 'modest derogation' from the *Campus Oil* principles, to examine the underlying strength of the parties' positions. He concluded that given that the plaintiff's case appeared to be particularly strong, it was only just and equitable that she be granted the interlocutory relief which she sought.

The principles set out in *NWL Ltd v Woods*[379] have been considered by Laffoy J in two decisions and it is clear that the courts in this jurisdiction have also accepted that where the grant or refusal of an interlocutory injunction will have the practical effect of putting an end to an action, 'the balance of the risk of doing an injustice'[380] is a more appropriate test. However, it was not possible in either case for various reasons to assess the plaintiff's likelihood of success if the matter had gone to trial and Laffoy J did not endorse such

377. [2013] IEHC 311.
378. [2012] 2 ILRM 345.
379. [1979] 1 WLR 1294.
380. *Cayne v Global Natural Resources plc* [1984] 1 All ER 225, 237 *per* May LJ. See also *Merck Sharp & Dohme Corporation v Clonmel Healthcare Ltd* [2018] IECA 177 at [87] *per* Whelan J.

an approach. In *Callanan v Geraghty*[381] the plaintiff sought an interlocutory injunction restraining the defendant coroner from carrying out a post-mortem on the body of her late husband in circumstances in which she contended that there was no uncertainty about the cause of his death. Laffoy J pointed out that if the interlocutory injunction were refused, the post-mortem was likely to be carried out, which would render it wholly impossible for the plaintiff to pursue the relief she contended she was entitled to. On the other hand, if the interlocutory relief were granted, while she accepted that the effectiveness of any post-mortem which would be carried out if the plaintiff was unsuccessful at the trial of the action would be compromised, she did not accept that the defendant would be wholly unable to perform his discretionary power in this regard. Laffoy J concluded that a consideration of those factors alone, without assessing the strength of the plaintiff's case, seemed to her to comply with the suggestion made by Lord Diplock in *NWL* to weigh up the risk that injustice might result from deciding the application one way rather than the other. She added that the reality was that, in the absence of medical evidence which had not been adduced, presumably because of time constraints, the strength or weakness of the plaintiff's case could not in any event be assessed. In the circumstances, Laffoy J granted an order restraining the defendant from causing a post-mortem to be carried out on the plaintiff's deceased husband pending trial.[382]

In *Jacob v Irish Amateur Rowing Union Ltd*[383] the plaintiff sought an order restraining the defendant from preventing him from competing in a regatta which provided the only remaining opportunity for him to qualify for a place in a rowing class competition in the 2008 Olympic Games. Laffoy J pointed out that if the court were to grant the injunction sought, the claim against the defendant would in reality be disposed of and she expressed the view that because of its nature and effect it was 'very much a case of balancing the risk of injustice'. She stated that given the conflicting evidence put forward, she did not think that it was possible to assess the relative strengths and weaknesses of the case put forward by each party. In her view the best that the court could do was to consider the question suggested by May LJ in the *Cayne* case, namely 'whether the plaintiff's case on the evidence is so strong that to refuse an injunction would constitute an injustice'.[384] She held that it was not possible to find that the plaintiff's case on his own evidence, leaving aside any conflicts, bore that necessary weight and she concluded that the proper exercise of the court's discretion, balancing the risk of injustice, was to refuse the interlocutory injunction sought.

---

381. [2008] 1 IR 399. See further Slattery (2008) 15(4) Comm LP 80.
382. The report of this case contains a reporter's note to the effect that following the delivery of the judgment on the interlocutory application, the proceedings were withdrawn by the plaintiff and struck out by order of the High Court.
383. [2008] 4 IR 731.
384. *Ibid.* at 741. See also *Morris v An Bord Pleanala* [2017] IEHC 354, where Barrett J applied this principle and refused the interlocutory relief sought.

The principles set out in *Jacob* have been applied by Keane J in two more recent decisions, *Rogers v An Post*[385] and *Byrne v Coyle*.[386] In *Rogers* the plaintiff sought an interlocutory injunction restraining the defendant from taking any further steps in a disciplinary process against him until the determination of related criminal proceedings. Keane J said that it was clear that in this case the grant of an interlocutory injunction would have the practical effect of determining the proceedings because if interlocutory relief were granted, the plaintiff would have obtained in advance of trial the form of relief that he would also be seeking at the trial of the action. He stated that it seemed to him to be appropriate to approach the application before him by reference to the principles identified by Laffoy J in *Jacob*. Keane J said that he was satisfied that this was a case in which, if the injunction sought were granted, the effective contest between the parties was likely to have been finally decided summarily in favour of the plaintiff. In these circumstances he was satisfied that it would lead to injustice to grant the injunction sought at the interlocutory stage, as there was a very great likelihood that this would effectively deprive the defendant of the opportunity of having its rights determined at a full trial. He added that he was unable to conclude that the case before him was an exceptional one in which the plaintiff's evidence was so strong that to refuse an injunction and allow the case to go to trial would be an unnecessary waste of time and expense, or that it would do an overwhelming injustice to the plaintiff.

Keane J applied similar principles in *Byrne v Coyle*,[387] which concerned an application by the owners of two mortgaged properties for an interlocutory injunction restraining a receiver from taking any steps in relation to those properties until the determination of a complaint that the applicants had made to the Financial Services Ombudsman against the mortgagee bank. Keane J said that it was clear that the grant of an interlocutory injunction would have the practical effect of determining the proceedings because the applicants would then have obtained at that stage the relief that they were seeking at the trial of the action. Having referred to the principles set out in *Jacob*, Keane J pointed out that the injunction sought on an interlocutory basis was in precisely the same terms as the injunction that formed the principal substantive relief sought at trial and said that this suggested that the case was not one that was likely to go to trial should the plaintiffs obtain interlocutory relief. He concluded that it would be an injustice to grant the injunction sought at the interlocutory stage, as this was very likely to effectively deprive the respondent of the opportunity of having his rights determined at trial and that in his view the matter before him was not an exceptional case in which the plaintiff's evidence was so strong that to allow the case to go to trial would be an unnecessary waste of time and expense, or would do an overwhelming injustice to the plaintiff.

385. [2014] IEHC 412.
386. [2014] IEHC 475.
387. [2014] IEHC 475.

The principles adopted by Laffoy J in *Jacob* and by the Court of Appeal in England in *Cayne v Global Natural Resources plc* were followed by Whelan J in the decision of the Court of Appeal in *Merck Sharp and Dohme Corporation v Clonmel Healthcare Ltd*,[388] where she was satisfied that the grant or refusal of the interlocutory application would be dispositive of the substantive claim as between the parties.[389] She expressed the view that '[t]he fundamental principle is that an interlocutory injunction is never intended to constitute a decision as to final rights but rather a decision as to what seems to be the best for the time being, in light of competing exigencies which are identified to the judge, in order to maintain, as far as practicable, a proper balance between the parties until their rights are finally determined at a substantive trial.'[390] Whelan J acknowledged that it is appropriate to a limited extent as part of the assessment of the balance of convenience to consider the respective merits of the claim and counterclaim and said that this is warranted having regard to the principle that the object of an interlocutory injunction is the avoidance of irreparable injury to rights.

In many respects the approach adopted by Laffoy J in *Jacob*, which has been consistently applied in other cases in which interlocutory relief of a prohibitory nature has been sought, mirrors the *Okunade* principles examined above, which also place emphasis on minimising the risk of injustice in cases which attract the application of the traditional *Cyanamid/Campus Oil* guidelines. However, in cases where the decision at the interlocutory stage will effectively determine the outcome in the case, the risk of injustice to the defendant if an interlocutory order is made is a more significant one and this will often affect the outcome. As against this, it must also be asked whether the requirement which Keane J seemed to impose on the plaintiffs in *Rogers* and *Byrne* of establishing that the case is an exceptional one in which the plaintiff's evidence is 'so strong that to refuse an injunction and allow the case to go to trial … would do an overwhelming injustice to the plaintiff' places too heavy a burden on a plaintiff in such cases. Admittedly the plaintiffs' claims in these cases appeared relatively weak and the decision to refuse interlocutory relief was readily supportable but it remains to be seen whether applying these principles will ensure fairness for both plaintiffs and defendants in future cases.

Finally, it should be noted that the issue of whether the *American Cyanamid/Campus Oil* guidelines should not be applied in a range of cases, namely those involving passing off and trademark infringement actions, on the grounds that in such cases the outcome of the interlocutory proceedings often determines

388. [2018] IECA 177.
389. However, it should be noted that when this matter was considered by the Supreme Court (see [2019] IESC 65), O'Donnell J made it clear (at [57]) that he did not agree that this was a case where there was no likelihood of a trial of the substantive issue taking place and the comments of Whelan J on this issue should be read in the light of this conclusion.
390. [2018] IECA 177 at [81].

the final outcome of the action, has been considered on a number of occasions in this jurisdiction but ultimately rejected.[391] It was suggested by McCracken J in *B. & S. Ltd v Irish Auto Trader Ltd*,[392] which concerned a claim of alleged passing off, that where the arguments are finely balanced, the court may consider the relative strength of each party's case at the interlocutory stage where the strength of one party's case is disproportionate to that of the other. However, in *Symonds Cider and English Wine Co. Ltd v Showerings (Ireland) Ltd*[393] the argument that the *American Cyanamid* principles should not be applied to all passing off actions was rejected. Laffoy J said that having regard to the decision of the Supreme Court in *Westman Holdings Ltd v McCormack*[394] – which applied the *American Cyanamid/Campus Oil* principles – it was not open to her, assuming that the plaintiff established that there was a fair and *bona fide* question to be tried, to express any view on the strength of the competing submissions. She concluded that she was satisfied that the plaintiff had shown that there were fair issues to be tried but that the balance of convenience lay in favour of refusing the interlocutory relief. Subsequently, in *Local Ireland Ltd v Local Ireland-Online Ltd*,[395] which also concerned a claim in relation to alleged passing off, despite the fact that counsel for both sides suggested that the outcome of the application for interlocutory relief was likely to determine the result of the dispute, Herbert J stated that having regard to the fact that there was no agreement to treat the hearing of the motion as the trial of the action, he was obliged to apply the *Campus Oil* principles.

In *Chieftain Construction Ltd v Ryan*[396] Edwards J acknowledged that it is certainly arguable that cases involving intellectual property rights in which injunctions are sought are perhaps in a special category, as very often the hearing of the interlocutory motion decides the case and they rarely proceed to a full hearing. However, he referred to the *dicta* of Laffoy J in *Symonds* and concluded that it was clear that: 'Irish law precludes a judge in most cases from having regard to the strength of the case after it has been decided that the plaintiff has raised a fair or substantial or serious issue to be tried.'[397] So, it would seem that the courts in this jurisdiction are still anxious to adhere to the *American Cyanamid/Campus Oil* guidelines even in intellectual property disputes involving allegations of passing off unless there is good reason for departing from them. There has clearly been a reluctance to extend the list of recognised exceptions to an entire class of proceedings, although undoubtedly there may be individual cases falling under this heading in which the facts may

391. A similar approach has been taken in England, see e.g. *Cowshed Products Ltd v Island Origins Ltd* [2010] EWHC 3357 (Ch).
392. [1995] 2 IR 142.
393. [1997] 1 ILRM 481.
394. [1992] 1 IR 151.
395. [2000] 4 IR 567.
396. [2008] IEHC 147.
397. *Ibid.* at 9.

warrant the conclusion that the trial of the action is unlikely to take place and that a wider consideration of the merits of both parties' cases is therefore justified.

Where an Interlocutory Injunction is Sought in a Public Law Context

The question of the specific principles which should be applied where an interlocutory injunction is sought in judicial review proceedings was considered in detail by Clarke J in the decision of the Supreme Court in *Okunade v Minister for Justice, Equality and Law Reform*,[398] which concerned an application for interlocutory injunctions restraining the applicants' deportation pending the hearing of their application for leave to seek judicial review.[399] He said that he was satisfied that the same underlying principle applies in any application taken in the context of judicial review which is designed to determine what the position should be until the substantive judicial review proceedings have been finally determined, namely that the court is required to make an order which minimises the risk of injustice. He added that it did not necessarily follow that the detailed rules for the implementation of the general principle of minimising the risk of injustice work in the same way in the context of the judicial review proceedings as opposed to in the context of injunctions sought in proceedings arising in other contexts. As Clarke J put it, '[t]he underlying principle is the same. The detailed application of that principle is likely to be different.'[400] He commented that the first question arising in the *Campus Oil* test, as to whether the plaintiff has established a fair or arguable question to be tried, remained the starting point in judicial review proceedings, but that questions relating to the adequacy of damages were less likely to be a significant feature in reaching an assessment as to how best to minimise the risk of injustice in the context of such proceedings. He added that in cases where the risk of injustice appears to be evenly balanced, it seemed that there might be greater scope in judicial review proceedings for the court to take into account the strength of the case. Clarke J set out the following principles which he suggested ought to be applied by the court in considering whether to grant a stay or an interlocutory injunction in the context of judicial review proceedings:

(a) The court should first determine whether the applicant has established an arguable case; if not the application must be refused, but if so then;
(b) The court should consider where the greatest risk of injustice would lie. But in doing so the court should:-

398. [2012] 3 IR 152.
399. Prior to the hearing of the appeal, the application for leave to seek judicial review was refused by the High Court (see [2012] IEHC 134), rendering the appeal moot. The first respondent applied for the appeal to proceed notwithstanding its mootness and the Supreme Court heard the matter and delivered judgment.
400. [2012] 3 IR 152, 185.

(i) Give all appropriate weight to the orderly implementation of measures which are prima facie valid;
(ii) Give such weight as may be appropriate (if any) to any public interest in the orderly operation of the particular scheme in which the measure under challenge was made; and
(iii) Give appropriate weight (if any) to any additional factors arising on the facts of the individual case which would heighten the risk to the public interest of the specific measure under challenge not being implemented pending resolution of the proceedings; but also
(iv) Give all due weight to the consequences for the applicant of being required to comply with the measure under challenge in circumstances where that measure may be found to be unlawful.

(c) In addition the court should, in those limited cases where it may be relevant, have regard to whether damages are available and would be an adequate remedy and also whether damages could be an adequate remedy arising from an undertaking as to damages.

(d) In addition, and subject to the issues arising on the judicial review not involving detailed investigation of fact or complex questions of law, the court can place all due weight on the strength or weakness of the applicant's case.[401]

These *Okunade* principles, which focus on minimising the risk of injustice, have been consistently applied in judicial review proceedings.[402] The relevance of these principles to public law cases generally was considered further by Clarke J in *Dowling v Minister for Finance*,[403] which concerned an application for an interlocutory injunction to prevent the respondent from selling off the Irish Life Group until the conclusion of related proceedings. An issue was raised by the appellants as to whether it was appropriate to apply the *Okunade* principles where issues of EU law are amongst those raised. Clarke J made it clear that these principles are the appropriate basis for considering domestic public law challenges in which an interlocutory injunction is sought but accepted that where a measure is challenged on the basis of EU law, the court should also have regard to the question of whether it can properly be said that a party might be deprived of an effective remedy by the court's decision in accordance with

401. *Ibid.* at 193.
402. See e.g. *Khan v Minister for Justice and Equality* [2013] IEHC 186; *K.N. v Minister for Justice and Equality* [2013] IEHC 566; *Viridian Power Ltd v Commission for Energy Regulation* [2014] IEHC 4; *P.T. v Wicklow County Council* [2017] IEHC 623; *Fitzpatrick v Minister for Agriculture, Food and the Marine* [2018] IEHC 77; *Friends of the Irish Environment Ltd v Minister for Communications, Climate Action and Environment* [2019] IEHC 555.
403. [2013] 4 IR 576.

the case law of the ECJ in *Zuckerfabrik* and subsequent decisions.[404] Clarke J noted that in applying the *Okunade* test in many public law cases, the question of damages or financial compensation will not arise but acknowledged that there may be some cases where differing considerations will apply because of the commercial or financial nature of the public law issues arising and that the matter before the court was one such case. He stated that 'the ultimate test is as to where the least risk of injustice lies'[405] and concluded that he was satisfied that the least risk of injustice would be met by not granting an interlocutory injunction.

The issue of whether particular considerations should apply where issues relating to the presumption of constitutionality are involved has been considered on a number of occasions. While Finlay CJ suggested in *Pesca Valentia Ltd v Minister for Fisheries and Forestry*[406] that he was not satisfied 'that there is any special principle applicable to an application for an interlocutory injunction of this kind', the presumption of constitutionality is an issue which must be weighed in the balance of convenience before interlocutory injunctive relief will be granted. In this case the plaintiff sought an interlocutory injunction restraining the defendants from enforcing a term in a licence granted pursuant to the Fisheries (Consolidation) Act 1959, as amended, which required that three-quarters of the crew of a trawler should be of Irish nationality. The Supreme Court considered whether any special principles applied to an application for an interlocutory injunction to prohibit the exercise of a statutory power presumed to be constitutional. Finlay CJ stated that he was satisfied that the presumption of constitutionality which applied to the legislation was material in relation to the determination by the court of whether the plaintiff had established a fair question to be tried at the hearing of the action. In addition, he was satisfied that the consequence arising from the making of an interlocutory injunction of preventing the executive from carrying out powers vested in it by a statute enjoying the presumption of constitutionality was a matter for consideration in assessing where the balance of convenience lay. However, as noted above Finlay CJ stated that he was not satisfied that any special principle applied to an application for an interlocutory injunction in this kind of case. The Supreme Court dismissed the defendants' appeal against the grant of an interlocutory injunction, but varied the terms of the order.

A similar approach was taken by Kelly J in *Controller of Patents, Designs and Trademarks v Ireland*,[407] in which the plaintiff sought, *inter alia*, an order restraining the defendant minister from implementing or bringing into operation sections 4 and 5 of the Intellectual Property (Miscellaneous Provisions) Act

404. Joined Cases C-143/88 and C-92/89 *Zuckerfabrik Süderdithmarschen AG v Hauptzollampt Itzehoe* and *Zuckerfabrik Soest GmbH v Hauptzollampt Paderborn* [1991] ECR I-415.
405. [2013] 4 IR 576, 639.
406. [1985] IR 193, 201.
407. [1998] IEHC 224.

1988 until further order of the court. He stated that it seemed to him that the mere existence of the presumption of constitutionality in favour of the impugned legislation did not mean that new or different rules should govern the application. Instead, Kelly J was of the view that he must weigh the presumption of constitutionality in the balance when deciding the question of whether a serious issue to be tried had been established and also in deciding where the balance of convenience lay. Applying these principles to the facts of the case before him, Kelly J concluded that the plaintiff had not established that there were any serious issues to be tried and said that in any event the balance of convenience would lie in favour of refusing the relief sought.

However, it should be noted that in *M.D. v Ireland*,[408] Clarke J commented that it had been argued, in his view correctly, that the jurisdiction to grant an injunction which would have the practical effect of preventing the operation of legislation pending the determination of proceedings in which its validity was under challenge was 'one which must be most sparingly exercised'.[409] He added that the reasons for this are obvious given that legislation which has been passed into law by the Oireachtas enjoys a presumption of constitutionality.

A decision which suggests that different considerations may apply in assessing where the balance of convenience lies in this context is *Crotty v An Taoiseach*.[410] In this case the plaintiff sought an interlocutory injunction to restrain the defendants from ratifying the Single European Act, a treaty which introduced a number of changes to the treaties establishing the European Communities. The Supreme Court reinstated interlocutory relief pending the hearing of an appeal in the matter. Finlay CJ found that the plaintiff had established a fair issue to be tried as to the effect of ratification of the treaty but expressed no view on the weight of the arguments. He continued as follows:

> As to the second question, whether the balance of convenience justifies the granting of an interlocutory injunction, the balance of convenience in the context of the Constitution is exceptional and considerations different to those of the ordinary injunction apply. If the interlocutory injunction sought by the plaintiff were not granted, then the Government's act of ratification would deprive this Court of its jurisdiction or power to grant to the plaintiff the remedies necessary to protect his constitutional rights. If that submission is correct, a fair argument has been made out and it constitutes what, in my view, would justify making an exception, given a reluctance to interfere with the Executive. I am satisfied that in order to do justice to the parties the injunction should continue.[411]

408. [2009] 3 IR 690.
409. *Ibid.* at 694.
410. [1987] IR 713.
411. *Ibid.* at 763.

As Clarke J subsequently pointed out in *Pringle v Ireland*,[412] the key point in the *dicta* of Finlay CJ was that the court would be deprived, in the absence of an interlocutory injunction, of any power to grant the plaintiff the remedies necessary to protect his constitutional rights if he were to succeed. The *Crotty* decision was distinguished by the Supreme Court in *Pringle*, in which the court had to consider whether to grant an interlocutory injunction restraining the defendants from ratifying or approving the European Stability Mechanism Treaty pending the final determination of the proceedings following a referral to the CJEU. Clarke J referred to the *dicta* of Finlay CJ in *Crotty* but said that the circumstances of the matter before the court were entirely different. He referred to the principles which he had set out in *Okunade v Minister for Justice, Equality and Law Reform*,[413] considered above, which focus on minimising the risk of injustice and said that similar, although not necessarily identical, considerations applied in determining the proper course to adopt at an interlocutory stage in proceedings involving constitutional issues. He added his agreement to the view expressed by O'Donnell J as to the significant weight to be attached in assessing the balance of justice to the fact that the decision-making power with which the case was concerned is specifically conferred by the Constitution on the government. As O'Donnell J put it, 'the proper functioning of the constitutional balance requires that considerable weight indeed should be accorded to the constitutional interest in ensuring that the government performs the executive functions assigned to it in the way it considers appropriate and for which it is accountable in the first place to the Dáil and through it to the People.'[414] Both O'Donnell and Clarke JJ were satisfied that whether principles of domestic law or the jurisprudence of the ECJ was applied, the balance of justice in the case before the court was decisively in favour of refusing the interlocutory injunction sought.

Principles Governing the Grant of Mandatory Injunctions

While a prohibitory injunction requires a defendant to refrain from doing certain acts, a mandatory injunction is one which compels a defendant to carry out an obligation or to perform a specified act. While this distinction may seem clear in principle, as Ní Raifeartaigh J has suggested in *Fitzpatrick v Minister for Agriculture, Food and the Marine*,[415] 'the dividing line between a mandatory and prohibitory injunction is not necessarily as obvious as might first appear, at least in some cases.' As she points out, it is the substance of the relief rather than how it is has been phrased in the pleadings which will determine how a court approaches applications for injunctive relief. So, as Clarke CJ has

412. [2013] 3 IR 1.
413. [2012] 3 IR 152.
414. [2013] 3 IR 1, 124.
415. [2018] IEHC 77.

reiterated in *Charleton v Scriven*,[416] the key issue in assessing the appropriate test for the grant of relief is whether the injunction can properly be said to be mandatory in substance.

Mandatory injunctions can be divided into two types, restorative and enforcing. The former type, which is granted more frequently, requires the party to whom it is directed to put right the consequences of his actions, e.g. by removing an offending structure. The enforcing mandatory injunction on the other hand requires the performance of some positive obligation, often of a continuing nature. To succeed in obtaining a mandatory order, particularly of the latter kind, it must be possible to specify with a sufficient degree of particularity precisely what action is required to comply with its terms and it must be quite clear 'what the person against whom the injunction or order is made is required to do or to refrain from doing.'[417] Maugham LJ laid down this requirement in *Fishenden v Higgs and Hill Ltd*[418] in the following terms:

> I think a mandatory injunction, except in very exceptional circumstances, ought to be granted in such terms that the person against whom it is granted ought to know exactly what he has to do.

This statement was quoted with approval by Murphy J in *Bula Ltd v Tara Mines Ltd (No.2)*,[419] in which he refused to grant mandatory interlocutory injunctions, *inter alia*, because in his opinion, if granted in the terms sought, the orders would not be certain enough in their terms to enable it to be ascertained whether the defendants were complying with the injunctions granted by the court.

In theory there may appear to be no difference between the principles which apply to the granting of a mandatory and prohibitory injunction at the trial of an action[420] and it has been suggested that care and caution must be exercised by a judge in either case and that no greater degree of caution is required in deciding to grant a mandatory order.[421] However, it must be recognised that in practical terms, the making of a mandatory order will usually impose an additional degree of hardship or expense on a defendant and is more likely to lead to difficulties in enforcement and supervision. Such factors may often influence a judge in deciding how to exercise his discretion and the reality is that it is often more difficult to obtain an order of a mandatory nature. One English authority which suggests that an additional degree of caution is required in the

416. [2019] IESC 28 at [4.6].
417. *Attorney-General v Staffordshire County Council* [1905] 1 Ch 336, 342.
418. (1935) 153 LT 128, 142. See also *Redland Bricks Ltd v Morris* [1970] AC 652, 666, where Lord Upjohn stated that the defendant must know what he has to do as a matter of fact, not as a matter of law. However, note the comments of Staughton LJ in *Channel Tunnel Group Ltd v Balfour Beatty Construction* [1992] QB 656, 678.
419. [1987] IR 95, 104.
420. *Davies v Gas Light & Coke Co.* [1909] 1 Ch 248, 259 *per* Warrington J.
421. *Smith v Smith* (1875) LR 20 Eq 500, 504 *per* Jessel MR.

context of mandatory orders is the decision of the House of Lords in *Redland Bricks Ltd v Morris*.[422] Land owned by the respondents, who carried on the business of strawberry farming, was affected by subsidence caused by quarrying work undertaken by the appellant on adjoining property. It was estimated that the cost of remedying the subsidence would be wholly disproportionate to the value of the land affected. The respondents were awarded damages and both prohibitory and mandatory injunctions to restrain further excavation, but the House of Lords, placing emphasis on the disproportionate cost of remedial work, allowed the appeal against the grant of a mandatory injunction. Lord Upjohn stated:

> A mandatory injunction can only be granted where the plaintiff shows a very strong probability upon the facts that grave damage will accrue to him in the future … It is jurisdiction to be exercised sparingly and with caution but, in the proper case, unhesitatingly.[423]

It was the view of Lord Upjohn that unlike in the case of a prohibitory injunction, the cost of the works which the defendant would be required to carry out must be taken into account except where the defendant has acted quite unreasonably. Where, as in the case before him, the defendant had acted reasonably, although wrongly, the cost of remedying his actions was a factor which should be taken into account. While these latter principles seem reasonable, Lord Upjohn's insistence on establishing a 'very strong probability … of grave damage' has been criticised and it has been said that this view cannot be accepted without qualification.[424] Spry suggests the following alternative, that 'whenever an injury to the plaintiff is shown, being an injury that might, before it took place, have been enjoined by a prohibitory injunction if the court thought fit, a mandatory injunction may be granted unless consequent prejudice to the defendant is so disproportionate that the course is unjust in all the circumstances'.[425]

While there may be no difference in theory between the principles which govern the grant of prohibitory and mandatory injunctions at trial, a court may be reluctant to grant interlocutory relief of a mandatory nature unless it is satisfied that 'the chances that it will turn out to have been wrongly granted are low'.[426] It has tended to have been accepted that different considerations apply to the granting of mandatory as opposed to prohibitory injunctions of

---

422. [1970] AC 652.
423. *Ibid.* at 665.
424. Spry, *The Principles of Equitable Remedies* (9th ed., 2014) p. 567. See also Heydon, Leeming and Turner, *Meagher, Gummow and Lehane's Equity: Doctrines and Remedies* (5th ed., 2015) p. 783, where the authors comment that the decision 'scintillates with dubious propositions'.
425. *Ibid.* p. 568.
426. *Per* Lord Hoffmann in *National Commercial Bank Jamaica Ltd v Olint Corporation Ltd* [2009] 1 WLR 1405, 1409.

an interlocutory nature.[427] It is also reasonable to conclude that the balance of convenience is unlikely to lie in favour of granting mandatory relief save in fairly exceptional cases and it is clear that the courts are more reluctant to grant an interlocutory injunction when it is of a mandatory nature. However, it has also been accepted that where mandatory relief sought by a plaintiff is in reality ancillary to the primary prohibitory relief claimed, it is not necessary to meet the higher standard of a 'strong case' required in the context of a mandatory injunction of an interlocutory nature.[428]

One of the most frequently quoted statements of the test which should be applied where a mandatory injunction of an interlocutory nature is sought in England is that of Megarry J in *Shepherd Homes Ltd v Sandham*,[429] where he made it clear that the court is far more reluctant to grant an injunction of a mandatory than a prohibitory nature. He said that the 'case has to be unusually strong and clear before a mandatory injunction will be granted'[430] and the court must 'feel a high degree of assurance that at the trial it will appear that the injunction was rightly granted.'[431]

It was pointed out in argument in *Locabail International Finance Ltd v Agroexport*[432] that the *dicta* of Megarry J in *Sandham* predated the revision of the principles relating to the grant of interlocutory injunctions effected by the House of Lords in *American Cyanamid*. However, Mustill LJ was satisfied that 'the statement of principle by Megarry J in relation to the very special case of the mandatory injunction is not affected by what the House of Lords said in the *Cyanamid* case.'[433] A more flexible approach was adopted by Hoffmann J in *Films Rover International Ltd v Cannon Film Sales Ltd*,[434] where he said that the 'high degree of assurance' test does not have to be satisfied in every case before an interlocutory injunction of a mandatory nature may be granted. Hoffmann J pointed out that in an exceptional case, where withholding such an injunction would carry with it a greater risk of injustice than granting it, even where the court does not feel a high degree of assurance about the plaintiff's

427. *Irish Shell Ltd v Elm Motors* [1984] IR 200, 217 *per* Costello J. However, note the comments of Lord Hoffmann's in *National Commercial Bank Jamaica Ltd v Olint Corporation Ltd* [2009] 1 WLR 1405, 1409 to the effect that the underlying principles are the same in both cases, namely that the court should take whichever course seems likely to cause the least irremediable prejudice to one party or the other. However, he acknowledged that mandatory relief is more likely to cause irremediable prejudice than would be the case where a defendant is merely prevented from taking or continuing with some course of action. See further *infra*.
428. *Kavanagh v Lynch* [2011] IEHC 348 at [7.6]; *Kavanagh v Murphy* [2016] IEHC 718 at [20].
429. [1971] Ch 340.
430. *Ibid.* at 349.
431. *Ibid.* at 351.
432. [1986] 1 WLR 657.
433. *Ibid.* at 664.
434. [1987] 1 WLR 670.

likelihood of succeeding at the trial, there cannot be any rational basis for withholding the injunction.[435]

This approach was also taken by Chadwick J in *Nottingham Building Society v Eurodynamics Systems plc*,[436] where he stated that even where the court is unable to feel a high degree of assurance that the claimant will establish his right at trial, it may still be appropriate to grant a mandatory injunction at the interlocutory stage where the risk of injustice if this injunction is refused sufficiently outweighs the risk of injustice if it is granted. However, he also stressed that in considering whether to grant a mandatory interlocutory injunction the court must bear in mind that an order which requires a party to take a positive step may well carry a greater risk of injustice if it turns out to have been wrongly made.

This latter principle was developed by Lord Hoffmann in delivering the opinion of the Privy Council in *National Commercial Bank Jamaica Ltd v Olint Corporation Ltd*.[437] He formulated a unified test to be applied in cases where either prohibitory or mandatory interlocutory injunctions are sought which focuses on avoiding causing irremediable prejudice. Having referred to the principles set out by Lord Diplock in *American Cyanamid* he continued as follows:

> There is however no reason to suppose that, in stating these principles, Lord Diplock was intending to confine them to injunctions which could be described as prohibitory rather than mandatory. In both cases, the underlying principle is the same, namely, that the court should take whichever course seems likely to cause the least irremediable prejudice to one party or the other: see Lord Jauncey in *R v Secretary of State for Transport, Ex p Factortame Ltd (No. 2)* (Case C-213/89) [1991] 1 AC 603, 682-683.[438] What is true is that the features which ordinarily justify describing an injunction as mandatory are often more likely to cause irremediable prejudice than in cases in which a defendant is merely prevented from taking or continuing with some course of action: see *Films Rover International Ltd v Cannon Film Sales Ltd* [1987] 1 WLR 670, 680. But this is no more than a generalisation. What is required in each case is to examine what on the particular facts of the case the consequences of granting or withholding of the injunction is likely to be. If it appears that

435. *Ibid.* at 681.
436. [1993] FSR 468, 474. See also *Zockoll Group Ltd v Mercury Communications Ltd* [1998] FSR 354, 366; *Shilmore Enterprises Corporation v Phoenix 1 Aviation Ltd* [2008] EWHC 169 (QB) at [7]; *AMEC Group Ltd v Universal Steels (Scotland) Ltd* [2009] EWHC 560 (TCC) at [5].
437. [2009] 1 WLR 1405.
438. This is also in line with the approach suggested by Clarke J in *Sabmiller Africa BV v East African Breweries Ltd* [2009] EWHC 2140 (Comm) at [48] to the effect that 'a fundamental principle is that the court should take whatever course appears to carry the lower risk of injustice if it should turn out to have been the "wrong" course'.

> the injunction is likely to cause irremediable prejudice to the defendant, a court may be reluctant to grant it unless satisfied that the chances that it will turn out to have been wrongly granted are low; that is to say, that the court will feel, as Megarry J said in *Shepherd Homes Ltd v Sandham* [1971] Ch 340, 351, 'a high degree of assurance that at the trial it will appear that the injunction was rightly granted'.
>
> For these reasons, arguments over whether the injunction should be classified as prohibitive or mandatory are barren: see *Films Rover* [1987] 1 WLR 670, 680. What matters is what the practical consequences of the actual injunction are likely to be.[439]

This is a logical approach and it removes the uncertainty which the need for the application of different tests has given rise to. Given the likely consequences of the grant of interlocutory relief of a mandatory nature, 'irremediable prejudice' is far more likely to be caused to a party against whom such an order is made and to this extent it is correct to continue to assert that it will be significantly more difficult to obtain relief of this nature. However, Lord Hoffmann's solution neatly avoids the difficulties of grappling with alternative tests depending on whether the relief sought is characterised as prohibitory or mandatory in nature.

The test to be applied where an application is made for a mandatory interlocutory injunction in this jurisdiction now seems reasonably settled although inconsistent approaches have been applied over the years.[440] Before examining the relevant decisions in detail, it should be pointed out that the decision in *Campus Oil Ltd v Minister for Industry and Energy (No. 2)*[441] itself dealt with an application for a mandatory interlocutory injunction.[442] In *Campus Oil* O'Higgins CJ made it clear that the likelihood of success at trial should not be a factor in the granting of interlocutory relief generally although he did go on to say that such relief will only issue in mandatory form in exceptional cases, such as that before the court. This first point is broadly in line with the view expressed by Murphy J in *Bula Ltd v Tara Mines Ltd (No. 2)*,[443] where he said that while he agreed with much of what had been said by Megarry J in *Shepherd Homes Ltd v Sandham*, he would be reluctant to accept the proposition

---

439. [2009] 1 WLR 1405, 1409-1410.
440. This lack of consistency has also been evident elsewhere in the common law world. So, in the decision of the Supreme Court of Canada in *R. v Canadian Broadcasting Corporation* (2018) 417 DLR (4th) 587, Brown J made reference to the fact that the Canadian courts have also been divided on the question of whether to apply a strong *prima facie* case or 'serious question to be tried' test in this context. He made it clear in that case that the Supreme Court of Canada favoured the strong *prima facie* case test.
441. [1983] IR 88.
442. See, e.g. the comments of Laffoy J in *O'Mahony v Examiner Publications (Cork) Ltd* [2010] IEHC 413 at 10.
443. [1987] IR 95.

that the granting or withholding of a mandatory interlocutory injunction should be related to or dependent on the strength of the applicant's case.[444]

In a number of High Court cases decided over the years since *Campus Oil*, the general guidelines laid down in that decision have been applied in the context of seeking mandatory interlocutory relief and a relatively low threshold imposed on plaintiffs. In *A & N Pharmacy Ltd v United Drug Wholesale Ltd*[445] the plaintiff, which had set up a new pharmacy in Limerick, sought a mandatory interlocutory injunction compelling the defendant, a wholesaler in its area, to supply it with non-generic pharmaceutical products. As a result of the refusal of the defendant and other major wholesalers to supply the plaintiff, it had been forced to import products from abroad at non-competitive prices. Carroll J held that there was a serious issue to be tried and that the balance of convenience favoured the plaintiff; in other words the ordinary test which applies to interlocutory injunctions of a prohibitory nature had been satisfied. She found that it was likely that damages would not be an adequate remedy because the plaintiff would be forced out of business if it could not obtain the supplies it required and decided to grant a mandatory injunction of an interlocutory nature compelling the defendant to supply the plaintiff on a cash-on-delivery basis.

Similarly in *Cronin v Minister for Education and Science*,[446] where the plaintiff sought a mandatory interlocutory injunction directing the defendant to provide for the cost of a specified number of hours of home tuition for him, Laffoy J stressed that whether the plaintiff was likely to succeed at trial was not a relevant factor in determining whether a mandatory interlocutory injunction should be granted and that it was not appropriate at the interlocutory stage for the court to make a judgment as to the strength of either party's case. In applying the *Campus Oil* guidelines, Laffoy J concluded that there was a fair *bona fide* issue to be tried, that damages were not an adequate remedy and that the balance of convenience lay in favour of granting the injunction sought as the plaintiff's parents could not, without incurring serious financial hardship, fund the educational programme themselves.

However, in many other High Court decisions following *Campus Oil*, it has been stressed that mandatory interlocutory injunctions will only issue in very limited circumstances and in some instances reference has been made to the likelihood of a plaintiff succeeding at trial. In *Boyhan v Tribunal of Inquiry into the Beef Industry*[447] Denham J declined to grant an interlocutory injunction of a mandatory nature in favour of the United Farmers Association directing that they should be granted full legal representation before the beef tribunal as she was satisfied that the limited representation granted to it by the tribunal was sufficient in the circumstances. In the course of her judgment Denham J

444. See also *De Burca v Wicklow County Council* [2000] IEHC 182; *Cronin v Minister for Education and Science* [2004] 3 IR 205.
445. [1996] 2 ILRM 46.
446. [2004] 3 IR 205.
447. [1992] ILRM 545. See also *O'Dea v O'Briain* [1992] ILRM 364.

described a mandatory injunction as a 'powerful instrument' and said that in seeking 'this exceptional form of relief … it is up to the plaintiffs to establish a strong and clear case — so that the court can feel a degree of assurance that at a trial of the action a similar injunction would be granted.'[448] Similarly, in *Boyle v An Post*,[449] while Lardner J decided to grant an interlocutory order of a mandatory nature directing An Post to pay the plaintiffs their wages after the payroll computer had to be shut down following the suspension of a number of staff, he stated that it was 'an exceptional case where one can say with assurance that at the hearing of the substantive action the plaintiffs are bound to succeed.'[450]

A greater onus has also been placed on plaintiffs in a series of cases where injunctions which are mandatory in substance have been sought in an employment context. In the decision of the Supreme Court in *Lingham v Health Service Executive*[451] Fennelly J stated as follows:

> [I]t is well established that the ordinary test of a fair case to be tried is not sufficient to meet the first leg of the test for the grant of an interlocutory injunction where the injunction sought is in effect mandatory. In such a case it is necessary for the applicant to show at least that he has a strong case that he is likely to succeed at the hearing of the action.[452]

These principles have been consistently applied in this context[453] and as McMahon J made clear in *Khan v Health Service Executive*,[454] in such cases the courts focus on the substance of the relief claimed rather than the form. As Clarke J commented in *Bergin v Galway Clinic Doughiska Ltd*:[455]

448. *Ibid.* at 556.
449. [1992] 2 IR 437.
450. *Ibid.* at 442.
451. [2006] ELR 137, 140.
452. See also *Coffey v William Connolly & Sons Ltd* [2007] IEHC 319 at 12; *Stoskus v Goode Concrete Ltd* [2007] IEHC 432 at 5; *Khan v Health Service Executive* [2009] ELR 178, 191; *Buckley v National University Maynooth* [2009] IEHC 58 at 9; *Keenan v Iarnród Eireann* [2010] IEHC 15 at 10; *Earley v Health Service Executive* [2015] IEHC 520 at [17]; *Brennan v Irish Pride Bakeries* [2015] IEHC 665 at [20]; *O'Leary v An Post* [2016] IEHC 237; *Quigley v Health Service Executive* [2017] IEHC 654; *Kearney v Byrne Wallace* [2017] IEHC 713. This test has also been applied in other contexts where the relief sought is mandatory in substance, see *Meade v Minister for Agriculture, Fisheries and Food* [2010] IEHC 105; *O'Leary v Volkswagen Group Ireland Ltd* [2013] IEHC 318; *Bank of Ireland v O'Donnell* [2015] IECA 73; *Jones v Coolmore Stud* [2016] IEHC 329; *Whooley v Merck Millipore Ltd* [2018] IEHC 725 at [28].
453. See, e.g. *Burke v Independent Colleges Ltd* [2010] IEHC 412 at 14; *O'Mahony v Examiner Publications (Cork) Ltd* [2010] IEHC 413 at 10.
454. [2009] ELR 178, 192.
455. [2008] 2 IR 205, 214.

> The basis for the higher standard is that the substance of the relief sought is a mandatory order requiring the employer to keep the employee in employment. The order remains a mandatory order, even though the plaintiff claims that a purported determination of his employment is unlawful by reason of a finding of a wrongdoing having been arrived at in breach of the principles of natural justice. However couched, the substance of the relief is the same.

Clarke J stated that he had reached the view that in any case in which an employee sought to prevent his dismissal, in whatever terms the claim was framed, the employee in question was seeking what was in substance a mandatory injunction. In those circumstances he said that it was necessary for the employee to establish 'a strong case'[456] in order to obtain interlocutory relief. On the facts of the case before him he was satisfied that the plaintiff had made out such a strong case and having considered where the balance of convenience lay, he granted the plaintiff an injunction which restrained his dismissal and prevented the defendant from appointing any other person to carry out the plaintiff's duties pending the trial.

Another example of these principles in operation is the decision of Edwards J in *Coffey v William Connolly & Sons Ltd*,[457] where the plaintiff sought interlocutory injunctive relief, *inter alia*, restraining the defendant from treating her as otherwise than continuing to be employed by it. Edwards J said that it was clear to him that the plaintiff was seeking to have her contract of employment positively enforced pending the trial of the action. Although the injunction she claimed was framed in prohibitory language, its practical effect if granted would be to require the defendant to treat the contract as continuing to subsist until the trial. While he was satisfied that the plaintiff had raised a fair issue to be tried, he made it clear that where she was in effect seeking a mandatory interlocutory injunction the threshold was higher and he concluded that he was not convinced that the plaintiff had discharged the onus of showing that she had a strong case that she was likely to succeed in her action. In the circumstances, he declined to grant the injunction in the terms set out above but did grant relief restraining the defendant from giving effect to the purported dismissal and from appointing any other person to the position held by the plaintiff. A similar approach was taken by Irvine J in *Stoskus v Goode Concrete Ltd*,[458] where the plaintiff sought an interlocutory injunction restraining the defendant from ceasing to pay his wages pending trial. She took the view that while the relief sought by the plaintiff was framed as prohibitory in nature, he was in effect seeking mandatory relief as he was asking the court to require the defendant to perform an obligation. Irvine J therefore held that the onus of proof on the

456. See also *Naujoks v National Institute of Bioprocessing Research and Training Ltd* [2007] ELR 25; *Turner v O'Reilly* [2008] IEHC 92.
457. [2007] IEHC 319.
458. [2007] IEHC 432.

plaintiff was to establish that he had a strong case and concluded that he had not made out such a case to support his application for interlocutory relief.

A slightly different approach, more in line with that adopted by Hoffmann J in *Films Rover*, was adopted by Kelly J in *Shelbourne Hotel Holdings Ltd v Torriam Hotel Operating Co. Ltd*,[459] which involves seeking to minimise the risk of injustice by making the 'wrong' decision at the interlocutory stage. The plaintiff sought an injunction to direct the defendant to grant it access to a hotel's books and records on foot of its rights under a management agreement. The plaintiff contended that the test for the grant of such an injunction was that prescribed by the Supreme Court in *Campus Oil Ltd v Minister for Energy (No. 2)*, while the defendant contended that the issue must be such as to allow the court to feel a high degree of assurance that the injunction would be granted at trial, or a strong likelihood of success. Kelly J referred to *Boyhan* and *Lingham* and said that the approach adopted in these cases seemed very different to that applied by the Supreme Court in the *Campus Oil* case, itself a decision on an application for a mandatory interlocutory injunction, as well as in cases such as *A & N Pharmacy* and *Cronin*. He noted that there has been an inconsistency of approach in relation to the standard that must be met in order to obtain an interlocutory injunction of a mandatory nature. He continued as follows:

> Faced with these conflicting approaches and pending a final determination of the issue by the Supreme Court, I am much attracted by the approach of Hoffmann J (as he then was) in the *Films Rover* case [1987] 1 WLR 670 where he took the view that the fundamental principle on interlocutory applications for both prohibitory and mandatory injunctions is that the court should adopt whatever course would carry the lower risk of injustice if it turns out to have been the 'wrong' decision. Whatever standard applies it is clear that the grant of mandatory interlocutory relief is exceptional. In many if not all cases, the mandatory nature of the relief will also be a factor to be taken into consideration when the balance of convenience falls to be considered.[460]

Kelly J concluded that he was satisfied on the basis of the evidence that the plaintiff had achieved the higher of the two tests, namely the demonstration of a clear case and that damages would not be an adequate remedy were the plaintiff to be further denied access to the information sought.[461] He also concluded that the balance of convenience lay in favour of granting rather than refusing the

459. [2010] 2 IR 52.
460. *Ibid.* at 67. See also *Brennan v Irish Pride Bakeries* [2015] IEHC 665 at [22]; See further *Quigley v Health Service Executive* [2017] IEHC 654 at [46], [50].
461. A similar conclusion was reached by Laffoy J in *ESB v Roddy* [2010] IEHC 158 where she said that irrespective of whether the test set out in *Lingham* or *Shelbourne* was applied, she was satisfied that the plaintiff had met the higher standard of showing that it had a strong case that was likely to succeed at trial.

injunction and he therefore made an order in the plaintiff's favour requiring the defendant to grant it access to the information sought.

In the Supreme Court decision of *Okunade v Minister for Justice, Equality and Law Reform*[462] Clarke J discussed the types of situations where 'refinements and variations' of the *Campus Oil* test have evolved 'as a response to the need to minimise the risk of injustice in the context of the particular types of issues which are likely to arise in special cases'. He instanced as an example of this the position in relation to mandatory interlocutory injunctions and reaffirmed that where the order sought in a case involves something which, in substance, is mandatory in nature, the courts have required the plaintiff to establish not just a fair or arguable case but rather the higher standard as set out by the Supreme Court in *Lingham.* Clarke J also acknowledged that there is something of a tension between the practical requirement which suggests that the court should not engage in a detailed analysis of the facts or complex legal questions at an interlocutory stage, and the requirement in cases such as *Lingham* that a higher standard than a 'fair issue to be tried' be established. However, he said that even in those cases where a higher threshold may need to be met, that requirement should not involve the court in a detailed analysis of the facts or complex questions of law. In his view, '[r]ather it obliges the plaintiff to put forward, in a straightforward way, a case which meets the higher threshold.'[463] It should also be reiterated, as noted above, that Clarke J made numerous references in his judgment to the importance of the overarching principle of seeking to minimise injustice.

Recent decisions show a more consistent application of the higher standard of a strong case that the plaintiff will succeed at trial. In *Albion Properties Ltd v Moonblast Ltd*[464] Hogan J acknowledged that the courts are very reluctant to grant a mandatory interlocutory injunction, save in the clearest of cases. He expressed the view that '[b]ecause the effect of such relief is generally to disturb the *status quo ante*, the granting of such an order is properly regarded as exceptional' and said that '[i]t would normally not be granted unless it was more or less inevitable that the plaintiff would succeed at the trial of the action or, at least, where a strong *prima facie* case had been made out.'[465] In addition, as he pointed out, the balance of convenience would have to favour the grant of such exceptional relief.

In *Tola Capital Management LLC v Joseph Linders*[466] Cregan J noted that what Clarke J described in *Okunade* as a 'refinement' or 'variation' of the *Campus Oil* test has been applied in determining whether to grant mandatory

---

462. [2012] 3 IR 152, 182.
463. *Ibid.* at 184.
464. [2011] 3 IR 563. See also *Wallace v Irish Aviation Authority* [2012] 2 ILRM 345 where Hogan J found that the plaintiff had established 'very strong grounds' in circumstances where the relief sought was mandatory in substance.
465. *Ibid.* at 570.
466. [2014] IEHC 316.

injunctions in the Supreme Court decision in *Lingham*. He commented that it appears from these decisions that where the order sought is a mandatory one, the appropriate test is that the plaintiff must establish, in the words of Fennelly J in *Lingham*, that he has 'a strong case that he is likely to succeed at the hearing of the action'. He added that where a mandatory interlocutory injunction is being sought, the court should also adopt, as suggested by Kelly J in *Shelbourne Hotel* and Clarke J in *Okunade*, 'whatever course would carry the lower risk of injustice'.[467] He concluded that the plaintiff in the matter before him had to establish a strong case that it was likely to succeed at the hearing of the action before it was entitled to an injunction and in the circumstances he found that it had not done so. A similar approach was adopted by Ní Raifeartaigh J in *Fitzpatrick v Minister for Agriculture, Food and the Marine*,[468] in the context of an application for relief which, after consideration, she concluded was best characterised as mandatory in nature, given that it sought to compel the State authorities to carry out their legal obligations in a particular way. In the view of Ní Raifeartaigh J the appropriate test in such cases was that the court should examine whether the applicants had met the threshold of a 'strong case' that they were likely to succeed at trial, subject to the caveat that 'this onus of proof would not be fatal if the withholding of the interlocutory injunction would carry with it a greater risk of injustice than granting it.'[469]

The fact that the 'strong case' test should be applied where relief which is mandatory in substance is sought was confirmed by Clarke CJ in the decision of the Supreme Court in *Charleton v Scriven*,[470] in a judgment in which he also placed considerable emphasis, as he had done in *Okunade*, on the importance of the court seeking to minimise the risk of injustice. He said that there was clear authority for the proposition that the assessment of whether an injunction could properly be said to be mandatory for this purpose was a matter of substance rather than one of form,[471] and that the reason why a higher standard is applied is 'not because of some technicality but because of the greater risk of injustice'. He added as follows:

> [This] greater risk is a function of the substance of the order sought and the consequences which it might have for an individual who became bound to obey the interlocutory injunction but ultimately succeeded. It is clear that, at least in general terms, requiring someone to do something which, it may ultimately transpire, they were not required to do may give rise to a greater risk of injustice than simply requiring someone to refrain from doing something which they may ultimately be found to be entitled to do.

467. See also *Brennan v Irish Pride Bakeries* [2015] IEHC 665 at [30].
468. [2018] IEHC 77.
469. *Ibid.* at [65].
470. [2019] IESC 28.
471. *Lingham v Health Service Executive* [2006] ELR 137; *Bergin v Galway Clinic Doughiska Ltd* [2008] 2 IR 205 and *Stoskus v Goode Concrete Ltd* [2007] IEHC 432.

> But that question is dependent on an analysis of the substance of the effect of the injunction if granted, rather than the language used in its terms.[472]

So, it now seems clear that the standard which will almost invariably be applied where an interlocutory injunction of a mandatory nature, either in form or substance, is sought is a strong case that the plaintiff is likely to succeed at trial. There is also considerable merit in taking the approach adopted by Kelly J in *Shelbourne*, which would allow a court not to insist on this higher onus of proof being met in such cases where withholding an interlocutory injunction would carry with it a greater risk of injustice than granting it.[473] While Hoffmann J spoke in *Films Rover* about this approach being taken in an exceptional case, Kelly J made no reference to the circumstances in which the courts should make such an assessment, but it is likely that this would only arise in such exceptional cases. For this reason it appears that the 'strong case' requirement must be complied with unless there is clear evidence that withholding the injunction in the event of this threshold not being met would lead to a higher risk of injustice. It should also be borne in mind, as Clarke CJ has made reference to in *Charleton v Scriven*, that the greater risk of injustice is often a function of the substance of the order sought and that it is more likely to affect a defendant who is required to do something, rather than refrain from doing it, if it subsequently turns out at trial that the interlocutory order was wrongly made. Therefore, the reality is that in all but exceptional cases, the initial threshold for seeking an interlocutory injunction which is mandatory in effect will be the 'strong case' test.

It should also be borne in mind that the balance of convenience is unlikely to lie in favour of granting mandatory relief save in fairly exceptional cases. In *Allied Irish Banks plc v Diamond*[474] Clarke J acknowledged that the balance of convenience is perhaps the factor most closely and directly associated with the risk of injustice. The court has to assess how serious the consequences for the parties would be if the decision made at the interlocutory stage is ultimately determined to have been the 'wrong' one. While there may be consequences which cannot be remedied for either party in such a situation, granting mandatory relief at the interlocutory stage is more likely to cause irremediable prejudice than would be the case where a defendant is merely prevented from taking or continuing with some course of action.

Clarke J summarised the factors which lie behind the approach taken by the courts well in the following terms in *Allied Irish Banks plc v Diamond*:[475]

---

472. [2019] IESC 28 at [4.8].
473. In her judgment in the Court of Appeal in *Merck Sharp & Dohme Corporation v Clonmel Healthcare Ltd* [2018] IECA 177 at [127], Whelan J stated that the approach of Kelly J in *Shelbourne* 'commends itself'.
474. [2012] 3 IR 549, 571.
475. *Ibid.* at 572. See also *Quigley v Health Service Executive* [2017] IEHC 654 at [47]; *Board of Management of St Patrick's School v O'Neachtain* [2018] IEHC 128 at [7].

> It is now well settled that in cases involving a mandatory injunction the court will normally require a higher level of likelihood that the plaintiff has a good case before granting an interlocutory injunction (see for example *Lingham v Health Service Executive)*. It may well be that the logic behind that departure from the normal rule can be found in the added risk of injustice that may arise where the court is asked not just to keep things as they were by means of a prohibitory injunction but to require someone to actively take a step which may, with the benefit of hindsight after a trial, turn out not to have been justified. The risk of injustice in the court taking such a step is obviously higher. In order to minimise the overall risk of injustice the court requires a higher level of likelihood about the strength of the plaintiff's case before being prepared to make such an order.

This means that if the court were simply to focus on asking which decision is least likely to lead to an injustice, as advocated by Lord Hoffmann in *National Commercial Bank Jamaica Ltd v Olint*,[476] such an approach would almost inevitably lead to a higher standard being applied where mandatory interlocutory injunctions are sought. However, in the interests of clarity, the standard of a strong case that the plaintiff is likely to succeed at trial, subject to the qualification that the court should not insist on this higher onus of proof being met in such cases where withholding an interlocutory injunction would carry with it a greater risk of injustice than granting it, may be the most appropriate test for the courts in this jurisdiction to apply.

Principles Governing the Grant of Quia Timet Injunctions

While an injunction will generally issue on the basis of an infringement of a plaintiff's rights, an order known as a *quia timet* injunction may also be granted before any injury or damage has actually been sustained, in circumstances where the injury to the plaintiff is merely threatened or apprehended. As Lord Upjohn stated in *Redland Bricks Ltd v Morris*,[477] 'to prevent the jurisdiction of the courts being stultified equity has invented the *quia timet* action, that is an action for an injunction to prevent an apprehended legal wrong, though none has occurred at present, and the suppliant for such an injunction is without any remedy at law.' This jurisdiction is preventative in nature and will be exercised either where a person threatens and intends to do an unlawful act or where the plaintiff's rights have already been infringed and he alleges that this infringement will be repeated.[478]

Spry suggests that the same general equitable principles are applied whether

476. [2009] 1 WLR 1405.
477. [1970] AC 652, 664.
478. *Proctor v Bayley* (1889) 42 Ch D 390, 398 *per* Cotton LJ; *Redland Bricks Ltd v Morris* [1970] AC 652, 665 *per* Lord Upjohn.

or not there has been a breach of the plaintiff's rights or merely a threatened violation of these rights: 'It may properly be said that wherever a court with equitable jurisdiction might enjoin an act if that act had been commenced, it may, in the exercise of its discretion, enjoin the act although it has not yet commenced, provided that its imminence is sufficiently clearly established in order to justify intervention in all the circumstances'.[479] However, as he points out, the fact that no breach has as yet occurred is of relevance as it may be more difficult to establish that there is a sufficient risk of future injury to justify the immediate grant of an injunction.[480] Therefore, it is important to consider how likely it is that injury will in fact occur and how severe the apprehended damage is required to be before a *quia timet* injunction will be granted. It is insufficient for a plaintiff merely to state that he harbours fears in this regard.[481] In the words of Chitty J in *Attorney-General v Manchester Corporation*,[482] 'he must show a strong case of probability that the apprehended mischief will, in fact, arise.'

The onus of proof which lies on a plaintiff seeking a *quia timet* injunction has been considered in this jurisdiction on a number of occasions. In *Attorney General (Boswell) v Rathmines and Pembroke Joint Hospital Board*[483] the plaintiff sought an injunction to restrain the defendant from building a smallpox hospital in a Dublin suburb. While there was conflicting expert evidence about the suitability of the site and the risk of the spread of disease, an injunction was refused on the ground that no real danger had been proved. Chatterton VC spoke in terms of having to establish 'a reasonable, well-grounded apprehension … [of] substantial damage' and Holmes LJ warned against accepting 'as a measure of danger, the fears of the timid and unreasonable'. However, it is the statement of Fitzgibbon LJ which has been most frequently referred to and he stated:

> To sustain the injunction, the law requires proof by the plaintiff of a well-founded apprehension of injury — proof of actual and real danger — a strong probability, almost amounting to moral certainty, that if the Hospital be established, it will be an actionable nuisance.[484]

479. Spry, *The Principles of Equitable Remedies* (9th ed., 2014) p. 391.
480. See, e.g. *McGrane v Louth County Council* High Court 1983 No. 28F (O'Hanlon J) 9 December 1983, where a *quia timet* injunction sought by the plaintiff to restrain the defendants from developing a rubbish dump was refused.
481. *Attorney-General for Dominion of Canada v Ritchie Contracting & Supply Co.* [1919] AC 999, 1005 *per* Lord Dunedin.
482. [1893] 2 Ch 87, 92. See also *Litchfield-Speer v Queen Anne's Gate Syndicate (No. 2) Ltd* [1919] 1 Ch 407, 412, where Lawrence J spoke of the plaintiff proving 'that he will certainly sustain substantial damage'.
483. [1904] 1 IR 161. See also *Attorney-General v Nottingham Corporation* [1904] 1 Ch 673.
484. *Ibid.* at 171. This test seems to have been accepted by Finlay P in *C. & A. Modes v C. & A. (Waterford) Ltd* [1976] IR 198, where he said that if the action before him was to be equated with an application for a *quia timet* injunction, which he did not necessarily so decide, the standard of proof laid down by Fitzgibbon LJ was the correct one. In the Supreme Court, Henchy J agreed that there were sufficient grounds for

This passage was quoted with approval by Judge Fawsitt in the Circuit Court decision of *Radford v Wexford Corporation*,[485] in which the plaintiffs failed in their application for a *quia timet* injunction to restrain the defendants from further proceeding with the construction of a public lavatory on a site adjoining the main street of Wexford town as they had not established a 'strong probability that the apprehended mischiefs will in fact arise'.

The slightly less stringent test of 'reasonable probability' was applied by Meredith J in *Independent Newspapers Ltd v Irish Press Ltd*,[486] in which the plaintiff company sought to restrain the defendant from publishing and passing off a newspaper with a title in which it claimed the property and goodwill. It was held by Meredith J that the plaintiff had failed to establish that damage would occur as it had not been able to show that the goodwill in the title was still an 'attractive force' and he refused to grant the injunction sought. Meredith J examined the onus which must be satisfied before a court would grant a *quia timet* injunction and said that it would not do so: 'unless it is satisfied that there is a reasonable probability that what is threatened to be done is calculated in the ordinary course of events, or according to the ordinary course of business, to cause damage to the plaintiff'.[487] Subsequently, in *Whelan v Madigan*[488] Kenny J spoke in terms of establishing a 'probability' *simpliciter* and granted a *quia timet* injunction to restrain the defendant from interfering with the plaintiffs' quiet enjoyment of their flats.

In view of the lack of consensus in relation to the degree of probability of injury required before a court will grant a *quia timet* injunction, perhaps the suggestion made by Russell LJ in *Hooper v Rogers*[489] has much to commend it. He said that 'the degree of probability of future injury is not an absolute standard: what is to be aimed at is justice between the parties having regard to all the relevant circumstances'.[490] In addition, it should be stated that the degree of probability of injury is not the only factor which should influence the court and the greater the damage or prejudice likely to be caused, the more justifiable the court's intervention may be.

Detailed consideration was given to the circumstances in which a *quia timet* injunction should be granted in the judgment of Geoghegan J in *Szabo v ESAT Digiphone Ltd*.[491] The plaintiffs, who were schoolchildren attending a national school, sought *quia timet* injunctions to restrain the erection and operation of a mobile phone base station in the grounds of a garda station located beside

the conclusion that this onus of proof had been discharged in the circumstances, but concluded that he was satisfied that what the plaintiffs claimed was not a *quia timet* injunction.

485. (1954) 89 ILTR 184.
486. [1932] IR 615.
487. *Ibid.* at 631.
488. [1978] ILRM 136.
489. [1975] Ch 43.
490. *Ibid.* at 50.
491. [1998] 2 ILRM 102.

their school. Geoghegan J referred to the test employed in *Attorney-General v Manchester Corporation*, namely that the plaintiff must show 'a strong case of probability that the apprehended mischief will, in fact, arise' and stated that he was inclined to think that it went too far, although he did say that for a *quia timet* injunction to be granted, there would have to be 'a proven substantial risk of danger',[492] a view which he said was supported by the decision of the Irish Court of Appeal in the *Boswell* case. In that case, Walker LJ had also expressed the opinion that where there was conflicting expert evidence, the judge himself could not form a view as an expert and if the conflict left him in doubt, he could not in a *quia timet* action decide that the case for the plaintiff had been made out.

Geoghegan J then went on to consider the correct principles to be applied in relation to applications for interlocutory *quia timet* injunctions and said that he would adopt the treatment of the subject in *Spry: Equitable Remedies*,[493] in which the author made it clear that there is no difference between the legal principles to be applied to interlocutory *quia timet* injunctions and any other kind of interlocutory injunction. However, as Spry pointed out in his consideration of *quia timet* injunctions in general, it should not be thought that it is never material that no breach of the applicant's rights has taken place at the time of the hearing of the application and if no breach has taken place, it may be more difficult to establish, as a matter of evidence, that there is a sufficient risk of a future injury to justify the immediate grant of an injunction. Geoghegan J concluded that it was highly improbable at the very least that any injury would ensue to the children before the hearing of the action and in these circumstances he did not think that it would be just or reasonable to grant a *quia timet* injunction.

The principles laid down by Geoghegan J in *Szabo* now seem firmly established and they have been applied in more recent decisions.[494] In *Ryanair Ltd v Aer Rianta cpt*[495] Kelly J referred to Geoghegan J's acceptance of the proposition that there was no difference between the principles applicable to an interlocutory *quia timet* injunction and any other kind of interlocutory injunction, but that the fact that no breach of the plaintiff's rights had taken place as of the date of the hearing was of relevance because it might be more difficult to establish as a matter of evidence that a sufficient risk of future injury existed to justify the grant of such an injunction. Kelly J stated that in cases of this nature the court must balance the magnitude of the evil against the chances of its occurrence and he expressed the view that in order to grant a *quia timet* injunction there would have to be 'a proven substantial risk of danger'.[496]

---

492. *Ibid.* at 110.
493. Spry, *The Principles of Equitable Remedies* (4th ed., 1990) p. 459. Now see Spry, *The Principles of Equitable Remedies* (9th ed., 2014).
494. E.g. *Murphy v Irish Water* [2016] IEHC 271 at [20].
495. [2001] IEHC 229.
496. See also *Minister for Arts, Heritage, the Gaeltacht and the Islands v Kennedy* [2002] 2 ILRM 94, 112.

Kelly J concluded that in the case before him he was not satisfied that there was a sufficient risk of future injury to the applicant to justify the immediate grant of an injunction.[497] Similarly, in *Garrahy v Bord na gCon*,[498] O'Higgins J stated that he would follow the approach of Geoghegan J in *Szabo* to the effect that there is no difference in the principles to be applied to interlocutory *quia timet* injunctions and any other kind of interlocutory injunction, although he also accepted, like Geoghegan J, that it may be more difficult to establish as a matter of evidence that there is a sufficient risk of a future injury to justify the immediate grant of an injunction in the former case. On the facts, O'Higgins J concluded that the plaintiff had shown a proven substantial risk of danger and that he had also established a strong case of probability that the apprehended mischief would in fact arise, that being the test laid down in *Attorney General v Manchester Corporation*.[499]

It is interesting to note that the notion of applying the *Campus Oil* guidelines has also been canvassed in a number of cases dealing with *quia timet* injunctions. In *Szabo* Geoghegan J said that he doubted whether their application was appropriate in a case such as that before him, but this was because he said there was something distasteful about balancing the convenience of the defendant in being able to carry on its business against alleged dangers to the health of the plaintiffs. In *National Irish Bank Ltd v RTE*[500] Shanley J stated that he was deciding the interlocutory application before him on the basis of the principles in *Campus Oil*, rather than on the basis of the test laid down in *Boswell*, even though the application was of a *quia timet* nature. He explained that he was doing so because he was dealing with a situation where the defendant had actually conceded that its aim was to publish confidential information belonging to the plaintiff and, in his view, in such a case the *Campus Oil* principles were 'a more appropriate guide than the more stringent evidential burden' that the test in *Boswell* would impose.

However, it would appear that even if the courts no longer insist upon the test of 'a proven substantial risk of danger' being satisfied in every case in which a *quia timet* injunction is sought, it will nevertheless remain more difficult to obtain an injunction of this nature, not least because, as Spry has pointed out, if no wrongdoing has yet occurred, it will be more difficult to establish, as a matter of evidence, that there is a sufficient risk of a future injury to justify the grant of an injunction.[501]

---

497. The applicant's appeal from the decision of Kelly J, which was solely concerned with the order for costs made against them, was dismissed by the Supreme Court in a decision delivered on 26 October 2001.
498. [2002] 3 IR 566.
499. [1893] 2 Ch 87.
500. [1998] 2 IR 465. Note that the Supreme Court upheld the refusal of an interlocutory injunction restraining the defendant from publishing information which the plaintiff asserted was confidential, see [1998] 2 IR 465, 479.
501. Spry, *The Principles of Equitable Remedies* (9th ed., 2014) p. 391.

Finally, it should be pointed out that before a *quia timet* injunction will be granted against a defendant, it is important to establish that it is the defendant himself who has threatened to carry out the action in question. So, in *Celsteel Ltd v Alton House Holdings Ltd*,[502] the Court of Appeal set aside an injunction granted against a lessor, and left in place the injunction granted against the lessee, who was the party actually threatening to erect the car wash to which the plaintiff objected.

SPECIFIC CIRCUMSTANCES IN WHICH AN INJUNCTION WILL BE GRANTED

To Restrain a Breach of Contract

While the usual method of enforcing a positive obligation in a contract is by an order of specific performance, an injunction may be granted to restrain the breach of a negative undertaking contained therein. It was suggested by Lord Cairns in *Doherty v Allman*[503] that an injunction will issue to secure enforcement of a negative contractual obligation almost as a matter of course. He stated as follows:

> If parties, for valuable consideration, with their eyes open, contract that a particular thing shall not be done, all that a Court of Equity has to do is to say, by way of injunction, that which the parties have already said by way of covenant, that the thing shall not be done; and in such case the injunction does nothing more than give the sanction of the process of the Court to that which already is the contract between the parties. It is not then a question of the balance of convenience or inconvenience, or the amount of damage or of injury — it is the specific performance, by the Court, of that negative bargain which the parties have made, with their eyes open, between themselves.

However, it has been said that this statement is 'the starting point, not a summation of equity's attitude to negative stipulations'[504] and it must not be read without some qualification. In England it has been stated that it must be applied in the light of the surrounding circumstances of each case,[505] and wider discretionary considerations have been taken into account where an order of a mandatory nature has been sought. In *Shepherd Homes Ltd v Sandham*[506] the

502. [1986] 1 WLR 512.
503. (1878) 3 App Cas 709, 720.
504. Heydon, Leeming and Turner, *Meagher, Gummow and Lehane's Equity: Doctrines and Remedies* (5th ed., 2015) p. 738.
505. *Shaw v Applegate* [1977] 1 WLR 970, 975 *per* Buckley LJ.
506. [1971] Ch 340. See also *Wrotham Park Estate Co. Ltd v Parkside Homes Ltd* [1974] 1 WLR 798.

plaintiff sought a mandatory injunction to compel the defendant to pull down a fence erected in breach of covenant. It was held by Megarry J in refusing the injunction that the court would exercise its discretion to withhold an injunction more readily if it were mandatory than if it were prohibitory and that even a blameless plaintiff could not as of right claim to enforce a negative covenant by means of a mandatory injunction. He commented that 'the enforcement of a negative covenant at the trial by a mandatory injunction is far more a matter of judicial discretion and not of right than in the case of a prohibitory injunction'[507] and that the statement of Lord Cairns, although it *prima facie* applies to mandatory injunctions, does not apply in its full width and is tempered by judicial discretion. This approach is in line with that put forward by Spry who points out that it is clear that, in proceedings for specific performance to enforce the performance of positive obligations in a contract, considerations of hardship and other discretionary factors are relevant and may induce the court to refuse relief, so there is no reason in principle why the same considerations should not apply to proceedings to enforce contractual rights by injunction.[508]

Where an interlocutory injunction is sought to restrain the breach of a negative covenant, there are conflicting authorities on the question of whether an injunction should issue as a matter of course. It has been held in England in *Hampstead & Suburban Properties Ltd v Diomedous*[509] that the principle in *Doherty v Allman* should apply where there is a 'plain and uncontested breach of a clear covenant.'[510] It seems to have also been accepted by the Supreme Court in *Dublin Port and Docks Board v Britannia Dredging Co. Ltd*,[511] in which the plaintiff sought an interlocutory injunction restraining the defendant from removing dredging equipment from a site where it had undertaken to carry out work. The court held that as the defendant had agreed to this negative term and as it was satisfied that a breach of the covenant was imminent, an interlocutory injunction should be granted. Ó Dálaigh CJ concluded that the principle in *Doherty v Allman* was accordingly applicable and said that the court was not concerned to examine either the balance of convenience or the amount of damage. In the circumstances where the parties had entered into a negative covenant, it was the duty of the court to hold the defendants to their bargain pending the trial.[512]

However, in *TMG Group Ltd v Al Babtain Trading and Contracting Co.*,[513]

---

507. *Ibid.* at 351. See also *Sharpe v Harrison* [1922] 1 Ch. 512, 520 *per* Astbury J and *Charrington v Simons & Co. Ltd* [1970] 1 WLR 725, 730.
508. Spry, *The Principles of Equitable Remedies* (9th ed., 2014) p. 608-609.
509. [1969] 1 Ch 248.
510. *Ibid.* at 259 *per* Megarry J. Although note the comments of Ungoed-Thomas J in *Texaco Ltd v Mulberry Filling Station Ltd* [1972] 1 WLR 814, 831.
511. [1968] IR 136.
512. *Ibid.* at 147. Applied by Costello J in *Irish Shell Ltd v Elm Motors Ltd* [1984] IR 200, 216.
513. [1982] ILRM 349.

Keane J distinguished the facts of the case before him from those in *Dublin Port and Docks Board* and stated as follows:

> The circumstances of the present case are wholly different: the defendants strenuously contend that neither of the transactions which the company proposes to enter into will constitute a breach of their contractual obligations under the shareholders' agreement. I do not think that Ó Dálaigh CJ in the passages to which I have referred, was laying down any general principle that, in all cases where the plaintiff establishes a *prima facie* case of a breach of a negative stipulation in a contract, the court could disregard any question of the balance of convenience as between the parties. His observations were clearly confined to a case where one party to a contract was proposing to act in breach of a negative contract (and indeed to repudiate the whole contract) in circumstances where the court was not satisfied on the evidence that they were entitled so to do.[514]

Subsequently, in *Irish Shell Ltd v Elm Motors Ltd*,[515] McCarthy J endorsed these views and said that save in the most exceptional circumstances, the determination of an application for an interlocutory injunction lies solely on a consideration of the questions of whether a fair case has been made out and where the balance of convenience lies. This question was addressed again by the Supreme Court in *Premier Dairies Ltd v Doyle*.[516] Delivering judgment in the High Court, Kinlen J held that the defendants, who had entered into distribution agreements with the plaintiff to deliver its products, should be held to the terms of the negative covenant contained in the agreements preventing them from competing with the plaintiff and he stated that the decision of the Supreme Court in *Britannia Dredging Co. Ltd* governed the case.[517] However, the defendants appealed against this order arguing, *inter alia*, that the clause in question was contrary to sections 4 and 5 of the Competition Act 1991. O'Flaherty J dismissed the appeal but it is interesting to note the comment which he made about the *Doherty v Allman/Britannia Dredging* principle. He was satisfied that if there had been no other factors in the case he would have held that it came 'four square within the *Britannia Dredging* decision'. However, O'Flaherty J stated that, as there was scope for an argument to be made as to the applicability of the Competition Act 1991 which he described as 'a rather complex piece of legislation which, so far, has not been judicially mined to any extent', it was not in his view appropriate to apply the *Britannia Dredging* principle to the case. O'Flaherty J accordingly went on to consider whether there was a fair case to be tried, which he was satisfied there was and to consider where the balance of convenience lay. While he disagreed with

514. *Ibid.* at 353.
515. [1984] IR 200.
516. [1996] 1 ILRM 363.
517. High Court 1995 No. 7008P (Kinlen J) 29 September 1995.

Kinlen J about the applicability of the *Britannia Dredging* principle, O'Flaherty J was satisfied that the former's conclusion that the balance of convenience favoured the plaintiffs was correct and for this reason affirmed his decision to grant the interlocutory relief sought.

The *Britannia Dredging* principle was considered again by Feeney J in *Tedcastles Oil Products v Sweeney Oil Retail Ltd.*[518] He was satisfied that there had been a 'plain and uncontested breach of a clear covenant'. Feeney J said that the matter before him was one in which the court should secure the enforcement of this negative contractual obligation and that the question of the balance of convenience or the amount of damage did not arise. However, he added that for the sake of completeness, he would go on to consider these issues and concluded that damages were not an adequate remedy and that the balance of convenience lay with the granting of an injunction. So, while some uncertainty remains about the applicability of the *Britannia Dredging* principle in this jurisdiction, even where a court proceeds to ask the traditional questions formulated in *Campus Oil*, in circumstances where a breach of a negative covenant has occurred the outcome is likely to favour the plaintiff. This is in line with the comments of Costello J in *Sports Direct International plc v Minor*,[519] where she said that where it is sought to ensure compliance with a negative covenant, 'the courts lean in favour of enforcement by injunction'.

The jurisdiction of the court to grant an injunction is wider than its jurisdiction to grant specific performance, and often a positive obligation in a contract may not be specifically enforceable.[520] It is therefore often of practical significance that even where a contract contains no express negative stipulation it may be possible to imply a negative undertaking which can be enforced by the grant of an injunction. As Lord Selborne stated in *Wolverhampton and Walsall Railway Co. v London and North-Western Railway Co.*,[521] in such circumstances the courts should look to the substance and not merely the form of the agreement and this approach has generally, although not universally,[522] been followed.[523] In *Catt v Tourle*,[524] where a publican agreed to procure all his beer supplies from a specified source, an injunction was granted restraining him from obtaining these supplies elsewhere. Similarly, in *Metropolitan*

518. High Court (Feeney J) 3 November 2010.
519. [2014] IEHC 546 at [41].
520. The courts have traditionally displayed a reluctance to grant specific performance of only part of a contract. See *Ryan v Mutual Tontine Westminster Chambers Association* [1893] 1 Ch 116, 125.
521. (1873) LR 16 Eq 433, 440.
522. See *Mortimer v Beckett* [1920] 1 Ch 571 where Russell J laid emphasis on the positive form of the agreement in declining to grant an injunction.
523. See, e.g. in relation to covenants affecting the use of land, *Tulk v Moxhay* (1848) 2 Ph 774.
524. (1869) LR 4 Ch App 654.

Electric Supply Co. v Ginder,[525] the defendant agreed to take all his electricity requirements from the plaintiff for a specified period. The court construed the contract as an undertaking not to obtain electricity from another supplier and granted an injunction to restrain the defendant from doing so. This principle has also been applied in this jurisdiction in *Irish Shell Ltd v Elm Motors Ltd*,[526] where injunctions were granted to compel the defendant to comply with the terms of covenants in a lease. As Costello J stated, once it was established that these covenants were enforceable it did not matter that they were expressed in the form of a positive rather than a negative obligation.

Particular Considerations which Apply to Contracts for Personal Services

In general the courts are reluctant to grant an injunction which would involve an element of ongoing supervision[527] and as Geoghegan J stated in *Ó Murchú v Eircell Ltd*,[528] they will be very slow to make orders of this nature in either service contracts or trading contracts because it will be difficult to assess whether they are being obeyed. A further compelling reason for the courts' reluctance to grant injunctions in respect of contracts for personal services is that as a matter of policy it is undesirable to force individuals to work together where a relationship of trust and confidence no longer exists between them.[529] While it was suggested by Lord Wilson JSC in *Geys v Société Générale*[530] that

525. [1901] 2 Ch 799. See also *James Jones & Sons Ltd v Earl of Tankerville* [1901] 2 Ch 440.
526. [1984] IR 200.
527. However, note the decision of Costello P in *Wanze Properties (Ireland) Ltd v Five Star Supermarket* High Court, 24 October 1997, in which he granted an interlocutory injunction compelling the defendant to comply with covenants in a lease requiring it to trade as a supermarket during normal business hours.
528. [2001] IESC 15. See also *Sheridan v Louis Fitzgerald Group Ltd* [2006] IEHC 125 at 14-15; *Relax Food Corporation Ltd v Brown Thomas & Co. Ltd* [2009] IEHC 181 at 9; *Health Service Executive v Keogh* [2009] IEHC 419 at 6.
529. It appears from *Lauritzencool AB v Lady Navigation Inc* [2005] 1 WLR 3686, 3704 that where the relationship is between business concerns which 'can be expected to continue to make [it] work in their own interests', the courts may be prepared to grant an injunction. So, in this case, the Court of Appeal upheld the granting of injunctive relief preventing the defendants from using their vessels outside a shipping pool pending the outcome of arbitration, even though Mance LJ acknowledged that the only realistic commercial course of action left to the defendants in the circumstances was to continue to provide vessels to the pools and perform charters. However, the comments of Lord Diplock in *Scandinavian Trading Tanker Co. AB v Flota Petrolera Ecuatoriana* [1983] 2 AC 694, 701, which suggested that injunctive relief will not be granted to restrain conduct inconsistent with a time charter if the practical effect will be to compel the party injuncted to perform the charter, should be noted. In *Lauritzencool*, the trial judge made no finding that the practical effect of the injunctions would be to compel performance and expressed confidence about the workable nature of the charter should the ship owners choose to perform it.
530. [2013] 1 AC 523, 553.

the 'more impersonal, less hierarchical, relationship of many employers with their employees' requires review of the traditional reluctance to make orders of a mandatory nature in this context, there has been little sign of a shift in judicial attitudes towards the issue.

While it has been acknowledged that an injunction may be a useful remedy where the positive obligations in a contract are not specifically enforceable, it is also generally accepted, particularly in the context of contracts for personal services, that an injunction should not be granted where this would indirectly provide for specific performance of the positive terms of the contract. As Kenny J stated in *Yeates v Minister for Posts and Telegraphs*[531] in the context of an application for an injunction which if granted would have indirectly amounted to specific performance, 'it is settled law that the courts never specifically enforce a contract for personal services'. Despite this principle, on occasion the courts have permitted the issue of an injunction to restrain a negative undertaking in a contract for personal services which may indirectly cause the contract to be performed; as O'Flaherty J stated in *Capital Radio Productions Ltd v Radio 2000 Ltd*,[532] 'while a person cannot be forced to work against his will for someone he can, if in breach of contract, be *prevented* from working for anyone else.'

This principle is well-illustrated by the decision of Lord St Leonards in *Lumley v Wagner*.[533] The defendant undertook to sing at the plaintiff's theatre for a specified period and not to perform elsewhere during this time. Subsequently, the defendant agreed another contract for a larger fee with a third party and the plaintiff sought an injunction to restrain her from singing for this person. Lord St Leonards held that the plaintiff was entitled to an injunction to restrain the breach of the negative stipulation in the contract. The decision may be criticised on the basis that it amounted to the equivalent of ordering specific performance of the original contract, although as Lord St Leonards pointed out, the defendant could not have been compelled to fulfil this obligation. This approach was followed in *Warner Brothers Pictures, Incorporated v Nelson*,[534] in which the defendant, Mrs Nelson, better known as the actress Bette Davis, agreed to act for a studio for a period of five years and undertook not to act for any other party during this time or to engage in any other occupation without the written consent of the studio. The plaintiff sought to enforce the obligation not to act for anyone other than itself and Branson J granted an injunction to restrain her from breaching this undertaking. He stated that where a contract of personal service contains negative covenants, the enforcement of which will not amount either to a decree of specific performance of the positive covenants of the contract or to a decree under which the defendant must remain idle or perform the positive covenants, the court will enforce those

531. [1978] ILRM 22, 24.
532. Supreme Court 1998 No.128 & 129, 26 May 1998.
533. (1852) 1 De G M & G 604.
534. [1937] 1 KB 209.

negative covenants. However, this will be subject to the consideration that an injunction is a discretionary remedy and the court in making an order of this nature may limit the terms of the injunction to what it considers reasonable in the circumstances. While an injunction covering all the negative covenants in the contract would have forced the defendant to perform her contract or to remain idle, that objection was removed by the limited form in which the order was sought. Branson J rejected the argument that the order made amounted to an indirect form of specific performance and said that while the defendant might be tempted to perform the contract in view of the fact that alternative work would be considerably less lucrative, she would not be driven to do so.

A related question is whether an employer can be compelled to continue to employ an employee and this issue was considered in *Page One Records Ltd v Britton*.[535] The plaintiffs had contracted with a group of musicians known as 'the Troggs' that they would act as their manager for a period of five years and the group agreed not to employ anyone else during this time. When the plaintiffs sought an injunction to prevent the employment of another manager the court refused to grant an injunction on the basis that as a practical matter it would force the group to continue to employ the plaintiffs. Stamp J said that it would be tantamount to ordering specific performance of a contract of personal services and it would be wrong to put pressure on the defendants to continue to employ someone in a fiduciary capacity in whom they had lost confidence.

The approach adopted by Stamp J is in many respects preferable to that of Branson J in that it was unrealistic to expect the defendants in either case to give up their chosen careers and the alternative was that they would find themselves compelled to perform a contract of personal services. The Court of Appeal in England confirmed this point and re-asserted the view that an injunction should not be granted if its indirect effect would be to compel performance of a contract for personal services. In *Warren v Mendy*[536] a boxer agreed that he would not be managed by anyone except the plaintiff for a three-year period but subsequently entered into a management agreement with the defendant. The plaintiff sought an injunction to restrain the defendant from inducing a breach of contract and from acting for the boxer. The effect of such an injunction would have been to restrain the boxer from receiving services from the defendant and would arguably have compelled him to perform his agreement with the plaintiff and the Court of Appeal held that no injunction should be granted. Nourse LJ commented that Branson J's approach in *Warner Brothers Pictures, Incorporated v Nelson* was 'extraordinarily unrealistic' and stated as follows:

> [T]he following general principles are applicable to the grant or refusal of an injunction to enforce performance of the servant's negative obligations in a contract for personal services inseparable from the exercise of some

535. [1968] 1 WLR 157.
536. [1989] 1 WLR 853. See McClean [1990] CLJ 28.

special skill or talent. In such a case the court ought not to enforce the performance of the negative obligations if their enforcement will effectively compel the servant to perform his positive obligations under the contract. Compulsion is a question to be decided on the facts of each case, with a realistic regard for the probable reaction of an injunction on the psychological and material, and sometimes the physical, need of the servant to maintain the skill or talent. The longer the term for which the injunction is sought, the more readily will compulsion be inferred … An injunction will less readily be granted where there are obligations of mutual trust and confidence, more especially where the servant's trust in the master may have been betrayed or his confidence in him has genuinely gone.[537]

McCutcheon has stated that 'the practical consequence of *Warren v Mendy* is to make it highly improbable that negative injunctions will be granted in sports cases, at least where the contract is for anything other than a short duration'[538] and has expressed the view that the approach of the English courts may be too lenient. In contrast he points out that the North American courts have placed a greater emphasis on ensuring that contracts of this nature are honoured and that individuals do not renege on their commitments simply because a more lucrative opportunity is presented to them.[539] There is clearly merit in his argument that 'if contractual obligations are to be taken seriously it is to be expected that the law would lean towards their enforcement rather than minimising the consequences of their breach to the wrongdoer'[540] and it will be interesting to see whether the approach adopted in North America will ultimately be taken on board either in England or in this jurisdiction.

A limited exception to the general principle that employer and employee should not be forced to work together has been recognised where a relationship of mutual trust and confidence still exists between them. This is illustrated by the decision of the Court of Appeal in *Hill v C.A. Parsons & Co. Ltd*,[541] where an injunction was granted against an employer to restrain an alleged wrongful dismissal after the employer had reluctantly been forced to terminate the contract of employment of an engineer who had refused to join a trade union. Lord Denning MR stated that '[i]f ever there was a case where an injunction should be granted against the employers, this is the case'[542] and the majority of the court justified its decision on the basis that a relationship of mutual trust

537. *Ibid.* at 867.
538. (1997) 17 LS 65, 74.
539. See, e.g. *Washington Capitols Basketball Club Inc. v Barry* (1969) 304 F Supp 1193; *Cincinnati Bengals Inc. v Bergey* (1974) 453 F Supp 129.
540. (1997) 17 LS 65, 100.
541. [1972] Ch 305. See also *Powell v London Borough of Brent* [1987] IRLR 466 and *Robb v Hammersmith and Fulham London Borough Council* [1991] ICR 514.
542. *Ibid.* at 316.

and confidence still existed between the parties. The importance of establishing continuing mutual confidence if a court is to intervene in an employment dispute is also clear from the decision of Taylor J in *Hughes v London Borough of Southwark*,[543] where he granted an interlocutory injunction restraining the defendants from seeking to enforce an instruction to the plaintiffs that they should carry out duties other than their normal work. Taylor J stated that 'the important criterion is as to whether there is mutual confidence, the point being that it would be inappropriate to grant an injunction against an employer requiring him to keep on in service on certain terms a servant who has lost the confidence of that employer.'[544] He said that the defendants continued to have 'great confidence' in the plaintiffs and added that it would be quite wrong to assume that mutual confidence has gone simply because there is a dispute between an employer and employee.

However, this concept of a continuing relationship of mutual trust has been arguably overstretched in some cases. In *Irani v Southampton and South-West Hampshire Health Authority*[545] Warner J granted an injunction to restrain the dismissal of an employee in circumstances where there were irreconcilable differences between him and the consultant in charge but no complaints of professional incompetence. He expressed the view that if he were to decline to grant an injunction in the circumstances he 'would in effect be holding that, without doubt, an authority in the position of the defendant is entitled to snap its fingers at the rights of its employees'.[546] Similarly, in *Powell v London Borough of Brent*,[547] the Court of Appeal granted an interlocutory injunction requiring the defendant to treat the plaintiff as if she were properly employed by them. Ralph Gibson LJ stated that a court would not by means of an injunction require an employer to let a servant continue in his employment unless it was clear not only that it was otherwise just to make the order but also that sufficient confidence in the servant's ability existed on the part of the employer. He added that 'sufficiency of confidence must be judged by reference to the circumstances of the case, including the nature of the work, the people with whom the work must be done and the likely effect upon the employer and the employer's operations if the employer is required by injunction to suffer the plaintiff to continue in the work.'[548] The court concluded that on the evidence before it there was 'clearly a good working relationship of mutual respect'[549] between the plaintiff and her colleagues and that it could not be accepted that the employers did not have full confidence in the plaintiff.

---

543. [1988] IRLR 72.
544. *Ibid.* at 73.
545. [1985] IRLR 203.
546. *Ibid.* at 209. See also *Robb v Hammersmith and Fulham London Borough Council* [1991] ICR 514, 523.
547. [1987] IRLR 466.
548. *Ibid.* at 473.
549. *Ibid.* at 474.

It is certainly arguable that in both *Irani* and *Powell* the finding of a continuing relationship of mutual trust and confidence was something of a fiction. In the former case, Warner J went as far as to state that the true position was that the defendant would have been willing to continue employing the plaintiff had it not been for the fact that his and the continued employment of the consultant in charge were incompatible. Similarly, in *Powell*, Ralph Gibson LJ spoke about 'strenuous opposition by her employers to [the plaintiff] continuing in her job'. Perhaps a more realistic approach is that adopted by Morland J in *Robb v Hammersmith and Fulham London Borough Council*,[550] where he granted an interlocutory injunction restraining the defendants from giving effect to a dismissal notice made against him. In his view the submission made by counsel for the defendants that unless trust and confidence between employer and employee remains, an injunction to preserve the contract of employment should never be granted, was 'far too sweeping'. However, he acknowledged that if an injunction is sought to reinstate an employee dismissed in breach of contract, clearly trust and confidence are highly relevant as without the confidence of his employer in his ability to do his job, an employee's position would be untenable. In his view 'the all important criterion is whether the order sought is workable'[551] and he concluded that despite the 'very cogent evidence of loss of trust and confidence,' the balance of convenience required him to grant the relief sought which was effectively confined to ensuring a resumption of the appropriate disciplinary procedure initiated against the plaintiff. The effect of the relief sought was fundamental to the court's decision, as it was in *Jones v Lee*,[552] where the Court of Appeal had granted an injunction to restrain the dismissal of a plaintiff without a hearing even in circumstances where his employers appeared to have lost trust and confidence in him.[553] In both these cases the plaintiff was essentially seeking to ensure that fair procedures were followed in the conduct of disciplinary proceedings rather than reinstatement.[554]

550. [1991] ICR 514.
551. *Ibid.* at 520.
552. [1980] ICR 310.
553. Carty comments that: 'the judgments reveal that the Court of Appeal saw this case as a simple contract point: the right to the correct pre-dismissal procedure should be upheld.' See Carty (1989) 52 MLR 449, 456.
554. In *Robb* the plaintiff undertook to carry out none of his duties or functions unless instructed to do so by the defendants and not to go the defendants' offices unless requested to do so by prior arrangement following the plaintiff's reasonable request. As has been suggested by Ryan in *Redmond on Dismissal Law in Ireland* (3rd ed., 2017) p.201: 'Trust and confidence in the plaintiff's ability to do the job had no relevance to the workability of the disciplinary procedure if ordered by the court'.

Employment Injunctions in this Jurisdiction

General Principles

The courts in this jurisdiction have traditionally accepted that as a general principle, a plaintiff will not be entitled to an interlocutory injunction which would amount to an indirect order of specific performance in respect of a contract of employment.[555] As Clarke J stated in *Yap v Children's University Hospital Temple Street Ltd*,[556] 'there are very limited circumstances in which the court will intervene to force a continuation of a contract of employment particularly where there is a serious controversy'. While the general principle and the reasons for it are well-established in this jurisdiction, it is also accepted that it may be subject to qualification in the interests of justice.[557] Clarke J aptly summarised the position in *Bergin v Galway Clinic Doughiska Ltd*,[558] where he said that 'it is fair to state that this area of the jurisprudence of the courts is in a state of evolution and the precise current state of that jurisprudence is far from clear'. He added that the situation is not helped by the fact that many cases do not proceed to trial and most of the authorities tend to be decisions made at an interlocutory stage rather than after a full hearing, where a court is required to approach issues on the basis of arguability or, where the injunction sought is mandatory in substance, likelihood of success.

Before examining in detail the types of situations in which employment injunctions are sought it may be useful to set out a number of overarching principles which have emerged from the recent case-law in this area. At the outset it should be noted that the courts in this jurisdiction have accepted that even where the relief sought is set out in prohibitory terms, where it is mandatory in effect, a plaintiff will have to meet the strong case requirement necessary for obtaining an interlocutory injunction of a mandatory nature. This principle, which can be traced back to the decision of the Supreme Court in

---

555. *Evans v IRFB Services (Ireland) Ltd* [2005] 2 ILRM 358, 364. See also *McNamara v Health Service Executive* [2009] IEHC 418 at 16; *Becker v Board of Management of St Dominic's Secondary School* [2005] 1 IR 561, 570. Clarke J went on to say that there may be exceptions to the general proposition, such as a case where an employer has failed to make out any arguable basis for a suspension, or has been guilty of an inordinate and unjust delay in concluding an investigation, as in *Martin v Nationwide Building Society* [2001] 1 IR 228.
556. [2006] 4 IR 298.
557. *Phelan v BIC (Ireland) Ltd* [1997] ELR 208, 212. Where the employer has not actually purported to terminate the contract or dismiss the employee, it may be relatively speaking easier to obtain an order of an interlocutory nature. So, in *Howard v UCC* [2000] IEHC 138 the plaintiff was granted interlocutory injunctions restraining the defendant from taking any steps to remove her from her post as head of the Department of German at University College Cork or from appointing a person other than her to the post in circumstances where she was apprehensive that the defendants would take steps to remove her from her post.
558. [2008] 2 IR 205, 212.

Lingham v Health Service Executive,[559] is well set out by Clarke J in *Bergin v Galway Clinic Doughiska Ltd*[560] in the following terms:

> I have, therefore, come to the view that in any case in which an employee seeks to prevent a dismissal or a process leading to a dismissal, as a matter of common law, and in whatever terms the claim is couched, the employee concerned is seeking what is, in substance, a mandatory injunction which has the effect of necessarily continuing his contract of employment even though the employer might otherwise be entitled to terminate it. In those circumstances it is necessary for the employee concerned to establish a strong case in order to obtain interlocutory relief.

While there has been evidence of some inconsistency in the application of this principle,[561] overall it is fair to say that in recent decisions it has proved more difficult for plaintiffs to establish the necessary preconditions for obtaining relief for this reason.[562]

The importance of considering broader issues relating to the protection of an individual's property rights in this context has also been highlighted by Hogan J in *Wallace v Irish Aviation Authority*[563] in the following terms:

> Moreover, if the courts were *de facto* debarred from giving interlocutory relief in employment cases merely because it involved the specific enforcement by means of mandatory interlocutory injunction of clauses contained in a contract of employment designed for the protection of employees, this would amount to a denial of effective access to this Court (as guaranteed by Article 34.3.1° and Article 40.3.1°) and a breach of the Court's duty (as imposed by Article 40.3.2°) to fashion a real (and not simply theoretical) remedy which would vindicate the infringement of a property right (namely, the breach of a contract of employment)…

So, as Hogan J subsequently commented in his judgment in the Court of Appeal in *Earley v Health Service Executive*,[564] 'the courts should ensure, where possible, that an effective – and not simply a theoretical – remedy should be available in employment cases where a clear breach of contract has been

559. [2006] ELR 137, 140. See also *Coffey v William Connolly & Sons Ltd* [2007] IEHC 319 at 12; *Stoskus v Goode Concrete Ltd* [2007] IEHC 432 at 5; *Khan v Health Service Executive* [2009] ELR 178, 191; *Buckley v National University Maynooth* [2009] IEHC 58 at 9; *Keenan v Iarnród Eireann* [2010] IEHC 15 at 10; *Earley v Health Service Executive* [2015] IEHC 520 at [17]. This principle is now well-established.
560. [2008] 2 IR 205, 214.
561. E.g. *Coffey v William Connolly & Sons Ltd* [2007] IEHC 319. See further *infra*.
562. E.g. *Stoskus v Goode Concrete Ltd* [2007] IEHC 432; *Buckley v National University of Ireland Maynooth* [2009] IEHC 58; *Keenan v Iarnród Eireann* [2010] IEHC 15.
563. [2012] 2 ILRM 345, 354.
564. [2017] IECA 207 at [16].

established.' However, there may be difficulties involved in granting relief, often of a mandatory nature, which will require parties to continue to work together. The significance of an ongoing relationship of mutual trust and confidence will be relevant to a greater or lesser extent depending on the nature of the relief sought. It is well-established that where this relationship has broken down the courts will decline to make an order of an interlocutory nature requiring reinstatement,[565] although in limited circumstances orders have been made in such cases restraining the implementation of a purported dismissal.[566] Where the courts are asked to intervene in order to ensure compliance with the rules of natural justice and the proper application of disciplinary procedures, there should be no need to establish an ongoing good relationship between the parties as it is not envisaged that they would continue to work together pending trial.

Orders Restraining Implementation of Dismissal or Requiring Reinstatement

The decision which is regarded as breaking new ground in terms of establishing an exception to the general principle that the courts tend not to grant injunctions in cases of termination of employment contracts is that of Costello J in *Fennelly v Assicurazioni Generali SPA*.[567] Costello J said that he accepted that the court should not require an employer to continue working with an employee where serious difficulties have arisen between them or where there is no work for the employee. However, in the case before him he was satisfied that the parties continued to have 'the highest regard for one another' and he made an order that the defendant should continue to pay the plaintiff his salary until the trial, leaving it to the defendant to decide whether to require the latter to carry out any duties he might be given or to grant him leave of absence. This precedent led to a number of decisions being made to grant interlocutory injunctions restraining implementation of purported terminations of appointments pending trial.[568] However, it is significant to note that in many of these cases the court specifically declined to order reinstatement.[569]

---

565. E.g. *Moore v Xnet Information Systems Ltd* [2002] 2 ILRM 278.
566. E.g. *Courtenay v Radio 2000 Ltd* [1997] IEHC 129; *Maher v Irish Permanent Ltd* [1998] ELR 77; *Coffey v William Connolly & Sons Ltd* [2007] IEHC 319; *Giblin v Irish Life and Permanent plc* [2010] IEHC 36; *Brennan v Irish Pride Bakeries* [2015] IEHC 665.
567. High Court, 12 March 1985. See (1985) 3 ILT 73.
568. *Shortt v Data Packaging Ltd* [1994] ELR 251; *Boland v Phoenix Shannon plc* [1997] ELR 113; *Harte v Kelly* [1997] ELR 125; *Phelan v BIC (Ireland) Ltd* [1997] ELR 208; *Courtenay v Radio 2000 Ltd* [1997] IEHC 129; *Maher v Irish Permanent plc* [1998] ELR 77; *Moore v Xnet Information Systems Ltd* [2002] 2 ILRM 278; *Naujoks v National Institute of Bioprocessing Research and Training Ltd* [2007] ELR 25; *Cahill v Dublin City University* [2007] IEHC 20; *Brennan v Irish Pride Bakeries* [2015] IEHC 665.
569. It should also be noted that in some cases, e.g. *Hennessy v St Gerard's School Trust* High Court 2003 No. 7556P (Smyth J) 30 July 2003 and *O'Malley v Aravon School Ltd* High Court (Costello P) 13 August 1997 neither reinstatement nor an order

In *Courtenay v Radio 2000 Ltd*[570] the plaintiff radio presenter sought a number of reliefs including an injunction restraining the defendant from implementing his purported dismissal until the trial of the action and an order requiring the defendant to reinstate the plaintiff to his position pending the trial. The defendant submitted that the plaintiff was employed to present live broadcasts and given that trust and confidence no longer existed on its part, it would be inappropriate for the court to grant the reliefs sought. Laffoy J agreed that it would not be appropriate to make an order requiring the defendant to reinstate the plaintiff but decided that the balance of convenience lay in favour of granting an injunction restraining the defendant from implementing the purported dismissal until the trial of the action. A similar conclusion was reached by Laffoy J in *Maher v Irish Permanent plc*,[571] where although she declined to order the plaintiff's reinstatement on the grounds that it would be inappropriate, she did order that the defendant be restrained from taking any steps to terminate the plaintiff's employment except in accordance with the principles of natural justice.

Another decision which confirms that the courts will be unwilling to grant an interlocutory injunction requiring an employee's reinstatement pending trial, at any rate where relations between the parties have broken down to a significant degree, is *Moore v Xnet Information Systems Ltd*.[572] The plaintiff sought interlocutory injunctions restraining the defendants from taking any further steps to terminate his employment and requiring them to reinstate him in his position and pay him pending the trial of the action. O'Sullivan J stated that the plaintiff had raised fair questions for determination at the trial and concluded that the balance of convenience favoured granting an order directing the defendant to continue paying the plaintiff's salary and other benefits until the trial, subject to an undertaking by the plaintiff to do any work he was required to do. However, while he was satisfied that the plaintiff had made out a fair argument that he had been wrongfully dismissed, having regard to the fact that relations between the parties had irretrievably broken down, O'Sullivan J stated that the balance of convenience did not favour an order directing the defendant to reinstate the plaintiff pending the hearing of the case.[573]

Two other decisions illustrate that in some instances orders allowing a form of reinstatment may be made at the interlocutory stage, although in both

---

restraining dismissal was granted where trust and confidence between the parties had broken down. It was suggested by Mallon and Bolger (1997) 3 Bar Rev 113, 114 that the decision in *O'Malley* can arguably be distinguished on the basis that the plaintiff had been dismissed with at least some regard for the principles of natural justice.

570. [1997] IEHC 129.
571. [1998] ELR 77.
572. [2002] 2 ILRM 278.
573. See also *Hartnett v Advance Tyre Co. Ltd* [2013] IEHC 615, where although Ryan J concluded that the plaintiff had established a strong case, he did not find that the balance of convenience favoured him in circumstances where 'any residue of trust that might have existed between the parties cannot be considered to be intact.'

cases specific factors probably influenced the outcome. In *Martin v Nationwide Building Society*[574] the plaintiff sought an order reinstating him in his position as branch manager of one of the defendant's offices and restraining the latter from appointing anyone other than the plaintiff to this position. Macken J acknowledged that where reinstatement has been sought at an interlocutory stage the authorities make it clear that if the employee does not enjoy the wholehearted support or confidence of his employer, the court will be very slow indeed to reinstate the employee pending the action. However, she stated that the case before her was not concerned with purported dismissal but with a suspension which had gone on for too long and the question was whether this suspension should be set aside because of the delay. Macken J concluded that the plaintiff had established a fair issue to be tried on the question of undue delay and that he would suffer irreparable loss and damage if relief were not granted. In the circumstances, even though she acknowledged that the defendant did not appear to have wholehearted trust in the plaintiff she decided to grant the interlocutory injunction sought. The most reasonable explanation for the decision in *Martin* is that what was at issue was the suspension of an employee rather than a purported dismissal and that the court simply wished to ensure that this overly lengthy suspension should not be allowed to continue.[575]

In *Cahill v Dublin City University*[576] the plaintiff, who was an associate professor at the defendant university, had indicated that it was highly probable that he would leave his post to move to another institution but had not formally resigned. The defendant subsequently purported to give the plaintiff three months' notice of termination of his employment and the plaintiff sought interlocutory injunctions restraining the defendant from treating him as having been dismissed and from interfering with the performance of his duties and responsibilities. At the interlocutory stage, the defendant indicated that it was prepared to continue paying the plaintiff's salary pending trial and Clarke J made an order that the plaintiff be permitted to continue to perform his duties until then. At the trial of the action, Clarke J concluded that the purported termination of the plaintiff's employment was invalid because it did not occur following appropriate procedures specified in the university's statutes so as to comply with the provisions of section 26(5) of the Universities Act 1997.[577]

---

574. [2001] 1 IR 228.
575. However, it should be noted that in *Joyce v Health Service Executive* [2005] IEHC 174 the court declined to grant an interlocutory injunction which would have permitted the plaintiff to return to work following a suspension in circumstances where the latter objected to agreeing to comply with certain conditions which the defendant sought to impose.
576. [2007] IEHC 20. See also *Naujoks v National Institution of Bioprocessing Research and Training Ltd* [2007] ELR 25 where Laffoy J granted an interlocutory injunction, *inter alia*, restraining the defendant from dismissing the plaintiff from his employment in circumstances where the notice provisions of his contract had not been complied with.
577. This decision was upheld by the Supreme Court, see [2009] IESC 80.

However, it should be noted that given that 'it was clear that much water ha[d] passed under the bridge' in the university since the difficulties between the parties had arisen, Clarke J said that it did not appear to him to be appropriate to make any order at that stage beyond declaring that the plaintiff remained in office and was entitled to the payment of his salary. Some explanation of the rationale behind the approach adopted by Clarke J at the interlocutory stage can be found in the following portion of his judgment where he stated as follows:

> It seems to me that it follows from the provisions of the 1997 Act, which limit the power to dismiss officers, and which require the court, in construing the statute, to lean in favour of a construction which favours the maintenance of academic freedom, that a court should, in turn, lean in favour, in an academic context, of making an order which preserves the entitlement of the academic office holder concerned to continue to operate as an academic in the university world. To take any other view would be to countenance a situation where, in an appropriate case, the university could exclude an academic and the ability to carry out his or her duties in the academic world in circumstances where the sanction imposed (either dismissal or suspension) was in breach of statute.[578]

Parallels can be drawn between this reasoning and the recognition of the need for an individual to maintain a special skill or talent identified in the judgment of Nourse LJ in the decision of the Court of Appeal in *Warren v Mendy*,[579] at any event which would support to some extent the conclusions reached at the interlocutory stage. However, given the tenor of Clarke J's judgment and his acknowledgement of the special circumstances of the case before him, it would probably be unwise to read too much into the conclusions which he reached.

The authorities therefore seem to confirm that while orders restraining the implementation of a purported dismissal or termination of appointment may be obtained, even where the relationship of mutual trust and confidence between the parties has broken down, such orders will be made on limited terms. While a plaintiff will often be required to give an undertaking that he will carry out such duties under his contract as may be required of him,[580] or as are reasonably appropriate, the courts have tended to make clear that 'whether the defendants wish to avail of the plaintiff's services is entirely a matter for them'.[581] Often the court will even concede that it will not be in the broader interest of the company to re-involve the plaintiff in its activities.[582] The reality that in the absence of a continuing relationship of mutual trust and confidence there is no

578. [2007] IEHC 20 at 24.
579. [1989] 1 WLR 853.
580. *Boland v Phoenix Shannon plc* [1997] ELR 113, 124.
581. *Shortt v Data Packaging Ltd* [1994] ELR 251, 255. See also *Phelan v BIC (Ireland) Ltd* [1997] ELR 208, 213.
582. *Harte v Kelly* [1997] ELR 125, 131.

basis on which to make an order requiring parties to continue to work together, even temporarily, has been generally accepted.

However, it is important to bear in mind that since the decision of the Supreme Court in *Lingham v Health Service Executive*[583] referred to above, an increasingly significant factor is whether orders sought by a plaintiff are construed as being mandatory in effect. In *Lingham*, the plaintiff's application for an injunction restraining the defendant from dismissing him from his post as a temporary orthopaedic surgeon was rejected on the basis that he had not established a strong case that he was likely to succeed at trial. In *Coffey v William Connolly & Sons Ltd*[584] Edwards J granted interlocutory injunctions restraining the defendant from giving effect to the plaintiff's purported dismissal or from appointing any other person to his position, but declined to grant an order restraining the defendant from treating the plaintiff otherwise than continuing to be employed on the basis that the plaintiff had not discharged the onus of establishing a strong case that she was likely to succeed at trial in obtaining such relief. However, in subsequent decisions such as *Bergin v Galway Clinic Doughiska Ltd*[585]and *Giblin v Irish Life and Permanent plc*[586] a stricter approach was taken towards the question of whether the relief sought was mandatory in substance and in both cases the plaintiffs were required to establish a 'strong case' in order to obtain interlocutory relief restraining their dismissal. Even where the strong case requirement can be met, as the decision of MacMenamin J in *Keenan v Iarnród Eireann*[587] shows, interlocutory relief restraining the defendant from taking steps to remove a plaintiff from his position may still be withheld on the ground that the balance of convenience lies in favour of such a result.

Orders Requiring Payment of an Employee's Salary Pending Trial

Another form of order which the courts in this jurisdiction have appeared willing to make notwithstanding a lack of a continuing relationship of trust and confidence between the parties is one which directs the employer to pay the employee's salary and other benefits pending trial. However, more recent decisions suggest that it has become increasingly difficult to obtain such orders, not least because they are mandatory in substance.

The making of such orders initially stemmed from the decision of Costello J in *Fennelly v Assicurazioni Generali SPA*,[588] where he noted that pending the trial the plaintiff would be left without a salary and with nothing to live on. He added that 'the situation in which he finds himself would be little short of

583. [2006] ELR 137.
584. [2007] IEHC 319.
585. [2008] 2 IR 205.
586. [2010] IEHC 36.
587. [2010] IEHC 15.
588. High Court, 12 March 1985. See (1985) 3 ILT 73.

disastrous' and that it would seem unjust if he were to be left virtually destitute with merely a prospect of damages at trial. In the circumstances, Costello J ordered that the defendant should continue to pay the plaintiff his salary and bonus pending the trial and that the plaintiff should undertake to carry out any duties under his contract which the defendant should ask of him.

While in *Fennelly* Costello J made it clear that the parties still had 'obviously the highest regard for one another,' this was far from being the case in some of the decisions which followed. In *Shortt v Data Packaging Ltd*[589] Keane J stated that he was satisfied that damages would not be an adequate remedy where the plaintiff would have to await the trial of the action in circumstances where he was totally without remuneration and where the trial would not take place for some time. In the circumstances he ordered the defendant to pay the plaintiff's salary and such other emoluments including pension as the plaintiff might be entitled to pending trial on the basis that the plaintiff would undertake to perform such duties on behalf of the defendant as were reasonably appropriate. An order of a similar nature was made by Barron J in *Boland v Phoenix Shannon plc*,[590] who commented that while in the case before him the plaintiff accountant had his profession and, to that extent, should be in a position to earn money, in practical terms his dismissal would leave him in the same situation as the plaintiff in *Fennelly's* case.

It was confirmed in both *Phelan v BIC (Ireland) Ltd*[591] and *Harte v Kelly*[592] that a plaintiff does not have to show a likelihood of virtual destitution in order to obtain an order of this nature. In the former case, while the plaintiff's pension entitlements had been preserved and his shareholding in the defendant company valued at £300,000, Costello P made an order that he continue to be paid his salary and other emoluments in circumstances where he suggested that the plaintiff had made out a case for exemplary damages at trial. Similarly, in *Harte*, an order for payment of salary was made in circumstances where the plaintiff was far from destitute, Laffoy J pointing out that in *Shortt* and *Boland* there had been no consideration of the value of the plaintiff's assets or his spending patterns. Laffoy J stated as follows:

> In my view, the entitlement to the type of order granted in the *Fennelly* case is not limited to a situation in which the plaintiff can establish that he will face penury if such an order is not made. The rationale of the decision is that it is unjust to leave a person who alleged that his dismissal has been

589. [1997] ELR 251. See also *Doyle v Grangeford Precast Concrete Ltd* [1998] ELR 260, where O'Donovan J granted an order that the plaintiff's salary should continue to be paid pending trial even though he was satisfied that: 'all trust and confidence between the parties…ha[d] broken down.'
590. [1997] ELR 113.
591. [1997] ELR 208.
592. [1997] ELR 125.

> wrongful without his salary pending the trial of the action and merely with his prospect of an award of damages at the trial of the action.[593]

In many of these cases where the relationship of trust and confidence between the parties had broken down, it was clear that an employer would not call on the employee to honour the undertaking, which developed as a result of the *Fennelly* decision, to carry out appropriate and reasonable duties associated with his work. However, there have also been examples of cases where no order for the payment of an employee's salary was made at least partly on the basis that the decisions where there had been no suggestion of any breakdown of trust or confidence had no relevance to the situation.[594]

It is also clear from the decisions of Clarke J in *Carroll v Dublin Bus*[595] and *Yap v Children's University Hospital Temple Street*[596] that where there is an issue which cannot be resolved at the interlocutory stage about the circumstances in which a plaintiff should be entitled to return to work, the court will not direct that he should be paid pending trial. In *Yap* Clarke J commented that 'in the ordinary course of events, an entitlement to be paid flows from carrying out the duties of one's employment'[597] although he acknowledged that in a limited number of cases an employee would be entitled to be paid even though he was not working.

In a significant number of more recent decisions a plaintiff has failed to obtain an interlocutory injunction requiring the continued payment of his salary pending trial because he has failed to establish the 'strong case' required due to the mandatory effect of such an order.[598] An example of this is *Stoskus v Goode Concrete Ltd*,[599] where the sole order sought was one restraining the defendant from ceasing to pay the plaintiff's salary pending trial. Irvine J said that while

---

593. *Ibid.* at 130. Quoted with approval by O'Sullivan J in *Moore v Xnet Information Systems Ltd* [2002] 2 ILRM 278, 286. See also the *dictum* of Laffoy J in *Courtenay v Radio 2000 Ltd* [1997] IEHC 129 that: 'relief should be granted if it would perpetrate an injustice to leave a person who alleges that he has been wrongfully dismissed without his salary, and only with the prospect of an award of damages at the trial of the action.' Orders that a plaintiff's salary should continue to be paid have been made in a number of more recent cases, see *Lonergan v Salter-Townshend* [2000] ELR 15; *Moore v Xnet Information Systems Ltd* [2002] 2 ILRM 278; *Sheehy v Ryan* High Court 2002 No. 10338P (Peart J) 29 August 2002; *Keane v Irish Amateur Swimming Association Ltd* High Court 2003 No. 8724P (Gilligan J) 4 August 2003; *Mullarkey v Irish National Stud Co. Ltd* [2004] IEHC 116; *Naujoks v National Institution of Bioprocessing Research and Training Ltd* [2006] IEHC 358; *Cahill v Dublin City University* [2007] IEHC 20.
594. *Orr v Zomax Ltd* [2004] 1 IR 486, 496.
595. [2005] 4 IR 184.
596. [2006] 4 IR 298.
597. *Ibid.* at 301.
598. See, e.g. *Nolan v Emo Oil Services Ltd* [2009] ELR 122; *Keenan v Iarnród Eireann* [2010] IEHC 15.
599. [2007] IEHC 432.

the relief sought by the plaintiff was framed in prohibitory terms, the plaintiff was in effect seeking mandatory relief as he was asking the court to require the defendant to perform an obligation which only existed in the context of an ongoing contractual relationship between the parties. She stated that the onus of proof on the plaintiff was to establish that he had a strong case to make at the hearing of the action and concluded that his case did not amount to a good arguable one and was certainly not a strong one. However, in *Brennan v Irish Pride Bakeries*,[600] where it was accepted by the High Court, in a decision upheld by the Court of Appeal[601] that the plaintiff had established a 'strong case', it was directed that he continue to be paid his salary in accordance with his contractual entitlements pending trial.

Injunctions to Restrain the Appointment of a Third Party

Even in cases where the court will refuse to order a plaintiff's reinstatement pending trial, it may grant an injunction to restrain the appointment of a person other than the plaintiff to his position or may prevent the advertising of a post which overlaps with the plaintiff's. So, in *Lonergan v Salter-Townshend*,[602] Macken J was willing to grant an order restraining the appointment of another person to a position which the plaintiff claimed to already occupy pending trial, although she would not order reinstatement on an interlocutory basis.[603] In addition, an order of this nature may readily be obtained where the court is prepared to go further and prevent steps being taken to remove the plaintiff from a post[604] or effectively terminate a suspension.[605] In both *Naujoks v National Institution of Bioprocessing Research and Training Ltd*[606] and *Coffey v William Connolly & Sons Ltd*[607] interlocutory injunctions were granted restraining the respective defendants from dismissing the plaintiffs from their employment and from appointing any persons other than the plaintiffs to their positions. An order of a slightly different nature was made by Clarke J in *Bergin v Galway Clinic Doughiska Ltd*[608] restraining the defendant from appointing any person to carry out the plaintiff's duties save in circumstances where the appointment of such a person contained terms sufficient to permit the plaintiff to return to his duties should the court be persuaded to make an order to that effect at the trial.

A similar situation arises where a defendant seeks to 'freeze out' a plaintiff

600. [2015] IEHC 665.
601. [2015] IECA 107.
602. [2000] ELR 15.
603. An order of this nature may even be made where a plaintiff claims to have been validly appointed to a post but has not yet taken it up, see *Keane v Irish Amateur Swimming Association Ltd* High Court 2003 No. 8724P (Gilligan J) 4 August 2003.
604. *Howard v UCC* [2000] IEHC 138.
605. *Martin v Nationwide Building Society* [2001] 1 IR 228.
606. [2006] ELR 25.
607. [2007] IEHC 319.
608. [2008] 2 IR 205.

by creating a new position very similar to the one which the plaintiff already occupies. An example of this arose in *Harkins v Shannon Foynes Port Company*,[609] where the plaintiff sought to restrain the defendant from advertising the position of operations manager which he was concerned would absorb his existing post as harbour engineer, which he had held for several years. The defendants asserted that the plaintiff would remain in his existing job if he did not secure the new appointment and that the only difference would be that he would be required to report to the appointed operations manager. O'Sullivan J was satisfied that if the defendant was permitted to continue with making the appointment the plaintiff's position at trial would be devalued, possibly in an irretrievable manner, and he made an order that the defendant be prohibited from advertising the position of operations manager unless and until the advertisement made it clear that it involved no overlap with or incorporation of the function of the post of harbour engineer held by the plaintiff.

However, as a number of other decisions show, an order restraining the appointment of a third party will not invariably be made in cases of this nature. In *Hennessy v St Gerard's School Trust*[610] the plaintiff teacher sought interlocutory injunctions restraining the defendant from dismissing her or from appointing anyone else to her teaching position in the school. Smyth J concluded that the 'mutuality of respect and trust' between the parties had been fractured and in the circumstances he declined to grant the plaintiff the relief sought. Similarly, in *Orr v Zomax Ltd*,[611] the plaintiff failed to obtain an injunction restraining the purported termination of his employment or an injunction restraining the performance of his functions and duties by any person other than him. Carroll J held that there was no justification for permitting the performance of functions and duties by the plaintiff or restraining the performance of those functions and duties by any person other than the plaintiff.

The decisions in *Hennessy* and *Orr* would seem to be exceptions to the general rule, which reflects the fact that an order restraining the advertisement of a post or the appointment of a third party will not have the direct effect of requiring parties to work together. However, as the decisions in *Page One Records Ltd v Britton*[612] and *Warren v Mendy*[613] show, injunctions granted in such cases will also have indirect effects and where an employer is prevented from proceeding to advertise and fill a post he may be forced to continue working with the plaintiff. To this extent the arguments made in favour of refusing relief in *Hennessy* and *Orr* should not be lightly dismissed and the nature of the working relationship between the parties may play a role despite the tenor of decisions such as *Harkins*.

609. [2001] ELR 75. Orders of a similar nature were made in *Garrahy v Bord na gCon* [2002] 3 IR 566; *Evans v IRFB Services (Ireland) Ltd* [2005] 2 ILRM 358.
610. High Court 2003 No.7556P (Smyth J) 30 July 2003.
611. [2004] 1 IR 486.
612. [1968] 1 WLR 157.
613. [1989] 1 WLR 853.

To Restrain the Commission or Continuance of a Tort

While Equity does not determine whether a tort has been committed or threatened, once it is established, a court may in its discretion grant or withhold an injunction on the basis of equitable principles.

Equity will commonly intervene and grant an injunction in the case of nuisance which is usually of a continuing nature and the remedy of an injunction will be the most appropriate form of remedy in the circumstances.[614] In relation to acts of public nuisance, i.e. acts or omissions which cause damage to the public generally, proceedings for an injunction may only be brought by the Attorney General either on his own motion or at the relation of an individual unless the individual can establish that he has suffered some special damage or that a private right of his has been infringed.[615]

An injunction is often sought to prevent a threatened or continued trespass to land, although if the trespass is of a trivial nature and involves no appreciable injury to the plaintiff,[616] an order will not be granted. Injunctions are also sought with increasing frequency in relation to alleged passing off,[617] and in the area of industrial relations. As noted above, the common law principles relating to the grant of an interlocutory injunction clearly favoured the employer where proceedings were brought seeking to restrain picketing by means of an interlocutory injunction and given the strict interpretation placed on the provisions of section 19 of the Industrial Relations Act 1990 it is open to question whether is has adequately redressed this imbalance.[618]

The circumstances in which an injunction may be granted to restrain alleged defamation are difficult to define with precision, although as noted above, the traditional reluctance on the part of the courts to interfere unduly with an individual's right to freedom of expression has been reflected in the rather onerous burden facing potential plaintiffs.[619]

To Restrain a Breach of Constitutional Rights

It is a well-established principle that damages will lie in respect of a breach of

614. See, e.g. *Bellew v Cement Ltd* [1948] IR 61; *Patterson v Murphy* [1978] ILRM 85.
615. *Boyce v Paddington Borough Council* [1903] 1 Ch 109, 113 *per* Buckley J.
616. *Fielden v Cox* (1906) 22 TLR 411; *Llandudno Urban District Council v Woods* [1899] 2 Ch 705.
617. See e.g. *Independent Newspapers Ltd v Irish Press Ltd* [1932] IR 615; *C.& A. Modes v C. & A. (Waterford) Ltd* [1976] IR 198; *Three Stripe International Ltd v Charles O'Neill & Co. Ltd* [1989] ILRM 124; *An Post v Irish Permanent plc* [1995] 1 ILRM 336; *B. & S. Ltd v Irish Auto Trader Ltd* [1995] 2 IR 142; *Symonds Cider and English Wine Co. Ltd v Showerings (Ireland) Ltd* [1997] 1 ILRM 481; *Local Ireland Ltd v Local Ireland-Online Ltd* [2000] 4 IR 567; *Metro International SA v Independent News and Media plc* [2006] 1 ILRM 414; *Jacob Fruitfield Food Group Ltd v United Biscuits (UK) Ltd* [2007] IEHC 368.
618. See *supra* pp. 670-674.
619. See *supra* pp. 674-688.

constitutional rights,[620] and that the amount of such an award may vary, from exemplary damages where the State has deliberately and without justification infringed a person's constitutional rights,[621] to a purely nominal sum where the breach has caused no real damage.[622] However, it has also been recognised that an injunction will lie to restrain unconstitutional activities, such as in *Murtagh Properties v Cleary*,[623] where an injunction was granted by Kenny J to restrain the picketing of a licensed premises on the basis that it amounted to unlawful interference with the constitutional right of the employees who worked there to earn their livelihood. This approach was followed by O'Hanlon J in *Parsons v Kavanagh*,[624] in which the plaintiff, who operated a passenger bus service on a route pursuant to a statutory licence, sought an injunction to prevent the defendants operating a bus service without a licence on the same route. O'Hanlon J held that having regard to the plaintiff's constitutional right to earn a livelihood, which carried with it the entitlement to be protected against any unlawful activity on the part of another person which materially infringed that right, the plaintiff was entitled to the injunction sought. Similarly, in *Lovett v Gogan*,[625] the Supreme Court granted an injunction restraining the defendants from operating an unlicensed coach passenger service in breach of the provisions of the Road Traffic Act 1932 on the basis that this activity constituted an actual and threatened interference with the plaintiff's constitutional right to earn a living by lawful means. However, it should be noted that Finlay CJ stressed that the plaintiff would be entitled to an injunction in such circumstances if he could establish that it was the only way of protecting himself from the threatened invasion of his constitutional rights. On the facts of the case before him, he was satisfied that an injunction was the only remedy which could protect the plaintiff given that the penalty which could be imposed on a person operating a passenger service without a licence was limited to £5 in respect of a continuing offence.

However, care should be exercised when the impugned activity constitutes a criminal offence, and the relevance of the statement made by Finlay CJ in *Lovett* becomes clear when one examines the judgment of Barron J in *O'Connor v Williams*,[626] in which the plaintiff taxi drivers sought an injunction to restrain the defendant hackney cab operators from carrying on their business in alleged breach of the Road Traffic (Public Service Vehicles) Regulations 1963, as amended, in a manner which the plaintiffs contended amounted to interference with their right to earn a livelihood. Barron J stated that the real issue was whether injunctive relief was the only way in which the plaintiffs could be

620. See, e.g. *Meskell v CIE* [1973] IR 121; *Hayes v Ireland* [1987] ILRM 651.
621. *Kennedy v Ireland* [1987] IR 587.
622. *Kearney v Ireland* [1986] IR 116.
623. [1972] IR 330.
624. [1990] ILRM 560.
625. [1995] 3 IR 132.
626. [2001] 1 IR 248.

protected from the invasion of their constitutional rights. He distinguished the decisions in *Parsons* and *Lovett*, stating that in the case before him the defendants were only one of several firms operating a service allegedly in breach of the regulations and the penalties for breaches of the relevant regulations were substantial.[627] In his view, the implementation of the criminal law was the most appropriate remedy and he refused the relief sought by the plaintiffs.

The importance of injunctive relief being available as a means of restraining a breach of constitutional rights is illustrated by a number of decisions of Hogan J. In *Albion Properties Ltd v Moonblast Ltd*,[628] in granting a mandatory interlocutory injunction requiring the defendant to yield up possession of property, Hogan J stressed that '[t]he courts are under a clear constitutional duty to ensure that the remedies available to protect and vindicate [the plaintiff's property] rights are real and effective.'[629] In *Sullivan v Boylan*[630] Hogan J granted an interlocutory injunction restraining a defendant from harassing the plaintiff and effectively picketing her house in breach of her constitutional right to the inviolability of her dwelling guaranteed by Article 40.5. A useful summary of the position is set out by Hogan J in his judgment in *Herrera v Garda Síochána*:[631]

> Article 40.3.2° obliges the courts to secure litigants an effective remedy to vindicate their constitutional rights to persons and property and not simply to afford a remedy which is purely theoretical or illusory in character …This is especially so where the grant of injunctive relief is necessary to secure to the plaintiff a core constitutional right and where the refusal of relief could prejudicially hinder the exercise of that right. In these circumstances the courts cannot be beguiled by legal formalism or corralled into the unthinking and uncritical application of rules governing the grant of interlocutory relief without taking proper account of these factors.

To Protect Public Rights

An injunction may issue to restrain activities which are detrimental to the public generally. As a general rule such an injunction may only be sought successfully by the Attorney General, either acting on his own initiative, or at the relation of another who seeks to prevent infringement of a right. As an exception to this general principle, an individual may seek an injunction to restrain interference

627. In the view of Barron J the decision which was more relevant was that of the Supreme Court in *Incorporated Law Society of Ireland v Carroll* [1995] 3 IR 145, in which the plaintiff's application for an injunction to restrain alleged breaches of the criminal law was refused.
628. [2011] 3 IR 563.
629. *Ibid* at 571. See also *Wallace v Irish Aviation Authority* [2012] 2 ILRM 345, 354.
630. [2012] IEHC 389.
631. [2013] IEHC 311. See also *Merck Sharp & Dohme Corporation v Clonmel Healthcare Ltd* [2018] IECA 177 *per* Hogan J at [11] in his dissenting judgment.

with a public right if this interference also amounts to an infringement of a private right or would cause special damage to this individual.[632] However, the traditional principles in this area were thrown into some doubt by a number of decisions of the Supreme Court in the late 1980s such as *Crotty v An Taoiseach*,[633] in which the plaintiff successfully sought an injunction to prevent the State ratifying the Single European Act, a treaty which introduced a number of significant changes to the treaties establishing the European Communities. In *SPUC v Coogan*[634] the Supreme Court held that the Attorney General did not have an exclusive right to commence proceedings seeking to secure compliance with the provisions of Article 40.3.3° of the Constitution of Ireland and that any citizen showing a *bona fide* interest and concern in its enforcement might do so. The Supreme Court held that the plaintiff, who was not in the position of an officious or meddlesome intervenient in the matter, had sufficient *locus standi* to maintain an action against individuals whom it claimed were acting in a manner contrary to Article 40.3.3° without being required to act in relator proceedings.

A question which has provoked considerable debate is whether an injunction may be granted to restrain the infringement of a public right even where a statutory remedy exists, in particular where the activity also constitutes a criminal offence. While the use of an injunction to restrain a breach of the criminal law has been described as a remedy of last resort,[635] it would appear that the Attorney General, in his role as guardian of the rights of the public, may obtain such a remedy. It has been stressed that an injunction will only be granted in these circumstances where the statutory remedy is inadequate and it has been established in England that an individual may not take such an action in the absence of interference with private rights or special damage. So, in *Gouriet v Union of Post Office Workers*,[636] the plaintiff failed to obtain an injunction to restrain a threatened boycott of postal communications between the UK and South Africa which amounted to a breach of the Post Office Act 1953 when the Attorney General declined to bring a relator action.

This issue has been considered in this jurisdiction on a number of occasions and in *Attorney General (O'Duffy) v Appleton*[637] the Attorney General was granted an injunction in a relator action in which it was sought to restrain the activities of a company formed for fraudulent purposes contrary to the Dentists Act 1878. The most important decision in this area is that of Costello J in *Attorney General v Paperlink*,[638] in which an injunction was sought to restrain the defendants from operating a courier service in breach of the statutory power

632. *Lonrho v Shell Petroleum Co. Ltd (No. 2)* [1982] AC 173.
633. [1987] IR 713.
634. [1989] IR 734.
635. *Waverly BC v Hilden* [1988] 1 WLR 246, 265 *per* Scott J.
636. [1978] AC 435.
637. [1907] 1 IR 252.
638. [1984] ILRM 373.

of the minister under the Post Office Act 1908. Costello J accepted as correct the statement of Professor Casey[639] to the effect that 'it is possible for [the Attorney General] to obtain an injunction to restrain someone from acting in breach of a statutory provision even where his action constitutes an offence,' and also the following statement of Lord Denning MR in *Attorney General v Chaudray*:[640]

> Whenever parliament has enacted a law and given a particular remedy for the breach of it, such remedy being in an inferior court, nevertheless the High Court always has reserve power to enforce the law so enacted by way of an injunction or declaration or other suitable remedy. The High Court has a jurisdiction to ensure obedience to the law whenever it is just and convenient to do so.

In the course of his judgment, Costello J laid down a number of important principles. He confirmed that the Attorney General has the right to seek an injunction to restrain a breach of statute, even where the statute prescribes alternative remedies including criminal sanctions. Costello J stressed that such a jurisdiction should only be exercised in exceptional circumstances and that the court must consider the adequacy of the alternative remedy but conceded that the fact that a criminal prosecution had not been brought did not in itself preclude the court from granting an injunction. Costello J was satisfied that there were exceptional circumstances justifying the granting of an injunction in the case before him and in answer to the defendant's argument stressed that the court was not trying a criminal charge but was merely exercising 'a distinct and different jurisdiction in civil proceedings'.

However, as the decision of the Supreme Court in *Incorporated Law Society of Ireland v Carroll*[641] makes clear, the only party who may bring civil proceedings to enforce a public right is the Attorney General. As Blayney J stated, there was no suggestion in the judgment of Costello J in *Attorney General v Paperlink* that anyone other than the Attorney General could seek an injunction in the public interest to restrain an offence being committed in breach of statute.[642]

639. Casey, *The Office of the Attorney General in Ireland* (1980) p. 149.
640. [1971] 1 WLR 1614, 1624.
641. [1995] 3 IR 145.
642. However, it should be noted that in his decision in the High Court in *Incorporated Law Society of Ireland v Carroll* [1995] 3 IR 145, 163 Murphy J stated that the right to maintain civil proceedings in respect of a criminal wrong where a constitutional right is in jeopardy may be described as one of the exceptional cases referred to by Costello J in *Attorney General v Paperlink* [1984] ILRM 373, 391 or as a distinct and separate exception to the rules laid down in that case. (See further *Parsons v Kavanagh* [1990] ILRM 560 and *Lovett v Gogan* [1995] 3 IR 132 considered *supra*.)

MAREVA INJUNCTIONS AND RELATED ORDERS[643]

Introduction

Traditionally, the courts would not grant an injunction to restrain a defendant from dealing with or dissipating his assets prior to the trial of an action.[644] However, a number of decisions of the English Court of Appeal in the mid-1970s resulted in a change in this position and a 'Mareva' injunction, or 'freezing order' as it now known as in England, may be granted to prevent a defendant from removing assets from the jurisdiction or from disposing of them within the jurisdiction in a manner likely to frustrate the plaintiff's proceedings. It has also been accepted that an injunction of this nature may even extend to assets held outside the jurisdiction on a worldwide basis.[645]

The genesis of Mareva injunctions can be traced to the decision of the English Court of Appeal in *Nippon Yusen Kaisha v Karageorgis*,[646] in which Denning MR stated that 'it seems to me that the time has come when we should revise our practice'. The plaintiff shipowners let a number of ships to charterers who defaulted after initially making some payments. Believing that the defendants had certain funds in London banks which would be sent out of the jurisdiction, the plaintiff sought an injunction to prevent this happening. The Court of Appeal held that where there is a strong *prima facie* case that a plaintiff is entitled to money from a defendant within the jurisdiction and the plaintiff has reason to believe that the defendant may remove these assets from the jurisdiction, the court may grant an interlocutory injunction on an *ex parte* basis restraining the defendant from disposing of these assets. This principle was confirmed several weeks later in *Mareva Compania Naviera SA v International Bulkcarriers SA*,[647] the decision which gave its name to the form of injunction granted in these cases.

A Mareva injunction will usually be sought initially on an interim *ex parte* basis and an order of an interlocutory nature may subsequently be sought.[648] Such orders are ancillary in nature so substantive proceedings should be in being or at least formulated when the application for a Mareva injunction is made.[649] This is clear from the decision of the House of Lords in *Fourie v*

643. See generally Capper, *Mareva Injunctions* (1988) and Courtney, *Mareva Injunctions and Related Interlocutory Orders* (1998).
644. *Lister & Co. v Stubbs* (1890) 45 Ch D 1.
645. *Babanaft International Co. SA v Bassatne* [1990] Ch 13; *Deutsche Bank Atkiengesellschaft v Murtagh* [1995] 1 ILRM 381; *Bennett Enterprises Ltd v Lipton* [1999] 2 IR 221.
646. [1975] 1 WLR 1093, 1095.
647. [1975] 2 Lloyd's Rep 509.
648. This is not always the case and sometimes, as in *O'Mahony v Horgan* [1995] 12 IR 411 an interlocutory order is sought in the first instance.
649. Kirwan in *Injunctions Law and Practice* (2nd ed., 2015) p. 385 suggests that if no

Le Roux[650] where it was stated that no Mareva injunction should be granted unless the claimant can identify the prospective judgment which he fears that the defendant may seek to frustrate by removing or dissipating his assets. As Lord Bingham stated, the claimant 'must at least point to proceedings already brought or proceedings about to be brought, so as to show where and on what basis he expects to recover judgment against the defendant.'[651]

The usual purpose of a Mareva injunction is to prevent the dissipation or removal of assets before the trial of an action to avoid a judgment remaining unsatisfied,[652] although it may be granted to prevent a defendant disposing of assets after the trial has taken place to avoid execution of a judgment.[653] Ancillary orders may be granted to require a defendant to disclose information relating to his assets, although the privilege against self-incrimination[654] may be invoked to undermine the effectiveness of such orders.[655] The jurisdiction to grant such injunctions is of general application[656] and the courts are loath to lay down any limitation in relation to the nature or subject matter of proceedings in which they can be sought, although they tend to be employed predominantly in the commercial sphere. While in theory an order of an unlimited nature can be made, this will often be unnecessary and will inflict disproportionate hardship on a defendant, so in practice a limited order is usually granted which will at least allow retention of sufficient funds to provide for living expenses, or in the case of a company, the costs of its day-to-day running. It has been stressed that the courts should not be too ready to grant relief in the form of a Mareva injunction in the context of an ordinary *bona fide* business transaction, but intervention is justified where an asset is being disposed of at an undervalue to a creditor's detriment, even where an independent valuation has been obtained.[657] A useful summary of the rationale underlying the grant of Mareva injunctions is provided by Clarke J in his judgment in *Bambrick v Cobley*[658] in the following terms:

> It is trite to say that a plaintiff is not entitled to security for every claimed liability. The Mareva injunction is not intended to provide plaintiffs with security in respect of all claims in relation to which they may be able to

---

proceedings seeking substantive relief are yet in being, a claim should at a minimum be formulated and entitled 'In the intended matter of' or a similar formula used.

650. [2007] 1 WLR 320.
651. *Ibid.* at 323. See also the comments of Lord Rodger at pp. 336-337.
652. So, the risk of a judgment remaining unsatisfied can be said to be the primary rationale, see *Fiona Trust Holding Corporation v Privalov* [2007] EWHC 1217 (Comm) at [70].
653. See e.g. *Walsh v Walsh (No. 2)* [2017] IEHC 177.
654. Considered *infra* in the context of Anton Piller orders.
655. *Den Norske Bank ASA v Antonatos* [1999] QB 271; *Memory Corporation v Sidhu* [2000] Ch 645.
656. *Z Ltd v A-Z and AA-LL* [1982] QB 558, 584 *per* Kerr LJ.
657. *Customs and Excise Commissioners v Anchor Foods Ltd* [1999] 1 WLR 1139.
658. [2006] 1 ILRM 81, 90. See also *Hughes v Hitachi Koki Imaging Solutions Europe* [2006] 3 IR 457, 464.

> pass an arguability test. The true basis of the jurisdiction is the exercise by the court of its inherent power to prevent parties from placing their assets beyond the likely reach of the court in the event of a successful action.

A Mareva injunction operates *in personam*[659] to restrain the defendant from dealing with the assets to which the order relates and it gives the plaintiff no proprietary right over these assets nor priority over other creditors.[660] Therefore, the rights of a third party with an interest in an asset will not be prejudiced and it was held by the English Court of Appeal in *Cretanor Maritime Co. Ltd v Irish Marine Management Ltd*[661] that the plaintiff was not entitled to a Mareva injunction in relation to funds owed by the defendant where a debenture holder had appointed a receiver over those funds. However, once a third party has been notified of an injunction, he will be restrained from dealing with assets in a manner contrary to its terms as otherwise he may be in contempt of court. As Clarke J commented in *Dowley v O'Brien*,[662] '[a] third party who, knowing of the terms of a Mareva injunction, willfully assists in the breach of that injunction, or in its frustration, is liable for contempt of court.' It is therefore in the plaintiff's interest to notify any third parties such as banks who may be holding assets belonging to the defendant of the terms of the order as soon as it is made.

However, it is also clear that such third parties may have a legitimate right to deal with an asset affected by a Mareva injunction in limited circumstances[663] given that the injunction is not intended to prevent a party using its assets in the ordinary course of business or paying its lawful debts in a *bona fide* manner. This issue was also considered by Clarke J in *Dowley v O'Brien*,[664] where he accepted that in principle a third party including a bank can only be affected by a Mareva injunction if it could be said that an action taken by that party amounted to either aiding and abetting a breach of the order or frustrating its effect in circumstances in which the bank had notice of it. However, he acknowledged that third party financial institutions may often have concerns about whether transactions are truly *bona fide* and will understandably take a conservative approach. Clarke J concluded that a typical Mareva injunction will not prevent a financial institution from *bona fide* exercising any power of set-off or security realisation which it may have had prior to being notified of the existence of the injunction.

---

659. See, e.g. *Mercedes Banz AG v Leiduck* [1996] AC 284, 306; *Masri v Consolidated Contractors International Co. SAL* [2007] EWHC 3010 (Comm) at [67]. Although note the rather ambiguous comments to the contrary of Lord Denning MR in *Z Ltd v A-Z and AA-LL* [1982] QB 558, 573.
660. See generally *Dowley v O'Brien* [2009] 4 IR 752, 764.
661. [1978] 1 WLR 966.
662. [2009] 4 IR 752, 760.
663. See, e.g. *Law Society v Shanks* [1988] 1 FLR 504; *Bank Mellat v Kazmi* [1989] QB 541.
664. [2009] 4 IR 752.

The issue of whether a Mareva injunction should be extended to cover the payment of the costs of the litigation has been considered on a number of occasions. In *Dowley v O'Brien*[665] Clarke J commented that a Mareva injunction restrains the defendant from removing his assets from the jurisdiction, 'at least to the extent that assets remaining in the jurisdiction cannot thereby be reduced below a threshold normally estimated by reference to the claim in respect of which the plaintiff has established a *prima facie* case, together with costs.' Reference was made to this statement when the issue was expressly considered by Humphreys J in *Walsh v Walsh (No.2)*.[666] The matter arose in the context of an application for a post-judgment order and he said that particularly in such a case, but potentially also in the case of a pre-judgment Mareva, he was of the view that provision for costs should be made by reason of the right to an effective remedy under Article 13 of the European Convention on Human Rights, a right which he would be inclined to consider should also be regarded as an unenumerated right under Article 40.3 of the Constitution. In the circumstances, Humphreys J therefore ordered that an injunction be granted restraining the defendant from reducing her assets below the figure identified in the earlier judgment until further order 'or until satisfaction of the judgment and costs'.

A useful summary of the criteria to be taken into account in determining whether a Mareva injunction should be granted were laid down by Lord Denning MR in *Third Chandris Shipping Corporation v Unimarine SA*[667] and summarised by Hamilton CJ in *O'Mahony v Horgan*[668] in the following terms:

(i) The plaintiff should make full and frank disclosure of all matters in his knowledge which are material for the judge to know.
(ii) The plaintiff should give particulars of his claims against the defendant, stating the grounds of his claims and the amount thereof, and fairly stating the points made against it by the defendant.
(iii) The plaintiff should give some grounds for believing that the defendant had assets within the jurisdiction.[669] The existence of a bank account is normally sufficient
(iv) The plaintiff should give some grounds for believing that there is a risk of assets being removed or dissipated.
(v) The plaintiff must give an undertaking in damages in case he fails.

---

665. [2009] 4 IR 752, 763.
666. [2017] IEHC 177.
667. [1979] QB 645, 668-669.
668. [1995] 2 IR 411, 416. See also *Bambrick v Cobley* [2006] 1 ILRM 81, 86.
669. It was suggested by Longmore LJ in *Ras al Khaimah Investment Authority and others v Bestfort Development LLP* [2018] 1 WLR 1099, 1114 that 'it is not enough for a claimant to assert that a defendant is an apparently wealthy person who must have assets somewhere' but that '[s]ince a claimant cannot invariably be expected to know of the existence of assets of a defendant, it should be sufficient that he can satisfy a court that there are grounds for so believing.'

The issue of whether an undertaking in damages is required where an application for an injunction of this nature is made post-judgment was considered by Humphreys J in *Walsh v Walsh (No.2)*.[670] He accepted that the law in this regard had been correctly set out by Gee in *Commercial Injunctions*[671] in the following terms:

> If Mareva relief is sought post-judgment, the purpose is to preserve assets so that the judgment can be satisfied. If such an injunction is sought *ex parte*, or whilst there is the possibility that it may be said that the injunction was wrongly granted, the cross-undertaking must be given. If the relief is granted *inter partes*, after the judgment debtor has had an opportunity to dispute the granting of the injunction if he wishes, then if there is no prospect of an issue about the injunction being 'wrongly granted' or improperly used, it may be appropriate to dispense with the cross undertaking in favour of the judgment debtor. This is because the judgment debtor has brought about the position by defaulting on the judgment

Therefore, where the application is made on an *inter partes* basis post-judgment, as was the case in the matter before the court, no undertaking in damages need be made.

Initially the Mareva injunction evolved as a remedy against foreign-based defendants who possessed assets within the jurisdiction of the court and while it was thought at one time that such injunctions could only issue against foreign-based defendants, this limitation was eroded by the courts.[672] So, in both *Fleming v Ranks (Ireland) Ltd*[673] and *Powerscourt Estates v Gallagher*[674] McWilliam J accepted that the types of cases in which Mareva injunctions may be granted are not confined to those where the defendant is resident outside the State.

A court may vary a Mareva injunction where it is causing undue hardship to allow a defendant to draw down sufficient funds from frozen assets to discharge living expenses and legal fees[675] or upon application by a third party which is affected by the order made by the court.[676] The circumstances in which such a variation will be made were considered by Murphy J in *Superwood Holdings plc v Sun Alliance and London Insurance plc*,[677] in which the first named plaintiff

---

670. [2017] IEHC 177.
671. 5th ed., 2004, p. 322.
672. See, e.g. *A.J. Bekhor & Co Ltd v Bilton* [1981] QB 923.
673. [1983] ILRM 541, 546.
674. [1984] ILRM 123.
675. *Director of Public Prosecutions v E.H.* High Court (Kelly J) 22 April 1997. See also *Criminal Assets Bureau v S.H.* High Court 1999 No. 235R (O'Sullivan J) 15 March 2000 where the court made an order varying the terms of a Mareva injunction to allow payment of legal expenses.
676. *Baltic Shipping Co. v Translink Shipping Ltd* [1995] 1 Lloyd's Rep 673.
677. [2002] IEHC 168.

sought to vary an existing Mareva injunction to pay the taxed costs of a third party. He referred to the *dicta* of Robert Goff J in *A. v C.*[678] to the effect that the court must be satisfied that there are no other assets available to meet the debt and as Murphy J stated 'a condition required for such variation is that the applicant has no other funds available'.[679] He also accepted that the court may vary an injunction of this nature on grounds of hardship, either to the defendant himself or to third party creditors of the defendant who are entitled to be paid in the ordinary course of business.[680] While Murphy J stressed that the authorities relating to the initial grant of injunctive relief and those dealing with variation should be distinguished, he stated that the requirement of full and frank disclosure applies equally to both and in his view it had not been complied with in the circumstances of the application before the court. In addition, he pointed out that the application was not for a variation to enable the plaintiff to pursue a legal appeal in the future but was to facilitate payment of a debt incurred in relation to litigation against a third party in the past. Murphy J concluded that in the circumstances he would refuse the application for variation on the basis of the evidence before the court.

Finally, it is important to distinguish an application to vary a Mareva injunction from an application to revisit the substantive basis for the granting of such an order, which is in reality a form of appeal. Smyth J drew this distinction in his judgment in *McMorrow v Morris*[681] in declining to set aside an order previously made by him in circumstances where he was satisfied that the defendant had had an opportunity to raise the issue of a failure to make full and frank disclosure and had not done so.

The Duty of Full and Frank Disclosure

Generally where a Mareva injunction is sought, due to considerations of urgency and secrecy it will be applied for on an interim *ex parte* basis.[682] As Balcombe LJ pointed out in *Brink's Mat Ltd v Elcombe*,[683] often it is the very fact of giving notice which may precipitate the action which the application is designed to prevent. However, given that proceedings of an *ex parte* nature deprive the defendant of the right to be heard and may expose him to the risk of serious and even irreparable harm, the court must seek to provide a mechanism for protecting the interests of the defendant.[684] In such cases one

678. [1981] 2 All ER 126.
679. [2002] IEHC 168 at 8.
680. See also *Powerscourt Estates Ltd v Gallagher* [1984] ILRM 123, 126.
681. [2007] IEHC 193.
682. Application may also be made to the court to serve short notice of motion pursuant to Order 52, rule 6. However, usually there is a risk of dissipation of assets or their removal from the jurisdiction if the defendant is put on notice of an impending application.
683. [1988] 1 WLR 1350, 1358.
684. As Isaacs J stated in *Thomas A Edison Ltd v Bullock* (1912) 15 CLR 679, 681 in a passage approved by Slade LJ in *Bank Mellat v Nikpour* [1985] FSR 87, 92, where

of the most effective means of achieving this aim is the imposition of a duty to make full and frank disclosure.[685] This principle was explained by Warrington LJ in *R. v Kensington Income Tax Commissioners, ex p. de Polignac*[686] in the following terms: 'It is perfectly well settled that a person who makes an *ex parte* application to the Court ... is under an obligation to the Court to make the fullest possible disclosure of all material facts within his knowledge'. This rule applies with particular force to applications for Mareva injunctions given the potentially adverse and often irreparable consequences for a defendant against whom an order is made. It has been characterised as the 'golden rule' by Browne-Wilkinson VC in *Tate Access Floors v Boswell*[687] in the following terms:

> No rule is better established, and few more important, than the rule, 'the golden rule', that a plaintiff applying for *ex parte* relief must disclose to the court all matters relevant to the exercise of the court's discretion whether or not to grant relief before giving the defendant an opportunity to be heard. If that duty is not observed by the plaintiffs, the court will discharge the *ex parte* order and may, to mark its displeasure, refuse the plaintiff further *inter partes* relief even though circumstances would otherwise justify the grant of such relief.

As Mummery LJ commented in *Memory Corporation plc v Sidhu (No. 2)*,[688] '[t]here is a high duty to make full, fair and accurate disclosure of material information to the court and to draw the court's attention to significant factual, legal and procedural aspects of the case.' This rule, as Slade LJ stated in *Brink's Mat Ltd v Elcombe*,[689] serves the purpose of encouraging litigants making *ex parte* applications to diligently observe their duty to the court to make full disclosure of all material facts and to deter them from any failure to observe this duty 'whether through deliberate lack of candour or innocent lack of due care'. An applicant is obliged to make all proper inquiries before making the

---

the court is asked to disregard the usual requirement of hearing the other side, 'the party moving incurs a most serious responsibility'. However, it would appear that the duty to make full and frank disclosure in proceedings relating to Mareva injunctions also applies to a defendant, see *Re Kelly's Carpetdrome Ltd* High Court (Costello J) 9 May 1983 in the context of an application by a defendant to vary the terms of an order.

685. It should be noted that in *Belair LLC v Basel LLC* [2009] EWHC 725 (Comm) at [44] Blair J rejected the suggestion that the duty of full and frank disclosure should in some way be reduced because notice of the application had been given to the respondent. In his view 'the duty is also of fundamental importance because of the drastic effect that such an order can have on the party against which it is made' and the fact that a few days' advance notice had been given did not alter this principle.
686. [1917] 1 KB 486, 509. See also *Bank Mellat v Nikpour* [1985] FSR 87, 90-91.
687. [1991] Ch 512, 532-533. See *Bambrick v Cobley* [2006] 1 ILRM 81, 86-87.
688. [2000] 1 WLR 1443, 1458. See also *Fourie v Le Roux* [2007] 1 WLR 320, 334; *Complete Retreats Liquidating Trust v Logue* [2010] EWHC 1864 (Ch) at [25].
689. [1988] 1 WLR 1350, 1359.

ex parte application and the duty of disclosure applies not only to material facts known to him but to any additional facts which he would have known if he had made such inquiries.[690] The extent of the proper inquiries which should be made will depend on all the circumstances including the nature of the case which the applicant is making.[691]

Material facts are those which it is material for the judge to know in dealing with the application and materiality is to be judged by the court and not by the applicant or his legal advisers.[692] This is borne out by the statement of Lord O'Hagan LC in *Atkin v Moran*[693] that 'the party applying is not to make himself the judge whether a particular fact is material or not'. This *dictum* was quoted with approval by Clarke J in *Bambrick v Cobley*,[694] where he also referred to the principle set out by Slade LJ in *Brink's Mat Ltd v Elcombe*[695] to the effect that particularly in commercial cases, the borderline between material and non-material facts may be somewhat uncertain. The latter went on to express the view that, while not discounting the heavy duty of candour and care which falls on persons making *ex parte* applications, he did not think that the application of the principle of disclosure should be carried to extreme lengths. Having considered these authorities, Clarke J concluded that 'the test by reference to which materiality is to be judged is one of whether objectively speaking the facts could reasonably be regarded as material with materiality to be construed in a reasonable and not excessive manner'.[696]

In some circumstances where injunctive relief is granted on an interim *ex parte* basis, a plaintiff may derive no real advantage in obtaining a remedy earlier than he might otherwise have done. However, this is not the case in relation to Mareva injunctions which will restrict a defendant's ability to deal with his property from the time the initial order is made. As Donaldson LJ commented in *Bank Mellatt v Nikpour*,[697] such an order 'confers tremendous advantage on the plaintiff who has been granted the order, and imposes a tremendous disadvantage on the defendant – the disadvantage of being fettered in dealing with your own property'. Applications to discharge *ex parte* orders are often made at the same time as the plaintiff's motion seeking to continue the relief initially granted comes before the court on an *inter partes* basis.[698] In this context it is therefore important to establish the principles on the basis of which the court will act where a case of material non-disclosure is brought to its attention.

690. *Brink's Mat Ltd v Elcombe* [1988] 1 WLR 1350, 1356 *per* Ralph Gibson LJ.
691. *Behbehani v Salem* [1989] 1 WLR 723, 737 *per* Nourse LJ.
692. *Brink's Mat Ltd v Elcombe* [1988] 1 WLR 1350, 1356 *per* Ralph Gibson LJ. See also *Complete Retreats Liquidating Trust v Logue* [2010] EWHC 1864 (Ch) at [26].
693. (1871) IR 6 Eq 79, 81. See also *F.McK. v D.C.* [2006] IEHC 185.
694. [2006] 1 ILRM 81, 87.
695. [1988] 1 WLR 1350, 1359. See also *Amedeo Hotels Ltd Partnership v Zaman* [2007] EWHC 295 (Comm) at [34].
696. [2006] 1 ILRM 81, 87.
697. [1985] FSR 85, 91.
698. *Dormeuil Freres SA v Nicolian International (Textiles) Ltd* [1988] 1 WLR 1362, 1368.

It is an accepted principle that if material non-disclosure is established, 'the court will be astute to ensure that a plaintiff who obtains an injunction… or any *ex parte* order without full disclosure … is deprived of any advantage he may have derived by that breach of duty'.[699] The traditional view was that if a plaintiff obtained a Mareva injunction or an Anton Piller order without full and frank disclosure, the order granted should be revoked.[700] However, it now seems to be accepted, as Dillon LJ suggested in *Lloyds Bowmaker Ltd v Britannia Arrow Holdings plc*,[701] that the court should have a discretion in an exceptional case not to revoke an *ex parte* order granted in the absence of full disclosure of material facts. A similar view was expressed by Flaux J in *Congentra AG v Sixteen Thirteen Marine SA*,[702] where he stated that while discharge of an order is not automatic on any non-disclosure of a material fact being established, in his view it would only be in exceptional circumstances that a court would not discharge an order where there had been deliberate non-disclosure or misrepresentation. A useful summary of the principles which are generally now being applied in England is contained in the judgment of Alan Boyle QC sitting as a Deputy High Court judge in *Arena Corporation Ltd v Schroeder*.[703] He stated that if a court finds that there have been breaches of the duty of full and fair disclosure on an *ex parte* application, the general rule is that it should discharge the order obtained and refuse to renew the order until trial. However, he accepted that notwithstanding this general rule, the court has jurisdiction to continue or re-grant the order, although he stressed that this jurisdiction should be exercised sparingly. He suggested that the court should assess the degree and extent of the culpability with regard to non-disclosure and the importance and significance to the outcome of the application for an injunction of the matters which were not disclosed to the court. He also stressed that there are no hard and fast rules as to whether the discretion to continue or re-grant the order should be exercised, and the court should take into account all relevant circumstances.

When this issue arose in this jurisdiction in *Bambrick v Cobley*,[704] Clarke J agreed that the discretionary approach was to be preferred. As he put it, '[t]herefore it seems to me that the court has a discretion, in cases where failure to disclose has been established, to refuse to grant the interlocutory

699. *Bank Mellatt v Nikpour* [1985] FSR 87, 91 citing *R. v Kensington Income Tax Commissioners, ex p. Polignac* [1917] 1 KB 486. See also *Brink's Mat Ltd v Elcombe* [1988] 1 WLR 1350, 1357.
700. *Bank Mellatt v Nikpour* [1985] FSR 87, 92. See also *Atkin v Moran* (1871) IR 6 Eq 79; *M'Donogh v Davies* (1875) IR 9 CL 300.
701. [1988] 1 WLR 1337, 1347.
702. [2008] EWHC 1615 (Comm) at [62]. See also *Belletti v Morici* [2009] EWHC 2316 (Comm) at [64].
703. [2003] EWHC 1089 (Ch) at [213]. See also *Dadourian Group International Inc v Simms* [2007] EWHC 1673 (Ch) at [29]; *Complete Retreats Liquidating Trust v Logue* [2010] EWHC 1864 (Ch) at [60].
704. [2006] 1 ILRM 81.

injunction and to discharge the already granted interim injunction but it is not necessarily obliged to do so.'[705] If it is accepted that the court retains a discretion in such cases, it must be asked what factors will influence the exercise of this discretion to decline to discharge an *ex parte* order even if it is obtained on the basis of some non-disclosure. In *Bambrick*, Clarke J stated that in exercising this discretion the court should have regard to all the circumstances of the case and he stressed that the factors he was setting out were only those which appeared to him to be the ones most likely to weigh heavily with the court in such circumstances. These were as follows:

1. The materiality of the facts not disclosed.
2. The extent to which it might be said that the plaintiff is culpable in respect of a failure to disclose. A deliberate misleading of the court is likely to weigh more heavily in favour of the discretion being exercised against the continuance of an injunction than an innocent omission. There are obviously intermediate cases where the court may not be satisfied that there was a deliberate attempt to mislead but that the plaintiff was, nonetheless, significantly culpable in failing to disclose.
3. The overall circumstances of the case which led to the application in the first place.[706]

Applying those criteria to the case before him, Clarke J concluded that it seemed to him that the non-disclosed facts were of significant materiality. In his view there was a very real possibility that the court would either have made no order or required short service and considered making an order in relation to a significantly lesser sum if it had been apprised of the full facts. While he was not prepared to hold on the evidence that the plaintiff had deliberately misled the court, he felt that as a solicitor he ought to have been aware of his duty to disclose all material facts and must be regarded as significantly culpable in failing to bring to the court's attention matters which on any objective view would have had the potential to influence its determination. Clarke J concluded that he should exercise his discretion in favour of the defendant's application to discharge the interim order and against any consideration of the merits of granting a further order.

Finally, it should be noted that in *Irish Bank Resolution Corporation Ltd v Quinn*[707] Kelly J held that the court may make an order that a defendant be called

705. *Ibid.* at 89.
706. *Ibid.* These principles were also applied by Clarke J in *F.McK. v D.C.* [2006] IEHC 185 in the context of the circumstances in which the court might exercise its discretion not to discharge an interim freezing order made pursuant to s. 2 of the Proceeds of Crime Act 1996. See also *Baínne Aláinn Ltd v Glanbia plc* [2014] IEHC 482 at [20]; *Murphy v Launceston Property Finance Ltd* [2017] IEHC 65 at [36].
707. [2012] 4 IR 381.

for cross-examination on his affidavit if it considers that the disclosure made is inadequate. As he commented, 'Mareva type orders are of little use unless the recipient of such an order knows the true asset position of the defendant'.[708] Kelly J referred to the judgment of Cumming-Bruce LJ in the decision of the Court of Appeal in *House of Spring Gardens Ltd v Waite*[709] and said that it supports the idea that cross-examination should be permitted 'not merely in circumstances of conflict on affidavit but in order to fill the vacuum alleged to exist in the disclosure affidavits'.[710] In his view that decision and the decision of the Court of Appeal in *Bekhor Ltd v Bilton*[711] demonstrated an entitlement on the part of the court to direct cross-examination in order to assist in the policing of a Mareva injunction and he made an order requiring the attendance of some of the defendants for cross-examination.

Prerequisites for the Granting of a Mareva Injunction

Although a Mareva injunction is a form of interlocutory injunction, it has been argued that the strength of the plaintiff's case is more important in Mareva proceedings than where other types of interlocutory order are sought,[712] and there is authority in England to the effect that 'a "good arguable case" is no doubt the minimum which the plaintiff must show in order to cross ... the "threshold" for the exercise of the jurisdiction.'[713] This standard also seemed to be required by McWilliam J in *Fleming v Ranks (Ireland) Ltd*,[714] although he declined to grant a Mareva injunction on the basis of the facts before him.

The standard of proof required has been considered further in more recent cases. In *Moloney v Laurib Investments Ltd*,[715] in which the plaintiff sought a Mareva injunction pending the trial of her action against the defendant for damages for personal injuries, Lynch J concluded that the plaintiff had a 'stateable case' against the defendant company and said that it was not appropriate that he should seek to establish anything more regarding the issue of liability at the hearing of the application. However, in the circumstances, Lynch J doubted that the grant of the order sought would improve the plaintiff's prospects of enforcing a judgment in her favour, and having regard to his findings that the grant of such an injunction would cause very serious loss to the defendant which could not be made good if the company were ultimately

---

708. *Ibid.* at 393.
709. [1985] FSR 173.
710. [2012] 4 IR 381, 394.
711. [1981] QB 923.
712. See Capper, *Mareva Injunctions* (1988) p. 34.
713. *The Niedersachsen* [1984] 1 All ER 398, 415. This standard is well-established, see e.g. *Fiona Trust Holding Corporation v Privalov* [2007] EWHC 1217 (Comm) at [17].
714. [1983] ILRM 541, 546.
715. High Court 1993 No. 3189P (Lynch J) 20 July 1993.

successful and also bearing in mind the probable prejudice to the rights of its *bona fide* creditors, Lynch J declined to grant the relief sought.

This question was given more extensive consideration by Murphy J in *Countyglen plc v Carway*,[716] in which he stressed that it would be wrong to require a plaintiff seeking a Mareva injunction to establish as a probability that his claim would succeed. The applicant company brought proceedings against the respondents seeking various orders including a declaration that they had been guilty of fraud and/or conspiracy to defraud, breach of trust and breach of duty and orders pursuant to section 12 of the Companies Act 1990 directing the respondents to repay sums which they had allegedly unlawfully and wrongfully removed from the company. The High Court granted an interim Mareva injunction and the issue of whether to grant an interlocutory order and ancillary relief then came before the court. Murphy J stated that he doubted that there was any significant difference between the expressions 'good arguable case' and 'substantial question to be tried', but he said that if such a distinction could be drawn he would prefer the latter formulation. He confirmed that the 'probability test' had been rejected by the Supreme Court in *Campus Oil* and stated 'in my view, it would be entirely inappropriate for the court on an interlocutory application to review such of the evidence as is available to it and attempt to forecast the outcome of the proceedings as a matter of probability or likelihood. What can and should be done is to determine that there is a fair and serious question to be tried.'[717] Murphy J stated that considerations different from those pertaining to conventional injunctions arose in relation to the risk of the defendant's assets being dissipated in advance of any judgment and also with regard to the general balance of convenience. On the basis of the evidence available to the court, Murphy J concluded that the proper inference to draw was that the defendants did have assets within the jurisdiction, that there was a real risk that these assets would be dissipated and that the defendants were not apprehensive of any real inconvenience being caused to them as a result of a Mareva injunction being granted and he made the order sought.

It is interesting to note that in *O'Mahony v Horgan*,[718] which will be considered in more detail below, the Supreme Court seemed to favour the 'good arguable case' test. While Capper suggests that it may be more difficult to establish this than that there is a serious or substantial question to be tried, he also says that the differences between the two tests should not be exaggerated.[719] In any event, as we will see, it is the other aspects of the proofs required to establish an entitlement to a Mareva injunction which clearly differentiate such applications from those in which an ordinary interlocutory injunction is sought.

A consideration of the balance of convenience between the parties will necessarily involve the weighing up of different factors to those which will

716. [1995] 1 ILRM 481.
717. *Ibid.* at 487.
718. [1995] 2 IR 411.
719. (1995) 17 DULJ 110, 114.

normally be of relevance where an interlocutory injunction is sought. In the first instance, the plaintiff will not usually be seeking an injunction at trial, but rather an award of damages which the Mareva order is designed to safeguard. Similarly, the question of the adequacy of damages as a remedy, which is often of considerable importance in deciding where the balance of convenience lies, will not be a factor. Instead the court will be required to weigh up the plaintiff's claim for relief against the likelihood of undue hardship or inconvenience being caused to the defendant. Finally, it should be borne in mind that a Mareva injunction, like any other form of equitable remedy, is granted on the basis of equitable principles and at the discretion of the court and will not be made in favour of a plaintiff whose conduct has been questionable in nature.[720]

Before a court will be satisfied that there is a real risk that a defendant is likely to frustrate the court's judgment by disposing of his assets, it will generally be necessary to establish either that they will be removed from the jurisdiction or that they will be dissipated within the jurisdiction.[721] Different considerations obviously apply to an extra-territorial Mareva injunction and these will be considered below. In relation to the risk of removal of assets from the jurisdiction, the defendant's domicile and place of residence or business may be of significance. In *Powerscourt Estates Ltd v Gallagher*,[722] in which McWilliam J granted a Mareva injunction against the defendants, the fact that they were directors of a group of companies, many of which were located outside the jurisdiction, was relevant as this would have facilitated the removal of assets from the jurisdiction of the Irish courts.

One of the most important issues which must be addressed in the context of Mareva injunctions is the extent to which it is necessary to adduce evidence that the defendant's intention is to frustrate the judgment of the court. This issue was considered by McWilliam J in *Fleming v Ranks (Ireland) Ltd.*[723] A union issued strike notice and the first defendant announced that its mills would have to close. The plaintiff employees sought a Mareva injunction restraining the defendants from dealing with their assets so as to reduce their value below a certain level. McWilliam J stated as follows:

> I am of opinion that, to justify such an injunction, the anticipated disposal of a defendant's assets must be for the purpose of preventing a plaintiff from recovering damages and not merely for the purpose of carrying on a business or discharging lawful debts.[724]

---

720. *The Assios* [1979] 1 Lloyd's Rep 331, 334 *per* Shaw LJ.
721. See *Larkins v National Union of Mineworkers* [1985] IR 671, 694.
722. [1984] ILRM 123. See Capper, *Mareva Injuctions* (1988) p. 40.
723. [1983] ILRM 541.
724. *Ibid.* at 546. Murphy J also drew attention to this point in *Countyglen plc v Carway* [1995] 1 ILRM 481, 488 and said that McWilliam J had declined to make the order sought in the *Ranks* case as he accepted that there had been no intention of disposing of assets with a view to evading any obligation to the plaintiff.

McWilliam J concluded that the balance of convenience clearly favoured the defendants, both on account of the perishable nature of the goods which they sought to dispose of and having regard to the fact that any undertaking in damages given by the plaintiffs would be of little value. Subsequently, in *Powerscourt*, McWilliam J echoed this view when he stated that a Mareva injunction may be granted where 'it appears to the court that dispositions are likely to be made for the purpose of preventing a plaintiff from recovering the amount of his award, as distinct from conducting the normal business or personal affairs of the defendant'.[725]

This issue was also addressed in some detail by the Supreme Court in *O'Mahony v Horgan*.[726] The applicant had been appointed liquidator of a company of which the respondents were directors. Murphy J granted an interlocutory injunction to restrain the second named respondent from disposing of or dissipating a sum of money payable under an insurance policy. The Supreme Court allowed the appeal of the second named respondent. It held that before a plaintiff will be entitled to a Mareva injunction, he must establish that there is a likelihood that the defendant's assets will be dissipated with the intention that they would not be available to meet any decree ultimately made in the proceedings and found that this intention had not been established in the case before the court. Hamilton CJ stated that:

> [T]he cases establish that there must be an intention on the part of the defendant to dispose of his assets with a view to evading his obligation to the plaintiff and to frustrate the anticipated order of the court. It is not sufficient to establish that the assets are likely to be dissipated in the ordinary course of business or in the payment of lawful debts.[727]

Commenting on this decision, Courtney stated that the Supreme Court had clarified the fact that an applicant for a Mareva injunction must adduce specific evidence of 'the requisite intention'[728] and he expressed the opinion that this requirement would be given greater emphasis in the future, a view borne out by two High Court decisions delivered soon afterwards. In *Production Association Minsk Tractor Works v Saenko*[729] McCracken J quoted the above passage from *O'Mahony* and stated that he did not think that there was any evidence before him to establish an intention on the part of the defendants to dispose of assets with a view to evading their obligations to the plaintiff or frustrating the anticipated order of the court. He stressed that a Mareva injunction is 'an extremely drastic remedy' and concluded that the plaintiffs had not satisfied the

725. [1984] ILRM 123, 126.
726. [1995] 2 IR 411.
727. *Ibid.* at 419. Quoted with approval by O'Sullivan J in *Bennett Enterprises Inc. v Lipton* [1999] 2 IR 221, 228. See also *Aerospares Ltd v Thompson* [1999] IEHC 76 at 4.
728. Courtney (1996) 3 Comm LP 3, 8.
729. [1998] IEHC 36.

criteria necessary to succeed in their application. Similarly, in *OBA Enterprises Ltd v TMC Trading International Ltd*,[730] Laffoy J quoted the same passage from *O'Mahony* and concluded that in her view the plaintiffs had not adduced evidence to show, or entitle her to infer, that the defendant was likely to dissipate its assets with the intention of evading its obligations, if any, to the plaintiffs.

In contrast, the approach of the English courts has tended to focus on the effect of the defendant's actions rather than on his intention. In *The Niedersachsen*[731] Kerr LJ accepted that no 'nefarious intent' was required and said that the plaintiff need only establish a real risk that a judgment in his favour would remain unsatisfied.[732] Similarly, in *Congentra AG v Sixteen Thirteen Marine SA*,[733] Flaux J stated that a claimant must establish first, that there is a real risk that a judgment or award will go unsatisfied, in the sense of a real risk that the defendant will dissipate or dispose of his assets other than in the ordinary course of business and secondly, that unless the defendant is restrained by injunction, assets are likely to be dealt with in such a way as to make enforcement of any award or judgment more difficult.

As Capper has pointed out, it may be unrealistic to expect a plaintiff to be in a position to adduce evidence of a defendant's intentions in this regard in making an *ex parte* application,[734] and a more flexible approach may be necessary when a Mareva injunction is sought on this basis, as will usually be the case in practice. He went on to suggest that 'an intention may be inferred from the risk that assets will be disposed of for no good reason'.[735] Courtney proposed that the court might be invited to draw an inference from the facts and circumstances of the case and from the disposition and conduct of the defendant.[736] He also expressed the view that where a plaintiff establishes a good arguable case of fraud or other nefarious activity, a court may be more inclined to accept that there is a likelihood that a defendant's future actions may be motivated by improper intentions.

A more pragmatic approach towards the issue of establishing the so-called 'requisite intention' was taken by O'Sullivan J in *Bennett Enterprises Inc. v Lipton*,[737] discussed in more detail below in the context of extra-territorial Mareva injunctions. He stressed that if any dissipation of assets were to occur in the ordinary course of business, this of itself would not justify the granting of a Mareva injunction and that the anticipated dissipation must be for the

---

730. [1998] IEHC 169. See Courtney (1999) 6 Comm LP 39.
731. [1984] 1 All ER 398.
732. See also *Derby & Co. Ltd v Weldon (Nos. 3 & 4)* [1990] Ch 65, 76; *Ketchum v Group Public Relations* [1997] 1 WLR 4, 13; *Cherny v Neuman* [2009] EWHC 1743 (Ch).
733. [2008] EWHC 1615 (Comm) at [49]. See also *Linsen International Ltd v Humpuss Sea Transport Pte Ltd* [2010] EWHC 303 (Comm) at [83].
734. Capper, *Mareva Injunctions* (1988) p. 48. See also Capper (1995) 17 DULJ 110, 117.
735. Capper (1995) 17 DULJ 110, 119.
736. Courtney, *Mareva Injunctions and Related Interlocutory Orders* (1998) para. 6.29.
737. [1999] 2 IR 211. See Courtney (1999) 6 Comm LP 39.

purpose of the defendant evading his obligation to the plaintiff. He then went on to state as follows:

> Equally, however, I consider that direct evidence of an intention to evade will rarely be available at the interlocutory stage. I consider it is legitimate for me to consider all the circumstances in relation to the case and I do not consider that this approach is in any way prohibited by or at variance with the principles set out in the Supreme Court judgment in *O'Mahony v Horgan*.[738]

A similar attitude was adopted by Clarke J in *Tracey v Bowen*,[739] where the defendant contended that the plaintiff had produced insufficient evidence for suggesting that there were grounds for believing that there was a risk that the defendant's assets might be removed from the jurisdiction or dissipated. However, counsel for the plaintiff relied on the *dictum* of O'Sullivan J in *Bennett Enterprises Inc. v Lipton*[740] set out above and Clarke J stated that it seemed to him that *Bennett* and the subsequent decision of Kearns J in *Aerospares Ltd v Thompson*[741] were authority for the proposition that:

> [I]n assessing the risk of dissipation the court is entitled to take into account all the circumstances of the case which can include, in an appropriate case, an inference drawn from the nature of the wrongdoing alleged which if fraudulent or unconscionable may lead to the establishment of a risk that further fraudulent or unconscionable actions will be taken so as to place any assets of the defendant outside the jurisdiction of the court.[742]

However, he added that it should be noted that the court is required to look at all the circumstances of the case and the above factors are likely to be of much greater significance in cases where the only assets of the defendant within the jurisdiction are liquid assets capable of being moved about with great ease and in particular where the defendant is 'experienced in intricate, sophisticated, international transactions involving movements of large sums of money'.[743] Clarke J stated that it seemed to him that the considerations referred to above are of significantly less weight where, as in the case before him, the plaintiff appeared to have real property within the jurisdiction which at least *prima facie* seemed sufficient to meet any claim which the plaintiff might have. He

738. *Ibid.* at 228. See also *Lehane v Dunne* [2017] IEHC 511 at [42].
739. [2005] 2 IR 528.
740. [1992] 2 IR 221.
741. [1999] IEHC 76.
742. [2005] IEHC 138 at 6. See also *McCourt v Tiernan* [2005] IEHC 268 at 16; *Hughes v Hitachi Koki Imaging Solutions Europe* [2006] 3 IR 457, 464.
743. Gee, *Mareva Injunctions and Anton Piller Relief* (4th ed., 1998) p.198. Now see Gee, *Commercial Injunctions* (5th ed., 2004).

concluded that many of these assertions made by the plaintiff in his affidavit were highly contentious and in all the circumstances of the case he was not satisfied that any of the factors referred to whether taken alone or collectively were sufficient to create a reasonable apprehension that the plaintiff would dissipate his assets in an inappropriate fashion.

Clarke J developed the approach adopted by O'Sullivan J in *Bennett* further in *Hughes v Hitachi Koki Imaging Solutions Europe*,[744] where he stated that the 'requisite intention' will in most cases have to be established by inference from other facts. He stated that while *O'Mahony v Horgan* was clear authority for the proposition that the payment of lawful debts in the course of an ongoing business should not give rise to any inference sufficient to justify the grant of a Mareva injunction, there was at least in principle a need to apply different considerations to a corporate entity which might be insolvent. Clarke J continued as follows:

> I am, therefore, satisfied that, in principle, it is open to a plaintiff to seek a Mareva type injunction in circumstances where it can be shown that an insolvent corporate entity intends to deal with its assets in a manner which would be in breach of the obligations on the company and its directors to ensure that those assets are maintained in a fashion which would enable them to be applied in accordance with corporate insolvency law.[745]

Therefore, where it could be demonstrated that the company in question intended to deal with its assets in a manner which would be in breach of its obligations and where such action was likely to affect the plaintiff's position, Clarke J said that it seemed to him that the 'requisite intention' required to justify the grant of a Mareva injunction would be established.

A further watering down of the test of establishing a risk of dissipation of assets was suggested by Keane J in *Bonice Property Corporation v Oakes*.[746] He stated that given that the matter before him was a case in which the underlying claim was one of fraud or dishonesty, involving a scheme for the misappropriation of the plaintiffs' funds through the unconscionable acts of the defendant, if the court were to find there to be a good arguable case to that effect, 'no further specific evidence of risk of dissipation of assets would be strictly necessary for the Court to be entitled to take the view that such risk has been established.'[747] However, he concluded in any event that, on the evidence, it was appropriate to draw the inference that there was a risk of dissipation of the defendant's assets with a view to defeating the plaintiffs' claim if the court did not restrain this conduct and he granted the Mareva relief sought.

So, in summary, while it is now clearly established that the so-called 'requisite intention' can be inferred from the circumstances of the case, the

744. [2006] 3 IR 457.
745. *Ibid.* at 464.
746. [2016] IEHC 461.
747. *Ibid.* at [30].

obiter comments of Keane J in *Bonice Property Corporation* should be treated with some caution. Given the potentially far reaching nature of the relief sought and the importance of balancing the rights of both plaintiffs and defendants in such cases, it is likely that the risk of dissipation of assets will still need to be established, even if this can be shown by the drawing of inferences from the underlying circumstances of the wrongdoing alleged.

It is clear from the judgment of Birmingham J in *Collins v Gharion*[748] that where the court is dealing with a defendant company which is a special purpose vehicle that has never traded or carried on a business as such, the phrase 'ordinary course of business' may not be a helpful one. In such circumstances he suggested that it might be useful to substitute a phrase such as 'in the ordinary way' or 'in the ordinary course of events' for 'in the ordinary course of business' and that the focus should be on whether the disposal of assets is proposed with the intention of evading obligations to the plaintiff and to frustrate anticipated court orders. On the facts of the case before him, he concluded that the plaintiff had not established an intention on the part of the defendant to put its assets beyond reach or frustrate future orders of the court and he refused the relief sought.

Finally, the relevance of the fact that a defendant may seek to remove assets from the jurisdiction to another country which is a party to what is now the Brussels I Regulation (recast)[749] with a view to evading his obligation to the plaintiff was considered by Clarke J in an *obiter* context in *Bambrick v Cobley*.[750] Clarke J stated that it seemed to him that where a defendant had readily identifiable assets which were held in a country to which the Brussels Regulation or Convention applied that was a factor which the court could properly take into account in assessing whether there was a real risk that the removal of further assets from this jurisdiction to another Convention country could be said to be 'with a view to evading obligations'. While the removal of assets from this jurisdiction to another could, of itself, be such as to give rise to an inference of a reasonable risk of evasion of obligation, that inference would weigh less strongly in a case where the second country was a Convention country and where the judgment of the court would be as enforceable as within the jurisdiction. Clarke J concluded that having regard to the weight which

---

748. [2013] IEHC 316.
749. The recognition and enforcement of judgments as between the Member States of the European Union is now governed by Regulation (EU) No. 1215/2012 on Jurisdiction and the Recognition and Enforcement of Judgments in Civil and Commercial Matters (Brussels I Regulation (recast)), which replaces Council Regulation (EC) No. 44/2001. Note that Denmark opted into the Brussels I Regulation by way of the 2005 Agreement between the European Community and the Kingdom of Denmark on jurisdiction and the recognition and enforcement of judgments in civil and commercial matters. See also the Lugano Convention 2007 on Jurisdiction and the Recognition and Enforcement of Judgments in Civil and Commercial Matters which replaced the Lugano Convention of 16 September 1988.
750. [2006] 1 ILRM 81.

should properly be attached to the removal of assets to the United Kingdom he was not satisfied that the plaintiff had discharged the onus of establishing that the removal of any further assets to the United Kingdom would be 'with a view to evading obligations'.

Extra-Territorial Mareva Injunctions

One of the most significant developments in relation to Mareva injunctions in recent years has been the willingness of the courts to make such orders in respect of assets outside the jurisdiction on a worldwide basis.[751] Originally Mareva injunctions were of a more limited nature and as Dillon LJ commented in *Ashtiani v Kashi*,[752] 'the basis of the jurisdiction, as it seems to me, is clearly limited to the assets within the jurisdiction of this court'. The reasons for this practice were far from compelling,[753] and in a series of decisions in the late 1980s, the English Court of Appeal extended the scope of Mareva injunctions to cover worldwide assets. However, in doing so the courts have had regard to the principle that '[c]onsiderations of comity require the [domestic] courts... to refrain from making orders which infringe the exclusive jurisdiction of the courts of other countries.'[754]

In *Babanaft International Co. SA v Bassatne*[755] such an order was granted against the defendants who held assets in a number of foreign jurisdictions as well as in England and against whom judgment in the sum of $15 million had been obtained. Kerr LJ concluded that 'in appropriate cases, though they may well be rare, there is nothing to preclude our courts from granting Mareva type injunctions against defendants which extend to their assets outside the jurisdiction.'[756] However, he stressed that unqualified Mareva injunctions covering assets abroad can never be justified as they involve an exorbitant assertion of jurisdiction of an *in rem* nature over third parties outside the jurisdiction of the court. It was therefore necessary to restrict such injunctions so as to bind only the defendant personally and to include a limiting proviso which made it clear that the order would not affect third parties.[757]

Extra-territorial Mareva injunctions are more likely to be granted after judgment has been obtained, as the risk that such an order will be made in favour of a party who is wrongly asserting a cause of action is removed, and it has been stressed that pre-judgment orders will be granted on a worldwide

---

751. See generally Capper (1991) 54 MLR 329.
752. [1987] QB 888, 899.
753. See Collins (1989) 105 LQR 262, 269.
754. *Derby & Co. Ltd v Weldon (Nos. 3 & 4)* [1990] Ch 65, 82. See also *Masri v Consolidated Contractors (UK) Ltd (No. 2)* [2009] QB 450, 465.
755. [1990] Ch 13.
756. *Ibid.* at 28.
757. Although it should be noted that Kerr LJ suggested (at 37) that it might be better to add 'unless and to the extent that it is enforced by the courts of the states in which any of the defendants' assets are located.'

basis less readily than after trial.[758] In *Republic of Haiti v Duvalier*[759] the Court of Appeal granted a pre-trial Mareva injunction against the assets of the defendants on a worldwide basis although Staughton LJ stressed that the cases in which it would be appropriate to grant such an injunction were 'rare — if not very rare indeed'.[760] The other notable feature of this decision is that the limiting proviso was extended to the effect that the order should not affect any third parties unless and to the extent that it is enforced by the courts of the state in which the defendants' assets are located. Similarly, in *Derby & Co. Ltd v Weldon*[761] the Court of Appeal granted a worldwide Mareva injunction prior to judgment in view of the large sums of money involved, the insufficiency of assets within the jurisdiction, the existence of foreign assets and the finding that there was a real risk that they would be dissipated before the trial. A point made by the Court of Appeal and subsequently reiterated by it in *Derby & Co. Ltd v Weldon (Nos. 3 & 4)*[762] is that a Mareva injunction should be limited to assets within the jurisdiction of the court if these are sufficient to meet the plaintiff's claim. However, there will often be insufficient domestic assets or even none at all and the court stressed in the latter case that this will not be a bar to obtaining an order on a worldwide basis.

A further attempt was made by the Court of Appeal in *Derby & Co. Ltd v Weldon (Nos. 3 & 4)* to clarify the position of third parties by putting forward a modified version of what had become known as the '*Babanaft* proviso'.[763] This new version of the proviso abolished what was seen as the rather artificial distinction drawn between legal and juridical persons and gave the order extra-territorial effect over persons who were subject to the jurisdiction of the court making the order who had been given written notice of it and who were in a position to 'prevent acts or omissions outside the jurisdiction of this court which assist in the breach of the terms of this order'. This modified proviso was developed further in the decision of *Baltic Shipping Co. v Translink Shipping Ltd*,[764] in which Clarke J suggested that in general and subject to the facts of a particular case, a proviso along the following lines should be adopted,[765] namely, that 'nothing in this order shall, in respect of assets located outside [the jurisdiction], prevent [the third party] or its subsidiaries from complying with…what it reasonably believes to be its obligations, contractual or otherwise

758. *Babanaft International Co. SA v Bassatne* [1990] Ch 13, 40 *per* Neill LJ; *Republic of Haiti v Duvalier* [1990] QB 202, 214 *per* Staughton LJ.
759. [1990] QB 202.
760. *Ibid.* at 215.
761. [1990] Ch 48.
762. [1990] Ch 65.
763. *Ibid.* at 84.
764. [1995] 1 Lloyd's Rep 673.
765. This suggestion was put forward by Saville J, the judge in charge of the Commercial Court, in his end of year statement on 30 July 1993. The relevant part of this statement is set out in *Baltic Shipping Co. v Translink Shipping Ltd* [1995] 1 Lloyd's Rep 673, 675 and *Bank of China v NBM LLC* [2002] 1 WLR 844, 849.

under the laws and obligations of the country or state in which the assets are situated or under the proper law of any bank account in question.' This form of proviso, sometimes referred to as the '*Baltic* proviso', has been approved by the Court of Appeal in *Bank of China v NBM LLC*[766] in upholding a decision to vary a Mareva injunction on the application of a third party by extending the proviso in this way. Tuckey LJ stated that the cases established two general principles: first, that the limits of the court's territorial jurisdiction and the principle of comity require that the effectiveness of freezing orders operating on third parties holding assets abroad should normally derive only from their recognition and enforcement by the local courts and secondly, that third parties amenable to the English jurisdiction should be given all reasonable protection. He concluded that the need to avoid unwanted extra-territorial jurisdiction and to provide reasonable protection for third parties affected by freezing orders will usually entitle them to have a proviso in the form set out above added unless the court considers that on the particular facts it is inappropriate.

A further important question is the circumstances in which the court's discretion should be exercised to permit a party to enforce a Mareva injunction, or worldwide freezing order as it is now known, in another jurisdiction. This issue arose before the Court of Appeal in *Dadourian Group International Inc. v Simms*,[767] in which the appellants sought to have an order granting permission to enforce a worldwide freezing order in Switzerland set aside. Given that this appeared to be the first time that this question had arisen directly in an appeal, Arden LJ stated that the court would set out guidelines which would apply when an application to enforce a worldwide freezing order abroad is made and it is useful to set these out in full.

> Guideline 1: The principle applying to the grant of permission to enforce a WFO abroad is that the grant of that permission should be just and convenient for the purpose of ensuring the effectiveness of the WFO, and in addition that it is not oppressive to the parties to the English proceedings or to third parties who may be joined to the foreign proceedings.
>
> Guideline 2: All the relevant circumstances and options need to be considered. In particular consideration should be given to granting relief on terms, for example terms as to the extension to third parties of the undertaking to compensate for costs incurred as a result of the WFO and as to the type of proceedings that may be commenced abroad. Consideration should also be given to the proportionality of the steps proposed to be taken abroad, and*Ibid.* at 388 in addition to the form of any order.
>
> Guideline 3: The interests of the applicant should be balanced against the

766. [2002] 1 WLR 844.
767. [2006] 1 WLR 2499. See further Meisel (2007) 26 CJQ 176.

> interests of the other parties to the proceedings and any new party likely to be joined to the foreign proceedings.
>
> Guideline 4: Permission should not normally be given in terms that would enable the applicant to obtain relief in the foreign proceedings which is superior to the relief given by the WFO.
>
> Guideline 5: The evidence in support of the application for permission should contain all the information (so far as it can reasonably be obtained in the time available) necessary to enable the judge to reach an informed decision, including evidence as to the applicable law and practice in the foreign court, evidence as to the nature of the proposed proceedings to be commenced and evidence as to the assets believed to be located in the jurisdiction of the foreign court and the names of the parties by whom such assets are held.
>
> Guideline 6: The standard of proof as to the existence of assets that are both within the WFO and within the jurisdiction of the foreign court is a real prospect, that is the applicant must show that there is a real prospect that such assets are located within the jurisdiction of the foreign court in question.
>
> Guideline 7: There must be evidence of a risk of dissipation of the assets in question.
>
> Guideline 8: Normally the application should be made on notice to the respondent, but in cases of urgency, where it is just to do so, the permission may be given without notice to the party against whom relief will be sought in the foreign proceedings but that party should have the earliest practicable opportunity of having the matter reconsidered by the court at a hearing of which he is given notice.[768]

Arden LJ concluded that the appellants had not pointed to any matter which, under the *Dadourian* guidelines set out above, should have been considered which would have prevented the exercise by the judge of his discretion to continue the permission given to enforce the worldwide freezing order in Switzerland. In these circumstances the respondents had discharged the onus of showing that there was a real prospect that the appellants had assets in Switzerland and the court concluded that in the light of the history of the matter it was reasonable and proportionate for the respondents to seek to enforce the worldwide freezing order in Switzerland in order to safeguard their rights in relation to those assets.

768. *Ibid.* at 2502-2503. See also *Belletti v Morici* [2009] EWHC 2316 (Comm) at [67].

The fact that Mareva injunctions may be made on a worldwide basis in this jurisdiction was confirmed by the High Court in *Deutsche Bank Atkiengesellchaft v Murtagh.*[769] The plaintiff sought an order restraining the defendants from dealing with extra-territorial assets. Costello J was satisfied that 'the court has jurisdiction to restrain the dissipation of extra-territorial assets where such an order is warranted by the facts'.[770] He said that it was well-established in England that a Mareva injunction may extend to foreign assets and that he believed the Irish courts had similar powers to avoid frustration of subsequent orders. It should be noted that the order made a month later by Murphy J in *Countyglen plc v Carway*[771] was confined to assets of the defendants within the jurisdiction, but this was the extent of the order sought by the plaintiffs. His comment that a Mareva injunction should be restricted to assets within the jurisdiction of the court must be viewed as purely *obiter*.

One of the most significant judgments in this context is that of O'Sullivan J in *Bennett Enterprises Ltd v Lipton.*[772] The plaintiffs instituted proceedings against the defendants for breach of contract and sought, *inter alia*, an interlocutory injunction restraining the defendants from reducing the monies in certain trust funds below a stated sum. O'Sullivan J stated that it was clear that the defendants had no assets within the jurisdiction but he did not consider that the plaintiffs' alleged failure to establish that there were assets within the jurisdiction was necessarily fatal to their application. On the contrary, he said that he could see the logic in the observation of Donaldson MR in *Derby & Co. Ltd v Weldon (Nos. 3 & 4)*[773] to the effect that the fewer the assets within the jurisdiction the greater the necessity for taking protective measures in relation to those outside it. O'Sullivan J also pointed out that in *Babanaft* Kerr LJ had stated that 'some situations, which are nowadays by no means uncommon, cry out — as a matter of justice to plaintiffs — for disclosure orders and Mareva type injunctions covering foreign assets of defendants even before judgment.'[774] The plaintiffs accepted that any order which the court might make would be subject to the '*Babanaft* proviso' and O'Sullivan J concluded that he would make an interlocutory order as sought by the plaintiffs and stated that he would discuss with counsel the precise form of the order.

A further important aspect of Mareva jurisdiction which has particular relevance in the context of worldwide orders is the power to make ancillary orders, for example requiring disclosure of the defendant's assets. This was adverted to by Ackner LJ in *Bekhor & Co. v Bilton,*[775] where he stated that the court has power to make 'all such ancillary orders as appear to the court

769. [1995] 1 ILRM 381.
770. *Ibid.* at 388.
771. [1995] 1 ILRM 481.
772. [1999] 2 IR 221. See Courtney (1999) 6 Comm LP 39.
773. [1990] Ch 65.
774. [1990] 1 Ch 13, 33.
775. [1981] QB 923, 940.

to be just and convenient, to ensure the exercise of the Mareva jurisdiction is effective to achieve its purpose'. Costello J also referred to this power to make ancillary orders in *Deutsche Bank Atkiengesellchaft v Murtagh* and said that in a suitable case the court will grant a disclosure order requiring the defendant to swear an affidavit in relation to assets outside the jurisdiction. It is certainly in the context of worldwide orders that ancillary powers take on the greatest significance and it may even prove to be of more significant practical importance than the Mareva injunction itself. As Collins has pointed out, if proper disclosure is made in relation to the defendant's foreign assets, the plaintiff will be able to seek an attachment order in relation to these assets in the relevant foreign jurisdiction.[776] The Court of Appeal re-emphasised the importance of disclosure orders in *Grupo Torras SA v Sheikh Fahad Mohammad Al-Sabah*.[777] The plaintiff obtained a Mareva injunction against the defendant together with an ancillary order requiring him to disclose the nature and extent of his assets both in England and abroad. The court rejected the defendant's application to have the disclosure order discharged and reaffirmed the importance of orders of this nature. As Steyn LJ commented, without such ancillary powers, the Mareva injunction itself 'would be a relatively toothless procedure in the fight against rampant transnational fraud'.

Provisional and Protective Measures

By virtue of the provisions of Article 35 of Regulation (EU) No. 1215/2012 on Jurisdiction and the Recognition and Enforcement of Judgments in Civil and Commercial Matters (Brussels I Regulation (recast)),[778] an application may be made to the courts of a Member State[779] for such provisional measures, including protective measures, as may be available under the law of that state, even if the court of another Member State has jurisdiction in relation to the substance of the matter. In addition, Article 40 provides that an enforceable judgment shall carry with it the power to proceed to any protective measures which exist under the law of the Member State addressed. The European Court of Justice made it clear in *Van Uden Maritime BV v Kommanditgesellschaft in Firma Deco-Line*[780] that 'the granting of provisional or protective measures on the basis of Article [35] is conditional on, *inter alia*, the existence of a real connecting link between the subject matter of the measures sought and the territorial jurisdiction

776. Collins (1989) 105 LQR 262, 297.
777. [2014] 2 CLC 636.
778. Regulation (EU) No. 1215/2012 replaces Council Regulation (EC) No. 44/2001. This article replaces Article 31 of Regulation No. 44/2001 which in turn replaced Article 24 of the Brussels Convention on Jurisdiction and the Recognition and Enforcement of Judgments in Civil and Commercial Matters 1968.
779. This regulation binds all Member States with the exception of Denmark which agreed to implement the contents of the Regulation.
780. [1999] 1 QB 1225, 1257. See also *Mietz v Intership Yachting Sneek BV* (Case C-99/96) [1999] ECR I–2277.

of the contracting state of the court before which those measures are sought'. In addition, it should be noted that it can be deduced from the decision of the Court of Appeal in *Banco Nacional de Comercio Exterior SNC v Empresa de Telecomunicaciones de Cuba SA*[781] that where a defendant is not resident in the jurisdiction and any assets within the jurisdiction may be protected by a domestic order, the courts will decline to grant a Mareva injunction of an extra-territorial nature on the basis that there is 'no connecting link'.

Article 8(1) of the European Communities (Civil and Commercial Judgments) Regulations 2015, which gives effect to the Brussels I Regulation (recast) in this jurisdiction, provides that the High Court may grant provisional, including protective, measures – which may include a Mareva injunction – where proceedings have been commenced or are to be commenced in another member state and the subject matter of the proceedings is within the scope of the Regulation.[782] This means that such measures may be granted by the courts here even where the plaintiff has no independent cause of action within this jurisdiction.[783] However, Article 8(2) goes on to provide that the High Court may refuse to grant the measures sought if, in its opinion, the fact that, apart from this provision, the court does not have jurisdiction in relation to the subject matter of the proceedings makes it inexpedient for it to grant the measure.

The equivalent provision in England, section 25(2) of the English Civil Jurisdiction and Judgments Act 1982, was fairly broadly interpreted in *Credit Suisse Fides Trust SA v Cuoghi*.[784] Millett LJ accepted that an ancillary jurisdiction ought to be exercised with caution and that care should be taken not to make orders which conflict with those of the court seised of the substantive proceedings. However, he did not accept that interim relief should be limited to that which would be available in the court trying the substantive dispute. Although the worldwide Mareva injunction sought would not have been available in Switzerland, where the substantive action had been initiated, Millett LJ was satisfied that there was no danger of conflicting jurisdiction and concluded that it was not inexpedient to grant the protective measures sought.[785] Bingham LJ reached the same conclusion and made the following

---

781. [2008] 1 WLR 1936. See further Merrett [2007] CLJ 495; Merrett [2008] LMCLQ 71.
782. This superseded the provisions of s.13 of the Jurisdiction of Courts and Enforcement of Judgments Act 1998 and regulation 10 of the European Communities (Civil and Commercial Judgments) Regulations 2002 (SI No. 52 of 2002). Order 42A of the Rules of the Superior Courts (substituted by the Rules of the Superior Courts (Jurisdiction, Recognition and Enforcement of Judgments 2016, SI No. 9 of 2016) sets out the procedure for making an application for provisional, including protective, measures.
783. This effectively reversed the finding of the Supreme Court in *Caudron v Air Zaire* [1985] IR 716 that a Mareva injunction could not be claimed as primary relief in an action but only as an ancillary order. See also *The Siskina* [1979] AC 210.
784. [1998] QB 818. See further Samad (2009) 27 ILT 135.
785. See also *Motorola Credit Corporation v Uzan (No. 2)* [2004] 1 WLR 113, where the

useful comments about the relationship between the substantive proceedings and applications for protective measures:

> It would be unwise to attempt to list all of the considerations which might be held to make the grant of relief under s. 25 inexpedient or expedient, whether on a municipal or a worldwide basis. But it would obviously weigh heavily, probably conclusively, against the grant of interim relief if such grant would obstruct or hamper the management of the case by the court seized of the substantive proceedings ('the primary court') or give rise to a risk of conflicting, inconsistent or overlapping orders in other courts. It may weigh against the grant of relief by this court that the primary court could have granted such relief and has not done so, particularly if the primary court has been asked to grant such relief and declined. On the other hand, it may be thought to weigh in favour of granting such relief that a defendant is present in this country and so liable to effective enforcement of an order made *in personam*, always provided that by granting such relief this court does not tread on the toes of the primary court or any other court involved in the case. On any application under s.25 this court must recognise that its role is subordinate to and must be supportive of that of the primary court.[786]

This reasoning was considered by the Court of Appeal in *Refco Inc. v Eastern Trading Co.*,[787] in which protective measures were refused in circumstances where the court was satisfied that no Mareva relief would have been granted even if the substantive proceedings had been brought in England. Morritt LJ advocated first considering whether the facts would warrant granting the interim relief sought if the substantive proceedings had been brought within the jurisdiction and, if the answer to that question was in the affirmative, then considering whether the fact that the court had no jurisdiction apart from under the section made it inexpedient to grant the relief sought.

Walker LJ also stressed in *Mobil Cerro Negro Ltd v Petroleos de Venezuela SA*[788] that a domestic court would only be prepared to exercise its discretion to grant an application in aid of foreign litigation for a freezing order affecting foreign assets if the respondent or the dispute had a sufficiently strong link with the jurisdiction or there was some other factor of sufficient strength to justify proceeding in the absence of such a link. He suggested that it should not be assumed that the presence of the respondent in the jurisdiction would necessarily be sufficient to warrant the exercise of discretion in favour of an applicant, although as Lord Bingham had observed in *Credit Suisse Fides Trust*

Court of Appeal accepted that provided that there was a sufficient connection to enable a Mareva injunction to be enforced it would not be inexpedient to grant such relief.

786. [1998] QB 818, 831-832.
787. [1999] 1 Lloyd's Rep 159.
788. [2008] 1 Lloyd's Rep. 684.

it may weigh in favour of granting relief. In the view of Walker LJ it should not be assumed that any particular factor will be sufficient to justify the making of an order and there should be 'a careful examination of the justification for any part of the proposed order which would tend to run counter to principles of comity with courts in other jurisdictions'.[789]

Conclusions

In the final analysis the effectiveness of Mareva injunctions, particularly those of an extra-territorial nature, will depend on the extent to which the courts can guarantee their observance. It appears to have been accepted that it would be wrong in principle for the courts in one jurisdiction 'to impose or attempt to impose obligations on persons not before the court in respect of acts to be done by them abroad regarding property outside the jurisdiction' on the basis that this would amount to an attempt to claim an 'exorbitant' extra-territorial authority.[790] However, defendants and in particular third parties will often be outside the jurisdiction of the court which has made the Mareva injunction and so will not be amenable to control by that court. As Collins has commented:[791]

> In practice the remedy is likely to be most effective where the defendant is an individual present within the jurisdiction (or a company with offices within the jurisdiction) or if the defendant has a real interest in defending the substance of the English action or (as the case may be) in appealing the English judgment. It is possible that these are the only cases in which the remedy will be effective, and this may be regarded as a cynical but realistic, conclusion.

The far-reaching and often draconian nature of Mareva injunctions is more readily recognised today than when the jurisdiction was first exercised.[792] However, as against this, the sophisticated fraudulent endeavours which can often extend into numerous different jurisdictions are also becoming increasingly difficult to control. There were signs in the decision of the English Court of Appeal in *Polly Peck International plc v Nadir (No. 2)*[793] that the judiciary are more willing to recognise the former consideration than the latter. While Millett J found that the plaintiff had shown an arguable case of liability and granted a Mareva injunction, the Court of Appeal concluded

---

789. *Ibid.* at 704.
790. *Babanaft International Co. SA v Bassatne* [1990] Ch 13, 44 *per* Nicholls LJ. See also the judgment of Neill LJ at 40.
791. Collins (1989) 105 LQR 262, 296.
792. See, e.g. the comments of Hamilton CJ in *O'Mahony v Horgan* [1995] 2 IR 411, 418 and of McCracken J in *Production Association Minsk Tractor Works v Saenko* [1998] IEHC 36 at 5 to the effect that a Mareva injunction is 'an extremely drastic remedy'.
793. [1992] 4 All ER 769.

that the balance of convenience was against its continuance and discharged the order. Scott LJ stressed that as a general principle, a Mareva injunction is not intended to give the plaintiff security in advance of judgment but merely to prevent the defendant from defeating the plaintiff's chances of recovery by dissipating or secreting away assets.[794] He stated that the court will not grant a Mareva injunction before any liability has been established if the injunction would interfere with the normal course of the defendant's business particularly if the cause of action which it was sought to have protected, as in the case before him, was no more than speculative. In his view, to grant a Mareva injunction in these circumstances would be 'not simply wrong in principle but positively unfair'.[795]

Zuckerman commented that the approach of the Court of Appeal in *Polly Peck* restored the Mareva jurisdiction to its true basis as a measure against abuse rather than a form of security for the plaintiff.[796] However, as Tomlinson LJ commented in *Energy Venture Partners Ltd v Malabu Oil and Gas Ltd*[797] 'in many cases … a freezing order has the practical if not theoretical effect of giving security to the Claimant for its claim.' More recently Saranovic has suggested that the courts 'need to avoid the temptation to promote a narrow, one-dimensional view that freezing injunctions are only the claimant's weapon against unscrupulous defendants' and instead argues that freezing injunctions should be seen as a reflection of the principle of 'equipage equality' in order to ensure a level playing field in litigation.[798] He has also argued for the introduction of a requirement of intention to avoid enforcement,[799] although as the analysis above shows, the courts in this jurisdiction appear to regard the requirement of establishing express intention as tipping the balance too far in favour of defendants.

In this jurisdiction there have been signs of a greater willingness to regard Mareva injunctions not as a form of security but rather as a measure against potential abuse. In *Moloney v Laurib Investments Ltd*[800] Lynch J appeared to place emphasis on the fact that the grant of the injunction sought would interfere with the normal course of the defendant's business and that it would cause serious loss which could not subsequently be made good if the defendant were ultimately successful. Signs of a more cautious approach are also evident in the Supreme Court decision of *O'Mahony v Horgan*;[801] as O'Flaherty J commented, 'it needs to be emphasised that the Mareva injunction is a very powerful

794. *Ibid.* at 782. See also *Dowley v O'Brien* [2009] 4 IR 752, 763.
795. *Ibid.* at 784.
796. Zuckerman (1992) 108 LQR 559, 561. As Lord Bingham stated in *Fourie v Le Roux* [2007] 1 WLR 320, 322, 'they are not granted to give a claimant advance security for his claim, although they may have that effect.'
797. [2015] 1 WLR 2309, 2324.
798. (2018) 37 CJQ 383, 388.
799. *Ibid.* at 393.
800. High Court 1993 No. 3189P (Lynch J) 20 July 1993.
801. [1995] 2 IR 411, 422.

remedy which if improperly invoked will bring about an injustice, something that it was designed to prevent'. In that case Hamilton CJ also emphasised that the common law has traditionally taken the position that a plaintiff is not entitled to require a defendant to guarantee satisfaction of a judgment that the former may ultimately obtain.[802] Clarke J addressed the security issue directly in *Bambrick v Cobley*,[803] where he stated that 'the Mareva injunction is not intended to provide plaintiffs with security in respect of all claims in relation to which they may be able to pass an arguability test.'

While it is arguable that the requirement of establishing an intention on the defendant's part to dispose of his assets with a view to evading his obligation to the plaintiff and to frustrate the anticipated order of the court imposes too great a burden on plaintiffs, the rationale behind such a requirement is understandable given the potentially far-reaching consequences of granting a Mareva injunction. What is clearly required in such cases is a careful balancing of the rights of both plaintiffs and defendants if this powerful legal weapon is not to be abused.

Anton Piller Orders

Anton Piller orders were developed as a means of dealing with cases where there is a serious risk that a defendant may destroy or otherwise dispose of material in his possession which may be of vital importance to the plaintiff if he is to establish his claim at a trial.[804] An Anton Piller order requires the defendant to consent to a plaintiff, attended by his solicitor, entering his premises to inspect and if necessary take away any documents or articles specified in the order. As Scott J commented in *Columbia Picture Industries v Robinson*,[805] 'Anton Piller orders are used to prevent a defendant, when warned of impending litigation, from destroying all documentary evidence in his possession, which might, were it available, support the plaintiff's cause of action.'

Where appropriate, an order may include directions that the defendant should provide discovery of documents or answer specified interrogatories. Such an order is obtained on an *ex parte* basis and applications are often heard *in camera*[806] as secrecy will be of the essence if the order is to have the required effect and if the defendant is forewarned he will in all likelihood take steps to frustrate the plaintiff's intentions.[807] As Smyth J made clear in *Microsoft*

802. *Ibid.* at 417.
803. [2006] 1 ILRM 81, 90.
804. As Paperny J commented in the decision of the Alberta Court of Queen's Bench in *Capitanescu v Universal Weld Overlays Inc* (1996) 141 DLR (4th) 751, 757, '[t]he primary aim of such an order is to preserve evidence to ensure that the pending civil action is not frustrated through lack of evidence'.
805. [1987] Ch 38, 71.
806. Section 45(1) of the Courts (Supplemental Provisions) Act 1961 makes provision for this.
807. See the comments of Templeman LJ in *Rank Film Distributors Ltd v Video Information Centre* [1982] AC 380, 418.

Corporation v Brightpoint Ireland Ltd,[808] the essence of an Anton Piller order is surprise and the publication of the existence of such an order in advance of its execution can weaken or deprive it of its element of surprise.

This remedy is of particular use in the context of the misappropriation of intellectual property, especially in the areas of infringement of copyright and patents and in relation to the exploitation of trade secrets. The practice of making orders of this nature developed in England in the mid 1970s,[809] and the jurisdiction to do so was confirmed by the Court of Appeal in *Anton Piller KG v Manufacturing Processes Ltd*,[810] the decision which gave its name to the form of order. The plaintiffs claimed that the defendants were selling confidential information to their competitors which they had obtained in their capacity as selling agents for the plaintiffs' electrical equipment and sought access to documents located on the defendant's premises. The Court of Appeal made an *ex parte* order permitting the plaintiffs to enter the defendant's premises to inspect, remove or make copies of documents relating to the equipment. Lord Denning MR stated as follows:

> It seems to me that such an order can be made by a judge *ex parte*, but it should only be made where it is essential that the plaintiff should have inspection so that justice can be done between the parties: and when, if the defendant were forewarned, there is a grave danger that vital evidence will be destroyed, that papers will be burnt or lost or hidden, or taken beyond the jurisdiction, and so the ends of justice be defeated: and when the inspection would do no real harm to the defendant or his case.[811]

In addition, Omrod LJ laid down a number of 'essential pre-conditions' which must be satisfied before an order of this nature will be granted; namely that the plaintiff must have an extremely strong *prima facie* case, the potential or actual damage must be very serious for the plaintiff, there must be clear evidence that the defendant has incriminating documents or articles in his possession and there must be a real possibility that these will be destroyed before any application *inter partes* can be made.

As Omrod LJ made clear in his judgment, the order operates *in personam* against the defendant and requires him to consent to its execution. While it is not equivalent to a search warrant and cannot be enforced by the plaintiff without the defendant's consent,[812] failure to comply with the order will constitute contempt

808. [2001] 1 ILRM 540, 545-546.
809. The first reported decision was in *EMI Ltd v Pandit* [1975] 1 WLR 302.
810. [1976] Ch 55, 61.
811. *Ibid.* at 61.
812. As Lord Denning MR stated in *Anton Piller KG v Manufacturing Processes Ltd* [1976] Ch 55, 61 if the defendants refuse the plaintiff permission to enter premises, the plaintiff must not force his way in but should bring this fact to the attention of the court.

of court. The terms of an order will usually require that in executing it, the plaintiff or his representatives afford the defendant the opportunity of obtaining legal advice provided that this is done forthwith. In assessing whether delay in complying with the terms of an order will constitute contempt, the courts may take a relatively lenient view, as in *Bhimji v Chatwani*,[813] in which Scott J stressed that something more than 'a mere technical breach of the obligation to allow entry forthwith' must be shown.

One issue which has provoked controversy is the extent to which a defendant should be penalised for failing to comply with an Anton Piller order which is subsequently set aside. In *Hallmark Cards Inc. v Image Arts Ltd*[814] Buckley LJ stated that, while a defendant who refuses to comply with the terms of an order pending his application to have it set aside is technically in contempt of court, he did not believe that such a defendant should be liable to any penalties if the order is subsequently discharged. However, in *Wardle Fabrics Ltd v G. Myristis Ltd*,[815] Goulding J stressed that disobedience of an order constituted contempt even if it was later set aside and in the case before him he required the defendants to meet the cost of the plaintiff's motion for contempt on an indemnity basis. While it cannot be disputed that failure to comply with the terms of an Anton Piller order in any circumstances technically amounts to contempt of court and should not be condoned, arguably the courts should be slow to impose penalties where the order is subsequently set aside in view of the potential for abuse inherent in this far-reaching and often draconian form of relief.

In view of this potential for abuse, a plaintiff will be required to give certain undertakings to the court before an Anton Piller order will be granted and, as Browne-Wilkinson VC commented in *Tate Access Floors v Boswell*,[816] failure to observe these undertakings 'should not be tolerated'. In view of the *ex parte* nature of the application, the plaintiff will be required to make full and frank disclosure of all material facts to the court and failure to do so may result in the order being discharged and a finding of liability in damages being made against the plaintiff.[817] In *Microsoft Corporation v Brightpoint Ireland Ltd*[818] Smyth J stated that an affidavit in support of an application for an Anton Piller order ought to err on the side of excessive disclosure because in the case of material which falls into the area of possible relevance, the judge and not the plaintiff should decide what is relevant.

As with other forms of orders of an interlocutory nature, the plaintiff will be required to give an undertaking in damages and where he has acted improperly,

---

813. [1991] 1 WLR 989, 1003.
814. [1977] FSR 150, 153. See also the judgment of Lord Donaldson MR in *WEA Records Ltd v Visions Channel 4 Ltd* [1983] 1 WLR 721.
815. [1984] FSR 263.
816. [1991] Ch 512.
817. See further *supra* in relation to Mareva injunctions.
818. [2001] 1 ILRM 540, 545-546.

either in the manner in which he made his application or executed the order, the court will not hesitate to enforce this undertaking or to award both compensatory and aggravated damages. This point is illustrated by the judgment of Scott J in *Columbia Picture Industries v Robinson*,[819] in which the plaintiffs brought proceedings against the defendants for breach of copyright relating to an alleged video piracy operation. The plaintiffs obtained an Anton Piller order but failed to disclose all material facts in making their application and in executing it they removed items not included in its terms. The defendants then brought a motion seeking to have the order set aside and Scott J found that the plaintiffs and their solicitors had failed to make full and frank disclosure of all material matters to the court and had acted oppressively and in abuse of their powers in executing the order. He made a finding that no purpose would be served by setting aside the order as it had already been executed but held that the plaintiffs were liable in damages to the defendants who had ceased trading as a result. Scott J was clearly acutely aware of the potential for abuse inherent in Anton Piller orders as can be seen from the following extract from his judgment:

> [A] decision whether or not an Anton Piller order should be granted requires a balance to be struck between the plaintiff's need that the remedies allowed by the civil law for the breach of his rights should be attainable and the requirement of justice that a defendant should not be deprived of his property without being heard. What I have heard in the present case has disposed me to think that the practice of the court has allowed the balance to swing much too far in favour of plaintiffs and that Anton Piller orders have been too readily granted and with insufficient safeguards for respondents.
>
> The draconian and essentially unfair nature of Anton Piller orders from the point of view of respondents against whom they are made requires, in my view, that they be so drawn as to extend no further than the minimum extent necessary to achieve the purpose for which they are granted, namely the preservation of documents or articles which might otherwise be destroyed or concealed.[820]

In *Microsoft Corporation v Brightpoint Ireland Ltd*[821] Smyth J had to consider, *inter alia*, an application brought by the defendant for reliefs arising out of the grant and execution of an Anton Piller order. On the facts Smyth J stated that he was satisfied that there had been full and proper disclosure by the plaintiff as to the circumstances of the case and that there was strong *prima*

---

819. [1987] Ch 38.
820. *Ibid.* at 76. The views of Scott J were subsequently echoed by Hoffmann J in *Lock International plc v Beswick* [1989] 1 WLR 1268, 1281 in which the latter stressed that there must be proportionality between the perceived threat to the plaintiff's rights and the remedy granted.
821. [2001] 1 ILRM 540.

facie evidence of dishonest conduct by the defendant which indicated a strong probability that they would destroy records. In relation to the defendant's argument that the Anton Piller order had been oppressively executed, Smyth J stated that the conflict of evidence as to what had happened in the course of its execution could only be resolved by an oral hearing and that he was not disposed to set the order aside given this conflict. He concluded on the basis of the documentary evidence before him that the making of the Anton Piller order had been justified and that the subsequent conduct of the plaintiff in the case was not such as could be regarded as contemptuous or as to warrant the relief sought by the defendant. While Smyth J did not explicitly set out the appropriate threshold test for seeking an Anton Piller order, by stating that he accepted that there was 'strong prima facie evidence' of dishonest conduct on the defendant's part, it seems clear that this was the standard which he considered had to be established.[822]

Capper has commented on the options facing a defendant when confronted with an Anton Piller order which he believes should not have been granted.[823] First, he may refuse to allow the order to be executed until he has had an opportunity to apply to the court for its discharge. This may be a potentially dangerous course of action as the defendant's refusal to comply with the order immediately constitutes contempt of court, although if the application to discharge the order is successful this will not necessarily have serious consequences. The second possibility is to apply for the order to be discharged after it has been executed, which is what happened in the *Columbia* case. However, as Capper points out, this is often of questionable value as the damage will already have been done, and the defendant will usually simply be seeking to force the plaintiff to comply with his undertaking in damages. The third option, which can be pursued where a plaintiff fails to serve a statement of claim or otherwise proceed with the action after the execution of an order, is for a defendant to apply for dismissal of the plaintiff's action. This option was followed by the plaintiffs in the Northern Irish case of *Group 4 Securitas (Northern Ireland) Ltd v McIldowney*,[824] which was decided by Girvan J. The defendant succeeded in obtaining a dismissal of the plaintiffs' action following the execution of an Anton Piller order even though the plaintiffs were only two weeks late in delivering their statement of claim. Nothing of substance had been found as a result of the execution of the order and, as Capper has commented, 'in giving the plaintiffs precious little indulgence, Girvan J was clearly (and

822. This is in line with the test applied elsewhere in the common law world, such as in Canada. See *Celanese Canada Inc v Murray Demolition Corp.* (2006) 269 DLR 193, 208 and *Secure 2013 Corp Inc v Tiger Calcium Services Inc* (2017) 417 DLR (4th) 509 at [58].

823. Capper (1998) 49 NILQ 210.

824. [1997] NIJB 23.

rightly it is submitted) influenced by a desire to warn practitioners and litigants against using the draconian remedy of the Anton Piller order in this way'.[825]

Another factor which has tended to swing the balance back in favour of defendants in recent years has been the increasing frequency with which the privilege against self-incrimination has been invoked. This issue was considered by the House of Lords in *Rank Film Distributors Ltd v Video Information Centre*,[826] in which it was held that a defendant could invoke this privilege to resist the making of an Anton Piller order. The appellants believed that unauthorised persons had pirated copies of their films and were selling videos of them and sought relief including Anton Piller orders which required the respondents, *inter alia*, to disclose certain information relating to these video cassettes. It was held by the House of Lords that disclosure of the information sought by the appellants would tend to expose the respondents to a charge of conspiracy to defraud and that there was no way in which the court could compel disclosure while at the same time protecting the respondents from the consequences of self-incrimination.

Lord Russell pointed out in the course of his judgment that because the privilege against self-incrimination could largely deprive the owner of copyright of his right to the protection of his property, legislation in this area would be desirable. This privilege was withdrawn in England by section 72 of the Senior Courts Act 1981, as amended,[827] in proceedings to obtain disclosure of information relating to the infringement of rights in the area of intellectual property which provided that matters disclosed would not be admissible in evidence against the defendant in proceedings against him for a related offence.[828] So, if a civil action is likely to lead to payment of damages it may be preferable to enforce the Anton Piller order but if the defendant has no assets, the plaintiff may lose out by enforcing the Anton Piller as the information obtained may not be usable in a criminal prosecution which might lead to the closing down of the operation.

The scope of section 72 was considered by the Supreme Court of the United Kingdom in *Phillips v News Group Newspapers Ltd*,[829] where Lord Walker JSC made it clear that there must be a sufficient connection between the subject matter of the claimant's civil proceedings and the offence with which the defendant has a reasonable apprehension of being charged. He also noted that in a case where the legislature had left no room for doubt that it intended the

825. Capper (1998) 49 NILQ 210, 212.
826. [1982] AC 380.
827. Originally enacted as the Supreme Court Act 1981.
828. See also s. 434(5) of the Companies Act 1985, s. 291 of the Insolvency Act 1986 and s. 2 of the Criminal Justice Act 1987 in England. As Lord Templeman commented in *AT & T Istel Ltd v Tully* [1993] AC 45, 55, '[p]arliament has thus recognised the unsatisfactory results of the common law privilege against self-incrimination and has been willing to abrogate or modify that privilege'.
829. [2013] 1 AC 1.

privilege to be withdrawn, there was no need for the court to lean in favour of the narrowest possible construction of the reach of the relevant provision.

However, the privilege against self-incrimination can still be invoked in other forms of action and as the decision of Browne-Wilkinson VC in *Tate Access Floors v Boswell*[830] shows, it can still provide a most effective weapon in a defendant's fight against the application of Anton Piller orders. In *Tate*, the plaintiffs alleged that the individual defendants who had formerly been senior employees of theirs, had in the course of their employment fraudulently obtained large sums from the plaintiffs and had created the defendant companies specifically for the purpose of fraudulently invoicing the plaintiffs. The individual defendants had then allegedly authorised payments to the invoicing companies for their own benefit. The plaintiffs were granted worldwide Mareva injunctions against all the defendants and Anton Piller orders compelling the defendants to disclose their assets and permitting the plaintiffs to enter premises to search and seize relevant documents. The defendants sought to have these orders set aside and while Browne-Wilkinson VC refused to discharge the Mareva injunctions, he did set aside the Anton Piller orders against the individual defendants. He held that the privilege against self-incrimination could properly be invoked in a case involving discovery in a fraud action where, as in the case before him, on the facts alleged by the plaintiff there was a real risk that a defendant might be prosecuted for conspiracy in the jurisdiction and the documents and information sought by the order might be incriminating.[831] Browne-Wilkinson VC stated that it was not wholly clear from the decision in *Rank Film* whether it had been held that the privilege against self-incrimination applied to the search and seizure aspects of an Anton Piller order. However, he confirmed that in the case before him, the privilege applied both to those parts of the order which required the defendants to produce and verify information and that part which required them to permit the plaintiffs to search their premises and seize material.

The privilege against self-incrimination can also be invoked in this jurisdiction in all contexts so where an intellectual property dispute arises, it may be preferable to make a complaint to the Gardaí who can obtain a warrant to search and seize pursuant to section 143 of the Copyright Act 2000. In the area of copyright infringement, plaintiffs have generally tended to choose this alternative method of informing the gardaí of their suspicions of piracy, which is a criminal offence. Pursuant to section 143 of the Copyright Act 2000, where a district judge is satisfied that there are reasonable grounds for suspecting that a copyright offence has been or is about to be committed, a warrant may be issued authorising the gardaí to search premises and seize material. In practice,

830. [1991] Ch 512.
831. It was accepted that there was no real risk of the corporate defendants which were overseas companies being prosecuted for conspiracy in England and it was held that the individual defendants could not object to the order made against the companies as there was no privilege against self-incrimination by a third party.

such a procedure is regarded as being preferable to seeking an Anton Piller order as it does not involve the copyright owner in any expense and entry can be enforced. In addition, in most piracy cases, the defendant is unlikely to be in a position to pay damages even if the plaintiff succeeds in a civil action, and a criminal prosecution is perceived to be a more effective means of closing down the operation.[832]

There have been signs of a growing judicial awareness in England of the 'profoundly unsatisfactory'[833] nature of the privilege against self-incrimination in this context and in *AT & T Istel Ltd v Tully*[834] the House of Lords, while acknowledging that it could only be altered by parliament, found that there was no reason to allow a defendant in civil proceedings to rely on the privilege, thus depriving a plaintiff of his rights, where the defendant's position could be adequately safeguarded by other means. In addition, it can be seen from the decision in *IBM (UK) Ltd v Prima Data International Ltd*[835] that a plaintiff may avoid the difficulties which emerge from *Rank Films* and *Tate* where an Anton Piller order contains a proviso which clearly safeguards a defendant's right to claim the privilege and if the order is not executed until he has been told of this right and expressly declines to claim it. However, in proceedings which do not come within the ambit of the statutory exceptions, the risk that a defendant may be able to invoke successfully the privilege against self-incrimination to frustrate the plaintiff's attempts to safeguard evidence to support his claim will remain.

A useful summary of the circumstances in which the privilege against self-incrimination can be invoked in this context is provided by Lindsay J in *O Ltd v Z*[836] in the following terms:

> [T]he privilege is available to be claimed even in civil proceedings. It is available as well before as after criminal proceedings have been launched. It can be used successfully to resist disclosure not only of that which, apart from the privilege, would definitely be admissible in criminal proceedings against the defendant but also….that which the prosecution *might* wish to rely upon and that which would be likely to set in train enquiries as to whether there had or had not been a criminal offence by, or should be proceedings against, a defendant.

---

832. It should be noted that an order may also be made by the District Court on the application of a copyright owner under s. 132 of the Copyright Act 2000 authorising the gardaí to seize infringing copies or articles without warrant and in addition, pursuant to s. 133, a copyright owner, in limited circumstances and subject to certain conditions, may seize infringing copies or articles where it would be impracticable to apply to the District Court under s. 132.
833. *AT & T Istel Ltd v Tully* [1993] AC 45, 53 *per* Lord Templeman. See also *Den Norske Bank ASA v Antonatos* [1999] QB 271, 295 *per* Waller LJ.
834. [1993] AC 45.
835. [1994] 1 WLR 719.
836. [2005] EWHC 238 (Ch) at [50].

The case raised an interesting issue, namely whether material obtained in the course of executing a search order made for the purpose of seeking to vindicate the claimant's intellectual property rights could be used for another purpose, viz. to incriminate the defendant when pornographic material was found on his computer.[837] Given the subject matter of the claimant's case, the defendant had not been informed of the privilege against self-incrimination either by the terms of the search order or by the supervising solicitor. Lindsay J examined the circumstances in which the privilege against self-incrimination may be lost and concluded that the better view of the authorities is that whether a defendant knows of the privilege and whether it is mentioned or explained to him, he will be taken to have lost the privilege if he does not claim it before he answers the questions posed or produces the documents in issue.[838] In the circumstances, Lindsay J concluded that the defendant had lost the privilege against self-incrimination before he had first claimed it and that his late claim conferred no retrospective protection.

The difficulties caused by the overuse of the privilege against self-incrimination are even more marked in this jurisdiction where it remains unaffected by legislation cutting down its effect. While there have been few cases involving Anton Piller orders in which written judgments have been delivered in this jurisdiction,[839] such orders are being sought with increasing frequency and legislative intervention to at least curtail the common law privilege may well be necessary if these orders are to be effective. The issue was raised but did not have to be determined in *Microsoft Corporation v Brightpoint Ireland Ltd*,[840] in which the defendant contended that the plaintiffs through their agents had failed to advise the defendant of its privilege against self-incrimination. However, given the assertion made on the defendant's behalf that the company was complying with the law, Smyth J stated that the issue of self-incrimination could not arise and he found that this was therefore not a basis for setting aside the Anton Piller order in the circumstances.

In an English context, Dockray and Laddie[841] suggested that unless the ambit of section 72 was extended, Anton Piller jurisdiction would to a large extent become incapable of being exercised and they commented that in their

---

837. *It is clear that the privilege does not* extend to documents which are independent evidence (see *Attorney General's Reference (No. 7 of 2000)* [2001] 1 WLR 1879) or to 'things' which are independent evidence (see *C plc v P* [2008] Ch 1).

838. Lindsay J stated that he could not interpret the decision in *IBM United Kingdom v Prima Data International Ltd* [1994] 1 WLR 719 as authority for the proposition that only where such a warning, explanation and adequate understanding is proved would the privilege be lost if not claimed as that would be to treat *IBM* as overriding earlier cases.

839. See *Microsoft Corporation v Brightpoint Ireland Ltd* [2001] 1 ILRM 540 and *Jobling-Purser v Jackman* High Court 1992 No. 3808P (Carroll J) 27 July 1999.

840. [2001] 1 ILRM 540, 545-546.

841. Dockray and Laddie (1990) 106 LQR 601.

view something more than 'limited legislative tinkering'[842] was required. They suggested that if legislation in this area is introduced it should also tackle the thorny question of potential abuse of this jurisdiction by plaintiffs and it would certainly appear that the 'inherently oppressive'[843] nature of the order is now more readily acknowledged by the judiciary. It is interesting to note that reference was made to some of their suggestions by Nicholls VC in *Universal Thermosensors Ltd v Hibben*.[844] While the issues in the case relating to the oppressive manner in which an Anton Piller order granted to the plaintiff was executed had been settled during the course of the trial of the action, Nicholls VC clearly felt that the procedure lent itself 'too readily to abuse' and laid down a number of safeguards in relation to the execution of Anton Piller orders which he felt should be observed. In his view such orders should only be executed during working hours and, if executed at a private house and where it is at all likely that a woman may be in the house alone, the solicitor serving the order must be, or must be accompanied by, a woman.[845] He also suggested that unless seriously impracticable, a detailed list of items removed from the premises should be prepared which the defendant should be given an opportunity to check at the time and that the order should not be executed at business premises in the absence of a responsible company representative unless there is good reason for so doing. Nicholls VC also recommended that, pursuing the suggestion made by Dockray and Laddie, judges should give serious consideration to the desirability of providing that the order should be served and its execution supervised by an experienced solicitor familiar with the workings of such orders other than a member of the firm of solicitors acting for the plaintiff and that a summary *inter partes* review of the manner in which the order is executed should then be conducted by the court. He concluded by saying that 'if plaintiffs wish to take advantage of this truly draconian type of order, they must be prepared to pay for the safeguards which experience has shown are necessary if the interests of defendants are fairly to be protected.'[846]

Davenport subsequently commented that these guidelines should 'go far towards correcting some of the more undesirable features of the manner in which this draconian order has been put into effect.'[847] It is interesting to note that as Lindsay J commented in *O Ltd v Z*,[848] the practice of having a supervising solicitor became 'virtually universal' following the observations made by Nicholls VC.

---

842. *Ibid.* at 603.
843. *Bhimji v Chatwani* [1991] 1 WLR 989, 1002 *per* Scott J.
844. [1992] 1 WLR 840.
845. Note that in Ireland there may be constitutional difficulties in executing an Anton Piller order at a private house in view of Article 40.5 of the Constitution which provides that: 'The dwelling of every citizen is inviolable and shall not be forcibly entered save in accordance with law.'
846. [1992] 1 WLR 840, 861.
847. Davenport (1992) 108 LQR 555.
848. [2005] EWHC 238 (Ch) at [35].

The issue of the type of guidelines which should be followed in executing an Anton Piller order has received little judicial attention in this jurisdiction, although in *Microsoft Corporation v Brightpoint Ireland Ltd*[849] a point was raised in relation to whether the plaintiff should be required to provide a list of the items and documents seized. Smyth J commented that while it might have been a sensible thing at the time of the inspection for an agreed list or inventory of the items taken to have been made and signed, there was no obligation on the plaintiffs to provide a list as requested by the defendant. However, he said that as there was an obligation to preserve all copies of documents taken under the Anton Piller order, the furnishing of a list was a courtesy which should have been accorded. In this regard Smyth J stated that the law on this issue was properly put by Scott J in *Columbia Picture Industries Inc. v Robinson*,[850] where the latter had said that it is essential that a detailed record of the material taken should be made by a solicitor executing an Anton Piller order before the material is removed from the premises.

Bayer Injunctions

As Fox LJ stated in *Bayer AG v Winter*,[851] 'the law in relation to the grant of injunctive relief for the protection of a litigant's rights pending the hearing of an action has been transformed over the past ten years by the Anton Piller and Mareva relief' and he added that: 'the court should not shrink, if it is of opinion that an injunction is necessary for the proper protection of a party to the action, from granting relief, notwithstanding it may be, in its terms, of novel character'. The 'novel' injunctive relief to which the *Bayer* decision gave its name is an order which restrains a defendant from leaving the jurisdiction and will usually be granted in circumstances where an existing Mareva injunction or Anton Piller order has not been complied with. In the *Bayer* case the plaintiffs claimed that the defendants were distributing a counterfeit product and although the plaintiffs had obtained Mareva and Anton Piller injunctions they were afraid that the defendant would evade the effect of these orders by leaving the jurisdiction. The Court of Appeal held that it had jurisdiction to grant the order sought, Fox LJ stating that 'the court has a wide discretion to do what appears to be just and reasonable in the circumstances of the case.'[852] Fox LJ relied on the *dictum* of Cumming-Bruce LJ in *House of Spring Gardens Ltd v Waite*[853] to the effect that 'the court has the power … to take such steps as are practicable upon an application of the plaintiff to procure that where an order has been made that the defendants identify their assets and disclose their whereabouts, such steps are taken as will enable the order to have effect as completely and

849. [2001] 1 ILRM 540, 545-546.
850. [1987] Ch 38, 76.
851. [1986] 1 WLR 497, 502.
852. *Ibid.* at 502.
853. [1985] FSR 173, 183.

successfully as the powers of the court can procure'. Fox LJ added that if such an order caused embarrassment or hardship to the defendant, he could apply to the High Court forthwith to seek its variation or discharge. He suggested that the order should be of very limited duration and should be in force for no longer than was necessary to enable the plaintiffs to serve the Mareva and Anton Piller orders which they had obtained and to endeavour to obtain from the defendant the information referred to in those orders.

It should be noted that it is clear from the decision of Wilson J in *B. v B.*[854] that the power to grant a '*Bayer* injunction' is an ancillary jurisdiction. So, while the court may grant an order to restrain a debtor from leaving the jurisdiction as an aid to its established procedures for the enforcement of a judgment, this type of order may not be used as a freestanding enforcement procedure in its own right. Wilson J stressed that there was no general power to detain a foreign debtor within the jurisdiction until the debt was paid and refused to grant an injunction to a wife to restrain her husband from leaving the jurisdiction until he had paid a sum outstanding under a costs order made arising out of family law proceedings between the parties.

The principles set out in *Bayer* were considered and applied in this jurisdiction in *O'Neill v O'Keeffe*.[855] The first named plaintiff had invested monies through the first named defendant who offered himself as a personal investment manager with particular expertise in trading foreign debt instruments through banks based in Switzerland. When the plaintiff sought repayment of his investment he failed to obtain it and he was apprehensive that his investment monies either had been or might be in the process of being dissipated or misappropriated altogether. On 1 February 2002, O'Higgins J made a number of orders on an *ex parte* basis including a Mareva injunction and an Anton Piller order to permit the plaintiff's solicitors to search a premises and seize listed items from it. Entry to the named premises to execute the Anton Piller order could not be effected. The plaintiff then sought to continue the existing reliefs and also sought an order that the defendant, whose whereabouts were unknown, be restrained from leaving the jurisdiction until a named date, and a further order that he deliver up his passport or other travel documents to the plaintiff's solicitors. Kearns J stated that it was clear from the decision in *Bayer* that the jurisdiction to make an injunction of this nature derived from the requirement to make court orders effective and was analogous to a disclosure order in aid of Mareva relief. However, he said that it went without saying that such relief could be granted in this jurisdiction only in 'exceptional and compelling circumstances'.[856] Any order of this nature was *prima facie* in breach of the constitutional right to travel, placing that right in abeyance for the specified period. However, Kearns J acknowledged that the right to travel

854. [1998] 1 WLR 329.
855. [2002] 2 IR 1.
856. *Ibid.* at 7.

might be curtailed in some instances and he referred to the decision of the High Court in *Lennon v Ganly*,[857] in which O'Hanlon J had stated that the defendants 'should only be restrained from exercising such right [to travel] if it was in some way unlawful for them to act in the manner in which they seek to act.' Kearns J stated that given that leaving the State with the intention of defrauding one's creditors was a criminal offence under section 124 of the Bankruptcy Act 1988, this requirement was capable of being met on the facts established on affidavit. He added that he was happy to adopt the criteria for granting such relief as enumerated by Courtney in *Mareva Injunctions*[858] where the author stated that such an injunction should only be granted where:

(1) The court is satisfied that there is probable cause for believing that the defendant is about to absent himself from the jurisdiction *with the intention* of frustrating the administration of justice and/or an order of the court.
(2) The jurisdiction should not be exercised for *punitive* reasons; a defendant's presence should be required in order to prevent a court hearing or process or existing order from being rendered nugatory.
(3) The injunction ought not to be granted where a lesser remedy would suffice.
(4) The injunction should be *interim* in nature and limited to the shortest possible period of time.
(5) The defendant's right to travel should be out-balanced by those of the plaintiff and the proper and effective administration of justice.
(6) The grant of the injunction should not be futile.

Kearns J concluded that he was satisfied that the case before him required the making of the orders sought both in relation to the restriction on the defendant leaving the country and in requiring him to hand over his passport. He added that a very substantial sum of money was unaccounted for in circumstances which gave rise to considerable suspicion and that he had a very real apprehension that the defendant might be about to absent himself from the jurisdiction with the intention of frustrating the orders of the court.

857. [1981] ILRM 84.
858. Courtney, *Mareva Injunctions and Related Interlocutory Orders* (1998) p. 457.

Chapter 15

Specific Performance

GENERAL PRINCIPLES

Where a court makes an order for specific performance, a party to a contract is compelled to carry out his contractual obligations.[1] As with the equitable remedy of the injunction, this remedy was developed by the Court of Chancery to provide relief where common law remedies were inadequate or inappropriate. It is based on the principle that a person should be entitled to have that which he has contracted for rather than merely an award of damages. If a claim for specific performance is to be entertained, it is essential to prove that a valid and enforceable contract exists between the parties[2] for which consideration has been provided. The terms of this contract must also be sufficiently certain before a court will decree performance and the onus lies on the plaintiff to establish this.[3] At one time it was felt that the expression 'specific performance' presupposed the existence of an executory as opposed to an executed agreement.[4] However, the Privy Council has made it clear that there is no reason why the 'equitable right to specific relief' should be governed by any different considerations in relation to executed as opposed to executory agreements[5] and the distinction would not appear to be of practical significance in this jurisdiction.[6]

Specific performance of a contract will not be granted where the plaintiff has an adequate remedy at common law. As Lord Selborne stated in *Wilson v Northampton and Banbury Junction Railway Co.*,[7] '[t]he court gives specific performance instead of damages, only when it can by that means do more perfect and complete justice.' It has come to be recognised that a more 'complete'

---

1. See generally Farrell, *The Irish Law of Specific Performance* (1994) and Buckley, Conroy and O'Neill, *Specific Performance in Ireland* (2012) for a comprehensive examination of all aspects of this remedy. See also Jones and Goodhart, *Specific Performance* (2nd ed., 1996).
2. *Holohan v Ardmayle Estates* Supreme Court 1966 No. 60, 1 May 1967 *per* Walsh J at 4.
3. *Williams v Kenneally* (1912) 46 ILTR 292, 294 *per* Barton J.
4. *Wolverhampton and Walsall Rly Co. v London & North-Western Railway Co.* (1873) LR 16 Eq 433, 439 *per* Lord Selborne LC.
5. *Australian Hardwoods Pty Ltd v Commissioner for Railways* [1961] 1 All ER 737, 743 *per* Lord Radcliffe.
6. Keane, *Equity and the Law of Trusts in Ireland* (3rd ed., 2017) p. 355 and Farrell, *The Irish Law of Specific Performance* (1994) p. 3.
7. (1874) 9 Ch App 279, 284.

form of relief can be afforded to a plaintiff by granting a decree for specific performance in certain types of situations, e.g. in relation to a contract for the sale of land, and that equally some forms of contract such as those that might involve a degree of supervision do not easily lend themselves to this type of remedy.

The Discretionary Nature of the Remedy

Like all equitable remedies, specific performance is granted only on a discretionary basis.[8] So, the court has a discretion to refuse to make an order for specific performance where, for example, a plaintiff comes to court otherwise than with clean hands.[9] However, the exercise of this discretion must not be arbitrary or capricious[10] and it is 'governed as far as possible by fixed rules and principles'.[11] This view has been echoed in numerous cases and as Romilly MR pointed out in *Haywood v Cope*,[12] 'what one person may consider fair another person may consider very unfair' and there must be some settled principles upon which to determine how this discretion is to be exercised. These points were well summarised as follows by Black LJ in *Conlon v Murray*:[13]

> The remedy of specific performance still retains the character of an equitable remedy. It is not granted as of right but is a discretionary remedy which may be withheld in cases of a type where the court, having regard to the conduct of the parties and all the circumstances of the case considers in its discretion that the remedy ought not to be granted. This discretion is not, of course, the arbitrary discretion of the individual judge but is a discretion to be exercised on the principles which have been worked out in a multitude of decided cases.

Despite his clear acceptance of the proposition that the discretion to grant or withhold the remedy of specific performance must be exercised in accordance

8. See, e.g. *Murphy v Ryan* [2009] IEHC 305 at 10.
9. *Kavanagh v Caulfield* [2002] IEHC 67 at 11; *McGrath v Stewart* [2008] IEHC 348 at 6 (reversed by the Supreme Court [2016] 2 IR 704).
10. *Smelter Corporation v O'Driscoll* [1977] IR 305, 310-311; *McGrath v Stewart* [2008] IEHC 348 at 6 (reversed by the Supreme Court [2016] 2 IR 704); *Kelly v Simpson* [2008] IEHC 374 at 6.
11. *Lamare v Dixon* (1873) LR 6 HL 414, 423.
12. (1858) 25 Beav 140, 151.
13. [1958] NI 17, 25. See also the *dicta* of Haugh J in *Nolan v Graves* [1946] IR 376, 391, where he emphasised that the jurisdiction to grant specific performance must be exercised with discretion and care and the *dicta* of Lord Hoffmann in *Co-Operative Insurance Co. Ltd v Argyll Stores (Holdings) Ltd* [1998] AC 1, 16 to the effect that the grant or refusal of specific performance remains a matter for the judge's discretion and that while there are no binding rules governing the exercise of this discretion, this does not mean that there cannot be settled principles to guide the court.

with settled principles, Black LJ rejected the suggestion that the types of cases in which the remedy will be refused should be categorised in any rigid manner.

Before examining in more detail some of the categories of contract which may be specifically enforced by the court, it is worth considering a few general principles which are observed in deciding whether to grant relief. First, the courts have traditionally been loath to grant specific performance of contracts which would require supervision, principally contracts to build and repair and contracts for services. While it has been accepted in both types of situation that this is not an inflexible rule,[14] it has certainly proved to be a relevant factor when a court is determining whether specific performance will lie.[15] Secondly, it is well accepted that an order of this nature will not be granted where to make it would be futile, e.g. if a plaintiff seeks specific performance of a lease for a term that has already expired,[16] or even where the lease is determinable by the defendant. Also for this reason, specific performance of a partnership agreement determinable at will would not be granted as it would not place the plaintiff in a more beneficial position. Similarly, in *Tito v Wadell (No. 2)*[17] Megarry VC declined to make the order of specific performance sought by the plaintiff to replant specified portions of an island with particular crops as it was highly unlikely that they would grow successfully and, because of problems relating to access, harvesting them would be difficult if not impossible. He concluded that he did not think that 'the court ever should, in its discretion, make an order which it is convinced would be an order of futility and waste'.[18]

Damages in Lieu of or in Addition to Specific Performance

Section 2 of the Chancery Amendment Act 1858, better known as Lord Cairns' Act, conferred power on the Court of Chancery to award damages either in addition to, or in substitution for, specific performance. Since the enactment of the Judicature (Ireland) Act 1877 jurisdiction has been conferred on the courts to make an award of damages in any case where this could have been done previously under common law, and often where it is felt that an order of specific performance is not a suitable remedy in the circumstances, a plaintiff will have a claim for damages at common law. However, it is in situations where a plaintiff may have no legal remedy that the jurisdiction conferred by Lord Cairns' Act is of such significance, e.g. where a contract for the sale of land has not been evidenced in writing as required by legislation but may be enforceable in equity because there have been acts of part performance.[19]

14. *Lift Manufacturers Ltd v Irish Life Assurance Co. Ltd* [1979] ILRM 277, 280; *Hill v C.A. Parsons & Co. Ltd* [1972] Ch 305.
15. See further *infra* pp. 811-823.
16. *Walters v Northern Coal Mining Co.* (1855) 5 De GM & G 629, 639.
17. [1977] Ch 106. See particularly 326-327.
18. *Ibid.* at 327.
19. This requirement was originally introduced by s. 2 of the Statute of Frauds (Ireland)

In order for a court to exercise this jurisdiction, there must be present 'all those ingredients which would enable the Court, if it thought fit, to exercise this power and decree specific performance'.[20] It is important to stress that damages may not be granted in equity where there is no valid contract which could be specifically enforced but are usually awarded where the court decides on discretionary grounds that damages are a more appropriate form of relief.

As Finlay CJ observed in *O'Neill v Ryan (No. 3)*,[21] there may well be cases where the courts will decide 'it is not fair to specifically perform this contract; we will award damages instead.' So, where delay has occurred, insufficient to establish the defence of laches, a plaintiff may on discretionary grounds be confined to a remedy in damages.[22] However, it is clear from the decision of the Supreme Court in *McGrath v Stewart*[23] that where the doctrine of laches does provide a defence and specific performance is refused on that basis, damages may not be awarded in lieu of specific performance. In this case Murphy J had concluded that the defence of laches had been established and that specific performance of a contract for the sale of lands should be refused on this basis. However, he awarded damages in lieu of specific performance and the defendant appealed, arguing that such an award could not be made where a defence of laches had succeeded in defeating a claim for a decree of specific performance. Laffoy J distinguished the decision in *Duggan v Allied Irish Building Society*,[24] in which damages had been awarded, as a case where an alternative claim for damages for breach of contract had also been made. She also agreed with the conclusion reached by Hogan J in *Meagher v Dublin City Council*[25] that the equitable doctrine of laches could not be utilised to defeat a claim for damages for breach of contract at common law which was otherwise not statute-barred. However, the key issue for the Supreme Court in the matter before it was whether the trial judge had been entitled to make an award of damages in lieu of specific performance in circumstances where he had found that the plaintiffs were not entitled to a decree of specific performance on the basis of a finding of laches. Laffoy J stated that where the court has determined that laches on the part of the plaintiff purchaser should operate as a bar to entitlement to an order for specific performance, it was difficult to see how the court could award damages *in lieu* of specific performance. She clarified that the situation in which the court will refuse to make an order for specific performance in favour of a plaintiff because laches on the part of the plaintiff purchaser has

---

1695 and is now contained in s. 51(1) of the Land and Conveyancing Law Reform Act 2009. See *infra* pp. 801-807.

20. *Ferguson v Wilson* (1866) 2 Ch App 77, 91 *per* Cairns LJ.
21. [1992] 1 IR 166, 196.
22. *White v McCooey* [1976-77] ILRM 72; *Lark Developments Ltd v Dublin Corporation* High Court 1992 No. 2888P (Murphy J) 10 February 1993 at 14-15.
23. [2016] 2 IR 704.
24. High Court (Finlay J) 4 March 1976.
25. [2013] IEHC 474.

been established is entirely different from the situation in which no finding has been made that the plaintiff has been guilty of laches but the court considers it appropriate to grant damages in lieu of specific performance, rather than specific performance itself. Laffoy J concluded that the trial judge had not had jurisdiction to award damages *in lieu* of specific performance where a finding of laches had been made and she allowed the defendant's appeal and vacated the order of the High Court awarding damages in lieu of specific performance.

If specific performance is no longer possible where, for example, another agreement is accorded priority over that which a plaintiff seeks to enforce, damages will be the appropriate remedy.[26] A further situation in which specific performance of a contract for the sale of land may be refused and damages awarded in lieu is where there is some element of uncertainty in the terms of the contract.[27] So, in *Duffy v Ridley Properties Ltd*,[28] Finlay Geoghegan J concluded that given the uncertainty surrounding the determination on the ground of the plot of land to be transferred, the court should exercise its discretion to refuse an order of specific performance and award the plaintiff damages in lieu thereof.[29] Where a court is required to determine the amount of an award of damages in lieu of specific performance, it will take into account, *inter alia*, the loss of bargain which is the difference in value of the property at the date of the contract and the date of judgment.[30]

It is clear from the decision of the House of Lords in *Johnson v Agnew*[31] that where a purchaser fails to complete, the vendor may claim damages for breach of contract or seek an order for specific performance. Lord Wilberforce stated that '[a]t the trial he will however have to elect which remedy to pursue' and added that 'if the vendor treats the purchaser as having repudiated the contract and accepts the repudiation, he cannot thereafter seek specific performance.'[32] However, it was held by the Court of Appeal in *Wyn Clons Development Ltd v Cooke*[33] that the actions of the respondent vendor in informing the purchaser that the property would be put on the market again after a completion notice

26. *O'Connor v McCarthy* [1982] IR 161, 178 *per* Costello J.
27. *Harnett v Yielding* (1805) 2 Sch & Lef 549, 555 *per* Lord Redesdale.
28. [2005] IEHC 314. A decision upheld by the Supreme Court [2008] 4 IR 282.
29. Finlay Geoghegan J added that it hardly seemed equitable to grant an order of specific performance in favour of a party who had resisted completing a contract for sale on the basis that the boundaries of the property were not adequately defined when the contract itself did not provide any mechanism or special condition as to how those boundaries should be defined.
30. *Duffy v Ridley Properties Ltd* [2005] IEHC 315 at 4. So, where a plaintiff contends that there has been an increase in the value of the property, it will be necessary to leave over evidence of this increase until after judgment on the claim for specific performance.
31. [1980] AC 367. See also *Flanagan v Forde* High Court (Feeney J) 6 March 2009, discussed in Buckley, Conroy and O'Neill, *Specific Performance in Ireland* (2012), p. 187.
32. *Ibid.* at 392.
33. [2016] IECA 317.

had expired did not amount to repudiation of its claim for specific performance. Hedigan J said that in the matter before the court the vendor was faced with an apparent attempt by the purchaser to repudiate the contract and that its response was to bring all due pressure to bear upon the purchaser, but also to attempt to market the property so as to mitigate its loss. Referring to the statement of Cooke J in the decision of the Court of Appeal of New Zealand in *McLachlan v Taylor*,[34] Hedigan J stated that 'it seems to me that any vendor in such a financially exposed situation, as here seemed to be the case, is entitled–and perhaps even obliged–to do everything he can to mitigate his potential loss.'[35] He therefore concluded that he did not find support for the appellant purchaser's assertion that the respondent had abandoned its specific performance claim.

A plaintiff may opt for damages in lieu of specific performance as was the case in *Collins v Duffy*,[36] where Finlay Geoghegan J found on the evidence that the purchasers would have been entitled to an order for specific performance of the agreement. In the circumstances, as they had opted for damages *in lieu* of specific performance, she exercised her discretion to award damages to them on the basis of seeking to put the plaintiffs in the position they would have been in if the contract had been performed.

It appears to be well-established, as Clarke J stated in *Mount Kennett Investment Co. v O'Meara (No.3)*,[37] that 'a party is not entitled as of right to have a decree of specific performance discharged and seek, instead, damages in lieu.' However, he acknowledged in that case that the court has a discretion to discharge an order for specific performance and direct that damages in lieu should be awarded where it considers it just to do so,[38] such as where a supervening event renders performance impossible or where there has been laches or acquiescence on the part of the plaintiff which renders continuance of the order unjust.

Finally, it should be noted that damages may also be awarded in addition to an order of specific performance and this jurisdiction may be exercised whenever the court believes it to be necessary to do so.[39]

---

34. [1985] 2 NZLR 277, 285.
35. [2016] IECA 317 at [11].
36. [2009] IEHC 290.
37. [2011] IEHC 210 at 17.
38. Referring to the list of circumstances set out in Spry, *The Principles of Equitable Remedies* (8th ed., 2010) pp. 319-321. Now see 9th ed., 2014.
39. *Grant v Dawkins* [1973] 3 All ER 897. See also *Duggan v Allied Irish Building Society* High Court 1974 No. 2302P (Finlay P) 4 March 1976 at 16.

SPECIFIC PERFORMANCE OF PARTICULAR TYPES OF CONTRACT

Contracts for the Sale of Land

An order of specific performance is often sought in relation to contracts for the sale of land. While it cannot be said that a plaintiff is entitled to a decree in these circumstances because of the discretionary nature of the remedy, in practice an order will usually be granted provided that a valid contract which complies with the necessary statutory formalities exists, and it has been stated that the onus lies on the defendant to establish why the remedy should be refused in such cases.[40] It is generally accepted that land is unique and will have a special value to a purchaser and that he cannot be adequately compensated by an award of damages which would enable him to buy other property instead.[41]

It is worth noting that specific performance may also be granted in relation to the assignment of a leasehold interest, or in relation to an option to purchase or re-purchase land. While traditionally specific performance of a lease of property for a short period or of a contractual licence to occupy land would not be granted, this would seem to no longer be the case. So, in *Verrall v Great Yarmouth Borough Council*,[42] the Court of Appeal granted specific performance of a contractual licence allowing the National Front to hold its annual conference in the defendant's hall.

There Must be a Concluded Agreement

It is important to emphasise that to successfully seek an order of specific performance of a contract for the sale of land, it is necessary to comply with certain requirements. In the first instance there must be a valid contract made for consideration. Once this is established, there must be compliance with the requirement originally introduced by section 2 of the Statute of Frauds (Ireland)

---

40. *McCrystal v O'Kane* [1986] NI 123, 132; *Broughton v Snook* [1938] Ch 505, 513; *Duffy v Ridley Properties Ltd* [2005] IEHC 314 at 22; *Mount Kennett Investment Co. v O'Meara* [2007] IEHC 420 at 3; *Murphy v Ryan* [2009] IEHC 305 at 11.
41. *Mungalsingh v Juman* [2015] UKPC 38 at [30]. There is authority in Canada to support the view that, where land is bought for investment or resale, an award of damages would provide adequate compensation, *Semelhago v Paramadevan* (1996) 136 DLR (4th) 1; *Southcott Estates Inc v Toronto Catholic School Board* (2012) 351 DLR (4th) 476. However, authority in Australia, *Pianta v National Finance and Trustees Ltd* (1964) 38 ALJR 232 and the dissenting judgment of Sir Garfield Barwick in *Loan Investment Corporation of Australasia v Bonner* [1970] NZLR 724, 745, supports the view that the motive of the purchaser should be irrelevant to the question of whether specific performance should be granted. See also Berryman [1984] Conv 130. Davies has recently argued [2018] Conv 324, 337 that '[t]he traditional position that each parcel of land is unique, such that specific performance of contracts for the sale of land will be granted as a matter of course, should be maintained in English law.'
42. [1981] QB 202.

1695 and now contained in section 51(1) of the Land and Conveyancing Law Reform Act 2009 which provides that no action shall be brought to enforce any contract for the sale or other disposition of land unless it is in writing, or there is a written note or memorandum of it, signed by the person against whom the action is brought or his authorised agent,[43] or there must be some good reason why equity will not insist on compliance, e.g. where to insist on compliance would facilitate a fraud or where sufficient acts of part performance[44] can be established.[45] As Barron J stated in *Jodifern Ltd v Fitzgerald*[46] in relation to contracts for the sale of land, '[i]n a claim for specific performance, a plaintiff must establish the making of an enforceable concluded agreement. Where the agreement is a verbal one, the plaintiff must establish not only the concluded agreement but also the existence of a note or memorandum of the agreement signed by the defendant or his agent.' However, as Henchy J made clear in the course of his judgment in *Lynch v O'Meara*,[47] if the negotiations between the parties have not culminated in a contract, the plaintiff's claim for specific performance will fail, 'not for want of the statutory evidence necessary for the enforcement of a contract for the sale of lands, but simply in default of the existence of any such contract.'[48]

It is clear that there cannot be a concluded agreement unless everything which the parties intend to be covered by the contract has been either expressly or impliedly agreed.[49] What will constitute all the material terms of an agreement may vary depending on the facts of a case.[50] Uncertainty has surrounded the issue of whether particular matters, for example the payment of a deposit or the completion date, must be addressed in order for there to be a concluded and complete agreement. However, as discussed further below, it may be more appropriate to ask whether all terms which the evidence suggests the parties treated as material have been agreed.[51]

In *Boyle v Lee*[52] Finlay CJ suggested that the amount of a deposit to be

---

43. As Ross J stated in *Lord Bellew's Estate* [1921] IR 174, 176 in relation to the requirement originally imposed by s. 2 of the Statute of Frauds 1695, the purpose of the statutory requirement is to guard against fraud and provide for a 'definite kind of proof' before the agreement can be enforced.
44. Section 51(2) of the Land and Conveyancing Law Reform Act 2009 provides that s. 51(1) does not affect the law relating to part performance or other equitable doctrines.
45. It is necessary for the defendant to plead absence of writing, and technically speaking if he does not, it cannot act as a bar to specific performance.
46. [2000] 3 IR 321, 330.
47. Supreme Court 1974 No. 12, 8 May 1975. Quoted with approval by Geoghegan J in *Supermacs Ireland Ltd v Katesan (Naas) Ltd* [2000] 4 IR 273, 288.
48. *Ibid.* at 4.
49. *Supermacs Ireland Ltd v Katesan (Naas) Ltd* [2000] 4 IR 273, 288 *per* Geoghegan J. See also *Globe Entertainment Ltd v Pub Pool Ltd* [2016] IECA 272 at [38].
50. *Globe Entertainment Ltd v Pub Pool Ltd* [2016] IECA 272 at [41].
51. See further *Supermacs Ireland Ltd v Katesan (Naas) Ltd* [2000] 4 IR 273, 286-287; *Globe Entertainment Ltd v Pub Pool Ltd* [2016] IECA 272 at [44].
52. [1992] 1 IR 555, 571.

made is too important a part of a contract for the sale of land to be omitted from a concluded oral agreement unless the parties had agreed that no deposit would be paid. However, as Hardiman J pointed out in *Supermacs Ireland Ltd v Katesan (Naas) Ltd*,[53] this statement represented a considerable development of what the position in this regard had previously been and earlier decisions[54] suggested that it was not essential for a concluded agreement that there should be a stipulation in relation to a deposit. Hardiman J suggested that while there is no doubt that an agreement in relation to the matter of a deposit is usual in contracts for the sale of land, there was at least scope for the contention that a deposit may not be considered essential and he added that it was also arguable that the opinion expressed by Finlay CJ in *Boyle v Lee* did not represent the view of the majority in that case. The better view would certainly seem to be that it is not essential that a term in relation to the payment of a deposit must invariably be included in order for there to be a concluded agreement. This is borne out by the terms of section 51(3) of the Land and Conveyancing Law Reform Act 2009 which provides that '[f]or the avoidance of doubt, but subject to an express provision in the contract to the contrary, payment of a deposit in money or money's worth is not necessary for an enforceable contract.' The crucial question is usually whether everything that there is evidence the parties intended to include in the contract has been addressed.[55] So, as Geoghegan J pointed out in *Supermacs Ireland Ltd v Katesan (Naas) Ltd*,[56] 'if the evidence is that there is going to be a deposit but that the amount of it is still to be negotiated, there cannot be a concluded agreement.'

Discussion has also taken place about whether there must be agreement on a completion date in order for there to be a concluded contract. In his judgment in *Boyle v Lee*[57] Egan J stated that 'it has long been established that where no

53. [2000] 4 IR 273, 279. Geoghegan J also considered the *dicta* of Finlay CJ in *Boyle v Lee* [1992] 1 IR 555, 571 and stressed (at 286) that it was important to bear in mind that the former Chief Justice, in considering the issue of agreement on a deposit, was dealing only with the question of whether there was a concluded agreement and not with the question of whether there was a sufficient note or memorandum to satisfy the Statute of Frauds. See also the *dicta* of Geoghegan J in *Shirley Engineering Ltd v Irish Telecommunications Investments plc* [1999] IEHC 204 at 12 and of O'Sullivan J in *Higgins v Argent Developments Ltd* [2002] IEHC 171 at 19.
54. *Barrett v Costello* High Court 1973 No. 703P (Kenny J) 13 July 1973; *Black v Kavanagh* (1974) 108 ILTR 91.
55. Although, as the decision in *Dore v Stephenson* High Court (Kenny J) 24 April 1980 makes clear, there may be features about a property which make it essential that the parties agree on terms in relation to them and the court may hold that failure to address or agree on a particular issue will prevent it concluding that an enforceable agreement has been reached.
56. So, as Geoghegan J pointed out in *Supermacs Ireland Ltd v Katesan (Naas) Ltd* [2000] 4 IR 273, 286-287 if the evidence is that there is going to be a deposit but the amount of it is still to be negotiated, there cannot be a concluded agreement.
57. [1992] 1 IR 555, 593.

time for performance is agreed the law implies an undertaking by each party to perform his part of the contract within a time which is reasonable having regard to the circumstances of the case'. Hardiman J agreed in *Supermacs Ireland Ltd v Katesan (Naas) Ltd*[58] that this 'is a long standing and, to my knowledge, unchallenged statement of the law'. However, it is also clear from the judgment of Finlay Geoghegan J in the Court of Appeal in *Globe Entertainment Ltd v Pub Pool Ltd*[59] that where the evidence shows that the parties intended that there should be agreement on a closing date, no concluded contract will come into being unless it is then stipulated. In reaching this conclusion she relied on the broader principle set out in the following terms in Farrell, *The Irish Law of Specific Performance*:[60]

> The question what is material or essential must be considered, at any rate primarily, from the point of view of the parties themselves. The test to be applied is a subjective one and the court is required to consider terms as essential to a contract which were so regarded by the parties themselves.

Finlay Geoghegan J expressed the view that the approach of Hardiman J in *Supermacs* was not inconsistent with the statement of principle set out by Farrell. She added that '[t]he question as to whether a term is material and must be agreed in order that a concluded agreement has come into existence depends upon a subjective assessment of the facts with particular regard being had to what the parties themselves considered to be material terms requiring express agreement.'[61] In her view this approach was also confirmed by the position adopted by Geoghegan J in *Supermacs* in relation to the issue of the payment of a deposit referred to above to the effect that if the evidence is that there will be a deposit but the amount of it is still to be finalised, there cannot be a concluded agreement. Finlay Geoghegan J therefore held that the trial judge had been correct in concluding that on the facts of the proceedings before the court, no concluded agreement had come into being. However, she also pointed out that the statement by the trial judge in relation to a closing date being an 'essential condition' was incorrect and that the issue was more nuanced, being dependent on what the parties considered material.

In summary, it appears that the key question to be answered in assessing whether there is a concluded contract is usually whether agreement has been reached on all terms regarded by the parties as material. Where, as in *Globe Entertainment*, the evidence suggests that the parties did regard reaching a consensus on a closing date as material, there will be no concluded agreement if this is not forthcoming. Finlay Geoghegan J is correct in suggesting that this approach is in line with the approach adopted by Geoghegan J in *Supermacs*

58. [2000] 4 IR 273, 280.
59. [2016] IECA 272.
60. Farrell, *The Irish Law of Specific Performance* (1994) para. 3.09.
61. *Ibid.* at [44].

and not inconsistent with the *dicta* of Hardiman J in that case and this principle might usefully be applied more broadly to other aspects of an agreement. Where difficulties arise in seeking to apply the subjective approach advocated by Farrell in this regard, in such cases it should be possible for the court to reach a view on the basis of the evidence of what was objectively considered necessary or material terms in the light of the dealings between the parties.

Requirements of Note or Memorandum of Agreement

It is important to distinguish the issues which arise in relation to the question of whether a concluded agreement has been reached from those which must be addressed in considering whether there is a valid note or memorandum of the agreement to satisfy the requirement originally introduced by section 2 of the Statute of Frauds (Ireland) 1695 and now contained in section 51(1) of the Land and Conveyancing Law Reform Act 2009. As Geoghegan J suggested in *Supermacs Ireland Ltd v Katesan (Naas) Ltd*,[62] '[o]nly the "material terms" need be included in a note or memorandum for it to be sufficient but all the terms, whether they be important or unimportant, must be agreed before there can be a concluded agreement.'

In order to comply with the statutory requirements, the note or memorandum must be in writing and signed by the person to be charged or by someone authorised by him to do so.[63] In addition, it must contain all the essential or material terms of the agreement,[64] and it has been suggested that what is essential or material in this context must be considered primarily from the point of view of the parties themselves.[65] The essential terms for the purpose of satisfying the statutory requirement have been described as 'the parties, the property and the consideration' but not the 'terms which the general law would imply'.[66] Consideration has been given in some cases to whether other terms, such as the amount of a deposit, should be set out in a note or memorandum in order for it to be valid. While what is material must depend on the circumstances of any given

62. [2000] 4 IR 273, 286.
63. Examples of cases where a sufficient note or memorandum has been held to exist include *McCarter & Co. Ltd v Roughan* [1986] ILRM 447; *Kavanagh v Delicato* High Court 1989 No. 7536P (Carroll J) 20 December 1996; *Higgins v Argent Developments Ltd* [2002] IEHC 171.
64. [1992] 1 IR 555, 588, *per* O'Flaherty J; *Higgins v Argent Developments Ltd* [2002] IEHC 171 at 20.
65. *Stinson v Owens* N.I. High Court 1973 noted 107 ILTSJ 239, *per* Lord MacDermott LCJ quoted by Geoghegan J in *Shirley Engineering Ltd v Irish Telecommunications Investments plc* [1999] IEHC 204 at 13. As Geoghegan J stated, the authorities establish that 'essential terms' means in this context 'the kind of terms that would always be regarded as essential, together with any special added terms which the parties in the particular case regarded as essential.'
66. *Godley v Power* (1961) 95 ILTR 135, 145.

case, in *Shirley Engineering Ltd v Irish Telecommunications Investments plc*[67] Geoghegan J stated that he did not think that the amount of the deposit was an essential term in the sense that it had to be included in a note or memorandum. In addition, in *Supermacs Ireland Ltd v Katesan (Naas) Ltd*[68] Geoghegan J stated that if there is an implied term as to a deposit it is well-established that there is no need for it to be expressed in the note or memorandum. He added that even if there had been, which there was not, an express agreement as to the amount of the deposit, there would 'still be plenty of room for argument' that it does not have to be referred to in the note or memorandum as it might not be regarded in the circumstances as a material term.

Another important prerequisite of a valid note or memorandum of an agreement is set out by Keane J in his judgment in *Mulhall v Haren*,[69] namely that either read alone or with other documents which can properly be read with it, it must contain a recognition, express or implied, of the existence of the oral contract sought to be enforced. Similar views were expressed by Finlay CJ in *Boyle v Lee*,[70] where he stated that a note or memorandum is not sufficient to satisfy the requirements of the statute 'unless it directly or by very necessary implication recognises, not only the terms to be enforced, but also the existence of a concluded contract between the parties'.

A further related issue which has caused considerable controversy over the years is the effect of the inclusion of the words 'subject to contract' in any document which is put forward to satisfy the statutory requirement of a note or memorandum in writing. Keane J put forward his view in *Mulhall v Haren*[71] in the following terms: 'A letter, which expressly states that a transaction is "subject to contract" cannot be a sufficient note or memorandum, since the use of those words is normally inconsistent with the existence of a concluded contract.' He added that it was only in 'certain rare and exceptional circumstances' such as those which arose in *Kelly v Park Hall School Ltd*[72] that the words could be treated as being of no effect. Subsequently, in *Boyle v Lee*[73] Finlay CJ reiterated this point stating that no note or memorandum which contains any term such as

67. [1999] IEHC 204 at 12. See also *Higgins v Argent Developments* Supreme Court, 13 May 2003 at 7; *Greenband Investments v Bruton* [2009] IEHC 67 at 16.
68. [2000] 4 IR 273, 297.
69. [1981] IR 364, 391. Quoted with approval by Morris J in *Aga Khan v Firestone* [1992] ILRM 31, 43. See also the *dictum* of Barron J in *Jodifern Ltd v Fitzgerald* [2000] 3 IR 321, 331 to the effect that 'there cannot be a valid note or memorandum in writing of an agreement when at the same time such note or memorandum denies that any such agreement exists'.
70. [1992] 1 IR 555, 574. See also *Shirley Engineering Ltd v Irish Telecommunications Investments plc* [1999] IEHC 204 at 11.
71. [1981] IR 364, 391. See further Fennelly (2011) 33 DULJ 1.
72. [1979] IR 340.
73. [1992] 1 IR 555. See also the *dictum* of O'Flaherty J (at 588) that expressions like 'subject to contract' are *prima facie* a strong declaration that a concluded agreement does not exist. This is also in line with the approach adopted by Laffoy J in *Liberty Asset Management Ltd v Gannon* [2009] IEHC 468 at 15. See also the *dicta* of O'Malley J

'subject to contract' can be sufficient for the purposes of satisfying the statutory requirement even if it can be established with certainty that the expression did not form part of the original orally concluded agreement.[74]

However, some doubt may have been cast on this position by the *dicta* of a number of Supreme Court judges in more recent decisions. In *Supermacs Ireland Ltd v Katesan (Naas) Ltd*[75] Hardiman J stated that it was plainly arguable that the use of the phrase 'subject to contract' did not preclude the existence of a 'done deal' between the parties. However, it should be borne in mind that the case before the Supreme Court concerned an application to dismiss a claim as being unsustainable and Hardiman J added that in so far as it was contended that the plaintiffs were estopped by the use of the phrase from asserting a completed agreement, this seemed to him to be a matter for evidence at the trial. In *Jodifern Ltd v Fitzgerald*[76] Barron J suggested that while a party might head any letter or other form of writing with the phrase 'subject to contract' when he wished to negotiate but not enter into an enforceable contract, he added that if these words are not placed at the head of the letter but are contained in the body of the document 'it is a matter of construction of the writing as a whole whether it is intended to deny the existence of a concluded agreement.' However, in the next paragraph Barron J went on to say that there cannot be a valid note or memorandum of an agreement when, at the same time, the note or memorandum denies that any such agreement exists.

The decision of O'Malley J in *Prunty v Crowley*[77] was that on the facts of the case before her, where the words 'subject to contract' had been used, there was no concluded contract between the parties and to this extent it involved a rejection of the argument put forward by counsel for the plaintiff to the effect that the *dicta* in *Supermacs* could be relied upon to support the proposition that the use of the phrase 'subject to contract' did not preclude the existence of a 'done deal'. However, while O'Malley J found that no concluded contract between the parties had arisen from the initial correspondence and discussions, in the circumstances of the case she was satisfied that an estoppel arose and on this basis, she made an order of specific performance in favour of the plaintiff. She interpreted a letter from the defendant's solicitor as an unequivocal inducement to the plaintiff to surrender his claim against a third party on the basis that once he did so the monies held in trust would be released to him and she expressed the view that it could only be seen as amounting to an implicit

on appeal in *JLT Financial Services Ltd formerly known as Liberty Asset Management Ltd v Gannon* [2017] IESC 70 at [55].

74. *Ibid.* at 574. Finlay CJ added that in so far as the decision in *Kelly v Park Hall School Ltd* [1979] IR 340 appeared to amend the note or memorandum by deletion by reference to the evidence of the oral agreements previously arrived at between the parties, it was not a decision which he thought the Supreme Court should follow.
75. [2000] 4 IR 273, 281. See also the *dicta* of Geoghegan J at 297; *O'Connor v P. Elliott & Co.* [2010] IEHC 167 at 17.
76. [2000] 3 IR 321, 331.
77. [2016] IEHC 293.

promise that the contract with the defendant would proceed and that the 'subject to contract' phrase would not be relied upon. O'Malley J referred to the judgment of Hardiman J in *Owens v Duggan*[78] and the *dicta* of Mummery LJ in *Cobbe v Yeoman's Row Management Ltd*,[79] in which he had considered the interaction between 'subject to contract' negotiations and the doctrine of proprietary estoppel in the following terms:

> Where that well understood expression is used an intention has been expressed to reserve the right for either party to withdraw from the negotiations at any time prior to the exchange of formal contracts. It is made clear that there are no legally enforceable rights before that happens. Even the use of the expression 'subject to contract' would not, however, necessarily preclude proprietary estoppel if the claimant established that the defendant had subsequently made a representation and had encouraged on the part of the claimant a belief or expectation that he would not withdraw from the 'subject to contract' agreement…

O'Malley J stated that in discontinuing the proceedings against the third party, the plaintiff had abandoned a strong case and in her view this constituted an act to the detriment of the plaintiff. She concluded that on the facts of the case it would be unconscionable to permit the result that the plaintiff would be left without either claim and in the circumstances she held that there should be an order for specific performance in favour of the plaintiff.

In conclusion, some doubt remains about whether the overall effect of the *dicta* of Hardiman J in *Supermacs* and Barron J in *Jodifern* will be to undermine the clear statement of the Supreme Court's position on this question in *Boyle v Lee*, but it is obviously undesirable that this element of uncertainty has been reintroduced. One solution advocated by O'Flaherty J in *Boyle v Lee*[80] is the introduction of a statutory requirement that all contracts for the sale of land should be in writing.[81] However, in the meantime it is to be hoped that the uncertainty created by the *dicta* of the members of the Supreme Court in both *Supermacs* and *Jodifern* may be put to one side in a decision where the issue of the validity of a note or memorandum purporting to satisfy the statutory requirement of written evidence is central to the case.

Doctrine of Part Performance

Often where an oral agreement is reached between parties, there may be no sufficient note or memorandum to satisfy the requirement originally introduced

---

78. High Court (Hardiman J) 2 April 2004.
79. [2006] 1 WLR 2964, 2978-2979.
80. [1992] 1 IR 555, 589.
81. As in England, see the provisions of s. 2(1) of the Law of Property (Miscellaneous Provisions) Act 1989.

by section 2 of the Statute of Frauds (Ireland) 1695 and now contained in section 51(1) of the Land and Conveyancing Law Reform Act 2009 and equity is faced with the dilemma of insisting on strict compliance with the formalities or allowing alternative evidence of the agreement in order to prevent the perpetration of a fraud. It is a well-established principle that a statute may not be used as an instrument of fraud and in the exercise of this equitable jurisdiction, the courts will prevent a defendant from relying on non-compliance with the statutory formalities where to do so would amount to fraud. Equally, a plaintiff may be able to obtain specific performance in the absence of a sufficient note or memorandum of an agreement by invoking the equitable doctrine of part performance, which allows a plaintiff to rely on his own actions as evidence of the existence of an agreement. However, it is clear that in order for a plaintiff to rely on the doctrine of part performance in an application for specific performance, a concluded agreement between the parties must have been reached.[82] As Clarke J stated in *Price v Keenaghan Developments Ltd*,[83] part performance 'was never intended to aid an incomplete oral agreement'. So, as he pointed out, 'if the parties are not yet *ad idem* on the essentials of a contract for the sale of land being the price, property, parties and other particulars such as the closing date, then there is no concluded agreement and the doctrine of part performance is irrelevant.'[84]

The rationale behind the operation of this doctrine was set out by Chatterton VC in *Hope v Lord Cloncurry*,[85] where he stated as follows:

> The principle upon which the rule in cases of part performance was engrafted on the Statute of Frauds is, that it would be a fraud on the part of the person who had entered into an agreement by parol for a lease or sale, to turn around and say that it did not legally exist.

Similarly, in *Lowry v Reid*,[86] Andrews LJ stated that the issue is 'whether the plaintiff has an equity arising from part performance which is so affixed upon the conscience of the defendant that it would amount to a fraud on his part to take advantage of the fact that the contract is not in writing.' The right to relief rests not so much on the contract as on what has been done in pursuance of it. There a mother undertook to make a will leaving her son two farms and thereby induced him to sell his farm to his brother. She made a will in those terms but subsequently revoked it leaving the plaintiff son with only a life interest. It

82. *J.C. v W.C.* [2004] 2 IR 312, 316-317. See also *Cosmoline Trading Ltd v D.H. Burke & Son Ltd* [2006] IEHC 38.
83. [2007] IEHC 190 at 7.
84. *Ibid.*
85. (1874) IR 8 Eq 555, 557.
86. [1927] NI 142, 154-155. See also the *dicta* of Lord Redesdale in *Bond v Hopkins* (1802) 1 Sch & Lef 413, 433.

was held that he was entitled to specific performance and that there were acts of part performance sufficient to take the case out of the reach of the statute.

It would appear, despite some suggestions to the contrary,[87] that the doctrine of part performance applies to all cases in which a court would entertain a claim for specific performance if the contract had been in writing and it is not confined to agreements for the sale of land.[88] This point would seem to have been confirmed in this jurisdiction by Palles CB in *Crowley v O'Sullivan*.[89] However, in practice the vast majority of cases in which the doctrine will be relied upon concern contracts for the sale of land.

The point was made by the House of Lords in *Maddison v Alderson*[90] that 'the acts relied upon as part performance must be unequivocally, and in their own nature, referable to some such agreement as that alleged.' A less strict requirement set out in *Fry on Specific Performance*[91] and approved by Andrews LJ in *Lowry v Reid*[92] is that 'the operation of acts of part performance seems only to require that the acts in question be such as must be referred to some contract, and may be referred to the alleged one'. This view appears to have been accepted by the majority of the House of Lords in *Steadman v Steadman*,[93] where it was suggested that it would be sufficient if the acts of part performance in question were, on the balance of probabilities, referable to some contract and not inconsistent with the contract in fact entered into.[94] This question was also considered by Keane J in *Silver Wraith Ltd v Siúicre Éireann Cpt*,[95] where he stated *obiter* that the acts should be 'unequivocally referable to the type of contract alleged'.[96] It was also addressed by the Supreme Court in *Mackie v Wilde*,[97] in which Barron J gave detailed consideration to the circumstances in which the doctrine of part performance operates. In his view '[w]hat is required is that the acts relied upon as being acts of part performance be such that on examination of the contract which has been found to have been concluded and to which they are alleged to refer show an intention to perform that contract'.

In *Mackie* the plaintiff and the first named defendant were the owners of a joint fishery on rivers in Co. Donegal. The original rules for the operation of

87. *Britain v Rossiter* (1879) 11 QBD 123.
88. *McManus v Cooke* (1887) 35 Ch D 681, 697 *per* Kay J.
89. [1900] 2 IR 478, 489-92. See also *Lowry v Reid* [1927] NI 142, 157.
90. (1883) 8 App Cas 467.
91. *Fry on Specific Performance* (6th ed., 1921) p. 278.
92. [1927] NI 142, 159.
93. [1976] AC 536.
94. Note that the High Court of Australia has recently held in *Pipikas v Trayans* (2018) 359 ALR 210 that the requirement that the acts of part performance relied upon should be unequivocally referable to the agreement alleged should continue to be enforced and *Steadman v Steadman* has not been followed in that jurisdiction.
95. [1989] IEHC 34 at 12.
96. See Farrell, *The Irish Law of Specific Performance* (1994) pp. 138-140 for a more detailed consideration of this question.
97. [1998] 2 IR 578.

the fishery had been laid down in an indenture but the plaintiff was dissatisfied with the arrangements relating to the number of people who could fish on the rivers and the parties met with a view to reaching agreement about the number of annual licences and daily tickets which would be issued. Subsequently, correspondence took place between the parties in which the plaintiff sought to obtain the defendant's written agreement to the limiting of the number of licences for the fishery. The plaintiff then instituted proceedings claiming that there was a binding agreement that each party would be limited to the granting of 25 annual licences and submitted that there had been part performance on foot of the agreement. Costello P held that a concluded agreement to this effect had been reached and that an additional term relating to the number of day tickets which could be granted had also been agreed upon. He therefore ordered that the first named defendant be restrained from issuing more than 25 annual licences and ten day tickets and this finding was appealed to the Supreme Court. The defendants submitted that the trial judge had been incorrect in finding that there had been a concluded agreement and that there were no sufficient acts of part performance to make the agreement enforceable. Barron J accepted the first submission and held that a concluded agreement had not been reached. However, he proceeded to consider whether there had been sufficient acts of part performance and his *dicta* on this issue provides a useful summary of the law in this area.

Barron J quoted extensively from the speech of Lord Simon in *Steadman v Steadman* and from those of Lord O'Hagan and the Earl of Selborne LC in *Maddison v Alderson* in relation to the nature of the doctrine and the acts which could be relied upon to constitute part performance. Barron J stated that ultimately the court seeks to ensure that a defendant is not, in relying upon statute, 'breaking faith' with the plaintiff. He stated that the doctrine of part performance is based on three things; the acts on the part of the plaintiff which are said to have been in part performance of the concluded agreement, the involvement of the defendant with respect to such acts and the oral agreement itself. Barron J stated that ultimately what is essential is that:

> (1) there was a concluded oral contract;
> (2) the plaintiff acted in such way which showed an intention to perform that contract;
> (3) the defendant induced such acts or stood by while they were being performed; and
> (4) it would be unconscionable and a breach of good faith to allow the defendant to rely on the terms of the Statute of Frauds to prevent performance of the contract.[98]

98. *Ibid.* at 587. See also *Liberty Asset Management Ltd v Gannon* [2009] IEHC 468 at 16-17.

Barron J stated that it is more logical to find out what the parties had agreed, since in the absence of a concluded agreement there is no point in seeking to find acts of part performance. As noted above, he stated that the doctrine requires that the acts relied upon as being acts of part performance should be such that on an examination of the contract which has been found to have been concluded and to which they are alleged to refer, they show an intention to perform the contract. He also said that in the earlier cases it had been assumed that the acts of part performance must necessarily relate to and affect land and nothing which he had said should be taken to suggest a modification of that position. Barron J continued by saying that the detriment to the plaintiff must be the result of what the plaintiff does with the defendant standing by and not detriment to the plaintiff as a result of what the defendant does with the plaintiff standing by. Barron J concluded that there was nothing in what was alleged which would in any way render it a breaking of faith with the plaintiff for the defendant to plead the Statute of Frauds. He therefore held that even if there had been a concluded oral agreement as claimed, there were no acts on the part of the plaintiff which showed an intention to perform the alleged contract.

The principles set out by Barron J in *Mackie* were applied by Laffoy J in *Liberty Asset Management Ltd v Gannon*,[99] in which the plaintiff sought specific performance of an agreement by the defendant to acquire its interest in a property which formed part of a wider transaction which involved the plaintiff taking the lease of another premises from the defendant. Laffoy J found that a concluded contract in relation to acquiring the lease of the property in question had come into existence but that there was no note or memorandum of this agreement to satisfy the Statute of Frauds and that it would be unenforceable unless the plaintiff could rely on the equitable doctrine of part performance or some other equitable principle. Having quoted the principles set out in *Mackie* she found that the plaintiff had not only acted in a way that showed an intention to perform his contractual liability, namely to enter into the lease of the other premises, but had actually done so. Moreover, it had vacated the property the subject matter of the claim before the court and had indicated its willingness to assign its existing leasehold interest to the defendant. In her view, the defendant had not merely induced and acquiesced in, but had actively participated in, the performance of the aspect of the contract by the plaintiff which it had carried out. She concluded that it would be unconscionable and a breach of good faith to allow the defendant to rely upon the terms of the Statute of Frauds to avoid having to fulfil what remained of his contractual liability to the plaintiff, namely, the acquisition of the plaintiff's interest in the property the subject matter of the claim. On appeal, O'Malley J agreed that Laffoy J had been entitled to find that the facts of the case gave rise to the application of the doctrine of part performance and she considered that the latter's conclusions in relation to the operation of the doctrine were a straightforward application

99. [2009] IEHC 468.

of the principles set out in *Mackie v Wilde*.[100] While she acknowledged that there was a lack of explicit reference to the doctrine of part performance in the pleadings, in her view the trial judge had been entitled to find that this issue was sufficiently covered by the statement of claim and the replies to particulars and she concluded that the appeal should be dismissed.

As Spry has stated, it should also be emphasised that 'an act of part performance must be judged, not in the abstract, but in the light of all the material circumstances, in order to establish whether it is sufficiently unequivocal'.[101] The acts upon which a plaintiff seeks to rely in establishing part performance must be his own acts and not those of the defendant, although often an action such as the taking and giving of possession of land may be attributable to both parties. Merely allowing a person who is already in possession of property to continue in possession cannot amount to an act of part performance whereas allowing someone to go into possession may, in an appropriate case, amount to part performance.[102]

Another common example of part performance which arises particularly in the context of an agreement for a lease is the carrying out of improvements or alterations to property.[103] In *Starling Securities Ltd v Woods*[104] McWilliam J held that entry onto land and the demolition of buildings thereon constituted sufficient acts of part performance.

While traditionally payment of purchase money was not a sufficient act of part performance,[105] this view must now be re-assessed in the light of the approach followed by the majority of the House of Lords in *Steadman v Steadman*.[106] As Lord Reid stated, 'to make a general rule that payment of money can never be part performance would seem to me to defeat the whole purpose of the doctrine and I do not think that we are compelled by authority to do that.'[107] In that case the House of Lords held that payment of arrears of maintenance by a husband to his wife and the incurring of other costs such as those involved in the sending of a transfer agreement to her were sufficient acts of part performance of a compromise reached between the parties whereby she would sell him her interest in the family home. Subsequently, McWilliam J in his judgment in *Howlin v Thomas F. Power (Dublin) Ltd*[108] said that he could not disagree with the reasoning of the majority in *Steadman* but stressed that

100. *JLT Financial Services Ltd formerly known as Liberty Asset Management Ltd v Gannon* [2017] IESC 70.
101. Spry, *The Principles of Equitable Remedies* (9th ed., 2014) p. 289.
102. *McManus v Cooke* (1887) 35 Ch D 681, 692; *Sheridan v Louis Fitzgerald Group Ltd* [2006] IEHC 125 at 9.
103. *Rawlinson v Ames* [1925] Ch 96.
104. High Court 1975 No. 4044P 24 May 1977.
105. *Clinam v Cooke* (1802) 1 Sch & Lef 22, 40-41; *Maddison v Alderson* (1883) 8 App Cas 467, 478-9.
106. [1976] AC 536.
107. *Ibid.* at 541.
108. High Court 1977 No.736P (McWilliam J) 5 May 1978.

the application of the doctrine was still confined to cases where it would be fraudulent or inequitable for a defendant to rely on the statute.

Finally, it should be noted that in England, the equitable doctrine of part performance is no longer recognised and section 2(1) of the Law of Property (Miscellaneous Provisions) Act 1989 now provides that contracts for the sale of land must be in writing. Some slight doubt on this issue remained as a result of the *dicta* of Neill LJ in *Singh v Beggs*,[109] in which he stated that the doctrine is an equitable one and 'it may be that in certain circumstances [it] could be relied on'.[110] However, as Swann pointed out, it has generally been assumed that section 2 succeeded in giving effect to the policy of abolishing the doctrine of part performance.[111] He expressed the view that 'the doctrine had become uncertain and confused and its abolition was a deliberate policy choice'.[112] The fact that the doctrine of part performance did not survive the enactment of section 2 of the Act of 1989 was confirmed by Robert Walker LJ in the course of his judgment in *Yaxley v Gotts*.[113] In this jurisdiction, section 51(2) of the Land and Conveyancing Law Reform Act 2009 specifically provides that section 51(1) of the Act, which sets out the requirement of a note or memorandum in writing of a contract for the sale of land, does not affect the law relating to part performance or other equitable doctrines.

Completion Notices

A further issue which may arise in specific performance actions relating to contracts for the sale of land is the circumstances in which a party will be required to comply with a completion notice. A party serving a completion notice must be ready, willing and able to complete the sale at the date of service of the notice. However, it should be noted that a party serving a completion notice is not obliged to be in a position to give vacant possession on the date of the service of the notice but rather is required to be able, ready and willing to deliver vacant possession 'upon being given reasonable advice of the other party's intention to close the sale on a date within the said period of twenty eight days...'.[114]

---

109. (1996) 71 P & CR 120.
110. *Ibid.* at 122. However, Neill LJ went on to reject the claim that the plaintiff's conduct could amount to part performance.
111. Swann [1997] Conv 293. See, e.g. *Firstpost Homes Ltd v Johnson* [1995] 1 WLR 1567, 1571.
112. Swann [1997] Conv 293, 295.
113. [2000] Ch 162, 172. However, it should be noted that an oral contract relating to an interest in property was held by the Court of Appeal to be enforceable on the basis of a constructive trust under s. 2(5) of the Law of Property (Miscellaneous Provisions) Act 1989 in circumstances where the doctrines of part performance or proprietary estoppel might previously have been relied upon.
114. *Windham v Maguire* [2009] IEHC 359 at [4.6]. See General Condition 40(g)(ii) of the Law Society General Conditions of Sale (2001).

It is clear from the judgment of Barrington J in *Keating v Bank of Ireland*[115] that a party cannot be forced by a court to close a sale before the issue of whether he is entitled to compensation under the original contract has been determined.[116] This was re-affirmed by McCracken J in *O'Brien v Kearney*,[117] where he stated that the defendant was only obliged to comply with a completion notice if the plaintiff was ready, willing and able to complete the sale in accordance with the terms of the contract. McCracken J stated that there was at least the possibility of an adverse claim which was within the knowledge of the plaintiff but not the defendant and that it was the plaintiff's duty to clear the title of the possible adverse claim before he could serve a completion notice.[118] Accordingly, he held that the defendant was not obliged to complete the sale in accordance with the completion notice and the plaintiff's claim for specific performance was dismissed, although McCracken J allowed the defendant's counterclaim for specific performance with an abatement of the purchase price.

It is clear from a number of decisions that a vendor is entitled to bring proceedings for specific performance after an agreed closing date has passed without serving a completion notice where the purchaser has indicated an unwillingness to complete as he had contracted to. In *Sidebottom Ltd v Leonard*[119] O'Keeffe P rejected the argument that before a vendor can institute proceedings for specific performance of a contract when the time for completion has passed and the completion date has not been insisted upon by the vendor, he must serve a notice making time of the essence. Subsequently, in *Collins v Duffy*,[120] the defendants contended that time was not of the essence in respect of the closing date specified in the contract and that in the absence of the service of a completion notice, the plaintiffs were not entitled to obtain an order for specific performance of the agreement. However, Finlay Geoghegan J, having referred to the position taken in relation to this issue in *Sidebottom*, rejected this argument. She stated that she had found on the evidence before her that the purchasers through their solicitors had made clear in correspondence that they were unwilling to complete the purchase and concluded that if the plaintiffs had pursued a claim for specific performance, they would have been entitled to an order to this effect. In the circumstances, the plaintiffs had opted for damages *in lieu* of specific performance and she held that she would exercise her discretion to award damages to them.

115. [1983] ILRM 295, 299.
116. See also the *dicta* of Finlay Geoghegan J in *Duffy v Ridley Properties Ltd* [2005] IEHC 314 at 22 that a purchaser is not obliged to comply with a completion notice where the question of compensation for mis-description has not been settled.
117. [1998] 2 ILRM 232.
118. See also *Horton v Kurzke* [1971] 1 WLR 769, 772.
119. High Court (O'Keeffe P) 18 May 1973.
120. [2009] IEHC 290.

Contracts for the Sale of Personal Property or to Pay Money

As a general principle a court will not exercise its discretion to award specific performance where damages would be an adequate remedy. Therefore, as a rule specific performance will not be granted in relation to a contract for the sale of goods because a breach of such a contract will usually be adequately remedied by an award of damages. However, it is important to stress that specific performance will not be refused merely because the object at the centre of the dispute is a chattel[121] and where the item in question is of 'unusual beauty, rarity and distinction',[122] an order to enforce the contract specifically may be made. Often goods will fall into this category because of their rarity or antiquity, such as, for example, an Adam door in a house.[123]

A further question which it has been suggested a court should ask itself is whether the object in question is of 'peculiar and practically unique value'[124] to the individual concerned. This involves a more subjective approach which may not always be followed and perhaps a better test would be to ask whether an award of damages would 'place the disappointed buyer or seller in as good a position as delivery of the article or receipt of the price'.[125]

There is certainly authority to suggest that specific performance will be refused where the subject matter of the contract is an 'ordinary article ... of commerce and of no special value or interest'. This point was made by McCardie J in *Cohen v Roche*,[126] in which he refused to order specific performance of a contract to deliver up eight Hepplewaite chairs and held that the plaintiff's remedy should be confined to damages for breach of contract. McCardie J also appeared to lay emphasis on the fact that the chairs were bought by the plaintiff 'in the ordinary way of his trade for the purpose of ordinary resale at a profit'.[127] While arguably this fact may be relevant as it will often suggest that an alternative to the item or items contracted for may be readily available, this will not always be the case and the question of whether the goods at issue are freely available elsewhere would seem to be a better test. While this approach was not accepted by the Court of Appeal in *Société des Industries Metallurgiques SA v Bronx Engineering Co. Ltd*,[128] in which an order of specific performance was refused despite the urgent need for the object in question and the likely delay in procuring an alternative, it is submitted that if the question of the adequacy of damages is properly applied, the availability of the goods should be of primary concern. This approach was followed by Goulding J in

121. *Falcke v Gray* (1859) 4 Drew 651, 657-658.
122. *Ibid.* at 658.
123. *Phillips v Lamdin* [1949] 2 KB 33.
124. *Behnke v Bede Shipping Co. Ltd* [1927] 1 KB 649, 661.
125. *Dougan v Ley* (1946) 71 CLR 142, 150 *per* Dixon J.
126. [1927] 1 KB 169, 181.
127. *Ibid.* at 179.
128. [1975] 1 Lloyd's Rep 465.

Sky Petroleum Ltd v VIP Petroleum Ltd,[129] albeit in the context of the grant of an injunction, where he granted an interlocutory injunction to restrain the defendant from withholding supplies of petrol from the plaintiff at a time when these were limited and the plaintiff would have had little chance of finding an alternative supplier.

It should be noted that section 52 of the Sale of Goods Act 1893 confers a discretion on a court to order specific performance of a contract for the sale of goods provided these goods are 'specific' or 'ascertained'. It was suggested by Lord Hanworth MR in *Re Wait*[130] that the section adds nothing to the equitable jurisdiction of the courts in this area and an examination of the case law would tend to confirm this view. Certainly in *Sky Petroleum Ltd v VIP Petroleum Ltd* Goulding J granted what amounted in substance to an order that a contract be specifically performed in respect of a commodity which might have been said to have been neither specific nor ascertained and the statutory power would seem to be in some respects less flexible than the equitable discretion which exists in this context.

The concept of free availability is also relevant in relation to contracts for the sale of shares or other securities. It would seem to be accepted on the authority of the *dicta* of Shadwell VC in *Duncuft v Albrecht*[131] that a contract for the purchase of shares which 'are not always to be had in the market' and are therefore not readily obtainable may be specifically enforced. However, this principle does not apply if 'anyone can go and buy them'[132] and damages will clearly be an adequate remedy where the purchaser can easily obtain the same amount of identical shares or securities elsewhere. One qualification to this principle is that even where the shares are freely available on the market, specific performance may be granted where the contract is for the sale of a quantity of shares which would give a controlling interest in a company,[133] or where it concerns a substantial holding which may alter the outcome of a takeover battle.[134]

As a general principle a contract to pay or lend money cannot be specifically enforced as damages will provide an adequate remedy.[135] However, where the contract is for the payment of an annuity or other periodic amount, or where the contract requires the payment of a sum to a third party, specific performance may be ordered.[136]

---

129. [1974] 1 WLR 576.
130. [1927] 1 Ch 606.
131. (1841) 12 Sim 189, 199.
132. *Re Schwabacher* (1908) 98 LT 127, 128 *per* Parker J.
133. *Dobell v Cowichan Copper Co. Ltd* (1967) 65 DLR (2d) 440.
134. *Pernod Ricard Comrie plc v FII (Fyffes) plc* [1988] IEHC 48 and [1988] IESC 7.
135. *Loan Investment Corporation of Australasia Pty Ltd v Bonner* [1970] NZLR 724.
136. *Beswick v Beswick* [1966] Ch 538. While there is some doubt about whether a contract to pay a lump sum to a third party, as opposed to a periodic payment would be specifically enforced, the better view is that it should, as the plaintiff in these circumstances is liable to recover only nominal damages. It should also be noted that

Contracts Requiring Supervision

Traditionally, the courts have been unwilling to order specific performance of a contract which would require supervision on an ongoing basis; as Dixon J stated in *J.C. Williamson Ltd v Lukey and Mulholland*,[137] 'specific performance is inapplicable when the continued supervision of the Court is necessary in order to ensure the fulfilment of the contract'. This principle could be said to underlie the courts' traditional reluctance to order specific performance of a contract to carry on a business,[138] and it is also a significant factor where it is sought to enforce contracts to build or repair and for services.

One of the main authorities illustrating equity's dislike of granting specific performance of contracts requiring supervision is the decision of the Court of Appeal in *Ryan v Mutual Tontine Westminster Chambers Association*.[139] The lease of a flat in a block of flats contained a covenant to the effect that the lessors should provide a porter who was 'constantly in attendance'. The lessors appointed a person who was frequently absent but the plaintiffs failed in their action for specific performance of the covenant on the basis that it would require 'constant superintendence by the court'.[140] More recent authorities would suggest that the difficulty of supervising the enforcement of contracts of this nature should not be a bar to specific performance but merely one of the factors to be taken into account in determining whether relief should be granted and a modification of the traditional position can be seen in the decision of Mervyn Davies J in *Posner v Scott-Lewis*.[141] The defendants owned a block of flats and the terms of the lease between them and the tenants contained a covenant that they would employ a resident porter. The person employed as a porter ceased to be resident in the building and the plaintiff tenants brought an action for specific performance of the covenant. Mervyn Davies J agreed that the arrangements which had been made were insufficient to ensure compliance with the clause in the lease and held that there had been a breach of covenant. He stated that the requirement that the defendants employ a resident porter required little

---

in England, the provisions of s. 1(5) of the Contracts (Rights of Third Parties) Act 1999 now provides that 'there shall be available to a third party any remedy that would have been available to him in an action for breach of contract if he had been a party to the contract (and the rules relating to damages, injunctions, specific performance and other relief shall apply accordingly).' Note that the Law Reform Commission has recommended that the privity of contract rule should be altered so as to allow third parties to enforce rights under contracts made for their benefit. See *Privity of Contract and Third Party Rights* LRC 88 – 2008, para. 2.66.

137. (1931) 45 CLR 282, 297-298. Quoted by Lord Hoffmann in *Co-Operative Insurance Society Ltd v Argyll Stores (Holdings) Ltd* [1998] AC 1, 12.
138. *Co-Operative Insurance Society Ltd v Argyll Stores (Holdings) Ltd* [1998] AC 1. However, see *Wanze Properties (Ireland) Ltd v Five Star Supermarket Ltd* High Court (Costello P) 24 October 1997.
139. [1893] 1 Ch 116.
140. *Ibid.* at 123 *per* Lord Esher.
141. [1987] Ch 25.

superintendence and decided to grant an order of specific performance in the circumstances. Mervyn Davies J listed the factors which in his opinion should be considered in deciding whether specific performance should be granted in such cases. First, it must be asked whether there is a sufficient definition of what has to be done in order to comply with the order of the court.[142] Secondly, the question of whether enforcing compliance would involve superintendence by the court to an unacceptable degree must be addressed, and thirdly, the prejudices or hardships which would be suffered by the parties if the order is made or not made must be considered.[143] Therefore, it would appear that where the terms of the obligation are sufficiently precisely defined and specific performance would seem to be the fairest remedy in the circumstances, it may be granted provided the order would not require an unacceptable degree of superintendence.

The issue of enforcing contracts which would require constant supervision was examined in detail by the House of Lords in *Co-Operative Insurance Society Ltd v Argyll Stores (Holdings) Ltd.*[144] The plaintiff landlord sought specific performance of a covenant in a lease requiring the defendant, which was the anchor tenant in a shopping centre, to keep its supermarket premises open for retail trade during usual business hours for the duration of the lease. The trial judge refused to order specific performance on the basis that there was a settled practice that an order which would require a defendant to run a business would not be made but the majority of the Court of Appeal ordered that the covenant be specifically performed. Leggatt and Roch LJJ were satisfied that the contract defined the tenant's obligations with sufficient precision to enable it to know what was required to comply with the order and both seemed to be heavily influenced by the fact that the defendant had acted 'with gross commercial cynicism'.[145] Millett LJ, who dissented, was satisfied that the existence of a practice not to grant specific performance in such circumstances was beyond dispute and also pointed to the fact that to compel a defendant to carry on a business which it considered was not commercially viable would be to expose it to 'potentially large, unquantifiable and unlimited losses which may be out of all proportion to the loss which his breach of contract has caused to the plaintiff'.[146] The House of Lords allowed the defendant's appeal and reversed the decision of the Court of Appeal to grant specific performance of the covenant in the lease. Lord Hoffmann referred to the fact that the 'settled and invariable

142. See also the *dictum* of Megarry VC in *Tito v Wadell (No. 2)* [1977] Ch 106, 322 to the effect that 'the real question is whether there is a sufficient definition of what has to be done in order to comply with the order of the court'.
143. These principles were applied by Laffoy J in *Ahmed v Health Service Executive* [2007] IEHC 312 at 20-21.
144. [1998] AC 1. See further Jones [1997] CLJ 488; Phang (1998) 61 MLR 421; McMeel (1998) 114 LQR 43; Tettenborn [1998] Conv 23; Luxton [1998] Conv 396.
145. [1996] Ch 286, 295 *per* Legatt LJ.
146. *Ibid.* at 304.

practice'[147] not to order a person to carry on a business had never been examined by the House of Lords[148] and proceeded to examine the rationale underlying it in some detail. He stated that the practice is not entirely dependent on damages being an adequate remedy[149] and that the most frequent reason given is that such orders would require constant supervision by the court. Lord Hoffmann pointed out that there has been some misunderstanding about what is meant by continued superintendence; supervision would in practice take the form of rulings by the courts and he said that it was the possibility of the court having to give an indefinite series of rulings in order to ensure the execution of the order which has been regarded as so undesirable. This was because the only means available to the court to enforce its order was punishment for contempt and this weapon was often so powerful as to be unsuitable as an instrument for resolving such disputes. Lord Hoffmann went on to distinguish between orders which require a defendant to carry on an activity such as running a business and orders which require him to achieve a result,[150] and stated that the possibility of repeated applications for rulings on compliance which arises in the former case does not exist to anything like the same extent in the latter.[151]

A further objection, which would apply in either case, is the likelihood of imprecision in the terms of the order and if the terms cannot be precisely drawn, the possibility of wasteful litigation over compliance is increased. The fact that the terms of a contractual obligation are sufficiently definite to escape being void for uncertainty or to found a claim for damages does not necessarily mean that they will be sufficiently precise to be capable of being specifically enforced. A final point, which would be relevant to an order requiring a defendant to carry on a business, is that which was emphasised by Millett LJ, namely that it may cause injustice by allowing the plaintiff to enrich himself at the defendant's expense and the loss which the defendant may suffer through having to comply with the order may be far greater than the plaintiff would suffer from the contract being broken. He therefore concluded that '[t]he cumulative effect of these various reasons, none of which would necessarily be sufficient on its own, seems to me

147. *Per* Slade J in *Braddon Towers Ltd v International Stores Ltd* [1987] 1 EGLR 209, 213.
148. Phang has commented (1998) 61 MLR 421, 423 that the principle is 'so well entrenched ... that it is seldom analysed and instead, is often repeated almost as a ritual incantation'.
149. McMeel has commented (1998) 114 LQR 43, 45 that both the dissenting judgment of Millett LJ and the speech of Lord Hoffmann make it clear that the true test is one of 'appropriateness of relief' and that the adequacy of damages is only one factor to be taken into account. Similarly Jones has stated [1997] CLJ 490 that: 'the formula of "adequacy of damages" is a chameleon one; specific performance should be granted if it is the more appropriate remedy'.
150. In *Capita Trust Co. (Channel Islands) Ltd v Chatham Maritime J3 Developments Ltd* [2006] EWHC 2596 (Ch) Pumfrey J also noted that in this context 'the distinction between result and process or activity is a fundamental one'.
151. See also the *dicta* of Peart J in *Dakota Packaging Ltd v APH Manufacturing BV* [2005] 2 IR 54, 92-93 where he contrasted orders requiring a business to be carried on with an order for specific performance is in respect of a single act.

to show that the settled practice is based upon sound sense'.[152] Lord Hoffmann stressed that the grant or refusal of specific performance remains a matter for the judge's discretion and that while there were no binding rules, this does not mean that there could not be settled principles which the courts would apply in all but exceptional circumstances. However, he pointed out that he could envisage cases of gross breach of personal faith, or attempts to use the threat of non-performance as blackmail, in which the needs of justice would override all the considerations which support the settled practice.

Academic reaction to the decision of the House of Lords was mixed; while Jones stated that 'on balance, the conclusion … is more to be welcomed than deplored',[153] Tettenborn characterised it as 'an unfortunate failure to liberalise the rules of specific performance' and expressed the view that it sits ill with the idea that it should be the function of the courts to ensure as far as possible that contracts should be performed rather than broken. As Phang has commented, the concept of constant supervision continues to constitute a major obstacle to the grant of specific performance in the context of continuous acts such as the running of a business.[154] However, as we shall see, in the context of obligations to achieve a result, which is what contracts to build or repair will often entail, lack of precision in the terms of the obligation has been the major stumbling block.

It should be noted that despite the decision of the House of Lords in *Co-Operative Insurance Society Ltd v Argyll Stores (Holdings) Ltd*,[155] Costello P subsequently reached what was effectively the opposite conclusion in *Wanze Properties (Ireland) Ltd v Five Star Supermarket*.[156] The defendant company held a lease of a premises in a shopping centre which contained a covenant that it would be used as a supermarket and that it would trade during usual business hours. In seeking an interlocutory injunction to enforce this covenant, the plaintiff submitted that the facts of the case before the court could be distinguished from those in *Argyll Stores*, in which the defendant had been running the supermarket business at a loss, and that it had made out a *prima facie* case that it would suffer very serious financial loss as a result of the defendant's decision to cease trading. Costello P made reference to the fact that in the case before him the defendant had taken a deliberate commercial decision to relocate its business to a new shopping centre being developed just 400 yards away.[157]

152. [1998] AC 1, 16.
153. [1997] CLJ 488, 491.
154. (1998) 61 MLR 421, 432.
155. [1998] AC 1.
156. High Court (Costello P) 24 October 1997.
157. However, it should be noted that in his dissenting judgment in the Court of Appeal in *Co-Operative Insurance Society Ltd v Argyll Stores (Holdings) Ltd* [1996] Ch 286, 304 Millett LJ expressed the view that to compel a defendant to carry on a business 'which for his own commercial reasons he has decided to close down' might expose him to potentially large and unquantifiable losses which might be out of all proportion to the loss which his breach of contract had caused to the plaintiff.

In his view, it was open to the plaintiff to argue that the financial loss which the defendant would suffer as a result of being required to carry on business in the plaintiff's centre would be brought about by the defendant's own actions. In these circumstances, Costello P decided to grant an interlocutory injunction to force the defendant to comply with the covenants in the lease requiring it to continue trading in the plaintiff's shopping centre during usual business hours, although he stressed that he was 'merely deciding that the plaintiff had made out a strong case that there was a reasonable probability that it would obtain the order it sought.'[158]

Breen has raised the issue of whether the factual distinction between the two cases, i.e. between breaching a trading covenant on the basis of non-viability of a business as in *Argyll* and breaching a covenant in pursuit of a deliberate commercial decision to obtain higher profits elsewhere as in *Wanze*, is sufficient to warrant the different conclusions reached[159] and she concludes that 'the compelling points raised by both Millett LJ and the House of Lords [in *Argyll*] remain to be answered by the Irish courts'.[160] It is in many respects unfortunate that the matter never proceeded to trial in *Wanze* as the case undoubtedly raised questions relating to the need for continuing supervision of any order made which the court would in all likelihood have felt compelled to address.[161]

One key point which should be noted is that where an interlocutory injunction is sought in this context, the courts in this jurisdiction now insist on a plaintiff meeting the 'strong case' test set out by the Supreme Court in *Lingham v Health Service Executive*[162] where the relief sought is mandatory in substance, rather than the '*prima facie*' standard applied by Costello P in *Wanze*. For this reason and as will be explored more fully below, the latter decision should be regarded with caution, and as a decision made in the exceptional circumstances of the case and on the basis of the test applicable to interlocutory injunctive relief at that time.

The reasoning adopted by the House of Lords in *Argyll Stores* is convincing in many respects and this view is supported by the *dicta* of Peart J and the conclusions which he reached in *Dakota Packaging Ltd v APH Manufacturing*

158. Note that Girvan J granted a mandatory interlocutory injunction in *Ravenseft Properties Ltd v Stewart's Supermarkets Ltd* Chancery Division (Girvan J) 6 May 1997 requiring the defendant to perform trading covenants in a lease where it had sought to close its supermarket business as its purchase figures had significantly declined when faced by competition from another shopping centre, although the order was to be reviewed by the court when the ruling of the House of Lords in *Co-Operative Insurance Society Ltd v Argyll Stores (Holdings) Ltd* became available.
159. Breen (1999) 50 NILQ 102.
160. *Ibid.* at 115.
161. This issue also arose but did not need to be decided in *Parol Ltd v Carroll Village (Retail Management) Services Ltd* [2010] IEHC 498, although note the *dicta* of Clarke J at [2.8].
162. [2006] ELR 137.

BV.[163] The background to this case was that the plaintiff had obtained a declaration that it was entitled to a minimum period of 12 months' notice of termination of the relationship of supplier and customer between the parties. The plaintiff then sought a mandatory order directing the defendant to purchase products from it during the notice period. As Peart J stated this order would in effect be akin to an order for specific performance. The defendants resisted the application on the basis that damages would be an adequate remedy and referred to the courts' traditional reluctance to grant mandatory orders by which parties would be ordered to continue doing business together. While Peart J did not refer to the decision of Costello P in *Wanze*, he made reference to the fact that Lord Hoffmann had made it clear in *Argyll* that difficulties will arise with an order requiring a business to be carried on as it will require constant supervision to ensure that it is complied with. In the case before the court, Peart J stated the order sought would not compel the running of a business as such, but would be restricted to how a portion of the business of the defendant was conducted with the plaintiff. However, in his view that distinction was not of sufficient significance to take it outside the scope of Lord Hoffmann's reasoning. He concluded that making the order sought would be entirely disproportionate to the result intended, which could in his view be far more easily achieved by an award of damages if this were necessary. Peart J added that it was up to the parties and in particular the defendant to work out what should happen during the notice period and that it would be open to the plaintiff to come back to court if it considered that the defendant had not complied with the notice requirement.

On appeal, the Supreme Court found that there was no contract between the parties and that accordingly, the defendant was not required to give the plaintiff reasonable notice of termination. However, the *dicta* of Peart J in the High Court gives a useful indication of how the issues raised in *Argyll Stores* are likely to be addressed in this jurisdiction.

This is also borne out by the decision of Hedigan J in *Thomas Thompson Holdings Ltd v Musgrave Group plc*,[164] in which the plaintiffs sought an interlocutory injunction to compel the anchor tenant in a shopping centre to comply with a 'keep open' covenant. He pointed out that the order sought was clearly mandatory in nature and that the test of 'a strong case that is likely to succeed at hearing' set out in *Lingham v Health Service Executive*[165] therefore applied. Hedigan J referred to the judgment of Costello P in *Wanze Properties* but pointed out that the defendants in that case were not trading at a loss and had taken a deliberate commercial decision to close the store and open another close by, matters which in his view Costello P had regarded as significant. He then made reference to the fact that in the matter before the court the defendants had invested heavily in the store over the previous four years in an effort to make

163. [2005] 2 IR 54.
164. [2016] IEHC 28.
165. [2006] ELR 137.

it financially viable. Hedigan J stated that Costello P in *Wanze* had referred to the *Argyll Stores* decision and had said that it 'indicated a rule of law which should be applied other than in exceptional circumstances' and suggested that Costello P seemed to deal with the matter before him on the basis that it was one of the exceptional cases to which Lord Hoffman had referred in *Argyll Stores*. Hedigan J also stated that he would have grave doubts about the wisdom of forcing companies which were trading at a loss to continue to do so and that this seemed to fly in the face of commercial standards of conduct and to be futile and impractical. He concluded that while the plaintiff had raised an arguable case and a *bona fide* question, it could not be considered a strong case likely to succeed at trial and on this basis he refused the interlocutory relief sought.

So, in summary, it seems clear from the decisions of Peart J in *Dakota* and Hedigan J in *Thomas Thompson Holdings Ltd* that the approach adopted by the House of Lords in *Argyll Stores* towards the issue of granting mandatory orders to enforce covenants in trading contracts of this nature is the one favoured too in this jurisdiction. As Hedigan J pointed out in *Thompson*, even the judgment of Costello P in *Wanze* could be interpreted as showing support for this view in all but exceptional cases, of which the matter before him was one. In addition, even if a case of a similar nature where a business was not being run at a loss were to come before the courts today, where the relief sought is a mandatory interlocutory injunction the higher burden of a 'strong case' will now apply, making it extremely unlikely that the result arrived at in *Wanze* would be replicated.

Finally, it is interesting to note the different position in Scotland in relation to the circumstances in which specific performance of contracts of this nature will be granted. In *Highland & Universal Properties Ltd v Safeway Properties Ltd (No. 2)*[166] the defender unsuccessfully appealed against an order that it was bound to keep open its store in a shopping centre for retail trade during normal business hours until the expiry of the lease in circumstances where it had decided for commercial reasons that it no longer wished to trade from the premises. Lord Kingarth stated that in Scotland, unlike in England, there is no doubt that a party to a contractual obligation is in general entitled to enforce that obligation by a decree for specific implement as a matter of right, subject to a residual discretion in the court to refuse such an order. He said that he was not persuaded that it could be said that the courts in Scotland should almost invariably exercise their discretion to refuse to grant orders for specific implement requiring a party to carry on business over a period of time. While it seemed clear from the authorities that a court has a discretion to refuse such orders, in his view it was equally clear that the discretion should be exercised only in exceptional circumstances where very cogent reasons existed to refuse the order and where to grant it would be inconvenient and unjust, or cause exceptional hardship. Lord Kingarth stated that the power to withhold an order

166. 2000 SC 297.

in such circumstances has rarely been used and then it seemed only in cases where to enforce the obligation would be to impose a burden upon the defender grossly disproportionate to any advantage to the pursuer.

Contracts to Build or Repair

By their nature building contracts will often be of an intricate and indefinite nature involving the performance of a variety of different obligations. As Porter MR noted in *Rushbrooke v O'Sullivan*,[167] the attitude of courts of equity towards their enforcement has not always been consistent, but the predominant view has traditionally been that they should rarely be enforced, particularly as their uncertain nature would make it difficult for a court to determine whether any order made has been complied with.[168] In addition, it is often argued that damages will be an adequate remedy where another builder can be found to carry out the work. In practice the likelihood of obtaining specific performance has tended to hinge on two main issues; primarily the certainty of the terms of the contract and, to a lesser extent, the degree of supervision which an order for specific performance would require.[169] One of the most important decisions in this area is that of the Court of Appeal in *Wolverhampton Corporation v Emmons*,[170] where Romer LJ laid down the principle that a court would order specific performance of a building contract if three conditions were satisfied. First, the work in question must be defined with sufficient precision in the contract; secondly, the plaintiff must have a substantial interest in the performance of the contract and damages must not be an adequate remedy and thirdly, the defendant must have 'by the contract obtained possession of the land on which the work is contracted to be done'. The plaintiff corporation sold land, which was part of a scheme for street improvement, to the defendant who agreed to build houses on the land. The court ordered specific performance of the covenant to build on the basis that the conditions outlined above were satisfied and held that the plaintiff's interest in having the contract specifically performed was such that it was not capable of being compensated by damages.

The first of these principles formed the basis of the court's decision in *Rushbrooke v O'Sullivan*,[171] in which Porter MR concluded that 'the exact nature of the work to be done [had] not been so specifically defined or ascertained as to justify a decree for specific performance'.[172] Similarly, in *Redland Bricks Ltd v Morris*[173] Lord Upjohn commented that 'the court must be careful to see that the defendant knows exactly in fact what he has to do and this means not

167. [1908] 1 IR 232, 234.
168. See the comments of Laffoy J in *Hannon v BQ Investments* [2009] IEHC 191.
169. See *Price v Strange* [1978] Ch 337, 359 *per* Goff LJ.
170. [1901] 1 KB 515, 525.
171. [1908] 1 IR 232.
172. *Ibid.* at 237.
173. [1970] AC 652, 666.

as a matter of law but as a matter of fact, so that in carrying out an order he can give his contractors the proper instructions'. It has been stated that this requirement of sufficient definition does not mean that the contract must be so specific that it leaves no room for doubt,[174] and Spry[175] has suggested that the requirement should be that: 'the obligations in question must be at least so clear that it will be possible for the court at any later application, upon the proper presentation of evidence, to determine whether the acts of the parties do or do not amount to due performance.' Provided the extent of the works which must be carried out to comply with the contract can be deduced from the evidence, it would seem that the courts have at times been willing to decree specific performance.[176]

The third requirement as laid down by Romer LJ has been qualified to a degree by Farwell J in *Carpenters Estates Ltd v Davies*,[177] in which the latter stated that it was not essential that the defendant had obtained possession of the land by virtue of the contract at issue provided that he is 'in possession of the land on which the work is contracted to be done'. In this case the court granted specific performance of a covenant entered into by the defendant to lay sewers on her land as she was in possession of this land and the plaintiffs could not proceed to build houses on the land which she had sold to them without these works being carried out.

Clearly, where the defendant is in possession of the lands specific performance may often be the preferred option as the plaintiff could not employ another builder without committing a trespass. While his qualification of Romer LJ's requirement would seem quite acceptable, Farwell J appeared to go on to suggest that the mere fact that the defendant does not have possession of the land on which the work is contracted to be carried out should not necessarily be a complete bar to relief in the form of specific performance.[178] This statement is definitely questionable for, as Farwell J himself acknowledged,[179] if the defendant is not in possession of the land, it may be impossible for him to carry out the works.

The requirements laid down in *Wolverhampton Corporation v Emmons* were applied to a situation in which a tenant sought to enforce a landlord's covenant to repair in *Jeune v Queens Cross Properties Ltd*.[180] Tenants alleged that their landlord was in breach of a covenant to repair by failing to reinstate a balcony at the front of the property after it had partially collapsed. It was accepted by Pennycuick VC that the court had a power which should be carefully exercised

174. *Molyneux v Richard* [1906] 1 Ch 34, 42 *per* Kekewich J.
175. Spry, *The Principles of Equitable Remedies* (9th ed., 2014) p. 119.
176. *Todd & Co. v Midland Great Western Rly of Ireland Co.* (1881) 9 LR Ir 85.
177. [1940] Ch 160. See also *Claystone Ltd v Larkin* [2007] IEHC 89 at 20-21.
178. *Ibid.* at 165.
179. *Ibid.* at 164-165.
180. [1974] Ch 97.

to make an order against a landlord to do specific work under a covenant to repair and an order of specific performance was granted in the circumstances.

Clearly the courts will be more willing to grant specific performance in contracts to build or repair where there is no need for ongoing supervision of any order it may make. As Lord Hoffmann stated in *Co-Operative Insurance Society Ltd v Argyll Stores (Holdings) Ltd*,[181] 'even if the achievement of the result is a complicated matter which will take some time, the court if called upon to rule, only has to examine the finished work and say whether it complies with the order'. This *dictum* was relied upon by Lawrence Collins QC, sitting as a Deputy High Court judge, in *Rainbow Estates Ltd v Tokenhold Ltd*,[182] where the plaintiff sought specific performance of a tenant's covenant to repair in circumstances where property was in a serious state of disrepair and there was no provision in the lease permitting the landlord to enter the premises to carry out repairs and no forfeiture clause for re-entry. Judge Collins made it clear that in his view a modern law of remedies requires specific performance of a tenant's repairing covenant to be available in appropriate circumstances and he stated that there were no constraints of principle or binding authority against the availability of that remedy. He added that the problems of defining the work and the need for supervision can be overcome by ensuring that there is a sufficient definition of what has to be done in order to comply with the order of the court. He therefore concluded, in granting the order sought, that subject to the overriding need to avoid injustice or oppression, specific performance should be available where appropriate in such cases, particularly if there is a substantial obstacle to the landlord effecting repairs and the condition of the premises may be deteriorating.

Finally, it should be said that while the result in cases such as *Jeune* and *Rainbow Estates* show an increased willingness to grant specific performance in cases of this nature, they should be treated with a degree of caution as the particular difficulties which faced the plaintiffs in these cases will not always be present. Equally, it should be stressed that the court must have sufficiently precise information before it about the works needed and their likely duration before it will grant an order requiring them to be specifically performed.[183] In addition, it should not be assumed that orders which require a defendant to achieve a result as opposed to those which require him to carry on an activity will necessarily be enforced by specific performance. In the last analysis, as Lord Hoffmann commented in *Co-Operative Insurance Society Ltd v Argyll Stores (Holdings) Ltd*, the grant or refusal of specific performance remains a matter within the judge's discretion and the level of precision which must be present if an obligation is to be enforced is difficult to predict with accuracy.

---

181. [1998] AC 1, 13.
182. [1999] Ch 64. See Pawlowski and Brown [1998] Conv 495 and Bridge [1999] CLJ 283.
183. *Jan v Torrance* [2002] EWCA Civ 431.

Contracts for Services

As a general principle, contracts which involve the performance of personal services will not be specifically enforced.[184] This is due partly to the fact that the courts would often be required to exercise a degree of supervision in relation to any order made[185] and partly due to a reluctance on the part of the judiciary as a matter of policy to compel individuals to work together in circumstances where the relationship of trust and confidence between them no longer exists. As stated above, McWilliam J accepted in the course of his judgment in *Lift Manufacturers Ltd v Irish Life Assurance Co. Ltd*[186] that the principle that specific performance of a contract for services will not be granted is not a rigid one and he acknowledged that where there does not seem to be any reason for the court to supervise performance of the contract, this argument against enforcement cannot apply. However, it is generally accepted that from a policy perspective it is undesirable to force parties to fulfil obligations arising under contracts for the provision of services and, as an examination of the relevant authorities in this area will show, it is usually only where a relationship of mutual trust still exists between the parties that the courts will be willing to grant specific performance or, where circumstances require it, an injunction.[187]

These issues were examined in some detail by Megarry J in his judgment in *C.H. Giles & Co. v Morris*,[188] where he commented that the so-called rule that contracts for personal services or involving the continuous performance of services will not be specifically enforced is plainly not absolute and without exception. He continued:

> I do not think that it should be assumed that as soon as any element of personal service or continuous services can be discerned in a contract the court will, without more, refuse specific performance. ... As is so often the case in equity, the matter is one of balance of advantage and disadvantage in relation to the particular obligations in question; and the fact that the balance will usually lie on one side does not turn this probability into a rule.[189]

184. As McCutcheon has commented (1997) 17 LS 65, 66 there is a 'near universal reluctance' to order performance of a contract for personal services.
185. See *supra Ryan v Mutual Tontine Westminster Chambers Association* [1893] 2 Ch 116; *Posner v Scott Lewis* [1987] Ch 25.
186. [1979] ILRM 277. See also *Ahmed v Health Service Executive* [2007] IEHC 312 at 7.
187. See *supra* Chapter 14.
188. [1972] 1 WLR 307.
189. *Ibid.* at 318. Quoted with approval by Goff LJ in *Price v Strange* [1978] Ch 337, 359-360. As McCutcheon has commented (1997) 17 LS 65, 67, Megarry J's judgment displays a 'willingness to depart from the traditional rule and to order performance where problems of superintendence would not arise and where the possibilities of evasion are not such as to render the order vain'. However, he points out that the

The *Giles* case concerned the issue of specific performance of a service agreement and the question arose whether the presence in the contract of a term in relation to the appointment of a third party prevented the court decreeing specific performance of the agreement. Megarry J accepted that there was a distinction between an order to perform a contract for services and an order to procure the execution of such a contract and held that, on the facts, the contract was specifically enforceable. As Megarry J said, specific performance may be granted of an agreement to execute an instrument even if the obligations which that instrument creates would not be specifically enforced.

In relation to contracts of employment, the policy arguments against enforcement are strong where a relationship of mutual trust and confidence no longer exists between the parties. However, as the decision of the Court of Appeal in *Hill v C.A. Parsons & Co. Ltd*[190] illustrates, in exceptional cases where such a relationship still subsists, the courts will enforce a contract of employment, in this instance by the grant of an injunction. In that case, the court granted an injunction restraining the dismissal of an employee where his employer had been coerced by a trade union into taking such a course of action when the employee refused to join the union and where the employer still retained confidence in the employee's ability to do his job.

The principles which need to be considered where a court is effectively being asked to order specific performance of a contract of employment were examined by Laffoy J in *Ahmed v Health Service Executive*,[191] in which the court had to determine whether there was a continuing breach of the defendant's contract with the plaintiff, a consultant surgeon, and, if so, whether the plaintiff was entitled to an order directing the defendant to make an offer of an alternative appropriate appointment to him. Counsel for the plaintiff submitted that the traditional view, that specific performance of a contract for services will not be decreed, is 'not rigid' on the authority of *Lift Manufacturers Ltd v Irish Life Assurance Co. Ltd*,[192] but counsel for the defendant submitted that there was no precedent for making an order of the type sought. Counsel for the defendant also relied on the following *dicta* from the judgment of Clarke J in *Carroll v Dublin Bus*,[193] in which a mandatory injunction in relation to a contract of employment had been sought:

> The extent to which there may be, notwithstanding the general policy of the courts to the contrary, a jurisdiction to make a mandatory order which would have the effect of entitling an employee to return actively

---

efforts of Megarry J have not provided a base from which a general jurisdiction to order performance in such circumstances has been developed.

190. [1972] Ch 305.
191. [2007] IEHC 312.
192. [1979] ILRM 277.
193. [2005] 4 IR 184, 210.

> to work after appropriate findings at a plenary hearing is, therefore, open to significant doubt.
>
> Even if such a jurisdiction exists, it seems to me that it could, in principle, only arise in circumstances where it was clear that no other difficulties could reasonably be expected to arise by virtue of the making of an order.

Laffoy J stated that for a variety of reasons the courts have refused to exercise discretion to compel performance of contracts of employment or their terms and that while the type of impediment which existed in *Carroll*, namely a breakdown of trust and confidence, did not exist in the case before her, other issues militated against making an order for specific performance such as the complex infrastructural, organisational and practical considerations which are involved in the provision of surgical services to the public. She added that she was not satisfied that, as a matter of practicality, an order compelling the making of an appointment which would allow the plaintiff to be involved in major surgery could properly be made and enforced and that the consequences of such an order were not foreseeable. In the circumstances she declined to make any form of mandatory order but awarded damages for breach of contract.

DEFENCES TO AN ACTION FOR SPECIFIC PERFORMANCE

Introduction

Having considered some of the types of cases in which a court will grant specific performance, it is now necessary to examine the various defences which may be put forward when a claim for specific performance is made. It is important to point out that while some of these defences may provide an absolute bar to relief (e.g. the fact that the contract is an illegal one), the majority are of a discretionary nature and such defences will often be merely one of a number of factors which the court will be required to consider in deciding whether to grant relief. In addition, it is necessary to draw a distinction between two types of cases; first, those where even if the defence is successfully established the validity of the contract itself remains unaffected and the defendant may still be liable in damages (e.g. where the defence of hardship is raised). These cases should be distinguished from those in which the defence (e.g. mistake or misrepresentation) is sufficient to secure rescission of the contract.

Before examining these defences under various headings it is also necessary to stress that the types of cases in which specific performance will be refused do not fall into 'rigid categories'[194] and the following examination is not intended to be exhaustive.

194. *Conlon v Murray* [1958] NI 17, 26.

Lack of Mutuality

It has traditionally been accepted that a court would not grant specific performance at the suit of one party when it could not do so at the suit of the other and that in order to obtain a decree of specific performance, the contract had to be mutually enforceable.[195] This point was summarised in the following manner by O'Connor LJ in *O'Regan v White*:[196]

> Generally speaking, at any rate, it would not be even-handed justice to compel specific performance against the one party, where the same remedy would not be available against the other party in respect of matters to be by him performed under the contract.

The operation of this principle can be seen in relation to the situation in which an infant seeks to enforce specifically a contract into which he has entered. So, in *Flight v Bolland*[197] a minor failed to obtain a decree of specific performance of a contract because such a decree could not be obtained against him. As Leach MR commented, '[i]t is a general principle of courts of equity to interpose only where the remedy is mutual.'

One question which has provoked considerable controversy is whether the question of mutuality is to be determined at the time the contract is entered into or at the date of the judgment. The former approach was favoured by Fry[198] and by Meredith J in *Murphy v Harrington*,[199] in which he stated that, in relation to the issue of mutuality, 'the material point in time to be considered is the time when the contract was entered into.' However, this point of view did not meet with the universal approval either of academic commentators,[200] or of members of the judiciary,[201] and the question was considered again by the English Court of Appeal in *Price v Strange*.[202] The plaintiff and the defendant agreed that the former should carry out certain repairs to the defendant's property in return for a new underlease. When the plaintiff had completed half the work, the

195. However, it should be noted that it seems to have been accepted by Brady LC in *Fennelly v Anderson* (1851) 1 Ir Ch R 706, 711 that lack of mutuality should not be a bar in cases arising under the Statute of Frauds and that a plaintiff may obtain specific performance of a contract signed by the defendant but not by him.
196. [1919] 2 IR 339, 393. See also his statement at 392 that 'equity will not aid one party to an agreement to have *in specie* that for which he bargained unless it can likewise aid (if necessary) the other party to have *in specie* that for which he bargained'.
197. (1828) 4 Russ 298.
198. Fry, *Specific Performance* (6th ed., 1921) p. 219: 'A contract to be specifically enforced by the Court must, as a general rule, be mutual — that is to say, such that it might, *at the time it was entered into*, have been enforced by either of the parties against the other of them' (emphasis added).
199. [1927] IR 339, 344. See *Bayley v Shoesmith's Contract* (1918) 87 LJ Ch 626.
200. Langdell (1887-88) 1 Harv LR 104; Saunders (1903) 19 LQR 341.
201. See the judgment of O'Connor LJ in *O'Regan v White* [1919] 2 IR 339, 395.
202. [1978] Ch 337.

defendant refused to allow him to continue and repudiated the agreement. When the plaintiff sought specific performance of the agreement this was refused by the trial judge on the grounds that the contract was not capable of mutual enforcement at the time it was entered into.

However, the Court of Appeal did not agree with this conclusion. Buckley LJ stressed that the time at which the mutual availability of specific performance must be considered is the time of judgment and said that the correct principle is that 'the court will not compel a defendant to perform his obligations specifically if it cannot at the same time ensure that any unperformed obligations of the plaintiff will be specifically performed, unless perhaps, damages would be an adequate remedy to the defendant for any default on the plaintiff's part.'[203] However, arguably the most important principle to emerge from the decision of the Court of Appeal is that a lack of mutuality does not result in the court being deprived of jurisdiction to entertain a claim for specific performance but is rather a matter to be taken into account in deciding whether to exercise its discretion in favour of granting the remedy.[204] In this case, the Court of Appeal held that specific performance of the agreement should be granted subject to the defendant being recompensed for any repair work carried out by her and concluded that, in any event, the defendant had waived any defence of want of mutuality by allowing the plaintiff to start the repair work and in accepting the increased rent payable under the new underlease.

It seems clear from the decision of Kelly J in *Desmond Murtagh Construction Ltd v Hannon*[205] that specific performance of a contract may be granted even where there are obligations on the plaintiff's part which have yet to be fulfilled, provided that the plaintiff undertakes to discharge these obligations. He quoted from *Spry on Equitable Remedies* to the effect that 'a defendant may in some circumstances be protected by a conditional order or by a special term inserted in the order.'[206] In the circumstances before the court, Kelly J held that no injustice would be done to the defendant if specific performance were granted provided that the order recited the undertaking of the receiver of the plaintiff company to ensure that a condition relating to planning permission was complied with and any necessary funds paid over.

Misrepresentation

The fact that a contract was induced by reason of a misrepresentation will usually be a defence to an action for specific performance. Certainly any misrepresentation which justifies rescission will suffice and specific

203. *Ibid.* at 367-368.
204. See also *Rainbow Estates Ltd v Tokenhold Ltd* [1999] Ch 64, 69.
205. [2011] IEHC 276.
206. Spry, *The Principles of Equitable Remedies* (8th ed., 2010) p. 111. Now see 9th ed., 2014.

performance may even be refused where there is no right to rescind. This point was made by Jessel MR in *Re Banister*,[207] where he stated as follows:

> I apprehend that the considerations which induce a Court to rescind any contract and the considerations which induce a Court of Equity to decline to enforce specific performance of a contract are by no means the same. It may well be that there is not sufficient to induce the Court to rescind the contract but still sufficient to prevent the Court enforcing it.

This point was reiterated by Lindley LJ in *Re Terry and White's Contract*,[208] where he said that 'a less serious misleading' of the defendant is sufficient to provide a defence in an action for specific performance than would be required to justify rescission. In practice successfully raising the defence of misrepresentation where specific performance is sought will be of less benefit to a defendant as he may still be liable in damages to the plaintiff, whereas if rescission of the contract is granted this will not be an option. In some cases, while a defendant in a specific performance action may have had good grounds for rescission, this right may have been lost for one reason or another,[209] and in these circumstances the misrepresentation should almost invariably still provide a good defence.

Misrepresentation will only provide a defence to an action for specific performance where it has induced the defendant to enter into the contract and he has been prejudiced as a result, although it may not be necessary to prove that the misrepresentation provided the sole motivation for the defendant's decision to enter into the agreement. It seems to have been accepted that even an innocent misrepresentation may suffice in this regard; as Brett LJ stated in *Re Banister*,[210] 'if there be a misrepresentation of facts however innocently made, the court of equity will not enforce the performance of the contract.' However, it would be fair to say that where the facts would never have warranted rescission or where the representation relates merely to a matter of opinion, a degree of caution should be exercised. Often where the misrepresentation can be classed as innocent in nature the question of whether it can provide a valid defence will depend on whether the court can find evidence of fundamental unfairness in the transaction. This point can be deduced from the decision of the Supreme Court in *Smelter Corporation v O'Driscoll*,[211] in which the plaintiff claimed an order of specific performance in relation to a contract for the sale of lands. The plaintiff's agent had told the defendant in the course of negotiations that if she did not agree to sell, the local authority would acquire the lands compulsorily

207. (1879) 12 Ch D 131, 142.
208. (1886) 32 Ch D 14, 29.
209. E.g. as a result of the doctrine of laches or because the parties cannot be restored to their original positions.
210. (1879) 12 Ch D 131, 147.
211. [1977] IR 305.

and although the agent believed this statement to be true, it was actually without foundation. The Supreme Court held that, while the plaintiff's agent had acted in a *bona fide* manner, by reason of the misrepresentation of the facts by the agent, the defendant had been under a 'fundamental misapprehension' as to the true position. O'Higgins CJ concluded that in these circumstances there was a fundamental unfairness in the transaction and that it would be unjust to grant a decree of specific performance. The general principles in this area are well summarised by Spry as follows:[212]

> If the defendant has entered into the material contract, or has elected not to rescind, in reliance on misleading statements or actions of the plaintiff, specific performance is refused either if circumstances of unfairness render it unreasonable to grant relief (and here it is generally of importance whether the plaintiff knew or ought to have known that his statements or actions might be relied upon) or if in view of the error or misunderstanding of the defendant and the hardship that may be suffered by him it is unreasonable to grant relief (and here it may be less important, though it is usually relevant, whether the plaintiff knew or ought to have known that his statements or acts would be relied upon), or if in view of both of these considerations it is unreasonable to grant relief.

A final point which should be made is that 'misrepresentation may arise as much from suppression of the material facts as from mis-stating them.' This point emerges from the judgment of Smith MR in *Geoghegan v Connolly*,[213] in which he found that there had been such a suppression of the facts in the particulars of sale of property as to disentitle the plaintiff to a decree of specific performance.

Mistake

In certain circumstances, mistake will constitute a defence to an action for specific performance. In determining whether specific performance should be refused on this ground, the court will often be primarily influenced by the unfairness or hardship caused by any misapprehension or mistake on the part of the defendant as to the nature of the contractual obligations.

The mistake may be of such proportions that it prevents a valid contract coming into existence at all; in these circumstances clearly no order of specific performance can be made. However, it is also necessary to consider the types of mistake, which although they do not prevent the contract being initially effective, may be of such a nature that a court will in the exercise of its discretion refuse to grant specific performance. Therefore, specific performance may be

212. Spry, *The Principles of Equitable Remedies* (9th ed., 2014) pp. 167-168.
213. (1859) 8 Ir Ch R 598, 609.

refused where the mistake is not such as to render the contract void at law, or even where there is no right to rescind in equity. In other words, as we have seen above in the context of misrepresentation, a less serious mistake is sufficient to provide a defence to an action for specific performance than would be required to justify rescission.

There will also be types of mistake which are neither serious enough to justify rescission nor to provide a good defence in an action for specific performance. This can be seen from an examination of the decision of Murphy J in *Ferguson v Merchant Banking Ltd*,[214] in which the plaintiff claimed specific performance of a contract for the sale of land. The defendant company was being wound up and the official liquidator contested the plaintiff's right to have the contract performed. It was claimed that the agreement between the parties was for the sale of specified residential estates and ancillary lands and that it was never intended that a vacant site with development potential should be included in the sale. The defendant sought rescission of the contract or rectification thereof to give effect to what it argued was the true intention of the parties. While Murphy J accepted that a mistake had been made in that the official liquidator had not intended to dispose of the property with development potential, he found that there had not been a fundamental error nor an absence of agreement on any fundamental term. He concluded that whether the matter was viewed as one of fundamental mistake or absence of consensus, the defendant was not entitled to deprive the plaintiff of the benefit of the contract which he had entered into and in the circumstances held that he was entitled to an order of specific performance and the defendant's counterclaim was rejected.

Where a defendant seeks to rely on mistake as a defence, often a crucial question will be whether the plaintiff contributed in any way to the misapprehension or misunderstanding. Certainly, where the plaintiff is aware of the mistake and seeks to take advantage of it, a court will not grant specific performance in his favour. In *Webster v Cecil*[215] a vendor offered property for sale for £1,250 instead of £2,250 as he had intended and the purchaser accepted the offer knowing that the former had made a mistake. Specific performance of the sale was refused on the basis that the mistake had been clearly proved and the defendant had immediately given notice of it. Romilly MR therefore concluded that the court would not compel the defendant to sell property for much less than its real value. On the other hand, where the mistake is solely that of the defendant and the plaintiff has in no way contributed to it, the courts are unlikely to refuse specific performance. This point is illustrated by the decision in *Tamplin v James*,[216] where property was offered for sale by reference to plans which correctly described the area of the site. The defendant did not look at the plans and mistakenly assumed that a piece of land behind the premises was

214. [1993] ILRM 136.
215. (1861) 30 Beav 62.
216. (1880) 15 Ch D 215.

included in the sale and agreed to buy on this basis. The plaintiff was granted a decree of specific performance when the defendant failed to complete the purchase. As James LJ stated, 'for the most part the cases where a defendant has escaped on the ground of a mistake not contributed to by the plaintiff have been cases where a hardship amounting to an injustice would have been inflicted upon him by holding him to his bargain, and it was unreasonable to hold him to it. … If a man makes a mistake of this kind without any reasonable excuse he ought to be held to his bargain.'[217]

This statement was quoted with approval by Costello J in *O'Neill v Ryan (No. 3)*[218] in a judgment which confirms the point that where a plaintiff has in no way contributed to the mistake it would not be unjust or unreasonable to require the defendant to carry out his contractual obligations. The plaintiff had instituted various proceedings against a number of defendants including an action under section 205 of the Companies Act 1963, claiming oppression and seeking damages for wrongful dismissal, fraud, misrepresentation and conspiracy. He claimed that the respondents in the section 205 proceedings had offered to buy his shares in the company at a stipulated price and to pay his costs and sought specific performance of this agreement. The defendants resisted the claim, contending that the agreement relied on had been entered into by mistake and that they had intended this offer to settle to apply to more than just the section 205 action and submitted that, as the parties had not been *ad idem*, there was no contract in existence which could be specifically enforced. Costello J said that he had to balance the hardship which the defendants contended they would suffer against the hardship which the plaintiff would be subject to if the contract was not specifically enforced. He held that a valid enforceable agreement had come into existence, that the plaintiff had in no way contributed to the situation which had arisen and concluded that the plaintiff was entitled to an order of specific performance. The conclusion reached by Costello J was upheld by the Supreme Court which held that he had properly exercised his discretion in granting specific performance.

While it would appear that even where the plaintiff has contributed to the mistake in an unintentional manner the defence may succeed,[219] it remains difficult to lay down any definite principles in relation to a situation where the plaintiff bears no responsibility for the mistake which has occurred. While specific performance has on occasion been refused where the mistake made is entirely attributable to the defendant,[220] the better view would seem to be that in such cases there must be other circumstances which would make it 'highly unreasonable' to decree performance of the contractual obligations. This approach is well set out by Lord Macnaghten in *Stewart v Kennedy*,[221] in

---

217. *Ibid.* at 221.
218. [1992] 1 IR 166, 192.
219. *Denny v Hancock* (1870) 6 Ch App 1.
220. *Malins v Freeman* (1837) 2 Keen 25.
221. (1890) 15 App Cas 75, 105.

which he acknowledged that while a court may refuse specific performance in cases of mistake not caused or contributed to by the plaintiff, it has acted in this manner because it would not be reasonable to compel the defendant to carry out his obligations.

In the last analysis perhaps the most realistic formula is that put forward by James LJ in *Tamplin v James*,[222] namely whether a 'hardship amounting to an injustice' would be caused to the defendant by not allowing him to resist a decree for specific performance on the basis of the mistake which has occurred. Spry[223] has captured the essence of the cases where the mistake may not be sufficiently grave to justify rescission and yet may be serious enough to persuade the court to refuse to decree specific performance. In his view it is necessary not to regard the mistake or misapprehension as an independent discretionary factor, but rather to treat it as a matter which, together with other considerations such as hardship or unfairness, may make it inequitable to grant specific performance of a contract.

Hardship

In the exercise of its discretion, a court may refuse to order specific performance of a contract where to do so would inflict unnecessary hardship on the defendant, even where the plaintiff is not responsible for this. This fact was acknowledged by Budd J in his judgment in *Lavan v Walsh*,[224] in which he said that it is well-established that a court 'will not enforce the specific performance of a contract the result of which would be to impose great hardship on either of the parties to it.'[225] However, it was conceded by counsel in that case that the question of hardship should generally be judged at the time the contract is entered into and, as Budd J commented, proof of subsequent hardship would have to be 'strong and above suspicion'. This issue was further considered by the Supreme Court in *Roberts v O'Neill*,[226] in which the plaintiff claimed specific performance of a contract for the sale of a licensed premises. The defendants claimed that to grant specific performance of the contract with the plaintiff would be to impose unreasonable hardship on them because of the large increase in the value of the property since the date of the contract. McCarthy J acknowledged that hardship might provide a good defence to an action for specific performance where an existing hardship was not known at the date of the contract. However, he clearly felt that subsequent hardship should operate as a defence only in exceptional cases:

> While recognising that there may be cases in which hardship arising after

222. (1880) 15 Ch D 215.
223. Spry, *The Principles of Equitable Remedies* (9th ed., 2014) p. 162.
224. [1964] IR 87.
225. *Ibid.* at 102.
226. [1983] IR 47.

> the date of the contract is such that to decree specific performance would result in great injury, there must be few such cases and, in my view, they should not include ordinarily cases of hardship resulting from inflation alone. To permit as an ordinary rule a defence of subsequent hardship, would be to add a further hazard to the already trouble strewn area of the law of contracts for the sale of land.[227]

In the circumstances the Supreme Court decided to grant a decree of specific performance and concluded that it was not a case in which the court should intervene to deny this remedy to a contracting party to what was 'at the time, a perfectly fair and proper transaction'.

However, it is clear from both the *Lavan* and *Roberts* cases that, where a serious injustice would otherwise result, supervening hardship may in an exceptional case provide a defence. A good example of the type of circumstances which might warrant such a conclusion is provided by *Patel v Ali*,[228] in which the claim of a purchaser of a house to an order of specific performance against the vendor was resisted on the grounds of hardship. After the parties had entered into the contract the vendor became seriously ill, necessitating the amputation of her leg. To compound her difficulties she gave birth to a second child and her husband, who had been adjudicated bankrupt, was sent to prison for a time. Evidence was adduced that she relied greatly on the help of neighbours and of members of her family living nearby to cope with looking after the household and that to enforce specifically the contract for sale would cause undue hardship. Goulding J stated that '[t]he important and true principle, in my view, is that only in extraordinary and persuasive circumstances can hardship supply an excuse for resisting performance of a contract for the sale of immovable property.'[229] However, he acknowledged that 'the court has sometimes refused specific performance because of a change of circumstances supervening after the making of the contract and not in any way attributable to the plaintiff'[230] and he refused to grant an order in the matter before him and instead awarded damages to the purchaser.

The principles set out in *Patel v Ali* were referred to in *Shah v Greening*,[231] in which it was reiterated that 'there must be extraordinary and persuasive circumstances such as to take the case away from the normal situation, in which the contracting parties undertake the risk of such hardship as may arise in the supervening period between exchange and completion.' On the facts of the case before the court, where the death of the defendant's husband had led to her suffering from depression and being unable to continue working, an

227. *Ibid.* at 64. See also *Kelly v Simpson* [2008] IEHC 374 at 4; *Leggett v Crowley* [2019] IEHC 182 at [59].
228. [1984] Ch 283.
229. Ibid. at 288.
230. *Ibid.* at 287.
231. [2016] EWHC 548 (Ch) at [84].

order of specific performance was granted on the basis that the case did 'not exhibit the extraordinary and persuasive circumstances which are required if the court is to refuse to order specific performance on account of hardship'.[232]

The circumstances in which hardship or impossibility may provide a defence to a claim for specific performance where the property which the plaintiff contracted to purchase had fallen significantly in value since the date the contract was concluded were considered by Clarke J in *Aranbel Ltd v Darcy*.[233] On the facts of the case before him Clarke J was satisfied that there was no realistic possibility of the defendants being in a position to complete the contracts in question and he found that impossibility provided a defence. He pointed out that hardship therefore did not arise. Clarke J stated that he would defer to a future case, in which the issue was determinative, any definitive ruling on the way in which hardship might provide a defence in cases where a purchaser could complete a contract, but only by disposing of assets such as a family home or business assets which would have significant practical consequences. Clarke J said that while there would be an obvious reluctance on the part of a court to require such a course of action, it also has to take into account the fact that the relevant defendant might be equally badly off as a result of a significant award of damages as from a decree of specific performance, particularly if a reasonable period of time was afforded for completion. These comments of Clarke J in this context were referred to by O'Connor J in *Leggett v Crowley*,[234] in which the defendant, who had entered into a contract for the sale of his family home, subsequently sought to argue that an order for specific performance would cause him hardship due to the loss of this property. He pointed out that the defendant had at all material times contemplated the sale of his home and that such a case was to be contrasted with a claim for hardship where a party might be forced to sell his family home to complete some other transaction. O'Connor J expressed the view that '[t]he hardship that is alleged must be external to the contract to preclude performance of the contract'[235] and reiterated that the court should assess the issue of hardship at the time the contract was entered into save in exceptional circumstances which in his view did not arise in the matter before him.

Clearly in deciding whether to exercise its discretion on this basis, the court must balance the hardship which the defendant contends he would suffer against the hardship which the plaintiff would sustain if the contract were not specifically enforced,[236] which may, for example, relate to the likelihood that the plaintiff may not be able to recover damages to compensate him for the defendant's wrongdoing.

---

232. *Ibid.* at [91].
233. [2010] 3 IR 769.
234. [2019] IEHC 182.
235. *Ibid.* at [64].
236. *O'Neill v Ryan (No. 3)* [1992] 1 IR 166, 192. See also *Beshoff Brothers Ltd v Select Service Partner Ireland Ltd* [1998] IEHC 122.

The predominant view is that hardship which may be caused to third parties as a result of a decision to grant specific performance is a factor which may be taken into account by a court.[237] So, in *Conlon v Murray*[238] Black LJ seems to have attached some weight at least to the fact that if the vendor's executors were compelled to proceed with a contract for the sale of her farm, her brother would have had nowhere to live. Whether hardship which may be suffered by the public generally will be relevant is less easy to predict but in either case the weight which a court will attach to it will depend largely on the probable extent of the hardship or prejudice which will ensue.

Closely related to the issue of the potential hardship which may be caused to the defendant are general considerations of unfairness which are more likely to concern the manner in which the plaintiff has behaved. So, where the plaintiff has acted in an unconscionable manner so as to take advantage of the weakness of a defendant's position, specific performance may be refused. A good illustration of the operation of this principle is the decision of the Northern Ireland Court of Appeal in *Conlon v Murray* to which reference has just been made. The plaintiff brought an action for specific performance of a contract for the sale of a farm against the vendor which was continued against her executors after her death. The vendor was an elderly lady who had agreed to the sale in a distressed state without taking any time for reflection and without the benefit of independent advice. While Black LJ acknowledged that specific performance of a contract will not be refused on the sole ground that one of the parties had not received legal advice, he stated that in view of the 'extraordinary and unexplained haste' with which the transaction had been rushed through, the court should hesitate to decree specific performance. He said that it is well-established that there is a class of case in which a contract may be of such a nature that the court will not order it to be rescinded, but at the same time, having regard to the substantial justice of the case, will not order that it be specifically performed. In the circumstances, in the exercise of its discretion, the Court of Appeal refused to grant specific performance. This result can be contrasted with that arrived at by Murray J in *McCrystal v O'Kane*,[239] in which *Conlon* was distinguished and suggestions that the plaintiff had taken unfair advantage of the defendant in concluding an agreement for the sale of land were rejected.

Laches or Delay

As a general principle, a plaintiff who delays unreasonably in bringing proceedings for specific performance may fail to obtain the relief which he seeks where by reason of his delay it would be inequitable to grant the remedy sought.

237. Although note the comments of Isaacs J in *Gall v Mitchell* (1924) 35 CLR 222, 230.
238. [1958] NI 17.
239. [1986] NI 123.

It is important to stress that delay alone will probably be insufficient without some further element of prejudice and it will tend to be necessary to show circumstances which, when considered in conjunction with the delay, would render the granting of a decree for specific performance unjust.[240] However, given that the circumstances of a case will vary so widely the courts have tended to stop short of laying down the requirement that detriment in addition to mere lapse of time is always essential. This point was made by Anderson J in the decision of the New Zealand Supreme Court in *Eastern Services Ltd v No.68 Ltd*,[241] where he said that he was cautious about endorsing an unqualified principle concerning mere delay without prejudice. He continued as follows:

> This is because the doctrine of laches requires a balancing of equities in relation to the broad span of human conduct. In the abstract, facts and the weight to be given to them are infinitely variable. But in a particular case they have to be identified and weighed for what they are, as a singular exercise.[242]

It is clear from the judgment of O'Connor J in *Guerin v Heffernan*[243] that where a plaintiff intends to seek relief in the form of specific performance he is bound to proceed without delay. As he stated, '[a] man who sleeps on his rights does not find favour in a court of equity.'[244] The defendant sought to repudiate a contract for the purchase of a farm and the plaintiff, after threatening to institute proceedings against him, did nothing for a period of over a year. O'Connor J concluded that during the intervening time the defendant might well have assumed that the plaintiff had abandoned his rights under the contract and had accepted the defendant's repudiation and held that on this basis the plaintiff was not entitled to relief in the form of specific performance.

It is difficult to lay down reliable guidelines about the length of delay which may disentitle a plaintiff to relief as the question is often governed by other factors such as the conduct of the parties. However, Spry[245] has stated that 'the general rule is that in order to establish that the delay of the plaintiff has been excessive it must appear that, in all the material circumstances, a reasonably assiduous person would have proceeded with substantially greater speed or diligence.'[246] In *Lazard Brothers & Co. Ltd v Fairfield Properties Co. (Mayfair) Ltd*[247] the plaintiff failed to issue proceedings for specific performance until

240. See also *Aranbel Ltd v Darcy* [2010] IEHC 272 at [2.13].
241. [2006] 3 NZLR 335.
242. *Ibid.* at 347.
243. [1925] 1 IR 57.
244. *Ibid.* at 68.
245. Spry, *The Principles of Equitable Remedies* (9th ed., 2014) p. 235.
246. These principles were quoted by Whelan J in *Barrington v ACC Loan Management DAC* [2018] IECA 31 at [16].
247. (1987) 121 SJ 793.

over two years had passed since the contract had been concluded. Megarry VC said that if specific performance was to be regarded as a prize 'to be awarded by equity to the zealous and denied to the indolent' the plaintiff might not succeed, but this was not the case and in the absence of any evidence of any other prejudice or circumstances which would make it unjust to grant relief, he made the order sought. More recently it has been suggested by Aldous LJ in the decision of the Court of Appeal in *Frawley v Neill*[248] that the modern approach in such cases should not require an inquiry as to whether the circumstances can be fitted within the confines of a preconceived formula derived from earlier cases. Instead the court should take a broad approach, directed to ascertaining whether it would in all the circumstances be unconscionable for a party to be permitted to assert his beneficial right.

Usually, unless the parties have stipulated otherwise, time will not be of the essence to a contract in equity,[249] and a plaintiff may still be entitled to an order for specific performance even after the date for performance of the contractual obligations has passed. So, in *O'Connor v McNamara*,[250] where the defendant had not made time of the essence in relation to an agreement for the dissolution of a partnership and the court accepted that the plaintiff had been unaware of the significance of having aspects of this agreement completed within a certain time frame, McGovern J held that the defendant was not entitled to claim that the contract was null and void. In the circumstances, where it appeared that the defendant had failed to complete because of a downturn in the market, he held that the plaintiff was entitled to an order for specific performance of the dissolution agreement.

However, where it is clear that time is of the essence, it is likely that a plaintiff will be entitled to relief in the form of an order for specific performance only in exceptional circumstances. Certainly a rigid approach to enforcing time stipulations in a contract was taken by the Privy Council in *Union Eagle Ltd v Golden Achievement Ltd*,[251] although a more flexible approach has been taken in a number of decisions of the High Court of Australia.[252] In *Union Eagle* relief in the form of specific performance was refused where a purchaser failed to complete a contract for the sale of property within the time stipulated by tendering the purchase price ten minutes after the time for completion had passed. It was clear as Lord Hoffmann stated that 'time was to be in every respect of the essence of the agreement'[253] and in the circumstances the vendor declared that the contract was rescinded and the deposit paid by the

248. [1999] EWCA Civ 875.
249. *Hopkins v Geoghegan* [1931] IR 135, 139; *Hynes v Independent Newspapers Ltd* [1980] IR 204, 218-219; *O'Connor v McNamara* [2009] IEHC 190 at 5.
250. [2009] IEHC 190.
251. [1997] AC 514. See Thompson [1997] Conv 382; Heydon (1997) 113 LQR 385; Stevens (1998) 61 MLR 255.
252. *Legione v Hateley* (1983) 152 CLR 406; *Stern v McArthur* (1988) 165 CLR 489.
253. [1997] AC 514, 517.

purchaser forfeited. Lord Hoffmann referred to the *dicta* of Viscount Haldane in *Steedman v Drinkle*[254] and stated that the courts in England, while ready to grant restitutionary relief against penalties, have been unwilling to grant specific performance where there has been a breach of an essential condition as to time.[255] While he acknowledged that the High Court of Australia has accepted that in exceptional cases specific performance may be granted at the instance of a purchaser who is in breach of an essential condition in a contract,[256] in his view these decisions could provide no assistance to the purchaser in the circumstances of the case before the court. He stated as follows:

> There is no question of any penalty, or of the vendor being unjustly enriched by improvements made at the purchaser's expense, or of the vendor's conduct having contributed to the breach, or of the transaction being in substance a mortgage. It remains for consideration on some future occasion as to whether the way to deal with the problems which have arisen in such cases is by relaxing the principle in *Steedman v Drinkle*, as the Australian courts have done, or by development of the law of restitution and estoppel.[257]

In the view of the Privy Council the case seemed to be one to which the full force of the general rule applied. As Lord Hoffmann stated, 'the fact is that the purchaser was late'[258] and any suggestion that he was only slightly late was bound to lead to arguments over how late was too late which could only be resolved by litigation. In the circumstances he concluded that there was a need for a firm restatement of the principle 'that in cases of rescission of an ordinary contract of sale of land for failure to comply with an essential condition as to time, equity will not intervene'. It remains to be seen whether in the circumstances referred to by Lord Hoffmann above, for example where the question of a penalty arises, or where it appears that the vendor has been unjustly enriched by improvements made at the purchaser's expense, the courts in this jurisdiction might be prepared to take a more lenient approach.

Illegality

A contract which is illegal will be void and cannot be specifically enforced. As

---

254. [1916] 1 AC 275.
255. However, earlier authorities showed that specific performance might be granted where time was of the essence where, e.g. a term providing for forfeiture of half the purchase price was regarded as a penalty, see *Re Dagenham (Thames) Dock Co., Ex p. Hulse* (1873) LR 8 Ch App 1022.
256. *Legione v Hateley* (1983) 152 CLR 406; *Stern v McArthur* (1988) 165 CLR 489.
257. [1997] AC 514, 523.
258. *Ibid.*

Jessel MR stated in *Sykes v Beadon*,[259] 'the principle is clear that you cannot directly enforce an illegal contract, and you cannot ask the court to assist you in carrying it out.'[260] Where the illegality inherent in the contract involves criminal or immoral conduct, as a general principle it will invalidate the entire agreement, although where the illegal element is of a lesser nature, for example, a clause in restraint of trade,[261] the contract may stand if the portion which the courts will not enforce on grounds of public policy can be severed.[262] In addition, a contract which appears valid on its face but which if carried into effect might achieve an underlying illegal purpose or be contrary to public policy will not be enforceable. So, in *Wroth v Tyler*[263] specific performance of a contract entered into by the defendant to sell his house to the plaintiff was refused in circumstances where the defendant's wife had the right not to be evicted from the property. The court was satisfied that if the order were made the plaintiff would be able to evict the husband and other members of his family apart from his wife and this would have the effect of splitting up the family which would be contrary to public policy.

As McWilliam J made clear in his judgment in *Starling Securities Ltd v Woods*,[264] the courts in this jurisdiction will not grant specific performance of a contract where there is an underlying illegal purpose. On the facts of the case before him he found that the only interpretation he could put on the 'very peculiar method adopted to conduct these transactions' was that both parties were trying to conceal their true nature from the Revenue Commissioners and he concluded that he would not countenance such attempted fraud on the Revenue by enforcing performance of the contract. In addition, it is clear from the *dicta* of Finlay P in *Whitecross Potatoes (International) Ltd v Coyle*[265] that the onus is on a defendant who asserts that a contract is illegal to establish as a matter of probability that it was at the time of its formation illegal in nature. This point has been reiterated in a number of more recent decisions in which the question of relying on illegality as a defence to an action for specific performance has been considered. In *Whelan v Kavanagh*[266] Herbert J stated that a party who has executed a contract which is regular and lawful on its face should not lightly be permitted to impugn it, particularly to his own advantage, by pleading

259. (1879) 11 Ch D 170, 197.
260. See generally the discussion in Chapter 7 in relation to the operation of the doctrine of illegality and in particular *Quinn v Irish Bank Resolution Corporation Ltd* [2016] 1 IR 1 and *Patel v Mirza* [2017] AC 467.
261. *S.V Nevenas & Co. v Walker* [1914] 1 Ch 413; *Goldsoll v Goldman* [1915] 1 Ch 292. However, note the comments of Younger LJ in *Attwood v Lamont* [1920] 3 KB 571, 595.
262. *Bennett v Bennett* [1952] 1 KB 249, 260; *Goodinson v Goodinson* [1954] 2 QB 118, 120.
263. [1974] Ch 30.
264. High Court 1975 No. 4044P (McWilliam J) 24 May 1977.
265. [1978] ILRM 31.
266. [2001] IEHC 14.

illegality as a defence to a claim for specific performance. He stressed that the onus of proving such illegality lies firmly on the party raising it, although he stated that extrinsic evidence outside the terms of the written contract was admissible to prove, for example as in the case before him, a smaller 'real' consideration inconsistent with the agreement itself. Herbert J was satisfied that there had been no proof placed before the court to support the defendant's claim to this effect other than his own oral evidence which was unsupported by any document or reliable corroborative evidence. He concluded that this evidence was 'altogether unreliable' and affirmed the order of the Circuit Court granting specific performance of the agreement for the sale of the premises in question.

Similarly, in *Kavanagh v Caulfield*[267] Murphy J reiterated that it is clear that the onus of proving illegality in a contract lies on the defendant. The parties had entered into a contract for the sale of a property, although the plaintiff claimed that the defendant had required her to pay a sum of money to a charity as an inducement to enter into the contract. In resisting the claim for specific performance, the defendant contended that if any agreement had been made, it was an illegal and unenforceable contract by reason of the fact that it did not reflect the true price paid by the plaintiff for the premises and that it had been agreed that the additional sum would be paid to the charity with the intention that it would not be disclosed to the Revenue Commissioners. Murphy J stated that, in deciding whether to grant the relief sought, the court must examine the quality of the illegality relied upon by the defendant and must look at all of the surrounding circumstances. It must assess whether there had been an illegality of which the court should take notice, whether it would be an affront to the public conscience if, by granting the relief sought, the court was seen to be indirectly assisting a criminal act, and it must also be satisfied that the contract has not been otherwise rendered ineffective. On the facts he found that the contract in the case before him was one which in accordance with the apparent intention of the parties at the time of its formation could and would be carried out in a legal manner. He concluded, in granting an order for specific performance, that there was insufficient evidence to establish that the plaintiff intended to carry the contract out in an illegal fashion and that there was therefore no illegality such as to render it unenforceable.

Impossibility and Frustration

A court will not make an order of specific performance compelling a party to a contract to perform his obligations where it will not be possible for him to comply with the order which the court proposes to make. As Brewster LC stated in *Sheppard v Murphy*,[268] 'a Court of Equity cannot compel him to do that which is impossible'. This point was reiterated by Murphy J in his decision

267. [2002] IEHC 62. See also *Leggett v Crowley* [2019] IEHC 182 at [41].
268. (1868) IR 2 Eq 544, 557.

in the High Court in *Neville & Sons Ltd v Guardian Builders Ltd*,[269] where he commented that 'if a contract is discharged by impossibility then clearly no court could compel its performance'. However, as Brewster LC also made clear in *Sheppard*, a party cannot take steps to make performance of his contractual obligations impossible and then seek to rely on this as a defence. As Farrell has stated, '[w]hile a court of equity will not compel a person to do something which is impossible it will have little sympathy for someone whose own neglect or default makes it impossible for him to perform his contract.'[270]

However, it appears from the judgment of Clarke J in *Aranbel Ltd v Darcy*[271] that impossibility arising from a purchaser's impecuniosity may provide a reason for a court to refuse to order specific performance. In this case, in which the plaintiff sought specific performance of contracts to buy apartments in circumstances where they had fallen significantly in value since the contracts had originally been entered into, Clarke J stated that '[i]t has often been said that equity will not act in vain'[272] and acknowledged that a court should be reluctant to order specific performance where there is no reasonable prospect of the order being complied with. In his view in order for a purchaser to be able to say that completion is impossible, it is necessary for him to demonstrate that he has no realisable assets or borrowing capacity that could be brought to bear to pay the contracted purchase price. Clarke J stated as follows:

> Where a party contends that they are unable to complete a contract for financial reasons and wishes to resist an order for specific performance on the basis of impossibility, then it seems to me to be clear that the onus of proof rests on that party to establish their inability to complete. In addition … it follows that that party must put before the court all reasonable evidence necessary to allow the court to assess whether there is a true case of impossibility.[273]

Having considered the evidence before him, Clarke J concluded that he was satisfied that that there was no realistic possibility of the defendants being in a position to complete the contracts in question, and it followed that an order for specific performance would not be appropriate.

Specific performance may also be refused for reasons of impracticability or futility falling short of impossibility. So, in *Duffy v Ridley Properties Ltd*[274]

---

269. [1990] ILRM 601, 616. Reversed by the Supreme Court [1995] 1 ILRM 1.
270. Farrell, *Irish Law of Specific Performance* (1994) para. 3.27. Quoted with approval by Smyth J in *Mount Kennett Investment Co. v O'Meara* [2007] IEHC 420. See also *Gibbons v Doherty* [2013] IEHC 109 at 16.
271. [2010] 3 IR 769.
272. *Ibid.* at 772. This principle was referred to by O'Connor J in *Leggett v Crowley* [2019] IEHC 182 at [53], although he added that the court will seek to 'fashion a remedy to ensure that the rule of law and justice applies.'
273. *Ibid.* at 779–780.
274. [2005] IEHC 314. A decision upheld by the Supreme Court [2008] 4 IR 282.

Finlay Geoghegan J refused to grant an order of specific performance and instead awarded the plaintiff damages in lieu in circumstances where uncertainty surrounded the boundaries of the plot of land to be transferred. In addition, in *Hannon v BQ Investments*,[275] although it should be acknowledged that the order sought related to the building of a road and was therefore of a nature which the courts are generally reluctant to enforce, specific performance was also refused by Laffoy J on the basis that the plaintiffs were asking the court 'to order the carrying out of what in all probability will be a waste of resources and a futile exercise.'

A contract may be rendered impossible to perform by reason of frustration and the circumstances in which this may occur were considered by the Supreme Court in *Neville & Sons Ltd v Guardian Builders Ltd*.[276] The plaintiff and defendant entered into an agreement whereby the plaintiff contracted to build houses on a site owned by the defendant. It was accepted that the only means of ensuring effective access to the site would be by the construction of a new roadway which involved the acquisition of a strip of land owned by the county council. Difficulties arose in acquiring this land; the plaintiff sought specific performance of the agreement and the defendant contended that by reason of the difficulties which had arisen in relation to access to the site, performance of the contract had been rendered impossible or possible only in circumstances so different from those contemplated that both parties were relieved from further performance. Murphy J accepted that performance of the contract had been frustrated by intervening circumstances and held that the plaintiffs were not entitled to specific performance, although this decision was reversed by the Supreme Court. In the course of his judgment Blayney J quoted with approval[277] from the speech of Lord Simon in *National Carriers Ltd v Panalpina (Northern) Ltd*[278] as follows:

> Frustration of a contract takes place when there supervenes an event (without default of either party and for which the contract makes no sufficient provision) which so significantly changes the nature (not merely the expense or onerousness) of the outstanding contractual rights and/or obligations from what the parties could reasonably have contemplated at the time of its execution that it would be unjust to hold them to the literal sense of its stipulations in the new circumstances; in such case the law declares both parties to be discharged from further performance.

Blayney J concluded that what had transpired could not be termed a supervening event which significantly changed the nature of the defendant's obligations and

275. [2009] IEHC 191.
276. [1995] 1 ILRM 1.
277. *Ibid.* at 7.
278. [1981] AC 675, 700. See also the judgment of Kenny J in *Browne v Mulligan* [1976-77] ILRM 327, 332-333 in relation to the possible basis for the doctrine of frustration.

while it made performance of the contract more onerous, he was satisfied that the defence of frustration should fail.

The principles set out by Blayney J are now well established in this jurisdiction and have been relied upon in a number of decisions.[279] In *Drocarne Ltd v Seamus Murphy Properties and Developments Ltd*[280] Finlay Geoghegan J also referred to the authorities considered in Treitel, *Frustration and Force Majeure*,[281] but said that there was no difference in the temporal approach in either case. As she stated, '[t]he Court in each is referred back to an examination of the agreement or bargain made between the parties at the time they entered into the contract alleged to be now discharged on the ground of frustration and a comparison between such agreement or bargain or its then performance and any future performance of the contract in the altered circumstances.'[282] In her view the only difference between the approaches appears to be in relation to what the court should examine at the two dates. In *National Carriers Ltd v Panalpina (Northern) Ltd*[283] Lord Simon made the comparison by reference to obligations or rights of the parties under the contract at the time it was entered into and the outstanding obligations and rights if they were to be held to its performance in the altered circumstances. In many of the decisions referred to by Treitel, comparisons were made between the performance intended by the contract when entered into with what would be achieved by the performance of the contract in the altered circumstances. Finlay Geoghegan J concluded that '[w]hether the court should consider the alleged frustration in terms of changed obligations or rights for the parties; change of bargain or change in what will be achieved by the performance of the contract in the altered circumstances seems to depend on the facts of the case. In some instances this may be different ways of considering very similar questions.'[284] On the facts of the case before her she was satisfied that notwithstanding the changed circumstances, this did not mean that the parties could not accomplish the objects they had had when they entered into the agreement and she concluded that the agreement had not been terminated by reason of frustration.

The manner in which the defence of frustration operates was also considered by Kelly J in *Ringsend Property Ltd v Donatex Ltd*[285] in the context of an application for summary judgment. He said that 'the defence of frustration is one of limited application and narrowness' and that '[i]t arises in circumstances where performance of a contract in the manner envisaged by the parties is rendered impossible because of some supervening event not within the

279. See e.g. *Collins v Gleeson* [2011] IEHC 200.
280. [2008] IEHC 99.
281. (2nd ed., 2004) pp. 67-68.
282. [2008] IEHC 99 at 18. See also *Collins v Gleeson* [2011] IEHC 200 at 15.
283. [1981] AC 675.
284. [2008] IEHC 99 at 18.
285. [2009] IEHC 568.

contemplation of the parties.'[286] Having quoted the passage from the speech of Lord Simon in *National Carriers* set out above, Kelly J commented that this demonstrated the narrow scope for invoking the doctrine of frustration. In the circumstances of the case before him, Kelly J stated that even if the defence were made out and the contractual obligations between the parties were at an end it would not benefit the defendants, as they would still remain liable to repay the funds advanced. He also rejected the defendants' claim that the concept of 'partial frustration' might be invoked and concluded that there was no arguable basis for seeking to avoid the provisions of the clause at issue by reference to either the doctrine of frustration or the concept of partial frustration.

It should be noted that it appears that a party cannot rely on the doctrine of frustration to provide a defence where the contract has been frustrated by an event which he anticipated or should have anticipated.[287] Kelly J also made it clear in *Murphy v Ryan*[288] that where the circumstances alleged to cause frustration of the contract have arisen from the act or default of a party, it cannot rely upon the doctrine. On the facts of the case before him, he concluded that the default was exclusively that of the defendants. As he put it, '[t]hey foolishly entered into an unconditional contract without the necessary finance to complete it. They cannot now walk away from their bargain.'[289]

286. *Ibid.* at 6.
287. *McGuill v Aer Lingus Teo* [1983] IEHC 71 at 13-14.
288. [2009] IEHC 305.
289. *Ibid.* at 9.

CHAPTER 16

Rectification

INTRODUCTION

Rectification is a discretionary equitable remedy which allows for the correction of an instrument which has failed to record the actual intentions of the parties to a contract.[1] It is important to stress at the outset that the task of the court in this regard 'is corrective and not speculative'.[2] So, in certain circumstances the court may rectify documents, such as deeds, in order to make them correspond with the pre-existing agreement of the parties. For example, in the case of a contract for the sale of land, where a deed did not reflect the agreement of the parties, equity would allow rectification so as to ensure that the final instrument gave proper effect to the prior contract. This jurisdiction is viewed as an exception to the parol evidence rule that oral evidence will not suffice to alter a written document.

It is important to stress that this does not constitute rectification of the contract, but only of the writing recording the contract. This point is well summarised in the following *dictum* of James VC in *Mackenzie v Coulson*[3] that while 'Courts of Equity do not rectify contracts; they may and do rectify instruments purporting to have been made in pursuance of the terms of contracts'. Similar sentiments have been expressed in a number of decisions in this jurisdiction. So, in *Irish Life Assurance Co. Ltd v Dublin Land Securities Ltd*[4] Griffin J commented that 'rectification is concerned with defects in the recording, not in the making, of an agreement',[5] a statement echoed by Barron J in *McD. v McD.*[6]

---

1. *Irish Pensions Trust Ltd v Central Remedial Clinic* [2006] 2 IR 126, 150. See also *Boliden Tara Mines Ltd v Cosgrove* [2010] IESC 62 at 11.
2. *Per* Binnie J in the decision of the Supreme Court of Canada in *Sylvan Lake Golf and Tennis Club Ltd v Performance Industries Ltd* (2002) 209 DLR (4th) 318, 330. He added that the court's role 'is to restore the parties to their original bargain, not to rectify a belatedly recognized error of judgment by one party or the other.'
3. (1869) LR 8 Eq 368, 375. See also the *dictum* of Buckley LJ in *Lovell and Christmas Ltd v Wall* (1911) 104 LT 85, 93 that 'the court does not rectify contracts, but what it rectifies is the erroneous expression of contracts in documents.'
4. [1989] IR 253, 260.
5. See also *Slattery v Friends First* [2015] 3 IR 292, 309.
6. [1993] ILRM 717, 722.

PREREQUISITES FOR RECTIFICATION

Originally, it was necessary to show that there was a valid and enforceable contract antecedent to the instrument sought to be rectified, and that such contract was inaccurately represented in the instrument. However, Clauson J suggested *obiter* in *Shipley Urban District Council v Bradford Corporation*[7] that it was not necessary to find a concluded and binding contract between the parties antecedent to the agreement which it was sought to rectify, provided that there was a common continuing intention with regard to a particular provision or aspect of the agreement. Thus if the parties were *ad idem* up to the point in time when they executed the formal instrument which, it transpired, did not correspond with their common agreement, the court might order rectification even though there was no concluded and binding contract between the parties up to the point when the formal instrument was executed. This approach was followed in this jurisdiction in *Monaghan County Council v Vaughan*.[8] The plaintiff county council invited tenders for demolition work and the removal of valuable materials from a derelict site. Dixon J found that it was the clear intention of both parties that the defendant would pay for the right to carry out the works. Thus when the county council executed a contract which provided that the defendant should be paid for the demolition work, this was an instance of mutual mistake, as the parties had agreed on matters which were not reflected in the written contract. Dixon J rejected the argument that there could be no rectification because there was no antecedent agreement between the parties which was capable of being enforced and granted the plaintiff's claim for rectification.

The reasoning of Clauson J in *Shipley* was followed in England in *Crane v Hegeman-Harris Co. Inc*,[9] where Simonds J stated that it was not necessary to find a concluded and binding contract between the parties antecedent to the agreement which it is sought to rectify provided there is a common continuing intention in relation to the particular provision of the agreement. Leaving aside questions about enforceability, doubts remained about whether an antecedent complete concluded agreement was necessary, particularly as a result of the views expressed by Denning LJ in *Frederick E. Rose (London) Ltd v William H. Pim Junior & Co. Ltd*,[10] which were quoted with approval in this jurisdiction in *Lucey v Laurel Construction Co. Ltd.*[11] The issue appears to have been resolved in England as a result of the judgment of Russell LJ in *Joscelyne v Nissen*,[12] where he stated that in his view the correct position was that enunciated by Simonds J in *Crane* subject to the qualification that there

7. [1936] Ch 375.
8. [1948] IR 306.
9. [1939] 1 All ER 662, 664.
10. [1953] 2 QB 450, 461-462.
11. High Court 1970 No. 3816 (Kenny J) 18 December 1970 at 10-11.
12. [1970] 2 QB 86.

should be some outward expression of accord between the parties. The court therefore concluded that as there was an accord between the parties on a specific term of the proposed contract, rectification of this provision could be ordered even though other aspects of the agreement might have been incomplete.

The question of the requirements which must be satisfied where the remedy of rectification is sought was considered in Northern Ireland by Lowry LCJ in *Rooney and McParland Ltd v Carlin*,[13] where he stated as follows:

> 1. There must be a concluded agreement antecedent to the instrument which it is sought to be rectified; but
> 2. The antecedent agreement need not be binding in law (for example, it need not be under seal if made by a public authority or in writing and signed by the party if relating to a sale of land) nor need it be in writing: such incidents merely help to discharge the heavy burden of proof; and
> 3. A complete antecedent concluded contract is not required, as long as there was prior accord on a term of a proposed agreement, outwardly expressed and communicated between the parties, as in *Joscelyne v Nissen*.

When the matter came before the Supreme Court in *Irish Life Assurance Co. Ltd v Dublin Land Securities Ltd*[14] Griffin J stated that he would adopt what had been said by Russell LJ in *Joscelyne* and by Lowry LCJ in *Rooney* and pointed out that in *Lucey v Laurel Construction Co. Ltd*, Kenny J did not appear to have been referred to the decision of Russell LJ. Griffin J concluded as follows:

> Applying those principles to the facts of this case, and bearing in mind the heavy burden of proof that lies on those seeking rectification, the question to be addressed is whether there was convincing proof, reflected in some outward expression of accord, that the contract in writing did not represent the common continuing intention of the parties on which the court can act …[15]

As a result it would now seem to be firmly established that an antecedent concluded agreement is not necessary provided there is a common intention to include or exclude a particular term which continues until the contract is executed and which is made manifest by the parties in some way. Edwards

---

13. [1981] NI 138, 146. See also *Irish Pensions Trust Ltd v Central Remedial Clinic* [2006] 2 IR 126, 150; *Boliden Tara Mines Ltd v Cosgrove* [2010] IESC 62 at 11; *King v Ulster Bank Ireland Ltd* [2013] IEHC 250 at [37].
14. [1989] IR 253.
15. *Ibid.* at 263. Quoted with approval by Murphy J in *Lac Minerals Ltd v Chevron Mineral Corporation of Ireland* [1995] 1 ILRM 161, 172. See also *Danske Bank A/S v Coyne* [2011] IEHC 234 at [18].

J explained the position well when he stated in *Leopardstown Club Ltd v Templeville Developments Ltd*[16] that:

> It is now well established that a common continuing intention, evidenced by an outward expression of accord, is all that is required for rectification for common mistake. There is no requirement that this outward expression of accord has been embodied in a legally binding contract. Nor is it necessary, that all matters between the parties have been agreed at the time of the outward expression of accord provided that there is a common intention on the particular provision or aspect of the agreement in respect of which rectification is being sought.

However, it is vital that this common intention can be ascertained with precision and a number of claims for rectification have failed on the grounds that the parties' exact intentions cannot be identified with sufficient certainty. This point emerges from the decision of the Supreme Court in *Irish Life Assurance Co. Ltd v Dublin Land Securities Ltd.*[17] The plaintiff company owned a large portfolio of ground rents and also valuable lands which had been made the subject of compulsory purchase orders. A contract of sale between the plaintiff and the defendant was drawn up and while it was the intention of the plaintiff to exclude the lands subject to the CPOs from the sale, due to a mix-up in its legal department, they were included in the contract. The plaintiff's intention to exclude these lands was communicated to an agent of the defendant in a rather imprecise way but was not passed on to the defendant. The plaintiff sought rectification of the contract, while the defendant sought specific performance of the agreement in its original form. Keane J found that the defendant did not know of the plaintiff's intention to exclude the properties in question and dismissed the plaintiff's claim on the grounds that there was no common intention between the parties to this effect. On appeal, the Supreme Court upheld the order of the High Court. Griffin J said that the party seeking rectification must establish by convincing proof that the instrument does not reflect the common intention of the parties and held that the plaintiff had failed to discharge this onus as the oral reference to the properties by the plaintiffs lacked the precision necessary to enable the court to conclude what the common intention of the parties had been.

The lack of precision in relation to the alleged common intention was even more pronounced in the subsequent decision of Murphy J in *Ferguson v Merchant Banking Ltd.*[18] The plaintiff claimed specific performance of a contract for the sale of land and the official liquidator of the defendant company contested the plaintiff's right to have the contract performed, claiming that it was

16. [2010] IEHC152 at [7.9].
17. [1986] IR 332 (HC); [1989] IR 253 (SC).
18. [1993] ILRM 136.

never the intention to include certain development lands in the sale. Murphy J commented that the case before him was far weaker from the defendant's point of view than that presented to the court by the plaintiff in *Irish Life Assurance Co*. In that case a conscious decision to exclude the lands in question had been made whereas in the case before the court, the liquidator simply did not know of the existence of the valuable vacant land. Murphy J also said that there was a striking similarity in that there was an 'absence of a pre-existing concluded agreement establishing the common intention of the parties with a sufficient degree of particularity'. He concluded that the bargain was too imprecise to constitute a contract and that the question of rectification of the agreement was wholly unstateable.

Lack of precision also proved to be fatal to the plaintiff's case in the decision of Barron J in *McD. v McD.*[19] The plaintiff wife and defendant husband signed an agreement following negotiations to settle proceedings relating to maintenance and the distribution of their property and custody of their children. The plaintiff sought rectification of the agreement to include the fact that the husband had agreed to pay her costs in all outstanding legal proceedings between them. Barron J accepted that: 'In order to rectify the contract the court must be satisfied that there was a common and continuing intention and that the agreement as recorded does not represent [the parties'] common intention'[20] and continued that it 'must also be satisfied as to precisely what that common intention was.' Applying these principles, Barron J said that it was necessary for the evidence to show that there was a common intention that the husband should pay the wife's costs and also the precise nature of such costs. He did not believe that the evidence established either of these matters and said that even if there had been an agreement that the husband was to pay the wife's costs, it was clear from the drafting of the subsequent documents that there was no *consensus ad idem* as to the matters to be dealt with on taxation.

An issue which was clarified by Edwards J in *Leopardstown Club Ltd v Templeville Developments Ltd*,[21] was 'the fact that various aspects of a deal not relevant to the matter in respect of which rectification was sought fell to be subsequently re-negotiated between the parties does not present a bar to rectification provided that there was no outward change in their common intention on the point in respect of which rectification is sought.'[22] So, in the matter before him, although certain further issues were negotiated and agreed between the parties subsequent to the time an outward expression of common continuing intention was established, and before the execution of the agreements in question, in his view this was not a relevant consideration. In the circumstances, he concluded that the plaintiff had established by convincing evidence on the balance of probabilities that the parties had reached agreement

19. [1993] ILRM 717.
20. *Ibid.* at 722.
21. [2010] IEHC 152.
22. *Ibid.* at 7.35.

on the issues in question and that the parties' common intention continued up until the relevant documents were executed, and that by reason of a common mistake these documents failed to accurately reflect the parties' common intention.

COMMON MISTAKE

A useful summary of the requirements for rectification on grounds of common mistake traditionally applied in England is set out in the judgment of Peter Gibson LJ in *Swainland Builders Ltd v Freehold Properties Ltd*[23] in the following terms:

> The party seeking rectification must show that: (1) the parties had a common continuing intention, whether or not amounting to an agreement, in respect of a particular matter in the instrument to be rectified; (2) there was an outward expression of accord; (3) the intention continued at the time of the execution of the instrument sought to be rectified; (4) by mistake, the instrument did not reflect that common intention.

However, albeit on an *obiter* basis, Lord Hoffmann in *Chartbrook Ltd v Persimmon Homes Ltd*[24] accepted that '[r]ectification required a mistake about whether the written instrument correctly reflected the prior consensus, not whether it accorded with what the party in question believed that consensus to have been', thereby reformulating the test for common intention to one based on what an objective observer would have thought the intentions of the parties to be.[25] When the Court of Appeal considered this issue in *Daventry District Council v Daventry and District Housing Ltd*[26] Etherton LJ summarised the position as follows:

---

23. [2002] 2 EGLR 71 at [33]. In *Chartbrook Ltd v Persimmon Homes Ltd* [2009] 1 AC 1101, 1123 Lord Hoffmann commented that these principles 'succinctly summarized' the requirements for rectification. See also *Tartsinis v Navona Management Co.* [2015] EWHC 57 (Comm) at [83]; *Murray Holdings Ltd v Oscatello Investments Ltd* [2018] EWHC 162 (Ch) at [172]. These principles were also endorsed by Edwards J in *Leopardstown Club Ltd v Templeville Developments Ltd* [2010] IEHC 152 at [7.31] and quoted by Whelan J in *Knockacummer Wind Farm Ltd v Cremins* [2018] IECA 252 at [56].
24. [2009] 1 AC 1101, 1125. See further McLauchlan (2010) 126 LQR 8; O'Sullivan [2009] CLJ 510; Nugee (2012) 26 Trust Law Int 76.
25. Davies [2016] CLJ 62, 74 is critical of the approach of Lord Hoffmann and suggests that the reasoning 'is unsatisfactory for reasons of principle, policy, and its use of precedent.' See further Davies (2012) 75 MLR 412.
26. [2012] 1 WLR 1333, 1354. See also *Persimmon Homes Ltd v Hillier* [2018] EWHC 221 (Ch) at [26].

> Lord Hoffmann's clarification was that the required "common continuing intention" is not a mere subjective belief but rather what an objective observer would have thought the intention to be: see the Chartbrook case, at para 60. In other words the requirements of "an outward expression of accord" and "common continuing intention" are not separate conditions, but two sides of the same coin, since an uncommunicated inward intention is irrelevant. I suggest that Peter Gibson LJ's statement of the requirements for rectification for mutual mistake can be rephrased as: (1) the parties had a common continuing intention, whether or not amounting to an agreement, in respect of a particular matter in the instrument to be rectified; (2) which existed at the time of execution of the instrument sought to be rectified; (3) such common continuing intention to be established objectively, that is to say by reference to what an objective observer would have thought the intentions of the parties to be; and (4) by mistake the instrument did not reflect that common intention.

The majority of the Court of Appeal, Toulson LJ and Lord Neuberger MR, allowed the claimant's appeal in *Daventry* on the basis of their conclusions that both parties had made a mistake from an objective perspective. However, Etherton LJ dissented and held that any common intention which the defendant held did not, objectively speaking, continue until the time the contract was executed. He also expressed the view that the approach adopted by Toulson LJ 'muddle[d] the distinction' between rectification for mutual and unilateral mistake and wrongly conflated elements of both these doctrines on the basis that the defendant's culpability was irrelevant for rectification for mutual mistake but essential in the case of unilateral mistake.

The courts in this jurisdiction have also endorsed an objective test of common intention where rectification is sought for common mistake. This issue was considered by Edwards J in *Leopardstown Club Ltd v Templeville Developments Ltd*,[27] who referred to decisions such as *Monaghan County Council v Vaughan*[28] and *Nolan v Graves*[29] as examples of the application of an objective test for establishing common intention. He stated that '[t]he requirement, that common intention be determined objectively, means that a subjective change of mind on the part of one party, following a common expression of outward accord, cannot be regarded, unless clearly communicated in a manner identifiable to the reasonable observer, as negating the prior common intention evidenced by this outward expression of accord.'[30] Edwards J also referred to the fact that the objective test of common intention had received judicial endorsement by the House of Lords in *Chartbrook Ltd v Persimmon Homes Ltd* and commented that 'the speeches of Lord Hoffman and his fellow

27. [2010] IEHC 152.
28. [1948] IR 306.
29. [1946] IR 376.
30. [2010] IEHC 152 at [7.40].

Law Lords, in so far as they endorse the application of the objective test of common intention to cases where rectification is sought on the basis of common mistake, display compelling logic.'[31] He added that he approved of them in that regard and stated that he considered that the objective test of common intention also represents the law in this jurisdiction.

However, there is ongoing judicial and academic debate about whether an objective test is appropriate in this context. Davies has been critical of the objective approach which, as he points out, may lead to rectification of a contract being ordered on the basis of 'an objective common mistake even where one party was not actually mistaken about the meaning of the document.'[32] He comments as follows:

> Such uncertainty about whether a court will *deem* a party to have made a mistake, even when that party was not, actually, in the least mistaken, stems from the objective test for common intention. As a result, rather than merely seeking to 'refine' this approach, (as Etherton LJ suggested in *Daventry* at [104]. See too Toulson LJ at [195]) it might be preferable simply to abandon it and return to the 'traditional' *subjective* approach to establishing common intention.[33]

Davies points out that focusing on the subjective intentions of the parties would further help to demarcate common and unilateral mistake rectification. As he notes, both Toulson LJ and Lord Neuberger MR indicated in *Daventry* that it might have been more satisfactory to consider the appeal on the basis of *unilateral* mistake,[34] but they indicated that they felt bound by Lord Hoffmann's analysis in *Chartbrook* to consider whether, objectively speaking, a common mistake had been made. Clearly both Toulson LJ and Lord Neuberger MR also had misgivings about accepting Lord Hoffmann's objective formulation of the test for common mistake,[35] with the latter commenting that it 'may have to be reconsidered or at least refined'.[36] In addition, as Davies points out, 'the difference in the approach between the majority and minority shows how malleable the objective test of mistake may be.'[37]

When this issue was considered by the High Court of Australia in *Simic*

31. *Ibid.* at [7.67].
32. (2012) 75 MLR 412, 413. See also Davies [2016] CLJ 62, 74-75.
33. *Ibid.* at 419.
34. [2012] 1 WLR 1333, 1378 *per* Toulson LJ; *per* Lord Neuberger at 1388. Although, as Etherton LJ pointed out (at 1358), the trial judge had expressly found that no dishonesty on the defendant's part had been proved.
35. *Per* Toulson LJ at 1375.
36. [2012] 1 WLR 1333, 1380. See also the comments of Leggatt J in *Tartsinis v Navona Management Co.* [2015] EWHC 57 (Comm) at [90]-[99]. He concluded that while he had 'very real misgivings' about the approach in *Chartbrook*, he would have felt bound to follow it if the issue had arisen.
37. Davies [2016] CLJ 62, 77.

v New South Wales Land and Housing Corp[38] the court applied a subjective test, holding that the relevant intention was that of the parties. French CJ stated that the objective test 'does not represent the common law of Australia as it presently stands'[39] and added that any change in the law would require full argument in a case in which the question was relevant to the outcome. Kiefel J also commented that the utility of the objective approach advocated by Lord Hoffmann in *Chartbrook* has been questioned and pointed out that rectification is an equitable remedy which is concerned with a mistake in relation to an aspect of what an instrument records and 'with the conscience of the parties'.[40] This is clearly an area of the law which would benefit from further consideration both in England and in Ireland and a convincing argument can be made to the effect that a return to a subjective test for rectification on the grounds of common mistake may be preferable.

For rectification to be available it is necessary to establish that the instrument in question does not accord with the actual terms agreed by the parties and that if rectified it will do so. In this context it is important to distinguish the actual terms from those the parties might have stipulated if they had not been under some misapprehension about what they were agreeing upon. As Spry has stated 'where there is no lack of conformity between the document and the concurrent intention, the basis for rectification does not exist'[41] so an instrument which truly reflects what the parties agreed cannot be altered even though those involved laboured under a fundamental misapprehension about the consequences of their agreement. This point is well-illustrated by the decision of the Court of Appeal in *Frederick E. Rose (London) Ltd v W.H. Pim Junior & Co. Ltd.*[42] The defendant agreed to supply the plaintiff with 'horsebeans', both parties mistakenly believing that the term was synonymous with 'feveroles'. When the defendant subsequently supplied another type of horsebean which was less valuable in nature the plaintiff sought rectification of the agreement to refer specifically to the term 'feverole' but failed on the basis that the contract as recorded accurately reflected the actual terms agreed.

Finally, it emerges from the decision of Murphy J in *Lac Minerals Ltd v Chevron Mineral Corporation of Ireland*[43] that a claim for rectification cannot succeed where it is not made by either of the parties involved in the original agreement, but by a party who although undoubtedly affected by it was in no sense privy to the manner in which it was negotiated, or the circumstances in which the error occurred. Murphy J concluded that the case law in the area demonstrated that while:

38. (2016) 339 ALR 200.
39. *Ibid.* at [19].
40. *Ibid.* at [48].
41. Spry, *The Principles of Equitable Remedies* (9th ed., 2014) p. 636.
42. [1953] 2 QB 450.
43. [1995] 1 ILRM 161.

> the action for rectification does not require that the parties to the litigation should be privy to the same contract, they must be privy to or affected by the same mistake in such a way that it would be unconscionable for the defendant in such proceedings to seek to rely on the document which erroneously recorded or mistakenly implemented the true agreement.[44]

UNILATERAL MISTAKE

Griffin J stated in *Irish Life Assurance Co. Ltd v Dublin Land Securities Ltd*[45] that 'as a general rule, the courts only rectify an agreement in writing where there has been a mutual mistake i.e. where it fails to record the intention of *both* parties'. However, he went on to acknowledge that this statement must now be qualified somewhat and that a party who has entered into an agreement by mistake may be entitled to rectification if he establishes that the other party concluded the agreement with knowledge of this mistake.[46] The basis for the exercise of this jurisdiction was set out by Kenny J in his judgment in *Lucey v Laurel Construction Co. Ltd*[47] in the following manner:

> The Court has jurisdiction to rectify a written agreement made between two parties only when either there is a mutual mistake made by the two parties in the drafting of a written agreement which is to give effect to a prior oral agreement or when one party sees a mistake in the written agreement and when he knows that the other party has not seen it and then signs the document knowing that it contains a mistake ….

Similar views were expressed by Pennycuick J in *A. Roberts & Co. Ltd v Leicestershire County Council*,[48] where he stated that 'a party is entitled to rectification of a contract on proof that he believed a particular term to be included in the contract and that the other party concluded the contract with the omission or a variation of that term in the knowledge that the first party believed the term to be included'. The plaintiff had undertaken to build a school for the defendant council. The agreement originally provided that the building should be completed within 18 months, but officers of the defendant changed the time for the performance of the contract to 30 months and the plaintiff signed without noticing the alteration. It was held that the defendant was aware of the mistake and rectification was ordered on this basis.

The circumstances in which the doctrine in *Roberts* will apply were

44. *Ibid.* at 178.
45. [1989] IR 253, 260.
46. *Ibid.* at 261. See also *O'Neill v Ryan (No. 3)* [1992] 1 IR 166, 185 *per* Costello J; *Knockacummer Wind Farm Ltd v Cremins* [2018] IECA 252 at [42].
47. High Court 1970 No. 3816P (Kenny J) 18 December 1970 at 9-10.
48. [1961] Ch 555.

considered in some detail by the Court of Appeal in *Thomas Bates & Son Ltd v Wyndham's (Lingerie) Ltd*.[49] The defendant tenant was aware of the plaintiff landlord's mistake in not including an arbitration provision in a rent review clause but did not draw its attention to it. The plaintiff realised the omission only when rent review was necessary although the defendant had at all times been aware of the mistake. The Court of Appeal ordered that an arbitration clause be inserted into the lease in accordance with the parties' original intention. Buckley LJ stated that for the doctrine to apply the following conditions must be satisfied:

1. One party, A, erroneously believed that the document to be rectified contained a particular term or provision, or mistakenly thought it did not contain a particular term or provision which mistakenly, it did contain.
2. The other party, B, was aware of the mistake and knew that it was due to an error on the part of A.
3. B omitted to draw the mistake to the notice of A.
4. The mistake must be one calculated to benefit B.

Buckley LJ commented that where these requirements are fulfilled, the court may regard it as inequitable to allow B to resist a claim for rectification to give effect to A's intention on the ground that the mistake was not a common one at the time of the execution of the document. One final observation made by Buckley LJ in *Bates* which is worth noting is his comment that while this 'inequitable conduct' may involve some element of sharp practice it depends more 'on the equity of the position'. The four necessary elements set out by Buckley LJ which a claimant has to establish in order to maintain a claim for rectification on the grounds of unilateral mistake were applied in *Traditional Structures Ltd v HW Construction Ltd*.[50] The claimant subcontractor sought rectification of a tender document sent to the defendant main contractor in which the last line had mistakenly been omitted. Judge Grant was satisfied that the defendant's managing director had actual knowledge, in the sense that he actually knew or appreciated that the claimant had made a mistake which led to the price quoted appearing as significantly less than had been intended. He also found that this behaviour was unconscionable and that it went beyond the bounds of fair dealing and he held that the claimant should succeed in its claim for rectification.

The conclusions reached in cases such as *Roberts*, *Bates* and *Traditional Structures* can be contrasted with that arrived at by the Court of Appeal in *Riverlate Properties Ltd v Paul*.[51] The parties executed a lease prepared by

49. [1981] 1 WLR 505.
50. [2010] EWHC 1530 (TCC).
51. [1975] Ch 133. See also *Yedina v Yedin* [2017] EWHC 3319 (Ch).

the solicitors for the lessor which obliged the lessor to bear all the costs of exterior and structural repairs to the demised premises. Although the lessor had intended that the lessee should be liable to make a contribution towards this expenditure, neither the lessee nor her solicitor were aware of this. The lessor sought rectification of the lease, or if the lessee would not accept this remedy, then rescission. The Court of Appeal held that rectification should not be granted since the lessee neither directly nor through her solicitor knew of the lessor's mistake. Similarly, in *George Wimpey UK Ltd v VI Construction Ltd*,[52] the Court of Appeal held, reversing the decision of the trial judge, that the claimant had failed to successfully invoke the 'exceptional jurisdiction' necessary to justify rectification for unilateral mistake. While Peter Gibson LJ accepted that the omission of part of a formula for calculating a selling price had serious consequences for the claimant and had brought an unexpected benefit to the defendant, he was satisfied that the claimant had failed to discharge the onus of providing convincing proof that the defendant had knowledge of this mistake.

Some consideration was given to the basis of a claim for rectification on the grounds of unilateral mistake in *Daventry District Council v Daventry & District Housing Ltd*,[53] which was decided by the English Court of Appeal by applying an objective test for common mistake.[54] Both Toulson LJ and Lord Neuberger MR, who formed the majority, expressed the view that if they had been deciding the appeal without the benefit of Lord Hoffmann's approach in *Chartbrook Ltd v Persimmon Homes Ltd*,[55] they would have allowed it instead on the basis of unilateral mistake.[56] However, Etherton LJ in a dissenting judgment made it clear that he would not have upheld the claim on the basis of unilateral mistake. He expressed the view that in such cases the 'critical broad distinction [is] between honesty and dishonesty'[57] and pointed out that the trial judge had expressly found that dishonesty had not been proven in the matter before the court. The approach of the majority is also open to question because, as Davies points out, previous decisions of the Court of Appeal[58] make clear that 'the defendant must *actually* know of his mistake or at least recklessly

52. [2005] EWCA Civ 77. See further Palser [2006] LMCLQ 139.
53. [2012] 1 WLR 1333.
54. See further *supra*.
55. [2009] AC 1101.
56. [2012] 1 WLR 1333, 1378 *per* Toulson LJ and at 1388 *per* Lord Neuberger MR. Davies [2016] CLJ 62, 82 also suggests that *Chartbrook* and *Daventry* should have been considered as potential cases for rectification on the basis of unilateral mistake since in both cases the trial judge had found as a matter of fact that one party to the contract was not actually mistaken as to its meaning.
57. *Ibid.* at 1358.
58. Davies refers to *A. Roberts & Co. Ltd v Leicestershire County Council* [1961] Ch 555; *Thomas Bates & Son Ltd v Wyndham's (Lingerie) Ltd* [1981] 1 WLR 505; *Commission for the New Towns v Cooper (Great Britain) Ltd* [1995] Ch 259.

turn a blind eye to the mistake, in order for his conscience to be affected.'[59] Arguably Davies is correct in suggesting that the intervention of equity can only be justified where the *actual* intentions of the parties are such that to stick to the written agreement would be unconscionable.[60]

A useful summary of the circumstances in which the court will permit rectification for unilateral mistake is contained in the judgment of Binnie J in the decision of the Supreme Court of Canada in *Sylvan Lake Golf and Tennis Club Ltd v Performance Industries Ltd*[61] in which he stated as follows:

> The plaintiff must establish that the terms agreed to orally were not written down properly. The error may be fraudulent, or it may be innocent. What is essential is that at the time of execution of the written document the defendant knew or ought to have known of the error and the plaintiff did not. Moreover, the attempt of the defendant to rely on the erroneous written document must amount to 'fraud or the equivalent of fraud'.

A similar approach has been taken in this jurisdiction and evidence of sharp practice has tended to be required. In *Irish Life Assurance Co. Ltd v Dublin Land Securities*[62] Keane J said that rectification could be granted in cases of unilateral mistake where it would be inequitable in the circumstances to allow the other party to retain a benefit derived from the mistake. In the case before him there was a mere unilateral mistake and no sharp practice or fraud on the part of the defendant. In his view, it would therefore not be equitable to grant rectification because the defendant was not aware of the plaintiffs' mistake when the contract was executed.

More recently, in *Slattery v Friends First*[63] the Irish Court of Appeal upheld the decision of the High Court to dismiss a claim for a declaration upholding the effect of a clause in a deed. Ryan P stated as follows:

> The first principle is that it is difficult for a party to a written contract to escape the effects of its provisions by reason of mistake … There is, however, an equitable jurisdiction in exceptional cases for a Court to order that the written formal document be rectified by removing, inserting or altering the provisions so as to reflect what the parties truly intended, understood and agreed.[64]

---

59. (2012) 75 MLR 412, 424. Toulson LJ in *Daventry* at 1374-1375 had referred to analysis put forward by MacLauchlan (see (2008) 124 LQR 608; (2010) 126 LQR 8) which favoured an objective approach.
60. *Ibid.* at 425.
61. (2002) 209 DLR (4th) 318, 330.
62. [1986] IR 332.
63. [2015] 3 IR 292.
64. *Ibid.* at 310. Quoted with approval by O'Connor J in *Fastwell Ltd v OCL Capital plc* [2018] IEHC 39.

In considering the circumstances in which rectification may be granted in cases of unilateral mistake, Ryan P stated that a claimant would have to establish that it executed the document under a mistake, that the other party or his agent were aware of this mistake, that there was an element of sharp practice in the other party's conduct or that the circumstances were such that it would be unconscionable for the court to enforce the terms of the document as executed.[65] In the circumstances he found that the defendants had been mistaken in thinking that the deed which was executed was the same as a previous draft, that the plaintiff and his agent knew of this and that the manner in which this had been achieved amounted to sharp practice. Ryan P therefore concluded that the conditions for rectification on the ground of unilateral mistake had been fulfilled.

The issue was also considered on an *obiter* basis by Edwards J in *Leopardstown Club Ltd v Templeville Developments Ltd*,[66] who commented that even where the requirement of outwardly expressed continuing common intention is not satisfied, there may still be rectification for unilateral mistake in certain circumstances. In his view, '[r]ectification for unilateral mistake differs from rectification for common mistake insofar as it is granted, not in order to give effect to a prior agreement of the parties, but rather, on the basis of an estoppel arising as a result of unconscionable behaviour by the non-mistaken party.'[67] On the issue of the degree of unconscionability required in order to justify rectification for unilateral mistake, Edwards J suggested that knowledge of the mistake by the non-mistaken party should be sufficient in that regard. When the issue of the nature of the mistaken conduct arose before the Court of Appeal in *Knockacummer Wind Farm Ltd v Cremins*,[68] Whelan J expressed the view that 'the court should be slow to amend an option to purchase in the absence of clear and compelling evidence of an error induced by unconscionable conduct or sharp practice.' In the circumstances of the matter before her she was satisfied that there was no such evidence and she concluded that the respondent had no entitlement to rectification for unilateral mistake. However, both Hogan and Peart JJ disagreed with the conclusion reached by Whelan J on this issue and directed that rectification should be granted. Peart J overturned the finding reached by the trial judge that there had been elements of sharp practice on the part of the defendant's solicitor and expressed the view that the latter had not been given a reasonable opportunity to address this issue. It should be noted, however, that he agreed with the conclusion reached by Hogan J that rectification should still be granted in these circumstances. Therefore, while there are some differences of opinion in the decisions of the Irish courts in relation to the type of behaviour which must be established in order to succeed in a claim for rectification based on unilateral mistake, it is

65. *Ibid.* at 311.
66. [2010] IEHC 152.
67. *Ibid.* at [7.90].
68. [2018] IECA 252 at [67].

generally a requirement to establish that there has been unconscionable conduct on the part of the defendant.

Davies has suggested that in this context, '[u]nilateral mistake should be very rare and very difficult to establish.'[69] However, McLauchlan has reasserted the view that rectification for unilateral mistake should not be viewed as a 'drastic or exceptional remedy'[70] and suggests that it 'serves essentially the same purpose as rectification for common mistake, namely, to ensure that the written contract reflects the true bargain between the parties as determined by ordinary principles of contract formation.'[71] On balance, Davies' view is preferable as it is difficult to justify rectification on grounds of unilateral mistake in equity in circumstances where the defendant's behaviour has not been shown to be unconscionable. This is also in line with the approach followed by the Irish Court of Appeal in *Slattery v Friends First*[72] and there is no reason to consider that the objective standards canvassed by the majority in *Daventry District Council v Daventry & District Housing Ltd*[73] would find favour in this jurisdiction.

THE ONUS OF PROOF

Clearly the rule that parol evidence is not admissible to add to or vary the terms of a written instrument does not apply to a claim for rectification as such a claim is based on the premise that the written agreement as recorded does not reflect the true intention of the parties. Oral evidence which expressly contradicts the terms of the written agreement may therefore be adduced and the onus lies firmly on the plaintiff to establish grounds for rectification. Traditionally, it was accepted that 'much vigilance and caution' was required in such cases, particularly where a claim was based entirely on oral evidence.[74] In *Fowler v Fowler*[75] Lord Chelmsford LC stated that evidence of the clearest and most satisfactory nature was necessary and that 'something more than the highest degree of probability' was required which would leave 'no fair and reasonable doubt' about the matter. Similar terminology was employed in this jurisdiction by Haugh J in *Nolan v Graves*,[76] where he spoke of an onus of proof 'beyond all reasonable doubt'.

Subsequently, however, the tendency has been to move towards a more

69. (2012) 75 MLR 412, 425.
70. (2008) 124 LQR 608, 639.
71. (2014) 130 LQR 83, 111.
72. [2015] 3 IR 292.
73. [2012] 1 WLR 1333.
74. *McCormack v McCormack* (1877) 1 LR Ir 119, 124.
75. (1859) 4 De G & J 250, 265. See also the *dictum* of Thurlow LC in *Countess of Shelburne v Earl of Inchiquin* (1784) 1 Bro CC 338, 341 that 'strong irrefragable evidence is required'.
76. [1946] IR 376, 389.

lenient approach to this issue. In *Joscelyne v Nissan*[77] Russell LJ, delivering the judgment of the Court of Appeal, stated that 'it is in our view better to use only the phrase "convincing proof" without echoing an old fashioned word such as "irrefragable" and without importing from the criminal law the phrase "beyond all reasonable doubt"'. The matter was also given consideration by the members of the Court of Appeal in *Thomas Bates & Son Ltd v Wyndham's (Lingerie) Ltd*,[78] where Brightman LJ stated that the standard of proof required in an action for rectification to establish the common intention of the parties is 'the civil standard of balance of probability'. However, he continued by saying that as the alleged common intention will necessarily contradict the written instrument 'convincing proof' is required to counteract the intention of the parties as displayed in the instrument itself.[79] In addition, he was of the opinion that the standard of proof should be no different in cases of unilateral mistake such as that before him. This is in line with the approach adopted by the Supreme Court of Canada in *Sylvan Lake Golf and Tennis Club Ltd v Performance Industries Ltd*,[80] in which Binnie J spoke in terms of 'convincing proof' which he described as 'proof that may fall well short of the criminal standard, but which goes beyond the sort of proof that only reluctantly and with hesitation scrapes over the low end of the civil "more probable than not" standard'.

In *Irish Life Assurance Co. Ltd v Dublin Land Securities Ltd*,[81] Griffin J also gave consideration to the general standard required in cases where a plaintiff seeks to establish the common continuing intention of the parties. He said that bearing in mind 'the heavy burden of proof'[82] that lies on a party seeking rectification, the question which the court must answer is whether there was 'convincing proof' that the written instrument did not reflect the parties' intention. Similar views were expressed by Edwards J in *Leopardstown Club Ltd v Templeville Developments Ltd*,[83] who reiterated that the standard of proof in rectification cases, whether for common or unilateral mistake, is proof on the balance of probabilities. However, he added that 'if the circumstances which need to be proved in order for the claim to succeed, are inherently unlikely, it will be necessary for the claimant to adduce particularly cogent evidence as to the existence of those circumstances before a court will be satisfied to act.'[84]

When this matter was considered by the Supreme Court in *Boliden Tara Mines Ltd v Cosgrove*[85] Hardiman J said that while he agreed with the general

77. [1970] 2 QB 86, 98. See also *Westland Savings Bank v Hancock* [1987] 2 NZLR 21.
78. [1981] 1 WLR 505, 521.
79. See also *George Wimpey UK Ltd v VI Construction Ltd* [2005] EWCA Civ 77 at [46].
80. (2002) 209 DLR (4th) 318, 333.
81. [1989] IR 253, 260-261.
82. *Ibid.* at 263. See also *Slattery v Friends First* [2015] 3 IR 292, 310.
83. [2010] IEHC 152.
84. *Ibid.* at [7.75]
85. [2010] IESC 62.

approach set out by Russell LJ in *Joscelyne v Nissen*, in his view no form of words other than 'proof on the balance of probability' should be used. He stated that the judgment of the Supreme Court in *Banco Ambrosiano v Ansbacher and Co.*[86] was authority for the proposition that there were only two standards of proof and that to introduce any intermediate standard would create uncertainty in the law. Hardiman J also referred to the comment of Buckley LJ in *Thomas Bates and Son Ltd v Wyndhams (Lingerie) Ltd*[87] that 'in every case the balance of probability must be discharged, but in some cases that balance may be more easily tipped than others' and said that this aptly summarised the position. He gave as an example a case where commercial parties had had their intentions expressed in a professionally drafted legal document, which was later said not to express these intentions, where a claim for rectification would call for evidence 'which is clear, coherent and convincing if the onus of establishing on the balance of probability that the parties' intention was not correctly expressed is to be discharged'.[88] Hardiman J expressed the view that the evidence of the witnesses who were officers or employees of the parties to the deed who had sworn affidavits showed an 'unusual degree of cogency and unanimity'. He also made reference to the fact that none of the witnesses whose affidavits had been relied on by the plaintiffs were cross-examined by the defendant, which in his view was a salient feature going to the weight of the evidence. He stated that while the trial judge had been quite correct to demand a high degree of cogency in the evidence, it was difficult to avoid concluding that the manner in which she dealt with the issue might have led her to adopt a standard which approached, if not mirrored, the criminal standard. Hardiman J concluded that there was ample cogent evidence about the manner in which the deed in question failed to express the mutual intentions of the parties and he granted rectification in the terms sought.

Therefore, the position would appear to be very similar now both in this jurisdiction and in England, namely that while it has been accepted that the ordinary civil standard of proof applies, the nature of the case being made inevitably demands that the proof adduced be 'convincing' in view of the fact that it will necessarily contradict the written agreement between the parties.[89]

DISCRETIONARY FACTORS

Rectification as an equitable remedy is discretionary in nature. Haugh J

86. [1987] ILRM 669.
87. [1981] 1 WLR 505, 514.
88. [2010] IESC 62 at 27.
89. Note that in *Knockacummer Wind Farm Ltd v Cremins* [2018] IECA 252 at [58] Whelan J quoted from the judgment of Gibson LJ in *Swainland Builders Ltd v Freehold Properties Ltd* [2002] EGLR 71 at [34], where he referred to the requirement of 'convincing proof'.

has commented in *Nolan v Graves*[90] that the jurisdiction of a court to grant rectification and specific performance 'is a delicate jurisdiction ... [which] must be exercised with discretion and care'. However, an examination of the case law in this area suggests that where a convincing case for a right to relief in this form is established, the remedy will only infrequently be withheld on discretionary grounds. The most obvious reason for this finding is that unlike other types of equitable remedy such as injunctions and specific performance, which may be withheld on discretionary grounds leaving the plaintiff to a remedy in damages, if rectification is refused the instrument in question remains effective in its original form and the plaintiff may have no remedy whatsoever.

One clear case in which rectification will not be granted is where a *bona fide* purchaser for value without notice has acquired some interest under the instrument which the plaintiff seeks to rectify.[91] In addition, an order will be withheld where granting it will serve no practical purpose, e.g. where the obligations arising under the agreement have already been performed in accordance with the common intention of the parties. Other more general discretionary grounds may relate to the conduct of the parties, such as an absence of clean hands on the part of the plaintiff, or laches or acquiescence on his part. Where a plaintiff has delayed unreasonably in seeking relief combined with circumstances which would make it inequitable or unjust to grant relief, such as where the defendant has altered his position on the basis of the plaintiff's statements or actions, relief in the form of rectification may be withheld. Equally, even where the plaintiff has in no way been at fault, he may still fail to obtain a remedy on discretionary grounds where the court is satisfied that to make the order sought would cause undue prejudice or hardship to the defendant.

TYPES OF INSTRUMENTS WHICH CAN BE RECTIFIED

Various types of *inter partes* agreements such as leases[92] and share transfers[93] can be rectified. However, where statute requires that an instrument be registered, relief may be refused once this has been done, particularly where a statutory mechanism exists for altering the document and a court will not make an order rectifying the articles of association of a company.[94]

90. [1946] IR 376, 391. See also the comments of Evershed MR in *Whiteside v Whiteside* [1950] Ch 65, 71 that rectification is a discretionary remedy 'which must be cautiously watched and jealously exercised'.
91. *Smith v Jones* [1954] 1 WLR 1089.
92. *Thomas Bates & Son Ltd v Wyndham's (Lingerie) Ltd* [1981] 1 WLR 505.
93. *Re International Contract Co.* (1872) 7 Ch App 485.
94. *Scott v Frank F. Scott (London) Ltd* [1940] Ch 794.

It is clear from the decision of Kelly J in *Irish Pensions Trust Ltd v CRC*[95] that rectification is not confined to bilateral agreements and that the remedy may be applied in the context of a pension scheme, although given the nature of the instrument a different approach must be taken. Kelly J referred to the decision of Lawrence Collins J in *AMP (UK) plc v Barker*,[96] who in considering this issue had commented that in the case of pension schemes it was not necessary to demonstrate the agreement or accord which would be required in bilateral transactions. Kelly J stated that it appeared to him that bilateral transactions were substantially different to those which created rights for persons other than the maker of the instrument but which were not the result of a bargain. He added that he could see good sense in drawing a distinction between the two as in the case of bilateral transactions some outward expression of accord or evidence of a continuing common intention was required. However, Kelly J stated that in the case of a pension scheme evidence of the intentions of both the trustees and the employer was required but not necessarily of their agreement or accord. In his view such an approach made sense having regard to the different nature of the transactions and appeared to be in line with the general approach taken towards the construction of pension schemes, which is purposive rather than literal. Kelly J concluded that the affidavit evidence satisfied him that there had been a continuing common intention between the plaintiff trustee and the employer and that they had made a mistake as to the legal consequences of adopting a rule in the form in which it was included in the scheme. He stated that it did not matter whether this mistaken belief could be described as oversight or negligence and that this was not relevant to the issue of whether rectification was an appropriate remedy. In these circumstances he concluded that the plaintiff trustee company was entitled to succeed on the claim for rectification.

In considering the principles which should be applied where rectification of a deed of amendment to a pension scheme was sought, Finlay Geoghegan J commented in *Boliden Tara Mines Ltd v Cosgrove*[97] that 'the essential nature of the jurisdiction being exercised by the court in a claim for rectification of a deed or other instrument appears to be the same whether the transaction is a bilateral contract, unilateral transaction or as in this instance a transaction which is a hybrid...'. However, she also stated that she agreed with the preference expressed by Kelly J in *Irish Pensions Trust Ltd v CRC* for the approach of Lawrence Collins J in *AMP (UK) plc v Barker* that in the context of rectifying a pension scheme it was not necessary to prove accord between the employer and trustees and an outward expression of that accord.

Rectification of a voluntary deed or settlement may be obtained where there is sufficient evidence to satisfy the court that the donor or settlor's intentions

95. [2006] 2 IR 126.
96. [2001] PLR 77.
97. [2007] IEHC 60.

were not accurately recorded in the terms of the instrument. As Brightman J stated in *Re Butlin's Settlement Trusts*,[98] there is no doubt that 'the court has power to rectify a settlement notwithstanding that it is a voluntary settlement and not the result of a bargain'. The circumstances in which rectification of a voluntary settlement will be ordered were also considered by the Court of Appeal in *Day v Day*.[99] Sir Terence Etherton C made it clear that what is relevant in such a case is the subjective intention of the settlor and said that '[i]t is not a legal requirement for rectification of a voluntary settlement that there is any outward expression or objective communication of the settlor's intention equivalent to the need to show an outward expression of accord for rectification of a contract for mutual mistake'.[100]

There has been some debate about the increasing scope of rectification of voluntary instruments in the context of tax planning mistakes in England. The traditional position, as set out by Mummery LJ in *Allnut v Wilding*,[101] was that no rectification could be granted where a provision in a trust was included based on incorrect advice as there was no mistake in recording the settlor's intentions in relation to the actual terms of the document as opposed to its effect. However, in some first instance decisions rectification has been granted in cases where the terms included in a trust accurately reflected the settlor's intention but not his motive or reason for the formulation of the term which he sought to rectify.[102] Douglas, in analysing these decisions, has suggested that they fall outside the scope of the traditional categories of rectification as the only mistake made by the settlor related to the reason for using the term or provision in question.[103] He argues that '[t]he use of rectification to cure tax planning mistakes represents a significant expansion in the scope of the doctrine, something which is at odds with Lord Walker's claim that it is a "strictly guarded" [104] remedy.'[105]

In *Fitzgerald v Fitzgerald*[106] the Irish Court of Appeal granted rectification of a marriage settlement to allow for the insertion of proper words of limitation where the deed itself afforded sufficient evidence of the parties' intention. While such applications will often be made by the settlor himself, a court may entertain

98. [1976] Ch 251, 260.
99. [2014] Ch 114. See also Dawson (2014) 130 LQR 356.
100. *Ibid.* at 122. See also *RBC Trustees Ltd v Stubbs* [2017] EWHC 180 (Ch) at [44].
101. [2007] EWCA Civ 412. See also *Racal Group Services Ltd v Ashmore* [1995] STC 1151.
102. See e.g. *Martin v Nicholson* [2004] EWHC 2135 (Ch); *Prowting 1968 Trustee One Ltd v Amos-Yeo* [2015] EWHC 2480 (Ch); *Bullard v Bullard* [2017] EWHC 3 (Ch). See further Douglas (2018) 134 LQR 138, footnote 34.
103. (2018) 134 LQR 138.
104. See *Pitt v Holt* [2013] 2 AC 108, 159, where Lord Walker JSC commented that '[r]ectification is a closely guarded remedy, strictly limited to some clearly-established disparity between the words of a legal document, and the intentions of the parties to it. It is not concerned with consequences.'
105. (2018) 134 LQR 138, 148.
106. [1902] 1 IR 477.

a claim by a beneficiary although it will be unlikely to be successful if made during the settlor's lifetime if his consent to the alteration is not forthcoming.[107] However, where the settlor is dead and it is proved either from his instructions or otherwise that the deed was not drawn up in the exact manner which he intended, rectification may be granted.[108] The circumstances in which a court may grant rectification of a voluntary settlement on the application of the settlor, where a trustee does not consent, were considered in *Re Butlin's Settlement Trusts*,[109] but it is clearly necessary for such a trustee to have reasonable evidence to support his opposition to the making of an order before he will succeed.

It has traditionally been accepted that a court has no jurisdiction to rectify a will apart from where as a matter of construction it finds that a manifest error has occurred.[110] In England, section 20 of the Administration of Justice Act 1982 provides that a will may be rectified where the instrument fails to give effect to the testator's intentions by reason of a clerical error or due to a failure to give effect to his instructions[111] although there is no equivalent provision in this jurisdiction. Section 20 was given a broad interpretation by Lord Neuberger PSC in the decision of the Supreme Court of the United Kingdom in *Marley v Rawlings*,[112] which concerned a claim for rectification of a will in circumstances where a husband and wife had each signed each other's wills in error as a result of a mistake made by their solicitor. He accepted that the expression 'clerical error' in section 20 can carry a wide meaning and could extend to a mistake arising out of office work of a routine nature.[113] The Supreme Court, in reversing the decision of the Court of Appeal, accepted that the corrections put forward by the claimant, which effectively involved transposing the entire text of the will signed by the wife into the will signed by the husband, were capable of being effected by rectification. It is also interesting to note that Lord Neuberger PSC stated that he would 'have been minded to hold that it was, as a matter of common law, open to a judge to rectify a will in the same way as any other document: no convincing reason for the absence of such a power has been advanced.'[114] He added that it was unnecessary to consider this matter further given the provisions of section 20 of the Act of 1982 and that in any event it would be wrong for a court to hold, at least in the absence of a compelling reason, that it actually had an inherent power which was wider than that conferred by legislation. However this comment might be of relevance if the issue were to arise in this jurisdiction.

---

107. *Thompson v Whitmore* (1860) 1 J & H 268.
108. *Lister v Hodgson* (1867) LR 4 Eq 30, 34 *per* Romilly MR.
109. [1976] Ch 251.
110. *Re Bacharach's Will Trusts* [1959] Ch 245.
111. This aspect of s.20 was considered on an *obiter* basis in *Royal Society v Robinson* [2015] EWHC 3442 (Ch) at [37].
112. [2015] AC 129. See further Haecker (2014) 130 LQR 360.
113. Such as a dictation error which arose in *Slattery v Jagger* [2015] EWCA Civ 953.
114. [2015] AC 129, 146.

However, it is clear from the *obiter* comments of Asplin J in *Reading v Reading*[115] that there are limitations to the manner in which the phrase 'clerical error' can be interpreted in this context. She stated that the fact that a solicitor drafting a will had overlooked the fact that 'issue' would not include stepchildren did not fall within the ambit of 'clerical error' in the sense outlined by Lord Neuberger in *Marley*. In her view, the inclusion of the term was part of the activity of drafting the will rather than its mere preparation. As she stated, '[t]he relevant activity here was not clerical. It related to [the solicitor's] professional judgment and expertise in the choice of the necessary phrases to encapsulate the instructions given.'[116]

115. [2015] EWHC 946 (Ch).
116. *Ibid.* at [53].

CHAPTER 17

Rescission

INTRODUCTION

The term 'rescission' can be used in a number of different contexts and it is important to appreciate this before examining the circumstances in which rescission in equity may be granted. Where one party has been in breach of a fundamental term of a contract, the innocent party may choose to either affirm it and sue for damages for its breach or, provided the breach goes to the root of the contract, he may treat this conduct as repudiation of the contract by the other party which relieves him from the performance of further contractual obligations and still allows him to sue for damages. This latter option of 'rescission' is a purely common law concept and the decision to pursue this course is essentially one for the innocent party to make. Alternatively, the terms of a contract itself may confer on a party the right to terminate or 'rescind' it in certain circumstances, e.g. on the occurrence of a specified event or where there is non-compliance with a condition precedent laid down in the contract.

Unlike the forms of rescission just described, rescission in equity involves the setting aside or avoiding of contracts and other instruments by the court, rather than as a result of a decision taken by a party to it, where, as Pettit states, 'the contract contains an inherent cause of invalidity'[1] often in the form of mistake, misrepresentation or undue influence. If a court orders the rescission of a contract in the exercise of this equitable jurisdiction the contract is treated as being voidable *ab initio*, so while it is treated as valid until rescission is ordered, it is then retrospectively invalidated from its inception.

The circumstances in which a court will intervene in the exercise of its equitable jurisdiction were summarised by Henchy J in *Northern Bank Finance Corporation Ltd v Charlton*,[2] where he said that relief in the form of rescission 'will be granted when the court considers that it would be just and equitable to do so in order to restore the parties, at least substantially to their respective positions' before the vitiating conduct occurred, a point which was echoed by Griffin J in his judgment in the same case.[3] As he went on to say, 'the primary purpose of all proceedings for rescission, as contrasted with that of actions for damages, is to restore the *status quo* and bring back the original position by

1. Pettit, *Equity and the Law of Trusts* (12th ed., 2012) p. 690.
2. [1979] IR 149, 197.
3. *Ibid.* at 206. See also the comments of Denning LJ in *Solle v Butcher* [1950] 1 KB 671, 696.

undoing all that has intervened between it and the present' and 'the object to be achieved by rescission is the restoration of *both parties* as nearly as may be to the position which each occupied before the transaction'.[4]

However, it should be noted that the attitude of equity towards the concept of *restitutio in integrum* in granting rescission is more flexible than that adopted by the common law and as Lord Blackburn commented in *Erlanger v New Sombrero Phosphate Co.*,[5] 'the practice has always been for a Court of Equity to give this relief whenever, by the exercise of its powers, it can do what is practically just, though it cannot restore the parties precisely to the state they were in before the contract.' This principle of what is 'practically just' was employed by Longmore LJ in the decision of the Court of Appeal in *Salt v Stratstone Specialist Ltd*,[6] in reversing a decision not to order rescission of a contract for the purchase of a car which had been represented by the seller as being 'brand new' when it was not. Longmore LJ held that the fact that the car had been registered was not a bar to rescission and that registration was a legal concept which did not change the physical entity which was the car. He added that neither depreciation nor intermittent enjoyment should be regarded as reasons for concluding that restitution was impossible and that '[i]t has always been the case that a court of equity, contemplating rescission, could order an account and/or an inquiry to determine the terms on which restitution should be made.'[7] He concluded that rescission is *prima facie* available if 'practical justice' can be achieved and that the purchaser should be entitled to rescind the contract.

MISTAKE

Introduction

While mistake alone is capable of justifying the refusal of a decree of specific performance, it would be incorrect to assume that it will always automatically justify rescission. However, as Flanagan J stated in *Gun v McCarthy*:[8]

> [W]here there being a clear undoubted mistake by one party in reference to a material term of the contract which he entered into with another, and the other party knowingly seeks to avail himself of that, and seeks to bind the other to the mistake, the law of this Court is, that it will not allow such a contract to be binding on the parties, but will give relief against it.

4. *Ibid.* at 206-207.
5. (1878) 3 App Cas 1218, 1278-1279.
6. [2015] 2 CLC 269.
7. *Ibid.* at [22].
8. (1883) 13 LR Ir 304, 310.

The type of mistake which will render a contract void in law was identified by Lord Atkin in *Bell v Lever Brothers Ltd*[9] as one 'as to the existence of some quality which makes the thing without the quality essentially different from the thing as it was believed to be'. However, for many years a well-established line of authority in England laid down the principle that equity would permit rescission of a contract on grounds of common mistake where the contract was valid at common law. While the Court of Appeal held in *Great Peace Shipping Ltd v Tsavliris Salvage (International) Ltd*[10] that there is no jurisdiction in equity to grant rescission of a contract on such grounds when it is valid and enforceable on ordinary principles of contract law, given the controversial nature of the decision and the fact that the courts in this jurisdiction may prefer to follow the previous authorities on this issue,[11] it remains necessary to trace how this equitable jurisdiction has been developed and applied.

Common Law and Equitable Jurisdiction

The starting point in examining the decisions in which relief was granted in equity on grounds of mistake in England is *Cooper v Phibbs*.[12] An individual agreed to take a lease of a salmon fishery from the trustee of a settlement in circumstances where, unknown to both parties, it already belonged to him and the House of Lords agreed to set aside the agreement subject to a lien on the fishery for such monies as had been expended on improvements. As Lord Westbury stated:

> [I]f parties contract under a mutual mistake and misapprehension as to their relative and respective rights, the result is, that that agreement is liable to be set aside as having proceeded upon a common mistake.[13]

This decision also illustrates the ability of equity to set aside a contract on such terms as the court sees fit to impose, in this instance involving the imposition of a lien, and shows the flexible nature of equitable rescission.

Perhaps the most extensive consideration of the circumstances in which rescission will be granted in equity on the grounds of common mistake is contained in the judgment of Denning LJ as he then was in *Solle v Butcher*.[14] In that case a lessee leased a flat for a period of years on the basis of an erroneous assumption made by both parties, that it had been so completely reconstructed that it constituted a new flat and as such was no longer controlled by the provisions of the Rent Acts. In fact the maximum permissible rent was

---

9. [1932] AC 161, 218.
10. [2003] QB 679.
11. See *O'Neill v Ryan (No. 3)* [1992] 1 IR 166, 185.
12. (1867) LR 2 HL 149.
13. *Ibid.* at 170.
14. [1950] 1 KB 671.

substantially less than that paid and the lessee sued to recover the overpaid rent. This action failed and the lease was set aside on the grounds of common mistake. Denning LJ stated as follows:

> It is now clear that a contract will be set aside if the mistake of the one party has been induced by a material misrepresentation of the other, even though it was not fraudulent or fundamental; or if the one party, knowing that the other is mistaken about the terms of an offer, or the identity of the person by whom it is made, lets him remain under his delusion and conclude a contract on the mistaken terms instead of pointing out the mistake.[15]

He continued:

> A contract is also liable in equity to be set aside if the parties were under a common misapprehension either as to facts or as to their relative and respective rights provided that the misapprehension was fundamental and that the party seeking to set it aside was not himself at fault.[16]

The suggestion made by Denning LJ that a contract which although not void as a result of mistake at law, may nevertheless be voidable in equity, was accepted by Goff J in *Grist v Bailey*.[17] The plaintiff agreed to buy the defendant's house at a reduced price because both parties mistakenly believed that it was the subject of a protected tenancy. The plaintiff claimed specific performance and the defendant counter-claimed and sought rescission of the contract. Goff J held that although the mistake did not suffice to nullify the contract at common law, equity could intervene. In relation to the statement made by Denning LJ in *Solle* he commented that this could not be dismissed as a 'mere *dictum*' and was in his judgment the basis of the decision and therefore binding on him. Goff J said that the essential questions to be decided were first, whether there had been a common mistake, secondly, whether it was fundamental and thirdly, whether the defendant was at fault. He was satisfied that in the case before him there had been a common mistake of a fundamental nature. While Goff J said that it was not absolutely clear what Denning LJ meant by the third requirement, namely that the party seeking to take advantage of the mistake must not be at fault, clearly there must be some degree of blameworthiness beyond the mere fact of having made a mistake. In the circumstances he did not feel that the defendant was at fault to the extent of disentitling herself to relief and he concluded that the plaintiff's action should be dismissed on terms that the

15. *Ibid.* at 692.
16. *Ibid.* at 693. See also *Magee v Pennine Insurance Co. Ltd* [1969] 2 QB 507, 514.
17. [1967] Ch 532.

defendant would enter into a new contract to sell the house at an appropriate price for vacant possession.

The reasoning in *Solle v Butcher* was applied again by Denning MR in *Magee v Pennine Insurance Co. Ltd*,[18] where he said that '[a] common mistake, even on a most fundamental matter, does not make a contract void at law; but it makes it voidable in equity'. In *Associated Japanese Bank (International) Ltd v Credit du Nord SA*,[19] while Steyn J accepted that a contract affected by mistake in equity is not void but may be set aside on terms, he added that in his view the principles enunciated by the House of Lords in *Bell v Lever Brothers Ltd*[20] clearly still governed mistake at common law. Subsequent decisions showed an acceptance of the principles enunciated by Denning LJ in *Solle v Butcher*. In *William Sindall plc v Cambridgeshire County Council*[21] Evans LJ stated that it must be assumed that there is a category of mistake which is 'fundamental' so as to permit the equitable remedy of rescission and wider than the 'serious and radical' mistake which means that the agreement is void in law. In his view the difference may be that the common law rule is limited to mistakes with regard to the subject matter of the contract while equity can have regard to a wider and perhaps unlimited category of 'fundamental mistake'.

However, in the decision of the Court of Appeal in *Great Peace Shipping Ltd v Tsavliris Salvage (International) Ltd*[22] Lord Phillips MR made it clear that the court found it impossible to reconcile *Solle v Butcher* with the decision of the House of Lords in *Bell v Lever Brothers Ltd* and stated that it was not possible to distinguish a mistake which was 'fundamental' from Lord Atkin's mistake as to quality which 'makes the thing contracted for essentially different from the thing that it was believed to be'. As Phillips MR stated:

> Thus the premise of equity's intrusion into the effects of the common law is that the common law rule in question is seen in the particular case to work injustice, and for some reason the common law cannot cure itself. But it is difficult to see how that can apply here.... We are *only* concerned with the question whether relief might be given for common mistake in circumstances wider than those stipulated in *Bell v Lever Brothers Ltd*. But that, surely, is a question as to where the common law rule should draw the line; not whether, given the common law rule, it needs to be mitigated by application of some other doctrine. The common law has drawn the line in *Bell v Lever Brothers Ltd*.[23]

18. [1969] 2 QB 507, 514.
19. [1989] 1 WLR 255, 266.
20. [1932] AC 161.
21. [1994] 1 WLR 1016, 1042. See also *Clarion Ltd v National Provident Institution* [2000] 1 WLR 1888; *West Sussex Properties Ltd v Chichester DC* Court of Appeal, 28 June 2000 at [42].
22. [2003] QB 679.
23. *Ibid.* at 725.

The Court of Appeal concluded that if coherence was to be restored to this area of the law it could only be by declaring that there is no jurisdiction to grant rescission of a contract on the ground of common mistake where the contract is valid and enforceable on ordinary principles of contract law. It has been suggested that the Court of Appeal in *Great Peace* was in fact bound to follow *Solle v Butcher*[24] and the decision itself has been the subject of considerable academic criticism.[25] Phang argues that the primary advantage of the doctrine of common mistake in equity is its great flexibility and that it allows a court to impose appropriate terms in a context where the contract is not automatically rendered void.[26] As he suggests, such flexibility is desirable 'not least to ensure that as much justice can be achieved under the circumstances as is possible'.[27]

It is submitted that it is unlikely that the Irish courts would agree with the conclusion reached by the Court of Appeal in *Great Peace*. Certainly, in *O'Neill v Ryan (No. 3)*[28] Costello J referred to the decision of Denning LJ in *Solle* as establishing that a court may set aside an agreement in the exercise of its equitable jurisdiction even though it is not void on the grounds of common mistake. Similarly, in *Intrum Justitia BV v Legal and Trade Financial Services Ltd*[29] O'Sullivan J, having concluded that the plaintiff was not entitled to rescission at common law on the basis of mistake, went on to hold that he would also not be entitled to rescission in equity in accordance with the principles identified in *Solle* and applied by Costello J in *O'Neill*. While no reference was made to the decision of the Court of Appeal in *Great Peace*, the approach adopted by O'Sullivan J shows a continued acceptance of a separate equitable jurisdiction to set aside a contract on the grounds of common mistake. There are strong grounds for arguing that this equitable basis for intervention should be allowed to continue as it allows for the setting aside of a contract where the justice of the case requires it and also permits this to take place on terms which appear just to the court.[30]

Unilateral Mistake

General Principles

Some uncertainty surrounds the question of whether a court will grant rescission

24. Midwinter (2003) 119 LQR 180, 182; Ryan (2003) 11 ISLR 3, 25; McMeel [2002] LMCLQ 449, 452.
25. Phang [2003] Conv 247; Midwinter (2003) 119 LQR 180; Ryan (2003) 11 ISLR 3; McMeel [2002] LMCLQ 449. Cf. Hare [2003] CLJ 29.
26. Phang [2003] Conv 247, 252-253.
27. *Ibid.* at 253.
28. [1992] 1 IR 166.
29. [2005] IEHC 190.
30. See also the comment of Ryan (2003) 11 ISLR 3, 27 that 'the parallel jurisdiction in equity, for all the confusion it has engendered in spite of its somewhat questionable origins, is worth retaining and defending'.

in equity in a case of unilateral mistake. It seemed to have been accepted in *Monaghan County Council v Vaughan*[31] that rescission for unilateral mistake might be granted in some circumstances, where Dixon J commented as follows: 'unilateral mistake arises where one of two or more parties is not *ad idem* with the other party or parties, and there is therefore, no real agreement between them. In such a case rescission may be appropriate… .' This statement was referred to by Griffin J in the course of his judgment in *Irish Life Assurance Co. Ltd v Dublin Land Securities Ltd*,[32] although as the Supreme Court was concerned solely with the issue of rectification in that case, no view was expressed on the circumstances in which the remedy of rescission would be granted.

This issue was considered by Russell LJ in *Riverlate Properties Ltd v Paul*,[33] where the parties executed a lease prepared by the lessor's solicitors which obliged the lessor to bear all the costs of exterior and structural repairs to the premises. Although the lessor had intended that the lessee should be liable to make a contribution towards this expenditure, neither the lessee nor her solicitor were aware of this. The Court of Appeal accepted that the mistake was in no way attributable to anything said or done by the lessee and held that it was a case of 'mere unilateral mistake' which could not entitle the plaintiff to rescission of the lease. In the course of his judgment, Russell LJ stated as follows:

> If reference be made to principles of equity, it operates on conscience. If conscience is clear at the time of the transaction, why should equity disrupt the transaction?
>
> If a man may be said to have been fortunate in obtaining a property at a bargain price, or on terms that make it a good bargain, because the other party unknown to him has made a miscalculation or other mistake, some high-minded men might consider it appropriate that he should agree to a fresh bargain to cure the miscalculation or mistake, abandoning his good fortune. But if equity were to enforce the views of those high-minded men, we have no doubt that it would run counter to the attitudes of much the greater part of ordinary mankind (not least the world of commerce), and would be venturing upon the field of moral philosophy in which it would soon be in difficulties.[34]

This statement was quoted with approval by Murphy J in *Ferguson v Merchant Banking Ltd*,[35] where a mistake had been made by one party to a contract by including land with development potential in a parcel of property which he did not appreciate were of significant value. The defendant's counterclaim for

31. [1948] IR 306, 312.
32. [1989] IR 253.
33. [1975] Ch 133.
34. *Ibid.* at 141.
35. [1993] ILRM 136.

rectification was refused,[36] as was the claim for rescission on the basis that the mistake was a unilateral one which had not been contributed to by the other party.

Voluntary Settlements and Similar Instruments

There is clearer authority supporting the view that a voluntary disposition may be set aside in equity on the grounds of unilateral mistake. The basis for the exercise of this jurisdiction was stated in the following terms by Lindley LJ in *Ogilvie v Littleboy*:[37]

> [A] donor can only obtain back property which he has given away by showing that he was under some mistake of so serious a character as to render it unjust on the part of the donee to retain the property given to him.

A different formula was adopted by Millett J in *Gibbon v Mitchell*,[38] who said that a voluntary disposition would be set aside 'so long as the mistake is as to the effect of the transaction itself and not merely as to its consequences or the advantages to be gained by entering into it'. The latter test was in a sense more restrictive as it envisaged only setting aside a transaction where there was a mistake as to its effect and not where the mistake related to its consequences. This distinction between effects and consequences has been criticised in some quarters. As Hilliard has commented, 'people tend to view the legal effects *in terms of the consequences they produce*.'[39]

Lloyd LJ sought to combine these two tests in his judgment in the Court of Appeal in *Pitt v Holt*,[40] in which the claimant, who had been appointed as receiver for her husband after he sustained serious injuries in an accident, settled money from a compensation award on a discretionary trust acting upon professional advice which she had obtained. On her husband's death, a liability to inheritance tax arose which could have been avoided if a clause had been included in the trust providing that half the fund would be applied for his benefit during his lifetime, which had been the case in any event. Lloyd LJ stated that for the equitable jurisdiction to set aside a voluntary disposition for mistake to be invoked, 'there must be a mistake on the part of the donor either as to the legal effect of the disposition or as to an existing fact which is basic to the transaction'[41] and this mistake must be of sufficient gravity to satisfy the *Ogilvie* test. He characterised the fact that the transaction had given rise to unforeseen fiscal liabilities as a consequence, not an effect, for this purpose,

36. See further Chapter 16.
37. (1897) 13 TLR 399, 400.
38. [1990] 1 WLR 1304.
39. Hilliard [2004] PCB 357, 363. See also *Wolff v Wolff* [2004] EWHC 2110 (Ch) at [25].
40. [2012] Ch 132.
41. *Ibid.* at 199.

and so the claimant could not succeed on the basis of mistake.[42] However, the Supreme Court of the United Kingdom allowed her appeal on this ground and held that the transaction could be set aside.[43] Lord Walker JSC set out a simplified test in the following terms:

> I would provisionally conclude that the true requirement is simply for there to be a causative mistake of sufficient gravity; and, as additional guidance to judges in finding and evaluating the facts of any particular case, that the test will normally be satisfied only when there is a mistake either as to the legal character or nature of a transaction, or as to some matter of fact or law which is basic to the transaction.[44]

He said that the test set out by Lindley LJ in *Ogilvie v Littleboy* requires the gravity of the causative mistake to be assessed in terms of injustice or unconscionableness and that what would be considered unjust or unconscionable must be evaluated objectively, but with an 'intense focus'[45] on the facts of the particular case. He continued as follows:

> The court cannot decide the issue of what is unconscionable by an elaborate set of rules. It must consider in the round the existence of a distinct mistake (as compared with total ignorance or disappointed expectations), its degree of centrality to the transaction in question and the seriousness of its consequences, and make an evaluative judgment whether it would be unconscionable, or unjust, to leave the mistake uncorrected. The court may and must form a judgment about the justice of the case.'[46]

Lord Walker JSC then went on to consider whether there are some types of mistake relating to tax liability which should not attract relief. He expressed the view that '[i]n some cases of artificial tax avoidance the court might think it right to refuse relief, either on the ground that such claimants, acting on supposedly expert advice, must be taken to have accepted the risk that the scheme would prove ineffective, or on the ground that discretionary relief should be refused on grounds of public policy.'[47] He concluded that the consequences, including the tax consequences, of a transaction will be relevant to the gravity

42. So, as Davies commented [2011] Conv 406, 407, the approach adopted by the Court of Appeal made it difficult for the doctrine of mistake to provide a remedy where a transaction, as in *Pitt v Holt*, gave rise to unforeseen financial consequences.
43. [2013] 2 AC 108. See further Nolan (2013) 129 LQR 469; Watterson [2013] CLJ 501; Etherton (2013) 27 Trust Law Int 159; Ng [2013] BTR 566; Lee [2014] Conv 175.
44. *Ibid.* at 156.
45. *Per* Lord Steyn in *Re S. (A Child)* [2005] 1 AC 593, 603.
46. [2013] 2 AC 108, 158.
47. *Ibid.* at 160.

of the mistake, whether or not they are basic to the transaction and that the loss of the tax advantage which would otherwise have been available was a serious matter for the claimant. Lord Walker JSC stated that the trust could have complied with the statutory provision necessary to obtain the tax relief 'without any artificiality or abusiveness' and was in fact the type of trust to which Parliament intended to grant relief. He therefore allowed the claimant's appeal on this basis and set aside the trust on the ground of mistake.

The principles set out in *Pitt v Holt* were applied by Sir Terence Etherton C in *Kennedy v Kennedy*,[48] where trustees of a settlement were granted an order of rescission correcting a mistake in the terms of the appointment of assets which had the effect of generating a significant tax liability. He found that he was satisfied that the principles set out by Lord Walker had been met in the case before him and expressed the view that the mistakes made by the trustees were 'causative and very serious'.[49] Sir Terence Etherton C concluded that the appointment made was not part of an artificial tax avoidance arrangement and that it would be unconscionable to leave it uncorrected.

The circumstances in which equitable principles will apply in this context were explained by Morgan J in *Van der Merwe v Goldman*[50] in the following terms:

> [T]he difference between the cases where the equitable rules apply and those where they do not turns on whether consideration has been given for the benefit conferred by the transaction. If the effect of rescission (or a declaration that a transaction is void) would deprive a party of a benefit for which he gave consideration, then the common law rules apply and there is no separate equitable jurisdiction to order rescission. Conversely, if the effect of rescission would deprive a party of a benefit for which he gave no consideration, then there is a separate equitable jurisdiction to order rescission, applying the principles in *Pitt v Holt*.'

In the matter before the court, Morgan J was satisfied that no consideration had been given for the benefits which would be taken away by an order for rescission and that, accordingly, the equitable rules as to rescission for mistake applied to the transactions. He concluded that, applying the equitable principles, the claimant and the first defendant were entitled to an order setting aside a transfer and settlement on the grounds of mistake.

An issue which a number of academics have commented on was Lord Walker JSC's failure in *Pitt v Holt* to address directly the relationship between the court's jurisdiction to set aside a voluntary disposition in equity

---

48. [2014] EWHC 4129 (Ch). See further Ng [2015] Conv 266. See also *Van der Merwe v Goldman* [2016] 4 WLR 71; *Rogge v Rogge* [2019] EWHC 1949 (Ch).
49. *Ibid.* at 38.
50. [2016] 4 WLR 71 at [31].

on the grounds of mistake and claims in unjust enrichment at common law.[51] Watterson suggests that it is difficult to reconcile the equitable jurisdiction to grant rescission of a voluntary transaction for mistake and the common law restitutionary remedy against donees for spontaneous causative mistake and rightly points out that the *Pitt* decision leaves the courts 'with more work to do, to integrate the common law and equitable perspectives, and secure a more "joined-up" coherent approach to the reversal of gift transactions for mistake.'[52] Etherton has also explored the basis for the different tests for imposing liability in equity and at common law in this context and has suggested that there is an explanation, given the distinction between a personal remedy for unjust enrichment and one which seeks to set aside a transaction which will give rise to proprietary consequences or at least the potential for such consequences.[53]

The circumstances in which a voluntary disposition, or other instrument of a similar nature, may be rescinded on the basis of a unilateral mistake has been the basis of some discussion in this jurisdiction. In *Irish Pensions Trust Ltd v Central Remedial Clinic Ltd*[54] Kelly J quoted the principle set out by Millett J in *Gibbon v Mitchell*,[55] referred to above, in relation to the circumstances in which a transaction would be set aside in equity on the grounds of mistake. He acknowledged that this principle had been set out in the context of a voluntary transaction but referred to the fact that Lawrence Collins J had expressed the view in *AMP(UK) Ltd v Barker*[56] that there was no reason why it should be so limited. The latter had stated that while occupational pension schemes were not voluntary settlements, they were similar to them and had taken the view that this form of relief would also be available in the context of such a scheme. Kelly J did not have to decide the issue on the facts of the case before him but stated that had he not found for the plaintiff on the claim for rectification, he would have been inclined to set aside the impugned provision under this jurisdiction or under the rule in *Re Hastings-Bass*.[57]

The principles set out by Millett J in *Gibbon v Mitchell* were also quoted by Finlay Geoghegan J in *Boliden Tara Mines Ltd v Cosgrove*.[58] She referred to the fact that both Lawrence Collins J in *AMP* and Kelly J in *Irish Pensions Trust* had considered that similar principles should apply to a mistake on the part of an employer as settlor in an occupational pension scheme. On the facts she concluded that the plaintiff had not adduced evidence that it had executed the impugned deed under a mistake and she dismissed its claim to set aside the

---

51. Watterson [2013] CLJ 501, 502-503; Ng [2013] BTR 566, 573; Lee [2014] Conv 175, 184.
52. *Ibid.* at 503.
53. Etherton (2013) 27 Trust Law Int 159, 169.
54. [2006] 2 IR 126.
55. [1990] 1 WLR 1304, 1309.
56. [2001] Pens LR 77.
57. [1975] Ch 25.
58. [2007] IEHC 60.

deed on this and other grounds. It remains to be seen whether the Irish courts will continue to apply the principles set out in *Gibbon v Mitchell* where a claim is brought to set aside a voluntary disposition on the grounds of mistake or whether they will adopt the revised test formulated by the Supreme Court of the United Kingdom in *Pitt v Holt.*[59] However, it seems clear that the equitable jurisdiction to set aside voluntary transactions, or other instruments of a similar nature such as occupational pension schemes, on the grounds of unilateral mistake is accepted in principle in this jurisdiction.

MISREPRESENTATION

Fraudulent Misrepresentation

A contract can be rescinded at common law and in equity where there has been a fraudulent misrepresentation. The most important Irish authority on the right to rescind in equity on grounds of fraudulent misrepresentation is *Northern Bank Finance Corporation Ltd v Charlton.*[60] The plaintiff bank loaned the defendants a sum of money to facilitate their objective of acquiring control of a public company. When the defendants defaulted on the loan repayments, the plaintiff claimed the balance and interest and the defendants counter-claimed that they had entered into the original transaction because of the fraudulent misrepresentations of the plaintiff. In the High Court, Finlay P made an order dismissing the plaintiff's claim and allowing the defendants' counter-claim on the basis that the defendants had been induced by a fraudulent misrepresentation to enter into the transactions. The Supreme Court agreed that the plaintiff's claim should be dismissed but the majority of the court held that the order of rescission granted by the High Court should be set aside because the principle of *restitutio in integrum* could not apply. Extensive consideration was given by a number of members of the Supreme Court to the circumstances in which rescission of a contract may be granted. O'Higgins CJ pointed out that in the case of a fraudulent misrepresentation, the fact that the contract has already been executed or the transaction completed is no bar to rescission unless *restitutio in integrum* has become impossible as a result. In his view it was the duty of the court to do what was 'practically just' in the circumstances, even though the precise restoration of the parties to their previous position was no longer possible. However, the majority view was to the contrary; as Henchy J put it, an order of rescission would in the circumstances run counter to the object of the restoration of the *status quo ante*.

59. [2013] 2 AC 108.
60. [1979] IR 149.

Innocent Misrepresentation

The principles which apply to rescission in cases of innocent misrepresentation are not as free from doubt.[61] The situation that arises where the contract has not yet been completed was examined in *Gahan v Boland*.[62] Murphy J said that where a false representation was made, even though made in good faith and with no intention to mislead, rescission could be granted where the plaintiff could establish that 'the representation was made by the defendant with the intention of inducing the plaintiff to act thereon and secondly, that the plaintiff did in fact act or rely on the representation.'[63] This view was echoed by Henchy J in the Supreme Court where he stated that an innocent yet false representation could suffice where it was a material one made with the intention of inducing a plaintiff to act on it and where it was one of the factors which induced the plaintiff to enter into the contract. It was also stated by Finlay Geoghegan J in *Leopardstown Club Ltd v Templeville Developments Ltd*[64] that there must be an intention that the other party rely on the representation and it must be a representation of a material fact, judged objectively.

It has been accepted that the misrepresentation need not be the 'sole cause of the transaction' and it is enough that it provides a material inducement to enter into the obligations in question.[65] It is also clear from the judgment of O'Sullivan J in *Intrum Justitia BV v Legal and Trade Financial Services Ltd*[66] that while the representation did not have to be 'the main or paramount consideration in the mind of the representee' it 'must be part of the underlying basis upon which the representee proceeds'. He concluded that there was no real sense in which the representations had been relied on given that the plaintiff had proceeded with its own thorough inquiries in exactly the same way after these had been made and he held that the plaintiff was not entitled to rescission on the basis of any misrepresentations made as it had not relied on them.

It would appear that in circumstances where the contract is complete rescission will only be granted in cases of fraudulent misrepresentation and not where the misrepresentation is innocent in nature. This point was made by Lord Selborne in *Brownlie v Campbell*[67] in the following manner: 'it is not … the principle of equity that relief should afterwards be given against [a] conveyance, unless there be a case of fraud, or a case of misrepresentation

---

61. As Keane J commented in *Doolan v Murray* High Court 1990 No. 7753 P, 21 December 1993, '[a]n innocent misrepresentation … may afford grounds for rescission of a contract'.
62. High Court 1981 No. 4995P (Murphy J) 21 January 1983 and Supreme Court 1983 No. 37, 20 January 1984.
63. *Ibid.* at 14.
64. [2015] IECA 164 at [18].
65. *Lecky v Walter* [1914] 1 IR 378, 384 *per* O'Connor MR.
66. [2005] IEHC 190.
67. (1880) 5 App Cas 925, 937. Quoted with approval by O'Connor MR in *Lecky v Walter* [1914] 1 IR 378, 385-386.

amounting to fraud, by which the purchaser may have been deceived'. This *dictum* was referred to by O'Connor MR in *Lecky v Walter*[68] in holding that where a contract has been completed and there has been no fraud, but only an innocent misrepresentation, the agreement cannot be set aside.[69]

General Principles

As a general principle, failure to disclose facts material to a contract will not constitute grounds for rescission unless by his silence a person implicitly alters the meaning of a representation previously made by him.[70] However, an exception to this general principle are contracts *uberrimae fidei* of which contracts of insurance and family settlements are the most common examples. In such cases failure to disclose any material fact may justify rescission.

A distinction which must be drawn between cases of fraudulent and innocent misrepresentation in the context of rescission, is that in the former case it is sufficient to show that the misrepresentation has been made 'as to any part of that which induced the party to enter into the contract which he seeks to rescind' whereas in the latter it is necessary to show that as a result there is 'a complete difference in substance' between what was contracted for and what was delivered.[71]

UNDUE INFLUENCE

Introduction

Gifts or agreements concluded on the basis of wholly inadequate consideration are liable to be set aside in equity where they have been given or made as a result of the exercise of undue influence over the donor or party of whom advantage has been taken.[72] As Lindley LJ made clear in *Allcard v Skinner*,[73] equity intervenes not to save individuals 'from the consequences of their own folly' but to prevent them from being victimised by others. He stated as follows in what has been described as a 'famous passage':[74]

---

68. [1914] 1 IR 378.
69. See also *Legge v Croker* (1811) 1 Ba & B 506, 514.
70. *Oakes v Turquand* (1867) LR 2 HL 325.
71. *Kennedy v Panama, New Zealand, and Australian Royal Mail Co. (Ltd)* (1867) LR 2 QB 580, 587. Quoted with approval by Joyce J in *Seddon v North Eastern Salt Co. Ltd* [1905] 1 Ch 326, 333; by O'Connor MR in *Lecky v Walter* [1914] 1 IR 378, 386 and by Fitzgibbon J in *Carbin v Somerville* [1933] IR 276, 288.
72. Referred to in *McCormack v Our Lady Queen of Peace Achill House of Prayer Ltd* [2018] IEHC 26 at [29].
73. (1887) 36 Ch D 145, 182.
74. By Lord Scarman in *National Westminster Bank plc v Morgan* [1985] AC 686, 705.

> It would obviously be to encourage folly, recklessness, extravagance and vice if persons could get back property which they foolishly made away with, whether by giving it to charitable institutions or by bestowing it on less worthy objects. On the other hand, to protect people from being forced, tricked or misled in any way by others into parting with their property is one of the most legitimate objects of all laws; and the equitable doctrine of undue influence has grown out of and been developed by the necessity of grappling with insidious forms of spiritual tyranny and with the infinite varieties of fraud.[75]

In general the courts have shied away from any attempt to define precisely what constitutes undue influence; but it has been described as where a person has exercised 'unfair, undue and unreasonable mental control'[76] over another. One of the most comprehensive formulations of the type of conduct which will amount to undue influence is that laid down by Lowry LCJ in *R. (Proctor) v Hutton*,[77] where he stated that 'the plaintiff must prove that an unfair advantage has been gained by an unconscientious use of power in the form of some unfair and improper conduct, some coercion from outside, some over reaching, some form of cheating.' Undue influence will therefore arise in circumstances where the defendant has caused the plaintiff's judgment to become clouded through the exercise of some form of domination and caused him to enter a transaction disadvantageous to him.

The question of what will amount to undue influence was also considered more recently by Lord Nicholls in *Royal Bank of Scotland v Etridge (No. 2)*,[78] where he acknowledged that the circumstances in which one person acquires influence over another and the manner in which this influence may be exercised vary too widely to be defined precisely. However, he made it clear that if the intention to enter into a transaction was secured by unacceptable means it will not be permitted to stand and the means used will be 'regarded as improper or "undue" influence whenever the consent thus procured ought not fairly to be treated as the expression of a person's free will.'[79] Lord Nicholls added that equity has identified broadly two types of unacceptable conduct: first, 'overt acts of improper pressure or coercion such as unlawful threats', which overlaps to an extent with the common law doctrine of duress,[80] and secondly, 'arising out of a relationship between two persons where one has acquired over another a measure of influence, or ascendancy, of which the ascendant person then takes unfair advantage.'[81] The meaning of this second form of unacceptable

75. (1887) 36 Ch D 145, 182-183.
76. *Harris v Swordy* High Court 1960 No 71 Sp (Henchy J) 21 December 1967 at 15.
77. [1978] NI 139, 146.
78. [2002] 2 AC 773, 795. See also *Wadlow v Samuel* [2007] EWCA Civ 155 at [48].
79. *Ibid.*
80. See also *Halpern v Halpern* [2008] QB 195, 221.
81. [2002] 2 AC 773, 795. See also *Hogg v Hogg* [2008] WTLR 35 at [42(v)]; *Wallbank*

conduct was considered by David Richards J in *Royal Bank of Scotland plc v Chandra*,[82] where he took the view that Lord Nicholls was not suggesting that there should be a general duty of disclosure. He expressed the opinion that non-disclosure as opposed to deliberate concealment or suppression of material facts is insufficient by itself to amount to undue influence, although he acknowledged that a deliberate suppression of information would be unconscionable and rightly categorised as unacceptable means.[83]

Actual and Presumed Undue Influence

Cases of undue influence have traditionally been divided into two broad categories, actual and presumed undue influence.[84] In cases of actual undue influence as Lord Browne-Wilkinson commented in *Barclays Bank plc v O'Brien*,[85] 'it is necessary for the claimant to prove affirmatively that the wrongdoer exerted undue influence on the complainant to enter into the particular transaction which is impugned'. In addition, undue influence is readily presumed in certain cases, whether because of the relationship of the parties to one another or because of the nature of the relationship in a particular case.

As Lowry LCJ pointed out in *R. (Proctor) v Hutton*,[86] the undue influence is of the same nature in both cases, the difference being that in cases of presumed undue influence it is deemed to have been exercised until this presumption is negatived on a balance of probabilities by evidence. The distinction between these two classes of cases was well-summarised by Costello J, as he then was, in *O'Flanagan v Ray-Ger Ltd*[87] as follows:

> The cases where a plaintiff seeks to set aside a gift or other transaction on the ground that it was procured by undue influence have been divided into two classes; firstly those in which it can be expressly proved that undue influence was exercised, in which circumstances the Court intervenes on the principle that no one should be allowed to retain any benefit arising

v Price [2008] 2 FLR 501, 511 (see further Brown [2008] Conv 336).

82. [2010] 1 Lloyd's Rep 677, 698.
83. *Ibid.* at 698, 700. See also *Hewett v First Plus Financial Group plc* [2010] 2 FLR 177, 184.
84. Although it should be noted that Lord Clyde has commented in *Royal Bank of Scotland v Etridge (No. 2)* [2002] 2 AC 773, 816 that on the face of it a division into cases of actual and presumed undue influence appears to be illogical. However, in her judgment in *Carroll v Carroll* [1999] 4 IR 241, 253 Denham J accepted this division. See also *O Síodhacháin v O'Mahony* [2002] IEHC 175 at 40.
85. [1994] 1 AC 180, 189. It should be noted that Lloyd LJ commented in *Smith v Cooper* [2010] EWCA Civ 722 at [58] that cases of actual undue influence are rare.
86. [1978] NI 139, 146.
87. High Court 1980 No. 2858P (Costello J) 28 April 1983 at 18. Quoted with approval by Shanley J in *Carroll v Carroll* [1998] 2 ILRM 218, 229. See also *Allcard v Skinner* (1887) 36 Ch D 145, 171 *per* Cotton LJ.

> from his own fraud or wrongful act; secondly those in which the relations between the donor and donee have at or shortly before the execution of a gift been such as to raise a presumption that the donor had influence over the donee.

In some types of relationship the law presumes that one party has influence over the other. As Lord Nicholls stated in *Royal Bank of Scotland v Etridge (No. 2)*:[88]

> The law has adopted a sternly protective attitude towards certain types of relationship in which one party acquires influence over another who is vulnerable and dependent and where, moreover, substantial gifts by the influenced or vulnerable person are not normally to be expected … In these cases the law presumes, irrebuttably, that one party had influence over the other. The complainant need not prove he actually reposed trust and confidence in the other party. It is sufficient for him to prove the existence of the type of relationship.

He referred to some of the types of relationship in which the presumption of undue influence arises as follows: 'parent and child, guardian and ward, trustee and beneficiary, solicitor and client,[89] and medical adviser and patient.' To this list could be added the relationship of religious adviser and pupil[90] but not the relationship of husband and wife[91] or of engaged couples.[92] However, as Gilligan J made clear in *Prendergast v Joyce*,[93] the categories of relationship to which the presumption applies are 'neither closed nor rigid'.

Some elucidation of the circumstances in which the presumption operates

---

88. [2002] 2 AC 773, 797.
89. See also *Danske Bank A/S trading as National Irish Bank plc v Madden* [2009] IEHC 319 at [13].
90. *Allcard v Skinner* (1887) 36 Ch D 145.
91. *Bank of Montreal v Stuart* [1911] AC 120. *Irish Bank Resolution Corporation v Quinn* [2011] IEHC 470 at [42] *per* Kelly J. Referred to by Birmingham J in *Ulster Bank (Ireland) Ltd v de Kretser* [2016] IECA 371 at [27]. See also *Royal Bank of Scotland v Etridge (No. 2)* [2002] 2 AC 773, 797, 842; *Royal Bank of Scotland v Chandra* [2010] 1 Lloyd's Rep 677, 699.
92. *Zamet v Hyman* [1961] 1 WLR 1442). While some doubt was cast on this assumption by the decision of the Court of Appeal in *Leeder v Stevens* [2005] EWCA Civ 50 (see further Enonchong (2005) 121 LQR 567), it is likely that the same reasoning which prevents a presumption of undue influence arising as between husband and wife applies in this context. In the decision of the High Court of Australia in *Thorne v Kennedy* (2017) 350 ALR 1, Kiefel CJ rejected the submission that the presumption should apply to an engaged couple and said (at [36]) that '[c]ommon experience today of the wide variety of circumstances in which two people can become engaged to marry negates any conclusion that a relationship of fiancé and fiancée should give rise to a presumption that either person substantially subordinates his or her free will to the other.'
93. [2009] 3 IR 519, 532. See also *McGonigle v Black* High Court (Barr J) 14 November 1988 at 9.

in the context of these various relationships is necessary. First, the case law suggests that where a person has assumed the role of adviser, whether in a legal sense or otherwise, even where the relationship has ended in the strict sense, the confidence which arises from it may still subsist in relation to matters previously within the scope of this arrangement.[94] Equally, in the context of the relationship of parent/child or guardian/ward, the presumption may continue even after the child has reached his majority or married,[95] or, provided some element of control remains, where the wardship has ceased,[96] although the view expressed by the English Court of Appeal in *Re Pauling's Settlement's Trusts*[97] was that it should not continue indefinitely.

One of the decisions most frequently referred to in this area of presumed undue influence is that of the English Court of Appeal in *Allcard v Skinner*.[98] The plaintiff joined a sisterhood of nuns and made her will in favour of the superior of the order and also transferred large amounts of money and stock to her. When she left the order, she revoked her will but made no attempt to reclaim her property until five or six years later when she instituted proceedings claiming that it had been transferred as a result of undue influence. The court held that the gifts were made by the plaintiff, who had received no independent legal advice, as a result of pressure which she could not resist and that they were recoverable in principle. However, the majority of the Court of Appeal held that, in the circumstances, the claim was barred by laches and acquiescence.

It is also clear from the opinion of Lord Nicholls in *Royal Bank of Scotland v Etridge (No. 2)*[99] that the types of relationship in which a presumption of undue influence arises cannot be listed exhaustively and he commented that Treitel has correctly noted that the question is whether one party has reposed sufficient trust and confidence in the other, rather than whether the relationship between them belongs to a particular type.[100] In his view even this test is not comprehensive and the principle is not confined to cases of abuse of trust and confidence and can extend to situations of 'reliance, dependence or vulnerability on the one hand and ascendancy, domination or control on the other.'[101]

So, a presumption of undue influence may also arise because of the particular circumstances of the relationship between the parties in that case. Lord Nicholls suggested in *Etridge* that, where the complainant places trust and confidence in the other party in relation to the management of the former's financial affairs and there is a transaction which calls for explanation, this will be sufficient to

94. See *McMaster v Byrne* [1952] 1 All ER 1362 in the context of a solicitor/client relationship.
95. *Lancashire Loans Ltd v Black* [1934] 1 KB 380.
96. *Hylton v Hylton* (1754) 2 Ves Sen 547.
97. [1964] Ch 303, 337.
98. (1887) 36 Ch D 145.
99. [2002] 2 AC 773, 795.
100. Treitel, *The Law of Contract* (10th ed., 1999) pp. 380-381. Now see Peel, *Treitel: The Law of Contract* (14th ed., 2017). See also *Hogg v Hogg* [2008] WTLR 35 at [42(vi)].
101. [2002] 2 AC 773, 795-796.

shift the evidential burden.[102] Commenting on this description of a complainant placing trust and confidence in the other party in relation to the management of his financial affairs, Lewison J subsequently stated in *Thompson v Foy*[103] that he did not think that it was intended to be exhaustive and he also suggested that the requisite trust and confidence could arise in the course of the impugned transaction itself.[104]

As Budd J made clear in *Gregg v Kidd*,[105] the courts have never attempted to delimit the categories of relationship in which this presumption may arise as 'to do so would fetter that wide jurisdiction to relieve against all manner of constructive fraud which courts administering equitable jurisdiction have always exercised.'[106] In that case the plaintiff executor succeeded in having a voluntary settlement made by the deceased in favour of his nephew set aside on the grounds that the relationship between the testator on the one hand, and the nephew and his mother on the other hand, was such as to raise a presumption of influence which had not been rebutted.

Once a relationship giving rise to a presumption of undue influence is established, and it is shown that a 'substantial benefit'[107] has been obtained, the onus lies on the donee to establish that the gift or transaction resulted from the 'free exercise of the donor's will.'[108] As Dixon J put it in *Johnson v Buttress*,[109] the evidence must establish that the gift was 'the independent and well-understood act of a man in a position to exercise a free judgment

---

102. *Ibid.* at 796. See also *Forde v Birmingham City Council* [2009] 1 WLR 2732, 2757; *Smith v Cooper* [2010] EWCA Civ 722 at [59]; *De Wind v Wedge* [2010] WTLR 795 at [12].
103. [2010] 1 P & CR 16 at [100].
104. See also *Turkey v Awadh* [2005] 2 P & CR 29 at [10]; *Hewett v First Plus Financial Group plc* [2010] 2 FLR 177, 184. Lewison J also stressed that even if a relationship of the requisite character is proved, the burden of proof does not shift unless the transaction itself is one that calls for an explanation and it is not satisfactorily explained (see also *Turkey v Awadh* [2005] 2 P & CR 29 at [15]).
105. [1956] IR 183, 194. So these categories can be added to as in *O'Sullivan v Management Agency & Music Ltd* [1985] QB 428 where the presumption of undue influence was found to arise in a relationship between an inexperienced and unknown composer and performer and his manager.
106. See also the comment of Shanley J in *Carroll v Carroll* [1998] 2 ILRM 218, 229 that 'the categories of relationship which will give rise to the presumption are never "closed"'.
107. *Johnson v Buttress* (1936) 56 CLR 113, 134. See also *Carroll v Carroll* [1998] 2 ILRM 218, 229 *per* Shanley J and *Mulcahy v Mulcahy* [2011] IEHC 186 at [10.5]. Lowry LCJ in *R. (Proctor) v Hutton* [1978] NI 139, 147 referred to the making of a 'substantial gift'.
108. *Gregg v Kidd* [1956] IR 183, 196. See also *M.C. v F.C.* [2012] 1 ILRM 1, 48. An alternative formula used in some recent English decisions is that the gift was made after 'full, free and informed thought'; see *Hammond v Osborn* [2002] EWCA Civ 887 at [29]; *Wright v Hodgkinson* [2005] WTLR 435 at [124]. See also *Goodchild v Bradbury* [2007] WTLR 463 at [27].
109. (1936) 56 CLR 113, 134-35.

based on information as full as that of the donee.' The manner in which this presumption may be rebutted relates to two main issues; first, the question of whether independent legal advice has been received and secondly, whether it can be shown that the decision to make the gift or transfer was 'a spontaneous and independent act'[110] or that the donor 'acted of his own free will.'[111] An alternative formula, put forward by MacMenamin J in the decision of the Supreme Court in *M.C. v F.C.*,[112] is that the onus can be discharged 'by evidence showing the gift was the independent and well understood act of a person in a position to exercise free judgment.'

Where independent legal advice has been given, it will tend to rebut the presumption of undue influence,[113] even where the donor is in a particularly vulnerable position *vis-à-vis* the donee.[114] On the other hand, while it would appear that it is not essential that independent legal advice be given in order to rebut the presumption,[115] the complete lack of any such advice may be a decisive factor in determining whether this will be achieved.[116] Black J made it clear in the course of his judgment in *Provincial Bank of Ireland v McKeever*[117] that in certain circumstances, even where independent advice has been given and

110. *Re Brocklehurst's Estate* [1978] Ch 14. See also *Carroll v Carroll* [1999] 4 IR 241, 264; *Moyles v Mahon* [2000] IEHC 197; *Ffrench-O'Carroll v Ffrench-O'Carroll* [2006] IEHC 220.
111. *Gregg v Kidd* [1956] IR 183, 196. See also *Inche Noriah v Shaik Allie Bin Omar* [1929] AC 127, 135. This analysis was adopted and applied by Denham J in *Carroll v Carroll* [1999] 4 IR 241, 254. See also *Lambert v Lyons* [2010] IEHC 29 at [11.4]; *Prendergast v Joyce* [2009] 3 IR 519, 537; *Mulcahy v Mulcahy* [2011] IEHC 186 at [10.4]; *Lynn v O'Hara* [2015] IEHC 689 at [247].
112. [2014] 1 ILRM 1, 48.
113. As Ward LJ stated in *Hammond v Osborn* [2002] EWCA Civ 887 at [49], 'independent advice is … usually the crucial evidence going to the rebuttal of the presumption' although he went on the stress that it is not the only way in which the presumption can be rebutted, see *Inche Noriah v Shaik Allie Bin Omar* [1929] AC 127, 135. However, as Lord Nicholls made clear in *Royal Bank of Scotland v Etridge (No. 2)* [2002] 2 AC 773, 798, 'proof of outside advice does not, of itself, necessarily show that the subsequent completion of the transaction was free from the exercise of undue influence.' See also *Wright v Hodgkinson* [2005] WTLR 435 at [125]: 'the mere fact that legal advice is obtained cannot suffice, unless it is proper to infer that it must have led to a decision based upon full, free and informed thought.'
114. See, e.g. *Leonard v Leonard* [1988] ILRM 245, where a transfer by a vulnerable elderly lady to her son was upheld despite a claim of undue influence in circumstances where she had obtained proper independent legal advice. It should also be pointed out that MacKenzie J stated that he was satisfied that 'the coercion on [the plaintiff] was because of her situation and was not of [the defendant's] making'. In his view she was alone, afraid and unable to work the land and needed the company and support which transferring the land to her son would bring her. See also *Elliot v Stamp* High Court (Murphy J) 7 November 2006.
115. *Provincial Bank of Ireland v McKeever* [1941] IR 471, 485.
116. *McMakin v Hibernian Bank* [1905] 1 IR 306.
117. [1941] IR 471, 485. Although note the comments of Farwell J in *Powell v Powell* [1900] 1 Ch 243, 246.

rejected, the fact of it having been given may suffice to rebut the presumption of undue influence, although this will not always be the case, as it may only have been rejected as a result of influence exerted. In the view of Black J, 'one cannot expect absolute disproof of undue influence' and he suggested that it is sufficient to establish 'a reasonable probability of the exercise of independent will founded upon adequate understanding'.[118] In *McKeever* the sons and widow of the deceased settlor were persuaded by trustees to execute a mortgage to secure an overdraft which these trustees had run up. Black J accepted that on the facts the presumption of undue influence had been rebutted although the only legal advice which they had received was from the trustees' solicitor, who was the sons' uncle. Black J stated that viewing the evidence as a whole, he was satisfied that the consequences of the mortgage transaction had been sufficiently understood and he allowed the claim of the plaintiff bank.

It was suggested by Barron J in *Carroll v Carroll*[119] that, where the full facts of a case are known, it is a matter for the court to determine whether there was undue influence and that in such cases, the presumption really plays no part.[120] However, in this case the Supreme Court accepted that there was clear doubt as to whether the donor knew what he was doing and what his real intentions were. The plaintiffs, who were the daughters and personal representatives of an elderly donor, sought to have a transfer of a pub and residential accommodation set aside on the grounds that it had been procured by undue influence and was an improvident transaction. After his wife's death, the donor had transferred the property to his son without disclosing this fact to his daughters. The donor and his son both subsequently died and tensions arose between the plaintiffs and the son's widow, the defendant, which led to the bringing of proceedings to have the original transfer set aside. The donor had discussed making the transfer to his son on two occasions with the solicitor who effected it, although the latter was, in reality, acting for both parties. While the donor was mentally alert at that time, he was subject to a number of physical infirmities which made him increasingly dependent on others. The plaintiffs submitted that the relationship between the donor and donee was such as to raise a presumption of undue influence, which they argued had not been rebutted. The defendant conceded that the relationship between the parties did give rise to a presumption of undue influence but submitted that it had been rebutted in the circumstances. The Supreme Court, upholding the decision of Shanley J, concluded that the relationship between the donor and donee was such as to raise a presumption of undue influence and that the presumption had not been rebutted in the circumstances.

In considering the submission made on behalf of the defendant that for the plaintiff to succeed it was necessary that there should be evidence that

118. *Ibid.* at 485.
119. [1998] 2 ILRM 218 (HC); [1999] 4 IR 241 (SC). See Dwyer (2001) 36 Ir Jur 324; Hourican (2001) 6 CPLJ 18.
120. See also *Prendergast v Joyce* [2009] 3 IR 519, 535.

the donee had exercised undue influence on the donor, Denham J pointed out that this was not a case of actual undue influence but rather one in which the relationship between the donor and donee raised a presumption of undue influence. It was therefore necessary for the defendant to rebut the presumption and, to this extent, she expressed the view that the appeal had been argued on the basis of a mistaken approach to the law. Denham J stated that the facts and circumstances of the case had been fully considered and determined by the learned trial judge and she was satisfied that he was correct in his finding that it was not necessary to prove specific acts of undue influence by the donee. Instead the evidence had to be considered to see whether the presumption of undue influence had been rebutted and Denham J stated that she was satisfied that this had been done most carefully by Shanley J and that she would affirm his decision on this aspect of the appeal. In relation to rebutting the presumption of undue influence, Barron J stated that it has to be shown that the 'gift was the spontaneous act of the donor acting in circumstances which enabled him to exercise an independent will'.[121] He was satisfied that there could have been no independent advice given by the solicitor in the case before him as he was at best acting for both parties and he agreed with the conclusion reached by Denham J that the presumption of undue influence had not been rebutted in the circumstances.

So, as Gilligan J commented in *Prendergast v Joyce*,[122] it is clear from the judgment of Denham J in *Carroll* that the existence of a relationship of a certain nature, combined with the conferring of a substantial benefit, gives rise to a presumption of undue influence without more. As Gilligan J stated:

> [T]he presumption arises from the actual relationship between donor and donee at or shortly before the time of the impugned transaction, coupled with the circumstances of the parties relevant to the acquisition of a position of influence, including the age, position in life, state of health and other particular vulnerabilities of the donor. This is probably because these and other vulnerabilities can give rise to a degree of influence over the donor in a relationship where no such influence would arise if both parties were of the same capacity and in the same position to protect their interests.[123]

On the facts of the case before him, where an elderly woman who was in a vulnerable and confused state had transferred monies into the joint names of herself and the defendant, her late husband's nephew, Gilligan J found that a presumption of undue influence arose. In the circumstances, he held that the defendant had not established that the gift resulted from the free exercise

121. [1999] 4 IR 241, 264. Quoting from the judgment of Cotton LJ in *Allcard v Skinner* (1887) 36 Ch D 145, 171.
122. [2009] 3 IR 519.
123. *Ibid.* at 533.

of the donor's will constituting the independent act of a person in a position to exercise a free judgment and he concluded that the presumption of undue influence had not been rebutted and that the transactions should be set aside. However, in contrast, in *Lynn v O'Hara*,[124] while O'Malley J accepted that the circumstances in which a farm had been transferred from elderly parents to their son gave rise to a presumption of undue influence, she was satisfied that this presumption had been rebutted. In proceedings brought by the mother against her late son's widow, O'Malley J found that the legal advice given to the parents had been independent and appropriate and that the transfer had been the result of the exercise of their free will.

It is important to stress that the presumption of undue influence does not arise in the context of all relationships which could be described as 'fiduciary' in nature,[125] and that whether a presumption will arise in a particular type of relationship may depend on the facts of the individual case. So, in *Lloyds Bank Ltd v Bundy*,[126] the presumption was held to apply to the relationship of banker and client in circumstances where a father had relied entirely on the advice of his bank manager in mortgaging his house as security for a guarantee relating to his son's debts. However, *Bundy* was distinguished by the House of Lords as turning on special facts in *National Westminster Bank plc v Morgan*,[127] in which a wife claimed that a bank manager had exerted undue influence over her to obtain her signature in relation to a mortgage agreement relating to the parties' house, which was concluded in order to secure a loan to her husband. The House of Lords was not satisfied that the relationship between Mrs Morgan and the bank went beyond the normal business relationship of banker and customer and held that the manager had never assumed a role which would raise the presumption of undue influence.

Undue Influence in the Context of Wills

It was stated by Costello J in *Healy v McGillicuddy*[128] that 'no presumption of undue influence…arises in the case of wills and the burden of proving undue influence in relation to wills always rests on the person alleging it.' This question of whether the presumption of undue influence can arise in the context of a gift in a will as opposed to one given *inter vivos* was also considered by Murphy J in *Lambert v Lyons*.[129] In his opinion, *Healy* was authority in Irish law for a 'longstanding distinction' between gifts in a will and transactions *inter vivos*. He stated that in the context of wills no presumption of undue influence can

124. [2015] IEHC 689.
125. E.g. *Re Coomber* [1911] 1 Ch 723.
126. [1975] QB 326.
127. [1985] AC 686.
128. [1978] ILRM 175, referring to *Boyse v Rossborough* (1857) 6 HLC 1; *Parfitt v Lawless* (1872) LR 2 P & D 462. See also *Gill v Woodall* [2009] EWHC 834 (Ch) at [483].
129. [2010] IEHC 29.

arise from the nature of the relationship between the parties and the burden is on the plaintiff to establish any undue influence alleged. Murphy J went on to conclude that even if a presumption of undue influence had arisen in the case before him, in the circumstances he was satisfied that it had been rebutted.

As the Law Commission in England has noted, the absence of the presumptions applied under the general doctrine of undue influence, combined with the high bar of establishing coercion, means that claims for testamentary undue influence often fail for lack of evidence.[130] However, where sufficient evidence exists, a finding of undue influence in relation to the making of a will may be made.[131]

It has been suggested by Mason that the scope of undue influence under probate law in England should be widened to encompass a presumption of undue influence where the testator-beneficiary relationship is one of trust and confidence and where the bequeathed gift is one which calls for an explanation.[132] However, Kerridge has argued that transposing the principles which apply to *inter vivos* gifts in this context to testamentary dispositions would not be appropriate,[133] although he acknowledges that he agrees with other commentators who suggest that the rules which apply to testamentary dispositions are unsatisfactory.[134] The Law Commission has also referred to the fact that stakeholders have expressed the view that it is too difficult to challenge a will on the basis of testamentary undue influence.[135] While it has rejected the approach of applying the general doctrine of undue influence in a testamentary context,[136] it has provisionally proposed the creation of a statutory doctrine of testamentary undue influence and has invited views on whether such a doctrine if adopted should take the form of a structured or discretionary approach.[137]

Undue Influence and Third Parties

The principles considered above also extend to cases where the party exerting undue influence does not benefit directly from his conduct and where the person over whom he has exercised this influence enters into obligations to a third party as a result. This issue has become very relevant in the context of obligations to financial institutions entered into by one party allegedly as a result of undue influence exerted over them by another. It has generally arisen in the context

130. Law Commission Consultation Paper No. 231, *Making a Will* (2017), para. 7.59.
131. E.g. *Re Edwards* [2007] EWHC 1119 (Ch); *Schrader v Schrader* [2013] EWHC 466 (Ch); *Schomberg v Taylor* [2013] EWHC 2269 (Ch).
132. Mason [2011] Conv 115, 122.
133. [2012] Conv 129, 143.
134. See Mason [2011] Conv 115; Ridge (2004) 120 LQR 617.
135. Law Commission Consultation Paper No. 231, *Making a Will* (2017), para. 7.94.
136. *Ibid.* at para.7.106.
137. See further Sloan [2017] Conv 440.

of relationships between spouses, co-habitees or a parent and child but it can also arise in other types of family or domestic relationships.

Several questions have arisen in this area including whether the husband/wife relationship gives rise to any presumption or whether wives should be treated as a 'specially protected class'. However, the primary focus of debate has been on what inferences may be drawn from the nature of the relationship between the debtor and guarantor and on the circumstances in which the financial institution, in the absence of actual knowledge of the debtor's improper conduct–generally but not invariably undue influence–will be fixed with constructive notice of this conduct. In addition, issues have arisen in relation to the steps which a financial institution should take where it is put on inquiry and about the adequacy or otherwise of legal advice which a party alleging undue influence has received.

The Position in England

In relation to the first of these questions, while it appears to be accepted that the relationship of husband and wife does not give rise to any presumption of undue influence,[138] there have been suggestions that wives constitute a special class which deserves protection in these circumstances. This approach was adopted by the majority of the Court of Appeal in *Barclays Bank plc v O'Brien*,[139] where Scott LJ made it clear that the likelihood of a husband exerting influence over his wife, which was the original justification for the 'tenderness of equity' towards married women who gave their property as security for their husband's debts, was still a relevant consideration.[140] This 'special equity' theory was referred to by Lord Browne-Wilkinson in the course of his speech in the House of Lords in *O'Brien* as meaning that 'equity affords special protection to a protected class of surety viz. those where the relationship between the debtor and the surety is such that influence by the debtor over the surety and reliance by the surety on the debtor are natural features of the relationship'. The approach adopted by Lord Nicholls in *Royal Bank of Scotland v Etridge (No. 2)*[141] towards this issue was to confirm that no presumption of undue influence arises as a result of the husband/wife relationship, although he did state that the court will note as a matter of fact the opportunities for abuse which flow from a wife's confidence in her husband. The boundaries of what will amount

138. *Bank of Montreal v Stuart* [1911] AC 120, 137; *Bank of Credit and Commerce International SA v Aboody* [1990] 1 QB 923, 953; *Royal Bank of Scotland v Etridge (No. 2)* [2002] 2 AC 773, 797, 842.
139. [1993] QB 109. See Dixon [1993] CLJ 24.
140. See also the reference made by Dixon J in the decision of the High Court of Australia in *Yerkey v Jones* (1930) 63 CLR 649 to the 'invalidating tendency' applied by the courts to transactions between husbands and wives. See further Burton (1997) 4 Comm LP 120.
141. [2002] 2 AC 773, 797.

to undue influence in the context of a husband and wife relationship were extended further by the decision of the Court of Appeal in *Hewett v First Plus Financial Group plc*,[142] in which it held that a husband's concealment of an affair from his wife amounted to the exercise of undue influence against her sufficient to vitiate a mortgage transaction.

The circumstances in which a financial institution may be unable to rely on a guarantee provided by a guarantor, even where it does not have actual knowledge of any improper conduct, has given rise to much debate. This involves a consideration of the circumstances in which a bank will be 'put on inquiry' and what steps it should take when in this situation. This in turn raises the issue of the content of the legal advice which should be given in such circumstances and the related question of the independence of this advice. These issues have been considered in numerous cases, particularly in England, most notably in two decisions of the House of Lords in *Barclays Bank plc v O'Brien*[143] and in *Royal Bank of Scotland v Etridge (No. 2)*.[144]

In *Barclays Bank plc v O'Brien* a wife had joined in a charge over the family home jointly owned by her and her husband as security for overdraft facilities extended by the plaintiff bank to a company in which the husband had an interest. The House of Lords found that as a general principle, where a wife was induced to stand as surety for her husband's debt as a result of his undue influence, misrepresentation or some other legal wrong, she had an equity against him to set aside the transaction and this right would be enforceable against a third party who had actual or constructive notice of the circumstances giving rise to the equity or for whom the husband was acting as agent. In the circumstances, it was held that the bank was fixed with constructive notice of the husband's wrongful misrepresentation and the wife was entitled as against the bank to set aside the legal charge on the matrimonial home securing the husband's liability to the bank. Lord Browne-Wilkinson said that constructive notice will exist when a creditor is put on inquiry, e.g. by the fact that the transaction is not on its face to the financial advantage of the borrower, and if having been put on inquiry, the lender fails to take reasonable steps to ensure that the borrower understands the nature of the transaction. In terms of what amounts to taking reasonable steps, Lord Browne-Wilkinson stated as follows:

> [A] creditor will have satisfied these requirements if it insists that the wife attend a private meeting (in the absence of the husband) with a representative of the creditor at which she is told of the extent of her liability as surety, warned of the risk she is running and urged to take

142. [2010] 2 FLR 177. See further Wood [2010] Cov LJ 52.
143. [1994] 1 AC 180. A number of commentators have written about this decision and its consequences, see Berg [1994] LMCLQ 34; Allen (1995) 58 MLR 87; Lawson [1995] CLJ 280; Sparkes [1995] Conv 250; Felhberg (1996) 59 MLR 675; Richardson (1996) 16 LS 368.
144. [2002] 2 AC 773.

> independent legal advice. If these steps are taken in my judgment the creditor will have taken such reasonable steps as are necessary to preclude a subsequent claim that it had constructive notice of the wife's rights.[145]

The alternative approach, namely the agency theory, was also considered by Lord Browne-Wilkinson although he criticised it as having developed in an artificial way. Essentially where it applies, the wrongdoing of the husband will be imputed to the creditor if the former can be regarded as being the agent of the latter in obtaining the wife's consent to the transaction.

It is important to note that in *O'Brien* the bank was held to have constructive notice of the husband's improper conduct[146] because the use of the wife's interest to secure a loan to a company in which she had no interest was *prima facie* not to her advantage, a fact which should immediately have put the bank on inquiry. It was this fact which distinguished the result in *O'Brien* from that in *CIBC Mortgages plc v Pitt*,[147] where the loan was on its face to both husband and wife for their joint benefit[148] and therefore not apparently to the wife's disadvantage. In *Pitt* the first named defendant persuaded his wife, the second named defendant, to execute a legal charge over their house in favour of the plaintiff in order to obtain a loan to purchase shares which he told her would improve their standard of living. After the stock market crash in 1987, the plaintiff brought proceedings for possession of the matrimonial home when the husband fell into arrears with the payments due under the loan. The Court of Appeal dismissed the wife's appeal against the finding of the trial judge in the plaintiff's favour and held that since the transaction was not manifestly disadvantageous to the wife, she could not establish undue influence and, in any event, since the plaintiff did not have any actual or constructive notice of any irregularity, the charge was valid as against the second named defendant. In the House of Lords, counsel for the wife argued that the Court of Appeal in *Bank of Credit and Commerce International SA v Aboody*[149] had erred in extending the need to show manifest disadvantage to cases of actual, as opposed to presumed, undue influence. Lord Browne-Wilkinson agreed and said that he had no doubt that this requirement, laid down in *National Westminster Bank plc v Morgan*,[150] did not extend to cases of actual undue influence.[151] However, the House of

145. [1994] 1 AC 180, 196-197.
146. It has been accepted that the principles which apply as to when a lender is put on inquiry and the reasonable steps it should take to avoid being affected by notice apply equally to cases of misrepresentation and undue influence, see *Annulment Funding Co. Ltd v Cowey* [2010] EWCA Civ 711 at [64].
147. See also the *dicta* of Lord Nicholls in *Royal Bank of Scotland v Etridge (No. 2)* [2002] 2 AC 773, 804.
148. [1994] 1 AC 200.
149. [1990] 1 QB 923.
150. [1985] AC 686.
151. However, Fehlberg has argued (1994) 57 MLR 467, 473 that by effectively saying that the transaction must not on its face be to the financial advantage of the wife in order

Lords held that as the transaction was not *prima facie* disadvantageous to the wife, the bank was not put on inquiry and was not affected by constructive notice of her husband's undue influence and could therefore enforce the security.[152]

The issue of whether it is a requirement to show manifest disadvantage in cases of presumed undue influence has troubled the courts in England on a number of occasions over the years. Millett LJ commented in *Dunbar Bank plc v Nadeem*[153] that 'a person who can prove the exercise of actual undue influence by another in respect to a transaction is entitled to have the transaction set aside without proof of manifest disadvantage … [b]ut such proof is required when the exercise of undue influence is only presumed'. Similarly, in *Cheese v Thomas*,[154] although the requirement of manifest disadvantage was given a fairly flexible interpretation, it was nevertheless insisted upon by the Court of Appeal. Subsequently, in *Barclays Bank plc v Coleman*,[155] Nourse LJ repeated that before a presumption of undue influence can be said to arise, a transaction must be shown to be manifestly disadvantageous to the party allegedly influenced.[156] However, he did concede that the views expressed by Lord Browne-Wilkinson in *CIBC Mortgages plc v Pitt*[157] placed a serious question mark over the future of the requirement of manifest disadvantage in cases of presumed as well as actual undue influence.[158] When the appeal in *Coleman* was heard by the House of Lords along with a number of others in *Royal Bank of Scotland v Etridge (No. 2)*,[159] Lord Nicholls, while he acknowledged that the label 'manifest disadvantage' has been causing difficulty and can give rise to misunderstanding, did not accept that the requirement could be dispensed with. In his view, in relationships where trust and confidence are reposed in another party, something more is needed before the law will reverse the burden

---

for constructive notice to arise, the 'manifest disadvantage' requirement rejected in *Pitt* is being resurrected in another guise. See also the comments of Lord Nicholls in *Royal Bank of Scotland v Etridge (No. 2)* [2002] 2 AC 773, 796.

152. See also *Chater v Mortgage Agency Services Number Two Ltd* [2003] EWCA Civ 490, where the Court of Appeal held that it was unable to detect anything about a transaction in which a mother mortgaged her house and used the funds to support her son's business sufficient to put the respondent on inquiry about undue influence.
153. [1998] 3 All ER 876, 882. See also *Mahoney v Purnell* [1996] 3 All ER 61, 82-83.
154. [1994] 1 WLR 129. See Mee [1994] LMCLQ 330; Chen-Wishart (1994) 110 LQR 173.
155. [2001] 1 QB 20. See Thompson [2000] Conv 444. The appeal was dismissed by the House of Lords [2002] 2 AC 773.
156. Nourse LJ stated that a manifest disadvantage must be one which is 'clear and obvious' and in deciding whether a transaction is manifestly disadvantageous an objective view must be taken of it and that view must be taken as at the date when the transaction is entered into (at 33).
157. [1994] 1 AC 200.
158. It has been suggested by Thompson [2000] Conv 444 that Nourse LJ was effectively saying that it was only judicial courtesy which restrained Lord Browne-Wilkinson in *CIBC Mortgages plc v Pitt* from stating that the introduction of a requirement of manifest disadvantage was wrong.
159. [2002] 2 AC 773.

of proof and 'when that something more is present, the greater the disadvantage to the vulnerable person, the more cogent must be the explanation before the presumption will be regarded as rebutted'.[160]

The issues of when a bank should be put on inquiry and what steps it should take when it has been were addressed in some detail by the House of Lords in *Royal Bank of Scotland v Etridge (No. 2)*,[161] a decision which has been described as representing a 'significant change in practice'.[162] However, the principles laid down in that case, particularly by Lord Nicholls, are now well established and as Lindsay J commented in *Hogg v Hogg*,[163] '[i]t is thus with confidence that one can look to that opinion for guidance at the most authoritative level on the subject of undue influence.'

In a number of cases heard prior to the decision of the House of Lords in *Etridge*, wives had charged their interests in their homes in favour of financial institutions as security for their husbands' indebtedness or the indebtedness of a company through which the latter carried on business. When the banks sought to enforce the charges, the wives raised the defence that they had signed them as a result of the undue influence of their husbands. The House of Lords heard a number of appeals together and set out the principles which should apply in such cases.[164] While Lord Nicholls acknowledged that the term 'put on inquiry' is strictly speaking a misnomer as the bank is not required to make inquiries but to take other steps, he stated that Lord Browne-Wilkinson's *dicta* in *O'Brien* has the effect that a bank is put on inquiry whenever a wife offers to stand surety for the husband's debts. He then explored the extent to which this obligation should arise in other contexts and came to the conclusion that there was 'no rational cut-off point, with certain types of relationship being susceptible to the *O'Brien* principle and others not.'[165] He therefore expressed the view that 'the only practical way forward is to regard banks as "put on inquiry" in every case where the relationship between the surety and the debtor is non-commercial.'[166]

This broad approach resolved the uncertainty which had lingered following the decision in *O'Brien*. In the course of his speech in that case, Lord Browne-Wilkinson stressed that the guidelines which he was laying down were not restricted to cases involving spouses and said that they also applied 'if and

160. *Ibid.* at 799.
161. [2002] 2 AC 773. However, as Lord Hobhouse pointed out at 822, situations will differ across a spectrum ranging from a very small risk to a risk verging on a probability and 'there has to be proportionality between the degree of risk and the requisite response to it'.
162. *Royal Bank of Scotland plc v Chandra* [2010] 1 Lloyd's Rep 677, 704.
163. [2008] WTLR 35 at [41].
164. See generally Andrews [2002] Conv 456; Oldham [2002] CLJ 29; O'Sullivan (2002) 118 LQR 337; Bigwood (2002) 65 MLR 435; Phang and Tijo [2002] LMCLQ 231; Capper [2002] RLR 100; Breslin (2002) 9 Comm LP 35; White (2002) 20 ILT 70.
165. [2002] 2 AC 773, 814.
166. *Ibid.*

only if, the creditor is aware that the surety is co-habiting with the principal debtor'.[167] This requirement of co-habitation was relaxed in *Massey v Midland Bank plc*[168] where, although the parties had never married or co-habited, they had enjoyed a stable 'sexual and emotional relationship' for many years and had had two children together. Steyn LJ, while recognising that it would constitute an extension of the approach laid down by Lord Browne-Wilkinson, said that he had no doubt that 'in terms of impairment of [the surety's] judgmental capacity, this case should be approached as if she was a wife or co-habitee of [the debtor]'.[169] It should also be noted that in *O'Brien*, Lord Browne-Wilkinson stated that the principles he was setting out applied 'where, to the creditor's knowledge, the surety reposes trust and confidence in the principal debtor in relation to his or her financial affairs'.[170]

An example of such a relationship is that which existed between an employer and a junior employee in *Credit Lyonnais Bank Nederland NV v Burch*.[171] As Nourse LJ commented, 'although the relationship between the debtor and the mortgagor was not that of persons living together but employer and employee, it may broadly be said to fall under *Barclays Bank plc v O'Brien*' and the court proceeded to apply these principles in order to determine whether the bank should be fixed with constructive notice of the employer's wrongdoing.

The test in relation to the steps which a bank should take if put on inquiry where this applies to past transactions was as set out by Lord Browne-Wilkinson in *O'Brien* namely, that it should reasonably be expected to take steps to bring home to the wife the risk she is running and to advise her to take independent advice. In relation to future transactions, a bank will fulfil its obligations if it insists that a wife attends a private meeting with a representative of the bank at which she is told of the extent of her liability, warned of the risk she is running and urged to take independent advice. Lord Nicholls in *Etridge* commented that the practice of banks generally is not to have a private meeting with the wife in such cases[172] and concluded that 'the furthest a bank can be expected to go is to take reasonable steps to satisfy itself that the wife has had brought home to her, in a meaningful way, the practical implications of the proposed transaction'.[173] In addition, he stressed that he did not understand Lord Browne-

167. [1994] 1 AC 180, 198. Lawson has suggested [1995] CLJ 280, 282 that this should be interpreted as meaning that a creditor should be put on inquiry only if he is actually aware that the surety is co-habiting with the debtor as otherwise it would require creditors to act as 'busybodies'.
168. [1995] 1 All ER 929.
169. *Ibid.* at 933. The approach in *Massey* was in line with that adopted by Lord Nicholls in *Royal Bank of Scotland v Etridge (No. 2)* where he stated that the principles will apply to unmarried couples, whether heterosexual or homosexual, where the bank is aware of the relationship and he agreed that cohabitation is not essential.
170. [1994] 1 AC 180, 196.
171. [1997] 1 All ER 144.
172. See further Pawlowski and Greer [2001] Conv 229.
173. [2002] 2 AC 773, 805.

Wilkinson to have stated in *O'Brien* that a personal meeting with the wife was the only way a bank could discharge its obligation to bring home to the wife the risks she was running.[174] This is in line with the approach previously adopted by the Court of Appeal in *Massey v Midland Bank plc*,[175] in which a bank was found to have been put on inquiry by the circumstances in which a woman had agreed to provide security for an overdraft granted to a business venture in which a man with whom she had a long-standing relationship was involved. However, the Court of Appeal was satisfied that the bank had taken reasonable steps to ensure that her agreement had been properly obtained and held that it was not fixed with constructive notice of the misrepresentation made in this case. Steyn LJ commented that the guidance provided by the House of Lords in *O'Brien* 'should not be mechanically applied'[176] and that, provided the lender had taken alternative steps to achieve Lord Browne-Wilkinson's aim, failure to follow his guidelines precisely would not be fatal to the lender's case. In this instance there had been no separate meeting between the surety and the creditor's representative unattended by the debtor but the creditor had required her to be independently advised. Steyn LJ was satisfied that she had received such independent legal advice[177] and that the creditor had therefore complied with the substance of Lord Browne-Wilkinson's guidance.[178]

Turning to the issue of the content of any legal advice which a solicitor may give wives in such a situation, the opinion of Lord Nicholls in *Royal Bank of*

174. However, note the *dicta* of Lord Hobhouse at 824 to the effect that Lord Browne-Wilkinson had stressed the need for the wife to be communicated with separately from her husband. Lord Hobhouse expressed the view that this was clearly appropriate since, if the purpose is to establish that the wife is acting freely, it is unlikely that an interview in the presence of the husband will achieve this if she has been improperly influenced by him.
175. [1995] 1 All ER 929. See Mee [1995] Conv 148.
176. *Ibid.* at 934. Steyn LJ stated that this guidance 'was intended to strike a fair balance between the need to protect wives (and others in a like position) whose judgmental capacity was impaired and the need to avoid unnecessary impediments to using the matrimonial home as security'.
177. However, it should be noted that earlier in his judgment (at 931) Steyn LJ mentioned that both debtor and surety had visited this independent legal adviser together and that the solicitor did not see the surety alone but explained the nature of the transaction to her and that she understood it. It should also be noted that Millett LJ has commented in the course of his judgment in *Credit Lyonnais Bank Nederland NV v Burch* [1997] 1 All ER 144, 156 that independent legal advice is 'neither always necessary nor always sufficient' and that the result in such cases 'does not depend mechanically on the presence or absence of legal advice'.
178. This can be contrasted with the decision of the Court of Appeal in *TSB Bank plc v Camfield* [1995] 1 All ER 951 where the bank was fixed with constructive notice of a husband's representation because it had failed in the view of the court to take reasonable steps to ensure that the wife understood the nature of the charge. While the bank had stipulated that the wife should be given independent advice, in fact she was not separately advised from her husband, and the wife executed the charge under the false impression that it was for a limited amount.

Scotland v Etridge (No. 2)[179] also provides useful guidance on this point. In his view the *dicta* of the Court of Appeal in *Etridge (No. 2)* went too far and he stated that the content of the advice required from a solicitor before giving the confirmation sought by the bank will inevitably depend on the circumstances of the case. He added that typically the advice which a solicitor can be expected to give should cover the following matters as a core minimum:

(1) He will need to explain the nature of the documents and the practical consequences these will have for the wife if she signs them.
(2) He will need to point out the seriousness of the risks involved and discuss her financial means with her, including whether there are other assets out of which repayments might be made.
(3) He will need to state clearly that the wife has a choice and that the decision is hers and hers alone.
(4) He should check whether the wife wishes to proceed and whether she is content that he should write to the bank confirming that he has explained the nature of the transaction to her.[180]

Lord Scott also listed a number of issues which he felt a solicitor should generally address which included a requirement that he should explain to the wife that he may need to give the bank written confirmation that he has advised her about the nature and effect of the transaction and obtain her written consent to his doing so.

A further issue which has provoked debate is whether a financial institution is entitled to rely on the fact that a solicitor has undertaken his task of advising a wife in a sufficiently independent manner. In general the Court of Appeal has held that a bank is entitled to assume that the solicitor has given her appropriate advice[181] even in circumstances where he has also acted for the company, owned and controlled by the husband, to whom the loan had been made.[182] So, in *Barclays Bank plc v Thomson*,[183] Simon Brown LJ commented: 'I can see no good reason whatever why a bank, perhaps conscientiously instructing solicitors to give independent advice to a signatory who might otherwise go unadvised, should thereby be disabled from relying on the solicitors' certificate

179. [2002] 2 AC 773. It should be noted that Lord Hobhouse has pointed out (at 825) that there is a risk of confusion about what the role of a solicitor should be in such cases and he has suggested that problems may arise in ensuring that the solicitor is in possession of any relevant facts known to the bank.
180. *Ibid.* at 808. These principles and Lord Nicholls' other observations about the appropriate approach to be taken where an individual seeks advice from a solicitor in this context were described as a 'very good guide' by Lord Neuberger MR in *Padden v Bevan Ashford* [2012] 1 WLR 1759, 1767.
181. *Bank of Baroda v Rayarel* [1995] 2 FLR 376.
182. *Banco Exterior Internacional v Mann* [1995] 1 All ER 936. See Dunn [1995] Conv 325.
183. [1997] 4 All ER 816, 826.

that such advice has been properly given'. It should be noted that a differently constituted Court of Appeal effectively held a few months later in *Royal Bank of Scotland v Etridge*[184] that a solicitor's certificate to the effect that he had explained the nature of the transaction to a surety wife was not conclusive. The essential difference between the reasoning employed in these two decisions is that in the view of Simon Brown LJ in *Thomson*, the solicitor is regarded as acting exclusively for the surety when advising her, although he may well have been retained by the bank to do so, whereas in *Etridge*, Hobhouse LJ was satisfied that the solicitor was acting as the bank's agent in so doing.

The view in *Thomson* seemed preferable[185] and this has been confirmed by the approach adopted by a number of the members of the House of Lords in *Royal Bank of Scotland v Etridge (No. 2)*,[186] where Lord Nicholls stated that 'ordinarily it will be reasonable that a bank should be able to rely upon confirmation from a solicitor, acting for the wife, that he has advised the wife appropriately'. Lord Nicholls stressed that when accepting instructions to advise the wife the solicitor assumes responsibilities directly to her and that in every case he must consider carefully whether there is any conflict of duty or interest and whether it would be in the wife's best interests for him to accept instructions from her. If he decides to accept the instructions, his assumption of legal and professional responsibilities towards her 'ought, in the ordinary course of things, to provide sufficient assurance that he will give the requisite advice fully, carefully and conscientiously'.[187] Lord Scott expressed the view that the fact that a solicitor is acting for the bank in arranging for the completion of the security does not prejudice his suitability to advise the wife. Where he is also acting for the husband, in his view this presents 'a little more difficulty' and if there is some particular reason known to the bank for suspecting impropriety on the husband's part, the bank should insist on advice being given by a solicitor who is independent of the husband. This is in line with the view expressed by Lord Browne-Wilkinson in *Barclays Bank plc v O'Brien*[188] where he stated that in an exceptional case where a creditor knows of additional facts rendering the presence of undue influence probable and not just possible, the creditor must insist that the surety be separately advised.[189]

However, in *Etridge (No. 2)* Lord Scott concluded that where the risk is no more than a possibility of impropriety, which he said would be present in all cases in which a wife provides a surety, there was no reason why the solicitor

---

184. [1997] 3 All ER 628.
185. See Price (1998) 114 LQR 186, 187. See also Draper [1999] Conv 176, 183-190.
186. [2002] 2 AC 773, 806. See also *Royal Bank of Scotland plc v Chandra* [2010] 1 Lloyd's Rep 677, 704.
187. *Ibid.* at 810.
188. [1994] 1 AC 180, 197.
189. The decision of the Court of Appeal in *Credit Lyonnais Bank Nederland NV v Burch* [1997] 1 All ER 144 would appear to be an example of this type of case. See Hooley and O'Sullivan [1997] LMCLQ 17; Tijo (1997) 113 LQR 10; Chen-Wishart [1997] CLJ 60.

advising the wife should not also be the husband's solicitor and that a bank is entitled to rely on the professional competence and propriety of the solicitor in providing proper and adequate advice in such circumstances. A further aspect of Lord Scott's speech which should be noted is his view that knowledge on the part of a bank that a solicitor is acting for a surety wife does not, without more, justify the assumption that the solicitor's instructions extend to advising her about the nature and effect of the transaction.[190] So, as the judgment of Jonathan Parker LJ in *UCB Corporate Services Ltd v Williams*[191] makes clear, a bank cannot avoid being fixed with constructive notice of a wife's equity to set aside a transaction by relying on an honest belief that she was represented in the transaction by a solicitor.

Reaction to the decision of the House of Lords in *Royal Bank of Scotland v Etridge (No. 2)* was generally favourable. While the predominant view was that it tipped the scales further in favour of lending institutions and against surety wives,[192] it was also heralded as a decision which went further than *O'Brien* in reducing the risk of undue influence.[193] The decision undoubtedly imposes a lower threshold of proof in relation to the circumstances in which a bank will be put on inquiry and ensures that the safeguards designed to protect the interests of those providing guarantees will frequently be required to be satisfied.

However, the 'reasonable steps' which a bank must take to avoid being fixed with notice appear less onerous than those contemplated in *O'Brien* and provided the bank requires that the wife receives independent legal advice, it may avoid liability. In a sense the responsibility has shifted to the solicitor advising the wife and overall it is probably fair to say that the principles laid down in *Etridge (No. 2)* are more favourable from the point of view of financial institutions than those laid down in *O'Brien*.

The Position in Ireland

Introduction

Before assessing how the courts in Ireland have considered the issues raised in *Etridge (No.2)* and the extent to which the principles set out in that case have been applied, a preliminary point should be made. Many of the judgments dealing with these issues in recent years have been delivered in the context of motions for summary judgment[194] where the net question before the court will

190. [2002] 2 AC 773, 844-845. See also the speech of Lord Hobhouse at 825.
191. [2003] 1 P & CR 168, 188. See also *Lloyds TSB Bank v Holdgate* [2002] EWCA Civ 1543 at [28] and [38].
192. Andrews [2002] Conv 456, 469; O'Sullivan (2002) 118 LQR 337, 350. Although Haley (2010) 61 NILQ 141, 161 has suggested that the change effected by *Etridge* 'does not disadvantage the surety'.
193. Oldham [2002] CLJ 29.
194. *ACC Loan Management Ltd v Sheehan* [2016] IEHC 818; *Ulster Bank (Ireland) Ltd v de Kretser* [2016] IECA 371; *Bank of Ireland v Curran* [2016] IECA 399; *ACC Loan*

be whether an arguable defence to the application has been established.[195] This threshold of arguability is much lower than the burden which will face a party at a full plenary hearing and this factor should be borne in mind in considering the Irish authorities in this area.

The first substantive question which needs to be addressed in cases where a party agrees to stand surety for the debts of another is whether there is sufficient evidence of undue influence or other misconduct. Even in the context of the low threshold for resisting summary judgment, it has been made clear that a bald assertion that undue influence has been exercised is insufficient.[196] In a number of recent cases there has been a failure to cross this first hurdle.[197] So, outside the category of relationships where a presumption of undue influence will arise, if there is no evidence which would give rise to such a presumption because of the particular circumstances of the relationship between the parties or of actual undue influence, a claim is likely to fail.[198] In the course of her judgment in *Barry v Ennis Property Finance DAC*[199] Stewart J set out a useful list of the type of questions which claimants should address in seeking to establish whether undue influence is to be considered as a serious issue in this context. These included any commercial experience–either generally or in relation to the matter at issue–possessed by the claimant, the relationship which it is alleged gave rise to the undue influence, the nature of the events which led to this influence being alleged, the circumstances surrounding the decisions which the claimant might have been motivated to make as a result and how these decisions contributed to the issues being considered by the court.

The Circumstances in which a Financial Institution will be put on Inquiry

A key issue is the circumstances in which a financial institution will be put on inquiry. If, where it is put on inquiry, it does not take the necessary precautionary steps, it may be fixed with notice of what these inquiries would have revealed. As McGovern J pointed out in *Danske Bank A/S trading as National Irish Bank*

Management Ltd v Connolly [2017] 3 IR 629; *ACC Bank plc v Walsh* [2017] IECA 166; *Barry v Ennis Property Finance DAC* [2018] IEHC 766.

195. The test set out in *First Commercial Bank plc v Anglin* [1996] 1 IR 75, endorsed by McGuinness J in *Aer Rianta cpt v Ryanair Ltd* [2001] 4 IR 607, is whether there is a fair or reasonable probability of the defendant having a real or *bona fide* defence.

196. *Bank of Scotland v Hickey* [2014] IEHC 202 at [34]; *Bank of Ireland v Curran* [2016] IECA 399 at [31]–[33]; *Ulster Bank (Ireland) Ltd v de Kretser* [2016] IECA 371 at [31] *per* Birmingham J; *ACC Bank plc v Walsh* [2017] IECA 166 at [29]; *Barry v Ennis Property Finance DAC* [2018] IEHC 766 at [28].

197. *Bank of Ireland v Curran* [2016] IECA 399 at [35]–[36]; *Ulster Bank (Ireland) Ltd v de Kretser* [2016] IECA 371 at [31] *per* Birmingham J; *ACC Loan Management Ltd v Connolly* [2017] 3 IR 629, 645.

198. However, note the views expressed in the dissenting judgment of Hogan J in *Ulster Bank (Ireland) Ltd v de Kretser* [2016] IECA 371, considered below.

199. [2018] IEHC 766 at [29].

plc v Madden,[200] where a party is seeking to set aside a contract on the basis that it was procured by the fraud or undue influence of a third party, it is necessary that the party seeking to enforce the contract had notice of the fraud or undue influence and the onus is on the defendant to establish that the plaintiff had actual or constructive knowledge of this. On the facts of the case before him, he was not satisfied that the plaintiff bank had actual or constructive knowledge of any fraud and he held that the defendant was liable to the plaintiff for the sum claimed.

Another issue which must be considered in this context is whether the fact that the parties are husband and wife is of relevance. It is now well established that no presumption of undue influence arises simply because of such a relationship.[201] It was suggested by Murphy J in his judgment in the Supreme Court in *Bank of Nova Scotia v Hogan*[202] that it may be possible to identify circumstances which would more readily raise a presumption of undue influence in favour of a wife than any other third party. Murphy J expressed the view that, notwithstanding the fact that the relationship between husband and wife has been held not to raise a presumption of undue influence,[203] some special status does appear to have been accorded to wives in a number of decisions. However, the better view, and one reiterated by Hogan J in *Ulster Bank (Ireland) Ltd v De Kretser*,[204] is that 'the fact that the parties are husband and wife does not *in itself* create any presumption of undue influence.'

The broader question of the circumstances in which a financial institution may be put on inquiry by the nature of the relationship between a surety and the person whose debts he has guaranteed has been the subject of changing attitudes in this jurisdiction. The narrow approach, which has now been effectively superseded, is as set out by O'Donovan J in *Ulster Bank Ltd v Fitzgerald*.[205] The plaintiff bank instituted proceedings claiming monies it alleged were owed to it by a company operated by the first defendant on foot of guarantees executed by him and his wife, the second defendant. The second defendant claimed that the guarantees were not enforceable against her on the grounds that she had no financial interest in them and that she had been persuaded to execute the guarantees as a result of undue influence exercised over her by her husband, a fact which she claimed the bank was or should have been aware of. While O'Donovan J said that he was prepared to accept that the first defendant may have exercised inordinate pressure on his wife to execute the guarantees, he

---

200. [2009] IEHC 319.
201. *Irish Bank Resolution Corporation v Quinn* [2011] IEHC 470 at [42] *per* Kelly J. Referred to by Birmingham J in *Ulster Bank (Ireland) Ltd v de Kretser* [2016] IECA 371 at [27].
202. [1996] 3 IR 239.
203. Although note that later in his judgment, Murphy J commented (at 249) that 'assuming, without deciding, that married women in this jurisdiction may in certain circumstances enjoy as against their husbands a presumption that undue influence was exercised…'
204. [2016] IECA 371 at [15].
205. [2001] IEHC 159.

concluded that he was not persuaded that the plaintiff bank had constructive notice of the fact that the wife might have executed the guarantees as a result of her husband's undue influence, if indeed this had been the case. He said that a presumption of undue influence did not arise merely because the parties were husband and wife and that he had heard no evidence to suggest that the bank had any inkling that there might be difficulties between the spouses or that there was any other reason why the wife might not have been acting of her own free will when she executed the guarantees. O'Donovan J added that he did not accept that the wife did not have a financial stake in the business, as she and her family relied on the income generated by it. So, in the absence of any actual or constructive knowledge on the part of the bank that the wife was not a free agent when she executed the guarantees, he was satisfied that the bank was not under any obligation to take any special steps to ensure that she had obtained independent legal advice.[206] In the circumstances, O'Donovan J therefore concluded that the guarantees were enforceable against the second defendant.

A key authority in this area, which sets out a broader approach to the circumstances in which a financial institution should be put on inquiry, is the decision of Clarke J in the High Court in *Ulster Bank Ltd v Roche*.[207] The plaintiff sought to enforce a guarantee over the liabilities of the first defendant's business which had been signed by the second defendant in circumstances where she was in a personal relationship with the first defendant and where, although she was a director of the business, she had an extremely limited role in it. Clarke J accepted that the second defendant had been under the undue influence of the first defendant at the time she signed the guarantee and proceeded to consider whether this could provide her with a defence to the plaintiff's claim to enforce its guarantee. He made reference to the fact that the decision in *Ulster Bank Ltd v Fitzgerald* had been made very shortly after the decision of the House of Lords in *Etridge* and that for understandable reasons the latter had not been referred to in the judgment of O'Donovan J. In these circumstances, Clarke J said that it seemed to him to be an appropriate case in which to consider whether the principles set out in *Etridge* were persuasive. Having reviewed these principles, Clarke J concluded that the criticism of the decision in *Fitzgerald* was well founded. He continued as follows:

> A regime which places no obligation on a bank to take any steps to ascertain whether, in the presence of circumstances suggesting a non-commercial aspect to a guarantee, the party offering the guarantee may

---

206. O'Donovan J stated (at [10]) that: 'the courts are not required to intervene to protect a contracting party from ill-advised action'.

207. [2012] 1 IR 765. The principles set out by Clarke J were referred to by Stewart J in *Barry v Ennis Property Finance DAC* [2018] IEHC 766 at [27] as 'the primary mechanism through which a claim of undue influence by a third party is assessed at plenary hearing.'

> not be fully and freely entering into same, gives insufficient protection to potentially vulnerable sureties.[208]

He said that while not necessarily accepting that the precise parameters identified in *Etridge* giving rise to an obligation on the bank to inquire represented the law in this jurisdiction, he was satisfied that the general principle which lay behind *Etridge* was to the effect that 'a bank is placed on inquiry where it is aware of facts which suggest, or ought to suggest, that there may be a non-commercial element to a guarantee.'[209] That general principle went far enough to cover the facts of the case before him, where the bank was aware that the parties were in a relationship and it was clear that the second defendant was not a shareholder in the company even though she was a director of it. While Clarke J suggested that the fact that the first defendant had conducted all the discussions with the bank was not of itself sufficient to put the bank on inquiry, he stated that 'where a person who is required to offer security is not a shareholder and where there is no evidence to suggest that the bank was aware of any active involvement of that party in the business, then it seems to me that the personal relationship between the parties emerges as a much more significant factor.'[210] Clarke J concluded that he was satisfied that the plaintiff bank was on inquiry on the facts of the case.

While the judgment of Clarke J in *Ulster Bank Ltd v Roche*[211] went some way towards strengthening the position of individuals who have entered into guarantees as a result of undue influence,[212] he made it clear on several occasions during the course of his judgment that nothing in it should be taken as implying that the law in this jurisdiction has gone as far as the position set out by the House of Lords in *Etridge*.[213] Clarke J accepted the criticism that the approach taken in *Ulster Bank Ltd v Fitzgerald* offered insufficient protection to vulnerable sureties, although he also commented that the principles set out by Lord Nicholls in *Etridge* in this context raised difficult questions and he concluded that it was not necessary for him to fully explore the precise parameters of the circumstances in which a bank should be put on inquiry.

A similar conclusion to that in *Ulster Bank Ltd v Roche* was reached by Peart J in the decision of the Court of Appeal in *ACC Bank v Walsh*,[214] albeit in the context of resisting a motion for summary judgment, where a wife had no

208. *Ibid.* at 780.
209. *Ibid.*
210. *Ibid.*
211. [2012] 1 IR 765.
212. Laffoy J expressed the view in *GE Capital Woodchester Home Loans Ltd v Reade* [2012] IEHC 363 at [35] that the decision in *Roche* did 'represent a development of the law in this jurisdiction'.
213. [2012] 1 IR 765, 779, 781. See also *Ulster Bank (Ireland) Ltd v de Kretser* [2016] IECA 371 at [23]; *Bank of Ireland v Curran* [2016] IECA 399 at [27]; *ACC Bank plc v Walsh* [2017] IECA 166 at [38].
214. [2017] IECA 166. In this case the wife was a joint borrower rather than a guarantor.

direct involvement in her husband's business and was only a nominal director of a company which he owned. Having accepted that a *prima facie* case of undue influence arose, he was satisfied that it was arguable that the bank had constructive notice of this undue influence and was required to ensure that the appellant had entered into the loan transaction freely, fully understanding the obligations she was undertaking. He added that one of the ways in which the bank could have discharged that onus would have been by ensuring that the wife had received independent legal advice, although there was no evidence that it had done so.

It is important to stress that Clarke J made clear in *Ulster Bank Ltd v Roche*[215] that the principles which underlie *Etridge* will only apply where the financial institution is aware of facts which suggest, or ought to suggest, that there may be a *non-commercial* element to a guarantee.[216] The significance of this non-commercial element is clear from the decision of Ryan J in *Bank of Scotland plc v Hickey*,[217] where the defendant sought to rely on the decision in *Roche* in relation to a guarantee which she and her partner had provided, but in a situation where there was a commercial purpose to the transaction. Ryan J found that there was nothing in the circumstances of the case that would attract the obligations recognised in *Etridge*. As he stated, '[t]he loan was for a commercial purpose. This was a case of joint borrowing by a person describing herself as a company director and confirming that she was acting in the course of her business or trade.'[218] In these circumstances, he held that the decision of Kelly J in *Irish Bank Resolution Corporation Ltd v Quinn*[219] applied, namely that a person who signs a potentially legally effective document without properly considering it or understanding it will be *prima facie* bound to accept any consequences which may later arise.

The significance of a non-commercial element to a guarantee is also clear from the judgment of Murphy J in *ACC Loan Management Ltd v Sheehan*,[220] in which the defendant had entered into a guarantee to facilitate a loan granted to a company owned and run by his brother, but of which he was also a director and 5% shareholder. The defendant claimed that he was under severe pressure to execute the guarantee and that he took no active role in the business and he relied on the *dicta* of Clarke J in *Ulster Bank Ltd v Roche* to support the argument that the plaintiff should have been put on inquiry in these circumstances. However, Murphy J concluded that there was no evidence of undue influence and said that

215. [2012] 1 IR 765, 781.
216. See also *Barry v Ennis Property Finance DAC* [2018] IEHC 766 at [26], where Stewart J referred to the decision of Clarke J in *Roche* and said that 'it seems clear that the bank would be put on inquiry when it becomes aware of facts which ought to suggest that there is a significant non-commercial element to the guarantee.' She added that 'such facts would include the guarantor having no active involvement in the business.'
217. [2014] IEHC 202.
218. *Ibid.* at [35]. See also *ACC Bank plc v McEllin* [2013] IEHC 454 at [30].
219. [2011] IEHC 470.
220. [2015] IEHC 818.

it was not necessary to express any view on whether the plaintiff should have had constructive notice of any wrongdoing, although she went on to comment that it would constitute 'a major evolution' of the principles laid down in *Etridge* and *Ulster Bank v Roche* to extend them to brothers who were both directors and participants in a commercial enterprise. Nevertheless, on the facts of the case before her, where the plaintiff lender had accepted the assurance of the solicitors' for the borrowers that the sureties had waived their entitlement to independent legal advice rather than requiring confirmation of this, she decided that there was a sufficient reason to provide the defendant with the arguable defence necessary to justify refusal of the motion for summary judgment.

Is Evidence of Undue Influence or Other Wrongdoing Necessary?

The question of whether a financial institution may be unable to enforce a guarantee where it has not taken steps to protect the position of a surety simply because of the nature of the relationship between the surety and debtor has led to some uncertainty in recent years. Although it is clear that the settled view of the Court of Appeal is now to answer this question in the negative, it is a significant issue which has arisen in a number of cases. In *Ulster Bank (Ireland) Ltd v de Kretser*[221] Birmingham J took the view that the debate about the circumstances in which a financial institution will be put on inquiry did not arise in the matter before the court as there was no evidence of undue influence or other wrongdoing on the husband's part. Although the wife had signed a guarantee in respect of a business of which her husband was the 99% shareholder and in which she only held a 1% share, Birmingham J took the view that she was an experienced businesswoman and he was not satisfied that the wife had established that her husband had exercised undue influence over her. Hogan J, who delivered a dissenting judgment, said that while he was satisfied that there was no actual evidence of undue influence, the fact remained that the bank had taken no affirmative steps to protect the wife prior to the execution of the guarantee. He stated that '[t]hose are the critical considerations so far as the decision *in Etridge (No.2)* is concerned, since that case is, in some respects, rather less about undue influence as such and rather more about ensuring that banks insist on independent advice where one spouse is guaranteeing the commercial debts of the other spouse, almost regardless of the personal circumstances of the spouse called upon to act as surety.'[222] Hogan J went on to refer to the *dicta* of Lord Nicholls in *Etridge* to the effect that 'quite simply … a bank is put on inquiry whenever a wife offers to stand surety for her husband's debts'. He concluded that the wife had raised an arguable case that the bank had been under an affirmative duty to insist that she obtain independent legal advice before she executed a guarantee of her

221. [2016] IECA 371.
222. *Ibid.* at [28].

husband's business debts. However, it should be noted that Hogan J stressed that nothing in his judgment should be interpreted as expressing any further views on the merits of the defence other than that the surety had in that respect met the threshold for resisting summary judgment.

The approach taken by Birmingham J in *de Kretser* of requiring evidence of undue influence or other wrongdoing was also adopted by Irvine J in a unanimous judgment of the Court of Appeal in *Bank of Ireland v Curran.*[223] This case concerned an application for summary judgment in circumstances where a guarantee had been provided by a mother in relation to the liabilities of a company managed by her son of which she was also a director. Irvine J concluded that the trial judge could not be faulted for concluding that the second defendant had failed to demonstrate a *bona fide* or credible defence based on acts of undue influence. She expressed the view that what was 'glaringly absent from her affidavits is evidence to demonstrate that any undue influence was brought to bear upon her by her son … or indeed by the bank itself.'[224] Irvine J concluded that there was no evidence that the bank should have been on inquiry to satisfy itself that the mother understood the nature of the guarantee proposed and that she was executing it otherwise than under her son's influence.

A similar, although slightly different factual scenario arose in *ACC Loan Management Ltd v Connolly*,[225] which also concerned an application for summary judgment but in a situation in which a guarantee had been provided by a father to enable his son to fund the purchase of a development property. At first instance Fullam J referred to the *obiter* comments of Birmingham J in *ACC Bank plc v McEllin*[226] in relation to the situation which might arise where elderly parents become guarantors for a child's commercial debts arising from a business enterprise with which they were not involved, and said that this would probably warrant the lender drawing the guarantor's attention to the desirability and importance of obtaining independent legal advice. Although no specific allegation of undue influence had been made, Fullam J found that the relationship between the defendants in the case before him placed the bank on inquiry and under an obligation to take some reasonable steps to ensure that the guarantees had been freely entered into by the second defendant. He concluded that there was no evidence that the plaintiff had taken any steps to satisfy itself that the second defendant had freely undertaken the obligations of a guarantor in relation to the second of two guarantees and Fullam J concluded that the issue of the second defendant's liability under the second guarantee should be remitted to plenary hearing. However, on appeal, Finlay Geoghegan

223. [2016] IECA 399.
224. *Ibid.* at [35]. Irvine J referred to the *dicta* of Ryan J in *Bank of Scotland plc v Hickey* [2014] IEHC 202 at [34] to the effect that a bald assertion of undue influence without supporting evidence was 'hopelessly inadequate' to provide a defence, even in the context of an application for summary judgment.
225. [2015] IEHC 188, [2017] 3 IR 629.
226. [2013] IEHC 454 at [30].

J concluded that the trial judge had been in error in considering that in the absence of any evidence of an arguable basis for a claim of undue influence, it was arguable that the bank had failed in any duty to ensure the appellant received independent legal advice or took other reasonable steps to ensure that the guarantees had been freely entered into by the appellant. In her view the decisions of the House of Lords in *Etridge* and of Clarke J in *Ulster Bank Ltd v Roche* were 'only concerned with the entitlement of a bank to enforce a guarantee where the guarantor has established, or in the case of an application for summary judgment has raised arguable grounds for contending, that the guarantee was entered into by reason of the undue influence or other wrongful act … of the principal debtor.'[227] She continued as follows:

> The judgment of Clarke J in *Ulster Bank v Roche* cannot in my view be considered as authority for a defence, independent of any allegation of undue influence or other wrong by the principal debtor, on the basis of a breach by a bank of a free standing obligation to take any measures to seek to ensure that a proposed surety is openly and freely agreeing to provide the requested guarantee or security.[228]

Significantly, Finlay Geoghegan J made it clear that the entire analysis in *Roche* was in the context of a prior finding of undue influence and she added that similarly, in her view, in *Etridge* the speeches of the House of Lords had been given in circumstances where all the appeals concerned claims where the wife had raised a defence of undue influence by the husband.

However, Hogan J took a different view on this issue. While he accepted that the decisions such as *Etridge* were based on a claim of undue influence on the part of a surety vis-à-vis her husband, he considered that it was necessary to appreciate the context in which claims such as that before the court were made. In his view there was every reason to suppose that the father reposed trust in his son in the management of the latter's business affairs and there was nothing to suggest that the father stood to gain personally by the giving of a guarantee for such large sums. Hogan J went on to say '[h]ere is a case plain and simple where the father offered to stand surety for the indebtedness of his son for large sums of money and, on at least one view of *Etridge*, I find it difficult to see why the bank was not put on inquiry to ensure that the father had understood and freely entered into the transaction and to take appropriate steps accordingly.'[229] He added that even independently of authorities such as *Etridge* and *Roche*, he considered that there was at least an arguable duty cast on a bank by equitable principles to take steps to ensure that a potentially

227. [2017] 3 IR 629, 639. This principle was applied in *Allied Irish Banks plc v Hiney* [2018] IEHC 325 at [6].
228. *Ibid.* at 642.
229. *Ibid.* at 651-652.

vulnerable surety is appropriately advised in a case of this kind.[230] However, Hogan J referred to the view taken by the majority of the Court of Appeal in *Ulster Bank (Ireland) Ltd v de Kretser* [231] and of a unanimous court in *Bank of Ireland v Curran*.[232] He stated that 'it is plain that the settled view of this Court is to the effect that, at least absent an express claim of undue influence or a claim of misrepresentation, a bank is under no such affirmative duty to ensure that a surety receives independent legal advice.'[233] In these circumstances, he said that while he adhered to the views which he had expressed in his dissent in *de Kretser* and in his judgment in the matter before the court, in his view in a collegiate court such as the Court of Appeal 'an individual member should ultimately submit to the settled views of the majority of that Court as reflected by *stare decisis*.'[234] For that reason, Hogan J stated that he agreed with the conclusions reached by Finlay Geoghegan J.

Reasonable Steps

Consideration has also been given in this jurisdiction to the 'reasonable steps' which a bank must take to avoid being fixed with constructive notice of any wrongdoing. In *Bank of Ireland v Smyth*,[235] a case which concerned a consent form signed for the purposes of the Family Home Protection Act 1976, Blayney J rejected the argument that the bank had a duty to explain a charge taken out on property fully to the wife or to suggest that she should obtain independent legal advice. However, he stated that in order to protect its own interests, the bank should have taken these steps, since if they had it was unlikely that the wife's consent could have been challenged.[236] In *Ulster Bank Ltd v Fitzgerald*[237] the evidence of the bank manager was that the second defendant's husband had not been present when he had explained the meaning of the guarantees to her and that he had told her 'that she could obtain legal advice' with regard to them, although she had signed them straight away. However, in view of the fact that

230. Hogan J took the view that if the matter had been *res integra*, he would have gone further than the trial judge and permitted the father to defend the claims in respect of both guarantees.
231. [2016] IECA 371.
232. [2016] IECA 399.
233. [2017] 3 IR 629, 657.
234. *Ibid.* at 658.
235. [1993] ILRM 790 (HC); [1995] 2 IR 459 (SC). See generally Sanfey (1994) 1 Comm LP 99; Doyle (1994) 88 GILSI 187; Sanfey (1996) 3 Comm LP 31; Mee (1996) 14 ILT (ns) 188; 209.
236. Sanfey (1996) 3 Comm LP 31, 34 commented that the reasoning in the decision could not be extended to the general situation where a spouse has acted as a guarantor of liabilities or created a charge over assets in respect of the other spouse's liabilities. Mee similarly commented (1996) 14 ILT (ns) 209, 210 that the Supreme Court decision threw little light on the impact of third party undue influence or misrepresentation on the validity of bank guarantees.
237. [2001] IEHC 159.

O'Donovan J concluded that the bank was not put on inquiry, the issue of the steps it might have taken to avoid being fixed with constructive knowledge of any undue influence did not arise.

In *Ulster Bank Ltd v Roche*[238] Clarke J commented that while nothing which he said should be taken as necessarily implying that the full rigours of the regime which applied in England represented the law in Ireland, he was 'satisfied that a bank which is placed on inquiry is obliged to take at least some measures to seek to ensure that the proposed surety is openly and freely agreeing to provide the requested security.'[239] As the plaintiff in the case before him had taken no such steps it was, in his view, unnecessary to consider the precise measures which a bank had to take.

This issue was also considered by Fullam J at first instance in *ACC Loan Management Ltd v Connolly*,[240] although as noted above, the Court of Appeal reached a different conclusion on the issue of the necessity of establishing evidence of undue influence. Fullam J referred to the fact that the plaintiff had obtained a declaration from the second defendant that he had been afforded independent legal advice in respect of the first guarantee he had entered into and he found that this was a sufficient 'reasonable step' on the part of the plaintiff. This issue was also referred to briefly by Stewart J in *Barry v Ennis Property Finance DAC*,[241] although she said that she did not intend to set out a list of steps which a bank should take in such circumstances in the matter before her, which concerned an application for summary judgment. She did add, however, that 'it is generally considered sufficient if the bank insisted the influenced party take independent legal advice before executing the agreement.'[242]

So, in terms of the obligations on a financial institution in this jurisdiction where it is put on inquiry, it now seems that it is obliged to take steps to ensure that the proposed surety is 'openly and freely agreeing'[243] to provide the guarantee. While a declaration by a guarantor that he has been given independent legal advice would appear to meet this requirement, it remains to be seen whether something short of this, such as a recommendation by the lender that such advice be obtained or a signed waiver, will suffice in this jurisdiction.

In *Bank of Ireland v Curran*[244] the surety had signed beneath a statement to the effect that she understood the nature of the liability she was undertaking and that she did not wish to obtain legal advice. However, whether this might have amounted to a 'reasonable step' was not tested in the circumstances of the case

238. [2012] 1 IR 765.
239. *Ibid.* at 781. See also *ACC Bank plc v Walsh* [2017] IECA 166 at [40].
240. [2015] IEHC 188, [2017] 3 IR 629.
241. [2018] IEHC 766.
242. *Ibid.* at [26]. Stewart J also noted (at [30]) that the loan account file can provide a contemporaneous record of steps taken by the bank which may be valuable in this context.
243. *Ulster Bank Ltd v Roche* [2012] 1 IR 765, 781 *per* Clarke J. Quoted by Fullam J in *ACC Bank plc v Connolly* [2015] IEHC 188 at [19].
244. [2016] IECA 399.

given the finding of Irvine J that there was no evidence that the bank should have been on inquiry. It should also be noted that in *ACC Loan Management Ltd v Sheehan*,[245] where the bank having stipulated that it required confirmation that the sureties had received independent legal advice then accepted an assurance from the borrower's solicitors that the defendant had waived this entitlement, Murphy J stated that 'one might have expected that, at a minimum, they would have required signed waivers from the proposed sureties'. In the circumstances she accepted that the lack of such waivers amounted to an arguable defence. However, the issue of whether insisting on a signed waiver might have amounted to a reasonable step did not need to be determined.

Adequacy of Legal Advice

The issue of the adequacy or otherwise of legal advice given to the party alleging undue influence has received consideration in this jurisdiction on a number of occasions. It has been made clear that a solicitor who acts for both parties to a transaction cannot be regarded as independent[246] and the importance of obtaining advice from 'an independent solicitor' was reiterated by Irvine J in *Darby v Shanley*.[247]

The meaning of the phrase 'independent legal advice' in this context was considered by McGovern J in *Danske Bank A/S trading as National Irish Bank plc v Madden*[248] who stated that, '[t]he usual meaning of such advice is that it is advice obtained by the party himself from a lawyer retained by him and not advice coming from the legal advisor of a third party with whom he is entering into a legal relationship.' Hogan J also suggested in *ACC Loan Management Ltd v Connolly*[249] that since the solicitors for the surety were also acting for the borrower, they could not be regarded as having provided an opportunity for '*independent* legal advice' to the former. This issue also arose peripherally in *ACC Loan Management v Sheehan*,[250] in which the same solicitor acted for both the defendant and his brother, whose company's debts were being guaranteed. Murphy J commented that '[i]t may transpire, on a full hearing, that the advice was perfectly adequate'.[251] However, in the circumstances, where the defendant had not signed a waiver and there was merely an assurance from the solicitors that the latter had waived his right to independent legal advice, she found that, given that the bank had effectively failed to enforce its own requirement in this

245. [2015] IEHC 818 at [37].
246. *Gregg v Kidd* [1956] IR 183, 201-202; *Carroll v Carroll* [1999] 4 IR 241, 265; *Prendergast v Joyce* [2009] 3 IR 519, 540.
247. [2009] IEHC 459 at [7.10].
248. [2009] IEHC 319 at [14]. See also *ACC Loan Management Ltd v Connolly* [2017] 3 IR 629, 655-656 *per* Hogan J.
249. [2017] 3 IR 629, 655.
250. [2015] IEHC 818.
251. *Ibid.* at [37].

regard, this was sufficient to establish an arguable defence. On balance it is, therefore, clear that in such cases at the time the advice is given, it is preferable that the solicitor should not also be acting for any other party to the transaction, and this includes the person for whom he agrees to stand surety.[252]

Some consideration was also given by Laffoy J to the issue of whether a financial institution is entitled to rely on the fact that advice has been properly given in *Tynan v County Registrar for Kilkenny*,[253] albeit in the context of a claim for an injunction to restrain the first defendant from evicting the plaintiff from a premises which were the subject matter of a possession order made in proceedings between the plaintiff and the second defendant as mortgagee. In considering the question of whether the mortgagee was entitled to rely on a letter from the plaintiff's solicitor as establishing that she had obtained appropriate independent legal advice, Laffoy J quoted from the judgment of Lord Nicholls in *Etridge*, to the effect that a bank is entitled to proceed on the assumption that a solicitor has done his job properly, and also from the judgments of Lord Hobhouse[254] and Lord Scott[255] in that case. She concluded that there was no doubt that the advice which the plaintiff received was independent, in the sense that it was obtained from a solicitor who was not acting for either the mortgagor or the mortgagee. In addition, Laffoy J said that she agreed with the suggestion put forward by counsel for the mortgagee that it would lead to 'utter chaos' if a mortgagee could not rely on a letter from an independent solicitor.

Conclusions

So, there has been an evolution from the position taken by Hogan J in *Ulster Bank (Ireland) Ltd v de Kretser*[256] and by Fullam J at first instance in *ACC Loan Management v Connolly*[257] to the approach adopted by the Court of Appeal in the latter case. Finlay Geoghegan J made it clear in her judgment on appeal in *Connolly* that the principles examined in *Etridge* and *Ulster Bank Ltd v Roche* were only concerned with the entitlement of a bank to enforce guarantees where the guarantor has established that 'the guarantee was entered into *by reason of the undue influence or other wrongful act* … of the principal debtor.'[258]

---

252. However, it should be noted that in *Bank of Nova Scotia v Hogan* [1996] 3 IR 239 a solicitor from a firm which had acted for the second named defendant and her husband in the past, and also for the bank from time to time, advised her in relation to the impugned transaction. Although Murphy J. held on the facts that she had no equity against her husband to have the transaction set aside and the issue did not arise, he stated that he was satisfied that the availability of 'appropriate legal advice' to the wife would have afforded the bank a defence in relation to any claim made by her.
253. [2011] IEHC 250.
254. See *Royal Bank of Scotland plc v Etridge (No. 2)* [2002] 2 AC 773, 828-829.
255. *Ibid.* at 845.
256. [2016] IECA 399.
257. [2015] IEHC 188.
258. [2017] 3 IR 629, 639. (Emphasis added).

So, it now seems clear that in this jurisdiction, financial institutions may be put on inquiry where there is a non-commercial element to a guarantee entered into by a surety, which will usually arise in the context of a family relationship or domestic partnership. However, despite the views put forward by Hogan J in his dissenting judgment in *Ulster Bank (Ireland) Ltd v de Kretser*[259] and in his judgment in *ACC Loan Management Ltd v Connolly*,[260] the nature of the relationship between the debtor and surety will not without evidence of undue influence or other wrongdoing be sufficient to provide grounds for an arguable defence. While some cases of this nature will involve a vulnerable surety which may lead to undue influence being fairly readily established, the approach of the majority of the Court of Appeal in *de Kretser* and of that court in *Bank of Ireland v Curran*[261] and *ACC Loan Management Ltd v Connolly*[262] make clear that a relationship giving rise to a presumption of undue influence or acts of undue influence or other wrongdoing must be established. The approach adopted by the Irish courts in this context[263] is arguably stricter from the surety's point of view than that of the House of Lords in *Etridge*, which is certainly open to the interpretation that a bank is put on inquiry whenever the relationship between the surety and debtor is non-commercial.

Overall, the balance adopted by the Irish courts as between the rights of financial institutions and vulnerable sureties seems fair. While some uncertainty remains as to whether the initial hurdle facing the latter in seeking to establish a claim is higher than that adopted by the House of Lords in *Etridge*, in other respects the law in this area now seems relatively clear in this jurisdiction. The principles set out in the case law in relation to the so-called 'reasonable steps' have not been examined in such detail as in England but would appear to be satisfied where the financial institution takes steps to ensure that the proposed surety is, in the words of Clarke J in *Ulster Bank Ltd v Roche*,[264] 'openly and freely agreeing' to provide the guarantee. Ensuring that the surety has obtained independent legal advice appears to be accepted as sufficing in this regard.

While the more recent decisions of the Court of Appeal have provided clarity about the significance of establishing evidence of undue influence or other wrongdoing on the part of the debtor, the judgment of Clarke J in *Roche* remains a key authority in this area. It provides useful guidance about the circumstances in which financial institutions may be placed on inquiry and illustrates the

---

259. [2016] IECA 371.
260. [2017] 3 IR 629.
261. [2016] IECA 399.
262. [2017] 3 IR 629.
263. There have been a number of references to the fact that Clarke J in *Ulster Bank Ltd v Roche* [2012] 1 IR 765, 779 said that nothing in his judgment should be taken as necessarily implying that the law in Ireland went as far as the position adopted in *Etridge* in relation to when a financial institution would be placed on inquiry. See *Ulster Bank (Ireland) Ltd v de Kretser* [2016] IECA 371 at [23]; *Bank of Ireland v Curran* [2016] IECA 399 at [27].
264. [2012] 1 IR 765, 781.

consequences for these institutions if they fail to take steps to protect vulnerable sureties where there is a non-commercial aspect to a guarantee. However, as the now settled position of the Court of Appeal makes clear, it is important to appreciate that the comments of Clarke J about the principles which underpinned *Etridge* were made in the context of a situation where the evidence established that the surety had been acting under the influence of the debtor. Where this is not the case it will not be possible for a surety to even cross the threshold of establishing an arguable defence in circumstances where a financial institution seeks to enforce a guarantee by seeking summary judgment.

Finally, at a practical level, from the perspective of financial institutions it will not always be clear at the time the transaction is entered into whether the surety might be characterised as vulnerable and whether evidence of undue influence may subsequently come to light. There is still lingering uncertainty about the extent to which the courts in this jurisdiction will embrace the *Etridge* principles about the circumstances which will lead to a lender being put on inquiry. Therefore, where there is any basis for concern about whether a surety is acting of his own free will, it may be prudent for a financial institution to consider taking the kind of reasonable steps which would avoid it being fixed with constructive notice of undue influence or other wrongdoing which might otherwise provide grounds for a defence in a case where it seeks to enforce a guarantee.

The Approach in New Zealand

The principles set out in *Etridge* have also been considered in other jurisdictions. In the decision of the Court of Appeal of New Zealand in *Hogan v Commercial Factors Ltd*[265] William Young J, delivering the judgment of the court, expressed the view that it was 'likely' that these principles would be adopted in New Zealand at least in banking cases, although it was not necessary for him to take a position on this as the matter before the court was found not to fall into the 'non-commercial' category.

More recently in *Gardiner v Westpac New Zealand Ltd*,[266] another decision of the New Zealand Court of Appeal, Lang J again stated that the court did not find it necessary to finally determine whether the principles set out in *Etridge* should be applied in New Zealand given its conclusion that even proceeding on the basis that there was no commercial element, the bank had taken sufficient steps to protect itself from the possibility that the appellants might have acted as a result of undue influence of their son. It was also not a case in which members of a family had agreed to guarantee the indebtedness of other family members when they were not deriving any benefit themselves from the transaction.

---

265. [2006] 3 NZLR 618, 627.
266. [2015] 3 NZLR 1.

UNCONSCIONABLE TRANSACTIONS

Introduction

A transaction may be set aside in equity where one party is at a serious disadvantage by reason of poverty, ignorance or some other factor such as old age, so that unfair advantage may be taken of that party.[267] Equity will intervene particularly where a transfer of property is made for no consideration at all[268] or at an undervalue and where the transferee acts without the benefit of independent legal advice.

The basis of this principle, which was set out by Lord Hatherley in *O'Rorke v Bolingbroke*,[269] was summarised as follows by Gavan Duffy J in *Grealish v Murphy*:[270] 'Equity comes to the rescue whenever the parties to a contract have not met upon equal terms'. A more specific summary of the circumstances which will warrant equitable intervention on this basis was provided by Kitto J in the Australian decision of *Blomley v Ryan*,[271] namely: 'whenever one party to a transaction is at a special disadvantage in dealing with the other party because illness, ignorance, inexperience, impaired faculties, financial need or other circumstances affect his ability to conserve his own interests, and the other party unconscientiously takes advantage of the opportunity thus placed in his hands.' In *Blomley* a sale of a property at an undervalue was set aside in circumstances where the same solicitor had acted for both parties and where the vendor was elderly and poorly educated and the purchasers had taken advantage of his liking for rum.

267. See generally Clark (1980) 31 NILQ 114; Capper 'Unconscionable bargains' in *One Hundred and Fifty Years of Irish Law* (eds. Dawson, Greer and Ingram,1996) p. 45 *et seq*. As Nourse LJ commented in *Credit Lyonnais Bank Nederland NV v Burch* [1997] 1 All ER 144, 151, 'Equity's jurisdiction to relieve against such transactions, although more rarely exercised in modern times, is at least as venerable as its jurisdiction to relieve against those procured by undue influence'.
268. Some doubt was raised about this point by the decision in *Langton v Langton* [1995] 2 FLR 890, in which A.W.H. Charles QC expressed the view that the doctrine of unconscionable bargains does not apply to gifts. However, as Capper has pointed out [1996] Conv 308, 314, 'the weight of principle and authority is against him' and he has commented (1998) 114 LQR 479, 492 that 'the better view … is that gifts are equally subject to the doctrine of unconscionability and that this concept rather than one of unconscionable bargain should be used in future to avoid confusion'.
269. (1877) 2 App Cas 814, 823.
270. [1946] IR 35, 49. See also *Haverty v Brooks* [1970] IR 214, 219; *Carroll v Carroll* [1999] 4 IR 241, 258-259; *Prendergast v Joyce* [2009] 3 IR 519, 547; *Keating v Keating* [2009] IEHC 405 at 25.
271. (1956) 99 CLR 362, 415. See also the *dicta* of Fullgar J at 405 and of Sullivan MR in *Slator v Nolan* (1876) IR 11 Eq 367, 386, where he spoke of undue advantage being taken 'by reason of distress or recklessness or wildness or want of care' and said that transactions resting on such unconscionable dealing would not be allowed to stand.

Elements of a Successful Claim

A comprehensive statement of the essential preconditions for setting aside a transaction on grounds of unconscionability in English law is set out in the judgment of Peter Millett QC, as he then was, in *Alec Lobb (Garages) Ltd v Total Oil (Great Britain) Ltd*:[272]

> First, one party has been at a serious disadvantage to the other, whether through poverty, or ignorance, or lack of advice, or otherwise, so that circumstances existed of which unfair advantage could be taken. Second, this weakness of the one party has been exploited by the other in some morally culpable manner … And third, the resulting transaction has been not merely hard or improvident, but overreaching and oppressive … In short, there must, in my judgment, be some impropriety, both in the conduct of the stronger party and in the terms of the transaction itself … which in the traditional phrase 'shocks the conscience of the court' and makes it against equity and good conscience for the stronger party to retain the benefit of a transaction he has unfairly obtained.

In considering the first of these requirements it is clear that some unfair advantage must have been gained 'by an unconscientious use of power by a stronger party against a weaker'.[273] So, in *Hart v O'Connor*,[274] the Privy Council rejected an application to have a contract set aside as an 'unconscionable bargain' on the basis that the defendant had not been guilty of unconscionable conduct. As Lord Brightman commented, '[t]here was no equitable fraud, no victimisation, no taking advantage, no overreaching or other description of unconscionable doings which might have justified the intervention of equity to restrain an action by the defendant at law.'[275]

On the second point set out above, as Hooley and O'Sullivan have confirmed, 'the courts have repeatedly stressed that it is not sufficient to show that a bargain was a harsh or unreasonable one – it must also be shown that the stronger party acted reprehensibly, exploiting the weaker position of the other party'.[276] So, as Lord Templeman made clear in *Boustany v Pigott*,[277] unconscionability in this context 'relates not merely to the terms of the bargain but to the behaviour of the stronger party which must be characterised by some

272. [1983] 1 WLR 87, 94-95. (Reversed in part [1985] 1 WLR 173). See also *Portman Building Society v Dusangh* [2000] 2 All ER (Comm) 221, 230-231.
273. *Morrison v Coast Finance Ltd* (1965) 55 DLR (2d) 710, 713 *per* Davey JA.
274. [1985] AC 1000.
275. *Ibid.* at 1028.
276. [1997] LMCLQ 17, 23.
277. (1995) 69 P & CR 298, 303. See also *Portman Building Society v Dusangh* [2000] 2 All ER (Comm) 221, 231; *Singla v Bashir* [2002] EWHC 883 (Ch) at [28]; *Strydom v Vendside Ltd* [2009] EWHC 2130 (QB) at [36]; *Fineland Investments Ltd v Pritchard* [2011] EWHC 113 (Ch) at [76].

moral culpability or impropriety'. Or, as Rimer J suggested in *Humphreys v Humphreys*,[278] this means that the party benefitting from the transaction 'must have imposed the objectionable terms in a morally reprehensible manner'.

The third requirement, that the transaction be overreaching and oppressive, necessitates a consideration of the transaction as a whole. So, in *Portman Building Society v Dusangh*,[279] where the defendant's understanding of English was poor and he was illiterate, Simon Brown LJ concluded that 'the transaction, although improvident, was not overreaching and oppressive' and that 'the conscience of the court [was] not shocked' by what had transpired.

Academic commentators have suggested that there remains a degree of uncertainty about the exact requirements which must be established to support a claim of unconscionability. As Bamforth has commented, 'the cases tend to leave the relative importance and requirements of each element unarticulated'[280] and in his view there is still an unacceptable degree of imprecision in the case law. Hooley and O'Sullivan have also raised this issue and suggest that the *dicta* of the members of the Court of Appeal in *Credit Lyonnais Bank Nederland NV v Burch*[281] provides an excellent illustration of Bamforth's point that the juridicial basis and elements of unconscionability as a vitiating factor should be more precisely defined and rooted in principle.[282]

Capper has commented that 'the English courts are much more insistent that the terms of the contract operate harshly against the weaker party, and also require that those terms be imposed in a morally reprehensible manner'.[283] He points out that the decisions of the High Court of Australia contain none of the rhetoric about the imposition of harsh terms in such a manner.[284] Similarly, the courts in New Zealand have also tended not to require elements of abuse of confidence or lack of good faith on the part of the individual seeking to uphold the transaction. As McMullin J stated in *Nicholls v Jessup*,[285] '[a]ccepting the benefit of an improvident bargain by an ignorant person acting without independent advice which cannot be shown to be fair, may be unconscionable'. Tipping J also made it clear in the decision of the Supreme Court of New Zealand in *Gustav & Co. Ltd v Macfield Ltd*[286] that equity will intervene where one party to a transaction unconscientiously takes advantage of the other in circumstances where the stronger party knows or ought to have known that

---

278. [2004] EWHC 2201 (Ch) at [106].
279. [2000] 2 All ER (Comm) 221.
280. Bamforth [1995] LMCLQ 538, 539.
281. [1997] 1 All ER 144.
282. Hooley and O'Sullivan [1997] LMCLQ 17, 22. In this case the transaction in question was set aside on the grounds of undue influence but both Nourse and Millett LJJ expressed views on the nature of unconscionable bargains.
283. Capper (2010) 126 LQR 403, 403-404.
284. See, e.g. *Bridgewater v Leahy* (1998) 194 CLR 457.
285. [1986] 1 NZLR 226, 234.
286. [2008] 2 NZLR 735, 741.

the weaker party is unable to look after his interests adequately and is acting to his detriment.

A more accurate summary of the elements which must be established before equity will intervene in this jurisdiction on the grounds of an unconscionable bargain are set out in the following terms in *Hanbury and Martin: Modern Equity*.[287] First, one party must be at a serious disadvantage to the other by reason of poverty, ignorance or otherwise, so that circumstances exist of which unfair advantage can be taken; secondly, the transaction must be at an undervalue; and thirdly there must be a lack of independent legal advice. A similar, albeit slightly different, list of factors was set out by Carroll J in *Secured Property Loans Ltd v Floyd*,[288] namely, was there inadequate consideration, was there some procedural impropriety on the part of the plaintiff and did the defendant have independent legal advice?

An example of the factors which may place a party at a serious disadvantage which were considered by Barr J as contributing towards what he regarded as an improvident transaction from the point of view of the vendor in *McGonigle v Black*[289] were 'a combination of bereavement, inability to cope, loneliness, alcoholism and ill-health', which made him vulnerable to manipulation.

As regards the requirement of undervalue or inadequate consideration, Gavan Duffy J stated in *Grealish v Murphy*[290] that a court will be 'very much slower to undo a transaction for value', although he stressed that the principles underlying intervention in either case remain the same. This issue was also considered by Baker J in *ACC Loan Management Ltd v Browne*,[291] who stated that '[w]hat is inadequate consideration in the context of perhaps two persons of unequal bargaining power depends on the relationship between those persons and the extent to which, if any, it might be considered reasonable or proper for one of them to support the other through a difficult time.'[292] She concluded that while consideration in the form of an advancement of money to a third party might be deemed inadequate in certain circumstances, when the parties were brothers, and one sought by his action to support the other, such consideration would not be inadequate.

In *Noonan v O'Connell*[293] a transfer of a half-share in a farm by an elderly man with limited mental capacity to his nephew for what appeared to be a nominal consideration was set aside, as was the disposition in *Slator v*

287. Glister and Lee, *Hanbury and Martin: Modern Equity* (21st ed., 2018) p. 868. These requirements, set out in an earlier edition, were quoted by Shanley J in his decision in the High Court in *Carroll v Carroll* [1998] 2 ILRM 218, 230. See also *Bank of Ireland v Curran* [2016] IECA 399 at [39].
288. [2011] 2 IR 652, 666-667.
289. High Court Circuit Appeal (Barr J) 14 November 1988.
290. [1946] IR 35, 49-50.
291. [2015] IEHC 722.
292. *Ibid.* at [114].
293. High Court 1986 No. 2135P (Lynch J) 10 April 1987.

Nolan[294] by a man to his brother-in-law for what was also a grossly inadequate consideration. These decisions can be contrasted with that of Pringle J in *Nyland v Brennan*,[295] in which a sale by an elderly lady at a reasonable price was upheld, albeit in circumstances where she had received comprehensive and independent legal advice, and with the decision of McLoughlin J in *Haverty v Brooks*,[296] where he found that 'substantial monetary consideration' had changed hands.

The receipt of full and independent legal advice becomes increasingly important where the consideration paid is low or non-existent[297] or where one party is negotiating from a position of relative weakness, although it will always be a factor which the court will consider in assessing whether a transaction has been improvident. In *Grealish v Murphy*[298] the plaintiff, an elderly farmer, who according to the medical evidence was mentally deficient, executed a settlement transferring his farm to the defendant subject to a life interest in his favour and charging the land with a right of residence and support for the defendant during the plaintiff's lifetime. While Gavan Duffy J declined to set aside the settlement on the grounds of undue influence, he accepted that the transaction was an improvident one and that it should be set aside on this basis. Gavan Duffy J laid emphasis on the plaintiff's weakness of mind and the deficiencies in the legal advice which he had received, pointing to the fact that his solicitor had been unaware of all the material facts and had failed to give the plaintiff a full explanation of the consequences of the settlement or to appreciate the latter's limited mental capacity. Lack of proper legal advice also appeared to be an important factor in the decision of Morris J in *McQuirk v Branigan*,[299] in which he set aside a deed executed by an elderly lady transferring land to her grandson so that he could build a house on the site. It became necessary to give the grandson an area larger than had been previously envisaged to make the site large enough to accommodate a house and this effectively divested the plaintiff completely of her back garden. Morris J pointed to the total lack of independent legal advice or indeed any advice given to the plaintiff and set aside the transaction as an improvident one from her point of view. Similarly, in *Carroll v Carroll*,[300] Denham J concluded that in view of the omissions in relation to the legal advice given, taken in conjunction with the donor's frail health and lack of other assets, there was clear evidence on which the trial judge

---

294. (1876) IR 11 Eq 367.
295. High Court 1970 No. 1548P (Pringle J) 19 December 1970.
296. [1970] IR 214, 219.
297. As in *Moyles v Mahon* [2000] IEHC 197, where it was acknowledged by Smyth J that a transaction was on its face improvident because the plaintiff had disposed of his interest in property without valuable consideration. However, he concluded that the plaintiff had exercised a 'spontaneous act of free will' and had had the benefit of independent legal advice and declined to set aside the transaction.
298. [1946] IR 35.
299. High Court Circuit Appeal (Morris J) 9 November 1992.
300. [1999] 4 IR 241.

could have concluded that this was a case in which the transaction should have been set aside on grounds of its improvidence.

It is clear from the judgment of Gilligan J in *Prendergast v Joyce*[301] that he did not believe that the requirements suggested by decisions such as *Alec Lobb (Garages) Ltd*, namely that in order to have a transaction set aside for improvidence it must be established that a defendant acted in a manner involving some element of moral turpitude, represented part of Irish law. On the facts of the case before him, where an elderly woman who was in a vulnerable and confused state had transferred monies into the joint names of herself and the defendant, Gilligan J was satisfied that the donor was at a serious disadvantage to the donee owing to her mental impairment, that the transaction had been at an undervalue and that the donor had not had independent legal advice. He therefore concluded that there were also grounds for setting aside the impugned transactions on the basis that they were improvident although he had already found that they should be set aside for undue influence.

Some doubt about the requirements which must be met in order to have a transaction set aside on the grounds of improvidence in this jurisdiction remain as a result of the decision of Laffoy J in *Keating v Keating*,[302] in which she referred to the fact that the criteria set out in *Alec Lobb (Garages) Ltd* provided helpful guidance in this respect.[303] Laffoy J concluded that on the facts before her, the plaintiff had been seriously disadvantaged because of his lack of understanding of the consequences of his decision to sell land to the first named defendant and that the second named defendant had exploited the situation. She was also satisfied that the plaintiff had not had the benefit of independent legal advice and she concluded that the transaction was improvident and also oppressive and unfair and should be set aside. However, other than the reference to the fact that the second named defendant had exploited the situation which had arisen, Laffoy J did not appear to attach significance to whether the defendants had acted in a morally reprehensible manner. It is therefore likely that the courts in this jurisdiction will continue to apply a less restrictive approach to the circumstances in which a claim based on an improvident transaction can be established than is the case in England.

Finally, one issue which has provoked considerable academic debate in recent years is whether the doctrines of undue influence and unconscionable transactions or unconscionability should continue to remain separate and distinct or whether they should be merged. This idea of a single thread based on inequality of bargaining power running through the case law was suggested by Lord Denning in *Lloyd's Bank v Bundy*[304] but was not developed. It should

301. [2009] 3 IR 519. Gilligan J referred to the fact that Shanley J in *Carroll v Carroll* [1998] 2 ILRM 218 had stated that there had been no suggestion from the plaintiffs that their brother had bullied or cajoled their father into making the impugned transaction.
302. [2009] IEHC 405.
303. See also *Mulcahy v Mulcahy* [2011] IEHC 186 at [11.2].
304. [1975] QB 326, 339.

be noted that the same facts will often cause a court to consider whether to grant relief under both or either heading,[305] and the two have even been combined on occasion.[306] Capper argues that the doctrines of undue influence and unconscionability are 'sufficiently similar in their objectives and effects that they can and may profitably be merged into one'[307] and that unconscionability as the broader of the two doctrines would allow undue influence to be subsumed into it. On the other hand, Birks and Chin have argued that the two doctrines are fundamentally distinct and that the existing analytical distinctions should be preserved.[308] In their view undue influence is concerned with the weakness of the plaintiff's consent owing to his excessive dependence on the defendant, while unconscionability is concerned with the defendant's exploitation of the plaintiff's vulnerability. More recently Capper has suggested that the common law should either differentiate between the principles of undue influence and unconscionable bargain or if this is not possible, consider merging them.[309] In his view a merged doctrine would not generate any more uncertainty than exists at present and he suggests that making a fresh start with conceptually clear principles could lead to a much more functional doctrine.[310] Despite this suggestion, to date the evidence points towards a judicial unwillingness to merge the doctrines, and Lord Walker commented in the decision of the Privy Council in *Laurence v Poorah*[311] that while they share a common root, namely equity's concern to protect the vulnerable from economic harm, they are generally recognised as distinct doctrines.

LOSS OF THE RIGHT TO RESCIND

Affirmation

If the party is aware of the facts giving rise to the right to rescind and nevertheless affirms the contract by taking some benefit under it he will be

305. *Grealish v Murphy* [1946] IR 35.
306. *McGonigle v Black* High Court Circuit Appeal (Barr J) 14 November 1988 in which a transaction was set aside as being a 'grossly improvident' one brought about by undue influence.
307. Capper (1998) 114 LQR 479, 480.
308. Birks and Chin, 'On the Nature of Undue Influence' in *Good Faith and Fault in Contract Law* (eds. Beatson and Friedmann, 1995) p. 57 *et seq.* See also Conaglen (1999) 18 NZULR 509.
309. (2010) 126 LQR 403, 417.
310. *Ibid.* at 419. See also Moore (2018) 134 LQR 257, who puts forward the view that a common principle of exploitation of constrained autonomy does exist and suggests that the law would benefit by consolidating the doctrines of duress, undue influence and unconscionability.
311. [2008] UKPC 21 at [20]. He referred to *National Westminster Bank plc v Morgan* [1985] AC 686, 707-708; *Credit Lyonnais Bank Nederland BV v Burch* [1997] 1 All ER 144.

taken to have waived his right to rescind.[312] Where a person seeks to rescind a contract he must do so within a reasonable time or he may be taken to have affirmed the contract and in this context the doctrine of laches may operate to defeat a claim. As we have seen, this involves a substantial lapse of time coupled with circumstances which make it inequitable to allow the plaintiff to succeed in his claim. The manner in which laches may defeat an action to have an agreement set aside in the context of an improvident transaction is illustrated by the decision of Keane J in *J.H. v W.J.H.*[313] As a result of delay by the plaintiff for four years and by reason of the time and money invested in the running of a farm by the defendant on the basis that the plaintiff had abandoned her claim, Keane J refused to grant the plaintiff relief although he held that the transaction in question was an improvident one which the courts would normally have set aside.

If Substantial Restitutio in Integrum is Impossible

As Lord Blackburn stated in *Erlanger v New Sombrero Phosphate Co.*,[314] 'as a condition to a rescission there must be a *restitutio in integrum*'. This principle was strictly enforced at common law but equity has taken a more flexible approach and as Lord Blackburn noted there is a considerable difference in the manner in which it has been applied at law and in equity. In the latter case it has not been applied as literally, the aim being to achieve practical justice even where precise restoration of the parties to their previous positions is no longer possible. The attitude of equity towards this concept was well summarised by Griffin J in *Northern Bank Finance Corporation Ltd v Charlton*[315] as follows: 'Therefore, the rule is that rescission cannot be enforced if events, which have occurred since the contract and in which the representee has participated, make it impossible to restore the parties substantially to their previous position.'

While any property or monies transferred under the contract must in theory be handed back, equity does not insist on precise restoration, and the wrongdoer may be asked to give up his profits in return for receiving compensation for work carried out in performance of his contractual obligations.[316] A further relevant factor may be whether the impossibility of restoring the parties to their previous positions is attributable to the nature of the subject matter of the agreement or whether it is due to the plaintiff's conduct.[317] Clearly where precise restoration of the parties is impossible the courts will take a more flexible approach if the plaintiff is not in any way responsible for this state of affairs.

312. See *Payman v Lanjani* [1985] Ch 457.
313. High Court 1977 No. 5831P (Keane J) 20 December 1979.
314. (1878) 3 App Cas 1218, 1278.
315. [1979] IR 149, 206. See also the *dicta* of O'Higgins CJ at 183.
316. See *O'Sullivan v Management Agency & Music Ltd* [1985] QB 428.
317. *Carbin v Somerville* [1933] IR 276, 289.

Third Party Rights

A contract will not be rescinded where this will prejudice the rights of innocent third parties who have acquired an interest for value in the subject matter of an agreement. So where a *bona fide* purchaser for value without notice has acquired good title to the property in the interim, an action for rescission will not succeed.[318] However, where the third party is a mere volunteer, the right to rescind will not be lost.

318. *Anderson v Ryan* [1967] IR 34.

CHAPTER 18

Equitable Estoppel

INTRODUCTION

Estoppel is not an exclusively equitable concept and it operates both at common law and in equity. Two main aspects of equitable estoppel are recognised, promissory and proprietary estoppel,[1] and both owe their origins to the concept of estoppel by representation.[2] The essential basis of the latter doctrine is the making of a representation by a person whether by words or conduct of an existing fact which causes another party to incur detriment in reliance on this representation. In these circumstances, the person making the representation will not be permitted to act subsequently in a manner inconsistent with that representation. This principle formed the basis of the decision of the House of Lords in *Jorden v Money*,[3] which limited the operation of estoppel to representations of existing fact rather than of a party's intentions. As Lord Cranworth stated:

> [I]f a person makes any false representation to another, and that other acts upon that false representation, the person who has made it shall not afterwards be allowed to set up that what he said was false.[4]

However, he continued by saying that he thought that the doctrine did not apply 'to a case where the representation is not a representation of fact, but a statement of something which the party intends or does not intend to do'. This approach was also followed in Ireland in *Munster & Leinster Bank Ltd v Croker*,[5] in which Black J agreed that this form of estoppel 'only applies to representation of existing facts'. While this reasoning did not appear to leave much scope for development, equity has eroded some of the limitations of this principle in a manner which shall be examined below.

At the outset it should also be noted that the courts in this jurisdiction have not been particularly careful about the use of different labels to describe various forms of estoppel. One of the most frequently quoted descriptions of

---

1. See generally Pawlowski, *Proprietary Estoppel* (1996); McFarlane, *The Law of Proprietary Estoppel* (2014).
2. See generally Spencer-Bower and Turner, *Estoppel by Representation* (3rd ed., 1977).
3. (1854) 5 HLC 185.
4. *Ibid.* at 210.
5. [1940] IR 185, 191.

the circumstances in which estoppel may arise is contained in the judgment of Griffin J in *Doran v Thompson*[6] in the following terms:

> Where one party has, by his words or conduct, made to the other a clear and unambiguous promise or assurance which was intended to affect the legal relations between them and to be acted on accordingly, and the other party has acted on it by altering his position to his detriment, it is well settled that the one who gave the promise or assurance cannot afterwards be allowed to revert to their previous legal relations as if no such promise or assurance had been made by him, and that he may be restrained in equity from acting inconsistently with such promise or assurance.

Although the principle was set out in that case in the context of an unsuccessful attempt to prevent reliance on the Statute of Limitations, it has been quoted or referred to in a variety of different circumstances.[7] Certainly compared with the principles established in case law in England, where the scope of the doctrine of proprietary estoppel in particular has been explored in detail, the jurisprudence in this area in this jurisdiction is not well developed.

PROMISSORY ESTOPPEL

The effect of the doctrine of promissory estoppel has been described as follows: 'if one party to a contract makes a promise to the other that his legal rights under the contract will not be enforced or will be suspended and the other party in some way relies on that promise, whether by altering his position or in any other way, then the party who might otherwise have enforced those rights will not be permitted to do so where it would be inequitable having regard to all of the circumstances.'[8] A useful summary of the key ingredients of a successful claim based on promissory estoppel is set out by McDermott in *Contract Law*[9] and referred to by Laffoy J in her judgment in *The Barge Inn Ltd v Quinn Hospitality Ireland Operations 3 Ltd*[10] in the following terms:

> (a) the pre-existing legal relationship between the parties; (b) an unambiguous representation; (c) reliance by the promisee

6. [1978] IR 223, 230.
7. See, e.g. *Ryan v Connolly* [2001] 1 IR 627, 632; *Courtney v McCarthy* [2007] IESC 58 at 19-20; *An Cumann Peile Boitheimeach Teoranta v Albion Properties Ltd* [2008] IEHC 447 at 64.
8. *MWB Business Exchange Centres Ltd v Rock Advertising Ltd* [2017] QB 604, 624 *per* Kitchin LJ.
9. *Contract Law* (2001) p. 137. Now see (2nd ed., 2017) p. 179.
10. [2013] IEHC 387 at [68]. See also *Danske Bank v Gillic* [2015] IEHC 375 at [24]; *Re Hoare, A Bankrupt* [2016] IEHC 345 at [11].

(and possible detriment); (d) some element of unfairness and unconscionability; (e) that the estoppel is being used not as a cause of action, but as a defence; and (f) that the remedy is a matter for the Court.

One of the guiding principles which arguably has circumscribed the development of the doctrine of promissory estoppel has been that it should not undermine the requirement of consideration. Its operation has been confined to situations where a pre-existing contractual relationship or at least a relationship which gives rise to legal rights and obligations exists.[11] For this reason promissory estoppel is often considered in a contractual context and a fuller treatment of it can be found in the leading texts in that area.[12] It is therefore proposed to briefly outline its early development and examine its main characteristics and later in the chapter to assess whether there is evidence of a move towards a unified doctrine of equitable estoppel.

While the effect of *Jorden v Money*[13] appeared to be to limit the doctrine of equitable estoppel to representations of existing fact, the decisions of *Hughes v Metropolitan Railway Co.*[14] and *Birmingham and District Land Co. v London and North Western Railway Co.*[15] showed that equity would give relief to a person in circumstances where the truth or accuracy of a representation of future intention might be denied in an unconscionable manner. These decisions were in turn employed by Denning J in his landmark judgment in *Central London Property Trust Ltd v High Trees House Ltd*,[16] which can be regarded as the decision in which the foundations of the doctrine known as 'promissory estoppel' were laid. In the view of Denning J, where a promise is made which is 'intended to create legal relations and which, to the knowledge of the person making the promise, was going to be acted on by the person to whom it was made, and which was in fact so acted on',[17] the court should ensure that such a promise is honoured. This reasoning was relied on in this jurisdiction by Kenny J in his decision in *Revenue Commissioners v Moroney*,[18] in which he held that a father, who had promised his sons that they would not have to pay the consideration referred to in a deed which they had signed, was estopped

---

11. E.g. *Durham Fancy Goods Ltd v Michael Jackson (Fancy Goods) Ltd* [1968] 2 QB 839, 847 *per* Donaldson J.
12. See, e.g. Clark, *Contract Law in Ireland* (7th ed., 2013); McDermott, *Contract Law* (2nd ed., 2017); Peel, *Treitel: The Law of Contract* (14th ed., 2015).
13. (1854) 3 HLC 185.
14. (1877) 2 App Cas 439.
15. (1888) 40 Ch D 268.
16. [1947] 1 KB 130.
17. *Ibid.* at 134. See also *Kenny v Kelly* [1988] IR 457, 463, where Barron J concluded that these elements, necessary to establish a claim based on promissory estoppel, were satisfied in the case before him.
18. [1972] IR 372.

from subsequently seeking this consideration.[19] In order to found a claim based on estoppel in this context, it has been stated by Clarke J in the decision of the Supreme Court in *Furey v Lurganville Construction Co. Ltd*[20] that there must be 'a clear unequivocal promise or representation'.

While this '*High Trees*' principle appeared to be potentially far-reaching in effect, its scope was circumscribed by the subsequent decision of the English Court of Appeal in *Combe v Combe*,[21] where Denning LJ himself stated that it did not 'create new causes of action where none existed before. It only prevents a party from insisting upon his strict legal rights, when it should be unjust to allow him to enforce them, having regard to the dealings which have taken place between the parties.' It was also in the *Combe* decision that Birkett LJ adopted the now famous expression used by counsel that the *High Trees* doctrine was one which should be 'used as a shield and not a sword'.[22] This reasoning was applied by Barron J in *Chartered Trust Ireland Ltd v Healy*,[23] where he held that estoppel could not confer a cause of action on a plaintiff.[24]

The *High Trees* principle also underpinned the decision of Kenny J in *Cullen v Cullen*.[25] The plaintiff purported to transfer his property and business to his wife in return for an undertaking that she would not seek to have him committed to a mental hospital. The plaintiff's wife won a portable house in a competition and gave it to her son. She suggested that he should erect it on the father's lands and the latter expressed the view that as he was transferring the property to his wife she could do as she liked. The son erected the house on these lands, rather than on his own as he had originally contemplated, and when the plaintiff instituted proceedings, *inter alia*, claiming injunctions to prevent the son trespassing on the land, the son counter-claimed for a declaration that he was entitled to the house and the site on which it was built. Kenny J held that he was satisfied that the son would have erected the house on his own property had the plaintiff not given his wife permission to erect the house on the disputed lands. However, he rejected the son's claim that he had acquired a right to compel the plaintiff to transfer the site to him although he held that the plaintiff was estopped by his conduct from asserting any title to the site.[26] As Kenny J stated, '[w]hile the estoppel created by the plaintiff's conduct prevents him asserting a title to the site, it does not give [the son] a right to require the

19. The Supreme Court dismissed the father's appeal but rested its decision on other grounds and made no comment on the estoppel argument.
20. [2012] IESC 38 at [5.3]. See also *Re Hoare, A Bankrupt* [2016] IEHC 345 at [12].
21. [1951] 2 KB 215.
22. *Ibid.* at 224.
23. High Court Circuit Appeal (Barron J) 10 December 1985.
24. These comments were referred to by Laffoy J in *The Barge Inn Ltd v Quinn Hospitality Ireland Operations 3 Ltd* [2013] IEHC 387 at [67].
25. [1962] IR 268. See Brady (1970) 5 Ir Jur (ns) 239.
26. At the end of a 12-year period the son could therefore bring an application under s. 52 of the Registration of Title Act 1891 for his registration as owner.

plaintiff to transfer the site to him: if I had jurisdiction to make such an order I would do so, but I do not think I have.'[27]

While the principle had certainly been employed in a defensive context in *Hughes v Metropolitan Railway Co.*,[28] as Jackson has commented, 'this does not imply that an action cannot be brought upon a representation'[29] and he argues that any attempt to restrict the effect of such a representation to a defensive mechanism ignores the principle on which it is based, namely that a promise may be enforced. As Mason CJ pointed out in *Waltons Stores (Interstate) Ltd v Maher*,[30] Denning LJ himself acknowledged in the *Combe* case that estoppel 'may be part of a cause of action' even if not a cause of action in itself. There have been signs in England of a more flexible approach being taken to this traditional limitation on the operation of the doctrine and in *Re Wyvern Developments Ltd*[31] Templeman J rejected the argument that estoppel could not confer a cause of action and said that it applies whenever 'the promissor knows and intends that the promisee will irretrievably alter his position on the promise'.[32]

High Court decisions in Ireland show that there is a lack of consensus on this question and it would be fair to say that there has been little real analysis of the issues underlying it. In *Re J.R.*[33] Costello J appeared to hold that promissory estoppel could give rise to a cause of action and indeed was capable of creating proprietary rights. However, this approach is at odds with the *dictum* of O'Hanlon J in *Association of General Practitioners Ltd v Minister for Health*,[34] in which he reasserted the traditional view that promissory estoppel should be regarded as providing a shield and not a sword. The question arose in the context of a claim by the plaintiffs based, *inter alia*, on the doctrine of legitimate expectation which Finlay CJ had described in *Webb v Ireland*[35] as 'but an aspect of the well-recognised equitable concept of promissory estoppel'. Relying on the position as laid down in *Combe v Combe*,[36] O'Hanlon J stated that 'the doctrine of equitable or promissory estoppel cannot create any new cause of action where none existed before'[37] and from this proposition he concluded that where a promise is made which is unsupported by consideration, the promisee cannot bring an action. While no detailed consideration was given by O'Hanlon J to this issue, his reiteration of the orthodox view of the limitations

27. [1962] IR 268, 292.
28. (1877) 2 App Cas 439.
29. Jackson (1965) 81 LQR 223, 242.
30. (1988) 164 CLR 387, 400.
31. [1974] 1 WLR 1097.
32. *Ibid.* at 1104.
33. [1993] ILRM 657. See further Coughlan (1993) 15 DULJ 188.
34. [1995] 2 ILRM 481.
35. [1988] IR 353.
36. [1951] 2 KB 215.
37. [1995] 2 ILRM 481, 492.

of the doctrine of promissory estoppel indicates at the very least that there is no coherent move towards broadening its parameters in this jurisdiction.

Another aspect of promissory estoppel which has provoked a degree of uncertainty is the need for a claimant to establish detriment. There have been suggestions made by Lord Denning to the effect that this is not an essential requirement,[38] however in *Lowe v Lombank Ltd*[39] Diplock J disagreed with this viewpoint and said that any representation made to a person must be acted upon by him to his detriment before an estoppel can arise. Similarly, in this jurisdiction in *Industrial Yarns Ltd v Greene*,[40] Costello J stated that to establish a claim of estoppel, 'the representee must show that what was said or done by the representor influenced both the belief and conduct of the representee to his detriment'. The approach adopted by Costello J in his judgment in *Re J.R.*[41] would tend to confirm the need to establish detriment if a claim based on promissory estoppel is to succeed. More recently, in *Bank of Scotland plc v Kennedy*[42] McGovern J stated that '[i]t is clear, therefore, that whether one is to characterise it as "detriment" or "reliance", there must be conduct on the part of the party seeking to raise a promissory estoppel such as to render it unconscionable for their counterparty to resile from representations purportedly altering the state of legal relations between them.'

PROPRIETARY ESTOPPEL

Introduction

The basis of the doctrine of proprietary estoppel is to prevent a person from insisting on his strict legal rights where to do so would be inequitable having regard to the dealings which have taken place between the parties.[43] It developed as an exception to the formalities required for the creation of interests in land and the rationale behind the doctrine could be said to be the prevention of unconscionable behaviour. It should be noted at this point that while proprietary estoppel is almost exclusively invoked in the context of rights in or over land, it can extend to other forms of property.[44] More recently it has been argued

38. *W.J. Alan & Co. Ltd v El Nasr Export and Import Co* [1972] 2 QB 189, 213. See also *Brikom Investments Ltd v Carr* [1979] QB 467, 482.
39. [1960] 1 WLR 196. Adopted as a correct statement of the law in this jurisdiction by Murphy J in *McCambridge v Winters* High Court 1983 No. 486Sp (Murphy J) 28 May 1984.
40. [1984] ILRM 15, 23 *per* Costello J. See also *Bank of Scotland plc v Kennedy* [2013] IEHC 420 at [14]. Note that in *Dunne v Molloy* [1976-77] ILRM 266 Gannon J pointed to the fact that there was no evidence of any detrimental act done by the plaintiff either with the encouragement or knowledge of the defendant.
41. [1993] ILRM 657.
42. [2013] IEHC 420 at [19].
43. *Crabb v Arun District Council* [1976] Ch 179, 187-188 *per* Lord Denning MR.
44. E.g. *Re Basham* [1986] 1 WLR 1498.

by McFarlane and Sales that English law has come to recognise a particular form of promise-based liability and that there are no grounds for restricting the operation of this principle to cases where the promise relates to land or other property owned or about to be owned by the promisor.[45]

As Lord Walker commented in *Thorner v Major*,[46] the doctrine of proprietary estoppel is based on three main elements: 'a representation or assurance made to the claimant; reliance on it by the claimant; and detriment to the claimant in consequence of his (reasonable) reliance.' However, as Robert Walker LJ made clear in the course of delivering his judgment in the decision of the Court of Appeal in *Gillett v Holt*,[47] the doctrine cannot be treated as if it can be 'subdivided into three or four watertight compartments.' As he stated, 'the quality of the relevant assurances may influence the issue of reliance' and 'reliance and detriment are often intertwined.'[48] While it must also be borne in mind that the doctrine of unconscionability has come to play an increasingly significant role, it is nevertheless useful to briefly examine these three traditional requirements at this point.

Assurance

The assurance given, while it need not necessarily have been express, must have been made by the party with the intention that it should be relied on and a mere expression of opinion would be insufficient in this context. It will usually consist of encouragement by words or deeds, although it has been suggested that 'in some circumstances passive conduct, even if unaccompanied by any words, may suffice to constitute the relevant encouragement'.[49] Support for this view may be derived from the *dicta* of Lord Walker in *Thorner v Major*,[50] where he

---

45. (2015) 131 LQR 610.
46. [2009] 1 WLR 776, 786. This statement of the necessary elements in a claim based on proprietary estoppel is increasingly relied upon. See *McGuinness v Preece* [2016] EWHC 1518 (Ch) at [61]; *Winkler v Shamoon* [2016] EWHC 217 (Ch) at [157]; *Gilpin v Legg* [2017] EWHC 3220 (Ch) at [96]; *West End Commercial Ltd v London Troacadero (2015) LLP* [2017] EWHC 2175 (Ch) at [38]; *James v James* [2018] EWHC 43 (Ch) at [21]; *Smyth-Tyrrell v Bowden* [2018] EWHC 106 (Ch) at [66]; *Gee v Gee* [2018] EWHC 1393 (Ch) at [5]; *Farrar v Miller* [2018] EWCA Civ 152 at [50]; *Wild v Wild* [2018] EWCA Civ 2197 (Ch) at [74].
47. [2001] Ch 210, 225. See also *Guest v Guest* [2019] EWHC 869 (Ch) at [128].
48. *Ibid.* See also *Henry v Henry* [2010] 1 All ER 988, 1000.
49. *Warnes v Hedley* Court of Appeal, 31 January 1984 *per* Slade LJ. In *Gilpin v Legg* [2017] EWHC 3220 (Ch) at [102] it was suggested as follows: 'that the "promise" element of proprietary estoppel may however be satisfied by a *failure* by the landowner to speak out. But this can happen *only* when there is otherwise a duty on the landowner to do so. However, for such a duty to arise it requires that the landowner should be aware of his own rights, and also aware that the "promise" mistakenly believes that the landowner is promising some interest, on the faith of which "promise" the "promise" is acting to his or her detriment.' This was not the case in the matter before the court.
50. [2009] 1 WLR 776, 793-794. He referred to the *dicta* of Lord Eldon LC in *Dann v*

stated that 'if all proprietary estoppel cases (including cases of acquiescence or standing-by) are to be analysed in terms of assurance, reliance and detriment, then the landowner's conduct in standing by in silence serves as the element of assurance.' This principle was referred to in *Guest v Guest*,[51] where Judge Russen suggested that acquiescence might suffice in circumstances where the claimant believes that he has already acquired an interest in the property in question. However, he suggested that 'where the proprietary estoppel claim is based upon the claimant's *expectation* of acquiring a proprietary interest at *some point in the future* then the owner cannot be estopped by mere passivity, or silence, in the absence of some prior representation or assurance by him which encouraged the expectation in the first place.'[52]

So, while it seems that mere acquiescence or 'conscious silence'[53] may suffice in certain circumstances, doubt has been cast on this proposition in this jurisdiction by McGuinness J in her judgment in *C.D. v J.D.F.*[54] In her view in order to establish an estoppel 'there must actually be a promise, or at least a reasonably clear direct representation or inducement of some kind'[55] and it is not sufficient to assert that something was permitted to happen or that third parties looking at the situation thought that a particular outcome was likely. McGuinness J distinguished the decision in *Salvation Army Trustee Co. Ltd v W. Yorkshire Metropolitan County Council*[56] on which counsel for the applicant relied as being a case where 'conscious silence' followed a period where very specific and detailed representations had been made to the plaintiff on which it had strongly relied. However, this approach is somewhat at odds with that taken in *Gill v Woodall*,[57] where it was stated that a representation can be sufficient to found proprietary estoppel even if it is not made expressly and that 'it may be made in oblique and allusive terms providing it was reasonable for the person to whom it was made, given his knowledge of the maker and the background circumstances, to have understood the maker to mean not merely that his present intention was to leave the property to the other but that he would definitely do so'.

Spurrier (1802) 7 Ves 231, 235–236 to the effect that 'this court will not permit a man knowingly, though but passively, to encourage another to lay out money under an erroneous opinion of title; and the circumstance of looking on is in many cases as strong as using terms of encouragement.' See also *Smyth-Tyrrell v Bowden* [2018] EWHC 106 (Ch) at [50].

51. [2019] EWHC 869 (Ch).
52. *Ibid.* at [141].
53. *Salvation Army Trustee Co. Ltd v W. Yorkshire Metropolitan County Council* (1981) 41 P & CR 179. Samet (2015) 78 MLR 85, 111 has suggested that the relative weakness of a claim based on acquiescence rather than active encouragement ought to be reflected in the remedy which might be granted to a successful claimant.
54. [2005] 4 IR 154.
55. *Ibid.* at 48. This approach of requiring a direct representation also appears to have been followed in *J.C. v W.C.* [2004] 2 IR 312.
56. (1981) 41 P & CR 179.
57. [2009] EWHC 834 (Ch) at [515].

A further interesting point was made by Robert Walker LJ in *Gillett v Holt*[58] to the effect that where assurances given were intended to be relied on, and were in fact relied on, it was not necessary to find an irrevocable promise as it is the other party's detrimental reliance on the promise which makes it irrevocable.[59] Wilson LJ made a similar point in *Lloyd v Sutcliffe*,[60] namely that equity intervenes to make a promise irrevocable not at the time it is made but only at a later stage where a promisee has acted to his detriment in reliance upon it and a promisor has sought unconscionably to withdraw from it. As he put it, '[t]he law requires that the promisor should make clear not that the promise *cannot* be revoked but that it *will not* be revoked'.[61] In addition, it should be noted that it has been accepted that assurances need not be the sole inducement for the conduct constituting the detriment and that it is sufficient if they are an inducement of some form.[62]

The nature and quality of any assurances made was one of the key issues in *Thorner v Major*.[63] The claimant, who was the deceased's cousin's son, had worked on an unpaid basis on the deceased's farm for a period of nearly 30 years. Over this time a number of oblique references had been made by the deceased to the fact that he had intended the claimant to inherit the farm, such as handing him an insurance bonus notice relating to life insurance policies and saying, 'that's for my death duties.' The deceased made a will in which he left his residuary estate, which included the farm, to the claimant, but after he fell out with one of the pecuniary legatees named in the will he destroyed it and he subsequently died intestate. The claimant sought a declaration that the defendants, the deceased's personal representatives, held the estate on trust for him and the trial judge found in his favour on the basis of proprietary estoppel. The Court of Appeal allowed the defendants' appeal on the grounds that there had not been a clear and unequivocal representation by the deceased upon which he had intended the claimant to rely. The House of Lords allowed the appeal and restored the decision of the trial judge.

Lord Scott, Lord Walker and Lord Neuberger gave consideration to the question of the clarity of any assurance made. Lord Scott referred to the fact that a representation, if it is to found a claim based on proprietary estoppel, must be 'clear and unequivocal.' He concluded that if at the time of the representor's death, evidence was available to identify the property in question with certainty, the appellant's claim to be entitled to it could not be rejected

58. [2001] Ch 210, 228-229.
59. See also *Q. v Q.* [2009] 1 FLR 935, 966; *Southwell v Blackburn* [2014] EWCA Civ 1347 at [20] which support the view that detrimental reliance can make a promise or assurance irrevocable.
60. [2007] EWCA Civ 153.
61. *Ibid.* at [38].
62. *Gill v Woodall* [2009] EWHC 834 (Ch) at [520].
63. [2009] 1 WLR 776. See further Dixon [2009] Conv 260; McFarlane and Robertson (2009) 125 LQR 535; Piska (2009) 72 MLR 998; Delany (2009) 31 DULJ 440.

on the basis of a lack of certainty of subject matter. Lord Neuberger, whilst he said he was not seeking to cast doubt on the proposition that there must be some sort of an assurance which is 'clear and unequivocal' before it can be relied on to found an estoppel, said that this principle must be read as subject to three qualifications. First, the effect of the relevant words or actions must be assessed in their context; secondly, it would be wrong to be unrealistically rigorous when applying the 'clear and unambiguous' test; and thirdly, it must be understood that there may be cases where the statement relied on to found an estoppel could amount to an assurance which could reasonably be understood as having more than one possible meaning.

Lord Walker took a more flexible approach towards this general issue and said that there is some authority for the view that the 'clear and unequivocal' test does not apply to proprietary estoppel. He stated that he would prefer to say that to establish a proprietary estoppel the relevant assurance must be 'clear enough' and that what amounts to sufficient clarity will greatly depend on the context.[64] Lord Walker then quoted the following passage from the judgment of Hoffmann LJ in *Walton v Walton*[65] and said that he would concur with this approach:

> The promise must be unambiguous and must appear to have been intended to be taken seriously. Taken in its context, it must have been a promise which one might reasonably expect to be relied upon by the person to whom it was made.[66]

So, as Hamblen LJ stated in *Liden v Burton*,[67] '[c]ontext is "hugely important" as to whether an assurance is sufficiently clear', and in the matter before the court he upheld the conclusion of the trial judge, who, as he pointed out, had had the advantage of seeing and hearing the witnesses, that the requisite assurance had been plainly made out.

A further issue which seemed clear from *Thorner v Major*, and was confirmed at first instance in *James v James*,[68] is that it may not be fatal to a claim if there is no evidence of a *specific* promise or assurance and that it is the effect of the evidence as a whole which will be decisive. So, in *James v James*[69] it was made clear that '[t]he court must look at the totality of the evidence of what passed between the parties and form a view as to whether it

---

64. See also the speech of Lord Rodger at 786. See also *Gill v Woodall* [2009] EWHC 834 (Ch) at [515]; *Thompson v Foy* [2010] 1 P & CR 16 at [90]; *Rawlings v Chapman* [2015] EWHC 180 (Ch) at [4]; *Liden v Burton* [2016] EWCA Civ 275 at [17]; *Smyth-Tyrrell v Bowden* [2018] EWHC 106 (Ch) at [69]; *Habberfield v Habberfield* [2018] EWHC 317 (Ch) at [48]; *Wild v Wild* [2018] EWHC 2197 (Ch) at [80].
65. Court of Appeal, 14 April 1994.
66. *Ibid.* at [16].
67. [2016] EWCA Civ 275 at [24]. See further Lower [2018] Conv 85.
68. [2018] EWHC 43 (Ch).
69. *Ibid.* at [22]. See also *Smyth-Tyrrell v Bowden* [2018] EWHC 106 (Ch) at [70].

was intended, or whether a reasonable man would have taken it to have been intended, to amount to such an assurance.' However, on the facts of the matter before the court, Judge Matthews concluded that there was no evidence with a sufficient degree of clarity to amount to an assurance. As he put it, 'a statement of *current intentions* as to future conduct is not a *promise* of that conduct, let alone a promise intended to be acted upon.'[70]

Where proprietary estoppel based on an assurance or representation is relied upon, this representation must have been made by all necessary parties to the transaction. So, it is clear from the judgment of Sir William Blackburne in *Fielden v Christie-Miller*[71] that where it is claimed that an obligation arises on this basis, it must be established that the trustees acted unanimously in giving the assurance or that the one who made the representation had authority to do so on behalf of his co-trustees. As he put it, '[e]lementary fairness requires that before a person can be bound by the acts of another purporting to act on his behalf, that other must have his authority to bind him in the matter. Whether he has will depend on the usual principles of agency. This applies, in my judgment, as much in the field of estoppel as it does in other contexts.'[72] O'Hanlon J referred to this principle in her judgment in *O'Rourke v O'Rourke*,[73] where she said that Sir William Blackburne had confirmed that 'it was not sufficient to plead that an individual appeared "to be speaking on behalf of all three trustees"'.

Finally, it should be noted that it is clear from *Thorner v Major* that changes to the character and extent of the property do not exclude a remedy in estoppel as long as it is still identifiable[74] and Lord Walker stated that in this case there was no reason to doubt that the parties' common understanding was that the deceased's assurance related to whatever the farm consisted of at the time of his death.[75] So, as James Allen QC, sitting as a Deputy High Court judge, stated in *Gill v Woodall*,[76] 'changes in the character or extent of the property the subject matter of the assurances will not exclude the application of the doctrine or the grant of equitable relief where the property is conceptually identified from the moment the equity comes into existence'. However, as he pointed out such changes may be relevant to the relief which the court may grant.

Reliance

Reliance would seem to be established once it is shown that a representation

---

70. *Ibid.* at [24]. See also *Habberfield v Habberfield* [2018] EWHC 317 (Ch) at [49].
71. [2015] EWHC 87 (Ch).
72. *Ibid.* at [26]. See also *Preedy v Dunne* [2015] EWHC 2713 (Ch).
73. [2018] IEHC 791 at [91].
74. [2009] 1 WLR 776, 780 *per* Lord Hoffmann.
75. *Ibid.* at 796. See also at 803 *per* Lord Neuberger. See also *MacDonald v Frost* [2009] WTLR 1815 at [12].
76. [2009] EWHC 834 (Ch) at [524].

'was calculated to influence the judgment of a reasonable man'[77] and there is authority for the proposition that once an assurance on the part of the legal owner has been established, there is a presumption of reliance.[78] The concept of reliance was considered by Balcombe LJ in *Wayling v Jones*,[79] in which he stated that '[o]nce it has been established that promises were made, and that there has been conduct by the plaintiff of such a nature that inducement may be inferred then the burden of proof shifts to the defendants to establish that he did not rely on the promises' but he added that 'there must be a sufficient link between the promises relied upon and the conduct which constitutes the detriment'.

The issue of reliance was also central to the decision of the House of Lords in *Thorner v Major*.[80] In the Court of Appeal Lloyd LJ was not satisfied that the trial judge's factual findings constituted a sufficient basis for a successful claim based on proprietary estoppel and as Lord Scott pointed out in his opinion in the House of Lords, this doubt appeared to have been based on the absence of an explicit finding that the deceased had intended the appellant to rely on his remarks. In the view of Lord Scott, there seemed to be an inconsistency between Lloyd LJ's acceptance of the judge's finding that it was reasonable for the appellant to have relied on the deceased's representations that he would inherit the property and his conclusion that 'no representation had been made by [the deceased] that it had been reasonable for [the appellant] to have taken as *intended* to be relied on.'[81]

Lord Scott concluded that the trial judge's factual finding that it was reasonable for the appellant to have relied on the deceased's representation that he would inherit the property carried with it an implicit finding that it was reasonable for the appellant to take the representation as intended by the deceased to be relied on. Lord Neuberger reached a similar conclusion on this point and said that if the statements were reasonably understood by the appellant to have the effect which the trial judge found, namely an assurance, and the appellant reasonably acted on that understanding to his detriment, then what the deceased intended was not really germane. Lord Walker also concluded that in his view the trial judge did find that the deceased's assurances, objectively assessed, were intended to be taken seriously and to be relied upon.

Further consideration was given to the concept of reliance in this context by Lord Hoffmann in *Thorner*, where he said that '[i]t was enough that the

77. *Brikom Investments Ltd v Carr* [1979] QB 467, 483 *per* Lord Denning MR.
78. *Greasley v Cooke* [1980] 1 WLR 1306. See also *Gillett v Holt* [2001] Ch 210, 228. Although note the comment of Lloyd LJ in *Cook v Thomas* [2010] EWCA Civ 227 at [77] that in this context such a presumption only plays a role in the absence of relevant evidence.
79. (1993) 69 P & CR 170, 173. See further Davis [1995] Conv 409; Cooke (1995) 111 LQR 389. See also *Ottey v Grundy* [2003] EWCA Civ 1176 at [56]; Thompson [2004] Conv 137, 145; *Culliford v Thorpe* [2018] EWHC 426 (Ch) at [67].
80. [2009] 1 WLR 776.
81. *Ibid.* at 782.

meaning … conveyed would reasonably have been understood as intended to be taken seriously as an assurance which could be relied upon.'[82] This principle was reiterated by Patten LJ in *Lester v Woodgate*,[83] where he added that in such cases it is not necessary to prove that the representor intended that his words or conduct would have that effect or was even subjectively aware that they did so but when such evidence does exist the reasonableness of the reliance is likely to be indisputable. However, it is necessary to establish that the assurance made was from an objective perspective *intended* to be relied on. So, where it is clear that the parties' intention was to enter into a contract and that they did not intend to be bound until that occurred, a claim based on proprietary estoppel will not succeed if no formal contract is subsequently entered into.[84]

The principles set out in *Thorner v Major* in relation to assurance and reliance appear to have been accepted in this jurisdiction. In his judgment in *Naylor v Maher*,[85] in which the plaintiff relied successfully on proprietary estoppel in establishing a claim to lands where he had worked on the deceased's farm on an unpaid basis for many years, O'Keeffe J stated that he accepted *Thorner v Major* as a 'persuasive authority' which was relevant to the case before the court. He concluded that the promises and representations made to the plaintiff by the deceased had been intended by the latter to be relied upon by the former, that they had in fact been relied upon by the plaintiff and that it had been reasonable for him to rely on them.

Further guidance about when reliance may be regarded as reasonable is provided in the judgment of McLachlin CJC in the decision of the Supreme Court of Canada in *Cowper-Smith v Morgan*,[86] where she expressed the view that whether, in a particular case, a claimant's reliance was reasonable in the circumstances is a question of mixed fact and law. She stated that, as Lord Scott had suggested in *Cobbe v Yeoman's Row Management Ltd*,[87] it may be that the party responsible for the expectation had such a speculative interest in the property that the claimant's reliance could not have been reasonable. However, she added that 'whether this is so will depend on context, not on *ex ante* doctrinal restrictions'.[88] In her view the position adopted by the majority of the Court of Appeal in the matter before the court, namely, that reliance on a promise by a party with no present interest in property can *never* be reasonable, 'is out of step with equity's purpose, which is to temper the harsh effects of strict legal rules.'[89] In the circumstances she concluded that the claimant had established reasonable reliance on an expectation that he would enjoy a benefit

82. *Ibid.* at 779.
83. [2010] EWCA Civ 199 at [26].
84. *Muhammed v ARY Properties Ltd* [2016] EWHC 1698 (Ch) at [48].
85. [2012] IEHC 408.
86. (2017) 416 DLR (4th) 1.
87. [2008] 1 WLR 1752, 1764.
88. (2017) 416 DLR (4th) 1 at [29].
89. *Ibid.*

in relation to property even when the party responsible for that expectation did not own an interest in the property at the time of his reliance.

Detriment

Detriment will be suffered where the assurance on which reliance is placed is withdrawn and it is the fact of detriment having been suffered which will render it unconscionable for the legal owner to insist on enforcing his rights. While the detriment suffered by the claimant will usually involve expenditure of money or the building of premises on another's land, it would appear that it need not consist of the payment of money or other quantifiable financial detriment so long as it is something substantial.[90] In *Re Basham*[91] Edward Nugee QC, sitting as a Deputy High Court judge, stated that 'the expenditure of A.'s money on B.'s property is not the only kind of detriment that gives rise to a proprietary estoppel' and in *McCarron v McCarron*[92] Murphy J commented *obiter* that 'in a suitable case it may well be argued that a plaintiff suffers as severe a loss or detriment by providing his own labours or services in relation to the lands of another and accordingly should equally qualify for recognition in equity'.[93]

This *dictum* was relied upon by counsel for the plaintiff in *Bracken v Byrne*,[94] although it is clear from the judgment of Clarke J that the requirement that the detriment suffered should be substantial in nature should be enforced. In *Bracken* the plaintiff contended that an arrangement had been entered into between herself and the first named defendant, her sister, that she would be provided with a plot of land on property belonging to the latter on which to build a house. Clarke J stated that the only detriment suffered by the plaintiff was the making of a planning application and some brief discussions with a builder and he concluded that he was not satisfied that any sufficient detriment had been incurred such as would require a court of equity to require a conveyance of the lands in reliance on the doctrine of proprietary estoppel.

The requirement that the detriment suffered by a plaintiff must be substantial in nature was also reiterated by O'Sullivan J in *McDonagh v Denton*,[95] in which the plaintiff sought, *inter alia*, a declaration that the defendants were

90. *Gillett v Holt* [2001] Ch 210, 232. See also *Lissimore v Downing* [2003] 2 FLR 308, 315. The fact that the detriment suffered must be of a substantial nature was reiterated in *Negus v Bahouse* [2008] 1 FLR 381, 389; *Stallion v Albert Stallion Holdings (Great Britain) Ltd* [2010] 2 FLR 78, 104.
91. [1986] 1 WLR 1498, 1509.
92. Supreme Court 1995 No. 181, 13 February 1997 at 13.
93. This view was confirmed by Kinlen J in *McGuinness v McGuinness* High Court 2001 Nos. 145CA and 147CA (Kinlen J) 19 March 2002, where he stated that the detriment must be substantial although it is not necessarily confined to monetary considerations and added that it must be tested against the principle that it would be unjust or inequitable to allow the assurance to be disregarded
94. [2006] 1 ILRM 91.
95. [2005] IEHC 127.

estopped from asserting that a disputed plot of land, which he believed he had previously purchased, was included in a deed of assignment registered by the defendants. The defendants' solicitor had not replied to an assertion of title made by the plaintiff's solicitor in a letter and O'Sullivan J was satisfied that this amounted in the circumstances to a representation on the defendants' behalf that this claim was not disputed. On the question of detriment which the plaintiff claimed to have suffered, O'Sullivan J concluded that the expenditure by the plaintiff and works of maintenance carried out by him on the disputed plot following the representation were not such as could amount to detriment for the purposes of the doctrine of estoppel. However, in reliance on the fact that the defendants had not disagreed with his assertion of title, the plaintiff had entered into a contract to sell the disputed plot to a third party and the latter had subsequently instituted proceedings for specific performance against the plaintiff. O'Sullivan J expressed the view that 'being involved as a defendant in specific performance proceedings is in itself a substantial detriment' and he concluded that the plaintiff in contracting to sell the disputed plot to a third party, thereby exposing himself to the specific performance proceedings, had acted to his detriment in the sense required to found an estoppel. More recently when the issue of detriment arose in *Naylor v Maher*,[96] O'Keeffe J concluded that the work done by the plaintiff over many years on the deceased's farm, often for little or no pay, amounted to 'serious and substantial detriment'.[97] Given the 'ongoing and lifelong commitment' which the plaintiff had made, detriment was clearly established on the facts of the case and there was no discussion of the standard which the court should require to be satisfied in this context.

It appears from the judgment of the Court of Appeal in *Joyce v Epsom and Ewell Borough Council*[98] that it is not necessary that the defendant should be aware of the detriment that the claimant has suffered in order for a claim to succeed.[99] Davies LJ stated that the alleged lack of knowledge on the part of the local authority of the works actually undertaken on which the claim of proprietary estoppel was based was not of crucial significance. He said that in cases of encouragement such as the one before the court, 'it was not an invariable requirement that the person encouraging necessarily must know exactly what the person encouraged might have actually done in reliance on the encouragement.'[100]

A comprehensive analysis of the manner in which the principle of detriment operates in the context of proprietary estoppel was undertaken by Robert Walker LJ in *Gillett v Holt*.[101] Referring to the judgment of Slade LJ in *Jones*

---

96. [2012] IEHC 408.
97. *Ibid.* at [409].
98. [2012] EWCA Civ 1398.
99. See also *Crabb v Arun Borough Council* [1976] Ch 179, 189.
100. [2012] EWCA Civ 1398 at [39].
101. [2001] Ch 211. While Thompson [2001] Conv 78, 83 has welcomed the decision as taking 'a wider and more principled view of the concept of detriment', Wells [2001]

v Watkins,[102] he said that there must be a sufficient causal link between the assurance relied on and the detriment asserted,[103] that the issue of detriment must be judged at the moment when the person who has given the assurance seeks to go back on it,[104] that whether the detriment is sufficiently substantial is to be tested by whether it would be unjust or inequitable to allow the assurance to be disregarded and that the detriment alleged must be pleaded and proved.[105] Robert Walker LJ stated as follows:

> The overwhelming weight of authority shows that detriment is required. But the authorities also show that it is not a narrow or technical concept. The detriment need not consist of the expenditure of money or other quantifiable financial detriment, so long as it is something substantial. The requirement must be approached as part of a broad inquiry as to whether repudiation of an assurance is or is not unconscionable in all the circumstances.[106]

Although the *dicta* of Robert Walker LJ in *Gillett v Holt*[107] referred to above suggests that the aim of seeking to prevent unconscionable conduct now 'permeates all elements of the doctrine', there is no sign of a move to dispense with the formal requirement of detriment as a prerequisite to establishing an estoppel. This was made clear by Judge McMahon in the Circuit Court decision of *Hardiman v Lawrence*,[108] in which he rejected an attempt by counsel to found a claim in estoppel based on the general principle of unconscionability. While Judge McMahon acknowledged that the law in this jurisdiction on proprietary estoppel is still evolving, he expressed the view that 'whatever formulation … the rule of unconscionability finally takes in our jurisprudence, it will not, I suggest, dispense with the requirement that he who invokes the doctrine will still have to show detriment to himself caused by unconscionable conduct by another.'[109]

Conv 13, 30 is more critical and suggests that the principles relating to detriment have not been clarified by it.

102. Court of Appeal, 26 November 1987.
103. See also *Capcon Holdings plc v Edwards* [2007] EWHC 2662 (Ch) at [40]; *Negus v Bahouse* [2008] 1 FLR 381, 389; *Gill v Woodall* [2009] EWHC 834 (Ch) at [519].
104. See also *Davies v Davies* [2014] EWCA Civ 568 at [32].
105. See also *McGuinness v McGuinness* High Court 2001 Nos. 145CA and 147CA (Kinlen J) 19 March 2002 at 7.
106. [2001] Ch 211, 232. See also *Lloyd v Dugdale* [2002] 2 P & CR 167, 177; *Clark v Clark* [2006] EWHC 275 (Ch) at [30]; *Gill v Woodall* [2009] EWHC 834 (Ch) at [518]; *Lester v Woodgate* [2010] EWCA Civ 199 at [40]; *Wild v Wild* [2018] EWHC 2197 (Ch) at [76].
107. [2001] Ch 211, 225. See also *Fisher v Brooker* [2009] 1 WLR 1764, 1780.
108. Circuit Court, 18 December 2002.
109. *Ibid.* at 8.

Categories of Cases in which Proprietary Estoppel may Arise

Gray and Gray[110] have suggested three categories of situation in which proprietary estoppel may arise: cases where an imperfect gift is made, cases based on common expectation and cases of unilateral mistake. These categories are clearly not mutually exclusive as the effect of the operation of the doctrine may well be to perfect an imperfect gift even in cases where the basis for its operation can be said to be expectation or mistake. An examination of the case law in this area over the last century or so shows that attempts were made to restrict the cases in which proprietary estoppel could arise to those falling into the mistake category and such an approach undoubtedly restricted the growth of the doctrine. More recently, it has come to be recognised that such categorisation is unnecessary and even unhelpful and a broader doctrine based on the general concept of unconscionability has evolved.[111] Nevertheless, it is still useful to build up a picture of how proprietary estoppel has developed by examining the case law by reference to these categories.

Where an Imperfect Gift is Made

While the general principle is that equity will not complete an imperfect gift,[112] in some circumstances the courts will allow the perfection of a gift in favour of a volunteer, usually in the context of a voluntary gift of realty. The main authority for this proposition is the decision of Lord Westbury in *Dillwyn v Llewelyn*.[113] A son built a house on his father's land with the latter's consent and an informal memorandum was signed which showed that the father's intention was that it should be given to the son for this purpose. After the father died, it was held by the House of Lords that the father's intention to convey the fee simple estate would be carried into effect by the court, although the land had been left in trust for the benefit of third parties by virtue of the provisions of the father's will. Lord Westbury pointed out that a promise of a gift had been made and on the strength of that promise and with the father's knowledge, the son had incurred substantial expenditure on the land. He stressed that a voluntary agreement would not be completed by a court of equity in the case of a mere gift and that it was instead the subsequent acts of the donor which gave rise to the claim. This decision was stated by Kenny J in *Cullen v Cullen*[114] to be authority for the proposition that 'a person claiming under a voluntary agreement will not be assisted by a court of equity but that the subsequent acts

110. Gray and Gray, *Elements of Land Law* (5th ed., 2009) p. 1202.
111. Pawlowski commented in the preface to his book *Proprietary Estoppel* (1996) that these three categories 'remain valid, notwithstanding the modern trend towards applying an underlying concept of unconscionability as the basis for proprietary estoppel claims'.
112. *Milroy v Lord* (1862) 4 De GF & J 264.
113. (1862) 4 De GF & J 517.
114. [1962] IR 268, 282.

of the donor may give the donee a ground of claim which he did not acquire from the original gift'.

The principle laid down in *Dillwyn* was applied by the English Court of Appeal in *Pascoe v Turner*.[115] The parties had lived together for a considerable period of time in a house owned by the plaintiff and when he moved out and went to live with another woman, he assured the defendant that she could remain in the house and that it would henceforth belong to her. On the basis of this assurance, the defendant carried out repairs and improvements to the property. When the plaintiff subsequently brought proceedings for possession, the Court of Appeal held that the fee simple estate in the house should be conveyed to the defendant.

Similarly, in *Smyth v Halpin*[116] the plaintiff had asked his father to provide him with a site on the latter's land so that he could build a house for himself. The father's reply was to the effect that the family house would be his after his mother's death and why would he want two houses, and suggested that the plaintiff instead build an extension onto the family home. The father made a number of wills during his lifetime but in the last of these he left the house to his wife for her life and thereafter to the second named defendant, one of his daughters. After the father's death the plaintiff instituted proceedings seeking, *inter alia*, a declaration that he was entitled to the reversionary interest in the property following the life interest in favour of his mother. Geoghegan J stated that the kind of proprietary estoppel invoked in this case has its origins in the decision of *Dillwyn v Llewelyn* and that the same principles have been applied in a number of other English decisions, including *Pascoe v Turner*. He stated that the plaintiff's clear expectation in this case was that he would have a fee simple interest in the entire house and concluded that the protection of the equity arising from the expenditure required that an order be made by the court directing a conveyance of that interest to him.

Common Expectation

Cases such as *Pascoe v Tuner* and *Smyth v Halpin* could equally be considered under the heading of 'common expectation', and the key feature in this class of case is the notion of reliance. So, proprietary estoppel may arise where parties have consistently dealt with each other in such a way as to reasonably cause one party to rely on a shared assumption that he would acquire rights in the other party's lands. The accepted classic formulation of this proposition was laid down by Lord Kingsdown in his dissenting opinion in *Ramsden v Dyson*[117] as follows:

115. [1979] 1 WLR 431.
116. [1997] 2 ILRM 38.
117. (1866) LR 1 HL 129, 170-171.

> If a man, under a verbal agreement with a landlord for a certain interest in land, or, what amounts to the same thing, under an expectation, created or encouraged by the landlord, that he shall have a certain interest, takes possession of such land, with the consent of the landlord, and upon the faith of such promise or expectation, with the knowledge of the landlord, and without objection by him, lays out money upon the land, a Court of equity will compel the landlord to give effect to such a promise or expectation. …
>
> If, on the other hand, a tenant being in possession of land, and knowing the nature and extent of his interest, lays out money upon it in the hope and expectation of an extended term or an allowance for expenditure, then, if such hope or expectation has not been created or encouraged by the landlord, the tenant has no claim which any Court of law or equity can enforce.

Lord Kingsdown's observations were approved of by the Privy Council in *Plimmer v Mayor of Wellington*,[118] where the landowner rather than merely encouraging the expenditure actually took the initiative in requesting it. A licensee of land had, at the government's request, spent a considerable sum of money on extending a jetty and constructing a warehouse. When the jetty was compulsorily acquired it was held that the appellants had an equity arising from their expenditure on the land and were entitled to 'an indefinite, that is practically a perpetual' right to the jetty for the purposes of the original licence. Similarly, in *Inwards v Baker*,[119] an estoppel arose on the basis of a common expectation that by reason of one party's expenditure on land, he should be entitled to an interest in it. A father had allowed his son to build a house at his own expense on the former's land, encouraging the son to believe that he would be allowed to remain there during his lifetime. When the father died, the Court of Appeal refused to allow the trustees of the father's will to obtain possession of the lands on the basis that the son had acquired an equity in the land by reason of his expenditure which bound the father and his successors in title. Instead, the court made an order that the son could remain in possession of the property as long as he wished to use the house as his home.

It is important to stress that before Lord Kingsdown's *dicta* will apply it is essential that the expenditure has been requested, or more commonly encouraged, by the landowner. As the second paragraph of Lord Kingsdown's statement makes clear, where the other party merely lays out money in the hope or expectation of acquiring an interest, which has not been encouraged by the landowner, no estoppel will arise. This point is well illustrated by the decision

118. (1884) 9 App Cas 699. The formulation set out by the Privy Council was quoted by Murphy J in *McCarron v McCarron* Supreme Court 1995 No. 181, 13 February 1997 at 12.
119. [1965] 2 QB 29.

of the Privy Council in *Attorney General of Hong Kong v Humphrey's Estate*.[120] It was agreed in principle between the Hong Kong government and a group of companies, which included the respondent, that the government would grant the group a lease of specific property in exchange for flats which belonged to the latter. The government took possession of the flats and fitted them out for civil servants but before the contract was concluded, the group withdrew from the transaction. When the government brought an action contesting the group's right to withdraw, the respondent sought a declaration that it was entitled to possession of the flats. The government contended that the group were estopped from withdrawing from what had been agreed in principle but the Privy Council rejected this claim. It was held that to found an estoppel it would have to be established not only that the government had acted to its detriment to the knowledge of the group in the hope that it would not withdraw from the agreement, but also that the group had created or encouraged a belief or expectation on the government's part that they would not withdraw, and that the government had relied on that belief or expectation. While it was accepted that 'the government acted in the confident and not unreasonable hope that the agreement in principle would come into effect,' it was held that the group had not encouraged or allowed a belief or expectation on the government's part that it would not withdraw from the agreement and that in the circumstances no estoppel arose.

The fact that a claimant must establish that the legal owner created or encouraged a belief that it would not change its mind was also of importance in the decision of *Taylor v Dickens*.[121] While the plaintiff asserted that he was confident that the defendant would not revoke the provision in her will in which she had left him her house as she had promised, there was no evidence that she had created or encouraged this belief on his behalf.[122] As Milne has commented, 'proprietary estoppel may prevent unconscionable conduct in respect of property, but it cannot operate unless there has been reliance on an encouraged belief in rights over that property'.[123]

The importance of the fact that any expectation or belief be created or encouraged by a landowner can also be seen in this jurisdiction from the decision of Blayney J in *Haughan v Rutledge*.[124] The plaintiffs, who were trustees of an association which promoted harness racing, sought to lease the defendant's land for the purpose of holding races. The parties agreed that the defendant would let a field for a trial period and the plaintiffs would construct a racetrack on it. It was further agreed that if at the end of this period the plaintiffs left the

---

120. [1987] AC 114.
121. [1998] 1 FLR 806. See Thompson [1998] Conv 210.
122. As Gray and Gray have commented in *Elements of Land Law* (5th ed., 2009) p.1218, 'detrimental reliance upon a self-generated expectation gives rise to no valid claim of estoppel'.
123. Milne (1998) 114 LQR 555, 558-559.
124. [1988] IR 295.

property, then they would pay no rent and the defendant would retain the benefit of the works carried out. Following a dispute, the defendant re-possessed the lands and the plaintiffs sought specific performance of the alleged agreement to grant a lease of the lands or alternatively an order requiring the defendant to let them into possession. Blayney J held that four conditions would have to be satisfied before an estoppel could arise, namely detriment, expectation or belief, encouragement and finally, that there be no bar to the equity. On the facts of the case before him, he held that the second and third requirements had not been satisfied. The second condition required that the plaintiffs had built the racetrack in the belief that they owned a sufficient interest in the land to justify the expenditure or that they would obtain such an interest and this had not been established. Blayney J added that even if he had been of the view that the plaintiffs had the required belief, he would not have been satisfied that this belief had been encouraged by the defendant. He referred to the *dicta* of Lord Kingsdown in *Ramsden* and said that the case before him came within the second limb of the latter's statement. Blayney J concluded as follows:

> I consider that the plaintiffs laid out money on the construction of the track in the hope and expectation that the defendant would continue to make lettings of the track to them, but as that hope and expectation was not created or encouraged by the defendant, the plaintiffs have no claim which can be enforced at law or in equity.[125]

Unilateral Mistake

Proprietary estoppel may also be invoked where one party has made an error as to the nature of his rights, the crucial factor being that detriment is suffered by the party who innocently relies on the mistaken assumption that he has rights in land. The following statement of Lord Cranworth in *Ramsden v Dyson*[126] provides a summary of the circumstances in which estoppel can arise in such cases:

> If a stranger begins to build on my land supposing it to be his own, and I, perceiving his mistake, abstain from setting him right, and leave him to persevere in his error, a Court of equity will not allow me afterwards to assert my title to the land on which he had expended money on the supposition that the land was his own. It considers that, when I saw the mistake into which he had fallen, it was my duty to be active and to state my adverse title, and that it would be dishonest in me to remain wilfully passive on such an occasion, in order afterwards to profit by the mistake which I might have prevented.

125. *Ibid*. at 303.
126. (1866) LR 1 HL 129, 140-141.

However, he continued as follows: 'If a stranger builds on my land knowing it to be mine, there is no principle of equity which would prevent my claiming the land with the benefit of all the expenditure made on it.' Therefore, it is necessary that the person spending the money thought that he was building on his own land and that the real owner knew at the time that the land in fact belonged to him;[127] no estoppel will arise under this heading where the 'stranger' knows that he has no rights over the land. This point is illustrated by the case of *O'Callaghan v Ballincollig Holdings Ltd.*[128] The plaintiffs claimed that they had acquired title to a house by adverse possession and this claim was rejected by the defendants and a notice to quit served. The plaintiffs sought a declaration of their title or alternatively a declaration that they had a lien on the house for monies spent on reinstating it while the defendant counter-claimed for possession. The plaintiffs' claim to a lien was based on the grounds of proprietary estoppel and unjust enrichment. They argued that the defendant had stood idly by while they had spent substantial sums of money reinstating the house and that this precluded it from recovering the property without compensating the plaintiffs for their expenditure. Blayney J was satisfied that this submission was not well founded; as long as the plaintiffs' tenancy continued to subsist, the defendant was not entitled to interfere and it was not a case of the defendant standing idly by. He quoted with approval the second limb of Lord Cranworth's *dicta* in *Ramsden* and concluded that the plaintiffs knew that they held the defendant's house as tenants and that they were reinstating a house to which the defendant was entitled subject to their tenancy. Therefore, they could not prevent the defendant from claiming the house with the benefit of their expenditure on it.

An attempt was made to rely on Lord Cranworth's principle in *Wilmott v Barber*,[129] although on the facts it was clear that both parties were mistaken as to their legal rights and the claim of estoppel was rejected. Neither the plaintiff assignee of a lease nor the lessor had realised that the lease prohibited assignment of the lease without the lessor's consent. Fry J concluded that the lessor could not, by his action in acquiescing in the expenditure incurred by the lessee, be estopped from asserting his right to refuse consent to the assignment since at the date of the purported acquiescence, he was not aware of the right of veto. However, the judgment of Fry J is important in view of the restrictive effect which it had on the development of the doctrine of proprietary estoppel. He laid down the proposition that a person should not be deprived of his strict legal rights unless he has acted in a manner which would make it fraudulent to assert those rights, fraud in this context being dependent on establishing five necessary elements. These were as follows:

127. In *Republic Bank Ltd v Lochan* [2015] UKPC 26 at [25] Lord Neuberger stated that '[b]uilding on another's land in the belief that it is one's land is a classic basis for a proprietary estoppel claim, but such a claim cannot be mounted unless the owner of the land in question was, or ought to have been, aware of the relevant facts.'
128. High Court 1987 No. E202 (Blayney J) 31 March 1993.
129. (1880) 15 Ch D 96.

1. The claimant must have made a mistake as to his legal rights.
2. The claimant must have expended some money or done some act on the faith of his mistaken belief.
3. The owner of the land must know of his own right which is inconsistent with the right claimed by the plaintiff.
4. The owner must know of the claimant's mistaken belief as to his rights.
5. The owner must have encouraged the claimant in relation to the expenditure incurred or other acts done, either directly or by refraining from asserting his legal rights.[130]

These five probanda came to be applied by the courts in cases where a claim of proprietary estoppel was made irrespective of the basis of such a claim and even where it did not involve a case of unilateral mistake. With a few limited exceptions, the most notable being the decision of the Privy Council in *Plimmer v Mayor of Wellington*,[131] in which a distinction was made between cases of unilateral mistake and common expectation, the courts often sought to construe situations so that they fell within the requirements laid down by Fry J, even where there was no mistake made, and where this was not possible, a claim might fail. So, in *Cullen v Cullen*,[132] Kenny J appeared to reject a claim based on proprietary estoppel on this basis. In *Hopgood v Brown*[133] Evershed MR recognised that these requirements should be limited to cases of unilateral mistake and commented that they were not intended to be a 'comprehensive formulation of the necessary requisites of any case of estoppel by representation.' However, because of the apparently general nature of the probanda, their application resulted in a very restrictive view of the circumstances in which estoppel could arise.[134] Nevertheless, by the 1980s the courts had begun to recognise that the *dicta* of Fry J did not constitute a formula which had to be rigidly adhered to, although the requirements continued to be applied in some cases which did not fall within the category of unilateral mistake.[135] A useful summary of the current position is contained in the judgment of Patten LJ in *Lester v Woodgate*[136] in the following terms:

> [I]n subsequent cases, the courts have held that it is not necessary for all five probanda to be satisfied in every case or (therefore) for the acts of the party seeking to rely on the estoppel to have been motivated by a

130. *Ibid.* at 105-106. Quoted with approval by Gannon J in *Dunne v Molloy* [1976-77] ILRM 266, 268.
131. (1884) 9 App Cas 699, 712.
132. [1962] IR 268.
133. [1955] 1 WLR 213, 223.
134. E.g. *E. & L. Berg Homes Ltd v Grey* (1979) 253 EG 473.
135. See, e.g. *Coombes v Smith* [1986] 1 WLR 808; *Matharu v Matharu* (1994) 68 P & CR 93. See Milne (1995) 58 MLR 412.
136. [2010] EWCA Civ 199 at [33].

> mistaken belief as to his rights. Those conditions are a useful test of what might amount to unconscionable behaviour in such a case but they are not intended to apply indiscriminately regardless of the particular facts or circumstances in question.

A Move Towards a Test of Unconscionability

A view that the five probanda should be used as a guide rather than as a strict requirement began to emerge in England during the 1970s. In *Shaw v Applegate*[137] Buckley LJ commented that his understanding of the *dicta* of Fry J in *Wilmott v Barber* was that where a party has a legal right, acquiescence will not deprive him of that right unless it would be dishonest or unconscionable of the plaintiff to seek to assert it, although he said that he doubted whether it was really necessary to comply strictly with all five requirements to establish unconscionability. Similarly, in *Crabb v Arun District Council*,[138] Scarman LJ, although he did refer to the probanda as a 'valuable guide',[139] expressed the view that it should be necessary to establish that a defendant by asserting a right is taking advantage of a plaintiff in a manner which is 'unconscionable, inequitable or unjust'.[140] However, it was not until the judgment of Oliver J in *Taylors Fashions Ltd v Liverpool Victoria Trustees Co. Ltd*[141] that any detailed consideration was given to the idea of a departure from the *Wilmott v Barber* approach. Oliver J pointed out that in the example given by Lord Kingsdown in *Ramsden v Dyson*[142] there was no room for the literal application of the probanda as the circumstances referred to did not presuppose a mistake but rather the fostering of an expectation in the minds of both parties. He said that more recent authorities seemed to support a much wider equitable jurisdiction to interfere in situations where the assertion of legal rights was found by a court to be unconscionable and suggested that the relevance of the probanda even in cases of unilateral mistake was now open to doubt. Oliver J concluded as follows:

> Furthermore, the more recent cases indicate, in my judgment, that the application of the *Ramsden v Dyson* principle … requires a very much broader approach which is directed rather at ascertaining whether, in particular circumstances, it would be unconscionable for a party to be permitted to deny that which, knowingly or unknowingly, he has allowed or encouraged another to assume to his detriment rather than to inquiring whether the circumstances can be fitted within the confines of some

137. [1977] 1 WLR 970.
138. [1976] Ch 179.
139. *Ibid.* at 194.
140. *Ibid.* at 195.
141. [1982] QB 133.
142. (1866) LR 1 HL 129.

preconceived formula serving as a universal yardstick for every form of unconscionable behaviour.[143]

This more flexible approach was not applied universally in England in the years following the decision in *Taylors Fashions*,[144] although a Privy Council decision suggested that the strictures of the *Wilmott v Barber* principles had been substantially relaxed and that the real question now seemed to be whether or not the assertion of strict legal rights would be unconscionable.

In *Lim Teng Huan v Ang Swee Chuan*[145] the parties entered into an agreement whereby the plaintiff acknowledged his consent to the building of a house by the defendant on land which they had originally purchased jointly[146] and agreed to exchange his share in the property for unspecified land which the defendant expected to acquire. After the defendant had completed the house and gone into occupation of it, the plaintiff sought a declaration that he was the owner of half the land and the defendant counter-claimed for a declaration that he was entitled to the sole beneficial ownership of the plaintiff's share or alternatively sought an injunction to restrain the plaintiff from entering the land. At the trial the plaintiff abandoned his claim and the defendant's counter-claim was dismissed. The Court of Appeal allowed the defendant's appeal and the Privy Council subsequently allowed the plaintiff's further appeal in part, ordering that on the payment of compensation by the defendant, the plaintiff must transfer his half share in the land to the defendant. The Privy Council inferred that the defendant had completed construction of the house in reliance on the agreement made between the parties and found that it would be unconscionable for the plaintiff to renege on the assumption that the defendant would have a sole absolute interest in the land upon paying compensation to the plaintiff. The plaintiff was therefore estopped from denying the defendant's title to the whole of the land. Lord Browne-Wilkinson referred to the decision of Oliver J in *Taylors Fashions* and said that it showed that in order to found a proprietary estoppel, 'it is enough if, in all the circumstances, it is unconscionable for the representor to go back on the assumption which he has permitted the representee to make'.[147]

Despite the attractiveness of such a straightforward formula, there has been a definite lack of consistency in the approach adopted by the English courts since the decision in *Lim*. In *Matharu v Matharu*,[148] despite the fact that

143. [1982] QB 133, 151-152.
144. See *Coombes v Smith* [1986] 1 WLR 808.
145. [1992] 1 WLR 113.
146. Shortly after the purchase the land was transferred into the name of their respective fathers who both died within a number of years and the plaintiff therefore instituted proceedings as administrator of his father's estate.
147. [1992] 1 WLR 113, 117. As a result of such decisions Halliwell (1994) 14 LS 15 commented that traditional orthodoxy was being challenged and asserted that it was now necessary to recognise that 'the organising concept for the doctrine of estoppel is unconscionability'.
148. (1994) 69 P & CR 93. See Milne (1995) 58 MLR 412; Welsted [1995] Conv 61.

adopting a narrow approach did not affect the outcome in the case, Roch LJ seemed to lay down the requirement that the probanda must be satisfied in all cases if proprietary estoppel is to be relied upon and did not refer to the broader approach based on the notion of unconscionability. However, in *Lloyds Bank plc v Carrick*[149] Morritt LJ made it clear that he agreed with the conclusion of Oliver J in *Taylors Fashions* that 'proof of all those elements or "probanda" is not necessary to found an estoppel.' Thompson, commenting on that decision, stated that 'it is to be welcomed as it continues the trend away from seeking to fit a flexible doctrine into a Procrustean bed, which is frequently not an appropriate thing to do, and should, it is hoped, prevent cases in the future being decided on a somewhat mechanical application of these probanda'.[150]

Subsequently, in *Taylor v Dickens*[151] Judge Weeks seemed decidedly hostile to a suggestion that the court might intervene merely where the assertion of strict legal rights was found to be unconscionable, although he stopped short of seeking to adopt the formulation in *Wilmott*. In his view, if one were to follow such an approach 'one might as well forget the law of contract and issue every judge with a portable palm tree. The days of justice varying with the size of the Lord Chancellor's foot would have returned'.[152] However, the decision in *Taylor v Dickens* met with considerable academic[153] and judicial criticism[154] and more recent decisions confirm that the concept of unconscionability is central to the modern doctrine of proprietary estoppel.[155]

One of the most important decisions in this area is *Gillett v Holt*,[156] in which the plaintiff spent his working life as a farm manager for the first named defendant whom he also regarded as a friend. The first named defendant repeatedly promised the plaintiff that he would succeed to the farming business and the house in which the plaintiff and his family had lived for over 25 years. After relations between the parties deteriorated and the plaintiff was dismissed from his job, the first named defendant made dispositions of the property to the second named defendant in whose favour he also altered his will. Carnwath J dismissed the plaintiff's claim based on proprietary estoppel finding that the representations made could not be construed as an irrevocable promise and that the claim would in any event have failed because the plaintiff had not proved himself to have suffered sufficient detriment in reliance on the first

149. [1996] 4 All ER 630, 640.
150. Thompson [1996] Conv 295, 298.
151. [1998] 1 FLR 806. This decision has been criticised by Thompson [1998] Conv 210, 217 as representing 'an unduly narrow approach to the doctrine of estoppel'.
152. *Ibid.* at 820.
153. Thompson [1998] Conv 210; Swadling [1998] RLR 220; Wells [1999] Conv 462.
154. *Gillett v Holt* [1998] 3 All ER 917 (ChD); [2001] Ch 210, 227 (CA). See further Dixon [2000] CLJ 453; Thompson [2001] Conv 78; Wells [2001] Conv 13.
155. See also *Lloyd v Dugdale* [2002] 2 P & CR 167, 179; *Jennings v Rice* [2003] 1 P & CR 8 at [21], [44]; *Turner v Jacob* [2006] EWHC 1317 (Ch) at [81]; *Harris v Kent* [2007] EWHC 463 (Ch) at [121].
156. [2001] Ch 210.

named defendant's assurances to give rise to proprietary estoppel. However, it is interesting to note that Carnwath J did agree that the overriding principle was that a defendant should be held to his representation 'only if it would be unconscionable to go back on it' although he stressed that estoppel must be founded on an expectation, created or encouraged by the party alleged to be bound by it, in reliance on which the other party has acted to his detriment.

The plaintiff's appeal to the Court of Appeal was allowed, Robert Walker LJ stating that where assurances were intended to be relied on and were in fact relied on it was not necessary to look for an irrevocable promise since it was the other party's detrimental reliance on the promise which made it irrevocable. In relation to the issue of detriment, Robert Walker LJ stated that the trial judge had not stood back and 'look[ed] at the matter in the round' and he was satisfied that if he had, he would have found that the plaintiff's case on this point was an unusually compelling one. Having found in the plaintiff's favour, the Court of Appeal concluded that the minimum equity to do justice to the plaintiff was to convey the farmhouse to him and award him a sufficient sum of money to compensate him for his exclusion from the rest of the farming business. While the approach adopted by Robert Walker LJ illustrates the importance of the traditional elements of assurance, reliance and detriment, his judgment also shows an acceptance of the increasing importance of the principle of unconscionability. As he stated, proprietary estoppel cannot be treated as if it can be subdivided into three or four watertight compartments, so the quality of the assurance may influence the issue of reliance and the concepts of reliance and detriment are often intertwined. In his view, 'the fundamental principle that equity is concerned to prevent unconscionable conduct permeates all elements of the doctrine. In the end the court must look at the matter in the round.'[157] Robert Walker LJ added that the requirement of detriment must be approached as part of a broad inquiry as to whether repudiation of an assurance is or is not unconscionable in all the circumstances and it is clear from the tenor of his judgment that he believed the concept of unconscionability to be fundamental to the imposition of liability.

The same judge in his decision in *Jennings v Rice*[158] adopted a similar approach towards this issue and said that the essence of the doctrine of proprietary estoppel is to do what is necessary to avoid an unconscionable result[159] and that the doctrine only applies if the elements of assurance and detrimental reliance make it unconscionable for the party making the assurance to go back on it.[160] Subsequently, in *Turner v Jacob*,[161] Patten J stated that the courts have emphasised that the central question is whether it would in all the

157. [2001] Ch 210, 225. See also *Ottey v Grundy* [2003] EWCA Civ 1176 at [52]; *Van Laethem v Brooker* [2005] EWHC 1478 (Ch) at [73]; *Q. v Q.* [2009] 1 FLR 935, 966.
158. [2003] 1 P & CR 8.
159. *Ibid.* at [56].
160. *Ibid.* at [44]. See also the *dicta* of Aldous LJ at [21].
161. [2006] EWHC 1317 (Ch).

circumstances be unconscionable for the maker of the representation to be allowed to go back on what he has promised.

However, this emphasis on the notion of unconscionability and lack of reference to the traditional elements of assurance, reliance and detriment has raised concerns. Pawlowski has commented that while 'the modern approach is to explain the doctrine in terms of a general concept of unconscionability, the courts do require the estoppel claimant to prove the three essential elements (i.e. assurance, reliance and detriment) as a prerequisite to a successful claim.'[162] It is important that this fundamental principle is not overlooked and it is perhaps the perception that this may increasingly be the case which partly prompted the House of Lords to take such a strong stand against the concept of unconscionability in its decision in *Cobbe v Yeoman's Row Management Ltd*.[163] In this case the claimant, who was an experienced property developer, entered into an oral agreement with the third named defendant, who was the sole director of the first named defendant, to purchase an apartment block with considerable development potential. The parties agreed that the claimant would apply for planning permission at his own expense and would then develop the property with the defendants obtaining a percentage of any amount by which the gross proceeds exceeded a stated sum. After planning permission was obtained, the defendants sought to renegotiate the terms of the agreement. The claimant brought proceedings alleging, *inter alia*, that the defendants were estopped from denying that he had acquired a beneficial interest in the property or that a constructive trust had arisen in his favour. Etherton J found that the defendants had encouraged the claimant to believe that if he succeeded in obtaining planning permission the oral agreement would be honoured even though it was not legally binding, that in reliance on that belief and with the knowledge and encouragement of the third named defendant he had acted to his detriment, and that in all the circumstances she had taken unconscionable advantage of him. The Court of Appeal dismissed the defendants' appeal but the House of Lords reversed this decision, limiting the claimant's relief to the *in personam* remedy of a *quantum meruit* payment for his services in obtaining planning permission for the property.

Undoubtedly the role which unconscionability plays in establishing a claim based on proprietary estoppel needed reassessment in the light of the decision of the House of Lords in *Cobbe*. However, as closer examination of the opinions of Lords Scott and Walker show, the decision was actually based on a total reappraisal of the circumstances in which proprietary estoppel may arise, particularly in a commercial context. Lord Walker expressed the view that it was not enough 'to hope, or even to have a confident expectation, that the person who has given assurances will eventually do the proper thing.'[164] As

162. Pawlowski (1998) 114 LQR 351, 352.
163. [2008] 1 WLR 1752. See further McFarlane and Robertson [2008] LMCLQ 449; Griffiths [2009] Conv 141; Delany (2009) 31 DULJ 440.
164. [2008] 1 WLR 1752, 1781.

he stated, 'hopes by themselves are not enough' and in his view in the cases in which an estoppel had been successfully established, the claimant had believed that the assurance on which he relied was binding and irrevocable. Lord Scott placed emphasis on the fact that the claimant was seeking to rely on what was from a contractual perspective an incomplete and non-binding agreement. He added that in any event, even if the agreement had been complete,[165] in the absence of the requisite statutory formalities proprietary estoppel could not be employed in order to render enforceable an agreement which was void for non-compliance with the provisions of section 2 of the Law of Property (Miscellaneous Provisions) Act 1989.

As Griffiths has pointed out, this view is difficult to reconcile with the position that the cause of action in an estoppel claim is based not on the unenforceable agreement, but on the defendant's conduct and that compliance with section 2 should not be an issue.[166] This reasoning, namely that the claim is not of a contractual nature and so not affected by section 2, had already been put forward by McFarlane.[167] However, as he and Robertson subsequently pointed out, if Lord Scott's analysis is accepted, proprietary estoppel can no longer be regarded as an independent means by which a party can acquire a right in these circumstances.[168] This leaves the alternative approach, that an agreement might nevertheless be enforceable by way of a constructive trust by virtue of the provisions of section 2(5) of the Act which exempts such trusts from the operation of section 2(1).[169] Yet this raises the spectre of the constructive trust being applied in an artificial manner where established proprietary estoppel principles would be conceptually preferable. As McFarlane and Robertson correctly point out, the reasoning of both Lord Scott and Lord Walker is based on what appears to be 'a dramatic re-interpretation of proprietary estoppel, as it has come to be commonly understood and applied.'[170] In their view Lord Scott's interpretation effectively denies the existence of proprietary estoppel as

165. As Arden LJ commented in *Herbert v Doyle* [2010] EWCA Civ 1095 at [57], if the agreement is incomplete, a claimant cannot utilise the doctrine of proprietary estoppel or a constructive trust to make it binding on the other party by virtue of s. 2(5) of the Law of Property (Miscellaneous Provisions) Act 1989.
166. Griffiths [2009] Conv 141, 144. Note that subsequently in *Herbert v Doyle* [2008] EWHC 1950 (Ch) Mark Herbert QC, sitting as a Deputy High Court judge, stated as follows at [15]: 'Lord Scott's statement of his present view was avowedly *obiter*, and in my view it remains the case that, if all the requirements are otherwise satisfied for a claim based on proprietary estoppel to succeed, the claim will not fail solely because it also consists of an agreement which falls foul of section 2. The analysis of such a case may be that the court gives effect to the proprietary estoppel by recognising or imposing a constructive trust, and it is this which enables section 2(5) to apply.'
167. McFarlane [2005] Conv 501, 521.
168. McFarlane and Robertson [2008] LMCLQ 449, 456.
169. This approach was adopted in cases such as *Yaxley v Gotts* [2000] Ch 162 and *Kinane v Mackie-Conteh* [2005] EWCA Civ 45.
170. McFarlane and Robertson [2008] LMCLQ 449, 453.

a distinct doctrine[171] and cannot be reconciled with its current operation.[172] The basis of Lord Walker's reasoning is also difficult to fathom, for as McFarlane and Robertson point out, proprietary estoppel has often been applied in cases where the claimant could not possibly have believed that the other party was bound to grant the interest promised.[173]

The following analysis set out by Etherton J in the High Court in *Cobbe* is in many respects a more accurate representation of the elements of proprietary estoppel as they have developed and of the role which unconscionability plays in this context:

> I have found as proven facts that Mrs Lisle-Mainwaring, on behalf of [the appellant], encouraged Mr Cobbe to believe that, if Mr Cobbe succeeded in obtaining planning permission in accordance with the Second Agreement, that Agreement would be honoured, even though it was not legally binding, and that, in reliance on that belief, Mr Cobbe, to her knowledge and with her encouragement, acted to his detriment. I have also concluded that, in all the circumstances, she took an unconscionable advantage of him.[174]

Lord Scott stated that both Etherton J at first instance and Mummery LJ in the Court of Appeal regarded the proprietary estoppel conclusion as justified by the unconscionability of the third named defendant's conduct. However, as the passage from Etherton J's judgment shows, the finding of unconscionability was only one aspect of his conclusion that the elements necessary to found a claim based in proprietary estoppel had been established. By re-adjusting the prerequisites to establishing a claim based in proprietary estoppel, the House of Lords has in a sense used the notion of unconscionability as a scapegoat. Lord Scott expressed the view that unconscionability of conduct may well lead to a remedy but, in his opinion, proprietary estoppel could not be the route to it unless the ingredients for such an estoppel were present. As he stated:

> To treat a 'proprietary estoppel equity' as requiring neither a proprietary claim by the claimant nor an estoppel against the defendant but simply

---

171. See also the comment of Etherton [2009] Conv 104, 116 that '[t]aken at face value, the analysis of Lord Scott...spells a severe restriction on the operation of the doctrine [of proprietary estoppel].'
172. See also the comments of Kitchin LJ in *Farrar v Miller* [2018] EWCA Civ 172 at [56] – [63], considered further below.
173. McFarlane and Robertson [2008] LMCLQ 449, 454 refer to cases such as *Re Basham* [1986] 1 WLR 1498; *Wayling v Jones* (1993) 69 P & CR 170; *Campbell v Griffin* [2001] EWCA Civ 990; *Ottey v Grundy* [2003] EWCA Civ 1176.
174. [2005] EWHC 266 (Ch) at [123]. See also the conclusions of Mummery LJ in the Court of Appeal [2006] 1 WLR 2964, 2979.

> unconscionable behaviour is, in my respectful opinion, a recipe for confusion.[175]

He concluded that a finding of proprietary estoppel, based on the unconscionability of the behaviour of the person against whom the finding was made but without any coherent formulation of the content of the estoppel or of the proprietary interest that the estoppel was designed to protect would inevitably invite criticism.[176] Lord Walker expressed similar sentiments and said that equitable estoppel is 'not a sort of joker or wild card to be used whenever the Court disapproves of the conduct of a litigant who seems to have the law on his side.'[177] He referred to the oft-quoted *dictum* of Oliver J in *Taylors Fashions Ltd v Liverpool Victoria Trustees Co. Ltd*,[178] and said while this passage certainly favours a broad or unified approach to equitable estoppel, 'it is emphatically not a licence for abandoning careful analysis for unprincipled and subjective judicial opinion.'[179]

However, it should be noted that there was no real evidence prior to the decision of the House of Lords in *Cobbe* that the traditional elements of assurance, reliance and detriment would be dispensed with and unconscionability has merely been viewed as an overarching concept in this context which does not obviate the need for assurance and detrimental reliance to be established. Lord Walker stated that in his view Etherton J and the Court of Appeal 'stretched the boundaries of the doctrine of equitable estoppel too far,'[180] but, with respect, the conclusions reached were similar to those arrived at in a number of non-commercial cases where assurances had been made and detrimental reliance established.[181] Perhaps the key factor was the commercial nature of the relationship between the parties in *Cobbe*. Lord Walker had voiced concerns about how the courts 'should be very slow to introduce uncertainty into commercial transactions'[182] and a narrow interpretation of his speech might be that his views were limited to a situation where an incomplete agreement which was not legally binding existed in a commercial situation. However,

175. [2008] 1 WLR 1752, 1762.
176. Lord Scott made reference to the comment of Deane J in his judgment in *Muschinski v Dodds* (1985) 160 CLR 583, 615-616 that a constructive trust should not represent 'a medium for the indulgence of idiosyncratic notions of fairness and justice' and suggested that similar criticism might apply in this context.
177. [2008] 1 WLR 1752, 1775.
178. [1982] QB 133, 151-152.
179. [2008] 1 WLR 1752, 1780.
180. *Ibid.* at 1786.
181. See e.g. *Gillett v Holt* [2001] Ch 210; *Jennings v Rice* [2003] 1 P & CR 8.
182. [2008] 1 WLR 1752, 1785. See also *A. v B.* [2008] EWHC 2687 (Ch) at [201]. Similarly, in *Reveille Independent LLC v Anotech International (UK) Ltd* [2016] EWCA Civ 443 at [42], Cranston J referred to the need for certainty in commercial contracts which 'applies as well in commercial negotiations and to the question of whether a contract has come into existence.'

the much more general condemnation of the role of unconscionability voiced by both Lord Walker and Lord Scott had the potential to undermine the scope of the doctrine of proprietary estoppel, even in a non-commercial context.[183]

The approach taken by the House of Lords in *Cobbe* was also adopted by the Privy Council in *Capron v Turks & Caicos Islands*,[184] in which the foundation of the appellant's claim based on proprietary estoppel rested on the assertion that both sides intended that they would be bound by an agreement. However, the Privy Council concluded that there was at most an intention or an aspiration that there would at some future time be a binding agreement. Lord Kerr stated that the application of the doctrine of proprietary estoppel depended on proof by the appellant that he has relied to his detriment upon a reasonable belief, arising from a clear representation by the defendant that he was entitled to acquire a certain interest in land. In this case the height of the appellant's expectation could only have been that a contract, the exact terms of which remained to be settled, would be entered into at some future unspecified date and the appellant could identify what 'certain interest' in land he claimed to have been entitled to receive. Lord Kerr stated that, as was clear from the decision in *Yeoman's Row*, unconscionable behaviour could not stand alone as the basis for a finding of proprietary estoppel. As he stated, '[w]here there is no ground for a belief that the claimant was entitled to acquire a certain interest in land, the fact that the behaviour of the person against whom proprietary estoppel is sought to be established was unconscionable cannot fill the gap that exists in the essential proofs required for the doctrine to come into play.'[185]

However, the decision of the House of Lords in *Thorner v Major*[186] suggests that a more flexible approach will be taken towards the use of the concept of unconscionability where proprietary estoppel is not invoked in a commercial context. Certainly McFarlane and Robertson have expressed the view that the decision in *Thorner*, by implicitly rejecting the limitations set out by the House of Lords in *Cobbe*, allows proprietary estoppel to continue to perform its role of protecting those who reasonably rely on assurances in relation to another's land.[187] However, as they point out, the inquiry in relation to whether

183. Lord Neuberger commented in *Thorner v Major* [2009] 1 WLR 776, 803 that the claimant's case failed in *Cobbe* because he was effectively seeking to invoke proprietary estoppel to give effect to a contract which the parties had intentionally and consciously not entered into and because he was simply seeking a remedy for unconscionable behaviour.
184. [2010] UKPC 2. See also *A. v B.* [2008] EWHC 2687 (Ch). However, *Cobbe* was distinguished in *Saunders v Al Himaly* [2017] EWHC 2219 (Ch).
185. *Ibid.* at [39].
186. [2009] 1 WLR 776.
187. McFarlane and Robertson (2009) 125 LQR 535, 542. See also *MacDonald v Frost* [2009] WTLR 1815 at [8].

an assurance has been made and whether reliance on it is reasonable will have to be sensitive to the background of the case.[188]

Clearly, different considerations will apply where the relationship between the parties is arm's length and commercial on the one hand and familial or personal on the other hand. In the former case, the parties would be expected to enter into a contract but may have chosen not to at that point in the transaction whereas in the latter, the entering into a formal contractual relationship may never have been envisaged at any stage. These distinctions have been explored in a number of decisions of the New South Wales Court of Appeal. In *DHJPM Pty Ltd v Blackthorn Resources Ltd*[189] Meagher JA stated that '[w]hether a representation or promise has created or encouraged an expectation which if relied upon will be sufficient to give rise to an equity obviously depends upon the circumstances including the nature of the relationship between the parties and whether they contemplate that any interest to be granted or promise to be performed is to be created by a binding contract.' So, as the subsequent decision of the New South Wales Court of Appeal in *Doueihi v Construction Technologies Australia Pty Ltd*[190] makes clear, an estoppel may arise where the evidence establishes that the parties expected that the respondent would be granted a lease without entering into a contract, unlike in *Cobbe*, which the Court of Appeal characterised as a case where the parties never expected that an interest in the property would be acquired otherwise than under a legally binding contract.

An excellent analysis of the role which unconscionability plays in the doctrine of proprietary estoppel is provided by Dixon, who suggests that it has a relatively narrow meaning when taken to be a defining feature of the doctrine and that it can be confined to predictable and coherent limits.[191] He puts forward the view that unconscionability may arise if a landowner makes a sufficiently definite assurance and this carries with it the further assurance that the right will be granted despite the absence of the normal formalities.[192] So, in his view unconscionability will exist when this 'formality assurance' is withdrawn after detrimental reliance.[193]

The Role of Unconscionability in this Jurisdiction

The concept of unconscionability also appears to be playing a role in this

188. As Lord Neuberger noted in *Thorner v Major* [2009] 1 WLR 776, 803, the claim of estoppel in *Cobbe* arose against a very different background.
189. (2011) 285 ALR 311, 325.
190. (2016) 333 ALR 151.
191. Dixon (2010) 30 LS 408.
192. Dixon suggests (at 417) that in the so called 'failed contract' cases, such as *Cobbe*, 'it is more difficult to establish unconscionability because the attempted use of formality usually will mean that no assurance was given that formality would not apply.'
193. *Ibid.* at 417.

jurisdiction, although very little detailed analysis has been devoted to it. In *McMahon v Kerry Co. Council*[194] Finlay P stressed the importance of assessing the consequences of the actions of the parties both from the point of view of the plaintiff and of the defendant. The plaintiffs bought a plot of land for the purpose of building a school, however, shortly afterwards they abandoned their plan and did not visit the site again for a further three years. They then discovered that the defendant council, which had originally known of their purchase, was preparing to build on the land and, upon a complaint being made, the work ceased. Four years later the defendant built two houses on the site and the following year the plaintiffs discovered this and instituted proceedings to recover possession of the site. Counsel for the defendant relied on *Ramsden v Dyson* but Finlay P concluded that the facts of the case did not fall within the principle laid down by Lord Cranworth LC in that case and said that there was no question of the plaintiffs remaining wilfully passive when the defendant commenced to build on their land. However, Finlay P held that in the circumstances, it would be unjust and unconscionable that the plaintiffs should recover possession and he held that they were only entitled to the market value of the site without the houses and to damages. With reference to *Ramsden*, Finlay P stated that the principles of equity set out in that case depended 'not exclusively on the action or inaction of the plaintiff or on the state of knowledge but have regard also to the action of the defendant.' He continued:

> If a court applying equitable principles is truly to act as a court of conscience then it seems to me unavoidable that it should consider not only conduct on the part of the plaintiff with particular regard to whether it is wrong and wilful but also conduct on the part of the defendant and furthermore the consequences and the justice of the consequences both from the point of view of the plaintiff and of the defendant.[195]

Unconscionability also appeared to provide the key to the imposition of liability in *Carter v Ross*,[196] where Murphy J stated that the courts will hold a promisor to his promise even if it is made without consideration where it would be unconscionable to permit him to resile from the promise which he had made. The defendant had already transferred a field in which the plaintiff had built his house to the latter. Murphy J concluded that he doubted whether there had ever been an assurance given by the defendant so that his decision to leave his farm to a third party could be deemed to be unconscionable or unacceptable. In his view the plaintiff's claim to the rest of the defendant's farm was based on a 'very vague promise and on minimal detriment to the plaintiff' and he concluded that his claim must be dismissed.

---

194. [1981] ILRM 419.
195. *Ibid.* at 421.
196. High Court (Murphy J) 8 December 2000.

However, an example of a successful claim in which the unconscionability principle played a role is the decision of Hardiman J, sitting as a judge of the High Court on a Circuit Appeal, in *Owens v Duggan*.[197] Hardiman J referred to the *dicta* of Finlay P in *McMahon* set out above and to the statement of Robert Walker LJ in *Gillett v Holt*[198] to the effect that the requirement of detriment must be approached as part of a broad inquiry as to whether repudiation of an assurance is unconscionable in all the circumstances of the case. He concluded that the plaintiffs had suffered detriment and expressed the view that the actions of the defendants in declining to release a right of way and transfer land to the plaintiffs was unconscionable. Reference was also made to the principle of unconscionability by Edwards J in *An Cumann Peile Boitheimeach Teoranta v Albion Properties Ltd*,[199] in which he upheld the defendants' counterclaim for relief on the grounds of proprietary estoppel and concluded that the plaintiffs held the lands in question on a constructive trust for the benefit of the defendants.

The concept of unconscionability also played a role in the judgment of Laffoy J in *Coyle v Finnegan*,[200] in which she commented that the decision of the Court of Appeal in *Gillett v Holt* might 'be properly characterised as a step in the evolutionary process of the development of the doctrine of proprietary estoppel'. Laffoy J found that there had been an express representation or assurance by the deceased to the plaintiff that, if the plaintiff assisted the deceased in running his farm, the deceased would leave the farm to the plaintiff in his will. She accepted that the plaintiff had acted in reliance on the assurances given to him by the deceased and that the plaintiff had suffered detriment in consequence of his reasonable reliance on the deceased's assurances. Laffoy J concluded that looking at the facts in the round, she was satisfied that it would be unconscionable if the plaintiff was not recompensed for the labours and services he had provided to the deceased over a period of years. She added that it would be unconscionable if the defendants were to acquire the deceased's farm under his will free from any entitlement of the plaintiff to be recompensed. Therefore, in her view, equity required that the plaintiff be reasonably remunerated for the labours and services which he had given the deceased and she held that he should have a charge or lien on the lands for a sum equivalent to such reasonable remuneration.

The Extent of the Remedy

The Minimum Equity

It has been recognised that 'of all doctrines, equitable estoppel is surely one

197. High Court (Hardiman J) 2 April 2004. These principles were referred to by O'Malley J in *Prunty v Crowley* [2016] IEHC 293 at [80].
198. [2001] Ch 210, 232.
199. [2008] IEHC 447.
200. [2013] IEHC 463 at [26].

of the most flexible'[201] and that the court must look at the circumstances of each case in order to determine how the equity which arises can be satisfied.[202] It is also important to appreciate that the raising of an estoppel does not give rise to a particular form of remedy and that 'the remedy required to satisfy an equity varies according to the circumstances of the case'.[203] One of the most striking features of proprietary estoppel is the wide range of responses open to the court.[204] An examination of the case law demonstrates that the remedies granted by the courts range dramatically and can extend to the conveyance of the fee simple interest[205] or be limited to a licence to occupy property for life.[206] In other cases, the equity has been held to be satisfied by the granting of a right of way[207] or by the mere denial of the legal owner's claim to possession.[208] Clearly flexibility is the hallmark of relief based on estoppel so, where appropriate, a fee simple interest in remainder has been granted[209] or a conveyance of the fee simple ordered subject to the payment of compensation.[210]

In *Crabb v Arun District Council*[211] Scarman LJ sought to lay down a general framework for determining the extent of the relief which should be granted where he stated as follows:

> The court, having analysed and assessed the conduct and relationship of the parties, has to answer three questions. First, is there an equity established? Secondly, what is the extent of the equity, if one is established? And, thirdly what is the relief appropriate to satisfy the equity?

Scarman LJ went on to say that having established that an equity arose in the plaintiff's favour, the court would then analyse the minimum equity to do

201. *Amalgmated Investment and Property Co. Ltd v Texas Commerce International Bank Ltd* [1982] QB 84, 103 *per* Robert Goff J.
202. *Plimmer v Mayor of Wellington* (1884) 9 App Cas 699, 714 *per* Sir Arthur Hobhouse. See also *Williams v Staite* [1979] Ch 291, 301 *per* Cumming-Bruce LJ; *Gillett v Holt* [2001] Ch 210, 235 *per* Robert Walker LJ. Blackburne J has commented in *Clark v Clark* [2006] EWHC 275 (Ch) at [38] that 'each case must turn on its own facts in what is a particularly fact-sensitive area of law'.
203. *Waltons Stores (Interstate) Ltd v Maher* (1988) 164 CLR 387, 419. See also *Voyce v Voyce* (1991) 62 P & CR 290, 296 *per* Nicholls LJ.
204. Cooke (1997) 17 LS 258, 266. As Mummery LJ commented in *McGuane v Welch* [2008] 2 P & CR 24 at [42], 'the remedies for proprietary estoppel are flexible'.
205. *Dillwyn v Llewelyn* (1862) 4 De GF & J 517; *Pascoe v Turner* [1979] 1 WLR 431; *Voyce v Voyce* (1991) 62 P & CR 290.
206. *Inwards v Baker* [1965] 2 QB 29; *Greasley v Cooke* [1980] 1 WLR 1306.
207. *Crabb v Arun District Council* [1976] Ch 179; *ER Ives Investment Ltd v High* [1967] 2 QB 379.
208. *Jones v Jones* [1977] 1 WLR 438.
209. *Smyth v Halpin* [1997] 2 ILRM 38.
210. *Lim Teng Huan v Ang Swee Chuan* [1992] 1 WLR 113.
211. [1976] Ch 179, 192-193.

justice to the plaintiff.[212] This minimum equity approach was also employed in *Pascoe v Turner*,[213] where the Court of Appeal considered the minimum equity to do justice to the defendant having regard to the way in which she altered her position to her detriment as a result of the acquiescence and encouragement of the plaintiff. In the circumstances, the Court of Appeal concluded that the equity could only be satisfied 'by compelling the plaintiff to give effect to his promise and her expectations' and the plaintiff was ordered to execute a conveyance of the property to the defendant.

However, the criticism that the Court of Appeal in *Crabb* and *Pascoe* failed to explain the significance of the word 'minimum' in this context is a fair one[214] and while the courts in England have made further attempts to explain the factors which should be taken into account in giving effect to the minimum equity,[215] there have also been examples of decisions in which relief has been granted without any reference to the concept.[216] In the decision of the Court of Appeal in *Gillett v Holt*[217] Robert Walker LJ stated that the court approaches its task of satisfying the equity in such cases 'in a cautious way' in order to achieve the 'minimum equity'.[218] He added that, having identified the maximum extent of the equity, the court's aim should be to determine the minimum required to satisfy it and do justice between the parties. It has also been suggested that the reference to 'minimum' in this context 'does not require the court to be constitutionally parsimonious, but it does implicitly recognise that the court must also do justice to the defendant'.[219] So, as will be explored more fully below, the court now tends to ask 'what…is the minimum equity necessary to do justice and to avoid an unconscionable and disproportionate result?'[220]

---

212. *Ibid.* at 198. See also *Waltons Stores (Interstate) Ltd v Maher* (1988) 164 CLR 387, 404. As Robertson has commented in (1996) 20 Melb Univ L Rev 805, 816, this reference to 'minimum equity' could be construed as a reference to the minimum necessary to prevent the representee suffering detriment as a result of his or her reliance, or as the minimum relief necessary to fulfil the representee's expectation.
213. [1979] 1 WLR 431.
214. See further Finn, 'Equitable Estoppel' in *Essays in Equity* (ed. Finn, 1985) p. 91.
215. *Baker v Baker* (1993) 25 HLR 408.
216. *Wayling v Jones* (1995) 69 P & CR 170.
217. [2001] Ch 210, 235.
218. See also *Flowermix Ltd v Site Development (Ferndown) Ltd* Chancery Divison (Arden J) 11 April 2000 at [37] and *Campbell v Griffin* [2001] EWCA Civ 990 at [30].
219. *Jennings v Rice* [2003] 1 P & CR 8 at [48] *per* Robert Walker LJ. See also *Sutcliffe v Lloyd* [2008] EWHC 1329 (Ch) at [4].
220. *Stallion v Albert Stallion Holdings (Great Britain) Ltd* [2010] 2 FLR 78, 105. However, the courts in Australia seem to have moved away from applying the 'minimum equity' approach. See *Sullivan v Sullivan* [2006] NSWCA 312 at [23] *Delaforce v Simpson-Cook (2010) 78 NSWLR 483* at [59]. See also *Ashton v Pratt* (2015) 318 ALR 260, 287 in the context of promissory estoppel.

The Expectation-based and Reliance-based Approaches

There has always tended to be a degree of uncertainty about what the doctrine of proprietary estoppel should seek to achieve. Is it designed to fulfil the expectations of a party which have arisen as a result of his dealings with another or is its role the more limited one of reversing any detriment suffered as a result of reliance on the promise of another?[221] Robertson has summarised these alternative approaches in the following terms:

> The court can protect the reliance interest in an estoppel case by compensating the claimant for the loss suffered as a result of his or her reliance on the relevant promise or representation. Alternatively, the court can protect the claimant's expectation interest, by providing a remedy which puts the claimant in the position he or she would have occupied had the relevant promise been fulfilled.[222]

Generally speaking, the expectation-based approach leads to the granting of a more extensive remedy and where a claimant's expectations are fulfilled this may often lead to more far reaching relief than that merited by the detrimental reliance.[223] Conversely, if the fulfilment of the expectation is the maximum extent of the remedy this may lead to a failure to fully compensate for any reliance,[224] although in practice this is unlikely to happen.

It has been suggested that the reliance and expectation-based interests overlap since the grant of expectation relief should also ensure that no detriment is suffered as a result of the representee's reliance.[225] As McHugh J commented in the decision of the High Court of Australia in *Commonwealth of Australia v Verwayen*,[226] 'often the only way to prevent the promisee suffering detriment will be to enforce the promise'. However, the important question is whether the application of these alternative approaches to a given situation will lead to different results. While Priestley has suggested that 'there may not in the end be any great difference'[227] between them, the better view is that while the approaches will only occasionally yield different results, there will be cases in which the distinction is a significant one.[228] This is well illustrated by the following example provided by Deane J in the course of his judgment in

221. For a discussion of the reliance-interest and expectation-interest in the context of damages for breach of contract, see Fuller and Purdue (1936) 46 Yale LJ 52.
222. Robertson (1998) 18 LS 360, 361.
223. See *Pascoe v Turner* [1979] 1 WLR 431 in which the defendant was awarded the fee simple interest in a property in circumstances where she had carried out repairs and improvements to it.
224. *Inwards v Baker* [1965] 2 QB 29 is possibly an example of this.
225. Robertson (1996) 20 Melb Univ LR 805, 808.
226. (1990) 170 CLR 394, 501.
227. Priestly, 'Estoppel: Liability and Remedy?' in *Equity, Fiduciaries and Trusts* (ed. Waters, 1993) p. 290.
228. Robertson (1996) 20 Melb Univ LR 805, 806 and (1998) 18 LS 360, 368.

Commonwealth of Australia v Verwayen.[229] If a party spends $100 erecting a shed on a piece of land belonging to another worth $1 million on the faith of a representation that the land will be his, clearly the expectation and reliance-based models will yield significantly different results. Under the former approach, the court would have to transfer the land in order to fulfil the expectation whereas in accordance with the latter all that would be necessary would be to compensate for the detriment suffered, namely the expenditure of $100.

The expectation-based approach can be traced back to decisions such as that of Lord Kingsdown in *Ramsden v Dyson*,[230] where he stated that in cases where a party has relied on a shared assumption that he would acquire rights in the land of another, 'a court of equity will compel the landlord to give effect to such a promise or expectation'. More recent examples of this approach include *Watson v Goldsbrough*,[231] where Browne-Wilkinson VC stated that in determining what remedy to grant, it could not be right 'to give the plaintiffs a right greater than that which they themselves expected to receive or thought they were going to receive when they incurred the expenditure which gave rise to the estoppel'. Similarly, in *Pascoe v Turner*,[232] Cumming-Bruce LJ stated that the equity to which the facts of the case gave rise could only be satisfied 'by compelling the plaintiff to give effect to his promise and [the defendant's] expectations' and in *Re Basham*,[233] Edward Nugee QC, sitting as a Deputy High Court judge, said that the extent of the equity was to make good 'so far as may fairly be done between the parties, the expectations which the deceased encouraged'.

The expectation-based approach may be subject to the criticism that it is more likely to lead to the creation of informal rights in land and that 'it threatens an improper outflanking of the requirement for contractual consideration'.[234] As Mason CJ stated in *Commonwealth of Australia v Verwayen*,[235] the breaking of a promise, while morally reprehensible, is not unconscionable in the sense that equity should necessarily remedy any consequential loss and he added that 'with estoppel, something more than a broken promise is required'.

It may be argued that, in addition to the expectation-based model, Lord Kingsdown in *Ramsden v Dyson*[236] also contemplated a reliance-based approach to granting a remedy 'in the shape of compensation for the expenditure' where the expectation interest was uncertain. However, the clearest statements in support of this model occur in a number of decisions of the High Court of

229. (1990) 170 CLR 394, 441.
230. (1866) LR 1 HL 129, 170.
231. (1986) 1 EGLR 265, 267.
232. [1979] 1 WLR 431, 439.
233. [1986] 1 WLR 1498, 1510.
234. Gray and Gray, *Elements of Land Law* (5th ed., 2009) p. 1242.
235. (1990) 170 CLR 394, 416.
236. (1866) LR 1 HL 129, 171.

Australia. In *Grundt v Great Boulder Proprietary Gold Mines Ltd*,[237] Dixon J stated that the purpose of the doctrine of estoppel is 'to avoid or prevent a detriment to the party asserting the estoppel by compelling the opposite party to adhere to the assumption upon which the former acted or abstained from acting. This means that the real detriment or harm from which the law seeks to give protection is that which would flow from the change of position if the assumption were deserted that led to it.' Subsequently, in *Waltons Stores (Interstate) Ltd v Maher*,[238] Brennan J stated that the equity is to be satisfied by avoiding a detriment suffered in reliance on an induced assumption, not by direct enforcement of the assumption, and that its satisfaction calls for the enforcement of a promise only as a means of avoiding the detriment and only to the extent necessary to achieve that object.[239] In his view, '[t]he object of equity is not to compel the party bound to fulfil the assumption or expectation; it is to avoid the detriment which, if the expectation goes unfulfilled, will be suffered by the party who has been induced to act or to abstain from acting thereon.'[240]

The majority of the High Court of Australia also advocated the application of a reliance-based approach in *Commonwealth of Australia v Verwayen*[241] and several members of the court considered its operation in some detail. Mason CJ stated that equity is concerned, not with making good the assumption, but with doing what is necessary to prevent the suffering of detriment; to do more would sit uncomfortably with the underlying foundation of the general principle which was the concept of unconscionability. In his view:

> [A] court of common law or equity may do what is required, but not more, to prevent a person who has relied upon an assumption as to a present, past or future state of affairs … which assumption the party estopped has induced him to hold, from suffering detriment in reliance upon the assumption as a result of the denial of its correctness. A central element of that doctrine is that there must be a proportionality between the remedy and the detriment which is its purpose to avoid. It would be wholly inequitable and unjust to insist upon a disproportionate making good of the relevant assumption.[242]

McHugh J added that the enforcement of promises is not the object of estoppel and that 'equitable estoppel is aimed at preventing unconscionable conduct

237. (1937) 59 CLR 641, 674. Cooke has commented in (1997) 17 LS 258, 278 that 'it is likely that Dixon J's words have added weight to the reliance loss theory although… it may be that no such idea was intended by him.'
238. (1988) 164 CLR 387, 433.
239. *Ibid.* at 427. See also *Commonwealth of Australia v Verwayen* (1990) 170 CLR 394, 475 *per* Toohey J.
240. *Ibid.* at 423.
241. (1990) 170 CLR 394.
242. *Ibid.* at 413.

and seeks to prevent detriment to the promisee'.[243] Brennan J agreed that the remedy is not designed to enforce the promise, although in some situations, the minimum equity will not be satisfied by anything short of giving effect to this promise.[244]

This reliance-based approach was welcomed by Robertson as providing a more coherent basis for the grant of relief[245] but it was criticised by others, such as Cooke, on the ground that it would 'confuse and emasculate' the law of estoppel.[246] However, Robertson concedes that the Australian courts have not really embraced this model following *Verwayen*[247] and he acknowledges that even where a reliance-based approach is applied, the circumstances of a case will often require the granting of expectation relief on the grounds that the detriment suffered may be difficult to quantify.[248] In the subsequent decision of *Giumelli v Giumelli*[249] the High Court of Australia rejected the argument that *Verwayen* was authority for the proposition that relief should not extend beyond the reversal of detriment.

In a sense the decisions in *Waltons Stores* and *Verwayen* marked the high water mark of the reliance-based approach in the common law world,[250] and the more recent Australian authorities have moved away from this model of relief. In its joint judgment in *Giumelli v Giumelli*[251] the High Court favoured a *prima facie* entitlement to fulfilling 'the assumed state of affairs'.[252] However, it suggested that this would be qualified if that relief would 'exceed what could be justified by the requirements of conscientious conduct and would be unjust to the estopped party'.[253] Similar principles were applied in a number of decisions of the Court of Appeal of New South Wales[254] and of Victoria.[255] The most important recent Australian authority, in which the approach adopted in *Giumelli* was applied, is the decision of the High Court of Australia in *Sidhu v Van Dyke*.[256] In a joint judgment, French CJ, Kiefel, Bell and Keane JJ acknowledged that there may be cases where it would be inequitable to insist upon a disproportionate making good of an assumption but concluded that in the circumstances, as in *Giumelli*, justice between the parties would not be

243. *Ibid.* at 501.
244. *Ibid.* at 429.
245. Robertson (1998) 18 LS 360, 363.
246. Cooke (1997) 17 LS 258, 280-281.
247. Robertson (1996) 20 Melb Univ LR 805, 828-847.
248. *Ibid.* at 835. See also Robertson (1997) 19 Syd L Rev 32, 46.
249. (1999) 196 CLR 101, 120.
250. See e.g. the survey of decisions in Australia following *Verwayen* conducted by Robertson, see (1996) 20 Melb Univ LR 805, 828-829.
251. (1999) 196 CLR 101, 123.
252. *Commonwealth of Australia v Verwayen* (1990) 170 CLR 394, 443 *per* Deane J.
253. *Ibid* at 442.
254. *Sullivan v Sullivan* [2006] NSWCA 312; *Delaforce v Simpson-Cook (2010) 78 NSWLR 483; Ashton v Pratt (2015) 318 ALR 260.*
255. *Harrison v Harrison* [2013] VSCA 170.
256. (2014) 308 ALR 232.

done by a remedy the value of which fell short of holding the appellant to his promises. While accepting that the court should go no further than is necessary to prevent unconscionable conduct, it concluded that 'where the unconscionable conduct consists of resiling from a promise or assurance which has induced conduct to the other party's detriment, the relief which is necessary in this sense is usually that which reflects the value of the promise.'[257]

An Approach Based on Proportionality

Prior to the decision of the Court of Appeal in *Jennings v Rice*,[258] there had been some signs, both in Australia and in England, of the increasing importance of the principle of proportionality in satisfying the equity which arises where an estoppel is raised. In *Waltons Stores (Interstate) Ltd v Maher*[259] Brennan J stated that in determining what remedy is appropriate, the court as a court of conscience goes no further than is necessary to prevent unconscionable conduct. Subsequently, in *Commonwealth of Australia v Verwayen*,[260] as noted above, Mason CJ developed this theme, stating that a court may do what is required, but not more, to prevent a person who has relied upon an assumption, which the party estopped has induced him to hold, from suffering detriment in reliance upon the assumption.[261] In his view, 'a central element of [the] doctrine is that there must be a proportionality between the remedy and the detriment which is its purpose to avoid'.[262]

In *Sledmore v Dalby*[263] Hobhouse LJ quoted extensively from the judgment of Mason CJ in *Verwayen*, which he said clearly emphasised the need for proportionality. In his view, '[t]his is to say little more than that the end result must be a just one having regard to the assumption made by the party asserting the estoppel and the detriment which he has experienced.'[264] In this context it is also worth referring to the *dictum* of Robert Walker LJ in *Gillett v Holt*[265] to the effect that the court's aim should be, having identified the maximum extent of the equity, to form a view as to what is the minimum required to satisfy it

257. *Ibid.* at [85]. See further Liew (2019) 39 OJLS 183, who suggests that the authorities in England and Australia are more closely aligned than might have been thought on this issue.
258. [2003] 1 P & CR 8.
259. (1988) 164 CLR 387, 419. See also *Commonwealth of Australia v Verwayen* (1990) 170 CLR 394, 501 *per* McHugh J.
260. (1990) 170 CLR 394, 413.
261. See also at 412 *per* Mason CJ and at 475 *per* Toohey J.
262. *Ibid.* at 413. Quoted with approval by Hobhouse LJ in *Sledmore v Dalby* (1996) 72 P & CR 196, 208.
263. (1996) 72 P & CR 196. See further Pawlowski (1997) 113 LQR 232 and Milne [1997] CLJ 34.
264. *Ibid.* at 209.
265. [2001] Ch 211, 237.

and do justice between the parties, in other words to avoid overcompensating the claimant.

However, it was not until the decision of the Court of Appeal in *Jennings v Rice*[266] that the role which the concept of proportionality can play in this context was analysed in any detail. The claimant had worked for the deceased for many years on a part-time basis as a gardener and subsequently ran errands and carried out maintenance work for her. During the last three years of her life, he also slept at her house to provide her with security and helped to care for her, although he had not been paid for many years. The deceased died intestate despite having made representations to the claimant that her house would be his one day and that she would 'see him right'. The trial judge held that the claimant was entitled to an award of £200,000 pursuant to the doctrine of proprietary estoppel on the basis that this was the minimum necessary to satisfy the equity in the case before the court. The claimant appealed contending that he was entitled to the deceased's whole estate (£1.285 million) or at least to a sum equal to the value of her house and furniture (£435,000), but the Court of Appeal dismissed his appeal. In considering how the equity in this case should be satisfied, Aldous LJ stated that '[t]he value of that equity will depend upon all the circumstances including the expectation and the detriment.' [267] In his view the task of the court is to do justice and the most essential requirement is that there must be proportionality between the expectation and the detriment.

Robert Walker LJ stated that if the claimant's expectations are uncertain their specific vindication cannot be the appropriate test. Equally, a problem will arise if the court is not satisfied that the high level of a claimant's expectations is fairly derived from the assurances given, which may have only justified a lower level of expectation[268] and in such cases he suggested that the court should merely take the claimant's expectations as a starting point. He continued as follows:

> It is no coincidence that these statements of principle refer to satisfying the equity (rather than satisfying, or vindicating, the claimant's expectations). The equity arises not from the claimant's expectations alone, but from the combination of expectations, detrimental reliance, and the unconscionableness of allowing the benefactor (or the deceased benefactor's estate) to go back on the assurances.[269]

Robert Walker LJ added that while it may be the natural response of the court to seek to fulfil the claimant's expectations, if these are uncertain, extravagant

---

266. [2003] 1 P & CR 8. See further Thompson [2003] Conv 225.
267. *Ibid.* at [36]. See also *Q. v Q.* [2009] 1 FLR 935, 980; *Malik v Kalyan* [2010] EWCA Civ 113 at [31].
268. See also the comment of Thompson [2001] Conv 78, 85 to the effect that '[t]he acts of reliance in question may be of considerably less value than the expectation and to fulfil the expectation in its entirety may be to overcompensate the claimant.'
269. [2003] 1 P & CR 8 at [49].

or out of all proportion to the detriment which he has suffered, the court can and should recognise that the claimant's equity should be satisfied in another and generally more limited way.[270] However, he stressed that this did not mean that the court should abandon expectations completely and look to the detriment suffered by the claimant as defining the appropriate measure of relief and he added that in many cases detriment may be even more difficult to quantify in financial terms than the claimant's expectations. Robert Walker LJ stated that while detriment can be quantified with reasonable precision if, for example, it consists solely of expenditure on improvements to another person's house, in which case an equitable charge for the expenditure may be sufficient to satisfy the equity, often it may be difficult to quantify in financial terms. While he accepted that compensation for reliance loss may sometimes be appropriate under English law, this would only be the case where, on the facts, a higher measure of relief would amount to overcompensation. Aldous LJ was more forthright in his rejection of the reliance-based approach and said that he did not believe it necessary to examine any of the Australian authorities which appeared to lean towards the view that an award should compensate detriment, as they 'did not reflect the law of this country'.

Having accepted that the court may exercise a wide discretion in such cases, Robert Walker LJ expressed the view that it would be unwise to attempt any comprehensive enumeration of the factors relevant to the exercise of this discretion or to suggest any hierarchy of factors. However, he went on to say that they included: misconduct on the claimant's part; particularly oppressive behaviour on the part of the defendant; recognition of the fact that people cannot be compelled to live peaceably together; alterations in the benefactor's assets and circumstances; the likely effect of taxation; and, to a limited degree, other legal or moral claims on the benefactor or his estate. Robert Walker LJ ultimately agreed with the view expressed by Hobhouse LJ in *Sledmore v Dalby*[271] that the principle of proportionality between remedy and detriment, emphasised by Mason CJ in *Commonwealth of Australia v Verwayen*,[272] is also relevant in England. In his view, 'the essence of the doctrine of proprietary estoppel is to do what is necessary to avoid an unconscionable result, and a disproportionate remedy cannot be the right way of going about that.'[273] In dismissing the appeal, both Aldous and Robert Walker LJJ concluded that the trial judge had exercised his discretion correctly in confining the claimant's award to £200,000 and they stated that they would not interfere with his finding.

A similar approach to that advocated in *Jennings* was also applied by the Court of Appeal in *Campbell v Griffin*, [274] where Robert Walker LJ stated that a court will be 'cautious' in approaching the issue of how the equity should be

270. *Ibid.* at [50]. See also *Moore v Moore* [2018] EWCA Civ 2669 at [29].
271. (1996) 72 P & CR 196, 208-209.
272. (1990) 170 CLR 394.
273. [2003] 1 P & CR 8 at [56]. See also *Hopper v Hopper* [2008] 1 FCR 557 at [104].
274. [2001] EWCA Civ 990. See further Thompson [2003] Conv 157.

satisfied in cases of estoppel. The appellant, who had initially been a lodger in the home of an elderly couple, looked after them as they became increasingly frail and was assured by them that he had a home for life. The Court of Appeal concluded that granting the appellant a life interest in the property would be disproportionate and instead held that he was entitled to a charge of £35,000 on the house which would have been worth about £160,000 unencumbered and with vacant possession. This principle that the extent of the remedy should be proportionate to the detriment suffered also found favour with the Court of Appeal in *Ottey v Grundy*,[275] where Arden LJ commented that the remedy should be no more than is necessary to protect against unconscionable conduct and must be proportionate to the detriment suffered.

A proportionate approach was also taken by the Court of Appeal in *Powell v Benney*,[276] in which the claimants, who had assisted the deceased with his day-to-day affairs over the years, sought to enforce his promise to leave two houses to them. Sir Peter Gibson said that he was left wholly unpersuaded that the trial judge had been wrong to form the view that the expectation of the claimants to receive the properties, which were worth £280,000, was out of all proportion to the detriment which they had suffered. In his view the trial judge could properly recognise that their equity should be satisfied in another and more limited way and he upheld the decision to grant them a monetary award of £20,000. However, it has also been accepted, as in the decision of the Court of Appeal in *Holman v Howes*,[277] that in some cases the minimum equity needed to do justice does require the making good of an assurance.

Pawlowski has suggested that the decisions in *Jennings* and *Campbell* confirm that 'the fundamental aim of proprietary estoppel is not necessarily to fulfil the claimant's expectations nor, for that matter, to compensate him for his detrimental reliance, but to satisfy the equity in a way which does justice to both parties having regard to all the circumstances and, in particular, the need for there to be proportionality between the expectation and detriment.'[278] It is submitted that this is an accurate summary of the reasoning adopted by the Court of Appeal and that it marked a change of emphasis on the part of the judiciary. As Robert Walker LJ made clear in *Jennings*, an unquestioning application of the expectation-based approach can be unsatisfactory: the claimant's expectations may be uncertain in nature, may not be fairly derived from the assurances made or may be out of proportion to the detriment suffered. Therefore, his suggestion that the expectations of the claimant should merely be taken as a 'starting point' is a useful one. However, the rejection by the Court of Appeal of the reliance-based approach is also to be welcomed: in many cases the detriment suffered may be difficult to quantify, for example the burden of caring for an elderly person as in *Jennings* or *Campbell*, and equally the detriment suffered

275. [2003] EWCA Civ 1176.
276. [2007] EWCA Civ 1283. See further Pawlowski [2008] Conv 253.
277. [2008] 1 FLR 1217.
278. Pawlowski (2002) 118 LQR 519, 519-520.

often cannot be adequately compensated without holding the representor to the expectations he induced.

In a number of respects the approach advocated by Robert Walker LJ in *Jennings* has much to recommend it, particularly his suggestion that the court should not abandon expectations completely but should seek to satisfy the equity based on an assessment of a combination of expectations, detrimental reliance and the unconscionability of allowing the representor to go back on his assurances. Gardner, in his analysis of *Jennings*, suggests that the aim of the jurisdiction is to rectify unconscionability and that the claimant's expectations and reliance are relevant because they are the essential ingredients of the unconscionability.[279] In a sense, this approach marks a return of the concept of the minimum equity but it is more carefully defined and structured. As Robert Walker LJ commented, 'Scarman LJ's reference to the minimum does not require the court to be constitutionally parsimonious, but it does implicitly recognise that the court must also do justice to the defendant'.[280] The key to satisfying the equity in such cases must be an element of flexibility provided that the grant of relief is based on established principles and proportionality can play an important role in ensuring that justice is done as between the parties.

Jennings v Rice remains the decision in which the most detailed consideration has been given to the issue of the appropriate remedy in cases of proprietary estoppel in England. When the case of *Thorner v Major*[281] came before the House of Lords, it restored the order of the trial judge that the claimant should inherit a farm and farming business, effectively giving effect to his expectations. Although no reference was made to the principle of proportionality in the course of the speeches of the members of the House of Lords, given the extensive detrimental reliance suffered by the claimant, who had worked on the farm on an unpaid basis for nearly 30 years, this outcome could be said to be proportionate in the circumstances. In the decision of the Privy Council in *Henry v Henry*,[282] Sir Jonathan Parker, who delivered the judgment of the Board, expressed the view that 'proportionality lies at the heart of the doctrine of proprietary estoppel and permeates its every application.' Although he did not state explicitly how the decision to award the appropriate relief to achieve the minimum equity was arrived at, the doctrine of proportionality appeared to be used in a positive way to achieve a fair result having regard to the claimant's expectations and the detriment suffered.

However, the manner in which the Court of Appeal employed the concept of proportionality in two subsequent decisions, *Suggitt v Suggitt*[283] and *Bradbury v Taylor*,[284] suggests that it was being applied in a purely negative way. In *Suggitt*

279. Gardner (2006) 122 LQR 492, 499.
280. [2003] 1 P & CR 8 at [48].
281. [2009] 1 WLR 776.
282. [2010] 1 All ER 988, 1002.
283. [2012] EWCA Civ 1140. See further Mee [2013] Conv 280.
284. [2012] EWCA Civ 1208.

the appellant daughter appealed against a decision that her brother was entitled to part of the estate of their deceased father, in circumstances where the son had assisted the latter with jobs around his farm without pay. The Court of Appeal upheld the decision of the trial judge that the son was entitled to a share of his deceased father's estate on the basis that repeated assurances of inheritance had been given to the son by the deceased. It concluded that the trial judge had been entitled to find that there had been sufficient reliance and detriment and that the relief granted could not be said to be disproportionate. Arden LJ, having referred to the principles set out by Robert Walker LJ in *Jennings v Rice*,[285] stated as follows:

> In my judgment, this principle does not mean that there has to be a relationship of proportionality between the level of detriment and the relief awarded. What Walker LJ holds in this paragraph is that if the expectations are extravagant or "out of all proportion to the detriment which the claimant has suffered", the court can and should recognise that the claimant's equity should be satisfied in another and generally more limited way. So the question is: was the relief that the judge granted "out of all proportion to the detriment" suffered?[286]

Arden LJ concluded that since the father had promised that the son should have the farmland unconditionally, granting it to him could not be said to be 'out of all proportion' and the decision to grant him the farmland and farmhouse was upheld.[287]

A similar approach was adopted by the Court of Appeal in *Bradbury v Taylor*,[288] in which it dismissed the appeal by the executors of the deceased's estate that the respondents were entitled to a property on the basis of proprietary estoppel. The appellants claimed that the trial judge had been wrong to treat it as a case in which it was appropriate to fulfil the expectation of inheritance and that to give the whole property to the respondents would be altogether disproportionate. They submitted that the trial judge had failed to address the question of whether the benefit to be provided would be disproportionate having regard to the detriment which had been suffered. However, Lloyd LJ concluded that he was satisfied that the trial judge had directed himself correctly in law and he dismissed the appeal.

Although the approach of Arden LJ in *Suggitt* purported to be based on the principles set out by Robert Walker LJ in *Jennings v Rice*, the latter had seemed to strive to achieve a proportionate result rather than simply asking whether the relief granted by the trial judge was 'out of all proportion' to the

---

285. [2003] 1 P & CR 8 at [50].
286. [2012] EWCA Civ 1140 at [44].
287. This approach was followed at first instance in *Davies v Davies* [2015] EWHC 1384 (Ch).
288. [2012] EWCA Civ 1208.

detriment suffered.[289] *Suggitt* and *Bradbury* therefore marked a shift towards a more expectation-based approach in which the proportionality, or rather the lack of proportionality, between the plaintiffs' expectations and the detriment they had suffered was unlikely to affect the outcome.

While there is acceptance of the view that an appellate court should be slow to interfere with a finding of whether, for example, there has been detrimental reliance on the facts of any given case unless it is satisfied that the trial judge's conclusions on this point are clearly wrong,[290] the approach of the Court of Appeal in *Suggitt* and *Bradbury* suggests that this deference should extend to the appropriateness of the remedy. Mee comments that in both these cases it appeared that 'the expectation remedy granted was disproportionate to the detriment incurred, so that on the basis of *Jennings v Rice* the court should have applied a lesser remedy.'[291] He suggests, quite rightly, that these cases illustrate a willingness on the part of the Court of Appeal to defer to the approach of the trial judge in relation to the appropriate remedy, even where this seems difficult to defend in principled terms. However, there was no evidence of this deferential approach on the part of the Court of Appeal in another decision made by it around the same time. In *Joyce v Epsom and Ewell Borough Council*[292] the claimant asserted that he was, as successor to a previous owner, entitled to a right of way over a private road. The trial judge accepted that he was entitled to the benefit of any proprietary estoppel, if one arose, in favour of the previous owner but his claim was dismissed because he found that the council had not acted unconscionably. The Court of Appeal, in allowing the claimant's appeal, held that it would be unconscionable for the local authority to resile from its encouragement and assurance on which the previous owner had relied to his detriment. However, Davies LJ stated that the overall focus of the court has to be on what is 'fair and proportionate as between the parties'[293] and limited the right of way to serving a single house on the property, although the claimant was a developer and had intended to develop the site.

It should be noted that Lloyd LJ commented in *Bradbury v Taylor* that the law was not in dispute in *Suggitt v Suggitt* or in the case before him. However, it would appear that different judges are drawing different conclusions from the *dicta* of Robert Walker LJ in *Jennings v Rice* referred to above. He undoubtedly stated in that case that the court should merely take the claimant's expectations as a 'starting point' and yet in both *Suggitt* and *Bradbury*, these

289. In *Jennings v Rice* [2003] P & CR 8 the Court of Appeal upheld an award equivalent to less than half the value of a property which the claimant asserted that he had been led to believe that he would inherit on the basis that this was a proportionate response given the detriment he had suffered in looking after the deceased over a period of many years.

290. *Suggitt v Suggitt* [2012] EWCA Civ 1140 at [37]; *Davies v Davies* [2014] EWCA Civ 568 at [33].

291. [2013] Conv 280, 281.

292. [2012] EWCA Civ 1398.

293. *Ibid.* at [48].

expectations appeared to count for significantly more than this. Perhaps more importantly, the reluctance of the Court of Appeal to conduct its own analysis of the proportionality between the claimant's expectations and the detriment suffered is a cause for concern. Merely asking the question whether the relief granted by the trial judge was out of all proportion to the detriment suffered leaves greater scope for a much broader range of remedy to be granted but also gives rise to uncertainty. Mee is arguably correct when he puts forward the view that '[d]espite much reverential talk on the part of legal commentators and judges about equitable flexibility and the prevention of unconscionability, it is not in the public interest for the legal system to tolerate an indulgent and confused proprietary estoppel jurisdiction.'[294]

A useful suggestion was adopted by Lewison LJ in *Davies v Davies*[295] in relation to how a court should approach the issue of how to satisfy an equity which has arisen in a plaintiff's favour in a claim based on proprietary estoppel. He set out a number of general principles which have subsequently been quoted with approval[296] and in so far as they relate to the assessment of an appropriate remedy they are as follows:

> i) Deciding whether an equity has been raised and, if so, how to satisfy it is a retrospective exercise looking backwards from the moment when the promise falls due to be performed and asking whether, in the circumstances which have actually happened, it would be unconscionable for a promise not to be kept either wholly or in part: *Thorner v Major* [2009] UKHL 18, [2009] 1 WLR 776 at [57] and [101]
>
> …
>
> vii) In deciding how to satisfy any equity the court must weigh the detriment suffered by the claimant in reliance on the defendant's assurances against any countervailing benefits he enjoyed in consequence of that reliance: *Henry v Henry* [2010] UKPC 3 at [51] and [53].
>
> viii) Proportionality lies at the heart of the doctrine of proprietary estoppel and permeates its every application: *Henry v Henry* at [65]. In particular there must be a proportionality between the remedy and the detriment which is its purpose to avoid: *Jennings v Rice* [2002] EWCA Civ 159 at [28] (citing from earlier cases) and [56]. This does not mean that the court should abandon expectations and seek only to compensate detrimental reliance, but if the expectation is

294. [2013] Conv 280, 297.
295. [2016] EWCA Civ 463.
296. *Moore v Moore* [2016] EWHC 2202 (Ch) at [16], [2018] EWCA Civ 2669 at [24]; *Habberfield v Habberfield* [2018] EWHC 317 (Ch) at [223]. See also *Gee v Gee* [2018] EWHC 1393 (Ch) at [140].

disproportionate to the detriment, the court should satisfy the equity in a more limited way: *Jennings v Rice* at [50] and [51].

ix) In deciding how to satisfy the equity the court has to exercise a broad judgmental discretion: *Jennings v Rice* at [51]. However the discretion is not unfettered. It must be exercised on a principled basis, and does not entail what HH Judge Weekes QC memorably called a "portable palm tree": *Taylor v Dickens* [1998] 1 FLR 806 (a decision criticised for other reasons in *Gillett v Holt*).[297]

Lewison LJ added that it is not entirely clear from the judgment of Robert Walker LJ in *Jennings v Rice* how the court should approach a case where a claimant's expectations are uncertain and are only a starting point. He agreed that the suggestion of counsel that 'there might be a sliding scale by which the clearer the expectation, the greater the detriment and the longer the passage of time during which the expectation was reasonably held, the greater would be the weight that should be given to the expectation'[298] was a useful working hypothesis. In the circumstances, Lewison LJ concluded that the trial judge had applied 'far too broad a brush', and although he said that he had taken the claimant's expectations as an appropriate starting point, he had not explained which out of the many sometimes mutually incompatible expectations held should be regarded as that starting point.

Some further clarification of the principles set out by Robert Walker LJ in *Jennings v Rice* has been provided by Lewison LJ in *Habberfield v Habberfield*.[299] He suggested that the explanation provided by Arden LJ in *Suggitt v Suggitt*[300] of the principles set out in *Jennings* was 'a difficult passage to understand' and stressed that the relevant comparison for the purposes of proportionality was between remedy and detriment. However, he added that '[n]evertheless, proportionality is not a question of mathematical precision. Like all cases in which the court decides how to satisfy an equity, it must exercise a judgmental discretion, and may do so in a flexible way.'[301] He also reiterated the point he had made in *Davies v Davies*,[302] that in a class of case in which the assurance and reliance had a consensual character not far short of a contract and the claimant has performed his part of this quasi-bargain, a

---

297. [2016] EWCA Civ 463 at [38].
298. *Ibid.* at [41]. See also the *dicta* of Birss J at first instance in *Habberfield v Habberfield* [2018] EWHC 317 (Ch) at [229], '[i]n other words it is not simply that an expectation reasonably held for a long time necessarily justifies giving greater weight to the expectation over the reliance loss, an important factor (if true) is that the long period of time amounts to fulfilling what the person promised was told they had to do in order to secure what they had been promised.'
299. [2019] EWCA Civ 890.
300. [2012] EWCA Civ 1140 at [44].
301. [2019] EWCA Civ 890 at [58].
302. [2016] EWCA Civ 463 at [40].

court is, subject to countervailing considerations, likely to seek to vindicate the claimant's expectations.[303]

Approaches Elsewhere in the Common Law World

Perhaps the most useful and comprehensive recent judgment in the common law world on this issue is the decision of the New Zealand Court of Appeal in *Wilson Parking New Zealand Ltd v Fanshawe 136 Ltd.*[304] Randerson J expressed the view that the three main elements relevant to relief stem from the ingredients necessary to establish equitable estoppel in the first place, namely the quality and nature of the assurances which give rise to the claimant's expectation; the extent and nature of the claimant's detrimental reliance; and the need for the claimant to show that it would be unconscionable for the promisor to depart from the assurances given. So, the clearer and more explicit the assurance, the more likely it is that a court will be willing to grant expectation-based relief. Similarly, the greater the degree and consequences of detrimental reliance by the claimant, the more likely it is that the court will be prepared to hold the defendant to the promise rather than make an award, which will generally be of a more limited nature, designed to compensate for reliance-based losses. Randerson J said that while some authorities continue to refer to relief as being the minimum necessary to satisfy the equity, the emphasis in more recent cases has been on a broad consideration of the relief necessary to achieve a just and proportionate outcome. He continued as follows:

> Where the claimant's expectation is seriously disproportionate to the detriment suffered, the court will be unlikely to grant expectation-based relief. To do so would be to overcompensate the claimant and would be unjust to the defendant. In such a case, the court would consider whether there may be a means of satisfying the equity in another way. But that does not mean the court will simply compare in an arithmetical manner the extent of any reliance-based losses with the value to the claimant of the expectation. A broad assessment of all the relevant circumstances is to be made including losses or other detriment which cannot be quantified or measured in monetary terms.[305]

Randerson J acknowledged that there is some support for the proposition that, subject to proportionality between the expectation and the detriment suffered, it will often be just to make an order to fulfil the expectation, but said that the court did not consider it appropriate to adopt a presumptive or *prima facie* approach one way or the other.[306] In the circumstances of the case the Court of

303. [2019] EWCA Civ 890 at [62].
304. [2014] 3 NZLR 567 at [113].
305. *Ibid.* at [118].
306. *Ibid.* at [119].

Appeal upheld the decision of Katz J to grant an expectation-based remedy. It concluded that the appellant had acted unconscionably in refusing to grant a waiver on an option to purchase which it had promised the respondents. The court did not accept the appellant's argument that payment of compensation for the direct financial loss suffered by the respondents in reliance on the waiver would be a sufficient remedy to address the appellant's unconscionable conduct in reneging on its promise and instead upheld the decision to hold the appellant to this promise.

The question of how to assess what is an appropriate remedy once a claim based on proprietary estoppel has been established has also been considered by the Supreme Court of Canada in *Cowper-Smith v Morgan*.[307] McLachlin CJC stressed the need for proportionality between the remedy sought and the detriment suffered. She stated as follows:

> [W]hile proprietary estoppel arises where the claimant's expectations are frustrated, the reasonableness of the claimant's expectations must be assessed in light of, among other things, the detriment the claimant has actually suffered ... Courts of equity must therefore strike a balance between vindicating the claimant's subjective expectations–which, in their full context, may or may not reflect a reasonable valuation of the claimant's detriment–and correcting that detriment, which may be difficult or even impossible to measure.[308]

Of the recent decisions in this area throughout the common law world, it is the judgment of Randerson J in *Wilson Parking* which appears to strike the fairest balance, eschewing support for a presumptive or *prima facie* approach for either an expectation or reliance-based model.[309] By assessing the quality and nature of the assurances made, the extent and nature of the claimant's detrimental reliance and the question of whether it would be unconscionable for the defendant to depart from the assurances given, the court has put forward a model which should prove sufficiently flexible to be employed in both commercial and non-commercial contexts. It also employs proportionality in a positive manner by embarking on a 'broad consideration of the relief necessary to achieve a just and proportionate outcome'.[310]

307. (2017) 416 DLR (4th) 1.
308. *Ibid.* at [48].
309. However, it should be noted that in the subsequent decision of the New Zealand Court of Appeal in *Hansard v Hansard* [2015] 2 NZLR 158, the court decided to adopt an expectation-based approach to the question of an appropriate remedy. It only explained this decision in very brief terms, on the basis that it would be impractical to do otherwise and that there was no justification for reducing the amount to be repaid in the circumstances.
310. [2014] 3 NZLR 567 at [117].

The Approach Adopted by the Irish Courts

Although there have been some decisions made by the courts in Ireland in recent years in which plaintiffs have succeeded in claims based on proprietary estoppel, little or no consideration has been given to the basis on which such relief ought to be granted in such cases. An example of the expectation-oriented approach being applied in this jurisdiction is *Smyth v Halpin*,[311] considered in more detail above, in which Geoghegan J ordered the transfer of a fee simple remainder interest to the plaintiff in circumstances where he found that it was his 'clear expectation' that he would have that interest. A similar approach was taken in *Naylor v Maher*,[312] where the plaintiff relied successfully on proprietary estoppel in establishing a claim to lands in circumstances where he had worked on the deceased's farm predominantly on an unpaid basis for many years. O'Keeffe J referred to the fact that the defendant had urged the court 'to measure in some equitable manner' the input and contributions of the plaintiff in the management of the farm. However, O'Keeffe J stated that he did not think such evaluation was appropriate in the case before him. In his view, given the plaintiff's lifelong commitment to the defendant, this method of compensation would be inappropriate and would not do justice to the plaintiff. Although some of the land had been sold to third parties since the promise to the plaintiff had been first made, O'Keeffe J concluded that the court 'can and will implement the promise in respect of the remaining lands'.

Another recent decision is that of Laffoy J in *Coyle v Finnegan*,[313] in which a claim made by the plaintiff, who had worked on an unpaid basis on the deceased's farm for a period of many years, was also upheld but to a more limited extent. For about five years prior to the latter's death, the defendants had carried out the bulk of the work on the farm. However, the plaintiff was unaware that the deceased had changed his will leaving the property to the defendants and a sum of only €5,000 to the plaintiff 'for assistance rendered' to him on the farm. Laffoy J concluded that it would be unconscionable if the plaintiff was not recompensed for the labours and services he had provided to the deceased and if the defendants were to acquire the deceased's farm under his will free from any entitlement of the plaintiff to be recompensed. Therefore, in her view, equity required that the plaintiff be reasonably remunerated for the labours and services which he had given the deceased and she held that he should have a charge or lien on the lands for a sum equivalent to such reasonable remuneration.

The decision in *Naylor v Maher* could be characterised as an example of a straightforward application of expectation-based approach to the granting of relief. However, the reasoning in *Coyle v Finnegan* appeared to be more nuanced in nature. There would have been difficulties in applying a purely

311. [1997] 2 ILRM 38.
312. [2012] IEHC 408.
313. [2013] IEHC 463 at [26].

expectation-based approach in any event, given the effect this would have had on the defendants, who had also suffered detriment over the years working on the farm. The approach adopted by Laffoy J took into account the plaintiff's detrimental reliance, but also the unconscionability of not giving effect in some way to his claim. Although she did not refer specifically to the concept of proportionality, she appeared to employ it is a positive way in arriving at a sum which was a fair reflection of the detriment suffered by the plaintiff. The fact that the sum arrived at was one which had not been challenged by the defendants if the claim had proceeded on a *quantum meruit* basis would seem to support the conclusion that it was a fair result in the circumstances.

So, although the Irish courts have yet to set out the principles which influence the conclusions that they have reached in relation to remedies, it seems clear that they are using an expectation-based model as a starting point, but also scaling this back where necessary in order to achieve a fair and proportionate outcome having regard to the plaintiff's detrimental reliance and other relevant factors such as the impact of any order on the defendant or on third parties.

The Relationship between Proprietary Estoppel and Constructive Trusts

It has been accepted that there is a close relationship between the concepts of proprietary estoppel and constructive trusts, in that both involve the application of the equitable principle that a party should not be allowed to enforce his strict legal rights when it would be inequitable to do so on the basis of the dealings which have taken place between the parties.[314] In the course of his judgment in *Grant v Edwards*[315] Browne-Wilkinson VC expressed the view that the principles underlying proprietary estoppel are 'closely akin' to those laid down in *Gissing v Gissing*[316] in relation to constructive trusts, and in his view while the two principles have been developed separately, they 'rest on the same foundation'. He stated as follows:

> In both, the claimant must to the knowledge of the legal owner have acted in the belief that the claimant has or will obtain an interest in the property. In both, the claimant must have acted to his or her detriment in reliance on such belief. In both, equity acts on the conscience of the legal owner to prevent him from acting in an unconscionable manner by defeating the common intention.[317]

314. Proudman J has referred to proprietary estoppel as the 'sister claim' of one based on a constructive trust in *Baynes Clarke v Corless* [2009] EWHC 1636 (Ch).
315. [1986] Ch 638.
316. [1971] AC 886.
317. [1986] Ch 638, 656. See also *Banner Homes plc v Luff Developments Ltd* [2000] Ch 372, 385.

Undoubtedly 'a common theme can be discerned'[318] in cases of proprietary estoppel and constructive trusts; they both allow for the creation of informal interests in land and the concept of unconscionability appears to underlie them both.[319] Nourse LJ commented in *Stokes v Anderson*[320] that 'there is no real reason for thinking that their assimilation would be unduly hindered by their separate development out of basically different factual situations', although in his view no such assimilation had yet taken place.[321] However, it has also been pointed out there are important differences between the two doctrines. It is clear that both doctrines developed with different aims; proprietary estoppel as a means of compensating detrimental reliance and giving effect to expectations, and constructive trusts as a flexible device for achieving justice in equity.[322] In addition, As Sir Andrew Park commented in *Lalani v Crump Holdings Ltd*,[323] cases involving a common intention constructive trust tend to focus on statements by the legal owner as to the current state of affairs, whereas proprietary estoppel cases are often concerned with promises that the legal owner will do something in future which will change the pre-existing state of affairs to the advantage of the claimant. Other differences arise in relation to the timing of the interest created[324] and the type of interest which will be acquired by a claimant.[325] While establishing a claim of estoppel may lead to the conferral of a less extensive property right than that which may arise where a constructive trust is imposed,[326] equally it will often lead to a more far-reaching form of relief.[327] So, as Lord Collins JSC suggested in *Southern Pacific Mortgages Ltd v Scott*,[328] '[i]t is likely that the difference [between the two doctrines] would only be crucial in terms of remedies.'

A decision which broke new ground in linking the two doctrines is *Re*

318. *Re Basham* [1986] 1 WLR 1498, 1504.
319. Hayton [1990] Conv 370. See further *Driver v Yorke* [2003] EWHC 746 (Ch) at [28].
320. [1991] 1 FLR 391, 399.
321. See also *Hyett v Stanley* [2003] EWCA Civ 942. However, it should be noted that in *Van Laethem v Brooker* [2005] EWHC 1478 (Ch) at [79] Lawrence Collins J stated, referring to *Oxley v Hiscock* [2004] 3 WLR 715, considered below, that 'matters have moved on since these decisions'.
322. Note that in *Haslemere Estates Ltd v Baker* [1982] 1 WLR 1109, 1119 Megarry VC rejected the argument that proprietary estoppel arises 'whenever justice and good conscience requires it'.
323. [2007] EWHC 47 (Ch).
324. As Moore points out (2000) 63 MLR 912, 915-916, it would seem that while a constructive trust arises at the time an agreement is made, a remedy in estoppel arises only on judgment which will potentially lead to different consequences where the rights of third parties intervene.
325. Warburton (1991) 5 Trust Law Int 9; Ferguson (1993) 109 LQR 114. See also Thompson [2004] Conv 496, 506.
326. See the comments of Black J in *Q. v Q.* [2009] 1 FLR 935, 968.
327. E.g. *Pascoe v Turner* [1979] 1 WLR 431. See also the comments of Sir Andrew Park in *Lalani v Crump Holdings Ltd* [2007] EWHC 47 (Ch) at [27].
328. [2015] AC 385, 404.

Basham,[329] in which Edward Nugee QC, sitting as a Deputy High Court judge, appeared to hold that proprietary estoppel will give rise to a constructive trust. The decision is also significant in that it showed that a claim of proprietary estoppel may succeed on the basis of acts undertaken not in reliance on the fact that the claimant had existing rights but on the faith of an undertaking that such rights would be granted in the future. The plaintiff helped to run her mother and stepfather's business for many years on an unpaid basis on the understanding that she would inherit her stepfather's estate and she and her husband also expended considerable time and money looking after her stepfather. The stepfather died intestate and the plaintiff sought a declaration against two of his nieces who were administratrixes of his estate that she was entitled to the deceased's house and to his furniture and other property. Judge Nugee held, in granting the declaration sought, that the principle of proprietary estoppel was not limited to acts done in reliance on a belief relating to an existing right, but extended to acts done in reliance on a belief that future rights would be granted. In addition, he accepted that estoppel could extend to non-specific property and held that since the plaintiff had established that she had acted to her detriment in reliance on the belief, which was encouraged by her stepfather, that she would ultimately benefit by receiving his property on his death, she was entitled to the residuary estate. Martin raises the question that if the plaintiff satisfied the requirements for proprietary estoppel, why was it necessary to introduce the concept of the constructive trust into the equation[330] and it should be pointed out that the reasoning in *Re Basham* has been characterised as 'somewhat dubious'.[331]

More recently there has been a return to the theme of the similarities between the doctrines of proprietary estoppel and constructive trusts, although as an analysis of the relevant decisions show, the equating of the concepts creates its own difficulties. In *Yaxley v Gotts*[332] the Court of Appeal held that an oral agreement whereby the plaintiff was promised an interest in a house in exchange for carrying out work on it, although unenforceable under section 2 of the Law of Property (Miscellaneous Provisions) Act 1989, was nevertheless enforceable on the basis of a constructive trust pursuant to section 2(5) of the Act, which provided that nothing in the section affected the creation or operation of resulting or constructive trusts. While Robert Walker LJ acknowledged that the trial judge had made no finding in relation to the existence of a constructive trust, on the findings of fact it had not been disputed that a proprietary estoppel arose and in his view such findings equally provided the basis for the conclusion that the plaintiff was entitled to an interest under a constructive trust. In the course of his judgment Robert Walker LJ stated that 'at a high level of generality there is much common ground between the doctrines of proprietary estoppel and the

329. [1986] 1 WLR 1498.
330. Martin [1987] Conv 211, 213.
331. Moore (2000) 63 MLR 912, 915.
332. [2000] Ch 162. See further Thompson [2000] Conv 245.

constructive trust'[333] and that in the area of a joint enterprise for the acquisition of land, the two concepts coincide.[334] He concluded that the species of constructive trust based on common intention is established by what Lord Bridge described in *Lloyds Bank plc v Rosset*[335] as an agreement or understanding reached between the parties and relied on and acted on by the claimant and that a constructive trust of this nature is 'closely akin to, if not indistinguishable from, proprietary estoppel'.[336] A common intention constructive trust was also held to be the appropriate remedy in *Dowding v Matchmove Ltd.*[337] In this case the court accepted that such a trust could arise where there was an express oral agreement which the parties intended to be binding which had been relied upon by the claimants to their detriment such that it would be unconscionable for the defendant to deny the claimants' ownership.

It should be pointed out that while the members of the Court of Appeal in *Yaxley v Gotts* appeared to consider it irrelevant whether the plaintiff succeeded on the basis of proprietary estoppel or a constructive trust, as in either case the result would be identical,[338] in another case the differences between the two doctrines could be significant.[339] For this reason further thought should be given to the consequences of the elision of what have traditionally been perceived to be distinct doctrines and it seems inevitable that cases will occur where the distinctions between them will be material to the outcome.

It should also be noted that the decision in *Yaxley v Gotts* led to some uncertainty about whether a failed agreement can only be enforced despite the provisions of section 2 of the Law of Property (Miscellaneous Provisions) Act 1989 when the circumstances which lead to the creation of an estoppel also give rise to a constructive trust. This uncertainty was fuelled by the decision of the Court of Appeal in *Kinane v Mackie-Conteh*,[340] in which Neuberger LJ suggested that if the facts of the case before him merely gave rise to proprietary estoppel, the provisions of section 2(5) might well not assist the claimant.[341]

---

333. *Ibid.* at 176.
334. See also *Banner Homes Group plc v Luff Developments Ltd* [2000] Ch 372, 384.
335. [1991] 1 AC 107, 132.
336. [2000] Ch 162, 180. See also *Lloyds Bank plc v Carrick* [1996] 4 All ER 630, 640; *Mollo v Mollo* Chancery Division, 8 October 1999 at [42]; *Beresford v Williamson* [2002] EWCA Civ 1632 at [10].
337. [2017] 1 WLR 749.
338. See also *Chan v Leung* [2002] EWCA Civ 1075 at [91].
339. Moore (2000) 63 MLR 912, 915. See also Smith (2000) 116 LQR 11, 12.
340. [2005] EWCA Civ 45; *Turner v Jacob* [2006] EWHC 1317 (Ch) at [80].
341. He added that the claim would run into the same difficulties as that of the party seeking to enforce the guarantee in *Actionstrength Ltd v International Glass Engineering SpA* [2003] 2 AC 541 (in which the House of Lords held that on the facts a claim of estoppel could not be relied on to challenge the unenforceability of a contract of guarantee due to failure to comply with s.4 of the Statute of Frauds). However, as McFarlane points out [2005] Conv 510, 514, 'the decision in *Actionstrength* has no relevance at all to proprietary estoppel and hence cannot alter the basic position that s. 2 has no effect on such claims.' See also McFarlane (2005) 16 KCLJ 174, 184.

Neuberger LJ expressed the view that 'the essential difference between a proprietary estoppel which does not also give rise to a constructive trust, and one that does, is the element of agreement, or at least expression of common understanding, exchanged between the parties, as to existence, or intended existence, of a proprietary interest, in the latter type of case.'[342] He concluded that this requirement had been satisfied in the case before him, that a constructive trust had been created and that section 2(5) could properly be invoked by the claimant. However, the reasoning in this decision has been rightly criticised as flawed[343] and it can be forcefully argued that the finding of a constructive trust was not necessary for the court to reach the conclusion which it did. As Arden LJ stated in her judgment, '[t]he cause of action in proprietary estoppel is thus not founded on the unenforceable agreement but upon the defendant's conduct which, when viewed in all relevant respects, is unconscionable'.[344] As Dixon points out, it is therefore not clear why the Court of Appeal deemed any saving from the provisions of section 2 relevant or necessary[345] and given that the basis of the estoppel claim was not the invalid agreement but the unconscionable conduct, he is surely correct in saying that there was no need to justify the fact that section 2 did not apply.

This logic seemed to commend itself to Etherton J at first instance in *Cobbe v Yeoman's Row Management Ltd*,[346] a judgment which is underpinned by much more satisfactory reasoning. He found that the estoppel which arose in the claimant's favour did not rest merely on the existence of a failed agreement but on the fact that the defendant had induced and encouraged the claimant to believe that it regarded the agreement as binding and on the unconscionability of the defendant's reliance on its strict legal rights.[347] The Court of Appeal, in dismissing the defendant's appeal, agreed with Etherton J that section 2 had no application to the proprietary estoppel claim before the court.[348] The House of Lords ultimately found in the defendant's favour and held that in the circumstances the doctrine of proprietary estoppel could not be relied upon.[349]

---

342. [2005] EWCA Civ 45 at [51].
343. Dixon [2005] Conv 247; McFarlane [2005] Conv 501.
344. [2005] EWCA Civ 45 at [29].
345. [2005] Conv 247, 253. See also McFarlane [2005] Conv 501, 521.
346. [2005] EWHC 266 (Ch).
347. Etherton J made it clear that in view of his decision in favour of the claimant based on proprietary estoppel it was not strictly necessary for him to consider the alternative claim to a constructive trust, although he concluded that the claimant would have been entitled to claim relief on this basis. However, he stated that a constructive trust was neither necessary nor appropriate in the case before him as in his view the lien he had ordered on the basis of the proprietary estoppel claim was a more suitable way of satisfying the equity which arose. As Dixon comments [2005] Conv 247, 254, 'the apparent subsumption of estoppel within constructive trusts in failed agreement cases by Neuberger LJ, arising from the confusion about the meaning of *Yaxley*, plays no part in the judgment of Etherton J in *Cobbe*'.
348. [2006] 1 WLR 2964.
349. [2008] 1 WLR 1752.

However, as referred to above, it should be noted that Lord Scott expressed the view that in the absence of the requisite statutory formalities, proprietary estoppel could not be employed in order to render enforceable an agreement which was void for non-compliance with the provisions of section 2 of the Law of Property (Miscellaneous Provisions) Act 1989.[350] Doubt has been cast in turn on this latter proposition by the comments of Kitchin LJ in the Court of Appeal in *Farrar v Miller*,[351] although it should be noted that this judgment was delivered at a preliminary stage in the proceedings and concerned an application to amend the particulars of a claim. He acknowledged that this issue raised a difficult question which would be better determined at trial but did express the view that there are 'strong arguments for saying that section 2 of the 1989 Act is concerned only with the requirements of a valid contract for the sale or other disposition of an interest in land'[352] and that the wording of section 2 does nothing to prevent arrangements over the sale or other disposition of land giving rise to another cause of action.

In *Jennings v Rice*[353] Robert Walker LJ again spoke of circumstances in which proprietary estoppel may become indistinguishable from a constructive trust. Further support for this view can be found in the *dicta* of Chadwick LJ in *Oxley v Hiscock*,[354] where he stated that once it is recognised that what the court is doing in family property disputes is to supply a common intention as to the parties' respective shares on the basis of that which is shown to be fair, 'it seems difficult to avoid the conclusion that an analysis in terms of proprietary estoppel will, necessarily, lead to the same result'.[355] In setting out his conclusions Chadwick LJ reiterated that 'the time has come to accept that there is no difference in outcome, in cases of this nature'.[356] Arden LJ also suggested in *Herbert v Doyle*,[357] that while the distinction between the two doctrines must be borne in mind, they both require completeness of agreement in relation to an interest in property at least in the context of commercial transactions. However,

350. This view has been criticised by Griffiths [2009] Conv 141, 144. See also McFarlane and Robertson [2008] LMCLQ 449, 456. However, it should be noted that in *Brightlingsea Haven Ltd v Morris* [2009] 2 P & CR 11, Jack J concluded that although the facts gave rise to a proprietary estoppel, it was open to the court to find a constructive trust in the defendants' favour which would not be barred by the provisions of s. 2 of the Act of 1989.
351. [2018] EWCA CIv 172.
352. *Ibid.* at [57].
353. [2003] 1 P & CR 8 at [45]. See also *Samad v Thompson* [2008] EWHC 2809 (Ch) at [129].
354. [2004] 3 WLR 715.
355. *Ibid.* at 748.
356. Although note that Gardner has commented (2004) 120 LQR 541, 546 that the problems associated with common intention constructive trusts 'cannot be solved by adopting the learning that proprietary estoppel has developed in response to a different set of considerations'.
357. [2010] EWCA Civ 1095 at [56].

it should be noted that in the decision of the House of Lords in *Stack v Dowden*[358] Lord Walker made reference to the encouragement he had given to the notion of the equating of proprietary estoppel and constructive trusts but said that he was now 'rather less enthusiastic' than he might previously have been about the idea that the two doctrines could or should be completely assimilated.[359]

The question of whether a constructive trust might provide the vehicle for conferring a proprietary interest in the disputed property on the claimant was considered but rejected by Lord Scott in *Cobbe*. He acknowledged that a constructive trust may arise out of a joint venture relating to property, the so-called *Pallant v Morgan*[360] equity, but said that it could not be imposed in the case before him in circumstances where the property had been owned by the defendant company before any negotiations for a joint venture had commenced. He stated that despite the unconscionability of the appellant's behaviour in withdrawing from the incomplete agreement immediately after planning permission had been obtained, this seemed a wholly inadequate basis for imposing a constructive trust over the property in order to provide the respondent with a remedy for his disappointed expectations. Lord Scott concluded that in these circumstances the imposition of a constructive trust on the property seemed to him 'more in the nature of an indignant reaction to…unconscionable behaviour than a principled answer to [the respondent's] claim for relief.'[361]

Lord Scott returned to the theme of the interaction between the concepts of proprietary estoppel and the constructive trust in *Thorner v Major*[362] and said that the case before him provided an example of the extent to which they have been treated as providing alternative and overlapping remedies. He stated that while he did not disagree with the conclusion that the appellant could establish his equity in the property by relying on proprietary estoppel, he found it 'easier and more comfortable'[363] to regard his equity as established through a remedial constructive trust. Lord Scott expressed the view that in cases where the representations relied upon related to the acquisition by the representee of an immediate, or more or less immediate, interest in property, then proprietary estoppel was the obvious remedy. However, he added that in cases where the relevant representation related to the prospect of an inheritance, it seemed difficult to square with the principles of proprietary estoppel established by the cases such as *Ramsden v Dyson* and *Crabb v Arun District Council*. He

---

358. [2007] 2 AC 432, 448. See also *Powell v Benney* [2007] EWCA Civ 1283 at [24]; *Q. v Q.* [2009] 1 FLR 935, 967-968.
359. However, as Etherton points out [2009] Conv 104, 123-124, in neither *Stack* nor *Cobbe* did Lord Walker or any other members of the Judicial Committee state that his analysis of the constructive trust in *Yaxley v Gotts* was wrong.
360. [1953] Ch 43. See also *Banner Homes Group plc v Luff Developments Ltd* [2000] Ch 372.
361. [2008] 1 WLR 1752, 1772.
362. [2009] 1 WLR 776.
363. *Ibid.* at 781.

said that he found such 'inheritance' cases easier to understand as constructive trust cases[364] and added that the possibility of a remedial constructive trust over property, created by the common intention or understanding of the parties regarding the property on the basis of which the claimant has acted to his detriment, is well recognised.[365] Lord Scott stated as follows:

> For my part I would prefer to keep proprietary estoppel and constructive trust as distinct and separate remedies, to confine proprietary estoppel to cases where the representation, whether express or implied, on which the claimant has acted is unconditional and to address the cases where the representations are of future benefits, and subject to qualification on account of unforeseen future events, via the principles of remedial constructive trusts.[366]

He concluded that he was satisfied that the case before him would, on the basis of the findings of fact made by the trial judge and accepted by the Court of Appeal, have justified a remedial constructive trust under which the appellant would have obtained the relief awarded to him at first instance.[367]

Given the result in *Cobbe*, it is likely that McFarlane and Robertson were correct in suggesting that it is inconceivable that the courts will ignore the impulse to protect a party who has reasonably relied to his detriment on an assurance that he will obtain a right over another's land to which he has no contractual entitlement.[368] They predict that attention may have to turn to the imposition of a constructive trust in such circumstances and that 'there is a clear risk that constructive trust principles will be extended and distorted'[369] in order to provide the necessary protection. This would seem to be borne out by the result in the decision of the Court of Appeal in *Dowding v Matchmove Ltd*,[370] in which a common intention constructive trust was held to arise in the context of a commercial venture.

Etherton has also pointed out that the decision in *Banner Homes plc v Luff Developments Ltd*[371] appears to be an example of circumstances in which

364. Lord Scott gave examples such as *Gillett v Holt* [2001] Ch 210 and *Re Basham* [1986] 1 WLR 1498 and said that it appeared from the latter case that the trial judge was of the same opinion.
365. He referred in particular to *Gissing v Gissing* [1971] AC 886, 905 *per* Lord Diplock.
366. [2009] 1 WLR 776, 785. See also *MacDonald v Frost* [2009] WTLR 1815 at [14].
367. Commenting on Lord Scott's views in *MacDonald v Frost* [2009] WTLR 1815 at [16], Geraldine Andrews QC, sitting as a Deputy High Court judge, said that while his approach had much to commend it, it had yet to command widespread support and that it remained a fertile ground for academic debate.
368. McFarlane and Robertson [2008] LMCLQ 449, 456. See also the comment of Etherton [2009] Conv 104, 120.
369. *Ibid.* at 457.
370. [2017] 1 WLR 749.
371. [2000] Ch 372.

a constructive trust has been imposed in a commercial context to provide a remedy of a proprietary nature where a party has reneged on a promise which was not part of a complete and legally binding agreement.[372] As he indicates, Lord Scott did not suggest in *Cobbe* that the decision in *Banner Homes* was suspect and it can be argued that there was no real difference in substance between the result arrived at in that case in the form of a constructive trust and the attempt to establish an entitlement to a remedy by employing proprietary estoppel in *Cobbe*. However, there were signs, both in the dissenting judgment of Etherton LJ and in the judgment of Arden LJ in *Crossco No. 4 Unlimited v Jolan Ltd*,[373] of a growing recognition of the undesirability of imposing a constructive trust in commercial situations.[374]

In many ways the constructive trust, particularly the post *Stack v Dowden*[375] and *Jones v Kernott*[376] version, stripped of its requirement of detrimental reliance, is ill-suited to providing a mechanism for achieving justice in a commercial context and in any event it lacks the inherent flexibility which a claim based on proprietary estoppel will give rise to. For this reason, it must be asked why the House of Lords in *Cobbe* saw fit to emasculate the doctrine which seemed the most appropriate in this context. As McFarlane and Robertson point out, '[i]t seems unfortunate that the legal doctrine best equipped to protect reliance may be prevented from fulfilling that role in the future.'[377]

There have also been some comments made in judgments delivered in this jurisdiction which suggest that successful reliance on estoppel principles will give rise to a constructive trust although there is little analysis to back up such a position. In *Reidy v McGreevy*[378] Barron J commented that 'where it would be unconscionable to disregard a promise such as that alleged here, the court will declare the existence of a constructive trust.' However, on the facts he concluded that the plaintiff's claim was statute barred and did not explore the issue further. This *dicta* was referred to by O'Keeffe J in *Prendergast v McLaughlin*,[379] in which the plaintiff sought to enforce a promise on which he alleged he had placed reliance by acting to his detriment. O'Keeffe J commented that the plaintiff's claim lay in equity and 'is long established as equitable/proprietary/promissory estoppel by giving rise to a constructive trust'.[380] However, he also concluded that the claim was statute barred and did not elaborate further on the link between estoppel and constructive trust principles. Similar reasoning was employed in a successful claim of estoppel in *An Cumann Peile Boitheimeach*

372. [2009] Conv 104, 123.
373. [2012] 2 All ER 754. See further Hopkins [2012] Conv 327; Lower [2012] Conv 379; Yip (2013) 33 LS 549.
374. See further Chapter 8.
375. [2007] 2 AC 432.
376. [2012] 1 AC 776.
377. McFarlane and Robertson [2008] LMCLQ 449, 460.
378. High Court (Barron J) 19 March 1993 at 5.
379. [2009] IEHC 250.
380. *Ibid.* at [22].

Teoranta v Albion Properties Ltd,[381] in which Edwards J upheld the defendants' counterclaim for relief on the grounds of proprietary estoppel and concluded that the plaintiffs held the lands in question on a constructive trust for the benefit of the defendants.

More recently reliance has been placed on the approach of Lord Scott in *Thorner v Major* in *Finnegan v Hand*[382] to support a finding of a constructive trust in circumstances where traditional proprietary estoppel principles might have seemed appropriate. The plaintiff brought proceedings against the defendant, who was the administratrix of the deceased's estate, seeking an interest in a farm which had been the property of the deceased. The plaintiff had worked on this farm on a full time basis for a period of 38 years and the objective evidence was that he had been substantially underpaid, and had made a significant sacrifice in giving up social housing and living with his family in substandard accommodation for some of this time. The plaintiff's evidence was to the effect that the deceased had indicated that he would leave the farm to the plaintiff and had told him that '[t]his will be yours after my day. The money in the Bank will be for my family.' While White J set out the essential elements in a proprietary estoppel claim, he then considered the principles relating to constructive trusts and referred to *Thorner v Major*, which he described as an important decision dealing with alleged assurances which were inexact in relation to future bequests. He specifically referred to the *dicta* of Lord Scott in *Thorner* to the effect that he would 'prefer to keep proprietary estoppel and constructive trust as distinct and separate remedies, to confine proprietary estoppel to cases where the representation whether express or implied on which the claimant has acted is unconditional and to address the cases where the representation are of future benefits, and subject to qualification on account of unforeseen future events, via the principles of remedial constructive trusts.'[383] He went on to state that the decision in *Thorner* would suggest that it is open to the court where it has concerns about the uncertainty of a promise, in particular a future promise of a bequest in a will, to hold that 'a constructive remedial trust' arises. White J stated that he was satisfied that the plaintiff thought that he had assurances that he would benefit under the deceased's will, although he acknowledged that there was a lack of certainty in relation to this, and that he had relied on the assurances to his substantial detriment. He expressed the view that because the deceased had led the plaintiff to believe that he would be rewarded in the future with an interest in the farm which led to him devoting a very substantial part of his adult life to working on it, it would be unconscionable that the deceased's estate should accrue entirely to the latter's family. He concluded that '[w]hile the court can hold that proprietary estoppel arises, because of the uncertain nature of the promises made as to the future

381. [2008] IEHC 447.
382. [2016] IEHC 255.
383. [2009] 1 WLR 776, 785.

intentions of the deceased, the court is of the opinion that a constructive remedial trust arises.'[384] In the circumstances, White J held that the appropriate remedy was that the plaintiff should be awarded half the farmland and half the value of the stock and machinery.

It appears from the judgment of White J that he, like Lord Scott in *Thorner*, favoured the use of constructive trust principles rather than proprietary estoppel where the claim made relates to a future benefit, which may be subject to qualification as a result of unforeseen events. However, there is little support for the drawing of such a distinction elsewhere and the circumstances which arose in *Finnegan v Hand* would equally have lent themselves to a straightforward application of the proprietary estoppel principles set out, for example, in *Coyle v Finnegan*. There has been no reference made in any of decisions in this jurisdiction to the complex issues explored above which an elision of proprietary estoppel and constructive trust principles may give rise to and it remains to be seen whether the courts here have any appetite to grapple with these questions.

The Relationship between Proprietary and Promissory Estoppel

Traditionally, a distinction has been drawn between cases in which promissory and proprietary estoppel may arise,[385] although there have also been suggestions to the effect that making such a distinction is not helpful.[386] A flexible approach towards the need to draw distinctions between the two doctrines was accepted in Australia by a number of the judges in the decisions of the High Court of Australia in *Waltons Stores (Interstate) Ltd v Maher*[387] and in *Commonwealth of Australia v Verwayen*.[388] However, subsequent decisions of the High Court of Australia showed no inclination to merge the two doctrines.[389] More recently, the distinction between the scope of the doctrines of promissory and proprietary estoppel has been maintained in a number of decisions of the Court of Appeal of New South Wales.[390]

The courts in this jurisdiction have on occasion used the labels promissory and proprietary estoppel in what appears to be a rather indiscriminate manner and it is necessary to consider what significance, if any, attaches to this development. One of the most controversial decisions in this context is that of Costello J in *Re J.R.*[391] The committee of an elderly ward of court, who was living in a psychiatric hospital and was unable to manage his own affairs, sought

384. [2016] IEHC 255 at [70].
385. For a useful analysis of the most significant differences between the two doctrines, see Mee (1998) 33 Ir Jur (ns) 187, 197-202.
386. *Crabb v Arun District Council* [1976] Ch 179, 193 *per* Scarman LJ.
387. (1988) 164 CLR 387. See in particular at 404 *per* Mason CJ; at 420 *per* Brennan J.
388. (1990) 170 CLR 394.
389. *Giumelli v Giumelli* (1999) 196 CLR 101; *Sidhu v Van Dyke* (2014) 308 ALR 232.
390. *Saleh v Romanous* [2010] NSWCA 274; *DHJPM Pty Ltd v Blackthorn Resources Ltd* (2011) 285 ALR 311; *Ashton v Pratt* (2015) 318 ALR 260.
391. [1993] ILRM 657.

to effect the sale of his house which had fallen into a dilapidated state. He had been living there with the respondent for many years and she maintained that when she went to live with him he had represented to her that he would look after her and that she would be sure of a home for the rest of her life. In his will the ward left everything to the respondent and at the time of its execution said to her that it was no longer his house but their house and that it would eventually be her house. Costello J concluded that the respondent had acted to her detriment on the representation made to her at the time she went to live with the ward that thereafter she could be sure of a home in his house for the rest of her life. He said that accordingly she had made out a case of promissory estoppel as she had acted on the representation made to her and '[i]t would be plainly inequitable for the ward now to deny that she has a right to live in his house and it seems to me that she has an equity which entitles her to stay in the house rent free for as long as she wishes to which the court must give effect.'[392] Costello J said that the respondent could not claim any enforceable rights by virtue of the ward handing her the will and saying the house was theirs as the gift was an imperfect one which the courts could not enforce – these actions did not confer an immediate beneficial interest under a constructive trust. Instead the ward had intended that she have a right to reside in the house during his life and ownership of it after his death. He concluded that the equity which the respondent had been able to establish was a right to reside in the house for her life. However, in the special circumstances of the case as the house was in a serious state of dilapidation, the respondent's equity could be satisfied by selling the house and buying another one suitable for her needs.

While the result achieved was clearly a fair and equitable one in the circumstances, there are a number of difficulties with the reasoning employed by Costello J. Essentially, he appeared to hold that promissory estoppel is capable of creating proprietary rights. While it has long been accepted that proprietary estoppel may give rise to a cause of action,[393] it would appear to be a novel approach to suggest that promissory estoppel is equally capable of doing so and it is clearly impossible to reconcile with the *dicta* of O'Hanlon J in *Association of General Practitioners Ltd v Minister for Health*,[394] in which he reasserted the traditional view that promissory estoppel should be regarded as providing a shield and not a sword.[395] Coughlan's comment that in *Re J.R.*[396] Costello J failed to address fully the implications of the step he was taking or

392. *Ibid.* at 663.
393. *Inwards v Baker* [1965] 2 QB 29, 38; *Crabb v Arun District Council* [1976] Ch 179, 187 *per* Denning MR. See also the comments of Geoghegan J in *Smyth v Halpin* [1997] 2 ILRM 38, 42, in which he pointed out that the granting of a remedy to the plaintiff would involve using estoppel 'as a sword and not merely as a shield'.
394. [1995] 2 ILRM 481.
395. See *Combe v Combe* [1951] 2 KB 215, 224; *Newport City Council v Charles* [2009] 1 WLR 1884, 1890. But see the judgment of Gresson J in *Thomas v Thomas* [1956] NZLR 785.
396. [1993] ILRM 657.

to consider the relevant authorities is a fair one.[397] In the context of the facts which were before the court in that case Coughlan's statement that 'it is difficult to envisage situations in which promissory estoppel will be of more utility than proprietary estoppel'[398] is particularly apt.

Similarly, Mee has commented in relation to *Re J.R.* that 'it is not readily apparent why Costello J chose to rest his decision on promissory estoppel rather than proprietary estoppel'[399] and this remark might equally be applied to a later decision in which the plaintiff sought to assert his entitlement to rights over land arising out of assurances allegedly made to him. In *Carter v Ross*[400] Murphy J concluded that the plaintiff's claim was based on a very vague promise and that there had been minimal detriment suffered and he concluded that there was no evidence to support a finding that promissory estoppel arose on the basis of the facts before the court. It should also be noted that in *McGuinness v McGuinness*,[401] although it differed significantly from the decisions considered above in that estoppel was raised as a defence rather than a cause of action, Kinlen J also spoke in terms of promissory estoppel. He concluded that 'to establish promissory estoppel, [the defendant] must prove a material detriment in reliance on a promise of entitlement to land'.

In his speech in the decision of the House of Lords in *Cobbe v Yeoman's Row Management Ltd*,[402] Lord Scott referred to estoppel becoming 'proprietary' estoppel if the right claimed is a proprietary right, usually a right to or over land and referred to it as 'a sub-species of a "promissory" estoppel'.[403] However, as Etherton subsequently commented, 'his characterisation of proprietary estoppel in that way would be viewed by some as surprising'.[404] In addition, Lord Walker expressed the view in his speech in *Thorner v Major*[405] that he had 'some difficulty' with Lord Scott's observation but added that he acknowledged that 'the terminology and taxonomy' in this area of the law are far from uniform.

Lord Walker also gave consideration in the course of his speech in *Thorner* to some of the distinctions between what he clearly viewed as separate doctrines. He said that there is some authority for the view that the 'clear and unequivocal' test does not apply to proprietary estoppel and that this has been expressed

---

397. Coughlan (1993) 15 DULJ 188. See also Lee & Ho (2009) 125 LQR 25 for an analysis of the decision of the Hong Kong Court of Final Appeal in *Luo v Hui* [2008] HKEC 996 which employed a similar approach.
398. *Ibid.* at 189.
399. Mee (1998) 33 Ir Jur (ns) 187, 218.
400. High Court (Murphy J) 8 December 2000.
401. High Court 2001 Nos. 145CA and 147CA (Kinlen J) 19 March 2002.
402. [2008] 1 WLR 1752.
403. *Ibid.* at 1761. It should be noted that Lord Scott referred to the claimant's 'promissory estoppel' claim later in his speech (at 1765) but it is likely that this was an oversight as the other surrounding references were all to the doctrine of proprietary estoppel.
404. Etherton [2009] Conv 104, 116. See also the comments of Griffiths [2009] Conv 141, 143.
405. [2009] 1 WLR 776, 797.

both by judges[406] and academics. He referred to the following passage from Treitel, *Law of Contract*:[407]

> Promissory estoppel arises only out of a representation or promise that is 'clear' or 'precise and unambiguous.' Proprietary estoppel, on the other hand, can arise where there is no actual promise: eg where one party makes improvements to another's land under a mistake and the other either knows of the mistake or seeks to take unconscionable advantage of it.

Subsequently, Lord Walker stated that in his opinion it is a necessary element of proprietary estoppel that the assurances given to the claimant, whether expressly or impliedly or even tacitly should relate to identified property owned, or about to be owned, by the defendant.[408] In his view, this is one of the main distinguishing features between promissory estoppel and proprietary estoppel. As he stated, promissory estoppel must be based on an existing legal relationship, usually a contract, but not necessarily a contract relating to land, and while proprietary estoppel need not be based on an existing legal relationship, it must relate to identified property, usually land, owned or about to be owned by the defendant.[409]

So, despite Lord Scott's attempt to characterise proprietary estoppel as a sub-species of promissory estoppel, there is little evidence in these recent decisions of any further move to assimilate them. On the contrary, Lord Walker's careful analysis of the differences between them would suggest that they will continue to co-exist as separate doctrines with their own particular characteristics. This approach is to a large extent borne out by the views expressed by Patten LJ in *Lester v Woodgate*.[410] While he acknowledged that in both cases the key to the intervention of equity is the making of a representation or promise about the enforcement of property or contractual rights in circumstances which make it unconscionable for the promisor subsequently to go back on his promise, he added that the distinctions between proprietary and promissory estoppel are justified either by the need to identify the conditions for the creation of the estoppel or in terms of the remedies available for its enforcement. As he stated, in cases of promissory estoppel, the existing contractual rights are modified by equity's refusal to allow the full terms of the contract to be enforced and it is

406. He referred to the judgment of Slade LJ in *Jones v Watkins* Court of Appeal, 26 November 1987.
407. Peel, *Treitel: The Law of Contract* (12th ed., 2007) para. 3-144. Now see 14th edition, 2015.
408. See also *MacDonald v Frost* [2009] WTLR 1815 at [11].
409. It was suggested by Snowden J when debate arose about this issue in *West End Commercial Ltd v London Trocadero (2015) LLP* [2017] EWHC 2175 (Ch) that 'given the authority of the decision in *Thorner v Major*, it is clear that only the Supreme Court or the legislature could remove the current proprietary limit to the operation of proprietary estoppel.'
410. [2010] EWCA Civ 199 at [25].

defensive only, whereas by contrast in cases of proprietary estoppel, the equity can be satisfied by the grant of permanent property rights over the estate of the person bound by the estoppel.

LIKELY FUTURE DEVELOPMENTS

As Robert Goff J commented in *Amalgamated Investment & Property Co. v Texas Commerce International Bank Ltd*,[411] '[o]f all doctrines, equitable estoppel is surely one of the most flexible'. While it has been recommended that the different species of estoppel should 'merge into one general principle shorn of limitation,'[412] it is questionable whether such an all-embracing doctrine based on the unifying concept of unconscionability would be desirable. Certainly, it has been suggested that there is no real authority to back up a development of this nature.[413] On the other hand, *dicta* in a number of Australian decisions did suggest that there is 'but one doctrine of estoppel'.[414] In *Waltons Stores (Interstate) Ltd v Maher*[415] Mason CJ stated as follows:

> One may therefore discern in the cases a common thread which links them together, namely the principle that equity will come to the relief of a plaintiff who has acted to his detriment on the basis of a basic assumption in relation to which the other party to the transaction has 'played such a part in the adoption of the assumption that it would be unfair or unjust if he were left free to ignore it' *per* Dixon J in *Grundt v Great Boulder Pty Gold Mines Ltd* (1937) 59 CLR 641 at p.675; see also *Thompson v Palmer* (1933) 49 CLR 507 at p. 547. Equity comes to the relief of such a plaintiff on the footing that it would be unconscionable conduct on the part of the other party to ignore the assumption.

In addition, in *Commonwealth of Australia v Verwayen*,[416] Mason CJ spoke of a single doctrine of estoppel which would provide that a court of common law or equity may do what is necessary to prevent a person, who has relied on an assumption as to a present, past or future state of affairs, which was induced by the party estopped, from suffering detriment in reliance on this assumption. However, as noted above, in its subsequent decision in *Giumelli v Giumelli*[417]

411. [1982] QB 84, 103. See also *Waltons Stores (Interstate) Ltd v Maher* (1988) 164 CLR 387, 419.
412. *Amalgamated Investment and Property Co. Ltd v Texas Commerce International Bank Ltd* [1982] QB 84, 122.
413. Evans [1988] Conv 346, 347.
414. *Commonwealth of Australia v Verwayen* (1990) 170 CLR 394, 412.
415. (1988) 164 CLR 387, 404.
416. (1990) 170 CLR 394.
417. (1999) 196 CLR 10, 112-113. See also *Sidhu v Van Dyke* (2014) 308 ALR 232, 234; *Crown Melbourne Ltd v Cosmopolitan Hotel (Vic) Pty Ltd* (2016) 333 ALR 384, 415,

the High Court of Australia made no further reference to a single doctrine of estoppel although it acknowledged that there was no reason in the matter before the court to consider whether the various principles and remedies in the field of estoppel should be brought under a single overarching doctrine. In New Zealand it has been suggested that 'as the traditional limitations on the doctrines of promissory and proprietary estoppel have been removed, New Zealand courts have drawn on cases from each stream of precedent without distinction' and that 'the end result has been the recognition of a unified doctrine of equitable estoppel'.[418] Bant and Bryan have also recently suggested that there is an opportunity to develop a 'coherent and unified doctrine of estoppel moulded around the requirement of reasonable reliance'.[419]

However, there have been no signs of a movement towards acceptance of a unified doctrine of estoppel in England.[420] As Millett LJ commented in *First National Bank plc v Thompson*:[421]

> Spencer Bower's valiant attempt to demonstrate that all estoppels other than estoppel by record are now subsumed in the single and all-embracing estoppel by representation and that they are all governed by the same requirements has never won general acceptance. Historically unsound, it has been repudiated by academic writers and is unsupported by authority.

Although it could be argued that the reasoning employed by Costello J in *Re J.R.* would support the view that a unified approach might be accepted in this jurisdiction, it would probably be unwise to assume such a conclusion based on a judgment which does not fully address the implications of such a step.[422] Realistically we are unlikely to see a unified doctrine of estoppel emerging in

---

although in the latter case it was acknowledged that 'broadly speaking … the categories of promissory and proprietary estoppel serve a common purpose of protecting a party from detriment.'

418. Every-Palmer, 'Equitable Estoppel' in *Equity and Trusts in New Zealand* (ed. Butler, 2nd ed., 2009) p. 609. While Mackenzie J commented in *Hawley v Rangitikei District Council* [2007] NZHC 1343 that the question of whether the previously separate forms of estoppel remain distinct was not one which the courts were required to address in the case before him, he suggested (at [8]) that: 'the requirements for the various forms of estoppel are sufficiently similar that the same result must follow in either case.'
419. (2015) 35 OJLS 427, 452.
420. Lunney [1992] Conv 239, 248-250 accepted that there is no direct authority in England which supports a unified doctrine of estoppel based on unconscionability raising equities which can be enforced by the other party, although he put forward the view that the approach advocated in Australia represented a logical advance.
421. [1996] Ch 231, 236.
422. Mee has commented (1998) 33 Ir Jur (ns) 187, 219 that 'one must conclude that *Re J.R.* was simply another example of an Irish judge reaching a conclusion which he regarded as just without paying much attention to strict legal doctrine'.

the near future either in this jurisdiction or in England.[423] Mee has suggested that 'there has been nothing resembling a carefully considered (or even conscious) decision to merge the estoppels in Ireland'[424] and suggests that the position in this jurisdiction appears to be that the doctrines of proprietary and promissory estoppel retain their separate identities.

It should be noted that the role which unconscionability plays in the doctrine of proprietary estoppel has given rise to considerable debate and uncertainty.[425] As Etherton comments, it is ironic that the House of Lords relaxed the requirements for a constructive trust in *Stack v Dowden*[426] while at the same time restricting the doctrine of proprietary estoppel in *Cobbe v Yeoman's Row Management Ltd*:[427] in his words, '[i]t might be said that they have shot the wrong beast.'[428] One of the primary criticisms of the doctrine of proprietary estoppel put forward by Lord Scott in *Cobbe* is that it can lead to uncertainty and unpredictability. He stated as follows:

> Proprietary estoppel requires, in my opinion, clarity as to what it is that the object of the estoppel is to be estopped from denying, or asserting, and clarity as to the interest in the property in question that that denial, or assertion, would otherwise defeat. If these requirements are not recognised, proprietary estoppel will lose contact with its roots and risk becoming unprincipled and therefore unpredictable, if it has not already become so.[429]

While certainty in commercial transactions is undoubtedly of importance, as noted above, the results achieved in decisions such as *Banner Homes* are not significantly different from that which might have been arrived at in *Cobbe* had the approach employed at first instance and in the Court of Appeal been allowed to stand. Proprietary estoppel with its well-established requirement to show detrimental reliance and its potential to provide flexibility as to the remedy to be imposed is in many ways a superior mechanism for intervention in cases of this nature. While it is difficult to argue with Etherton's conclusion that there is a real need for a coherent legal framework across the boundaries of trusts, estoppel and restitution to provide remedies for unconscionable conduct in relation to the acquisition and ownership of land,[430] in one sense proprietary estoppel as it had developed prior to *Cobbe* provided that framework. In some

423. See generally *National Westminster Bank v Somer International* (UK) Ltd [2002] QB 1286, 1303-1304.
424. Mee (1998) 33 Ir Jur (ns) 187, 219.
425. See Balen and Knowles [2011] Conv 176, 181 who go as far as to suggest that 'unconscionability should not form part of the estoppel inquiry'.
426. [2007] 2 AC 432.
427. [2008] 1 WLR 1752.
428. [2009] Conv 104, 125.
429. [2008] 1 WLR 1752, 1768-1769.
430. Etherton [2009] Conv 104, 125.

ways it is hard to reconcile the decisions of the House of Lords in *Cobbe* and *Thorner*, other than by acknowledging that the former related to a commercial transaction, while the latter did not.[431] It is to be hoped that future decisions may restore proprietary estoppel to the high ground which it formerly occupied, as a principled, coherent and yet flexible solution in situations calling for judicial intervention in relation to dealings in land whether of a commercial or non-commercial nature.

Finally, it is worth pointing out that Mee has commented that the courts appear to be willing to assume that a person who has explicitly declined to enter into a contract 'is merely excluding legal liability of a contractual kind but is still assuming potential liability under the law of proprietary estoppel.'[432] However, he suggests that such a person may be indicating that he does not wish to take on legal liability of any kind and expresses the view that 'the development of proprietary estoppel should not undermine the important distinction between the moral concept of promise and the legal concept of contract.'[433] While this is undoubtedly true, the challenge for the courts in applying and developing the doctrine of proprietary estoppel is to be mindful of this distinction but also willing to intervene where the claimant's detrimental reliance requires it, and where it would be unconscionable not to provide a remedy of a proportionate nature.

431. Piska has commented (2009) 72 MLR 998, 1012 that the decisions in *Cobbe* and *Thorner*, as well as *Stack v Dowden* [2007] 2 AC 432 illustrate the growing emphasis on context in equity, particularly between commercial and domestic settings.
432. [2013] Conv 280, 290-291.
433. *Ibid.* at 291. See further Mee, 'Proprietary Estoppel, Promises and Mistaken Belief' in *Modern Studies in Property Law Volume 6* (ed. Bright, 2011) p. 175 at 195-197.

Chapter 19

Tracing

TRACING AT COMMON LAW

At common law while a person who was wrongfully deprived of his property could follow it into the hands of another party, he could only do so in circumstances where this property was still identifiable and had not been mixed with other funds. Millett J has summarised the principles which apply to this form of tracing in his judgment in *Agip (Africa) Ltd v Jackson* as follows:[1]

> Tracing at common law, unlike its counterpart in equity, is neither a cause of action nor a remedy but serves an evidential purpose. The cause of action is for money had and received. Tracing at common law enables the defendant to be identified as the recipient of the plaintiff's money and the measure of his liability to be determined by the amount of the plaintiff's money he is shown to have received.

So, at common law the legal owner of property was entitled to follow it into the hands of another even where it had changed in form provided that there was a means of identifying the asset in its original or converted form. As Lord Ellenborough stated in *Taylor v Plumer*,[2] '[i]t makes no difference in reason or law into what other form, different from the original, the change may have been made'. He pointed out that 'the product of or substitute for the original thing still follows the nature of the thing itself, as long as it can be ascertained as such'[3] but this right to follow at common law will cease when the means of identifying the original is lost, e.g. when the assets are converted into money and 'confounded into a general mass of the same description'.[4] These principles were reiterated by the Court of Appeal in *Re Diplock*,[5] where Lord Greene MR

---

1. [1990] Ch 265, 285. See also *Armstrong DLW GmbH v Winnington Networks Ltd* [2013] Ch 156, 178.
2. (1815) 3 M & S 562, 575. For an alternative interpretation of what this decision established, see Smith [1995] LMCLQ 240.
3. *Ibid.* at 575.
4. However, note the comments of Virgo, 'Re Hallett's Estate' in *Landmark Cases in Equity* (2012) p. 357 at 386-387, where he suggests that there is no difference between the tracing rules at common law and in equity but rather that in the latter case, a claimant would be confined to a personal claim against a recipient for the value of what was received.
5. [1948] 1 Ch 465, 518. See also the comment of Millett J in *Agip (Africa) Ltd v Jackson*

commented that the common law 'could only appreciate what might almost be called the "physical" identity of one thing with another'. So, the common law could treat money as identifiable provided it was not mixed with other money and could also treat as identifiable other kinds of property acquired with these funds alone.[6]

The inability of the common law to trace into a mixed fund in a manner which would lead to a proprietary form of remedy is undoubtedly its greatest limitation. This means that it cannot assist a plaintiff in what is probably the most common situation in practice where tracing may be required, namely where a defendant has mixed the plaintiff's money with his own and subsequently gone bankrupt.[7] The other major limitation of this form of tracing is that because the common law did not recognise equitable rights and interests, a beneficiary could not follow trust property into the hands of a trustee.[8]

Consideration was given to tracing at common law by the English Court of Appeal in *F.C. Jones & Sons (Trustees) v Jones*,[9] in which the plaintiff was held to be entitled to trace not only the property but also any profit made from it. As Nourse LJ commented, the decision went further than previous cases 'in that it holds that the action for money had and received entitles the legal owner to trace his property into its product, not only in the sense of property for which it is exchanged, but also in the sense of property representing the original and the profit made by the defendant's use of it'.[10] In considering the rules which apply to tracing at law and in equity Millett LJ stated as follows:

> There is no merit in having distinct and different tracing rules at law and in equity, given that tracing is neither a right nor a remedy but merely the process by which the plaintiff establishes what has happened to his property and makes good his claim that the assets which he claims can properly be regarded as representing his property. The fact that there are different tracing rules at law and in equity is unfortunate though probably inevitable, but unnecessary differences should not be created where they are not required by the different nature of legal and equitable doctrines and remedies. There is in my view, even less merit in the present rule which precludes the invocation of the equitable tracing rules to support a common law claim; until that rule is swept away unnecessary obstacles to the development of a rational and coherent law of restitution will remain.[11]

[1990] Ch 265, 285 that 'it can only follow a physical asset … from one person to another'.

6. *Ibid.* at 518.
7. See Glister and Lee, *Hanbury and Martin: Modern Equity* (21st ed., 2018) p. 726.
8. See the judgment of Lord Greene MR in *Re Diplock* [1948] Ch 465, 519-520 where this and other limitations were discussed.
9. [1997] Ch 159.
10. *Ibid.* at 172.
11. *Ibid.* at 169-170.

These views were reiterated by Lord Millett in his speech in *Foskett v McKeown*,[12] where he added that given its nature there is nothing inherently legal or equitable about the tracing exercise and that there is thus no sense in maintaining different rules for tracing at law and in equity. However, Stevens has argued that once the proprietary nature of tracing is accepted,[13] it should be recognised that the historic distinction between legal and equitable tracing cannot be abandoned and that the rules in each case differ because the incidents of ownership at common law and in equity also differ.[14]

TRACING IN EQUITY

Introduction

While a trustee or a party liable to account in Equity may be personally liable to beneficiaries, where, e.g. he has transferred the trust property to another in breach of trust and has disposed of the proceeds of sale, this remedy will be of little value if the trustee has insufficient assets to meet the claim. Where he no longer has the trust property in his possession and cannot meet any personal claim against him, the alternative of a proprietary remedy must be considered. It is also important to remember that a liability to account in equity will only be imposed where trust property becomes vested in a person in a manner which amounts to a breach of trust and where property is transferred to an innocent volunteer no personal liability can be imposed. In both these situations tracing will provide a process whereby a beneficiary may identify property belonging to him which has been wrongly disposed of. As Lord Millett stated in *Foskett v McKeown*:[15]

> A beneficiary of a trust is entitled to a continuing beneficial interest not merely in the trust property but in its traceable proceeds also, and his interest binds every one who takes the property or its traceable proceeds except a *bona fide* purchaser for value without notice.

The proprietary tracing process has a number of advantages; first, where the trustee is insolvent, the claimant will take in priority to his general creditors.[16] Secondly, where trust property comes into the hands of an innocent volunteer, who takes subject to the trust but has neither actual nor constructive knowledge

12. [2001] 1 AC 102, 128. See also the views expressed by Lord Steyn at 113 and by Birks in 'The Necessity of a Unitary Law of Tracing' in *Making Commercial Law, Essays in Honour of Roy Goode* (ed. Cranston, 1997) p. 257.
13. As it was by Lord Millett and the other law lords in the majority in *Foskett*, Lord Browne-Wilkinson and Lord Hoffmann.
14. Stevens [2001] Conv 94, 100.
15. [2001] 1 AC 102, 127.
16. *Re Hallett's Estate* (1880) 13 Ch D 696.

of it, the volunteer will not be liable to account in equity but tracing may enable a beneficiary to identify property belonging to him in the hands of a recipient prior to asserting a proprietary claim against the latter.

Tracing has taken on a new significance as a means of recovering the proceeds of international fraud. While, as we have seen, the common law cannot trace into a mixed fund, equity does not require the existence of a physical asset and can identify funds even where they have been the subject of electronic transfer.[17] As Lord Greene MR commented in *Re Diplock*,[18] 'Equity adopted a more metaphysical approach' and 'found no difficulty in regarding a composite fund as an amalgam constituted by the mixture of two or more funds each of which could be regarded as having, for certain purposes, a continued separate existence.'

Some debate has also developed about the nature of the tracing process.[19] In the course of his speech for the majority in *Foskett v McKeown*,[20] Lord Millett stated as follows:

> Tracing is thus neither a claim nor a remedy. It is merely the process by which a claimant demonstrates what has happened to his property, identifies its proceeds and the persons who have handled or received them, and justifies his claim that the proceeds can be properly regarded as representing his property.

Lord Steyn, although he was in the minority, agreed that tracing was a process of identifying assets and that it belonged to the realm of evidence.[21]

General Principles

Tracing in equity is usually sought where property has come into the hands of trustees and other persons in a fiduciary relationship. It is 'a claim to follow and recover property with which, in equity at all events, [a person] had never really parted'.[22] The right to trace in equity also exists against third parties into whose hands the funds may have come. Although it does not extend to

17. Millett (1991) 107 LQR 71, 74.
18. [1948] Ch 465, 520. Quoted by Budd J in *Shanahan's Stamp Auctions Ltd v Farrelly* [1962] IR 386, 436.
19. See generally Smith, *The Law of Tracing* (1997). See also O'Dell (1999) 21 DULJ 131.
20. [2001] 1 AC 102, 128. See also Grantham and Rickett (2000) 63 MLR 905. As Lewison J stated in *Ultraframe (UK) Ltd v Fielding* [2005] EWHC 1638 (Ch) at [1464], it follows that the tracing exercise must be carried out first, '[o]nly then can the court consider what rights (if any) the claimant has in the assets that have been identified as trust property or their identifiable substitutes'.
21. However, Stevens [2001] Conv 94, 101 has questioned whether such an approach is consistent with the proprietary nature of tracing.
22. *Sinclair v Brougham* [1914] AC 398, 418.

purchasers for value of the property without notice of the right to trace, it will apply to an innocent volunteer who comes into possession of the trust property. It should also be noted that traditionally it has been accepted that in order to trace in equity, a plaintiff should possess an equitable proprietary interest.[23]

The decision in which the parameters of tracing in equity were first explored in detail and which illustrated the potential for tracing into a mixed fund was that of the English Court of Appeal in *Re Hallett's Estate*.[24] As Atkin LJ was later to comment in relation to this decision,[25] 'if in 1815 the common law halted outside the banker's door, by 1879 equity had had the courage to lift the latch, walk in and examine the books'. In *Hallett* a solicitor had lodged funds from a trust of which he was trustee and those belonging to a client to his own bank account. He made various payments from and into the account and after his death it emerged that there were insufficient funds remaining to pay these monies back and to meet his personal debts. In an action brought to decide how his estate should be administered, the question arose whether the trust and the client could claim priority over the solicitor's general creditors. It was held by the Court of Appeal that the beneficiaries under the trust and the client were entitled to trace the misappropriated funds and that they were entitled to a lien or charge on the monies in the bank account in priority to the general creditors. One important principle to be derived from the judgment to which we shall return is that the solicitor was presumed to have spent his own money first and not to have drawn on the trust monies irrespective of the order in which these funds were paid into his account.[26] It should be noted that one aspect of the conclusion reached by Jessel MR in *Hallett* was disapproved by Lord Millett in *Foskett v McKeown*,[27] where he noted that the former appeared to suggest that in the case of a mixed substitution, the beneficiary is confined to a lien. Lord Millett stated 'in my view the time has come to state unequivocally that English law has no such rule'[28] and that it conflicts with the principle that a trustee must not benefit from his trust.

It has also been established that the equitable tracing remedy is not confined to claims as between a trustee and beneficiary but will extend to any persons in fiduciary relationships and it has become clear that this relationship need not exist between the parties to the action. In *Sinclair v Brougham*[29] a building society which had operated an *ultra vires* banking business was wound up and a dispute arose in relation to the respective claims of the shareholders and the depositors. The House of Lords found that there was a sufficient fiduciary

23. Although note the decision of the English Court of Appeal in *Aluminium Industrie Vassen BV v Romalpa Aluminium Ltd* [1976] 1 WLR 676.
24. (1880) 13 Ch D 696.
25. *Banque Belge pour l'Etranger v Hambrouck* [1921] 1 KB 321, 335.
26. See also *Carroll Group Distributors Ltd v G. & J.F. Bourke Ltd* [1990] 1 IR 481, 484.
27. [2001] 1 AC 102.
28. *Ibid.* at 131.
29. [1914] AC 398.

relationship between the depositors and the directors of the building society 'by reason of the fact that the purposes for which the depositors had handed their money to the directors were by law incapable of fulfilment'.[30] It was held that the depositors had a right to trace the funds into the hands of the society and ranked *pari passu* with the shareholders as regards entitlement to the funds. As Viscount Haldane LC commented, 'I see no reason why either set of claimants should have priority over the other.'[31] Oakley has stated that 'the decision was unquestionably authority for the availability of an equitable proprietary claim to the transferor of property under a transaction which is void *ab initio*'.[32] However, it should be pointed out that the decision in *Sinclair v Brougham* was effectively overruled by the House of Lords in *Westdeutsche Landesbank Girozentrale v Islington London Borough Council*,[33] which will be considered in more detail below, where the majority of the House of Lords held that an equitable proprietary claim is not available to a transferor of property under an *ultra vires* transaction which is void *ab initio*.

It was established in *Re Diplock*[34] that an innocent volunteer who receives money or property *bona fide* is in the same position as regards entitlement to this property as an equitable owner who has a right to trace.[35] Mr Diplock left the residue of his estate on trust for 'such charitable institutions or other charitable or benevolent object or objects in England as my executors may in their absolute discretion select'. The executors of the will, thinking that it was a valid charitable gift, paid out a large part of the residue amounting to over £200,000 to various charitable institutions. Subsequently, it became clear that the gift was not a valid charitable one,[36] and the next of kin, having exhausted their remedies against the executors, sought to recover these monies from the charities. It was held by the Court of Appeal[37] that they were entitled to trace the funds into the hands of the charities which were innocent volunteers,[38] with whom they had to share rateably. So, as Lord Greene MR stated, '[w]here the contest is between two claimants

30. *Per* Lord Greene MR in *Re Diplock* [1948] Ch 465, 540-541.
31. [1914] AC 398, 425.
32. Oakley [1997] Conv 1, 2.
33. [1996] AC 669. Lord Browne-Wilkinson (at 713) described it as a 'bewildering authority' and commented that all the reasoning in the decision was 'open to serious objection'.
34. [1948] Ch 465.
35. As Lord Greene MR commented at 539, '[i]t would be inequitable for the volunteer to claim priority for the reason that he is a volunteer: it would be equally inequitable for the true owner of the money to claim priority over the volunteer for the reason that the volunteer is innocent and cannot be said to act unconscionably if he claims the equal treatment for himself.'
36. The use of the word 'or' was interpreted to mean that the words of the gift were wide enough to allow the trustees to dispose of the fund or an unascertainable part of it to non-charitable purposes.
37. The appeal to the House of Lords, (*sub nom Ministry of Health v Simpson* [1951] AC 251) related only to the *in personam* claims of the next of kin.
38. Lord Greene MR went on to stress (at 544) that although 'equity may operate upon

to a mixed fund made up entirely of moneys held on behalf of the two of them respectively and mixed together by the fiduciary agent, they share *pari passu.*'[39]

This view was reiterated by Lord Millett in *Foskett v McKeown*,[40] where he stated that innocent contributors must be treated equally *inter se* and that where a beneficiary's claim is in competition with the claims of other innocent contributors, there is no basis upon which any of the claims can be subordinated to any of the others. *Foskett v McKeown*[41] has been described as 'without doubt the most important recent decision of the law of tracing'[42] and needs to be considered in some detail. A trustee fraudulently used money entrusted to him for a property development scheme to pay a number of the premiums on a life insurance policy. When the trustee died, a dispute arose in relation to entitlement to the death benefit on the policy. A majority of the House of Lords held that the purchasers in the property development scheme were entitled to a share of the proceeds of the policy proportionate to the premiums which had been paid out of trust monies,[43] although there was disagreement about the manner in which the proportions were to be calculated.[44] Lord Millett stated the 'basic rule' as follows:

> Where a trustee wrongfully uses trust money to provide part of the cost of acquiring an asset, the beneficiary is entitled *at his option* either to claim a proportionate share of the asset or to enforce a lien upon it to secure his personal claim against the trustee for the amount of the misapplied money. It does not matter whether the trustee mixed the trust money with his own in a single fund before using it to acquire the asset, or made separate payments (whether simultaneously or sequentially) out of the differently owned funds to acquire a single asset.[45]

---

the conscience of a volunteer, it will not operate upon the conscience of a purchaser for value without notice.'

39. [1948] Ch 465, 539.
40. [2001] 1 AC 102, 132.
41. [2001] 1 AC 102.
42. Stevens [2001] Conv 94. See also Jaffey (2000) 14 Trust Law Int 194; Walker [2000] RLR 573; Grantham and Rickett (2000) 63 MLR 905; Rotherham [2000] CLJ 440; Berg (2001) 117 LQR 366.
43. This view is in line with the approach suggested by Ungoed-Thomas J in *Re Tilley's Will Trusts* [1967] Ch 1179, 1193, where he commented as follows: 'If…it appears that the trustee has in fact, whatever his intention, laid out trust moneys in or towards a purchase, then the beneficiaries are entitled to the property purchased and any profits which it produces to the extent to which it has been paid for out of trust moneys.'
44. While Lord Browne-Wilkinson and Lord Hoffmann held that the purchasers' shares should be calculated on a pro rata basis, Lord Millett suggested a more complicated approach, although he ultimately conceded that he would be content if the money were divided between the parties in the proportions in which they had contributed to the premiums.
45. [2001] 1 AC 102, 131. See also *Ultraframe (UK) Ltd v Fielding* [2005] EWHC 1638 (Ch) at [1469]; *Director of the Serious Fraud Office v Lexi Holdings plc* [2009]

The alternative to claiming a proportionate share, namely a lien for the amount of the misapplied money, may be useful where the mixed fund is ultimately deficient. However, Lord Millett stressed that the right of a beneficiary to claim a lien is available only against a wrongdoer and those deriving title under him otherwise than for value; as he stated 'it is not available against competing contributors who are innocent of any wrongdoing'.[46]

It is the reasoning underlying the difference between the conclusions reached by the majority and minority in *Foskett* which has attracted most academic comment. While the majority clearly felt that tracing was a process of a proprietary nature, the minority were in favour of a restitutionary-based approach. Lord Millett stated that the purchasers sought to vindicate their property rights and not to reverse unjust enrichment and Lord Browne-Wilkinson agreed that '[w]e are not dealing with a claim in unjust enrichment'.[47] Similarly, Lord Hoffmann stressed that the claim was 'not based upon unjust enrichment except in the most trivial sense of that expression'[48] and was instead the vindication of a proprietary right. However, Lord Hope placed emphasis on the fact that the beneficiaries of the policy had not been enriched by the payments made and he and Lord Steyn concluded that the purchasers were merely entitled to a lien to secure payment of the monies expended on the policy.

Another important decision in this area is *Westdeutsche Landesbank Girozentrale v Islington London Borough Council*.[49] The parties had entered into a ten-year interest rate swap agreement whereby the plaintiff paid a lump sum to the defendant and the defendant was then obliged to make 'interest' payments to the plaintiff. The House of Lords had held in *Hazell v Hammersmith and Fulham LBC*[50] that such interest rate swap agreements were *ultra vires* the powers of local authorities and following this decision the council made no more payments to the bank. The Court of Appeal held that the bank was entitled to recover the balance owed as money had and received and in equity on the basis of its equitable proprietary interest in the monies advanced and awarded compound interest on this sum. Before the House of Lords the council contested its liability to pay compound interest, the traditional view being that the existence of a claim in equity is a prerequisite to the award of compound as opposed to simple interest. The majority of the House of Lords adhered to this view and held that the type of interest payable depended on whether

---

QB 376, 389. So, in *Clark v Cutland* [2004] 1 WLR 783, counsel for the petitioner submitted on the authority of *Foskett v McKeown* that it had an option whether to claim a proportionate share of a pension fund to which money had been diverted or a lien on its assets and elected to pursue a proprietary remedy by seeking a charge over the fund assets, which Arden LJ held was an appropriate form of remedy.

46. *Ibid.* at 132.
47. *Ibid.* at 110.
48. *Ibid.* at 115.
49. [1996] AC 669. See Cope (1996) 112 LQR 521; Jones [1996] CLJ 432; Oakley [1997] Conv 1; Birks [1997] RLR 3.
50. [1992] AC 1.

the bank had a continuing equitable proprietary interest in the sum advanced. They held, overruling *Sinclair v Brougham*, that an equitable proprietary interest cannot exist in favour of a transferor of property under an *ultra vires* transaction which is void *ab initio* and concluded that as a result only simple interest should be awarded to the bank. The minority disagreed and held that equitable jurisdiction to award compound interest could exist even in relation to personal claims at common law and dismissed the council's appeal. Lord Browne-Wilkinson summarised the effect of overruling *Sinclair v Brougham* in the following terms:

> [T]he law can be established in accordance with principle and commercial common sense: a claimant for restitution of moneys paid under an *ultra vires*, and therefore void, contract has a personal action at law to recover the moneys paid as on a total failure of consideration; he will not have an equitable proprietary claim which gives him either rights against third parties or priority in an insolvency; nor will he have a personal claim in equity, since the recipient is not a trustee.[51]

One of the few cases in which general equitable tracing principles have been considered in this jurisdiction is *Shanahan's Stamp Auctions Ltd v Farrelly*.[52] A company which grouped investors into syndicates and used their funds to buy stamps went into liquidation. Some of these investors had been allocated to syndicates at the time and the liquidator sought directions from the court about priority of payments as between the general creditors and the syndicated and unsyndicated investors. Budd J held that at all material times a fiduciary relationship existed between the company and the investors and that both classes of investors were entitled to trace their money. The stamps allocated to the syndicates were held to be subject to a charge in favour of the syndicated investors for the amount of the investment and the remaining stamps were held by the company subject to a charge in favour of the unsyndicated investors on a rateable basis.[53]

Tracing into a Bank Account

Where the mixed fund in which trust monies have been lodged is an active bank account, in certain circumstances a principle known as the rule in *Clayton's* case[54] may apply, although its application is being increasingly rejected both

51. [1996] AC 669, 714.
52. [1962] IR 386.
53. In *Re Money Markets International Stockbrokers Ltd* [2006] IEHC 349 Laffoy J rejected the claim of the applicant investors that the manner in which the court had treated the syndicated investors supported their claim to a better equity than other clients of the company.
54. (1816) 1 Mer 572. See generally O'Dell (2000) 22 DULJ 161.

in this jurisdiction, in England and throughout the common law world. In theory it applies to competing claims of beneficiaries of different trusts and of beneficiaries and innocent volunteers and the effect of the rule is 'first in, first out'. So, if a trustee pays €1,000 from one trust fund into a bank account and then pays a further sum of €1,000 from another fund into the account and later withdraws €1,000, the loss is borne wholly by the first trust on the basis of the principle of 'first in, first out'.[55]

It is important to stress that the rule in *Clayton's* case will not apply to the type of situation which arose in *Re Hallett's Estate*[56] as the trustee was presumed to be acting honestly and to have drawn on his own money in the account first. This is sometimes referred to as the rule in *Re Hallett's Estate* and can be summarised as follows:[57] 'the trustee is presumed to be honest rather than dishonest and to make payments out of his own private moneys and not out of the trust fund that was mingled with his private moneys'.[58] However, this principle will not always be strictly adhered to where this would lead to injustice. In *Re Oatway*[59] a trustee withdrew misappropriated trust monies from a mixed fund and invested them and subsequently dissipated the remainder of the fund. Joyce J refused to apply the *Hallett* principle strictly as this would have led to the conclusion that the money withdrawn initially and invested was the trustee's own, and held instead that the beneficiaries were entitled to the assets represented by the investments.[60]

The rule in *Clayton's* case was applied in relation to some of the claims in *Re Diplock*,[61] although Lord Greene MR did not seem to suggest that it should be automatically applied in such circumstances[62] and said that it was a 'rule of convenience based upon so-called presumed intention'.[63] Similar views were expressed by Woolf LJ in *Barlow Clowes International Ltd v Vaughan*,[64] where he made it clear that 'the rule need only be applied when it is convenient to do so and when its application can be said to do broad justice having regard to the

55. See *Headstart Global Fund Ltd v Citco Bank Nederland NV* [2011] IEHC 5 at [4.4].
56. (1880) 13 Ch D 696.
57. *Per* Sargant J in *James Roscoe (Bolton) Ltd v Winder* [1915] 1 Ch 62, 67. See also the *dictum* of Budd J in *Shanahan's Stamp Auctions Ltd v Farrelly* [1962] IR 386, 428: 'If the person holding the money in a fiduciary capacity mixed it with his own the rule in *Clayton's case* does not apply; such person must be taken to have drawn out his own monies in preference to the trust monies … .'
58. Applied in *FHR European Ventures LLP v Mankarious* [2016] EWHC 359 (Ch).
59. [1903] 2 Ch 356.
60. See also the comments of Rimer J in *Shalson v Russo* [2005] Ch 281, 329, where he acknowledged that while this method amounts to a 'cherry-picking' exercise, if the beneficiary is not permitted to make a claim to the assets represented by the investments, 'the wrongdoing trustee may be left with all the cherries and the victim with nothing'.
61. [1948] Ch 465.
62. *Barlow Clowes International Ltd v Vaughan* [1992] 4 All ER 22, 38 *per* Woolf LJ.
63. [1948] Ch 465, 554.
64. [1992] 4 All ER 22, 39.

nature of the competing claims.'[65] In this case companies which had promoted and managed certain investment plans ran into severe financial difficulties and the amount of money owed to investors far exceeded the funds available for distribution. The receivers sought directions as to how the assets in their hands should be distributed. The trial judge held that the rule of 'first in, first out' should be applied to the distribution of assets so that the investors who could trace into the funds were to be paid in the reverse order to that in which they had made deposits. The Court of Appeal was of the view that, while the first in first out rule would be applied where it provided a convenient method of determining competing claims as between several beneficiaries, where its application would be impractical or would result in injustice between the investors it would not be applied if a preferable alternative method of distribution were available. It was held that it would be contrary to the presumed intention of the investors to distribute the remaining monies in accordance with the 'first in, first out' rule so that those who had invested first could expect least. While it was accepted that the rolling charge or 'North American' solution[66] would in theory be the most logical and just method of distributing the remaining assets, it was held that in the circumstances it would be impractical to apply as, in the view of Woolf LJ, the costs involved in carrying out the necessary calculations would be out of proportion to the sums involved. Instead, it was held that the available assets and moneys should be distributed *pari passu* among all the unpaid investors rateably in proportion to the amounts due to them regardless of the dates on which investors had made their investment.

The suggestion made by Woolf LJ in *Barlow Clowes* that the rule should only be applied where it can be said to do 'broad justice' was heralded as 'a welcome relaxation'[67] of what has been labelled a 'capricious and arbitrary'[68] rule. Subsequently, in *El Ajou v Dollar Land Holdings plc*,[69] Robert Walker J pointed out that the members of the Court of Appeal in *Barlow Clowes* had recognised that the rule may be applied as between rival claimants seeking to trace through an active bank account, although he did acknowledge that the court had accepted that it is 'perhaps *prima facie* not appropriate for those who

---

65. Oliver has commented (1995) 9 Trust Law Int 78, 79 that 'it is at least clear as a result of the *Barlow Clowes* case that the rule in *Clayton's case* is a rule of convenience and not a rule of law, and accordingly it seems unlikely that the courts will use it where it is impracticable or likely to produce inequitable results'.
66. This was described in *Barlow Clowes* (at 28) by Dillon LJ in the following terms: 'where funds of several depositors, or sources, have been blended in one account, each debit to the account, unless unequivocally attributable to the moneys of one depositor or source (eg as if an investment was purchased for one), should be attributed to all the depositors so as to reduce all their deposits pro rata, instead of being attributed, as under *Clayton's* Case, to the earliest deposits in point of time.'
67. Goff and Jones, *The Law of Restitution* (7th ed., 2007) p. 116.
68. *Ibid.* at 108.
69. [1995] 2 All ER 213.

have the common misfortune of being victims of a large scale fraud'.[70] The approach adopted in *Barlow Clowes* was endorsed by Lindsay J in *Russell-Cooke Trust Co. v Prentis*,[71] in which he commented that the modern view has been generally not to challenge the binding nature of the rule in *Clayton's* case but rather to permit it to be distinguished by reference to the facts of the particular case.[72] Lindsay J expressed the opinion that it is clear from all three judgments of the Court of Appeal in *Barlow Clowes* that the rule can be displaced by even a slight counterweight and added, 'indeed, in terms of its actual application between beneficiaries who have in any sense met a shared misfortune, it might be more accurate to refer to the exception that is, rather than the rule in, *Clayton's* case'.[73] Similarly, in *Commerzbank Atkiengesellschaft v IMB Morgan plc*,[74] Lawrence Collins J concluded that the rule in *Clayton's* case had no application to the facts of the case before him, because it would be 'both impracticable and unjust'[75] to apply it. More recently, Etherton C has commented in *National Crime Agency v Robb*[76] that the principle in *Clayton's* case is 'one of convenience and will be displaced if, for example, another approach is more practical or more consistent with the intention of those contributing to the fund.'

In this jurisdiction, consideration was given by Budd J to the circumstances in which the rule in *Clayton's* case should be applied in *Shanahan's Stamp Auctions Ltd v Farrelly*.[77] He accepted that the rule is generally applicable to determine the competing claims of beneficiaries, 'that is the first drawings out are to be attributable to the first payments in'.[78] He then went on to state that it may be that the rule does not apply beyond tracing in a bank account and that it may have no application to property acquired by means of a mixed fund.[79] However, Budd J was satisfied that on the facts of the case it could have no application as there had been a 'second mixing of the investor's funds into a second mixed amalgam of property'.[80]

Further consideration was given to the rule in *Clayton's* case by Laffoy J

70. *Ibid.* at 222.
71. [2003] 2 All ER 478.
72. Pawlowski [2003] Conv 339, 345 draws attention to the fact that the judiciary has declined the invitation to disregard the rule altogether.
73. [2003] 2 All ER 478, 495.
74. [2004] EWHC 2771 (Ch).
75. *Ibid.* at [50].
76. [2015] Ch 520. See also the comment of Henderson J in *Charity Commission for England and Wales v Framjee* [2015] 1 WLR 16, 30 that while the rule in *Clayton's* case is probably still the default rule, 'it may be displaced with relative ease in favour of a solution which produces a fairer result.'
77. [1962] IR 386.
78. *Ibid.* at 442.
79. Although he added that he would 'prefer to deal with the situation, for safety's sake, as if the principle can properly be applied to the case of property acquired with such a mixed fund' (at 442).
80. [1962] IR 386, 442.

in *Re Money Markets International Stockbrokers Ltd*[81] and while her decision has not fully clarified the circumstances in which the rule will be applied, it nevertheless gives a useful indication of judicial thinking on the issue in this jurisdiction. The applicant instructed a stockbroking firm to buy shares on the Irish Stock Exchange on his behalf and the sum due was transferred and credited to the company's bank account several days before the settlement date. The following day the Irish Stock Exchange suspended the right of the company to transact business on the exchange and it was subsequently wound up and an official liquidator appointed. The liquidator acknowledged that the applicant's situation was different to that of other clients of the company as he had transferred monies to the company before the settlement date and these were identifiable in the client account of the company. It was agreed that the company stood in a fiduciary relationship to the applicant and that the funds transferred by the applicant to the company's account were held by the company as trust funds. These funds had been mixed with other funds and the dispute between the parties was in broad terms whether the rule in *Clayton's* case should be applied to determine who was entitled to the monies represented by the credit balance in the company's account.

Having referred to the decisions in *Shanahan's Stamp Auctions Ltd v Farrelly* and *Barlow Clowes International v Vaughan*, Laffoy J stated as follows:

> The conclusions I draw from the authorities are that, as far as this Court is concerned, in the case of a current account such as the account in issue here where trust funds sourced from various beneficiaries are mixed or pooled in the account, it is settled law that as a general proposition the rule in *Clayton's* case is applicable in determining to whom the balance on the account belongs. However, the application of the rule may be displaced in the particular circumstance of a case, for instance, if it is shown or to be inferred that it does not accord with the intention or the presumed intention of the beneficiaries of the trust funds.[82]

Laffoy J stated that having regard to the uniqueness of the applicant's position, she did not think that applying equitable principles, the applicant should be bound by a *pari passu* distribution. She concluded that if the rule in *Clayton's* case was applied in determining entitlement to the monies, it was clear that the applicant would be entitled to repayment of the entirety of the funds transferred by him. Equally if the rule in *Clayton's* case was not applicable, in her view the equity of the applicant was superior to the equity of any other client creditor so that he could not be bound by a rateable distribution. Therefore, irrespective of whether the rule in *Clayton's* case was applied, Laffoy J was satisfied that an order should be made directing the liquidator to repay to the applicant the sum

81. [1999] 4 IR 267.
82. *Ibid.* at 276-277.

transferred to the company. The decision in *Re Money Markets International Stockbrokers Ltd* has been welcomed as 'a good start on the journey towards the repudiation of the rule in *Clayton's* case'[83] and as upholding a strong tradition of the courts deciding cases having regard to the justice of the case as between the parties.[84]

The application of the rule in *Clayton's* case was further considered by Murphy J in *Re W. & R. Murrogh*,[85] in which the court was asked, *inter alia*, to give directions to a receiver about the distribution of the remaining assets of a stockbroking firm which had ceased to trade. As regards the monies in the firm's bank accounts, Murphy J pointed out that if the rule in *Clayton's* case were applied, it would greatly benefit those whose funds had passed through the firm's accounts in a relatively brief period prior to the appointment of a receiver and all other claimants would lose out. In the circumstances Murphy J stated that he agreed with the submissions made by the majority of the parties that the application of the rule was not appropriate in the case before him. In his view the approach adopted by the Court of Appeal in *Barlow Clowes* was more suitable, namely that the rule would not be applied where it would result in injustice and there was a preferable alternative, and he made a declaration that the monies should be distributed rateably to those claimants who could prove their entitlement to repayment. Murphy J stated that it is clear that the rule in *Clayton's* case can be displaced and he pointed out that the monies in the accounts were 'very much in the nature of a mixed pool'. In his view, a compelling case had been made out by all those appointed to argue against the application of the rule who had stressed that its application would result in injustice between clients as it would favour those whose monies had entered the accounts in the days immediately prior to the appointment of the receiver. He concluded that it did not seem to him that those whose monies had entered the accounts in that week had a greater equity than those whose monies had been lodged earlier; as he put it: '[t]he equities between the competing claimants to the account would seem to be equal'.

Similarly, in *Re Custom House Capital Ltd*,[86] while Finlay Geoghegan J accepted that the rule in *Clayton's* case was potentially applicable to the distribution in the matter before the court, she expressed the view that it should not be applied as it would not be just or convenient to do so. She noted that the rule was based on a presumed intention as to how a bank account would operate and that it was not suggested that the contractual documents between the clients and the company supported any such presumed intention. On the contrary, she said that funds had been given to the company for investment purposes to be used in accordance with the relevant client mandate and the timing of the transfer of the funds out of the account to the relevant investment

83. O'Dell (2000) 22 DULJ 161, 198.
84. McGrath (2000) 5 Bar Rev 393, 395.
85. [2003] IEHC 95.
86. [2017] IEHC 484.

would depend upon the mandate and investment vehicle. Finlay Geoghegan J stated that the equities between all client claimants appeared to be equal and she concluded that *pro rata* distribution appeared to do justice as between all the claimants.

However, the rule in *Clayton's* case was applied by Clarke J in *Headstart Global Fund Ltd v Citco Bank Nederland NV*.[87] He said that while the rule in *Clayton's* case was an appropriate way for assessing a series of largely unconnected transactions passing through the same bank account, a question arose as to whether an exception to the rule should be recognised where there was a clear connection between specific payments in and out which ought to lead the court to treat the payment out as being of the same monies, even though there were other monies in the account at the relevant time. Clarke J concluded that while there were certain advantages to adopting such a course of action, on balance he felt that it would be inappropriate and would create a degree of uncertainty about which money was which, and could add unnecessary complications to the tracing process. In his view the better course of action was to rely on the application of the established rule, of 'first in, first out'.[88]

Whether the courts in this jurisdiction follow the approach adopted in other parts of the common law world in rejecting the application of the rule in *Clayton's* case to the claims of competing contributors remains to be seen,[89] but it is clear that it may now be easily displaced. As Conaglen has commented, its application to competing claims between multiple beneficiaries requires a thorough review and he argues convincingly that, '[i]f there is sufficient information to conduct the analysis required by *Clayton's* case, there should be sufficient information to perform a rolling charge analysis or, at the very least, a simple *pari passu* sharing.'[90]

Tracing Through an Overdrawn Bank Account or a Debt

While it has generally been accepted that it is not possible to trace into an overdrawn bank account, the principles in this area may need to be reassessed in the light of the decision of the Privy Council in *Brazil v Durant International Corporation*,[91] which will be considered in more detail below.

Traditionally, a beneficiary's right to trace into a mixed fund in a bank account only applied to the extent that the trust monies could be shown to

87. [2011] IEHC 5.
88. See also *Allied Irish Banks plc v Smith* [2015] IEHC 707 in the context of an 'overdraft debt incurred, overdraft debt repaid' arrangement.
89. *Re Registered Securities Ltd* [1991] 1 NZLR 545, 553; *Keefe v Law Society* (1998) 44 NSWLR 451; *Ontario (Ontario Securities Commission) v Greymac Credit Corporation* (1989) 52 DLR (4th) 767 (see also (1986) 30 DLR (4th) 1 Ont CA); *Law Society of Upper Canada v Toronto-Dominion Bank* (1998) 169 DLR (4th) 353; *Easy Loan Corp. v Wiseman* (2017) 412 DLR (4th) 155.
90. Conaglen [2005] CLJ 45, 48.
91. [2016] AC 297.

be still there and if the account fell below the sum said to constitute the trust funds, they were then deemed to have been spent. This point is illustrated by the decision of Sargant J in *James Roscoe (Bolton) Ltd v Winder*,[92] where an agreement for the sale of the goodwill of a business provided that the purchaser should collect certain book debts and pay this money over to the vendor. The purchaser collected some of these debts and paid part of the money amounting to about £455 into his own account. Subsequently, this balance was reduced to approximately £25 although by the time of the purchaser's death, the balance had risen again to just over £358. Sargant J considered the principles laid down in *Re Hallett's Estate*[93] and said that the general view of that decision was 'that it only applied to such an amount of the balance ultimately standing to the credit of the trustee as did not exceed the lowest balance of the account during the intervening period'.[94] He therefore concluded that the purchaser held the money as trustee but found that the charge was limited to the sum of around £25, which was the lowest intermediate balance after the money had been appropriated.[95]

It is clear from the decision in *Roscoe* that subsequent payments into an account will not generally be treated as repayments of the trust fund. However, this presumption can be displaced by evidence which establishes that the trustee intended to replace the misappropriated funds. So, in *Re Hughes*,[96] where a solicitor lodged funds to an account after the Law Society had initiated an investigation into his professional activities, Kenny J held that the only possible inference was that he had intended the lodgement to be a replacement for the monies he had withdrawn from the client account.

The question of whether it is possible to trace into an overdrawn bank account was considered on a number of further occasions in both England and Ireland and the consensus was that it is not possible. In *Bishopsgate Investment Management Ltd v Homan*[97] the liquidators of a company which was the trustee of the assets of pension schemes from which monies had been improperly paid into the bank account of another company sought to establish an equitable charge in priority to this company's other unsecured creditors. Their claim was rejected by the Court of Appeal on the basis that equitable tracing could not be pursued through an overdrawn, and therefore non-existent, fund. Similarly, in *Shalson v Russo*[98] Rimer J concluded that the claimant could not show that

92. [1915] 1 Ch 62.
93. (1880) 13 Ch D 696.
94. [1915] 1 Ch 62, 69. See also *Campden Hill Ltd v Chakrani* [2005] EWHC 911 (Ch) at [79]; *Turner v Jacob* [2006] EWHC 1317 (Ch) at [88].
95. It should be noted that the Ontario Court of Appeal declined to apply the lowest intermediate balance rule in *Law Society of Upper Canada v Toronto-Dominion Bank* (1998) 169 DLR (4th) 353, a decision criticised by O'Dell (2000) 22 DULJ 161, 188-194.
96. [1970] IR 237.
97. [1995] Ch 211. See also *Re Goldcorp Exchange* [1995] 1 AC 74.
98. [2005] Ch 281.

his money had become represented by an asset into which it was possible to trace. As he stated, '[i]t is not possible to trace into and through an overdrawn account, because such an account is not an asset at all; it is a liability.'[99] The same conclusion was reached by Murphy J in this jurisdiction in *PMPA Ltd v PMPS Ltd*,[100] in which the plaintiff had made an *ultra vires* payment of £450,000 to the defendant which the latter had lodged in an overdrawn account. Murphy J was satisfied that the plaintiff could not trace as the monies had been dissipated and no longer existed as such, although he concluded that the defendant had no right to these monies in the first instance and that the plaintiff was entitled to restitution. It seemed therefore that once the balance in an account falls below a certain level or becomes overdrawn, the capacity to trace is limited to the lowest intermediate balance and in the case of an overdrawn account, ceases altogether.

However, over the years there have also been a number of *obiter* statements suggesting that it should be possible to trace through a debt or through property which the defendant had already acquired at the time the claimant's assets were received, sometimes referred to as 'backward tracing'. The clearest statement to this effect is contained in the judgment of Scott VC in the Court of Appeal in *Foskett v McKeown*,[101] where he stated as follows:

> I would wish, for my part, to make it clear that I regard the point as still open and, in particular, that I do not regard the fact that an asset is paid for out of borrowed money with the borrowing subsequently repaid out of trust money as being necessarily fatal to an equitable tracing claim by the trust beneficiaries. If, in such a case, it can be shown that it was always the intention to use the trust money to acquire the asset, I do not see why the order in which the events happen should be regarded as critical to the claim.[102]

Some support for this approach can also be seen in the *dicta* of Lord Millett in the House of Lords in *Foskett v McKeown*,[103] where he refers to what is traced as 'not the physical asset itself but the value inherent in it'. Opinion amongst academics was similarly divided. Smith is in favour of permitting 'backward tracing', suggesting that 'it seems clear that money which is used to pay a debt can be traced into what was acquired in exchange for the assumption of that

99. *Ibid.* at 328.
100. High Court 1992 No. 702Sp (Murphy J) 27 June 1994. See also *Carroll Group Distributors Ltd v G. & J.F. Bourke Ltd* [1990] 1 IR 481, 486-7.
101. [1998] Ch 265, 284-284. See also *Bishopsgate Investment Management Ltd v Homan* [1995] Ch 211, 216-217 *per* Dillon LJ.
102. However, note the *dicta* of Hobhouse LJ at 289 that '[t]he doctrine of tracing does not extend to following value into a previously acquired asset' and of Morritt LJ at 296.
103. [2001] 1 AC 102, 128.

debt.'[104] In his view the incurring of the debt is the means of acquisition of the item and the money being traced is the means of acquisition or extinguishment of the debt. However, Conaglen has suggested that there are weaknesses in the conceptual justification for this approach, and puts forward the view that 'the acquisition and extinguishment of debts are very different things'.[105] He argues that 'when trust money is used to pay a debt, there is no value inherent in the debt which is capable of being acquired because the debt is a liability.'[106]

In delivering the judgment of the Privy Council in *Brazil v Durant International Corporation*,[107] Lord Toulson considered the *dicta* from previous decisions and the views of academic commentators. He said that the Privy Council would reject the argument put forward by the respondents, relying on the views of Smith, that money used to pay a debt can in principle be traced into whatever was acquired in return for the debt, which in his opinion was a very broad proposition which would take the doctrine of tracing far beyond its limits in the case law to date. However, Lord Toulson acknowledged that there may be cases where there is a close causal and transactional link between the incurring of a debt and the use of trust funds to discharge it.[108] He expressed the view that '[t]he development of increasingly sophisticated and elaborate methods of money laundering, often involving a web of credits and debits between intermediaries, makes it particularly important that a court should not allow a camouflage of interconnected transactions to obscure its vision of their true overall purpose and effect.'[109] In his view if the court is satisfied that the steps taken are part of a coordinated scheme, it should not matter that either deliberately or because of the incidents of the banking system, a debit appears in the bank account of an intermediary before a reciprocal credit entry. Similarly, he stated that it should not matter whether the account used for the purpose of providing bridging finance was in credit or in overdraft at the time. He concluded as follows:

> The Board therefore rejects the argument that there can never be backward tracing, or that the court can never trace the value of an asset whose proceeds are paid into an overdrawn account. But the claimant has to establish a coordination between the depletion of the trust fund and the acquisition of the asset which is the subject of the tracing claim, looking at the whole transaction, such as to warrant the court attributing the value of the interest acquired to the misuse of the trust fund. This is likely to

104. [1995] CLJ 290, 293.
105. (2011) 127 LQR 432, 448.
106. *Ibid.*
107. [2016] AC 297. See further Turner [2016] CLJ 462; Fong (2017) 133 LQR 389.
108. Referring to the decision of Saskatchewan Court of Appeal in *Agricultural Credit Corpn of Saskatchewan v Pettyjohn* (1991) 79 DLR (4th) 22 as an example of this.
109. [2016] AC 297, 312.

depend on inference from the proved facts, particularly since in many cases the testimony of the trustee, if available, will be of little value.[110]

While the courts in this jurisdiction have yet to directly address the policy considerations both in favour of and against permitting backward tracing, some issues should be borne in mind. Conaglen has suggested that '[w]hen the already precarious position of unsecured creditors is weighed against the concomitantly far better protected position of trust beneficiaries, it is suggested that the law ought not to recognise the possibility of tracing backwards.'[111] Lord Toulson in delivering the judgment of the Privy Council in *Brazil v Durant International Corporation*[112] also commented that the courts should be very cautious about expanding equitable proprietary remedies in a way which might have an adverse effect on other innocent parties. As he said, '[i]f a trustee on the verge of bankruptcy uses trust funds to pay off an unsecured creditor to whom he is personally indebted, in the absence of special circumstances it is hard to see why the beneficiaries' claim should take precedence over those of the general body of unsecured creditors.'[113] However, his focus on the question of whether there is a 'sufficient transactional link' is a useful one and should allow for 'backward tracing' in limited circumstances which may lessen the risk to innocent third parties.

Another key issue, which seemed to underlie the decision of Kenny J in *Re Hughes*[114] and was also identified by Dillon LJ in his *obiter* comments in *Bishopsgate Investment Management Ltd v Homan*,[115] is whether there was a pre-existing intention to pay back the debt owed with the funds in question. However, given the important policy issues at stake and the authorities which suggest otherwise,[116] it is still far from clear whether, and if so in what circumstances, 'backward tracing' may be permitted by the courts in this jurisdiction.[117]

The Requirement of a Fiduciary Relationship

While the decision in *Re Hallett's Estate*[118] concerned the relationship of trustee and beneficiary, Jessel MR made it clear in the course of his judgment that he

110. *Ibid.* at [40].
111. (2011) 127 LQR 432, 455.
112. [2016] AC 297.
113. *Ibid.* at 311.
114. [1970] IR 237.
115. [2005] Ch 211, 217. See also *Foskett v McKeown* [1998] Ch 265, 284 *per* Scott VC.
116. *PMPA Ltd v PMPS Ltd* High Court 1992 No. 702Sp (Murphy J) 27 June 1994. See also *Carroll Group Distributors Ltd v G. & J.F. Bourke Ltd* [1990] 1 IR 481, 486-7.
117. Writing in 2017, Penner has suggested that '[a]ny conclusion at this stage of the development of backwards tracing is necessarily inconclusive' in '"Sort of" Backwards Tracing' in *Equity, Trusts and Commerce* (eds. Davies and Penner, 2017) p.123 at 149.
118. (1880) 13 Ch D 696.

intended that the principles which he laid down should be extended to other types of fiduciary relationships.[119]

The requirement of a fiduciary relationship was also stressed by Kenny J in *Re Shannon Travel Ltd*,[120] where he stated as follows:

> The general principle is that when a person receives money as a trustee or as one occupying a fiduciary relation to another, the person who transferred the property or paid the money may recover the property and has a charge on the account to which the money or cheques have been lodged or on property on which the monies received have been spent provided that the property or money can be traced through the accounts of the debtor into the bank account etc., and provided that there is money to the credit of the account on which the charge can operate.[121]

In *Shannon*, Kenny J held that an equitable charge over a bank account containing funds held in trust by an insolvent was liable to abatement so that the liquidator's expenses and remuneration could be paid. This result is in some respects unsatisfactory, as Kenny J failed to address adequately the question of why the proprietary remedy should be qualified in such a manner.

In England, as a result of the decision of the House of Lords in *Sinclair v Brougham*,[122] it became clear that tracing in equity would extend to any persons in fiduciary relationships even where this relationship did not exist between the parties to the action.[123] This requirement of a fiduciary relationship was accepted unquestioningly by the Court of Appeal in *Re Diplock*[124] and it was regarded in principle as a pre-requisite by Goulding J in *Chase Manhattan Bank NA v Israel-British Bank (London) Ltd*,[125] although it would appear that this 'fiduciary element can be satisfied at the moment the payment is made'.[126] The plaintiff made a duplicate payment of $2,000,000 in error into another bank for the benefit of the defendant. The defendant's bank became insolvent and the question arose whether the plaintiff was entitled to trace this money into the bank's assets or whether it had to prove with the other creditors. Goulding J held that the fact that the payment had been mistakenly made gave rise to a constructive trust and that the plaintiff was entitled to trace these funds.[127] He

---

119. *Ibid.* at 709.
120. High Court 1970 No. 3849P (Kenny J) 8 May 1972.
121. *Ibid.* at 8-9.
122. [1914] Ch 398.
123. However, note that in *Dublin Corporation v Ancient Guild of Incorporated Brick and Stone Layers and Allied Trades Union* High Court 1991 No. 1556P, 6 March 1996 Budd J questioned (at 41) whether *Sinclair* was authority for the proposition that a fiduciary relationship is essential before a claim to trace in equity may be established.
124. [1948] Ch 465.
125. [1981] Ch 105.
126. Collins (1994) 1 Comm L P 211, 213.
127. It should be noted that Lord Browne-Wilkinson in *Westdeutsche Landesbank v Islington*

stated that it was common ground that a right to trace money paid by mistake exists in English law and reiterated that: 'an initial fiduciary relationship is a necessary foundation of the equitable right of tracing'.[128] However, it is hard to disagree with the criticism that Goulding J was effectively by-passing the requirement of a fiduciary relationship and he appeared to hold that the payment into the wrong hands itself gave rise to the relationship. His reasoning was approved by Carroll J in *Re Irish Shipping Ltd*,[129] in which a bank made a duplicate payment in error to the bank account in Citibank of Irish Shipping Ltd which subsequently went into liquidation. Citibank, the former bankers of Irish Shipping, claimed to be entitled to set off debts due by the company to them against the mistaken payment. However, it was held by Carroll J that where monies are paid by mistake into the account of a company such monies do not form part of the assets of the company at the date of the liquidation and she concluded that the bank which had made the duplicate payment was entitled to trace the money into the account.

Further comments were made about the requirement of a fiduciary relationship by Millett J at first instance in *Agip (Africa) Ltd v Jackson*,[130] where he stated as follows:

> The only restriction on the ability of equity to follow assets is the requirement that there must be some fiduciary relationship which permits the assistance of equity to be invoked. The requirement has been widely condemned and depends on authority rather than principle, but the law was settled in *In re Diplock* [1948] Ch 465. It may need to be reconsidered but not, I venture to think, at first instance. The requirement may be circumvented since it is not necessary that the fund to be traced should have been the subject of fiduciary obligations before it got into the wrong hands; it is sufficient that the payment to the defendant itself gives rise to a fiduciary relationship: *Chase Manhattan Bank NA v Israel-British Bank London Ltd* [1981] Ch 105.[131]

London Borough Council [1996] AC 669, 715 stated that while he did not accept the reasoning of Goulding J, *Chase Manhattan* may well have been correctly decided. As Jones has pointed out [1996] CLJ 432, 434-435, '[t]he retention of the money once the [defendant] learnt of the mistake may well have given rise to a constructive trust'. However, Oakley has commented [1997] Conv 1, 3 that although the decision has not been formally overruled, 'it appears unlikely that an equitable proprietary claim will now be available to a transferor of money acting as a result of a mistake of fact'. See also Cope (1996) 112 LQR 521, 523.

128. [1981] Ch 105, 119.
129. [1986] ILRM 518.
130. [1990] Ch 265, 290.
131. Fox LJ also suggested in delivering his decision in the Court of Appeal [1991] Ch 547, 566 that the requirement of a fiduciary relationship remained.

In *Boscawen v Bajwa*[132] Millett LJ reiterated that: '[i]t is still a prerequisite of the right to trace in equity that there must be a fiduciary relationship which calls the equitable jurisdiction into being'. However, a subsequent pronouncement which has been interpreted as having relevance to this issue is less clear, namely Lord Browne-Wilkinson's statement in *Westdeutsche Landesbank Girozentrale v Islington London Borough Council*,[133] that their Lordships 'should not be taken to be casting any doubt on the principles of tracing as established in *Re Diplock*'. As Oakley has commented, '[s]ince it is generally thought that in this case the Court of Appeal interpreted *Sinclair v Brougham* as establishing the controversial proposition "that an initial fiduciary relationship is a necessary foundation of the equitable right of tracing" this remark appeared to indicate that Lord Browne-Wilkinson was in favour of the requirement'.[134] As a result of Lord Browne-Wilkinson's statement Cope has commented that 'the extent to which a trust or other fiduciary relationship is still essential to maintain an equitable proprietary claim is not made clear'[135] and Jones has stated that '[t]he condition that there must be a fiduciary relationship to support an equitable proprietary claim is still alive but appears to be increasingly meaningless'.[136]

While the issue did not arise for decision in *Foskett v McKeown*[137] because, as Lord Millett pointed out, even on the traditional approach equitable tracing rules were available to the plaintiffs, Lord Millett did express some views on this issue. He stated that there was no logical justification for allowing any distinction between the rules governing tracing at common law and in equity 'to produce capricious results in cases of mixed substitutions by insisting on the existence of a fiduciary relationship as a precondition for applying equity's tracing rules'.[138] However, he added that the existence of a fiduciary relationship may be relevant to the nature of the claim which the plaintiff can maintain, whether personal or proprietary.

There are certainly signs elsewhere in the common law world of alternative approaches being adopted towards this issue, as in New Zealand where it was suggested by Cooke P in *Elders Pastoral Ltd v Bank of New Zealand*[139] that

---

132. [1996] 1 WLR 328, 335. See Birks (1995) 9 Trust Law Int 124; Andrews [1996] CLJ 199.
133. [1996] AC 669, 714.
134. Oakley [1997] Conv 1, 3-4. However, Oakley went on to point out that at a seminar in Oxford in September 1996, Lord Browne-Wilkinson indicated that he had only made that remark to forestall any argument that the whole framework of equitable proprietary claims had been swept away and that he regarded the requirement of establishing a fiduciary relationship as wholly misconceived.
135. Cope (1996) 112 LQR 521, 523.
136. Jones [1996] CLJ 432, 435. Oliver had expressed the hope that the House of Lords would soon eliminate the fiduciary requirement, see (1995) 9 Trust Law Int 78, 83.
137. [2001] 1 AC 102.
138. *Ibid.* at 128.
139. [1989] 2 NZLR 180. See Watts (1990) 106 LQR 552.

unconscionability is the key to establishing a right to trace in equity and not the presence of a fiduciary relationship.

The best summary of the likely approach of the courts in this jurisdiction to the question of the need to establish a fiduciary relationship is provided by Collins in the following terms:[140]

> The fiduciary relationship requirement may not be expressly abandoned but the definition of that relationship is proving sufficiently flexible that it no longer seems to represent a real bar to exercising an equitable tracing remedy if the other conditions for that remedy are satisfied.

Loss of the Right to Trace

In certain circumstances, many of which were referred to by the Court of Appeal in its judgment in *Re Diplock*,[141] the right to trace in equity may be lost. The first example is the obvious one that if the property has been dissipated it cannot be traced. As Lord Greene MR stated in *Re Diplock*:

> The equitable remedies presuppose the continued existence of the money either as a separate fund or as part of a mixed fund or as latent in property acquired by means of such a fund. If, on the facts of any individual case, such continued existence is not established, equity is as helpless as the common law itself. If the fund mixed or unmixed is spent upon a dinner, equity, which dealt only in specific relief and not in damages, could do nothing.[142]

Secondly, where property comes into the hands of a *bona fide* purchaser for value without notice, any equitable tracing claim will be extinguished,[143] and an alternative remedy must be pursued.[144] Thirdly, where it would be inequitable to allow a tracing claim to proceed, such a remedy will not be available. This will happen most frequently where a volunteer uses trust funds to alter or improve property already owned by him. This occurred in *Re Diplock* where some of the charities who received trust funds had used them to carry out improvements to their property. As Lord Greene MR stated, '[i]n the case of adaptation of property of the volunteer by means of trust money, it by no means necessarily

140. Collins (1994) 1 Comm LP 211, 214.
141. [1948] Ch 465.
142. *Ibid.* at 521.
143. *Re Diplock* [1948] Ch 465, 539. It would appear that in Ireland the equitable right to trace is regarded as a mere equity and thus a *bona fide* purchaser for value of an equitable estate will take free of it. See *Re Ffrench's Estate* (1887) 21 LR Ir 283 and *Scott v Scott* [1924] 1 IR 141 and see *infra* Chapter 2.
144. E.g. a claim against the trustees personally.

follows that the money can be said to be present in the adapted property.'[145] In such circumstances, he concluded that the trust money could not be traced. The reasoning behind such an approach is that it would be inequitable to allow beneficiaries a charge over the property which would be enforceable by sale. This can be contrasted with the situation where a volunteer has purchased an asset with a mixed fund in which case there would be nothing inequitable in forcing a sale and dividing up the proceeds as he would recover what he invested.

Although there is little evidence of how it would operate in relation to equitable proprietary claims, it would appear that the defence of change of position should also be referred to.[146] In *Lipkin Gorman v Karpanale Ltd*[147] Lord Goff stated that 'the defence is available to a person whose position has so changed that it would be inequitable in all the circumstances to require him to make restitution, or alternatively to make restitution in full'. He commented that whilst he recognised the different functions of property at law and in equity, in his view 'there may also in due course develop a more consistent approach to tracing claims, in which common defences are recognised as available to such claims, whether advanced at law or in equity'.[148] As Oakley[149] has commented, it is clear from this statement that Lord Goff envisaged the application of the defence of change of position to both legal and equitable proprietary claims, although for the present the principles which have been developed relate to the former situation.

It has been accepted that the defence, while available to an innocent defendant, is not open to a wrongdoer or to a person who has changed his position in bad faith.[150] As Laddie J commented in *Barros Mattos Junior v MacDaniels Ltd*,[151] '[t]he recipient cannot put up a tainted claim to retention against the victim's untainted claim for restitution.' In this context it would seem that a defendant who ought to have been aware of the fact that the property in question did not belong to him may not be classified as innocent.[152] It was suggested by Clarke LJ in *Niru Battery Manufacturing Co. v Milestone Trading*

145. [1948] Ch 465, 546-547.
146. See generally Mitchell, Mitchell and Watterson, *Goff and Jones' The Law of Unjust Enrichment* (9th ed., 2016) Chapter 27; Nolan in *Laundering and Tracing* (ed. Birks, 1995) p. 135 *et seq*. and Birks in *Laundering and Tracing* (ed. Birks, 1995) pp. 323-332.
147. [1991] 2 AC 548, 580.
148. *Ibid*. at 580. However, Lord Goff stated that nothing should be said by him which would inhibit the development of the defence on a case by case basis and Lord Bridge commented that in acknowledging the defence for the first time, 'it would be unwise to attempt to define its scope in abstract terms'.
149. Oakley [1995] CLJ 377, 425.
150. *Lipkin Gorman v Karpanale Ltd* [1991] 2 AC 548, 580 *per* Lord Goff.
151. [2005] 1 WLR 247, 257.
152. *South Tyneside Metropolitan Council v Svenska International plc* [1995] 1 All ER 545, 569.

Ltd (No. 1)[153] that the emphasis in Lord Goff's speech in *Lipkin Gorman* was on whether it would be unjust or inequitable to allow restitution and that he did not maintain that the defence of change of position is only lost where the defendant is guilty of dishonesty or other wrongdoing. He summarised the underlying principles to be derived from Lord Goff's speech in the following terms:

> (i) The question is whether it would be unjust to allow restitution, or restitution in full. (ii) It will be unjust to allow restitution where an innocent defendant's position has so changed that the injustice of requiring him to repay outweighs the injustice of denying the claimant restitution. (iii) The defence of change of position is not, for example, available to a defendant who has changed his position in bad faith, as where he has paid away the money with knowledge of the facts entitling the claimant to restitution. (iv) Nor is it available to a wrongdoer. (v) In general terms, the defence is available to a defendant whose position has so changed that it would be inequitable to require him to make restitution or to make restitution in full.[154]

153. [2004] QB 985.
154. *Ibid.* at 999-1000.

CHAPTER 20

Equitable Doctrines

THE DOCTRINE OF CONVERSION

Introduction

The doctrine of conversion is based on the maxim that equity looks on that as done which ought to be done.[1] It operates by regarding one form of property as being another because an obligation to convert it exists. The effect of the doctrine is that in certain circumstances the nature of property is notionally changed so that realty may be treated as personalty with the legal incidents of personalty and vice versa. The reasoning behind the doctrine is that where a person is under a duty to convert realty into personalty or personalty into realty, the property should not be regarded as still being in its original form because the individual concerned has failed to perform his obligations.

Traditionally, the doctrine had an important effect on the passing of property where an individual died intestate, because real estate devolved to the heir-at-law and personalty to the next of kin. However, the practical significance of the doctrine has greatly diminished since the enactment of the Administration of Estates Act 1959 and the Succession Act 1965 which abolished these principles, although it remains relevant where a testator makes separate residuary dispositions of his real and personal property.

The basis of the doctrine was outlined by Sir Thomas Sewell MR in *Fletcher v Ashburner*:[2]

> [N]othing was better established than this principle, that money directed to be employed in the purchase of land, and land directed to be sold and turned into money, are to be considered as that species of property into which they are directed to be converted; and this in whatever manner the direction is given.

There are a number of situations in which the doctrine of conversion will be applied and these will be examined in turn.

1. *McDonnell v Stenson* [1921] 1 IR 80, 86 *per* Ronan LJ.
2. (1779) 1 Bro CC 497, 499.

Trusts for Sale

Where trustees are directed to sell or purchase realty and there is some person who can insist on their doing so, the property is treated as being converted from the moment when the instrument comes into force.[3] So, in the case of a will, conversion takes place from the date of the testator's death and, in the case of a deed, from the date of its execution. However, as Stirling J stated in *Goodier v Edmunds*,[4] 'nothing short of an absolute and effective trust for sale can in equity create the conversion of realty into personalty'. In order to effect the conversion, the direction to sell or buy must be imperative and a trust for sale, which is mandatory and imposes a duty to sell and which produces an immediate notional conversion, must be distinguished from a power of sale, which merely confers a discretion to sell. As Porter MR stated in *McGwire v McGwire*,[5] the question which arises is 'whether there is to be found in the settlement an express and imperative direction to convert [the property], or a trust for [its] conversion'. In this case, he concluded that no immediate conversion was effected or intended and that the lands which remained unsold should pass as realty. Similarly, in *Re Tyndall's Estate*[6] where a testator directed that after his wife's death his trustees should invest his residuary personalty in the purchase of realty, it was held by Gavan Duffy J that such a direction did not create an imperative trust for such a conversion. As a matter of construction, it must be shown that the testator intended the conversion to take place and as Sullivan MR made clear in *Norreys v Franks*[7] this intention must be discerned from the language which he has employed.

It should be noted that in England the Trusts of Land and Appointment of Trustees Act 1996 abolishes the doctrine of conversion in relation to trusts for sale which are now replaced by a 'trust of land', in relation to which trustees have a power of sale, which may be exercised.[8]

Contracts or Conditional Contracts for the Sale or Purchase of Land

Where there is a valid contract to sell realty, the realty is treated as part of the vendor's personalty from the time the contract is concluded.[9] Traditionally,

---

3. See Boyle [1981] Conv 108.
4. [1893] 3 Ch 455, 462.
5. [1900] 1 IR 200, 203. See also *Owen v Owen* [1897] 1 IR 580 and the *dicta* of Chatterton VC in *McDonogh v Nolan* (1881) 9 Lr Ir 262, 270.
6. [1941] Ir Jur Rep 51.
7. (1874) IR 9 Eq 18, 35.
8. Pettit submits (1997) 113 LQR 207 that the Act does not abolish the trust for sale completely and argues that s. 3 of the Act clearly assumes that a trust for sale can still exist. Section 3(1) provides: 'Where land is held by trustees subject to a trust for sale, the land is not to be regarded as personal property; and where personal property is subject to a trust for sale in order that the trustees may acquire land, the personal property is not to be regarded as land.'
9. See *Hillingdon Estates Co. v Stonefield Estates Ltd* [1952] Ch 627, 631 *per* Vaisey J.

it was accepted that a contract must be specifically enforceable in order for the doctrine to apply, but this would no longer appear to be the case.[10] Where a vendor dies before completion of the contract, his representatives must convey the realty or will be entitled to enforce specific performance against the purchaser, and the proceeds of the sale will form part of the vendor's estate as personalty. If a purchaser dies before completion, his interest passes to those entitled to his realty, but subject to the obligation to pay the balance of the purchase price.

This principle has been extended to conditional contracts. As Holmes LJ commented in *Re Sherlock's Estate*,[11] 'if the making of an absolute agreement to sell is fixed by judicial authority as the time of conversion, it seems to me that it is both logical and desirable to apply the same rule to a conditional agreement.' The most common example of such a conditional contract is where an option to purchase is created. The operation of this principle is illustrated by the decision of *Lawes v Bennett*,[12] in which a testator leased a farm to an individual for a period of seven years and gave him an option to purchase the reversion on giving written notice before a specified date. This individual assigned the lease to another party who exercised the option and paid the purchase money after the testator's death. It was held that the purchase money formed part of the testator's personalty. The effect of the rule in *Lawes v Bennett* is therefore that the exercise of an option to purchase after a testator's death will retrospectively convert the property into personalty.

The rationale behind the application of this principle is that a testator is presumed to be aware of the legal result which will flow from granting an option of this nature.[13] However, as the principle is based on the presumed intention of the testator, it will not apply where a contrary intention can be deduced. So, as Johnston J stated in *Miley v Carty*,[14] 'whenever in a will or codicil the testator indicates an intention that, notwithstanding a contract for the sale of the lands, the devisee shall take whatever interest in the lands that the testator may have had at the time of his death, then that intention is to be carried out, and the general rule as established in *Lawes v Bennett* is not to be followed.' In addition, it has been held that the application of the principle 'should be limited

10. Keane suggests that all that is necessary is that there is a 'valid contract for sale' (see *Equity and the Law of Trusts in Ireland* (3rd ed., 2017) p. 392) and Wylie states in *Irish Land Law* (5th ed., 2013) p. 148-149 that 'arguably all that is needed is a "valid" contract or "binding contract *simpliciter*"'. Pettit also points out (1960) 24 Conv 47, 64-65 that it is doubtful whether the availability of specific performance can be regarded as a satisfactory criterion for determining whether conversion should occur and concludes that: 'there do not appear to be any decisions directly and necessarily based on the availability or non-availability of the remedy of specific performance'.
11. [1899] 2 IR 561, 608.
12. (1785) 1 Cox 167.
13. See *Miley v Carty* [1927] IR 541, 543. See also *Weeding v Weeding* (1861) 1 J & H 424.
14. [1927] IR 541, 544.

to cases where there was no specific disposition of the property made after the date of the contract giving the option to purchase'.[15] This point was made in the following terms by Page-Wood VC in *Weeding v Weeding*:[16]

> When you find that, in a will made after a contract giving an option of purchase, the testator, knowing of the existence of the contract, devises the specific property which is the subject of the contract without referring in any way to the contract … it is considered that there is sufficient indication of an intention to pass that property, to give the devisee all the interest, whatever it may be, that the testator had in it.

Therefore, in the case of a general or residuary devise, the rule operates even where the option cannot be exercised until after the death of the grantor but in the case of a specific devise of the property, it will not operate if the will is made subsequent to the creation of the option or contemporaneously with it. The exception operates not only where a specific devise is made after the granting of the option but also where a will is republished after such grant by the execution of a codicil. These principles were conveniently summarised in *Snell's Equity*[17] in the following terms:

> Where … there is a specific devise, the operation of the rule depends on the relative dates of the will and the grant of the option. If the will was made before the option was granted, the devise is adeemed by the exercise of the option, just as if the testator had sold the land in his lifetime. But if the will was made or confirmed by codicil after the grant of the option, or substantially contemporaneously with it, the specific devisee is entitled to the proceeds of sale; for the testator will be taken to have been aware of the option and to have intended the devisee to take the property whether it was land or purchase-money.

Where the option can be construed as a gift subject to the payment of the purchase price, it may subsequently be exercised by the personal representatives of the lessee to whom the option was given in the first instance.[18] Finally, the rule in *Lawes v Bennett* will only be applied as between the competing claims of those entitled to the real and personal property of a grantor on an option and will not apply as between a vendor and purchaser.[19]

---

15. *Duffield v McMaster* [1896] 1 IR 370, 379.
16. (1861) 1 J & H 424, 431. Quoted with approval by Porter MR in *Duffield v McMaster* [1896] 1 IR 370, 381 and by Palles CB in *Steele v Steele* [1913] 1 IR 292, 305.
17. (29th ed., 1990, Baker and Langan), p. 493. This passage was omitted from the 30th and later editions.
18. *Belshaw v Rollins* [1904] 1 IR 284.
19. *Re Sherlock's Estate* [1899] 2 IR 561.

Order of the Court

Conversion may occur by reason of a court order directing that property should be bought or sold[20] and such conversion takes effect from the date of the order[21] and not from the date of the sale. This principle is illustrated by the decision of Monroe J in *Re Beamish's Estate*,[22] in which he held that an order for sale of an unencumbered estate operated as a conversion into personalty.

An absolute order for the sale of realty made on the petition of an incumbrancer operates as a conversion of only so much of the lands as it is necessary to sell to discharge the incumbrance. This conclusion was reached by Ross J in *Sheane v Fetherstonhaugh*,[23] in which part only of an owner's lands had been sold to discharge incumbrances on the property. After his death the question arose whether the unsold lands had been converted by the order made by the court or whether they remained as real estate. As Ross J concluded: 'because only so much of the land is to be sold as is required for the discharge of incumbrances, no valid order can be deemed to exist for the sale of the remainder … It can never become operative in respect of the unsold lands'.[24] In reaching this conclusion, Ross J distinguished his previous decision in *Re Stinson's Estate*,[25] where he had held that if more property is actually sold than is necessary to pay off incumbrances, then it must pass as personalty to the next of kin.

It should be noted that a court order will not always effect a conversion and section 67 of the Lunacy Regulation (Ireland) Act 1871 provides that any surplus remaining on the sale or mortgage of a lunatic's estate will be treated as if it were of the same character and nature as the property sold.[26] If an order is not made under this section, but is made in the ordinary course of the management of the estate of a person of unsound mind, conversion will be effected unless the court makes a direction to the contrary. However, where an order for sale is made outside the ordinary course of managing the estate, the property will retain its original character.

Partnership Property

Section 22 of the Partnership Act 1890[27] provides that unless the contrary

20. Pettit suggests (1997) 113 LQR 207, 210 that the courts have treated such cases as analogous to the situation where there is a trust for sale, but states that it is not a trust for sale and would not appear to come within the terms of s. 3 of the Trusts of Land and Appointment of Trustees Act 1996.
21. *Re Henry's Estate* (1893) 31 LR Ir 158, 165.
22. (1891) 27 LR Ir 326. See also *Steed v Preece* (1874) LR 18 Eq 192.
23. [1914] 1 IR 268.
24. *Ibid.* at 270.
25. [1910] 1 IR 13.
26. See the *dicta* of Kennedy CJ in *O'Connell v Harrison* [1927] IR 330, 337-338.
27. It should be noted that s.22 has been repealed in England by the Trusts of Land and Appointment of Trustees Act 1996. Pettit argues (1997) 113 LQR 207, 210-211 that

intention appears, land which has become partnership property shall be treated as personalty and not as realty as between the partners themselves and those entitled to their estates. The reason for this provision is that on the dissolution of a partnership, the land will have to be sold to be divided amongst the partners.

Settled Land

Section 22(5) of the Settled Land Act 1882 provides that capital money arising from the disposition of property pursuant to the Settled Land Acts 1882-1890 is to be treated as realty.

Failure of Conversion

Where property is subject to a duty to convert but before or at the same time as the direction to convert becomes effective, a total failure of the objects of the conversion occurs, there will be a resulting trust of the property in its actual form. So, if A devises realty on trust for sale for the benefit of B and B dies before the sale takes place, a resulting trust of the property, which remains as realty, arises in favour of the settlor. However, where there is a partial failure of the objects for which conversion was directed, the outcome depends on whether the property is left by will or settled by deed. Where the direction to convert is contained in a deed, the property will result subject to the trust for conversion.[28] On the other hand, if the direction is in a will, it will go to the person entitled to the property in its unconverted form, although he will receive it in its converted form because the trustees will be under an obligation to carry out the objects which have not failed.[29]

THE DOCTRINE OF RECONVERSION

In certain circumstances, property which has notionally been converted may be reconverted or theoretically returned to its actual physical form. Reconversion may either occur by act of the party or by operation of law.

By Act of the Party

Where a party is absolutely entitled to property and expresses the desire to take this property in its original unconverted form, it would make no sense for equity to compel the trustees of the property to convert it as the owner

---

as the section effectively put a pre-existing equitable principle into statutory form, the pre-Partnership Act equitable rule may continue to apply. However, he points out that the effect of this repeal is not entirely clear.

28. *Griffith v Ricketts* (1849) 7 Hare 299.
29. *Re O'Connor's Estate* [1923] 1 IR 142.

could immediately reverse this process. Therefore, on the basis that 'Equity, like nature, will do nothing in vain', the doctrine of reconversion intervenes. So, where beneficiaries who are of full age and capacity and between them absolutely entitled to trust property choose to take property in its actual form, notional reconversion occurs. The decision to reconvert may be expressly stated or it may be inferred from 'evidence of acts and circumstances'.[30] Minors and persons of unsound mind cannot make an election of this nature although where it is necessary to do so, the court may make the decision for such persons or sanction a decision already made.

Normally, 'all persons having interests must concur to effect conversion',[31] although in a limited manner a remainderman may elect to reconvert. Clearly, no election made by him can prejudice the interests of those with interests in possession and any decision made may be affected subsequently by any actual conversion which occurs before his interest falls into possession.

In the case of tenants in common, one of them may reconvert without the concurrence of the other(s) in the case of money to be invested in land,[32] but it would appear not in the case of land to be converted into money on the grounds that land would not be as valuable if divided up in such a manner.[33]

By Operation of Law

Reconversion may also be effected by operation of law where property which has been notionally converted in equity becomes reconverted without any declaration or act of the party entitled. This will occur where, e.g., property which was subject to an obligation to convert comes into the possession of some person who is absolutely entitled, without having been converted, and he dies without making any declaration of intention in relation to it. The important factor here is that there must no longer be anyone who can enforce the obligation to convert and this is illustrated by the decision of Chatterton VC in *McDonogh v Nolan*.[34] By virtue of a marriage settlement, a sum of money was vested in trustees for the purchase of realty to be held on certain trusts. The realty was never purchased and the parties' only son became absolutely entitled and died unmarried and intestate. It was held that the money should be regarded as personalty and therefore passed to his next of kin.

30. *Hart v McDougall* [1912] 1 IR 62, 75 *per* Barton J. See also the *dicta* of Byrne J in *Re Douglas and Powell's Contract* [1902] 2 Ch 296, 312 to the effect that evidence may be derived from 'declarations or acts and conduct'.
31. *Hart v McDougall* [1912] 1 IR 62, 72 *per* Barton J.
32. *Seeley v Jago* (1717) P Wms 389.
33. *Holloway v Radcliffe* (1857) 23 Beav 163.
34. (1881) 9 LR Ir 262.

THE DOCTRINE OF ELECTION

Introduction

The doctrine of election can be explained in terms of the principle that 'a man shall not be allowed to approbate and reprobate',[35] in other words one cannot take a benefit and reject an associated burden. The doctrine comes into operation where a testator or donor purports to confer a benefit on a donee and in the same instrument purports to transfer some of this donee's property to a third party. A useful recent summary of the effect of the doctrine of election is set out by Histed in the following terms:[36]

> Where a beneficiary receives a gift under a will or deed which also disposes of some of his own property and where the circumstances of the case permit the court to conclude that the donor would not have wanted the beneficiary to receive the gift and keep his own property, then the court will imply a condition that the beneficiary so give up his property before receiving the gift.

As Walsh MR stated in *Williams v Mayne*,[37] '[i]n giving effect to an election, the Court professess to enforce a duty; there being two benefits which it is inequitable in the party electing to claim together, it compels him, on the condition of obtaining one, to relinquish the other.' This principle was more fully set out by Lord Hatherley in the course of his judgment in *Cooper v Cooper*:[38]

> There is an obligation on him who takes a benefit under a will or other instrument to give full effect to that instrument under which he takes a benefit; and if it be found that that instrument purports to deal with something which it was beyond the power of the donor or settlor to dispose of, but to which effect can be given by the concurrence of him who receives a benefit under the same instrument, the law will impose on him who takes the benefit the obligation of carrying the instrument into full and complete force and effect.

35. *Re Lord Chesham* (1886) 31 Ch D 466, 473 *per* Chitty J. See also the comments of Lord Redesdale in *Birmingham v Kirwan* (1805) 2 Sch & Lef 444, 449 that 'a person cannot accept and reject the same instrument' and of Lord Robertson in *Douglas-Menzies v Umphelby* [1908] AC 224, 232 that 'it is against equity that any one should take against a man's will and also under it'.
36. Histed (1998) 114 LQR 621, 634. Histed comments at 637 that the doctrine is based on the intention of the testator and the willingness of the court to imply a conditional gift where it can be convinced that the intention would be defeated without the condition being placed on the gift.
37. (1867) IR 1 Eq 519, 530.
38. (1874) LR 7 HL 53, 70.

This statement was quoted with approval by Ronan LJ in *Re Sullivan*.[39] In that case, a testator gave his wife a legacy of £3,000 to be paid in cash or out of his own or their joint shares as she should select. The Irish Court of Appeal held that the widow was bound to elect between the benefits conferred by the will and any claim to the stocks and shares invested in the joint names of herself and the testator.

It is important to distinguish such a situation from one in which the gift to the donee is expressly made conditional upon his transferring his property to a third party. Where this condition is not complied with, the gift to the donee cannot take effect and it will fall into residue.

This example provided by Hanbury and Martin[40] best illustrates the operation of the doctrine in practice:

> A is owner of Blackacre. T in his will devises Blackacre to B and bequeaths £10,000 to A. A cannot, of course, be compelled to transfer Blackacre to B. A is put to his election. This means that he can choose to take with the will or against the will. If A takes with the will, he will release Blackacre to B and get his £10,000. If A takes against the will, he will retain Blackacre but the £10,000 will be subject to an equity in B to claim compensation out of it to the extent of the value of Blackacre.

The doctrine has traditionally been described as being based on the implied intention of the testator or donor that effect should be given to every part of the instrument drawn up.[41] However, the view has been expressed that the principle does not depend on 'a conjecture of a presumed intention'[42] and as pointed out in *Equity: Doctrines and Remedies*,[43] 'any such intention will usually be fictional or constructive for ordinarily the donor will have been mistaken'. In practice where a contrary intention is expressed, the operation of the doctrine may be excluded, although it would not be sufficient merely to show that the testator or donor had not contemplated the circumstances which would give rise to an election. As Buckley LJ pointed out in *Re Mengel's Will Trusts*,[44] 'the case in which the testator frames his will with the conscious intention of bringing the doctrine into play must be very rare' and in the vast majority of cases it will come into effect due to an oversight or mistake on the testator's part.[45]

However, it is necessary to establish an intention on the part of the testator

39. [1917] 1 IR 38, 42.
40. *Modern Equity* (15th ed., 1997) p. 852. This chapter was omitted from subsequent editions.
41. *Re Vardon's Trusts* (1885) 31 Ch D 275, 279 *per* Fry LJ.
42. *Cooper v Cooper* (1874) LR 7 HL 53, 67 *per* Lord Cairns. See also *Re Sullivan* [1917] 1 IR 38, 43.
43. Heydon, Leeming and Turner, *Meagher, Gummow and Lehane's Equity: Doctrines and Remedies* (5th ed., 2015) p.1133.
44. [1962] Ch 791, 796-797.
45. *Ibid.* and see Crago (1990) 106 LQR 487, 489.

or donor to dispose of the property in question, although it is irrelevant that he did not realise that the property was not in fact his.[46] This point was considered by Porter MR in *Minchin v Gabbett*,[47] where he stated as follows:

> But the question is, what was the intention of the testator? and that is to be gathered from the whole will, not by speculating, but by an honest endeavour to discover what the testator meant, seeing the language used and what it fairly means. No doubt, in approaching such a question, the Court must *prima facie* construe the words as applying to an estate which the testator had, if the words will fairly apply to it, nay, more than that, in order to raise a question of election, it must be clearly seen that the words used point to an estate which is not the testator's own but another's.

This reasoning was developed by Porter MR in *Galvin v Devereux*,[48] in which it was held that the testatrix intended to dispose only of her own estate and interest in lands and not to dispose of property which was not her own, and that therefore no case of election arose.

Requirements for Election

The doctrine of election applies both to wills and deeds,[49] although it operates more frequently in relation to wills. In circumstances where it applies, the donee is faced with a choice; he may either take under the instrument, in which case he may take the benefit of the gift to himself but must also consent to the transfer of his own property to a third party. Alternatively, he may take against the instrument, in which case he will retain his own property but will lose the benefit of the gift which the donor directed that he should have to the extent to which it is required to compensate the third party for failing to receive the donee's own property. As Sugden LC stated in *Hamilton v Jackson*,[50] in these circumstances 'the property goes in compensation to the persons disappointed' and in the event of delay, such compensation may carry interest.[51] However, it should be noted that the obligation to compensate is only to the extent of the benefit derived; as Jessel MR pointed out in *Pickersgill v Rodger*,[52] no more compensation can be required than the value of the testator's own property given to the person called upon to elect, even though this may be inadequate to compensate for the disappointment.

---

46. *Re Harris* [1909] 2 Ch 206, 209; *Re Sullivan* [1917] 1 IR 38, 43.
47. [1896] 1 IR 1, 12.
48. [1903] 1 IR 185.
49. *Birmingham v Kirwan* (1805) 2 Sch & Lef 444, 449.
50. (1845) 8 Ir Eq R 195.
51. *Re Saul's Trust* [1951] Ir Jur Rep 34.
52. (1876) 5 Ch D 163, 174. As Jessel MR stated: 'the obligation is only to the extent of the benefit [which the donee] derives: it cannot go beyond that'.

As Crago points out, whatever choice the electing party decides to make, he will not be as well off as the testator in all likelihood intended that he should be.[53] Where the value of the benefit which he is given is no more than the value of his own property, then irrespective of whether he takes under or against the instrument he will derive no net benefit. Even where the value of the benefit is greater than that of his own property, he will only receive a benefit amounting to the difference between these two values. The only circumstances in which the donee will benefit as much as the third party to whom he must give his own property is where the gift made to him by the donor is worth at least twice the value of his own property.

In order to give rise to an election, the testator or donor must not only make a gift to the donee but must also *in the same instrument* make an effective disposition of the donee's property to a third party. It has been accepted in England that a will and any codicils to it will be regarded as the same instrument in this context[54] and a deed and a will have even been treated as one for this purpose. In *Re Woodleys*[55] Palles CB was satisfied that the two documents taken together 'carry out and effectuate one entire and indivisible intention', although he made it clear in the course of his judgment that had they been 'separate and independent', no question of election would have arisen.

The essentials for election were set out as follows by Jenkins LJ in *Re Edwards*:[56] 'there should be an intention on the part of the testator or testatrix to dispose of certain property; secondly, that the property should not in fact be the testator's or testatrix's own property; and, thirdly, that a benefit should be given by the will to the true owner of the property.' So, in order for election to be necessary, it is essential that the donor has conferred a benefit on the donee with which he can compensate the third party if he elects to take against the instrument. As Loughborough LC commented in *Bristow v Warde*,[57] 'in all cases there must be some free disposable property given to the person, which can be made a compensation for what the testator takes away.' In addition, in order for a case for election to arise, it is necessary that the donee's property be directly disposed of to a third party by the terms of the same instrument. This point was laid down as follows by Christian LJ in *Lewis v Lewis*,[58] 'in order to raise a case of election, a testator must directly by his will assume to dispose of that which is not his; if he merely recites that it *has been* already disposed of in a particular way, and then proceeds to distribute his property on that assumption, and it turns out that he was mistaken, that does not raise a case of election.'

53. Crago (1990) 106 LQR 487, 488.
54. *Cooper v Cooper* (1874) LR 7 HL 53.
55. (1892) 29 LR Ir 304.
56. [1958] Ch 168, 175.
57. (1794) 2 Ves 336, 350.
58. (1876) IR 11 Eq 313. Quoted with approval by Palles CB in *Re Woodleys* (1892) 29 LR Ir 304, 313.

A further requirement is that the donee's property, which the donor purports to give to the third party, must be freely alienable. Election presupposes that the donee will have a choice and if his property cannot be alienated, he will not be required to make an election and will take the donor's gift free from any obligation. This point is illustrated by the decision in *Re Lord Chesham*.[59] A testator bequeathed his residuary estate to his eldest son and purported to dispose of chattels, in relation to which this son enjoyed a life interest but over which he had no power of disposition, in favour of his younger sons. It was held that the eldest son was not put to his election as he had no power to alienate this property and that he was entitled to take the residue of the testator's estate without compensating his younger brothers. However, in this context, it has been held that the application of the doctrine will only be excluded where the donee cannot by any relevant means comply with the testator's intentions and that it will apply even where the donee merely has a contingent interest in the property which he is required to alienate. So, in *Morgan v Morgan*[60] it was held that the doctrine applied even where the interest in question was a remainder expectant on an estate tail. Equally, the doctrine will apply to property which is subject to a special power of appointment so 'as a general rule when the donee of a power purports to give the property, the subject-matter of the power, to a person not an object, and gives property of his own to the object of the power, the latter is put to his election, and cannot dispute the disposition of the trust property if he takes the benefit out of the donee's own property'.[61]

A further important prerequisite for the application of the doctrine is that title to the electing party's property must arise independently of the instrument which gives rise to the need for the election to be made. So as James VC stated in *Wollaston v King*,[62] 'the rule as to election is to be applied as between a gift under the will, and a claim *dehors* the will and adverse to it, and is not to be applied as between one clause in a will and another clause in the same will'. This principle seems to have been accepted in England,[63] although it was not applied by Neville J in the decision of *Re Macartney*[64] which has admittedly been criticised as 'aberrant'.[65] The better view would seem to be that no case for election arises where the electing party acquires title to both properties under the same instrument and this approach is supported by the *dictum* of Chatterton VC in *Sweetman v Sweetman*,[66] where he said that the property

59. (1886) 31 Ch D 466. See also *Brown v Gregson* [1920] AC 860.
60. (1853) 4 Ir Ch R 606.
61. *Re Handcock's Trusts* (1888) 23 LR Ir 34, 46-47. See also *Moriarty v Martin* (1852) 3 Ir Ch R 26 and *Fearon v Fearon* (1852) 3 Ir Ch R 19.
62. (1869) Lr 8 Eq 165, 174.
63. See e.g. *Bate v Willats* (1877) 37 LT 221.
64. [1918] 1 Ch 300.
65. Heydon, Leeming and Turner, *Meagher, Gummow and Lehane's Equity: Doctrines and Remedies* (5th ed., 2015) p. 1130.
66. (1868) IR 2 Eq 141, 153.

which the testator purported to devise to a third party must belong 'not by the will, but by an earlier title, to the person who is called upon to elect'.

Making an Election

Romilly MR expressed the view in *Worthington v Wiginton*[67] that two requirements had to be satisfied in order for a valid election to be made under a will; first, there must be clear proof that the person making the election was aware of the nature and extent of his rights and secondly, it must be shown that having this knowledge, he intended to elect. Chatterton VC expanded these requirements in the following terms in the course of his judgment in *Sweetman v Sweetman*:[68]

> The requisites for holding a party bound by an election as concluded are, I think, these: first, he must have a knowledge of his rights, that is to say, he must know that the property, which the testator attempted to give to another person, was not the testator's property, and that it would, upon the testator's decease, become independently of the testator's will, the property of the party called upon to elect. It must be known by him, as a matter of fact, that the testator had not the power to give the property which he purported to devise, and that it belongs, not by the will, but by an earlier title, to the person who is called upon to elect. Next he must know the relative values of the properties between which he is called upon to elect; and further, he must know, as a matter of fact, and not as a presumption of law, that the rule of equity exists, that he cannot, under such circumstances, take both estates, but must make an election between the two. And further, the Court must be satisfied that he made a deliberate choice with the intention of making it.

Election may either be express or may be implied from a party's conduct,[69] provided that a clear choice was made with a full knowledge and understanding of the issues involved. When an election is made it relates back to the date of the gift and so any compensation payable in the case of election against the terms of a will depends on the valuation of the property in question at the date of the testator's death. It would appear that where a specified time limit is laid down by the instrument within which election must be made, failure to do so within this time will be considered as election against the instrument. However, where no limitation is expressed, a person is unlikely to lose the right to make

67. (1855) 20 Beav 67, 74.
68. (1868) IR 2 Eq 141, 152-153.
69. Note that in *Padbury v Clarke* (1850) 2 McN & G 298 it was found by Lord Cottenham LC that mere receipt of rents and profits of properties could not be construed as election. See also *Morgan v Morgan* (1853) 4 Ir Ch R 606, 614.

an election, even if he has knowledge of his right to do so, merely by reason of lapse of time unless serious prejudice would be caused to third parties as a result.

Disabilities, namely infancy or mental incapacity, will prevent a person exercising a right of election. In such cases an election will generally be made on behalf of the individual once the court has conducted an inquiry as to the most appropriate course of action to take,[70] although in the case of infants, the election may be deferred until majority is attained.

Conclusion

In practice the application of the doctrine of election may lead to rather anomalous results. Although the donee alone has an effective gift under a will, where the doctrine comes into operation, he will generally receive less of a net benefit than a third party to whom he must give either his own property or that which he appeared to be entitled to under the terms of the will, and in some circumstances he may receive no net benefit at all. It has been argued[71] that the doctrine is a 'mischievous' one which tends to defeat the testator's real intentions and that it is being applied in conditions which no longer correspond to those which may have justified its adoption in the first instance. Any application of the doctrine today will almost inevitably be as a result of a mistake made on the testator's part and the question must be asked whether equity should continue to intervene in a manner which arguably does not give effect to a testator's actual intentions and which so often produces an unfair result from the perspective of the person whom he expressly sought to benefit.

THE DOCTRINE OF SATISFACTION

This equitable doctrine is an illustration of the maxim that 'Equity imputes an intention to fulfil an obligation' and depends on a party's presumed intention to carry out an obligation. Where the doctrine of satisfaction applies, the act performed is of a different nature to that which it had been agreed should be carried out. The question which must be addressed is whether it can be presumed to have been intended to satisfy the original obligation. Cases in which the doctrine may operate are usually grouped into the following classifications.

1. Satisfaction of debts by legacies.
2. Satisfaction of portion debts by legacies.
3. Satisfaction (or ademption) of legacies by portions.
4. Satisfaction of legacies by legacies.

---

70. *Moore v Butler* (1805) 2 Sch & Lef 249, 266-267 *per* Lord Redesdale.
71. See Crago (1990) 106 LQR 487, 505.

Satisfaction of Debts by Legacies

Where a testator leaves a legacy to a creditor the question arises whether the creditor can claim both the legacy and the debt. The position is straightforward if the legacy is expressed to be in reduction of the debt. However, even if there is no such stipulation, equity presumes that if a debtor leaves a legacy in his will to his creditor of a sum which equals or exceeds the amount of the debt without making any mention of it, the legacy should be treated as being in satisfaction of the debt.[72] The general principle in this area was set out by Trevor MR in *Talbot v Duke of Shrewsbury*[73] as follows:

> [T]hat if one, being indebted to another in a sum of money, does by his will give him as great, or greater sum of money than the debt amounts to, without taking any notice at all of the debt, that this shall nevertheless be in satisfaction of the debt, so as that he shall not have both the debt and legacy.

Being based on a presumption, the doctrine will not apply where there is an indication of a contrary intention. In practice the presumption may be rebutted where there are any reasonable grounds for doing so and the general trend has been to circumscribe the scope of the circumstances in which it may apply.[74] The doctrine has been held not to apply for a number of different reasons. First, the presumption of satisfaction of a debt by a legacy does not apply where a will contains a direction to pay the testator's debts.[75] Most well-drafted wills now contain such a direction and in practice the application of the doctrine is usually excluded on this basis. Secondly, its application may be excluded for reasons relating to the nature of the debt and the time when it was incurred. Because the doctrine is based on presumed intention, the debt must have existed before the making of the will.[76] In addition, it does not apply to a continuous running account where the debt would have been uncertain at the time of drawing up the will. So, in *Buckley v Buckley*[77] the testator and another party were involved in ongoing business dealings and their practice was to settle their accounts from time to time. The amounts owed by the testator fluctuated after the date when the will was made and it was held by Porter MR that the testator's indebtedness to the other party at the time of his death was not satisfied by a legacy left in his will. As Porter MR stated:

---

72. *Garner v Holmes* (1858) 8 Ir Ch R 469, 476.
73. (1714) Prec Ch 394, 394-395.
74. See the comments of Stirling J in *Re Horlock* [1895] 1 Ch 516, 518 that: 'no sooner was [the doctrine] established than learned Judges of great eminence expressed their disapproval of it, and invented ways to get out of it'. But note also the comments of Romer J in *Re Stibbe* (1946) 175 LT 198, 201.
75. *Re Manners* [1949] Ch 613, 618 *per* Evershed MR.
76. *Cranmer's Case* (1701) 2 Salk 508.
77. (1888) 19 LR Ir 544.

> The debt here was on a running account, to which the ordinary presumption of satisfaction of debts by legacies does not apply … The reason is that the testator could not be presumed to know how the account would stand at his death and therefore he is not deemed to have intended the legacy in satisfaction of it without express words.[78]

Finally, it is important to stress that the presumption of satisfaction of a debt by a legacy applies only if the legacy is equal to or greater than the debt. In *Ellard v Phelan*,[79] where the testator owed small sums of money in respect of wages to his employees and left them more substantial legacies in his will, Ross J held that these bequests should be held to be a satisfaction of the sums owed by him at the time of his death. This can be contrasted with the situation which arose in *Coates v Coates*,[80] where it was held that where the amount of the legacy was less than the amount of the debt the presumption could not operate. Chatterton VC stressed in the course of his judgment that *pro tanto* satisfaction is not possible either in such cases; as he stated 'a legacy cannot operate in satisfaction of a debt of greater amount, even *pro tanto*'.[81] Therefore, it is even doubtful whether a legacy can be regarded as being in satisfaction of a debt which is for exactly the same amount but subject to the payment of interest.

The presumption will not apply where the legacy is of uncertain amount and satisfaction is not possible where the gift under the will is the whole or part of the residue of an estate because its value cannot be definitely fixed. So, even where the residue of the testator's estate may clearly exceed the amount of the debt, such a gift will not be regarded as satisfaction of the debt. In *Re Keogh's Estate*[82] the testator mortgaged his land and in his will directed that the mortgagees, who were relatives and had resided with him prior to his death, should be entitled to remain in his house for a year after his death. The testator also appointed them joint residuary legatees but Monroe J held that these benefits were not to be regarded as being in satisfaction of the mortgage debt.

In order for the presumption to apply, the legacy must be in every way as beneficial as the debt and where the legacy is different in character to the debt, this will not be the case. So, in *Coates v Coates*,[83] a bequest of the use of a house and furniture for life could not satisfy an obligation to pay a sum of money on a weekly basis. As Chatterton VC stated, 'the nature of the gift must correspond with the nature of the obligation'.[84]

---

78. *Ibid.* at 558.
79. [1914] 1 IR 76.
80. [1898] 1 IR 258.
81. *Ibid.* at 261. See also *Reade v Reade* (1880) 9 LR Ir 409.
82. (1889) 23 LR Ir 257.
83. [1898] 1 IR 258.
84. *Ibid.* at 261.

Satisfaction of Portion Debts by Legacies

The presumption in favour of the satisfaction of portion debts by legacies is an aspect of the principle that 'equity leans against double portions'.[85] The effect of the presumption is that where a father, or another person *in loco parentis* to a child undertakes to make a gift of a substantial nature or incurs an obligation to do so and subsequently makes provision in his will in the nature of a portion for this child, the portion debt is deemed to be satisfied by the obligation contained in the will. As Lord Cottenham LC stated in *Thynne v Earl of Glengall*,[86] 'Equity leans in favour of a provision by will being in satisfaction of a portion by contract feeling the great improbability of a parent intending a double portion for one child, to the prejudice generally … of other children.'

A number of aspects of this principle require further elaboration. A 'portion' in this context means that the gift must be of a substantial nature, relative to the means of the parent and child, and intended to set a child up in life. As Jessel MR commented in *Taylor v Taylor*,[87] 'I have always understood that an advancement by way of portion is something given by the parent to establish the child in life, or make what is called a provision for him – not a mere casual payment … .' The mere bestowing of a gift by a parent on a child will not suffice to make this gift a portion and equally a number of small gifts or advancements cannot be construed together as amounting to a portion.[88] The most common examples of a 'portion' would be a substantial gift made to a child on the occasion of his marriage or to enable him to set up in business.

The presumption of the satisfaction of portion debts by legacies in this context will only apply where the person making the provision for the child is his father or stands *in loco parentis* to him. Authority would suggest that it does not apply to provision made for a child by his mother[89] or other close relative unless that person can be considered to be *in loco parentis*. The exact interpretation of this phrase has caused difficulties,[90] but it is generally accepted as meaning where a person has assumed 'the office and duty of the parent to make provision for the child'.[91] In *Preston v Greene*[92] Meredith MR commented that: 'the difference between a father and a mother is this, that in the one case there is a moral obligation to [advance the child] recognised in equity, while in the case of a mother the moral obligation is there, but the Courts of equity do not recognise it.' While it is unlikely that the courts in this jurisdiction would continue to approve of drawing a distinction between fathers and mothers in

85. See *Keays v Gilmore* (1873) IR 8 Eq 290, 295 *per* Sullivan MR.
86. (1848) 2 HL Cas 131, 153.
87. (1875) LR 20 Eq 155, 157.
88. *Suisse v Lord Lowther* (1843) 2 Hare 424, 434 *per* Wigram VC; *Watson v Watson* (1864) 33 Beav 574.
89. *Re Ashton* [1897] 2 Ch 574.
90. See, e.g. *Fowkes v Pascoe* (1875) 10 Ch App 343, 350 *per* James LJ.
91. *Powys v Mansfield* (1837) 3 My & Cr 359, 377 *per* Lord Cottenham LC.
92. [1909] 1 IR 172, 177-178.

this context,[93] until the matter falls to be considered, no definite conclusion can be reached. Where a child's father is still alive it may be more difficult to establish that another individual is acting *in loco parentis*, although it will be easier to do so where this individual is a close relative, and in *Pym v Lockyer*[94] a grandfather was held to be acting *in loco parentis* to his grandchildren even though their father was still alive. The question of whether a person is acting *in loco parentis* must be answered on the basis of whether there has been 'the assumption of a parent's responsibility'.[95] While Barton J suggested in *Smyth v Gleeson*[96] that the actions of a brother in making a gift to his older sister were more those of 'an affectionate brother' and said that it was at least doubtful whether the former has ever placed himself *in loco parentis*, he was prepared to assume for the sake of argument that this might have been the case. However, this can be contrasted with the decision of the Supreme Court in *Re Bannon*,[97] where it was held that the facts proved did not support the inference that the testator stood *in loco parentis* to his nephew.

It would appear that the question of whether a portion debt may be satisfied by a legacy is one of intention to be determined from the terms of the instrument in the absence of evidence to the contrary. This point was made by Monroe J in *Re Battersby's Estate*[98] in the following terms:

> The question whether a portion given by a settlement is satisfied by a legacy in a subsequent will is entirely one of intention to be gathered in the absence of other evidence from the terms of the two instruments, subject to the consideration, that the presumption of law is against double portions. If the provision made by the later limitations are substantially the same, double portions will not be allowed; the parties entitled will be put to their election. If the limitations are widely different, the presumption is that the provisions were to be cumulative.

Unlike in the case of satisfaction of debts by legacies *pro tanto* satisfaction is possible, so if the legacy is of less value than the portion, it is deemed to be a satisfaction *pro tanto*.[99] Although the *dicta* of Monroe J in *Re Battersby*[100] might have suggested otherwise, this was confirmed by Laffoy J in her judgment in *Hickey v O'Dwyer*.[101] In this case the testator took out a policy of assurance on his life and executed a declaration of trust in a standard form. He conferred

93. See also *supra* Chapter 7 in relation to the presumption of advancement.
94. (1841) 5 My & Cr 29.
95. *Smyth v Gleeson* [1911] 1 IR 113, 119. See also *Monck v Monck* (1810) 1 Ba & B 298.
96. [1911] 1 IR 113.
97. [1934] IR 701.
98. (1887) 19 LR Ir 359, 363-364.
99. *Warren v Warren* (1783) 1 Bro CC 305.
100. (1887) 19 LR Ir 359, 363-364.
101. [2006] 2 ILRM 81.

a power of appointment upon himself which provided that, in default of and subject to any such appointment, the entire trust fund should be held for the absolute benefit of his daughter, the fourth defendant. The testator did not exercise the power of appointment over the trust fund and after his death the sum of £223,350, being the proceeds of the policy, was paid out to two trustees appointed by the court on behalf of his daughter. In his will, made subsequently to the taking out of the life assurance policy, the testator bequeathed the sum of £100,000 to the first three defendants to be held by them in trust for his daughter until she reached the age of 25 years and then to her absolutely. He also devised and bequeathed the residue of his estate to the plaintiff, his widow, for her own use and benefit. In a special summons the court was asked whether the testator by the bequest in his will in favour of his daughter had exercised the power of appointment in relation to the proceeds of the policy. If the answer to this question was in the negative, the court was asked whether the bequest in the testator's will to set up a trust in favour of his daughter in the amount of £100,000 was intended to be in whole or in part satisfaction of the monies held on trust for her pursuant to the terms of the trust funds. The case made by the plaintiff was that by operation of the equitable doctrine of satisfaction the testator's daughter was not entitled to both the provision made in the trust and the bequest.

Laffoy J stated that she was satisfied that the provision made in the trust was a portion in the sense of being a gift of a substantial nature relative to the means of the testator and intended to set his daughter up in life. In addition, she concluded that the provision made in the trust and the provision made by the testator in his will for his daughter were substantially of the same nature. Although the provision in the will was considerably smaller than what the policy had yielded, she confirmed that the doctrine of satisfaction allowed a lesser provision in a will to be satisfaction *pro tanto* of an earlier portion. Laffoy J concluded that the circumstances of the case gave rise to a presumption that the testator had not intended his daughter to take both provisions. She concluded that the totality of the relevant evidence in relation to the testator's age, marital status and personal circumstances and the state of his assets when he made his will supported the presumption that the testator did not intend that his daughter should receive both the entirety of the proceeds of the policy and the bequest contained in his will and so the presumption stood. Laffoy J therefore held that the provision in the testator's will in favour of his daughter was intended to be in part satisfaction of the proceeds of the policy the subject of the trust.

As a general principle the property left by will must be of 'substantially the same nature'[102] as the property to which the beneficiary is entitled by virtue of the existing obligation and the interest in the property taken by the beneficiary must be as beneficial to him as this interest. While a greater degree of flexibility may be exercised than in the case of ordinary debts and legacies, generally

102. *Hickey v O'Dwyer* [2006] 2 ILRM 81, 85 *per* Laffoy J.

speaking they 'must be of the same nature and attended with the same degree of certainty'.[103] So, in *Smyth v Gleeson*[104] the presumption of satisfaction of a portion debt by a legacy was rebutted by the difference in certainty and value between the two benefits.

If the father or person *in loco parentis* has actually advanced a portion to a child and subsequently gives a legacy to the same child, the latter will not be regarded as satisfaction and the child will be entitled to take the benefit of the legacy.[105] The reasoning behind this approach is clear, as, if the father has already given the child the gift in the nature of a portion, he would undoubtedly intend that child to benefit in addition from any provision made for him in a subsequent will.

Unlike in the case of ordinary debts, once it is found that the presumption applies, the child is put to his election between the gift under the will and the *inter vivos* portion obligation.[106] So, in *Hickey v O'Dwyer*[107] referred to above, the consequence of the conclusion that the doctrine of satisfaction applied was that an election had to be made on behalf of the testator's daughter between the provision contained in the trust and the provision under the will. On the facts of the case before the court where the former was greater in value, Laffoy J stated that it must be assumed that the election would be to take the provision under the trust.

Although designed to promote equality between children, the application of the doctrine of satisfaction has been criticised for penalising an only child in an unfair manner while not applying to more distant relatives of a testator. However, it has been expressly preserved by section 63(9) of the Succession Act 1965. The subsection provides that section 63, which requires that advancements made to a child must be taken into account when determining the child's share on an intestacy, is not to affect the principle of the satisfaction of portion debts by legacies.

Satisfaction of Legacies by Portions and the Doctrine of Ademption

This is essentially a case of ademption, meaning in this context the writing off of a legacy by an advance made during the intended legatee's lifetime. There are two aspects of this principle which must be considered; first the ademption of a legacy by a subsequent portion where the parties are father and child or where the donor is *in loco parentis*, and secondly the ademption of a legacy

103. *Bellasis v Uthwatt* (1737) 1 Atk 426, 427-428.
104. [1911] 1 IR 113.
105. *Smyth v Gleeson* [1911] 1 IR 113, 119.
106. See the *dicta* of Monroe J in *Re Battersby's Estate* (1887) 19 LR Ir 359, 363-364. This choice must be distinguished from the operation of the doctrine of election discussed above.
107. [2006] 2 ILRM 81.

given for a specific purpose by a subsequent gift made during the donee's lifetime for the same purpose.

The principle of the ademption of a legacy by a portion was set out in the following terms by Lord Selborne LC in *Re Pollock*:[108]

> When a testator gives a legacy to a child, or to any other person towards whom he has taken on himself parental obligations, and afterwards makes a gift or enters into a binding contract in his lifetime in favour of the same legatee then (unless there be distinctions between the nature and conditions of the two gifts) there is a presumption that both gifts were made to fulfil the same natural or moral obligation of providing for the legatee and consequently that the gift *inter vivos* is either wholly or in part a substitution for or an ademption of the legacy.

The operation of these principles can be seen in the decision of Sugden LC in *Barry v Harding*,[109] in which he held that an absolute gift in a will to a child would be adeemed by a portion of the same amount subsequently given on her marriage, even though this sum was settled on her and her husband. The presumption against double portions forms the basis for this principle, as was made clear by Sullivan MR in his judgment in *Curtin v Evans*:[110]

> There is a presumption raised by the law against double portions; and accordingly, when a parent, or one standing *in loco parentis*, gives by will a sum of money to a child, and afterwards a like or greater sum is secured by a settlement on the marriage of that child, the law presumes the legacy to be adeemed.

However, Sullivan MR went on to stress that this principle is only a presumption and may be rebutted by evidence of intention to the contrary. He stated that the burden of proving the intention necessary to rebut the presumption rests on the person claiming the double portion and said that parol evidence will be admitted with a view to establishing whether the presumption is well founded. However, he stressed that where the claim rests on oral evidence, 'the Court ought to view and examine it with scrupulous care and great discrimination' and ought not to act on it unless it is free from suspicion and clearly shows the real intention of the person making the advancement.

As ademption of a gift by will by way of a later *inter vivos* gift is a working out of the intention of the donor it would appear that there is no need for the donee either to know of the prospective gift by will or to be party to or to know of the *inter vivos* gift.[111] It is therefore not necessary for the donor to

108. (1885) 28 Ch D 552, 555.
109. (1844) 7 Ir Eq R 313.
110. (1872) IR 9 Eq 553, 557.
111. *Re Cameron* [1999] Ch 386, 410; *Re Eardley's Will* [1920] 1 Ch 397, 410.

communicate his intention to the donee and the fact that the matter was not discussed does not of itself rebut the presumption.[112]

Where a devise or bequest in the will is followed by a subsequent *inter vivos* gift to the same beneficiary, ademption may operate *pro tanto* if the amount of the gift is less than the value of the legacy.[113] The corollary of this principle is that where a child is left a legacy and is subsequently advanced a smaller sum, he can claim the balance under the terms of the will.[114]

If the portion is paid before the will is drawn up, there can be no question of ademption, as there will be no legacy in existence at the time to be adeemed.[115] Where ademption does take place, equity deems the devise or bequest in the will to have been cancelled. It is therefore no longer treated as being an operable part of the will and the beneficiary cannot claim under it. Thus, unlike in the case of the satisfaction of portions by legacies considered above, there can be no election between the will and the *inter vivos* portion and the beneficiary must take the latter.[116]

The legacy and the portion must be of the same general nature for the presumption of ademption to apply, e.g. there can be no ademption of a pecuniary legacy by a portion consisting of land.[117] However, this requirement will be less strictly applied than in the case of satisfaction and the presumption of ademption will only be displaced by more substantial differences in subject-matter.[118]

As noted above, the doctrine of ademption can operate in a more general context, and a legacy given for a specific purpose may be adeemed by a subsequent gift made during the donee's lifetime for the same purpose. The operation of this principle is well illustrated by the decision of *Griffith v Bourke*.[119] A legacy was given to a parish priest for the purpose of erecting a new chapel. It was held by Porter MR that this legacy was adeemed by the gift of a like sum for the same purpose to the archbishop of the diocese by the testator during his lifetime. As Porter MR stated: 'Where there is a gift in a will for an expressed object and afterwards a donation by the testator in his lifetime for the *same* object, the law presumes that he did not intend that both should take effect but that the latter should be in substitution for the former gift.'[120] However, he went on to stress that the object in question must be clearly expressed and it must be plain that the reason for making the *inter vivos* gift

112. *Barraclough v Mell* [2006] WTLR 203, 221.
113. *Edgeworth v Johnston* (1877) IR 11 Eq 326.
114. *Pym v Lockyer* (1841) 5 My & Cr 29. See also *Re Pollock* (1885) 28 Ch D 522.
115. *Re Peacock's Estate* (1872) LR 14 Eq 236.
116. See the *dicta* of Lord Cranworth in *Chichester v Coventry* (1867) LR 2 HL 71, 87.
117. *Re Wall's Estate* [1922] 1 IR 59.
118. *Chichester v Coventry* (1867) LR 2 HL 71, 87 *per* Lord Cranworth.
119. (1887) 21 LR Ir 92.
120. *Ibid.* at 95.

was the same as that which motivated the testator to give the legacy; both gifts must be for the 'same identical object'.

It is the requirement of a specific purpose which distinguishes this form of ademption from the variety applying to father and child. A fairly liberal interpretation of the requirement of a specific purpose was given by the English Court of Appeal in *Re Pollock*,[121] where Lord Selborne LC stated that the legacy may be adeemed by the subsequent gift where it is expressed to be made 'in fulfilment of some moral obligation recognised by the testator' even though this obligation is not of a kind which the law will recognise. In this case a testatrix bequeathed a sum of £500 to a niece of her deceased husband stating that she was doing so in accordance with the latter's wishes. Subsequently, during her lifetime, she paid the niece the sum of £300 and entered in her diary that this was a legacy from her uncle. It was held by Lord Selborne LC that there was a presumption that the legacy was adeemed to the extent of £300.

Satisfaction of Legacies by Legacies

This process has been described as only 'superficially akin'[122] to the doctrine of satisfaction and is probably better described as an instance of construing a will so as to avoid duplication of legacies which a testator is not likely to have intended. The underlying principle is the desire of the courts to attempt to construe the testamentary documents so as to give effect where possible to the testator's actual intention.

Where two or more legacies are given to the same person either in the same will or more usually in a will and a codicil, the question arises whether these should be regarded as cumulative or substitutional. If the two legacies which are given to the same person are of the same value and are given in the same instrument, equity presumes that they are substitutional and the legatee can take one only.[123] However, where the two legacies given by the same instrument are for different amounts, the presumption is that they are cumulative. This point was made in the following terms by Smith MR in *Brennan v Moran*:[124]

> [I]t is a rule of construction that; where two legacies are given by the same testamentary instrument to the same person, of different amount, the legacies are to be considered cumulative, unless a contrary intention appears on the will.

In addition, if the two legacies are given by different instruments, usually by a will and a codicil, it is presumed that they are cumulative irrespective of their

121. (1885) 28 Ch D 552.
122. Heydon, Leeming and Turner, *Meagher, Gummow and Lehane's Equity: Doctrines and Remedies* (5th ed., 2015) p. 1030.
123. *Garth v Meyrick* (1779) 1 Bro CC 30.
124. (1857) 6 Ir Ch R 126, 130.

value; as Smith MR stated in *Brennan v Moran*[125] in such a case 'as the testator has given twice, he must *prima facie* be intended to mean two gifts'. This principle was re-iterated by O'Sullivan MR in *Quin v Armstrong*[126] as follows:

> [W]here a testator by his will gives a benefit to a person, and by a codicil to his will gives a benefit to the same person, the presumption of law is that he means to give twice; and it lies on the party who disputes it to show why that construction of them should not be adopted.

However, this presumption may be rebutted and the legacies may be regarded as substitutional if they are for the same amount and are given for the same motive. So, in *Re Armstrong*[127] it was held that the presumption that legacies given to the same person in a will and in a subsequent testamentary instrument are cumulative was rebutted by the testatrix's intention 'to take away one gift and leave … one gift instead of that one which is taken away'.[128]

Despite the guidelines laid down above, the question will ultimately be one of construction of the instruments concerned and, as stated, the primary aim is to give effect as far as possible to the testator's intentions. So, in *Bell v Park*[129] legacies in a second will were taken as being in substitution for those in the first because, on an overall reading of the instruments, it appeared that this was the intention of the testatrix. As Cherry LJ stated, '[s]uch gifts are undoubtedly *prima facie* cumulative, but it is always permissible to show by the terms of the two instruments that the gifts by the later document were intended to be substitutional and not cumulative'.[130]

If gifts are presumed to be cumulative parol evidence is not admissible to rebut this presumption. However, if gifts are presumed to be substitutional parol evidence is admissible.

THE DOCTRINE OF PERFORMANCE

This equitable doctrine is also based on the maxim that 'Equity imputes an intention to fulfil an obligation' and reflects the principle that 'a person is presumed to do that which he is bound to do'.[131] However, performance can be distinguished from satisfaction because while satisfaction involves fulfilling an obligation by means of an act different in form from the one originally contemplated, performance involves the carrying out of the obligation itself.

125. *Ibid.* at 130. See also *Walsh v Walsh* (1870) IR 4 Eq 396.
126. (1876) IR 11 Eq 161, 168.
127. (1893) 31 LR Ir 154.
128. *Ibid.* at 156.
129. [1914] 1 IR 158.
130. *Ibid.* at 174.
131. *Tubbs v Broadwood* (1831) 2 Russ & M 487, 493 *per* Lord Brougham LC.

So, where a person is under an obligation to carry out a particular act and subsequently does an act which can be considered as performance of his obligation, in certain circumstances equity will presume that this subsequent act was done in performance of the earlier obligation. This principle was stated in the following terms by Walker LJ in *Bannatyne v Ferguson*:[132]

> The principle of performance is that when a person covenants to do an act, and he does that which may either wholly or partially be converted to or towards a completion of the covenant there will be a presumption that he had done the act with the intention to perform his covenant.

The situations in which the doctrine of performance operates can be divided into two categories.

By Act of the Party

The most common example of the operation of the doctrine by act of the party is where a person covenants to purchase land and settle it on certain trusts and subsequently purchases land but fails to settle it. In these circumstances, equity may consider that the purchase amounted to performance of the covenant and the land will be considered as being held on the trusts of the settlement. This point is illustrated by the decision of Talbot LC in *Lechmere v Lechmere*.[133] Prior to his marriage, a husband covenanted to lay out £30,000 in the purchase of freehold land within one year of his marriage. These lands were to be conveyed to trustees and each purchase was to be approved by them. After his marriage but not within the time stipulated and without the consent of the trustees, the husband purchased various interests in land, some of a fee simple nature but others of a reversionary or leasehold character, and also contracted to purchase fee simple estates. The husband died intestate and was survived by his wife. It was held that the freehold land purchased and contracted to be purchased after his marriage, although not amounting to £30,000 in value, should go towards performance of the covenant. However, any lands purchased by the husband before the date of the covenant and the interests which were not of a fee simple nature could not regarded as having been purchased in performance of his obligations. This decision established that where the lands are of lesser value than the lands covenanted to be purchased, they will be considered to have been purchased in part performance of the obligation and it also shows that property of a different nature from that covenanted to be purchased will not be available for this purpose.

However, for the doctrine to apply in this context, the act done must be essentially the same as that which the individual has covenanted to do and in

132. [1896] 1 IR 149, 179.
133. (1735) Cas t Talb 80.

Bannatyne v Ferguson[134] the Irish Court of Appeal held that the appointment of a jointure by deed was not performance of an obligation to secure an annuity.

The operation of the doctrine may have important practical consequences in this context because where a covenant to purchase or settle property in the future is deemed to be performed, it may create a specific charge or lien over the property.[135]

By Operation of Law

Where a person covenants to leave a sum of money to another person or covenants that his executors will pay that person such a sum and then dies intestate, with the other person taking a share in his intestate estate, that share may be regarded as performance, or *pro tanto* performance, of the covenant to leave money. While provision for this individual may be expressly made to be in substitution for any claim which the covenantee may have in relation to an estate,[136] the more common situation is that which arose in *Re Finegan's Estate*.[137] A husband executed a bond which provided that in the event of his death in his wife's lifetime, a sum of money was to be paid to trustees in trust for her. When he predeceased his wife leaving no issue it was held that the sum secured by the bond was to be regarded, in the absence of any contrary intention being expressed, as satisfaction *pro tanto* of the widow's share in her husband's estate. Where there is evidence of a contrary intention, the doctrine will not apply and the covenantee will be entitled to the benefit of the gift and the distributive share.[138]

134. [1896] 1 IR 149.
135. *Creed v Carey* (1857) 7 Ir Ch R 295.
136. See *Re Hogan* [1901] 1 IR 168.
137. [1925] 1 IR 201. See also *Blandy v Widmore* (1716) 1 P Wms 323.
138. *Re Hood* [1923] 1 IR 109.

Index

Absolute present gift
donatio mortis causa distinguished, 144
Academic research
gift for, 426–427
Accessory liability *see* **Third party liability to account**
Accounts
charitable trust, 404
inspection by beneficiary, 561–562
trustee's duty to keep, 561
Acquiescence *see* **Laches and acquiescence**
Action for money had and received, 372, 993–995
Actual notice *see also* **Notice, doctrine of**
nature of, 60–61
Ademption, doctrine of, 1037–1040
Administration of deceased's estate
trust distinguished, 80–82
Administration of trusts
accounts and information, 561–569
breach of trust *see* Breach of trust
charitable trusts, 402–406
legislation, 517
pension trusts, 614–615
possible future developments, 612–616
trustees' powers and duties *see* **Trustees**
variation of trust *see* **Variation of trust**
Administrative unworkability, 110–111
Advancement
presumption of *see* **Presumption of advancement**
trustee's power, 583
Advertisement
potential beneficiaries, 559
Affirmation of contract, 919–920
After-acquired property, 153–156
Aged persons
gift for, 423, 460–464
Agency
trust distinguished, 72
Agent
appointment, 577
delegation of trustee's functions to, 575–579
fiduciary position, 285–288
liability to account, of agent of trustee, 375–376
***Allhusen v Whittel*, rule in**, 556–557
Amateur sport
gift promoting, 472–474, 482–483
***American Cyanamid/Campus Oil* principles**
adequacy of damages, 651–654, 656–658, 658–662
approval in *Campus Oil* case, 652–653
balance of convenience, 651–653, 656–658, 662–663
departure from
defamation or freedom of expression case, 674–688
no arguable defence, 669–670
public law context, 699–703
trade dispute, 670–674
trial of action unlikely, 691–699
winding-up petition, 688–691
guidelines only, 667–669
interlocutory injunction, test for grant, 650–654
pending appeal, 665–667
preservation of *status quo*, 663–665
risk of injustice, 668–669

***American Cyanamid/Campus Oil* principles**—*contd.*
serious or fair question to be tried, 652–653, 654–656
strength of plaintiff's case, 654–656
summary of, 653
Amnesty International
trust created by, 478
Anchor tenant
specific performance of contract, 812–818
Animals
charitable trust
anti-vivisection, 394, 459, 468–469, 477–478
examples, 466–467
performing animals, 468
protection from cruelty, 469
rationale for enforcing, 465–466
vegetarianism, 457, 467
purpose trust for particular animal, 388–389, 465–466
Annuity payment
specific performance, 810
Anonymous donations
failure to exhaust beneficial interest, 164–165
Anti-vivisection society
gift to, 394, 459, 468–469, 477–478
Anton Piller order
defendant's options, 779–780
full and frank disclosure, 777–779
in personam effect, 776
legal advice, defendant's right to seek, 777
list of items seized, 784, 785
nature and effect, 775–776
non-compliance
contempt of court, 776–777
order subsequently set aside, 777
origin of, 776
pre-conditions, 776
privilege against self-incrimination, 780–783
procedural safeguards, 784–785
supervising solicitor, 784
surprise of the essence, 775–776
undertaking in damages, 777–778
Appeal
injunction pending, 665–667
Appointment of trustees *see* **Trustees**
Apportionment of trust property
accumulated profits distributed as bonus shares, 558
capital profit distributed, 558
conversion of trust property, on, 555–556
debts payable out of estate, 556–557
purchase or sale of shares cum dividend, 558
repairs or improvements carried out, 557–558
rule in *Allhusen v Whittel*, 556–557
rule in *Re Atkinson*, 557
sale of mortgage security, 557
wasting, hazardous or unauthorised assets, 555–556
valuation date, 555–556
Art appreciation
gift for, 428–429
Association *see* **Unincorporated association**
***Atkinson*, rule in**, 557
Attorney General
charitable trust functions, 403
proceedings enforcing public rights, 744–746
Automatic resulting trust
definition, 83, 157–158
distribution of surplus on dissolution of association, 166–169
failure of the trust, 160–161
failure to exhaust beneficial interest, 162–165
Quistclose trust, 169–175
theoretical basis, 158–160

***Babanaft* proviso**, 766, 769
***Baden* categories of knowledge**, 344–345
Bailment
definition, 71
trust distinguished, 71
Balance of convenience
injunction, 651–653, 656–658, 662–663

Baltic **proviso**, 767
Bank account
distribution of mixed funds, 46n
joint account, presumed resulting trust, 180–191
legal and beneficial ownership of money paid in, 359–360
Quistclose trust, 169–175
tracing into
first in, first out, 1001–1007
overdrawn account, 1007–1011
trust of credit balance, 102
Banker
receipt of insurance monies, 578
undue influence, 887
Bankruptcy
voidable settlements, 513–515
Bare trust, 84n
Bayer injunction, 785–787
Beddoe **order**, 540
Beneficial interest
failure to exhaust, 162–165
family property dispute *see* **Family property dispute**
right *in personam* or *in rem*, 52–54
Beneficiaries of trust
definition, 70–71
administrative unworkability and capriciousness, 110–111
advancements out of trust capital, 583
advertisement for potential beneficiaries, 559
certainty as to, 79–80, 103–111
conceptual and evidential certainty, 108–109
concurrence or acquiescence in breach of trust, 593–594
discretionary trust, 75–76, 105–108
distribution of trust property, 559–561
education and maintenance, 581–582
equality between, 553–558
fixed trust, 103–104
information to be made available to, 561–569
inspection of trust accounts, 561–562
Beneficiaries of trust—*contd.*
instigating or consenting to breach of trust, 27–28, 591–593
missing beneficiary, 559–561
notice of existence of trust, 568–569
purpose trust, 381–382
trustee, as, 518
unborn or minor, 571, 608–609, 610
unpaid or underpaid beneficiary's remedy, 559
volunteer's position, 152–153
Beneficiary principle, 82, 381–382
Benefits fraud, 32–33, 197–198
Benevolent construction, 135, 139–140
Benjamin order, 559–560
Bodily integrity
interlocutory injunction, 684–685
Bona fide **purchaser**
priorities and doctrine of notice, 56–57, 58–64
rectification of contract, 860
tracing, 1015
Bona vacantia, 164–165, 166–168
***Bonnard v Perryman*, rule in**, 676
Bonus shares, 558
Breach of confidence
'clean hands' principle, 30, 625–626
damages, 11
injunction, 625–626, 683, 684, 692–693
Breach of contract
damages where no financial loss, 641–643
delay in claiming damages, 15–16
equitable remedy, laches, 39
estimate of damage or penalty, 48
injunctive relief
contract for personal services, 725–730
employment injunction, 731–741
general principles, 721–725
limitation period, 38
specific performance *see* **Specific performance**
Breach of fiduciary duty *see* **Fiduciary relationship**

Breach of statute
injunction restraining, 745–746
Breach of trust
beneficiary instigating or consenting to, 27–28, 591–593
causation, 588
charitable trust, 405
concurrence or acquiescence of beneficiary, 593–594
constructive trust *see* **Constructive trust**
damages, 11, 586
date for assessing loss, 588–589
equitable compensation, 13–15, 586–588
examples, 584–585
extent and measure of trustee's liability, 584–589
indemnity of co-trustees, 590–591
interest on sum due, 589
joint and several liability, 589–590
liability of trustees inter se, 589–591
liability to account, 585, 586
limitation period, 37–38, 594
prior to appointment or after retirement, 585–586
protection of trustees from personal liability, 591–594
statutory defence (UK), 592
third party liability *see* **Third party liability to account**
tracing trust property *see* **Tracing**
trustee exemption clause, 595–607
unauthorised investment, 586
Brehon law, 7
Bribe
fiduciary receiving, 50, 278–285
Broker
employment by trustee, 576–578
Brussels I Regulation (recast)
provisional and protective measures, 770–773
rights *in rem* in immovable property, jurisdiction, 52–54
Building contract
specific performance, 818–820
Building maintenance and improvement
trust for, 395
Capital acquisitions tax
charitable trust, 400–401
Capital gains tax
charitable trust, 400
Capital profit
distribution of, 558
Capriciousness, 111
Carrying on business
specific performance of contract, 812–818
Cemetery
trust for upkeep, 385n, 387, 448
Certainty
creation of trust *see* **Three certainties**
Chancery Division, 8
Change of position, 1016–1017
Charitable purposes
definition, 406–408
advancement of education
academic research, 426–427
aesthetic education, 428–429
Charities Act 2009, 425
'founder's kin', 434–436
meaning of education, 425–430
personal connection with donor, 431–436
physical education, 428, 470
private school, 431–434
professional body, 429–430
public benefit requirement, 412, 430–436
Royal College of Surgeons, 429–430
self-help group, 428
Worth Library, 427–428, 434
advancement of religion
celebration of masses, 384n, 441–444
Charities Act 2009, 436–437
church buildings etc, 447–449
ecclesiastical office holders, 439–441
gift in general terms, 438–439

Charitable purposes—*contd.*
advancement of religion—*contd.*
missionary purposes, 439
organisation or cult employing psychological manipulation, 438
public benefit requirement, 411–412
religious denominations, 437–438
religious orders, 392–394, 444–447
residence for priests etc, 449
Roman Catholic religion, 438–439
upkeep of churchyard or cemetery, 448–449
evolving concept, 409
failure of, cy-près doctrine *see* **Cy-près doctrine**
Macnaghten categories, 407–408
other purposes of benefit to the community
aged, disabled and sick, 460–464
animals, 465–469
Charities Act 2009, 449–450
community development, harmonious relations etc, 464–465
general public utility, 450–451
law reporting, 451
non-exhaustive list, 450, 459–460
objective or subjective test, 457–459
personal connection with donor, 456
political purposes, 474–482
public benefit requirement, 412–413, 451–456
sports and recreation, 469–474
Worth Library, 454–456
prevention or relief of poverty
aged and sick, 423
Charities Act 2009, 414
degree of poverty, 414–416
economic hardship, 418
general or particular terms, 417
gift must be directed to poverty, 416–417

Charitable purposes—*contd.*
prevention or relief of poverty—*contd.*
poor relations/employees, 411n, 418–425
prevention of poverty, 417
public benefit requirement, 411, 418–425
relevance of existing case law, 414
public benefit requirement, 409–414
Statute of Charitable Uses, 406–407

Charitable trust
definition, 408–409
accounts, 404
administration of charities, 402–406
advantages of charitable status, 398–402
annual report, 404
Attorney General's functions, 403
charitable purposes *see* **Charitable purposes**
Charities Act 2009
commencement, 398n, 402n
measures proposed but omitted, 405–406, 449n
Charities Regulatory Authority, 403–404
Charity Appeals Tribunal, 404
Commissioners of Charitable Donations and Bequests, 403
cy-près doctrine *see* **Cy-près doctrine**
excluded bodies, 409, 481
fiscal immunity, 400–402
investigation and report, 405
investment policy, 552–553
Macnaghten categories, 407–408
non-charitable purposes, 380, 399–400
perpetual duration, 400
production of books and documents, 405
public benefit requirement, 409–414
Register of Charitable Organisations, 404
sign manual procedure, 499–500
tax exemptions, 400–402

Charitable purposes—*contd.*
trustees
grounds for disqualification, 404n
liability for breach of trust, 405
order authorising disqualified person, 404–405
Charities Regulatory Authority, 403–404
Charity Appeals Tribunal, 404
Child *see also* **Minor; Parent and child**
illegitimacy *see* **Illegitimate child**
maintenance or education out of trust income, 581–582
presumption of advancement
father and child, 209–211
mother and child, 212–215
person *in loco parentis*, 211–212
religious upbringing, 504–506
testator's moral duty to make proper provision, 47
Childcare
beneficial interest in family property, 233–236
Christian Brothers
gift to, 391, 439
Church
gift to *see* **Religion, trust for advancement**
Churchyard
trust for upkeep, 387, 448
Civil partner
property adjustment order, 224, 235–236
***Clayton's* case, rule in,** 1001–1007
'Clean hands' principle
adultery, 30
application for injunction, 624–626
connection between conduct and subject-matter of dispute, 29–30
conveyance of land, 28–29
element of turpitude, 32
equitable maxim, 27–36
exclusive licensing agreement, 31–32
fraudulent misrepresentation of age, 27
Charitable purposes—*contd.*
illegal agreement, 33–34
last resort defence, 27n
presenting case to court, 31
public conscience test, 34
Revenue fraud, 35
social security fraud, 32–33
specific performance, 28
Clergy's residence
gift for repair or upkeep, 449
Cohabitee
beneficial interest in mortgaged property, 225–227, 255–256
no presumption of advancement, 215
property adjustment order, 224, 235–236
qualified cohabitant: 224n
undue influence, 894
Coke, Edward (Chief Justice of England), 7
College
gift to, 425, 435–436
Commercial transactions
constructive notice, 62–63, 363–364
equitable principles, 5–6
fiduciary relationship, 267–269
Pallant v Morgan equity, 304–307, 981
presumption of advancement, 215
proprietary estoppel, 949–950, 952–954, 980–981, 982–983, 991–992
Commissioners of Charitable Donations and Bequests, 403
Common expectation
proprietary estoppel, 939–942
Common intention constructive trust
family property
ambulatory constructive trust, 252
background, 236–239
circumstances giving rise to trust, 239–243
direct and indirect contributions, 236–238
doctrinal issues, 247–251
express or implied common intention, 237–238

Common intention constructive trust—*contd.*
family property—*contd.*
extent of beneficial interest, 243–251
joint or sole legal ownership, 239–243
fraud or illegality, 197
other circumstances, 236n
Pallant v Morgan equity and, 305–307
Common injunctions, 7
Common law
equity and, 1, 8–9, 10–19
shortcomings giving rise to equity, 6
Common mistake
rectification, 848–852
rescission of contract, 867–870
Common Pleas Division, 8
Communication and acceptance
half secret trust, 120–126
Community development
gift for, 464–465
Company
director *see* **Director of company**
pre-incorporation commission payments, constructive trust, 320–321
Competition with trust business, 276–278
Completely constituted trust
definition, 83, 129
declaration of trust by settlor, 136–141
enforceability, 129
modes of constitution, 130
transfer of trust property, 130–136
Completion notice
sale of land, 807–808
Compounding of liabilities
trustee's power, 583–584
Compromise of disputes
variation of trust, 609
Conditions precedent and subsequent, 85, 502
Conflict of interest
fiduciary relationship *see* **Fiduciary relationship**
Conflict of interest—*contd.*
removal of trustee, 522–526
Conspiracy to injure
injunctive relief, 683–684
Constitution of Ireland 1937
carrying forward of existing laws, 5
equality of spouses, 209, 225n
rights under *see* **Constitutional rights**
same-sex marriage, 207, 209, 215
Constitution of trust
complete *see* **Completely constituted trust**
incomplete *see* **Incompletely constituted trust**
volunteer's position, 129, 152–153
Constitutional rights
condition precedent violating, 502, 506
fair procedures, 37, 38
freedom of expression, 674–688
injunction restraining breach, 742–744
inviolability of the dwelling, 744
livelihood, right to earn, 743–744
parental rights, 505
property rights, 744
right to marry, 504
Constitutionality of legislation
Charities Act 2009, 443–444
presumption, and interlocutory injunction, 701–703
Constructive notice *see also* **Notice, doctrine of**
knowing receipt, 362, 363–364, 366–367, 370, 371
nature of, 61–63
undue influence, 890–892
Constructive trust
definition, 83, 257
common intention *see* **Common intention constructive trust**
contractual rights for benefit of third party, 73–75
family property dispute *see* **Common intention constructive trust**

Constructive trust—*contd.*
fiduciary relationship *see* **Fiduciary relationship**
general principles, 257–258
institutional constructive trust, 258–259
intermeddling, 308–309
killing of co-tenant, 315–316
mortgagee as constructive trustee, 314–315
mutual wills, 297–303
nature and purpose, 257–258
Pallant v Morgan equity, 303–308
proprietary estoppel and, 975–985
remedial constructive trust *see* **Remedial constructive trust**
resulting trust distinguished, 83–84
secret commission or bribe, 278–285
secret trust as, 126–128
trustee de son tort, 308–309
vendor as constructive trustee, 309–314
Contemplative religious order
gift to, 392–394, 444–447
Contempt of court
Anton Piller order, non-compliance, 777
equitable relief, non-compliance, 51
Contract
affirmation of, 919–920
breach *see* **Breach of contract**
illegality, 836–838
impossibility and frustration, 838–842
rectification *see* **Rectification**
rescission *see* **Rescission of contract**
specific performance *see* **Specific performance**
third party rights, 73–75
trust distinguished, 72–75
Contract-holding theory, 394–395
Contractual licence
new model constructive trust, 318–319
specific performance, 794
Convent
gift to, 391–394, 445–447, 449, 486
Conversion, doctrine of
contract for sale or purchase of land, 1019–1021
court order, 1022
equity looks on that as done which ought to be done, 50, 1018
failure of conversion, 1023
nature and effect, 1018
option to purchase, 1020–1021
partnership property, 1022–1023
reconversion, 1023–1024
settled land, 1023
trust for sale, 1019
vendor as constructive trustee, 309
Conversion of trust property, 553–555
Conveyance of land
bankruptcy, voidable settlements, 513–515
'clean hands' principle, 28–29
defrauding creditors, 506–512
defrauding subsequent purchasers, 512–513
presumed resulting trust, 177–179
purchase on behalf of another, 191–193
setting aside for fraud or mistake, 56–57
trustee's power, 580
Copyright infringement *see also* **Intellectual property dispute**
Anton Piller order *see* **Anton Piller order**
injunctive relief, 627, 636
search and seizure powers, 781–782
Corporation
trustee, as, 518
Corporation tax
amateur sporting body, 474
charitable trust, 400
Costs of legal proceedings
Mareva injunction, 750
trustee's position, 538–541
Court of Chancery
court of conscience, 1, 7
damages, jurisdiction to award, 8
historical background, 6–7

Court of conscience, 1, 7, 26, 51–52, 257, 955, 963
Covenant to repair
specific performance, 819–820
Cradock v Piper, **rule in**, 571
Creation of trust
by will, 90–91
equity looks to intent rather than form, 48
formalities *see* **Formalities for creating trust**
inter vivos, 86-90
precatory words, 48, 93–96
three certainties *see* **Three certainties**
Creditors
Quistclose trust, 169–175
settlement defrauding, 506–512
Criminal law
injunction restraining breach, 743–744, 745–746
Cy-près doctrine
advantage of charitable status, 399, 484
amalgamation of institution with another, 489–490
as near as possible to original purposes, 498–499
Charities Regulatory Authority function, 497–498
consent of intended recipient not given, 490
discriminatory provision, 487
general charitable intention, 485–490
initial failure of charitable purpose, 484–485, 485–490
legislative reform, 492–498
manner of exercising jurisdiction, 498–499
misdescription of institution, 490
non-existent institution, 488–489
property given for non-charitable purposes, 165
rationale for, 483–485
sale of trust property, 495–496
schism in religious organisation, 496–497
Cy-près doctrine—*contd.*
subsequent failure of charitable purpose, 484–485, 490–492
surplus funds, 491–492

Damages
breach of confidence, 11
breach of constitutional right, 742–743
breach of fiduciary duty, 11
breach of trust, 11, 586
equitable compensation distinguished, 11, 13–16
inadequacy, as basis for injunction, 621–624, 651–654, 656–658, 658–662
injunction, in addition to or in lieu of
jurisdiction under Lord Cairns' Act, 8, 617, 637–641
measure of damages, 641–644
Patterson principles, 639–640
Shelfer principles, 637–639
passing off, 640–641
specific performance, in addition to or in lieu of, 790–793
undertaking as to, 25, 645–649, 751, 777–778
De Worchley, John, 7n
Death
gift in contemplation of *see* ***Donatio mortis causa***
presumption, 560
Debt
apportionment under rule in *Allhusen v Whittel*, 556–557
future debts, settlement defrauding creditors, 511–512
portion debt, satisfaction by legacy, 1034–1037
satisfaction by legacy, 1032–1033
trustee's power to compound, settle etc, 583–584
Declaration of trust
certainty of intention or words, 92–96
complete constitution of trust, 136–141

Declaration of trust—*contd.*
'money is as much yours as mine', 141
written or oral, 86–87
Defamation
interlocutory injunction, 674–688
justification defence, 676, 677, 678–682
s.33 order, 687–688
Definitions *see* **Words and phrases**
Delay *see also* **Laches and acquiescence**
application for injunction, 628–633
constitutional right to fair procedures, 37, 38
defeats equity, 36–44
limitation periods, 37–39
rectification of contract, 860
specific performance claim, 41–42, 791–792, 833–836
undue influence claim, 40
Delegation of trustee's functions, 575–579
Destruction of documents
Anton Piller order, 775–785
Detriment
promissory estoppel, 927
proprietary estoppel, 935–937
Director of company
disqualification proceedings, injunction, 690–691
fiduciary position, 288–296
Disabled persons
gift for, 460–464
Disclosure of trust documents, 563–569
Discretionary nature of equity, 2
Discretionary powers of trustees
court intervention, 527–528
duty to properly exercise, 527–528
improper motive, 535–536
reasonableness, 536–537
relevant and irrelevant considerations, 528–535
rule in *Re Hastings-Bass*, 528–535
Discretionary trust
definition, 84
accounts and information, 562–568
Discretionary trust—*contd.*
administrative unworkability and capriciousness, 110–111
certainty test, 79–80, 105–108
exhaustive or non-exhaustive, 84
fixed trust distinguished, 84
nature of, 75–76, 84
power of appointment distinguished, 75
Dishonest assistance in misappropriation of trust property
causation, 358
dishonesty of person assisting in breach of trust, 343–344
formulation of third party liability, 343
knowing receipt distinguished, 360–361
knowledge/dishonesty requirement, 344–357
liability to account, 357–358
nature of remedies, 357–358
partner's liability, 376–379
trustee's dishonesty not required, 343–344
Dismissal
injunctive relief, 733–737
Disposition of beneficial interests held under trust, 90
Dissipation of assets *see* **Mareva injunction**
Distress, 9
Distribution of trust property, 559–561
Divorce
property adjustment order, 224, 235–236
property dispute *see* **Family property dispute**
Documents
Anton Piller order, 775–785
trust documents, disclosure, 563–569
Donatio mortis causa
definition, 144
conditional upon death, and revocable, 150
delivery of subject matter, 148–150

***Donatio mortis causa*—contd.**
essential elements, 144
exception to principle against perfecting incomplete gift, 144
gift *inter vivos* distinguished, 144
in contemplation of death, 147–148
land, 150–151
Law Commission Consultation Paper, 146
onus of proof, 145
property capable of forming subject matter, 150–152
revocation, 150
savings bank book, 151
stocks and shares, 151
strict approach taken by courts, 144–146
suicide, 147–148
testamentary gift distinguished, 144
Double portions
presumption against, 1034
Duress, 879
Duties of trustees
accounts and information, 561–569
appointment, on, 526–527
delegation, 575–579
distribution of trust property, 559–561
fiduciary duties *see* **Fiduciary relationship**
investment of trust property, 541–553
maintaining equality between beneficiaries, 553–558
non-profit, 569–575
proper exercise of discretion, 527–537
safeguarding trust assets, 537–541
Duty of care of trustees
English law, 517n, 595n
exemption clause *see* **Trustee exemption clause**
generally, 517
investment of trust property, 544–550
Dwelling, inviolability of, 744
***Earl of Chesterfield's Trusts*, rule in**, 556
Ecclesiastical office holder
gift to, 439–441
Economic hardship, 418
Education and maintenance, trust for
failure to exhaust beneficial interest, 163–164
general principles, 581–582
trust property carries the intermediate income, 581
Education, trust for advancement
academic research, 426–427
aesthetic education, 428–429
Charities Act 2009, 425
'founder's kin', 434–436
meaning of education, 425–430
personal connection with donor, 431–436
physical education, 428, 470
private school, 431–434
professional body, 429–430
public benefit requirement, 412, 430–436
Royal College of Surgeons, 429–430
self-help group, 428
Worth Library, 427–428, 434
Elderly persons
gift to, 423, 460–464
Eldon, Lord (Lord Chancellor, 1801-**1806 and 1807-1827)**, 8
Election, doctrine of
he who seeks equity must do equity, 26
infant or mentally incapable person, 1031
intention of testator, 1026–1027
making an election, 1030–1031
nature and effect, 1025–1027
requirements for election, 1027–1030
time for making election, 1030–1031
Electronic signature, 86n
Electronic transfer of funds
tracing, 996
Ellesmere, Lord (Lord Chancellor), 7
Emergency or salvage jurisdiction, 609

Employment contract
injunctive relief *see* **Employment injunction**
specific performance, 821–823
Employment injunction
appointment of third party, 740–741
apprehended removal from post, 731n
delay in concluding investigation, 731n
dismissal and reinstatement cases, 733–737
general principles, 731–733
he who seeks equity must do equity, 25–26
indirect order of specific performance, 726–727, 731
payment of salary pending trial, 737–740
relationship of mutual trust and confidence, 728–730, 733, 734, 736–737
strong case requirement, 731–732, 734n, 737, 739–740
Endowment for benefit of association, 390
Engaged couple
undue influence, 881
Equality between beneficiaries
apportionment of trust property, 555–558
conversion of trust property, 553–555
trustees' duty to maintain, 553
Equality is equity
distribution of surplus on dissolution of association, 45–46
division of matrimonial property, 46–47
joint tenancy, 45
power of appointment, 47
testator's moral duty to provide for children, 47
Equitable doctrines
conversion, 1018–1023
election, 1025–1031
performance, 1041–1043
reconversion, 1023–1024
Equitable doctrines—*contd.*
satisfaction, 1031–1041
Equitable estoppel *see* **Estoppel**
Equitable interest
definition, 55
mere equity distinguished, 54–58
Equitable maxims *see* **Maxims of equity**
Equitable mortgage
priority, 57–58, 65, 66–67
Equity
definition, 1
certainty versus flexibility, 2–5
commercial transactions, 5–6
common law and, 1, 8–9, 10–19
court of conscience 1, 7, 26, 51–52, 257, 955, 963
discretionary nature, 2
doctrines *see* **Equitable doctrines**
fusion of law and, 8–9, 10–19, 617–618
general principles, 1–6
historical background, 6–9
maxims *see* **Maxims of equity**
ongoing development, 3–5
precedent, 2–5, 7–8, 20
property disputes, 5n
role and scope, 1–6
rule of law and, 3
unconscionability, 2–3
Equity of redemption
cohabitee's beneficial interest, 225–227
he who seeks equity must do equity, 26
Equity prevails, 9
Estoppel
definition, 923
by representation, 922
equitable concept, 922–923
he who seeks equity must do equity, 26
likely future developments, 989–992
promissory estoppel *see* **Promissory estoppel**
proprietary estoppel *see* **Proprietary estoppel**
unified doctrine, 990–991

Ethical investment policy, 550–553
European Convention on Human Rights
  freedom of speech, 682, 686
  reputation, 682
European Stability Mechanism, 703
Ex turpi causa, 32, 198
Exchequer Division, 8
Executed trust, 23–24, 83
Executory trust, 23–24, 83
Exemption clause *see* **Trustee exemption clause**
Exhaustive discretionary trust, 84
Expenses of trustee, 570–572
Express trust
  definition, 82–83
  constitution, 130
  essential elements, 91–92
  failure giving rise to resulting trust, 160–161
  formalities, 86–87
  Quistclose trust, 170
  secret trust as, 126–128
Extra-territorial assets
  Mareva injunction, 747, 765–770

Failure of the trust, 160–161
Failure to exhaust beneficial interest, 162–165
Fair-dealing rule, 265, 574–575
Fair procedures
  constitutional right, 37, 38
Faith healing group
  gift to, 407n, 462
Family assets, doctrine of, 236
Family home
  consent to conveyance, 55n
  constructive notice of spouse's rights, 61–63
  contributions to purchase price
    cohabitee's beneficial interest, 225–227, 255–256
    direct contributions, 227–229
    housework or caring for children, 233–236
    improvements to property, 231–233
    indirect contributions, 229–231
Family home—*contd.*
  presumption of advancement, 205–209
  property dispute *see* **Family property dispute**
  undue influence between husband and wife *see* **Undue influence**
Family property dispute
  alternative models, 251–256
  application of equitable principles, 223–227
  cohabitees, 225–227
  common intention constructive trust (UK), 236–251, 252
  constructive trust, 253–254, 321–322
  direct contributions, 227–229
  doctrinal issues, 247–251
  equality is equity, 46–47
  housework or caring for children, 233–236
  improvements to property, 231–233, 252
  indirect contributions, 229–231
  legislation governing, 223–224
  purchase in the name of another, 192
  property adjustment order, 224, 235–236
  reasonable expectation (New Zealand), 254–255
  resulting trust, 223–227
  unconscionability (Australia), 254
  unjust enrichment (Canada), 254
Father and child
  portion debt, satisfaction by legacy, 1034–1037
  presumption of advancement, 209–211
Fiduciary relationship
  agent, 285–288
  categories, 261–262
  commercial relationship, 267–269
  company director, 288–296
  constructive trust, 270
  liability to account, 269–271
  nature of, 259–261
  no-conflict and no-profit rules
    fully informed consent, 265–266

Fiduciary relationship—*contd.*
no-conflict and no-profit rules—*contd.*
nature and scope, 262–265, 569–570
strict application, 266–267
remedies for breach of fiduciary duty, 269–271
secret commission or bribe, 50, 278–285
tracing, requirement for, 997–998, 1011–1015
trustee
competition with trust business, 276–278
duty not to profit, 569–570
generally, 271–272
purchase of reversion in lease, 275–276
renewal of lease, 272–275
undue influence, 887
Fieri facias, 51
Fixed trust
definition, 84
certainty of objects, 103–104
discretionary trust distinguished, 84
'Founder's kin', 434–436
Foreign charity
tax exemption, 401
Foreign immovable property
jurisdiction as to, 52–54
Formalities for creating trust
by will, 90–91
declaration of trust, 86–87
disposition of beneficial interests held under trust, 90
electronic signature, 86n
equity looks to intent rather than form, 48
express trust of land, 86–87
express trust of personalty, 86
inter vivos, 86–90
Statute of Frauds
not to be used as instrument of fraud, 87–90
requirements, 86–87
written evidence, 86–87
Fraud
'clean hands' principle, 27–36, 624–626
constructive trust *see* **Constructive trust**
creditors, settlement defrauding, 506–512
dishonest assistance in misappropriation of trust property, 343–358
equity follows the law, 23
presumption of advancement, rebutting, 218–223
purchasers, settlement defrauding, 512–513
resulting trust, rebuttal of presumption, 194–204
social security fraud, 32–33, 197–198
Fraud on a power, 535–536
Fraudulent misrepresentation
age of beneficiary, 27
rescission of contract, 876
Freedom of expression
interlocutory injunction and, 674–688
Freezing order *see* **Mareva injunction**
Frustration
defence to specific performance, 840–842
Fully secret trust
definition, 112
beneficiary predeceasing testator, 114
communication of testator's intention, 114–116
dehors the will, 113–114, 126
enforceability, 23, 113
equity follows the law, 23
essential elements, 114–115
joint tenant and tenants in common, 116–118
juridical nature, 126–128
renunciation or disclaimer, 114n
revocation during testator's lifetime, 113n
standard of proof, 116
witness to will, 114

Fusion of law and equity
court reforms, 8
grant of injunctions, 617–618
Judicature Acts, 8–9, 10–19, 617–618
whether procedural only, 10–19
Future testamentary gift
intention to make, 142

General power of appointment, 75
Gold bullion, 99–100
Graft, doctrine of, 273–274
Grave
trust for maintenance, 386–388, 448–449
Greenpeace
registration as charity, 479–480
Gross negligence
trustee exemption clause, 596, 598, 603, 605–606
Guardian
application to make maintenance payments out of trust income or capital, 582
undue influence, 881, 882

Half secret trust
definition, 112, 119
communication and acceptance, 120–126
enforceability, 23, 119–120
equity follows the law, 23
failure of, resulting trust, 161
inconsistency, 120n, 123, 124, 125, 126n
juridical nature, 126–128
Hardship
defence to specific performance, 830–833
***Hastings-Bass*, rule in**, 528–535
He who comes to equity must come with clean hands, 27–36, 624–626
He who seeks equity must do equity, 24–26, 626–627
High Court of Justice
divisions, 8
establishment, 8, 9

Hospital
charitable status, 462–464
Housework
beneficial interest in family property, 233–236
***Howe v Earl of Dartmouth*, rule in**, 554–555
Human rights
charitable purpose, 480n, 481–482, 483
Husband and wife *see also* **Marriage**
division of matrimonial property, 46–47
equality within marriage, 209, 225n
family home *see* **Family home**
joint bank account, 189–191
marriage settlement *see* **Marriage settlement**
mutual wills, 297–303
presumption of advancement, 205–209, 225
property dispute *see* **Family property dispute**
trust encouraging separation, 504
undue influence *see* **Undue influence**

Illegality
'clean hands' principle, 27–36, 624–626
defence to specific performance, 836–838
presumption of advancement, rebuttal, 218–223
presumption of resulting trust, rebuttal, 194–204
re-assessment of defence, 198–204
void trust, 502, 503
Illegitimate child
future illegitimate children, trust in favour of, 503
marriage consideration, 153n
presumption of advancement, 212
secret trust, 112
Immoral object
trust having, 503
Imperfect gift *see* **Incompletely constituted trust**

Implied trust, 83n, 157
Impossibility
defence to specific performance, 838–842
Improper motive of trustee, 535–536
Improvements to property *see* **Repairs and improvements**
Improvident transaction
laches and acquiescence, 40–41
setting aside *see* **Unconscionability**
Imputed notice, 63
In personam maxim, 51–54
Inalienability, rule against, 384–386, 400, 501
Income tax
amateur sporting body, 474
charitable trust, 400–401
Incompletely constituted trust
definition, 83, 129
equity will not perfect in favour of volunteer, 129
exceptions to principle against perfection in favour of volunteer
donatio mortis causa, 144–152
proprietary estoppel, 152, 938–939
rule in *Strong v Bird*, 141–143
possible alternative remedies for volunteer, 153–156
Independent school
gift to, 431–434
Inducement theory
secret trust, 118
Industrial action
injunction, 626–627, 670–674
secret ballot, 670–674
Infant *see* **Child; Minor; Parent and child**
Information
trustee's duty to provide, 561–569
Inheritance tax
charitable trust, 400–401
tax planning errors, 528–535, 862, 872–874
Injunction
definition, 617
Anton Piller order, 775–785

Injunction—*contd.*
auxiliary jurisdiction, 617
Bayer injunction, 785–787
breach of constitutional rights, 742–744
breach of contract, 721–725
breach of statute, 745–746
classification, 618–619
'clean hands' principle, 28, 624–626
conduct of parties, 624–628
contract for personal services, 725–730
damages in addition to or in lieu, 8, 617, 637–644
employment cases *see* **Employment injunction**
exclusive jurisdiction, 617
full and frank disclosure, 619, 627–628
he who seeks equity must do equity, 25–26, 626–627
historical background, 7, 617
insolvency, real risk, 623–624
interim injunction, 618–619
interlocutory injunction *see* **Interlocutory injunction**
Judicature Act, effect of, 617–618
laches and acquiescence, 42, 628–633
mandatory injunction *see* **Mandatory injunction**
Mareva injunction *see* **Mareva injunction**
nature and effect, 617
perpetual injunction *see* **Perpetual injunction**
prohibitory injunction, 618
public convenience, 634, 636
public rights, protecting, 744–746
quia timet injunction *see* ***Quia timet* injunction**
State or public authority, against, 648–649
third parties, effect on, 634–636
tort, restraining, 724
undertaking as to damages, 25, 645–649
variation or discharge, 645

Innocent misrepresentation
defence to specific performance, 826–827
rescission of contract, 877–878
Insolvency
risk of, inadequacy of damages, 623–624
Inspection of trust accounts, 561–562
Institutional constructive trust *see also* **Constructive trust**
definition, 258
remedial constructive trust distinguished, 258–259
Insurance
trustee's power, 584
Intangible asset
certainty of subject matter, 100–102
Intellectual property dispute
Anton Piller order *see* **Anton Piller order**
inadequacy of damages, 660–662
interlocutory injunction, 697–699
privilege against self-incrimination, 780
Intention
certainty of intention or words, 92–96
creation of trust, 86
doctrine of election, 1026–1027
equity imputes an intention to fulfil an obligation, 50–51, 1031, 1041
equity looks to intent rather than form, 47–48
mere power or trust power, 76–80
rectification of contract, 844–848
testator's intention, 91–92
Interest
apportionment of trust property, 556
breach of trust, 589
Interim injunction, 618–619
Interlocutory injunction
adequacy of damages, 621–624, 651–654, 656–658, 658–662
American Cyanamid/Campus Oil principles, 650–669
balance of convenience, 651–653, 656–658, 662–663
Interlocutory injunction—*contd.*
breach of constitutional rights, 742–744
breach of contract, 721–725
'clean hands' principle, 624–626
defamation or freedom of expression case, 674–688
departure from *American Cyanamid/Campus Oil* principles, 669–703
effect on third parties, 634–636
full and frank disclosure, 619, 627–628
judicial review proceedings, 699–700
just and convenient, 649
he who seeks equity must do equity, 25–26, 626–627
laches and acquiescence, 628–633
nature and effect, 618–619, 644–645
no arguable defence, 669–670
nuisance *see* **Nuisance**
passing off *see* **Passing off**
pending appeal, 665–667
picketing, 654, 663–664, 670–674, 742, 743, 744
preservation of *status quo*, 663–665
presumption of constitutionality cases, 701–703
prima facie test, 650–651
principles governing grant, 644–645, 649–669
public law context, 699–703
public rights, protecting, 744–746
real risk of insolvency, 623–624
risk of injustice, 668–669
serious or fair question to be tried, 652–653, 654–656
State or public authority, against, 648–649
strength of plaintiff's case, 654–656
terminology, 618n, 649n
tort, restraining, 724
trade dispute, 670–674
trespass, 659–660, 669–670, 742
trial of action unlikely, 691–699
undertaking as to damages, 25, 645–649

Interlocutory injunction—*contd.*
variation or discharge, 645
winding-up petition, 688–691
Intermeddling, 308–309
Intestacy
doctrine of conversion, 1018
doctrine of performance, 1043
Investment of trust property
absolute discretion, 547
advice, duty to seek, 544n, 549
authorised investments, 542–543
charitable trust, 552–553
compensation for loss, 549–550
consultation with beneficiaries, 541
ethical and other non-financial considerations, 550–553
investment clause, 542, 543
real securities, 543–544
review of investments, 543
standard of care and prudence, 544–550
statutory scheme, 542–543
unauthorised investment, liability for, 586

Jesuit Order
gift to, 393–394, 444
Joint and several liability
trustees, for breach of trust, 589–590
Joint bank account
deposit account, 180–189
husband and wife, 189–191
Joint tenancy
constructive trust where co-tenant killed, 315–316
equality is equity, 45
equity follows the law, 23
secret trust, 116–118
Joint venture
fiduciary relationship, 269
Pallant v Morgan equity, 304–306, 981
termination, 254
Judicature Acts, 8–9, 10–19, 617–618
Judicial review proceedings
interlocutory injunction, 699–700
Judicial separation
property adjustment order, 224, 235–236
property dispute *see* **Family property dispute**
Jurisdiction
equity acts in personam, 51–54
foreign immovable property, 52–54
Just or convenient, 16–17, 618, 645

Knowing assistance *see* **Dishonest assistance in misappropriation of trust property**
Knowing receipt of and inconsistent dealing with trust property
agent of trustee, 375–376
Australia, 368
Canada, 367–368
dishonest assistance distinguished, 360–361
English threshold for liability, 361–367
Irish position, 368–371
liability to account, 358–361, 367
nature of remedies, 367
New Zealand, 367
possible future developments, 372–375

Laches and acquiescence
acquiescence, 42–43, 631–633
application for injunction, 42, 628–633
claim for damages for breach of contract, 15–16
detriment, 43–44
equitable concepts, 36–37, 39–44
factors to be considered, 43–44
improvident transaction, 40–41
laches, 39–42, 628–631
rectification of contract, 860
single defence, 43, 44
specific performance claim, 41–42, 791–792, 833–836
undue influence claim, 40
Lack of mutuality
defence to specific performance, 26, 824–825

Land
conveyance *see* **Conveyance of land**
doctrine of conversion, 1018–1023
donatio mortis causa, 150–151
recovery of, limitation period, 37
sale *see* **Sale of land**
secret trust, 126–127
transfer constituting trust, 130–136
Land Registry, 66, 132–133, 150n
Law reporting
gift for purpose of, 451
Lease
covenant to repair, specific performance, 819–820
purchase of reversion by fiduciary, 275–276
rectification, 860
renewal by trustee, 272–275
specific performance, 794
transfer constituting trust, 132–133
Legacy
doctrine of ademption, 1037–1041
doctrine of satisfaction, 1031–1041
Legitimate expectation, 926
Liability to account
fiduciary relationship, 269–271
third party *see* **Third party liability to account**
trustee, for breach of trust *see* **Breach of trust**
Life
perpetuity period, 384n, 388–389, 501
risk to, interlocutory injunction, 684–686
Limitation periods
application by analogy, 38–39
breach of trust, 37–38, 341–342, 594
breach of trust by company director, 295–296
inordinate and inexcusable delay, 38
recovery of land, 37
Livelihood, right to earn, 743–744
Loan
Quistclose trust, 169–175
specific performance, 810
Locus poenitentiae, 195n
Lord Cairns' Act
damages under, 8, 617, 637–644, 790–791
Lord Chancellor of Ireland
creation of office, 7
Lourdes pilgrimages
gift for, 462
Lunatic's estate
doctrine of conversion, 1022
doctrine of graft, 273
Maintenance and education, trust for
failure to exhaust beneficial interest, 163–164
general principles, 581–582
trust property carries the intermediate income, 581
Maintenance payments
trustee's power to make, 581–582
Malum in se, 502
Malum prohibitum, 502
Management agreement
injunction restraining breach, 727–728
Mandatory injunction
breach of contract, 721–722
departure from *American Cyanamid/ Campus Oil* principles, 693–694
employment injunction *see* **Employment injunction**
high degree of assurance test, 706–707, 712
irremediable prejudice, 707–708
laches and acquiescence, 633
nature and effect, 618
principles governing grant, 703–716
prohibitory injunction distinguished, 703
restorative or enforcing, 704
'strong case' test, 706, 710–716
Manslaughter
co-tenant, constructive trust, 315–316
Mareva injunction
ancillary nature, 747–748
approach of courts, 773–775

Mareva injunction—*contd.*
assets held in Brussels Regulation or Convention county, 764–765
balance of convenience, 758–759
bank's position, 749
costs of litigation, 750
criteria for grant, 750
cross-examination on disclosure affidavit, 756–757
disposal of asset at undervalue, 748
foreign-based or local defendant, 751
full and frank disclosure, 752–757
good arguable case, 757–758
in personam operation, 749
just or convenient, 17
limited order, 748
living expenses and legal fees, 748, 751–752
nature and effect, 747–752
origin of, 747
post-judgment order, 750–751
privilege against self-incrimination and, 748
provisional and protective measures under Brussels I Regulation (recast), 770–773
requirements for grant, 757–765
risk of dissipation of assets/requisite intention, 759–765
security, use as, 773–775
standard of proof, 757–758
substantial question to be tried, 757–758
third party rights, 749
undertaking in damages, 751
variation, 751–752
worldwide basis, 747, 765–770

Market overt, 71n

Marriage *see also* **Husband and wife**
constitutional right to marry, 504
division of matrimonial property, 46–47
equality of spouses, 209, 225n
same-sex marriage, 207, 209, 215
settlement *see* **Marriage settlement**
trust in restraint of, 503–504

Marriage consideration, 152–153

Marriage settlement
after-acquired property, 153–154
bankruptcy, exception to voidable settlements provision, 515
equity follows the law, 24
failure of, resulting trust, 160–161
failure to exhaust beneficial interest, 162
rectification, 862–863
valuable consideration, 152–153
volunteer's position, 152–153
written evidence, 87

Mass cards
sale of, 443–444

Masses
gift for celebration of, 384n, 441–444

Matrimonial property
division of, 46–47

Maxims of equity
delay defeats equity, 36–44
equality is equity, 45–47
equity acts in personam, 51–54
equity follows the law, 22–24
equity imputes an intention to fulfil an obligation, 50–51, 1031, 1041
equity looks on that as done which ought to have been done, 49–50, 1018
equity looks to intent rather than form, 47–48
equity will not suffer a wrong to be without a remedy, 20–22
generally, 20
he who comes to equity must come with clean hands, 27–36, 624–626
he who seeks equity must do equity, 24–26, 626–627
where equities are equal, the first in time prevails, 54–67
where equities are equal, the law prevails, 54–67

Medical adviser
undue influence, 881

Mere equities, 54–58

Mere power *see* **Power of appointment**
Minor *see also* **Child**
beneficiary of trust, 571, 608–609
personal injury claim, 38
specific performance of contract, 824
trustee, as, 518
Misrepresentation
'clean hands' principle, 27–28
defence to specific performance, 825–827
rescission of contract, 876–878
voidable trust, 506
Missing beneficiary
Benjamin order, 559–560
insurance policy, 560–561
presumption of death, 560
Mistake
defence to specific performance, 827–830
proprietary estoppel, 942–945
rectification, 848–857
rescission of contract, 866–876
Mobile phone base station
quia timet injunction, 718–719
Monument
trust for erection or maintenance, 386–388, 448–449
Moral duty to provide for children, 47
Mortgage
apportionment under rule in *Re Atkinson*, 557
constructive notice of leasehold interest, 62
contributions to repayment
cohabitee, 225–227
direct contributions, 227–229
housework or caring for children, 233–236
improvements to property, 231–233
indirect contributions, 229–231
equity looks to intent rather than form, 48
equity of redemption *see* **Equity of redemption**
investment of trust funds, 543–544
Mortgage—*contd.*
redemption *see* **Redemption of mortgage**
undue influence *see* **Undue influence**
Mortgagee
equitable duties, 13
liability as constructive trustee, 314–315
Mortmain, 68
Mother and child
portion debt, satisfaction by legacy, 1034–1037
whether presumption of advancement, 212–215
Museum
gift to, 428
Musical appreciation
gift for, 428–429
Mutual wills
English Law Commission recommendations, 303
evidence of agreement not to revoke, 297–301
prerequisites for constructive trust, 297–301
time when trust arising, 301–302
usefulness of doctrine, 302–303

Naked equity, 55, 58–59
Negative covenant
contract for personal services, 726–728
injunction restraining breach, 721–725
Negligence
mortgagee and receiver, 13
New model constructive trust, 22, 318–319
Non-charitable purposes
trust for *see* **Purpose trust**
Notice, doctrine of
actual notice, 60–61
bona fide purchaser's position, 56–57, 58–64
constructive notice, 61–63
imputed notice, 63
onus of proof, 64

Notice, doctrine of—*contd.*
registration of deeds, 64–66
statutory provisions, 59–60
Notice of existence of trust, 568–569
Nottingham, Lord (Lord Chancellor, 1673–1682), 7
Nuclear disarmament
gift promoting, 476–477
Nuisance
damages in lieu of injunction, 637–641
injunctive relief, 21, 621, 634–635, 742
public nuisance, 742
Nuncupative will, 186

Objects of trust *see also* **Beneficiaries of trust**
certainty, 103–111
Option to purchase
doctrine of conversion, 1020–1021
rectification, 856
specific performance, 794
Overreaching, 60

***Pallant v Morgan* equity**, 35, 303–308
Parent and child
portion debt, satisfaction by legacy, 1034–1037
presumption of advancement
father and child, 209–211
mother and child, 212–215
person *in loco parentis*, 211–212
trust interfering with parental duties, 504–506
undue influence, 881, 882
Park or playing field
gift for, 470
Part performance, 801–807
Partner
dishonest assistance, 376–379
Partnership property
doctrine of conversion, 1022–1023
Passing off
damages in lieu of injunction, 640–641
delay in applying for injunction, 630–631

Passing off—*contd.*
inadequacy of damages, 660–662
interlocutory injunction, 664, 668, 697–699, 742
Passport
Bayer injunction, 785–787
injunction compelling return, 694
Patent infringement *see* **Intellectual property dispute**
Payment of money
part performance, as, 806–807
specific performance, 810
Peace
gift promoting, 475-477
Pension scheme
administration of, 614–615
exercise of trustees' discretion, 533–534, 567, 614–615
rectification, 861
rescission, where unilateral mistake, 875–876
Performance, doctrine of
act of party, 1042–1043
equity imputes an intention to fulfil an obligation, 50–51, 1041
nature and effect, 1041–1042
operation of law, 1043
satisfaction distinguished, 1041
Periodic payments
specific performance, 810
Perpetual injunction
conduct of parties, 624–628
discretionary remedy, 620
effect on third parties, 634–636
inadequacy or inappropriateness of damages, 621–624
laches and acquiescence, 628–633
nature and effect, 619
principles governing grant, 620
rights protectable, 620
Perpetuities, rule against, 384–386, 501
Perpetuity period, 384n, 388–389, 501
Person *in loco parentis*
portion debt, satisfaction by legacy, 1034–1037
presumption of advancement, 211–212

Personal property
bailment, 71
creation of *inter vivos* express trust, 86
sale of, specific performance, 809–810
voluntary transfer, resulting trust, 179–180
Personal representative
claims by and against, limitation periods, 37
joint and several authority, 81
trustee distinguished, 80–82
Personal services, contract for
injunctive relief, 725–730
specific performance, 821–823
Physical education
gift for, 428, 470
Picketing
injunction, 654, 663–664, 670–674, 742, 743, 744
Planning injunction
'clean hands' principle, 28
Political purposes
gift promoting, 474-482
Portion debt
satisfaction by legacy, 1034–1037
Post-mortem
injunction restraining, 694–695
Poverty, trust for prevention or relief
aged and sick, 423
Charities Act 2009, 414
degree of poverty, 414–416
economic hardship, 418
general or particular terms, 417
gift must be directed to poverty, 416–417
poor relations/employees, 411n, 418–425
prevention of poverty, 417
public benefit requirement, 411, 418–425
relevance of existing case law, 414
Power fiduciary, 104n
Power in the nature of a trust, 76–80
Power of appointment
capriciousness, 111
certainty test, 79–80, 104–105
Power of appointment—*contd.*
equality is equity, 47
general and special powers, 75
trust distinguished, 75–80, 104
Powers of trustees
advancement, 583
compounding liabilities, 583–584
delegation, 575–579
discretionary powers *see* **Discretionary powers of trustees**
insurance, 584
legislation, 579
maintenance of infant beneficiary, 581–582
sale and receipts, 580–581
Pre-nuptial agreement, 152
Precatory trust, 93n
Precatory words, 48, 93–96
Precedent in equity, 2–5, 7–8, 20
Presumed resulting trust
definition, 83, 157
basis of presumption, 175–176
equity intends bargains not gifts, 175
family property *see* **Family property dispute**
joint bank account
deposit account, 180–189
husband and wife, 189–191
purchase in name of another, 191–193
rebuttal of presumption
evidence of intention to benefit, 193–194
fraud or illegality, 194–204
generally, 176–177
theoretical basis, 158–160
voluntary conveyance or transfer
conveyance of land, 177–179
generally, 176–177
transfer of personalty, 179–180
Presumption of advancement
definition, 192, 204
abolition abroad, 205
cohabitant, 215
commercial relationship, 215
current status, 204–205
father and child, 209–211

Presumption of advancement—*contd.*
husband and wife, 205–209, 225
mother and child, 212–215
person *in loco parentis*, 211–212
rebuts presumption of resulting trust, 175
rebuttal
fraud or illegality, 196n, 198n, 218–223
nature of evidence admissible, 217–218
no gift intended, 215–216
Presumption of constitutionality
interlocutory injunction, 701–703
Presumption of death, 560
***Prima facie* test**
injunctive relief, 650–651
Prior restraint on publication, 674–688
Priority
doctrine of notice and, 58–64
equitable interests and mere equities, 55–58
registration of deeds, 64–66
registration of title, 66–67
where equities are equal, the first in time prevails, 54–67
Private school
gift to, 431–434
Private trust, 82
Probate and Matrimonial Division, 8
Professional advice to trustees
incorrect advice, 531–532
investment advice, 544n, 549
Professional body
gift to, 429–430
Professional trustees
definition, 607
controlling influence, 590–591
exemption clause *see* **Trustee exemption clause**
remuneration, 570
standard of care, 545–547, 549, 602–604, 613
unsuitability of equitable rules, 613–614

Profit by trustee *see also* **Fiduciary relationship**
duty not to profit, 569–570
Prohibitory injunction, 618
Promissory estoppel
cause of action, 926, 986
contractual context, 924
detriment, 927
development of doctrine, 924–926
essential elements, 923–924
High Trees principle, 924–926
nature and effect, 923
proprietary estoppel distinguished, 985–989
shield not a sword, 926, 986
Property adjustment order, 224, 235–236
Proprietary estoppel
definition, 927
assurance or representation, 928–932
categories of cases, 938
change in character or extent of property, 932
clear and unequivocal promise, 930–931
common expectation, 939–942
constructive trust and, 975–985
detriment, 935–937
development of doctrine, 927
essential elements, 928
extent of remedy
expectation or reliance-based approach, 959–963
Irish approach, 974–975
minimum equity, 956–958
other common law jurisdictions, 972–973
proportionality approach, 963–972
imperfect gift, 152, 938–939
irrevocability of promise, 930
land or other property, 927–928
passive conduct or silence, 928–929
promissory estoppel distinguished, 985–989
reasonable reliance, 932–935
unconscionability, 945–956, 991–992

Proprietary estoppel—*contd.*
unilateral mistake, 942–945
Proprietary versus personal remedies, 51
Protective trust, 84–85
Provisional and protective measures
Brussels I Regulation (recast), 770–773
Public benefit, 409–414
Public facilities
gift for, 464
Public law proceedings
interlocutory injunction, 699–703
Public nuisance, 742
Public policy
trust contrary to, 503–506
Public rights
injunction protecting, 744–746
Public trust, 82
Public works
gift for, 464
Purchase money resulting trust
family property dispute *see* **Family property dispute**
presumption, 208–209
Statute of Uses and, 191n
Purchase of property *see* **Sale of land**
Purpose trust
animals, 388–389, 465–466
charitable purposes *see* **Charitable purposes; Charitable trust**
enforceability, 82n, 380, 396–397
'enforcer' approach, 396–397
invalid trust construed as power, 396
rationale for non-enforcement
beneficiary principle, 381–382
clarity and certainty, 382–384
rules against perpetual trusts and inalienability, 384–386
tombs and monuments, 386–388, 448–449
unincorporated association, 389–395

Queen's Bench Division, 8
Quia timet **injunction**
degree of probability of injury, 717–718
nature and effect, 21, 619, 716
Quia timet **injunction**—*contd.*
onus of proof, 717–718
party against whom granted, 721
principles governing grant, 716–721
risk of future injury, 719–720
Quistclose trust, 169–175

Radcliffe Commission, 402, 456
***Re Hallet's Estate*, rule in**, 997, 1002
Reasonableness
exercise of trustee's discretion, 536–537
Receipts
trustee's power to give, 581
Receiver
equitable duties, 13
Receiver by way of equitable execution, 16–17, 21
Reconversion, doctrine of
act of party, 1023–1024
nature and effect, 1023
operation of law, 1024
Recovery of land
limitation period, 37
Recreational and leisure facilities
gift for, 469–474
Rectification
bona fide purchaser's position, 860
common continuing intention, 844–848
common mistake, 848–852
concluded antecedent agreement, 844–846
delay in applying for, 860
discretionary factors, 859–860
equity looks to intent rather than form, 48
instruments which can be rectified, 860–864
marriage settlement, 862–863
nature and effect, 843
onus of proof, 857–859
oral evidence, 857
pension scheme, 861
prerequisites for, 844–848
standard of proof, 857–859
tax planning errors, 862
unilateral mistake, 852–857

Rectification—*contd.*
voluntary deed or settlement, 861–863
will, 863–864
written record of contract, 843
Redemption of mortgage
cohabitee's beneficial interest, 225–227
equitable interest, 55
equity of redemption *see* **Equity of redemption**
he who seeks equity must do equity, 26
limitation period, 37
Registered land
prior equitable interests, 59, 66–67
Registration of deeds
priority and notice, 64–66
Registration of title
priority, 66–67
Reinstatement
injunction requiring, 733–737
Relator proceedings, 744–746
Reliance principle
illegality defence and, 33–34, 196–198, 198–204, 222–223
Religion, trust for advancement
celebration of masses, 384n, 441–444
Charities Act 2009, 436–437
church buildings etc, 447–449
ecclesiastical office holders, 439–441
gift in general terms, 438–439
missionary purposes, 439
organisation or cult employing psychological manipulation, 438
public benefit requirement, 411–412
religious denominations, 437–438
religious orders, 392–394, 444–447
residence for priests etc, 449
Roman Catholic religion, 438–439
upkeep of churchyard or cemetery, 448–449
Religious adviser
undue influence, 881
Religious order
gift to, 392–394, 444–447
Religious order—*contd.*
transfer of property to, 40
undue influence, 882
Religious upbringing
trust interfering with, 504–506
Remedial constructive trust
definition, 258, 316
Australia, 327
Canada, 326
conclusions, 336–337
England, 328–331
institutional trust distinguished, 258–259
Irish approach, 319–325
judicial reluctance to impose, 316–317
new model constructive trust, 22, 318–319
New Zealand, 327–328
unconscionable conduct, 327, 328, 335–336
unjust enrichment, 324, 326, 327, 328, 331–335
Removal of trustee, 521–526
Remuneration of trustee, 570–572
Rent review clause, 11–12
Repairs and improvements
family property, 231–233, 252
specific performance of covenant to repair, 819–820
trust property, apportionment of cost, 557–558
Rescission of contract
common law concept, 865
equitable concept, 865–866
he who seeks equity must do equity, 25
loss of right
affirmation of contract, 919–920
substantial restitution impossible, 920
third party rights prejudiced, 921
misrepresentation
failure to disclose material facts, 878
fraudulent, 876
general principles, 878
innocent, 877–878

Rescission of contract—*contd.*
mistake
common mistake, 867–870
general principles, 866–867
unilateral mistake, 870–872
voluntary settlement, 872–876
nature and effect, 865–866
restitutio in integrum, 866
unconscionable transaction, 913–919
undue influence *see* **Undue influence**
Research
charitable trust, 426–427
Restitutio in integrum
rescission of contract, 866
substantial restitution impossible, 920
Restraint clause
injunction enforcing, 693
Restraint from leaving jurisdiction
Bayer injunction, 785–787
Resulting trust
definition, 83, 157
automatic *see* **Automatic resulting trust**
categories, 157–158
factual situations, 157
family property dispute *see* **Family property dispute**
general principles, 157–158
illegality defence, 194–204
implied trust, 157
presumed *see* **Presumed resulting trust**
restitution and, 159
theoretical basis, 158–160
Retirement of trustee, 521, 585–586
Revenue fraud, 35
Risk, passing of, 311–312
Roman Catholic religion
gift for the advancement of, 438–439
Royal College of Surgeons
gift to, 429–430
Royal Kilmainham Hospital, 491
Rule of law
equity and, 3

Safeguarding of trust assets, 537–541
Salary
payment pending trial, 737–740
Sale of goods
specific performance, 809–810
Sale of land
bona fide purchaser's position, 56–57
completion date, agreement as to, 796–798
completion notice, 807–808
Conditions of Sale, 311n, 312, 807n
deposit, 795–796, 798–799
doctrine of conversion, 1018–1023
equity looks on that as done which ought to have been done, 49
failure to complete within time stipulated, 48
impecuniosity of purchaser, 839
Pallant v Morgan equity, 303–308
part performance, 801–807
passing of risk, 311–312
priorities and doctrine of notice, 58–64
purchase in name of another, 191–193
reasonable time for completion, 48
settlement defrauding purchaser, 512–513
specific performance, 794–808
subject to contract, 799–801
trust property, to trustee, 572–575
trustee's power, 580
vendor as constructive trustee, 309–314
vendor's lien, 313
written note or memorandum of agreement, 795, 798–801
Sale of trust assets, 538
Same-sex marriage, 207, 209, 215
Satisfaction, doctrine of
debt by legacy, 1032–1033
equity imputes an intention to fulfil an obligation, 50–51, 1031
legacy by legacy, 1040–1041
legacy by portion, and doctrine of ademption, 1037–1040
nature and effect, 1031
performance distinguished, 1041

Satisfaction, doctrine of—*contd.*
portion debt by legacy, 1034–1037
***Saunders v Vautier*, rule in**, 608
School
gift to, 431–434
Secret ballot, 670–674
Secret commission, 278–285
Secret trust
definition, 112
fully secret *see* **Fully secret trust**
half secret trust *see* **Half secret trust**
historical origins, 112–113
juridical nature, 126–128
whether express or constructive trust, 126–128
Self-dealing rule, 572–575
Self-incrimination, privilege against, 748, 780–783
Separation of husband and wife
property adjustment order, 224, 235–236
property dispute *see* **Family property dispute**
trust encouraging, 504
Settled land
doctrine of conversion, 1023
doctrine of performance, 1042–1043
Sham trust, 96–97
Shares
bonus shares, 558
certainty of subject matter, 100–102
donatio mortis causa, 151
presumption of advancement, 204, 215, 216, 217, 220
purchase or sale cum dividend, 558
sale, specific performance, 810
self-dealing rule, 573
transfer constituting trust, 130–136
Sick persons
gift for, 423, 460–464
Sign manual procedure, 499–500
Simple trust, 84
Single European Act, 702–703, 745
Social security fraud, 32–33, 197–198
Solicitor
liability to account *see* **Third party liability to account**

Solicitor—*contd.*
receipt of purchase and insurance monies, 578
undue influence, 881, 882
Solicitor-trustee
breach of trust, 596
remuneration, 571
Special power of appointment, 75
Special trust, 84
Specific performance
building or repair contract, 818–820
'clean hands' principle, 28
common law remedy, effect of, 788–789
contract for personal services, 821–823
contractual licence, 794
damages in lieu of or in addition to, 790–793
defences
general principles, 823
hardship, 830–833
illegality, 836–838
impossibility and frustration, 838–842
laches or delay, 41–42, 791–792, 833–836
lack of mutuality, 26, 824–825
misrepresentation, 825–827
mistake, 827–830
delay in claiming, 41–42, 791–792
development of equitable remedy, 788
discretionary nature of remedy, 2, 789–790
employment contract, 821–823
executed or executory agreement, 788
futile or wasteful effect, 790
general principles, 788–789, 790
he who seeks equity must do equity, 26
illegal contract, 34
lease, 794
loan, 810
part of contract, 724n
payment of money, 810
sale of land

Specific performance—*contd.*
completion date, agreement as to, 796–798
completion notice, 807–808
concluded agreement required, 794–798
damages in lieu of specific performance, 792–793, 794
deposit, stipulation as to, 795–796, 798–799
doctrine of part performance, 801–807
general principles, 794
subject to contract, 799–801
written note or memorandum of agreement, 795, 798–801
sale of personal property, 809–810
supervision, contract requiring
building or repair contract, 818–820
contract for personal services, 821–823
resident porter, 811
strong case test, 815
trading contract, 812–818
terms of contract uncertain, 792
trading contract, 812–818
Sport
gift promoting, 469–474
Sports management agreement
injunction restraining breach, 727–728
Spouse *see* **Husband and wife; Marriage**
Standard of care
professional trustees, 545–547, 549, 602–604, 613
Statute of Chantries, 442
Statute of Charitable uses, 406–407
Statute of Frauds
disposition of beneficial interests held under trust, 90
express trust of land, 86–87
lease longer than 3 years, 9n
not to be used as instrument of fraud, 87–90
part performance, 801–807
sale of land, 795, 798–801
Statute of Limitations 1957, 37–39, 594
Statute of Uses, 68–70, 177, 191n
Statute of Westminster II 1285, 6
Strict liability, 372–374, 572
***Strong v Bird*, rule in**, 141–143
Subject-matter of trust
certainty, 98–103
Subject to contract, 799–801
Suicide, 147–148
Supreme Court of Judicature Acts, 8–9, 10–19, 617–618
Survivorship, right of, 45, 182, 183, 184, 187–188, 300, 316
Suretyship
undue influence *see* **Undue influence**

Tax exemption
amateur sports body, 474, 482–483
charitable trust, 400–402
Tax planning errors, 528–535, 862, 872–874
Tenancy in common
doctrine of reconversion, 1024
presumption, 45
secret trust, 116–118
Tenant for life and remainderman
apportionment of trust property, 555–558
conversion of trust property, 553–555
equality between, 553
Termination of trust, 608
Testamentary gift
doctrine of ademption, 1037–1041
doctrine of election, 1025–1031
doctrine of satisfaction, 1031–1041
donatio mortis causa distinguished, 144
secret trust *see* **Secret trust**
Testamentary trust
formalities, 90–91
Third party liability to account
agent of trustee, 375–376
constructive trusteeship distinguished, 338–339

Third party liability to account—*contd.*
dishonest assistance in misappropriation of trust property, 343–358
knowing receipt of and inconsistent dealing with trust property, 358–371
partner, 376–379
rationale for remedy, 338
terminology, 339–342

Third party rights
contract, under, 73–75
injunction, effect of, 634–636
loss of right to rescind contract, 921
Mareva injunction, 749
specific performance, 810

Three certainties
definition, 91
essential elements of trust, 91–92
intention or words
precatory words, 93–96
question of construction, 92–96
sham trust, 96–97
objects
administrative unworkability and capriciousness, 110–111
conceptual and evidential certainty, 108–109
discretionary trust, 105–108
fixed trust, 103–104
general principle, 103
mere power, 104–105
subject-matter
'bulk of my … residuary estate', 98
certainty of words and, 102–103
definite but unidentified portion, 99–100
effect of failure due to uncertainty, 98–99
intangible assets, 100–102
objective criterion applicable, 99
reasonable income, 99

Time of the essence
rent review clause, 11–12
specific performance where, 835–836

Tomb
trust for erection or maintenance, 386–388, 448–449

Tort
equitable remedy, laches, 39
injunction restraining, 724
limitation period, 38

Tracing
definition, 996
advantages, 995–996
alterations or improvements made, 1015–1016
backward tracing, 1009–1011
bank account
first in, first out, 1001–1007
overdrawn account, 1007–1011
bona fide purchaser's position, 1015
common law, 993–995
debt, through, 1007–1011
defence of change of position, 1016–1017
dissipation of property, 1015
electronic transfer, 996
equitable remedy, 995–996
fiduciary relationship, 997–998, 1011–1015
general principles, 996–1001
loss of right, 1015–1017
mere equity or equitable interest, 57–58
priority of beneficiary's right, 57–58, 995
proportionate share or lien, 999–1000
rule in *Clayton's* case, 1001–1007
rule in *Re Hallet's Estate*, 997, 1002
syndicates, 1001
ultra vires transaction void *ab initio*, 998, 1000–1001
unjust enrichment distinguished, 1000
volunteer's position, 995–996, 997, 998–999, 1015–1016

Trade dispute
injunction, 626–627, 670–674

Trademark infringement *see also* **Intellectual property dispute**
delay in applying for injunction, 630–631

Trademark infringement—*contd.*
interlocutory injunction, 697–699
Trading contract
specific performance, 812–818
Transfer of property
remedial constructive trust, 323–324
Travel
Bayer injunction, 785–787
return of passport, 694
Trespass
injunctive relief, 659–660, 669–670, 742
Trust
definition, 2, 70–71
administration of deceased's estate distinguished, 80–82
administration of trusts *see* **Administration of trusts; Trustees**
agency distinguished, 72
bailment distinguished, 71
beneficiaries *see* **Beneficiary of trust**
breach of trust *see* **Breach of trust**
charitable trust *see* **Charitable trust**
classifications, 82–85
completely constituted trust *see* **Completely constituted trust**
constitution *see* **Constitution of trust**
constructive trust *see* **Constructive trust**
contract distinguished, 72–75
creation *see* **Creation of trust**
declaration *see* **Declaration of trust**
discretionary trust *see* **Discretionary trust**
equitable device, 2, 21
essential elements, 91–92
express trust *see* **Express trust**
family property *see* **Family property dispute**
fixed trust *see* **Fixed trust**
formalities *see* **Formalities for creating trust**
historical background, 68–70
implied trust, 83n, 157

Trust—*contd.*
incompletely constituted trust *see* **Incompletely constituted trust**
objects *see* **Beneficiaries of trust**
origin of concept, 68–70
pension trust *see* **Pension scheme**
powers distinguished, 75–80
private trust, 82
property *see* **Trust property**
protective trust, 84–85
public trust, 82
purpose trust *see* **Purpose trust**
Quistclose trust, 169–175
rectification, 861–863
resulting trust *see* **Resulting trust**
secret trust *see* **Secret trust**
sham trust, 96–97
simple trust, 84
special trust, 84
tax planning errors, 528–535, 862, 872–874
three certainties *see* **Three certainties**
trustees *see* **Trustees**
use system, 68
variation *see* **Variation of trust**
void trust, 501–506
voidable trust, 506–515
Trust for sale
doctrine of conversion, 1019
trustee's duty to sell, 553–554
Trust power, 47, 76–80, 106, 108
Trust property
accounts and information, 561–569
action to recover, limitation period, 37
advancements out of capital, 583
apportionment, 555–558
best price on sale, 538, 580
conversion, 553–555
demand for payment of monies owed to trust, 537–538
dishonest assistance in misappropriation, 343–358
distribution, 559–561
education and maintenance payments, 581–582

Trust property—*contd.*
emergency or salvage jurisdiction, 609
equity acts in personam, 52–54
foreign immovable property, jurisdiction as to, 52–54
insurance, 584
investment, 541–553
knowing receipt and inconsistent dealing, 358–371
litigation to safeguard, 537–541
purchase by trustee, 572–575
repairs and improvements, 557–558
sale and receipts, 580–581
tracing *see* **Tracing**
transfer constituting trust, 130–136

Trustee de son tort, 308–309

Trustee exemption clause
English law, 595–598
Irish law, 598–600
irreducible core obligations of trusteeship, 600–602
Law Reform Commission recommendations, 600–602
lay and professional trustees distinguished, 596–597, 602–604
need for statutory regulation, 604–607

Trustees
definition, 70–71
accounts and information, 561–569
active or passive, 590
additional trustees, 519–521
agent of
appointment, 577
delegation of functions to, 575–579
liability to account, 375–376
appointment
disclaimer, 521
duties on, 526–527
eligible persons, 518
first trustees, 519
new or additional trustees, 519–521
number of trustees, 518
beneficiary as, 518

Trustees—*contd.*
breach of trust *see* **Breach of trust**
charitable trust *see* **Charitable trust**
competition with trust business, 276–278
conflict of interest, 522–526
constructive trustee *see* **Constructive trust**
corporation as, 518
costs of litigation, 538–541
delegation of functions, 575–579
disclaimer of appointment, 521
discretionary powers, exercise of, 527–537
duties *see* **Duties of trustees**
duty of care *see* **Duty of care of trustees**
exemption clause *see* **Trustee exemption clause**
fiduciary position, 271–278
improper motive, 535–536
investment of trust property, 541–553
irreducible core obligations, 600–602
legislation governing, 517
minor as, 518
new trustees, 519–521
non-professional, 517
non-resident, 518
number of trustees, 518
office of trustee, 516–518
personal representative distinguished, 80–82
powers *see* **Powers of trustees**
professional *see* **Professional trustees**
purchase of reversion in lease, 275–276
purchase of trust property, 572–575
removal, 521–526
remuneration and expenses, 570–572
renewal of lease in own name, 272–275
retirement, 82, 521, 585–586
safeguarding trust assets, 537–541
self-dealing rule, 572–575
tax planning errors, 528–535
undue influence, 572–575, 881

Unborn beneficiary of trust, 571, 608–609, 610
'Unclean hands' principle *see* **'Clean hands' principle**
Unconscionability
equitable principle, 2–3
family property dispute, 254
knowing receipt, 365–367, 370–371
laches and acquiescence, 631–633
perfecting imperfect transactions, 134–136
proprietary estoppel, 945–956, 991–992
remedial constructive trust, 327, 328, 335–336
setting aside unconscionable transaction
elements of successful claim, 914
equitable remedy, 913
independent legal advice, 917–918
transaction at undervalue, 913, 916–917
undue influence distinguished, 918–919
Undertaking as to damages, 25, 645–649, 751, 777–778
Undue influence
definition, 879
actual, 880
banker and client, 887
cohabitees, 894
delay in claiming, 40
engaged couple, 881
equitable doctrine, 878–880
fiduciary relationship, 887
guardian and ward, 881, 882
husband and surety wife
agency theory, 891
circumstances when bank put on inquiry, 893–895, 899–904
concealment of an affair, 890
constructive notice of wrongdoing, 890–892
English law, 889–898
independent legal advice, 895–898, 904–907, 907–909, 909–910
Undue influence—*contd.*
Irish law, 898–912
manifest disadvantage, 891–893
New Zealand law, 912
reasonable steps by bank, 890–891, 894–895, 907–909
special equity theory, 889
whether evidence of undue influence required, 904–907
husband and wife, 881, 889
independent legal advice, 884–885
laches and acquiescence, 40
medical adviser and patient, 881
non-disclosure and, 880
parent and child, 881, 882
presumed undue influence
actual undue influence distinguished, 880–881
rebuttal of presumption, 883–887
relationships giving rise to presumption, 881–883
religious adviser, 881
religious order, 882
rescission of contract, 878
solicitor and client, 881, 882
spontaneous and independent act, 884, 885–887
third party's position, 888–889
trust and confidence in another's management of financial affairs, 882–883
trustee and beneficiary, 572–575, 881
two types, 879–880
unconscionability distinguished, 918–919
wills context, 887–888
Unilateral mistake
proprietary estoppel, 942–945
rectification, 852–857
rescission of contract
general principles, 870–872
voluntary settlement, 872–876
Unincorporated association
definition, 389–390
distribution of surplus on dissolution, 45–46, 166–169
gift to

Unincorporated association—*contd.*
contract-holding theory, 394–395
endowment for benefit of association, 390
gift to members for time being, 390–394
legal difficulties, 390
Unjust enrichment
essential elements, 331–332
family property dispute (Canada), 254
fiduciary's liability to account, 270
illegality defence and, 200, 202–203
knowing receipt, 373–374
remedial constructive trust, 324, 326, 327, 328, 331–335
res judicata and, 323
tracing distinguished, 1000
Unlawful conduct *see* **Illegality**
Urban council
gift to, 471
Ut res magis valeat quam pereat, 139

Variation of trust
compromise of disputes, 609
emergency or salvage jurisdiction, 609
opposition by Revenue Commissioners, 610
rule in *Saunders v Vautier*, 608
statutory mechanism, 609–612
tax reasons, 607–608, 610
with court approval before legislative reform, 608–609
without court approval, 608
Vegetarian society
gift to, 457, 467
Vendor
liability as constructive trustee, 309–314
lien, 313
Vigilantibus, non dormientibus jura subveniunt, 36
Vivisection
trust for abolition, 394, 459, 468–469, 477–478
Void trust
conditions precedent and subsequent, 502
consequences, 501
contrary to public policy, 503–506
marriage, trust in restraint of, 503–504
parental duties, trust interfering with, 504–506
rule against inalienability, 501
rule against perpetuities, 501
voidable trust distinguished, 501
Voidable trust
bankrupt, settlement by, 513–515
creditors, settlement defrauding, 506–512
effect, 501, 506
grounds, 506
purchasers, voluntary settlement defrauding, 512–513
void trust distinguished, 501
Voluntary transfer resulting trust *see* **Presumed resulting trust**
Volunteer
equity looks on that as done which out to have been done, 49–50
equity will not perfect incomplete gift
equitable principle, 129
exceptions, 141–152, 938–939
possible alternative remedies, 153–156
position generally, 152–153
tracing of trust property, 995–996, 997, 998–999, 1015–1016

Wasting, hazardous or unauthorised assets
apportionment, 555–556
conversion, 553–555
***Wednesbury* principles**, 536
Where equities are equal, the first in time prevails, 54–67
Where equities are equal, the law prevails, 54–67
Wife *see* **Husband and wife; Marriage**

Wilful default
trustee's liability for, 577–578, 585, 599–600
Will (testament)
clerical error, 863–864
creation of trust by, 90–91
formalities, 90
intention of testator, 91–92
mutual wills, 297–303
rectification, 863–864
secret trust *see* **Secret trust**
undue influence, 887–888
Winding-up of company
injunction, 688–691
remedial constructive trust, 324–325
Wine, 99
Wish letter, 567–568
Witness to will
beneficiary under secret trust, 114
formalities, 90
may not benefit under will, 114n
Words and phrases
acquiescence, 42, 631
actual notice, 60–61
advancement, 583
Anton Piller order, 775
automatic resulting trust, 83, 157–158
bailment, 71
Bayer injunction, 785
beneficiary, 70–71
charitable purpose, 406–408
charitable trust, 408–409
completely constituted trust, 83, 129
conditions precedent and subsequent, 502
constructive notice, 61
constructive trust, 83, 257
cy-près doctrine, 483
discretionary trust, 75–76, 84
doctrine of conversion, 1018
doctrine of election, 1025
doctrine of performance, 1041–1042
doctrine of reconversion, 1023
doctrine of satisfaction, 1031
donatio mortis causa, 144
education, 425–430
equitable interest, 55
Words and phrases—*contd.*
equity, 1
estoppel, 923
estoppel by representation, 922
executed trust, 23–24, 83
executory trust, 23–24, 83
exhaustive discretionary trust, 84
express trust, 82–83
fiduciary relationship, 259–261
fixed trust, 84
frustration of contract, 840
fully secret trust, 112
general power, 75
half secret trust, 112
imputed notice, 63
incompletely constituted trust, 83, 129
injunction, 617
institutional constructive trust, 258
interim injunction, 618–619
interlocutory injunction, 618–619, 644
laches, 39, 628
mandatory injunction, 618
Mareva injunction, 747
maxim, 20
mere equity, 55
mutual wills, 297
non-exhaustive discretionary trust, 84
Pallant v Morgan equity, 303–304
perpetual injunction, 619
poor, 414–417
presumed resulting trust, 83, 157
presumption of advancement, 192, 204
private trust, 82
professional trustee, 607
prohibitory injunction, 618
promissory estoppel, 923
proprietary estoppel, 927
protective trust, 84–85
public benefit, 409–414
public trust, 82
purpose trust, 380
quia timet injunction, 619, 716
Quistclose trust, 169–170
rectification, 843

Words and phrases—*contd.*
religion, 437–438
remedial constructive trust, 258, 316
rescission, 865
resulting trust, 83, 157
rule against inalienability, 384–385
secret trust, 112
simple trust, 84
special power, 75
special trust, 84
specific performance, 788
subject to contract, 799–801
three certainties, 91
tracing, 996
trust, 2, 70–71

Words and phrases—*contd.*
trust power, 76
trustee, 70–71
trustee de son tort, 308–309
unincorporated association, 389–390
unjust enrichment, 331–332
void trust, 501
voidable trust, 501
wilful default, 577–578

Words of limitation
executed or executory trust, 23–24

Worldwide Mareva injunction, 747, 765–770

Worth Library, 403, 427–428, 434, 454–456, 491